The Careless Technology

ECOLOGY AND INTERNATIONAL DEVELOPMENT

The Natural History Press, publisher for The American Museum of Natural History, is a division of Doubleday and Company, Inc. Directed by a joint editorial board made up of members of the staff of both the Museum and Doubleday, the Natural History Press publishes books and periodicals in all branches of the life and earth sciences, including anthropology and astronomy. The Natural History Press has its editorial offices at Doubleday & Company, Inc., 277 Park Avenue, New York, New York 10017, and its business offices at 501 Franklin Avenue, Garden City, New York 11530.

THE CONSERVATION FOUNDATION, established in 1948 under the leadership of the late Fairfield Osborn, became the first non-profit organization dedicated to carrying out balanced programs of research, planning, education, and public information in the field of natural resources and environmental quality. Its basic mission today is to serve as a bridge between ideas and action in the environmental field—by determining important gaps in environmental understanding, by seeking to reduce those gaps, and by making its findings widely available. With a staff of some twenty professionals, the Foundation conducts environmental law and policy studies programs and provides training and other services to a wide range of citizens and officials concerned with environmental problems.

Although much of it work has been in the domestic field, the Foundation has been involved in international activities from the time of its founding, usually through specific research in specific countries. Its international activities since the conference on which this book is based have included advisory work for a variety of agencies in the international development field; interdisciplinary research on the impact of various technologies in developing nations; film and educational efforts related to developing country problems; the preparation of environmental principles for use in the planning of development projects; and the conduct of demonstration surveys in East Africa, Peru, and Dominica.

THE CENTER FOR THE BIOLOGY OF NATURAL SYSTEMS (at Washington University, St. Louis, Missouri 63130), which was created in January 1966, is based on collaboration among specialists in a wide range of basic sciences who have an interest in inherently complex systems and a concern for solving the growing problems which threaten the capacity of the environment to support human life. The Center conducts a research and training program to develop the knowledge and the competence to illuminate the basic scientific problems arising from the impact of technology on the environment especially in relation to human health. It is composed of faculty and graduate fellows from diverse fields ranging from computer science to biology who have joined to pursue a common interest in the intrinsic complexity of natural systems while continuing to work in their own areas of specialization.

The Program on Ecology and International Development is one example of the Center's approach to the study of science and technology's repercussions in the environment. Since 1967 it has helped organize a number of conferences on the scientific aspects of international development and environmental problems. The Program also encompasses a unique Reference Center on Ecology and International Development which has acquired a large body of documentation and case histories. The information is organized systematically for convenient use by scholars researching environmental parameters affecting development. The work of the Program also includes active interdisciplinary field research on the effects of the introduction of modern technology into less developed countries. Through this and other programs and task forces, the Center co-ordinates the efforts of faculty and graduate fellows from diverse scientific fields, and works actively toward environmental solutions at local, national and international levels.

The Careless Technology

ECOLOGY AND INTERNATIONAL DEVELOPMENT

EDITED BY

M. TAGHI FARVAR
CENTER FOR THE BIOLOGY OF NATURAL SYSTEMS
WASHINGTON UNIVERSITY

JOHN P. MILTON
INTERNATIONAL PROGRAMS
THE CONSERVATION FOUNDATION

THE RECORD OF THE CONFERENCE ON THE ECOLOGICAL ASPECTS OF
INTERNATIONAL DEVELOPMENT CONVENED BY THE CONSERVATION
FOUNDATION AND THE CENTER FOR THE BIOLOGY OF NATURAL
SYSTEMS, WASHINGTON UNIVERSITY, DECEMBER 8-11, 1968,
AIRLIE HOUSE, WARRENTON, VIRGINIA

 The Natural History Press / Garden City, New York
1972

CONTENTS

FOREWORD   *M. Taghi Farvar and John P. Milton*   xiii

INTRODUCTION TO THE CONFERENCE   *Russell E. Train*   xvii

SUMMARY OF THE CONFERENCE   *Barry Commoner*   xxi

(*Abstract precedes each paper*)

I. HEALTH AND NUTRITIONAL CONSEQUENCES OF SELECTED DEVELOPMENT PROGRAMS.   *Carter L. Marshall,* Chairman   1

A Ballad of Ecological Awareness   *Kenneth E. Boulding*   3

1. Some Exercises in Social Ecology: Health, Disease, and Modernization in the Ryukyu Islands   *Carter L. Marshall*   5

2. Influence of Environmental Transformation in Changing the Map of Disease   *Jacques M. May*   19

3. Transferable Drug Resistance and the Ecologic Effects of Antibiotics   *LaVerne C. Harold*   35

4. Biological Disorders in the Genito-Urinary System Following the Introduction of New Technologies and Lifeways in the Less Developed Countries   *Boyouk Farvar*   47

5. Aggravation of Vitamin A Deficiency Following Distribution of Non-Fortified Skim Milk. An Example of Nutrient Interaction   *George E. Bunce*   53

6. Lactose Intolerance in Southeast Asia   *A. E. Davis and T. D. Bolin*   61

7. The Role of Technological Development in Promoting Disease in Africa   *Charles C. Hughes and John M. Hunter*   69

8A. The Impact of Agricultural Development on Aquatic Systems and Its Effect on the Epidemiology of Schistosomes in Rhodesia   *C. J. Shiff*   102

8B. The Effects of Molluscicides on the Microflora and Microfauna of Aquatic Systems   *C. J. Shiff*   109

9.   World Health Organization Project Egypt 10: A Case History of a
     Schistosomiasis Control Project   *Henry van der Schalie*   116

     DISCUSSION   137

II. **IRRIGATION AND WATER DEVELOPMENT.**
                                                   Thayer Scudder, Chairman   155

     A Ballad of Ecological Awareness (continued)   *K. E. Boulding*   157

10. The Role of the Aswan High Dam in Changing the Fisheries of the
     Southeastern Mediterranean   *Carl J. George*   159

11. Impact of River Control Schemes on the Shoreline of the Nile Delta
                                                              M. Kassas   179

12. The Nile Catchment—Technological Change and Aquatic Biology
                                                   E. Barton Worthington   189

13. Ecological Bottlenecks and the Development of the Kariba Lake Basin
                                                           Thayer Scudder   206

14. Some Ecological Implications of Mekong River Development Plans
                                                          John E. Bardach   236

     DISCUSSION   245

15. The Impact of Modern Irrigation Technology in the Indus and Helmand
     Basins of Southwest Asia   *Aloys A. Michel*   257

16. Salinization and Water Problems in the Algerian Northeast Sahara
                                                            Kamel Achi   276

17. Salt Cedar and Salinity on the Upper Rio Grande   *John Hay*   288

18. Consequences of Uncontrolled Human Activities in the Valencia Lake
     Basin   *Alberto Böckh*   301

19. The Anchicayá Hydroelectric Project in Colombia: Design and Sedi-
     mentation Problems   *Robert N. Allen*   318

     DISCUSSION   343

20. On Irrigation—Induced Changes in Insect Populations in Israel
                                                             E. Rivnay   349

     DISCUSSION   365

III. **ECOLOGICAL CONSEQUENCES OF INTENSIFICATION OF
     PLANT PRODUCTIVITY.**
                                   Ray F. Smith and E. W. Russell, Co-Chairmen   369

     A Ballad of Ecological Awareness (continued)   *K. E. Boulding*   371

21. Effects of Manipulation of Cotton Agro-Ecosystems on Insect Pest
     Populations   *Ray F. Smith and Harold T. Reynolds*   373

22. The Relationship between Insect Pests and Cotton Production in Central Africa *F. E. M. Gillham* 407

23. Ecological Consequences of Pesticides Used for the Control of Cotton Insects in Cañete Valley, Peru *Teodoro Boza Barducci* 423

24. Some Ecological Implications of Two Decades of Use of Synthetic Organic Insecticides for Control of Agricultural Pests in Louisiana *L. D. Newsom* 439

DISCUSSION 460

25. Ecological Aspects of Pest Control in Malaysia *Gordon R. Conway* 467

26. Toxicity of Insecticides Used for Asiatic Rice Borer Control to Tropical Fish in Rice Paddies *L. T. Kok* 489

27. Locust Control: Ecological Problems and International Pests *P. T. Haskell* 499

28. Ecological Effects of Chemical Control of Rodents and Jackals in Israel *H. Mendelssohn* 527

DISCUSSION 545

29. Problems in the Use of Chemical Fertilizers *John Phillips* 549

30. The Impact of Technological Developments on Soils in East Africa *E. W. Russell* 567

31. Nitrate Problems and Nitrite Hazards as Influenced by Ecological Conditions and by Fertilization of Plants *W. Schuphan* 577

32. Lateritic Soils in Distinct Tropical Environments: Southern Sudan and Brazil *Mary McNeil* 591

33. Problems of Tropical Settlement—Experiences in Colombia and Bolivia *Harold T. Jorgenson* 609

34. Plant Germ—Plasm Resources and Utilization *David H. Timothy* 631

DISCUSSION 657

IV. **INTENSIFICATION OF ANIMAL PRODUCTIVITY.**
F. Fraser Darling, Chairman 667

A Ballad of Ecological Awareness (continued) *K. E. Boulding* 669

35. Ecological Consequences of Sedentarization of Nomads *F. Fraser Darling and Mary A. Farvar* 671

36. Ecological Consequences of Bedouin Settlement in Saudi Arabia *Harold F. Heady* 683

37. Ecological Consequences of Rangeland Development in Masailand, East
     Africa   *Lee M. Talbot*   694

38. The Ecological Impact of the Introduction of Domestic Cattle into
     Wild Life and Tsetse Areas of Rhodesia   *Oliver West*   712

39. The Tsetse Fly: A Blessing or a Curse?   *Frank L. Lambrecht*   726

40. The Sheep and the Saltbush: The Utilization of Australia's Arid Lands
                                                  Peter Crowcroft   742

41. Ecological Aspects of Protein Feeding—the Case of Peru
                                                 Georg Borgstrom   753

DISCUSSION   775

V. SPECIAL PROBLEMS OF ENVIRONMENTAL DEGRADATION.
                                          Gilbert F. White, Chairman 791

     A Ballad of Ecological Awareness (continued)   *K. E. Boulding* 793

42. Ecological Hazards from Nuclear Power Plants
                                              Dean E. Abrahamson   795

43. Atomic Waste Disposal in the Sea: An Ecological Dilemma?
                                               Joel W. Hedgpeth   812

44. Enviromental Quality and the Thermal Pollution Problem
                                                John Cairns, Jr.   829

DISCUSSION   854

45. An Ecological Overview of Caribbean Development Programs
                                              Carl A. Carlozzi   858

46. Man's Effects on Island Ecosystems   *F. R. Fosberg*   869

47. Some Ecological Factors in Development Projects in the Dominican
     Republic   *Wolfram U. Drewes*   881

DISCUSSION   892

48. Experiments with the Use of Case Histories in an Ecology Seminar
                                                   Thane Riney   903

49. Organizing Scientific Investigations to Deal with Environmental Impacts
                                                Gilbert F. White   914

50. An Ecological Approach to International Development: Problems of
     Policy and Administration   *Lynton K. Caldwell*   927

DISCUSSION   948

VI. THE IMPLICATIONS OF THE CONFERENCE FOR INTERNATIONAL DEVELOPMENT PROGRAMS.

Barry Commoner, Chairman

A Ballad of Ecological Awareness (conclusion)   *K. E. Boulding*   955

DISCUSSION   959

GENERAL INDEX   984

INDEX OF SCIENTIFIC NAMES   1019

BIOGRAPHICAL INFORMATION   1022

FOREWORD

This conference was designed to investigate the question: "To what extent have the ecological costs of introducing technology affected the less-developed countries?" As this record of the conference shows, the environmental side effects of technology are often even more serious in the less-developed than in the developed countries. Those responsible for international development can no longer afford to ignore these ecological problems. The very validity of the values, goals and methods of development are challenged here. One emerging implication is that the post-World War II idea that traditional societies can and should be overhauled overnight has not only proved virtually unachievable, but perhaps undesirable. The profound scientific, social and ethical issues involved are discussed in this volume.

When we first conceived of commissioning a series of special studies to explore the past role of ecology in international development, we had hoped to elicit both positive and negative case histories. As we investigated possible topics and contributors, it became apparent that little concern had ever been given to anticipating ecological costs and side-effects, to say nothing of having such factors serve as inputs to decision-making in development projects. In example after example, we found that large dams, irrigation projects, oil and mineral developments, industrial plants, nomadic settlement efforts, resettlement programs, heavy agricultural machinery, medical aid, food distribution efforts, chemical pesticides and fertilizers, animal husbandry projects, road construction efforts, and programs to build fossil fuel and atomic energy plants were being promoted throughout the world with little or no attention to their environmental consequences. One of the central elements affecting the productivity of any region—the specific character of its ecosystems—had almost always been ignored. As a consequence, the bulk of international development to date has often been destructive.

The problems of man's careless use of development technologies tend to fall into two general categories. In one, the fault is intrinsic to the technology on a global scale: the environmental problems of application are present in the developed (source) countries and have been exported along with the technology to less developed countries, where similar environmental impacts then have occurred. In the other category, there is a "transfer" problem: a technology which has been developed to suit conditions of temperate zone ecosystems will fail operationally when imposed on alien, usually tropical environments.

Private industry and international agencies have also been negligent in guiding the development and application of man's tools. They have failed to study and understand the complex interdependency of the biosphere and the many local ecosystems that make it up. They have failed to give science and its application in technology the goal of coming into harmony with the natural systems that sustain life on earth. There has been considerable discussion recently by various bilateral and multilateral agencies on how to include ecological factors in their decision-making. We are encouraged by the rhetoric, but await the most important test of all: effective action.

As the power, variety and cumulative impacts of development technologies continue to grow and exert ecological influence, the need for a major reassessment of development goals becomes urgent. We hope that this book, the case studies and discussion of their implications, will help toward that end. This well-documented record of serious environmental failures suggests a number of specific changes; in particular, it suggests we must plan for a major restructuring of the criteria used by international agencies and others in the selection and design of development projects if we are to avoid making future ecological mistakes. The case histories also indicate that careful environmental research should be included at most levels of the development process, particularly in preinvestment surveys, project planning, actual development on the site and post-project evaluation. There are other clear needs for the future suggested by the conference. Of particular importance is the necessity to undertake immediately a series of interdisciplinary research projects (perhaps through the establishment of a network of environmental studies centers) to understand the complex ecological problems that have followed technological development, in order to learn from past mistakes, and to begin the difficult discipline of predicting the impacts of various man-induced changes, including pollution.

For success in these goals, however, the nations of the world must soon allocate a substantial investment to the development of relevant interdisciplinary science, in expanded training not only of tropical and arid lands ecologists, but also of other relevant scientists. Such training should take place in both the highly-developed and less-developed nations. The world now faces a serious shortage of culturally sensitive interdisciplinary scientists familiar with and capable of handling the problems unique to less-developed regions. Similarly, there is an obvious need to include relevant ecological subjects as a basic part of every country's general educational program. Improved environmental education for many international civil servants is also badly needed. For example, area study programs now emphasizing political science, economics and sociology might do well to include in their training knowledge of the environmental sciences applicable to each region studied.

The population issue is a very controversial one that was not covered *per se* in this volume. The main reason was that it would have taken a volume equal in size to do justice to the complex and often difficult problems involved. Many other efforts have explored this difficult issue more thoroughly than would have been possible at this conference.

Nor does this book attempt to provide a complete synthesis of all the ecological, social, economic, political, anthropological and many other factors involved in the process of international development. The analysis of such factors, particularly the political, economic and demographic, have been scrutinized in many other studies. The purpose of this book is rather to explore the much-neglected ecology involved and to provide a framework for understanding its relevance to the development process.

We hope the lessons of this book contribute to a fundamental re-evaluation of global environmental relationships and to the development of sound values and goals. Human societies must begin learning how to halt the historically careless application of technology and begin to create a new technology to replace the old: a technology in equilibrium with the biosphere and with man's biological potentials.

We have maintained all the scientific detail necessary to defend the positions taken by each author. At the same time we have tried to see that the papers are comprehensible to the non-technically oriented public. In a few cases, the paper actually presented at the conference was considerably longer than that given here. Abridgements are indicated in the text. We hope that this effort will be of interest to concerned laymen and of particular usefulness to students of international development, to those already involved in introducing alien technologies to the less-developed countries, and to politicians, conservationists, natural scientists, lawyers, and various other professionals connected with the global development process.

Innumerable individuals have helped make a task of this magnitude possible, and thanks are due here to more than we can list. We owe a special debt to Stephanie Hoar, Linda Mattison, Laura O'Sullivan, Howard Boksenbaum, Diane Wilkins, Cynthia Vander Veen, Shelley Culver, and Susan Schechter who devoted many months of arduous attention to the organizational and linguistic details of papers so varied in style and ethnic origin. Thanks are due to Artis Bernard who meticulously prepared the index. We also appreciate the assistance of Sydney Howe and Marvin Zeldin of the Conservation Foundation, and Barry Commoner of the Center for the Biology of Natural Systems, in shepherding the manuscript through its many stages.

The Smithsonian Institution, the International Union for the Conservation of Nature, the International Biological Programme and the St. Louis Committee for Environmental Information (and its staff of the magazine *Environment*), all deserve thanks for generous assistance in various stages of the work. Roland Clement, Dale Newsom, Gilbert White, John Bardach, Georg Borgstrom, Harold Coolidge, and Lee Talbot made many helpful suggestions which led to topics and contributors. We also wish to express our gratitude to the Conference Steering Committee, especially to its Chairman, Raymond Dasmann, for his generous contribution of thought and working support throughout our efforts. We appreciate the efforts of Sheldon Novick and Lawrence Moss in reviewing the papers on side effects of atomic energy, of Albert Bradford, who wrote many of the abstracts, of Kevin Shea in commenting on the pesticide papers and of Lindsay Mattison in supplying critical advice and support during the seminal stages of the conference.

Many other individuals helped in determining the composition of the Conference. A detailed acknowledgement would be impossible.

The Rockefeller Foundation's generous support, a special grant from the Conservation Foundation, a gift from the Joseph van Vleck family in memory of William Vogt, and several anonymous grants from individuals, made the conference possible financially. We are sincerely grateful to all of them for their financial assistance.

Finally, the patient cooperation of individual authors with the editors is gratefully acknowledged.

M. TAGHI FARVAR   JOHN P. MILTON
March 1971

INTRODUCTION TO THE CONFERENCE

Russell E. Train

It is a great pleasure to welcome each and every one of you on behalf of Dr. Barry Commoner and myself to this conference on the Ecological Aspects of International Development.

As you know, this conference is sponsored jointly by the center for the Biology of Natural Systems, Washington University, St. Louis, Missouri, and the Conservation Foundation, Washington, D.C.

A glance at the program will, I think, convince anyone that we have not only a very fascinating program spread before us but also a very full and demanding schedule to meet. Meeting that schedule is going to require the cooperation of all of us and, in particular, very firm control and direction on the part of the section chairmen.

The procedure we expect to follow in each session is to have each member present a short summary of his paper, hopefully not longer than three minutes. We shall assume that everyone here has read every paper. Then, each session chairman will give a brief summary of the papers of those participants who were unable to get here. Following these presentations, there will be discussions and questions open to all participants in the conference.

We have purposely built this conference on the case history method, and it is important that discussion focus on the specific case histories and subject matter of the session and not wander over into broad generalizations.

In the final session, chaired by Dr. Commoner, we will seek to identify those general principles to be derived from the conference as a whole and relate them to the specific problems which have been discussed in the case histories.

Like most conference chairmen, I share little credit for the planning and arrangements which have brought us to Airlie House from all parts of the world. Credit in large and generous measure is due to our co-secretaries, John Milton of The Conservation Foundation and Taghi Farvar of the Center for the Biology of Natural Systems. These men for the most part conceived and carried through the idea of this conference, and both have spent over a year and a half in preparation for today. They will act as the co-editors of the published proceedings.

I also wish to mention and thank our Steering Committee and its chairman, Ray Dasmann.

We are indebted to several sources for the funding of this conference, notably the

Rockefeller Foundation. We are grateful to all of them, not only for their money but also for their vision in seeing the importance of the subject matter before us.

In the spring of 1965 The Conservation Foundation sponsored the Conference on the Future Environments of North America here at Airlie House.[1] Several of you are veterans of that earlier meeting and will provide a valuable linkage between the two sessions. One scholar from that earlier meeting, who would have been with us but for his death earlier this year, is William Vogt. Years ago, Bill saw and understood with prophetic clarity the needs toward which this conference is pointed. We will miss his brilliant intellect and sharp wit. I am sure he wishes us well, although perhaps with characteristic pessimism about the results.

As we turn from the environments of North America to those of the rest of the world, it is certainly not because we have solved at home the problems of technological intrusion into the environment. Far from it. Indeed, with the possible exception of some of the health consequences of development programs, most of the problems of the developing countries which we will be discussing here occur perhaps to an even greater degree in the developed countries. And even that one exception would become questionable if we were to shift our emphasis from physical to mental health.

Thus, it seems to me that we are not meeting just to point a finger at the development process and its inadequacies but to hold up a mirror in which we and others can see clearly reflected the growing crises of our own technology. The adverse environmental consequences of much well-accepted technological progress is perhaps most readily and dramatically seen in international development programs where

alien technology and alien goals interact with traditional cultures and values.

Furthermore, the relative lack of sophistication on the part of the responsible officials and agencies in the developing countries means that those countries are defenseless—perhaps a better word would be "naked"—before the self-assured wisdom of Western planners. Therefore, if we had no other reason, we have a very heavy moral obligation to assess the full range of consequences of those international development programs, both bilateral and multilateral, which we have undertaken so confidently.

We are not attempting here to examine the overall development process. Our immediate purpose is to build the clearest possible case for the inclusion of ecology in the development planning and decision-making process. We shall do this not by generalization but by presenting a carefully documented body of evidence of the adverse consequences which have followed in real situations from the failure to include ecological considerations in development planning. The evidence will be scientific and expert. It will not be in the nature of hearsay but will represent the direct personal observations of highly trained individuals, based upon actual situations in which they themselves have participated.

However, our task here will not be completed simply by developing a record of this sort. Case histories necessarily deal with things past. Our concern must be for the future. Our purpose must be to identify the lessons to be learned from past mistakes and current failures in order that we may do a better job in the future.

If we agree on the need to build more ecological expertise into the planning of development projects, the preinvestment surveys and the projects themselves, how is this need to be met? Ecologists tend to be

---

[1] F. Fraser Darling and J. P. Milton, eds., *Future Environments of North America* (New York: Natural History Press, 1966).

free in their criticism of complex development programs for their failure to consider ecological implications but not always equally helpful in suggesting solutions to the problem. I hope our conference will keep this need for action in mind.

One clear prerequisite to improved performance certainly lies in education. I was particularly struck by the statement in Gilbert White's paper that a sense of efficacy in handling complexity may be a powerful aid to awareness. Thus, I hope that our closing panel in particular will address itself to such needs as those for expanded support for environmental science centers abroad and for building ecological training into regional study centers now emphasizing sociology, economics and political science.

Of course, training is not the only problem; new institutional arrangements should also be an important consideration. For example, how does an organization such as the Agency for International Development or the World Bank insure the consideration of ecology in its planning and operations? In this connection, it is interesting to note the recent establishment of an Office of Environmental Impact by the U. S. Department of Transportation which has responsibility for federal highway construction and also the establishment of an environmental branch by the Army Corps of Engineers which has massive dam-building and other water management responsibilities. These new functions have been located at the highest level in their respective agencies. These are only signs, but they strike me as important ones.

It seems to me that the timing of this conference is most opportune. A new Administration is about to take office in Washington and will doubtless be reappraising old programs and seeking new initiatives. Our proceedings could provide at least a small stimulus to that process.

Finally, I hope that we will not limit our thinking here just to the need for including ecology in development planning. Ecology has a larger and more significant role than simply to fill a gap in development thinking. An ecological awareness in both the highly developed and the developing nations is a primary key to understanding the options we possess, the alternative courses of action we face and the implications of each.

I suspect that a major reason ecology is so often ignored is not so much lack of expertise as the fact that an ecological awareness leads to the questioning of goals—and this is something few wish to do. The time has come when questions must be asked about the validity of development goals here and abroad. I hope that our conference can contribute to that need.

SUMMARY OF THE CONFERENCE

On the Meaning of Ecological Failures in International Development

Barry Commoner

The conference has recorded a long roster of ecological mistakes which have accompanied the introduction of new technological advances into underdeveloped countries. Some of the problems have been small, transitory and remediable, such as the plight of Malaysian villages where cats ingested insecticide-laden pests and died. Infestations by disease-bearing rats followed and were finally controlled by the timely arrival of new troops of parachute-borne cats. Other problems, however, such as the shoreline erosion caused by dam projects on the Nile, have been massive and essentially irreversible. Some of the ecological difficulties have intruded directly on the physiology of man: for example, the untoward effects of introducing milk among peoples with inappropriate enzymatic constitutions. Others have affected man through a chain of biological events such as the devastating invasions of schistosome worms due to the build-up of infected snail populations in permanent irrigation systems.

Are these difficulties, large or small, only accidents of progress—the random perturbations to be expected in any complex and massive undertaking? If so, little more need be said about them. For, given the enormous benefits which have already accrued from the new power plants, irrigation systems and health programs, a further recitation of accidents would be graceless. On the other hand, if these widespread ecological mistakes are not the random accidents of progress, but rather the *systematic* consequences of some deep fault in our approach to technological development, the matter becomes much more serious. For if the system of technological advance already exhibits such a pervasive fault, the failing may become fatal as we expand international development to avert the impending world famine.

In my view, the ecological mistakes that have been reported in this conference reflect a grave and systematic fault in the overall approach which has thus far guided most international development programs. Although each new technology that is introduced into an underdeveloped country impinges on a complex natural system, we have generally failed to take into account the effects of this technological intrusion on the properties—indeed, the very stability—of the system as a whole. Given the complex feedback networks in even the simplest ecosystem, these intrusions have nearly always led to unforeseen effects, often sufficiently deleterious to counterbalance significantly the good derived from the intended program. In some cases, such *ecological backlash* has destroyed the effectiveness of the intended program itself. There are many examples of this general failure:

1. Nearly every irrigation project reported to the conference has been followed by outbreaks, some of them disastrous, of waterborne diseases of human (in particular schistosomiasis) or of animals (such as tsetse-borne trypanosomiasis of cattle). Some irrigation projects, such as the pervasive system of dams on the Nile, have induced large-scale geophysical changes which have, in turn, reduced the agricultural potential of the region. Small-scale irrigation projects, as in Israel, have generated new insect pest problems.

2. Nearly every reported instance involving the introduction of chemical control of agricultural pests in newly developed agricultural areas has been characterized by serious ecological hazards. With awesome regularity, major outbreaks of insect pests have been *induced* by the use of the modern contact-killing insecticides—by stimulating the development of resistant strains and destroying the natural predators which ordinarily regulate the densities of pest populations.

3. Case histories of technological improvements in animal husbandry and fisheries, while less numerous, yield the same picture: unexpected hazards resulting, for example, from ecological interactions in the food chain (as in Peruvian fisheries) or in host-parasite relationships (as in the several tsetse fly problems in Africa).

4. The introduction of modern health programs has in some cases involved specific intrusions on human physiology with untoward effects on aspects of nutrition and health.

Thus, while nearly all of the projects described in the conference were conceived as specific technological advances—the construction of a hydroelectric plant, the de-

velopment of an irrigation system, enhancement of crop yields by chemical control of insect pests—they were in operational fact powerful intrusions on large-scale geophysical and ecological systems. Most of the difficulties which have been recounted result from the failure to recognize this basic fact.

Such failures are exemplified by many of the specific case histories which we have heard. Lake Kariba is the largest man-made body of water in the world; surely its creation must be regarded as a huge and intricate ecological operation. Yet, Scudder reports that ". . . no ecological surveys of the lake basin or the relocation areas were initiated, let alone completed, prior to the decision to proceed with the construction of the dam in 1955." Van der Schalie reports that he had great difficulty in obtaining support for a study of the ecological consequences of the Aswan High Dam designed ". . . to obtain the data necessary to show whether the prediction that the new dam might prove to be a liability rather than an asset" was correct. Perhaps the most authoritative evidence is that provided by Riney's account of FAO experience:

> Much of the assistance which has been given to developing countries has used criteria found within the teacup perimeter of various single disciplines. Within this limited horizon decisions have often been well meaning and seemingly logical, but catastrophic in their ultimate effect on the environment. The danger comes from not realizing that the virtuous activity of giving outside advice often triggers the most profound effects on the environment extending far outside the scope of the single discipline responsible for the original advice. The decisions in fact quite often guarantee failure rather than success.

I believe that we must conclude, then, that the ecological failures recounted at this conference are not the random accidents of progress. They are, rather, evidence that (a) regardless of its conceived purpose, the introduction of new technology into developing countries is always an *ecological* operation which must be expected to affect the complex network of physical and biological processes that characterize natural systems; and that (b) with rare exceptions, development programs were planned, put into operation, and sometimes closed down in failure, before their ecological consequences were appreciated.

This conclusion leads to a second question: Is this general failure the result of some circumstance peculiar to the introduction of new advances into underdeveloped regions of the world, or is it rather a fault inherent in the very nature of the instruments themselves—modern science and technology? This is, of course, an especially painful issue for those of us who represent "advanced" science and technology. It forces us to consider the possibility that we may be in the position of the good Samaritan who comes to the aid of a drowning man with what proves, in the breach, to be a rotten rope.

Yet we must face this issue. Indeed, I must record my own very strong conviction that the rescue rope offered to developing nations by modern science and technology is intrinsically unsound. I believe that science generally, and biology in particular, have been dominated by an intensely reductionist approach; scientific analyses engendered by this reductionist approach are a poor guide to the understanding of those realms of nature which are stressed by modern technology. This fault is the cause, not only of the ecological failures in international development, but also of the grave and unwitting deterioration of the environment in advanced nations, for example, the United States. These are strong claims, but the evidence is, I believe, of sufficient force to support them.

That modern science is a dangerously faulty foundation for technological interventions into nature becomes evident if we apply the so-called "engineering test"—that is, how well does it work in practice? Science represents our understanding of the natural world in which man must live. Man, like any other living thing, can survive only in a given set of environmental conditions. At the same time, like all living things, man influences the very environment on which he depends, and human survival hangs on the maintenance, at a suitable ecological balance, of this reciprocal interdependence. Since man consciously acts on the environment through technology, the compatibility of such action with human survival will, in turn, depend on the degree to which our technological practices accurately reflect the nature of the environment. We may ask, then: Is the understanding of nature which science gives us an effective guide to technological action in the natural world?

We in the "advanced" nations are proud of our science and technology. One of the striking features of modern life is a deep and widespread faith in the efficacy of science and the usefulness of technological progress. The United States is widely envied as an advanced nation not merely for its magnificent material wealth, but because it possesses the marvelous instruments—science and technology—which are the continuing source of more wealth. It is these wealth-producing instruments which less developed nations are eager to acquire.

There is now at least one good reason to question this faith—environmental pollution. It is my contention that environmental pollution reflects the failure of modern science to achieve an adequate understanding of the natural world, which is, after all, the arena in which every technological event takes place.

The roster of the recent technological mistakes in the environment which have been perpetrated by the most scientifically advanced society in the history of man—the United States of 1968—is appalling:

—We used to be told that radiation from the fallout produced in nuclear tests was harmless. Only now, long after the damage has been done, do we know differently. The bombs were exploded long before we had even a partial scientific understanding that they could increase the incidence of harmful mutations, thyroid cancer, leukemia and congenital birth defects.

—We built the maze of highways that strangles almost every large city and filled them with hordes of automobiles and trucks long before it was learned—from analysis of the chemistry of the air over Los Angeles—that sunlight induces a complex chain of chemical events in the vehicles' exhaust fumes, leading eventually to the noxious accumulation of smog.

—For more than forty years massive amounts of lead have been disseminated into the environment from automotive fuel additives; only now has concern developed about the resultant accumulation of lead in human beings at levels that may be approaching toxicity.

—Insecticides were synthesized and massively disseminated before it was learned that they kill not only insects, but birds and fish as well, and accumulate in the human body; and that they also stimulate the development of insecticide-resistant pests and kill off natural predators and parasites.

—Billions of pounds of synthetic detergents were annually drained into U.S. surface waters before it was learned—more than ten years too late—that such detergents are not degraded by bacterial action and therefore accumulate in water supplies. Nor were we aware until a few years ago that the phosphates added to improve the cleansing properties of synthetic detergents would cause overgrowths of algae, which on their death pollute surface waters.

—In the last twenty-five years the amount of inorganic nitrogen fertilizer used on U.S. farms annually has increased about twelve-fold. Only in the last few years has it become apparent that this vast elevation in the natural levels of soil nutrients has so stressed the biology of the soil that harmful amounts of nitrate have been introduced into surface waters.

—The rapid combustion of fossil fuels for power, and more recently, the invasion of the stratosphere by aircraft, are rapidly changing the earth's heat balance in still poorly understood ways. The effects of these processes may drastically influence the climate and the level of the sea.

—And for the future, if we make the catastrophic blunder, the major military powers are prepared to conduct large-scale nuclear warfare, even though no one knows how our societies could survive.

Each of these problems is a technological mistake, in which an unforeseen consequence has seriously marred the value of the undertaking. Each stems directly from misconceptions which are engendered by a specific fault in our system of science and in our understanding of the natural world. This fault is reductionism, the view that effective understanding of a real, complex system can be achieved by investigating the properties of its isolated parts. The reductionist methodology, which is so characteristic of much of modern biological research, is not an effective means of analyzing the vast natural systems which are threatened by modern technology. Water pollutants stress the total ecological web which ties together the numerous organisms that inhabit rivers; their effects on the whole natural system are not adequately described by laboratory studies of pure cultures of separate organisms. Smog attacks the self-protective mechanism of the human lung; its noxious effects on man are not accountable by the influence on a single enzyme or even a single tissue. If, for the sake of analytical detail, molecular constituents are isolated from the smashed remains of a cell or single organisms are separated from their natural neighbors, what is lost is the network of interrelationships which crucially determines the properties of the natural whole.

Modern technologies, being massive and

novel, inevitably intrude upon the natural environment on a large scale and in unfamiliar ways. However, viewed through the blinders of reductionism we see this inherently complex environment only in terms of separate parts. As a result, new technologies are designed, not to fit into the environment *as a whole,* but only to enhance a singular desired effect.

Thus a new synthetic chemical is designed to kill insects; its value is determined by testing the substance against this singular target. But this target—the insect pest—is, in nature, an interconnected part of an elaborate whole, the ecosystem. As a result, it comes as a surprise that synthetic chemicals destroy the predators which normally regulate the pest population, and so nullify the original aim of controlling the pest.

Similarly, synthetic detergents were designed as cleansing agents; the accommodation of the resultant waste water in the environment was ignored. As a result, no one was aware—until too late—that the detergents, being branched molecules, would resist bacterial degradation in waste disposal systems and accumulate in surface waters.

This bias has had a particularly adverse effect on knowledge about the biological systems which are at risk in the environment. Biology has become a flourishing and well-supported science in the United States; it is producing a wealth of new knowledge and is training many scientists skilled in its new methodology. But modern biological research is now dominated by the conviction that the most fruitful way to understand life is to discover a specific molecular event which can be identified as "the mechanism" of a particular biological process. The complexities of soil biology or the delicate balance of the nitrogen cycle in a river, which are not reducible to simple molecular mechanisms, are now often regarded as uninteresting relics of some ancient craft. In the pure glow of molecular biology, studying the biology of sewage is a dull and distasteful exercise hardly worth the attention of a "modern" biologist. This approach leads to the substitution of molecular biology for the biology of natural systems. It leads sociologists to become psychologists, psychologists to become physiologists, physiologists to become cellular biologists, and turns cellular biologists into chemists, chemists into physicists and physicists into mathematicians.

It is not surprising then, that in contrast to the rapid increase in our knowledge of the molecular features of life, research on environmental biology has been slow. Thus, although it is now known that the increase in nitrate and phosphate in surface waters causes new pollution problems by fostering the rapid growth of algae, there are, as yet, no reliable data to assess the contributions of the various possible sources—urban wastes, industrial wastes, fertilizer runoff— to this stress. Little is known about the processes which trigger the growth of such algal blooms; only recently have we begun to detect the toxic substances which they can release into the water. The fundamental biology of soil nitrogen is still so poorly understood that we cannot, even today, draw up a reliable balance sheet to describe the fate of the huge tonnage of nitrogen fertilizer added yearly to the soil —much of which runs off the soil and contaminates the water.

A related source of difficulty in understanding environmental problems arises from the failure of communication among the various specialized basic sciences. Thus, the chemists who developed the processes for synthesizing branched-chain detergents might have been forewarned about the ultimate failure of their products if they were in close contact with biochemists and bacteriologists—who already knew that such branched molecules tend to resist enzymatic attack and would therefore persist in disposal systems. The natural environment is itself an integrated system, a complex web, which if stressed at a specific point, usually responds as a whole. Isolated knowledge of one of its separate parts is an unreliable guide to the behavior of the whole system.

The parallels between the ecological mistakes made in the United States and abroad are striking. In the United States, we get into trouble because our narrow, single-valued approach conflicts with the intrinsic complexity of the environment; we are often concerned only with commercial value and ignore effects on the environment as a whole. In the region of Kariba Lake in Africa the same kind of outlook prevailed. Following an account of the multiple, unanticipated, ecological hazards that accompanied the formation of the lake, Scudder points out:

This project was essentially a unipurpose scheme. The population to be relocated were seen not as a resource, but as an expensive nuisance, whose very existence was unfortunate. As for the future lake, it was strictly a dam by-product, whereas the needs of down-river inhabitants were considered only where backed up by political power, and then were seen as constraints by those who viewed the Kariba Project almost entirely as a means for generating power.

We come, then, to a final question: What are the origins of the reductionist bias in science and what can be done to restore an outlook that would give adequate weight to the importance of intrinsically complex systems, such as the environment?

It would take us too far afield to undertake even a moderately complete answer to this question, and I shall restrict my comments to a single source of the reductionist bias which is, I believe, of crucial importance. We are concerned not so much with the nature of science and technology in the abstract, as with the form which these activities take in connection with very large scale economic enterprises—the introduction of a hydroelectric project in Africa or of a new detergent in the United States. For our purposes, it is particularly relevant, there-fore, to examine the interface between economics and technology.

A major school of economics, at least in the United States, is deeply concerned with the nature of technology, which it regards as the crucial determinant of the nature of "the new industrial state," to use the term made popular by the chief proponent of this view, J. K. Galbraith. Galbraith's definition of technology is useful for this discussion:

Technology means the systematic application of scientific or other organized knowledge to practical tasks. *Its most important consequence, at least for purposes of economics, is in forcing the division and subdivision of any such task into its component parts. Thus, and only thus, can organized knowledge be brought to bear on performance.* Specifically, there is no way that organized knowledge can be brought to bear on the production of an automobile as a whole or even on the manufacture of a body or chassis. It can only be applied if the task is so subdivided that it begins to be coterminous with some established area of scientific or engineering knowledge. Though metallurgical knowledge cannot be applied to the manufacture of the whole vehicle, it can be used in the design of the cooling system or the engine block. While knowledge of mechanical engineering cannot be brought to bear on the manufacture of the vehicle, it can be applied to the machining of the crank-shaft. While chemistry cannot be applied to the composition of the car as a whole, it can be used to decide on the composition of the finish or trim. . . .

Nearly all of the consequences of technology, and much of the shape of modern industry, derive from this need to divide and subdivide tasks. . . .

However, the subdivision of tasks to accord with area of organized knowledge is not confined to, nor has it any special relevance to, mechanical processes. It occurs in medicine, business management, building design, child and dog rearing and every other problem that involves an agglomerate of scientific knowledge.[1]

These are very explicit statements. They

[1] J. K. Galbraith, *The New Industrial State* (New York: New American Library, 1967), pp. 24–25; the indicated emphasis is my own.

define technology as intrinsically reductionist, and indeed, assert that technology can be applied to the modern productive process only because it *is reductionist*. Clearly, Galbraith's description of how technology is applied to the production of an automobile— fragment by fragment—is precisely the way in which it has been applied to hydroelectric plants in Africa and to the use of detergents in the United States. Technology, according to this view, is designed to construct an efficient power plant, a safe dam, or an effective cleansing agent; it cannot cope with the *whole* system on which the power plant, the dam, or the detergent intrudes; hence disastrous ecological surprises—schistosomiasis, agricultural failures, water pollution— become inevitable. Ecological failure is apparently a necessary consequence of the nature of modern technology, as Galbraith defines it.

Perhaps the most damaging consequences of the reductionist bias of modern science and technology is that it leads us to act massively on nature *before* we can be reasonably aware of the consequences; we have become the Sorcerer's Apprentice on a global scale. This, too, according to Galbraith, is a basic feature of modern technology:

It is a commonplace of modern technology that there is a high measure of certainty that problems have solutions before there is knowledge of how they are to be solved. As this is written in 1966, it is reasonably certain that a man can be landed on the moon within the next five years. However, many of the details of the procedure for doing so are not yet worked out. It is certain that air and water pollution can be more effectively controlled for those who, for better or worse, must remain on this planet. Uncertainty continues as to the best methods of doing so.[2]

If the technology exported from advanced countries to underdeveloped nations does, in fact, have the properties attributed to it by Galbraith, then the pattern of mistakes

[2] *Ibid.*, pp. 30–31.

which this conference has discussed is quite understandable. We have, indeed, in these discussions, learned of numerous instances in which massive development programs were undertaken in the faith ". . . that there is a high measure of certainty that problems have solutions before there is knowledge of how they are to be solved." Where our experience differs from Galbraith's is that some of the problems—for example, schistosomiasis—have in fact stubbornly resisted solution and that in many instances even the existence of the problems was unknown until it was too late.

No one can deny that despite the reductionist technology used to construct it, the modern mass-produced automobile is a technological triumph—up to a point. The dividing line between success and failure is the factory door. So long as the automobile is being constructed, reductionist technology is admirably successful. However, once the automobile is allowed out of the factory and into the environment, it is a shocking failure. It becomes the agent which has rendered urban air carcinogenic, burdened human bodies with nearly toxic levels of carbon monoxide and lead, embedded pathogenic particles of asbestos in human lungs and contributed significantly to the nitrate pollution of surface waters.

We tolerate the operational failure of the automobile and other technological hazards to the environment only because of a peculiar social and economic arrangement; the high costs of such failures (for example, the lives lost to lung cancer or the medical cost of smog-induced emphysema) are not charged to any given enterprise but are widely distributed in society. As a result, these costs become so intermingled with the costs due to other agents (for example, air pollution from power plants) as to become effectively hidden and unidentifiable. This suggests that the "success" of modern technology is largely determined by its ability to meet the economic requirements of the manufacturer. Measured against the economic interests of those who bear its costs in environmental deterioration—society as a whole—technology is by no means as successful.

Let me simply reiterate the position. When we develop a detergent, our tubular vision makes us concentrate on its immediate properties. Is it a good washing agent? Is it soft on milady's hands? Will it turn linen whiter than white? Will it sell? What is forgotten is what happens when it goes down the drain. Many tests were performed on detergents—consumer acceptability tests. The ultimate consumer of the detergents, the bacteria in the sewage disposal system, was forgotten. No one asked whether they were ready to receive the detergents.

Modern technology, it seems to me, is an instrument admirably suited to the economic needs of manufacturers, but poorly suited to the economic needs of those of us who must live in the natural environment. I believe that modern technology has had imposed on it the reductionist bias which Galbraith describes and which is so evident in its environmental effects. Thus people who have to judge the balance between cost and benefit, which is a political, social and moral judgment, don't have the raw material to exercise their conscience. They don't know the full costs and in some cases they may not know the full benefits. In other words, science as it is now construed, doesn't give our social system the raw material on which to base its decisions.

In seeking a remedy for the pervasive errors in international development I suggest that we reverse the order of relationships which now connect economic need, technology, engineering and the biology of the natural world. What is called for, I believe, is a new technology, designed to meet the needs of the human condition and of the natural environment rather than of "the new industrial state." In the present scheme

of priorities relatively narrow economic needs dictate the reductionist organization of technology; in turn, a given technological capability—construction of a hydroelectric plant, dissemination of insect-killing chemicals or the provision of irrigation waters—is translated into a specific engineering operation; when this operation is imposed upon the natural world, a myriad of ecological and biological problems arise—leaving the biologists, physicians and others concerned with the survival of living things, to cope with these hazards as best they can.

As long as the scale of technological intrusion into the environment remained small relative to the scale of the biosphere itself, this kind of haphazard arrangement could perhaps be tolerated. But that stage in the human occupancy of the earth has now come to an end. There is now simply not enough air, water and soil on the earth to absorb the resultant man-made insults without effect. If we continue in our feckless way to destroy the living systems which support us, this planet will soon become an unsuitable place for human habitation.

I believe that if we are to assimilate modern science into a technology which is suited to operate in a real, natural system, whether the valley of the Nile or the Hudson, we shall need to reverse the present relationships among biology, engineering technology, and economics. We ought to begin with an *ecological* evaluation of a region, its problems and potentials, in which man is regarded, as Scudder has urged, as the dominant species. Within this broad context, a given engineering task can then be defined with the constraint that it fit suitably into the properties of the system as a whole. Thus, if hydroelectric power is desired and is to harmonize—as it does not at Kariba—with the agricultural potential of the lake border and the downstream plains, auxiliary power plants can be specified in order to stabilize the river's flow and the lake's level. In turn, the engineers who need to design their works as integral parts of a natural system will need to turn for guidance to a new technology—one governed not by a narrow reductionist bias, but by a holistic view of nature. Finally, and most difficult, the economic value of such an operation would be defined not first—as it is now—but last. In effect I suggest that we need to proceed from an evaluation of human needs and desires, and the potential of a given environment to meet them, and *then* determine what engineering operations, technological processes, and economic resources are needed to accomplish these desires in harmony with the demands of the whole natural system.

We need to reassess our attitudes toward the natural world on which our technology intrudes. Among primitive people, man is seen as a dependent part of nature, a frail reed in a harsh world, governed by immutable processes which must be obeyed if he is to survive. The knowledge of nature which can be achieved among primitive peoples is remarkable. The African Bushman lives in one of the most stringent habitats on earth; food is scarce, water even more so, and extremes of weather come rapidly. The Bushman survives because he has an incredibly intimate understanding of his environment. A Bushman can, for example, return after many months and miles of travel to find a single underground tuber, when he needs it for his water supply.

We who call ourselves advanced claim to have escaped from this kind of dependence on the environment. While the Bushman must squeeze water from a searched-out tuber, we get ours by the turn of a tap. Instead of trackless wastes, we have the grid of city streets; instead of seeking the sun's heat when we need it or shunning it when it is too strong, we warm ourselves and cool ourselves with man-made machines. All this tends to foster the idea that we have made our own environment and no longer depend on the one provided by nature. In the eager search for the benefits of modern science and technology, we have become enticed into a nearly fatal illusion—that we have at last escaped from the dependence of man on the balance of nature.

The truth is tragically different. We have become, not less dependent on the balance of nature, but more dependent on it. Modern technology has so stressed the web of processes in the living environment at its most vulnerable points that there is little leeway left in the system. As the population of the world continues to increase and the already bitter need for food intensifies, the stress on the biology of the earth may reach the breaking point.

We are still in a period of grace. In that time, let us hope, we can learn that the proper use of science is not to conquer the world, but to live in it.

I HEALTH AND NUTRITIONAL CONSEQUENCES OF SELECTED DEVELOPMENT PROGRAMS

Carter L. Marshall, Chairman

1. Some Exercises in Social Ecology: Health, Disease, and Modernization in the Ryukyu Islands   *Carter L. Marshall*   5

2. Influence of Environmental Transformation in Changing the Map of Disease   *Jacques M. May*   19

3. Transferable Drug Resistance and the Ecologic Effects of Antibiotics   *LaVerne C. Harold*   35

4. Biological Disorders in the Genito-Urinary System Following the Introduction of New Technologies and Lifeways in the Less Developed Countries   *Boyouk Farvar*   47

5. Aggravation of Vitamin A Deficiency Following Distribution of Non-Fortified Skim Milk. An Example of Nutrient Interaction   *George E. Bunce*   53

6. Lactose Intolerance in Southeast Asia   *A. E. Davis and T. D. Bolin*   61

7. The Role of Technological Development in Promoting Disease in Africa   *Charles C. Hughes and John M. Hunter*   69

8A. The Impact of Agricultural Development on Aquatic Systems and Its Effect on the Epidemiology of Schistosomes in Rhodesia   *C. J. Shiff*   102

8B. The Effects of Molluscicides on the Microflora and Microfauna of Aquatic Systems   *C. J. Shiff*   109

9. World Health Organization Project Egypt 10: A Case History of a Schistosomiasis Control Project   *Henry van der Schalie*   116

DISCUSSION   137

A BALLAD OF ECOLOGICAL AWARENESS

Kenneth E. Boulding

Ecological awareness leads to questioning of goals:
This threatens the performance of some old established roles.
So to raise the human species from the level of subsistence
We have to overcome Covert Political Resistance.
So we should be propagating, without shadow of apology,
A Scientific Discipline of Poleconecology.

Among the very saddest of developmental tales
Is the indestructibility of fluke-infested snails.
Development is fluky when with flukes the blood is crammed,
So the more we dam the rivers, then the sooner we are damned.

Schistosomiasis has conquered—for the sad Egyptian fails
In six thousand years of history to eliminate the snails;
Yet in spite of all the furor of ecologist's conniptions
The Snail has failed completely to eradicate Egyptians.

In use upon the water of a good molluscicide
We really don't know what is true, but only what is tried.
For snails are pretty clever and climb upon the bank;
So if any good is done at all, we don't know what to thank.

Development must be successful, O, my darling daughter,
So keep your clothes on all the time, and don't go near the water.
The best advice we have is—for developmental tactics,
Don't wash or swim or go to bed without your prophylactics.

Bacteria have learned the trick of formal education—
They can transfer drug resistance with a shot of information.
So perhaps our universities should go in new directions,
And give their education by a series of injections.

The more we move around the world to where the prospect pleases,
The more we will communicate deplorable diseases.
Yet there may be a solution if we do not choose to flout it,
If we also can communicate just what to do about it.

Development will conquer the diseases of the poor,
By spraying all the houses and by putting in the sewer.
And we'll know we have success in our developmental pitch,
When everybody dies from the diseases of the rich.

A BALLAD OF ECOLOGICAL AWARENESS

Kenneth E. Boulding

1. SOME EXERCISES IN SOCIAL ECOLOGY: HEALTH, DISEASE, AND MODERNIZATION IN THE RYUKYU ISLANDS

Carter L. Marshall

The process of modernization is not a smooth one but rather one that proceeds in fits and starts. With respect to health and health programs, these fits and starts can result in an incomplete adaptation to what is considered "new," "scientific," and "modern"—with results which are rarely beneficial and often harmful. It is this failure of adaptation that accounts for the familiar dictum that to a very great extent, each society creates its own health problems.

During the past two decades, the Ryukyu Islands have experienced unparalleled economic advancement. The archipelago has been transformed from a peasant, agrarian society into one which is increasingly urban and dominated by light industry. The Ryukyuan sky, once the domain of the mosquito vectors of malaria and filariasis, is now filled with the smoke and gases of new factories. The water supply no longer abounds with the organisms of typhoid and dysentery; these have been replaced by detergents and chemical wastes. The great communicable diseases so characteristic of developing countries have given way to the chronic diseases prevalent in the industrialized world. Like the United States, the most common causes of death in the Ryukyus are now heart disease, cancer, stroke, and accidents.

There are several documented cases in which the rapid alteration of environmental conditions coupled with more or less rapid alteration of human habits can effect, for better or worse, the health of the population. Thus, government attempts to educate school children to personal hygiene by insisting on hand-washing before lunch resulted indirectly in a probable increase in trachoma transmission because the schools provide supervision, soap, and water, but no paper towels for drying. Similarly, older Ryukyuans who still drink boiled tea in preference to tap water were spared in a local dysentery outbreak. More complex examples involve national health programs such as filariasis eradication and tuberculosis control. The differing natures of the offending organisms in both of these diseases, coupled with similar programs of control, led to overwhelming success in one case and dismal failure in the other. Meanwhile, in the immediate future looms the threat of massive environmental pollution resulting from the process of industrialization and demanding enormous alterations in the area of government and public policy—nothing less than a new adaptation by an entire social system.

Most of the world's population today finds itself part of a vast aggregate of different races and contrasting cultures conveniently lumped under the title "developing countries." While this division of the globe into "developed" and "developing" implies a homogeneity within each group which may be more apparent than real, there seems to be little doubt that what distinguishes the one from the other is the elusive process known as "modernization." The "modern" countries are thus considered "developed," and the process of modernization is widely identified as the great need of the "developing areas." Basically this process is one through which a relatively stable, rural, agrarian society is transformed into a more mobile, urbanized, industrialized state. As Black (1966) has pointed out, it is an agonizing process involving the destruction of old institutions, the creation of new ones, and fundamental alterations in the function if not the structure of those institutions which manage to survive. Modernization is thus a process of social revolution, the goals of which are usually stated in economic terms.

Government officials spend much of their time pondering over problems of foreign exchange, gross national product, balanced growth, and the vexing question of consumption vs. investment. At the level of sophistication of most citizens, however, modernization has a meaning far more concrete and specific than the abstract economic concerns of government. After extensive travel in Asia and less extensive travel in Latin America, I am convinced that the meaning of modernization to the vast bulk of these people can be adequately summarized by almost any billboard that advertises Coca-Cola, washing machines, refrigerators, televisions, or other consumer items. Modernization is consumer hardware and consumer services. The proverbial house in suburbia may still be a century away for most Asians, but bicycles and transistor radios are often meaningful substitutes.

For these citizens then, modernization is seen, not as a dynamic process, but rather as a static entity characterized by the general availability of goods and services unavailable to them at the present time. There is little or no awareness of the enormous changes which must occur as prerequisites to a more bountiful life. What is desired is, to a great extent, determined by observing resident Americans or Europeans and by the growing use of mass media advertising. The people want commodities rather than an uprooting of their entire social system. This is not to suggest that a people would not deliberately destroy their social system to obtain higher living standards, but it does point out that the prime concern is apparently materialistic rather than ideological. In my experience, there seems to be no great admiration or respect in Asia for American (i.e., Western) institutions such as democracy, free enterprise, or Christianity. On the other hand, American technology is greatly admired. It is as if the goal were the grafting of Western technology onto a society that is to remain basically unchanged.

If we can accept scientific technology and its material fruits as the essence of modernization for most Asians, it is not difficult to understand the ready acceptance in many of these countries of whatever is perceived to be "modern" and "scientific." While the wearing of Western clothes may not seem very "scientific" to us, it may seem to be to an Asian for whom no real distinction exists between these two terms. That which is "modern" is necessarily also "scientific." The adoption of new habits, customs, or behavioral standards because of the convenient label, "modernization syndrome," can produce unpredictable and potentially tragic consequences. Viewed in ecological terms, this grafting-on process often alters the ecosystem by changing man without producing a compensatory change in his environment. Of course the converse, in which the application of technology alters the environment while man remains essentially unchanged, also occurs. In either case, the equilibrium of the ecosystem is disrupted, manifesting all too often the emergence of new problems more difficult to solve than the old ones.

Perhaps the disruptive impact of the more superficial aspects of modernization have been most apparent in nutrition. Two of the most widely publicized examples deal with changes in food habits. It has been pointed out, for example, that millions of Asians now refuse to eat unpolished rice, insisting on the more expensive, less nutritious white variety. Millions of Asians also exist at the brink of starvation and their rejection of unmilled rice robs them of a valuable source of dietary protein. While they may be acting in a modern way, it is difficult to see how they are better off. Similarly, Latham

(1965) has recently condemned the growing trend among African mothers to switch from breast to bottle feeding. The bottle is considered "scientific," the breast anachronistic. Yet the African mother has no facilities for sterilization or refrigeration of bottled milk, and the added cost in an already marginal budget usually also means a poorer quality diet for other members of the family. An equally disturbing trend in Africa is the increasing rejection of traditional foods which, while bizarre to Western tastes, provide a substantial part of the protein in the African diet. Thus the consumption of rats, dogs, flies, locusts, animal blood, and curdled milk is falling into disfavor even though no equivalent protein sources are presently available as replacements. In each of these cases, man has altered his relationship to his environment without compensatory environmental changes. What is too often ignored is the manner in which such changes may operate in more complex situations involving nationwide programs or even entire social systems. Even in less obvious cases, the basic problem is one in which a change in one part of the ecosystem is not accompanied by compensatory changes in another.

The object of this paper is to discuss some of these less apparent interactions between man and his social environment and to point out how these relationships can exert a preponderant influence on the health and welfare of a population. While the examples cited are all taken from the Ryukyu Islands, it is probable that similar examples can be found in any country.

THE RYUKYU ISLANDS:
HISTORICAL PERSPECTIVE

The Ryukyus comprise seventy-three islands lying on the China perimeter between southern Japan and Taiwan. The history of the island people, who prefer to be called

Okinawans, is a chronicle of the relations between a small, weak country and three great powers, China, Japan, and (most recently) the United States. Okinawa was first visited by a delegation from China in 608 A.D. and for the five hundred years between 1372 and 1870 the Chinese emperor was recognized as overlord of the Ryukyus. The Chinese were displaced by the Japanese in 1872 when the Ryukyus became a Japanese prefecture. This situation lasted until 1945 when Okinawa fell to advancing American forces in the most savage battle of the war in the Pacific. During the period of Japanese dominance, the monarch of the Ryukyus was disparagingly given the status of viceroy, and the central government was dominated by civil servants from the Japanese mainland. Self-government was limited largely to the local level, and an important tradition of village and regional autonomy developed which still persists.

This traditional localism was encouraged by the Americans in the early years of occupation. Between 1945 and 1952 central government disappeared entirely; it had been replaced by three separate bodies, each controlling the internal affairs of an island group. Central government was vested in the United States Civil Administration of the Ryukyu Islands. In 1952 this Civil Administration created, by executive decree, a counterpart national governing body known as the Government of the Ryukyu Islands. During its sixteen-year history GRI has gradually assumed more and more autonomy, and at present USCAR's role is primarily restricted to foreign affairs and advisory services in the various governmental functions.

In spite of long experience with foreign domination, the Ryukyus today differ in many respects from the "typical" developing area. First and foremost, the Ryukyus are prosperous, at least by Asian standards. The economy has been booming since the late fifties. Since 1960, the average annual rate of economic growth has been 19% and annual per capita income has risen from $202 to $426. The process of urbanization, which began immediately after World War II with the influx of almost 100,000 displaced Okinawans from every part of the Japanese empire, continues at a brisk rate. More than 50% of the people now live in cities, and in recent years light industry has developed at a rapid rate. Unlike virtually every other developing country in Asia, the Ryukyus do not have a significant population problem. The annual rate of population growth, which approached 3.0% in 1955, had fallen to 1.6% by 1966, and economic planners are increasingly concerned about a growing shortage of labor.

Steady, if not spectacular, progress has been made against the communicable diseases so prevalent in the developing world. Malaria eradication was achieved in 1961 and other important insect-borne diseases such as filariasis and Japanese encephalitis are under vigorous attack. Water-borne diseases have declined with the increasing availability of treated water. In 1966 a broad health insurance program was established which dwarfs anything now operating in the United States. The disease patterns of the Ryukyus have increasingly come to resemble those of Japan and the United States. While data on morbidity are scant, the leading causes of death in 1965 were heart disease, cancer, stroke, and accidents, the same afflictions so prevalent in industrialized countries.[1]

The control of the various communicable diseases is a continuing process, and as of December 1966 there were thirteen separate programs in operation, some more successful than others. Each of these programs,

[1] All of the information pertaining to the Ryukyu Islands is available from two sources, both of which appear annually. These are the *USCAR Fact Book* and the *High Commissioner's Report,* both available for various years from the U. S. Civil Administration of the Ryukyu Islands, APO San Francisco 96248.

viewed ecologically, involves the alteration of the existing ecosystem through the manipulation of man or the environment or both. The remainder of this discussion is devoted to a brief description of the manner in which these alterations often produced unpredictable results and directly influenced the eventual success of the program in question.

FILARIASIS ERADICATION: PRESERVING HEALTH BY FILLING A SOCIAL VACUUM

Filariasis (sometimes known as elephantiasis) is a disease transmitted by certain species of *Culex* mosquitoes. While rarely fatal, it is a significant cause of low productivity because it is chronic and debilitating. Surveys carried out in the early sixties revealed a prevalence rate of 19% in the southernmost island group of the Ryukyus, the Miyako Gunto. A mass campaign to eradicate filariasis in this area began in early 1965.

The Miyako Gunto consists of eight small islands with a total land area of eighty-five square miles and a population of about 73,000. There is one urban trade center, but the way of life is largely rural and agricultural. Sugar cane is the most important crop. Like most Okinawans, the people are very receptive to applied Western technology and their attitudes toward health programs are favorable.

The mechanics of filariasis eradication are virtually identical to those of malaria. In both cases the attack is a dual one aimed at identifying and treating human cases while spraying each home with residual insecticide to reduce the mosquito population. Yet the conquest of malaria required fifteen years of more or less constant effort. In contrast, the prevalence of filariasis was reduced from 19% to less than 3% in fifteen months.

There are many possible reasons for the rapid success of the filariasis program. Fifteen years of prior experience with the methodology is certainly an important consideration. The extensive use of Okinawan instead of American personnel, better organization, more money, an effective drug, and less mosquito resistance to insecticides are only a partial list of the many factors which played an important role. Yet in the final analysis, the great limiting factor in any mass campaign is its ability to reach the target population, i.e., popular support of and cooperation with the program. It was this consideration, more than any other, which distinguished the filariasis program. Ninety-nine per cent of the population volunteered for examination and the cooperation with home spraying was 100%. More than 90% of those tested to be positive for the filarial parasite completed the prescribed course of therapy, and 82% were cured (Marshall and Yasukawa, 1966). When I left the Ryukyus in June of 1967, examination figures were still over 99% and the prevalence of filariasis had fallen to about 1%.

Those of us who worked in this program were amazed at its success. The actual reasons for its remarkable popular acceptance remain a mystery, and no specific research into this question has been carried out. For this reason, it must be kept in mind that the proposed explanation which follows, while perhaps correct, remains speculative.

Unlike any other disease vulnerable to mass campaign attack, filariasis requires that people be examined at night. The reason for this is a peculiar property of the parasite; it is nocturnally periodic and disappears from the bloodstream by day. Given the rural, semi-isolated setting of the program, the nocturnal habits of the parasite proved to be a boon rather than a burden.

Life in Miyako tends to be cyclic, and these cycles are dictated by the process of sugar-cane cultivation. Life is busy and difficult during planting and harvesting and quite dull during the growing season. The population lives in ninety-two separate villages, and social contacts are minimal except during the six-month growing period. The eradication program began at the beginning of the harvest season and, while it was recognized that evening examinations were perhaps preferable in view of the family's total immersion in the daytime harvesting work, there was, nevertheless, great concern about the view the farmer and his family would take to leaving their home after a hard day and submitting to an unpleasant procedure such as bloodletting. In fact, the farmers and their families were delighted and, as we have already seen, highly receptive.

The examination sessions became social occasions, furnishing a legitimate excuse for what turned out to be a series of parties. Women prepared food; children brought toys; men brought alcohol; and in general everyone seemed to immensely enjoy these sessions. Unwittingly, this program filled a social vacuum at a difficult and dreary time of year. By this manipulation of the social ecosystem, those of us whose main concern was the collection of thirty cubic millimeters of blood and the distribution of diethylcarbamazine tablets had unintentionally built a specific, tangible reward into a health program.

TRACHOMA: A PARADOX OF SANITATION

Trachoma is an infectious disease of the eyes which, in untreated cases, can lead to permanent blindness. It is caused by a virus and is thought to spread from man to man either by direct contact or indirectly by way of water, towels, or even clothing. It is widely considered to be one of several diseases whose prevalence is inversely related to the degree of personal hygiene and to the level of general community sanita-

tion. Trachoma has virtually disappeared from the Western world, with the exception of those groups whose living standards are far below the norm, such as American Indians in the southwestern United States.

Generally the Ryukyus fall into a similar pattern. In areas with treated water, adequate waste disposal, and generally higher living standards, trachoma prevalence is relatively low. In contrast, 40% or more of the people suffer from this disease in areas with no water supply and low standards of community and personal hygiene (Marshall, 1968).

In view of the strong association between trachoma and sanitation, one of the more curious aspects of this disease in the Ryukyus is the strong possibility that the insistence on personal hygiene in the schools actually facilitates the transmission of trachoma from child to child. This process is related to different patterns of water use in certain areas, and these patterns in turn depend on the local availability of water.

People living in areas without piped water must rely on wells often located some distance from the home. Because the water collection is laborious, residents of such areas usually build rain catchments attached to the home and depend on this water as their primary source of supply. Yet it is an uncertain source, especially in summer. For this reason, water is very carefully preserved. Well water is also preserved because its collection is laborious. In both cases, circumstances dictate that the whole family use a single bowl of water for bathing purposes. Because of dirty bath water, trachoma virus is easily passed from one family member to another. It is fairly accurate to say that hygienic bathing under existing conditions is impractical and that one of the prime determinants in trachoma transmission is the scarcity of water in these areas.

Most Okinawans, however, now enjoy a piped-in water supply. These people are usually located in urban areas where prevailing standards of sanitation are usually higher than those in rural areas. Residents of cities rarely share bath water because water is plentiful and collected without effort. In these areas, the transmission of trachoma most probably occurs primarily in the school system, where the factor of personal hygiene takes its bizarre twist. All school children receive a hot lunch in the Ryukyus, and in water-scarce areas stringent standards of personel hygiene are not demanded of the children before eating. In water-rich areas, however, each child must wash his hands and face and be inspected by the teacher before he is allowed to eat. This hand-washing process takes place at long, multi-fauceted troughs capable of accommodating a dozen or more children at a time. But while the schools insist on this procedure, they lack the funds to provide individual paper towels for drying the hands and face. Usually one or two children volunteer the use of their handkerchief, and I have seen one handkerchief used to dry the hands and faces of ten children. Thus it is almost certain that trachoma is transmitted from child to child in this manner. What is at fault here is not bathing per se, but the inability of the schools to provide the means of completing the process in a sanitary manner. Like white rice in Asia and bottle-fed babies in Africa, hand-washing in the Ryukyus represents a superficial acceptance of something considered modern. But new dietary protein sources in Asia, adequate refrigeration in Africa, and paper towels in the Ryukyus are missing, and their lack negates whatever benefits these procedures may offer. Modernization itself is a system which depends not only on pure water and personal hygiene but on the existence of a governmental framework capable of maximizing rather than undermining the effects of improved hydrology and personal hygiene. In this case, we are dealing with an item as mundane as a

paper towel, yet its absence in this context proved to be a crucial determinant in the transmission of a serious disease. The manipulation of the environment through an improved water supply was accompanied by an incomplete and therefore inadequate alteration in man himself.

DYSENTERY: THE PROTECTIVE EFFECTS OF OLD HABITS

Kin Son (Son means "county") is a semi-rural area in northern Okinawa whose population is increasingly shifting toward a preponderance of children and old people as the young adults migrate to the cities. In July of 1966, Kin was the scene of an extensive outbreak of dysentery. Like so many health problems in the Ryukyus and developing countries generally, this one involved water. It also involved a selective attack pattern because all of the more than four hundred reputed cases were children or young adults. Bacillary dysentery is a very common problem in the Ryukyus, and this outbreak more or less followed the general pattern in that cases were mild, no deaths occurred, and the disease was waterborne. While dysentery symptoms usually predominate in young people, the total lack of cases among older people in Kin was quite peculiar, and for several days this curious distribution impeded the epidemiologic investigation.

The village affected is on a large hill with houses built up along its sides and at the top. At the base of the hill, an underground spring reaches the surface, and this spring has been used as the community water source for centuries. Until quite recently, the collection of water for home use was most difficult, involving a trip down the hill to the spring and the long trek back up with several heavy buckets filled with water. Women were required to go to the spring to wash clothes. Here again we are dealing with a situation in which water becomes quite a precious commodity. Water was rarely consumed raw, probably because of its value. It was almost always served as tea. Of course, tea is served hot and the brewing process requires several hours of boiling and simmering before drinking. In all likelihood, this habitual heating of water for long periods tended to protect the residents from many a water-borne pathogen; this benefit may indeed be the original reason for drinking tea since it makes hot water potable.

In 1964, the ancient water source was converted into a simple water system. A pump was installed which drove the water through a pipeline to a large storage tank at the top of the hill. From this tank, water was piped by gravity flow to individual homes. At the bottom of the hill provision was made to divert some of the water into two concrete-lined enclosures, one for washing clothes and the other for swimming. An important result of these changes was a rapid change in the community attitude toward water. Suddenly it was accessible without effort, and it existed in such abundance that the villagers could now enjoy the luxury of a swimming pool. Although the water was supposed to be chlorinated, this was rarely done by village officials; at the time of the outbreak the chlorinating apparatus had not been used for six months. The hill itself was largely porous coral rock, and any contaminants such as human fecal matter readily found their way into the spring below. The stage was set for an outbreak of water-borne disease, but it should be remembered that this same stage had been set for centuries. The changes of 1964 made the water easier to obtain but did nothing to change its quality for, as we have seen, the chlorinator was rarely, if ever, used. Yet what seemed to trigger the outbreak was a change in the way water was consumed.

With a new water system, younger adults abandoned the use of tea and began to drink water directly from the tap. The decline of tea drinking is general in the Ryukyus as this ancient drink yields increasingly to a formidable modern rival, Coca-Cola. At Kin, children emulated their parents and, in the two years between the construction of the water system and the dysentery outbreak, tea was preferred only by the old people who continued to drink it out of long habit. And so it was that the distribution of dysentery was largely restricted to children and young adults.

In this case, the outbreak of disease might have been averted in one of two ways. The people would have been protected if they had continued the old tea-drinking habit. Of course, they would have been equally well protected if the chlorinator were used properly. In the earlier case of trachoma, the problem was created by a complete environmental change (treated, piped water) accompanied by an incomplete, inadequate human response (hand-washing but no towels). In the dysentery example, the problem is the reverse, for the environmental change was only partial (no chlorination) while the change in human habits for a large segment of the population was total.

TUBERCULOSIS: THE INADEQUATE INSTITUTIONAL RESPONSE

Health officials in the Ryukyus are increasingly called upon to deal with a new array of chronic illnesses such as heart disease and cancer, even though their entire previous experience had been in the area of acute, communicable diseases such as malaria, filariasis, trachoma, and dysentery. As these "tropical" diseases become less important, the entire emphasis of health delivery and medical care must be shifted from mass campaigns against epidemics to the creation of a system for the long-term care of people whose disease can be managed but never cured. Unlike filariasis or malaria, cancer or diabetes has no eradication program. In a very real sense, applied medical technology finds that its great successes against communicable diseases lead to a confrontation with chronic illness against which a totally new technology, backed up by a totally new organizational framework, must be applied. Yet meeting this challenge is a difficult process which represents a major crisis in health care.

At the root of this crisis lies the continuing commitment of the health care system to an orientation toward communicable disease which becomes less and less relevant as chronic illnesses become increasingly important. To a greater or lesser degree, fighting communicable diseases involves mass campaigns and relatively short-term patient contact with an emphasis on a diagnostic and therapeutic blitzkrieg. The focus is on the disease rather than on the system of medical care delivery because the latter is designed to accommodate the peculiarities of the former. Thus there is no general health care system. Instead there are multiple systems, one for malaria, one for filariasis, one for water-borne disease, one for trachoma. Because each system exists only as long as the particular disease remains under attack and because the mass campaign methodology tends to overshadow more routine functions of health departments, opportunities for the development of a viable general delivery system are lacking. For these reasons, the Ryukyus now face the chronic disease challenge without a realistic system of health services delivery and, what is more important, little appreciation of the need for one.

Tuberculosis serves as an excellent example of the application of mass campaign techniques to a disease which is only partly susceptible to this methodology. Tuberculosis is without question the major communicable disease problem in the Ryukyus. It is the most common cause of death from communicable diseases, and a major cause of economic embarrassment both to the government and to individual families. Eighty per cent of the working time of the 162 public health nurses is devoted to TB, and it is the single great preoccupation of the six regional health centers. Tuberculosis control is an open-ended mass campaign which began in 1952 with the inauguration of a case-finding program relying primarily on Mantoux testing. Between 1960 and 1965, for example, 1,877,000 skin tests and 675,000 chest films were administered to persons of all ages and occupations. Since 1965 almost one-half of the population (about 430,000) has been skin-tested each year. While the prevalence of positive reactors of Mantoux testing has declined steadily, the 8.2% positive rate among fourteen-year-old children is far greater than the W.H.O. target of less than 1% (W.H.O., 1964). Furthermore, there is no reason to believe that the goal will ever be achieved under the present control program. As a result of this massive case-finding effort, an average of 2500 new cases are identified each year. While this is a successful mass case-finding campaign, it raises the important question of what should be done once the disease is uncovered, for TB, unlike many other communicable diseases, does not yield to a short-term therapeutic blitz.

Here the mass campaign approach breaks down. Each year 2500 new cases of TB are fed into a medical care system which is not, in fact, a system at all. It is much like pouring water into a container with a hole in the bottom—most of the water immediately leaks out. The basic problem is, of course, the hole, and what is needed is a new container, not more water. In 1966, 41% of the 904 available general hospital beds were given over to tuberculosis, and 700 additional beds were available in the three tuberculosis hospitals. One thousand more patients were hospitalized in Japan. The remaining 11,000 to 12,000 patients were part of the home care program which is administered by the 162 public health nurses mentioned above.

The cost of treatment for tuberculosis (i.e., hospitalization and drug therapy) is borne by the government and in 1966 came to about $1.25 per capita per day, an amount considered high for Asia. Hospitalized patients receive an allowance to provide for their families during the period of incapacitation. Patients on home care, even though their working is limited by law and often by physical impairment, receive no compensation except for the cost of drugs. It is not unusual, therefore, for home care patients to move from one village to another in search of work. This is quite expedient because, if the move takes the individual out of the jurisdiction of the regional health center to whom he is known, he drops out of the home care system. Because each regional health center is completely independent, there is no central record system for tuberculosis. The same is true for hospitals, and a patient discharged from one institution is free to seek hospitalization at another; no record will follow him. Since hospitalization assures a family subsidy, the rotation of individual patients from hospital to hospital is not uncommon. Both the patients who move to a new locale and those who move from hospital to hospital are quite likely to turn up as a "newly diagnosed case," the former through compulsory examination at his new job and the latter simply by presenting himself for examination at a second or third or fourth hospital. It is estimated that perhaps 25% of all "new" cases are actually renegade patients previously diagnosed. Thus incidence cannot be distinguished from prevalence, and the true status of this disease remains uncertain even after sixteen years of intensive mass case-finding.

To make matters worse, hospitals tend to select only those persons whose disease may be amenable to surgical intervention. This practice varies somewhat among the eight hospitals providing TB care because, like the health centers, each is entirely independent of the others with respect to admission practices, diagnostic procedures, therapeutic regimens, and record keeping. Generally speaking, however, chronic excretors of tubercle bacilli with extensive lesions are not admitted, and no institution exists for the isolation of such patients. These people are placed on home care along with the less serious cases, and, as we have seen, they may or may not stay in the program. As we have also seen, seriously ill patients often attempt to secure hospitalization at another institution to insure the security of their families while those who are more or less asymptomatic often move to another jurisdiction to find work. Six months is the maximum period of hospitalization in all eight hospitals and patients at various stages of arrest are automatically released at the end of this period to make room for new patients. These discharged patients also end up on home care.

Meanwhile, the home care system is about to completely collapse because the size of the nursing staff has remained constant while the patient load has greatly increased. Nursing is losing ground in the Ryukyus because new fields are now open to women and because nurses are underpaid and have very little status in the eyes of the general public and the health care hierarchy. It is not unusual for a single nurse to be responsible for as many as one hundred patients over a wide area. There is no transportation provided for the nurse who is nevertheless expected to visit each patient once every four to eight weeks in addition to her other duties, one of which is the never-ending case-finding campaign. She is also called upon to involve herself in mass campaigns to immunize school children against the usual diseases—recently the "usual" list has included the use of BCG (tuberculosis vaccine)—and to do contact-tracing for venereal disease control. There is also a growing leprosy home care program for which she is responsible. Few nurses, if any, are able to devote their full time to TB.[2]

Such is the state of tuberculosis control in the Ryukyus. It is perhaps supreme irony that much of this situation is caused by a very successful mass case-finding program. Yet this approach cannot solve the medical care problem inherent in TB therapy, and it is largely the failure to deal with this problem which undermines the best efforts of the mass campaign to accurately define the incidence and prevalence of the target disease. It is unfortunate that the very success of mass campaigns against some diseases tends to suggest the same approach to diseases like TB which are only partially susceptible to this technique. Ultimately, the control of TB is a problem in chronic disease care which requires a highly sophisticated organizational framework which considers not only the disease but also the people needing care, the providers of care, and the institutions for care. These considerations must all be coordinated on a permanent basis yet retain the flexibility required to change the system as new needs arise.

The present tuberculosis program is plagued by overloaded facilities, a growing manpower deficit in home care, an unrealistic system for the support of patients and their families, a decentralized, uncoordinated network of hospitals and health centers, and little apparent concern about the release of chronic active cases into the community. None of these problems applies to those communicable diseases susceptible to

mass campaign methods. Long-term medical care facilities have no real place in the mass campaign, and because vast resources are diverted into mass campaigns, the entire hospital system tends to remain anemic and underdeveloped. At the same time, skilled manpower deficits are not of primary concern as the emphasis is on the use of unskilled workers who can be trained on the job. The system of family support which places what amounts to a 100% tax on home care patients is of little relevance in the era of rapid cure without long-term patient involvement. The decentralized, autonomous network of regional health centers springs naturally from the strong tradition of localism. Also, enormous efforts such as malaria or filariasis eradication, while highly centralized in themselves, operate as programs entirely outside the jurisdiction of regional centers. To these centers fall the less exciting, lower-priority tasks of putting down "brush-fire" outbreaks of dysentery, immunizing the local children, and sporadically attempting to convince the local people to abandon the use of night soil. Jobs of this kind are best done through a decentralized system because each center is responsive primarily to local problems.

Unfortunately, the prevailing tendency has been to regard the morass of tuberculosis control as the failure of individual, independent entities—too few hospital beds, not enough nurses, uncooperative home care patients, etc.—when what is involved is an inadequate system of care. Curiously enough, there is very little concern about the economic penalties imposed upon home care patients because home care is regarded as a welfare rather than a health problem. Yet this economic penalty is a major reason for the failure of the home care program. A failure to appreciate the importance of welfare legislation is characteristic of a disease-specific outlook. Indeed, the health establishment is so indifferent to this problem that the national health in-

[2] For a more detailed description of the tuberculosis program in the Ryukyus, see J. C. Tao, Report on a Field Visit to the Ryukyu Islands, W.H.O. document W PR/TB/FR/25, 28 May, 1962. It is unpublished but available from the W.H.O. Regional Office for the Western Pacific, United Nations Avenue, Manila, Philippines.

surance scheme was drawn up by the labor department with minimal assistance from the health department.

Interestingly enough, the present program represents an attempt to integrate tuberculosis control into general health services as recommended by the World Health Organization (W.H.O., 1964). But neither the general health services nor the TB control program is organized to cope with the chronic aspects of this disease. For this reason, integration has simply superimposed a mass campaign requiring centralized administration on a network of decentralized regional health centers whose administration is locally autonomous. Thus the very process of integration has confounded the situation and produced a hybrid program in which the mass case-finding component is continuously negated by a fragmented system of patient care. The very nature of tuberculosis and of chronic diseases in general requires a medical care system which is centralized, countrywide, and permanent. The Ryukyus, in contrast, enter an era of chronic diseases with a system which is decentralized, regional, and sporadic.

The limitations of mass campaigns have been well known for many years and have been a constant theme of the World Health Organization. Most recently, Gunnar Myrdal (1968), in his monumental work on Asian development, has re-emphasized the restricted applicability of this technological approach even in countries still burdened with great communicable disease problems. The more care people require, the more crucial become the economic, social, and legal environments in which care is provided. Health systems which cannot or will not address themselves to this widening sector of concern will find themselves increasingly irrelevant to the health care needs of the people the system is supposed to serve. Yet the health department has never requested funds to evaluate these problems. It continues, however, to request and to

spend large amounts on diseases such as Japanese encephalitis, of which there were twenty-two cases in 1967. The Labor Department has already moved into the health care field by championing the national health insurance plan, and this may well signal the beginning of more extensive involvement. The importance of all these events in the Ryukyus lies in the very real possibility that similar difficulties lie ahead for other developing areas. The incipient need for improved medical care organization and administration is perhaps the least recognized health problem of the developing world.

CONCLUSION: THE EMERGING PROBLEM OF ENVIRONMENTAL POLLUTION

Each of the examples discussed in this paper has focused on a recognized problem where man's interaction with his environment contributed to the success or failure in seeking a solution. The case of tuberculosis, which is very complex and involves virtually every facet of Okinawan social and economic life, is nevertheless essentially similar to the less complex cases discussed previously. In all cases, either man or the environment or both is altered, and the results of these changes are sometimes beneficial and sometimes harmful, depending on a wide range of determinants—social isolation, long-established habits, local traditions, or an increasingly irrelevant system of medical care delivery.

In sharp contrast to these recognized health problems is an incipient one which, at least for the moment, seems a distant menace of little immediate concern. Nevertheless, the assertion that each society creates its own health problems is to a great extent correct, and one can predict with near certainty that environmental pollution is the next great health crisis the Ryukyus will be forced to confront. The mosquito vectors of filariasis are being driven from the skies only to be replaced with smoke and gases from new industry. The chronic water supply problem will add a new and quite different dimension as the few remaining dysentery organisms are either destroyed by chemical wastes or floated away in a sea of detergent.

If the experience of the industrial countries can be used as a guide, coping with pollution problems will prove extraordinarily difficult in the Ryukyus. Tuberculosis control has been difficult because this control demands a change in the ecosystem involving health care delivery and the broader social system. Nevertheless, tuberculosis is a specific disease entity and although its control is quite difficult, it does not present itself as an unsolvable problem.

Environmental pollution, on the other hand, is quite unlike anything which preceded it. Air and water pollution are not diseases; they are terms used to describe an environmental situation. Furthermore, epidemiologic studies to confirm the association between disease and, let us say, air pollution are very difficult to carry out because exposure is hard to quantify. Yet such studies are crucial in an area which finds itself totally committed to economic development through industrialization, where costly pollution control devices are not likely to enjoy wide popularity.

Presently there is little interest in pollution within Okinawan governmental circles. Lay officials are only dimly aware of it and health officials are overwhelmingly oriented to communicable disease control through tried and true methods. Thus, an objective assessment of this problem has never been carried out. This should not come as a surprise if one considers that virtually nothing specific to the Ryukyus is known about the epidemiology of the four leading causes of death and relatively little of the fifth,

tuberculosis. A health care system slow to adjust itself to the widening role demanded by the chronic diseases is unlikely to respond readily to the still wider dimensions of environmental pollution, which is not only biological, social, and economic but very political as well. It is perhaps the supreme irony that the Okinawan health system, floundering and inadequate as it now seems, finds itself in this situation largely because of its past victories. Thus it is victimized by its own success. Called into existence to cope with the communicable disease and sanitation problems of a developing country, the health system has remained unchanged in outlook and methodology even though its society has entered the industrial era and is no longer underdeveloped.

It is very difficult in a paper of this kind to avoid what might be interpreted as criticism of the Ryukyus and of its health officials. However, criticism is not my intent. The Okinawan people in two decades have transformed a poor, infertile country devastated by war into a dynamic economy with a standard of living in their part of the world second only to Japan. The communicable disease and population problems which plague other developing countries are rapidly receding in the Ryukyus, and although the Okinawans have received assistance from both the United States and Japan, this fact need not detract at all from what must be considered a great achievement. Few people have accomplished as much with foreign aid as the Okinawans. If, therefore, we now find the Ryukyus somewhat slow in responding to new problems such as chronic diseases and industrial pollution of air and water, we should be neither surprised nor critical. Those of us who might be inclined to criticism need only consider the present status of these problems in the United States. Our own efforts have been equally slow and our own errors equally apparent.

Rather than criticize, this paper, by using

examples from the health field, seeks to point out that a community's problems represent the disturbance of an ecosystem and that, if studied properly, the lessons from one part of the developing world may be applied to other areas to avoid endless repetition of the same mistakes. Once it is

appreciated that each challenge met creates or unmasks still new challenges, those of us who are concerned with the process of international development (i.e., "modernization") should begin to widen our focus to include not only existing problems but also the new problems created by our solutions.

REFERENCES

Black, C. E., *The Dynamics of Modernization.* New York: Harper and Row, 1966, pp. 26–34.

Latham, M., *Human Nutrition in Tropical Africa.* Rome: Food and Agriculture Organization of the United Nations, 1965, pp. 11–20.

Marshall, C. L., "The Relationship Between Trachoma and Piped Water in a Developing Area." *Arch. of Environ. Health*, 17:8 (August, 1968), 215–20.

Marshall, C. L., and Yasukawa, K., "Control of Bancroftian Filariasis in the Ryukyu Islands: Preliminary Results of Mass Administration of Diethylcarbamazine." *Amer. J. Trop. Med. and Hyg.*, 15:6, Pt. 1 (November, 1966), pp. 934–42.

Myrdal, Gunnar. *Asian Drama*, Vol. III. New York: Pantheon Books, 1968, pp. 1575–76.

W.H.O. Expert Committee on Tuberculosis. *W.H.O. Techn. Report Ser.* No. 290. Geneva, 1964, 24 pp.

2. INFLUENCE OF ENVIRONMENTAL TRANSFORMATION IN CHANGING THE MAP OF DISEASE

Jacques M. May

The transformation of the environment is the major factor modifying the relationships of all the possible stimuli with which man has to contend in order to survive. Any discussion of disease as an alteration of living cells or tissues which jeopardizes their survival in the environment, must be based upon the global system of what we know of environmental stimuli and man's adjustment to these stimuli.

The data we have concerning the relationships between the malaria parasite, its two hosts, man and mosquito, and the environment in which these hosts live together illustrate clearly the three aspects of environmental stimuli—physical, biological, and cultural—which modify the dominance of this parasite and any other of the vast number of stimuli with which man has to contend. There are many gaps in our knowledge about the nature of these three factors and their intricate interrelationships with changing disease dominance.

In the diseases of man, the cultural factor is crucial, since cultural traits either bring stimulus and host together or erect barriers to keep them apart. Each culture brings about its own set of diseases. We should try to recognize the birth of new stimuli to disease, the changes that occur among dominance patterns of agents and vectors, and the changes in the maps of immunities and susceptibilities. With this wide perspective, we must assess the development programs that we so liberally and often so foolishly encourage throughout the world. Widespread changes in the habitat will bring about changes in the map of disease and challenges to human adaptation which could in some instances be impossible to manage. For example, the manipulation of the environmental complex in Southeast Asia by means of drugs for parasite control and insecticides for control of the vector, has created a serious situation. Mosquito resistance to insecticides on the one hand, and parasite resistance to chemotherapeutic agents on the other, have caused an apparently insurmountable dilemma. There are large areas in Southeast Asia where any military force entering the area will almost certainly contract *Plasmodium falciparum* malaria at infection rates approaching 100%.

The study of all the environmental factors we have mentioned and their mapping on an area basis form the structure of global epidemiology. As the map of disease changes, we must study all the stimuli discussed above and then study all the factors that govern responses from the host.

I

The topic first suggested for my contribution to this conference was "Influence of Environmental Transformation in Promoting Dominance of *Plasmodium falciparum*." This subject is intriguing, and I gave it much thought, having all my life wondered about the way natural forces compete or conjoin to create the global picture of living things or dying things we observe and are part of.

Dominance is an ecological term that indicates the greater importance of one species of a living thing in a given habitat. *Plasmodium falciparum,* the parasite responsible (in part) for the most severe form of malaria, has two habitats: the blood and hematopoietic (blood cell producing) organs of man; and the digestive and, as far as we know, the connective tissue of certain species and strains of anopheline mosquitoes. Since the mosquito is the definitive host of *P. falciparum* and man the intermediate one, we must discuss not only factors affecting the ecology of *P. falciparum* as it relates to other parasites competing for dominance in the human economy, but also the ecology of competitive strains of anopheline mosquitoes which might ingest *P. falciparum* during a blood meal (Fig. 2–1).

PLASMODIUM-RELATED FACTORS

These two facets of the assignment were, of course, of fascinating interest. They raised problems of considerable obscurity, such as, What are the needs of *P. falciparum* for survival in the mammal economy? While some facts are known on the subject, the relationship with other parasites competing for dominance has been little explored. It is known that *P. falciparum* synthesizes its proteins from the amino acids of the erythrocytes of the host. It is also known that a certain degree of immunity or rather imperviousness to *P. falciparum* exists among people endowed with Hemoglobin S (sickle-cell anemia) (Allison, 1954). Undoubtedly, an essential requirement of *P. falciparum* is absent from the erythrocytes of these people.

In all likelihood, other chemical or biophysical properties are required for *P. falciparum* survival in human blood. Is it possible that there are normal or near-normal components of the human erythrocytes that might either hinder or assist its survival and development in the human cycle of the parasite? Could competition in the biotic world of the "internal milieu" result in arresting the development of *P. falciparum?* We have no evidence of such competition and the attempts made to treat malaria due to *P. falciparum* with the better-known antibiotics have given no indication that these drugs influence the survival of the parasite. We know, of course, that certain chemicals are effective in doing this, and form the basis of the eminently successful chemotherapy of malaria. But there is surely more

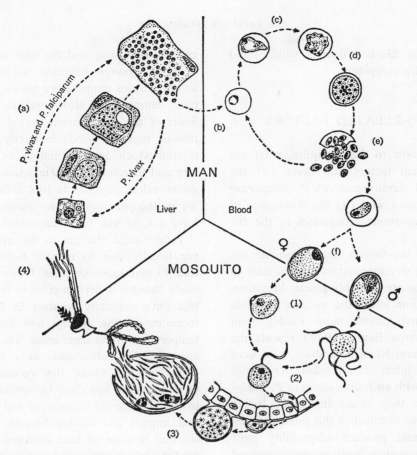

Figure 2–1   LIFE CYCLE OF MALARIA PARASITE   *P. falciparum cycle* (simplified)

Anopheline Sexual Phase

1. The mosquito picks up blood containing a mature "gametocyte" (sexual form of the parasite).

2. In the stomach of the mosquito fecundation takes place.

3. An "egg" (oocyst) is formed and grows in the wall of the mosquito's stomach.

4. At maturity the "egg" hatches, freeing several hundred motile individuals (sporozoites) that migrate through the tissues of the mosquito. Eventually some of them reach the salivary glands of the insect ready to be injected into a new host.

Human Asexual Phase

a. The injected parasite reaches the liver or spleen of man and multiplies there by division (schizogony).

b. The new form resulting from the schizogony (merozoite) returns to the bloodstream and invades the red cells.

c. The merozoite grows inside the red cell to an active, motile, full-grown parasite (trophozoite).

d. This subdivides successively until it fills the red blood cell with merozoites.

e. The red blood cell explodes, the merozoites are let loose into the bloodstream, other red cells are invaded.

f. At one point, the parasite in the red cell grows into a mature gametocyte (male or female) which is picked up by an anopheline mosquito.

Drawing from: Richard Fiennes, *Man, Nature and Disease* (London: Weidenfeld and Nicolson, 1964).

to learn and this is a field in which I did not feel fully competent.

MOSQUITO-RELATED FACTORS

Turning now to the mosquito, what are the ecological factors that favor (a) the growth and development of *P. falciparum* in the mosquito, and (b) the dominance of *P. falciparum*-prone mosquitoes in the environment?

Some of the factors that determine the growth and development of the parasite in the mosquito are probably genetic in nature. Certain strains infect the vectors available in their environment more readily than others. Marston Bates (1949) reports the work of James, Nicol, and Shute, who were unable to infect an English *Anopheles atroparvus* with an Italian strain of *P. falciparum* while they could infect an Italian strain. The mechanism of this mosquito susceptibility and parasite adaptability must have genotypical as well as environmental cases. Conversely, mosquito species vary in their susceptibility to strains of parasites; susceptibility to *P. falciparum* seems also to be related to genetic factors (Bates, 1949). Bates also states (p. 236) that as far as he is aware, "there is no evidence that the cycle with a given strain of *Plasmodium* varies with the species of mosquito host."

However, authors agree that the most important factor governing the development of *P. falciparum* inside the mosquito is environmental temperature. Very high or very low temperatures prevent the establishment of mosquito infectiousness. The local temperature governs the time required for the mosquito to become infective after its blood and plasmodial meal. This relationship to temperature explains the predominance of *P. vivax* and *P. malariae* in the Temperate Zone and that of *P. falciparum* in the tropical belt. It may also explain the earlier occurrence of *P. vivax* and *P. malariae*

cases in the spring and the later appearance of *P. falciparum* infection in summer or autumn. Since temperature varies with altitude, temperature also regulates the time limits of the transmission period in mountainous regions. Winds indirectly influence rainfall which, in turn, influences temperature and therefore affects infectiousness. No doubt other physical factors influence the life of the parasites in the vector but these have not, as yet, been discovered.

Temperature changes in the environment are usually due to natural factors rather than to man-made changes. However, manmade changes in certain cities in the tropical belt have definitely resulted in the transformation of the average and extremes of temperature in the same areas. The phenomenon is easily observable in a metropolis like Bangkok, where the maximum level of temperature has risen by several degrees in the last decade because of tall buildings that impede the cooling breezes from the sea and because of heat reflected from extended asphalt surfaces. Concurrently, however, the filling of the marshes and klongs has reduced the chances for mosquito breeding, making it difficult to assess the respective importance of these coincidental factors in modifying *Plasmodium* dominance.

Environmental factors influence the parasites through the physiology of the mosquito vector and its survival rather than through influence on the parasite itself. For instance, the relative humidity of the environment influences the survival of the mosquito to a great extent but seems to have no effect on the parasite inside the mosquito host. The survival of the mosquito is then the key to *Plasmodium* dominance and obscures the *Plasmodium*-related factors which, however, combine to create the range between high and low endemicity.

Given this close relationship between *Plasmodium* dominance and mosquito survival, the study of environmental changes that can influence the map of plasmodia through the map of mosquitoes is the most rewarding. Mosquitoes, like men, are concerned with food, breeding, and shelter, but as with men, their tastes differ. They can feed on human or animal blood or both. All mosquitoes require water for breeding, but it can be clear or turbid, sunlit or shaded, running or stagnant, warm or cold, salty or fresh, acid or alkaline. At certain hours mosquitoes seek shelter. Some prefer to dwell indoors, others outdoors. Some cruise high under the canopy of the forest, others low above the ground. Rainfall and temperature, as well as the topography of the soil, combine to create situations in which mosquitoes either multiply or stop breeding. Heavy downpours increase occurrence of malaria throughout the tropics because of the multiple breeding sites they create, but droughts in the equatorial tropics also increase occurrence because small depressions hold accumulations of stagnant water that favor the breeding of certain species. Rainfall under certain circumstances promotes the growth of plants such as bamboos or epiphytes (e.g., bromeliads) whose physical structures create water receptacles where physical and chemical conditions favor certain species of vectors. Temperature influences the mosquito, and breeding does not occur unless the temperature is appropriate.

Winds may help or hinder the flights of the mosquito vector. Some vectors, such as *Anopheles pharoensis,* have been known to fly more than twenty miles across the desert. In certain parts of the Trobriand Islands of the South Pacific, the transmission season corresponds to the periods of northwest winds (Black, 1952). Localities of the south, being more sheltered than those in the north, have less malaria, which implies that if a house or a village or a city is built away from the flight path of the mosquitoes, chances of malaria epidemics are lessened. If, on the contrary, these factors are not taken into consideration and the village, city,

factory, or camp is erected within the flight path of the mosquitoes, the change in the environment will be accompanied by an increased malaria transmission. The requirements of *P. falciparum*-susceptible strains of mosquitoes vary both with the larva and with the adult.

Because the requirements of the larva are more limited than those of the adult, the dominance of *P. falciparum* will also be limited by the spectrum of environmental factors which govern larval survival. The larvae of all known species need water and oxygen for survival. They almost always confine their habitats to the upper layers of the bodies of water they occupy whence they can get at the air. It is interesting to note that no breeding occurs on open waters. The breeding places of the effective vector *Anopheles gambiae melas* are almost entirely confined to parts of the coastal swamps flooded by high spring tides and characterized by the presence of *Avicennia* mangroves and wide stretches of coarse marsh grass, *Paspalum vaginatum* (May, 1961). Any new transformation of the environment that would make this vegetation unavailable or modify the current of the spring tides might well have an influence on the breeding of *A. gambiae melas* and hence on the predominance of *P. falciparum*.

The characteristics of the water and possibly of the air above the surface, especially in terms of temperature and chemical composition, govern the presence or absence of mosquito larvae. The temperature of the waters is related, for the most part, to climatic conditions that seem permanently established, but the settlement of man can transform the temperature of waters. Should a factory be established in the vicinity of breeding sites, the temperature of the waters enriched by sewage of all kinds will change. The larval habitat may become uninhabitable both because of temperature changes and chemical transformation through industrial waste and pollution. *Anopheles quad-*

rimaculatus has been found to disappear from certain areas where nascent industry has brought about that kind of change (Bates, 1949). It has also been found that the degree of light and shade influences the breedings of *Anopheles albimanus*. It also influences the adult form of the vector *A. funestus,* which enters houses after midnight, especially during moonlight (WHO, 1951). Since light seems to be essential to survival of these larvae, it has been recommended that trees be planted in order to control breeding. Other species (e.g., *A. darlingi*) prefer shade, but it is difficult to identify whether this factor acts upon the larva itself or upon the organic life in the medium on which the larva feeds. The movements of the waters also influence the species prevailing in an environment; modifying the dynamism of a stream—either by slowing it down above a dam or accelerating it below—may favor the growth of a larval type. Yet, most anophelines prefer still water to running water for their breeding.

Since the larva usually breathes the air from the surface, it is to be expected that access to the surface must be unhindered; hence, the surface tension modified by artificial (oil spreads) or natural (pollen, leaves) factors will also govern the dominance of certain anopheline species and the plasmodium most adapted to each strain.

Opinions vary as to the importance of alkaline versus acidic composition of waters depending on the authors' locations of observation. It is not known whether, in nature, the degree of acidity directly influences the larva or the other organisms whose presence creates or negates the existence of a survival-worthy environment for the species.

The requirements of the adult mosquito should be added to those of the larva as factors governing *P. falciparum* dominance. These requirements will play an important role in qualifying a species of mosquito as an effective or weak vector of *P. falciparum*. It is interesting to note that the species that can be an effective malaria vector in one area may not be effective in another. With Russell (1952), we can list the characteristics of an effective vector as follows:

a. The mosquito must enter human dwellings and be "domestic" (example: *Anopheles minimus*).

b. The mosquito must prefer human to animal blood; in other words, it must be anthropophilic (example: *A. gambiae*).

c. The mosquito must be long-lived, since the vector must remain alive long enough to allow the sporogony (sexual phase) to take place so that the vector harbors the agent in a form transmissible to man.

d. The mosquito must possess the constitutional characteristics (genotype) that make it a desirable host for *P. falciparum*. All these characteristics of the adult mosquito are dependent upon environmental conditions, most of which may undergo transformation for many causes.

The characteristics of human dwellings that are attractive to the vector will vary with light, the composition and mobility of the air inside the house (drafts, closeness, smoke, smells, etc.), availability of resting places after the blood meal, and a multitude of home factors best known to the mosquitoes themselves. Any changes occurring in the site and characteristics of the house will influence the mosquito presence and will thus enhance or limit the effectiveness of a species in promoting *P. falciparum* dominance.

The anthropophilic tendencies of the mosquito are linked to some unknown need of the insect's physiology and to some unidentified ability to provide for the needs of the *Plasmodium*. These tendencies will make a certain anopheline species a promoter of *P. falciparum* or of some of the other three malaria agents, or of none of them.

The longevity of the mosquito depends, of course, on two orders of factors. Some are totally unknown because they are inherent to the genetic constitution of the mosquito. Others depend again on environmental circumstances such as temperature, humidity, winds, and light. A presence or absence of some lethal element—natural or artificially added to the environment by the presence of a competing animal, insect, or human—will also influence mosquito longevity.

Finally, the ecology of the human host influences to a considerable degree the dominance of *P. falciparum* in an area. It affects the chances of contact between the host and the vector. If the houses are built on the ground or on pilings, infection will depend upon the flight level of the vector. If the cooking is done indoors or outdoors, the smoke will either chase the mosquitoes away or keep them inside. The presence of animals in the vicinity or at a distance would respectively increase or diminish the risk of man being bitten.

The example of the farmers of North Vietnam is illustrative of these human factors (May, 1958). In the delta region of the Red River, these people live in one of the two or three most densely crowded areas of the world. The density of population is around nine hundred per square mile. The houses and the villages they form represent, from the point of view of construction, a compromise between the material that is available and the need to save as much soil as possible for food crops. The materials available are mud and rice straw which do not lend themselves to skyscraping architecture. Thus, there are very few two-story houses in the villages of the Red River Delta. The dwelling place usually consists of a mud bungalow with the pigsty on one side and the kitchen on the other. There are no fierce effective malaria vectors in the area.

Some sixty miles to the north, in the hills, we find a different cultural trait, also very much influenced by the physical environment. In these hills lumber is abundant but there is little rice straw and mud. The people, for reasons that are not as yet fully understood, build their houses on wooden pilings which place what we would call their living room at an elevation of 4, 5, and sometimes 6 or 7 meters above the ground. In these hills, *A. minimus,* a very fierce malaria vector, abounds, its breeding enhanced by the network of mountain streams. However, it so happens that *A. minimus* does not fly much higher than 3 meters above the ground. As a result, although it is essentially a man-biting insect wherever possible, it feeds on the cattle herded under the house between the pilings because it finds them at its normal flight altitude. Furthermore, the cooking takes place in the house, not outside as in the delta. This fills the living room with smoke and chases away any stray vector.

Due to congestion of the delta, several schemes have been carried out at different times in history to try to relocate delta people in the hills. These people carried their culture to the new location and started to live at ground level, to cook outside the house and to shelter their pigs away from the dwellings. The results have been disastrous. Malaria epidemics decimated the newcomers, and the reputation of the hilly regions among the lowland dwellers is that it is full of evil spirits and that no man of the delta should ever go to the hills—a belief which is, given the above circumstances, essentially correct!

The type of agriculture also has an effect. In rice cultivation, seeds sown by broadcasting require a longer period of irrigation than do transplanted nursery shoots. This longer period of irrigation and the resulting transformation of the environment increases malaria transmission and the predominance of *P. falciparum* in the tropical belt.

The habit of watching the crops at night, to guard against thieves (as in Turkey), birds (as in Liberia), or just to be on the spot for work the next day (as in

Madagascar, Sarawak, and many other places), also influences the chances of being bitten and of spreading the dominance of *P. falciparum* (May, 1961). The type of walls used in house building, mud or bamboo, rough or smooth, influences the efficiency of DDT house-spraying, as does the habit of washing the walls with lime or frequently replastering them. Finally, and perhaps more than anything else, economics, implying various levels of ability to train public health workers, to practice sanitation, to sleep under mosquito nets permanently, and to understand the value of prophylactic measures, combine with the other factors listed to create a suitable habitat for *P. falciparum.*

In the light of the above, it seems that the dominance of *P. falciparum* in a given environment is dependent upon a number of factors: parasite-related, vector-related, and man-related. In addition, the environment is in constant change, both as a result of natural causes and as a result of man's actions.

Under the constant changes of the environment, from those involving the minute amount of organic matter in the water that makes the life of a larva possible, to the erection of eighty-story buildings, the dominance of *P. falciparum* will change. Most of the significant factors governing these changes are unknown, and those that are not known are obviously the most intriguing.

This is probably the time to focus on the fact that *P. falciparum* is not one parasite but many parasites whose various strains are gradually being identified in increasing numbers by malariologists. As our knowledge of the "microbiochemistry" or "microphysiology" of living things increases, we discover that there may be as many genotypes of *P. falciparum* as there are genotypes of men. Up to 1948, the existence of drug-resistant strains of malaria parasites was not recognized and malariologists the

world over believed that the existing therapeutic armamentarium would eradicate the disease.

During the decade 1948 to 1958,[1] cases of resistance to a number of drugs hitherto believed almost 100% effective in eradicating the parasite began to appear in such widely scattered parts of the world as South America, tropical Africa, the Middle East, the South Pacific, and Southeast Asia.[2]

In 1960, the first instance of *P. falciparum* resistance to chloroquine was reported (WHO, 1965). In 1962, a British Commonwealth unit that was operating in the jungle of north Perlis State, on the Thai-Malayan border, had 10% of its personnel affected in spite of strictly enforced malaria prophylaxis (Forbes, unpublished data). Ten cases of *P. falciparum* malaria were identified as resistant to chloroquine. The unit replacing this force suffered the same fate during the following three months.

A similar experience befell a Walter Reed Army Institute research team working in the Chonburi province of southeastern Thailand in 1963–64 (Young *et al.,* 1963).

Since that date, cases of *P. falciparum* resistance to most usually used drugs, including quinine, at commonly accepted doses, have multiplied so that there is little doubt that any military force entering certain areas of Southeast Asia will contract *P. falciparum* malaria at infection rates approaching 100%.

There is now evidence that *P. falciparum* drug-resistant strains occur, for example, among the native populations of Southeast Asia. The problem now is to find the mechanism of drug resistance and to devise a way to work around it.

That there exist various strains of *P. fal-*

[1] I am indebted to my learned friend Dr. Allan Forbes for much of the following information.
[2] Drug resistance is that property of a strain of parasites that causes it to remain unaffected by doses of a drug that would normally destroy it.

ciparum and of other parasites could have been suspected from a number of known facts. Prominent among these is the diversity of disease intensity in different areas of the world. While this diversity can be ascribed to differences in host-parasite relationship, some of it must be inherent to a difference in virulence of each strain. Yet these strains are not distinguishable from each other by their morphology or by the biological assays used.

It is also known that various strains can infect the same host; but their relationship to each other within the host's environment and the scope and area of their competition for survival from the host's resources, are not known.

It is known that a patient immune to an Indian strain of *P. falciparum* can be susceptible to a Romanian one and that the infectivity of the mosquito varies with the strain of the mosquito as well as with the strain of the parasite.

Let us not forget that, from an anthropomorphic bias, resistance to our drugs is by far the most important biological trait of the strain under study. However, there must be many other traits that, when known, will allow a broader definition and understanding of these strains and conceivably offer an opening for their destruction. These other traits determine to a large extent the geographical extension of a strain of parasite because of the parasite's affinities with its vectors and their dependence on climatic and other factors; thus all factors involved in the spread of any *Plasmodium* may be involved in the spread of a resistant strain. These factors involve the gametocyte density in the host, the vector capability for transmission, and host factors such as the possible degree of immunity.

We can hypothesize about the reasons that have caused the dominance of these strains to appear. We should remind ourselves, however, that the words "develop-

ment of drug resistance" are misleading, as they may imply that the *same* parasite individual can at one time be drug-sensitive, learn how to resist the toxic effect of a drug, and then transmit this acquired property to the next generation. There is no need for such an unorthodox hypothesis since more plausible genetic explanations are available.

We could be confronted with a recent mutation induced by drugs or by another as yet unidentified mutagenic factor resulting from an adaptive response of *P. falciparum* characterized by the formation of new enzymes in the parasite that allow it to neutralize the toxicity of our drugs. Or we could be faced with the emergence into visibility of a very ancient mutant?

A number of strains coexist in a given host, some drug-sensitive, some drug-resistant. As long as the drug-sensitive strains are more numerous, the parasite density of the resistant strains remains low and the vector feeds on the more abundant susceptible strains which he transmits to the human host. As the susceptible strains disappear under treatment, the density of resistant strains increases and the vectors in a given area transmit more and more of them. The chance of recently introduced populations becoming infected with resistant forms increases accordingly. This is quite possibly what has happened in Southeast Asia. For millennia the resistant strains were kept at a low level by the greater numbers of susceptible strains which were not treated. As populations and governments became more and more public health conscious, more and more untreated patients were diagnosed and treated, causing the susceptible strains to disappear.

In the past twenty years two important changes have modified the environment of Southeast Asia: (1) antimalarial treatments were intensified; and (2) native populations began to move from one area to another more than they ever had. In Vietnam, for instance, refugees from the north moved south; people from the coastal areas went into the hills on political missions intended to assimilate the "Moi"[3] into the Vietnamese culture. To a lesser but nevertheless significant degree, similar migrations in both directions occurred in Malaysia and Thailand. Resistant strains that might have existed as isolated pockets overstepped their limits and got mixed with susceptible strains common throughout the land. Drugs were distributed in ever greater amounts, destroying most of the susceptibles, and leaving the resistant *P. falciparum* strains without competitors and free to multiply many times.

In addition to these two hypotheses a host of unanswered questions remain concerning these fundamental problems:

1. What are the factors that have caused the mutation?
2. Could it be the chemical action of our drugs?
3. What are the mechanisms of drug action on the parasite?
4. What is the mechanism of *P. falciparum* immunity to man?
5. What are the host factors involved in this immunity?
6. Does the molecular nature of hemoglobin play a role in immunity of strains of *P. falciparum?*
7. What are the natural enemies of certain *P. falciparum?* Are some of them innocuous to man and is there a future in the biotherapy of malaria?

The list of questions could be extended indefinitely. The problem remains: For each resistant strain of the parasite, what is the minimal lethal dose of the drug or of the biotic that will destroy it while remaining harmless to the host?

The solution to these problems will necessitate a deep understanding of the body

[3] Vietnamese word meaning "savages." Americans in Vietnam call them "Montagnards."

composition of the parasite and of its physiology as well as the screening of countless new substances or compounds. By 1966, sixty thousand new components had been synthesized and U. S. Army research proposals in biology and chemistry amounted to more than thirty million dollars (Forbes, unpublished data).

II

After reviewing the data available I felt compelled to enlarge my topic. The transformation of the environment modifies not only the dominance of one man-oriented lethal parasite but of all possible stimuli with which man has to contend to survive. Thus, I felt compelled to relate my observations to the global system of man's adjustment to the environment.

Before analyzing the phenomenon described as the "map of diseases," it may be good to define once more what we call "disease." It is surprising how many students of medicine limit their concept of disease to "the opposite of health." I suggest that what we call disease *is that alteration of living cells or tissues which jeopardizes their survival in the environment.* As its criterion, this definition stresses survival, which is, of course, the basic dynamic force of any living thing. I believe it is better to define disease in terms of survival than to define it in terms of health, since health is also a very relative concept.

Disease must be understood on an area basis. The immediate environment provides stimuli with which living things have to cope in order to survive and to which they must provide a response. This response as we evaluate it depends upon the amount of stimulus in relation to the genetic makeup of the host and upon the acuity of the physician's ability to detect.

The disease pattern is also governed by the operation between stimuli and host in the edifice of customs, habits, and techniques that we call "culture." Cultural traits either bring stimulus and host together, creating the chance for disease occurrence, or keep them separate, thus preventing the disease. Thus, at any place considered there is a disease potential which is replaced by actual disease if and when the cultural trait separating stimulus and host breaks down or disappears. It is on this three-cornered basis —stimulus, host, and culture—that the science of the ecology of disease is established. It is the study of these disease factors— their geography, their mapping—that gives us our understanding of disease occurrence on an area basis and forms the subject of global epidemiology.

All three factors are intimately related to the environment, and the transformation of the environment will automatically bring about a change in the mutual relationship of these closely-knit complexes. Environmental stimuli can be arbitrarily but conveniently classified as physical, biological, and cultural.

PHYSICAL STIMULI

Physicists and geographers of the last fifty years have gone very deeply into the study of the component elements of the environment in which man lives. Physicians, however, have taken only cursory interest in these relationships. As a result, our knowledge of the influence of these components on the survival of our cells and tissues and on the survival of the cells and tissues of other living things closely related to us is amazingly small.

Taking first the physical stimuli in the human environment, Lee (1957) established an interesting diagram based on the combined plotting of temperatures and humidity. Within this chart Lee defines several zones: a zone of comfort below or beyond which nobody is comfortable; a zone where muscular performance begins to deteriorate; a

zone where mental performance deteriorates; and a zone of distress. It is possible to superimpose on this chart another chart based on the range of mean monthly temperature and humidity for sample locations. Thus it can be seen on which days of the year the people of Rio de Janeiro, Brazil, or of Basra, Iraq, are in comfort or discomfort and under what conditions they can function well. Beyond such measurements, loosely expressed in the terms "comfort" and "distress," our lack of knowledge about the effects of climate on man is considerable.

An important reason for our ignorance on matters of climatic influence on man is that it is impossible to separate in nature the physical elements of climate from the living things that have established their habitats in this climate. When our grandfathers used to speak of a "good" climate, they meant, without realizing it, a climate where no outside bacterias, parasites, or viruses attacked the body; whereas a "bad" climate was one where such aggressions did occur. The considered climates were, in fact, unrecognized disease agents. When climates are reproduced in artificial chambers, devoid of aggressive living things, the result is nevertheless distorted because many elements existing in the outside world, such as radiation and cosmic rays, are not included among the variables used in the experiments.

We are just beginning to realize the existence and possible importance of such unknown variables as cosmic rays, static electricity, radiation, and other material forces that are as yet nameless. If it is possible that flares in the sun may disrupt "macroscopic" electronic communications on earth, as happens on airplanes and with submarines, it is also likely that they produce changes in the microscopic electronic communications that occur in our cells, and are probably infinitely involved in the makeup of what we call life.

The forces of climate may conceivably influence resilience to disease in us as they do in chickens. Pasteur, experimenting with these animals, had to lower their body temperature by plunging them into an icy bath to be able to inoculate them with a number of pathogenic agents. The conditions of "stress" thus created resulted in a susceptibility to the agents that had not existed before.

Further, the physical elements of climate —those we know how to measure and those we do not—influence the things we eat as well as the agents, vectors, intermediate hosts, and reservoirs of pathogens that bring us our transmissible diseases. The whole field of climatically-induced mutations in agents, vectors, and intermediate hosts that could modify virulence, susceptibility, and immunity is practically unexplored and will be alluded to below when we discuss biological stimuli.

So far, we physicians have done little to explore the fields of geology, geography, climatology, meteorology, and physics, with the purpose of relating the findings of these sciences with disease occurrence. Let us agree once more that investing in the organization of interdisciplinary research would, in all likelihood, yield large dividends.

BIOLOGICAL STIMULI

Let us come now to a second group of environmental stimuli challenging human survival, comprising all the living things which have elected to inhabit the macroclimates and microclimates surrounding man. An important aspect of the coexistence agreement developed by these living things, which the physician and even the public health officer often forgets, is that these living things, like men, live in societies. I like to think of a society as *a pattern of mutual tolerance that occurs temporarily among living things when the dynamism of reciprocal exclusion has been exhausted.* The idea stressed in these words is that

a social structure is essentially temporary, based on mutual tolerance, which implies dominance and submission. The moment anything happens to disturb the equilibrium of this compromise, the pattern is upset— new dominants come to the top with unpredictable results. The reason for all this, of course, is that whatever size they are living things always compete for food and shelter and organize themselves temporarily on a pattern of mutual strength and power.

I believe that it is profitable for the medical ecologist studying the occurrence of transmissible diseases throughout the world to remember that, in all likelihood, bacteria, snails, mosquitoes, rodents, and mammals all live in societies. It is on this concept that modern therapy with antibiotics and disease control is based. Indeed, in a room loaded with aerosols of *Penicillium notatum,* the transmission of pneumonia among human hosts would not occur for lack of a live pneumococcus. In a paddy field sown with "gambusia," the mosquito *Anopheles jeyporiensis candidiensis* would have a difficult time surviving and so would the parasite *Plasmodium vivax* for lack of adult mosquito habitat in which to spend its sexual life. It has been shown that it is difficult to have the yellow fever virus multiply in an *Aedes aegypti* previously fed on dengue virus (Sabin, 1948). Could it be that these two viruses cannot belong to the same social structure because of some competition that is not yet understood?

The social structures of living things are closely dependent upon the geographic factors and the food availability discussed above, which is why we find these societies closely integrated and almost identified with the map of the geographical area in which they occur. Hence, a good understanding of the map of disease should be based on an in-depth study of the relationship in time and space between physical environmental factors, biological environmental factors, and the cells, tissues, and organs of the host.

Health and disease, in the final analysis, should be conceived solely as a function of the ability of a living thing to adjust to the environment in which it lives. Sometimes these adjustments are orderly and unconscious; sometimes they shake the tissues, disturb the functions, and upset the whole organism beyond the range of unconscious integration and the individual is made aware of the change. Until adjustment is eventually made, this change can be called "disease." If adjustment is not made, death occurs. If it is made, a scar is left which will play its role in the future behavior of the tissues and in future adjustments to new stresses. A study of the changing map of disease implies first a study of all the stimuli we have discussed and then a study of the factors that govern responses from the host. These are all important.

Given many aggressive stimuli, the living hosts respond according to their respective genius in a way that modifies the map of disease. Very little is known about this subject. We have paid scant attention in the past to the factors governing the attitudes of the hosts. Our textbooks and our literature are full of studies on the living stimuli but offer very little information on the host structure, the genetic makeup of the man who presents the symptoms we study, and the relationship between genetics and the development of human disease. No discussion of the changing map of diseases can afford to ignore the changes that occur in the host as a result of insults from the environment; neither can such a discussion afford to ignore changes occurring in the emotional system as a result of significant environmental changes. Crowding of a habitat, for example, strongly influences the adjustment of both man and animal, not solely through the physical problems of spatial occupancy but conceivably by affecting susceptibility or immunity through the obscure pathway of emotional changes.

Because the relationship between genetics

and response to environmental stimuli is not known, so far we have not been able to manage any classification of hosts on the basis of these responses to environmental stimuli. We have no map of susceptibilities and immunities. Obviously, the genetic makeup of the individual lies at the basis of the responses any individual or any population offers to environmental challenges. We all know that the genetic makeup of an individual is represented by the sum total of his genes (his genotype) and by the appearance of his genotype at a given time (his phenotype). If it is true that the concept of one gene, one enzyme, has value, then we can understand why certain people or animals are susceptible to certain diseases and others are not. Why is leprosy essentially a human disease? Why is foot-and-mouth disease essentially a cattle pathology? Why do cholera *Vibrios* multiply in the intestines of guinea pigs without causing them any harm? Why cannot birds catch human malaria? The enzymes controlling these agent-host relationships, governed by the genes that support the enzymes, might be the field in which answers to these questions could be found.

Interesting possibilities have recently been brought to light: some studies seem to indicate that individuals belonging to the blood group "O" are particularly susceptible to the stimuli that result in the development of peptic ulcers (Aird *et al.,* 1954), and, as already mentioned, the pathological significance of certain types of hemoglobin is certainly worth exploring thoroughly (Allison, 1954a; Allison, 1954b).

The genetic constitution of an individual or of a population is more closely linked with the environment than we currently realize. I have already hinted at this relationship: the present and future genotype of a population is dependent upon the presence of environmental stimuli which cause mutations and on the pressures which force living things into migrations. Mutagenic factors are little known; however, heat, chemicals, radiation, and probably others are specific to environmental niches: the way these factors combine determines the microclimates or macroclimates for all living things. These climates exert their influence on the genes of plants and animals alike, causing mutations that upset the social patterns referred to above, causing dominants to lose their dominance and submissive elements to acquire dominance. When we say, "This year was a bad year for cholera; there was too much heat and humidity," we may be giving only a partial description of what occurred because it could very well be that the cholera *Vibrios* living in that area have mutated from a mild strain into a virulent one through the effects of heat, humidity, or radiation. This, of course, can also be true of the influenza virus or of any other agent, vector, or reservoir we can think of.

When the environment exerts its pressure and when that pressure becomes too painful for a living group to accept, the group usually flees that environment. This has happened when animals migrate and when European populations came to America to escape political pressures in the Old Continent. These migrations (at every level, from disease agent to man) result in the mixing of genes and the creation of new genotypes in the environment to which the refugees have fled. Thus are disease patterns genetically linked with geographic pressures.

In the same way, the environment in which man lives pressures his genotype, and brings about new shapes and new phenotypes that may be useful or detrimental to the continuation of his living in that same place. If a man has lived for a certain time in a certain environment, he has been bitten and hurt; he has suffered emotions that are specific to that place. All these stimuli have left scars, the sum of which form his personality and govern his future

response to future stimuli. Some of these scars are beneficial, such as immunities and education; some are detrimental, such as allergies and neuroses; and it is the total of these scars that governs the disease pattern by governing responses to the stimuli present in the environment.

CULTURAL STIMULI

The third group of forces that intervenes in the disease pattern is the "culture" of the various human groups that grow in the infinite variety of physical and biological environments. To the global epidemiologist, culture is the sum total of the concepts and techniques that individuals or populations devise and use in order to survive in a given environment. Of course, not all cultural traits are survival-worthy. It is quite possible that many cultural traits will lead the group to its destruction rather than to its survival. A case probably could be made to show that cultural traits originally developed because they were thought to promote survival or because they did promote survival when they were adopted, but that they often have ceased to do so under changing circumstances.

People do not give up their culture easily. They often like to feel the protection of their ancestors around them and they often would rather die doing something that has always been done than survive by not doing it or trying something that has not been tried before. The origin of culture is truly the job of anthropologists; I am not competent to discuss it. My point of view is that of the epidemiologist, and I am only interested in whether a particular cultural trait promotes disease or prevents it.

III

We have discussed the various factors that combine to pressure any host in its environment. It seems that a transformation of the environment will bring about changes that will modify the adaptation of man to his milieu. These environment changes occur as follows: alluviums fill up estuaries; isolated villages are replaced by large cities; vast populations multiply and create crowded situations; people migrate; genes segregate; and new genotypes are created which result in new responses to the environmental stimuli.

The diseases prevalent among the sparse population of Manhattan when Captain Hudson sailed to these shores are not the same as those that prevail there today. When jungles are cleared, as in parts of Malaya, or are allowed to reconquer the land, as on the site of the dead city of Angkor, new societies of agents, vectors, and hosts nestle themselves in new niches. Each culture brings about its set of diseases; we have just now begun to study the diseases brought about by radiation. Thus, at all times the health of tomorrow is prepared and hatched in the remotest corners of the world, as shown, for instance, by the spread of Asian flu which may have started with a few sneezes in some obscure countryside of the Chinese mainland. There is no doubt that we must increase our information about these events. We should try to recognize the birth of new stimuli to disease, the changes that occur among social structures of agents and vectors, and the changes in the maps of immunities and susceptibilities. We must keep abreast of the cultural changes that either create new links between agents and hosts or erect protective shields between them. We must gauge the development programs that we so liberally and, perhaps, so foolishly encourage throughout the world. Drainage, irrigation, pest control, deforestation, afforestation, pollution, and destruction of cities create changes in the habitat which eventually and inescapably will bring about challenges to human adaptation, and hence changes in the map of diseases.

REFERENCES

Aird, Ian; Bentall, H. H.; Mehigan, J. A.; and Roberts, J. A. F. "Blood Groups in Relation to Peptic Ulceration and Carcinoma of Colon, Rectum, Breast and Bronchus; Association Between ABO Groups and Peptic Ulceration." *Brit. Med. J.,* 2 (August 7, 1954), 315–21.

Allison, A. C. "Protection Afforded by Sickle-Cell Trait Against Subtertian Malaria Infection." *Brit. Med. J.* 1 (1954a), 290–94.

Allison, A. C. "Distribution of Sickle-Cell Trait in East Africa and Elsewhere and Its Apparent Relationship to Incidence of Subtertian Malaria." *Brit. R. Soc. Trop. Med. and Hyg.,* 48 (July, 1954b), 312–18.

Augustine, D. L., and Smillie, W. G. "The Relation of the Types of Soils of Alabama to the Distribution of Hookworm Disease." *Amer. J. Hyg.,* 6 (March Supplement, 1926), 36–62.

Bates, Marston. *The Natural History of Mosquitoes.* New York: Macmillan, 1949.

Black, R. H. *Malaria in the Trobriand Islands (Territory of Papua and New Guinea).* Technical Paper No. 33. Noumea, New Caledonia: South Pacific Commission, 1952.

Faust, E. C. *Human Helminthology.* Philadelphia: Lea & Febiger, 1949.

Ferreira, M. de O., and Almeida, D. "Geographical Distribution of the Strain of *P. falciparum* Resistant to Chloroquine." Paper read at the Seventh International Congress on Tropical Medicine and Malaria, Rio de Janeiro, Brazil, Sept. 1–11, 1963.

Forbes, A. "Proposed Acceleration of the Army Research Program on Drug Resistant *falciparum* Malaria." Unpublished.

Lee, Douglas H. K. *Climate and Economic Development in the Tropics.* New York:

Council on Foreign Relations Publications, Harper & Brothers, 1957. Pp. 97–98.

May, Jacques M. "Ecology of Disease in World Health," *U. S. Armed Forces Med. J.,* Vol. 9, No. 6 (June, 1958a), pp. 232–34.

May, Jacques M. *Ecology of Human Disease,* Vol. 1. New York: M.D. Publications, 1958b.

May, Jacques M. *Studies in Disease Ecology,* Vol. 2. New York: Hafner Publishing Co., 1961.

Rogers, L. "The Incidence and Spread of Cholera in India; Forecasting and Control of Epidemics." *Indian J. of Med. Rec. and Memoirs,* Vol. 9 (March, 1928).

Russell, P. F. *Malaria—Basic Principles Briefly Stated.* Oxford: Blackwell Scientific Publications, 1952.

Sabin, Albert B. *Proceedings of the 4th International Congress on Tropical Medicine and Malaria.* Department of State Publication 324b. Washington, D.C.: U. S. Government Printing Office, 1948. Pp. 534–35.

World Health Organization. *Malaria Conference in Equatorial Africa.* Techn. Report Ser. No. 38. Geneva, 1951.

———. *Techn. Bull. No. 296.* Geneva, 1965.

Young, M. D.; Contacos, P. G.; Stitcher, J. E.; and Miller, J. W. "Drug Resistance in *Plasmodium falciparum* from Thailand." *Amer. J. Trop. Med. and Hyg.,* 12 (1963), 305–14.

3. TRANSFERABLE DRUG RESISTANCE AND THE ECOLOGIC EFFECTS OF ANTIBIOTICS

LaVerne C. Harold

Transferable drug resistance, discovered by Japanese workers in 1959, is a most important type of drug resistance of the Gram-negative enterobacteria. It can transfer multiple resistance quickly and effectively from one bacterial cell to another of the same or different species simply by cell-to-cell contact—a feature distinguishing it from all other known forms of resistance.

Transferable drug resistance is confined principally to the Enterobacteraceae and can be transferred to some of the other Gram-negative bacteria. Some that inhabit the alimentary tract also invade the genito-urinary tract. R-factors are prevalent in strains of *Salmonella, Shigella,* and *Escherichia coli* and can be found throughout the world. There have been reports of transferable drug resistance in Europe, the Middle East, Southeast Asia, North and South America and Africa.

Each year reports of multi-resistant strains of bacteria appear with increased frequency. Also, resistant factors are being found to confer resistance to more and more antibacterial drugs. As a result, infections once considered susceptible to effective treatment by antibiotics are becoming all the more troublesome to treat. In countries where there are medical or sanitation problems, this development of transfer resistance, unless controlled, can be particularly serious.

Antibiotics were first introduced as chemotherapeutic agents in the early 1940s with the advent of penicillin for the treatment of human infections. They have since grown in number to some fifty different types. Approximately twenty of these antibiotics are commonly used with man and animal.

An antibiotic is defined as a chemical

substance, derived from a mold or bacteria, which has the capacity, in dilute solution, to inhibit or destroy microorganisms. Antibiotics are used to control infectious diseases of man, to treat and control diseases in animals and food crops, to stimulate the growth of animals and to preserve foods. They are the "wonder drugs."

Large as the benefits may be from the use of antibiotics, certain risks threatened their effectiveness from the beginning. The greatest of these risks was the emergence of resistant bacteria. As resistance developed, an antibiotic would become less effective at initially established doses. Dosages, therefore, had to be greatly increased.

It has long been known that resistance to drugs may be produced by bacteria. The commonly known methods by which resistance develops are mutation, replacement of drug-sensitive bacteria strains by resistant strains, or transduction in which genes are carried from one bacterial cell to another by infecting phages or bacterial viruses. Normally, resistance by these means develops at a relatively low frequency.

In 1959, the Japanese scientists Ochiai and Akiba and their coworkers were able to show that a more efficient and more disturbing mechanism for drug resistance was at work in Gram-negative[1] enterobacteria[2]—the mechanism of transferable drug resistance (Akiba *et al.,* 1960; Mitsuhashi, 1965; Watanabe, 1963).

By this mechanism, bacteria suddenly become resistant to several antibacterial drugs at once and are able to transfer this resistance to other susceptible bacteria of the same species or different species simply by cell-to-cell contact. In vitro, it has been shown that this process of transferring re-

[1] Gram-negative bacteria are those bacteria that lose the stain or are decolorized by alcohol in Gram's method of staining: this decolorization is a primary characteristic of certain microorganisms.
[2] Enterobacteria are those bacteria found in the intestines.

sistance continues until nearly all of the organisms coming into contact with the infectious bacteria become resistant.

Since the discovery of transferable drug resistance in Japan, it has been detected in many countries. Other names given transferable drug resistance are infectious drug resistance, multiple drug resistance and multiply drug resistance.

TRANSFERABLE DRUG RESISTANCE

Transferable drug resistance is brought about by conjugation—a transfer of genetic information from one bacteria cell to another through direct cell contact (Falkow, 1965). Exactly how this genetic information or drug resistance moves from the donor cell to the recipient cell by conjugation is not definitely known. Investigators agree, however, that resistance to antibiotics transmitted by conjugation does occur, both in vitro (Akiba *et al.,* 1960; Harada *et al.,* 1960; Watanabe and Fukasawa, 1960, 1961a, 1961b), and in the intestinal tract of man and animal (Guinee, 1965; Kasuya, 1964; Walton, 1966a; Watanabe, 1963).

In theory, transferable drug resistance concerns an element in the cell called the R-factor (for "resistance") (Watanabe, 1963). It is postulated that the R-factor has two components: one component is the Resistance Transfer Factory (RTF), which may be extrachromosomal (Watanabe and Fukasawa, 1960, 1961b; Watanabe, 1963) and contains DNA (Falkow, 1965; Falkow *et al.,* 1965), the genetic material that specifies the design and construction of future generations. The other component, which may also be extrachromosomal, is called the Resistance Determinant (R-d), the genetic fragment that determines the specific drug's resistance (Anderson, 1965a) (Fig. 3–1).

The RTF component or episome units receive and transmit the drug resistance

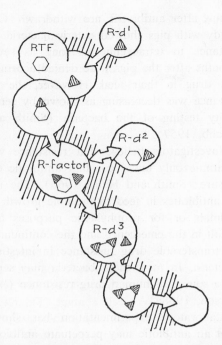

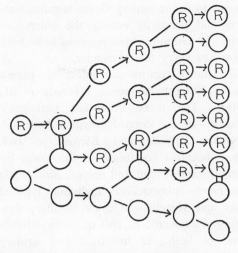

Figure 3–2 Schematic drawing of chain reaction occurring in transferable drug resistance. Resistance cell R comes in contact with sensitive cell O. Sensitive cell receives a copy of the R-factor. The process is repeated as cell comes in contact with cell to increase the number of cells that are resistant. Sometimes an R-factor is lost.

Figure 3–1 Schematic drawing of transferable drug resistance involving transfer of the resistance factor (R-factor). It is postulated that the R-factor has two components: resistance transfer factor (RTF) and resistance determinant (R-d). The R-d activates the RTF for drug resistance. This process is thought to be maintained as long as there is constant antibiotic pressure.

(Watanabe and Fukasawa, 1960). However, the RTF is not activated for drug resistance until it comes in contact with the R-determinant. Both are needed for the transfer of drug resistance (Anderson, 1965a).

The RTF itself may transfer the R-determinants, or the R-determinants may be present in the cell in the absence of the RTF (Anderson, 1965a, 1965b). How the R-d actually gets into a bacterial cell is academic when we consider that one such donor cell will activate the RTF in any recipient cell it contacts, and the recipient cell then becomes a donor cell, thus continuing a chain reaction (Fig. 3–2). This process is thought to be maintained as long as there is constant antibiotic pressure.

When one adds a small number of bac-teria with R-factor to a culture of drug-sensitive cells, there is a rapid increase in the relative number of drug-resistant cells. Within twenty minutes, a transfer of resistance can be completed between cells. In twenty-four hours or so, the culture may become almost completely resistant. This rapid spread of R-factors or resistance to the once-sensitive bacteria occurs at a much faster rate than the overall growth of the culture. (Kontomichalou, 1967; Watanabe and Fukasawa, 1960, 1961a).

The defense system set up by bacteria carrying the R-factor is very sophisticated. They can ward off attack not only to one but to several antibiotics simultaneously (Kontomichalou, 1967). In turn, the R-factor can transfer this resistance to bacteria of other strains—nonpathogenic bacteria can transfer their resistance to bacteria that are pathogenic (Harada *et al.,* 1960; Watanabe and Fukasawa, 1961a).

Transferable drug resistance is only

known to occur among Gram-negative bacteria and primarily among the enterobacteria. No Gram-positive bacteria have been shown to carry this resistance.

Resistance factors can infect all genera of the Enterobacteriaceae (Harada et al., 1960). The more important pathogenic members of the Enterobacteriaceae are *Salmonella, Shigella* and *Escherichia coli*. These bacteria are found in the lower intestinal tract of man and animal. *Salmonella* can cause salmonellosis including typhoid fever and *Shigella* can cause bacillary dysentery. Pathogenic *E. coli* may cause infections of both the intestinal and urinary tracts.

Other Gram-negative bacteria to which multiple drug resistance can be transferred include: *Serratia* (Falkow et al., 1961; Suzuki et al., 1961), *Vibrio* (Baron and Falkow, 1961; Kuwabara et al., 1963), *Pasteurella* (Ginoza and Matney, 1963) and *Pseudomonas* (Smith and Armour, 1966). Transferable drug resistance can occur between species of genera in Enterobacteriaceae, Brucellaceae, Pseudomonadaceae and Spirillaceae.

The drugs to which transferable drug resistance most frequently develops are: streptomycin, chloramphenicol, tetracyclines, and the sulfonamides. Resistance has also been reported to penicillin (Anderson and Datta, 1965), ampicillin (Anderson and Datta, 1965; Datta and Kontomichalou, 1965), furazolidone (Smith and Halls, 1966), kanamycin, neomycin, paromomycin (Watanabe, Ogata and Sato, 1964), celphaloridine and gentamycin.

The frequency in nature with which antibiotic resistance is transferred from one bacterial cell to another is not definitely known. It is known that any contact with antibiotics will bring about an increase in resistance. In general, the more frequently a drug is used the higher the incidence of the corresponding resistance.

It is not known how long resistance remains after antibiotics are withdrawn. One study with pigs showed enteric bacteria resistance to tetracycline as long as seven months after the pigs were denied access to the drug in their feed. However, the resistance was decreasing as shown by sensitivity testing of the bacteria (Smith and Crabb, 1957).

Investigators believe that resistance will continue only under constant antibiotic exposure (Smith and Halls, 1966). The use of antibiotics in feed to promote growth in animals or for prophylactic purposes can result in the emergence and the continuance of transferable drug resistance in intestinal bacteria. In turn, these bacteria may serve as a source of human drug resistance (Anderson, 1968a).

Laboratory experimentation has shown that an antibiotic may perpetuate antibiotic resistance to another unrelated antibiotic (Lebek, 1963). That is, an organism may become resistant to one antibiotic and the resistance may be perpetuated for an indefinite period of time by the presence of another antibiotic.

Bacteria may spontaneously lose the R-factor[3] or lose the capacity to transfer the R-factor and yet retain the resistance itself (Watanabe, 1963). This failure to transfer resistance has been observed among R-factors associated with *Salmonella* (Anderson, 1968b; Smith and Halls, 1966) and other enteric bacteria (Smith and Armour, 1966; Watanabe, 1963).

In vitro, the resistance factors of multiple drug resistance can be eliminated by treating the resistant cells with acridines although the frequencies of loss are rather low. Ultraviolet irradiation of the resistant cells before acridine treatment was found to increase the frequency of elimination (Watanabe and Fukasawa, 1960, 1961b). Such studies have not been carried out in animals.

[3] See references for further details: Datta, 1962, 1965; Lebek, 1963a; Smith, 1966; Watanabe and Fukasawa, 1961b.

The phage type[4] may be changed by transfer factors. This change has been observed in *Salmonella*. When infected, the phage type of one strain of bacteria can be converted and resemble the phage type of another (Anderson and Lewis, 1965b; Anderson, 1966). No studies have been reported on serotype[5] changes accompanying R-factor resistance. Such studies are needed because serotypes in *Salmonella* are germane to epidemiological investigations.

OCCURRENCE AND DISTRIBUTION

Scientists do not know the origin of the R-factors, nor how far back in history they go. Neither do they know the mechanism of developing new types of R-factors (Mitsuhashi, Egawa *et al.,* 1967; Watanabe, 1966).

In Japan, the R-factor can be traced back to 1955 but no further. This is true in spite of the extensive use of sulfanilamide since 1945 and of dihydrostreptomycin, tetracycline and chloramphenicol since 1950 (Mitsuhashi, Egawa *et al.,* 1967).

In the United States, R-factors have been demonstrated in bacteria isolated and stored for a number of years. In fact, an *E. coli* isolated in the 1930s and lyophilized[6] in 1946 was found to contain an R-factor mediating resistance to tetracycline and streptomycin (D. H. Smith, 1967).

It has been suggested that R-factors may have come about from gene pickup by the resistance-transfer factor. That is, the transfer factor picked up resistance genes from the chromosome of some unknown bacteria, first picking up one resistance gene, then

another, and finally another until bacteria were resistant to a number of drugs (Watanabe, 1963, 1966).

On the other hand, epidemiological surveys suggest that multiple drug resistance has not developed step by step but has existed from the beginning or has developed all at once (Mitsuhashi, 1965). The first isolation of R-factor in Japan was resistant to four drugs.

Distributions of R-factors are world-wide. Multi-resistant strains of bacteria have been found with increasing frequency in many different parts of the world.

JAPAN:

Transferable resistance was first brought to light in Japan in 1959. Strains of *Shigella* resistant to streptomycin, chloramphenicol, tetracycline, and sulfanilamide were found in 1955. Subsequently, Japanese workers isolated *Escherichia coli* strains resistant to the same four drugs during an epidemic caused by *Salmonella flexneri* in 1957 and in a patient afflicted with *S. flexneri* in 1958. In another patient, *S. flexneri* and *E. freundii* resistant strains were isolated (Mitsuhashi, 1965).

To account for the increasing number of antibiotic-resistant bacteria they were finding, Japanese scientists advanced the R-factor theory. The antibiotic-resistant *Shigella* prevalent in Japan were investigated (Mitsuhashi *et al.,* 1961). Their studies showed that the dysentery-causing bacteria *Shigella,* which were resistant, could pass this resistance to *E. coli*. In turn, they found that *E. coli* could pass the resistance to sensitive Shigellae (Akiba *et al.,* 1960; Mitsuhashi, 1965; Watanabe, 1963).

GREAT BRITAIN:

The first isolation of multiple transferable drug resistance reported outside of Japan was made in Great Britain in 1962. Strains

---

[4] Phage type is a classification of bacteriophage (bacteria virus) reproduced by bacteria and resulting in a characteristic plague used for identifying strains of bacteria.

[5] Serotype is a subdivision or type of bacteria as determined by the kinds and combination of constituent antigens present in the bacteria cell.

[6] To lyophilize is to dry in a frozen state under high vacuum.

of *Salmonella typhimurium* that had been isolated during an outbreak of gastroenteritis in London in 1959 were found to be resistant to streptomycin, tetracycline, and sulfathiazole. This triple resistance could be transferred to a strain of *Shigella sonnei* and back again to *S. typhimurium* (Datta, 1962).

In 1965 resistance to ampicillin and penicillin were reported in strains of *S. typhimurium* isolated in 1962 (Anderson and Datta, 1965). Also, outbreaks of enteric infections due to strains of *E. coli,* (Anderson, 1968a), and *Shigella* (Lewis, 1967) were found to be carrying transferable drug resistance.

WEST GERMANY:

In West Germany, in 1963, resistance of Salmonella strains to four antibiotics was reported in the course of a *Salmonella* infection in an infant treated with chloramphenicol. The resistance pattern bore no relation to the drug therapy used since only chloramphenicol had been administered in treatment. This gave rise to the assumption that there had been a transfer of multiple resistance to the *Salmonella.* On investigation, an R-factor was found in an enteropathogenic[7] strain of *Escherichia coli* that was responsible for the resistance (Lebek, 1963b).

These findings, like the observations made by the Japanese and British, showed that in pathogenic intestinal bacteria, resistance can arise in an indirect manner by transfer. Isolates of drug resistance in pathogenic *E. coli* have become prevalent in Germany (Linzenmeier *et al.,* 1962).

HUNGARY:

In Hungary, in 1965, the episomal nature of drug-resistant strains of *Shigella* was studied and verified. This study was prompted

[7] Enteropathogenic bacteria pertain to or are effective in causing disease of the intestinal tract.

by the remarkably high incidence of multiple resistant strains. A majority of the isolated *Shigella* strains were found to be carrying episomal resistance. This helped to explain the rapid increase in the incidence of multiple resistance in that country (Ketyi and Vertenyi, 1965–66).

ISRAEL:

In Israel, multiple drug-resistant strains of *Shigella* rapidly appeared in 1956. It has been postulated that the marked increase in resistance may be due to the spread of R-factors since they have been found in strains of Shigellae (Datta, 1965; Gill and Hook, 1965; Watanabe, Nishida *et al.,* 1964). Transferable resistance to chloramphenicol in a strain of *S. typhi* has also been observed in a typhoid carrier treated with the drug (Anderson, 1968b).

UNITED STATES:

In the United States, bacteria carrying transferable antibiotic drug resistance were first reported in 1966 (Kabins and Cohen, 1966). Resistance was found in isolates of *Salmonella, E. coli,* and *Shigella* bacteria taken from humans in the Chicago area between September 1964 and February 1966. Also, reports of transferable resistance were published in 1966 in isolations of *E. coli, Proteus, Pseudomonas* and *Klebsiella* bacteria from humans in the New England area (Smith and Armour, 1966; Smith, 1966) and on clinical isolations of *Salmonella* furnished by laboratories in New York, Massachusetts and Pennsylvania (Gill and Hook, 1966). Transferable resistance to multiple antibiotics have since been associated with outbreaks of shigellosis in Georgia (Farrar and Dekle, 1967) and New York (Salzman *et al.,* 1967).

Evidence indicates that resistance transfer factors are widespread in the United States. They have been found not only in the large metropolitan areas of the United States but also in the less populated regions (Smith and Marymont, 1967).

OTHER COUNTRIES:

Other countries and areas reporting incidence of infectious or transferable drug resistance include: the Netherlands (Manten *et al.,* 1964, 1966), Czechoslovakia (Schuh and Aldova, 1966), Canada (Datta, 1965; Dulaney *et al.,* 1968), Brazil (Watson, 1967), Greece (Datta and Kontomichalou, 1965; Kontomichalou, 1967), Switzerland (Datta and Kontomichalou, 1965) and South Africa (Watson, 1967). No country appears to be exempt. Wherever R-factors have been looked for, they have been found.

THE WORLD-WIDE SIGNIFICANCE

The immediate importance of transferable resistance to the world is that it poses a serious threat to effective treatment and control of enterobacterial diseases of both animal and man. Many of the organisms affected are notorious pathogens. Infections of the genito-urinary tract caused by enteric bacteria resistant drugs are a serious therapeutic problem (Smith and Armour, 1966).

Enteric pathogens resistant to antibiotics emerge during treatment. The administration of a single antibiotic to a patient with shigellosis has been followed by the appearance of multiple drug resistance (Watanabe, 1963). The administration of low-level antibiotics in livestock feeds can cause and perpetuate drug resistance (Smith and Crabb, 1957).

In diseases of the intestinal tract where the most common pathogen is *E. coli,* antibiotic-resistant strains may multiply rapidly during antibiotic therapy. Resistant strains can become the dominant microorganisms and transfer RTF to all available Entero-

bacteriaceae (Kabins and Cohen, 1966).

From the onset one of the most striking pictures was the early period of susceptibility of bacteria to antibiotics (Gill and Hook, 1965). This was the period of early clinical use. Since then there has been a marked increase in the number of resistant enterobacterial strains (Datta, 1965; Watanabe, 1963). This increase in resistance has been associated with the greater use of antibiotics. In 1966, the most recent year for which data are available, in the United States alone production of antibiotics as therapeutic agents totaled 9,652,000 pounds (U. S. Tariff Commission, 1967). Compared with 1965, this was an increase of 2,194,000 pounds (U. S. Tariff Commission, 1968).

Because of resistance, infections are becoming more and more difficult to treat. Resistance by R-factors may be so high that the infections caused by the bacteria infected with the R-factors are not amenable to antibiotic therapy. Disease outbreaks due to the emergence of enteric pathogens resistant to antibiotics have occurred with increasing incidence with *Shigella, Salmonella,* and *E. coli.*

In Atlanta, Georgia, in 1966, an outbreak of dysentery due to *Shigella flexneri* type 2a, involved eleven out of eighteen individuals in four households. Six of the individuals were found to be excreting organisms resistant to ampicillin, streptomycin, tetracycline, chloramphenicol and sulfisoxazole (Farrar and Dekle, 1967).

In 1965, at the Sherwood Hospitals, Nottingham, England, an outbreak of infection by *Shigella flexneri* type 2a started in a ward of mentally subnormal children. Strains of *Shigella flexneri* were isolated with eight different patterns of sensitivity to antimicrobial drugs, from strains sensitive to all agents tested to one resistant to six different drugs (Lewis, 1967). For several months thereafter the outbreak appeared to be under control. Eventually, however, there was a recrudescence of the infection. When strains of *Escherichia coli* from the patients during the *Shigella flexneri* infection were examined, 33.8 percent were found to be resistant to one or more antibacterial drugs and 21.1 percent could transfer their resistance (Lewis, 1968).

In 1967, at the Albert Einstein College of Medicine, Bronx, New York, an outbreak of shigellosis due to *Salmonella sonnei* occurred in a nursery for premature infants. The outbreak originated with a mother, involved at least one of her twin infants, and was transmitted to a nurse. The strain of *S. sonnei* causing the outbreak was resistant to tetracycline, chloramphenicol, streptomycin, and sulfonamides. Resistance to these antibiotics was transferable by an R-factor (Salzman *et al.,* 1967).

At the Children's Hospital Medical Center, Boston, Massachusetts, bacteria isolated from thirty-two patients with *Salmonella* infection during a three-month period in 1966 were studied. Twenty-four strains were sensitive to each of nine drugs tested and one was resistant only to streptomycin. Seven strains were resistant to streptomycin and one or more other drugs, and six of these strains were able to transfer the resistance factor (Smith, 1966).

An outbreak of infantile enteritis reported in 1968 due to pathogenic *E. coli* occurred in the Middlesbrough area of England. There were fourteen deaths. Strains of *E. coli* isolated from patients were tested and found resistant to ampicillin, chloramphenicol, neomycin, tetracycline, streptomycin and sulfonamides. Transferable drug resistance occurred with all except ampicillin (Anderson, 1968a).

The incidence of enterobacteria with transferable drug resistance has increased in direct proportion to the use of antibacterial drugs. In Japan, where antibiotics are widely used, the incidence of antibiotic-resistant strains of *Shigella* has increased enormously (Mitsuhashi, 1965). In 1956 al-

most no cases of *Shigella* resistance were reported. In 1964, hospitals in three major cities reported that some 50 percent of the *Shigella* isolates were resistant to streptomycin, chloramphenicol, the tetracyclines and the sulfonamides (Watanabe, 1966).

In England, through RTF, resistance is rapidly increasing (Datta, 1965). Antibiotic resistance first demonstrated in *Salmonella typhimurium* in 1962 increased from 2.9 percent in 1961–62, to 21 percent in 1963–64, to 61 percent in 1964–65 (Anderson, 1968b). Chloramphenicol and furazolidone resistance appeared in 1964 (Anderson, 1968b).

In 1966 a high incidence of transferable drug resistance was found in England among strains of *E. coli* isolated from human beings suffering from neonatal diarrhea; from calves and lambs suffering from neonatal diarrhea or bacteremia; from pigs suffering from neonatal or post-weaning diarrhea or bowel edema; and from fowl suffering from "coli-septicemia." The drugs studied included tetracyclines, streptomycin, sulfonamides, chloramphenicol, ampicillin, neomycin, furazolidone, polymixin, and nalidixic acid. Of all these drugs only two, polymixin and nalidixic acid, were active against all the strains of *E. coli* tested. Both drugs had been used very little in humans and not at all in domestic animals in England. The incidence of drug resistance appeared to be directly related to the extent that the drug was used. This resistance was found to be increasing. The incidence of resistance was twice as great in pigs isolated in 1965 as in those isolated in 1960–62. Also, neomycin and furazolidone resistance was found among the 1965 strains but not among the 1960–62 strains (H. W. Smith, 1967).

Extensive and sometimes indiscriminate use of antibiotics in agriculture creates a dual problem. Strains of bacteria emerge which are resistant to antibiotics or which harbor R-factors (Mitsuhashi, Hashimoto and Suzuki, 1967; Walton, 1966b). It is reported that these bacteria are not only a hindrance to the effective treatment or control of the animal infection but are also a potential source of human infection or drug resistance (Anderson and Datta, 1965; Anderson and Lewis, 1965a; Anderson, 1968b). *Escherichia coli* strains from animals which received therapeutic drugs or low levels of antibiotics in their feed may possibly serve as vectors of drug resistance to humans (Anderson and Datta, 1965; Anderson, 1968b; Smith and Halls, 1966).

The Enteric Reference Laboratory in Britain reported that of 2544 human *S. typhimurium* cultures examined, drug-resistant type 29 comprised 22 percent of the most common type in man in 1965. There were six deaths. Many times a connection could be demonstrated between the bovine and human infection caused by type 29. Where a connection was not demonstrated, it could usually be deduced because of resistance to furazolidone, a drug used only in calves. Of all the 2544 *S. typhimurium* cultures, 63 percent or more represented types (including type 29) predominantly of bovine origin (Anderson, 1968b).

Increases in drug resistance have been noted in the general population. In Great Britain, *E. coli* strains isolated at random from healthy people in a small survey conducted in 1965 showed a high incidence of multiple-drug resistance (Smith and Halls, 1966). In 1968, three hundred strains of *E. coli* isolated from a normal population were examined to determine their resistance to antibacterial drugs. Twenty-four percent of the strains were drug-resistant and 10 percent carried transferable resistance. It

has been estimated that in Great Britain, where antibiotics are used extensively, the incidence of strains with transferable drug resistance in the population at large is about 1 person in 10 (Lewis, 1968).

Extrapolating from data available, the incidence of resistance to antibiotics can be expected to increase in any country as the use of antibiotics increases. This could become serious.

In many countries, salmonellosis has increased in the last two decades and may be considered a public health threat. In the underdeveloped countries, shigellosis, or bacillary dysentery, presents a most serious threat to the health of mankind. Also, epidemics occur most frequently in overcrowded populations with inadequate sanitation. Resistance to antibiotics in these countries could have serious consequences.

The World Health Organization Expert Committee on Antibiotics in its second report (1961) made the following observations:

Bacterial resistance to antibiotics is the principal obstacle to their successful therapeutic use. When resistance develops during the course of treatment, it may deprive an antibiotic of its proper therapeutic effect in the patient being treated. More important in the long run is the effect on the general community, since the elimination of sensitive strains and the dissemination of resistant ones lead to a situation in which many infections are resistant *ab initio* and alternate treatment must be adopted. For this reason, the estimation of bacterial sensitivity or resistance to antibiotics has assumed great importance. Such estimations are an essential prerequisite for the rational use of antibiotics and for preserving the efficacy of this important group of therapeutic substances.

ACKNOWLEDGMENT

The author wishes to thank Dr. Robert A. Baldwin, Bureau of Veterinary Medicine, Food and Drug Administration, who was a consultant in the preparation of this manuscript.

REFERENCES

Akiba, T.; Koyama, K.; Ishiki, Y.; Kimura, S.; and Fukushima, T. "On the Mechanism of the Development of Multiple Drug-Resistant Clones of Shigella." *Jap. J. Microbiol.*, 4 (April, 1960), 219–27.

Anderson, E. S. "Origin of Transferable Drug-Resistance Factors in the Enterobacteriaceae." *Brit. Med. J.*, 2 (Nov. 27, 1965a), 1289–91.

———. "A Rapid Screening Test for Transfer Factors in Drug-Sensitive Enterobacteriaceae." *Nature* (London), 208 (Dec. 4, 1965b), 1016–17.

———. "Influence of the Delta Transfer Factor on the Phage Sensitivity of Salmonellae." *Nature* (London), 212 (Nov. 19, 1966), 795–99.

———. "Middlesbrough Outbreak of Infantile Enteritis and Transferable Drug Resistance." *Brit. Med. J.* [Preliminary Communications], 1 (Feb. 3, 1968a), 293.

———. "Transferable Drug Resistance." *Science Journal* (London), 4 (1968b), 71–76.

Anderson, E. S., and Datta, N. "Resistance to Penicillins and Its Transfer in Enterobacteriaceae." *Lancet*, 1 (Feb. 20, 1965), 407–09.

Anderson, E. S., and Lewis, M. J. "Drug Resistance and Its Transfer in Salmonella typhimurium." *Nature* (London), 206 (May 8, 1965a), 579–83.

———. "Characterization of a Transfer Factor Associated with Drug Resistance in Salmonella typhimurium." *Nature* (London), 208 (Nov. 27, 1965b), 843–49.

Baron, L. S., and Falkow, S. "Genetic Transfer of Episomes from Salmonella typhosa to Vibrio cholera." *Genetics*, 46 (1961), 849; abstr.

Datta, N. "Transmissible Drug Resistance in Epidemic Strain of Salmonella typhimurium." *J. Hyg.* (Cambridge), 60 (September, 1962), 301–10.

———. "Infectious Drug Resistance." *Brit. Med. Bull.*, 21 (September, 1965), 254–59 (59 ref.).

Datta, N., and Kontomichalou, P. "Penicillinase Synthesis Controlled by Infectious R-factors in Enterobacteriaceae." *Nature* (London), 208 (Oct. 16, 1965), 239–41.

Dulaney, E. L.; Carey, M. J.; and Glantz, P. J. "Extrachromosomal Drug Resistance in Escherichia coli from Diseased Animals." *Amer. J. Vet Res.*, 29 (May, 1968), 1067–72.

Falkow, S. "Nucleic Acids, Genetic Exchange and Bacterial Speciation." *Amer. J. Med.*, 39 (November, 1965), 753–65 (89 ref.).

Falkow, S.; Citarella, R. V.; Wohlhieter, J. A.; and Watanabe, T. "The Molecular Basis of R-factors." *Bact. Proc.*, 65th Meeting (1965), p. 14; abstr.

Falkow, S.; Marmur, J.; Carey, W. F.; Spilman, W. M.; and Baron, L. S. "Episomic Transfer between Salmonella typhosa and Serratia marcescens." *Genetics*, 46 (July, 1961), 703–06.

Farrar, W. E., Jr., and Dekle, L. C. "Transferable Antibiotic Resistance Associated with an Outbreak of Shigellosis." *Ann. Intern. Med.*, 67 (December, 1967), 1208–15.

Gill, F. A., and Hook, E. W. "Changing Patterns of Bacterial Resistance to Antimicrobial Drugs." *Amer. J. Med.*, 39 (November, 1965), 780–95 (157 ref.).

———. "Salmonella Strains with Transferable Antimicrobial Resistance." *J.A.M.A.*, 198 (Dec. 19, 1966), 1267–69.

Ginoza, H. S., and Matney, T. S. "Transmission of a Resistance Transfer Factor from Escherichia coli to Two Species of Pasteurella." *J. Bact.*, 85 (May, 1963), 1177–78.

Guinee, P. A. M. "Transfer of Multiple Drug Resistance from Escherichia coli to Salmonella typhimurium in the Mouse Intestine." *Antonie Leeuwenhoek*, 31 (1965), 314–22.

Harada, K.; Suzuki, M.; Kameda, M.; and Mitsuhashi, S. "On the Drug-Resistance of Enteric Bacteria. 2. Transmission of Drug-Resistance Among Enterobacteriaceae." *Jap. J. Exp. Med.*, 30 (August, 1960), 289–99.

Kabins, S. A., and Cohen, S. "Resistance-Transfer Factor in Enterobacteriaceae." *New Eng. J. Med.*, 275 (Aug. 4, 1966), 248–52.

Kasuya, M. "Transfer of Drug Resistance Between Enteric Bacteria Induced in the Mouse Intestine." *J. Bact.*, 88 (August, 1964), 322–28.

Ketyi, I., and Vertenyi, A. "Episomic Antibiotic Resistance Among Shigella Strains Isolated in Hungary." *Acta Microbiol. Acad. Sci. Hung.*, 12 (1965–66), 305–17.

Kontomichalou, P. "Studies on Resistance Transfer Factors. II. Transmissible Resistance to Eight Antibacterial Drugs in a Strain of Escherichia coli." *Path. Microbiol.* (Basel), 30 (1967), 185–200.

Kuwabara, S.; Koyama, K.; Akiba, T.; and Arai, T. "Transmission of Multiple Drug-Resistance from Shigella flexneri to Vibrio comma through Conjugation." *Jap. J. Microbiol.*, 7 (August, 1963), 61–67.

Lebek, G. "Der spontane Verlust episomal übertragener Mehrfachresistenz gegen Antibiotica bei Populationen gramnegativer Darmkeime in Kulturen mit und ohne Antibiotica." *Z. Hyg. Infektionskr.*, 149 (Oct. 25, 1963a), 255–66 (Ger.).

————. "Über die Entstehung Mehrfachresistenter Salmonellen. Ein experimenteller Beitrag." *Zbl. Bakt.* [orig.], 188 (1963b), 494–505 (Ger.).

Lewis, M. J. "Multiple Transmissible Drug Resistance in an Outbreak of Shigella flexneri Infection." *Lancet*, 2 (Nov. 4, 1967), 953–56.

————. "Transferable Drug Resistance and Other Transferable Agents in Strains of Escherichia coli from Two Human Populations." *Lancet*, 1 (June 29, 1968), 1389–93.

Linzenmeier, G.; Scheppe, K.; and Schuster, W." [Colistin in Infant Enteritis Due to E. coli 0 114]." *Deutsch. Med. Wschr.*, 87 (Feb. 2, 1962), 246–49 (Ger.).

Manten, A.; Guinee, P. A. M.; and Kampelmacher, E. H. "Incidence of Resistance to Tetracycline and Chloramphenicol among Salmonella Bacteria Found in the Netherlands in 1963 and 1964." *Zbl. Bakt.* [orig.], 200 (May, 1966), 13–20.

Manten, A.; Kampelmacher, E. H.; and Guinee, P. A. M. "Frequency of Resistance to Tetracycline and Chloramphenicol among Salmonella Strains Isolated in the Netherlands in 1962." *Antonie Leeuwenhoek*, 30 (1964), 10–16.

Mitsuhashi, S. "Transmissible Drug-Resistance Factor R," *Gunma J. Med. Sci.*, 14 (September, 1965), 169–209.

Mitsuhashi, S.; Harada, K.; Hashimoto, H.; and Egawa, R. "On the Drug-Resistance of Enteric Bacteria. 4. Drug-Resistance of Shigella Prevalent in Japan." *Jap. J. Exp. Med.*, 31 (February, 1961), 47–52.

Mitsuhashi, S.; Hashimoto, H.; Egawa, R.; Tanaka, T.; and Nagai, Y. "Drug-Resistance of Enteric Bacteria. IX. Distribution of R-Factors in Gram Negative Bacteria from Clinical Sources." *J. Bact.*, 93 (April, 1967), 1242–45.

Mitsuhashi, S.; Hashimoto, H.; and Suzuki, K. "Drug-Resistance of Enteric Bacteria. XIII. Distribution of R-Factors in Escherichia coli Strains Isolated from Livestock." *J. Bact.*, 94 (October, 1967), 1166–69.

Salzman, T. C.; Scher, C. D.; and Moss, R. "Shigellae with Transferable Drug-Resistance: Outbreak in a Nursery for Premature Infants." *J. Pediat.*, 71 (July, 1967), 21–26.

Schuh, V., and Aldova, E. "Multiple Drug-Resistant Shigellae." *Zbl. Bakt.* [orig.], 200 (August, 1966), 460–67.

Smith, D. H. "Salmonella with Transferable Drug-Resistance." *New Eng. J. Med.*, 275 (Sept. 22, 1966), 625–30.

————. "R-Factor Infection of Escherichia coli Lyophilized in 1946." *J. Bact.*, 94 (December, 1967), 2071–72.

Smith, D. H., and Armour, S. E. "Transferable R-Factors in Enteric Bacteria Causing Infection of the Genito-urinary Tract." *Lancet*, 2 (July 2, 1966), 15–18.

Smith, H. W. "The Incidence of Infective Drug-Resistance in Strains of Escherichia coli Isolated from Diseased Human Beings and Domestic Animals." *Vet. Rec.,* 80 (Apr. 15, 1967), 464–69.

Smith, H. W., and Crabb, W. E. "The Effect of the Continuous Administration of Diets Containing Low Levels of Tetracyclines on the Incidence of Drug-Resistant Bacterium coli in the Faeces of Pigs and Chickens: The Sensitivity of Bact. coli to Other Chemotherapeutic Agents." *Vet. Rec.,* 69 (Jan. 12, 1957), 24–30.

Smith, H. W., and Halls, S. "Observations on Infective Drug-Resistance in Britain." *Brit. Med. J.,* 1 (Jan. 29, 1966), 266–69.

Smith, J. P., and Marymont, J. H., Jr. "Infectious Drug-Resistance: A New and Important Cause of Antibiotic-Resistant Bacteria." *J. Kans. Med. Soc.,* 68 (November, 1967), 425–27, 431.

Suzuki, M.; Kameda, M.; Harada, K.; and Mitsuhashi, S. "Drug Resistance of Enteric Bacteria. 16. Transmission of Transmissible Drug-Resistance (R) Factor to Serratia marcescens by Conjugation and Inhibition of Its Expression by Streptomycin." *Gunma J. Med. Sci.,* 11 (1961), 69–74.

United States Tariff Commission. "Synthetic Organic Chemicals. United States Production and Sales, 1965." TC Publication No. 206. Washington: United States Government Printing Office, 1967. Pp. 32–35.

———. "Synthetic Organic Chemicals. United States Production and Sales, 1966." TC Publication No. 248. Washington: United States Government Printing Office, 1968.

Walton, J. R. "In vivo Transfer of Infectious Drug Resistance." *Nature* (London), 211 (July 16, 1966a), 312–13.

———. "Infectious Drug-Resistance in Escherichia coli Isolated from Healthy Farm Animals." *Lancet,* 2 (Dec. 10, 1966b), 1300–02.

Watanabe, T. "Infective Heredity of Multiple Drug Resistance in Bacteria." *Bact. Rev.,* 27 (March, 1963), 87–115.

———. "Infectious Drug Resistance in Enteric Bacteria." *New Eng. J. Med.,* 275 (Oct. 20, 1966), 888–94.

Watanabe, T., and Fukasawa, T. "Resistance Transfer Factor" an "Episome in Enterobacteriaceae." *Biochem. Biophys. Res. Commun.,* 3 (December, 1960), 660–65.

———. "Episome-Mediated Transfer of Drug Resistance in Enterobacteriaceae. I. Transfer of Resistance Factors by Conjugation." *J. Bact.,* 81 (May, 1961a), 669–78.

———. "Episome-Mediated Transfer of Drug Resistance in Enterobacteriaceae. II. Elimination of Resistance Factors with Acridine Dyes." *J. Bact.,* 81 (May, 1961b), 679–83.

Watanabe, T.; Nishida, H.; Ogato, C.; Arai, T.; and Sato, S. "Episome-Mediated Transfer of Drug Resistance in Enterobacteriaceae, VII. Two Types of Naturally-Occurring R-Factors." *J. Bact.,* 88 (September, 1964), 717–26.

Watanabe, T.; Ogata, C.; and Sato, S. "Episome-Mediated Transfer of Drug Resistance in Enterobacteriaceae, VIII. Six-Drug-Resistance R-Factor." *J. Bact.,* 88 (October, 1964), 922–28.

Watson, C. E. "Infectious Drug Resistance in Shigellae in Cape Town." *S. Afr. Med. J.,* 41 (Aug. 5, 1967), 728–31.

World Health Organization. Expert Committee on Antibiotics: "Standardization of Methods for Conducting Microbic Sensitivity Tests." *WHO Techn. Report Ser.* No. 210 (1961).

4. BIOLOGICAL DISORDERS IN THE GENITO-URINARY SYSTEM FOLLOWING THE INTRODUCTION OF NEW TECHNOLOGIES AND LIFEWAYS IN THE LESS DEVELOPED COUNTRIES

Boyouk Farvar

The introduction of new kinds of technology from alien environments into that of a less developed country, together with the complex of factors involved in the usual change that follows such introductions, can cause certain definite dysfunctions in the normal man-environment relationships. In this paper an effort is made to present the mounting clinical evidence that disturbances in these relationships can cause disorders with definite clinical symptoms in the genito-urinary system.

1. The introduction of new dyes such as beta-naphthylamine in the chemical industry has increased the rate of deadly bladder tumors in dye workers in less developed countries. The tumor is produced by ingesting this compound or by inhaling its fumes.

2. The increase in dam-building operations has caused a tremendous increase in vesical (urinary) schistosomiasis, primarily affecting the bladder. This, in turn, has been blamed as a significant cause of cancer of the bladder.

3. Protein supplementation programs can lead to urinary tract stone formation. There are several instances, one of them from post-World War II Japan, where complex interactions following a protein supplementation program led to urinary tract stone formations. Such problems are of prime significance in international development programs involving protein supplementation in a population adapted to a low protein diet (a quite common practice).

4. It has been shown that vitamin B_6 (pyridoxine) deficiency causes oxalate

stone formation in the urinary tract. The introduction of new formulas (poor in Vitamin B_6 because of the evaporation process) for infant feeding, which causes an increasing tendency toward bottle feeding of infants (versus natural breast feeding) in the less developed countries, has predisposed these infants to stone formation.

5. Popularization of fast transportation, particularly the increased use of automobiles, instead of walking even for short distances, in the less developed countries, means that there has been an increase in obesity, causing metabolic disorders and producing mostly urate and acid uric stone formations in the urinary tract. These stones, which usually form quiescently, at times cause irreparable kidney damage in patients from the developing nations. The author's personal experience and research since 1960 shows a considerable increase in the incidence of this type of stone formation in Iran.

6. Hypertension and cases of coronary diseases have increased tremendously in the less developed countries in recent years. There is evidence that one factor which is at least as important as any other in this complex change in the demographic disease pattern is the introduction of the modern factory techniques requiring harder work in longer hours, rush, and nervousness. These dangerous diseases cause renal damage in due term.

New technology has introduced or imposed changes upon less developed nations. Despite many useful effects, numerous biological changes have occurred, producing serious problems and hazards to human health. It is my intention in this paper to present a few of the many problems in the genito-urinary system which are caused by the advent of new technologies and new ways of life.

CHEMICAL DYES AND BLADDER TUMORS

The most important and serious problem among urological disorders in newly developing countries is the increasing incidence of bladder carcinoma. For more than sixty years it has been known that tumors of the bladder often occur among certain groups of dye workers in the chemical industry. Many investigators have demonstrated conclusively that beta-naphthylamine causes bladder tumors when fed to dogs (Hueper *et al.*, 1938; Gehrmann *et. al.*, 1948; and

others). Furthermore, it has been shown that similar tumors developed after a while in dye workers who have ingested this compound or have inhaled its fumes. Bonser *et al.* (1954) have furnished evidence that beta-naphthylamine is metabolized to 2-amino-1-naphthol-sulfuric acid. They believe this end product stimulates the bladder mucosa to undergo malignant change.

The carcinogen is now known to be transported by the urine and not by the blood: the material reaches the kidneys through the blood, but it can only be "activated" in the presence of urine. This is why the carcinogen does not seem to spread to other parts of the body. Melick and associates (1955) have found that xenylamine (4-amino-diphenyl) is carcinogenic for the human bladder. Xenylamine and beta-naphthylamine, then, are up to the present the only compounds *indisputably* capable of producing bladder cancer in man under ordinary working conditions.

The established carcinogenicity of these compounds for the human bladder has caused speculation regarding the etiology of the bladder tumors in the general population. It is suspected that other compounds, as yet unidentified, may produce tumors of the bladder by their introduction into the body through ingestion, inhalation, or cutaneous applications. Certain foodstuffs, medicines, cosmetics, and clothing may provide the vehicle for their transport. In less developed countries such as those of the Middle East, naturally derived dyes (usually of botanical origin) have been employed for many centuries. In some remote villages such practices may still be observed, but recently there has been a wide-scale substitution of the new synthetic dyes for the traditional materials. This has predisposed people to bladder carcinoma.

WIDESPREAD EFFECT OF DAM CONSTRUCTION AND IRRIGATION ON BILHARZIASIS AND BLADDER CARCINOMA

Other papers in this volume establish the role of water development and irrigation projects in the spread of schistosomiasis (see the articles by van der Schalie, Shiff, and Hughes and Hunter). Urinary schistosomiasis, due to the trematode *Schistosoma haematobium,* causes extensive damage to the bladder. This in turn is caused by the action of the schistosome eggs passing through the bladder walls. Many of them do not succeed in completing this journey, and this is the main reason for any complications resulting from this disease. It is now thought probable that urinary schistosomiasis is ultimately responsible for many deaths due to cancer of the bladder.

Cancer is said to occur in about 5 percent of the persons with bladder infestation due to schistosomiasis (also known as bilharziasis). It is preceded by inflammatory changes associated with the extrusion of worms and the passage of eggs through the bladder mucosa. Dimmette *et al.* (1956),

however, state that carcinoma is a common complication of schistosomiasis in Egyptian patients, and that of 96 cases of bladder carcinoma studied by them, vesical (urinary) schistosomiasis due to *S. haematobium* was present in 90. In 75 of these cases, schistosome eggs were present in sections made from the bladder and chronic inflammatory changes in the mucosa could often be seen adjacent to these sections as well as in the remaining bladder wall.

METABOLIC CAUSE OF STONE FORMATION IN THE URINARY TRACT: uric acid and urate stones

The popular use of the automobile, even for traveling short distances, has increased the incidence of metabolic diseases in newly developing nations. These include obesity, gout, and urate stone formations. Because people living in large cities have to depend on motor vehicles, they are unable to get enough physical exercise. The ensuing changes in the regime of living account for the metabolic disorders. The incidence of urinary stones (urate and uric-acid type) has increased tremendously during the past twenty years in Iran. According to the author's personal studies on metabolic factors in urinary stone formation in Iran since 1960 (Farvar, unpublished data; Farvar and Mohammadiha, 1963), 20 percent of all chemically analyzed urinary stones consisted of urate or uric acid. This figure is even higher than that reported in the Western world, which is about 10 percent (Wardlaw, 1952).

METABOLIC CAUSES OF STONE FORMATION: vitamin B_6 (pyridoxine) deficiency and stone formation

It has been observed in Japan that in the immediate post-World War II period the human incidence of oxalate-type urinary stones increased remarkably (Zinsser, H. H., personal communication). It has been postulated that during the war there was some degree of vitamin B_6[1] deficiency in the general population, presumably due to rationing. Shortly after the war ended, the people who had been deprived of high protein diets consumed large amounts of meat products which then became available. A hyperoxaluria (excess excretion of oxalate in urine) therefore occurred, causing calcium oxalate stone formation.

The author, taking this event into consideration, has completed a study in human subjects, both normal ones and those with a propensity to form urinary oxalate stones. The subjects were deprived of vitamin B_6 (pyridoxine), by giving them a diet poor in vitamin B_6 and administering a "tryptophan load" and glycine and deoxypyridoxine, which is an antimetabolite of vitamin B_6. We were able to produce high oxalic acid excretion in their urine.[2] The exact mechanisms of these interactions are not understood, but it seems virtually certain that there is a causal relationship at work here: the addition of good quality protein to the diet of a people otherwise not accustomed to it, in the presence of vitamin B_6 deficiency, may result in hyperoxaluria and oxalate stones in the urinary tract. The situation is quite analogous to the case history of dried skim milk (devoid of vitamin A) in northeast Brazil which was held responsible for epidemics of keratomalacia and irreversible blindness, as related in the chapter by G. E. Bunce.

Vitamin B_6 deficiency has been demonstrated in infants fed formulas in which vitamin B_6 had been greatly reduced due to the processing in evaporated milk. It is logical to think that a vitamin B_6-deficient diet in infants fed meat and high-protein products may well predispose them to urinary stone formation. There is evidence that this has already happened in less developed countries where mothers are now feeding their babies formulas instead of breast feeding them (Boyouk Farvar, unpublished data). In an area extending from Southeast Asia through the Middle East into southern Europe, primary urinary (bladder) stones are common, particularly in young boys. There is a strong possibility that poor nutrition is of major importance in the etiology of these calculi.

Data obtained in the Nutrition Survey of Burma (1963) conducted by the Interdepartmental Committee on Nutrition for National Defense (U.S.A.) suggest that there is a tendency toward oxaluria in groups of Burmese showing high urinary xanthurenic acid and low vitamin B_6 excretion levels. Since numerous nutrition surveys have shown that children in the stone belts of Asia show a high incidence of signs of thiamine, riboflavin, and other nutritional deficiencies, it is possible that vitamin B_6 levels may also be relatively low in some of these areas and that this may be a factor in the development of vesical calculi in children. More precise studies are obviously lacking and needed. Nevertheless, many signs help support the possibility that conditions such as those described for wartime and postwar Japan prevail. For example, per capita protein consumption is declining; mothers are increasingly relying on bottle feeding, and new strains of rice and wheat are replacing old ones along with the Western habit of discarding the vitamin-rich grain shells—not to mention the results of increasing hunger, starvation, and social strife. It is reasonable to speculate in the absence of precise data that in such areas

[1] Major sources of Vitamin B_6 are: cane molasses, beef, grain products, milk, and wheat.
[2] This work was done in Columbia Presbyterian Medical Center's Department of Urology in New York City in 1960. Similar studies were done by Andrus *et al.* (1960), Gershoff and Prien (1960), and Faber *et al.* (1963).

a sudden augmentation of high-quality proteins (e.g. a dried milk distribution program) may precipitate a complex series of reactions culminating in urinary stones.

CONCLUSION AND DISCUSSION

The introduction of new kinds of technology from alien environments into that of a less developed country, together with the complex of factors involved in the usual change that follows such introduction, can cause certain definite dysfunctions in the normal man-environment relationships. There is mounting clinical evidence that disturbances in these relationships can cause disorders in the genito-urinary system with definite clinical symptoms. Prolonged contact with chemical dyes has caused bladder tumors in dye workers under ordinary working conditions. Building dams, especially in Egypt, has increased the incidence of bilharziasis in the human bladder, sometimes ending with carcinomatous changes in the bladder.

Introduction of new machinery to the less developed countries and widespread use of the automobile, even for short distances, have replaced walking and physical exercise, normally practiced in these countries. These changes have led to a high incidence of metabolic disorders, including urinary stone formation, in man.

Hard work, lack of physical exercise, nervous tension, short vacations and leisure time, are all replacing more relaxed regimes of living, and are causing psychosomatic problems including diminished libido and potentia even in young men.

The introduction of technology into the underdeveloped countries has produced widespread, serious disruptions. Even in the most developed countries, these disruptions have not been adequately controlled. In the less developed world, such problems of control are even more complex; technology involves the destruction of traditional ways of life without providing adequate solutions and alternatives for coping with this destruction. Thus, the panaceas of technological development have produced widespread modifications, drastically altering the biological order which forms the basis for public health. Science is only now beginning to uncover some of the manifold changes that accompany technological change. Most of the problems remain undetected. The general lack of a scientific infrastructure in the less developed countries makes it difficult to detect, let alone remedy, the majority of these problems.

Scientific inquiries must be organized now to elucidate the harmful side effects of technological innovations in the less developed countries.

REFERENCES

Andrus, S. B.; Gershoff, S. N.; and Faragalla, E. L. "Production of Calcium Oxalate Renal Calculi in Vitamin B$_6$ Deficient Rats. Study of the Influences of Urine pH, *Lab. Invest.,* 9 (1960), p. 7.

Bonser, G. M.; Clayson, D. B.; Jull, J. W.; and Pyrah, L. L. "Experimental Aspects of Industrial Bladder Cancer." *Brit. J. Urol.,* 26 (1954), p. 49.

Dimmette, R. M.; Sproat, H. F.; and Sayegh, E. S. "The Classification of Carcinoma of the Bladder Associated with Urinary

Schistosomiasis and Metaplasia." *J. Urol.,* 75 (1956), p. 680.

Faber, S. R.; Feitler, W. W.; Bleiler, R. E.; Ohlson, M. A.; and Hodges, R. E. "The Effect of an Induced Pyridoxine and Pantothenic Acid Deficiency on Excretions of Oxalic and Xanthurenic Acids in the Rine," *Amer. J. Clin. Nutr.* 12 (1963), p. 406.

Farvar, B. Unpublished data and results (1968).

Farvar, B.; Chase, T. N.; Meyer, G. G.; and Zinsser, H. H. "The Effect of Vitamin B_6 (Pyridoxine) on the Excretion of Calcium, Phosphorous, Oxalic Acid and the Other Urinary Constituents in the Urine of Oxalate Stone Forming Patients." *Abstr. Internat. Congr. Nutr.,* 5th. Wasington, D.C., 1960. P. 34.

Farvar, B., and Mohammadiha, H. "Urolithiasis in Iran. A Study of 137 Cases." *Revue de la Faculté de Médecine.* Université de Téhéran, Vol. 2 (1963).

Gehrmann, G. H.; Foulger, J. H.; and Fleming, A. J. *Proc. 9th Internat. Congr. Indust. Med.* London, 1948.

Gershoff, S. N., and Prien, E. L. "Excretion of Urinary Metabolites in Calcium Oxalate Urolithiasis. Effect of Tryptophan and Vitamin B_6 Administration," *Amer. J. Clin. Nutr.,* 8. (1960), p. 812.

Hueper, W. E.; Wiley, F. H.; and Wolfe, H. D. "Experimental Production of Bladder Tumors in Dogs by Administration of Beta-naphthylamine." *J. Industr. Hyg. and Toxicol.,* 20 (1938), p. 46.

Melick, W. F.; Escue, H. M.; Naryka, J. J.; Mereza, R. A.; and Wheeler, E. P. "The First Reported Cases of Human Bladder Tumors Due to a New Carcinogen: Xenylamine." *J. Urol.,* 74 (1955), p. 760.

Wardlaw, H. S. H. "Observations on Incidence and Composition of Urinary Calculi." *Med. J. Australia,* 1 (1952), p. 180.

Zinsser, Hans H. Professor of Clinical Urology, Columbia University, College of Physicians and Surgeons (personal communication).

5. AGGRAVATION OF VITAMIN A DEFICIENCY FOLLOWING DISTRIBUTION OF NON-FORTIFIED SKIM MILK
An Example of Nutrient Interaction*

George E. Bunce

Nutrients are interrelated to one another in a variety of ways. The relationships are usually not readily apparent to the non-specialist. Disturbance of these relationships may have a profound effect upon the recipient of the food.

One example of the potentially tragic results of alteration of dietary patterns is discussed in this paper; namely the aggravation of vitamin A deficit following the distribution of a high protein supplement with a consequent epidemic outbreak of keratomalacia and irreversible blindness. Several other examples are given to illustrate that complex nutrient interactions are more the rule than the exception. Thus even the seemingly harmless measure of food supplementation may yield undesirable, unexpected and serious problems.

Malnutrition is one of the most serious problems facing the world today. In its Third World Food Survey, the FAO estimated that at least 20% of the population of the developing countries receive too few calories and are undernourished and that about 60% consume diets that are inadequate in nutritional quality because of a deficiency of protein, thiamine, vitamin A, and other essentials. One of the most ominous aspects of the problem is that in spite of considerable efforts which have already been

* The material in this paper was originally published in different form as "Milk and Blindness in Brazil" in *Natural History* magazine, Copyright © 1969 by The American Museum of Natural History.

mounted, we are failing. Today there are more hungry persons than ever before in the history of the world.

In May 1967 the President's Science Advisory Committee (PSAC) published a three-volume report entitled *The World Food Problem*. The report of this panel of experts is one of the most comprehensive and sobering résumés yet assembled about the magnitude of the world food problem and the possible solutions. The panel began by noting the immense complexity of the current situation. No one group of specialists has the capacity to defeat world malnutrition and hunger. Prevention of widespread famine and malnutrition will require the joint efforts of experts in nutrition, agriculture, family planning, economic development and many other fields. Massive funding on a worldwide basis will be necessary to insure sound programs. The needs are critical and the time is short.

There is the very real danger, however, as the organizers of this conference realize, that these urgent needs may produce projects whose overall impact on a region or its population have not been reviewed carefully. This may happen when the potential dangers are not readily visible to the reasonably well educated layman. In such circumstances, much harm may be done before corrective measures can be applied.

Most laymen are aware of the need for adequate daily supplies of the various macronutrients and micronutrients. Most are unaware, however, of the relationships among nutrients or between nutrients and environmental factors. Moreover, conventional medical training and practice may also ignore many of these interdependencies. These interdependencies, however, markedly affect the physiology of the consuming organism. Such interactions are the rule rather than the exception.

In order to illustrate this point more fully let us consider the case of the interrelationship of protein and vitamin A, two nutrients which are in deficient supply in many populations and which produce profound deficiency symptoms.

Vitamin A is one of the class of fat soluble vitamins. It participates in a number of biochemical processes and is necessary for a normal rate of growth, for night vision and for the maintenance of the healthy state of epithelial structures of the eye, respiratory tract and gastrointestinal tract. A mild deficiency of vitamin A may result in loss of vision in dim light, the retardation of growth, and a dermatosis characterized by dryness, roughening and itching of the skin. If the deficiency is more severe, the conjunctiva and para-ocular glands become abnormal and are unable to produce their usual supply of lubricating fluids. This condition, xerophthalmia, may be readily followed by secondary infection, ulceration, softening of the cornea (keratomalacia) and perforation. If therapy is begun at the stage of uncomplicated xerophthalmia, the prognosis is good. If not, partial or total blindness is likely to result.

Protein, on the other hand, is one of the macronutrients. Proteins are large polymeric molecules formed from smaller compounds called amino acids. Protein serves a structural role as the primary material of muscle and other cells. It is also required for the production of enzymes, the regulators of biochemical processes.

Protein deficiency (kwashiorkor) and protein-calorie malnutrition (marasmus) are the two most widespread nutritional deficiencies in the world today. Failure to consume adequate amounts of protein and calories leads first to growth failure; it is then followed by wasting and ultimate death and is often complicated by secondary infections. Between the two extremes there are, of course, many degrees of deficiency. Vitamin A deficiency is also common in underdeveloped regions. Almost all of the countries of south and east Asia and certain parts of the Near East, Africa and Latin

America are affected. It is particularly prevalent in urban slums where neither whole milk or green or yellow vegetables (two major sources of vitamin A) are available in good supply. The most susceptible age group is the preschool child, whose dietary deficiency of vitamin A accounts for the major proportion of blindness and makes a considerable contribution to mortality.

The relationship of deficiencies of vitamin A and protein is complex. In studies with experimental animals, the amount of dietary protein provided influences the pathological picture. Animals fed a good protein diet apparently consume their body stores of vitamin A rapidly and develop eye lesions more quickly than their slower-growing litter mates fed rations low in protein (McLaren, 1959). Clinical evidence with human infants suggests that they behave in a similar fashion (Oomen *et al.,* 1964). Children with grossly retarded growth often have no ocular lesions despite low vitamin A intakes and low blood levels, but they may develop xerophthalmia if vitamin A supplements are not included with the treatment for protein malnutrition. The picture is further complicated by the fact that serum proteins act as carriers for vitamin A in the blood. Thus, mobilization as well as utilization of stored vitamin A may be stimulated by protein supplements in children previously receiving low protein diets.

With this background information, one may speculate that prolonged intake of a marginal level of both vitamin A and protein could result in a juvenile population in which growth retardation was present but not severe, and in which the body reserves of vitamin A were minimal. Sudden famine, brought on by drought, flood or revolution, would precipitate protein calorie malnutrition, but the concurrent acute growth restriction or weight loss would prevent the outbreak of visible signs of vitamin A deficiency. The distribution of a high-quality protein, low in vitamin A, to children in

this condition would spur growth and rapid mobilization and consumption of the remaining meager body stores of vitamin A. The acute stage of vitamin A deficiency with its potential for partial or total blindness could then follow.

J. H. deHaas (1958) was one of the first persons to draw attention to the danger of feeding a high protein, low vitamin A food to human infants as a major food item. His observations in Java between 1935 and 1940 convinced him that the sale and consumption of sweetened skimmed condensed milk was a principal cause of vitamin A deficiency.[1] Although his major concern was probably with the low intake of vitamin A imposed by this regimen rather than with the potentiating effect of simultaneous consumption of a good-quality protein, his observations were sound and were implemented in the distribution policies of the major post-World War II relief agencies. Although these agencies (UNICEF, etc.) did utilize dry skim milk powder as a major item in famine relief, they were careful to insist upon the distribution of vitamin A capsules along with the milk powder. They warned that the children might lose their sight if the capsules were not consumed as directed. They also restricted distribution to responsible groups such as health centers rather than allowing sale of the product on the open market. What is not known is the number of children who actually received the recommended amounts of vitamin A. Lacking data on this point, one may presume it likely that, despite the conscientious efforts of the distributors, their warnings were either ignored or forgotten by many uneducated and destitute parents.

Fortunately, it appears that few instances of widespread and serious complications have occurred. Perhaps the populations which received the supplements were not in

---

[1] Skimmed milk products have been treated to remove lipids so as to improve their stability in storage. Vitamin A, being a lipid-soluble compound, is also removed by this treatment.

the state of balance that would make them susceptible in large numbers. Perhaps the instructions concerning the consumption of the vitamin A capsules were carried out more faithfully than one might anticipate. It is also possible, however, that the difficulties of obtaining reliable medical statistics in underdeveloped countries has obscured the true incidence of the problem. Documentation of the incidence of xerophthalmia and keratomalacia in a given region requires the efforts of physicians specifically alerted to the problem and actively seeking cases away from the hospital population (Oomen et al., 1964). Without this special emphasis, a significant increase in eye lesions induced by vitamin A deficiency might easily go unnoticed.

There is reason to believe that protein supplements low in vitamin A were related to the aggravation of a chronic vitamin A deficit in Recife in northeast Brazil. Recife, the capital of the state of Pernambuco, is a city of approximately one million people and is located on the coastline of the eastern bulge of South America. It is the major population center for eleven states covering a total land area of some 476,000 square miles. About 70% of this total land area is within the so-called "drought polygon." The population of the drought region was approximately thirteen million in 1960, or about 20% of the total population of Brazil. Most of these people live in small villages and engage in subsistence agriculture. Rainfall within this area is extremely irregular. During the past four hundred years, there have been some fifty-five droughts, an average of a major drought every seven years (Nutrition Survey of Northeast Brazil, March–May, 1963). These droughts have caused widespread crop failure. In times of crop failure, large numbers of persons migrate to Recife to find work and famine relief. Thus the misery of the entire region comes into focus in

the squatter's slums of Recife. Under such circumstances, malnutrition is inevitable and the deficits of protein and vitamin A are serious, well-established and long-standing (Oomen et al., 1964).

A series of particularly severe droughts occurred in northeast Brazil during the 1950's, resulting in an unusually large influx of indigents into Recife and other major urban centers. The resources of UNICEF and other relief agencies were mobilized to meet this crisis. Following the usual practice, skim milk powder was dispensed accompanied by vitamin A capsules with warnings of the consequences of failure to follow instructions. On this occasion, however, reports soon began to circulate from the major hospitals that noted a sharp increase in keratomalacia and xerophthalmia following the distribution of the skimmed milk.

Unfortunately, as far as the author knows, the only written records describing this outbreak are in the archives of the Recife newspapers and possibly in hospital records. I know of no scientific publication in which the incidence of keratomalacia and xerophthalmia was recorded during the "epidemic" months and evaluated in terms of the dietary history of the patients. Two sources may be cited, however, that provide supporting evidence. One source, entitled "A Global Survey on Xerophthalmia," is a summary of the findings during an extensive survey of the worldwide problem of hypovitaminosis A (Oomen et al., 1964). Based upon their interviews with local physicians, the authors concluded that an epidemic of xerophthalmia had occurred at the time of the skimmed milk distribution and that it appeared likely to be a result of the recipients' failure to use the vitamin A capsules correctly. The second source of information is the interviews conducted in 1963 with Recife physicians by members of the ICNND Nutrition Survey Team, to which the author belonged. The team members are listed in the agency report (ICNND, Nutrition Survey of Northeast Brazil, March–May, 1963). The reliability of such evidence is always subject to question. In view of the known relationship of vitamin A and protein and the uniform agreement among experienced local physicians, however, it would seem reasonable to conclude that in this instance the problem probably did exist.

The necessity of separate distribution of the skim milk powder and vitamin A supplements imposed potential hazards, and UNICEF was not unaware of this. For example, the Joint FAO/WHO Expert Committee on Nutrition at its fourth meeting (FAO Nutr. Meetings Report Svc. No. 9, 1955) urged the continuation of investigations already sponsored by FAO on the development of additives which could be mixed with the milk powder before distribution to the consumers. This became technically feasible in the early 1960's with the development of a stable, water-dispersible vitamin A derivative by chemists at Hoffman-LaRoche (Bauernfeind and Parman, 1964). Tests with rats showed the additive to be effective even with low fat intakes. The possibility still remained, however, that humans in the affected area might respond differently because of unsuspected variations in conditions (parasite loads, chronic deficiencies, etc.). It seemed advisable, therefore, to carry out studies on recipient subjects to assure safety and effectiveness under field conditions. Such a project began in 1965 and ended in 1967. Dr. Fernando Figueira and his coworkers of the Instituto de Medicina Infantil de Pernambuco and Dr. Nelson Chaves and his associates at the Instituto de Nutrição of the Federal University of Pernambuco, under the joint sponsorship of the AID mission to Brazil and the Nutrition Section of the Office for International Research, conducted the study in Recife.[2] The data obtained from these studies supported the animal tests and encouraged the widespread employment of the additives in human feeding programs.

It is not my purpose to find fault with any of the agencies involved in the food relief programs for northeast Brazil. I believe that they were cognizant of the possibilities and made a reasonable effort to minimize the danger. I do believe, however, that this example points out the necessity for careful planning and consultation with nutrition experts before the implementation of relief or development projects dealing with food commodities. Suppose, for example, that an administrative decision had been made to economize. Vitamin A supplements could have been eliminated on the grounds that they were unnecessary because few cases of xerophthalmia were being reported. Such a decision would probably have seemed quite sound and safe to a person unfamiliar with the nutritional history of northeast Brazil and the interrelationship of these two nutrients. Yet it would have caused immense medical havoc and suffering.

Nutrient and environment interdependencies are not rare in the study of nutrition. Several more examples might be instructive. One such example is the relationship between the amino acid tryptophan and the vitamin niacin. The studies of Goldberger, Elvehjem and many others during the period of 1915 to 1935 on pellagra in humans and blacktongue in dogs established that these diseases were responsive to dietary supplements of the vitamin niacin. These investigations as well as those of other major contributors have been clearly and completely chronicled by McCollum (1957). Having shown the importance of

[2] The author participated in these studies as a consultant in biochemistry to the two laboratories. John W. Reynolds, M.D., of the Department of Pediatrics of the University of Minnesota Medical School, served as the clinical adviser.

niacin in the treatment of pellagra, nutritionists found it difficult to understand why there was a high incidence of the disease among maize-eating people when it was discovered that several other staple cereal grains never associated with pellagra were actually lower in niacin content than corn. This situation was clarified, however, by the subsequent finding that a small proportion of the amino acid tryptophan could be converted to niacin by a metabolic process. Thus the condition of pellagra was not the result of a single deficiency but of a dual deficit in both niacin and tryptophan.

A second example is the recent series of reports by Caddell (1967) and Caddell and Goddard (1967) of the benefit of magnesium supplements for children suffering from protein-calorie malnutrition. These researchers as well as a number of others have determined that magnesium deficiency may occur in such patients as a conditioned deficiency; that is, the body magnesium deficit is a result of excessive losses associated with the muscle wasting, diarrhea and vomiting of protein-calorie malnutrition. During the treatment and recovery phase the children require magnesium supplements in excess of the normal requirements in order to compensate for the previous high losses. This conditioned deficit was not recognized earlier because the patients failed to develop classical signs of magnesium deficiency. Quite frequently, however, dual deficiencies will present a syndrome in which the classical symptoms are obscured. Inclusion of magnesium as part of the therapy of protein-calorie malnutrition was found to improve clinical recovery by a substantial degree.

The third example I have chosen is a case of interaction between nutrition and parasitology. Infestation with a heavy parasite load is quite common among lower economic classes in underdeveloped nations. Considering the lack of sanitation and education, it could hardly be otherwise. If parasites cause only minimal residual damage to the host, some of them are not regarded as particularly dangerous organisms by physicians. One organism of substantial concern, however, is *Entamoeba histolytica*. This organism ordinarily invades the intestinal wall of the host, causing scarring and functional loss of the affected areas. A patient suffering from the effects of this invasion is said to have clinical amebiasis, a very serious condition.

In view of the usual behavior of this organism, a joint team from Tulane University and the Universidad del Valle, in Cali, Colombia, engaged in a parasitological survey in Colombia, were surprised to find only occasional cases of amoebiasis among a population of about one thousand persons with approximately 40% infestation of *E. histolytica* according to fecal examinations (Faust and Read, 1959). The sample population was found to have a daily nutrient intake which was deficient by U.S. standards in practically all of the macronutrients and micronutrients tested. As is frequently the case, locally available foods low in protein but high in starch (plantain, yucca, potato) were the major dietary staples.

In the course of the fecal examinations, the investigators also noted the appreciable amount of undigested starch grains in the stool specimens. They concluded that a major factor contributing to the indigestibility of the starch was the poor protein intake of the subjects and the subsequent low production of starch-digesting enzymes. This point has been explored by Platt (1958) in a paper on malnutrition and the pathogenesis of disease.

Considering all these factors, Faust and Read (1959) hypothesized that the protozoan organisms in the large intestine were being provided with a much greater supply of starch in subjects with poor dietary protein intakes as compared to well-fed persons. The organism was therefore utilizing the starch as an energy source in preference to invading the intestinal wall. The authors also described their evidence that *E. histolytica* readily digested in vitro the starchy foods typical of the local dietary pattern. By such a mechanism, a normally highly pathogenic organism was carried as an essentially asymptomatic infection. Obviously, this hypothesis would need to be considered as part of a protein feeding program in any underdeveloped nation.

In conclusion, an attempt has been made in this paper to show that nutrient interrelationships are common and may have profound effects if ignored. The experience in northeast Brazil of aggravation of a vitamin A deficit by the feeding of high-protein supplements has been cited as a specific example of this situation. Emphasis has also been placed on the fact that such interactions are not readily obvious to the reasonably well educated lay public.

It should be evident that there are many factors to be considered before any changes in dietary patterns are recommended or effected. In order to minimize the potential for tragic unsuspected results, any agency considering a dietary supplementation or alteration, however minor it may appear on the surface, should seek the services of appropriately trained and experienced nutrition experts before any action is begun. The American Institute of Nutrition[3] can provide a list of qualified individuals to serve in this capacity. It would also seem reasonable to encourage the continued support of research in basic biochemistry and nutrition as a means of providing fundamental knowledge of nutrient interrelationships and the pathological consequences of faulty nutrition.

[3] American Institute of Nutrition, 9650 Rockville Pike, Bethesda, Maryland 20014.

REFERENCES

Bauernfeind, J. C., and Parman, G. K. "Restoration of Nonfat Dry Milk with Vitamins A and D." *Food Technology*, Vol. 18, No. 2 (1964), pp. 174–79.

Caddell, J. L. "Studies in Protein-Calorie Malnutrition. II. A Double-Blind Clinical Trial to Assess Magnesium Therapy." *New Eng. J. Med.*, 276 (1967), 535.

Caddell, J. L., and Goddard, D. R. "Studies in Protein-Calorie Malnutrition. I. Chemical Evidence for Magnesium Deficiency." *New Eng. J. Med.*, 276 (1967), 533–34.

deHaas, J. H., and Meulemans, O. *Geneesk. Tydschr. Ned. Indie.*, 78 (1938), 847, as cited by W. R. Aykroyd in Conference on Nutritional Disease, *Federation Proc.*, Suppl. No. 2, Vol. 17, No. III (1958), p. 105.

Faust, E. C., and Read, T. R. "Parasitologic Surveys in Cali, Departamento del Valle, Colombia. V. Capacity of *Entamoeba histolytica* of Human Origin to Utilize Different Types of Starches in Its Metabolism." *Amer. J. Trop. Med. and Hyg.*, 8 (1959), 293–303.

Interdep'tl. Comm. on Nut. for Natl. Devel. *Nutrition Survey of Northeast Brazil, March–May 1963.* A Report of the Interdepartmental Committee on Nutrition for National Development. Bethesda, Md.: National Institutes of Health, 1963.

McCollum, E. V. *A History of Nutrition.* Boston: Houghton Mifflin Co., 1957.

McLaren, D. S. "Influence of Protein Deficiency and Sex on the Development of Ocular Lesions in Survival Time of the

Vitamin A-Deficient Rat." *Brit. J. Oph-thalmol.*, 43 (1959), 234.

Oomen, H. A. P. C.; McLaren, D. S.; and Escapini, H. "A Global Survey on Xeroph-thalmia. Epidemiology and Public Health Aspects of Hypovitaminosis-A." *Trop. and Geog. Med.*, 16 (1964), 271.

Platt, B. S. "Malnutrition and the Pathogenesis of Disease." *Trans. R. Soc. Trop. Med. Hyg.*, 52 (1958), 189–210.

Pres. Sci. Adv. Comm. *The World Food Problem*, Vols. I, II and III. A Report of the President's Science Advisory Committee; the Panel on the World Food Supply. Washington: U. S. Government Printing Office, 1967.

6. LACTOSE INTOLERANCE IN SOUTHEAST ASIA

A. E. Davis and T. D. Bolin

There has been increasing interest in the phenomenon of lactose intolerance, especially in adults who usually suffer abdominal pain and diarrhea following ingestion of milk. An increased racial incidence of lactose intolerance has been described in Negroes and Australian aborigines and has been suggested for Greek Cypriots and Indians.

We have found that lactose intolerance is common in peoples from Southeast Asia. This finding has great importance when one considers the increasing part played by milk and milk products in food aid programs to underdeveloped countries both during normal times and periods of famine. Milk distribution to people who are intolerant of lactose, especially when they are debilitated, may, in addition to having little if any nutritional value, be positively harmful.

Controversy exists as to whether lactose intolerance is an acquired defect or a genetically determined trait. Both human and animal studies have been conducted. Whereas the general agreement is that the trait is genetically determined, we are of the opinion that it is an adaptive phenomenon due to the lack of sufficient substrate challenge. If the fault is an adaptive one then milk and milk products could be introduced successfully into an Asian community, provided their introduction was preceded by a suitable educational program.

It would seem crucial to prove the etiology of lactose intolerance in peoples from Asia before large sums of money are spent on developing a dairy industry.

The phenomenon of lactose (milk sugar) intolerance, due to a deficiency of the intestinal enzyme lactase, which is essential for the absorption and utilization of lactose, is drawing increasing attention as its implications in food aid programs become clear. Lactose intolerance is manifest by abdominal pain, flatulence and diarrhea following the ingestion of milk or milk products. (See Appendix A.)

Lactose intolerance can be either primary or secondary. The secondary form occurs commonly in association with many gastrointestinal diseases (Table 6–1). The primary

Table 6–1

CONDITIONS ASSOCIATED WITH
SECONDARY DISACCHARIDASE DEFICIENCY

1. Gastroenteritis
2. Protein-Calorie malnutrition (Kwashiorkor)
3. Coeliac Disease
4. Tropical Sprue
5. Idiopathic Steatorrhea
6. Ulcerative Colitis
7. Whipple's Disease
8. Regional Enteritis
9. Cystic Fibrosis
10. Intestinal Lymphangiectasia
11. Beta-lipoprotein Deficiency
12. Drugs — Neomycin
              Conovid
13. Giardia Lamblia Infestation
14. Infectious Hepatitis
15. Postsurgical: Postgastrectomy
                Gastroenterostomy
                Blind Loop
                Shortened Small Intestine

form occurs in otherwise healthy adults and has a varying incidence in different ethnic groups. There is a high incidence in American (Bayless and Rosensweig, 1966) and African (Cook and Kajubi, 1966) Negroes, Australian aborigines (Elliott *et al.,* 1967) and Greek Cypriots (McMichael *et al.,* 1965). The initial report of Davis and Bolin (1967) describing a high incidence of lactose intolerance in Asian students has been confirmed in other Asian populations (Chung and McGill, 1968; Bayless *et al.,* 1968; Matsunaga, 1968).

The high incidence of lactose intolerance in Asian and other ethnic groups has important socio-economic implications when we realize the important role of milk and milk products in food aid programs to underdeveloped countries. This aid may consist of the establishment of milk-processing plants in Asian communities by government or international agencies, or the direct distribution of powdered milk. The United

Nations Economic and Social Council has reported the technical and economic difficulties of starting milk-processing plants in underdeveloped countries. The cost is high and establishment of a dairy industry is particularly difficult in a tropical climate (Whyte, 1967).[1] One attempt to avoid these problems is to "tone" the extremely high fat content of the native buffalo milk with powdered milk from milk-producing countries such as Australia and New Zealand.

When there is co-existence of primary and secondary lactase deficiency, particularly in times of famine, milk in amounts contributing a significant part of the diet may induce or exacerbate diarrhea. This could be particularly serious in malnourished and debilitated children. It is especially in this situation that aid tends to be given in the form of milk.

The pathogenesis of primary lactose intolerance is disputed. It could be a hereditary enzyme defect occurring with varying frequency in different ethnic groups. Another, and it would seem to us more likely possibility, is an acquired defect, due to lack of continued substrate challenge in the form of low level of milk consumption, resulting in a gradual adaptive decline in enzymatic activity. It is known that there is very little milk consumption after weaning in most of the population groups reported to have a high incidence of lactose intolerance.

Results of studies on both animals and humans are inconclusive but seem to us to favor the theory that lactose intolerance is due to a gradual decline in enzyme activity because of the lack of a continued substrate challenge. This theory would account for the earlier appearance of the condition in some ethnic groups whose milk consumption after weaning is minimal, compared

[1] For an appraisal of UNICEF/FAO-assisted milk conservation programs see the Milk Conservation Program (1948–66) E./I.C.E.F./1257.

with Caucasians whose milk consumption declines at a later age. A direct relationship of age to an increased incidence of lactose-induced cramps and diarrhea in Negroes (Bayless et al., 1968) supports this theory. However, a detailed survey of milk-drinking habits of the various ethnic groups is needed to verify it.

If lactose intolerance is a late manifestation of a genetically predetermined condition, it might be expected to occur in association with congenital lactose intolerance (a rare form of lactose intolerance occurring in infancy). There appears to be no such association, and there is also no convincing familial incidence of the condition, at least in Caucasians. A congenital defect should be manifest in childhood when the load is maximal. As compared to the congenital syndrome, these people tolerate milk well in infancy. Finally, the condition occurs too frequently to be explained as a genetic mutation.

There have been numerous attempts to induce intestinal lactase in the rat and other animals.[2] The results remain conflicting and controversial. Protagonists of the genetic etiology of adult lactase deficiency rely largely on early reports of failure to adapt lactase in various animals to support this theory. However, many of these experiments were performed before reliable methods of enzyme assay became available. Only Girardet et al. (1964) have shown adaptation to occur in the adult rat, but this paper is rarely quoted. As the problem of adaptation assumes importance in relation to human lactase deficiency, we thought it essential to confirm their work. In summary, it was found that after five to eight weeks on a 30% lactose diet a significant increase in jejunal lactase activity was obtained (Bolin, Pirola, and Davis, 1969). Intestinal lactase

[2] See References for further details: Plimmer, 1906; Heilskov, 1951; Fischer and Sutton, 1953; Fischer, 1957; Groot and Hoogendoorn, 1957; Alvarez and Sas, 1961; Doell and Kretchmer, 1962; Koldovsky and Chytil, 1965; Huber et al., 1964; Girardet et al., 1964.

in the rat is thus seen to be an adaptive enzyme and presumably such adaptation can occur in the human.

Studies of human subjects again illustrate the controversy over the genetic or acquired nature of lactose intolerance. Cuatrecasas et al., (1965) showed in a group of sixty patients, 67% Negro, a strong correlation between milk consumption and lactose absorption. Of the "non-drinkers" of milk 86% were lactose "non-absorbers," while only 13% of milk "drinkers" were "non-absorbers." An attempt to increase lactose absorption in seven "non-absorbers" was made by giving 150 grams of lactose daily for up to forty-five days. There was no increase in lactose absorption or jejunal lactase activity.

· However, animal experiments suggest that at least eight weeks are required with lactose loading to result in enzyme induction. It is also possible that lactose alone is insufficient to provoke enzyme induction in humans. Lactose is a component of oligosaccharides in milk (Clamp et al., 1961) and it may be that these or some other fractions of whole milk are essential for continued enzyme production.

A significant fall in "lactose absorption" was found in two patients deprived of milk for five months (Cuatrecasas et al., 1965), suggesting a decline in enzyme activity with the disappearance of continued substrate challenge.

McMichael et al. (1965) concluded that there is an inherited basis for lactase deficiency because they found lactase deficiency in fifteen of seventeen Greek Cypriots. Two of these patients had a family history of milk intolerance. No details of milk consumption were given.

Cook and Kajubi (1966) found an "inherited congenital" difference in lactase levels between different African tribes. Lactase deficiency is very common in the Baganda, occurring in 89%. However, their diet is largely vegetable and mainly banana.

Milk consumption was either nil or less than one-fourth pint daily. In contrast, the Bahima tribe "took between 2 and 7 pints of milk daily and little else." Only one of eleven Bahima patients had a flat lactose curve. Intestinal lactase levels were not measured. Here, then, are two tribes, one of milk drinkers who are lactose-tolerant and the other of non-milk drinkers who are nearly all lactose-intolerant. We would interpret this as evidence more in favor of an acquired rather than of a congenital defect.

The differences between other tribes were not as marked, but Cook and Kajubi (1966) point out that "although every effort was made to obtain accurate histories of milk intake, limitations inherent in nutritional assessment in Africa must be appreciated." (This difficulty did not apply to the Baganda and Bahima tribes.)

Cook (1967) found a gradual fall in the mean maximum rise of blood glucose after a lactose load in the first four years of age in an African population. These results were related to the previous paper and, as "some infants with flat curves were breast-fed and most of the infants had milk for many weeks before the test," a hereditary basis was again favored. However, precise details of milk consumption were not obtained.

Bayless and Rosensweig (1967) consider lactose intolerance to be hereditary because of the similar incidence in American and African Negroes. Huang and Bayless (1967) reach the same conclusions. Four of twenty Negro children and no white children had a maximum rise of blood sugar of less than 20 mg./100 ml. after lactose. The difference in incidence compared to older Negro groups is unexplained, but the majority of the children in this study consumed at least one glass of milk per day.

We have carried out an investigation on lactose intolerance in various ethnic groups in Southeast Asia (Bolin *et al.*, 1970) and this study revealed lactose intolerance to be common in Chinese students, New Guineans, and a small group of Indians. A total of twenty-nine out of thirty Chinese students, or 97%, were found to have lactose intolerance. After lactose the only Chinese subject without diarrhea had a maximum rise in blood sugar of 25 mg./100 ml. and her jejunal lactase activity was 1 unit per gram wet weight—low limit of normal. All the New Guinean men and four of the five Indians were lactose-intolerant. None of the well-recognized causes of secondary lactase deficiency were evident in any of our subjects. Therefore, in these Asians we are dealing with primary lactose intolerance.

As we have stated, we feel that the evidence favors the adaptive theory rather than the genetic. This evidence is as yet insufficient. Regardless of which theory is correct, because of the increasing importance of milk aid programs to underdeveloped countries, particularly in times of famine, it is imperative to assess the over-all incidence of lactose intolerance in recipient countries. What is required is a survey of lactose intolerance among Asian peoples in their own environment. This survey must ask certain questions. What is the over-all incidence of lactose intolerance in the various communities? What is the incidence in relation to age and previous milk-drinking habits? Is the defect congenital or acquired? The results of such a survey would show which communities (and which groups within an individual community) would benefit most from the introduction of milk products into the diet. If the defect could be shown to be an adaptive phenomenon, then milk could be introduced into the diet under a planned scheme which aimed at gradually increasing the lactose content of the various milk products. If, on the other hand, the defect is genetically determined, then it would appear better to concentrate on other ways of improving the value of the basic diet.

Such a survey has now been carried out in Singapore (Bolin *et al.*, 1970). In summary, lactose intolerance was found to be universal after the age of ten years. Before this there was an increasing incidence of intolerance with age, particularly after the age of four years. A secondary cause for lactase deficiency was excluded in all but six of the ninety-eight subjects. The association between proportion of life as a milk drinker and lactose tolerance was statistically significant, and intolerance appeared at an earlier age in non-milk drinkers. The relationship of lactose tolerance to continued milk drinking after weaning found in this study would therefore support a theory of adaptation.

If the theory of adaptation is correct, it should be possible to forecast which populations are likely to be lactose-intolerant by referring to the known per capita milk consumption (F.A.O. Year Book, 1967). Table 6–2, which shows examples of per capita milk consumption in various countries, reveals that those populations that are lactose-tolerant have a per capita milk consumption of approximately 600 grams per day, while those that are lactose-intolerant have a per capita milk consumption of approximately 100 grams per day or less.

Therefore, other countries with a per capita milk consumption of approximately 100 grams per day are likely to have a high incidence of lactose intolerance. The majority of these are in underdeveloped areas of the world and it seems essential that surveys such as the above are carried out in these countries to assess the value of future milk aid programs.

We are presently continuing our work on lactose intolerance by carrying out experiments on human volunteers and animals. Our aim is to prove whether the defect is acquired or genetic. In addition a survey has begun in Singapore to show whether lactose feeding will reduce the high incidence of lactose intolerance. (We are being supported in this work by the Australian Dairy Produce Board and the National Health and Medical Research Council of Australia.)

Table 6–2

EXAMPLES OF PER CAPITA
MILK CONSUMPTION IN
DIFFERENT COUNTRIES
(F.A.O. Yearbook, 1967)

A. *Lactose Tolerant*

COUNTRY	PER CAPITA MILK CONSUMPTION (G/DAY)
U.S.A.	673
Canada	646
U.K.	593
Australia	614
New Zealand	771
Denmark	728

B. *Lactose Intolerant*

Uganda	63
Nigeria	18
Ghana	8
China (Taiwan)	11
India	110
Japan	100
Malaysia	112
Korea	5

APPENDIX A

Lactose Absorption and Pathogenesis of Diarrhea in Lactose Intolerance.

Before being metabolized, lactose must undergo hydrolysis into its component monosaccharides, glucose and galactose. Formerly it was believed that lactase, the enzyme responsible for this hydrolysis, together with the other disaccharidases sucrase and maltase, was

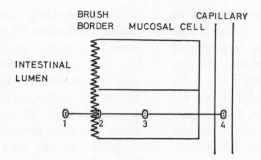

1 UNHYDROLYZED LACTOSE IN INTESTINAL LUMEN
2 HYDROLYSIS OCCURRING IN BRUSH BORDER OF MUCOSAL CELL
3 COMPONENT MONOSACCHARIDES TRANSPORTED THROUGH
   MUCOSAL CELL AFTER HYDROLYSIS
4 TRANSPORT OF MONOSACCHARIDES INTO CAPILLARY BLOOD

Figure 6–1   Mechanism of lactose hydrolysis and absorption

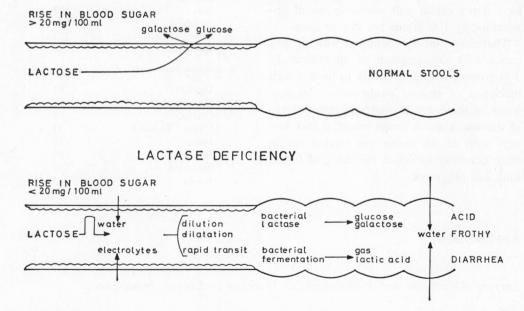

Figure 6–2   Pathogenesis of diarrhea in lactose intolerance

secreted by unspecified cells of the intestinal mucosa into the lumen of the gut where hydrolysis of the respective disaccharides occurred. However, recent studies indicated that hydrolysis takes place in the intestinal wall.[3] A variety of methods also demonstrated that the hydrolytic enzymes are localized in the brush border, or microvilli, of the epithelial cells facing the intestinal lumen. After hydrolysis the component monosaccharides are transported through the cell and into the blood stream (Figure 6-1).

Two mechanisms produce the symptoms of lactose intolerance (Figure 6-2). When lactose remains unsplit in the small intestine, there is a considerable flux of water into the lumen of the small bowel. In experiments in which lactose had been perfused into the small bowel of lactase-deficient subjects, volumes of up to 2,200 ml. have been recovered from the aspirate

[3] See References for further details: Fridhandler and Quastel, 1955; Borgstrom *et al.,* 1957; Dahlqvist and Borgstrom, 1961; Miller and Crane, 1961.

100 cm. distally when only 780 ml. of a 90% solution have been instilled, a net flux of 1,400 ml. (Kern and Struthers, 1966).

This aspirate remains isomolar due to diffusion of sodium, chloride, and to a lesser extent potassium into the gut lumen. Symptoms of cramps and nausea started five minutes after the infusion began and may be caused by distention of the small intestine. This large volume of fluid containing unsplit lactose is rapidly transported to the colon, where the second mechanism comes into action when the lactose contacts the colonic bacterial flora. Some bacteria, especially *Escherichia coli,* have marked lactase activity and split lactose into glucose and galactose. However, the greater part of the non-absorbed lactose undergoes bacterial fermentation and thus produces lower-molecular-weight organic acids and subsequently forms gas. These breakdown products exert a marked osmotic effect in the colon and a massive inpouring of fluid again occurs. The combination of fluid and gas causes bloating, abdominal distention, wind, and diarrhea.

REFERENCES

Alvarez, A., and Sas, J. "B-Galactosidase Changes in the Developing Intestinal Tract of the Rat." *Nature* (London), 190 (1961), 826.

Bayless, T. M., and Rosensweig, N. S. "A Racial Difference in Incidence of Lactase Deficiency." *J. Amer. Med. Ass.,* 197 (1966), 968.

———. "Incidence and Implications of Lactase Deficiency and Milk Intolerance in White and Negro Populations." *Johns Hopk. Hosp. J.,* 121 (1967), 54.

Bayless, T. M.; Huang, S. S.; Rosensweig, N. S.; and Christopher, N. L. "Milk and Lactose Intolerance." *Gastroenterology,* 54 (1968), 1220.

Bolin, T. D.; Pirola, R. C.; and Davis, A. E. "Lactose Intolerance in Various Ethnic Groups in South-East Asia." *Aust. Ann. Med.,* 17 (1968), 300.

Bolin, T. D.; Crane, G. G.; and Davis, A. E. "Adaptation of Intestinal Lactase in the Rat." *Gastroenterology,* 57 (1969), 406.

Bolin, T. D.; Davis, A. E.; Seah, C. S.; and Chua, K. L. "Lactose Intolerance in Singapore." *Gastroenterology* (1970).

Borgstrom, B.; Dahlqvist, A.; Lundh, G.; and Sjovall, J. "Studies of Intestinal Digestion and Absorption in the Human." *J. Clin. Invest.,* 36 (1957), 1521.

Chung, M. H., and McGill, D. B. "Lactase deficiency in Orientals." *Gastroenterology,* 54 (1968), 225.

Clamp, J. R.; Hough, L.; Hickson, J. L.; and Whistler, R. L. "Lactose." *Advanc. Carbohyd. Chem.,* 16 (1961), 159.

Cook, G. C. "Lactase Activity in Newborn and Infant Baganda." *Brit. Med. J.* (1967), 527-30.

———, and Kajubi, S. K. "Tribal Incidence

of Lactase Deficiency in Uganda." *Lancet*, 1 (1966), 725.

Cuatrecasas, P.; Lockwood, D. H.; and Caldwell, J. R. "Lactase Deficiency in the Adult. A Common Occurrence." *Lancet*, 1 (1965), 14.

Dahlqvist, A., and Borgstrom, B. "Digestion and Absorption of Disaccharides in Man." *Biochem. J.*, 81 (1961), 411.

Davis, A. E., and Bolin, T. D. "Lactose Intolerance in Asians." *Nature*, 216 (1967), 1244.

Doell, R. G., and Kretchmer, N. "Studies of Small Intestine During Development. 1. Distribution and Activity of B-Galactosidases." *Biochim. Biophys. Acta.* (Amsterdam), 62 (1962), 353–62.

Elliot, R. B.; Maxwell, G. M.; and Vawser, N. "Lactose Maldigestion in Australian Aboriginal Children." *Med. J. Australia*, 1 (1967), 46.

F.A.O. Year Book. 1967.

Fischer, J. E. "Effects of Feeding a Diet Containing Lactose upon B-D-Galactosidase Activity and Organ Development in the Rat Digestive Tract." *Amer. J. Physiol.*, 188 (1957), 49.

——, and Sutton, T. S. "Effect of Previous Lactose Feeding upon Intestinal Absorption of Lactose in the Rat." *J. Dairy Sci.*, 36 (1953), 7.

Fridhandler, L., and Quastel, J. H. "Absorption of Sugars from Isolated Surviving Intestine." *Arch. Biochem.*, 56 (1955), 412.

Girardet, P.; Richterich, R.; and Antener, I. "Adaptation de la lactase intestinale a l'administration de lactose chez le rat adulte." *Helv. Physiol. Pharmacol. Acta*, 22 (1964), 22.

Groot, A. P., and Hoogendoorn, P., "The Detrimental Effect of Lactose. 11. Quantitative Lactase Determinations in Various

Mammals." *Neth. Milk Dairy J.* 11 (1957), 290.

Heilskov, N. S. C. "Studies on Animal Lactase. 1. Lactase Activity Determination." *Acta. Physiol. Scand.*, 22 (1951), 267.

Huang, Shi-Shung, and Bayless, T. M. "Lactose Intolerance in Healthy Children." *New Eng. J. Med.*, 276 (1967), 1283.

Huber, J. T.; Rifkin, R. J.; and Keith, J. N. "Effect of Level of Lactose upon Lactase Concentrations in the Small Intestines of Young Calves." *J. Dairy Sci.*, 47 (1964), 789.

Kern, F., and Struthers, J. E. "Intestinal Lactase Deficiency and Lactose Intolerance in Adults." *J.A.M.A.*, 195 (1966), 927.

Koldovsky, O., and Chytil, F. "Postnatal development of B-Galactosidase Activity in the Small Intestine of the Rat. Effect of Adrenalectomy and Diet." *Biochem. J.*, 94 (1965), 266.

Lowry, O. H.; Rosebrough, N. J.; Farr, A. L.; and Randall, R. J. "Protein Measurement with the Folin Phenol Reagent." *J. Biol. Chem.*, 193 (1951), 265.

McMichael, H. B.; Webb, J.; and Dawson, A. M. "Lactase Deficiency in Adults. A Cause of Functional Diarrhea." *Lancet*, 1 (1965), 717.

Matsunaga, F. "A Study of Intestinal Lactase Deficiency in Japanese Adults." *Abstract International Gastroenterology Congress*, Prague, 1968.

Miller, D., and Crane, R. K. "Digestive Function of Epithelium of Small Intestine." *Biochim. Biophys. Acta.* (Amsterdam), 52 (1961), 281.

Plimmer, R. H. A. "On the Presence of Lactase in the Intestines of Animals and on the Adaptation of the Intestine to Lactose." *J. Physiol.* (London), 35 (1906), 20.

Whyte, R. O. *Milk Production in Developing Countries.* London: Faber & Faber, 1967.

7. THE ROLE OF TECHNOLOGICAL DEVELOPMENT IN PROMOTING DISEASE IN AFRICA[1]

Charles C. Hughes and John M. Hunter

For most countries of the world, this is an "age of development," of planned endeavors to intervene into the *status quo ante* with the purpose of initiating change, both economic and social. But developmental activities often produce unexpected and sometimes vitiating consequences. The very nature of change itself (being an intervention in the physical and human environment) is predispositional to disease, although not necessarily causative of it, because it disrupts established ecologic patterns at many levels of interrelationship. This idea can be extensively corroborated in contemporary Africa.

Field evidence relating to malnutrition and three selected infectious diseases (viz. sleeping sickness, bilharziasis and malaria) is reviewed. In each case, the evidence is replete with examples of development interventions that inadvertently increase disease hazards. In regard to the infectious diseases, examples of such evidence are: (1) increased incidence of trypanosomiasis (sleeping sickness) along new road networks in Liberia and Nigeria; the cycling of trypanosomes by migrant labor between Ghana and the Upper Volta Republic; and an outbreak of trypanosomiasis near the man-made Lake Kariba; (2) increased incidence of bilharziasis (schistosomiasis), especially the more serious intestinal form, *Schistosoma mansoni,* around irrigation schemes, with examples ranging from the Gezira cotton scheme in Sudan to sugar schemes in Nigeria and Tanzania, and tobacco farms in Rhodesia, with the dangers of further spread of the disease through presently planned agricultural schemes; and (3) an increasingly complex epidemiology of malaria in which, as a result of development activities and the

---

[1] This paper draws heavily from another discussion of this topic, including the psychosocial consequences of modernization. See References for Hughes and Hunter.

emergence of insecticide-resistant vectors, sociocultural factors are playing a more involved role.

Ironically, nutritional deficiencies and diseases often accompany substantial regional agricultural development. The transition to a cash-crop economy (e.g., cocoa, rubber, cotton, groundnuts, coffee) in many cases has led to the neglect of food farming and the declining use of protein-rich sorghums and similar nutrients. Purchased foodstuffs such as protein-poor cassava, yam or plantain have become food staples, causing rural malnutrition.

Africa's burgeoning towns are both a vehicle for, and a product of, development activities. And, as has been the case everywhere else in human history, the towns are also very effective as disease-fostering environments. Despite the provision of certain amenities, such as clinics, urban health standards are often lower than rural standards. For one thing, gross overcrowding and lack of sanitation cause deterioration in health status, and infectious diseases, such as tuberculosis and infant gastroenteritis, are rampant in towns. With regard to nutrition, the overwhelming impact of urbanization has been negative. Nutritional standards among urban migrants are unsatisfactory for a variety of reasons explained in this paper. Children are particularly prone to nutritional problems. It is well known, for example, that protein deficiency in early childhood (kwashiorkor) can cause irreversible intellectual impairment. Furthermore, for each case of kwashiorkor in African towns, diagnosed or not, there are countless other cases of subclinical malnutrition in which health deterioration is insidious and persistent.

The conclusion seems obvious, but inescapable. Because development activities have not been coordinated within a comprehensive ecologic framework, there has been a drastic deterioration in the social and economic conditions of life.

Our purpose in this paper is to focus on some of the disease consequences of technological development activities in Africa. This discussion will underscore the need to emphasize an ecologic frame of reference in research and planning.

Development programs, being an intervention into the affairs of nature, will have both intended and unintended consequences; that is to say, they enter the scene as elements in the ecologic dialectic in which all life is enmeshed, and they must be examined as such. In his *Man Adapting*, René Dubos has in a sense expressed the basic philosophy of this paper:

All technological innovations, whether concerned with industrial, agricultural, or medical practices, are bound to upset the balance of nature. In fact, to master nature is synonymous with disturbing the natural order. While it is desirable in principle to maintain the "balance of nature," it is not easy to define the operational meaning of this idea. Nature is never in a static equilibrium because the interrelationships between its physical and biological components are endlessly changing. Furthermore, man placed himself apart from the rest of nature when he began to farm the land and even more when he became urbanized. The survival, let alone growth, of his complex societies, implies that he will continue to exploit and therefore upset nature. The real problem, therefore, is not how to maintain the balance of nature, but rather how to change it in such a manner that the overall result is favorable for the human species. (1965, p. 416)

Dubos is, of course, echoing Hippocrates' ancient observation that change itself, creating the necessity for readaptation to a complex of conditions, is *predispositional* to disease although not necessarily causative of it.

It is changes that are chiefly responsible for diseases, especially the greatest changes, the violent alterations both in the seasons and other things. But seasons which come on gradually are the safest, as are gradual changes of regimen and temperature, and gradual changes from one period of life to another. (Dubos, 1959, p. 116)

In this connection, let us note some of the associated alterations in life conditions affecting man-environmental relationships which, while they may not in all cases be part of the explicit goal of any given development scheme, are nevertheless involved in the course of the implementation of the scheme. Aside from major purposes abstractly stated (e.g., "to raise agricultural productivity"), what other kinds of changes which have obvious relevance to the health status of the population often come about under the aegis of "development"?

(1) overall changes in man-habitat relationships (e.g., working in new farmland or under other new geographical and geozoological conditions; relocation to different climatic and zoonotic areas)

(2) increased population movement, mixing, and concentration (e.g., building roads, railways, and other transportation networks; migration to towns and sites of economic opportunity such as mines, factories, hydroelectric or irrigation projects; relocation of communities, etc.)

(3) change of patterns of water flow and use (e.g., building irrigation schemes, dams and ponds; use of polluted water resources in undersanitized and overcrowded towns)

(4) change of vegetation cover (e.g., cutting down forest or bush, altering ground cover; denudation of landscape)

(5) changes in micro-environmental conditions (e.g., changes in housing, neighborhood, and settlement patterns; in house style and construction materials; in location

with respect to modes of transportation, sources of water, kinsmen, etc.)

(6) changes in value systems and social sanction systems (e.g., conjunction of alternative ways of life in urban environments or socially heterogeneous populations, as in large-scale economic schemes; the erosion of traditional systems in conditions of economic deprivation, as in urban slums, etc.)

This listing of what might be called the "hidden costs" of development is clearly incomplete at this stage and unquestionably could be expanded with additional comprehensive data on change projects. But let us review the extent to which a change in disease patterns has ensued from such changes in ecological situation as those suggested above. While the following selected illustrations make the point that frequently such consequent relationships do exist with some of the major pathological conditions in Africa, it should be clear that systematic epidemiological data are rare, and the data that do exist for regions or for the continent as a whole, are not comprehensive in their coverage. But they are compelling in their import—viz., that often the ecologically unenlightened introduction of a given scheme will result largely in a "robbing of Peter to pay Paul" as far as the overall improvement of health status is concerned.

THE ROLE OF DEVELOPMENT IN FOSTERING DISEASE

Trypanosomiasis (Sleeping Sickness). Sleeping sickness is a protozoan disease caused by the genus *Trypanosoma,* which can infect not only domesticated and wild animals, but also man.

The Kissi tribal region of northern Liberia, bordering upon Sierra Leone and Guinea, is a prime focus of sleeping sickness in Liberia. Surveys in the early 1940's showed that the infection rate had been pushed down by treatment from 26% to 2.5% (Veatch, 1946), but recent evidence shows that infection has increased, reaching 10% in many places. In some areas, 79% of the population are carrying *Trypanosome gambiense* in their blood, although advanced cases are rare (Vaucel *et al.,* 1963).

There are two sets of reasons for this endemic focus. The first deals with the traditional way of life. For one thing, the Kissi raise swamp rice in a tsetse habitat. Secondly, their migratory habits make adequate treatment difficult and many cases relapse. In addition, they live in small settlements whose surroundings are kept insufficiently cleared of vegetation, so that tsetse can breed in the immediate area. Finally, they keep pigs, which may be a reservoir of *T. gambiense* (Veatch, 1946).

Another set of reasons for the endemicity is based on "modernizing" trends and sociopolitical developments. The Kissi tribe lives in adjoining sections of three countries: Liberia, Guinea and Sierra Leone, and much movement takes place across the international borders for purposes of trade and of visiting relatives. Political changes in Guinea following independence caused the control practices originated by the French to be dropped, and now Liberia is open to the ingress of new cases from that country (Foster, 1963). Of late, such movement has been greatly facilitated by improved road linkages. Reintroduction of trypanosomiasis into areas which were once clear of the disease has resulted. Such diffusion of the disease is illustrated, for example, in the case of the new road through Kissi country in northern Liberia, which was constructed in 1960. Because *Glossina palpalis* is found at every river crossing, a particular hazard arises wherever a road is intersected by a stream or river; vehicles often stop at such places for water and to refresh passengers, who thereby become highly

susceptible to the bite of the tsetse fly. To compound the jeopardy, tsetse flies are attracted to moving vehicles and may therefore be carried by them for some miles, a fact instrumental in spreading the disease into former tsetse-free areas (Abedi and Miller, 1964; Bequaert, 1946).

Among the Ashanti in Ghana, there is a clear illustration of the role of migrant labor, another aspect of population movement, in the dissemination of the disease and the reinfecting of controlled areas. From the 1920's into the 1940's many laborers from the savanna areas of northern Ghana and from other northern countries such as the (now) Upper Volta Republic, Mali, and Niger moved into southern Ghana for work. As they migrated, they passed through the tsetse belt immediately north of the forest, where they picked up the infection. Upon reaching their destination, Ashanti country in central Ghana, they became the source for spreading the disease. It spread to such an extent that Ashanti foci began to have higher rates than the north. At the same time, eradication campaigns in the northern areas were effective in reducing somewhat the incidence of infection there. With the periodic return of (infected) migrant laborers from the south, however, the process of reinfection began. Such migratory movements continue today. One of the consequences is the recycling of trypanosomes in the northern savanna (Scott, 1957).

The case of the Moshie of the Upper Volta Republic provided some supporting statistics for this phenomenon (Scott, 1957). A sleeping sickness survey in Ashanti from 1952 to 1954 showed an incidence of 1.05% among adult male Moshie. The rate for the general Ashanti population was 0.18%, that is, one-sixth of the Moshie infection rate. A concomitant survey at the Yeji ferry on the north-south migration route in 1952 to 1954 clearly shows the degree of reinfection northward. The rate among Moshie males of ages 16 to 44, on their initial entry to Ashanti, was 0.14%; on leaving Ashanti, it was 1.44%. To a certain extent an increased risk of morbidity accompanied employment in Ashanti. While the difference in infection rates is not great in absolute terms, its demographic implication could be of much more significance, especially when coupled with the rest of the disease load under which most Africans labor. Davey (1948), for example, has estimated that in a population with a 6% trypanosomiasis infection rate, a stable population equilibrium is attained, while an infection rate as low as 3% allows only some natural increase. Other surveys, conducted along the road network connecting Ashanti with the north, show clearly that the highest incidence of sleeping sickness occurs along the major highways because such lines of communication facilitate man-fly contact (Scott, 1957).

In Nigeria transmission has increased sharply in localized pockets along the main Jos-Wamba road, a road used by migrant laborers going to the tin workings in the plateau (Thomson, 1967). Another, almost textbook, illustration of a man-made transmission site also comes from northern Nigeria, the area of Kanawa. In 1961, as a precautionary measure for laborers working on the Bornu railway extension, Kanawa was surveyed for prevalence of sleeping sickness. It was found to be free of the disease. Later, however, there was a sharp outbreak of sleeping sickness. Subsequent investigation indicated the source to be man-made; a small forest reserve was deliberately planted along the banks of a stream at the point where it was crossed by the main road—a place where people gathered to wash, drink and relax. In this case the trypanosome strain was one of high transmissibility but low virulence (Thomson, 1967).

Roads are thus linear-type transmission sites. Although systematic epidemiological data are not numerous, modern roads built for economic development seem to constitute a major health hazard in endemic regions, their very purpose being to encourage movement and mixture of peoples and goods but having, as implicated effects, the facilitation of manvector contacts for several different kinds of insect-borne diseases. With the expanding road and physical communication networks in Africa, all of which facilitate population movement, the risks of rapid reinvasion of areas by tsetse (and consequent reinfection) are great. One obvious suggestion from the public health point of view would be the imposition of strict vigilance and control measures (Thomson, 1967; Scott, 1957).

Settlement relocation is often an etiological factor. In pre-colonial Africa, many traditional settlements were located in refuge areas, on mountaintops, on ridges, on high plateaus—inaccessible, easily defensible sites. These sites were elevated and therefore tended to be freer of fly-borne diseases than lowland sites. However, with the coming of the various European colonial regimes and the law and order they brought, settlements have tended to move down from the hills to better agricultural land on the plains. Agricultural developments of this sort have often led to a significant increase in sleeping sickness.

The Rukuba tribe of the Bauchi Plateau of northern Nigeria illustrates the point. This virile tribe came to the verge of extinction because of an epidemic of sleeping sickness. *Glossina palpalis* had inhabited the dense vegetation on the Rukuba escarpment long before the introduction of the trypanosomes themselves. After the Pax Britannica, homesteads were moved down onto the lowlands from the hilltop fortresses which had once repelled human invaders, thus bringing man and flies into ever increasing contact. During 1931 and 1932, farmers returning from Piti brought trypanosomes first into Ikala and then into Kakkek, thus providing the one biological necessity which had been lacking. Man, fly and parasite were thus brought together and a transmission cycle began, resulting in a devastating and cataclysmic epidemic. Ruins of once-prosperous compounds and farms became a feature of the Rukuba landscape (Duggan, 1962).

Another illustration of sleeping sickness as a result of opening up new farmland occurred in Nigeria. Movement onto the plains west of the Jos escarpment resulted in one thousand cases of diagnosed sleeping sickness from 1960 to 1965 (Thomson, 1967).

In 1956, the people from Muyama in the Kasulu District of Tanzania, a barren and heavily eroded area on the hillside above the Milangilizi Valley, obtained permission to go down into the valley to cultivate new fields because of pressure on available agricultural land. The valley was fertile and well watered, but much of the riverine thicket contained large concentrations of *G. morsitans.* For a year nothing happened, and then, in 1958 and in 1959, after man, fly, and parasite contact had been established, an epidemic outbreak of sleeping sickness occurred (Apted *et al.,* 1963).

From the Dodos country in northern Uganda, another illustration shows how government action can trigger off an epidemic of sleeping sickness with repercussions in settlement, land use, economy and ecological balance. The government evacuated numbers of the Napore and Nyangeya tribes in 1924–25 in order to stop tribal warfare. As a result, a barrier to tsetse was removed because wild animals began to enter the territory formerly occupied (and extensively hunted in) by the Napore and Nyangeya. With the game the tsetse arrived. The advancing game and tsetse began to put pressure on the neighboring Dodos peoples. Tsetse advanced eighty miles and infested 1500 square miles of Dodos territory in the

1920's. In the face of this tsetse hazard, cattle-keeping Dodos people were forced to migrate toward the south and west into a much more limited territory. This caused overpopulation, overgrazing, and soil deterioration, and seriously affected the health and demography of the Dodos people. However, in 1946, a tsetse clearance program was started and in three years two-thirds of the fly belt was cleared. The land which was reclaimed was in good condition after the long fallow (Deshler, 1960).

Another example of ecologically uninformed government action that resulted in an epidemic of sleeping sickness is from East Africa, in the endemic region around Lake Edward and Lake George, near the Semliki Valley in the (then) Belgian Congo. Native tradition holds that sleeping sickness had been present in the Semliki long before its occupation by the Belgians in 1896, and that it had decimated successive tribes who had tried to occupy this fertile plain. Soon after the European occupation, for greater ease of administration, the scattered agricultural population was moved into more compact settlements, which were placed on rivers to provide permanent water. In this part of the valley, the whole length of the Semliki and all its tributaries holding permanent water are infested with *Glossina palpalis,* the vector of *Trypanosome gambiense.* Consequently, the great amount of movement called for by the concentration of the inhabitants, and the position of the settlements, brought about so much increased contact between the population and the tsetse that the existing endemic was rapidly turned into a fierce epidemic which literally wiped out many of these new villages. It was especially severe in the southern end of the Semliki Valley and around the shores of Lake Edward. Mortality was appalling. The epidemic reached its height between 1915 and 1923. In 1924 and 1925 the Belgian authorities took drastic action. The whole population of the valley was moved up onto the higher fly-free ground of the Mitumba and Ruwenzori Mountains and even deep into the Ituri forest along the new road being built from Beni to Irumu. In evacuating the Semliki Valley the Belgians eventually completely eliminated human trypanosomiasis (Morris, 1960).

Another example of population transfer forced by economic development occurred in Rhodesia, the Bumi River area, in 1958. The changes brought about by the Kariba dam produced an outbreak of sleeping sickness as well as a decline in nutritional standards (Apted *et al.,* 1963) and overall health status (Scudder, 1966). A section of the Tonga tribe was displaced by the rising waters of Lake Kariba. They were moved to a dryer region in which their traditional crops would not ripen, but they were reluctant to use the new seed varieties given to them by the government. They therefore suffered from food shortage. When the group lived on the banks on the Zambesi River they had supplemented their diet with fish and rodents, which were not available in their new homeland. Severe malnutrition followed. A government grain store was established to help them, but because of its location, the store became a transmission site for sleeping sickness and a sharp outbreak occurred (Apted *et al.,* 1963).

Bovine as well as human trypanosomiasis is a major disease obstacle to economic and social development in Africa. Huge areas on the African continent are infested by the tsetse fly, and the various trypanosomes which they carry are not only fatal and debilitating to man but also to domestic cattle. In the most highly infested fly belts, it is impossible to raise cattle. This produces a chronic shortage of animal protein; and protein deficiency, especially in early childhood, is one of the major health problems of Africa. As population increases, the problem will become more severe. Yet if the problem of tsetse infection could be solved in practical terms, the fly belts of

Africa could be turned into productive cattle-ranching lands, thus in turn helping to solve the severe protein deficiency problem.

An experiment conducted in Nigeria illustrates the obstacles to development created by such bovine trypanosomiasis. In 1963, a herd of 28 Zebu cattle was trekked some 415 miles from a tsetse-free area in north Nigeria to Ilorin in the south. Although the sample size in this experiment was small, the implications are significant. Such a trek is typical of the pattern for the whole of West Africa, whereby cattle raised in the tsetse-free areas of the far north are trekked or conveyed by truck through the fly belt to the southern zone where there is a shortage of animal protein. The journey through the fly belt took twenty-eight days, and measurements were taken daily of the increasing load of trypanosome infection. On arrival at their destination, 39% of the herd were infected. Typical trade cattle surveyed in other studies had an infection rate of 42% (Jordan, 1965).

At their terminus, the herd of 28 Zebu were held over for a seventeen-day observation period. Within this seventeen-day period, 19 of the cattle died and of the 9 survivors only 1 was in good condition. The others were dying of sleeping sickness—illustrating the very high infectivity of sleeping sickness in the south and the obvious unfeasibility of raising cattle there (Godfrey *et al.,* 1965).

In view of the vulnerability of the big Zebu cattle to trypanosomes and the great shortage of animal protein in the southern part of West Africa, it has been suggested that the N'dama dwarf cattle (which have some resistance to trypanosomes) should be developed for meat production in the fly belt. Veterinary opinion does not support this policy, however, because these cattle are slow-maturing, low-milk-yielding and low-meat-yielding. One further aspect of this situation is that the tolerance of the dwarf cattle to infection is broken down when the animals are subjected (as they often are) to adverse conditions such as malnutrition, overwork, mineral and vitamin deficiencies, and intercurrent infections such as piroplasmosis, anaplasmosis, helminthiasis and rinderpest, or exposure to heterologous strains and species of the trypanosomes. At present in the fly belt and in lightly infested fly areas the only way to raise cattle is to use a supporting regimen of chemotherapy and chemoprophylaxis (Stephen, 1966).

Bilharzia (*Schistosomiasis*). Schistosomiasis is the disease caused by the worm *Schistosoma haematobium* or *S. mansoni*. The worm uses human beings as a primary host and snails as a secondary one. One of the chief ways of improving agricultural production in many parts of Africa is manipulation and control of water resources by dam construction and irrigation schemes. However, the reliability of water resources is not all that is ensured. In addition to creating dependable water resources, transmission networks are often produced for the diffusion of snails, which are the intermediate host of the schistosome. Indeed, the World Health Organization commented: "The incidence of bilharzia has increased but it is of man's doing. As he constructs dams, irrigation ditches, etc., to alleviate the world's hunger, he sets up the ideal conditions . . . for the spread of the disease" (WHO, 1961, p. 431). Such schemes also tend to foster dense populations—both human and snail—and thereby increase rates of transmission. Because many new projects serve as foci for migrations of labor forces, they result in population concentration, and often the introduction of the schistosome itself (by workers from endemic areas). And, in passing, it may be noted that of the two types of schistosomiasis—the urinary or vesical (due to *Schistosoma haematobium*), and the more severe form, intestinal bilharzia (due to *Schistosoma mansoni*), it is the latter

which is mainly increased by the irrigation schemes (Alves, 1958). Thus irrigation, as an example of a technological improvement oriented to increasing agricultural yield, poses many health problems. Closer attention to bilharzia implications of expanding irrigation schemes is necessary in Africa (Waddy, 1966).

Insofar, then, as the opening up of Africa means, in part, the tapping of considerable hydroelectric potential for the development of irrigation systems, it should be recognized that with every mile of water the bilharzia snail will very often appear.

Its debilitating effects will strike man down and make him an unproductive worker. And as the World Health Organization noted with respect to the planning, and therefore preventive, phase, "The successful attack on the disease will be accomplished by a team: the engineer, the malacologist, the parasitologist, the sanitarian, the physician, and the chemist, widely divergent in training, speaking in the beginning different technical languages, but with a common purpose in mind" (WHO, 1953, quoted by Odei, 1961 c). Such a plea for interdisciplinary coordination and planning is echoed by Lanoix (1958), who notes that irrigation systems have also been indicted by epidemiologists and other health authorities as the causal agents of several other diseases of man, such as enteric bacterial infections, diarrheas, cercarial dermatitis, guinea worm, polio and possibly histoplasmosis; such irrigation systems also provide suitable breeding places for dangerous insect vectors of malaria, dengue, encephalitis and filariasis. Thomas (1965), in dealing with the ecology of a small man-made lake in Ghana, has studied the great variety and number of potentially dangerous pathogenic parasites, of both man and domestic animals, for which an aquatic environment is necessary. The numerous possibilities for the inadvertent spread of disease created by the spread of irrigation systems or the impounding of water can be seen in Appendix.

As far as general prevalence is concerned, it may be noted that bilharzia data on fourteen selected African countries collected by McMullen (1963) show that out of a population of 100 million persons, there were some 34 million infected. More than 50% of the population is infected in five of these countries: Egypt, 14 million out of 26 million; Ivory Coast, 1.75 million out of 3.1 million; Mozambique, 4.5 million out of 6.5 million; Rhodesia, 2.2 million out of 3.12 million; Tanzania, 5 million out of 9.5 million.

Other more specific rates and incidence patterns are those for French West Africa in 1952, which showed case mortality rates from vesical schistosomiasis of 0.3%, i.e., 3 per 1000, and that from intestinal schistosomiasis of 1.46%, i.e., 14.6 per 1000 (Odei, 1961 c).

Egypt, with its vast irrigation network, is the most heavily infected country in the continent. A study in 1949 claimed that "since the erection of the [first] Aswan dam, bilharzia has spread out and health and mentality of the individual deteriorated." For example, in four selected areas in a three-year period bilharzia infection rates increased as follows: from 10% to 44%, from 7% to 50%, from 11% to 64%, from 2% to 75% (Lanoix, 1958).

Bilharzia is spreading gradually toward the west in Uganda. One study reports that *S. mansoni* is most prevalent in the Nile valley and along the shores of Lake Albert. In this disease, as in others, seasonal migration plays a role in the transmission (Nelson, 1958). In Kenya, the Lake Victoria area is one of the hyperendemic areas of Africa, with percentages for school children running up to 100%. Tanzania is likely to become a classic example of the dangers inherent in the economic opening up of Africa by irrigation and water conservation projects. It appears that infection is already

fairly widespread throughout the country, but rates are not yet very high. However, irrigation schemes are certain to increase snail populations so that considerable epidemic bilharzia can be expected in the future (Alves, 1958).

In the Upper Volta Republic, about 50% of the population, more than 1.5 million people, are infected at some time during their life with *S. haematobium*. Yet here, as an example of a general point of this paper, an analysis in public health terms indicates that programs of bilharzia control are usually not of much practical value. One reason for this failure is that they are not combined with an integrated approach to general problems of environmental and urban sanitation. Ouagadougou, for example, has two public lavatories for a population of seventy thousand. Pollution by human waste along with refuse from houses and markets accumulate and offer harbor for flies and rats (McMullen and Francotte, 1962).

In the southwest Gambia coastal village of Kartung, the infection rates for the various age groups were as follows: 3 to 10 years, 59%; 11 to 12 years, 91%; 21 to 30 years, 52% (Odei, 1961a). The decline in rates was probably due both to mortality and development of immunity. It may be predicted that the Volta River irrigation scheme in Ghana will result in the spread of the snail hosts and convergence of infected peoples. In north Nigeria, in the Wulago region near Lake Chad, important irrigation works have been built, but in a location that reinforces an existing focus of bilharzia (Odei, 1961a).

The Gezira area of the Republic of the Sudan provides a particularly good example of the dangers of lack of ecological foresight. The welfare and prosperity of this area is significant to the country as a whole because the Gezira provides nearly one-third of the total revenue of the country. Before 1925, the people of the Gezira lived under primitive conditions, wholly dependent upon grain cultivation (mostly millet). Drinking water was scarce and drought was common. In 1918, work began on the dam at Sennar and it was completed after World War I. When the irrigation works were completed, cotton was planted and yielded abundantly. Prosperity came to the region.

Approximately three years after the establishment of irrigation, however, disease-transmitting snail vectors began to appear in the irrigation canals. The snail population increased from 1931 to 1953. The influx of migratory workers to the cotton fields, first from neighboring areas, then from western Sudan, and finally from West Africa, also increased. By 1954, half a million people worked regularly in the Gezira area. The total number of temporary migrants fluctuated between 150,000 and 200,000 per annum.

In 1942, attention was drawn to the ever increasing incidence of bilharzia, which, it is believed, was introduced into the area by the migrant workers from West Africa. In 1947, field investigations in northern Gezira showed a mean incidence of 21% among adults and 45% among children. Another survey showed that infection rates among males were twice as high as infection rates among females. Much of the bilharzia in Gezira is the more virulent intestinal variety, S. mansoni (El-Nagar, 1958).

In Nigeria, an irrigated sugar-cane scheme was recently instituted at Bacita on the river Niger east of Jebba. It attracted large numbers of people to an already endemic area. At the beginning of the season, the recruited labor force had a S. haematobium rate of 6.5%. At the end of the season, the rate was 20%. A preliminary morbidity survey showed the prevalence of not only S. haematobium but also S. mansoni in the area. It seems clear, therefore, that the Bacita scheme will increase the rate of transmission of intestinal as well as urinary bilharzia in this area by exposing a large number of people who are drawn there by economic opportunity (Thomson, 1967).

Another example is found in Yo, northern Nigeria in the Lake Chad Basin, where the River Yobe separates Nigeria from the Niger Republic to the north. The irrigation system functions for only four months of the year, but is sufficient to serve as a transmitter of both S. haematobium and S. mansoni. Here S. mansoni infected 15% of the irrigation staff and 10% of the local population. Liver enlargement was found in 18% of the adult villagers examined, and spleen enlargement in 17%. The possibility that schistosomiasis can produce serious liver damage may also be considered in this area. Here, as at Bacita, the main effect of irritation appears to have been the attraction of more people to natural transmission sites as well as the creation of new modes of transmission through the network of irrigation (Thomson, 1967).

Irrigation schemes are being rapidly developed in Tanzania, and there is fear of increased bilharzial infection. Until recently, the only large-scale scheme was at Arusha Chini where sugar has been grown for several decades. But, between 1955 and 1961, nine new schemes were started, and, in addition, another fifteen are now proposed. Since both forms of bilharzia, S. mansoni and S. haematobium, are endemic in many areas of Tanzania, it seems inevitable that the disease will spread and become severe as irrigation networks are developed and concentrations of human populations around them increase. And in many cases, migrant workers carry infection into the new irrigation scheme and establish a focus of transmission. For example, in one particular scheme, when the labor force was examined in an initial data setting survey, it was found that 1425 (86%) out of a total sample of 1652 came from areas where *S. haematobium* is endemic, and 320 (19%) came from areas where *S. mansoni* is endemic (Sturrock, 1965).

In the Mbarali irrigation scheme, Rufiji Basin, Tanzania, development began in 1950 and settlement started in 1961. Surveys of bilharzial infection were made in 1962, 1963, and 1965. In the four-year period from 1962 through 1965, the *S. haematobium* rate remained stable, ranging from 9.5% in 1962 to 8.7% in 1965. The *S. mansoni* infection rate, however, increased from 14.5% in 1962 to 28.9% in 1965. In the age group 5 to 9 years, the infection increased from 16.3% to 39.5%; age group 20 to 39 years, 17.3% to 26.4%; age group 40 years and over, 24.0% to 35.0%. The *S. mansoni* rates were also differentiated according to occupation. Senior African Supervisors' infection increased from 2.5% to 12.8%, while Tenant Laborers' rose from 34.7% to 63.7%. Intestinal bilharzia is thus seriously increasing at both socioeconomic levels, and its prevalence is five times greater among tenant laborers, who work more in water on the irrigation scheme itself and whose villages are badly situated in relation to the irrigation scheme. The planned villages, in which the tenant laborers live, are all in the irrigated area and consist of mud huts which lack sanitation and depend for water on the secondary canal system of the irrigation scheme itself. This scheme provides numerous transmission sites. One of the obvious conclusions to be drawn is that all people moving into a new irrigation scheme should be examined for bilharzia, and infected persons treated (Sturrock, 1965).

In Tanzania, some five million people are infected. From northwest Tanzania, on the shores of Lake Victoria, figures from an unselected community sample indicate that *S. mansoni* infections are light but *S. haematobium* is rampant in the area, giving rise to hydronephrosis, ureteric lesions or non-functioning kidneys in more than 20% of the children and in over 10% of the adults (Forsyth and Bradley, 1966).

In 1954, the Department of Health in Rhodesia warned that large-scale irrigation projects might well wreck the health of the country and bring the most grandiose of schemes to an end. For example, one of the first irrigation schemes established in that country after World War II has been a complete failure and is now largely abandoned because the effects of malaria and bilharzia were not calculated (Lanoix, 1958).

In Rhodesia, a study of parasitic infection among 80 laborers on a tobacco farm showed that 45 had *S. haematobium*, 18 had *S. mansoni*, and 11 had hookworm. The investigator, however, did not feel that these parasite loads impaired the performance of these laborers to any great degree (Young, 1955). But this observation was impressionistic rather than based on systematic data.

In the Republic of South Africa, bilharzia is well known in Natal and is now also being reported in the Transvaal, particularly in the eastern low veld and in the north. It is likely that the extension of irrigation schemes in these areas will make the Transvaal a much more dangerous area than Natal. The *S. haematobium* incidence was only slightly higher among Africans on European farms in the north and east of Transvaal than in the African reservations (Anneche, 1955). However, the *S. mansoni* infection rate was 68.5% on the European farms, as compared to 33.4% on the reserves. The difference presumably resulted from the irrigation on the European farms.

Again in the Transvaal, on protected farms in the irrigated low veld the infection rates for Africans were 29.3% and 49% for *S. mansoni* and *S. haematobium*, respectively. On farms without control, the *S.*

mansoni rate was 68.5% and the *S. haematobium* rate was 66.7%. On the African reserves the *S. haematobium* rate was comparable to that of the unprotected farms, but the *S. mansoni* rate was lower (Anneche, 1955).

It appears that bilharzia is spreading into Southwest Africa: *S. haematobium* and *S. mansoni* have been found in the east Caprivi Strip next to Zambia. The disease has also been found in the Okovango swamp at Maum, where previous surveys had been negative. The swamp provides an ideal snail habitat, and therefore the disease dangers are very considerable in this area. No bilharzia is found at present in Ovamboland, but a major water diversion scheme is planned whereby the Kunene River water in Angola will be conveyed through canals into Ovamboland for water supplies and possible irrigation in this densely populated area. When it is completed, bilharzia, which is present in the southern Angola rivers, will probably spread into Ovamboland (Geldenhuys *et al.*, 1967).

Other kinds of occupational activity or development schemes which involve manipulation of water resources may also assist the spread of bilharzia. In the southern part of Cameroon, for example, it is noted that rice cultivation is eminently favorable for the spread of infection, since dangerous transmission sites include slow-moving streams, ponds and marshes (Odei, 1961a). Liberia serves as another example. There, bilharzia is an occupational disease among women who spend a great deal of their time washing clothes along riverbanks. In the marshes of the coastal areas in Portuguese Guinea women grow the main crop, rice. They consequently develop a high rate of vesical bilharzia (Odei, 1961c). At another development project in a low-lying area of eastern Kenya, a rice scheme was developed which was a focus for bilharzia; in this case, however, attempts are being made to control the snail habitat. In rural areas where bilharzia infection is endemic, such scattered foci present a very difficult problem for public health planners because any water-connected development activity, such as a rice scheme, or the construction of fishponds, compounds the problem immeasurably (Fendall and Grounds, 1965b).

Numerous other deleterious effects of the disease can also be noted. On the basis of a study in Dakar, it is believed that schistosomiasis may give rise to cirrhosis (Charmot, 1954). Furthermore, it is possible that bilharzial infection can adversely affect nutrition. Disorders in the conversion of the amino acid tryptophan to nicotinic acid (the vitamin niacin) have been encountered in bilharzial cases. This would be significant in the upset of protein metabolism and in the increased likelihood of pellagra, another extensive public health problem in Africa (Mousa *et al.*, 1967). Regarding another complication, King (1965) reports that Bantu mineworkers in South Africa who have schistosomiasis develop irreversible urinary lesions with genito-urinary complications.

In this discussion, we cannot further develop the associated physiological concomitants of the disease. That is more properly done by specialists in the field. We would, however, with Farooq (1964), point to the widespread problem of decreased labor output in areas of endemicity.

During 1962 and 1963, an attempt was made to assess the economic effect of chronic schistosomiasis among a labor force of young male African adults employed on an irrigated estate at Arusha Chini in northern Tanzania. Some 75% of recruits in 1963 had current or previous experience with schistosomiasis. Workers lived in camps provided with bore-hole water, washing places, and latrine facilities. But where irrigation water ran close to habitation, it was used for domestic purposes. Because latrine facilities were available in the camp but not in the fields, contamination of canals and reservoirs by infected persons was widespread. Transmission continued. Data on daily absenteeism indicated that schistosomiasis was second only to injury among principal causes of lost working time (Foster, 1967a).

Estimates were made of the annual cost in lower productivity ascribable to schistosomiasis. Without control, the cost of schistosomiasis is £ st. 2.6 per worker per annum. The cost is made up of the following four items: direct treatment, additional absenteeism, additional inpatient treatment, and additional outpatient treatment. With control, the annual cost of schistosomiasis per worker is £ st. 5 per worker per annum. Control costs are made up as follows: molluscicide, additional staff, transport and application, treatment of new labor and dependents. With control, and the resulting increase in worker productivity, the saving is £ st. 1 per worker per annum (Foster, 1967b).

In Africa, the distribution of the snail hosts of bilharzia is more widespread than the distribution of schistosomes. Therefore, the disease can easily spread over a much wider area than it covers at present. Since man is the primary carrier of the disease, its spread is greatly fostered by migration, by concentration around water holes, and by development of new ways of farming which implicate surface water resources (Odei, 1961c). A technique for measuring the spread of bilharzia that might be of help to epidemiologists in the development of preventive measures is to ascertain the incidence of the disease by age groups. Normally, the measurable incidence, if not the actual incidence, is highest in young persons and somewhat lower in the adult population. In areas where it is believed that the disease has been recently introduced, measurable adult infection rates are significantly higher. Figures on incidence by age groups would help to portray the geographical spread of the disease.

Malaria. There are three types of malaria in Africa, caused by three different but closely related parasites: *Plasmodium falciparum, Plasmodium malariae,* and *Plasmodium vivax. Plasmodium falciparum* is the most common. The vector of the disease is the anopheline mosquito; two varieties are widespread and relevant to the dissemination of the parasite in Africa: *Anopheles gambiae* and *Anopheles funestus.*

When malaria does not kill, it debilitates. Victims develop a variety of symptoms: anemia, fever, high blood parasite level, and spleen enlargement. Populations in malarious regions are also characterized by high infant mortality and a greater susceptibility to many kinds of infection; in addition, pregnant women frequently suffer miscarriage as a result of the disease (Cannon, 1958). Thus, malaria contributes to the severity and exacerbation of a variety of morbid conditions in a population.

With malaria, as with bilharzia, the construction of irrigation schemes and expansion of agricultural programs has facilitated the spread of the disease; indeed, the spread of malaria in Africa was probably facilitated from the beginning by man's own constructive activities. Livingstone, for example, notes that the clearing of tropical forest for agricultural purposes and the establishment of thatched-roofed permanent villages provided ideal habitats for *Anopheles gambiae* (1958). Similar processes, and similar effects, continue today. Wilson (1957) made a plea for coordinated environmental planning in this respect. The fears he expressed were realized in the Taveta area of Kenya and Tanzania when water from springs in the Kilimanjaro area was diverted for irrigation purposes and thereby provided ideal breeding sites for mosquitoes (Smith and Draper, 1959).

The fact that mosquitoes cannot transmit malaria directly to each other makes man's role in its diffusion a primary one; and widespread population movements in Africa, both those linked with traditional patterns such as pastoral nomadism and those linked with modern developments such as labor migration, are among the outstanding contributory features in this respect. As such, migrations both facilitate the spread of malaria and create serious difficulties in its eradication. Since most of these population movements are essentially uncontrolled and many are interterritorial and international, they often hamper effective eradication and control programs through the reinfection possible in uncontrolled areas. In fact, the eradication and control of malaria in Africa today increasingly has more to do with understanding and control of the human relations aspect of the problem than with the biological aspects. The techniques of the malariologists and entomologists are well established, as are methods of eradication (the main purpose of which is to interrupt the transmission cycle); but what remains is the articulation of these techniques within widely differing physical and sociocultural environments. Population instability and movement is only one consideration; the ways in which a population is distributed, its settlement patterns, house types, farming practices, communication patterns, and water-use patterns, are also important aspects of a malaria eradication campaign. It is in the area of the complex interrelationships among the parasite, the vector, and man that further data and studies are needed (Prothero, 1961; Fonaroff, 1963).

Malaria and attempts to control or eradicate the disease prove that the quest for health is continuous and that there is only temporary respite. Malarial programs are waging a continual fight to keep ahead of the proliferation of insecticide-resistant strains of the insect vectors which, through processes of natural selection, adaptive capabilities, and enormous reproductive capacity, are multiplying the disease threat. In a sense, the more control is attempted,

the more the problem is exacerbated because of the need for new research to develop more effective and more specific insecticides. It might almost be said that unless the transmission cycle is broken at other points, insecticide spraying of the insect vector creates a new environment, an environment of "development," and is an attack on a problem which itself has been created by earlier spraying—a "disease of development."

This point has been documented in a number of studies. The study by Bruce-Chwatt (1956) with regard to DDT and dieldrin is a good example. After a four-year spraying campaign in the region of Thies, Senegal, the parasite rate among children under age fourteen was reduced from 22% to only 1%. However, the disease rebounded to 16% within only a year. In the opinion of the researcher, this rebound occurred because of the adaptation of the mosquito vector to the new environmental conditions (Escudié and Abonnenc, 1958). In the Para area of Tanzania, there was another outbreak of malaria transmission based on similar factors. The spraying campaign ceased in 1959, and thirteen months after the final round of dieldrin spraying, parasite rates had sharply increased, from a low figure of about 5% only six months after the cessation of the spraying campaign, to an average rate of 30% for children from 2 to 9 years. The factor causing the rebound was the development of a new strain of *Anopheles gambiae*. Because the transmission cycle was not completely broken by the spray campaign, human susceptibility to the disease actually increased rather than diminished (Pringle, 1967).

Resistance of mosquito vectors to insecticides has three forms: (1) simple behavioristic, (2) excito-repellency, (3) physiological. Behavioristic resistance occurs when an insect population changes its habits to avoid contact with the insecticide. For example, mosquitoes may try to rest on clothing or furniture or leave the house immediately after taking a blood meal, instead of resting on the walls of a room. Excito-repellency is a form of hypersensitivity to an insecticide. When a mosquito comes into contact with the poison, it may take off again before it has received a lethal dose. Physiological resistance arises when strains of mosquitoes emerge which are genetically tolerant to doses of toxicants which would be lethal for the majority of the mosquito population of the same species. It is this latter kind of resistance which poses such a severe problem and which has developed as a result of man's own activities in spraying campaigns. In 1967, the WHO Expert Committee on malaria reported that twenty-four vector species of Anopheles show resistance to dieldrin, DDT, or both. In sixteen countries, eleven of these twenty-four vector species showed double resistance, which is much more difficult to counter than single resistance.

It is therefore clear that no single method will rid the world of malaria. Combination programs incorporating techniques such as spraying, draining marshland, clearing of the bush, and mass chemotherapy and chemoprophylaxis have the best chance of success although even with these measures it should be recognized that there may be a serious problem of drug resistance to the chemicals. Although such programs might be expensive to mount and complicated to administer, there is no question of the overall gain in terms of worker well-being and productivity. In the Transvaal and Natal, for example, malaria control programs decreased worker absenteeism by at least 30%; and in Rhodesia an antimalaria campaign reduced absenteeism during the harvest season in the Mazoe Valley from 25% to almost nothing (Winslow, 1951, pp. 24, 25; quoted in Taylor and Hall, 1967).

It is not appropriate here to enter into complicated matters of the economics of labor supply; but insofar as much of the worker absenteeism in developing countries is of an erratic and aperiodic nature (thereby making permanent replacement of trained workers from the unemployed pool difficult to accomplish), one further observation is relevant to the general issue. Calculations by Mushkin are reported to the effect that in a hypothetical developing country, with 80% of its population affected by malaria, for example (which would decrease productivity of agricultural workers by 30% during a three-month period), the output loss in the agricultural sector would be 6%. If agriculture accounted for one-third of the total output, the gross national product would be diminished by 1% for that period alone; and over a twelve-month period the loss would be 4% (Taylor and Hall, 1967). Of course, the specifics of such calculations might well vary; but what is quite clear is that sick workers simply do not work as well, nor as regularly, as those who have their health. Even an effective antimalarial campaign brings other problems. First, the complete eradication of malaria from holoendemic areas will increase susceptibility so that any attacks that do occur after the campaign will tend to be more crippling to adults. Thus, in the long run, partial control may prove to be a social detriment. Secondly, the demographic effects of an antimalarial campaign will include a rise in the rates of population increase. In fact, the rate of increase may exceed that of food resources. Other problems, such as malnutrition, may arise because antimalarial campaigns lead to a sharp increase in birth rates and sharp decrease in death rates (Learmonth, 1954; Cannon, 1958). In the short run, too, it is foreseeable that a sharp reduction of infant mortality rates (as, for example, from a successful antimalarial program) will lead to protein-calorie malnutrition because more surviving infants are competing for limited supplies of breast milk and other protein supplies. Thus, even an effective antimalaria campaign may at best substitute complex new problems for old ones.

Rural Malnutrition. Many traditional African diets provide an excellent and well-rounded nutritional regime, especially where there is no population pressure and no cash-cropping. For example, the Karamojong of Uganda possess many cattle, which are the mainstay of their economic and social life. Sorghum, milk and blood are the main foods and meat is eaten in times of famine. In this situation, protein-calorie malnutrition is rare (Jelliffe *et al.,* 1964). The Mabaans occupy the bush country in the southeastern part of Sudan near the Ethiopian border, and they, too, have an excellent nutritional status; there are no nutritional deficiencies. Their major foods, all rich in protein, are guinea fowl, rodents, game, millet, sorghum, nuts, and dried fish (Rosen *et al.,* 1962). In short, many indigenous diets are good diets which include a high proportion of protein-rich foods. Considerably more research, however, is needed in this area (Jelliffe, 1955).

On the other hand, it should also be noted that in numerous cases culturally-based food taboos prevent consumption of animal protein which is available for either an entire group or for special classes of persons in the group. These food taboos play a part in denying children some of the vital nutritional elements required. In the Ankole area of Uganda, for example, many weaned children are deprived of goat milk because the goats are not used for this purpose; of eggs, because they are believed to be unsuitable for human consumption; and of meat and fish, or even an adequate quantity of cow's milk, because of the expense. The value of vegetable protein, as in beans, peas, and ground nuts, is likewise not appreciated (Cook, 1966).

The introduction of cash crops in the colonial period often led to the neglect of traditional diets and proper food production. In many African countries, a high proportion of the men engaged in farming are still concerned primarily with cash-crop production, and the vigorous efforts to increase cash-crop yields have often been at the expense of subsistence farming. This is observable, for example, in the cocoa and coffee-growing districts of West Africa, where the best lands are used for cash-crop purposes. In many areas such a concentration on cash-crop production has reduced the quantity of locally produced food. Meanwhile, income derived from cash crops is subject to wide fluctuations and is not in every case wisely spent or wisely spread out. Lump sums derived from bulk sales tend to be quickly spent on items such as education fees or clothes and status symbols, leaving little for food purchases (Hendrickse, 1966).

In this connection, a study of the effects of cocoa production in West Africa are pertinent:

Economically, the most important finding for the country which came out of our survey concerns the cocoa villages. Cocoa is one of the best cash crops in the world, giving the highest cash yield for the smallest energy output. One might therefore expect the cocoa villagers to be well off, well fed, happy and gay. We found exactly the reverse. The people were dull, apathetic and unhappy. Their villages were run down, dirty and dilapidated and their children naked, pot-bellied and sickly. The reason for this is that it is not enough to introduce a highly paying cash crop to an illiterate peasantry and expect them to profit by it. What happens is that it tends to kill their traditional life, merely putting money in their pockets for a short period in the year, during which time they enjoy themselves. When the money gets scarce, months before the next harvest, they find themselves short of everything. In a pure cocoa village they have given up most of their land for cocoa and are no longer able to till the ground for food. . . . Hence, with their money running out they can only buy the cheapest of food, e.g. cassava and yam. . . . At Igun [West Nigerian cocoa village] the villagers are apathetic, complaining if asked questions, and appear devitalized and sick. (Collis *et al.*, 1962b, pp. 223–24)

Cash-crop production of mainly coffee and cotton in the Kilimanjaro District of Tanzania, mostly by the Chagga people, leads to some neglect of local diets. The main crops are bananas, pulses, maize and yams. The diet is very high in starch and, not surprisingly, kwashiorkor is the main form of protein-calorie malnutrition (PCM) found in this area. It is observable in 2% of the children (Marealle and Kazungu, 1964). The real incidence of PCM will probably be much higher than the 2% figure for kwashiorkor, since subclinical PCM and post-PCM cases should be taken into consideration for such an assessment.

There are other examples of deleterious effects on diet and nutritional health following government programs. The Hadza (or Watindiga) are a small hunting and gathering tribe living in the tsetse-infested savanna adjacent to Lake Eyasi in northern Tanzania. It is believed that they may be related to the Bushmen of South Africa. Their diet consists of grain and gathered fruits, seeds and berries. Intercourse is forbidden during the prolonged lactations. At five months children are given bone marrow, seeds and pre-chewed meat. Overall, their nutritional status is excellent, and dental caries are almost absent. But tsetse clearance programs are changing the ecologic and nutritional status of this group. Because of tsetse clearance, surrounding tribes are encroaching upon Hadza territory, and diet changes are inevitable. Corn meal, which can bring PCM and pellagra, is starting to make inroads on the diet (Jelliffe, Bennett *et al.*, 1962).

The Lugbara, a large tribe living on both sides of the Congo-Uganda border, traditionally had a high-protein diet. Feeding and weaning of infants was satisfactory. The tribe had a high intake of beans, milk, peas, ground nuts, and sesame seeds; and their main food crops were millets and sorghum. Such a diet kept PCM incidence low. Following famines in the West Nile District, however, a law was introduced in 1950 requiring every householder to plant half an acre of cassava, a plant with very low protein content. The crop has now become a secondary staple, and if its cultivation further increases, as it may well do, the nutritional implications are obvious (Jelliffe, Bennett *et al.*, 1962b). With mounting population pressure in rural areas, there is an inevitable tendency to change from protein-rich staples, such as millet and sorghum, to carbohydrate staples, such as cassava, yams and plantain. Areas of high rural population density are usually characterized by a dependence upon starchy staples, which yield more calories but less protein to the acre. For example, cassava produces four to five times the calories per unit area as does millet:[2]

Table 7–1

CALORIES PER HECTARE OF AFRICAN CROPS

Cassava	7090
Maize	2845
Rice	2151
Sorghum	1854
Millet	1530

However, from the nutritional point of view, protein supplies are vital. Comparative protein content of various African foods are shown in Table 7–2.[3]

In such areas with considerable dependence upon starchy staples lacking supplementation, PCM is usually found. For example, in the Kayonza District of Kigezi, Uganda, a densely populated area in which the major food staple is plantain, a high incidence of PCM is found among the

[2] Table from J. F. Brock and M. Autert, 1952.
[3] *Ibid.*

Table 7–2

GRAMS OF PROTEIN PER 100 CALORIES

Dried fish	15.3
Soya (whole dry seed)	11.3
Beef	9.6
Beans or Peas	6.4
Ground nuts	4.7
Millet (*Pennisetum*)	3.4
Sorghum vulgare	2.9
Maize (whole meal)	2.6
Yams	2.3
Plantain	1.0
Cassava (fresh)	0.83
Cassava (flour)	0.44

Bachiga children. This has occurred because of pressure on the land (Jelliffe *et al.*, 1961).

When regional surveys of foodstuffs are taken into consideration with population density, they give a good indication of patterns of nutritional risks. In the Buganda region of Uganda, for example, there is a heavy dependence upon plantains (46%), at the expense of cereals (11.3%), pulses (9.7%), and animal products (4.2%). These figures express the percentage of total calories derived from the sources indicated. In Buganda therefore, protein intake is low, especially when compared to the northern region of Uganda, where total calories derived from cereals, pulses, and animal products were 39.3%, 24.1%, and 5.2% respectively. While the protein intake in the northern region is much better, cassava has recently spread into northern Uganda and at present accounts for 24.2% of total calories (Burgess, 1962).

The development of hybrids is often hailed as the agriculturists' answer to the problem of population increase. And although hybrids do produce spectacular increases in yields, it is sometimes the case that protein content in hybrids is lower than in unimproved varieties. For example, Japanese hybrid rice has a 5% protein content (as compared to 10% for other rice), and U.S. hybrid maize has a 6% to 8% protein content (as compared to Nigerian or Brazilian maize with 10%). Allowances should be made for these differences in rural development planning; in particular, the amino acid composition of those food crops selected for promotion in rural areas should be carefully considered.

Much of the acute rural poverty on the South African reserves, where there is heavy soil erosion and serious malnutrition, is a consequence of the phenomenon of urbanization, for the rural hinterlands of towns serve as labor reservoirs. Government restrictions on movement mean that wives and children are left on the reserves, in many instances to fend for themselves, while the men work in the towns. Food production, consequently, has fallen rapidly behind food needs on the Bantu reserves (Fox, 1954).

A study of an African reserve in northeast Transvaal (Sekhukuniland) clearly shows some of the severe social and nutritional problems. Soil is poor and rainfall is highly seasonal and sparse—averaging only 23 inches per year. Women and children form the bulk of the population because the able-bodied men have migrated to the cities. Child wastage because of malnutrition is an important problem. This study, among numerous others, illustrates the nutritional stress of the transition from tribal life to wage-economy in South Africa (Waldmann, 1960).

In one health survey of a rural Zulu community in southwest Natal, in the Polela District, it was shown that about three-fourths of the males between 25 and 40 years are absent from the community most of the time. Although from 1945 to 1955, health, education and welfare services aimed at improving the nutritional status of infants and at developing preventive measures pushed down the infant annual mortality rate from 202 to 86, the present high mortality levels caused by poverty and malnutrition cannot be reduced without economic assistance (Bennett, 1960).

THE ROLE OF URBANIZATION

The relationship between "development" and urbanization is obviously not a simple one. But that there is a relationship of evolving complexity in today's context of accelerating urbanization all over the continent is quite clear (Steel, 1961). Many of the tangible instances of "development" schemes (schools, amenities, multifarious goods, occasional wage-jobs, health clinics, etc.) are concentrated in towns and cities, and whether accurately or not, the city or town is taken as the exemplar of the process of betterment. It thus serves as the magnet drawing population from a hinterland, and creates that mix of peoples and ideas which, in the absence of ameliorating influences, is commonly predispositional to diverse pathology (Brockington, 1958, Chap. 10). The growth of urban areas in many parts of Africa today may therefore be taken as at least a corollary, if not a simple result, of developmental ideologies and programs. But it is a corollary which includes many ecologically based conditions conducive to widespread pathology. Such pathology is both physically rooted (as in crowded and unsanitary living conditions) and psychosocially rooted (as in widespread conditions of anxiety and stress deriving from economic deprivation, unemployment, physical threats, insecurity and social alienation).

Recalling the pathogenic conditions accompanying the industrial development of the Western world, a fairly recent summation (1959) by the World Health Organization of African urban conditions is pertinent, and essentially unchanged in its gross details today:

The situation created by the rapid urbanization of Africa was examined by the WHO Regional Committee for Africa at its ninth session in Nairobi in September 1959. The influx of immigrants into the towns leads to overcrowding, which in turn produces water shortages, overloading of existing sewage disposal systems, the creation of fresh sanitary problems in towns without such systems, and the risk of spread of infectious diseases. The rural immigrant . . . is the least adequately protected of all town dwellers from the standpoint of environmental sanitation because of his poverty and his ignorance of the ways of the town. He is poorly housed and badly fed; he is without access to a wholesome water supply; his personal hygiene is of the lowest standard. Sanitary measures seem to be designed less to protect his health than to protect the town community from any infection he might carry. His attempts to earn a living by hawking food and drink, for example, are frowned upon. Householders are prevented by anticrowding measures from giving him cheap shelter. His very presence in the town is discouraged, not only by the health authorities but also by the police. He accordingly settles outside the town, entering it daily to look for employment; and the overcrowded, unsanitary hovels in which he and his fellow-immigrants live form the peri-urban slums, the "shanty towns," of modern Africa. From the sanitary aspect Engels' description of the Manchester slums in 1844 is applicable to these shanty towns. Sanitation is non-existent, and open drains run down what passes for streets. The shanties are built of mud and wattle, old packing-cases, or kerosene tins, with tattered blankets as doors. Children crawl among the uncollected rubbish or in the drains. Water has to be fetched from a pump, well or tap, and may be contaminated. The atmosphere is unlikely to be polluted, as it was so often in Industrial Revolution towns, and the warmer climate leads to life being spent out of doors to an extent not possible in more northern latitudes; but the climate also encourages vast numbers of flies and mosquitos and, in places, the snails which transmit bilharziasis. Occasional floods convert the ground into a quagmire. Malaria, the diarrhoeal diseases, tuberculosis, bilharziasis, and the helminthiases all abound. Malnutrition is common, with its train of deficiency diseases and kwashiorkor. The destruction of tribal traditions and the general social disorganization lead to alcoholism, prostitution, and venereal disease; and mental disorders are frequent. Morbidity and mortality are both high. (WHO, 1960, p. 176)

Urbanization is perhaps the most salient social and economic feature in the life of

Africa today. While populations of African countries are doubling in a period of from twenty-five to forty years, African urban populations are doubling in less than fifteen years. The towns in Senegal have increased by more than 100% in a decade. Enugu, in Nigeria, was an empty site in 1914 and now has a population of more than eighty thousand; Ibadan, also in Nigeria, has trebled its population in twenty years. And much of this population concentration is packed into the peri-urban fringes, slums and shantytowns. A recent housing survey in Jinja, Uganda, for example, showed that one-third of the workers live in mud-and-thatch- or metal-roofed huts on the fringe of town, and such peri-urban slums are a constant feature of the large cities and towns (Fendall, 1963). Migrants to these slums often lack a good understanding of how to operate in a monetary economy, and face the stresses of unemployment and social heterogeneity often without the support of traditional relationships (Fendall, 1963; Little, 1966).

Such social heterogeneity—particularly in the "new" towns and cities of Nairobi, Johannesburg, Abidjan, Dakar, Freetown, Accra, Lagos, and Kumasi—is manifested not only in economic and wealth differentials, but also in considerable tribal and linguistic diversity (H. Kuper, 1965). In Accra, for example, more than sixty ethnic groups are represented. Many people are strangers to each other; they huddle together in areas where there are kinsmen who speak their languages; they feel a sense of estrangement from much of their environment. An additional socially disruptive feature is that many towns (especially in industrial or mining areas) have an excess of males, particularly single males, or married men without their families.

The stresses which affect life are therefore not simply those relating to the traditional concerns of public health; they also derive from the psychosocial dimension of a human environment. For man lives not only in terms of physical parameters; he is also enmeshed in a framework of social relationships which constitute varying patterns of threat and support. He functions within a symbolically transmitted framework of values and orientations which define the nature of legitimate goals, means, and aspirations. One salient feature of the widespread phenomenon of urbanization in Africa today is the disruption of these frameworks of social relationships and value systems. This social aspect of the urban context is described by us in another work. (Hughes and Hunter, 1968). Here we shall review some of the primarily organic pathogenic conditions, focusing on communicable diseases and malnutrition.

Nonpsychological Disorders and Pathogenic Conditions: Tuberculosis and Other Communicable Diseases. The association between health status and overcrowded, unsanitary conditions is well known in public health literature. Africa's towns are no exception to this maxim; they serve as the breeding ground and reservoir for many diseases of mass contact: whooping cough, smallpox, polio, malaria, typhoid, gastroenteritis. Many examples of overcrowding can be cited. There is the case of Kericho, a small town in Kenya, where two-fifths of all families live in single rooms (Fendall, 1959).

Tuberculosis is commonly associated with other diseases such as malnutrition, anemia, helminth diseases, and malaria. Not unexpectedly, then, tuberculosis in Africa is primarily an urban slum disease. In Kenya it is of fairly recent origin. Reports of the disease from the coast early in this century describe it as "galloping consumption," of acute onset and rapid fatality. Immediately after World War II the disease assumed primarily an urban locale, and in the last twenty years the most prevalent type of tuberculosis has changed from tuberculosis septicemia to chronic pulmonary tuberculosis. A 1948 survey estimated a rate of proved and suspected cases at 11.1 per 1000 for the country as a whole.

A WHO survey of 1958 and 1959 in Kenya confirmed that the disease was more prevalent in central and coastal regions than elsewhere. Except for the Lake Victoria region, these regions have higher humidity and greater population densities than anywhere else in the country (Fendall and Grounds, 1965a). Indeed, the disease is most closely tied to the density of population rather than to any other single feature of the urban milieu. A study in Kenya corroborates the finding of the highest rural rates in areas of highest population concentration: the Myeri district, an area in which the population has almost doubled in the last twenty years, is associated with a concomitant precipitous increase in tuberculosis (Turner, 1962). Another study similarly reports the highest prevalence in the Zambian countryside in those areas of highest population density (Grave and Ililonga, 1962).

A TB study of forty-four thousand African children in Rhodesia showed the highest rates in urban areas (Shennan, 1960). Another study of children in the Kano area of Northern Nigeria showed an infection rate in the congested central area almost twice as high as the infection rates in the better-quality housing of the suburbs and villages (McArdle, 1961). And a general WHO summary of TB surveys in African countries shows that the highest rates are found among men rather than women, and in urban rather than rural areas. These data support the inference of a close relationship between the migration of labor to congested urban areas and the prevalence of the disease (Roelsgaard *et al.*, 1964).

Through migration, especially labor migration, TB, originating in urban slum areas, is being transmitted to the rural areas in Africa. These areas then become additional foci (e.g., Fendall and Grounds, 1965a).

Migrants, for example, come to town for work and contract TB there, and then often return to their rural homeland because they are too sick to work. One study traces the diffusion of the disease from Abidjan to rural areas in the Ivory Coast (Delormas, 1960). Another example of TB spread by such migrant labor occurs in Gao. Many farmers of Gao apparently contracted the disease while they were working or searching for work in Ghana. One practical implication would be the imposition of control and inspection of migrants returning from Ghana to Gao (Plessis *et al.*, 1959).

Urban Malnutrition. Protein-calorie malnutrition is emerging as a significant force in the rapidly growing towns of Africa as well as in rural areas. Urban diets, in fact, are often deficient in vitamins, minerals, and proteins. These deficiencies occur, in part, when important nutritional elements are lost in the processing of grains and cereals (Jelliffe, 1962; Mead, 1955). Traditional methods of preparing these plants for consumption in the countryside do not result in comparable vitiation of nutritional elements. One study of polyneuropathy (a condition strongly related to pellagra) in Dar es Salaam, Tanzania, indicates that the condition is probably of nutritional origin and could be based on the use of highly refined (and therefore niacin- and thiamine-deficient) maize flour (Ebrahin and Haddock, 1964). Kwashiorkor and marasmus were found in some 2% of the children in a sample in Dar es Salaam. These diseases occurred because of high starch diets and, in some cases, early weaning followed by poorly administered artificial feeding (Marealle *et al.*, 1964).

The Acholi peoples inhabit the north central part of Uganda. In a study comparing rural Acholi with urban Acholi the latter were found to have a higher rate of PCM, presumably because of the substitution of maize flour and other foods for traditional vegetable proteins, including millet, sesame seed and ground nuts (Jelliffe, Bennett *et al.*, 1963). In Durban, where 1565 cases of kwashiorkor in children admitted to clinics were studied, the peak age of prevalence was 1 to 3 years. Fifty-three per cent of the children died, and in some instances their condition was complicated by pneumonia and gastroenteritis. Excessive use of starch products was judged to be the main reason for the poor diets of these urban Africans (Scragg and Rubidge, 1960).

Several factors are implicated in urban malnutrition. One of the chief culprits is money and the high cost of protein-rich foods. The urban environment, to a much greater extent than the rural, revolves, of course, around a money economy. This factor is the core of many aspects of the malnutrition often found as a concomitant of the shift from rural to urban areas (Mead, 1955). A study done in West Africa, for example, indicates that malnutrition is more common in urban and peri-urban areas than in rural areas. It states that the value of money income in the towns is diminished by (1) obligatory expenditures such as rents, transportation expenses, and clothing; (2) by higher food prices; and (3) by having limited and even no access to home-produced foodstuffs (Hendrickse, 1966). But there are other features in a monetary economy which are detrimental to nutritional standards. One study, for example (Fendall, 1963), shows that twice as much is spent on food in the first ten days immediately after payday than in the last ten days of the month. Similarly, three times as much is spent on alcohol in the first ten days than in the last ten days.

When men work in towns and live without their families, they frequently feed themselves much less adequately than when they live in the rural areas. They lack women's expertise in food preparation and purchase. They often eat in canteens which provide monotonous and poor-quality diets.

Living in towns also frequently leads to extramarital liaisons which involve a man in a new set of familial obligations under which either his village family or his city family will suffer financially (Hendrickse, 1966).

Because of less effective child care in the towns, urbanization frequently results in infant malnutrition. In the towns considerable pressure is placed on young mothers to go to work. In their mother's absence, babies from two to three months old are often cared for by children from seven to ten years old. The diet for such babies is often poorly prepared canned foods. This poor diet can produce gastroenteritis and eventual malnutrition (Fendall, 1963). Kahn (1962) also reports kwashiorkor in children of working mothers.

Not only are there fewer relatives to help care for the children in towns and cities, but there is also less sunlight and therefore more rickets. In addition, there tends to be earlier weaning in the town than the country, with consequent intake of less protein. Subsistence depends mainly on expensive and poorly carried out artificial diets (Jelliffe, 1962).

Ignorant and uninformed adoption of European-type baby bottle-feeding also contributes to infant malnutrition in the towns. The practice of feeding powdered milk to babies is rapidly growing in urban areas, but this practice is being used by women with no knowledge of hygiene, no ability to read the instructions on the can, and no money with which to buy sufficient powdered milk. Thus, diluted powdered milk from dirty bottles and dirty teats is substituted for breast milk. This leads to malnutrition and dietary disorders such as marasmus, diarrhea, or vomiting (Cook, 1966). Welbourn (1958) also comments on the uninformed use of bottle-feeding and its deleterious effects. In Uganda, bottle-fed children were two pounds lighter in average weight than breast-fed children.

It is worth looking at some specific studies of relationships between overall physical and mental development and early protein deficiency. For eleven years, Stoch and Smythe studied twenty Cape colored infants who were grossly undernourished during infancy. The undernourished group lived under unhealthful slum conditions in one-room shanties built on sand without any sanitary facilities. Those who lived in houses were crowded into unventilated dark back rooms. Thirteen were illegitimate and, in another three cases, the fathers had deserted. Mothers appeared too apathetic to care for their children. Social workers and district nurses repeatedly requested the mothers to take their children to municipal soup kitchens or to clinics for meals but there was little cooperation. Compared to matched controls, the head circumference, height, weight, intellectual and psychological assessment and encephalograms of these children show that undernutrition during the period of active brain growth has resulted in a significant reduction in brain size and impairment of intellectual development (Stoch and Smythe, 1963, 1967).

In brief the findings are as follows (1967):

Table 7-3

	CONTROL GROUP	UNDER-NOURISHED GROUP	MAGNITUDE OF DIFFERENCE
Average head Circumference	52.04 cm	49.58 cm	2.46 cm smaller
Average height	133.68 cm	125.73 cm	7.95 cm shorter
Average weight	29.45 kg	24.38 kg	5.07 kg lighter

In addition, electroencephalogram data indicate that twelve of the undernourished children had poorly formed low-voltage alpha waves with poor response to eye opening, whereas seventeen of the controls had well-formed high-voltage alpha waves, especially posteriorly, with an excellent response to eye opening. In terms of the New South African Intelligence Scale (not standardized for Cape colored children), the mean for the control group was 76.70, and that for the undernourished group, 61.15—some 15.5 points lower.

Another study points to the same result—i.e., long-term crippling effects from nutritional deficiencies in early infancy, the period of maximum brain growth. From 1953 to 1964, data were collected on 1094 autopsies performed at the Mulago Hospital at Kampala, Uganda, on children from the age of birth to fifteen years old. The children were divided into two groups: those who had suffered from malnourishment and those who had not. The malnourished children had been afflicted with kwashiorkor or marasmus. In each autopsy the child's brain was weighed. The findings for the age group 4 to 5 years indicated that the non-malnourished brain weight was 1127 grams, and the malnourished brain weight, 985 grams. The malnourished brain was 13% lighter than the non-malnourished brain (Brown, 1965).

At birth the human brain is approximately 40% of its adult weight; it increases to 70% after one year and to 80% by the age of two years. The brain increases in weight in incremental stages, but because of the metabolic stability of many of its constituents, once these constituents are laid down they may be inaccessible to the general metabolic pools of the body in times of shortage. Therefore, even good nutrition in later life cannot repair the irreversible damage done to the brain in infancy, damage which may well result in poor learning capacity in adult life (Brown, 1965; Scrimshaw, 1968). Such an assertion is supported not only by clinical experience with human beings, but also by experimental data on animals such as the pig and the rat (Barnes, 1967). A recent article covering studies of this kind notes that they

. . . indicate that poverty and the poor nutrition that almost invariably accompanies it may bring into the world children who are less able to learn and to earn than their genetic potential would otherwise allow.

The studies give the expression "food for thought" a new dimension. They have shown that children who receive inadequate nourishment both before and shortly after birth suffer a diminished capacity for intellectual achievement.

In fact, studies of infants and laboratory animals have indicated that children inadequately nourished while still in the womb may start life with a subnormal number of brain cells—a deficit which can never be made up. (Brody, 1968)

Thus, the concept of a close, reciprocal interrelation between aspects of organic growth and psychological capacity, influenced by both a social and an ecologic context, is a critical area for further research. Indeed, the spiraling effect, once set in motion, is difficult to break. Cravioto, after commenting on the pervasive and permanent psychobiological effects of protein malnutrition in Central America, another "underdeveloped" area, says of the "PCM spiral":

A low level of adaptive capacity, ignorance, social custom, infection, or environmental paucity of foodstuffs appears to result in malnutrition, which may produce a large pool of individuals who come to function in sub-optimal ways. Such persons are themselves more ready to be victims of ignorance and less effective than would be the case in their social adaptations. (1966, p. 320)

A concept like the PCM spiral would seem to be particularly useful in understanding many aspects of the social history of West and Equatorial Africa. Vansina (1966) discusses the rise and fall of traditional political-military empires in the Congo in terms of the spread of cassava, a very-low-protein staple. Dependence on cassava is predispositional to the development of kwashiorkor and other deficiency diseases. Such a "cassava belt" stretches along the coast of West Africa where kwashiorkor was first clinically described. And the tragic events of today in eastern Nigeria and Biafra are only too

compelling in their underscoring of the close relationship between a protein-adequate diet and effective bodily and psychological functioning. On the latter note—that of the interpenetration of "social" or "political" events and nutritional health—one may recall the pessimistic appraisal by the African pediatrician Hendrickse, who said:

The high incidence of nutritional disorders in Africa today reflects the seriousness of the social and economic problems of the people of Africa. Current trends in African affairs offer little hope of improvement. On the contrary, the direction of social change and the long-term effects of economic policies currently in operation will inevitably result in deterioration of the present position. Meanwhile, the unstable political situation in the continent threatens constantly to disrupt the existing economic structure and to precipitate disaster. (Hendrickse, 1966, p. 346)

Beyond the obvious clinical cases of protein deficiency in African children in the towns, there are numerous cases of *subclinical* protein-calorie malnutrition, sometimes known as mild-moderate malnutrition. It is difficult to diagnose. Children suffering from mild-moderate malnutrition are not suffering from kwashiorkor nor are they visibly emaciated, yet they are completely outside of the normal range of body weight for age, and they have an increased susceptibility to disease. How common this nutritional growth failure is can be judged by field surveys of preschool children and records of young-child clinics that often show that between 15% and 30% of children weigh below 75% of that which is normal for their age, and therefore fall into this mild-moderate malnutrition group (Cook, 1966).

Thus, it would appear that the major benefit of urbanization for child nutrition is the provision of clinics and other health facilities in which mothers can eventually be educated and severe cases of malnutrition can be treated. But thus far the overwhelming impact of the urban environment on child and adult nutrition has been negative.

In conclusion, we firmly assert that programs of economic or agricultural development, population relocation, industrial construction, or any program which either deliberately or inadvertently changes pre-existing relationships between man and any aspect of his environment must be viewed from the outset in an ecologic framework. We must realize the serious hidden costs of a new "ecologic contract" between man and his surroundings. Perhaps it would be useful for public health specialists to start talking about a new category of diseases analogous to the "iatrogenic" diseases known in medicine. Such diseases could be called the "diseases of development" and would consist of those pathological conditions which are based on the usually unanticipated consequences of the implementation of developmental schemes.

Appendix

SOME PARASITES OF MAN AND DOMESTIC ANIMALS IN AFRICA FOR WHICH AN AQUATIC ENVIRONMENT IS OBLIGATORY
(Thomas, 1965)

PARASITES OF MAN

PARASITES	INTERMEDIATE HOST	METHOD OF INFECTION	MOST COMMON DIS-EASES TRANSMITTED
Viruses:			
About 32 mosquito-borne viruses are associated with human infections	Mosquito	Mosquito bite	Yellow fever, dengue fever
Protozoa:			
Trypanosoma gambiense Dutton	*Glossina palpalis* and *G. tachinoides* (found near water)	Tsetse bite	Trypanosomiasis (Gambian sleeping sickness)
Plasmodium spp.	Mosquitoes	Mosquito bite	*P. vivax:* benign tertian malaria
			P. malariae: quartan malaria
			P. ovale: mild tertian malaria
			P. falciparum: malignant subtertian malaria
Nematoda:			
Wuchereira bancrofti (Cobbold)	Mosquitoes	Insect biting man	Bancroftian filariasis (elephantiasis)
Setaria equina (Abildgaard)	Simulium, mosquitoes	Insect biting man	
Dipetalonema perstans (Manson)	Mosquitoes, *Culicoides, Simulium,* tabanids, *Pulex,* ticks	Insect biting man	
Dipetalonema streptocerca (Macfie and Carson)	*Culicoides*	Insect biting man	
Mansonella ozzardi (Manson)	*Culicoides, Simulium*	Insect biting man	
Dirofilaria repens (Railliet and Henry)	Mosquitoes	Insect biting man	
Loa loa (Guyot)	*Chrysops*	Insect biting man	Loiasis (calabar swelling)
Onchocerca volvulus (Leuckart)	*Simulium*	Insect biting man	Onchocerciasis (river blindness)
Dracunculus medinensis (L.)	Copepods	Drinking water containing infested copepods	Dracunculiasis (Guinean worm)
Trematoda:			
Fasciola gigantica Cobbold	Aquatic snail	Infective stage on water plants	Fascioliasis (river fluke)

PARASITES OF MAN

PARASITES	INTERMEDIATE HOST	METHOD OF INFECTION	MOST COMMON DIS-EASES TRANSMITTED
Trematoda: (continued)			
Fasciolopsis fuelleborni Rodenwaldt	Aquatic snail	Infective stage on water plants	
Heterophyes heterophyes (Siebold)	Aquatic snail, fish	Infective stage in fish	Intestinal fluke
*Stictidora tridactyla Martin and Kintz	Aquatic snail, fish	Infective stage in fish	Intestinal fluke
*Echinostoma revolutum (Froelich)	Aquatic snail	Infective stage in snail or second intermediate host	Intestinal fluke
Echinoparyphium recurvatum (Linstow)	Aquatic snails, frogs	Infective stage in snails or frogs	
Paragonimus westermani (Kerbert)	Aquatic snail, crustacean	Infective stage in crustacean	Paragonimiasis (lung fluke)
Schistosoma mansoni Sambon	Aquatic snail	Infective larvae enter through skin of man	Intestinal schistosomiasis
Schistosoma haematobium (Bilharz)	Aquatic snail	Infective larvae enter through skin of man	Genitourinary schistosomiasis
Watsonius watsoni (Coryngam)	Aquatic snail	Infective stages on water plants	Intestinal fluke
Cestoda:			
Diphyllobothrium sp. larva	Copepod, man	Infective stage in copepod	Broad fish tapeworm
*Spirometra pretonensis (Baer)	Copepod, reptiles, amphibia, mammals (including man)	Infective stage in intermediate host	

PARASITES OF DOMESTIC ANIMALS

PARASITES	INTERMEDIATE HOST	METHOD OF INFECTION
Protozoa:		
Trypanosoma brucei	Glossina palpalis and other Glossina sp. Mechanically by tabanids or mosquitoes	Biting of cattle, sheep, goats, camels, pigs, dogs, etc., by flies
Trypanosoma vivax	Glossina palpalis, etc. Also mechanically by tabanids	Biting of cattle, sheep, goats, camels, pigs, dogs, etc., by flies
Trematoda:		
Fasciola gigantica Cobbold	Snail	Eating infested vegetation
Paramphistomum cervi	Snail	Eating infested vegetation
Paramphistomum microbothrium Frischoeder	Snail	Eating infested vegetation
Cotylophoron cotylophorum (Frischoeder)	Snail	Eating infested vegetation

*Recorded in Africa but in mammalian hosts other than man. However, man is a potential host.

PARASITES OF DOMESTIC ANIMALS

PARASITES	INTERMEDIATE HOST	METHOD OF INFECTION
Trematoda: (continued)		
Gastrodiscus aegyptiacus Cobbold	Snail	Eating infested vegetation
Schistosoma bovis (Sonsino)	Snail	Infective stages penetrate skin
Schistosoma mattheei Veglia and la Roux	Snail	Infective stages penetrate skin
Schistosoma leiperi (la Roux)	Snail	Infective stages penetrate skin
Schistosoma margrebowiei (la Roux)	Snail	Infective stages penetrate skin
Schistosoma curassoni Brumpt	Snail	Infective stages penetrate skin
Nematoda:		
Setaria equina (Abildgaard)	*Simulium*, mosquitoes	Fly biting horse
Setaria digitata (Linstow)	Mosquitoes	Fly biting sheep, horse
Setaria labiato papillosa (Alesc)	Mosquito	Fly biting cattle, sheep
Dipetalonema ruandae Fain and Herin		Fly biting cattle
Brugia patei (Buckley et al.)	Mosquitoes	Fly biting dog
Dirofilaria immitis (Leidy)	Mosquitoes, ticks	Fly biting dog, cat, etc.
Dirofilaria repens (Railliet and Henry)	Mosquito	Fly biting dog
Onchocerca armillata (Railliet and Henry)	?	Fly biting cattle
Onchocerca fasciata Railliet and Henry	?	Fly biting camel
Onchocerca gibsoni (Cleland and Johnston)	*Culicoides*	Fly biting cattle
Onchocerca gutturosa (Neumann)	*Simulium*	Fly biting cattle
Elaeophora poeli (Vryburg)	?	Fly biting ox
Dracunculus medinensis (L.)	Copepods	Cattle, dog, etc., drinking water containing infested copepods

REFERENCES

Abedi, Z. H., and Miller, Max J. "Roadside Tsetse Hazard in Liberia." *Amer. J. Trop. Med. and Hyg.,* 13 (1964), 499–504.

Alves, William. "The Challenge of Bilharzia in a Developing Africa." *Optima,* 8 (1958), 139–46.

Anneche, D. H. S. "Bilharzia in Transvaal." *Pub. Health* (Johannesburg), 18 (1955), 2–7.

Apted, F. I. C.; Ormerod, W. E.; Smyly, D. P.; Stronach, B. W.; and Szlamp, E. L. "A Comparative Study of the Epidemiology of Endemic Rhodesian Sleeping Sickness in Different Parts of Africa." *J. Trop. Med. and Hyg.,* 66 (1963), 1–16.

Barnes, Richard H.; Moore, A. Ulric; Reid, Ian M.; and Pond, Wilson G. "Learning Behavior Following Nutritional Deprivations in Early Life." *J. Amer. Dietetic Assn.,* 51 (1967), 34–39.

Bennett, F. J. "Mortality in a Rural Zulu Community." *Brit. J. Preventive and Soc. Med.,* 14 (1960), 1–8.

Bequaert, Joseph C. "Tsetse Flies in Liberia: Distribution and Ecology; Possibilities of Control." *Amer. J. Trop. Med.,* 26 (1946), 57–94.

Brock, J. F., and Autert, M. *Kwashiorkor in Africa,* Geneva: WHO, 1952.

Brockington, F. *World Heath.* Harmondsworth, England: Penguin Books, 1958.

Brody, Jane E. "It Really May Be 'Food for Thought.'" *New York Times,* July 28, 1968, p. 10E.

Brown, Roy E. "Decreased Brain Weight in Malnutrition and Its Implications." *E. Afr. Med. J.,* 42 (1965), 584–95.

Bruce-Chwatt, L. W. "Problems of Insecticide Resistance in Relation to Malaria Control in Africa." *W. Afr. Med. J.,* 5 (1956), 47–54.

Burgess, A. P. "Calories and Proteins Available from Local Sources for Uganda Africans in 1958 and 1959." *E. Afr. Med. J.,* 39 (1962), 449–63.

Cannon, D. S. H. "Malaria and Prematurity in the Western Region of Nigeria." *Brit. Med. J.,* Oct. 11, 1958, pp. 877–88.

Charmot, G. "L'étiologie des cirrhoses afri-caines." *Med. Trop.,* 14 (1954), 689–702.

Collis, W. R. F.; Dema, J.; and Omololu, A. "The Ecology of Child Health and Nutrition in Nigerian Villages: Part 1, Environment, Population and Resources." *Trop. and Geogr. Med.,* 14 (1962a), 140–63.

———. "The Ecology of Child Health and Nutrition in Nigerian Villages: Part II, Dietary and Medical Surveys." *Trop. and Geogr. Med.,* 14 (1962b), 201–29.

Cook, R. "The General Nutritional Problems of Africa." *Afr. Affairs,* 65 (1966), 329–40.

Cravioto, Joaquin; Delicardie, Elsa R.; and Birch, Herbert G. "Nutrition, Growth and Neurointegrative Development: an Experimental and Ecologic Study." *Pediatrics,* 38 (1966), 319–72.

Davey, T. H. *Trypanosomiasis in British West Africa.* London: Colonial Office, H.M. Stationery Office, 1948.

Delormas, M. P. "Orientation de la lutte anti tuberculeuse en Côte d'Ivoire. *Méd. Afrique Noire,* 7 (1960), 281–82.

Deshler, Walter. "Livestock Trypanosomiasis and Human Settlement in Northeastern Uganda." *Geogr. Rev.,* 50 (1960), 541–54.

Dubos, René. *Mirage of Health.* New York: Harper, 1959.

———. *Man Adapting.* New Haven: Yale University Press, 1965.

Duggan, A. J. "The Occurrence of Human Trypanosomiasis among the Rukuba Tribe of Northern Nigeria." *J. Trop. Med. and Hyg.,* 65 (1962), 151–63.

Ebrahin, G. J., and Haddock, D. R. W. "Polyneuropathy of Probable Nutritional Origin in Dar es Salaam, Tanganyika." *Trans. R. Soc. Trop. Med. and Hyg.,* 58 (1964), 246–54.

El-Nagar, Hadi. "Control of Schistosomiasis in the Gezira, Sudan." *J. Trop. Med., and Hyg.,* 61 (1958), 231–35.

Escudié, A., and Abonnenc, E. "Sur le comportement de quelques anophèles de la région de Thiès (Sénégal), en zones traitées par les insecticides à effet rémanent." *Med. Trop.,* 18 (1958), 286–303.

Farooq, M. "Medical and Economic Importance of Schistosomiasis." *J. Trop. Med. and Hyg.,* 67 (1964), 105–12.

Farooq, M.; Samaan, S. A.; and Nielsen, Y. J. "Assessment of Severity of Disease Caused by Schistosoma haematobium and S. mansoni in the Egypt—49 Project Area." *Bull. WHO,* 35 (1966), 389–404.

Fendall, N. R. E. "Housing, Health and Happiness." *E. Afr. Med. J.,* 36 (1959), 473–85.

———. "Public Health and Urbanization in Africa." *Pub. Health Reports,* 78 (1963), 569–84.

Fendall, N. R. E., and Grounds, J. G. "The Incidence and Epidemiology of Disease in Kenya: Part I, Some Diseases of Social Significance," *J. Trop. Med. and Hyg.,* 68 (1965a), 77–84.

———. "The Incidence and Epidemiology of Disease in Kenya: Part II, Some Important Communicable Diseases." *J. Trop. Med. and Hyg.,* 68 (1965b), 113–20.

Fonaroff, L. Schuyler. "Malaria Geography: Problems and Potentials for the Profession." *Professional Geographer,* 15 (1963), 1–7.

Forsyth, D. M., and Bradley, D. J. "The Consequences of Bilharziasis: Medical and Public Health Importance in North-West Tanzania. *Bull. W.H.O.,* 34 (1966), 715–35.

Fossati, C. "Osservazioni sulla patologia delle parassitosi intestinali nei lattani e nei bambini della città di Bengasi (Libia) e sobborghi" (Intestinal Parasitic Infections in Children and Infants in Bengasi, Libya). *Giorn. di Malattie Infettive e Parassit.,* 16 (1964), 521–27.

Foster, R. "Contributions to the Epidemiology of Human Sleeping Sickness in Liberia." *Trans. R. Soc. Trop. Med. Hyg.,* 57 (1963), 465–75.

———. "Schistosomiasis on an Irrigated Estate in East Africa: Part I, The Background." *J. Trop. Med. and Hyg.,* 70 (1967a), 133–40.

———. "Schistosomiasis on an Irrigated Estate in East Africa: Part II, Epidemiology." *J. Trop. Med. and Hyg.,* 70 (1967b), 159–68.

———. "Schistosomiasis on an Irrigated Estate in East Africa: Part III, Effects of Asymptomatic Infection on Health and Industrial Efficiency." *J. Trop. Med. and Hyg.,* 70 (1967c), 185–95.

Fox, F. W. "Agricultural Foundations of Nutrition." *S. Afr. Med. J.,* 28 (1954), 97–98, 178–89, 267–68, 361–63, 441–44, 542–46, 649–53, 770–73, 897–99, 1019–22; 29 (1955), 63–66, 282–84.

Geldenhuys, P. J.; Hallet, A. F.; Visser, P. S.; and Malcolm, A. C. "Bilharzia Survey in the Eastern Caprivi Strip, Northern Bechuanaland and Northern South West Africa." *S. Afr. Med. J.,* 41 (1967), 767–71.

Godfrey, D. G.; Killick-Kendrick, R.; and Furguson, W. "Bovine Trypanosomiasis in Nigeria: IV, Observations on Cattle Trekked along a Trade Cattle Route through Areas Infested with Tsetse Fly." *Ann. Trop. Med. and Parasit.,* 59 (1965), 255–69.

Grave, G. F., and Ililonga, M. K. "The Problem of Tuberculosis in Balovale and Kabompo Districts." *Cent. Afr. J. Med.,* 8 (1962), 216–24.

Hendrickse, R. G. "Some Observations on the Social Background to Malnutrition in Tropical Africa." *Afr. Affairs,* 65 (1966), 341–49.

Hughes, Charles C., and Hunter, John M. "Disease and 'Development' in Africa." Paper presented at First International Conference on Social Science and Medicine, Aberdeen, Scotland, September 4–6, 1968. To appear in *Social Science and Medicine,* Vol. 4 (1970), 1–51.

Jelliffe, D. B. *Infant Nutrition in the Tropics and Subtropics.* Geneva: WHO, 1955.

———. "Urbanization and Child Nutrition in Africa." *Internat. Child Welfare Rev.,* 16 (1962), 67–73.

Jelliffe, D. B.; Bennett, F. John; Jelliffe, E. F. P.; and White, Richard H. R. "The Ecology of Childhood Disease in the Kavamajong of Uganda." *Arch. Environ. Health,* 9 (1964), 25–36.

Jelliffe, D. B.; Bennett, F. J.; Stroud, C. E.; Novotny, M. E.; Karrach, H. A.; Musoke, L. K.; and Jelliffe, E. F. P. "Field Survey of the Health of Bachiga Children in the Kayonza District of Kigezi, Uganda." *Amer. J. Trop. Med. and Hyg.,* 10 (1961), 435–43.

Jelliffe, D. B.; Bennett, F. J.; Stroud, C. E.; Welbourn, Hebe F.; Williams, M. C.; and Jelliffe, E. F. P. "The Health of Acholi

Children." *Trop. and Geogr. Med.,* 15 (1963), 411–21.

Jelliffe, E. G., and Jelliffe, D. B. "Plasmodium Cullinan, T. R.; and Jelliffe, E. F. P. "The Children of the Lugbara." *Trop. and Geogr. Med.,* 14 (1962), 33–50.

Jelliffe, E. G., and Jeliffe, D. B. "Plasmodium in Ugandan Children." *Amer. J. Trop. Med. and Hyg.,* 12 (1963), 296–99.

Jelliffe, D. B.; Woodburn, J.; Bennett, F. J.; and Jelliffe, E. F. P. "The Children of the Hadza Hunters." *J. of Pediat.,* 60 (1962), 907–13.

Jordan, A. M. "Bovine Trypanosomiasis in Nigeria: V, The Tsetse Fly Challenge to a Herd of Cattle Trekked along a Cattle Trade Route." *Ann. Trop. Med. and Parasit.,* 59 (1965), 255–69.

Kahn, E. "Protein Malnutrition (Kwashiorkor) in Children of Working Mothers." *S. Afr. Med. J.,* 36 (1962), 177–78.

King, B. A. "Urinary Bilharziasis and Morbidity, with Special Reference to the Genito-urinary Surgical Complications." *S. Afr. Med. J.,* 39 (1965), 1044–48.

Kuper, Hilda, ed. *Urbanization and Migration in West Africa.* Berkeley and Los Angeles: University of California Press, 1965.

Kuper, L. "Sociology: Some Aspects of Urban Plural Societies." In *The African World: A Survey of Social Research,* Robert A. Lystad. New York: Frederick A. Praeger, 1965.

Lanoix, Joseph N. "Relation between Irrigation Engineering and Bilharziasis." *Bull. WHO,* 18 (1958), 1011–35.

Learmonth, A. T. A. "Malaria: Some Implications of Recent Revolutionary Progress." *Geography,* 39 (1954), 37–40.

Little, Kenneth. "Some Social Consequences." *Afr. Affairs,* 65 (1966), 160–69.

Livingstone, Frank B. "Anthropological Implications of Sickle Cell Gene Distribution in West Africa." *Amer. Anthropologist,* 40 (1958).

Mabogunje, Akin L. *Yoruba Towns.* Ibadan, Nigeria: Ibadan University Press, 1962.

McArdle, E. J. "A Survey of the Tuberculin Reaction of School Children in Kano Province, N. Nigeria." *W. Afr. Med. J.,* 10 (1961), 98–100.

McMullen, Donald B. "Schistosomiasis Control in Theory and Practice." *Amer. J. Trop. Med. and Hyg.,* 12 (1963), 288–95.

McMullen, Donald B., and Francotte, Jean.

"Report on a Preliminary Survey by the WHO Bilharziasis Advisory Team in Upper Volta, *Bull. WHO,* 27 (1962), 5–24.

Marealle, A. L. D.; Kazungu, M.; and Kondakis, X. G. "Cross-sectional Studies on Protein-Calorie Malnutrition in Tanganyika." *J. of Trop. Med. and Hyg.* 67 (1964), 222–29.

Mead, Margaret, ed. *Cultural Patterns and Technical Change.* New York: Mentor Books, 1955.

Morris, K. R. S. "Studies on the Epidemiology of Sleeping Sickness in East Africa: III, The Endemic Area of Lakes Edward and George in Uganda." *Trans. R. Soc. Trop. Med. and Hyg.,* 54 (1960), 212–24.

Mousa, A. H.; Abdel Wahab, A. F.; and Mousa, W. "Tryptophan Metabolism in Hepatoplenic Bilharziasis." *Trans. R. Soc. Trop. Med. and Hyg.,* 61 (1967), 640–47.

Nelson, G. S. "Schistosoma mansoni Infection in the West Nile District of Uganda: Part II, The Distribution of S. mansoni with a Note on the Probable Vectors." *E. Afr. Med. J.,* 35 (1958), 335–44.

———. "Schistosoma mansoni Infection in the West Nile District of Uganda: V, Host-Parasite Relationships." *E. Afr. Med. J.,* 36 (1959), 29–35.

Odei, M. A. "A Review of the Distribution and Snail Hosts of Bilharziasis in West Africa: Part I, Gambia, Ghana, Sierra Leone, Nigeria and British Cameroons." *J. Trop. Med. and Hyg.,* 64 (1961a), 27–41.

———. "A Review of the Distribution and Snail Hosts of Bilharziasis in West Africa: Part II, French Guinea, Ivory Coast, Senegal, Togo, Dahomey, Niger, Haute Volta and Sudan." *J. Trop. Med. and Hyg.,* 64 (1961b), 64–68.

———. "A Review of the Distribution and Snail Hosts of Bilharziasis in West Africa: Part III, Liberia and Portuguese Guinea." *J. Trop. Med. and Hyg.,* 64 (1961c), 88–97.

Plessis, J.; Ducloux, M.; Gentillini, M.; and Sankalé M. "La tuberculose en zone Sahelo—saharienne (Cercle de Gao, République Soudanaise)." *Med. Afrique Noire,* 6 (1959), 365–68.

Pringle, G. "Malaria in the Pare Area of Tanzania: Part III, The Course of Malaria Transmission since the Suspension of an

Experimental Programme of Residual Insecticide Spraying." *Trans. R. Soc. Trop.
Med. and Hyg.,* 61 (1967), 69–79.

Prothero, R. Mansell. "Population Movements
and Problems of Malaria Eradication in
Africa." *Bull. WHO,* 24 (1961), 405–25.

————. *Migrants and Malaria.* London: Longmans, Green, 1965.

Roelsgaard, E.; Iversen, E.; and Blocher, C.
"Tuberculosis in Tropical Africa: an Epidemiological Study." *Bull. W.H.O.,* 30
(1964), 459–518.

Rosen, Samuel; Bergman, Moe; Plester, Die-
trich; El-Mofty, Aly; and Satti, Mohamed
Hamed. "Prebycusis Study of a Relatively
Noise-Free Population of the Sudan." *Ann.
Otol. Rhinal. Laryngal.,* 71 (1962), 727–
43.

Scott, David. "The Epidemiology of Human
Trypanosomiasis in Ashanti, Ghana."
J. Trop. Med. and Hyg., 60 (1957), 205–
14, 238–49, 257–74, 302–15.

————. *Epidemic Disease in Ghana, 1901–
1960.* London: Oxford University Press,
1965.

Scragg, Joan, and Rubidge, Carol. "Kwashiorkor in African Children in Durban." *Brit.
Med. J.,* Dec. 17, 1960, pp. 1759–66.

Scrimshaw, Nevin S. "Infant Malnutrition and
Adult Learning." *Saturday Review,* March
16, 1968, pp. 64–66.

Scudder, T. "Man-Made Lakes and Population Resettlement in Africa." In *Man-
Made Lakes,* ed. R. H. Low-McConnell.
London and New York: Academic Press,
1966.

Shennan, D. H. "The Evolution of Tuberculosis in Southern Rhodesia: Part III, Examination: a Comprehensive Tuberculin
Survey of the African School Children
of Manicaland." *Cent. Afr. J. Med.,* 6
(1960), 432–46.

Smith, A., and Draper, C. C. "Malaria in
the Tareta Area of Kenya and Tanganyika: Part I, Epidemiology." *E. Afr. Med.
J.,* 36 (1959), 99–113.

Steel, Robert W. "The Towns of Tropical
Africa." In *Essays on African Population,*
eds. K. M. Barbour and R. M. Prothero.
London: Routledge and Kegan Paul, 1961.

Stephen, L. E. "Observations on the Resist-
ance of the West African N'dama and
Zebu Cattle to Trypanosomiasis Following
Challenge by Wild *Glossina morsitans*

from an Early Age." *Ann. Trop. Med. and
Parasit.,* 60 (1966), 230–46.

Stoch, M. B., and Smythe, P. M. "Does Undernutrition during Infancy Inhibit Brain
Growth and Subsequent Intellectual Development?" *Archives of Disease in Childhood,* 38 (1963), 546–52.

————. "The Effect of Undernutrition during
Infancy on Subsequent Brain Growth and
Intellectual Development." *S. Afr. Med.
J.,* 41 (1967), 1027–30.

Sturrock, R. F. "The Development of Irrigation and Its Influence on the Transmission
of Bilharziasis in Tanganyika," *Bull. WHO,*
32 (1965), 225–36.

————. "Bilharzia Transmission on a New
Tanzanian Irrigation Scheme." *E. Afr.
Med. J.,* 43 (1966), 1–6.

Taylor, Carl E., and Hall, Marie-Françoise.
"Health, Population, and Economic Development." *Science,* 157 (1967), 651–57.

Thomas, John D. "Some Preliminary Observations on the Ecology of a Small Man-Made
Lake in Tropical Africa." In *Ecology and
Economic Development in Tropical Africa, ed.* David Brokensha. Berkeley: Institute of International Studies, University
of California Press, 1965.

Thomson, K. D. B. "Rural Health in Northern
Nigeria: Some Recent Developments and
Problems." *Trans. R. Soc. Trop. Med.
and Hyg.,* 61 (1967), 277–95.

Turner, P. P. Home Treatment of Tuberculosis in the Nyeri District of Kenya." *Tubercle,* 43 (1962), 76–82.

Vansina, Jan. *Kingdoms of the Savanna.* Madi-
son; University of Wisconsin Press, 1966.

Vaucel, M. A.; Waddy, B. B.; De Andrade
da Silva, M. A.; and Pons, V. E. "Try-
panosomiase Africaine chez l'homme et
les animaux." *Bull. WHO,* 28 (1963),
545–94.

Veatch, Everett P. "Human Trypanosomiasis
in Liberia 1941–44." *Am. J. Trop. Med.,*
26 (1946), 5–56.

Waddy, B. B. "Frontiers and Disease in West
Africa." *J. Trop. Med. and Hyg.,* Vol.
61 (1958).

————. "Medical Problems Arising from the
Making of Lakes in The Tropics." *Man-
Made Lakes, ed.* R. H. Lowe-McConnell.
London and New York: Academic Press
Inc., 1966, 87–94.

Waldmann, E. "Child Wastage, Due to Malnutrition in Sekhukuniland." *Cent. Afr. J. Med.*, 6 (1960), 298–301.

Welbourn, Hebe F. "Bottle Feeding: a Problem of Modern Civilization." *J. Trop. Pediat.*, 3 (1958), 157–66.

Wilson, D. Bagster. "Construction, Irrigation and Malaria." *E. Afr. Med. J.*, 34 (1957), 479–85.

World Health Organization. "Health Aspects of Urbanization in Africa." *WHO Chronicle,* 14 (1960), 173–79.

———. "Bilharzia." *Bull., WHO,* 25 (1961), 431–740.

Young, C. N. "Parasitic Infection on a Tobacco Farm in the Umvukwes District." *Cent. Afr. J. Med.*, 1 (1955), 288.

8A. THE IMPACT OF AGRICULTURAL DEVELOPMENT ON AQUATIC SYSTEMS AND ITS EFFECT ON THE EPIDEMIOLOGY OF SCHISTOSOMES IN RHODESIA[1]

C. J. Shiff

In the past the indigenous population of Central Africa was nomadic, practicing transient agriculture with no regard for conservation. Unstable water systems carried heavy floods in the short rainy season and dried out over the rest of the year. Aquatic snail populations, the essential link in the transmission of schistosome parasites, led a tenuous existence in these waters.

Recently, agricultural development has concentrated on soil and water conservation and resulted in the construction of a multitude of dams of various capacities which tend to stabilize water flow in rivers and provide a significant amount of permanent and stable bodies of water. Concurrently, the population has become settled and expanded, leading to increased human contact with, and pollution of, the water systems. With the increase in the extent of the water biotope there has been an increase in aquatic snail populations, particularly the pioneer species, some of which are intermediate hosts for human schistosomes. This has disrupted the previously stable and almost benign host-parasite relationship between schistosome, aquatic snail and man.

---

[1] The material in this paper was originally published in different form as "Host & Parasite in Rhodesia" in *Natural History*, copyright © 1969 by The American Museum of Natural History.

Evidence from two irrigation settlement schemes is produced to show details of the increase in severity of schistosomiasis in the human population. This has produced dangerous and even fatal sequelae. Documented evidence showing this increase is given.

It is reasonable to presume that the schistosomes have been parasites of man for a considerable part of his evolutionary history. Under the ecological conditions which prevailed in the past, the interrelationship among both primary and secondary hosts and the parasite itself had evolved toward an equilibrium; thus the schistosomes were in a position to maintain their numbers among the sparse, nomadic populations of man and the temporary, rather unstable populations of aquatic snails without causing excessive stress on the infected hosts.

This pattern of host-parasite relationship probably existed in Rhodesia until modern times. Recently, however, rapid economic and agricultural developments have resulted in the settlement and massive increase of the human population. Of late, the need to conserve natural resources and the implementation of soil and water conservation procedures in the country have produced major changes in the overall hydrological picture. The construction of dams has stabilized water flow and resulted in fewer flash floods in the streams and rivers, most of which are now of a perennial nature. Thus there has been an increase in the extent of snail habitat throughout the country. Because the water bodies are more durable, aquatic snail populations can increase as a result of the general amelioration of the environment.

Where agricultural projects are based on irrigation, large populations live in close relationship with stable water systems; snails invade and breed; water contact and pollution increase, and in turn produce a major upsurge in the prevalence of bilharzia (schistosomiasis) and, what is probably more serious, an increase in the worm load of infected persons.

THE AQUATIC ENVIRONMENT AND SCHISTOSOME TRANSMISSION

An association between the level of schistosome transmission and the geographical extent of surface water was noticed as early as 1915 when Orpen (1915) recorded a 31% infection among 592 jail prisoners, the majority of those infected coming from the damper northern parts of the country. This pattern was strikingly demonstrated more recently by Clarke (1966) who analyzed the age prevalence of both *Schistosoma haematobium* and *S. mansoni* in several different communities in Rhodesia. In Table 8–1 the association between climate, topography, extent of water availability, and prevalence of the parasite (*S. haematobium*) is clearly shown. In particular, the high prevalence at Chipoli, an established irrigation scheme some forty years old in the hot lowveld approximately two thousand feet above sea level, shows the degree of transmission which can develop. Under these conditions there is no appreciable falloff in parasite prevalence among the older age groups, such as is characteristic of all the other populations surveyed, including those from the newly established irrigation scheme, Triangle and Hippo Valley.

The pattern of transmission seen in Table 8–1 is further accentuated in Table 8–2, which deals with the prevalence of *S. mansoni* in the same localities. Where water bodies are inclined to be unstable and temporary, as with communities at Bikita

Table 8-1

PREVALENCE OF SCHISTOSOMA HAEMATOBIUM INFECTIONS IN SEVERAL COMMUNITIES IN RHODESIA

After Clarke (1966)

COMMUNITY NUMBER	OCCUPATION	HYDROLOGY	ALTITUDE		AGE GROUPS							
					Under 4	4-6	7-9	10-12	13-15	16-20	21-40	Over 40
1. Iron Duke Mine	Rural Mineworkers	Well watered Perennial[b]	Middle veld[a] 2000-4000'	No. examined	25	49	58	46	26	15	68	41
				% positive	16	61	78	80	88	80	24	5
2. Arcturus Mine	Rural Mineworkers	Well watered Seasonal[b]	Highveld over 4000'	No. examined	32	62	74	54	52	33	45	52
				% positive	3	16	34	63	69	52	29	8
3. Bikita Minerals Mine	Rural Mineworkers	Well watered Seasonal	Middle veld 2000-4000'	No. examined	18	40	66	106	77	78	22	20
				% positive	6	20	33	57	53	44	18	10
4. Turk Mine	Rural Mineworkers	Poorly watered Seasonal	Highveld Over 4000'	No. examined	18	25	100	76	13	15	114	102
				% positive	Nil	12	13	13	39	29	13	1
5. Chipoli Estate	Irrigation (Old)	Well watered Perennial	Lowveld Under 2000'	No. examined	9	76	55	25	13	21	101	35
				% positive	89	96	98	96	92	90	72	57
6. Triangle and Hippo Valley Sugar Estates	Irrigation New	Well watered Perennial	Lowveld Under 2000'	No. examined	30	87	66	38	42	106	237	116
				% positive	30	30	54	74	67	55	33	7

[a] As Rhodesia is a tropical country, prevailing temperatures increase as altitude decreases.

[b] The distinction between perennial and seasonal is based on availability of water from permanent sources or temporary ponds filled by seasonal rains.

Table 8-2

PREVALENCE OF *SCHISTOSOMA MANSONI* INFECTIONS IN RHODESIA.
SURVEYS MADE IN THE SAME COMMUNITIES AS IN TABLE 1 AND AT THE SAME TIME.

After Clarke (1966)

COMMUNITY	NUMBER	AGE GROUPS							
		Under 4	4-6	7-9	10-12	13-15	16-20	21-40	Over 40
1. Iron Duke Mine	No. examined	6	27	45	50	24	Not done	29	11
	% positive	Nil	41	78	58	58		38	18
2. Arcturus Mine	No. examined	33	61	73	53	52	33	106	51
	% positive	3	7	10	43	44	18	15	20
3. Bikita Minerals Mine	No. examined	20	37	60	84	67	59	21	20
	% positive	5	3	5	6	3	12	14	5
4. Turk Mine	No. examined	14	26	100	75	14	9	95	95
	% positive	Nil	Nil	5	3	Nil	Nil	6	6
5. Chipoli Estate	No. examined	8	70	51	23	15	24	95	32
	% positive	50	83	92	87	67	50	59	50
6. Triangle and Hippo Valley Sugar Estates	No. examined	30	87	66	38	42	106	237	116
	% positive	13	11	17	50	24	16	10	7

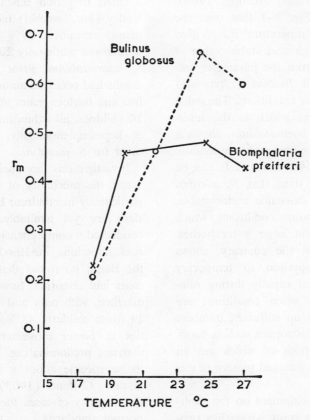

Figure 8–1 Values for r_m obtained from snails cultured at different temperatures

Minerals and Turk Mines, the parasite is rare. It becomes more common in those communities associated with stable water bodies, especially where temperature and contact increase. Again the prevalence at Chipoli shows a particular and high rate of transmission.

The close association between *S. mansoni* and the communities living near stable water systems is a direct result of the ecology of *Biomphalaria pfeifferi,* the intermediate host snail involved in its transmission cycle. The response of a species to a set of environmental conditions can be measured by rearing individuals under those particular conditions and calculating a parameter from the age-specific birth and death rates, namely, the intrinsic rate of natural increase. The influence of temperature on the intrinsic rate of natural increase (r) of this species has been investigated (Shiff and Garnett, 1967; Shiff and Husting, 1966). It will be seen in Fig. 8–1 that over the optimal range of temperature *B. pfeifferi* has a moderately high and stable value of r. This is different from the parameter calculated for the snail *Bulinus* (*Physopsis*) *globosus* under similar conditions. The value for r in this species, which is the intermediate host for *S. haematobium,* shows a high peak value at the optimum temperature of 25° C (Shiff, 1964a, 1964b). It can be inferred from these data that *B. pfeifferi* is better adapted to existence under stable, well-buffered temperature conditions, which normally are found in large water bodies. *Bulinus globosus,* on the contrary, shows a characteristic adaptation to temporary habitats. It can breed rapidly during relatively short periods when conditions are ideal and thus build up sufficient numbers to survive ensuing catastrophes such as flooding or desiccation, both of which are an annual feature of the seasonal pattern in this latter biotope.

The impact of development on the problem of bilharziasis in rural Africa has pro-

duced illness of increasing severity. The effects of increasing *S. haematobium* infections, with concomitant kidney and bladder damage, are slowly being superseded in the population by an increase in the more dangerous parasite, *S. mansoni.* This occurs because populations of *B. pfeifferi* are becoming more widespread in the increasing number of stable water bodies appearing over the country. The changing picture can be seen in two different ways. White school children from rural areas are inclined to swim and fish in farm dams, while black school children have more contact with river water in the rural areas. In a recent survey of 490 white children in the Victoria province, the ratio of *mansoni* to *haematobium* was 3 to 1. In Bantu children from the same province the *mansoni* to *haematobium* ratio was 1 to 9.6.

A recent survey among the population of a small irrigation scheme in the Zambesi Valley (hot, lowveld) indicated that of 193 people examined, 89% were infected with *S. mansoni* while only 20% showed signs of *S. haematobium.* Prior to the survey, 11 deaths had occurred among children between five and thirteen years of age; and a further 16 children, all exhibiting similar symptoms of hepatosplenomegaly, were given treatment for *S. mansoni.*

Investigations are being undertaken to assess the morbidity of bilharzial infection, particularly in children; however, no precise ,data are yet available. Gelfand (1963) conducted a comprehensive study of *S. mansoni* infections in Rhodesian children. In the Bantu he found that 33% of infected cases had abnormal bowel function, mainly diarrhea, with pain and blood in the stool. In white childern, 48% showed abnormalities in bowel movement, with pain and diarrhea predominating. While it is difficult to be specific about a general debilitating disease, Gelfand (1963) stressed that "in the majority of cases there is a lowering of normal standards. . . . the great tiredness, listlessness and lack of energy that so many children openly admit," are direct results of the disease. Gross liver damage, uretal strictures and hydronephrosis are concomitant with bilharzial infection, but these seldom produce death, although they may often be contributory causes. The most common and serious effect in any community is the debilitating nature of the disease, producing a general listlessness and lack of energy, inability to work and lower productivity and earning capacity of the affected community.

As can be expected, with the more intense cycle of infection, people are now carrying increasingly heavier burdens of the adult schistosome worms. As a result of this an increased number of unusual symptoms and sequelae of bilharzia are being noticed. Bird (1965) in reporting on cases of spinal complications in bilharziasis mentions that, up to 1963, literature on this subject reported a total of twenty-six cases of *S. mansoni* and eleven of *S. haematobium*. In 1964 Bird himself examined a total of eight cases, one of which was terminal. Later Zilberg (1967) noted a case of *S. mansoni*-induced paraplegia in a child, while cerebral abnormalities were seen in three other cases (Zilberg *et al.*, 1967). Gelfand (1965) has given details of a suspected bilharzial lesion of the spinal cord which produced rapid paralysis of the lower limbs; *S. mansoni* was diagnosed and the patient responded slowly to treatment. Stephens (1966) reported a case representing a bilharzial granuloma as an abdominal

mass in an eighteen-year-old African girl. Certainly clay pipestem cirrhosis and liver granulomata represent a serious and not uncommon phase in this disease. Gelfand has recorded (1963) evidence of this damage in 4.3% of cases examined. A further seven undocumented cases of paraplegia, presumed to be of bilharzial origin, were reported to the Rhodesian Ministry of Health in 1967. This indicated that in the four years between 1963 and 1967 almost as many cases of spinal complications due to schistosomes were reported in southern Africa alone, as were reported for the whole globe up to 1963 (excluding *S. japonicum* infections).

FUTURE OUTLOOK

With the rapid increase in population in central and southern Africa, development of agriculture will depend more and more on irrigation, especially in the drier parts of the country where rainfall is unreliable. In Rhodesia from 1964 until recently, the amount of irrigated land has increased by close to 100,000 acres. There are now 126 irrigation schemes ranging in area from 20 to 3,000 acres in rural areas reserved for Bantu settlement. These derive water from dams of various sizes, perennial rivers, or from subterranean sources. However, regardless of the water source, the overall stabilization of the aquatic biotope is occurring, and with it the increased problem of bilharziasis.

REFERENCES

Bird, A. V. "Spinal Cord Complications of Bilharziasis." *S. Afr. Med. J.,* 39 (1965), 158–62.

Blair Research Laboratory. Unpublished reports and surveys.

Clarke, V. de V. "The Influence of Acquired Resistance in the Epidemiology of Bilharziasis." *Cent. Afr. J. Med.,* 12 (1966), Supplement No. 6.

Gelfand, M. "Clinical Features of Intestinal

Bilharziasis in Rhodesia." *Cent. Afr. J. Med.*, 9 (1963), 319–27.

———. "A Possible Case of Paraplegia Caused by *Schistosoma Mansoni.*" *Cent. Afr. J. Med.*, 11 (1965), 75–76.

Orpen, L. J. J. *Annual Report,* Public Health Department, Salisbury, Southern Rhodesia (1915).

Shiff, C. J. "Studies on *Bulinus* (*Physopsis*) *globosus* in Rhodesia, I. The Influence of Temperature on the Intrinsic Rate of Natural Increase." *Ann. Trop. Med. Parasit.*, 58 (1964a), 94–105.

———. "Studies on *Bulinus* (*Physopsis*) *globosus* in Rhodesia, III. Bionomics of a Natural Population Existing in a Temporary Habitat." *Ann. Trop. Med. Parasit.*, 58 (1964b), 240–55.

Shiff, C. J., and Garnett, B. "The Influence of Temperature on the Intrinsic Rate of Natural Increase of the Freshwater Snail *Biomphalaria pfeifferi* (Krauss) (Pulmonata; Planorbidae)." *Archiv für Hydrobiol.*, 62 (1967), 429–38.

Shiff, C. J. and Husting, E. L. "An Application of the Concept of Intrinsic Rate of Natural Increase to Studies on the Ecology of Freshwater Snails of the Genera *Biomphalaria* and *Bulinus* (*Physopsis*) in Southern Africa." *Proc. Trans. Rhod. Sci. Assn.*, 51 (1966), 2–8.

Stephens, R. R. "Bilharziasis as Differential Diagnosis for Abdominal Tumours." *Cent. Afr. J. Med.*, 12 (1966), 28–29.

Zilberg, B. "Bilharzial Paraplegia in a Child: A Case Report." *S. Afr. Med. J.*, 41 (1967), 783–84.

Zilberg, B.; Saunders, E.; and Lewis, B. "Cerebral and Cardiac Abnormalities in Katayama Fever." *S. Afr. Med. J.*, 41 (1967), 598–602.

8B. THE EFFECTS OF MOLLUSCICIDES ON THE MICROFLORA AND MICROFAUNA OF AQUATIC SYSTEMS

C. J. Shiff

The events discussed above produced a public health problem which demanded immediate action. Initial experiments involved the application of unselective biocides such as copper sulphate and sodium pentachlorophenate to aquatic systems to destroy snail populations; there was some success, but lack of knowledge resulted in instances when the biotope was completely disrupted and remained imbalanced for extended periods. Comparative trials with several molluscicides in small water systems have shown new chemicals to be more selective. They destroy less of the biotope, leaving plants and the fauna—other than snails—largely unharmed.

Experiments were undertaken in which selective molluscicides were applied only to those regions of bodies of water where intermediate host snails were found. The system of searching for snails, and judicious application of chemicals, known as snail surveillance, is described. These experiments have been in operation for six years, and assessments on various ecological aspects have been carried out. Data are presented to show how surveillance depresses the population of species of host snails while not interfering with other molluscs; analysis of general biota within treated areas shows no other apparent changes. Data are presented to show reduction in prevalence of human schistosomiasis in the controlled areas.

The situation outlined in the case histories on schistosomes and development requires immediate preventive action to avert the growing menace to public health. As there is yet no prophylaxis, people cured by chemotherapy are immediately vulnerable once treatment ceases. The best solution is to reduce the infectivity of natural water bodies colonized by intermediate host snails of the schistosomes. Because snails once infected will produce cercariae for several months, and because it is almost impossible to exclude human contact with the water at this stage in Africa, the strategy has been to attack the aquatic snail populations with chemical poisons.

Initial experiments using copper sulphate were carried out in Rhodesia as early as 1950 (Clarke *et al.*, 1961). They showed that it was feasible to reduce the snail populations by spraying the chemical into water bodies at approximately 20 to 30 parts per million (ppm). The desirability of adding a stable biocide to water systems, particularly static water bodies, was disputable, but when sodium pentachlorophenate (NaPCP) became available, large-scale experiments were undertaken. Early reports indicated that this chemical was more selective and, being organic, would not be so stable as copper sulphate (Hiatt *et al.*, 1960); furthermore, it was to be applied at the lower concentration of 5 ppm. At this stage experimental application of molluscicides to natural water systems in Rhodesia was expanding over four different geographical regions covering some four thousand square miles of territory.

A wide variety of water bodies was treated with chemicals, particularly with sodium pentachlorophenate, and some of the results produced immediate concern. The effects were frequently noticeable in small lakes and ponds, particularly if there was an abundance of "soft" aquatic vegetation such as *Nymphaea, Otellia,* and *Potamogeton.* With the molluscicidal doses these plants were quickly killed by both sodium pentachlorophenate and copper sulphate, and in the hot weather soon rotted. This decaying organic material increased the biological oxygen demand on the water, and, as there was no longer a source of tran-spiratory oxygen for the water system, the system tended to become anoxic. As a result numbers of fish and other aquatic fauna died, and their rotting bodies made the situation much worse, the ponds sometimes remaining almost sterile until rejuvenated by the next rains. The writer personally investigated nine such water bodies—two affected by copper sulphate, and the rest by sodium pentachlorophenate.

One of these water bodies, the Karoi dam, contained approximately 100 million gallons of water and supplied the nearby village. In August 1962 the periphery was treated to a depth of approximately six feet using sodium pentachlorophenate: 50 lbs. (23 kg) of chemical were applied. Several days after spraying, power boats used on the lake caused considerable disturbance. Over the next six days the oxygen status of the water decreased until large numbers of fish began to die. At this stage the water became anoxic and developed a strong odor of decay, and large quantities of rotting fish were evident in parts of the lake. The water was completely unpalatable and remained so, in spite of expensive filtration techniques, for four months, until rejuvenated by heavy seasonal rains.

EXPERIMENTAL EVIDENCE

Clearly the effect of these chemicals had to be studied in detail, and we did so, studying also a new molluscicidal product called Baylucid. Shiff and Garnett (1961) selected four trial ponds 4×4 m in area and 60 cm deep which were normally interconnected by water furrows, but for the duration of the experiment they were completely isolated from each other and any inflowing water. The ponds were essentially similar in macro-vegetation, containing growths of *Potamogeton pusillus, Polygonum salicifolium* and the alga *Chara* sp. The ponds were numbered 1 to 4: pond

1 was treated with copper sulphate at 20 ppm, pond 2 with sodium pentachlorophenate at 5 ppm, pond 3 with Bayluscid at 1 ppm, and pond 4 left untreated as a control. They were sampled for plankton just before treatment and again on day 2, day 11 and day 32 after treatment. It was possible to classify the plankton collected as follows: Cladocera; Insecta (larval Diptera, Trichoptera, Coleoptera, Neuroptera, Odonata, and Ephemeroptera; adult Gyrinidae, Gerridae and Dytiscidae); acarines; Copepoda; copepod nauplii; Ostracoda (*Cypris* sp. and others) and Spirogyra. A few Rotifera were seen, but as they appeared

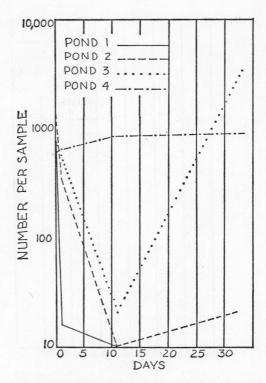

Figure 8–3 Showing numerical fluctuations of individuals of the order Cladocera

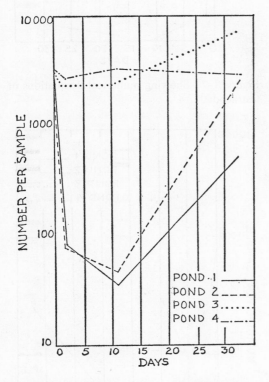

Figure 8–2 Showing the numerical fluctuations of the total number of individuals collected in each sample. Samples were made on Day 0, Day 4, Day 11, and Day 32. Pond 1 was treated with copper sulphate at 20 ppm, Pond 2 with sodium pentachlorophenate at 5 ppm, Pond 3 with Bayluscid at 1 ppm. Pond 4 is the untreated control. After Shiff and Garnett (1961). (For Figures 8–2 through 8–8 the vertical scale is logarithmic.)

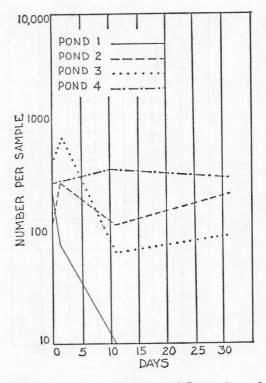

Figure 8–4 Showing numerical fluctuations of aquatic insect larvae

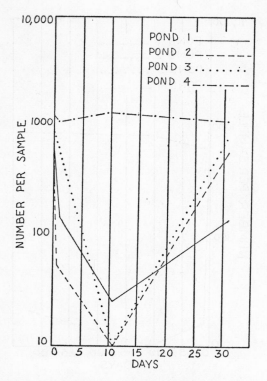

Figure 8–5 Showing numerical fluctuations of Copepoda

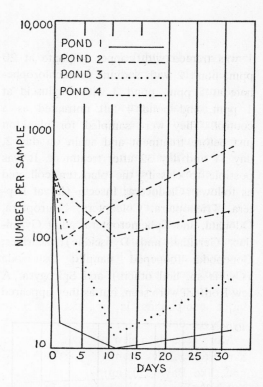

Figure 8–7 Showing numerical fluctuations of Ostracoda

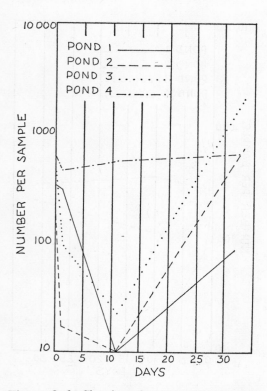

Figure 8–6 Showing the numerical fluctuations of copepod *nauplii*

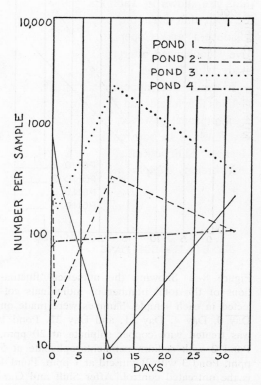

Figure 8–8 Showing numerical fluctuations of various Spirogyra

only sporadically their numbers were excluded; this was also the case with some diatoms.

The overall short-term effect is clearly demonstrated in Fig. 8–2, which records the population fluctuation of the total number of individuals in all groups. The immediate effect of both copper sulphate and sodium pentachlorophenate was to reduce the population very considerably, while only a slight reduction was apparent after treatment with Bayluscid. The Cladocera and copepods appear to be highly sensitive to the molluscicides, particularly to the more stable chemicals. The phytotoxicity of these latter compounds is apparent from the Spirogyra data.

More recently a new molluscicidal chemical, Frescon, has been tested (Shiff, 1966) and, like Bayluscid, appears to have very little effect on the plankton normally found in small ponds and dams in Rhodesia. The data are shown in Table 8–3, where it can be seen that even the sensitive forms, the Cladocera and Copepoda, remained relatively unchanged after treatment of a water body with Frescon.

It would thus appear that the two compounds Bayluscid and Frescon are selective snail poisons; however, most species of fish are sensitive to both compounds in varying degrees. Shiff *et al.* (1967) have shown that bream, *Tilapia mossambica,* can tol-

erate a higher concentration of Frescon than the related *T. melanopleura,* while personal observation shows that *Clarias* sp. (barbel) are sensitive to all molluscicides.

The latter observations were carried out in small, static water bodies. However, in an anti-bilharzia campaign, much of the water treated is flowing and application can either be blanket, to effect total coverage, or focal, i.e., only where snails are found. Harrison (1966) has studied the effects of blanket spraying on two streams from source downward with Bayluscid. One stream flowed with soft water over stony runnels and small pools and after spraying retained chemical from 2 to 24 hours. The second stream, a somewhat larger one, carried hard water with a longer retention time up to three days. Blanket spraying produced concentrations of 0.2 to 0.4 ppm of Bayluscid. Harrison recorded the following effects:

IMMEDIATE

1. Gastropod snails were virtually eliminated.

2. All fish were killed. Fish died more rapidly in soft water (5–10 minutes) than in harder water (2–6 hours).

3. The rest of the invertebrate fauna, especially insects, was not seriously affected. In the soft-water stream some were excited and others became mori-

Table 8-3

RESULTS OF *SCHISTOSOMA HAEMATOBIUM* SURVEYS CARRIED OUT IN THE
KYLE CATCHMENT SNAIL CONTROL AREA FROM 1960 TO 1966. CONTROL ORIGINATED IN 1960
After Shiff and Clarke (1967)

YEAR OF ASSESSMENT		AGE GROUPS						
		0-4	4-5	6-7	8-9	10-11	12-13	14-15
1960	No. examined	403	590	611	578	209	144	106
	% positive	5	5	32.6	55.6	70.8	63.9	65.1
1962	No. examined	117	160	367	504	657	731	441
	% positive	0	3.1	22	35	43.7	46.1	56.9
1966	No. examined	17	20	75	187	276	275	113
	% positive	0	0	17.3	20.3	31.5	47.6	42.5

bund, but, at least in some cases, these effects were temporary and reversible. There was no reduction in density of invertebrate predators such as crabs and Odonata.

SUBSEQUENT EFFECTS

4. Recolonisation by snails which are hosts to schistosomes *Bulinus* (*Physopsis*) spp. and *Biomphalaria pfeifferi* was slow. In the stream with hard water they began to reappear 10 months after treatment but in the soft water none was found 22 months after treatment. Other snails, especially smaller species, returned more rapidly.

5. There were local increases in density of insect larvae including mosquitoes during the first three months after treatment.

The technique evolved in Rhodesia of applying molluscicides to aquatic systems is based on snail surveillance. When a stream or water body is brought into a bilharzia control scheme, it is initially blanket-sprayed using a suspension of molluscicide applied by means of a stirrup pump or pressure sprayer. Subsequently water bodies are inspected every 6 to 8 weeks by rangers trained to look for snails, and chemical is applied only to those foci where intermediate host snails occur. No attempt is made to eradicate snails, but artificial pressure is maintained upon the population of those species which transmit schistosome parasites. As soon as they increase in density and become obvious within the biotope, the focus is dosed with chemical. Harrison and Mason (1967) studied two streams which had been under surveillance for two years and matched each stream with a similar untreated one nearby. The invertebrate fauna of all four was studied periodically over a year. They recorded the following results of the application of Bayluscid under the system of snail surveillance:

1. No schistosome host snails were found in the treated streams until surveillance was discontinued. Other snail species were found.

2. The surveillance treatment appeared to have no significant effect on the invertebrate fauna, including those arthropods known to prey on snails.

3. Fish were not eliminated from the one treated stream which was sampled for them.

4. When surveillance treatment was discontinued, host snails returned within two or three months and, in one case, an abnormally high density built up.

This latter instance refers to an increase of *Bulinus* (*Physopsis*) *globosus* in a pool on the Mutoraseka Stream, lat. 17°13′ S., long. 31° E. (Harrison and Mason, 1967). There are two factors which probably contributed to this phenomenon. The species has a high intrinsic rate of natural increase in warm weather, and this is when spraying stopped. Second, there is evidence that snails produce some metabolic product which has a density-dependent population effect. Berrie and Visser (1963) have shown that it will reduce growth and reproduction in *Biomphalaria*. This mechanism is not operative after a castastrophe such as drying out of the pond or the suppression of snail populations by surveillance. When conditions ameliorate, it can be expected that particularly *B. globosus* will increase rapidly until the regulatory mechanisms begin to operate.

The application of such a toxic chemical to any water system should not be lightly undertaken as it must have some disrupting effects on the flora and fauna, although they have not been detectable in the study reported here. However, in the face of severe public health problems some control must be achieved, and it would appear that this has been done with minimum interference of the biotope. The reduction in populations of intermediate host snails produced by snail surveillance has been shown to reduce the incidence of urinary bilharzia (*Schistosoma haematobium*) in a rural population. Shiff and Clarke (1967) have published the results of surveys carried out in a rural population living in an area protected by snail surveillance over a period of seven years, 1960 to 1966. The data in Table 8–3 show an overall reduction in the prevalence in each age group during the period 1960 to 1962 and 1963 through 1966, together with the progressive absence of infection in the younger age groups. This gives some indication of the real impact of the campaign as practiced in Rhodesia.

ACKNOWLEDGMENT

The author wishes to thank the Secretary for Health for permission to submit these case histories. Grateful thanks to Dr. V. de V. Clarke, Director, Blair Research Laboratory, for criticism and help.

REFERENCES

Berrie, A. D., and Visser, S. A. "Investigations of a Growth-Inhibiting Substance Affecting a Natural Population of Freshwater Snails." *Physiol. Zool.*, 36 (1963), 167–73.

Clarke, V. de V.; Shiff, C. J.; and Blair, D. M. "The Control of Snail Hosts of Bilharziasis and Fascioliasis in Southern Rhodesia." *Bull. WHO*, 25 (1961), 549–58.

Harrison, A. D. "The Effects of Bayluscid on Gastropod Snails and Other Aquatic Fauna in Rhodesia." *Hydrobiol.*, 28 (1966), 371–84.

Harrison, A. D., and Mason, M. H. "The Effects on the Fauna of Natural Waters of Surveillance Treatment with Bayluscide in Rhodesia." *Hydrobiol.*, 29 (1967), 149–55.

Hiatt, C. W.; Haskins, W. T.; and Olivier, L. "The Action of Sunlight on Sodium Pentachlorophenate." *Amer. J. Trop. Med. and Hyg.*, 9 (1960), 527–31.

Shiff, C. J. "Trials with *N*-tritylmorpholine (Shell WL8008) as a Molluscicide in Southern Rhodesia." *Bull. WHO*, 35 (1966), 203–12.

Shiff, C. J., and Clarke, V. de V. "The Effect of Snail Surveillance in Natural Waterways on the Transmission of *Schistosoma haematobium* in Rhodesia." *Cent. Afr. Med. J.*, 13 (1967), 133–37.

Shiff, C. J.; Crossland, N. O.; and Millar, D. R. "The Susceptibilities of Various Species of Fish to the Molluscicide *N*-tritylmorpholine." *Bull. WHO*, 36 (1967), 500–07.

Shiff, C. J., and Garnett, B. "The Short-Term Effects of Three Molluscicides on the Microflora and Microfauna of Small, Biologically Stable Ponds in Southern Rhodesia." *Bull. WHO*, 25 (1961), 543–47.

9. WORLD HEALTH ORGANIZATION PROJECT EGYPT 10:

A Case History of a Schistosomiasis Control Project[1]

Henry van der Schalie

The great increase in irrigated areas in Egypt and the Sudan and the replacement of the ancient simple techniques of irrigation by modern perennial irrigation systems have created conditions whereby the incidence of bilharziasis has risen dramatically. Formerly, low percentages of the population were affected; now, with a permanent supply of water, well over one-half of the population, sometimes up to almost 100%, has contracted the disease over wide areas. The disease is almost impossible to cure, and the available drugs and treatments are often too dangerous and too expensive for most of the population to use.

The disease poses a very serious problem in both Egypt and the Sudan. Programs of bilharziasis control, such as the medical, sanitation, education, and snail control programs of WHO, are designed to attack the immediate aspects only and have not been successful when promoted in isolation. Few diseases demand more collaboration in more fields at every level. International programs,

---

[1] The material in this paper was originally published in different form as "Schistosomiasis: Control in Egypt and the Sudan" by Henry van der Schalie in *Natural History,* Copyright © 1969, The American Museum of Natural History. Much of the original planning for the Egypt 10 project of the World Health Organization was initially by Drs. Claude Barlow and Abdel Azim, then of the Egyptian Ministry of Public Health. A good summary analysis of the situation was given by Abdel Azim (1948); Barlow (1951) also reported on the nature of the problem for the public at large (*Egyptian Gazette,* 1951).

particularly irrigation projects, too often fail to make their programs mesh with bilharziasis control, and inadvertently encourage the spread of this scourge, which soon enters practically every field of human endeavor.

In brief, the need for integration and planning seems overwhelming, but the prospects for obtaining relief are dim. In the meantime, the emerging countries in Africa face frightening increases in the incidence of bilharziasis.

One of the best summary statements of the dilemma in the control of schistosomiasis (bilharziasis) appeared in the article "Bilharziasis as a Man-Made Disease" (Weir, 1959):

It is a tragic irony that in many parts of the world the vast irrigation schemes constructed with the aim of improving the standard of living have had the effect of undermining the health of the areas they serve. The network of canals designed to carry water to arid territories have proved ideally suited for carrying bilharziasis—and sometimes other diseases—to the inhabitants. Still more important is the fact that before the introduction of perennial irrigation, bilharziasis was unknown in many of these areas. For this reason, bilharziasis has been termed a "man-made" disease.

At present, human blood fluke is one of the most serious parasitic human afflictions. The debilitating nature of this disease and its occupational hazards place it at the heart of many economic and social problems in countries where it is prevalent. Since Pharaonic times Egypt has been known to have had incidence of this blood fluke disease among the villagers in farm communities, but since the spread of modern irrigation the disease has taken astronomic proportions; in the Sudan this disease and cattle liver fluke increased as agricultural schemes were introduced.

Blood fluke, as it relates to humans, has a cycle in which the adult worms live in the mesenteric veins surrounding the intestine (in *Schistosoma mansoni*) or in the blood vessels around the urinary bladder (in *Schistosoma haematobium*). The sexes of this trematode worm are separate, with the slender and longer female carried in a special groove in the body of the male. The female is a virtual egg-laying machine, producing eggs by the thousands. Many of the chitonous and spined eggs find their way out of the human body with the feces or with the urine; too many others fail to leave their human host and are the cause of most of the pathology associated with the disease. Those eggs that do reach the water of a canal or a drain, often during a normal course of human elimination, hatch and must find a suitable snail to continue the life cycle. In the intestinal variety (*Schistosoma mansoni*) the snail host is a planorbid form called *Biomphalaria,* while the bladder parasite (*S. haematobium*) must enter a spired *Bulinus* snail. In the snail, the parasites develop bag-like reproductive structures nourished by the snails' digestive gland. After about a month under normal regional temperatures the infective larvae of the parasite, called cercariae, emerge from the snails; cercariae are often "shed" in prodigious numbers. Humans become infected when their skin is placed in contact with water contaminated with the cercariae. Once infected, a human may pass eggs of this schistosome parasite for many years.

The suffering caused by blood flukes (schistosomiasis) has been known and recorded since ancient times. An excellent description and a good historic account of the disease is given by Leonard Greenbaum (1961) in his article titled "Bilharziasis/Schistosomiasis," in which he traces the problems in Egypt as chronicled from the ancient (Pharaonic) period to the time when the French expeditionary force was in Egypt and Syria; he also indicates the role of the pioneers in blood fluke studies such as Drs. Theodore Bilharz, Leiper and Barlow. It was the latter who, as a medical doctor, infected himself and carefully described the symptoms of the disease (Barlow and Meleney, 1949). In the early stages the patient experiences irritation of the skin which is later followed by a cough, headaches, loss of appetite, various aches and pains, and often difficulty in breathing. When the disease reaches a more advanced stage nausea is common, accompanied by dysentery, with bloody stools, in intestinal schistosomiasis; or by bloody urine (haematuria), in the urinary variety. The liver becomes enlarged, as does the spleen, and the abdomen often becomes bloated, while the body is emaciated. It is in the advanced stages that the patients often develop cancerous growths. The intense suffering and the difficulty involved in bringing about a cure is well documented by Dr. Barlow, who clearly indicated that the cure involves suffering more intense at times than that caused by the disease.

The World Health Organization program (documented as "Egypt 10") was designed essentially to carry out four phases of schistosomiasis control in one area, the Qaliub tract. These programs were previously carried out by different agencies in the country, in different places and at different times.

The WHO program determined the incidence of schistosomiasis among the thirty-two thousand people living in the six villages of the five-thousand-acre tract. A house-to-house survey established that at least half the population was infected in most of the villages (in one, Barada'a, the incidence was 70%). The project then undertook: (1) a sanitation program designed to provide potable water by building 150 wells and pumps; also five thousand borehole latrines were to be built to assist in preventing eggs of the schistosomes from getting to the canals and drains; (2) a government medical program in which the patients found to be positive were given Fouadin intramuscularly: seventy thousand shots were given; (3) a program of health education to inform the people of the nature of the disease and what they would need to do to prevent becoming infected; (4) a snail control program, since it was well established that a preventive campaign would constitute the best possible defense. This latter phase of the program best displays some of the ecological consequences and reveals the need for better coordination and cooperation.

SCHISTOSOMIASIS AND THE NILE

It has long been known (Barlow, 1937) that a direct correlation exists between the kind of irrigation practiced by people in endemic areas and the incidence of human blood fluke (schistosomiasis). The Delta with its *perennial* irrigation has a fabulously high incidence of both *Schistosoma mansoni* and *S. haematobium*. In contrast, the Nile above Cairo has *basin* irrigation, and there the incidence of *S. mansoni* (Scott, 1937) is very spotty and low (imported from the Delta), while *S. haematobium* was estimated at only 5%. The change projected for the upper Nile when the new High Dam project is completed warrants some real concern (van der Schalie, 1960). An effort was made to obtain some basic information before the change, so that appraisals could be made as the new system of perennial irrigation becomes established. The recent war in the Middle East, however, prevented the development of an evaluation program. Too little assessment has been made of the effect of building large dams, the attendant irrigation schemes that they promote, and the slow and steady rise in schistosomiasis that usually follows such developments (Abdel Azim, 1948; Wright, 1951; and others). One such case is the development of the Gezira "Scheme" in the Sudan, an irrigation system running parallel to the Blue Nile south of Khartoum. One of the best exposés of the relation of perennial irrigation to the increased incidence of schistosomiasis is a description of this case by W. H. Greany (1952). That region was a vast savannah in the Sudan until the Sennar Dam was built, transforming some 900,000 acres into a large agricultural scheme, the Gezira Irrigated Area. Three years after irrigation was introduced, both *S. mansoni* and *S. haematobium* were well established and on the rise among the population.

In his study of the Gezira, Greany verified (as was previously discovered in Egypt) that the density of the pulmonate snail hosts was usually correlated with the growth of aquatic vegetation. Since copper sulphate was used as the molluscicide, it was necessary to remove the aquatic vegetation before the chemical was applied. Copper ions are adsorbed by both vegetation and mud. Hence, in any such venture herbiciding and mollusciciding should be carried out jointly. In 1954 Dr. Naguib Ayad and the author surveyed a program to reduce the snail populations in the canals of the Gezira tract. The program was designed to apply 30 ppm of copper sulphate and to maintain a concentration of .125 ppm by keeping bags with copper sulphate immersed in the canals. It was evident that this program not only eliminated the snails, but, where the copper ions were held in solution, there was an equally beneficial reduction of aquatic vegetation which augmented the flow of water in the canals. This program was to cost a quarter of a million dollars and there was naturally some concern since it would cost more than malaria control. In any case, the program seems to have produced some beneficial results as a method for controlling schistosomiasis.

If one compares the Sudan to Egypt in terms of possible methods of control, some interesting differences appear. Perhaps some very important similarities in the two regions should first be stressed. Among them are: (1) the people are culturally alike in that they are mainly Islamic and similarly practice the rites of their religion (ablutions, *wadu* or washing before prayers, etc.); (2) they often use the canal water for bathing, washing clothes, tending the *gamoosa* (water buffalo) which youngsters almost daily take into the canals, etc.; and (3) they work in the fields in similar irrigation systems designed to grow cotton and other staple crops. However, in several ways the areas are so strikingly different that there appears more hope for protecting the health of the people in the Sudan than in Egypt. The Sudanese have room to build homes and sanitary facilities; they enjoy a higher standard of living and, with the much lower incidence of blood fluke, are more vigorous in coming to grips with their problems.

Over hundreds of years Egypt has become unbelievably infested with blood fluke. The seriousness of the health conditions in rural Egypt was documented in the Delta region by John Weir and his associates in 1952 at Sindbis (near the Qaliub Egypt 10 tract). They provided the first meaningful mortality and morbidity data; they also showed that the life expectancy of women in the region was 27 years and that of men was 25.

It is interesting to compare the Sudan with Egypt in the functional aspects of blood fluke control. The Sudan in many ways typifies the emergent countries of Africa where schistosomiasis remains at a low ebb until irrigation is developed and then snail hosts and aquatic vegetation flourish. Migrant labor carrying blood fluke infections move to the area, and the habits of the people encourage a steady rise in the incidence of schistosomiasis. In Egypt, this process has reached a stage where the countryside of the Delta is virtually rotting with the disease. The overpopulated condition of the area with its farm population in horribly crowded villages, the lack of sanitation and the near impossibility of building proper facilities for potable water and waste disposal, the many unfortunate daily practices that allow for an amazing exposure to infection—all contribute to make the conditions almost impossible to control in the areas where perennial irrigation exists. The amazing ramifications as they relate to politics, economics, education, agricultural practices, etc., compound the problems. In the Sudan, the problem of control is serious and difficult, but there the prospects look brighter. The fact that there is room not only for people to live, but also for facilities such as wells and latrines makes control easier. The Gezira scheme has proven to be a very successful venture economically, not only providing most of the funds used for operating the government but also sufficiently raising living standards for the tenant farmers to enable them to procure some of the facilities needed to cope with the problems on their own. While roughly a million acres are now cultivated, the area between the White and Blue Nile will allow for the development of two million more acres.

The potentials in the Gezira of the Sudan are good for several reasons. The disease has not spread as widely as it has in the lower Nile or Delta of Egypt. Greany (1952, p. 261) indicated that about 9% of the population was infected with both *S. mansoni* and *S. haematobium* in the Sudan; I found (van der Schalie, 1958, p. 265) that in Egypt the incidence in villages is at least 50%. Consequently, people in the Sudan are apt to be more vigorous with a more positive attitude toward initiating constructive reforms. The programs relating to key aspects such as education, medica-

tion, sanitation and potential snail control, etc., seem to be kept more in focus in the areas where support for collateral and integrated activity is needed.

METHODS FOR SCHISTOSOMIASIS CONTROL

HEALTH EDUCATION

This undoubtedly serves as one of the best ways to inform the people of the endemic area about the nature of the disease and the conditions that expose them to infection. In the Sudan, in 1954, there were some excellent village councils made up of people active in the community. The village council at Hassa Hessa in the Sudan was most impressive; the paucity of leaders available in the Egyptian villages (usually only the mayor (the sheik), the imam (religious leader), the schoolteacher, and an occasional person from another profession) made work in the community very difficult. Yet, the adults and children were aware of the program and available means were mustered for the benefit of the protective aspects of the work.

SANITATION

In an Egyptian village it is almost impossible to provide sanitary facilities. In Egypt 10, bore-hole latrines were installed. They soon became open cesspools because the water table was so high. People were obviously not able to cope with them even in the few houses where they could be installed. Few planners seemed to realize that those latrines can serve only about nine months, that they become frightfully putrid in summer where the temperatures are so high, and that it is well-nigh impossible to reestablish the latrine once it has filled up. Again, coordination between the several aspects of the project failed, and this project could have profited from assistance available in parallel programs such as those now sponsored by AID. The evidence, then, indicates that bore-hole latrines are not the answer to the sanitation problem in rural Egypt, especially when they are placed within the limited confines of already substandard housing units. One must bear in mind that the people and their animals all remain in the house together at night. The *gamoosa* are apt to step too close to the walls of the latrine, causing it to crumble away at the edges; other inconveniences arise simply because there is just no room for a latrine. It was not until the second year of the project that the WHO was able to recruit a capable sanitary engineer (Max Aroaz) who later developed some good models of pit latrines that were used outdoors and showed promise for better disposal of human wastes. Obviously the great difficulty of coping with a rapidly filling bore-hole latrine placed within a house during a hot summer drove the people back to their usual haunts of elimination at the edge of the canal (or drain) where conditions were far more tolerable, although fraught with great danger of infection.

MEDICAL ASPECTS

In terms of the medical aspects, the control of schistosomiasis is proving very difficult for several reasons. Many drug companies have been working for a number of years to find a suitable drug for treatment. Most drugs used today have serious side effects and it is generally conceded that attaining a cure is often questionable. Two major obstacles appear in the medical approach to control: (1) When the eggs fail to find their way out of the body, they cause serious pathological changes in organs such as the liver, spleen, and colon. Drugs are of little help to those with heavy and advanced cases. (2) Poverty is so great in endemic regions that few can obtain medication unless the government is prepared to provide

such help. The government provides, but in the process of being treated it is too onerous an experience for the people to wait and to lose fifteen whole days of the month and be sick the intervening days; they end up losing about twenty days. While the programs are usually administered by medical personnel, the first line of defense obviously is not within the medical field. Since many well-meaning but uninformed doctors are in charge of all phases of the control programs, errors often occur when they make decisions without consultation in fields other than their own.

Data on the prevalence of schistosomiasis were obtained from people registered and called to the medical centers after the house-to-house survey (Fig. 9–1). When these data are considered, the incidence of blood fluke in the villages is alarmingly high. The survey area will be shown later to harbor largely *Bulinus* snails with a relatively small sector in the northern part of the tract harboring *Biomphalaria,* usually in terminal canals or drains in association with water hyacinth. However, as shown in Table 9–1, the villages did have a wide range of difference in the incidence of the two species of schistosomes carried by the inhabitants. As for the most prevalent blood fluke, *Schistosoma haematobium,* Qanater Town had a relatively light incidence of 17%. But many of the people in that village traveled to Cairo to work, so that they were not as likely to be engaged in farming with its high potential for occupational hazard. On the other hand, Barada'a had 72% infection and most of the other villages showed at least half of the population carrying blood flukes (Table 9–1). One does not always find eggs in the urine to indicate a positive on a single urine examination; consequently, those previously negative were recalled for additional testing. As shown in Table 9–2 between 20% and 30% of those supposedly negative turned positive.

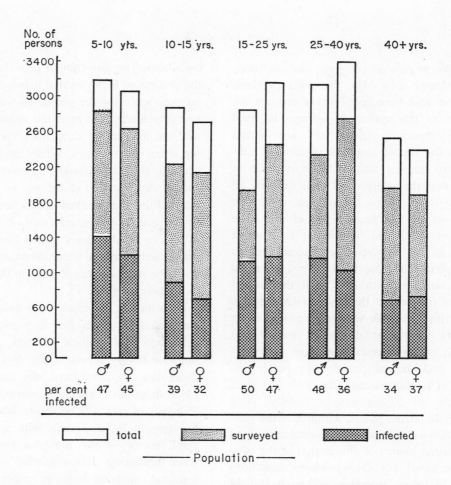

Figure 9–1 Human survey for *Bilharzia haematobia* according to age and sex in Qaliub area

Table 9-1

HUMAN SURVEY FOR BILHARZIASIS IN THE TOWNS, VILLAGES AND FARMS OF THE PROJECT AREA
(Figures from March 15, 1953, to June 25, 1954)*

LOCALITY	URINES			STOOLS		
	PERSONS EXAMINED†	*SCHISTOSOMA HAEMATOBIUM*	% INFECTED	PERSONS EXAMINED	*SCHISTOSOMA MANSONI*	% INFECTED
Qanater Town	7,862	1,356	17	7,643	1	0.01
Shalaqan, Kafr el Harith and Farms	6,944	2,918	42	4,935	6	0.12
Hallaba and Farms	1,993	1,164	58	1,261	1	0.08
Sanafir and Farms	3,807	1,939	51	2,713	4	0.15
Barada'a and Farms	4,734	3,429	72	3,711	317	8.54
Total	25,340	10,806	43%	20,263	329	1.62%

S. mansoni eggs were not found in the urines but *S. haematobium* were found in the stools on 19 occasions.
†The urines of 1,440 negative persons were examined twice; the distribution by age groups is shown in Fig. 9-1.

Table 9–2

RE-EXAMINATION OF URINES FOR *Schistosoma haematobium* IN
PERSONS FOUND NEGATIVE IN THE FIRST EXAMINATION,
from September 1, 1953, to June 25, 1954

LOCALITY	PERSONS EXAMINED	POSITIVE	%
Shalaqan, Kafr el Harith and Farms	859	171	20
Hallaba and Farms	298	38	13
Sanafir and Farms	194	37	19
Barada'a and Farms	89	25	28
Total	1,440	271	19%

Table 9–3

HUMAN TREATMENT OF BILHARZIASIS CASES WITH FOUADIN
IN THE QALIUB PROJECT AREA
from September 1, 1953, to June 25, 1954

LOCALITY	CALLS SENT	PATIENTS BEGINNING TREATMENT	PATIENTS ENDING TREATMENT*	NUMBER OF INJECTIONS RECORDED
Qanater	1,356	622	596	6,342
Shalaqan, Kafr el Harith and Farms	2,914	2,909	1,898	22,137
Hallaba and Farms	1,389	993	745	7,967
Sanafir and Farms	1,997	1,632	1,161	13,275
Barada'a and Farms	3,698	2,839	2,169	20,861
Total	11,354	8,995	6,569	70,582

* A course of nine injections of Fouadin given on alternate days.

More precise tests over more extended periods would probably show that the whole population in most of those villages had either active cases or were chronically harboring blood fluke.

In the medical phase of the work some seventy thousand injections of Fouadin were given to almost nine thousand patients (Table 9–3). These treatments were given by a special medical team supplied by the Egyptian government. The treatment is drastic; and with its serious side effects (so ably described by Dr. Barlow), many patients fail to complete the course of treatment. It has been indicated by medical authorities that the relapse rate is very high and relatively few people are cured in such courses of treatment. More serious is the fact that, in their daily activities, the patients are bound to become reinfected within a short time even though they may have had some relief from the medication.

Sanitary engineering has held a high place in the control programs, and properly so. When one realizes that *in the winter practically all of the snails in Egypt lose their schistosome infections,* it would obviously be a great boon if the canals and drains were not polluted as soon as the winter period of closure ends. In two consecutive years of observations, for which there are good data, the team in Egypt 10 found that there were practically no snails shedding cercariae until the middle of May (Table

Table 9-4

MONTHLY EXAMINATIONS OF *BULINUS TRUNCATUS* FOR CERCARIAE OF
SCHISTOSOMA HAEMATOBIUM: AUGUST 8, 1953, TO JULY 6, 1954
(Van der Schalie, 1958)

YEAR AND MONTH	SAMPLES			*BULINUS*		
	NUMBER EXAMINED	NUMBER INFECTED	PERCENT-AGE INFECTED	NUMBER EXAMINED	NUMBER INFECTED	PERCENT-AGE INFECTED
1953						
August	22	0	0	49	0	0
September	65	1	1.6	106	1	1.0
October	265	1	0.4	488	1	0.2
November	104	2	2.0	259	2	0.8
December	5	0	0	9	0	0
1954						
January	14	0	0	39	0	0
February	99	1	1.0	466	1*	0.2
March	89	0	0	204	0	0
April	164	0	0	394	0	0
May	645	6	0.9	3,421	9	0.3
June	1,111	21	1.8	7,648	27	0.3
July	226	25	11.0	1,206	30	2.4
Total	2,809	57	2.0	14,289	71	0.4

*This infected snail was found in a drain not subject to closure of water.

9–4)! This observation obviously has great significance in all planning in epidemiology. Yet, in an excellent series of reports by the teams in Egypt 49 near Alexandria (Dazo *et al.,* 1966) there is virtually no mention of this very important functional relationship in the epidemiology of this disease. Perhaps drains near Alexandria do have a little overwintering of infection since they probably never dry out.

SNAIL CONTROL

The five-thousand-acre Qaliub tract was surveyed by the WHO Egypt 10 team to determine the distribution of the host snails. Even in this relatively small area in this system of perennial irrigation there were more than 450 kilometers of canals and drains. When plotted, the collection of snails shows that *Biomphalaria* snails with possible *Schistosoma mansoni* infections occurred only in the northern sector of this tract and mostly above a line shown in the snail distribution map. It should be emphasized that the *Bulinus* snails, which carry *S. haematobium,* were widely distributed throughout the sample area. While this limited distribution of *Biomphalaria* was fortuitous, it is interesting to note (as will be emphasized later in connection with the High Dam at Aswan) that this demarcation line actually extends across the whole Delta area. *Schistosoma mansoni,* as a corollary of perennial irrigation, should become common throughout the whole length of the Nile in Egypt when the pattern of irrigation is changed from basin, as it now exists throughout Upper Egypt, to perennial when the High Dam is completed.

It should be noted that the onset of infective cercariae shed by the snails takes place largely in late May. Also, agencies often fail to realize that the actual number of snails infected *in nature* is surprisingly low. In the studies of the Egypt 10 project

Table 9-5

MONTHLY EXAMINATIONS OF *BIOMPHALARIA BOISSY** FOR CERCARIAE
OF *SCHISTOSOMA MANSONI*: AUGUST 8, 1953, TO JULY 6, 1954

YEAR AND MONTH	SAMPLES			*BIOMPHALARIA*		
	NUMBER EXAMINED	NUMBER INFECTED	PERCENT-AGE INFECTED	NUMBER EXAMINED	NUMBER INFECTED	PERCENT-AGE INFECTED
1953						
August	1	0	0	1	0	0
September	4	0	0	7	0	0
October	59	2	3	126	3	2.3
November	11	0	0	24	0	0
December	0	0	0	0	0	0
1954						
January	4	1	25.0	78	1†	1.2
February	22	0	0	26	0	0
March	49	0	0	482	0	0
April	0	0	0	0	0	0
May	7	0	0	45	0	0
June	147	3	2.0	1,944	3	0.2
July	89	11	12.0	530	12	2.3
Total	393	17	4.0	3,263	19	0.6

*Now called *B. alexandrina*.
†This infected snail was found in a drain not subject to closure of water.

(van der Schalie, 1958, p. 277), the highest rate of infection among snails infected with *S. haematobium* brought in from the field was 0.4%! This low incidence appeared in a sample of more than fourteen thousand snails collected from many stations in the five-thousand-acre tract. Yet, the incidence among humans in the six villages ran over 50% for most of them and over 70% for Barada'a. Evidently a few widely scattered infected snails (not necessarily located near the villages) produce enough cercariae sometime *after the middle of May* to infect almost the whole population because of the tremendous amount of contact people in the countryside have with infested water. If these facts were mentioned in later reports they seem somehow hard to uncover!

The loss of infection among the snail hosts between December and May of each year has been attested to both in Egypt and the Sudan. The work of the Snail Control Section of the Ministry of Health and especially

the studies of Dr. C. W. Barlow (1939) and his associates indicated that few infected snails could be found in the Delta of Egypt in the cold period during and following winter closure. The significance and regularity in the appearance of infected snails as they are found in nature was clearly shown in two years of observation in the Egypt 10 project. In our survey of the Qaliub tract (van der Schalie, 1958) the effects of cold weather and aestivating conditions on the infections in the snails are evident, as shown in Tables 9–4 and 9–5. Most of the infected snails are found in May, June and July, whether they are infected with *S. mansoni* in the snail *Biomphalaria boissyi* (now called *B. alexandrina*) or with *S. haematobium* in *Bulinus truncatus*. It is just this lateness in the appearance of cercariae in Egypt that led Dr. Barlow to emphasize that he was not concerned about getting infected if exposed to canal water prior to May since the emergence or shed of cercariae usually comes about the middle of May, as is clearly shown in the number of infected snails that appear in these tables seasonally by months. Another striking and important bit of evidence in these tables is the low incidence in the snails even during the seasons of highest infection. Yet, the populations in the villages have such a tremendous amount of exposure to natural and infested waters that the incidence in humans involves almost all the people of some villages. The failure to find infected snails which shed cercariae before the climate turns quite hot in May also has historic significance. Dr. Looss in 1910 decided that the human schistosomes in Egypt completed their life history without passing through snails! Dr. Leiper, in 1915, after two years without finding infected snails, discovered infected ones only after he remained longer than usual in Egypt (because of illness) and was able in the late spring to find the infections.

In a recent WHO Expert Report (1965) insufficient stress was given a paper by C. H. Barlow (1939) in which he stated: ". . . For 5 years the writer and his men have worked barehanded in the El Marg area during January, February and March without becoming infected. Constant crushing and dissecting of snails have presented a picture of such inactivity of whatever cercariae exist that an assumption of security seems warranted." This loss of infection at low temperatures in snails that are cold-stressed has been proven experimentally by Stirewalt (1954). Evidently most snails in Egypt lose their infections in the winter. This fact was confirmed in the laboratory at Ann Arbor when loss of infection occurred after snails in the aquaria were chilled when the windows of an aquarium room were accidentally left open in the fall of the year.

In the last analysis snail control has been considered by most authorities as the most promising method for reducing the incidence of schistosomiasis in the populations exposed to infection. Both in Egypt (van der Schalie, 1958) and in the Sudan (Greany, 1952),

Table 9-6a

PREVALENCE OF *SCHISTOSOMA HAEMATOBIUM* – KOM ISHU AND KOM EL BIRKA COMBINED

Age at Time of Survey	1962		1963		1964		1965		%	%	%	%
	No. Examined	No. Positive	No. Examined	No. Positive	No. Examined	No. Positive	No. Examined	No. Positive	1962	1963	1964	1965
1	14	0	29	0	57	0	35	0	0	0	0	0
1-2	9	1	58	7	34	0	54	0	11.1	12.1	0	0
2-3	24	5	40	2	54	4	23	0	20.8	5.0	7.4	0
3-4	29	5	59	11	34	1	62	2	17.2	18.6	2.9	2.9
4-5	28	10	64	10	59	4	33	0	35.7	15.6	6.8	0
5-6	29	15	52	19	60	9	55	9	51.7	36.5	15.0	16.4
6-7	35	14	70	30	51	21	61	18	40.0	42.9	43.1	29.5

PREVALENCE OF *SCHISTOSOMA HAEMATOBIUM* IN AKRISHA SECTION (CONTROL DIVISION)

Age at Time of Survey	1962		1963		1964		1965		%	%	%	%
	No. Examined	No. Positive	No. Examined	No. Positive	No. Examined	No. Positive	No. Examined	No. Positive	1962	1963	1964	1965
1	31	3	No Survey		34	0	46	0	9.7		0	0
1-2	28	1			25	2	29	2	3.6		8.0	6.9
2-3	33	4			29	3	28	7	12.1	No Survey	10.3	25.0
3-4	41	5			28	8	28	5	12.2		28.6	17.5
4-5	32	8			35	7	28	7	25.0		20.0	25.0
5-6	42	13			31	15	35	12	31.0		48.4	34.3
6-7	35	17			42	19	31	18	48.6		45.2	58.1

copper sulphate has been used as a molluscicide for many years. More recently, some of the newer chemicals have been tested, and among them sodium pentachlorophenate and Bayluscide appear most promising (Dawood, Dazo and Farooq, 1966). Bayluscide seems to be preferred because NaPCP (sodium pentachlorophenate) is more irritating to the dispenser and, therefore, may be a dangerous chemical to handle. The recent surveys by the WHO team working with the Egypt 49 project near Alexandria, and specially the studies of M. Farooq and his associates (1966), provide a wide variety of detailed data on prevalence, relation of schistosomiasis to personal habits, environmental factors, and incidence, of this disease. In that same project information is given on methods for the control of snails and the lowering of disease incidence in populations in areas where control was maintained with molluscicides (Bayluscide and sodium pentachlorophenate). Similar work previously done by E. G. Berry working near Cairo, and more recently M. Farooq *et al.* (1966) working near Alexandria, also showed that incidence in children was reduced when a molluscicide was applied to eliminate the snail hosts in an experimental area (Tables 9–6a and b).

The data in Tables 9–6a and b indicate that molluscicides, when applied for an extended period to an area where schistosomiasis is prevalent, will bring about a reduction in the transmission of the disease. For the villages of Kom Ishu and Kom el Birka, M. Farooq *et al.* (1966, p. 43) reported:

The evidence is very strong, particularly when it is realized that no one born in the two years since the start of mollusciciding operations has become positive for either parasite.

The work on which this assessment was based is of a high order of excellence, but one wonders what is gained by the statement at the end of this article:

The authors believe this to be the first scientifically acceptable demonstration of the interruption of transmission of bilharziasis in the Nile Valley or Delta.

Table 9-6b

PREVALENCE OF *SCHISTOSOMA MANSONI* – KOM ISHU AND KOM EL BIRKA COMBINED

Age at Time of Survey	1962		1963		1964		1965		%	%	%	%
	No. Examined	No. Positive	No. Examined	No. Positive	No. Examined	No. Positive	No. Examined	No. Positive	1962	1963	1964	1965
1	14	0	29	3	57	0	35	0	0	10.3	0	0
1-2	9	0	58	6	27	2	54	0	0	10.3	7.4	0
2-3	24	7	40	4	54	3	23	0	29.2	10.0	5.6	0
3-4	29	8	59	8	34	2	62	0	27.6	13.6	5.9	0
4-5	27	4	64	8	59	4	33	0	14.8	12.5	6.8	0
5-6	29	11	52	8	60	10	55	4	37.9	15.4	16.7	7.3
6-7	35	16	70	27	51	10	61	3	45.7	38.6	19.6	4.9

PREVALENCE OF *SCHISTOSOMA MANSONI* IN AKRISHA SECTION (CONTROL DIVISION)

Age at Time of Survey	1962		1963		1964		1965		%	%	%	%
	No. Examined	No. Positive	No. Examined	No. Positive	No. Examined	No. Positive	No. Examined	No. Positive	1962	1963	1964	1965
1	31	1	No Survey		34	0	46	0	3.2		0	0
1-2	28	1			25	2	29	0	3.6	No Survey	8.0	0
2-3	33	1			29	1	28	3	3.0		3.4	10.7
3-4	41	6			28	3	28	4	14.6		10.7	14.3
4-5	32	8			35	3	28	6	25.0		8.6	21.4
5-6	42	9			31	6	35	3	21.4		19.4	8.6
6-7	35	9			42	5	31	9	25.7		11.9	29.0

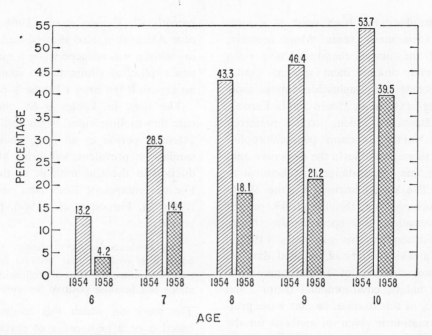

Figure 9–2 (a) *Schistosoma haematobium.* Comparative infection rate found in Warraq El Arab school children age 6 to 10, 1954 and 1958

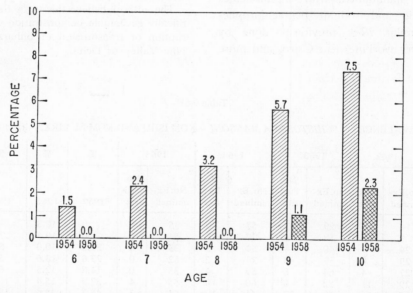

Figure 9–2 (b) *Schistosoma mansoni.* Comparative infection rate found in Warraq El Arab school children age 6 to 10, 1954 and 1958

They evidently did not bother to take into account work published by their sponsor, the World Health Organization, done a decade earlier and appearing under the title "Field Trials of Various Molluscicides (chiefly sodium pentachlorophenate) for the Control of Aquatic Intermediate Hosts of Human Bilharziasis." This study was reported by Wright, Dobrovolny and Berry (1958). The work was done mainly in an area near the Pyramids southwest of Cairo where *Schistosoma haematobium* predominates. Graphs are here presented (through the courtesy of Dr. Elmer G. Berry) clearly indicating that the incidence is reduced in areas where molluscicides can be applied for several years. In Fig. 9–2a the reduction of *S. haematobium* in school children in each of the age classes from six to ten years old is clearly indicated; in Fig. 9–2b a similar and marked reduction is shown for *S. mansoni* in the same Warraq el Arab region even though the incidence of this parasite is usually comparatively low in that region. In Gelfand's "A Clinical Study of Intestinal Bilharziasis in Africa," E. Lee Husting (1967, p. 195) indicated that snail eradication ". . . is one fifteenth of its original level, by mollusciciding or other means." It would "reduce the worm load to zero in about twenty-three years, thus achieving eradication." However, in most regions where blood fluke is widespread and represents a serious problem, the prospects for using large quantities of a molluscicide over extended periods are not good. Consequently, it is almost certain that snail eradication with molluscicides alone will never be

achieved and plans must be made for the use of chemicals with measures designed specifically for each situation.

The snail survey of the Qaliub tract was carried out by the WHO Egypt 10 team in a manner developed by previous investigators working with the Snail Control Section of the Ministry of Health. Small canals and drains were usually sampled with a dip net. The snails were placed in marked containers for spot recording purposes and then brought to the field laboratory at Qaliub for study. The larger canals were surveyed with the use of palm leaf traps which were placed in the lower bank of the canal, left there for a week or ten days and then recovered and examined for snails (usually *Bulinus*) on the fronds. As many as 80 or 100 may be found on a single trap. The snails were placed in marked bags and brought to the laboratory for the determination of the sites that produce infected or uninfected snails. Those snails that did not show infection when placed in water for such observation were later crushed to determine whether they were infected but not in the shedding state. The data accumulated from these field surveys and the laboratory

Table 9-7

LABOR REQUIRED FOR CLEARANCE OF VEGETATION
FROM CHANNELS IN PROJECT AREA PRIOR TO SULFATION: APRIL 1953 TO JUNE 1954
(Van der Schalie, 1958)

SEQUENCE OF CLEARANCES	NUMBER OF CHANNELS CLEARED	LENGTH OF CHANNELS (KM)		LABOR REQUIRED (MAN-DAYS)	TIME SPENT (DAYS)
		TOTAL	CLEARED PORTIONS		
Before First Sulfation in 1953 (April-August)	8	29	12	302	16
Between First and Second Sulfations in 1953 (August-December)	82	53	39	1,400	47
Before Third Sulfation of area* (December 1953-June 1954)	50	25	23	688	36
Total	140	107	74	2,390	99

*This was the first sulfation in 1954.

examination were plotted on maps which not only showed an enormous amount of snail production, but also indicated that the two intermediate host snails, *Biomphalaria* and *Bulinus,* lived under different ecological conditions, shown by their patterns of distribution. It was surprising also to note that foci of infected snails in this tract were not nearly as numerous as one might expect. In keeping with the low incidence of infection within the host snails, the infested localities were relatively few and widely scattered. There was no evidence that infested areas were necessarily in the neighborhood of inhabited places.

When the distribution of the intermediate host snails was established and the infested areas had been determined, the tract was treated with copper sulphate. It had been established previously that vegetation in canals and drains tended to remove the copper ions by adsorption. Consequently, programs of removal of vegetation were undertaken prior to sulphation. This process is arduous and expensive, as is shown in Table 9–7, which indicates that the labor required was close to 2,400 man-days (see also Barlow, 1937). The amount of copper

sulphate necessary for even so small a tract is shown to be 71 tons (Table 9–8). Calculations made on the relative costs of just the chemical used indicate that more than thirteen thousand dollars were spent to complete one sulphation in an area with 450 kilometers of canals and drains. If one projects this cost to the area (roughly five million acres) to be treated in Egypt as a whole, the costs for the chemical alone would be prohibitive. As conditions developed, it was not possible to maintain programs of sulphation in the tract in subsequent years. The following year there were about half the number of snails but as many foci of infestation; by the third year the tract reverted to its original state of high infestation with infective snails. The population pressures of snails in surrounding regions are so great that reinfestation takes place very rapidly when eradication methods are discontinued.

However, there are conditions and methods for control that have been recommended by previous investigators in the WHO itself but which were not considered in subsequent programs. For example, infections occur in both *Bulinus truncatus* (carrying *S.*

Table 9-8

AMOUNT OF CHEMICAL AND LABOR REQUIRED FOR SULFATION OF MAIN AND BRANCH CANALS AND DRAINS IN PROJECT AREA: JULY 1953 TO JUNE 1954*
(Van der Schalie, 1958)

TYPE OF CHANNEL	NUMBER OF CHANNELS TREATED	LENGTH OF CHANNELS (KM)		AMOUNT OF CUSO$_4$ USED (TONS)†	LABOR REQUIRED (MAN-DAYS)	TIME SPENT (DAYS)
		TOTAL	TREATED PORTIONS			
Main Canals	21	106	72	15.1	414	18
Branch Canals	754	355	349	13.3	636	34
Main Drains	12	75	54	6.1	238	10
Branch Drains	318	153	149	5.0	181	9
Total	1,105	689	624	39.5	1,469	71

*The figures are cumulative and represent the total amount of work done since the inception of the project.
†Excluding 6.3 tons used in treatment of infested channels upstream of project area.

haematobium) and in *Biomphalaria alexan-drina* (carrying *S. mansoni*) usually after the middle of May, so that a single molluscicing, taking into account not only the life cycle of the snails but also their time of infection, would seem most efficacious.

Another observation that would warrant more attention than it has received, is the possibility that snails could be eliminated from the canals during the latter's winter closure and cleaning. This could possibly be accomplished by bringing the canals back to a proper gradient by removing accumulations of silt and mud (WHO, 1965, p. 94). It is specifically indicated that snails thrive in canals where silt accumulates. Silt removal improves the flow of water in the channels and curbs snail populations.

During the Egypt 10 program it was observed that the snails do *not* burrow when the canal dries. The *Bulinus* remain exposed with epiphragms (a mucous membrane across aperture of shell) in place on the surface mud; the *Biomphalaria* secrete epiphragms and remain in the surface litter awaiting the return of water to their habitat. If a small mechanical scraper could be devised and used along with a conveyor belt, the mud (or bottom material) could then be dug in such a way as to take the soil and the snails away from the site they occupy during hibernation. With the small amount of rain (in some places less than 25 millimeters a year) the snails removed would be deposited away from the canal. While this process may not completely eliminate the snails from the canals, it would certainly greatly reduce the populations. A study using this technique has long been needed since it is another area in which argricultural practices and health programs could well be meshed. Space will not permit a review of a very informative paper by C. H. Barlow (1937), but essentially he has shown that "the use of canal clearance is proposed as a prime factor in a scheme for the control of human schistosomiasis in Egypt because it is efficient, inexpensive, and requires no teaching of new methods for its execution."

One of the most interesting recent developments suggesting a probable increase in schistosomiasis is the building of the new High Dam at Aswan. The nature of this problem was previously discussed (van der Schalie, 1960) and an effort was made two years ago to obtain some support for a study to obtain field data. Such data are necessary to test the prediction that the new dam might well prove to be a liability rather than an asset. It is quite certain that the incidence of urinary schistosomiasis (*S. haematobium*) would greatly increase and the intestinal form (*S. mansoni*, now *not* widespread) would eventually invade the five-hundred-odd miles of river flood plain converted to perennial irrigation. Assistance was requested from three agencies: (1) the Ford Foundation, which was involved in improvement of fishing to provide protein in that region; (2) the Rockefeller Foundation, which had a long history of work designed to improve health there; and (3) the PL 480 source for funding since it appears that those funds may eventually be used for ventures other than archaeology. Progress in getting support was discouraging and slow. Most agencies were interested and saw the need for the study but there was a reluctance that discouraged work in what already appeared to be a difficult program. All projected programs became prohibitive because of the outbreak of war in that area.

The high incidence of schistosomiasis is closely related to the distribution of the intermediate snail hosts. It has already been shown from the distribution patterns in the Qaliub tract that there is a definite break in the range of the *Biomphalaria* snails (carrying *S. mansoni*) and the *Bulinus* (hosts for *S. haematobium*), in such a way that the former are found only in the northern sector of this tract while the latter are distributed throughout the tract. From what

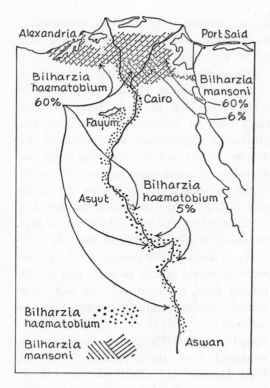

Figure 9–3 Incidence and distribution of both species of Bilharziasis in Egypt. Showing correlation of high incidence (60%) of both Schistosomes (*S. mansoni* and *S. haematobium*) in the Delta with perennial) (4-Crop) irrigation; from Cairo to Aswan, where irrigation is the Basin (1-Crop) type, incidence is low (5%) and limited to only one species (*S. haematobium*), which is the less dangerous of the two. (After J. Allen Scott, 1937)

is known of the ecology of *Biomphalaria* it is apt to become established in areas where the irrigation system is of the *perennial* type. A 1937 map (Fig. 9–3) prepared by J. Allen Scott reveals that the high incidence of both *S. mansoni* and *S. haematobium* is correlated with the type of irrigation practiced in the area. In this case the two prevalent schistosomes are shown to have an incidence of at least 60% in the Delta with its perennial irrigation. The rest of the Nile upstream for approximately five hundred miles has mostly the basin (or one-crop) system of irrigation. In that region only *S.*

haematobium is common, at a rather low incidence of about 5%.

The purpose of the new High Dam at Aswan, in addition to power that it will supply, is to provide the water necessary to establish the perennial (or four-crop rotation system) throughout the five hundred miles of flood plain along the Nile from Cairo to Aswan. Actually little additional land will be provided, but on the basis of increased land potential it will add the equivalent of another two million acres to the approximately six million now available for agriculture. On the basis of what is known about the snail hosts, their ecology, and the relation of perennial irrigation to human blood fluke in Egypt, the prospects are good that this new agricultural development will produce a tremendous increase in schistosomiasis.

FASCIOLIASIS

In the realm of snail control, a key problem in the Sudan (and elsewhere in Africa) is the propagation of Lymnaeid snails that carry fascioliasis of cattle and sheep. The Gezira agricultural project (see Fig. 9–4) occupies about a million acres below the Sennar Dam along the west shore of the Blue Nile. It has been a very successful *economic* venture. But it also has some of the characteristic problems that are found in most such schemes in Africa. Reference should be made to the studies of Greany (1952) reporting essentially the same basic pattern of incidence of schistosomiasis as was shown for the Delta region by the Egypt 10 team. In Greany's study (Table 9–9) he reported only 0.06% of about 5,000 *Bulinus* snails carrying *S. haematobium;* among the 6,600 *Planorbis* (now called *Biomphalaria*) only 1.2% were positive. It should be emphasized that eradication would benefit both fascioliasis as well as schistosomiasis control.

In addition to the increase in the trend of schistosomiasis, the problem of controlling

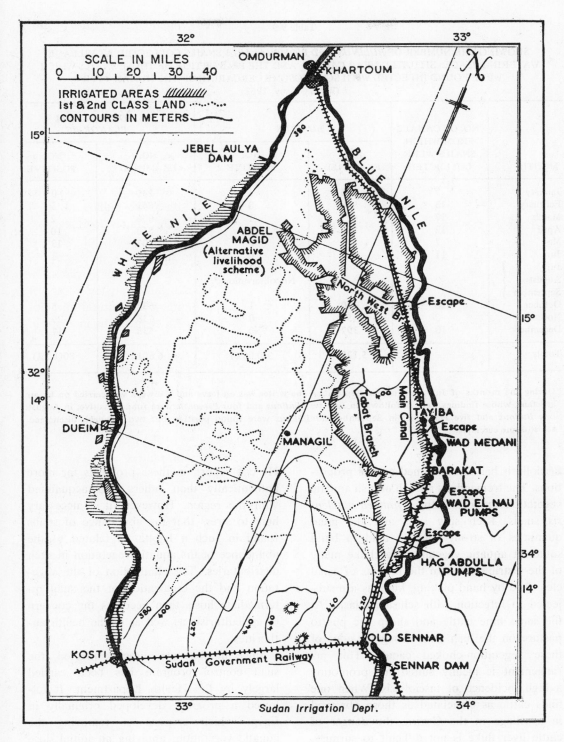

Figure 9–4 The Gezira agriculture tract, below Sennar Dam, in the Sudan

Table 9-9

SHOWING THE NUMBER OF *BULINUS* AND *BIOMPHALARIA* SNAILS COLLECTED AT VILLAGE
WATERING PLACES SITUATED NEAR CANALS, AND THE PROPORTION OF THOSE SNAILS WHICH
WERE FOUND INFECTED WITH SCHISTOSOME CERCARIAE OF THE HUMAN TYPE
(W. H. Greany, 1952)

MONTH	NO. OF CANALS FROM WHICH SNAILS WERE COLLECTED	*BULINUS*		*BIOMPHALARIA PLANORBIS*	
		NO. EXAMINED	NO. POSITIVE	NO. EXAMINED	NO. POSITIVE
January	9	336	1	246	0
February	13	936	0	841	3
March	17	697	1	606	2
April	12	886	0	850	10
May	7	535	0	1,007	13
June	11	397	0	1,238	1
July					
August		No observations*			
September					
October	10	480	1	637	5
November	6	457	0	638	29
December	10	397	0	538	17
Totals		5,121	3(0.06%)	6,601	80(1.2%)

*During the months of July, August and September, the writer was on leave and the work was carried on by an
assistant, whose findings were as follows: in July two *Bulinus* and four *Planorbis* were found positive; in August
one *Bulinus* and five *Planorbis*; in September no *Bulinus* were found positive, but two *Planorbis* discharged
schistosome cercariae.

fascioliasis has also assumed crucial proportions. The tremendous growth of lush aquatic
vegetation supports many *Lymnaea natalen-
sis* snails. Rich silty soils and the great
quantities of strong sunlight tend to build
sufficient aquatic vegetation to choke many
of the distributaries. In the process of canal
clearance by hand picking, humans are subjected to infection with schistosomiasis. At
the same time cattle and sheep are put to
pasture on the lush grass along the edge of
these vegetation-choked canals. This arrangement is ideally suited for promoting
a high incidence of fascioliasis. When one
finds cattle as emaciated as those observed
in a village in the Gezira, the danger of
cattle liver fluke is not difficult to surmise.
While serving as a professor in the University of Khartoum at Shambat, Dr. Emile
A. Malek studied fascioliasis in the Sudan.

He can report on these problems far more
authentically than others less acquainted
with the region. However, it is necessary
here to stress that the abundance of snails
found in such a habitat is related to the
abundance of the aquatic vegetation in such
distributaries. The elimination of the vegetation and the eradication of the snail intermediate hosts then becomes the concern
of agriculturists as well as of the health authorities.

Since humans are directly affected, the
snail control program has been carried
largely by the Health Department. It followed a program developed originally in
Egypt which consists of removing the
aquatic vegetation, applying an initial dose
of 30 ppm of copper sulphate to kill most
of the snails. To keep the canals free of
reinvasion by snails a small residual (0.125

ppm) of copper ions is maintained in the canals by placing bags with copper sulphate suspended in the water.

SUMMARY

To summarize, schistosomiasis, or bilharziasis, poses a very serious problem both in Egypt and the Sudan. While both regions share many ecological relationships, the areas are also strikingly different in the position they hold with respect to the developmental stage of the disease and its implications. A number of studies and programs have been initiated and some good basic information is available. Few diseases demand more collaboration in more fields and at every level. International programs fail to include the areas where their programs mesh with blood fluke control. Within the country involved the scourge of this disease enters practically every field of human endeavor. Programs within an agency such as the WHO concentrate on the immediate aspects (usually medical, sanitary, education and snail control) but many important other fields must of necessity be involved. Only when the control of schistosomiasis can receive total commitment will there be any hope for alleviating suffering and improving economy.

In the Egypt 10 project interest was focused on educating the people, improving sanitary conditions, providing some drug therapy (in this case Fouadin), and attempting snail control with copper sulphate. But these measures became ineffective as a result of their incompatibility with long-established cultural patterns. Religious practices such as ablution, the lack of available facilities due to extreme poverty within rural communities, the impossibility of enforcing helpful legislation, and the unconcern of government agents whose lot is not in the filthy villages but largely in the metropolitan areas of Cairo and Alexandria have virtually made a failure of such control projects.

In conclusion, it is clear that the *perennial* system of irrigation is most explosive in producing a high incidence of blood flukes—as is well exemplified in the Sudan. Problems become difficult because in the conditions of rural Egypt, all facets of living have their own special relation to the control problem. Although the need for integration and planning is overwhelming, the prospects for obtaining relief are dim. In the meantime the emerging countries in Africa face frightening increases in the incidence of blood fluke.

REFERENCES

Abdel Azim, M. "Problems in the Control of Schistosomiasis (Bilharziasis) in Egypt." *Proc. 4th Internat. Congr. Trop. Med. and Malaria,* Washington, D.C., May 10–18, 1948, pp. 1013–21.

Abdel Malek, Emile. "Distribution of the Intermediate Hosts of Bilharziasis in Relation to Hydrography with Special Reference to the Nile Basin and the Sudan." *Bull. WHO,* 18 (1958a), 691–734.

———. "Factors Conditioning the Habitat of Bilharziasis Intermediate Hosts of the Family Planorbidae." *Bull. WHO,* 18 (1958b), 785–818.

Barlow, C. H. "The Value of Canal Clearance in the control of Schistosomiasis in Egypt." *Amer. J. Hyg.,* 25 (1937), 327–48.

———. "Seasonal Incidence of Infestation of the Snail Hosts with Larval Human Schistosomes." *Amer. J. Hyg.,* 30 (1939), 73–81.

Barlow, C. H., and Meleney, H. E. "A Voluntary Infection with *Schistosoma haematobium*." *Amer. J. Trop. Med.*, 29 (1949), 79–87.

Chandler, A. C. "A Comparison of Helminthic and Protozoan Infections in Two Egyptian Villages Two Years after the Installation of Sanitary Improvements in One of Them." *Amer. J. Trop. Med. and Hyg.*, 3 (1954), 59–73.

Dazo, B. C.; Hairston, N. G.; and Dawood, I. K. "The Ecology of *Bulinus truncatus* and *Biomphalaria alexandrina* and Its Implications for the Control of Bilharziasis in the Egypt-49 Project Area." *Bull WHO*, 35 (1966), 339–56.

Farooq, M.; Hairston, N. G.; and Samaan, S. A. "Preliminary Report on the Effect of Area-Wide Snail Control on the Incidence of Bilharziasis in Egypt." *Pflanzenschutz-Nachrichten*, 19 (1966), 41–48.

Gelfand, Michael. *A Clinical Study of Intestinal Bilharziasis*, (Schistosoma mansoni) *in Africa*. London: Edward Arnold, Ltd., 1967, 230 pp.

Greany, W. H. "Schistosomiasis in the Gezira Irrigated Area of the Anglo-Egyptian Sudan. I. Public Health and Field Aspects. II. Clinical Study of *Schistomiasis mansoni*." *Ann. Trop. Med. and Parasit.*, 46 (1952), 250–67, 298–310.

Greenbaum, Leonard. "Phoenix: Bilharziasis/ Schistosomiasis." *Magazine Phoenix*, I (1961), 1–16.

McMullen, D. B., and Harry, H. W. "Comments on the Epidemiology and Control of Bilharziasis." *Bull. WHO*, 18 (1958), 1037–47.

Scott, J. Allen. "The Incidence and Distribution of Human Schistosomes in Egypt." *Amer. J. Hyg.*, 25 (1937), 566–614.

Stirewalt, M. A. "Effect of Snail Maintenance Temperatures on Development of *Schistosoma mansoni*." *J. Parasit.*, 40 (1954), 35.

van der Schalie, Henry. "Vector Snail Control in Qualiub, Egypt." *Bull. WHO*, 19 (1958), 263–83.

———. "Egypt's New High Dam—Asset or Liability." *The Biologist*, 42 (1960), 63–70.

———. "People and Their Snail-Borne Diseases." *Mich. Quart. Review*, 2 (1963), 106–14.

Weir, John. "An Evaluation of Health and Sanitation in Egyptian Villages." *J. Egyptian Pub. Health Assn.*, 27 (1952), 55–114.

———. *WHO Chronicle*, 13 (1959), 19.

World Health Organization. "Molluscicides." *WHO Techn. Report Ser.* No. 214 (1961), pp. 1–50.

———. "Snail Control in the Prevention of Bilharziasis." *WHO Monog. Ser.* 50 (1965), 1–255.

Wright, W. H. "Medical Parasitology in a Changing World. What of the Future?" *J. Parasit.*, 37 (1951), 1–12.

Wright, W. H.; Dobrovolny, C. G.; and Berry, E. G. "Field Trials of Certain Molluscicides (chiefly Sodium Pentachlorophenate)." *Bull. WHO*, 18 (1958), 263–83.

DISCUSSION

CALDWELL: Efforts have been made to improve the yields of rice in Southeast Asia and elsewhere by genetic methods. Is there any evidence that the improved strains are in any way less adequate from a nutritional point of view, or has the nutritional quality of the rice improved? Is there any effect that has been observed other than merely the larger yields of rice? In other words, have there been any nutritional side effects from the change in the nature of the rice?

BUNCE: I think the rice you are referring to is the strain that was developed by the group in the Philippines. It is much more resistant to the effects of climate. This rice is a stockier, sturdier plant, so it is more resistant to storm effects, and the yields are improved because there is less destruction.

However, in areas where vitamin A deficiency is chronic, one ought to be aware of the potential problems in making more rice protein available. Are you then satisfying the other nutritional needs that might result from this?

COMMONER: We know in the development of these new grains a very careful ecological agricultural analysis was used as backup in order to provide a highly productive, economically efficient crop. But was the overall nutritional usefulness of the grain a parameter in the research used to develop the new material? Do we know or are we guessing what the nutritional consequences of eating the new rice will be? Is there anyone who knows whether there were nutritional studies with these grains?

SMITH: I don't have an answer, but I can make the question even more complicated by mentioning that there is some evidence that there is limited cultural acceptance of the rice by the people who are supposed to eat it.

COMMONER: The lactose story tells us that acceptability may be a very important sign of a nutritional disharmony. And so this is again the question.

PHILLIPS: It is interesting to read the contributions on the interplay of schistosomiasis and irrigation. I believe many authorities have been rather slow in foreseeing this problem.

In Natal and Zululand, where I have worked for the last five years on potential development of land, medical authorities have found among European, Asian, and Zulu children some increase in the incidence of *S. haematobium,* associated with an extension of irrigation. This is in keeping with experiences in North, East, West, and Central Africa.

We should ask ourselves, of course, the question: Is it worthwhile extending irrigation if we are unable to control the related increase in schistosomiasis?

MARSHALL: In the Ryukyu Islands, malaria control was undertaken initially in 1946 because 100,000 people out of a population of 600,000 had malaria.

But beyond this, one of the hopes of malaria control was that it would open certain island groups to the south of the main island of Okinawa to the raising of cattle. At that time these islands were economically useless because of malaria. In the process of eradicating this disease, which took some fifteen years, these islands were, indeed, freed from malaria. However, while these fifteen years were passing, people were beginning to move to the cities. Now the islands have lands that could support a cattle industry, but people are no longer living there. Is it worthwhile to undertake these things when you aren't really able to foresee what the consequences will be?

WORTHINGTON: I would like to pursue that point, and to hear some discussion specifically on schistosomiasis.

When I was first researching on the East African lakes in the late 1920's and early thirties, there was no obvious schistosomiasis. My colleagues and I were in and out of every kind of water, and no doctor that I met so much as mentioned the problem; there were no cases in the hospitals.

Now, anywhere around those lakes near a village you can be fairly certain that you will catch a dose of schistosomiasis even if you paddle, let alone work in the water. The cause is certainly not irrigation; I think it is primarily the development of the fishery industry which means that more people are in and out of the water, coupled with the movement of African peoples all over the continent which didn't start seriously until the thirties.

Whether or not schistosomiasis has always been there, it has become Africa's number one disease only during the last twenty or thirty years.

These papers on the subject, in which I have been extremely interested, suggest one definite fact: that the known cures are quite inadequate and that the known molluscicides are equally inadequate. I have seen molluscicides, particularly copper sulfate, used on a huge scale in many places: a great wastage of chemicals and a terrible destruction of aquatic life, not only snails.

It seems to me that in the course of the next ten or twenty years, we are going to have a whole succession of new molluscicides shoved out into the environment. We badly need some reliable standardized methods of trying them out. We need an experimental area in some convenient part of the tropics where the variables of aquatic biology can be reduced to a minimum and you can really test the effects of old and new chemicals, not only their effectiveness as molluscicides, but also their ancillary effects on aquatic flora and fauna, including man himself.

WHITE: Dr. Worthington has pointed out that the spread of schistosomiasis is a consequence partly of technological development, but also of the shifts in population movements which have accompanied technological development. Thus in the Gezira scheme, the fact of large migrations of population into and out of the scheme going east and west from West Africa and on to Arabia means that what happens in a small irrigated area has tremendous influence beyond. Similarly the movement of workers in and out of city areas from rural areas has changed the effect of small developments in scattered parts of the African continent. Likewise, the capacity of fishermen to navigate on Lake Victoria, as Bradley has shown, has had great influence on the spread of schistosomiasis around the borders of the lake into areas that hadn't been touched by it before.

As one begins to try to assess what the full effect of these technological and economic changes may be, both on human ecology and on human behavior, one is struck by the fact that for no area do we have an adequate assessment of the total environmental impact of any one of these interventions.

Dr. van der Schalie has talked about effects in a control area in Egypt and in the Gezira scheme in the Sudan, but he hasn't been able to give us, as I understand it, a genuine assessment of the full consequences, in terms not only of schistosomiasis, but of all aspects of health and productivity.

If one goes into East Africa today, one will find that there is conscious planning of new irrigation, as in the Arushashini scheme, including systematic efforts to curb schistosomiasis. The assumption is that, although there will be a modest spread of the disease, the other effects on the population in improved health services, improved productivity, nutrition and so on, will offset the adverse consequences. For example, one sees in the Mweya project in Kenya a conscious development of new rice on irrigated lands accompanied by applications of the molluscicide, Frescon, with a horseback judgment that the costs on one side will be more than offset by the benefits on the other.

You could raise the same question of total costs versus benefits about nutrition in Recife or pollution in the Ryukyu Islands. I wonder whether anybody has any evidence of a systematic effort to canvass the total consequences of any one of these major interventions before it is undertaken. I don't know of any really systematic venture in this direction. The studies of African reservoirs are on the right track. Until such efforts are standard and until effective methods of carrying them out are common it will do little good to lament the unforeseen consequences.

VAN DER SCHALIE: A couple of years ago I went to Liberia. As many of you know, Liberia is going to rice culture. Dr. Belai, a very seasoned and experienced Indian worker, was there and took me around.

So I said to Dr. Belai, "What do you know about schistosomiasis?"

And he said, "Nothing."

I asked: "Don't tell me you were sent here on a mission without being briefed?"

It also happens that one of my students, Dr. Harry Walter, went to the same area for two years to collect snails. Harry came back infected with both schistosomes!

I said, "Harry, how could this happen? You know better than that."

He said, "Well, Van, to get snails in that area, I worked very hard for four hours. I wear waders. I sweat so profusely that I don't know whether I am in contact with water half the time or not."

Let's come back to dear old Michigan for a few minutes—you won't believe this, but for three years I have tried in both NIH [National Institute of Health] and NSF [National Science Foundation] and several other agencies to get a few dollars to study animal schistosomes, what we call "swimmer's itch."

For two years running, we have had swimmer's itch recorded from at least one hundred lakes in Michigan. And I know the problem is greater than this because most people don't know swimmer's itch when they see it. This holds for physicians too, by the way.

So I have been trying to get some money to see if we could study schistosomiasis in our country's own back yard. If you can study it in Michigan, you may obtain the fundamental concepts that often can be applied in Africa. If you first go to Africa or other less-developed areas, you are up against the problem of research facilities and well-prepared students.

Now, why can't I get money in a place like Michigan to study swimmer's itch? The answer is very simple. We have a thing called tourism. On our license plates, you will see that Michigan is the great water wonderland. Don't you mention swimmer's itch. It is a naughty word.

As a consequence, I can't even get a decent article in a journal to feature what swimmer's itch is all about. "In Michigan, you see, we don't have it. They have *that* in Wisconsin and Minnesota!"

Can you explain to me why in Michigan, with a multimillion-dollar industry that goes hand in hand with automobiles and tourism, we can't get a few measly dollars to do some basic studies? And foreign countries don't even begin to have the economy we have. It is rather disturbing to me. Another major problem is that not only are we losing the opportunity for new knowledge, but also we are failing to train students to solve these difficult problems.

Why do we fail to train students? Our University of Michigan over the years has had an outstanding international reputation in natural history. It might interest you to know I can't get a parasitologist in my department. But why can't I get a parasitologist? The reason I can't get a parasitologist is that he must be biochemically oriented. And we don't train people this way easily. I don't know of anyplace where they do.

I would love to have somebody who is a basic field ecologist who knows a great deal about systematics (you have to if you are going to work with insects or mollusks) and who also can go to the lab and do all the biochemistry, but I can't find such a person. We have to come to grips with these training problems because, as I see it, matters aren't getting better; they are getting worse. The sort of diseases that our friends in Africa are fighting are becoming extremely serious.

DAVIS: I would like to comment on the effect of molluscicides on mollusks and fish and flora, and say that I am particularly concerned about their effect on humans. I must admit I was rather appalled by the use of copper sulfate in canals. There is a well-known hereditary disease called Wilson's disease, related to the overabsorption of copper. It can affect the liver and also the central nervous system. Are the effects of copper on man for snail control being noted?

VAN DER SCHALIE: The copper is very soon absorbed in both mud and vegetation, and it has also proved to be a good herbicide in the canals. How much of that gets back into man and how damaging it is, I don't know. I do know of areas that are being molluscicided with copper today. It goes on day after day, hour after hour. They now have about seven thousand parts per million of bound copper. I hate to think what could happen if we ever put in a chemical which would have a synergism with the copper sulfate.

CARLOZZI: I would like to go back to something Gilbert White said a moment ago. He asked if anything was being done in which a comprehensive environmental analysis of all possible impacts was taken before changes were made. It seems to me that very little gets done that way, even when you put together teams of people who represent various disciplines. I think we suffer from the whole historical mentality of science, if I can put it that way. Science to me has been in large measure learning how to hold a whole lot of other things as constants while I proceeded to involve myself in some highly speculative variable, and how well I did was related to how neatly I could do this. As you pursue the course of science through history one finds that we have evolved much neater devices for holding more and more things constant.

Now what we are asking for is a reversal of scientific procedure. We seek a way to open up proposed action to all of the variables involved and then proceed from this point of view to better delineate what kind of action people ought to take.

There is a great resistance to this approach. It is counterposed to everything that the scientific mentality has been working toward for hundreds of years. I can just imagine this group as a team going out to some place prior to the day when any action was to take place. In the attempt to bring together our singular or several points of view, we might better discover the necessary process for making some overall determination of what should be done. I don't know how long it would take us to achieve that synthesis, but I can tell you it would be something to see.

COMMONER: I agree completely with the generalizations that have been made about the importance of the reductionist bias in our science. The force necessary to correct this bias can come from the accumulation of the ecological consequences which we are investigating here. As people see the consequences of reductionism—the bias in our science which converts, for example, parasitologists into biochemists (an exchange which means that one gets schistosomiasis) —as they see the importance of this problem, we will begin to see a shift. It seems to me we ought to try to hold our discussion to the accumulation of this evidence until it hurts. The very weight of this information then may begin to do what you would like to see done, what we all feel must be done.

FRASER DARLING: I would like to question Dr. LaVerne Harold on a particular point. Is there circulation of antibiotics among people who really haven't a very good reason for using them? I am thinking particularly of chloramphenicol which I believe is one of the very few antibiotics which can be employed against typhoid fever and salmonellosis. Is that right?

HAROLD: That's right.

FRASER DARLING: Well, I believe that the so-called farmers of debeaked hens and broiler chickens are using this material. Considering the growing problem of transferable resistance, shouldn't we consider very carefully whether chloramphenicol or any other antibiotic should be used for this kind of thing? These broiler-chicken farmers are getting rid of their wastes in just whatever way they can. It seems to me there are great possibilities that these waste materials will contact the germs against which medical science would wish to use them and produce drug-resistant strains. Have you any views on this?

HAROLD: As you say, the use of antibiotics in agriculture and particularly in feeds is very widespread. In fact, you can hardly buy any feed in this country for animals that does not have an antibiotic in it.

You mentioned chloramphenicol. Fortunately, that is one of the antibiotics that is not added to livestock feed in this country. It is restricted to use by professional veterinarians and the medical profession. But the antibiotics—chlortetracycline, oxytetracycline, tetracyline, streptomycins, and the bacitracins—are widely used in the field and will cause resistance to develop.

FRASER DARLING: I believe that chloramphenicol is not legally debarred as yet from feeds in Britain. And if certain feed merchants wish, apparently they can use it.

MARSHALL: Chloramphenicol in humans carries a serious liability which in some cases can produce granulocytopenia, which is a cessation of the synthesis of certain kinds of white cells. For this reason it is less indiscriminately used than certain other antibiotics.

HAROLD: The main problem is that many drugs have been cleared primarily because of their effectiveness in treating disease and their safety to the animal. There has been little or no regard for the development of resistant organisms or to the potential harm that may develop from the transmission of these organisms with their drug-resistance to the human population.

BUNCE: I would like to comment on one of the examples in my paper that really was a corollary to the main theme. It discussed the interaction of nutrition and parasitology. This summer a team of parasitologists doing a survey in Cali, Colombia, were surprised to find a very high incidence of the parasite, *Entamoeba histolytica,* but a very low incidence of clinical cases of amebiasis due to this parasite. And they were really startled at this because amebiasis is a very critical disease that usually appears in a very high percentage of people who are infected with the parasite.

Subsequent research indicated it was very likely that the protective factor was the low protein intake of this population. These people were consuming a low protein diet, and the enzymes needed for digesting starch were present in low quantities; therefore, the starch was not being properly digested, and there was a high content of starch in the intestinal tract. The infecting organisms were making use of that starch as their food supply rather than invading the intestinal tract and causing the clinical condition of amebiasis.

I may be admitting to a deficiency of my own, but if I had been in the area, I probably would have said offhand that the parasitological condition is going to improve if you improve the nutrition. As you add more food, the people will be better able to fight off infections. However, here is an example where nutritional improvement would have had just the opposite effect. Very likely the clinical incidence of amebiasis would have greatly increased in this area had there been an increase in protein intake. It is where disciplines interact that you really begin to get into problems in predicting what is going to be beneficial or in predicting what might be harmful.

I think I would have been very naive in this also had I been in the area. I think I could have easily run afoul of a problem like this. I think other people feel the same way.

M. T. FARVAR: Do you think clinical amebiasis due to added protein may have actually occurred in some places, such as northeast Brazil, where protein supplementation was taken up?

BUNCE: The clinical proof for this would have to come from taking such a population, increasing their protein intake, and watching them in a controlled fashion. Of course, it is morally unacceptable to run this kind of test.

But certainly the authors who wrote a paper on this subject, the two being Faust and Read from Tulane, felt it was suffi-ciently possible that they wanted to point out the potential dangers.

SCHUPHAN: Dr. Bunce's paper poses a question of how we can provide an adequate source of vitamin A in the dried whole milk regime. In Germany, the pediatrician, Dr. Kubla Kiel, in collaboration with our Institute, found that carrots cooked and well smashed with whole milk gave a better supply of vitamin A than capsules. Carotene in carrots, even given in excess, remains in the blood as reserve vitamin A to be metabolized when needed. No hypervitaminosis occurred. In addition carrots have a distinct antibiotic effect on dysentery.

SCUDDER: I want to bring up two additional cases which now are only partially documented, but which could have very serious implications for health; both arise directly out of development projects.

The first and the most important case concerns massive population relocation. For various reasons, for example population imbalances, large numbers of people are being relocated throughout the tropics, and particularly in connection with development. One per cent of the total population of Africa, over two million people, have been relocated in the last ten years.

The few studies that have been made—and unfortunately there are very few baseline studies before relocation—indicate that, even where health benefits supposedly increase in terms of medical services, both morbidity and mortality rates go up in the years immediately after relocation. This points out, I think, the kind of complex variables that many scientists are not trained to deal with. We are not dealing just with isolated individual physiological and psychological stress in these cases, but we are dealing with the cultural stress of being moved. What is the impact of this movement on public health and mental health?

Also, most relocation projects result in increased population densities and seem to be followed by, for example, epidemics of dysentery and often increased parasite loads. We are dealing with very large numbers of people. Often these people are being moved from their familiar environment to a fairly dissimilar one which means such problems as nutritional deficiencies are appearing because the development is based on new, unfamiliar crops and insufficient overall diets.

There has been virtually no adequate base-line survey of this kind of problem, let alone good follow-ups in relocation projects to see what has happened. I think that we can expect increased morbidity and mortality in this particular kind of situation unless the problem is emphasized and the necessary research initiated.

The second case is a more specific one and gets back to our earlier discussion of schistosomiasis.

At Lake Kariba, there was no schistosomiasis ten years ago simply because Lake Kariba did not exist. We now have the world's largest artificial reservoir. Recently it has been reported that schistosomiasis has cropped up in this area. I see no reason why it will not spread around the entire lake. And bear in mind, this is a huge lake with wave action ten feet or higher. I find it very difficult to foresee how we can eliminate the disease-bearing snails after they have become established. I fully suspect that in Kariba and in other major man-made lakes in Africa you will find bilharzia over the entire lake area.

Again, there have been very inadequate base-line surveys, let alone a realization of and concern for the problem.

KASSAS: Could I, Mr. Chairman, go back to the story of Dr. van der Schalie?

My first point is that when we talk about the control of these disease problems, we at once talk about chemical control. I would like to question whether chemical control through herbicides, insecticides, mollusci-cides or any other such elements have actually succeeded in eradicating any pest. Did chemical control rid a continent like Australia of its rabbits or did they find some more biological means of controlling that pest?

I mention this because Dr. van der Schalie mentioned that there is seasonal variation in the development of foci in these snails. I think this should lead us to do more studies on the biology of the snails themselves, in order to find some more biologically sound means of controlling them.

The second point I would like to make concerns the impact of bilharziasis (schistosomiasis) on the human population. We can say that Egypt has a population that has lived with bilharziasis for thousands of years. Bilharzia eggs were discovered in ancient Egyptian mummies dated to the second or third dynasties. We might say at the minimum, then, that the Egyptians as a population have failed in several thousand years to eradicate and rid themselves of bilharziasis. But I can look at this fact another way and say that the Egyptian has managed to live with bilharziasis and bilharziasis has failed to eradicate Egyptians for thousands of years.

In Dr. van der Schalie's paper, we are told that bilharziasis kills one out of every five people who die in Egypt. I wonder whether it is more painful to die of bilharziasis or die of hunger. I believe it is more demoralizing to die of hunger than to die of bilharziasis.

I wouldn't like this conference to give the impression that we are advising all these developing countries to beware of developing their agriculture and irrigation by saying to them, "Wherever you develop irrigation, you will get bilharziasis." I would prefer to say that if people develop more agriculture and perennial irrigation, they will have more bilharziasis, but in the meantime, they may be able to raise their standard of living.

Indeed, raising their standard of living may be the only means of combating bilharziasis.

I know there have been epidemics all over the world, including the countries that are at present described as developed. These countries have rid themselves of their epidemics after their development, not before it.

M. T. FARVAR: Professor Kassas's points are interesting, but they do not point out both sides of the dilemma. Unfortunately for the peasants in the countryside they are the victims of schistosomiasis. These are also the people who produce the "food" which urban people consume. Thus, assuming that irrigation and technological development are indeed used to produce more food, we have the urban dwellers who make the decision to exchange food (for themselves) with disease (for the peasants). Naturally, from the point of view of the urbanite it is more demoralizing for him to die of hunger than for the peasant to die of schistosomiasis. The actual situation is even worse because the irrigation and the technology are not even used to produce food as they are to produce cash crops like cotton, and electricity (again for the enjoyment of the city people). How much should the peasants have to suffer in order to fulfill the whims of those who are ruling them from the cities? Who asks the peasants what price *they* are willing to pay? And when the cost is finally pointed out, the answer is invariably: "The solution is being field-tested just around the corner!"

MILTON: I would add a cautionary note to this discussion of Aswan. To wait for indirect economic factors to have an impact on slowing population growth would mean to risk depending on the ancient controls of war, disease, starvation and malnutrition. Each one of our "assistance agencies," whether bilateral or multilateral, must begin to build direct population control assistance into every program—or in relation to every program. Unless the problem of population growth is attacked directly and solved wherever our development efforts flow, our other solutions, be they economic, social or ecological, must ultimately fail.

Starvation and disease (such as bilharziasis in Egypt) have long been a control on population growth. But it is also true that both starvation and bilharziasis cause demoralizing deaths. I don't feel mankind should condone either form of natural population control by such deaths; rather, in such areas the emphasis must and should be on birth control. In addition, we should also attempt to prevent starvation by developing systems of increased agricultural production that are free of causing the spread of parasitic diseases and other negative effects on the human ecology.

MENDELSSOHN: Of what use are molluscicides for controlling a snail like *Bulinus,* which is able to survive out of the water for several days and in the soil even for months? I would like to cite a case I witnessed.

Near Tel Aviv is a small river which transmitted schistosomiasis for many years. From the point of view of public health, it was hardly a problem because less than five cases a year occurred; people knew that it was forbidden to bathe in this river due to the danger of infection.

Notwithstanding these facts, a large campaign was undertaken to eradicate *Bulinus* which is a vector of *Schistosoma haematobium* in this river. Several applications of molluscicide were made. All aquatic life was effectively eradicated except *Bulinus,* because at least part of the population left the water to sit on the stems of reeds or dug into the soil along the banks only to return later after the molluscicide diminished. A year after this campaign the river contained almost nothing other than *Bulinus.*

I should perhaps add that eventually *Bulinus* was also effectively controlled by heavy pollution of the river; I wouldn't recommend this, however, as an ideal cure.

GEORGE: The Sterling-Winthrop Laboratories in Troy, New York, are now field-testing a new drug which is directed toward the control of the adult parasite of *Schistosoma mansoni* and *Schistosoma haematobium*. Their tests as thus far conducted in South Africa, Brazil and the Nile Delta, suggest this drug is 95 per cent effective on a one-dose basis, with what they have thus far suggested are rather minor side effects—the side effects being nausea in a certain percentage of those treated from four to six hours after application.

If the field-testing of this drug is successful, they feel that bilharzia could be controlled almost completely within a two- to three-year period.

Now, if that were to come to pass, and it is utopian I grant, what effect would this have on a population whose size is now partially controlled in the Nile Delta and other areas? What are the sociological implications?

We have continually seen that application of remarkably therapeutic drugs has had serious consequences. I think we now must go one step further and consider in advance what these consequences will be.

MARSHALL: If I may just add a point of my own here—generally speaking the most difficult thing one can undertake in public health is getting the pill, regardless of its effectiveness, from the hand of the person into his gut. No matter how good the drug is, it may not be effective due to lack of compliance.

However, even if we assume a compliance of 100 per cent, there are remaining questions which are very relevant ones. Take, for example, the Ryukyu Islands. This is a small place with a population of about one million people. It has had available to it all kinds of money and technically-trained manpower from the United States and from Japan. They also have some very good public health people of their own. And as a result, the great communicable diseases have declined in importance. Malaria has been eradicated; filariasis is on the run; dysentery doesn't occur much any more. They don't even have a population explosion. But what they do have, as of 1965, is a mortality pattern which is exactly the same as that of the United States—heart disease, cancer, stroke and accidents being leading causes of death. And yet they enter this chronic disease era with a health care system which is set up specifically to cope only with communicable diseases and which is totally inadequate for long-term patient care.

One can't help wondering whether they are really a lot better off, particularly when one reflects on the experience of the United States in dealing with the same problem. I don't think that we have responded to the diseases of industrial society very well either. Our chronic diseases may represent in economic terms an even greater drain than some of the communicable diseases which we have worked so hard to overcome.

CONWAY: I would like to remark on some of the comments made by Dr. Kassas and do this by reference to the International Rice Research Institute's new rice.

I was recently in Asia, looking at the new cereals and the problems that arise from them. The people who developed these new crops said, "We had to develop a new rice. To get a new rice, we had to concentrate on a few small aspects which could result in gains. We had to concentrate on a short stalk that will allow you to take up nitrogen without lodging. We had to get lack of sensitivity to photoperiod. We had to get a plant that would effectively use irrigation water." This is what they had to work toward, and they achieved it. In five years, they produced a rice which now will yield ten thousand pounds to the acre, and grow in multiple cropping. This, in a limited sense, is probably one of the greatest scientific achievements since the last war. Their view is now: "We have accomplished this, now we will look at the other related problems, such as pests and diseases, which continue to cause massive losses. We will look at nutritional problems, at cultural acceptability, and at how we can best integrate these new crops into various natural and social systems.

Dr. Carlozzi suggested, I don't know whether flippantly or seriously, that perhaps this whole group should go out to a developing country and begin work on a problem in an integrated fashion. I wonder whether or not we still would be looking for a new rice if this whole group had gone out to the Philippines at that time.

Is Dr. Kassas correct in saying that development comes first and then you attempt to solve the problems that follow from it? We certainly have massive problems in the United States. Dr. Marshall has shown clearly how Okinawans now have substituted industrialization-related medical problems for their earlier more primitive medical problems.

But how does this balance out? Are more or fewer people dying from these new diseases than were dying from the older ones? If ecologists are going to have an impact on development programs, they must be able to show not only that they can analyze all the factors relevant to development, but also that they can suggest positive courses of action.

When I was working in what was then the colony of North Borneo, it was deliberate government policy that all investment of time, money, and skills should go into agriculture and public works, while forestry and health should be neglected for a period. This was a deliberate policy. Were they right?

I would like to hear Dr. Myrdal's views on this question. As I understand it, many economists today believe that development can only come about through a limited number of specific thrusts for change. There is a big argument about this. However, some economists say that you can't advance simultaneously in a number of interrelated problem areas; however, in a sense this is what ecologists *are* saying needs doing. Have we ever tried it?

MYRDAL: My friends, I am a displaced person who knows very little about the problems you are discussing. I thought I was a broad-minded economist like my friend Mr. Boulding, but this conference is already giving me a new education in the historical narrowness of development economics. In my opinion we have a basic moral imperative to cure a man from illness and to try to prevent death. To me the problem which has been raised here is not a problem. When we change one factor in a society, we must take on the responsibility for all the other changes which result and try to deal with them intelligently. When we introduced death control technology and then got the population explosion, we should have simultaneously begun to work on birth control. I do not believe that any assembly of people would ever reject control of disease, and I feel it is our moral imperative not only to cure disease, but also to prevent the starvation, malnutrition and diseases that come from overpopulation.

BOULDING: I think the dilemma of what in economics we call balanced versus unbalanced growth is at the heart of a lot of these problems. The real problem is what you might call the total dynamics of society.

There is a whole school of economists which argues that the way you get growth is to upset things and that the great problem of subsistence societies is their stability. As Dr. Myrdal knows all too well after having studied Asia, the great problem of Asia is the homeostasis of the village, the fact that you go in and try to change it and then you go away and "blup," it all slumps down to where it was before—largely due to this extraordinary social homeostasis. Development is profoundly a process of disequilibrium.

This is one reason why I think you have to be a little careful of ecologists; they are still very equilibrium-minded. If there is any change that is very good in the world, it causes disequilibrium. I think ecology will make its greatest contribution as it moves toward dynamics, as economics has to do, too.

MYRDAL: It is absolutely true that all development implies disequilibrium. However, our ideal must be to have it in dynamic balance.

In other words, we need to have as much equilibrium as we can have. Development planning really should involve analyzing and acting on a great number of things at the same time in a coordinated way to get maximum positive results.

BOULDING: I am more modest about this. All I really want is to avoid irretrievable disasters. This is the most modest level of achievement. We all agree that irretrievable disasters are very bad. If you have retrievable disasters, however, there may be a learning process. Mistakes may be part of the total process of development. Nevertheless, handling such problems is very tricky.

I think we have to be careful of the man who says we have to know everything before we can do anything. This leads to a Hamlet kind of being.

On the other hand, I must say all these ecological horror stories that we have before us are extremely valuable, and have important lessons that I hope we will plug into the international development process. I would suggest an appropriate title for the conference volume might be: *Developmental Horror Stories or, Is Man a Fugitive Species?*

However, the real trouble is that no science really knows very much about dynamics. We have an enormous impact of science on the world, halfway through the development of science itself. I think science will come to an end in less than five hundred

years. I wouldn't give it more than that. In one hundred years, we will know so much we won't be able to transmit it; in fact we are already running into this problem. You will have to live to be seventy to get a Ph.D. Research time will be all gobbled up by time spent on education.

But the impact on our present world is being made by half-baked science, and all science is half-baked at the moment. We are all in a stage where we have extremely imperfect understanding of dynamic processes.

On the other hand, we can't just stop. We have set in motion an absolutely irreversible disequilibrium process. There is no question about it.

MYRDAL: Do you agree with my fundamental assumption for all development thinking: that we have a moral imperative to do our best to cure illnesses and prevent premature death?

BOULDING: No. I think death is absolutely essential to mankind. The greatest disaster that the human race could ever face is immortality. By the time our molecular biologists are finished, they may find out what it is that creates aging and tweak it out. This would be an unprecedented and unspeakable disaster.

I may not be being academic, but who wants to be an assistant professor for five hundred years? I feel the only thing that makes human life tolerable is death at a reasonable age.

COMMONER: Dr. Myrdal made the point that equilibrium is ultimately absolutely essential. We have to ask ourselves whether or not we believe that. Is it true that the biosphere is a closed system which must be in equilibrium or fail to survive? I myself am quite convinced of his position, and I think this is something we need to discuss in a hard, factual way.

Dr. Boulding intimated that the problem of immortality is soluble. To me, as a biologist, this is nonsense. It is an intrinsic feature of life that it moves toward death, that in living it transforms itself in a way which leads to its dissolution and death. That which is immortal would not be alive.

Now, why do I raise this question? Not because there is time to discuss it, but simply because in this conference it is important to keep the hard facts in front of us. I think we will have to take life with death and deal with the ultimate necessity of equilibrium.

BOULDING: This part of the universe has been in strong disequilibrium for at least six billion years. Evolution always involves ecological disequilibrium. We have always had to live with profound and continuing disequilibrium.

I say the thing we have to avoid is irretrievable disaster, because that would stop the evolutionary process.

Unless we do fall into such disaster, I think it is extremely likely that man could produce his evolutionary successor in one hundred years, including the possibility that evolutionary process can produce immortality.

TIMOTHY: There are several kinds of equilibrium, both static and dynamic. Over any given period of time, you may have a dynamic or changing equilibrium which in a more restricted sense of time can appear quite static. Other seemingly static equilibriums, when given another variable, may go through a process of evolution to another stage of relatively static equilibrium. In this process, you do have dynamism and evolutionary process which in the shorter range appears static.

MARSHALL: I think we have gotten away from the case histories that we were trying to discuss. I am largely responsible because I called on Dr. Boulding to begin with.

BOULDING: Back to the snails.

M. T. FARVAR: I also want to bring us back to the snails! There are some interesting questions with respect to the new varieties of rice. This new kind of rice depends very much on irrigation. In fact, one of its major purposes was to try to make the best use of available irrigation by developing a variety of rice that would best respond to it.

One of the problems is that there are now rats in the Philippines that get to the rice before it is ready for man. The sort of irrigation that goes with this rice is particularly favorable for rat infestation and spreading, for the animals utilize the raised mud banks for burrowing. This seems to be one of the most serious problems this rice is facing. They have tried all kinds of control methods, but the only successful one so far has been a contraption they have come up with which electrocutes any rat who would dare approach the rice. So far as I know this has only been tried around the experiment station.

Obviously, this is not a suitable control method for the backwoods of the Philippines or Iran. One would need rural electrification to make it practical!

The second irrigation factor is schistosomiasis. Some of the earliest experiments on snail control in bilharziasis were developed in the Philippines by Harsten. Extensive studies were done on the ecology of swamps with respect to snails; in fact, many control measures depended on eliminating the swamps in order to eliminate the snails. In other words, environmental control. Now the development of irrigated rice usually encourages snails. I would like to ask Dr. van der Schalie to comment on what is known about the possibility that schistosomiasis will become a major health problem in the irrigated areas of the Philippines. Do we know the various host reservoir for schistosomes?

VAN DER SCHALIE: There are surprising situations with regard to reservoir hosts. When I worked in Japan, the cow was the great reservoir host. When you go to the Philippines, you would assume the carabas would be, but this isn't the case. We know very little about reservoir hosts. And we need to know a great deal more. In our laboratory, we find we can't use guinea pigs as reservoirs for the parasites, but we can use hamsters. We have maybe five or six hundred hamsters infected with all three of the human schistosomes. Some of these, particularly *S. japonicum,* are very prevalent in Southeast Asia.

COOLIDGE: About fifteen years ago I visited a so-called slum clearance project in Saigon which had been funded by the United States. Filthy, thatch-type units, infested with rats and insects, which housed 150 families, had been cleared away and replaced by neat rows of one-room, cinderblock, tin-roofed houses, with toilets at the end of the block. In front of the houses was an open parklike area, and behind them a narrow strip of land between the back door and an open drainage ditch.

The families went into the houses only to escape a hard tropical shower, preferring to live, cook, eat, and play in the narrow strip between the back of the house and the drainage ditch where they had assembled all their belongings. The drainage ditch was a smelly, open cesspool with children playing around it, and the smaller ones falling into it. We were told that the toilet facilities were too far away to be given much use, and the ditch was used instead.

Two rows of new houses backed on the ditch from both sides, making this a high-density living area. The inhabitants refused to sit out in front of their houses, and from the front it looked like a deserted village. We were told it was difficult to persuade even very poor families to make use of this model housing area.

If a cultural anthropologist with a knowledge of Vietnamese city and village life and customs had been included in the planning process for this slum clearance project, I am confident that a much healthier and happier solution to the problem could have been arrived at for all concerned.

The lesson noted here was not lost on planners of similar future slum clearance projects in the Saigon area, but unfortunately social and cultural anthropologists are still in most instances not consulted in the development process (especially housing planning) where their cultural knowledge could supply required wisdom.

MARSHALL: Great efforts have been directed toward getting the floating population of people living on boats in the bay of Hong Kong to move into high-rise public housing. These efforts have had little success. I have visited both the floating population and the housing developments, and I would personally prefer to live on a boat. The overcrowding, the stench, the one bathroom per floor, which may be accommodating twenty or twenty-five families, certainly doesn't make such public housing a desirable place to live.

GILLHAM: I would like to come back, Mr. Chairman, to what Dr. Al Kassas had to say about the situation in Egypt and the survival of the people in view of six thousand years of schistosomiasis.

Is this a situation of dynamic equilibrium? As I understand it, although there is no strict immunity built up by the presence of these schistosomes in the body, when an infected individual comes into contact with heavily infested water, the attack is not as severe as it would be in an individual who is completely free of schistosomes. In a place like southern Africa we have one section of the community living almost entirely in urban areas with complete control of water supplies and sanitation. Some individuals who get better education can be kept free of bilharzia. The other section of the community, even though part of their life may be lived under the same health conditions, are almost certain to go to urban areas where they are bound to come into contact with infected water. Would they, in fact, be better off by first having light attacks of bilharziasis? If I am correct in this, is this problem an engineering one, a medical one, or an educational one? Or all of them?

CONWAY: To what extent can medical ecologists take part in a development program? If, for example, you are faced with a river which is going to be dammed, can you predict what is going to be the health hazard? The economist and the engineer need tangible figures to build into their cost-benefit ratios. Can a medical ecologist predict what is going to happen and say what you need to do to prevent health hazards?

VAN DER SCHALIE: My argument is: at the Aswan Dam for example, why don't we take a little time before initiating development and find out what the initial conditions are and how they may change after the dam is built? We now have about 5 percent schistosomiasis infection due to *haematobium* around the Aswan area. In the past we have found a high disease incidence with perennial irrigation. My prediction is that soon the whole Aswan region is not going to have any different infection rates than the Delta. If you compare the upper Nile with its former basin irrigation, schistosomiasis incidence is low. It is low anywhere you have basin irrigation. In the Delta, however, where we have had perennial irrigation, schistosomiasis rates are very high.

I think we can predict trouble pretty well if we know there are people and the potential snail host in a region, and we know we are going to create an ideal situation for snails, and hence for the disease. Our trouble too often has been that after they get the dam and canals built and they are right in the middle of trouble, then somebody has to go in and see what they can do about rescuing the situation. I just don't believe that this is sensible.

Someone says, "Here we will build the dams and we will create a condition, and then we will go ahead and fix it up." Don't forget *this is irreversible*. You don't fix it up. You are ruining something that was built over millions of years, perhaps. And what are we going to do? "We are a great people, we can fix it up!"

MILTON: I want to ask several questions, Dr. Marshall, relating to your case history on the Ryukyu Islands.

I wonder to what degree it would be possible now to provide built-in controls for the many pollution problems which are typical of new industrial centers. Why not require pollution controls as an integral part of the various assistance programs and aid we are giving to industrialization abroad? At present, North America, Europe, Russia and Japan together consume raw materials and pollute the global environment at tremendously higher per capita rates than the other peoples of the earth. The "advanced" nations form a minority group on this planet and yet we devour and degrade the great majority of the planet's environmental resources. Inevitably, a better distribution of the world's available resources must be fostered, and this may mean the rich countries giving up most of their luxuries. A stable world population, a shift into non-polluting energy sources, and creation of a technology that recycles what are now "wastes" and pollutants must also be achieved. I feel that these privileged rich nations also must pioneer the control of the multiple pollutions their technology has spawned and see to it these mistakes are not repeated elsewhere. They must begin to create and export a truly ecological technology in harmony with the places they affect.

Usually it is significantly cheaper to build pollution controls into the process of industrialization early in the game. But what attempts are our assistance and lending agencies making now to learn from the past health and pollution problems of the over-developed nations, as I like to call them, and to prevent repetition of the same environmental problems abroad? International

Unplanned modernization often produces changes in man's behavior without producing compensatory changes in his environment. Conversely, it sometimes changes the environment but fails to provide the people with the means of adaptation to these changes. Naha (Photo 1-1), capital of the Ryukyu Islands, is a good example of this. In **SOME EXERCISES IN SOCIAL ECOLOGY** (Page 5), Carter Marshall shows how efforts to improve the health standards in the Ryukyus had unforeseen results, some negative, some positive. For example, a filariasis control project, shown in Photo 1-2, was successful because it "accidentally" manipulated the social ecosystem in such a way as to obtain mass support from the population. Another effort to improve health standards involved persuading school children to wash their hands before lunch (Photo 1-3). Although school officials instituted this program of personal hygiene, their failure to supply drying facilities demonstrates that their acceptance of something they consider to be modern is only superficial. The children improvised by passing around borrowed handkerchiefs; this facilitated the transmission of trachoma, which can lead to blindess.

1-1

1-2

1-3

Malnutrition is one of the most serious problems in the world today. Many attempts to alleviate this problem have met with disastrous results because the interrelationships of nutrients are not considered. In his paper, subtitled **AN EXAMPLE OF NUTRIENT INTERACTION** (Page 53), George Bunce shows that, although food supplement programs may be started with the best intentions, without thorough study and research in complex nutrient interactions, which are more the rule than the exception, these programs can do more harm than good. An example of this occurred in Northeast Brazil, where dried milk distributed by UNICEF and other food aid programs led to an aggravation of vitamin A deficiency in children, producing blindness from keratomalacia (softening of the cornea).

5-1

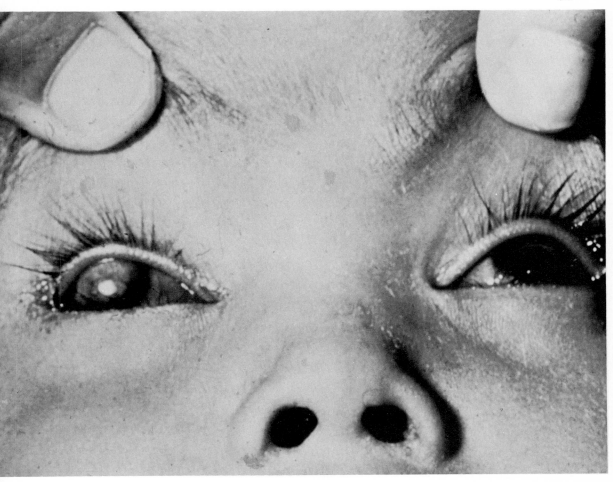

Technological advancement always upsets the man/environment relationship, but, as René Dubos points out, "the real problem is not how to maintain the balance of nature, but rather how to change it in such a manner that the overall result is favorable for the human species." Developing a country may mean building new roads, providing more water, increasing urbanization, and constructing factories. Consideration, however, should also be given to what increased migration, lack of water purification facilities, overcrowded towns, and the breakdown of a homogeneous community may mean to the people in the country.

Hunter and Hughes in their paper **THE ROLE OF TECHNOLOGICAL DEVELOPMENT IN PROMOTING DISEASE IN AFRICA** (Page 69), discuss these problems in terms of malnutrition and disease.

Photo 7-1 shows an urban slum in Freetown, Sierra Leone. The African shantytown shown in Photo 7-2 is the result of an influx of migrants from the rural areas.

Clean water pipes can significantly lower morbidity. Photo 7-3 shows villagers in Suhum, African Ghana. In contrast, many streams are still used for drinking water, washing, personal hygiene, laundry, and for playing by children, thereby becoming potential sites for bilharzia.

In Suhum (Photo 7-4), outside food preparation and vending risks gastroenteritis infection carried by flies. Unhygienic market conditions are also seen in Photo 7-5. The dry fish being sold here is a valuable source of animal protein in West Africa's forest zone. It is imported from the coast and from the Niger River Delta in Mali.

7-1

7-2

7-3

7-4

7-5

In the past, the indigenous population of Central Africa was nomadic, practicing only transient agriculture with no regard for conservation. Unstable water systems carried heavy floods in the short rainy season and dried out over the rest of the year. Aquatic snail populations, the essential link in the transmission of schistosome parasites, led a tenuous existence in these waters.

Recently, however, agricultural development has concentrated on soil and water conservation. Dams have been constructed to stabilize the water flow in rivers and provide a significant amount of permanent water. At the same time, the population has become settled and expanded, thus increasing human contact with and population of the water systems.

THE IMPACT OF AGRICULTURAL DEVELOPMENT ON AQUATIC SYSTEMS by C. J. Shiff (Page 102) describes how the irrigation of sugar and other crops (Photo 8-1) increases the snail-water-man contact and produces heavy infections of bilharzia and other diseases.

The recently constructed Manjirenji Dam in Rhodesia provides water for irrigation to some twenty thousand acres of previously arid lands (Photo 8-2).

In the past, rivers like that shown in Photo 8-3 carried very seasonal flash floods. Now, permanent pools persist throughout the year and provide ideal snail habitats, thus facilitating transmission of water-borne disease.

Photo 8-4 shows a typical stream with perennial flow as a result of water stabilization in Rhodesia. Such conditions are ideal for bilharzia transmission. (Photographs courtesy of the Ministry of Information, Rhodesia.)

8-1

8-2

8-3

8-4

agencies and the less-developed countries must take advantage of the lessons we have learned in Europe and the United States where we have such severe urban problems of air and water pollution; they have the opportunity to learn from our failures and to try to build better controls into their own urbanizing areas.

In traveling around Latin America, however, I have already found terrible problems of air and water pollution in places like Rio, Lima, and Mexico City. It is a great tragedy that so few people are aware or even interested in such problems. Many cars and buses are old and in very poor shape. The amount of pollutants they help dump into the urban air of Latin America may be even higher than we get in some of the worst-polluted U.S. cities. What are we doing about this problem?

MARSHALL: In the Ryukyu Islands this is a difficult problem to deal with because of the diffusion of authority in the present setup of the government. There are really three governments involved—the governments of the United States, of Japan and of the Ryukyu Islands itself.

Thus far, the Japanese government is not interested in the industrialization of the Ryukyu Islands per se. I think that of the two governments, the United States is more interested in that. In the Japanese scheme of things, it is my impression that the Ryukyus fit in as a market for Japanese products and as a source of labor. It is difficult to find anybody who has responsibility for pollution. And it is not just environmental pollution; it goes all the way back to the manufacturing process itself.

There is very little concept of occupational health or hygiene. The Health Department, as I have mentioned in my case history, is preoccupied. The Labor Department is very much involved in health matters, though only from the insurance standpoint. The only other resource which is supposedly readily available is the Army Environmental Hygiene Agency, from which we were unable to get any cooperation during the two years that I was there because they are preoccupied with other things.

HARDOY: To help answer John's questions I can say that in Latin America we are not learning the lessons of environmental pollution; we are repeating the mistakes of the United States and Europe.

I don't know if the attendees of this conference are aware of the problem posed by urbanization in Latin America. We recently thought that we were jumping from 90 million urban dwellers to 360 million urban dwellers between 1960 and 2000. However, the last estimate shows that the urban dwellers in the year 2000 will be close to 430 million.

This means a fivefold growth of urban population in a little bit more than a generation. About 150 million of the 430 million will be crowding the shantytowns.

To make things worse, urbanization in Latin America is taking place without even the minimum financial investments and with a minimum of human resources. Last year I researched the problem of urban land policies in South America for the United Nations. There is not a single country in Latin America outside Cuba that at the national or regional level has any idea about what to do and they just don't know how to cope with the problem of urbanization.

In a continent where municipalities are extremely weak, and where the direction that urbanization is taking is a consequence of uncoordinated public and private investments, there is little chance to control local environmental problems unless the national governments decide to act.

Industry is relatively new to Latin America. With the exception of relatively small areas of the Argentine, Mexico, Venezuela and Brazil, the rest of Latin America is practically in an early phase of industrialization. Because of historic and geographical circumstances, many of our industries in Argentina were located close to the Paraná Plata River. Up to now the problem of pollution has largely been prevented because of the strong current of both rivers. But pollution now is becoming a very important factor in the areas north of Valparaiso where many new Chilean industries are located. Pollution is becoming a problem in places like Córdoba, in Argentina, like São Paulo and in many of the cities and many of the interior countries where industries and mines are polluting rivers and lakes.

What is being done about this? We have a Ministry of Planning or a National Planning Commission in every one of our countries, but they are sectorially oriented and mainly concerned with long-range economic developments. As a consequence, they have always failed. Of course, there is now an awareness of the need to plan, and this is an improvement. But we have little knowledge of how to cope with the problems of urban development in a country like Brazil that has to build a new town of almost two and a half million people per year to absorb the new urban population. We just don't have the resources to do it.

This suggests the problem that has already been posed concerning the role that ecology can play in development. The problem to us is: What is the role that all disciplines can play in development? To date each discipline continues to act completely separately and independently, with no awareness, no concern and no respect for what the other disciplines have to say.

Let me finish by mentioning a very interesting case study. Argentina has had a National Council for Scientific and Technical Research since 1956. The Council has done a good job of promoting research. Sixty per cent of its budget is spent in medical research. The country has one doctor per seven hundred people. So health

services have never been, for the last generation, a general problem in Argentina. However, they only spend about 5 percent per year on social sciences and about 5 percent per year on natural sciences. Countries in an early stage of development have to develop policies for research. We just cannot go on using most of our relatively limited human and financial resources just to promote one field of research. Research should be concentrated on those aspects which are really strategic for the development of the country, and this is not happening.

MARSHALL: I want to summarize in general terms what has been said here this morning.

Development programs in all cases seem to involve the initiation and the continuation of a set of activities which are considered necessary to the achievement of some predefined objective. From the selection of papers prepared for this discussion and most of the comments made here this morning, various objectives of various programs can be identified, each one involving the carrying out of widely differing activities. While objectives are often more general than specific, the activities themselves are always quite specific.

The central theme presented so ably in the paper by Hunter and Hughes has been that each of these sets of objective-oriented activities has ramifications that go far beyond the desired objective itself. Indeed, it was the importance of these often unforeseen effects and the need to anticipate them that has made up the essence of this session.

One starts out by doing this or that to achieve Objective A. And while it may or may not be achieved by the activities, it seems quite certain that along with A will come B, C, D, E, F, G, *ad nauseam*. And each of these latter results may present problems in their own right.

The papers dealing with schistosomiasis

and its predictable increases with the attainment of a specific objective—that is, boosting agricultural output through an ever expanding irrigation system—have been very much on our minds this morning. Dr. May's paper deals with malaria more or less from the point of view of the parasite itself, whose own objective, survival and propagation is elaborately dependent upon the activities of men, mosquitoes and inanimate phenomena such as temperature and rainfall. Were we to have a paper representing the objectives and viewpoint of the schistosome itself, the paper would doubtless report man's irrigation activities with great satisfaction.

Three papers have concerned the untoward side effects of attempts to improve the nutritional status of semistarved people. All such case histories point out the problems and the complex interactions involved in such work.

Dr. Harold's paper on transferable drug resistance to antibiotics presents similar problems and stresses the continuing problems involved in using one of medicine's most potent weapons in an attempt to achieve final dominance over communicable diseases.

In all these cases, the objectives are noble, worthy, and humanitarian, and the activities were at first apparently assured of success—except that success never quite seemed to arrive.

One other important problem is the inability of medicine alone to achieve an objective, even when medicine itself has defined that objective in its own terms. The objective cannot be achieved because a single discipline acting unilaterally lacks the expertise and skill required to carry out or even identify the necessary activities.

My paper describes the interaction between health programs, all of which are very single-purpose oriented, and the various cultural, economic, political and administrative influences which not only affect the success of the health program itself, but also act as important determinants of whether a disease occurs or not.

Throughout our discussion of these problems, one important element has recurred: training. We have talked about the need to train populations to behave in their own self-interest. Dr. van der Schalie has commented on the lack of trainees in what might be called classical (or real world) parasitology as opposed to a purely biochemical orientation. Dr. Carlozzi criticized the kind of scientific training which teaches us to restrict our interest to one variable while trying to hold all the others constant. The scientists can do this in the laboratory. However, we are dealing with problems which are multivariant by their very nature. Perhaps there is a need for new techniques to deal with multivariant environmental problems. We might borrow profitably from the social scientists who have dealt with such problems for a long time.

II IRRIGATION AND WATER DEVELOPMENT

Thayer Scudder, Chairman

10. The Role of the Aswan High Dam in Changing the Fisheries of the Southeastern Mediterranean   *Carl J. George*   159

11. Impact of River Control Schemes on the Shoreline of the Nile Delta   *M. Kassas*   179

12. The Nile Catchment—Technological Change and Aquatic Biology.   *E. Barton Worthington*   189

13. Ecological Bottlenecks and the Development of the Kariba Lake Basin   *Thayer Scudder*   206

14. Some Ecological Implications of Mekong River Development Plans.   *John E. Bardach*   236

DISCUSSION   245

15. The Impact of Modern Irrigation Technology in the Indus and Helmand Basins of Southwest Asia   *Aloys A. Michel*   257

16. Salinization and Water Problems in the Algerian Northeast Sahara   *Kamel Achi*   276

17. Salt Cedar and Salinity on the Upper Rio Grande   *John Hay*   288

18. Consequences of Uncontrolled Human Activities in the Valencia Lake Basin   *Alberto Böckh*   301

19. The Anchicayá Hydroelectric Project in Colombia: Design and Sedimentation Problems   *Robert N. Allen*   318

DISCUSSION   343

20. On Irrigation—Induced Changes in Insect Populations in Israel   *E. Rivnay*   349

DISCUSSION   365

The cost of building dams is always underestimated—
There's erosion of the delta that the river has created,
There's fertile soil below the dam that's likely to be looted,
And the tangled mat of forest that has got to be uprooted.

There's the breaking up of cultures with old haunts and habits loss,
There's the education program that just doesn't come across,
And the wasted fruits of progress that are seldom much enjoyed
By expelled subsistence farmers who are urban unemployed.

There's disappointing yield of fish, beyond the first explosion;
There's silting up, and drawing down, and watershed erosion.
Above the dam the water's lost by sheer evaporation;
Below, the river scours, and suffers dangerous alteration.

For engineers, however good, are likely to be guilty
Of quietly forgetting that a river can be silty,
While the irrigation people too are frequently forgetting
That water poured upon the land is likely to be wetting.

Then the water in the lake, and what the lake releases,
Is crawling with infected snails and water-borne diseases.
There's a hideous locust breeding ground when water level's low,
And a million ecologic facts we really do not know.

There are benefits, of course, which may be countable, but which
Have a tendency to fall into the pockets of the rich,
While the costs are apt to fall upon the shoulders of the poor.
So cost-benefit analysis is nearly always sure,
To justify the building of a solid concrete fact,
While the Ecologic Truth is left behind in the Abstract.

KENNETH E. BOULDING

10. THE ROLE OF THE ASWAN HIGH DAM IN CHANGING THE FISHERIES OF THE SOUTHEASTERN MEDITERRANEAN

Carl J. George

During the past millennia and at an ever increasing rate, the original hydrology of the Nile has been changed by man. The most notable of events today is the construction of the new High Dam at Aswan, which is now near completion and will eventually impound a five-hundred-kilometer-long body of water called Lake Nasser. This lake will hold the annual flood and then release it slowly throughout the year for irrigation and navigation purposes. The floodwaters used to have both a freshening and a nourishing effect on the Levant Basin because of the quantities of fresh water and plant nutrients they carried.

A research project conducted by me at the American University of Beirut from spring 1963 to fall 1965 helped establish a base line of ichthyological and hydrological data against which ecological changes can be measured. My expedition in November 1968 to the U.A.R. provided further data on the impact of these changes on marine (Mediterranean), brackish water (the Delta lakes), and fresh-water (Lake Nasser) fisheries.

Since 1965, Egypt has suffered a great decline in the eastern Mediterranean fisheries. In 1962, the total fish catch was 30,600 metric tons (excluding shrimp). The impoundment of the rich floodwaters has all but eliminated the 18,000 metric tons of sardines (a loss of nearly 60% of the 1962 total fisheries intake). This eastern Mediterranean decline has caused a destabilization of the Egyptian fishery. An Atlantic trawler fleet has been developed, for the first time enabling Egypt to tap the fishery resources of the high seas.

In the Delta lakes similar trends are observable. The area of these lakes has shrunk considerably because land reclamation schemes cause a decline in available fish protein. Periodic massive fish kills have been reported in the Delta lakes as a result of runoff insecticides, herbicides, and molluscicides, such as the copper sulfate used for snail control. Overfertilization of these shallow, brackish waters is another danger from the use of fertilizers in agriculture; the lakes are trophically so rich that areas of anaerobic waters are becoming an increasing problem.

The fresh waters of Lake Nasser on the other hand have been yielding increasing quantities of fish (now up to 2,000 metric tons) and with additional impoundment, this is expected to reach some 10,000 metric tons by the mid-1970's. Experience elsewhere, however, indicates that the initial "boom" in fisheries should not warrant overoptimism, because as the environmental conditions of the lake are further stabilized, increase in populations of predator species and other factors will cause a remarkable decline in yields of edible fish.

This paper surveys the ecological circumstances of the eastern Mediterranean with special reference to the influence of the Aswan High Dam (Sadd-el-Aali) on the fisheries of the Levant and deltaic coast. The subject falls naturally into three areas: the marine fishery, the brackish water fishery of the Delta lakes, and the freshwater fishery of Lake Nasser as a compensatory development following the decline of dispersal of sardine stocks.

Completion of the Aswan High Dam has resulted in an alteration of the hydrological and sedimentary regimes of the Nile River, the influence being most notable on the Delta and in the sea. The decline in the flow of fertilizing waters and the interruption of the moving sands essential to the maintenance of coastal features appear to be two of the most influential aspects of change.

HYDROGRAPHY AND HYDROLOGY

The Mediterranean Sea is distinctive, being nearly landlocked and situated in a zone of atmospheric subsidence. The settling air warmed adiabatically has low relative humidity and produces more evaporation than precipitation for the basin. Saltier and denser waters result. They settle beneath the euphotic zone to move westward over the sill of Sicily and Gibraltar into the Atlantic Ocean. Less saline waters of relatively low fertility enter the Mediterranean and sweep eastward along the coast of North Africa. These waters proceed into the Levant sector of the eastern basin past the Egyptian coast and then northward past Israel to Lebanon where the current becomes more variable. Waters from the Adriatic are believed to enter the western depths of the basin to reinforce the generally counterclockwise movement pattern.

The deepest waters of the basin are well oxygenated, having concentrations almost invariably greater than 3.75 milliliters per liter. Temperatures are usually in excess of 13° C at the maximum depths encountered (i.e. 4,000 meters), a temperature nearly ten degrees warmer than comparable depths in the open Atlantic.

As might be expected from the hydrography, fertility is quite low. Superficial waters have less than 0.10 microgram atoms of phosphorus per liter, a level one-sixth of that commonly encountered in the open ocean of the same latitude. Salinity is high, approximating 38 to 40 parts per thousand (ppt), in contrast to salinities of 35 to 36 ppt in the Atlantic. The highest salinities appear to be generated in the fall with the evaporative cooling of summer-warmed waters. Because of the low fertility, transparency is high, producing the rich blue and indigo waters so characteristic of the Mediterranean.

Tides in the eastern basin are low, rarely exceeding 50 centimeters, while barometric influence on sea level may seasonally produce tidal changes of 15 centimeters or more. Wind-generated currents generally support those created by density differences and benthic relief. Atmospheric low-pressure cells generated over the Atlantic and the western portion of the Mediterranean move eastward, frequently pausing over the island of Cyprus to create a system of prevailing winds; those that reach Lebanon are out of the southwest; those that strike the U.A.R. come out of the northwest, and so on. The wind systems are noticeably modified by sea breezes generated by differentials in heating and cooling over land and sea. This "thermal bufferring" of the Mediterranean is a feature of the Near Eastern meteorology.

We can thus see that until the closing of the Sadd-el-Aali or Aswan High Dam, a complex of events tended to accent the importance of the Nile outflow on the Levant and eastern Delta region. The counterclockwise gyre, the prevailing winds, and the low density of Nilotic waters produced a tongue of relatively low salinity and high fertility that adhered to the eastern Mediterranean coast of the U.A.R., Israel and Lebanon. The great quantity and richness of the Nile flood entering a sea of such low fertility amplified its fertilizing significance. Liebman (1935), Halim (1960), and Oren and Komarovsky (1961) among others have described the character and the movement of the floodwater. At the Damietta mouth Halim has determined phosphorous levels (August 21, 1968) of 6.38 microgram atoms per liter, which led him to approximate, using a figure of 30 thousand million tons water outflow, an elemental phosphorous contribution of about 5,800 tons for the four months (August–November) of the flood.

Oren and Komarovsky (1961) have illustrated a tongue of water having a salinity of 37 ppt reaching as far as Rubin, a town south of Tel Aviv and the 38 ppt isohaline reaching Haifa. They assessed the northward extension of this influence to be about 8.6 km per 24 hours. Earlier, Liebman (1935) had approximated a speed of about 10 km for each 24 hours. In Beirut we were able to determine a slight but apparently significant decline to 37.42 ppt on September 25, 1963, and a barely detectable fall to 38.95 ppt on September 16, 1964. The absence of rain during the preceding weeks (i.e. the summer drought period) removes fresh-water runoff as a complicating factor. Salinities determined by D. Dinsmore and myself for samples taken at Beirut from September 22 through October 5, 1966, were all in excess of 39 ppt, suggesting the absence of any flood freshening. These observations relate to the fact that in 1964 the cofferdams of the Sadd-el-Aali were in place, acting to hold part of the annual flood. In 1965 only the Rosetta barrage was opened partially; in 1966 the flood was effectively contained at Aswan and the other dams and barrages. We must thus look upon 1964 through 1965 as the dawn of a new nutrient regime for the southeastern Mediterranean Sea.[1]

A number of figures are quoted for the sediment load of the Nile, but it seems accurate enough to say that anywhere from 50 to 100 million tons have been carried past Cairo each year, until the last few years. These sediments have spilled over the Delta to nourish the soil and have moved through the distributaries and irrigation system of the Delta to reach the sea. On mixing with saltier waters, colloidal materials and other finer particles are precipitated out to build the sedimentary platform (*ca.* 25–75 km wide) which then courses eastward along the deltaic and the southern

[1] The hydrographic conditons off the Nile Delta have recently been reviewed by Dr. Samy Gorgy (1966), Director of the Institute of Oceanography and Fisheries, Alexandria.

coast to eventually reach, in attenuated form, Lebanon. The aeolian sandstones of Israel (Emery and Neev, 1960; Emery and Bentor, 1960) and beach rock mark the long-standing accumulation of Nilotic sediments. The presence of what are probably turbidity-current-cut canyons off the coast of northern Israel and Lebanon and the rockiness of the coastline further suggest the route of Nile sediments into the depths of the basin.

We are well aware that much of the sedimentary load of the Nile is derived from the rich basaltic-volcanic highlands of Ethiopia entering the main Nile via the Atbara and the ill-named Blue Nile, but it does seem tenuous to assume that this source has always been so generous. It seems likely that with the ancient development of agriculture on the slopes of Ethiopia, stabilizing vegetation that once held both sediment and water has been lost. Further we must visualize a naturally much more verdant Nile with papyrus and several dozen other species of aquatic plant forming great swamps, like those existing today in the Sudd, dominating the flood plain and the delta. Again, as in the Sudd, this vegetation must have done much to reduce the velocity and sediment load of the flood and to spread its influence over a much longer period of time. Such conditions would have yielded a relatively well-filtered water to the Mediterranean, less in volume and richer in dissolved materials. With the coming of man as hydrologist and agriculturist, sediments were released, at first in relatively small amounts. With the acceleration of population and cultural complexity more sediments were released to produce the sedimentary tongues of the several distributaries which have in turn been swept eastward as sand bars to produce the five major lakes of the Delta. So, we may not be justified in thinking of the Nile flood as a particularly long-standing fertilizing influence of the type prevailing at the turn of the last century.

Furthermore, if R. Said and other geologists are correct in their thesis that the Nile broke through into the Sudd Basin only some forty thousand years ago, we may be forced to abbreviate even further our concept of the ancient flood.

THE FISHERIES

The fisheries of the southern Levant Basin[2] are poorly developed and based on relatively feeble stocks. Although modern techniques have been introduced to the area, the fishery is characterized by its low level of capital investment, and by overfishing that depends upon relatively young and small fish.

The fishery is traditionally divided into the pelagic, trawl, and inshore categories. The former is dominated by such species as *Sardinella aurita, S. maderensis, Sardina pilchardus, Seriola dumerili, Trachurus trachurus,* and *Pomatomus saltatrix.* Prominent species of the trawl fishery are *Saurida undosquamis, Merluccius merluccius, Mullus barbatus, M. surmuletus, Solea vulgaris, Pagellus erythrinus, Pagrus erythrinus, Pagrus ehrenbergi,* and *Epinephelus aeneus.* Important fishes of the inshore fishery are *Sciaena aquila, Mullus* of several species, *Lithognathus mormyrus, Sphyraena chrysotaenia, S. sphyraena, Oblada melanura, Diplodus sargus,* and *Sarpa salpa.* The categories become ill-defined in Lebanon where the coastal shelf is narrow and shore seines routinely harvest species falling into all three categories. The pelagic species such as the jacks, small tuna, horse mackerel, and sardines, are most regularly available.

The most common techniques include set line, gill and trammel nets, purse seines (especially one form set at night with lights called the *lamparo*), trawl, and the shore

---

[2] That sector of the eastern Mediterranean east of a line drawn southward through the western end of Crete and south of Cyprus.

seine. In Israel, the Italian purse seine, the *chianchola,* a longer and deeper net than the *lamparo,* has been used since the early 1950's. Syria and Turkey use trawlers in the northeastern sector of the basin while the Egyptians and the Israelis trawl in the southeastern region, harvesting the fertile area associated with the sedimentary plains of the Delta. Lebanon has consistently failed to acquire trawlers because of the aggressiveness of fishermen applying other techniques.

Today there are about 3,600 fishermen in Lebanon using one thousand small and open boats, rarely exceeding six meters in length (Boulos, 1967). It is approximated that some 2,300 tons of fish are harvested annually, but as one might suspect, landings of catches are spread along the entire coast, making more precise inventory techniques impossible. This tonnage results in an approximated 1,000 Lebanese pounds (*ca.* $300) of income per fisherman per year or an average of something less than £L 3 per day (*ca.* $1). At the same time, fish on the market is expensive. One may visit the Souk Abu Ali in downtown Beirut or a small roadside stand away from the larger coastal cities and still be required to pay from $2 to $5 per kg for better-quality fish. By comparison, in the tri-city area of New York State (with an average per capita income some twenty times higher) during a period of storm and consequent short supply, we are still required to pay only about $2 per kg for fillets of excellent quality of haddock, cod, and halibut.

The Israeli fishery is the most advanced of the region, having relatively high investment, good catch per unit effort, a number of more advanced techniques, and a good statistical survey. The average annual catch of the present decade for all methods is about 2,000 MT (metric tons).

The Gaza fishery formerly under Egyptian administration yielded about 1,000 MT annually with the *lamparo* usually contributing more than 60% of the catch. Hook, gill nets or *maltush,* shore seine or *jarufi, bashlooli,* and trawl or *grirah* contribute in decreasing order. Today few, if any, trawlers land catches in the Gaza area. With the inception of the Israeli administration the *chianchola* has been introduced, successfully displacing the *lamparo* and producing a harvest of 980.5 MT for the ten months of 1967, excluding the two months of hostilities, June and July (Landau, 1968). Again, there is little evidence of changes due to the loss of the Nile flood with the possible exception of a notable increase of the sardine catch of Gaza in 1965, the year the Egyptian harvest fell.

Turning now to the statistics of El Zarka and Koura (1965): for the U.A.R. we see a yield during 1962 of 12,429 MT of fish other than sardines and 18,166 MT of sardines, producing a total of 30,595 MT. When 7,237 MT of shrimp are included, the total rises to 37,832 MT. But since 1965 the catch has been effectively halved with the loss of the sardine.

In summary, the 2,500 MT of Lebanon, 2,000 MT of Israel, 1,000 MT of the Gaza area, and 37,800 MT of the U.A.R. produced a total of about 43,300 MT annually for the southeastern sector of the basin prior to 1965.

Because sardines show the indications of change most clearly, it is appropriate to give them special attention. Three species enter the fishery, *Sardina pilchardus, Sardinella aurita,* and *S. maderensis.* Their bionomics are complex, and it is expected that a number of rather well segregated stocks for each species will eventually be determined. This expectation is borne out by the fact that U.A.R. fishermen have detected a serious decline in the abundance of *S. aurita* and *S. maderensis,* while Israeli fishermen have yet to experience any notable alteration in their harvests.

During my visit in the U.A.R. (November 1968) I interviewed a number of fisher-men in Al Burg, Baltim, Rosetta, and Alexandria regarding the sardine fishery. Without any doubt whatsoever it has al-most completely collapsed. Eighteen thou-sand tons (El Zarka and Koura, 1965) is one approximation of the annual sardine catch prior to the closing of the Sadd-el-Aali. Today the catch is at most only 500 tons![3] I searched the fish markets of the Delta coast and found not a single sardine at a time of year when they were previously abundant. At 20 piasters per kilogram (100 piasters to the Egyptian pound) and as-suming a conversion of two dollars to the pound, the loss may be approximated at about seven million dollars annually. In light of the fact that sardines formerly con-stituted about 48% by weight of the marine catch (El Zarka and Koura, 1965), the fish-ery has suffered seriously.

Fishery practice at Al Burg is already readjusting to the sardine absence and di-recting its large fleet of sardine net boats to shallow-water trawling and seining. Dr. Abdul Rahman Al Kholy, Director of the Institute of Oceanography and Fisheries of the U.A.R., has made the valuable point that the expected increased transparency of Egyptian waters following the full curtail-ment of the Nile flood may allow the ef-fective use of the *lamparo* or *chianchola* technique (using night lights), a method relatively unused in the fishery. An earlier attempt has been judged unsuccessful but future attempts may match the success of areas such as those of the Gaza and Leb-anese coasts.

The U.A.R. fish trade statistics further illustrate the influence on the fishery. In 1963, 2,438 MT of fish products (includ-ing shrimp) valued at £E 895,000 (Egyp-tian pounds) were exported; in 1967 these figures had fallen to 1,117 MT and £E

603,000. Political events have probably had relatively little influence on these fig-ures. The Arab-Israeli encounter of 1967 took place in June; however, 95% or more of the sardine catch occurs during the three months of September, October, and November.

In the Israel-Gaza sector, May–June and October peaks in the catch of these species are observed. Along the Delta coast the bulk of the catch is made during the three months of September, October, and No-vember.

At Beirut, *S. pilchardus* appears irregu-larly during the months of April, May, June, and July, constituting a relatively stable source. Individual fish are small, however, and enter the market in fried form called *bisri,* or *seed. Sardinella aurita* is particularly important, occurring almost all year and in relatively large size. This spe-cies is the mainstay of the sardine fishery. *Sardinella maderensis* is marginal at Beirut. Fine, large specimens do appear but they rarely contribute much by weight or num-bers.[4]

Of all schooling groups appearing in the Levant basin the sardines appear to play a critical role in harvesting the burst in primary productivity associated with the flood. Halim (1960) counted the number of phytoplankters per liter at the mouth of the Rosetta distributary prior to the flood on August 12, 1956, and determined the presence of about 35,000 cells per liter, while seven days later, after the arrival of the turbid brown waters, the count had risen to 1,240,000 cells per liter. Slightly less than a month later, on September 11, the count had risen still further to

---

[3] Because of poor yields fishermen have gen-erally abandoned the sardine fishery, dropping this figure even further to less than 10 MT (March, 1970).

[4] The synopses of Adam Ben-Tuvia (1960a, 1960b) on *S. maderensis* and *S. aurita* are good sources here. Wimpenny (1931) makes special references to the incidence of *S. maderensis* at the time of the Nile flood, and other authors (Dieuzeide, 1950; Heldt, 1950) have determined the time of spawning to be late summer, just preceding the flood. We see still another ad-aptation to the flood regime with its tolerance to lower salinities (Fage, 1920).

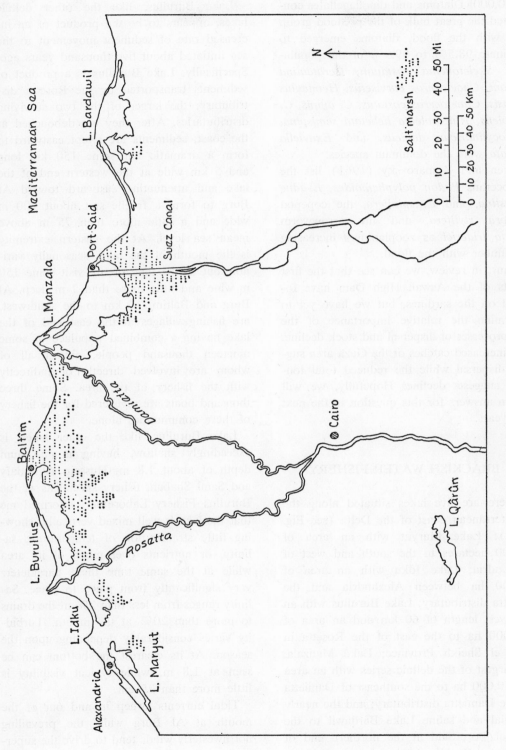

Figure 10-1 Lakes of the Nile Delta

2,400,000! Diatoms and dinoflagellates constituted the great bulk of the preflood group but, with the flood, diatoms emerged to dominate 98.5% to 99.9% of the population. *Skeletonema costatum, Cerataulina bergoni, Chaetoceros curvisetus, Hemiaulus sinensis, Chaetoceros costatus, C. affinis, C. decipiens, Rhizosolenia hebetata semispina, Leptocylindricus danicus,* and *Exuviella cordata* were the dominant species.

Oren and Komarovsky (1961) list the cladocerans *Podon polyphemoides, Evadne tergestina,* and *E. spinifera,* the copepod *Temora stylifera,* and the arrowworm *Sagitta friderici* as zooplankters increasing in number with the flood.

Thus, in review, we can see that the first effects of the Aswan High Dam have focused on the sardines, but we have yet to determine the relative importance of the two processes of dispersal and stock decline. The increased catches of the Gaza area suggest dispersal while the reduced total tonnage suggests decline. Hopefully, we will obtain answers for this question in the next few years.

THE BRACKISH WATER FISHERY

There are five lakes situated along the Mediterranean coast of the Delta (see Fig. 10–1): Lake Maryut with an area of 15,000 hectares to the south and west of Alexandria; Lake Idku with an area of 20,000 ha between Alexandria and the Rosetta distributary; Lake Burullus with an east-west length of 60 km and an area of 100,000 ha to the east of the Rosetta in Kafr el Sheikh Province; Lake Manzala, the largest of the deltaic series with an area of 150,000 ha to the southeast of Damietta on the Damietta distributary; and the nearly vestigial and saline Lake Bardawil to the east of Port Said at the northern end of the Suez Canal with an area of about 80,000 ha (Gorgy, 1966).

Lake Burullus, like the other deltaic lakes, appears to be the product of an increased rate of sediment movement to the sea initiated about five thousand years ago. Specifically, Lake Burullus is a product of sediments transported by the Rosetta distributary, the larger of the two surviving distributaries. After they are debouched at the coast, sediments are swept eastward to form a dramatic bar some 150 km long and 5 km wide at the western end of the lake and attenuating eastward toward Al Burg to form a fragile spit about 200 m wide and a little more than 75 m above mean sea level. At the eastern extremity is the mouth of the lake, seasonally variable but at the time of my visit some 150 m wide and little more than 2 m deep. Al Burg and Baltim, 10 km to the southwest, are fishing villages at the east end of the lake having a combined populace of some nineteen thousand people, almost all of whom are involved directly or indirectly with the fishery of the area. Some three thousand boats are registered for the fishery of these communities alone.

Lake Burullus, like the other lakes, is exceedingly shallow, having a maximum depth of about 1.8 m. Hussein Al Sidafy and Sami Shaban, fishery specialists of the Burullus Fishery Laboratory, informed me that the lake is well mixed vertically, showing little stratification of temperature, salinity, or nutrients over much of its area while at the same time these parameters vary significantly from place to place. Salinity ranges from less than 2% at the drains to more than 20% at the mouth. Turbidity varies considerably depending upon the season. At its clearest the bottom can be seen at 1.8 m, while typical visibility is little more than 25 cm.

Tidal currents sweep in and out of the mouth at Al Burg while the prevailing northwesterly winds tend to drive the superficial and more saline waters of the northern margin southeastward to mix with the fresher waters of the irrigation drainage. These same winds return sands to the beaches to establish a system of migratory dunes oriented in a predominantly south-easterly direction.

The waters at the ends of the drainage canals are below the level of the lake surface and must be lifted a meter or more by pumping stations to enter the lake. This point becomes critical with the possibility that the sand bars separating the lake from the open sea may diminish with a reduced supply of Nile sediments and eventually open, allowing sea waves to broach the low dikes protecting the reclaimed land. Talking with Egyptian ecologists, it was my impression that this possibility could be one of the most unfavorable consequences of the Aswan High Dam project.

The southern shore of the lake is dominated for much of its extent by commercial salt flats and shallow enclosed basins that are seasonally opened and closed for the capture and rearing of fish. To the south of these "fish farms" is an east-west oriented belt of several kilometers of unreclaimed brackish water marsh. Prominent halophytes of this area are *Suaeda fruitocosa, Salicornia fruitocosa, Inula crithmoides, Phragmites communis, Juncus acutus,* and a number of other species composing what might be considered the most virginal community of the Delta.

South of this *"Suaeda-Salicornia* marsh" a band of recently reclaimed lands begins to stretch some fifteen to twenty kilometers southward. This area is dissected with a new and growing complex of irrigation channels, roadways, high tension lines, and telephone and electrical wires. A million acres is a rough approximation of the extent of these lands reclaimed during the last decade.

The characteristic perennial irrigation system, beginning to the south of the marshes, with three or more rotated crops of rice, cotton, *birseem* (*Trifolium alexandrinum*),

fool (*Vicia faba*), cabbage, radish, *dohra* (*Zea mayz*), eggplant, and other crops, is quickly penetrating the area following the solution and drainage of salts from the soil. This agriculture depends heavily upon DDT, BHC, and other insecticides, and occasional mass fish kills suggest that these chemicals constitute an important influence on the fisheries of the area.

New windbreaks and canal bank trees of *Casuarina equisetefolia, Eucalyptus* spp., *Populus euphratica, Acacia nilotica, Ficus sycamorus, Salix tetrasperma, Salix subserrata,* and others are beginning to rise from the flat expanse of the newly reclaimed lands.

The drains reaching northward to the lake range in size from less than a meter wide to some fifty meters, such as the Kitchener Drain. The drains commonly have steep margins maintained by work gangs who move the unwanted silt by hand basket to adjacent banks. Some five thousand men were engaged in this activity and canal enlargement along the route of my trip to Baltim on November 26, 1968.

The smaller drains are inhabited by the snail hosts and parasites associated with the disease bilharziasis, and control efforts using molluscicides and herbicides such as copper sulfate constitute another detrimental feature of the aquatic environment.

Lake Idku, although smaller than Lake Burullus, shares many of the same characteristics of depth and salinity and has a seasonal connection with the open sea. It differs in having a broader protective bar. The bar carries a number of villages, including the larger community of Idku, and an extensive sea salt industry. Another distinctive feature is the presence of raised agricultural platforms extensively fenced with the stems of the marsh grass *Phragmites communis,* interspersed with evaporation basins.

Lake Maryut is unique in being 2.5 to 3 meters below sea level. During the summer months evaporation proceeds at a rate equal to or even exceeding the drainage into the lake, while during the cooler months the excess waters must be raised to sea level by the pumping facilities at Al Mex, a district to the west of Alexandria. The below-sea-level situation of Lake Maryut has come about through land reclamation efforts which have recovered nearly half of the lake's original 24,800 hectares (approx.). The western sector of the depression is devoted to evaporation pans associated with the salt industry. At the time of my visit the shallow waters of this area were stained a deep purple-red with what I assume to be *Rhodospirillum* sp. The northern portion near Al Mex is devoted to a few hectares of shallow basins used for the holding and rearing of mullet fry which are caught in the seaward side of the discharge channel. For years millions of young mullet have been captured for transfer to Lake Maryut and Lake Qârûn to support the fishery.

Lake Manzala, the largest of the Delta lakes, is at sea level and remains in contact with the sea all year via a number of different mouths.

Lake Bardawil, the most easterly of the lakes, long ago lost the freshening influence of the now extinct Pelusaic branch of the Nile and exhibits salinities at or above those of the sea. This lake plays a negligible role in the Egyptian fishery for both ecological and political reasons.

Land reclamation has reduced the areas of all the lakes. Lake Maryut has declined from 25,000 hectares to the current 15,000, Lake Idku from 15,000 to 13,000 hectares, Lake Burullus from 59,000 to 56,000 hectares and Lake Manzala from 171,000 to 145,000 hectares. I must admit that these figures are very approximate and need confirmation. But land reclamation has definitely generated considerable friction between the fishermen and the agricultural fellaheen.

THE FISHERY

One may divide the fishes of the Delta lake fishery into three groups: fresh water, brackish, and marine. Listed in the increasing order of their importance in the northern delta area,[5] prominent species of the fresh waters are the *lahfash*, or Nile perch, *Lates niloticus;* the large *cormoot* catfish, *Clarias lazera;* the *bayat, Bagras bayad;* the *lehbeece, Labeo niloticus; Barbus benni;* and the *boulti, Tilapia nilotica, T. zilli,* and *T. galilaea.*

This group especially has suffered under the influence of modern perennial irrigation and public health practice. Toxaphene and other insecticides appearing on the local market have been used for the last twenty years in ever increasing quantities, resulting in a decline that seems to have gone undetailed. The manual clearing of vegetation from the waterways and the use of the herbicide 2, 4-D along with the application of copper sulfate for bilharziasis control have been further steps in the curtailment of the fish fauna.

Still another force has been the intensive harvesting made possible through "pulsed irrigation" in which large volumes of water are allowed to enter a specific area and then isolated for application to cultivated lands. As the water is consumed, fishes are restricted to more confined areas where they can be almost completely harvested with seines, thrown nets, and traps. Here is the basis for the implication that with the fuller control gained over the Nile flood, overharvesting will increase to the detriment of the resident stocks. Greater implementation of rice field culture of fish could counter this suspected trend. Some 218,000 hectares of lotic surface (i.e., canals, drains, and

[5] Boulenger (1907) has described the fishes of the Nile in a manner unsurpassed by modern ichthyologists and the illustrations of his work may be consulted to assist the reader.

rivers) are available but support a trivial and at best "accidental" fishery.

The brackish water group consists primarily of the *bour* or Mugilidae, *Mugil cephalus, M. capito, M. saliens, M. chelo,* and *M. auratus;* and the *boulti, Tilapia nilotica, T. zilli,* and *T. galilaea.* During the periods of flood, the previously listed species extend from their preferred freshwater habitats into the brackish waters of the Delta lakes, while during the spring and early summer months a number of more marine species such as the *marmur, Lithognathus mormyrus;* the *deneece, Chrysophyrys auratus;* and the *noct* (meaning "spotted"), *Morone punctata* enter the lake for spawning or feeding.

The marine group is more diverse, having several dozen more-or-less regular contributors. The *sardina mabatat* (*Sardinella maderensis*) and the *sardina mabrooma* (*S. aurita*) have been of primary importance until only recently.

Other important fishes of the marine group are the *loot, Sciaena aquila;* the *wakar, Epinephelus aeneus;* the *shefish, Umbrina cirrhosa;* the barbooni, *Mullus barbatus, Spicara smaris;* the *begha, Lichia amia;* the *sphyrnih, Sphyraena chrysotaenia* (=*S.* spet?); the *baccala, Saurida undosquamis* (=*S.* tumbil); and a number of other species (see Fig. 10–2).

Another feature of the fish fauna is the ever increasing number of Indo-Pacific (Erythraean) species. Examination of specimens at the Burullus Fisheries Laboratory indicates the presence of the Red Sea *Dussumieria acuta,* known to the Arab fisherman as the *Sardine ingleezi. Leiognathus klunzingeri* is another Erythraean form along with the halfbeak, *Hemiramphus far;* and the rabbit fishes or *Sigan, Siganus rivulatus* and *S. luridus,* reported for the first time here. The common small barracuda identified as *S. spet* reported by El Zarka and Koura (1965) may in reality be *S.*

chrysotaenia, another Red Sea species. Similarly, *Saurida tumbil* is almost surely equivalent to *S. undosquamis,* and the goatfish, *Upeneus asymmetricus,* is another, new to the record for the U.A.R.

The importance of Indo-Pacific crustaceans in the fishery, especially that of the Delta lakes, is striking. Of the seven commercially significant shrimp species, fully six are of Red Sea origin. *Penaeus semisulcatus, Penaeus japonicus, Metapenaeus monoceros,* and *Metapenaeus stebbingi,* as identified by Dr. El Zarka of the Institute of Oceanography and Fisheries, Alexandria, are four of the more notable species. The many basketfuls of the Indo-Pacific crab, *Portunus pelagicus,* seen on my visits to the markets in Alexandria further accent the importance of such introduced species.

In addition to the Red Sea immigration one North American species, the blue crab, *Callinectes sapidus,* has become established in Lake Burullus, Lake Idku, and Lake Manzala, assuming an active role in the local markets.

A. Sidafy and Sami Shaban, biologists of the Burullus Laboratory, have kindly provided statistics on the fishery of the lake. Fifteen thousand metric tons of fish are taken yearly, a figure based on a system of daily and weekly assessment of entire catches conducted jointly by the Coast Guard and Fisheries Laboratory.

The *boulti* or *Tilapia* spp. compose 60% of the total with *T. nilotica* contributing 30%, *T. zilli* 18%, and *T. galilaea* 12%. The *bouri* or Mugilidae supply 25% of the catch, *Mugil capito, M. cephalus,* and *M. saliens* ranking respectively. The first and second are taken year around; the third occurs during the five months from May through September. The *Nihili* or Nile fishes, *Lates niloticus, Clarias lazera, Bagrus bayad, Labeo nilotica,* and *Barbus benni,* in approximately this order, constitute the remaining 15%. The more marine fishes

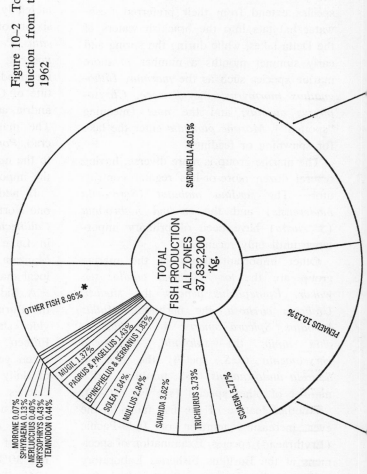

Figure 10–2 Total commercial fish production from the Mediterranean Sea, 1962

TOTAL FISH PRODUCTION ALL ZONES 37,832,200 Kg.

SARDINELLA 48.01%

PENAEUS 19.13%

SCIAENA 5.77%

TRICHIURUS 3.73%

SAURIDA 3.62%

MULLUS 2.64%

SOLEA 1.84%

EPINEPHELUS & SERRANUS 1.83%

PAGRUS & PAGELLUS 1.43%

MUGIL 1.37%

OTHER FISH 8.96% *

MORONE 0.07%
SPHYRAENA 0.13%
MERLUCCIUS 0.40%
CHRYSOPHRYS 0.43%
TEMNODON 0.44%

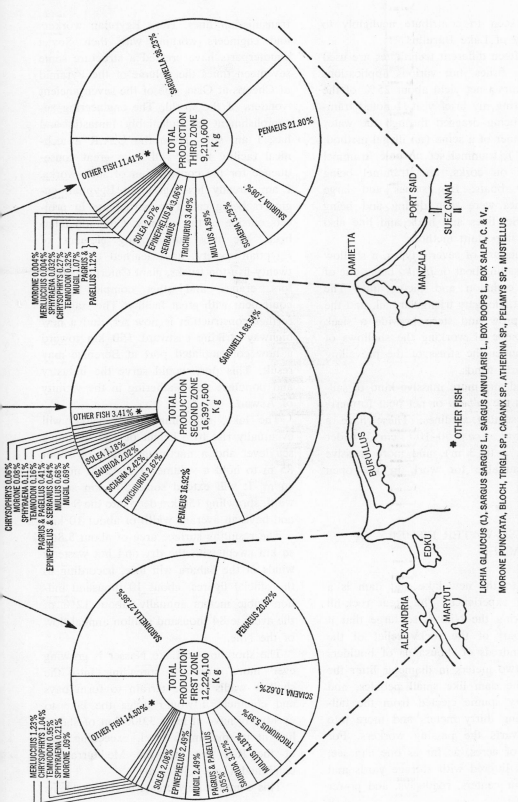

TOTAL PRODUCTION
THIRD ZONE
9,210,600
Kg

SARDINELLA 38.23%
PENAEUS 21.80%
SAURIDA 7.08%
SCIAENA 5.29%
MULLUS 4.89%
TRICHIURUS 3.49%
EPINEPHELUS & SERRANUS 3.06%
SOLEA 2.67%
OTHER FISH 11.41% *

MORONE 0.004%
MERLUCCIUS 0.004%
SPHYRAENA 0.032%
CHRYSOPHRYS 0.27%
TEMNODON 0.32%
MUGIL 1.07%
PAGRUS & PAGELLUS 1.12%

TOTAL PRODUCTION
SECOND ZONE
16,397,500
Kg

SARDINELLA 68.54%
PENAEUS 16.92%
TRICHIURUS 2.62%
SCIAENA 2.42%
SAURIDA 2.02%
SOLEA 1.18%
OTHER FISH 3.41% *

CHRYSOPHRYS 0.06%
MORONE 0.08%
SPHYRAENA 0.11%
TEMNODON 0.16%
PAGRUS & PAGELLUS 0.41%
EPINEPHELUS & SERRANUS 0.64%
MULLUS 0.68%
MUGIL 0.69%

TOTAL PRODUCTION
FIRST ZONE
12,224,100
Kg

SARDINELLA 27.86%
PENAEUS 20.62%
SCIAENA 10.62%
TRICHIURUS 5.39%
MULLUS 4.18%
SAURIDA 3.12%
PAGRUS & PAGELLUS 3.05%
MUGIL 2.49%
EPINEPHELUS 2.49%
SOLEA 2.08%
OTHER FISH 14.50% *

MERLUCCIUS 1.23%
CHRYSOPHRYS 1.04%
TEMNODON 0.95%
SPHYRAENA 0.21%
MORONE .09%

PORT SAID
SUEZ CANAL
DAMIETTA
MANZALA
BURULLUS
EDKU
ALEXANDRIA
MARYUT

* OTHER FISH

LICHIA GLAUCUS (L), SARGUS SARGUS L., SARGUS ANNULARIS L., BOX BOOPS L., BOX SALPA, C. & V.,
MORONE PUNCTATA, BLOCH, TRIGLA SP., CARANX SP., ATHERINA SP., PELAMYS SP., MUSTELLUS
VULGARIS, MULL & HENI, RHINOBATUS COEMICULUS GEOFFR.

are thus seen to contribute negligibly to the fishery of Lake Burullus.

Some fifteen different techniques are used to capture fishes, but various applications of the trammel net yield about 25% of the catch. During my brief visit, I noted trammel nets being dragged through the water in the manner of a seine (an illegal method, I am told!), trammel set on pole, trammel suspended on corks, and trammel being pulled by boats. Bag seines and large shore seines were seen drying and being repaired. Set lines and hook and line also constitute important methods.

The boats are of several types, a shallow scow-like sailing boat or *fuluka* being one of the most common and picturesque. The raked mast, elongate triangular sail, and the extended prow and stern provide a sleek design capable of working the shallows of the lake under the stress of the prevailing northwesterly winds.

A second and more massive kind of sailing boat is the *m'botn* or net boat formerly used for seining sardines. These have a deeper draft (*ca.* 50–100 cm), wider beam (*ca.* 2 to 3 m), and more massive planking suitable for work in the open sea.

THE FRESH-WATER FISHERY OF LAKE NASSER

A visit to the new lake and dam is a benumbing experience. The great rock-fill mass blocking the Nile is so large that it seems a part of the rocky relief of the region. Hundreds of thousands of boulders well over two meters in diameter litter the faces of the dam like small pebbles, and the feathery spume ejected from the tailraces arching thirty meters and more into the air dwarfs the passing workers. For thousands of acres, as far as one can see, the land is littered with storage yards and sheds, repair centers, roadways, and power transmission lines. Here Egyptian workers and engineers working with their Soviet counterparts have erected a structure some seventeen times the volume of the Pyramid of Cheops at Giza, one of the seven ancient wonders of the world. The engineering accomplishment is undeniably fantastic and has, I am sure, given the U.A.R a technical facility which will have great consequence for the construction of such works. I am already hearing about Egyptian engineers being called to participate in projects outside of the country. Common fellaheen, the most unchanging element of Egyptian society, have learned to operate twenty-five-ton trucks, giant Caterpillar tractors, cranes, and other complex power equipment with great facility. The stage for further construction is now set, and a new highway striking eastward 150 km toward a now contemplated port at Berenice may result. This port would serve the industry and populace now gathering in the vicinity of Aswan.

The lake, still filling since 1964, will eventually rise to a height of 183 m above sea level and a maximum depth of about 85 m to hold a volume of 164,300 million cu m. It will extend some 500 km southward, sprawling 150 km deep into the Sudan, and have an average width of about 10 km.

The resulting surface area of about 5,860 sq km swept with the dry and hot westerly winds of the Sahara will lose, according to the official figures, about 10 thousand million cubic meters annually, about 12% of the average 84 thousand million annual flow of the Nile.

The shoreline of Lake Nasser is growing ever more tortuous, spreading into the shallow wadis of the terrain to form bays and channels. I would judge the lake to eventually have at least 3,000 km of shoreline at its maximum level, exceeding that of the Red Sea and the Mediterranean combined (i.e., 2,500 km).

This complex may create health problems

unless watched closely. In 1942 *Anopheles gambiae* introduced malaria to the area from the Sudan, and resulting in about 100,000 deaths, 10,000 of which occurred in Upper Egypt. *Culex pipiens,* the vector for filariasis, is present along with the newly reported *Phlebotomus* spp., vector of the disease kalazar (leishmaniasis), and several species of the black fly, *Simulium,* active in the transmission of river blindness (onchocerciasis).

The water hyacinth, not yet present in the lake, remains a threat, judging from the serious problems this species is causing in the Sudan.

The waters at the northern end of the lake are relatively clear of suspended sediments, these being lost in the upper Sudanese reaches. Instead, the waters are now turning a deep turquoise green with phytoplankton, the organic base for the fishery.

THE FISHERY

The fishery of Lake Nasser, like that of the Delta lakes, depends heavily on the Cichlidae, with *Tilapia nilotica* constituting about 70% of the catch. The other two species, *T. zilli* and *T. galilaea,* do not occur. Judging from the excellent growth (i.e., up to 55 cm total length and 3.5 kg weight), the *boulti nili* is well adapted to the lake. Its preference for shallow nearshore waters, omnivorous diet, and mouth-breeding habits have all been suggested as reasons for its success.

Labeo nilotica and *L. hori,* grouped together by the fishermen as *lebeece,* rank second. *Bagrus bayad* and *B. docmac,* again grouped under a single name, *bayat,* rank third in the fishery. The large catfish, *Clarius lazera,* reaching weights of 100 kg, is the next ranking contributor. Then comes the *lafash,* or Nile perch, *Lates niloticus,* another species reaching large size. *Cynodontis* spp., or *calf; Schilbe* spp., or *shilba,* notable for their habit of swimming upside down at the surface; and the *sardine nili, Alestes dentex, A. baremosa,* and *A. nurse,* also exist. *Barbus bynni,* or *binni;* and the tiger fish *Hydrocyon* spp., or *kelb,* close out the list of prominent species (El Zarka, 1965). It can be seen that the species composition is quite similar to that occurring in the fresher parts of the Delta lakes.

The trammel net, gill net, long line, beach seine, throw nets, and a variety of traps are the prominent instruments and are usually operated from small (4–6 m length) wind-driven and oar-driven craft.

A number of predictions have been made regarding the fishery. Ibrahim Al Gueddawi, in a mimeographed report for the Regional Planning Center of Aswan, compares Lake Nasser to the reservoir of the Jebel Aeulia Dam in the Sudan. The 136,000 hectares of this water body exist for the six months of August through March, producing at least five pounds of fish per acre during this period. If we use this figure we would expect 6,000 MT per half-year or 12,000 MT per entire year for the lake at full level. If Al Gueddawi's figure of 18.5 kilograms per hectare is used as a more optimistic approximation, 24,000 MT may be expected. Data for 1936–1941 for Lake Manzala give a yield of 90 kg/ha. Lake Burullus yields 69 kg/ha, and the harvest of Lake Idku is about 133 kg/ha. Eutrophic shallow water lakes of brackish character are well known for their high productivity, and thus the lower approximation for the deeper and fresher Lake Nasser seems justified.

Lagler and El Zarka (1967) have also given attention to the productivity of Lake Nasser. They report a catch of 1,430 MT for October 1965 through September 1966 with a harvest area of 443 sq km, about one-third of the 1,330 sq km area available at the time. This is equivalent to a catch of 1 MT per sq km or 17.5 kg/ha, a figure approximating the larger one by Al Gueddawi. Lagler and El Zarka go on to suggest a harvest of 12,870 MT per year when the lake reaches its maximum area in 1975 or after.

The harvestable productivity for the various usable fish stocks of the lake will probably illustrate a relaxed oscillation during the next decade or so as the lake ecosystem establishes some drifting equilibrium, but it will most likely fail to sustain the high productivity of the first honeymoon years due to the growing strength of higher trophic levels. But, judging from case histories of other impoundments, the development of the several hundred thousand hectares of lake foreshore, the fishery innovations, and the physical-chemical character of the lake will be most influential. Heavy use of insecticides and fertilizers could induce a serious decline through either toxification or excessively rapid eutrophication. Light fishing, electric fishing, or trawling may prove especially successful, and the current limitation on the importation of nylon filament and thread and the accent on locally manufactured cotton materials as an economic measure may eventually be abandoned.

The lake may develop an appreciable anaerobic zone. Today thermal stratification is observable, with deeper waters approximating 18°C and surface waters reaching 30°C or more during the warmer months of August through October. Dr. P. C. Raheja has brought to my attention the high sulfur content of the silts, which may result in exceptionally high H_2S levels when O_2 is depleted. If a series of exceptionally cool years are followed by a number of warm years, the anaerobic layer could thicken, accumulating a heavy load of H_2S. If this situation were followed by a cold period when mixing occurred throughout the depths of the lake, serious mortality could take place. Biologists of the fishery station at Aswan are following the thermal stratification of the lake closely.

Thus the lake may conservatively be ex- pected to eventually yield 10,000 to 12,000 MT per year under relatively undependable and evolving circumstances. At present the catch approximates 2,000 MT.

The most serious problem today centers on the vastness of the growing lake. Enough fishermen are not present to harvest the available production. Further, the catch now suffers serious spoilage because of high temperatures, the slowness of the fishing craft, the large distances which must be traveled to reach adequate refrigeration facilities, and the absence of adequate roads surrounding the greater part of the lake. Circumstances now force a large percentage of the catch to be made into a salted and less desirable preparation called *fiseekh*. Presently a number of refrigerated mother ships are being considered, possibly to be provided by the U.S.S.R.

The current paucity of fishermen and fishing craft may be remedied by the return of some of the residents of the sixty villages vacated at the inception of flooding. There is also the very real possibility that there will be a movement from the deltaic coast. I have been informed that some thirteen hundred families have indicated their willingness to move to the lake area. The areas apparently most suitable for settlement are: the west-bank lands of the peninsula immediately south of Kalabsha, the lands on the east bank of the southern shores of the El Okka basin—named after the El Dokka Temple, and the lands just north of the Sudanese-Egyptian border on the west bank in the vicinity of the Abu Simbel Temple and Ballana Tombs. These sites are appropriate because they are adjacent to areas having agricultural potential.

READJUSTMENT

In light of the nearly complete loss of the sardine fishery and the anticipated decline of the productivity of the Delta lakes we must give attention to the planned rehabilitation of the thousands of coastal persons who are now entering a crisis period.

Two approaches are now being considered and in some measure implemented. First, new techniques are being introduced. The sardine fleet is readapting to the capture of more demersal species such as the hake, *Merluccius merluccius,* and the Indo-Pacific (Erythraean) lizard fish, *Saurida undosquamis.*

As has already been mentioned, light fishing, generally successful both to the east and west of the Delta, is potentially successful with the anticipated reduction in turbidity.

But the most current scheme is the development of a fleet of oceanic trawlers. Three such ships of Spanish design (type AXA-B) and manufacture, 90 m in length and 1,000 MT in capacity, have already completed their maiden voyages to the waters of West Africa with general success (*ca.* 600 MT each) and have returned for a second fishing effort. The ships were financed by the U.S.S.R. and their crews were trained by Soviet specialists working in the Atlantic and Indian Oceans. About 40 days of fishing at a minimum of about 20 MT per day and 45 days of travel are routinely planned. Thirteen more trawlers of smaller size and wooden construction are planned for manufacture at Alexandria following Russian design.

Dr. Abdul Rahman Al Kholy, Director of the Institute of Oceanography and Fisheries, conservatively suggests that some 5,000 MT may be harvested annually by the existing fleet, which will assist considerably in replacing the loss due to the decline of the Nile flood. A more optimistic viewpoint, assuming an average catch of 800 MT per cruise and four trips annually for each of the three ships, would result in about a 9,600 MT production annually. This venture is particularly notable because it represents the first high-seas fishery effort of any Middle Eastern country. Its as yet unproven success would produce a stimulus for renovation that would prove immensely therapeutic to the archaic and poorly developed fishery. We may thus see that the High Dam has induced an improved restructuring of the fishery. A simple tonnage equivalent alone is thus not a sufficient means of comparison.

Eel fishing in the lakes is another, though much smaller, element of late date. The Cook Co., a Dutch firm, has constructed a weir several hundred meters long perpendicular to the north shore of Lake Idku. Eels traveling along shore pass through a number of gates into fyke nets where they are collected for live shipment to Holland. I was informed that two shiploads of live eels of about 15 MT each leave monthly for Europe during the active season, thus producing a harvest of about 200 MT. Though the tonnage is small, the cash value is high, and apparently because of fear of competition the industry has an aura of secrecy about it that was quickly demonstrated when I attempted to take photographs of the Idku weir. We may well expect this fishery to expand into the other Delta lakes, and I was led to believe first efforts have already been made at the mouth of Lake Burullus.

Second, and perhaps most important of all, we must look to the new fishery of Lake Nasser. We have already noted approximations of about 10,000 MT for this fishery, and coupling this figure with a conservative prediction of 5,000 MT for the high sea fishery we have already recouped a significant part of the fishery lost with the decline of the flood. If the eel fishery continues to develop along with "readjustments" in the existing marine industry such as the introduction of light fishing and an increased harvest from the Red Sea, we may well see the lost tonnage eventually balanced or even exceeded. But this will not occur until at least the mid-1970's when

Lake Nasser reaches its full extent; the fishermen, however, are in trouble now.

As Dr. Worthington has so well emphasized in another paper in this volume (Chapter 12), it is a frightening thing to undertake a project such as the Aswan High Dam with the full realization that the consequences will influence millions of people. It also takes courage, but for the projects of the future and those under way, it should also take the interest and involvement of the ecologist. And, whether we like it or not, failures of dramatic projects are the fault of the ecologist more than any other person because he was unable to see the inevitability of such ventures as the Aswan High Dam and because he was not able to respond sufficiently well after the fact. Beyond this criticism of the ecologist, I am led to question the validity of the unilateral acts of any country which

may have influence on the ecology of a region shared by a group of countries. The High Dam is not unique. Dams of nearly comparable influence are planned for the Mesopotamian Valley and Iran. The new sea-level canal presently being considered for the isthmus of Central America is another example. The influence of such acts is invariably more accentuated when the marine waters involved are partially landlocked such as the Mediterranean, Persian Gulf, and the Caribbean. Mid-latitude and low-latitude gulfs and bays having a high evaporation-precipitation ratio are particularly susceptible because of the sinking of waters fertilized by terrestrial runoff below the euphotic zone.

International regional ecological studies and planning seem an essential feature if there is to be any hope of avoiding an enduring misuse of natural resources.

ACKNOWLEDGMENTS

Special thanks are due Dr. Abdul Rahman Al Kholy, Director of the Institute of Oceanography and Fisheries of the Ministry of Scientific Research of the United Arab Republic, for his kind assistance in making much information available to the author and in providing a general orientation as to fishery research efforts currently under way in the U.A.R.

Dr. M. Al Kassas, Professor of Botany of the University of Cairo, Dr. Said Hassan, former Director of the Red Sea Institute at Ataka, Dr. Sami Gorgy, Director of the Institute of Oceanography and Fisheries at Alexandria, Dr. Salah el Din El Zarka, Professor of Fishery Biology at the I.O.F.A., and Dr. P. C. Raheja, Project Manager, Lake Nasser Development Centre at Aswan, have all offered generously of their time and experience during my brief stay in the U.A.R. Thanks are also due to the many fishery biologists who gave so freely of their time during my visits to their laboratories.

Finally, I would like to thank the officers of the Center for the Biology of Natural Systems (Washington University), the Department of Oceanography of the Smithsonian Institution, and the Smithsonian Research Foundation for making my recent trip to the U.A.R. possible. Appreciation is again expressed to the Rockefeller Research Foundation for supporting work performed in the Republic of Lebanon (George and Athanassiou, 1967).

REFERENCES

Ahmed, Abdel Aziz. "An Analytical Study of the Storage Losses in the Nile Basin, with Special Reference to Aswan Dam Reservoir and the High Dam Reservoir (Sadd-el-Aali)." *Proc. Inst. Civ. Eng.,* 17 (1960a), 181–200.

———. "Recent Developments in the Nile Control." *Proc. Inst. Civ. Eng.,* 17 (1960b), 137–80.

Anonymous. "A map of Lake Nasser, Aswan Development Project, Scale 1:50,000, Showing the Original Course of the River, the 133 and 180 m above s.l. Contours and Cultivable Lands." N.d.

———. *Aswan High Dam, Commissioning of the First Units, Transmission of Power to Cairo.* Aswan High Dam Authority, Ministry of the High Dam. Cairo: Rose El Youssef Press, 1968. With 60 photos, 13 schematics, diagrams and models, 11 line drawings and sketches, 4 tables and 1 map. 84 pp.

Ben-Tuvia, Adam. *Synopsis of Biological Data on* Sardinella aurita *of the Mediterranean Sea and Other Waters.* FAO Fisheries Biology Synopsis No. 14, Fisheries Division, Biology Branch. Rome: FAO of the U.N., 1960a.

———. *Synopsis on the systematics and biology of* Sardinella maderensis *(Lowe).* FAO Fisheries Biology Synopsis No. 19, Fisheries Division, Biology Branch. Rome: FAO of the U.N., 1960b, 7–519.

Boulenger, G. A. *The Fishes of the Nile.* London: Rees Ltd., 1907. 578 pp.

Boulos, Ismat. *La Pêche moderne, méthodes pratiquées au Japon: possibilités d'adaptation au Liban.* Éditions du Centre d'Études Techniques. Beyrouth: Imm. Gouraeb. 1967. 260 pp.

Dieuzeide, R. *"Sardinella maderensis* Lowe (= *S. granigera* C.V.) sur les Côtes Nord-Africaines." *Rapp. Cons. Explor. Mer.* 126 (1950), pp. 21–22.

Emery, K. O., and Bentor, Y. K. "The Continental Shelf of Israel." *Bull. Sea Fish. Res. St.* (Israel), No. 28 (1960), pp. 25–41.

Emery, K. O., and Neev, D. "Mediterranean

Beaches of Israel." *Bull. Sea Fish. Res. St.* (Israel), No. 28 (1960), pp. 1–14.

Fage, L. "Engraulidae. Clupeidae." *Rep. Danish Oceanogr. Exped. 1908–1910,* 2 (A9), (1920), 1–140.

Fisher, W. B. *The Middle East, a Physical, Social and Regional Geography.* London: Methuen and Co., 1963. 568 pp.

Furuskog, Valter, and Kennedy, Geoffrey Farrer. "The Aswan Hydro-electric Scheme." *Proc. Inst. Civ. Eng.,* 17 (1960), 201–18.

George, Carl J., and Athanassiou, Victoria. "A Two Year Study of the Fishes Appearing in the Seine Fishery of St. George Bay, Lebanon." *Annali del Museo Civico di Storia Naturale di Genoa,* 76 (1967), 237–94.

Gorgy, Samy. *Les pêcheries et le milieu marin dans le secteur méditerranéen de la République Arabe Unie.* Thèse prés. La Fac. Sci., Univ. Paris., Inst. Sci. Tech. Pêch. Mar. Série A, No. 1140, Ord. 1164. 1966. 76 pp.

Greener, Leslie. *High Dam over Nubia.* London: Cassell and Co., 1962. 198 pp.

Grosvenor, M. B., ed. *National Geographic Atlas of the World.* Washington: National Geographic Society, 1966. 343 pp. Specifically, see p. 156.

Gueddawi, I. Al. "The Fish Wealth in Lake Nasser." Regional Planning of Aswan, Lake Nasser Development Center. N.d., mimeographed report. 20 pp.

Halim, Y. "Observations on the Nile Bloom of Phytoplankton in the Mediterranean." *J. Cons. Internat. Explor. Mer,* 26 (1) (1960), 57–67.

Heldt, J. H. "Sardinella granigera (*S. granigera* C.V.) Espèce nouvelle por la Faune Ichtyologique Tunisienne." *Ann. biol., Copenhague* 6 (1950), pp. 69–70.

Herodotus. *The Histories* as translated by Aubrey de Selincourt. Harmondsworth, England: Penguin Books Ltd., 1953. 599 pp.

Hurst, H. E. *The Nile, a General Account of the River and the Utilization of Its Waters.* London: Constable, 1957. 331 pp.

Keller, Anton, and Kalff, P. Baudoin. "Contribution aux études de l'utilisation optimum des eaux du Nil." *Travaus Publics et Entreprises* (Paris), 53 (1965), 1–42.

Lagler, Karl F., and Zarka, Salah El. *Preliminary Considerations on the Fish Production, Lake Nasser.* FAO Fisheries Misc. No. 67. Rome: FAO of the U.N., 1967. 5 pp.

Landau, R. "Pelagic Fisheries, 1966, and Summary of Trends in Recent Years." *Fisheries and Fishbreeding in Israel*, 2 (1) (1967). (A translation was kindly supplied by the author.)

Larraneta, M. Gomez. *Synopsis of Biological Data on Sardina pilchardus of the Mediterranean and Adjacent Sea.* FAO Fisheries Biology Synopsis No. 9, Fisheries Division, Biology Branch. Rome: FAO of the U.N., 1960.

Liebman, E. "Some Oceanographical Observations on the Palestine Coast." *Comm. Int. Explor. Sci. Mer Medit.*, 9 (1935). (My copy without page numbers.)

Oren, O. H., and Komarovsky, B. "The Influence of the Nile Flood on the Shore Waters of Israel." *Comm. Int. Explor. Sci. Mer Medit.*, 16 (3) (1961), 655–59.

Saab, Gabriel S. *The Egyptian Agrarian Reform, 1952–1962.* London: Oxford University Press, 1967. 236 pp.

Simmons, Daryl B. *Evaluation of Degradation and Related Problems Downstream of Aswan Dam.* Hydraulic Research and Experimentation Station, Delta Barrage, U.A.R. Mimeographed report. 4 pp. plus 6 figures.

Walker, D. S. *The Mediterranean Lands.* London: Methuen and Co., 1960. 524 pp.

Wimpenny, R. S. Report on the fisheries of Egypt for the year 1929. Cairo, 1931. 92 pp.

Zarka, Salah el Din El, and Fahmy, Fahmy K. "Experiments in the Culture of the Grey Mullet, *Mugil cephalus* in Brackish Water Ponds in the U.A.R." *Proc. World Symp. on warm-Water Pond Fish Culture,* FAO Fish Rep., 5 (44) (1968), 255–66.

Zarka, Salah el Din El, and Kamel, Fahmy. "Mullet Fry Transplantation and Its Contribution to the Fisheries of Inland Brackish Lakes in the United Arab Republic." *Proc. Gen. Fish. Counc. Medit.*, 8 (1965), 209–26.

Zarka, Salah el Din El, and Koura, Riad. "Seasonal Fluctuations in Production of the Principal Edible Fish in the Mediterranean Sea off the United Arab Republic." *Proc. Gen. Fish. Counc. Medit.*, 8 (1965), 227–59.

11. IMPACT OF RIVER CONTROL SCHEMES ON THE SHORELINE OF THE NILE DELTA

M. Kassas

There is now an active process of coastal retreat of the Nile Delta. Comparative study of maps, review of historical documents concerning the sites of old coastal fortresses and lighthouses, and personal observations of shoreline changes show the rate of coastal erosion. The retreat is the sum of two opposite processes: (a) the natural process of building the Delta by the annual load of sediments brought to the shoreline by the river flood; (b) the erosion action of waves and a westward shoreline current that prevails throughout the main part of the year.

This coastal retreat represents a substantial departure from the history of the area. A building process had continued throughout the Pleistocene and recent time, but began to lessen during the nineteenth and twentieth centuries as a result of river control schemes, such as the Delta Barrages (1881) and the Aswan Dam (1902). The establishment of the High Dam (1967) brings the delta building process to an end.

The rate of erosion varies locally, and is associated with the distribution of bodies of coastal sand dunes (related to old channels of the Nile Delta). These dunes are mobile and proceed inlandward, burying villages on one side and exposing the shoreline on the other side.

The immediate effect of this phenomenon on the fishing villages and summer resorts is described. The future—and more alarming—effects on the agricultural lands reclaimed and cultivated as a result of drainage schemes established during the period 1925–1967 is also discussed.

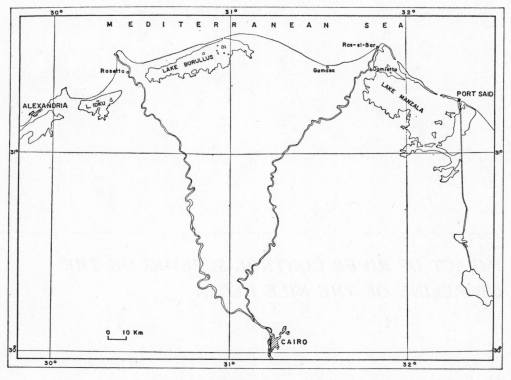

Figure 11–1   Nile Delta location map

GEOMORPHOLOGY OF THE DELTA SHORE

The Mediterranean coastline from Port Said (longitude 32 degrees 19 minutes E.) to Alexandria (longitude 29 degrees 53 minutes E.) is an undulating line that bears the features of an advancing delta (Fig. 11–1).

Three shallow lakes occupy the northern part of the Delta: Lake Manzala (east), Lake Burullus (middle), and Lake Idku (west). These lakes receive the main bulk of the drainage water collecting from the Delta; they are separated from the sea by strips of land that are very narrow in several places, and they are connected with the sea through outlets. The Delta shoreline is dotted with villages and summer resorts such as Ras-el-Bar, Gamasa, and Baltim.

Along the shore there are sand dunes seemingly associated with the eastern banks of present and past Nile branches. Two promontories are associated with the mouths of the Damietta and Rosetta branches of the Nile. The land between the two mouths extends into the sea to latitude 31 degrees 36 minutes, 12 and 5 latitudinal seconds farther than the tips of the Rosetta and Damietta promontories respectively. This middle part is the site of the mouth of an old branch of the Nile: the Sebennytic. The coastal land to the east of the Lake Burullus exit is covered by sand dunes that extend for about fifteen kilometers east of the outlet. The strip of land to the west of this outlet has no dunes comparable to those of the east side. The Lake Burullus exit is the site of the mouth of the Sebennytic branch.

This pattern is repeated at the sites of all the several branches of the Nile that emptied directly into the Mediterranean until

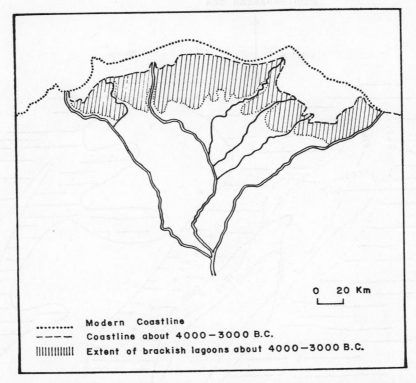

Figure 11–2   The Delta in predynastic and early historical times (After Butzer, 1959)

the ninth century.[1] The sand was obviously brought to the shoreline with the Nile sediments debouched at the mouth points. Softer silts and clays traveled further into the sea or were transported along the shoreline for long distances by littoral currents. Sand was deposited at the shoreline and pushed to the eastern sides of the mouths by the eastward current that prevails throughout the main part of the year.

That the Nile sediments travel eastward is proved by studies of Shukri and his associates. Shukri *et al.* (1956) compare the mineralogy of recent shoreline sediments with that of the Nile sediments analyzed by Shukri (1950 and 1951) and show that only little of the Nile sediments spread westward of Rosetta reaching Alexandria.

[1] According to maps produced by O. Tosson, Egyptian Geographical Society; see also maps of Egypt in classic times reproduced by Ball (1942), and map of the Delta in predynastic times by Butzer (1959), quoted herein Fig. 11–2.

Shukri and Phillip (1960) show that Nile sediments travel eastward reaching the whole of the Sinai coast and beyond. Coastal dunes of the Delta and the country to its east are formed of continental sand (siliceous) whereas dunes of the country west of the Delta are formed of maritime sand (calcareous oolitic grains).

THE PROBLEM

The Delta shoreline that had obviously been advancing throughout the history of the Delta formation is now retreating. Villages, small farms, and seaside resort establishments (notably Ras-el-Bar at the Damietta mouth and Baltim east of the Burullus exit) are gradually losing ground. The silting of the lake exits deprives fish migrations necessary to fish propagation from their natural passage. Thus silting, together with other factors, is causing gradual im-

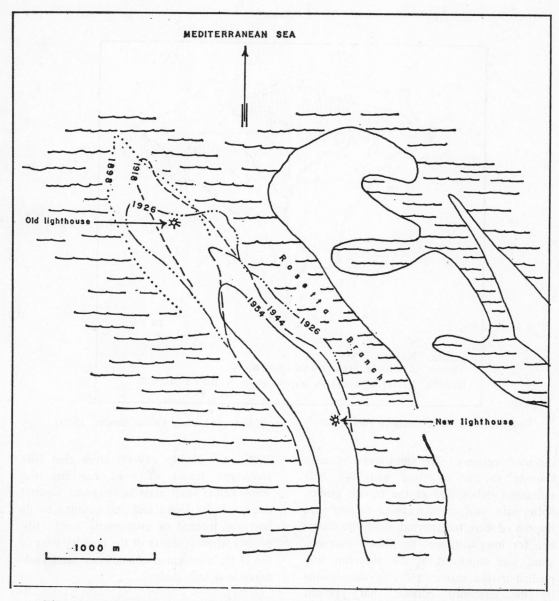

MEDITERRANEAN SEA

Old lighthouse

Rosetta Branch

New lighthouse

·1000 m

Figure 11–3   Rosetta mouth of Nile changes from 1898 to 1954 (After F. Wassing)

poverishment of the lake fisheries. The silting and instability of lake exits deprive the marine fishing industry of its natural harbors throughout the long stretch between Port Said and Alexandria.

The map in Fig. 11–3 shows the shoreline at the western side of the Rosetta mouth in 1898, 1918, 1926, 1944, and 1954. It is obvious that this promontory has lost about 1650 meters of its length in

sixty-five years; the average yearly retreat is about 29 meters. Wassing (1964) produces the following figures for the rates of shoreline retreat:

Table 11–1

PERIOD	1898–1918	1918–26	1926–44	1944–54
Retreat (meters)	300	620	375	350
Average per year	15	81	21	35

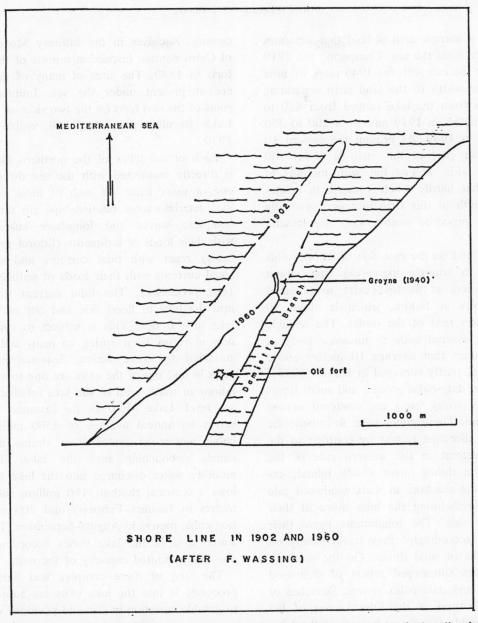

MEDITERRANEAN SEA

1902

1960

Damietta Branch

Groyne (1940)

Old fort

1000 m

SHORE LINE IN 1902 AND 1960

(AFTER F. WASSING)

Figure 11–4 Ras el Bar on the west side of the mouth of Damietta Branch shoreline in
1902 and 1960 (After F. Wassing)

In 1898 the old lighthouse was 950 meters inland from the tip of the promontory; in 1926 it was merely a few meters from the tip. In 1942 the lighthouse became isolated from the mainland, and in 1954 a new lighthouse was built 2350 meters south of the site of the old lighthouse.

The western side of the Damietta mouth

is the site of the Ras-el-Bar summer resort. From Wassing's drawing (1964), reproduced here in Fig. 11–4, it is evident that during the fifty-eight years from 1902 to 1960 the length of the Ras-el-Bar peninsula has decreased by about 1800 meters, an average of 31 meters per year.

On the western side of the Lake Burullus

exit is a narrow strip of land that separates the lake from the sea. Comparing the 1919 map of the exit with the 1949 map, we note that the width of the land strip separating the sea from the lake ranged from 850 to 1000 meters in 1919 and from 200 to 350 meters in 1949. At present the eastern 10 kilometer part of this strip is about 100 meters wide, almost flat with mounds of sand that hardly reach 1 meter in height. The width of this strip increases gradually as one proceeds west toward the Rosetta mouth.

The land on the east side of the Burullus exit is a triangle increasing from about 300 meters at its tip (exit) to about 8 kilometers at Baltim, which is about 10 kilometers east of the outlet. The triangle area is covered with an immense body of sand dunes that average 10 meters above sea level, partly surveyed in Hume (1925). Villages, date-palm groves, and small farms (melons, fruits, etc.) are scattered among the dunes. These dunes seem to impede the rate of shoreline retreat by contrast to the active retreat in the western side of the exit. The dunes move slowly inland, exposing the seashore at their windward side and overwhelming the lake shore at their leeward side. The inhabitants move their villages accordingly: they travel slowly on the backs of sand dunes. On the seashore one notes submerged relicts of destroyed villages and date-palm groves. Stretches of clayey bottom of the littoral zone of the sea resemble the clayey bottom of the lake.

The village of Borg-el-Borollos, home village of the writer, was moved to its present site some eighty years ago. The old site is now about 2 kilometers out to sea, and the present site on the eastern side of the Lake Burullus exit is protected by a concrete wall supported by a number of short groynes. These constructions require yearly maintenance and repair.

A chain of coastal forts dotted the Delta coast in the late part of the nineteenth century. Archives in the Military Museum of Cairo contain inspection reports of these forts in 1880. The sites of many of these are at present under the sea. Inundated ruins of the two forts on the two sides of the Lake Burullus exit were still visible in 1930.

Each of the lakes of the northern Delta is directly connected with the sea through one or more exits. At each of these exits the material-energy relationships are rather complex: waves and longshore currents with their loads of sediments (littoral processes) react with tidal currents and seasonal currents with their loads of sediments (exit processes). The tidal current flows into the lake in flood tide and out of the lake in ebb tide. This is subject to variation in range from spring to neap and is modified by wave action. Seasonal currents in and out of the exits are due to variations in water level of the lake relative to sea level. Lake Manzala, for instance, receives an annual average of 4500 million cubic meters of water from drains and canals debouching into the lake. The monthly water discharge into the lake follows a seasonal rhythm: 100 million cubic meters in January–February and 700 million cubic meters in August–September. The water level in the lake varies accordingly due to the limited capacity of the exit.

The sum of these complex and varied processes is that the lake exits are subject to notable variation in size and position. We may quote the historical account of the Lake Manzala exit as summarized in Report No. 18 (1964) of the Research Laboratory, Suez Canal Authority. In 1887 there was one exit 100 meters wide and more than 5 meters deep. In 1890 the exit was 50 meters east of the old fort; in 1921 it was 1000 meters east of the fort: it moved eastward at an average of 30 meters per year. In 1922 the exit was 75 meters wide with a channel 3 meters deep in its eastern side. In this year an artificial exit 20 meters wide and 3 meters deep was dug immediately west of the fort. In 1926 the newly dug exit had moved eastward, causing the destruction of the fort. In 1942 this artificial exit was silted and a new exit was naturally formed further east of the original (first mentioned) exit. This new exit was deepened and a barrage was built across it to control the outflow of the lake water. In 1953 the original exit was silted; it was artificially cleared in 1955, but silted again in 1956. The instability of the Lake Man-

zala exit is similar to that noted of the Lake Burullus exit.

The outflow current from the lake exit may be an effective factor in lowering the rate of beach erosion through its effect on the longshore current. The silting of these exits hinders the movement of fish from lake to sea and vice versa and disturbs the migratory movements associated with fish propagation. The maintenance of these exits is part of the general problem of beach protection.

Figure 11–5 The Nile Delta in the Pleistocene (After Shukri *et al.*, 1956)

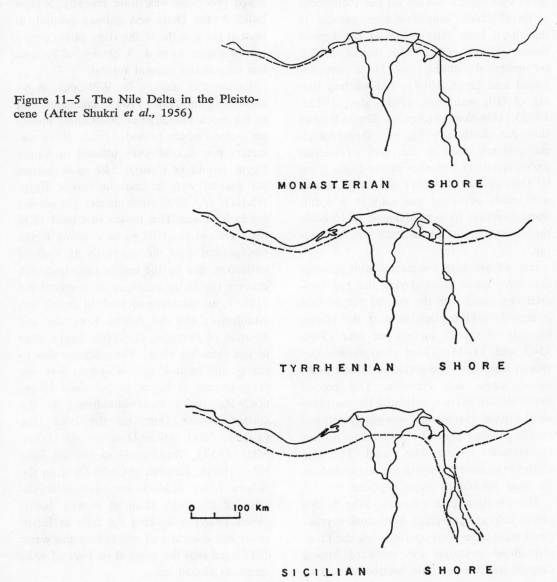

MONASTERIAN   SHORE

TYRRHENIAN   SHORE

0   100 Km

SICILIAN   SHORE

CAUSES OF SHORELINE RETREAT

The history of the Nile Delta is closely related to the relative levels of land and sea. This could be visualized by correlating and integrating information from studies on levels and histories of river terraces in parts south of Cairo (Sandford, 1934; Sandford and Arkell, 1929, 1933, 1939), deposit stratigraphy of the Delta (Judd, 1897; Fourtau, 1915; Attia, 1954; Yousri, 1962), geomorphological studies on the Pleistocene series of oolitic limestone bars parallel to the shore from Alexandria to the Libyan border (Shukri et al., 1956; Butzer, 1960), palynological studies on Delta deposits (Saad and Sami, 1967), radiocarbon dating of Nile sediments (Fairbridge, 1962a, 1963), historical studies on Greco-Roman sites Audebeau (1919), etc. Archaeological evidence such as the sites of ancient towns and river branches in the Delta given by Daressy (1928–1934) show that human settlements advanced gradually in a northward direction from predynastic to Hellenic times; that is, the Delta itself was advancing.

But we are here concerned with changes that have taken place during the last hundred years and with the coastal retreat that is actively taking place now at the alarming rate of several meters per year (Figs. 11–3 and 11–4). These changes are obviously due to erosive action of littoral processes: waves and currents. The eroded materials are carried eastward by the prevalent littoral current and are partly trapped by the groynes built at Port Said to protect the entrance of the Suez Canal. The area of the Port Said township has expanded on the land formed by these deposits.

The question that arises is: Why is this recent retreat occurring? The erosion processes must have been operative all the time: throughout centuries the eastward littoral current has moved Nile sediments east of the river mouths, wave action is universal; the rate of sea-level changes (Fairbridge, 1962b) does not seem to have been radically modified during the last hundred years; yet the shoreline morphology, even in its present form, bears features indicative of building (Fig. 11–1). The answer may be sought in the material-energy balance concerned in the two processes: building by sediments brought to the shoreline by the river, especially in flood season, and erosion agents. The net outcome of these two opposed processes was, until recently, a slow building; the Delta was gaining ground, at least at the mouths of the river where promontories were formed. A change of balance has caused the present retreat.

Earlier this century W. Willcocks, in his account of the Nile (1904), calculated that of the mean discharge of 3040 cubic meters per second which passed Aswan, 400 cubic meters per second were utilized in Upper Egypt (south of Cairo), 540 cubic meters per second were utilized in Lower Egypt (Delta), and 2100 cubic meters per second reached the sea. This means that until 1904 two-thirds of the Nile water entering Egypt was poured into the sea with its load of sediments. But by the end of the nineteenth century the Delta Barrages were completed (1861), an extensive network of canals was established; and the Aswan Reservoir and a series of barrages in Upper Egypt were in the planning stage. The purpose was to change the basin-irrigation system that was preponderant in Egypt to perennial irrigation. Reservoirs were established in the Sudan: Sennar Dam on the Blue Nile (1925), Jebel Aulia Dam on the White Nile (1937), Roseires Dam on the Blue Nile (1964), Khashm el-Girba Dam on the Atbara River (1962), etc. The establishment of the High Dam at Aswan (completed 1968) will bring the Nile in Egypt under full control and will reduce the water discharged into the sea and its load of sediments to almost nil.

Before the elaboration of these irrigation and Nile-control constructions that started on a large scale by the end of the nineteenth century, the load of sediments reaching the shoreline was much greater.

Quantities of sediments carried in suspension by the Nile water are calculated by Ball (1939). He gives these in millions of tons past Wadi Halfa (Sudano-Egyptian border) and Cairo during flood seasons of three years as follows:

Table 11–2

	WADI HALFA	CAIRO
1929	136.13	73.81
1930	75.69	41.62
1931	118.27	57.30

The suspended material diminishes in the journey from Wadi Halfa to Cairo by about half of its quantity. Part of the load is further lost through the journey from Cairo to the sea. This loss is due, in part at least, to the interception of sediments through irrigation canals and at the Aswan Reservoir.

The deposition of the full load of flood sediments was enough to compensate for the erosion and to build the Delta shores further northward at least in parts where river branches debouched into the sea. The flow of Nile water into the sea must have formed currents perpendicular to the prevalent littoral current pushing it farther from the shoreline and hence saving the beach from its erosion action. This protective influence of the river flow has gradually been diminished; it will be completely nullified by the completion of the Aswan High Dam.

DANGERS OF SHORELINE RETREAT

The narrow bars separating Lake Manzala and Lake Burullus from the sea, especially the parts west of the exits, are likely to collapse. If this is allowed to happen, the two lakes will be transformed into sea bays extending into the northern Delta. Land reclamation endeavors during the last fifty years, and recent reclamation schemes that will bear fruit during the next five years, will have gained about one million acres of land for Egyptian agriculture. But these large stretches of land are at, or only little above, sea level. The reclamation of these areas was made possible through pump-drainage into the lakes. The transformation of these lakes into marine bays will endanger the hydrology of the northern Delta drainage systems. The southern shores of the present lakes will become marine beaches, and in case of storms the high waves are likely to cause marine inundation and salt-water sprays.

The lakes are at present bodies of brackish water separating the northern Delta from the sea. The change of these bodies of brackish water (salinity 0.8–1% in Lake Manzala; Montasir, 1937) presently in contact with the Delta lands to salt water (salinity 3.5–3.9% in the Mediterranean) will increase the salinity of the near-surface underground water with obvious repercussions on the fertility of these lands.

This prospective danger is the yet-to-be-seen finale of a story. Armed by modern technology, Egyptians ceased to worship the Nile as a god and the benevolent giver of their fertile land, and started in the middle of the eighteenth century to harness the mighty river till they brought it under almost full control by the establishment of the Aswan High Dam. But the complexity an ecosystem such as this river represents is often beyond the engineer's genius. The land reclaimed by sustained effort throughout a century is being endangered by shoreline retreat; and if not alert to the repercussions we may face the finale of a story that amounts to the first man-made marine transgression.

REFERENCES

Attia, M. I. *Deposits in the Nile Valley and the Delta*. Geological Survey of Egypt, special publication, 1954.

Audebeau, C. "Note sur l'affaissement du nord du Delta égyptien depuis l'Empire romain." *Bull. Inst. d'Egypte,* 1 (1919), 118–34.

Ball, J. *Contribution to the Geography of Egypt*. Survey and Mines Dept., special publication, 1939.

———. *Egypt in the Classical Geographers*. Ed. by G. W. Murray. Survey of Egypt, special publication, 1942.

Butzer, K. W. "Environment and Human Ecology in Egypt during Predynastic and Early Dynastic Times." *Bull. Soc. Géogr. d'Egypte,* 32 (1959), 43–87.

———. "On the Pleistocene Shore Lines of the Arabs' Gulf, Egypt." *Journ. Geol.,* 68 (1960), 626–37.

Daressy, G. "Les Branches du Nil sous la XVIIIᵉ dynastie." *Bull. Soc. Géogr. d'Egypte,* 16:225–54, 293–329; 17:81–115, 189–223; 18:169–202 (1928–1934).

Fairbridge, R. W. "New Radiocarbon Dates of Nile Sediments." *Nature* (London), No. 4850 (1962a), pp. 108–10.

———. "World Sea-Level and Climatic Changes." *Quaternaria,* 6 (1962b), 111–34.

———. "Nile Sedimentation above Wadi Halfa during the last 20,000 Years." *Kush,* 11 (1963), 96–107.

Fourtau, R. "Contribution à l'étude de dépôt nilotiques." *Mém. Inst. d'Egypte,* 8 (1915), 57–94.

Hume, W. F. *Geology of Egypt,* Vol. 1. Survey of Egypt, special publication, 1925.

Judd, J. W. "Second Report on a Series of Specimens of the Deposits of the Nile Delta Obtained by Boring Operations Undertaken by the Royal Society." *Proc. R. Soc.,* 61 (1897), 32–40.

Montasir, A. H. "Ecology of Lake Manzala." *Bull. Fac. Science, Egypt. Univ.,* No. 12 (1937).

Saad, S. I., and Sami, S. "Studies of Pollen and Spores Content of Nile Delta Deposits (Berenbal Region)." *Pollen et Spores,* 9 (1967), 467–503.

Sandford, K. S. "Paleolithic Man and Nile Valley in Upper and Middle Egypt." *Univ. Chicago Orient. Inst. Pubn.,* No. 18 (1934).

Sandford, K. S., and Arkell, W. J. "Paleolithic Man and the Nile-Faiyum Divide." *Univ. Chicago Orient. Inst. Pubn.,* No. 10 (1929).

———. "Paleolithic Man and the Nile Valley and Upper Egypt." *Univ. Chicago Orient. Pubn.,* No. 17 (1933).

———. "Paleolithic Man and the Nile Valley in Lower Egypt." *Univ. Chicago Orient. Inst. Pubn.,* No. 46 (1939).

Shukri, N. M. "The Mineralogy of Some Nile Sediments." *Quart. J. Geol. Soc. London,* 105 (1950), 511–34; 106 (1950), 466–67.

———. "Mineral Analysis Tables of Some Nile Sediments." *Bull. Desert Inst. Egypt,* 1 (1951), 39–67.

Shukri, N. M., et al. "The Geology of the Mediterranean Coast between Rosetta and Bardia." *Bull. Inst. d'Egypte,* 37 (1956), 377–86, 395–427, 445–55.

Shukri, N. M., and Philip, G. "The Mineralogy of Some Recent Deposits in the Arish-Ghaza Area." *Bull. Fac. Science Univ. Cairo,* 35, (1960), 73–85.

Wassing, F. "Coastal Engineering Problems in the Delta Region of U.A.R., Memoranda *W1–W6*." Reports of U.N. Expert to the Department of Ports and Lighthouses, (1964).

Willcocks, W. *The Nile in 1904*. London, 1904.

Yousri, F. Studies on Four Wells Drilled in the River Nile Flood-Plain near Cairo. M.Sc. Thesis, *Cairo University,* 1962.

12. THE NILE CATCHMENT—TECHNOLOGICAL CHANGE AND AQUATIC BIOLOGY

E. Barton Worthington

The Nile catchment is shared by eight countries and hydrologically is among the best-known international rivers in the world. The aquatic ecosystems encompass two of the five major freshwater regions of Africa, the two being divided by the Murchison Falls and Semliki Rapids.

The controlled Nile is traced in this paper from mouth to source, since most of the stimulus for development has come from Egypt. This country has suffered land hunger at intervals in its history, and since 1800 population growth is well documented, approximately doubling each fifty years. To meet the needs of the growing population, major works of river control were started early in the nineteenth century. Now progressively more interest is being paid to the river's control by countries which hold the headwaters.

The five barrages of Egypt and the six Nile dams, only one of which is in Egypt, are sketched with reference to their purposes and their influences on the aquatic ecosystems. More control will certainly be effected in the future. The development of fisheries in relation to the works of river control, including the man-made lakes, is outlined.

It is concluded that

1. The holistic view of the Nile is illuminating, but in this study, by limitation to aquatic ecosystems, we see only one side of the crystal.
2. Every project has had to be undertaken with limited background knowledge; but this should not deter the scientist from a major part in decision-making.
3. In prediction the ecologist is rightly diffident, compared, for example,

with the engineer. We need more ecologists with the courage of their convictions.

4. Each project has one, or at most two, primary objects, it has also numerous other effects, but project plans are not generally equipped now to give the effects all due weight.

5. However, in spite of mistakes, the progressive steps in the control of the Nile provide an outstanding example of how the scientific and technical approach can open the door for international collaboration.

The Nile catchment includes the river Nile with its barrages, dams and reservoirs, all its tributaries, the great and small lakes and swamps, and the mountain streams from which its water originates. The aquatic ecosystem of this great complex shows examples of development without due regard to the possible benefits and malpractices of modern technology and also cases in which ecological considerations have been successfully applied. This ambitious case study will emphasize the importance of treating freshwater environments on the scale of entire catchment areas rather than individual water bodies such as particular lakes, rivers or reservoirs. It will also show the importance of linking developments affecting the aquatic ecosystems with other ecosystems on the land or even in the sea, for the influences of large-scale modern developments on a great river are rarely limited to the particular purpose for which each development was designed.

That development of the Nile catchment presents a truly international problem is vouched for by the fact that the river is shared by no fewer than eight countries. One thinks first of Egypt as the main receiving country, wholly dependent for its economy and the safety of its people on the controlled flow of the river. Next is the Sudan, both a receiver and giver since the northern Sudan depends largely on the river while the southern Sudan provides all the tributaries of the Bahr-el-Ghazal and some of those which flow to the Sobat and Blue Nile; moreover, it gives passage for the waters of the Bahr-el-Jebel and the Atbara. Ethiopia is the principal origin of water for the Atbara, Blue Nile and Sobat; and as such it has, by massive soil erosion, repeatedly renewed the Delta and the fertile soil of Middle and Upper Egypt—that is, until the High Dam was constructed at Aswan. The waters of the White Nile, on the other hand, flow from five countries— Kenya, Uganda, Tanzania, Congo (Kinshasha) and Rwanda, the first three sharing Lake Victoria and its tributaries, the last two sharing the Semliki system with Uganda (Fig. 12–1).

Technological changes which have influenced the Nile's ecosystem during the past century include the series of barrages designed to lift the water level at particular points and the dams designed to store water or to produce hydroelectric power. Their effects have been manifold, including barring the distribution of flora and fauna up and down the river and, more importantly, the creation of large man-made lakes. Coupled with the barrages and dams has been, in certain cases, the drainage of swamps to ensure more rapid runoff and the creation of intricate systems of canals and drains in the irrigated lands commanded by the barrages.

Another change has been the development of fisheries of great importance throughout much of the Nile catchment owing to the lack of animal protein in a country which has but a meager animal industry because of trypanosomiasis and other diseases.

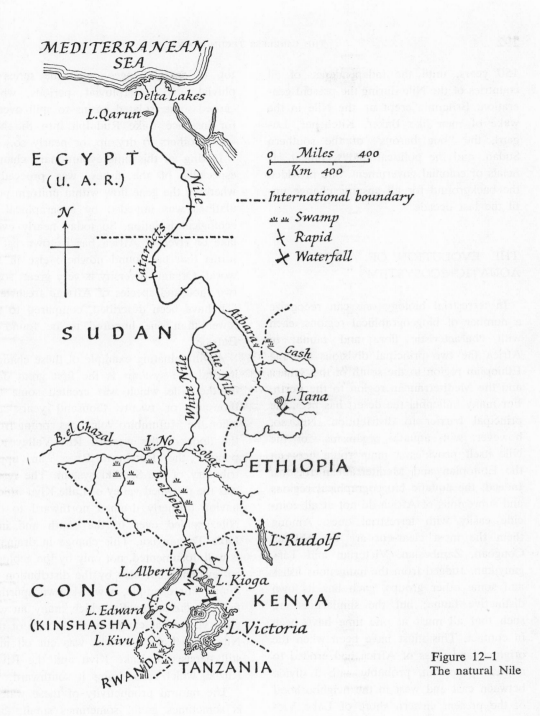

MEDITERRANEAN
SEA

Delta Lakes

L. Qarun

E G Y P T
(U. A. R.)

Nile

Cataracts

S U D A N

White Nile

Blue Nile

Atbara

Gash

L. Tana

B. el Ghazal

L. No

Sobat

B. el Jebel

ETHIOPIA

L. Rudolf

L. Albert

U G A N D A

L. Kioga

C O N G O

L. Edward

(KINSHASHA)

L. Kivu

KENYA

L. Victoria

RWANDA

TANZANIA

0   Miles   400

0   Km   400

------- International boundary

⊌⊌ Swamp

⅄ Rapid

⅃ Waterfall

Figure 12–1
The natural Nile

Transport has involved much technological change which, by bringing about massive human traveling, has had both positive and negative influences. The latter is particularly noticeable in the spread of schistosomiasis, now probably the most important human disease in the catchment area. The technology of transport has also allowed the importation and escape of certain alien species, including aquatic plants, which have caused great trouble and expense.

Pax Britannica made all technological changes possible. Gradually, during the last

150 years, until the independence of all countries of the Nile during the present generation, Britannia crept up the Nile in the wake of men like Baker, Kitchener, Lugard, the "bog barons" of the southern Sudan, and the political and technical officials of colonial government. She provided the background for all ensuing change until the last decade.

THE EVOLUTION OF AFRICAN AQUATIC ECOSYSTEMS

In terrestrial biology one can recognize a number of biogeographical regions, each with characteristic flora and fauna; in Africa the two principal divisions are the Ethiopian region to the south of the Sahara and the Mediterranean region to the north. For many millennia the desert has been the principal barrier to distribution. Not so, however, with aquatic organisms, for the Nile itself provides a main route between the Ethiopian and Mediterranean regions. Indeed, the aquatic biogeographical regions and subregions of Africa do not at all coincide easily with terrestrial ones. Among them the most clear-cut are the Nilotic, Congoan, Zambesian, Victorian and Tanganyikan. Judged from the indigenous fishes and some other groups, each has its own distinctive fauna; but the similarities are such that all must at one time have been in contact. This must have been when the original land mass of Africa had eroded to a great peneplain, probably with a divide between east and west in the neighborhood of the present eastern shore of Lake Victoria. Then came tectonic movements—the eastern and western Rift Valleys and the saucer-like depression of Lakes Victoria and Kioga between them were created. The original drainage pattern of consequent rivers was drastically altered and was further diverted and dammed by volcanic activities associated with the rift faulting. On top of such changes came the series of pluvial and interpluvial periods which caused some isolated basins to spill over—for instance Lake Rudolph into the Nile—and others to dry up, or nearly so.

During all this time evolutionary change, especially of the fishes, was proceeding wherever the gene flow within uniform populations was impeded by geographical or ecological isolation. So today nearly every lake or river of Africa has its own list of forms that are found nowhere else in the world. Organic diversity is very great; some two thousand species of African freshwater fish have been described, compared to the fewer than one hundred to be found in Europe.

An illuminating example of these changes in drainage systems is the first great dam on the Nile which was created some ten thousand or twenty thousand years ago when the Mufumbiro volcanoes sprang from the floor of the western Rift Valley and ponded the Rutchuru River, an upper tributary of the Semliki system. The result was the drowned valley of Lake Kivu which, having formerly drained northward to the Nile, spilled over to the south and into Lake Tanganyika. This change in drainage is well documented, not only by the geological evidence but also by the distribution of fauna. For example, a well-known sporting fish, *Barbus altianalis,* which many an angling visitor has caught at the source of the Nile from Lake Victoria, was cut off and still persists in Lake Kivu and the River Ruzizi, which now drains it southward.

The natural productivity of these waters is sometimes great, sometimes small, dictated by a combination of physical and biological factors which are dependent on this geological history. In general the deep lakes have a much lower productivity than the shallow ones, because in the tropics a permanent thermocline is generally formed at about 100 meters below the surface, locking the nutritive salts in the depths beneath. For this reason Lakes Tanganyika, Malawi and Edward have a much lower productivity per unit area than Lakes Kioga and George, which are so shallow that the nutrients are continually in circulation.

FAUNA AND FLORA OF THE NILE

The Nile catchment today includes two quite distinct aquatic regions, the Nilotic and the Victorian. The former extends from the Delta upstream to the Murchison Falls above Lake Albert on the Victoria Nile, and to the Semliki Rapids on the branch which drains from Lake Edward. Below these barriers the fauna of fishes is very rich in families and genera and includes important large predators such as the Nile perch (*Lates*) and the tiger fish (*Hydrocynus*). Above the barriers, i.e., in Lakes Kioga and Victoria and their tributaries and in Lakes Edward and George, the fish fauna are greatly impoverished in families and genera but with a wealth of closely related species, most of them unique to this part of the world, having come into existence through local speciation in recent geological times. The reasons for this great distinction between Nilotic and Victorian fauna make a long story, but fossil evidence shows that once the fauna of the whole Nile was one. Disaster overcame the lakes at the headwaters, probably through drought during an interpluvial period, though some say it was through the heat and toxic chemicals of volcanic activity; and most of the original fauna was destroyed. The present fauna of the Victorian region, poor in families and genera but rich in species, has come into being largely through very recent evolution.

Associated with this difference in fauna is another factor of importance, namely the length of the food chains. In the Nilotic region, with abundant and varied predators, a typical food chain may consist of six links —from microflora through microfauna; insect larvae; small, intermediate and large fish; and finally man and crocodile, competing at the top. At each link productivity is reduced to about one-sixth, so that one cannot expect very heavy fish crops from such waters—20 or 30 kilograms per hectare would be good. By comparison the principal food chain of Lake George is simple: algae to *Tilapia* fish to man; this vast, natural fishpond has one of the highest natural productivity rates known anywhere in the world—over 100 kilograms of fish per hectare.

In all such matters there is much scope for research and for argument. For instance, specialists are by no means agreed whether the presence of crocodiles is good or bad for fish production. Apart from damage they cause to nets, some conclude that, by eating more piscivorous than herbivorous fishes, they allow a larger crop to be available to man (Cott, 1961). However, a quirk of geological history which obliterated the original fishes of Lakes Edward and George also obliterated the crocodiles which, as shown by fossils, formerly inhabited these lakes. Thus a natural experiment was started and the ecologists can now draw the results. The present-day fish of Lakes Edward and George are closely comparable to those of similar habitats in Lake Victoria; but the fisheries of the former, in the absence of crocodiles, run at a consistently higher level of productivity than those of the latter, in the presence of crocodiles.

This, however, is no good argument for the persistent destruction of the crocodile populations which has been going on throughout Africa during the past twenty years. The crocodile has proved to be an important natural resource in its own right with a high value in the skin trade. Moreover, in certain national parks, notably that surrounding Murchison Falls in Uganda, the crocodile, though even here sadly reduced in numbers by poachers, is a major attraction to tourists. Indeed, so important is the crocodile in certain conditions, that I am sure we shall see crocodile farms being established soon, and from these it should be possible to restock certain waters where this reptile could, or should, be a resource of importance.

Another interesting problem in productivity, obvious to those who have visited national parks within the Nile system, relates to the hippopotamus. To what extent do these animals benefit fish production by eating vegetation on the land by night and dumping it as faeces into the water by day? Like the crocodile, the hippopotamus was exceedingly abundant through all the upper Nile catchment until about thirty years ago, when its population was drastically reduced. However, protection in certain national parks and reserves has shown how rapidly this great animal, which has few enemies, can multiply in favorable conditions. The result is that, to avoid gross overpopulation by hippos, some thousands are now cropped each year from the reserved areas and contribute significantly to local meat supplies. By consuming great quantities of swamp and grass vegetation which would otherwise be wasted, the hippo is a most useful creature. I hope we shall see hippo rearing encouraged and a policy adopted of restocking many of the swampy coastlines, such as those around Lake Victoria and Lake Kioga, in the double interest of providing meat supplies and improving fisheries.

THE CONTROLLED NILE FROM MOUTH TO SOURCE (Fig. 12–2)

HYDROLOGY AND POPULATION

From the hydrological point of view the Nile is the best known of all big rivers, at least in its lower reaches. Four or five millennia ago, the ancient Egyptians recorded river levels on nilometers, some of which can still be seen today. Passing to more recent times there is a fairly complete series of maximum and minimum annual levels from 641 A.D. to 1450 A.D., and onward with interruptions, on the Roda Island gauge in Cairo. At Aswan, levels have been recorded since 1870. During the present century, especially since World War I, the study of the Nile and its tributaries has been greatly intensified. This study has been the great work of Dr. H. E. Hurst who, having handed it over to his Egyptian colleagues many years ago, at the age of eighty-eight, is still retained as hydrological advisor to the U.A.R. and spends a month there each year. His ten volumes and twenty-one supplements on the Nile Basin (1931–1966), written with various collaborators, will continue as the standard work for many years to come.

In the ancient past and until the present century, control of the Nile was the concern of only one country, Egypt, whose population has always been almost totally dependent on the river. We are accustomed to think of overpopulation problems as a modern trouble, but Egypt, which has been since time immemorial one of the richest and at the same time one of the smallest countries —the inhabited area even today is only the size of a large English county—has been through it before. Indeed, the history of ancient Egypt shows cycles of prosperity followed by disaster, and there is not much doubt that they were accompanied by, and perhaps caused by, big increases in population.

The population of Egypt at the beginning of the nineteenth century was estimated at about 2.5 million, but by 1850 it had doubled to 5 million. The first modern census of 1897 gave a figure of 9.75 million, and by 1950 it was put at 19 million. The latest census of 1960 gave a total of almost

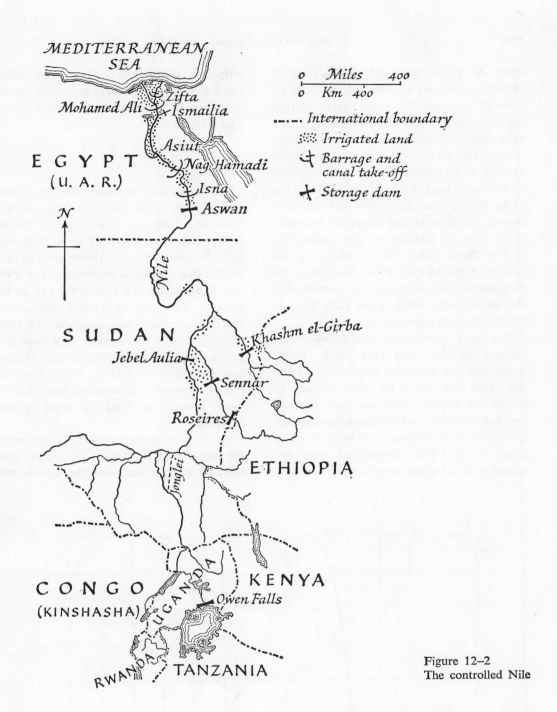

Figure 12–2
The controlled Nile

26 million. The population seems to have about doubled each half century, with the rate of increase showing a still steeper upward trend recently. The density on the arable land is now about 730 per square kilometer.

THE BARRAGES

Early in the nineteenth century, Mohammed Ali Pasha, a farsighted man, became governor of Egypt. He started the great series of barrages which function not to store water but to lift the level of the river in order to command a system of canals at all times of the year. The canal system started the changeover from the old basin or annual "slosh" irrigation to perennial irrigation, so that instead of one crop, two, three or even more crops a year could be grown on the same land. Mohammed Ali built the Delta Barrage just below (north) Cairo to control the Rosetta and Damietta branches of the Nile. Its architecture was reminiscent of a medieval castle, but it served well and was not replaced until 1940. Since then the Mohammed Ali Barrage has commanded the whole Delta, aided by the Zifta Barrage on the Damietta branch.

The next barrage, at Asiut, was constructed in 1902 and enlarged in 1938; it provides for perennial irrigation in Middle Egypt with one of its canals running as far as the Fayum. Next the Isna Barrage was built in 1908, and the latest barrage was completed at Nag-Hamadi in 1930. Both of these are in Upper Egypt and were designed to improve the water supply for basin

irrigation. Their function can now be altered since the High Dam at Aswan enables the whole of Egypt to change over to perennial irrigation.

ASWAN

We must now consider the great dams which have a function entirely different from the barrages. The need for storing Nile water when the river is at high stage with the Blue Nile and Atbara both in flood so that more could be available at low stage, was appreciated well before the end of last century. That mighty granite edifice, the first Aswan Dam, was completed in 1902. The capacity of its reservoir was more than doubled by the first heightening in 1912 and was multiplied fivefold in 1934. The final dam contained a little more than half as much masonry as does the great pyramid of Giza.

After each storage period the sluices of the old Aswan Dam were opened to drain most of the lake and wash the accumulated

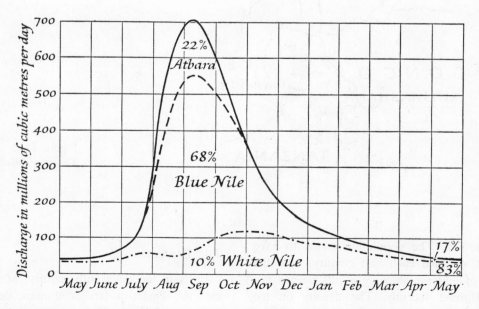

Figure 12–3 The average flow of the Atbara, Blue Nile, and White Nile. The percentages relate to peak flow and minimum flow (From H. E. Hurst)

silt downstream, much of it deposited in the basins where agriculture benefited from this annual contribution of fertile topsoil. The new High Dam, impounding behind it the vast Lake Nasser of some 5,000 square kilometers which will never be drained, must cause a revolution in Egyptian irrigation. Practically all the fertile silt from Ethiopia will be deposited in the lake, not on the agricultural land below the dam. This will have the disadvantage that the silt will build up the floor of the lake instead of the agricultural land, and the annual addition of nutrients from it will have to be made up in other ways. Nevertheless, the extra water in store and the reduction of silt in the irrigation canals will allow a total changeover from basin to perennial irrigation as well as a significant increase in the irrigated area.

Although the great engineering works on the Nile are thought of primarily as providers of water for irrigation, they also function in flood control, which is of supreme importance in a flat country that lies at a level below that of its waterways. The disasters of last century, particularly in 1863 and 1878, when breaches in the Damietta branch caused heavy loss of life in the Delta, are no longer fresh in people's minds, but there have been several potentially dangerous occasions since then. In the autumn of 1946 when the Blue Nile and Atbara were having their second-highest flood on record (Fig. 12–3), I happened to visit the Physical Department in Cairo. For several nights few of the engineers had slept because they were lining the banks with sandbags. All available water storage space was filled to capacity, and yet the Nile kept rising. Telegrams and telephone calls poured in from minute to minute. On that occasion the upstream pressure was relieved by the river flooding over its banks below Khartoum and little damage was caused, but the threat brought home the need for strict working of every control point on the

best hydrological advice. Now the Aswan High Dam provides storage against flood control as well as for irrigation and for that reason is never allowed to fill up. But woe betide Egypt if ever its storage capacity should be overstretched before a season of exceptional Blue Nile and Atbara flow.

EFFECTS ON AQUATIC LIFE

In this paper I am concerned primarily with the effect of control on aquatic ecosystems, which can be divided into the influences on the waters of the irrigated lands on the one hand and of the impounded lakes on the other.

In the past, one of the biological problems of the canals has been the growth of water weeds, nurtured by the deposition of fertile silt, and thereby providing an ecosystem highly favorable to those kinds of water snail which are the intermediate hosts of schistosomes. Schistosomiasis in its urinary and intestinal forms has been, and still is, the bane of Egypt and of most other irrigated lands in warm climates. Vast tonnages of copper sulphate and other herbicides and molluscicides have been dissolved in the canals of Egypt to partially control the disease. This has killed or starved out most of the fish and other aquatic life as well as snails. Let us hope that the change in quality of the canal waters, and particularly the absence of silt, consequent on their storage in Lake Nasser, will help create a new approach to schistosomiasis control.

The great basins of Upper and formerly also of Middle and Lower Egypt, the last of which will disappear now that the new Aswan Dam is in operation, were important as temporary sites for aquatic life. Submerged for a period under a foot or two of water, they produced quantities of algae, a rich insect fauna and rapidly-growing fish crops from the fry washed in with the irrigation water. The algae may well have contributed to fertility through the fixation of atmospheric nitrogen; the insects were mostly eaten by fish which, in their turn, were collected and consumed by the people as the waters drained away. From a health point of view, although some medical authorities consider that the basins contributed in the past to epidemics of malaria in Upper Egypt transmitted by *Anopheles gambiae*, the aquatic habitats of the basins did not last long enough to be a major hazard. Perennial irrigation, however, provides permanent aquatic ecosystems which encourage the debilitating, though not usually fatal, diseases of schistosomiasis and hookworm.

Interest in the aquatic ecosystem of Lake Nasser itself centers around the potential fishery, and here, as in all other large man-made lakes, there are great opportunities for the ecologists to predict the changes involved by impoundment. Lake Nasser is unique among the great man-made lakes in that, being formed largely on desert, there are no problems of submerged trees which in other areas interfere seriously with fish netting. The lake provides new opportunity for the Nilotic fauna which in Lake Albert and Lake No is already well adapted to lake conditions. However, the interests of fishery development and of the irrigation engineers may sometimes come into conflict. When I was at the High Dam during its construction, the engineers were talking about the possibility of saving a huge amount of water, which would otherwise be evaporated from the surface of Lake Nasser, by attempting to keep it covered with a film of cetyl alcohol. This technique has been used effectively on small reservoirs, but the practicality of its application to a huge water area is doubtful. Although cetyl alcohol is nontoxic to aquatic organisms, to break the gaseous exchange between hydrosphere and atmosphere must have a deleterious influence on biological productivity and fisheries.

Another interesting interaction between biology and hydrology may perhaps be predicated in the growth of emergent aquatic vegetation around the margins of Lake Nasser. If, as seems possible, vegetation grows with vigor to form a floating mat, it could cover hundreds of square kilometers. According to information provided by Professor Kassas in this volume (see Discussion following Chapter 14), transpiration from experimental plots of sudd in the Sudan was much higher than evaporation from equal areas of free water surface. Any increase of water loss over a significant proportion of the area of Lake Nasser would upset calculations concerning the use of the stored water.

THE WHITE NILE

The dam at Jebel Aulia on the White Nile was completed in 1937. Its function is to hold back part of the White Nile while the Blue Nile is in flood; but since the valley above Jebel Aulia is very flat and open (at maximum capacity the reservoir extends some 480 kilometers upstream), a great deal of water is lost by evaporation and seepage. Fortunately, through the excellent scientists available in the Sudan during the past thirty years, the Jebel Aulia Lake has been studied from the viewpoints of insects of medical importance and the other fauna and flora. The fisheries have proved to be highly productive and profitable, and, once the lake had settled down to its annual regime, the health risk from mosquitoes breeding along its margin was less than had been feared.

The Jebel Aulia dam undoubtedly impedes the movement of migratory fish. A fish ladder was installed, but it does not provide good access, and numerous Nile perch remain below the dam instead of proceeding upstream to their spawning areas. From the viewpoint of commercial fisheries this may not be bad, for the scarcity of large predators in the Jebel Aulia reservoir is likely to result in larger crops of herbivorous and microphagous species.

The whole complex of the White Nile upstream of Jebel Aulia has great possibilities of control and wide implications for agriculture, fisheries, and hydroelectric power. Before the High Dam at Aswan became practical politics, the hydrology of this region was studied in detail by H. E. Hurst (Vol. 7 of *The Nile Basin* and elsewhere). The urgency for such control works has been reduced by the huge storage in Lake Nasser, but there is no doubt that proposals will be made again in the future, though perhaps with rather more emphasis on the advantages to the countries of the upper Nile and rather less on Egypt's role.

OWEN FALLS

At the outfall of Lake Victoria itself, her Majesty Queen Elizabeth pressed a button in April 1954, and thereby made the dream of a great British Colonial Secretary come true: "What fun to make the immemorial Nile begin its journey by driving through a turbine!" (Winston Churchill, 1908).

The Owen Falls Dam, the first control work on the White Nile system which is in the interest of the local countries as well as of Egypt, has hydrolectric power as its primary function but, at the same time, controls the outflow of Lake Victoria, which it thereby converts into a reservoir of 67,000 square kilometers. This project was put forward in 1946 in connection with the first ten-year Uganda development plan (Worthington, 1947), and was designed to bring the requirements of Uganda into line with those of Egypt.

The effect of the Owen Falls Dam on the aquatic flora and fauna was to convert the partial barrier of the Ripon Falls, now under water, into a total barrier. The question of installing a fish ladder was carefully considered, but the biologists advised against it on the grounds that only a few species of

fish of minor ecological and economic importance were capable of surmounting the former Ripon Falls.

THE MURCHISON FALLS

By 1966, the rising demand for electricity in Uganda, together with a quantity exported under arrangement with Kenya, indicated that the full capacity of 175,000 KW at Owen Falls would soon be needed. Accordingly, following site studies, the government authorized a second dam and installation at Bujagali, not far downstream from Owen Falls, where no amenity interests were involved. However, in July 1968 it was announced that the next major scheme would not be at Bujagali but at Murchison Falls, in the center of a world-famed National Park. This raised a storm of protest, for the ecological effects of the project would be substantial, and the Murchison Falls, in its natural setting, is perhaps the most important tourist attraction that Uganda possesses.

Since 1962, the climate of Lake Victoria catchment has been exceptionally wet and the discharge over the Falls has been high, averaging around 1500 cumecs. Previously, for some forty years, the average discharge was less than half this, around 600 cumecs, and it must be assumed that, in due course, the river will return to similar low flows. The full project provides for nine tenths of the average low flow to pass through turbines, leaving only one tenth to flow over the Falls. The World Bank has recently indicated that it would need a thorough assessment of the ecological and other ancillary effects before deciding on the application for finance.

Murchison Falls offers a challenge to the engineer far greater than five other sites on the Upper Nile in Uganda, two in the north and three in the south, any one of which could produce more electricity than the Owen Falls Dam. If the Murchison

Falls scheme is in fact pushed through, it will be a sad thing for Uganda, an example of the "ribbon-cutting complex" referred to by M. Batisse on page 254.

THE BLUE NILE

On the Blue Nile, the Sennar Dam, which was completed in 1925, serves the Sudan more than Egypt. Its main function is to provide water for the Gezira irrigation scheme which still provides the basis for the Sudan's economy. It does this by raising the water level to command the Gezira Canal during the time of high Nile and by storing water in the period of falling flood for use in the season of low water. A fish ladder was originally provided but was soon destroyed and has never been rebuilt.

Further upstream, near the Sudano-Ethiopian border, is the Roseires Dam and reservoir. This was completed in 1966 and has the primary purpose of greatly increasing the Blue Nile storage, previously possible only at Sennar, and also has a hydroelectric installation. The reservoir is over 80 kilometers long with a maximum depth of about 50 meters and is under study by the hydrobiological research unit of the University of Khartoum. The water stratified soon after filling, with complete deoxygenation of the lower layers, and in 1967 there was a heavy fish mortality when deoxygenation affected all the water temporarily. An interesting biological event here has been the elimination of large beds of the Nile oyster (*Etheria eliptica*) which have been smothered by enormous quantities of silt deposited in the upper reaches of the lake. This oyster, however, has almost no economic importance.

FISHERIES

Fisheries throughout the Nile system have always been important. Even those inhabit-ants of the Delta who have access to the sea get a large proportion of their fish from the Delta lakes which, in production per unit area, were among the most productive fisheries in the world until the High Dam at Aswan reduced the flow of nutrients to these lakes, thereby damaging their fisheries (see Carl J. George's paper, Chapter 10, this volume).

There have been setbacks such as this example and the fish kill at Roseires through deoxygenation mentioned above, but generally in the Nile basin flooding land for water storage leads to higher usable production from the area concerned. Desert, savannah and swamp, which are the kinds of land used for this purpose, are far less productive in terms of human needs than water with its fisheries and opportunities for transport. Of course when developed agricultural land is flooded as in the case of the Wadi Halfa agricultural settlement now under the waters of Lake Nasser, and the agriculture of the Zambezi's floodwater land submerged or ruined by that river's control at Kariba, as described in the paper by Dr. Scudder in this volume (Chapter 13), there is a different story to tell.

INTRODUCED AND INDIGENOUS METHODS

European methods of fishery technology and fishery management began to penetrate Egypt in the latter part of the nineteenth century. Upstream of Khartoum, however, the fisheries, though they had undoubtedly existed in almost every lake, river and swamp since time immemorial, relied entirely on indigenous methods until this century and, in most of the waters, until after about 1930. Many of these indigenous fishing methods, based as they were on local materials, were efficient. The combination of many varieties of basket trap, fished alone or in association with seines made of papyrus stems or banana leaves, with fish weirs across the rivers, and even something similar to the trawl, reveal a surprising knowledge of fish ecology. One fishing tribe, the Luo of Lake Victoria, had separate names for many kinds of fish, and the distinction of native names gave clues to scientific distinction between closely related species. It was the distinction by Luo fishermen, for example, of two kinds of *Tilapia*, which they called *ngege* and *nibiru*, which led to the discovery in 1927 of *Tilapia esculenta* in spite of the fact that this species had been eaten on the breakfast and dinner tables of Nairobi for decades.

The technology of boat building throughout the Nile system was likewise locally adapted to available materials: the papyrus-bundle craft of ancient Egypt, for instance, had its counterpart in the papyrus-bundle fishing canoe of the Luo, although there is every reason to believe that this came from independent invention rather than from culture contact.

When modern fishing nets of imported material were introduced to the upper Nile and the lakes, the results were often dramatic in that the catch of fish per unit effort was increased manyfold. Some of the indigenous methods survived. One was even exported, for during the war we started a food fishery for freshwater perch in British lakes based on a Luo design of nonreturn trap; this still combines as a means of controlling perch in many British waters. Of the methods imported to the upper Nile, the gill net of hemp or cotton twine, which consists of about five inches of mesh stretched, which is used mainly for *Tilapia*, was the most important. Sometimes it has led to serious overfishing, the Kavirondo Gulf of Lake Victoria providing a classic example.

In 1905 a Dutchman introduced the gill net to the northeast corner of Lake Victoria, and it was quickly taken up by the native fishermen. To begin with, the new fishery was very productive, and each net during one night in the water caught an average of about 30 fish. By the 1920's, however, this fishing index had dropped alarmingly to 10 or even less. This could be expected following exploitation of an almost virgin population of fish, but how much further would it drop? To find the answer a fishery survey of Lake Victoria was organized in 1927 (Graham, 1929). By then the index in the Kavirondo Gulf had dropped as low as 5. The survey lasted almost a year, used a tug as a research vessel, and examined the lake in all its parts, though concentrating especially on the Kavirondo Gulf. I was privileged to be a member of this survey. Our recommendations were designed to conserve the stock and maintain a permanently productive fishery. The recommendations were acted on only in part, and about 1940 the fishing index had dropped further, to 2. It is now running at a little more than 1 per net per night, and such a low return continues to be economic, since hemp and cotton were replaced by nylon, which lasts much longer.

RESEARCH

This example of what may result from the introduction of modern technology is fortunately not typical of all the Nile waters. For many of them the ecology was studied and recommendations for fishery management were made before the introduction of modern techniques. A major recommendation of the Lake Victoria fishery survey was that a permanent hydrobiological and fishery research institute should be established on Lake Victoria. After a respectable gestation period of twenty years, such an institute was opened at Jinja in 1947, and the era of intensive team research inaugurated. Meanwhile, however, fishery surveys had been conducted on most of the other great lakes (Worthington, 1929 and 1931). During these surveys, which were conducted during two expeditions from Cambridge, England, the physiography, depths, shorelines and biological content of these lakes were determined, and many kinds of European fishing gear were tried out for the first time. The most successful methods, adaptable to local peoples with simple technology, were various kinds of gill net, seine net and long lines. Based on the recommendations of these surveys, fisheries using such techniques were developed and supervised by a growing cadre of fishery officers.

In the Sudan there were also developments. The Game Department took a particular interest in fisheries and in 1953 a hydrobiological research unit was established at the University of Khartoum. Egypt, meanwhile, had built up a network of fishery research, first under the direction of British scientists, later under their Egyptian colleagues. The mullet and *Tilapia* fisheries of the Delta lakes were developed with appropriate nets and craft on sound conservation lines to very high productivity; the fish production of Lake Qarun and in many other Egyptian freshwaters was stimulated by stocking with mullet fry and elvers. The changes in quality and quantity of water now reaching these lakes, consequent on the new Aswan Dam, are now causing changes to these fisheries, mostly, it seems, for the worse.

Now there is opportunity for more sophisticated research, and in this connection I would like to refer to one of the research projects under the International Biological Programme, which is currently operating on Lake George at the headwaters on the Semliki branch of the Nile. Here, as a joint project between Uganda and the United Kingdom, a group of young scientists, financed through the Royal Society, are devoting a number of years to a comprehensive study of biological productivity. Lake George has been chosen because of its very high fish production, and the new research is designed to discover the reasons for this production rate. Thus it is concerned with primary production by algae,

secondary production by zooplankton and insects, as well as fish studies. This is not the only IBP project on fisheries on the Nile catchment. For instance, by arrangements with FAO, the intention is to include within the IBP the research components of several United Nations Development Program schemes, one of which is now devoted to the productivity and fishery potential of the open waters of Lake Victoria, basing itself on the Research Institute at Jinja.

INTRODUCTION OF EXOTIC SPECIES

The contrast between the fish fauna of Lakes Victoria and Kioga, with no large predators which could be caught on a rod, and the Nilotic fauna below the Murchison Falls, where such fish were abundant, stimulated repeated suggestions that the Nile perch should be introduced up above. These were resisted by most biologists on the grounds that damage might be done to the economic fisheries, but in the end the introduction took place, first to Lake Kioga about 1957 and to Lake Victoria a year or two later. The result to date in Lake Kioga has been somewhat unexpected. A flourishing fishery with gill nets and long lines had been developed there and the annual catch had crept up to about 11,000 tons. As the voracious Nile perch, each capable of growing to fifty or one hundred pounds, rapidly colonized the lake, the prospect looked poor for the other fishes. During the past seven years, however, the total catch of other fish has continued to increase, and on top of that the catch of Nile perch has risen rapidly to more than 12,000 tons a year. If this remarkable production is maintained, it will confound the Jeremiahs, and the numerous fishermen of Lake Victoria, where the Nile perch is taking longer to get established, will look forward with some optimism. These introductions of Nile perch to the upper lakes provide major experiments in economic ecology, and warrant close and continuous scientific examination so that in due course the full story can be told. On the one hand, there is substantial and almost immediate economic gain; on the other hand, there is the unpredictable effect of a very large and rapacious predator on the species flocks of Cichlidae and other endemic forms.

A more gloomy story must be told about the introduction of the water hyacinth (*Eichornia crassipides*). A native of South America, this ornamental plant is assumed to have escaped in Africa from garden pools or aquaria. It spread with rapidity in southern Africa and caused extensive damage to fisheries and water transport by blocking up the waterways. During the 1950's it invaded the Congo system where it flourished exceedingly, became a hazard to transport and made fishing impossible over hundreds of square kilometers. Millions of dollars were expended in attempts at control. There were grim forebodings as to what this pest would do if it got across the watershed into Lake Victoria. In fact *Eichornia* has not yet reached Lake Victoria, but it appeared in the Nile below the Sudd region about 1958 and vast quantities soon accumulated in the Jebel Aulia Lake where it caused great trouble to the water engineers by partially blocking the sluices. Fortunately it has proved possible to get the pest under some form of control with hormone weed-killers, but their use involves continuous, expensive and troublesome operations. Whether there are ecological side effects of importance has yet to be determined.

THE MEDITERRANEAN

There is one other matter in which Nile control has an important bearing on fisheries, namely, on fisheries in the sea. In the old days of the natural Nile, large quantities of water, well-laden with silt and nutrient salts, poured across the Delta into the eastern Mediterranean which, except for this annual fertilization, is a sea of low biological productivity. There was a sizable fishery, particularly in the inshore waters near the Delta and up the Levant coast. Nile control steadily reduced the supply of nutrients; and the situation was complicated by the Suez Canal, which allowed the passage of some Red Sea water and some Red Sea fauna into the Mediterranean. Now the Aswan High Dam has cut off the supply of water and nutrients almost completely. The Levant fishery is at a low ebb. To replace the water, which of course continues to be evaporated from the eastern Mediterranean, the flow of water from the Red Sea along the Canal has increased. This might be expected to enhance the invasion of the Mediterranean by Red Sea fauna, but the partial blockage and consequent silting and shallowing of the Canal, caused by the Israel-Arab troubles, has so far delayed this effect.

This is a complex of man-made change which is scientifically of deep interest and economically of importance to a number of countries which are concerned in the eastern Mediterranean fishery.[1]

CONCLUSIONS

What are the main lessons to be learned from this multiple case history?

The first conclusion is that, by limiting this paper to aquatic ecosystems, and not at the same time taking full account of the interactions between the control of the Nile and terrestrial ecology, we have seen only one side of the crystal. The terrestrial ecology which also needs to be considered includes the wild lands and tame lands. It includes animal industry, plant industry and

---

[1] The IBP plans to convene an international meeting to discuss all aspects of the problem and to recommend a course of action. Some of these changes are considered in detail in the papers in this book by Dr. Carl George (Chapter 10) and Professor M. Kassas (Chapter 11).

irrigated agriculture, and it includes human ecology, that is, the activity and inactivity of the human being in health and disease. Human ecology in turn includes the tourist industry, which is of ever-growing importance to international development.

We cannot go into all these matters here, but a second conclusion arises, namely that every project in Nile control has had to be undertaken with a strictly limited background of knowledge. As a scientist who has participated in development I have sometimes found it positively frightening to make decisions which will affect the lives of millions of people when the basic facts were unknown. It felt a bit like writing the conclusions of a scientific paper before settling down to do the research!

A third conclusion is concerned with prediction. Here we have a rather marked difference between the approach of the engineer and that of the ecologist, for engineers *must* predict the future of the works they create, otherwise they could not start the designs. Ecologists are rather apt to say that prediction is hardly worth the paper it is written on because there will always be so many unknown factors.

Each of the projects of Nile control, from Mohammed Ali's barrage onward, involved many kinds of prediction, concerning not only the future of the engineering works, but their effects on land and water use, agriculture, health and social change. In developing countries, at least, there will never be enough funds or enough scientists to cover all aspects of information needed for thorough prediction, so it seems to me that the art of the ecologist is to pinpoint those features of the total ecosystem where the limited effort can most effectively be applied. We need more ecologists with the courage of their convictions.

A fourth conclusion derives from every major work of Nile control and is similar to that brought out by Dr. Thayer Scudder and Professor Gilbert White in their papers, namely that in the original design and working out of projects the viewpoint has been unduly narrow. Usually there are but one or two primary objectives, especially irrigation, or hydroelectric power or both—and obviously the designers, financers and executors must keep these to the fore. However, every project influences a great many other subjects which may be of general importance to the country concerned or of overriding importance to small groups of people: they have often to do with food-producing activities such as fisheries and agriculture, or with health. Each project, moreover, brings up new opportunities such as cultivation on the drawdown margins of a reservoir. The existing system of planning, however well intentioned, is not generally equipped to give all such matters due weight.

When all is said and done, however, there is still a fifth conclusion, that the progressive steps in the control of the Nile during the seventy years or so since Sir William Willcox presented his plan for the first Aswan Dam, provide an outstanding example of how the scientific and technical approach can open the door for international collaboration. This history presents a sequence, from the collection of basic knowledge about the river's hydrology, chemistry, and biology (albeit sometimes meager), the working-out of projects, international agreement, financing, construction and finally adaptation to the new regime. It is surely not too much to hope that, under the independent countries which now own the catchment, the future may hold opportunities for ecology and international development no less than those demonstrated by the past.

REFERENCES

Balls, W. L. In a contribution to a conference on Middle East Agricultural Development, Cairo, 1944. Sponsored and published by Middle East Supply Centre, 10 Sharia Tolumbat, Cairo, 1944.

Churchill, Winston S. *My African Journey.* London, 1908.

Cott, H. B. "Scientific Results of an Enquiry into the Ecology and Economic Status of the Nile Crocodile." *Trans. Zool. Soc. London,* 29, (4) (1961).

Graham, M. *The Victoria Nyanza and Its Fisheries.* London: Crown Agents, 1929.

Hurst, H. E., *et al. The Nile Basin.* 10 vols. and 21 supplements. Cairo, 1931–66.

Jonglei Investigation. Report in 4 vols. plus Introduction and Index. Sudan Government, 1954.

Worthington, E. B. *Fishery Surveys of Lakes Albert, Kioga, Edward, George, etc.* London: Crown Agents, 1929, 1931.

———. *A Development Plan for Uganda.* Entebbe, Uganda, 1947.

13. ECOLOGICAL BOTTLENECKS AND THE DEVELOPMENT OF THE KARIBA LAKE BASIN*

Thayer Scudder

When it reached its maximum extent in 1963, Lake Kariba on the Zambezi River was the world's largest artificial reservoir with a surface area of approximately 2000 square miles and a storage capacity of over 120 million acre feet.

The total population displaced was about 57,000 people. To provide new occupations for these people the government of Northern Rhodesia made an ambitious attempt to develop lake fisheries while local extension officers in the resettlement areas tried to improve agriculture through intensification, cashcropping and the expansion of cattle husbandry. A major problem confronting planners was the lack of knowledge of the ecological implications of the new lake. In my paper I wish to examine some of these as they relate to subsequent

---

* The material in this paper was originally published in different form as "The Ecological Hazards of Making a Lake," by Thayer Scudder in *Natural History*, Copyright © 1969. The American Museum of Natural History.

This paper is based on information gathered by my colleague, Dr. Elizabeth Colson, and myself, in 1956–57, 1962–63, 1965 and 1967 as part of our long-term study of those Gwembe Tonga who were relocated in connection with the Kariba Dam scheme. It is not intended to be an exhaustive overview of all the ecological implications of Kariba for the dislocated population. Indeed, certain important topics have been intentionally omitted. One of these is the health implications of resettlement on the people and of the formation of Kariba on the distribution and severity of schistosomiasis, malaria and human trypanosomiasis. This omission is a serious one. In large part it results from the inadequacy of medical research carried out within the Kariba Lake Basin before, during and following dam construction.

developments. Specifically, I will examine the present depressed fisheries in terms of the appearance and spread of the aquatic water fern *Salvinia auriculata* and the behavior of fish populations under the new lacustrine conditions and in response to partial bush clearing. I will also discuss the response of the tsetse species *Glossina morsitans* to inundation and the implications of this response for cattle keeping.

Because of insufficient land, the carrying capacity of the resettlement areas under existing techniques of cultivation was exceeded for the relocated people. In this case the planners were well aware of the ecological implication of overcultivation, overgrazing and clearance of catchment areas and riverbanks. Here their problem was not lack of knowledge (as was the case with the lake itself) but rather an inability to produce ecologically acceptable systems of land use which were also acceptable to the farmers. Today, no farmers practice the recommended crop rotation and very few apply fertilizer or manures. Extensive clearing, even down to the edge of rivers, continues. Though the farmers themselves are also aware of the ecological implications of their actions, they find the ecologically adequate alternatives suggested by the government to be unacceptable for economic and other reasons. This example will stress the need for developing compromise systems that include both ecological and economic considerations. Needless to say, a workable ecological "solution" is worthless if unacceptable to the human population involved.

The formation of Lake Kariba in Central Africa began on December 2, 1958, when the sluice gates of the first dam across the Zambezi were closed. During the next few weeks the water rose rapidly; deserted villages 100 feet above the normal river level were inundated within two months. The subsequent rise was more gradual; the encroaching water did not reach the proposed shore line until the middle of 1963. With a storage capacity of approximately 130 million acre feet and a surface area of over 1700 square miles, the new reservoir was by far the largest man-made lake in the world. The first of the major African impoundments, its creation also initiated a trend which can be expected to play a major role in altering portions of the African landscape as well as the lives of millions of people.

Our first two studies were sponsored by the Rhodes-Livingstone Institute, now the Institute for Social Research of the University of Zambia. Though the Institute also provided assistance and hospitality during our more recent restudies, Dr. Colson's six-week visit in 1965 was financed with a grant from the Social Science Research Council, while my four-month visit in 1967 was financed partially by the Food and Agriculture Organization of the United Nations, with the rest of my support being provided by the California Institute of Technology. From the beginning, most of our research has been carried out within Gwembe District on the north bank of the Zambezi, although we also visited the Southern Rhodesian portions of the Middle Zambezi Valley in 1957 and 1963. Except where otherwise mentioned, however, the analysis in this paper relates to that portion of the Kariba Lake Basin and hinterland which lies in what was formerly Northern Rhodesia and is now the Republic of Zambia. The author takes sole responsibility for all views expressed.

Since the completion of the Kariba Dam, approximately 75,000 people, or one per cent of the population of Ghana, have been relocated in connection with the Volta Dam at Akosombo. In Egypt and the Sudan, over 100,000 people have been shifted as a result of the Aswan High Dam. When filled, the lakes backed up behind these dams will each have a surface area one and one half times as large as that of Lake Kariba, although their storage capacity will be slightly less. Looking to the future, we can expect all of the major African rivers, as well as many of the lesser ones, to be dammed within the next generation. At Kainji in northern Nigeria, the first dam on the Niger was sealed in 1968. Some 500 square miles in surface area, the new lake will probably fill within a single year, flooding an area which formerly contained the residences of approximately 50,000 people. In the Ivory Coast, construction on the Kossou Dam will begin early in 1969. Elsewhere, surveys currently being undertaken on other river systems, including the Senegal, Mono (Dahomey-Togo), Congo, Tana (Kenya), Kafue (Zambia), and Orange (southern Africa), can be expected to lay the basis for new dams. With only a few exceptions, new construction can be expected to lead to the inundation of large areas and the relocation of thousands of people.

The creation of major man-made lakes in Africa presents the scientist with an exceptional research opportunity. Provided appropriate studies are made before, during and after inundation, the impact of flooding on the physical and biotic environment, as well as on the lifeways of the associated human populations, can be monitored. Dam construction and population relocation, for example, accelerate change in certain areas of human behavior. During the months preceding and following resettlement, relocation also increases physiological, psychological, social and ideological stress among the populations involved (Scudder, 1968). The

behavioral scientist who wishes to study this change, and to learn how the population attempts to manage the accompanying stress in adjusting to a new habitat, is presented with what amounts to a quasi-laboratory situation. While obviously it is not possible to repeat the process of lake formation and relocation in the same area, it is possible to choose another river basin where approximately the same sequence of events is about to occur and to observe the processes of change there. Provided the studies involved are properly designed, executed and analyzed, it is my belief that they can make a major contribution to our understanding of human behavior.

While man-made lakes research in a wide range of disciplines, including meteorology, geophysics, hydrology, limnology and the biological and social sciences, can make major contributions to our understanding of what occurs when extensive areas are inundated, it also has important implications for regional development which could raise the living standards of millions of Africans. Although the primary purpose of African dam projects is usually the provision of hydroelectric power, they also provide an opportunity to improve flood control and transportation and to develop river and lake basins with a program which could include, for example, agriculture and fisheries, conservation areas and national parks, tourist and recreational facilities, and residential and industrial townships. To date, this opportunity has only been partially realized. Though the reasons involved are many and lie beyond the scope of this paper (Scudder, 1966a), it is obvious that one basic problem concerns our lack of knowledge of the ecological implications of large-scale man-made lakes as they relate to the development of the lake basin and its hinterland. In this paper I should like to review some of the events that accompanied the filling of Lake Kariba and comment on their implications for the lives of the residents of the area.

There is also another type of problem which I wish to stress, which relates to our inability to relate current ecological knowledge to human populations, in this case the 57,000 people relocated in connection with the Kariba scheme. While it is true that no ecological surveys of the lake basin or the relocation areas were initiated, let alone completed, prior to the decision to proceed with the construction of the dam in 1955, it was known that there was insufficient land, under the present system of agriculture, for the approximately 36,000 Tonga-speakers who required relocation on the north bank of the Zambezi. It was also known that their present agricultural practices would lead to serious erosion along the tributary systems and to inland degradation unless certain changes were made. While those changes suggested by government personnel made sense ecologically, they were unacceptable to the Tonga, so that today the type of erosion and degradation that was predicted is occurring in a number of areas. The problem arises because the land management system proposed by the agriculturalists was incompatible with the farming system and current values of the Tonga. For this reason the current predicament was quite predictable. What was needed from the beginning, and is still needed, was a compromise system which would not only be acceptable to the Tonga, but also would make sense ecologically.

ECOLOGICAL ASPECTS OF THE LAKE KARIBA FISHERIES

Since this topic has already been well documented in the literature, my intention in this section is to briefly summarize the situation, while referring the interested reader to more detailed sources.[1] On the north bank of the new lake the first Tonga

[1] For a recent though brief review on which I have drawn heavily in parts of this section, see Coulter (1967).

began to fish with gill nets as soon as impoundment began. Within a year a government survey reported 407 fishermen, with this number increasing to over 2000 in 1962. Using over four thousand gill nets, they caught an estimated 3000 short tons of fish during the year, with the 1963 estimated yield being nearly 4000 short tons. Throughout this rapid buildup, the Provincial Administration and the Departments of Fisheries, Forestry and Community Development played an important role.[2] In 1964, however, annual production dropped sharply (to 2100 short tons), and since then production has continued to drop,[3] with the lake supporting fewer than 500 fishermen during 1967. The reasons behind this decline are not connected with the fishing industry as such. Rather they are of a primarily ecological nature.

FISH POPULATIONS: DISTRIBUTION AND DENSITY

Before Kariba, the free-flowing Middle Zambezi was poor in fish species. Jackson (1961) listed 28 species as contrasted to over 100 species observed on the Middle Niger within the area to be flooded by the Kainji Dam. Furthermore, owing to a difficult environment with a short breeding season and predation by the tiger fish (*Hydrocynus vittatus*), especially during the period that the Zambezi was restricted to its primary channel, the density of most species was low.

During the years immediately after im-

[2] This is described in Scudder (1965), which deals with the development of the Kariba Lake fisheries through 1963.

[3] Although no statistics are available, the Chief Fisheries Officer is of the opinion that local consumption of fish, especially at the Siankandoba coal mine, is increasing (communication to E. Colson, 1968). Since some of the catch involved would not be exported through established markets, this increase is probably not reflected accurately in production figures. The decline in the number of fishermen, however, is well documented, while current yields per fisherman are low in comparison with 1963.

poundment, a much more favorable environment prevailed. Not only were predators dispersed, but herbivores profited from a greatly increased food supply including flooded vegetation in the shallower waters and a bloom of phytoplankton. According to Coulter, not only were the 1958–59 and 1959–60 breeding seasons apparently longer, but survival rates among fry were "very high." As they matured, these generations formed the basis for the new fisheries rather than succeeding generations in which recruitment was lower. Aside from the chemical and biological stabilization of the lake, which could have led to a reduced biomass after the termination of bloom conditions, the reasons behind this drop in productivity are not clear. Of a number of possibilities, several are probably significant. One is a buildup in the numbers of tiger fish so that today, as predators, they may play the same role as they did in the undammed river. Another possibility is that commercial species may have moved to a greater extent into shallow uncleared areas (see below) or into deeper uncleared waters which formerly were deoxygenated to a greater extent.[4] Yet another reason concerns the ecology of the most desirable species in the lake fisheries. This is a riverine cichlid, *Tilapia mortimeri* (formerly *T. mossambica*), which may be unable to adjust to lacustrine conditions. Regardless of the reasons, however, production has dropped. As for *Tilapia* catches, they "have consisted mostly of larger fishes each year, with relatively very little recruitment of smaller sizes, and the fishery apparently de-

pends upon the successful generations spawned between 1958 and 1960" (Coulter, 1967).

FISH POPULATIONS: STOCKING

In hopes of building up a lacustrine population of *Tilapia*, 28 tons of *T. macrochir* were stocked between 1959 and 1962. To date there is little evidence of success with only the occasional *macrochir* being caught either by fishermen or Department of Fisheries personnel. More recently, the United Nations Development Program–Food and Agriculture Organization–Zambian Central Fisheries Research Institute has initiated a program to stock the lake with the Lake Tanganyika clupeid (*Limnothrissa miodon*), along with other species, such as a freshwater shrimp and a Nile perch (*Lates* sp.), necessary for the creation of an open-water community. Needless to say, this is a long-term and hazardous enterprise which may or may not have a profound effect on the future fisheries.

BUSH CLEARING

In large-scale man-made lakes extensive bush clearing, though expensive, is desirable for a number of reasons relating to fisheries, the formation of aquatic weed mats, and health and aesthetic considerations. At Kariba nearly one-quarter of a million acres was cleared at a cost of approximately £10 per acre. Of these, 126,-000 acres were cleared along the north bank, with the main pitches concentrated on either side of Sinazongwe harbor. As Fig. 13–1 shows, most of the lake basin was uncleared. Furthermore, within fishing pitches, clearing extended from approximately the 1590-foot contour (close to the upper margin of the drawdown area) to 1530 feet, so that the deeper areas remained uncleared. These uncleared areas are very difficult to fish, especially when the crowns of the trees project beyond the surface and hence form

---

[4] In 1960 a thermal discontinuity formed at about 30 meters depth, below which deoxygenation occurred as the result of the decomposition of vegetation on the lake bottom, oxygen being replaced by high concentrations of hydrogen sulphide. In recent years, the degree of deoxygenation has grown less while concentrations of hydrogen sulphide are "now found only in the deeper, bottom valleys towards the end of the annual stratification period" (Coulter, 1967). For more detailed information on the hydrology of Lake Kariba, see Harding (1966).

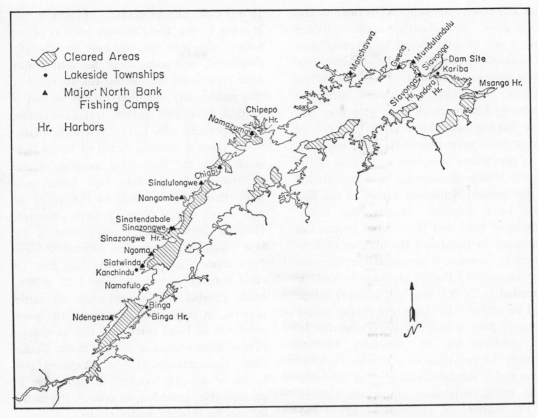

Figure 13–1   Kariba Lake. After a 1962 map drawn by the irrigation division of the government of Southern Rhodesia

anchors for mats of *Salvinia auriculata* and other sudd components. While it is to be hoped that the Central Fisheries Research Institute will be able to develop better techniques for use in these areas, underwater snags will continue to shred nets which the fishermen of today cannot afford to lose. On the other hand, many fishermen must fish the uncleared areas because the principal fish populations are now congregated there, no doubt because of a better food supply and a greater degree of protection.

THE INVASION OF AQUATIC PLANTS

The rapid buildup of the aquatic fern, *Salvinia auriculata,* on Lake Kariba and its role in facilitating the colonization of other plants and thus creating a "sudd" community, is well documented (see Boughey, 1962). The "weed" was first observed on the lake in 1959. By 1962 it covered more than one-tenth of Kariba's surface area, although thereafter the extent declined significantly.[5] Nevertheless, the weed continues to present a formidable problem to the fishermen. Except in sheltered areas which were never cleared, the problem is least severe at the lower end of Kariba, in part because the prevailing wind blows up the lake throughout most of the year. It is most severe in Mwemba, which is particularly unfortunate since there is insufficient land in

[5] Quoting Mitchell, who made periodic surveys of the degree of weed infestation, Little (1966) mentions 400 square miles as the extent of greatest coverage. Coulter (1967), on the other hand, mentions 250 square miles.

that chieftaincy to support its agricultural population. Periodically, certain fishing camps are literally closed by floating mats of *Salvinia,* which make the movement of boats extremely difficult, if not impossible. In other, more fortunate camps, fishermen venturing out to check their gear may find that floating mats have either covered or swept away their nets during the night.

In conclusion, it is obvious that all of the factors briefly summarized have contributed to the present depressed nature of the Kariba Lake fisheries. During the heady months of 1962 and 1963, when production continued to spiral and the number of fishermen to increase, it appeared that the earlier estimates of Kariba productivity (which extended to 20,000 tons per annum) might well be realized. In that event fishing would certainly play a critically important role in the development of Gwembe District through the provision of a reliable cash income and a substantial number of jobs, the latter being particularly important because of the scarcity of cultivable land in the relocation areas. Unfortunately, events have turned out otherwise, although it appears unlikely that productivity will drop much lower.

LAKE FORMATION, THE DISTRIBUTION OF TSETSE FLIES, AND ANIMAL TRYPANOSOMIASIS

There are two species of tsetse, *Glossina morsitans* and *Glossina pallidipes,* resident in the Middle Zambezi Valley. Of these, the second is not common, having first been identified in 1942 in the Southern Rhodesian portion of the valley, while north of the Zambezi its presence was apparently not documented until about 1964. In the opinion of some, only *G. pallidipes* is a carrier of human sleeping sickness in this area although elsewhere in Zambia *G. morsitans* is "the outstandingly important vector."[6]

[6] J. A. Gledhill, written communication, 1968.

In any case, human sleeping sickness is rare in what is now the Zambian portion of the valley, with only the odd case occasionally diagnosed, and even then the victim may have contracted the disease elsewhere.[7] For this reason, my intention in this section is to deal only with animal trypanosomiasis, and especially with bovine trypanosomiasis, which poses a constant threat to Tonga livestock near the fluctuating margins of the fly areas.[8] Though there have never been more than 30,000 cattle in the valley at any time during the present century, Gwembe District does contain some of the best ranching country in Central Africa. Furthermore, in spite of the fact that its rural population controls over 1.25 million head, Zambia is still dependent on cattle imports, in large part because of the poor condition of local stock and the unwillingness of their owners to market them. Under these circumstances, the development potential of a cattle industry in the valley is considerable, provided, of course, the tsetse fly can be brought under control.

The distribution of *G. morsitans* in the Northern Rhodesian portion of the Middle Zambezi Valley was mapped between 1949 and 1955 as part of a territory-wide survey of *Glossina* species. Two main concentrations, along with two smaller foci, were found, which are shown in Fig. 13–2, a map upon which the future lake shore margin

[7] The position in regard to human sleeping sickness in the Rhodesian portion of the Valley is quite different. As a result of the disease in 1912 in the Lubu Valley of Sebungwe District, an unknown number of Tonga were resettled in 1913. Thereafter the threat of renewed outbreaks remained a problem. This was especially the case at the time of Kariba resettlement when some Tonga wished to move back to areas of former infection. After the lake began to form, an outbreak of the disease, which apparently assumed serious proportions, did occur in Sinakatenge and adjacent resettlement areas. Though I do not know if the distribution of the fly involved had been influenced by the rise in lake level, the situation definitely deserves careful analysis in connection with the subject material dealt with in this paper.

[8] See Scudder (1962, pp. 164–73) for background information on animal trypanosomiasis in the Gwembe Valley.

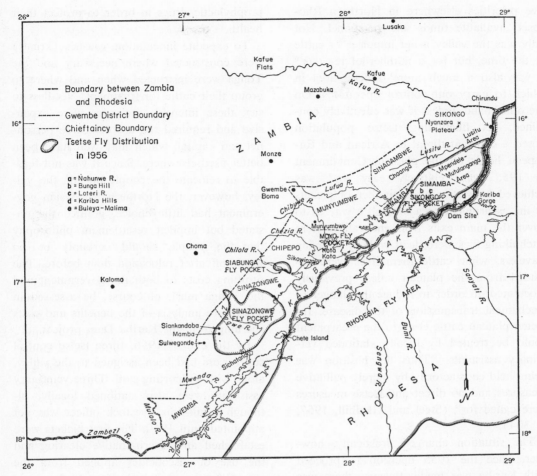

Figure 13–2 Gwembe District and Kariba Lake Basin. Courtesy of Manchester University Press, Manchester, England

has been superimposed. Within these pockets the distribution of the fly often formed a dentritic pattern, the preferred fly habitat being associated with changes (ecotones) between vegetation zones, especially in river and stream valleys, but also in connection with thickets and *dambo* (hardpan) margins, and the foot of the escarpment and the base of Karroo and granitic formations throughout the valley.[9]

[9] According to Steel and Gledhill (on whose undated manuscript I have drawn heavily in the paragraphs that immediately follow), "none of the main vegetation types to be found in the Valley itself comprises a complete fly habitat." By contrast Pilson (oral communication, 1963) was impressed by the number of *G. morsitans*

Prior to the decision to proceed with Kariba, no tsetse or veterinary personnel were stationed in the valley. While this situation was obviously hard on those residents who tried to build up herds of cattle and small stock, it was realistic in terms of rela-

in Brachystegia savannah woodland near the Lusulu research station in the Rhodesian portion of the Middle Zambezi Valley. Gledhill (written communication, 1968) believes that game density probably is the distinguishing factor, game populations being greater in the Rhodesian areas. Whether or not mopane and other vegetation zones along the Kariba Lake shore margin, with their more equitable climate and more favorable game conditions, form a complete fly habitat today remains to be substantiated.

tive priorities elsewhere in Northern Rhodesia, available funds and personnel. Not only was the valley a net importer of cattle at the time, but for a number of reasons[10] it was also a much more difficult area in which to carry out control operations. On the other hand, unless it was effectively contained, its fluctuating tsetse population posed a constant threat to African and European herds on the plateau. Containment in 1955 was relatively easy and was achieved by stationing a number of pickets in the escarpment area in such a way as to cover the main exits from the valley. Here hitchhiking flies were dealt with by spraying travelers, while cattle themselves were excluded from the plateau unless previously inoculated, in order to reduce the danger of mechanical transmission of the disease. Infected plateau cattle close to the escarpment could be treated by locally stationed veterinary assistants. "Thus the position was being held satisfactorily by merely palliative measures and no direct anti-tsetse measures were called for" (Steel and Gledhill, 1957, p. 304).

The situation changed drastically, however, once the 1955 decision to proceed with Kariba was made. Because there was insufficient land within the valley available for the resettlement of 36,000 north-bank Tonga, it was essential that the more desirable areas be opened up for occupation. Since a number of these were tsetse-infested, extensive eradication and control measures were now necessary for the first time in the valley's history. Furthermore, as cattle were moved from fly-free areas into relocation areas recently cleared of tsetse, they would have to be placed on a fixed regime of

prophylactic drugs in order to protect their health.[11]

To expedite inoculation, crushes (kraals) were constructed where necessary and the Tonga were instructed when and where to group their cattle for treatment. Needless to say, these intensive measures were expensive and required the use of scarce personnel and capital, which may well have been better used elsewhere. Since it was not feasible to relocate the people outside the valley, however, the Northern Rhodesian government had little choice, granted the unstated but implicit resettlement philosophy that the people should certainly be no worse off after relocation than before. The resulting costs to both the government and the Tonga must, of course, be assessed in any future analysis of the benefits and costs accruing from the Kariba Dam project.

By the end of 1956, three tsetse control supervisors had been assigned to the valley, along with supporting staff. Three veterinary assistants were also stationed locally, although a full-time livestock officer was not appointed until 1960. The first pickets were established and discriminative clearing and the use of insecticides applied from the ground[12] were initiated after further sur-

---

[10] The following are listed by Steel and Gledhill: isolation, difficulty of communications during at least half of each year, the large proportion of areas unsuitable for human settlement, inclement climate, famine conditions (with those seeking food elsewhere carrying fly with them), larger game populations, and the large proportion of virtually useless agricultural land, which is either uninhabited or only sparsely inhabited.

[11] In 1962, drug instructions from the livestock officer to his veterinary assistants in the valley were as follows: where heavy fly, poor communications and few cattle—use prothidium three times yearly; where heavy fly and many cattle—use anthracide every two months; where no fly but diseased cattle as shown by blood smear tests—use novidium selectively; and where cattle to be exported to the plateau—use dimidium bromide. (In all cases berenil to be held in reserve as a precaution against drug resistance in certain strains.)

[12] To the best of my knowledge, the only aerial spraying used in the valley in connection with resettlement occurred on the Southern Rhodesian side. This was in the Lubu area, which had been evacuated in 1913 as a result of human sleeping sickness. Following aerial spraying around 1957, there was a radical drop in fly numbers, after which the evacuees arrived and began to clear new gardens. Though a gradual increase in fly was noticed at first, as the garden area became more extensive, the fly population began to drop. By the end of 1962, the number of cattle had increased from 300 to over 1000, although they remained dependent on anthracide

veys to pinpoint the main fly concentrations. During 1957, a fourth supervisor was appointed and eradication efforts continued on a large scale, with special stress placed on the Sinazongwe area. By the end of 1958, when the dam wall was sealed and the lake began to form, the situation in the various resettlement areas being prepared for cattle appeared satisfactory. It improved during the next year as tsetse operations continued and as the evacuees began to open up new gardens, hence consolidating the gains made by reducing the extent of regeneration and clearing further areas.[13] Because of its isolation and light fly density, the Siabunga pocket was easily eliminated. In the Sinazongwe pocket, the situation was quite different, the concentration of fly being heavy in certain areas. These areas required a major effort which continued through 1961, when the last major concentration was brought under control. Indeed, by 1963 the tsetse control supervisor stationed at Sinazongwe believed (oral communication, 1963) that the tsetse problem was largely over in the southern portion of the Gwembe District (from the Chibuwe to the Mulolo), provided that surveys and pickets were continued so that a new buildup in any area could be spotted and treated before the fly had time to spread outward.

More difficult to handle was the Simamba-Sikongo pocket. Not only was this larger in size, but it also contained a number of relatively waterless and unpopulated areas (in particular, Bunga Hill, the Kariba Hills, and the Nyanzara Plateau). These areas were

not only hard to get at, but were also areas in which temporary eradication could not be followed up by human settlement. Furthermore, the danger of reinfestation from Southern Rhodesia below the exit of Kariba Gorge was an unmanageable problem under existing conditions. The small Moyo pocket in the southwestern corner of Simamba was ignored. No doubt there were a number of reasons for the lack of attention paid to this concentration, including isolation and the fact that the entire pocket not only lay outside of the areas set aside for relocation, but also would eventually be inundated by the rising lake.

During 1960 and 1961, reports dealing with the tsetse situation tended to be rather optimistic. Throughout the Kariba Lake Basin it was assumed to be only a factor of time before the fly was eliminated entirely (or at least contained in small pockets remote from human habitation), whereas downriver from Kariba Gorge the assumption was that a combination of clearing, spraying, human settlement and selective game elimination would control the threat of serious encroachment from across the Zambezi. In the meantime, the number of cattle in Gwembe District continued to increase (see Table 13–1). This was an altogether desirable situation. Not only were the cattle seen by the government as an integrated part of agricultural development leading to better husbandry and to cash cropping, but also a cattle industry in certain parts of the valley seemed a distinct possibility. This was especially the case in the southern half of Mwemba chieftaincy and in the Mpendele-Mutulanganga area, which lay between the Kariba Hills, the southeast corner of the lake, and the Lusitu.

In comparison to the neighboring plateau, the valley, except for tsetse, provided a much better habitat for cattle. The reasons for this were simple: better water and better feed, the latter including both grazing and browsing. Though a definite stress pe-

---

injections every two months (oral communication from J. Ford, sometime director of Southern Rhodesia's Tsetse and Trypanosomiasis Control and Reclamation Department; 1963). The cost of this operation was high and involved £42,000 and the loss of one aircraft with its pilot.

[13] Wherever possible, tsetse control operations were closely correlated with human settlement. Otherwise, as in the Mpendele-Mutulanganga area below the dam, costly clearing and spraying operations had to be repeated as the fly moved back into its former habitats.

Table 13–1

GWEMBE DISTRICT CATTLE FIGURES[1]

	1951	1956	1959	1962	1964	1966
Mwemba	3,061	5,766	5,355	6,586	7,410	n/d
Sinazongwe	407	351	935	2,403	3,840	n/d
Chipepo	338	1,167	1,199	1,862	2,166	2,630
Munyumbwe	5,420	8,356	7,484	8,139	4,399[2]	3,977[3]
Sinadambwe	6,141	4,264	1,881	2,867	2,145	2,061
Simamba[4]	156	n/d	79	169	18	41
Chipepo (Lusitu)	—	—	562	1,562	2,177	2,524
Sikongo	1,383	602	435	629	353	560[5]
	16,906	20,506	17,930	24,217	22,509	n/d

[1] Information provided by the District Commissioner, Gwembe (1951–1956) and the Livestock Officers, Gwembe (1962) and Mazabuka (1964–1966).
[2] Not including ten Chambwe villages which are included in Sinadambwe total.
[3] Not including ten Chambwe villages which are included in Sinadambwe total (Chambwe total was 472).
[4] Simamba figures questionable throughout (some stock may be included within Sinadambwe totals).
[5] Two sets of figures available; other is 908.

riod often came toward the end of the dry season, the potential pastures were there, provided early burning by the Tonga could be controlled and provided the herders could be persuaded to move their stock back into the escarpment country or down toward the lake (in Mwemba) or to specially selected grazing areas (Mpendele-Mutulanganga) during the drier months. While such problems would not be easily overcome, they appeared no less manageable than in other livestock areas. Certainly the Tonga wished to build up their herds, had shown a desire in Munyumbwe and Sinadambwe to sell cattle to traders as early as 1951 if not before, and had cooperated closely with the local veterinary assistants in connection with prophylactic and curative inoculations. Against this background, most tsetse and livestock officers who were familiar with the valley saw no reason why a profitable cattle industry could not be developed. This would be especially appropriate for south Mwemba, where a human population of over 5000 in 1963 did not have sufficient land for cultivation. In

the Mpendele-Mutulanganga area, which had some of the best cattle country in the valley, and which was currently unpopulated, some officials even discussed the possibility of fenced grazing schemes which would support, under proper management, roughly one cow for every ten acres.

The first sign that all might not be well appeared in the 1960 Annual Report of the Department of Veterinary and Tsetse Control Services. It was noted that fly had spread to previously fly-free Kota Kota Hill in the mid-lake area. Though the source of the spread was not noted, presumably this was the Moyo pocket which was now largely, if not totally, under water, the fly being forced to move from a favored habitat into a less favored one as a result of flooding. No doubt, whatever spread occurred was facilitated by two other types of movement: one of game, which also had to seek new habitats as the water rose, and the other of fishermen, who moved to and fro throughout the area.

During 1961 and 1962, none of the reports that I have read refer again to the

Kota Kota situation. By 1963, however, the situation had deteriorated drastically, with fly now present in an area extending from the Nahunwe (east of the Lufua) to the Chibuwe River west of Kota Kota. Apparently expanding outward from Kota Kota Hill and perhaps also Bunga Hill, tsetse encroachment was now a definite threat to the sizable cattle populations along the Chaanga-Munyumbwe road and in Chipepo. By this time the lake had reached its highest level and the lake shore margin was beginning to stabilize. Formerly an incomplete tsetse habitat because of extremely high temperatures during the dry season, much of the vegetation along the lake's edge was now retaining its leaves for a longer period of time. This was especially the case with mopane (*Colophospermum mopane*), which might retain a partial leaf cover throughout the dry season, hence creating a lakeside tsetse refuge where none existed before.

Another serious factor was a continuing buildup of the new lake fisheries, which reached its peak on the north bank during 1963. In seeking out new fishing grounds along the lake shore margin and on islands, fishermen doubtless facilitated the spread of fly. Perhaps even more important were the movements of fish traders to and from outlying camps. This would be especially true of those who hawked both fresh and dry fish to the nearest villages, moving through the intervening bush either on foot or on bicycles. According to Steel and Gledhill, "in . . . Northern Rhodesia, it may be stated that somewhere in the region of 90% of the cases of Bovine Trypanosomiasis recorded in a year are initially the direct outcome of carried Tsetse Fly." As far as carriers were concerned, they suggested that the fish trade was of particular importance, with dried fish perhaps even luring the fly from its resting places. As an example from the plateau, they noted bicycle traders connected with the Kafue fisheries in parts of

Namwala District who traveled to and from fly and fly-free areas, hence seriously threatening the substantial herds of Ila cattle. Suggesting that possibly a fishing and a cattle industry were incompatible under such conditions, they went on to state that "it is no exaggeration to say that with uncontrolled traffic, the marginal fly area has now been increased to perhaps thirty to forty miles outside the true fly habitat."

Though the rapid buildup in lake shore fly between the Nahunwe and the Chibuwe is tied up with the formation and recent stabilization of Lake Kariba, its rapid encroachment inland, as in the Kafue case, was no doubt facilitated by the movement of fish traders. While pickets established along the roads leading from the major fish camps and markets were able to inspect and spray travelers, including motorized fish traders, those traveling on small trails would not be intercepted. And between the Chibuwe and Manchavwa camp (just east of the Lufua), trail and water travel were the main means of transport, there being no roads serving this extensive area at the time.

Table 13–1 suggests the impact of fly encroachment during 1963 and 1964 on cattle in Munyumbwe's chieftaincy, which before Kariba was the only chieftaincy in the district thought to be fly-free. In 1962, 8139 cattle (slightly over one per capita) were recorded, while the district livestock officer in his annual report stated that the health of valley cattle in general was excellent. Furthermore, the export of cattle from the valley seemed to be picking up, with 249 of the 283 sales recorded taking place in Munyumbwe. The next two years, however, were catastrophic for the Munyumbwe cattle industry, with the number of cattle dropping to less than 5000 by the end of 1964. By the end of 1966, cattle were still dying, although the rate of decrease had fallen off, with the total cattle reported from Munyumbwe being 4449 at the end of the year.[14] While the pastures of this chieftaincy had been overgrazed at the time of the sudden decline and cattle were suffering from poverty, especially toward the end of the dry season, nonetheless there can be little doubt that the primary cause of death was bovine trypanosomiasis carried by flies moving inland from the Kota Kota and the Lufua-Nahunwe areas. Having crossed the Munyumbwe-Chaanga road from the south, fly had established themselves in the Munyumbwe neighborhoods of Lumbo, Bondo and Lukonde, apparently for the first time in the district's history. Moving up the escarpment, they even threatened cattle in Chona's plateau chieftaincy until extensive spraying was carried out in 1966 and 1967.

In Sinadambwe, the picture is not as clear, since a significant decline in the cattle population began there prior to the formation of Kariba Lake. In my 1962 volume on the Gwembe Tonga, I have suggested that bovine trypanosomiasis was the most likely cause of this decline owing to both mechanical transmission of the disease from infected cattle outside of the Simamba-Sikongo pocket and to fly-encroachment from within this pocket. I see no reason for changing this view, believing that the even more significant decline between 1956 and 1959 represented a continuation of the same process. While it is true that control operations were initiated during 1957 in the Simamba portion of the pocket, it was not until late in 1958 that a concentrated attack was begun on the major fly concentrations. This is probably significant in regard to the reversal of the decline in the number of Sinadambwe cattle during the early 1960's, with 2371 reported in 1960, 2742 in 1961, and 2867 in 1962. Unfortunately, by 1964 numbers were once again dropping, the totals being even less than those entered in Table 13–1, since the 1964 and 1966 Sinadambwe figures include several hundred cattle from the ten Chambwe villages inside the eastern boundary of Munyumbwe and perhaps a few Simamba beasts. Indeed, by the end of 1966 the total had fallen below the 1959 low point. This reversal presumably is also tied to the buildup in fly along the lake shore margin, which we have already discussed in connection with the Munyumbwe livestock industry—Sinadambwe being at the eastern end of the new lake shore fly zone extending from the Nahunwe to the Chibuwe.

By the end of 1963, it was quite evident that the stabilization of the lake shore margin was associated with unexpectedly favorable conditions for the buildup and spread of fly in Simamba. It was also clear that this development greatly increased the area requiring tsetse control operations. On the other hand, the belief continued that it was "still practicable to aim at tsetse eradication in the Gwembe Valley as a short-term policy" (Department of Veterinary and Tsetse Control Services, 1963 section 60).

In the Simamba area the strategy had been to move gradually west or up the lake from the Simamba-Chaanga road, along which small concentrations of fly were virtually eliminated by clearing in 1957. During 1958 and 1959, effort was concentrated on the Loteri system and Bunga Hill with good results. Between 1960 and 1963, residual insecticides were applied throughout the area between Bunga Hill and the Lufua estuary, with nearly 1000 lineal miles of habitat sprayed during the latter year. At that time some areas had to be resprayed

---

[14] The first government-sponsored sale in the valley occurred in 1951 in the Lukonde area of Munyumbwe's chieftaincy. In 1964, the Cold Storage Board organized its first sales in Gwembe District. Between October 1963 and September 1964, 408 valley cattle were sold to all buyers, of which 236 were from Munyumbwe (1963–64 Annual Report of the Chief Agricultural Supervisor, Gwembe). According to the technical assistant-in-charge, Gwembe Boma, in 1966 and 1967 Cold Storage Board buyers were no longer making Munyumbwe purchases during their occasional trips there, primarily because of deaths from bovine trypanosomiasis. Farmers who lose oxen were particularly hard-hit, with some using cows for traction for the first time.

(especially south of Bunga Hill) because of the buildup of fly along the lake shore.[15] During 1964 the entire area sprayed the previous year had to be resprayed. Though it was clear of fly immediately after the 1963 treatment, subsequently massive encroachment from the still-untreated lake shore areas west of the Lufua occurred. Reinfestation from this area also threatened the peninsulas jutting out into the lake immediately east of the Lufua and the Nahunwe rivers, fishermen en route to Gwena camp being potential carriers.

As a result of the danger of reinfestation from west of the Lufua, the first access roads were cut on the west bank during 1964, with both sides of the Lufua sprayed from the lake upstream to the Lufua-Lusengazi confluence. By the end of the year, the fly position east of the Lufua was satisfactory, although the costs of 1964 control operations were heavy, the major item (£28,696) being spraying.[16] The year was also hard on staff, with supervisory personnel in North Gwembe cut back from three to one. Furthermore, though vehicular spraying remained the main means of attack, the proportion of knapsack spraying rose because of the roughness of the terrain. In 1965, a pontoon was established on the Lufua and further access roads on the west bank were opened. Heavy fly concentrations were found and sprayed. Again district costs were high, with the cost of spraying, most of which was again in the Simamba area, coming to £43,552. A record 1338.1 lineal miles were treated with 100,265 gallons of Dieldrax 15T 3 per cent emulsion and 13,454 gallons of DDT 75 per cent W.P. at 5 per cent strength.

[15] The insecticide most commonly used was a 3 per cent Dieldrin emulsion, which must be applied to 1.5 to 2 lineal miles per square mile of tsetse infestation for effective control in Gwembe District (J. A. Gledhill, Assistant Director for Tsetse Control Operations, oral communication, 1967).

[16] While these costs refer to Gwembe District as a whole, most of the spraying during the year occurred in the Simamba area.

During 1966, no major spraying of a new area was undertaken, the services of the Insecticide Unit being required outside the valley. However, from the new holding line on the Nangandwe River (nearly halfway between Kota Kota Hill and the Lufua), a major effort was made to extend the road system into the area linking the Nangandwe system with the Chibuwe system to the west. The strategy here was first to contain Kota Kota Hill (hence protecting the cattle in Munyumbwe and Chipepo), and then to eradicate the fly on Kota Kota itself. Containment was programmed for 1967, setting the stage for the first spraying of Kota Kota Hill during the current year. If successful, fly would be eliminated for the first time in recent history from the Simamba area, although, as we shall see, the danger of reinfestation from without remains a serious danger.

Simamba was not the only area which provided a new habitat for tsetse fly as a result of the stabilization of Lake Kariba. In Chipepo, fly was found to have re-established itself in the isolated Sikowinzala area during 1967. Encroachment from here would pose a very serious threat to the substantial herds in the Tonga neighborhoods of Chezia and Chilola. Eradication would require surveys and the opening of new spray lanes and tracks, and then the application of residual insecticides. Further up the lake, occasional fly were found in otherwise fly-free Sinazongwe, presumably having been brought in by boat from Chete or other islands close to the heavily infested Rhodesian side of the lake. In Mwemba, the rapid buildup of lake shore fly in the Sichitando peninsular area in 1963 required extensive spraying late that year. Inland, a number of cattle died of bovine trypanosomiasis in the upper Mweenda area at the base of the plateau. Kraaled within a fly-free area, these cattle perhaps were victimized by traveling fly or perhaps they became ill as a result of mechanical transmission from an infected beast imported from a fly area. One possibility was the Sichitando area; another was the Sinankumbe-Sulwegonde area to the east. Here fly appeared in 1967 and required the application of insecticides in an area which apparently had been fly-free in the past, although it lay only a short distance southwest of the outer margin of the former Sinazongwe pocket. Hence the 1967 presence of fly probably represented a previously unknown extension of that pocket rather than a new establishment of fly from a lakeside population.

Though the Sikongo portion of the Simamba-Sikongo pocket falls largely outside of the Kariba Basin, it nonetheless warrants some attention. For our purposes this portion can be divided into three sections, including the Kariba Hills to the south, the Mpendele-Mutulanganga area in the middle, and the Lusitu area to the north. Just inland from the damsite, the Kariba Hills contained a fly population which in 1963 encroached on the lake shore at Mundulundulu fish camp, hence creating a possible means whereby the lake shore margin of the Simamba portion could be reinfested. Fortunately, at the time, the danger was identified and the threat temporarily removed through control operations. These were continuing during 1967 through discriminative clearing in the tributary valleys of the Kariba Hills.

The northernmost area of the Sikongo portion extended into the Lusitu area, which had been chosen for the relocation of some 6000 Tonga who could not be resettled within the actual lake basin because of land scarcity. Fly eradication here had high priority in 1957 and was successful to the extent that 243 of the immigrants' cattle were able to join them within a month of their relocation in 1958. During the next year a major effort was continued to completely eradicate the fly between the Lusitu River and the Chirundu-Lusaka road. By 1967

this aim had not yet been achieved. Standing in the way were at least three problems. One was the persistence of a small number of fly in the remote, rugged and unpopulated Nyanzara Plateau in the northeast corner of the area. Another was the movement of fly from Rhodesia directly across the Zambezi into the resettlement areas. Though this movement is hard to document, its significance was brought home to me in 1962 when Tonga told me of a herd of elephant that had crossed the Zambezi to feed in the Lusitu delta area. While there they mixed with some cattle, one of which was trampled to death. When subsequently found by Tonga herders, its mutilated body was the focal point of a small number of tsetse. The third problem relates to the fly still present in the Mpendele-Mutulanganga system. In spite of two pickets along the tracks exiting from this area, infection is still spread across the Lusitu. In some cases cattle owners are themselves directly to blame, as when one villager took two oxen into the Mutulanganga area during 1966 to bring back poles for building purposes. Subsequently both sickened and died. In other cases hitchhiking flies are probably responsible for infection, coming in on game, hunters and fish traders.

In spite of the use of both prophylactic and curative drugs in the Lusitu, during March 1967 a serious outbreak of bovine trypanosomiasis occurred. It had run its course by August, but at least 454 cattle had died out of a total population of less than 3500. This was a terrible loss for a society which is becoming increasingly dependent on oxen for plowing. Prior to the epidemic, some cattle owners had begun to sell stock to traders. Now the emphasis would be placed on rebuilding one's herds. External sales, as in the Munyumbwe and Sinadambwe areas in recent years, would probably become almost insignificant.

Looking to the future, there is little room for miscalculation. The original strategy of the Department of Tsetse Control within the Kariba Lake basin was to eliminate the fly in areas of human settlement, with the Tonga themselves consolidating departmental gains through the practice of their extensive agricultural system. Elsewhere in the valley, eradication was also to be attempted, although in some of the remoter areas a policy of containment based on periodic checks, spraying and discriminative clearing, would be the best that could be achieved.

Though initially this policy did not take into consideration the possible relationship of the stabilized lake shore margin to tsetse ecology, it has been remarkably successful in achieving its aims, with over 3500 square miles cleared of fly within Gwembe District by the end of 1966. (J. A. Gledhill, oral communication, 1967.) Continued vigilance, however, is absolutely necessary if current gains are to be maintained. There are at least four reasons for this statement. First, low density and isolated pockets of fly still exist in some of the more rugged portions of the valley, and it is probably impossible to completely eliminate these. Rather, periodic checks and surveys are necessary so that any buildup in fly can be dealt with before it presents a serious threat to valley cattle. It must be borne in mind that the 1967 epidemic in the Lusitu, which took the lives of nearly 500 cattle, probably was derived, at least in part, from the isolated fly population of the Nyanzara Plateau. Second, the risk of fly crossing the Zambezi from Rhodesia in the area between the end of Kariba Gorge and the Zambezi-Kafue confluence is ever present. While the present pioneer settlement in the Mpendele and Mutulanganga areas, along with the extensive spraying and clearing operations of the Department of Tsetse Control, have probably nearly eliminated resident fly from the lower portion of the drainage systems of these two rivers, windblown and game-carried movement across

the Zambezi will, of course, continue to threaten cattle in those areas and in the Lusitu. Where human settlement does not exist, discriminative clearing will continue to be necessary as regeneration occurs, and potential fly habitats will have to be periodically sprayed.[17] Third, the danger of fly movement across the lake from Rhodesia or from islands near the Rhodesian shore line can be expected to continue indefinitely. Here the unintentional carriers will be fishermen and other boat users. Again, the only recourse is periodic surveys backed up by the potential to eliminate reinfestation by whatever means necessary. Fourth, the danger of encroachment from Rhodesia upriver from the far end of Kariba may present as serious a threat as spread of tsetse across the Zambezi below the dam. Although there was no south bank fly in this area before lake formation, recent information suggests that fly is spreading up the lake on the Rhodesian side for the same reasons that tsetse in Simamba spread up the lake to Kota Kota Hill. Although no fly apparently have yet been found in Zambia at the junction of the lake with the inflowing Zambezi, it would appear to be only a matter of time before fly begin to cross the river. Here again, periodic surveys backed up by an ability to control invasion are necessary.

Current tsetse-control operations in the Middle Zambezi Valley are expensive in terms of capital, personnel and equipment. On the other hand, a serious cut in any one of these factors could lead to a very rapid deterioration of the situation and the eventual elimination of cattle from all, if not most, of the valley. At the same time, containment methods would be once again nec-

[17] In the opinion of the assistant director for tsetse control operations, spraying along the uncleared riverine ecotone will be necessary four times a year, in connection with other methods, such as game elimination and control of human movements (oral communication). It is unfortunate for control operations that the pioneer settlers took their cattle with them.

essary, although on a larger scale than before, to protect cattle on the adjacent plateau. So long as the valley is relatively fly-free, these methods are unnecessary.

From the point of view of the Gwembe Tonga themselves, the eradication of fly is of immense importance. With the beginning of the cash-cropping of cotton and sorghum in the past few years, cattle are playing an increasingly important role in agricultural development, which would be set back if ox traction was restricted by fly encroachment. At the same time, the Gwembe Tonga from Mwemba to the Lusitu have shown a willingness to sell cattle for export, provided their herds are sufficiently large to meet their immediate agricultural needs. With the major exception of Munyumbwe prior to the recent epidemic, most of the valley has always been understocked with cattle. Aside from the south Mwemba and Mpendele-Mutulanganga areas already mentioned, the entire lake shore margin would appear to have a considerable potential for a developing cattle industry, a potential which is denied to agriculture because of the extreme irregularity in lake drawdown. Between 1962 and 1967, the number of cattle in Chiabi increased from 260 to 498. With a higher per capita average (slightly over one) than the rest of Chipepo, presumably the villagers here have profited directly from easy access to an extensive lake shore margin—especially during the dry season—when before Kariba, grazing was particularly short. Because of their relative remoteness from the main road system, farmers in this area are still looking for a profitable cash crop which could well be cattle, unless, of course, tsetse encroachment from Sikowinzala or elsewhere was allowed to occur.

As an employer of labor on both a full-time and seasonal basis, the Department of Tsetse Control has made a different kind of positive contribution to the economy of Gwembe District. According to the chief tsetse control supervisor (oral communica-tion) and my own rough calculations, at least 87 full-time staff were employed in the valley during 1967, while the number of casual laborers employed during the dry season fluctuated between 200 and 300, making the department one of the major employers of valley labor. Not only are those seasonally employed working during the nonagricultural season, but some at least are putting their earnings into the purchase of cattle. Finally, the development of a mining township in the Sinankandobo-Maamba area of Mwemba, a pilot project in village regrouping in the Kanchindu area, and other residential townships along the lake shore margin at Sinazongwe and Siavonga make it desirable to keep the fly situation under control, since the danger of human sleeping sickness in the Middle Zambezi Valley continues to be a serious one on the Rhodesian side, and hence presumably is a possibility on the north bank.[18]

In the future, it is also possible that current research will provide results which will reduce the costs of control operations. According to the assistant director for tsetse control operations (1966 Annual Report), "under the hot dry conditions in the Zambezi Valley the effective persistence on tree boles of a deposit from a 5% DDT wettable powder formulation is at least as good as that obtained using a 3% dieldrin emulsion formulation." If so, the use of DDT will reduce the costs of insecticides, although in the cases of all such chemicals enough is not yet known about the long-term ecological effects of extensive use. In this regard, biological control through the release of sterile males is particularly promising, especially in isolated pockets with a low tsetse population. Located in rough terrain, these pockets are particularly difficult and costly to treat effectively with insecticides, yet such conditions are quite typical of Gwembe

[18] According to J. Ford, some eight cases of sleeping sickness were diagnosed near Kariba Township between December 1961 and April 1962 (oral communication).

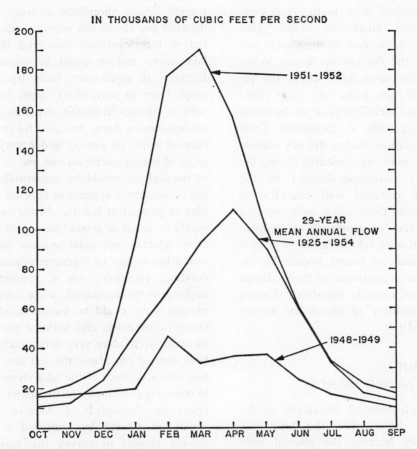

Figure 13–3 Annual pre-lake flow regime of the Zambezi River in comparison with selected wet and dry years. Calculated for Kariba by the Hydrological Branch, Division of Irrigation, former Central African Federation. Courtesy of Manchester University Press, Manchester, England

District. Yet another promising technique for reducing costs, though one which is hardly appealing to ecologists, is the application of arboricides such as 2,4,5=T, which have already been used in Zambia in combination with late burning, with good results.

AGRICULTURE, THE LAKE SHORE MARGIN AND RIVER FLOW BELOW THE DAM

Before Kariba, most Tonga lived within a mile of the Zambezi and the lower reaches of its major tributaries. The people were farmers, producing two crops during the

agricultural season. These were grown primarily for local consumption, the valley having been a serious famine area throughout its recorded history (Scudder, 1962). Indeed, no farmers grew cash crops in lieu of food crops, although the more enterprising intentionally grew some cereals, hemp and tobacco for sale. They also tried to sell the unexpected food surpluses that occasionally occurred.

The Zambezi system played a major role in the agricultural economy. With the advent of the rains, tributary deltas and the more fertile alluvia immediately inland from the primary channel of the Zambezi were planted with crops of cereals, legumes and cucurbits harvested prior to the river's expected annual flood in April (see Fig. 13–3). The second alluvial crop was planted after the floodwaters began to recede, with seed sown just behind the retreating water line from late April until September, and harvested prior to the initial rise of the Zambezi in December. Only alluvia were planted during the dry season, although they were supplemented during the rains (usually November-March) by the cultivation of colluvial soils and Karroo sediments. While these latter soils were of major importance to a majority of farmers just prior to Kariba relocation, in large part this was because of recent population increase and the degradation of those alluvia which were not annually inundated. Karroo soils were definitely of secondary importance before 1950.

AFTER KARIBA:
THE LAKE SHORE MARGIN

The situation changed drastically in the Kariba Lake basin after the lake was formed, simply because the alluvial soils were completely inundated except along the middle and upper reaches of the tributary system, where the extent of alluvial deposits has always been limited. As a result, the agricultural system of most evacuees was now primarily dependent on the less fertile and more easily erodible Karroo sediments. An unknown factor was the agricultural potential of these soils within the drawdown area of the lake. While the situation was such that one could not expect the lake to gradually build up an extensive layer of silt along its margin to increase soil fertility, the action of water on the soils and the presence of a high water table might well allow a continuation of the Tonga practice of growing two crops per year—provided, of course, fluctuations in lake level were consonant with agricultural demands.

In large-scale man-made lakes in the tropics, whose shorelines measure in hundreds if not thousands of miles, the potential of the drawdown area and the inner lake shore margin could be considerable. In terms of agriculture, both dry and wet crops (rice in particular) might be grown with or without irrigation, depending on the circumstances. Areas not used for crop agriculture could be grazed under varying degrees of management. At one end of a range of possibilities would be uncontrolled grazing on whatever vegetation appears—as occurs at present at Kariba. At the other end would be aerial or ground sowing of ecologically selected perennial grasses and their utilization as part of a grazing scheme. Fishponding, preferably on a peasant basis, might also be developed, while certain unutilized areas could be incorporated within conservation zones and national parks. Unfortunately, to date very little research has been carried out about the soil and vegetation characteristics of the lake shore margin in connection with any of the major African reservoirs, although P. M. Ahm of the University of Ghana has initiated a much-needed project to survey the agricultural potential of the drawdown area of Lake Volta, the intention being to provide information for the intelligent utilization of the most promising locations.

At Kariba, study of lake vegetation was restricted to the Southern Rhodesian side, where Boughey and Mitchell concentrated on the sudd aspects and ecology of *Salvinia auriculata,* and at least one university researcher dealt with phytoplankton. To the best of my knowledge, however, no one has documented through time the development and composition of fixed vegetation within the drawdown area or along the margin of the high-water level, or related this to the possibility of a cattle industry using the lakeside area during the dry season. While certain grasses with a high nutrient value have been observed at Kariba (for example,

Vossia sp. and *Echinochloa* sp.), the relative proportions of these through time (and especially since lake stabilization) are unknown.

As for the agricultural potential of the drawdown soils, it took experimentation by the Tonga to provide a partial answer. While the lake was gradually filling between the end of 1958 and the 1963 dry season, no drawdown cultivation was possible, with all lake basin Tonga dependent on a single rain crop for the first time in their lives. In October 1963, the high point was reached, with the water level dropping thereafter over twenty feet before it began to rise again in March 1964. During this time, up to two miles of shore line was exposed in certain areas because of the gentle gradient. Though without prior experience, some lake shore Tonga responded to this situation by planting ninety-day maize in the drawdown area in November. The results were excellent, with "some of the best maize ever reaped in the Valley" harvested in February and March. (March, 1964,

communication from the Chief Agricultural Supervisor, C. Mitchell).

While this result was most encouraging, the major problem was to regularize it on an annual basis. The problem was entirely man-made, and derives from the fact that the annual regime of Lake Kariba since 1963 has been more irregular than that of the Zambezi before damming (see Fig. 13–4). For drawdown agriculture in the Middle Zambezi Valley, it is desirable to have a four-month growing season for most crops. It is also desirable that this season occur at roughly the same time each year and at a time when the population is not involved in other labor-intensive tasks. Unfortunately, these conditions are less satisfactory today than before Kariba. Prior to relocation, the dry-season cultivation of the riverine drawdown fell within the period April–November, although a small proportion of the crop might be harvested as late as December. Aside from the harvest of giant sorghum in April–May and the preparation of garden land for planting in Octo-

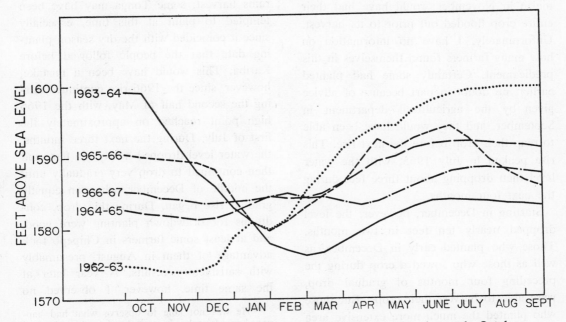

Figure 13–4   Lake Kariba water levels on the 1st and 15th day of each month, October 1962 to September 1967. Data provided by the Central African Power Corporation

ber–November, the agricultural activities involved did not overlap with those practiced during the rains. Today this is not the case, since the most reliable drawdown season extends from August to December, and hence overlaps with the rainy-season plowing, sowing and first weeding of inland gardens. But even more serious than this is the annual variation in the lake drawdown with the resultant uncertainty of the farmer about planting time.

The extent of this uncertainty can be seen by briefly reviewing the drawdown situation since the record February–March 1964 harvest. During the latter month, the water level began to rise again, reaching its 1964 peak in June–July. Thereafter, a gradual drop of slightly over two feet (as opposed to twenty the year before) occurred, with the low point of the 1964–65 season in December, as opposed to March in 1963–64. Furthermore, by the middle of January, the rising lake had already passed its 1964 peak. In other words, any Tonga who had tried to repeat the successful 1963–64 experiment by again planting maize in November would have had their entire crop flooded out prior to its harvest. Unfortunately, I have no information on how many farmers found themselves in this predicament. Certainly some had planted earlier, no doubt in part because of advice given by the agricultural department in September, and they would have been able to reap their crop before the next rise. This rise peaked in July 1965, with the water level then dropping about three feet during the next four months.

Starting in December, however, the level dropped nearly ten feet in two months. Those who planted early in December, as well as those who sowed a crop during the preceding four months of gradual drop, were able to harvest their crops. But those who planted the much more extensive area that emerged during the latter part of December and January would have lost out,

since the lake level began to rise quite rapidly during February and March. The agricultural season in question (1965–66) was poor at the southern end of the valley because of inadequate rainfall in December. Because of reports of possible famine in Mwemba, an agricultural officer and a livestock officer with previous experience in the valley were asked to carry out a reconnaissance in January and February. During the first month they reported that the only good stands of cereals observed were "odd spots" along the lake shore. The next month, the livestock officer noted that the January rise had flooded out drawndown crops planted in both Chipepo and Sinazongwe.[19] Because of the drought it is likely that planted areas had been quite extensive, with concerned farmers sowing the drawdown *after* the failure of the rains in December–January. Their subsequent total loss of this drawdown planting must have been most discouraging.

The 1966 rise continued until about the first of May, after which the water level fell approximately a foot. Because of the poor rains harvest, some Tonga may have been tempted to plant at this time, especially since it coincided with the dry season planting date that the people followed before Kariba. This would have been a mistake, however, since the 1966 rise continued during the second half of May, with the 1966 high point reached on approximately the first of July. During the next three months, the water level dropped nearly ten feet, and then continued to drop very gradually until the middle of December, when an equally gradual rise began. During this drop, conditions for drawdown planting were good, and at least some farmers in Chipepo took advantage of them in August, presumably with satisfactory results. A year later at the same time, however, I observed no

---

[19] He was not able to observe what had happened in Mwemba, because by then the rains had finally set in, with the result that the Mwemba river crossings were impassable (communication from C. Furse).

planting along the lake shore margin. Moreover, by October still no planting had taken place along the land-starved southern end of the lake. Although the water level had in fact begun to drop in August, the drawdown was very gradual, being only about two feet by the first of November.

It is too early to know how the Tonga will respond to a continuation of this type of uncertainty. One possibility is that they will consider the risks too great, so that in the future virtually no crops will be grown in the extensive drawdown even during years when a large harvest might be possible. This is what occurred along the Nile after the second heightening of the Aswan Dam in 1933. There, after a number of disappointing seasons when crops were prematurely flooded out, the Nubian population ceased cultivating cereal crops almost entirely within the drawdown area (Scudder, 1967).

A second, perhaps more likely possibility, is that some Tonga, for a wide variety of reasons which need not concern us here, will be willing to put up with the uncertainties involved. For these, early planting (July–August) would appear to be the wisest, but if the lake level drops sharply thereafter, there is the danger that crops will be above the water table during the hottest portion of the year. On the other hand, late planting on recently exposed soils either just before or just after the advent of the rains, may be flooded out by a rise in lake level which in some years may begin as early as December and in others be delayed until February or March.

Regardless of the alternative chosen by the Tonga, the potential of the lake shore margin will be underutilized in terms of both productivity and the provision of jobs.[20] This situation was unplanned, since

[20] In terms of population projections, far too little attention has been placed on increasing job opportunities throughout the Third World. Systems of lake shore agriculture which will provide a means of livelihood for thousands of rural residents should definitely be built into future benefit-cost analyses.

no one in a position of responsibility considered the relative merits of the drawdown area as a resource for development. Looking to the future, planners should think more in terms of creating more productive ecosystems rather than simply in terms of kilowatt hours and other statistical indices. More specifically, they should pay more attention to the food-producing potential of the lake shore margin as opposed to the river system below the damsite. In some cases it may well be that this potential is sufficiently great to warrant establishing a fixed drawdown regime which does not exist for any of the major African projects now in operation or under construction. Under these circumstances, the power-producing potential of the dam generators would have to be integrated with other power-producing facilities, such as thermal stations, so that conflicts between power and agricultural uses of water would not always be at the sacrifice of the latter. In other words, if power needs could not be met by the dam without seriously altering a fixed drawdown regime, they could be met by increasing output from another installation built into a nationally or regionally organized system.

AFTER KARIBA: RIVER FLOW BELOW THE DAM

The impact of the Kariba dam on agriculture below the damsite is an excellent example of how man's engineering capacities can drastically reduce the productivity of an existing ecosystem. Figure 13–5 shows river flows from October 1958 through September 1963, while Fig. 13–6 deals with the period October 1963 through September 1967. A glance at these is sufficient to show the extreme irregularity that has been introduced into the annual regime of the Zambezi between Kariba gorge and the Kafue River as a result of the dam. Though fortunately commercial agriculture is of virtually no im-

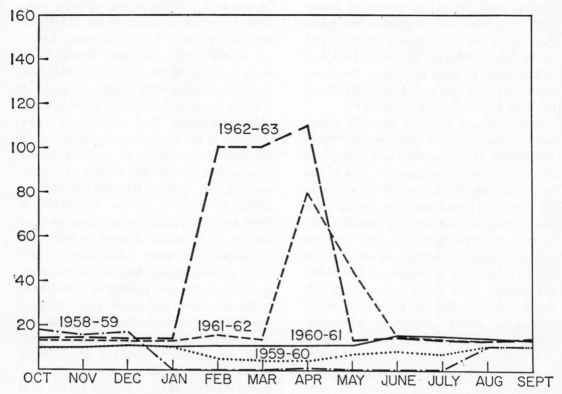

Figure 13–5 Zambezi River flows below Kariba Dam, October 1958 to September 1963. Average monthly flows in thousands of cubic feet per second. Data provided by the Central African Power Corporation

portance at present in the stretch of river involved, this is of little comfort to those thousands of Africans who desire to cultivate the fertile alluvia on a biannual basis. Once again, we have the same pattern of increased risks for the farmer in an already high-risk environment. Once again, it is too early to predict how the farmer will respond, although it is already obvious that he has suffered far more loss from man's manipulation of the Zambezi than he ever did during any equivalent time period in the past.

During the first three years (October 1958–September 1961), there was no Zambezi flood at all between the dam and the Kafue; indeed, during the first seven months that the dam was sealed no water was released except for a small trickle in March–April 1959. During the rainy season, the

agricultural implications of having the Zambezi restricted to its primary channel throughout this period were inconsequential for alluvium previously cultivated. On the other hand, the area that could be cultivated during the dry season was greatly reduced because of the absence of annual flooding. During the 1961–62 season, the dam-controlled regime approximated the original flow pattern for the first time since impoundment began. While this must have been a relief to those farmers who had suffered during the previous three dry seasons, it proved disastrous for those who had begun to cultivate rainy season gardens on the lower-level alluvia. This land had never been cultivated during the rains in the past because of flooding during the annual rise of the Zambezi. When this pattern was ap-

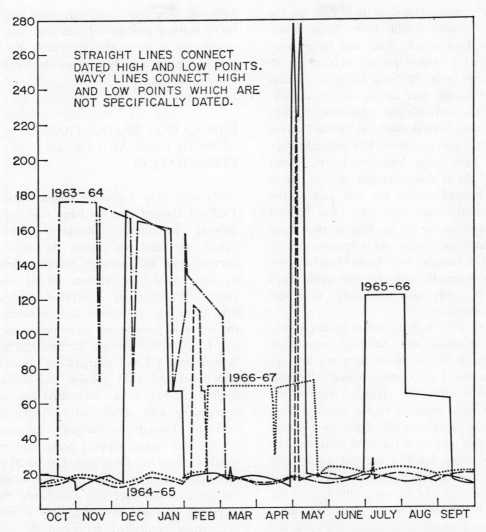

Figure 13–6 Zambezi River flows below Kariba Dam, October 1963 to September 1967. In thousands of cubic feet per second. Data provided by the Central African Power Corporation

proximated in April 1962 through nearly a sixfold increase in river flow over the previous month, these new gardens were inundated by over ten feet of water within a single day.[21] The next year the man-made flood of the Zambezi came in February, again destroying crops within these lower-terrace alluvial gardens, but fortunately not

[21] The loss of crops at that time subsequently led to a food shortage in the Lusitu village of Kadabuka, which was most dependent on the gardens concerned (the District Assistant, Lusitu, oral communication, 1963).

rising sufficiently high to destroy the extensive maize gardens planted in the Lusitu delta.

The case was altogether different, however, during 1963–64. Then three sluice gates were alternately opened and shut throughout most of the rains, so that virtually none of the Zambezi and tributary delta alluvia could even be planted during the most important agricultural season. Furthermore, since the river dropped rapidly in March, and no rain fell during April, "dry season" crops planted at that time on the higher alluvia would have been subsequently heat struck. The next three years continued a similar pattern of extreme irregularity, with 1965–66 being a particularly disastrous year for the alluvial cultivator. Then early-planted rainy-season crops would have been flooded out by the December rise, whereas most late-planted crops would have been destroyed by the April peak.[22] As if this were not enough, those crops planted during the first part of the dry season would have also been flooded out, this time by the opening of two sluice gates in June. Under the circumstances, it is hard to imagine how those regulating the flow of water through the dam could have acted in a way more detrimental to downriver agriculture.

At this point it is important to emphasize, in all fairness, that Zambian population densities in the downriver area are low except in the Lusitu area, where relocation was responsible for creating one of the highest rural densities in the country. Furthermore, practically all of the food grown on riverine alluvia is for local consumption. On the other hand, I am not aware that those planning for Kariba even considered the implications of alternate outflows for the future development of the downriver area. Nor am I aware that they considered the costs of possible food shortages for the local people and for the government arising from the present regime. I am not so much protesting against what happened as against the narrow viewpoint of those responsible for planning installations like Kariba. This project was essentially a unipurpose scheme. The population to be relocated was seen not as a resource but as an expensive nuisance, whose very existence was unfortunate. As for the future lake, it was strictly a dam by-product, whereas the needs of downriver in-

habitants were considered only when backed up by political power, and then were seen as constraints by those who viewed the Kariba Project almost entirely as a means for generating power.

POPULATION RELOCATION, AGRICULTURE AND LAND DEGRADATION

My own study of a single Tonga village in 1956–57 showed that the large majority of farming households cultivated approximately one acre per capita, the expected harvest from this acreage being sufficient to support the population during most years.[23] Unfortunately, just prior to relocation, there was insufficient land in much of the valley to provide this minimum, in large part because of population increase and land degradation. ("Land degradation" includes both sheet and gully erosion and reduced fertility arising from overcultivation and overgrazing with or without accompanying erosion.) Though the annually inundated alluvial soils could support permanent cultivation for an indefinite period, over 20 per cent of the farmers in our five river villages did not have any access to such lands. Furthermore, of those who did, only a small proportion controlled large-enough acreages to meet their consumption needs. In other words, most of the population also relied on the cultivation of less-fertile upper-level alluvia and on colluvial and Karroo soils which had to be periodically fallowed. Though the Tonga were quite familiar with the amount of fallowing that their various garden types required to restore fertility, lack of additional land was responsible for the overcultivation and hence exhaustion of certain alluvial gardens by the 1930's. This process continued during the

---

[22] Planting during the middle of the season, of course, would have been impossible, because the water level remained up during most of December and January.

[23] See pp. 218–19 and Appendix B in Scudder (1962). Information collected by the Department of Agriculture ranged, on the average, from one acre to one and one half acres per capita.

Table 13–2

CULTIVABLE LAND AND POPULATION IN GWEMBE DISTRICT
RELOCATION AREAS (1958)[1]

CHIEFTAINCY	POPULATION TO BE RELOCATED	LAND AVAILABLE FOR RELOCATION	TYPE[2]
Mwemba	9,000	20,000	Mostly category 2
Sinazongwe	9,000	30,000	At least 14,000 acres, category 1
Chipepo	9,300	8,000 (8,281)	Mostly category 2
Sinadambwe	none	4,550	Mostly category 2
Simamba	2,200	7,800	Mostly category 2
Lusitu	none	25,000	Mostly category 1
Mpendele-Mutulanganga	none	7,500	Categories 1 and 2
	29,500	102,850	Approx. 40,000 acres Category 1

[1] Information provided by the District Commissioner, Gwembe.

[2] Category 1: Supports "semipermanent agriculture" (5–10 years cultivation followed by 5–10 years fallowing).

Category 2: Supports "bush-fallow agriculture" (2–10 years cultivation followed by 20 years fallowing).

1940's, when certain farmers began to pioneer less fertile Karroo soils well back in the bush. By 1957, most of the better Karroo soils within walking distance were under cultivation, while extensive areas of upper-terrace alluvium were so degraded as to be under indefinite fallow. While the situation would have continued to deteriorate, since the exhaustion of the Karroo soils was only a matter of years, relocation intervened. The overtaxed lands were flooded and the people were moved back toward the outer margin of the valley or into the Lusitu area below the damsite.

Resettlement, however, did not solve the land problem. In fact, for many villages in the southern portion of the valley, it only made it worse, since those soils least susceptible to degradation through cultivation had been permanently flooded along the banks of the Zambezi and the lower reaches of the major tributaries. Table 13–2 shows the amount of land available for relocation within the valley. Under the local system of agriculture, less than 40 per cent of this land could support semipermanent cultivation (category 1),[24] which involves five to ten years of continuous cropping, followed by a fallow period of approximately equal length. The rest (category 2), ranging in quality from fair to poor, could support at best cultivation for about six years, followed by a twenty-year fallow. With almost all of the arable land in the valley surveyed, this meant that semipermanent cultivators needed an absolute minimum of two acres per capita, whereas bush fallow cultivators needed five or more. The situation in Mwemba was by far the worst; 9000 people had access to approximately 20,000 acres of category 2 soil, much of which fell in the less fertile and more easily erodable grades. To meet their needs, at least 40,000 more acres were necessary. In Sinazongwe, the 4000 people who moved into the Buleya-Malima area were in a much

[24] This land consists mainly of deep woodland soils which had been only partially cultivated prior to relocation. Though their origin is still in doubt apparently, Bainbridge and Edwards (1962) believe that they were derived from non-Karoo parent material, being transported into the valley from the adjacent escarpment and plateau. Mostly sandy clays, they are quite susceptible to erosion.

better position, since they had access to perhaps 14,000 acres which could be cultivated semipermanently. The 6000 people relocated in the Lusitu were in an equally favored position, with access to at least 20,000 acres of category 1 land. As for the remaining 10,500 people, they fell between the Mwemba and Lusitu-Buleya-Malima extremes. Worse off were the 3300 relocated within Chipepo, since they had access to only 8281 acres of fair to poor quality (category 2).

The problem of land shortage presented by relocation was obvious from the start to all government officials concerned. After resettlement had been completed, it was known that approximately one-third of the population would find themselves in serious straits within ten years. The rest were more fortunate, although there was little room for population increase in some areas and all areas could easily become degraded in the years ahead through erosion, overcultivation, and overgrazing.

The response of the Department of Agriculture to this situation was to push erosion control and intensification, although there was general agreement that the situation in the southern portion of Mwemba was hopeless unless further relocation occurred. Two types of erosion control were stressed. The first would involve a prohibition of cultivation within twenty-five yards of the banks of major tributaries. The need for such an ordinance was obvious to all ecologically-oriented personnel who were familiar with the tributary system on the plateau, in the escarpment and in the valley. Referring to Mazabuka District on the plateau, Bainbridge and Edwards reported that "the amount of run-off, coupled with sheet and gully erosion that takes place during the heavy rains is quite frightening." With much of their grass cropped right down to the roots, *dambos* along the upper reaches of rivers like the Lusitu are increasingly subject to abnormal flash floods.

In the escarpment country leading down into the valley, the same authors refer to air photographs which "show clearly the denudation of the protective strips of woodland along the stream banks and the spreading of the cultivation away from the streams up the steep slopes." Without a protective cover, flash floods each year remove more of the soil, with the authors estimating that within ten to fifteen years "there will no longer be sufficient soil left in the escarpment to carry the present population." In the valley, flash floods periodically sweep the now unprotected banks of the major tributaries. When the Lusitu rose to record heights in a matter of hours in March 1963, the extensive riverbank areas under cultivation since relocation were severely eroded. Clearly this would not have occurred if the riverine fringe vegetation had not been systematically removed through the upper, lower, and perhaps middle reaches of the Lusitu. For the second type of erosion control, the stress was on the construction of contour ridges to keep *in situ* relocation area soils. Initially, £25,000 were allocated for this task, the hope being that eventually the Native Authority (now the Gwembe Rural Council) would take over responsibility for the financing, construction and maintenance of ridges, with the Department of Agriculture's responsibility being restricted to locating and pegging them.

Turning to intensification in relationship to the control of land degradation, the core of the program was a two- or four-crop rotation supplemented by the use of cattle manure. This system was carefully worked out by a research man with long valley experience on experimental plots cleared from the different valley soils. It was then applied on departmental demonstration gardens and on the holdings of Peasant Farmers and Native Authority Improved Farmers. The first ten Peasant Farmers were selected by the district commissioner in 1959. After receiving credit from a revolving fund under the district commissioner's jurisdiction for their equipment and cattle needs, they became the responsibility of the Department of Agriculture. At first, each Peasant Farmer was restricted to a 20-acre holding. While building this up, he was supposed to follow a four-crop rotation involving equal acreages of maize, sorghum, cotton, and a green manure crop. Supplemental manure (at three tons per acre) was to be applied annually to half the acreage planted in grain, with each farmer told to build up a herd of twenty cattle to meet his ox-traction and manure needs. As for the NA Improved Farmers, they had much smaller holdings on which they could receive a one pound sterling bonus per acre, provided they followed a simple grain-legume rotation and manured half the grain plot each year.

If actually practiced, the recommended measures most likely would have been effective in maintaining soil fertility and preventing erosion. The degree of acceptance, however, by the farmer has been minimal. No ordinance prohibiting cultivation within twenty-five yards of tributary beds was enacted. Even if it had been, it is unlikely that enforcement would have been possible. Throughout their known history, the Tonga have always cleared tributary banks, except for occasional shade and fruit trees, in order to cultivate the fertile alluvial soils. After relocation and the loss of Zambezi and delta alluvia, these soils became even more desirable, with tributary bank clearing extended throughout much of the valley. This was especially the case in Mwemba, where other soils were not only extremely limited but also of generally poor quality. While those Tonga involved were well aware of the resulting dangers of erosion, they saw no option but to continue as in the past.

The alternative suggested by the Department of Agriculture was seen as no alternative at all, since no acceptable substitute for riverbank cultivation was presented to

them. While contour ridging was not actively opposed, the Native Authority was unwilling to publicly back it through its own regulations and sponsorship. Well aware that the valley residents did not really understand the basis for contouring, the Native Authority did not wish to associate itself with a potentially unpopular measure. After all, their support had always been minimal and this was especially so after relocation, which the NA councilors and chiefs had been pressured into supporting by the central government. Though some 1230 miles of ridges (protecting 14,247 acres) were dug under the jurisdiction of agricultural staff by October 1964 (communication from the Chief Agricultural Supervisor, C. Mitchell), they never received popular understanding, let alone sufficient support to provide for their maintenance. A year later, construction apparently stopped in the Lusitu, and thereafter I recall seeing only occasional references to ridges in agricultural reports. Though I do not know how these ridges are faring today, some Lusitu farmers have broken them down in the cultivation and extension of their own gardens.

Intensification in the valley has fared no better as a degradation control device. Out of a total district farming population of well over 10,000 males, to the best of my knowledge there have never been over twenty-five Peasant Farmers and seventy-five Improved Farmers. Moreover, the degree of intensification among these has decreased, if anything, through the years. According to the agricultural assistant, at the Lusitu, in 1965, those wishing to become Rural Council Improved Farmers wanted to grow unrotated cotton. In 1967, most Peasant Farmers had sown cotton or maize in plots that they were supposed to plant in green manure crops.

In the Kayuni block of the Lusitu, the most enterprising of the five Peasant Farmers was mono-cropping cotton during a four-year period, after which he planned to carry on a cotton-maize rotation.[25] He had also stopped applying manure, although the reason, as with other progressive farmers, was the breakdown of his Scotch cart, for which it was literally impossible to get parts because of the Rhodesian crisis. Moreover, he had substantially increased his acreage with twenty acres planted in cotton and nine in maize, compared to only three in sun hemp and one in groundnuts during the 1966–67 season.

As for the application of manure at the village level, no one in the village that I have been following over the past ten years had applied it during the previous season, or any other season for that matter. No form of rotation was used either. Indeed, I doubt that it is an exaggeration to state that no more than one per cent of the valley farmers have ever practiced either animal manuring or crop rotation on a regular basis.

The present relocation areas cannot support the existing population under these agricultural practices. In South Mwemba, the population has exceeded the carrying capacity of the land and is once again subjected to periodic food shortages which are bound to get worse. To prevent this, the government has decided to re-relocate at least 6000 people, and it is only a matter of time before this resettlement occurs. Elsewhere, the situation is still within the control of the local population, since exhausted fields can still be replaced by uncultivated land around the margins of the relocation areas or in the few areas which have yet to be settled. On the other hand, I expect all available land to be utilized within the next ten years unless there is a major reduction of population or change in agricultural techniques. In the highly favored Lusitu area, the surplus population is already crossing into the previously unsettled Mpendele-Mutulanganga area. Though no one in my own Lusitu study village had

joined this movement by 1967, some of the men had begun to clear distant gardens on the far side of the Lusitu. In all cases, no intensification was occurring; rather pioneer farmers were simply re-establishing the same extensive system of bush fallow cultivation.

Though the problem outlined in the last few paragraphs is a severe one, it is not my purpose in this paper to propose possible solutions. Rather I wish to emphasize in closing that what we are dealing with are two incompatible systems of agriculture. One, proposed by the Department of Agriculture, is satisfactory from an ecological point of view, but is not acceptable to the farming population. The other, while satisfying to the farmer, has serious, indeed catastrophic, ecological implications under the present population conditions. The problem is to design a compromise system which is acceptable to all involved. Throughout Africa, research stations have tended to develop new techniques without taking into consideration the total context within which the farmer, for whom these techniques are designed, lives.

Ecologists, I think, tend to make a similar mistake when they propose alternative land-use systems without asking the questions, "Can these support the existing human population which, after all, is the ecological dominant in the area?" And, "If not, is there an alternative way of life available for the people which they are likely to accept?" If, for example, cattle pastoralists are to be driven out of an area to be used for game-cropping or conservation purposes, the same concern must go into planning an acceptable future for them as for other communities within the habitat concerned. Failure to do this is not only morally indefensible but is also apt to be politically unacceptable. In other words, a technical or ecological solution to problems of environmental degradation is useless unless it is understood and implemented by the relevant people at the local and national levels.

[25] This schedule warrants testing under valley conditions as a possible basis for a compromise rotation.

REFERENCES

Bainbridge, W. R., and Edmonds, A. C. R. *Northern Rhodesia Forest Department Management Book for Gwembe, South Choma and Mazabuka Districts.* 1963.

Boughey, A. S. "The Explosive Development of a Floating Weed Vegetation in Lake Kariba." *Adansonia,* Vol. III, No. 1 (1962), pp. 49–61.

Coulter, G. W. "What's Happening at Kariba?" *New Scientist,* Dec. 28, 1967.

Harding, D. "Lake Kariba: The Hydrology and Development of Fisheries." In *Man-Made Lakes,* R. H. Lowe-McConnell, ed. New York: Academic Press, 1966.

Jackson, P. B. N. *Ichthyology: The Fish of the Middle Zambezi.* Kariba Studies. Manchester-Manchester University Press for National Museums of Southern Rhodesia, 1961.

Little, E. C. S. "The Invasion of Man-made Lakes by Plants." In *Man-Made Lakes,* R. H. Lowe-McConnell, ed. New York: Academic Press, 1966.

Scudder, T. *The Ecology of the Gwembe Tonga,* Kariba Studies, Vol. II. Manchester-Manchester University Press for Rhodes-Livingstone Institute, 1962.

———. "The Kariba Case: Manmade Lakes and Resource Development in Africa."

Bulletin of the Atomic Scientists, December, 1965.

———. "Manmade Lakes and Social Change." *Engineering and Science,* Vol. XXIX, No. 6 (1966a).

———. "Man-Made Lakes and Population Resettlement in Africa." In *Man-Made Lakes,* R. H. Lowe-McConnell, ed. New York: Academic Press, 1966b.

———. "The Economic Basis of Egyptian Nubian Labor Migration." In *A Symposium on Contemporary Nubia,* R. Fernea, ed. New Haven: HRAF Press, 1967.

———. "Social Anthropology, Manmade Lakes and Population Relocation in Africa." *Anthropological Quarterly,* Vol. 41, No. 3 (1968).

UNPUBLISHED GOVERNMENT REPORTS

Department of Veterinary and Tsetse Control Services. Annual Reports, 1960, 1963.

Steel, W. S., and Gledhill, J. A. A Survey of the Distribution of *Glossina* Species and Factors Influencing Their Control in the Territory of Northern Rhodesia. Ca. 1957.

Republic of Zambia. Department of Veterinary and Tsetse Control Services. Annual Report, 1966.

14. SOME ECOLOGICAL IMPLICATIONS OF MEKONG RIVER DEVELOPMENT PLANS

John E. Bardach

The Lower Mekong River Basin is about to undergo many alterations as a result of a comprehensive water resources development project supervised by the United Nations and the governments of Cambodia, Laos, Thailand, and Vietnam (South). The planners of the various dams and other river developments intend to change a seasonally variable water supply to one controlled by man, to curb destructive floods, and to make energy cheap and abundant. But there are many drastic effects which will occur on the Basin's nonhuman and human ecology. At present, overall ecological changes are being given little serious consideration in weighing the benefits and the true costs of the river control program. The project is proceeding, yet little planning or research has occurred to help the region and its people attempt to make an abrupt transition smoothly and productively.

The effects on fish and on fishing are likely to be serious; spawning grounds and river environments will be made inaccessible or unsuitable and several important food fish species may actually become extinct, although proper planning might ameliorate this effect by providing proper environments for some of these fish. Large lakes created by the dams could provide a large new source of fish, yet no planning has been done on selecting species, helping the farmers and forest-dwelling peoples learn to become fishermen, adapting the lake to encourage fish culture, or setting up extension services and marketing plans.

Agriculture will also be revolutionized, with accompanying serious dangers and problems. The regulation of the river flow will deprive the river valleys of the annual natural land improvement caused by flooding. Mineralization will accelerate; the soil temperature will increase; and fertility will decline. However, properly planned irrigation systems, crop diversification, soil management, and other changes in food culture could more or less prevent a decline in agricultural prosperity. In contrast, the highlands are already areas of poor land and increasing population, and careful soil management and irrigation would be needed. In these areas, dramatic cultural changes would have to occur if the highly individualistic upland peoples were to successfully cooperate to maintain the new irrigation-based agriculture; the many factors and new institutions which would be needed to attempt such change are at present not being planned, yet they are crucial if the altered land is to be made useful for its inhabitants.

The new irrigation and mass agriculture will themselves create serious problems. Diseases and their aquatic intermediate hosts will have a chance to spread widely, and there can easily be a sharp increase in schistosomiasis, liver fluke infections, eosinophilic meningitis, paragonimiasis, malaria, and Bancroftian filariasis, all debilitating or fatal diseases. The use of pesticides can have serious effects on local fish culture in the rice fields; pesticide use would be effective and minimally damaging only if the local tropical ecology of the pests were carefully considered in spraying schedules.

All these and other strains in the relation of man to the land on which he has to live are inevitable when such rapid changes are initiated. If those who plan and execute the changes attempt an assessment of optimal social and ecological rates of change, these consequences may be less painful and less destructive.

The Mekong, one of the great rivers of the world, rises in the mountains of China and flows through China, Burma, Laos, Thailand, Cambodia, and South Vietnam, entering the South China Sea some 2700 miles from its origin. The Lower Mekong Basin whose planning is considered here includes the river's watershed in the four riparian countries, Laos, Thailand, Cambodia and Vietnam, an area inhabited by twenty million people (United Nations, 1966).

To harness the heretofore undeveloped river, the governments of Cambodia, Thailand, Laos, and the Republic of Vietnam established a Committee for Coordination of Investigations of the Lower Mekong Basin, to work under the auspices of the U. N. Economic Commission for Asia and the Far East (ECAFE) "to promote, coordinate, supervise and control the planning and investigation of water resources development projects in the Lower Mekong Basin" (United Nations, ibid.). This project has now entered the implementation stage.

Several tributary projects have been completed and major mainstream projects are well advanced. It will take many decades for the development scheme to fully materialize, but considerable support has been forthcoming from outside countries. The "Mekong Committee" has thus far made good progress because of a spirit of cooperation among the member nations; the long-run success of the Mekong scheme will depend on a continuation of this spirit.

The planners and executors of the various phases intend to change a seasonally variable water supply to one controlled by man, to curb destructive floods and to make energy cheap and abundant.

In 1959, I flew over many square miles of the Mekong valley with an FAO team. Our first task was to decide what studies were necessary to select dam sites and to devise plans for contingent investigations (FAO, 1959). At the time of this survey over the main stream and a number of tributaries I was impressed by how strong and ubiquitous a stamp man has already put on this land, despite the low population density of certain regions. Even in what at first glance appeared wilderness there were many telltale signs of human occupancy. I have since viewed these signs from close up and marveled at the way they represent man's adjustment to a complex monsoon-dominated ecosystem.

This mutual adjustment of man and nature took place at a rate far slower than that engendered by *Homo faber occidentalis,* whose presence, heralded by our plane overhead, presaged that man's relationship to the land and its waterways would soon be channeled into new directions rapidly. This paper will explore some changes that the dams of the Mekong project are likely to cause in the nonhuman components of the Mekong ecosystem, but I cannot refrain from believing that the repercussions on the human coactors are equally important. As I firmly believe that it is easier to move earth than to move men and that dams can be built faster than new attitudes toward water and land use, I will also speculate on some approaches to improving the newly-to-be-created, dam-dominated ecology.

EFFECTS OF THE NEW DAMS ON FISHERIES

Fish and rice are the staff of life in Southeast Asia, and the Lower Mekong watershed encompasses some of the world's most productive freshwater fisheries. Contributing to this abundance are the yearly inundations of low-lying areas in Cambodia and Vietnam at the onset of the monsoon rains. Two large groups of freshwater fishes, the minnows (Cyprinidae) and the catfishes (Siluriformes), are represented by hundreds of species, a result of their evolutionary proliferation in Southeast Asia.

The total freshwater fish harvest in all Mekong-related waters is probably greater than 200,000 metric tons (F.A.O., 1966). Important components of this harvest are contributed by the fisheries of the Great Lake of Cambodia, by the fisheries of the Mekong River itself from Luang Prabang to the China Sea, and by a seasonal sea fishery off the Mekong Delta where certain species congregate at the time of the silt-laden, nutrient-rich high water flow.

While the natural histories of most species are incompletely known, our knowledge is sufficient to predict that the mainstream dams proposed at Pa Mong near Vientiane (for river control), and at Sambor or Stung Treng in northern Cambodia (for power production) would have several undesirable effects on the native fish.

The projected dams would certainly block the spawning migrations of a number of species. For instance, the largest true freshwater fish known, *Pangasianodon gigas,* which spawns above the Pa Mong dam site, would be kept from its breeding sites and almost certainly become extinct. Studies of its unknown migration patterns have not been carried out. Such studies might lead to artificial propagation below the dam. The economic value of the fish is uncertain although its roe, prepared like caviar, is a high-priced delicacy. Lifting devices such as fish ladders cannot be used here because of the unusual size and little-known habits of this species. Preservation for its own sake appears unlikely under the circumstances (Chevey, 1930b; Smith, 1945). The major dams will also bar some fish from access to important tributaries. Among the fish so affected would be the sardine-like *Hilsa* species caught in great numbers in northern Cambodia and in the Nong Han Lake of northeastern Thailand. Another highly prized food fish, *Cirrhinus* sp., ascends the Mekong and its larger tributaries above Sambor, the Se Kong, and the Se

San, side streams with great seasonal water fluctuations; this system might also be interrupted (Bardach, 1959).

These large dams will alter seasonal flow rates and bring subtle changes in the river bottom and in the interplay between flow and temperature at certain seasons, thereby altering the conditions upon which spawning physiology is based. The projected Pa Mong dam is a large structure and will certainly alter the stream flow below it and thus change the fish fauna (Chevey, 1930a, Chevey and LePoulain, 1940). Moreover, this portion of the river supplies protein to a region where it is scarce, thus making it imperative to avoid unfavorable impact on the fish population.

Seasonal inundation in low-lying areas of Cambodia and Vietnam is due in part to local excesses of rainwater and in part to flooding from the main river and its tributaries. Sediments carried onto land in this manner maintain fertility for both agriculture and fish production. Construction of the dams will prevent much of this sediment from reaching the agricultural lands. Eventually, control of the river implies that only irrigation agriculture will be practiced and that many swamps and lakes will disappear; with them will go the harvest from the untended fish populations that used to inhabit them. Additionally, since the dam-altered Mekong will carry less silt, the sea fish concentration in the river's effluent cone in the sea is bound to decrease, thereby lowering the harvest from another sector of the fishery economy.

All the preceding facts suggest that the dams will reduce the fish harvest from the Mekong ecosystem unless certain management measures not now planned are taken. Studies in various regions of India, China, and Soviet Russia have shown that large reservoirs can produce fish yields far greater than those previously harvested from the rivers they have modified. Requirements include the selection of species best suited

for each specific reservoir, the establishment of facilities for artificial propagation of certain desired species, and intensive management and regulation of the reservoirs. A team of biologists, technicians, and extension experts is desirable for each reservoir (Pantulu, 1966).

One of the planned major dams is to cross the outlet of the Great Lake of Cambodia and may permit application of such measures. In fact, one of the main benefits hoped for from this project is increased fish production. This now-shallow lake would be stabilized by the dam at a low-water depth of 2.5 meters, about one meter deeper than at present. At this water level there would be less stirring of sediments by the wind and more photosynthesis. The area of the new lake will be approximately three times its present size. It is hoped that the dam will allow fish to enter the lake with the rising water but will retain them at will when the water falls.

Fishing in the lake is now practiced by highly mobile fishermen who shift their abodes with the advancing and receding water. The fish harvest has declined over the past two decades due to changing land use around the lake, silt interfering with primary fish production, and heavy fishing. It is hoped that the overall effect of the dam will be one of increasing primary production in the aquatic ecosystem, although the species composition of the lake biota may change, with some species declining and some increasing. Since the present lake is being changed only to a larger but similar version of itself, one may expect the fishermen to adjust also (Fily and d'Aubenton, 1966).

Matters are different for both fish and men when new reservoirs are created. The story of the tributary reservoir built at Nam Pong in northeastern Thailand is an example to be heeded by planners of other and larger dams. When the new lake had been formed in 1966, extending over approximately 410 square kilometers, a fishery had also sprung up, unplanned, in expectation of fish proliferation. Middlemen and organizers for what promised to be a profitable venture were attracted, as were some settlers and outsiders displaced from their former homes, all of whom had to learn fishing as a new full-time or part-time trade. No extension services were provided for these new fishermen, and no rearing station for suitable high-yield fish species was established, but instead the new reservoir went untended and became top-heavy with predators. Although the predators, the snakeheads (*Ophiocephalus* sp.), are prized food fish, harvesting them is like cropping wolves instead of deer or cattle, and consequently the fish yield is considerably less than it might be.

It may, however, be argued that since fisheries were not included in planning the reservoir, even the limited output of the Nam Pong fishery (a yield of about 30 kilograms per hectare) was a success. In fact, optimal use of the reservoir's fish potential would have involved anticipatory attention to transportation, storage, and distribution facilities for sites a hundred or more kilometers away, in addition to the biological management of the reservoir. Now that a market is created, and growing rapidly, there should be concern for early changeover from the predator-dominated waters to a properly harvested and stocked fishery of herbivores, omnivores, and a few predators. Although the riparian countries' mutual agency has a fishery expert, his powers are advisory only. However, the proper planning of fisheries during dam and reservoir development, making them locally feasible, spells the difference between ecologically sound and unsound uses of a reservoir.

Only 150 kilometers to the northwest of Nam Pong is the proposed site of one of the world's largest dams, the Pa Mong, to contain a lake surface behind it of more than 1500 square kilometers. Like Nam Pong, it will cover forest land and displace thousands of people (few of them now are fishermen) from existing agricultural lands. If no advance planning is done for protein production, its now vaunted fishery potential is not likely to be realized. Under proper management the reservoir might produce between 10,000 and 20,000 metric tons of fish annually, an estimate based on yields from the Great Lake of Cambodia ecosystem and some well-managed Indian reservoirs. At a yearly per capita consumption rate of 20 kilograms, as in Cambodia, most of the animal protein needs of between a half-million and a million people could be supplied by this source. This amount far exceeds what is now caught in the river a hundred kilometers above and below the dam site. If the irrigation system to be created with the dam were shaped to include pond culture, this aquatic protein production could be multiplied: each one-hectare pond in Southeast Asia can yield a fish harvest of a ton per year, under even moderately intensive management.

It must be stressed, however, that realization of such potentials requires advance planning and early execution of adaptive research. These activites should include selection of species, propagation trials, and the devising of fishing methods and management techniques applicable to smaller reservoirs. Planning should cover such topics as where and how to clear trees and anticipation of distribution and marketing needs.

Furthermore, the problems to be anticipated in turning the present residents into fishermen may be even more difficult. While the prospect of changing the habits of traditional farmers has received attention from rural sociologists, anthropologists, and economists, parallel problems in fisheries have hardly been considered. It would be worthwhile to do so in planning the best fishery uses of the reservoirs now to be created on the Mekong.

POSSIBLE IMPACTS OF NEW DAMS ON MEKONG ECOLOGY

This section will be an overview and therefore suffers almost by definition from the same disregard of details that besets macro models such as the Mekong development scheme. Some possible consequences of dams appear clear, however.

In the present hydrological pattern certain low-lying areas near the river and its larger tributaries, especially in Cambodia and Vietnam, are flooded annually. A French colonial administrator wrote of them in the early 1900's: "This rhythmical movement of the waters, regular, like breathing, furnishes much of what is needed to improve the land. High waters deposit on the soil a layer of rich silt and spare the farmer the drudgery of transporting fertilizer to the fields, and when the water recedes he finds the ground all ready to support rich and remunerative crops" (Chevey and LePoulain, 1940).

These regions of rich river-valley fields on alluvial soils are the sites of the most diversified agriculture practiced in the valley and would certainly be endangered by a more regulated river flow. Mineralization would be accelerated; the soil temperature would increase; and their fertility would decline. However, due to their topography these lands could easily be irrigated; their cultivators are settled, and it may not take too much change in the farmer's outlook or reorganization of their practices to adapt to a new and also prosperous regime. I would also expect further crop diversification, the introduction of high-yield varieties, and some mechanization soon after irrigation water can be supplied.

In contrast to the fertile river valleys, most of the watershed of the Mekong has poor to medium-grade soils; they are dry, often leached, overused, and sometimes acid,

especially in northeastern Thailand with its low humic gleys, its gray and red-yellow podsols. Cultivation has been attempted where forests should have remained. Slash-and-burn agriculture is practiced in remote areas, as well as the burning of forests for driving game. The use of manure or fertilizer is virtually nonexistent. This type of land use is logical and perhaps even economically justifiable in an economy with a vast surplus of land. But given demographic trends, it must sooner or later conflict with other land-use patterns and lead to deleterious runoff and erosion. Eventually the shifting cultivators will settle and compete with small villages for suitable soil to grow crops. Without irrigation they would be limited to one crop a year, but their growing season could be nearly year-round if water were available. Given the trends of modern agriculture, the soils will inevitably be built up, rotation practiced, and fertilizers and probably insecticides employed for higher-yielding crop varieties, planted in terraces or strip-cropping patterns (Moorman *et al.,* 1964). The consequences of such practices will need to be studied. Let us hope that the new irrigation canals will be built with more regard for natural drainage patterns than those that now exist.

Theoretically, then, by building dams, vast areas of soil could be improved and changes in agricultural practices could occur. However, in the human ecology of the region formidable obstacles exist to attaining this utopian state. Transition to irrigation agriculture requires a complex social organization with cooperation between social units such as villages, delegation of authority, and a well-functioning central or provincial government extension service. Agriculture in much of the basin, and certainly in northeastern Thailand, is a family affair with each family autonomous in decision-making; help is traded between families only occasionally. The needs of irrigation agriculture are not compatible with the social units, and the kind of cooperation such techniques impose is virtually unknown among the villagers. The creation of irrigation districts with common funds to be administered would cause severe cultural dysfunctions.

All is not rosy either with the government representatives or officials who would have to help bring about the needed social and technical changes. There are still not enough of them with adequate training, especially in managerial techniques; there also is a lack of capability to adapt these techniques to the situation at hand. Consequently, there is little cooperation between numerous offices and departments, each concerned with one aspect of the problem. Also, there is heavy culturally engendered "capital dominance" in a few major population centers, such as Bangkok and Vientiane.

The traditional distance between the government officials and farmers also makes sound environmental administration difficult, though it must be said that many young technicians in the riparian countries are attempting to break this barrier; they are hampered in this by cultural resistances in their own ranks as well as by those between them and the farmers; there is also graft which works against any establishment of trust. In some regions there are language barriers, which can present an additional problem. Finally, present facilities for farm credit are rudimentary at best and the beneficiaries of such credit are not prepared, culturally, to plan over time spans of several years.

These obstacles are not insuperable, as has been shown occasionally in other parts of the world. Nevertheless, the macro-model builder's cost-benefit ratios for Mekong development are probably not attainable, at the least not as soon as they would hope to attain them. The main difficulties lie partly in relations between people and partly on an overemphasis upon purely technological solutions to problems. Assist-

ing technicians and the riparians have cultural license to converse about flow, rainfall, soil types, fertilizer, proper material for pipes, etc., but not about how officials are appointed and what their attitudes to the farmers might be to ease and speed needed transitions. Similarly there is little chance to develop sound extension that is necessary to encourage a farmer scarcely removed from subsistence cropping to go into debt over several years for the sake of a possible future benefit. Clearly there is a one-sided emphasis in Mekong development planning.

It is perhaps not germane to this conference to speculate on how to redress this imbalance, but it is important to stress that ecologists and sociologists must be given a stronger voice both in the planning process and in the execution of the various schemes, because they can be instrumental in bridging at least a few of the gaps in understanding that now exist.

As a result of dams many square kilometers of new water surfaces and many kilometers of new shorelines will emerge in the Mekong Valley. Many watercourses will have new connections such as the new canal from Pa Mong to Nam Pong. Diseases and their aquatic intermediate hosts will have an opportunity to spread. Snails and mosquitoes are probably of greatest concern as vectors. Snails are known to carry a liver fluke (the snail host is *Bythnia* spp.) and three species of schistosomes (*S. japonicum, S. spindale,* and *Trichobilharzia* spp.). Opisthorchiasis (liver fluke) infection is reasonably high in certain portions of northeastern Thailand; in the makeshift village where the fish from Nam Pong reservoir are landed, it is suspected to have reached a hundred percent. The incidence of schistosomiasis is, at present, low, but snails are also hosts of the worm parasite *Angiostrongylus cantonensis,* manifesting itself mainly in brain damage. As snails have greatly increased at Nam Pong, are harvested copiously and are eaten raw in a light pickle, central nervous system damage due to this parasite is believed to have risen in the reservoir area. Paragonimiasis is also endemic in northern Thailand; its metacercariae have been located in freshwater crabs. Diseases carried by water-dependent insects include malaria and Bancroftian filariasis, both now having low incidence levels in the area.

There is a reasonably good chance that the intermediate hosts of these diseases may undergo proliferation when permanent waters are increased through mainstream or tributary reservoirs as some of them already have at Nam Pong. The health authorities of the riparian countries are at present ill-equipped to carry out an evaluation of the probable results from changes in the aquatic ecology. To my knowledge, inadequate attention is paid to the problem on the part of international organizations. Strategies for increased mosquito eradication and the use of mollusk poisons are the least measures that should be anticipated. The ecological consequences of both water development programs and of disease control projects have been discussed by other participants in the Conference.

The new dams will also affect wildlife habitats throughout the region. Presently the largest planned dam is Pa Mong. No bird and mammal survey has been done in the area to be flooded; it is not certain if any unique habitats or truly endemic species exist in the extensive reservoir site. Nevertheless, such a faunistic survey would be well worth making.

Another potential dam development centers on Khone Falls and Stung Treng in northern Cambodia; while no feasibility studies of this project have been made as yet, preliminary reconnaissance indicates that considerable areas of savannah habitat would be flooded. The water would cover a region known to harbor not only the rare primitive cattle, the kouprey (*Bos sauveli*),

already threatened by uncontrolled hunting, but also a large number of other ungulates. Their density is reported to rival that of ungulates on the African plains, and game farming in northern Cambodia appears as a distinct wildlife management possibility. It is highly recommended that an intensive survey of the larger vertebrates of this region be made and that, should the findings warrant it, a good conservation land use such as game farming be considered in the planning for river modifications in this area.

If irrigation is practiced in some portions of the basin as a result of dams and reservoirs, farming will become intensified and with it the use of insecticides. It is hoped that by that time chlorinated hydrocarbons will have been replaced universally by nonpersistent varieties. Fishes are very susceptible to certain insecticides. Some adaptive research may be necessary to safeguard fish harvests, and certainly to make possible fish culture either in conjunction with the growing of rice or in ponds close to areas where other crops need insecticide treatment. It should be stressed that insecticide use in the tropics can lead to aggravated problems in pest control because of the insects' year-round growing season and their consequent ability to develop resistant strains faster than insects of the temperate zone. Attention also must be paid to the peculiar nature of tropical soils, both wet and dry.

CODA

Under any political system the population of the Mekong basin is sure to increase, and its aspirations will rise. Increased power and improved agriculture are therefore desirable, as are the other benefits of dams such as flood control and the improvement of navigation. Dysfunctions in even the nonhuman ecology may result from a planning process that relies too much on what man can do with bulldozers and cement. Strains in the relation of man to the land on which he has to live are inevitable when such rapid changes are initiated. If those who plan and execute the changes attempt an assessment of optimal social and ecological rates of change, these consequences may be less painful. For this assessment studies now not undertaken are needed, as is the advice at all levels of ecologists and sociologists, representatives of disciplines sometimes but not sufficiently frequently consulted.

I thank my colleagues at the Center for Southeast Asian Studies of Kyoto University, where this paper was written, and R. V. Pantulu of the Mekong Committee for much counsel and advise.

ACKNOWLEDGMENTS

REFERENCES

Bardach, J. *Report on Fisheries in Cambodia.* United States Operations Mission in Cambodia, 1959. mimeo., 80 pp.

Chevey, P. "Sur divers rhythmes autres que les rhythmes thermiques susceptibles de marquer les écailles de poisson de la zone intertropicale." *C. R. Acad., Sci.* (Paris), 1 90:(1930a), 280–81.

———. "Sur un nouveau silure géant du Basin du Mékong (*Pangasianodon gigas*), nov. g. nov. sp." *Bull. Soc. Zool. Franc.*, 55 (1930b), 536–42.

Chevey, P., and LePoulain, C. *La Pêche dans les eaux douces du Cambodge.* Trav. Inst. Oceanogr. Indochine, 5ᵉ mem. Saigon, 1940. 193 pp.

Food and Agriculture Organization. *A Survey of the Investigations Required for Planning Development of Agriculture, Forestry and Fisheries in the Lower Mekong Basin.* Rome, 1959. mimeo., 40 pp.

———. *Yearbook of Fisheries Statistics, Catches and Landings,* Vol. 22, Rome, 1966.

Fily, M., and d'Aubenton, F. "Cambodia, Report on Fisheries Technology in the Great Lake and the Tonle Sap, Pt. 2." *Min. For. Aff. Dep. Tech. Coop. Republ. Française.* Paris: Nat. Mus. Hist. Naturelle, 1966. Esp. pp. 475–509.

Moorman, F. R.; Montrakun, J.; and Panichapong, S. *Soils of Northeastern Thailand, a Key to Their Identification and Survey.* MSR 9. Bangkok, Thailand: Land Dev. Dept. Soil Surv. Div., 1964. 32 pp.

Pantulu, V. R. "Studies of Fisheries Aspects of Lower Mekong Basin Development." *Ind. J. Power and River Valley Devel.*, (Calcutta, India), *Mekong Project Number* (1966), pp. 65–67.

Smith, H. M. "The Freshwater Fishes of Siam or Thailand." *Bull. Dep. Fish.* (Washington, D.C.), No. 188 (1945). 622 pp.

United Nations. *A Compendium of Major International Rivers in the ECAFE Region.* Water Resources Series No. 29. New York, 1966.

DISCUSSION

MARSHALL: In both of the past two sessions we have heard a lot about the Aswan High Dam. I for one would like to know what the expectations were for increased agricultural output, etc., resulting from this dam.

KASSAS: The High Dam is a source of power first and foremost. Second, it will give Egypt water enough to cultivate 1 million new acres and change the 700,000 acres presently cultivated under basin irrigation to perennial irrigation.

MYRDAL: How large is the total cultivated acreage now?

KASSAS: Total acreage now cultivated within Egypt is about 7 million acres.

DASMANN: To follow up on the last question, what is the loss of land that you predict in the Nile Delta as a result of construction of the Aswan High Dam? How does that compare with the projected gain in irrigated land? Is land already going out of production as a result of shoreline erosion?

KASSAS: Not yet. The northern part of the Delta which is cultivated and drained mechanically, is made up of fields having a ground level varying from 50 centimeters to 1.5 meters above sea level. These lands are already below, at least seasonally, the water level in the brackish water lakes of Burullus and Manzala. At present Lake Burullus and Lake Manzala are separated from the Mediterranean Sea by narrow and very fragile bars of sand. This is all that remains of much broader belts of land that once separated these lakes from the sea.

We think that if these bars collapse, the lakes would be transformed into marine bays; this would bring the sea next to cultivated land, and if the embankments now protecting the cultivated land eroded and broke, then the agricultural areas would be inundated by sea water. Even if these embankments didn't break, there is the danger of salt spray, which may travel inland as far as several kilometers. I cannot tell you for certain what is going to happen. I am only saying that there is a real danger of marine inundation of certain areas.

SCUDDER: What might be some of the technical mechanisms for reducing the risks here?

KASSAS: It all depends on whether we start today or whether we had started ten years ago or whether we will actually start five years from now.

Ten years ago we had a good deal of sediment movement along the shoreline, at least in the flood season. It would have been easy to build a series of short, inexpensive groynes perpendicular to the shore. These would have trapped a good deal of sediment and built up the shoreline. At present, there is little sediment movement along the shoreline; we will have to devise, not groynes, but more expensive sea walls. If these sea walls were constructed now we would still have the thin bars of sand to make the construction easier and less expensive.

If we wait until these bars are completely destroyed, we will probably have to build these sea walls in the sea itself, which would be frightfully expensive.

BATISSE: Dr. Kassas refers to the fact that the sediments of the Nile no longer build up the barriers that protect Egypt from the sea. But perhaps there is an equally dangerous situation, referred to in Dr. Worthington's paper, affecting the soils of the whole Nile Valley downstream. For the first time in history all the sediments will now be retained behind the High Dam and will no longer be deposited on the fields of Egypt. Is not this a most serious consequence of the High Dam? Another obvious consequence, of course, is the loss of water by evaporation: about one cubic meter will be lost out of every eight cubic meters of the Nile flow, which is a very high proportion due to the geographical location and the size of the lake.

KASSAS: Certainly, there will be a loss of mineral nutrition for the soil, but with modern fertilizers this may be compensated for.

The intense evaporation, I understand, was taken into consideration by people who planned the High Dam. This is of the order of 10 or 15 billion cubic meters per year. But what they probably did not consider is the danger of this lake being infested by water plants such as reeds and water hyacinths.

I calculate that if only 10 per cent of the surface area of the water behind the High Dam be covered with a mixture of phragmites, *Cyperus* or water hyacinth, the increase in water loss by evapotranspiration would amount to 10 billion cubic meters.

MILTON: I do think it is important to emphasize that formerly sediments provided free basin fertilization. Now, below Aswan and the barrages, artificial fertilizers

can be used, but who will pay for them? And was this expense built into the cost/benefit ratio for the dam? I doubt it.

RUSSELL: Can I ask a question of geomorphology? I presume the Nile Valley must be sinking slowly because silt has been deposited on the Nile Valley now for thousands of years, and the levels have remained more or less the same. Presumably, then, the rate of sinking of the valley has been more or less the same as the deposition of silt.

I assume the construction of the High Dam, in the period of centuries, will mean that the valley will continue to sink, and so we will get a transgression of the sea, because the valley will sink without being made good through additional silt deposits. Is that a bit of sound prediction, or a bit of nonsense?

KASSAS: Whether the Nile Valley or the Nile Delta is sinking, or whether the Mediterranean is rising, it amounts to the same thing. But it is true from the terrace formations that the base line of the river has been going down compared with the Mediterranean during the last 500,000 years, with only minor oscillations up and down. This has caused the terraces in the upper region of the Nile. There is evidence showing that during the last 2000 years the sea level has been rising.

These are long-term processes. But here we are dealing with a short-term process that began just in the last hundred years. The dam building started in about 1840 when Mohammed Ali started his barrages. Then came the Aswan Dam, then the dams on the Blue Nile, the White Nile, the Atbara River, the Khashm el-Girba, and lastly, the High Dam. The High Dam has put a finishing touch on a long story.

The marine transgression due to receding shorelines of the Delta has been going on for at least one hundred years, a very brief span of time. The fact that the Mediterranean Sea is rising relative to the ground level (or that the ground level is dropping relative to the Sea) by some 12 or 14 centimeters per century is not enough to explain the marine transgression that is taking place. The transgression, therefore, is to a great extent the work of man, not of natural factors.

CARLOZZI: Has anyone made any estimates of what is going to happen to the normal channel of the Nile with the flow of water that is freed from sediments? What is the rate of channel closing going to be?

Our experience below dams in the United States shows a very rapid rate. And since this lowers the whole stream, any water that has to come out of the stream requires a higher lift if it is going to be used for irrigation below the dam. Has this been investigated at all?

KASSAS: I understand that they have to put some thirty thousand tons of gravel at the foundations of some of the barrages to secure the foundation from increased erosion, and that a series of new barrages will be built across the Nile from Aswan to Cairo.

VAN DER SCHALIE: I don't want to complicate this, but it appears to me that if we get more marine waters coming inland, we might develop a *Heterophyes* problem that might be quite severe. *Heterophyes* is a parasitic trematode that people get from eating small fish. We thought it had a very low incidence, but when Dr. Kuntz studied it in Balteem he found that almost the whole population was quite heavily infested. If the fisheries there must be developed to counteract what you are losing in agricultural productivity, and we don't have some way of curbing this disease either with snail control or some other medical approach, I can see where we might develop some serious problems with the disease.

GEORGE: *Heterophyes*, I think, is being transmitted in two ways now. The first is in a salted preparation called *fiseekh*. If it is not allowed to cure long enough, the parasite is not killed; it is carried on. The second way is just through direct eating of *samak nayye*, or raw fish. So this is perhaps one point of control: giving greater attention to the proper curing of the *fiseekh*—at least by advertising the problem of *Heterophyes* when you eat raw fish.

But the important hosts for this parasite now are the *Mugilidae* of some four or five different species. It is likely that with the increased salinization of the four lakes the reproductivity of the *Muglidae* will be decreased. And thus, I think you will have fewer of the host animals there to carry the parasite. In a way, this may improve the *Heterophyes* problem rather than worsen it.

MENDELSSOHN: The gray mullet moves and is born in salt water. In fact the increasing salinization of the lakes is what makes it possible for the fish to spawn in the lakes. They may also spawn in the sea and migrate into the brackish water to grow.

GEORGE: The very important stage, of course, is when the young fish migrate into the lakes to grow.

MENDELSSOHN: They carry the *Heterophyes* with them.

GEORGE: Apparently so.

MENDELSSOHN: Do they acquire it in the sea?

GEORGE: I don't know where they acquire it.

MENDELSSOHN: They probably do because one can get infested with *Heterophyes* by eating raw fish caught in the sea.

GEORGE: Do they pick up the infection in the sea or in the brackish water lakes?

MENDELSSOHN: Yes, in the sea. The transmitting host snail is *Pirenelle*.

VAN DER SCHALIE: This snail can stand quite a lot of salinity. It is quite an adaptable snail, but it is more marine than brackish. This is why my question was directed to the fact that you are creating more marine conditions, you see.

I think here again, we have a host-parasite relationship that really hasn't been studied very well. All I was trying to interject was the question: "Are we looking at some of the attendant problems of the new High Dam?"

MILTON: I wonder what the causes were for the disappointing fish production behind the Kariba Dam. As I recall, there was an expectation that the production would be fairly high, and this prediction was built into the cost-benefit ratio, I suppose, in supporting the case for the construction of the dam.

What are the arguments for predicting high fish production in the case of Lake Nasser? Could also we have some problems similar to the nutrient loss and waterlogging at Kariba?

Also, what problems are the Egyptians having with salinization, in the area being irrigated with waters from Lake Nasser?

SCUDDER: On the Kariba question, let me emphasize that Kariba was conceived largely as a unipurpose scheme. I would say that power was the only consideration in the cost-benefit analysis. All of the other costs and benefits, and they appear to be primarily costs, were not taken into consideration either during the feasibility study or subsequently. The hope is, of course, that subsequent evaluations will take these costs into consideration and one will better be able to appraise whether or not Kariba was a net benefit or loss.

The problems relating to the decreased fish yield in Kariba are almost entirely ecological, and probably apply very specifically to Kariba; I don't think too much generalization can be made for Aswan from this case.

In Kariba about a quarter of a million acres of bush were cleared at tremendous cost—2.5 million pounds. That was only half of the acreage that could have been cleared if the entire area had been cleared from high-water line to a hundred-foot depth.

This means that half of the lake is a fish preserve with fish protected in the areas which are still heavily vegetated. The trees are not decaying as you might expect to be the case in this area. The crowns in the shallow waters still stick above the surface of the water, especially during the drawdown. So it is very difficult to get into these uncleared areas of over a quarter of a million acres for fishing purposes. An effective technology has not yet been worked out to fish these particular areas, granted the weed problem and granted the unclearing of the trees and hence the net-snagging of gill net fishermen.

Another problem is that originally Kariba was stratified at about 13 meters; during the first five or six years it was completely anaerobic below the thermocline, but more recently evidence has appeared that the thermocline will eventually vanish over much of the area. If this happens, fish populations may be going into deeper, uncleared waters where, again, they are unavailable.

One other problem is that the most important commercial species, *Tilapia mossambica,* although observed to breed during the years immediately after inundation, is apparently not breeding today. The fish now being cropped mostly are the larger ones which were present as fry at the time the area was flooded. The reasons why *Tilapia* are not breeding are not known. Nevertheless, yields on the north bank decreased from over 3000 tons in 1963 to the present figure somewhere between 1000 and 2000 tons, and we expect a similar situation on the south bank.

WORTHINGTON: In the case of Aswan we are creating a new lake with a fish fauna already adapted to lake living—for Lake No and Lake Albert have almost exactly the same fish fauna. So one can predict that when Lake Nasser has settled down, perhaps five to ten years hence, its fish production will be not dissimilar to the proved fish production in the fisheries of Lake Albert, which runs about 20 pounds per acre.

When you consider Kariba, however, you are dealing with a fish fauna which is adapted to living only in the River Zambesi which has no natural lakes. So you have a situation in which at present much potential open-water habitat is not used fully by fish.

GEORGE: I think I would like to challenge you a bit on this, Dr. Worthington. I think Lake Albert is much more constant in its level, isn't it? What is the level variation in Lake Albert around the year? A couple of meters?

WORTHINGTON: The level variation in Lake Albert is two to three meters. Yes, there will be a greater level variation in Lake Nasser, but my prediction is that this will not have a very pronounced influence on fish production.

SCUDDER: What will be the drawdown in Lake Nasser approximately?

GEORGE: It is supposed to be seven meters from one authority, but I think it will be more than that. This is bound to have considerable influence on the fisheries.

HASKELL: I understand that a lot of the *Salvinia* in Kariba is concentrated around the inlets. Isn't it possible that it is filtering out a lot of nutrients that should go to support fish food?

SCUDDER: I think this is a valid assumption, but perhaps Dr. Worthington can say more on it.

WORTHINGTON: This is a valid comment. The point is now being studied intensively by Rhodesian scientists. Their work does indicate that the *Salvinia* is using up a great deal of nutrients.

On the other hand a great deal of that *Salvinia* mat is dead. And when it is dead, it reduces very substantially the amount of evaporation from free water surface, so that you have a possible beneficial effect from weed cover as well as a deleterious one.

KASSASS *Salvinia* is a submergent plant.

A weed type like *Cyperus* is much more important in evapotranspiration.

SCUDDER: Given that the conditions are not anaerobic below these mats, as people feared at first, is it not possible that you may also have a more complex associated plankton and thus edible fauna such as snails and such things?

WORTHINGTON: No, because these weed mats are opaque. And as soon as you cut out the light of the sun, you cut out most biological productivity.

BORGSTROM: What are the economics of the mineral nutrients of the Egyptian farmer? Some four or five years back, I came to the conclusion that the natural gain through the deposition of river silt, which brought fertility free of charge to the average Egyptian farmer, had not been regained following flood control. In other words, he now has to buy fertilizer. But how is this really to be judged economically? Since he is now having to pay for the fertilizers which used to come free, specifically, in terms of potassium and phosphate, what has he gained?

GEORGE: When you shift from basin to perennial irrigation, you are already working the soil too hard. And so the moment you shift, you are required automatically to go to application of artificial fertilizers. But fertilizers apparently are available and will become more available with the completion of new chemical factories producing nitrogen, ammonium nitrite, and other fertilizers. The mineral resources of the country yield an average phosphate rock. In fact, phosphate is the second leading mineral product of the country. So the fertilizer aspect of the Egyptian situation is perhaps not as difficult or as complex, as it was originally thought to be.

BORGSTROM: Is all this true also for the poor farmer?

WORTHINGTON: A basic point in the agricultural economics of the change from basin irrigation to perennial irrigation has not been mentioned. With perennial irrigation the region will change automatically from one crop per annum to two, three, or even four crops per annum. This alters the whole basis of the economics and the potential to buy fertilizer.

SCUDDER: But this wouldn't apply in the Delta which presumably is the larger acreage involved. There the farmer is going to have to put on a greater amount of fertilizer, and this is going to increase his cost. As the price of fertilizer goes down or is somehow subsidized from the point of view of the individual peasant, he still is going to be paying more than before, isn't he, to get the same? Because there won't be any transition there: only the rich flood waters will cease to come, without compensation.

RUSSELL: I think I can say that Egypt has probably got the most efficient extension service of any country in Africa. The speed with which the results of research go into practice is quite phenomenal.

SCUDDER: But isn't the question how the poor farmer is going to pay for the increased fertilizer?

BORGSTROM: Yes.

SCUDDER: That has nothing to do with extension service efficiency!

COMMONER: Since the question of the replacement of natural fertility by means of chemical fertilizers, particularly nitrogen, has come up here, I want to mention that there is a cost associated with the use of inorganic nitrogen fertilizer: the appearance of oxidized forms of nitrogen in the environment in places where it ordinarily doesn't belong.

In the United States, we have now forced nitrogen (nitrates) into rain, into surface waters, into plants (this is something that Dr. Schuphan is going to be talking about) because we have consumed much of the soil's original organic nitrogen and have replaced it with inorganic nitrogen to continue getting high yields. But in the corn belt, at least half of the fertilizer nitrogen draws

into surface waters where it is responsible for pollution.

Perhaps some of you who are familiar with the situation in Egypt may be able to make some remarks about the organic content of the soil which, in turn, relates to the efficiency of nutrient absorption by the roots. What will happen to that efficiency as you switch from an input of organic nitrogen to inorganic nitrogen.

M. T. FARVAR: Apparently not very much is known about the exact contribution of organic versus inorganic nutrients from the floodwaters. Although there is a rich inorganic supply from the volcanic basalt highlands of Ethiopia, it is probable that in the course of a very long journey down the Nile a good deal of these nutrients may have become converted to organic compounds. This depends on the path of these nutrients in the hydrobiological cycles. One thing is certain: that there is visible deterioration in the farmlands below the High Dam, with a good deal of loss of formerly productive land to dry uselessness. Aerial photography would reveal only patches of green within the boundaries of formerly cultivated areas. These boundaries are increasingly hard to distinguish, as the sand invades and covers them up. It is clear that the opportunity for assessing many of these problems has already been lost, for there is a lack of good base-line data against which to compare the new regime of the river.

RUSSELL: I think—Dr. Kassas could correct me—about one-third to a half of the Egyptian soils in the wintertime carry Berseem clover. Berseem clover is an extremely important crop for fixing nitrogen in Egyptian soils; it certainly adds a great deal to the soil.

KASSAS: Of course, with the practice of agriculture, the Egyptian fellaheen always put organic manure into the fields. And this, I must say, costs almost nothing.

COMMONER: Except labor. Is that being continued?

KASSAS: Yes. They mix the cow droppings with silt and clay from the riverbanks to make their own compost.

BORGSTROM: I think it is essential that we not lose sight of the magnitude of the needs we are facing. I find particularly disturbing our approach to discussing the fishing potential of Africa or discussing, as Dr. Bardach does in his paper, the potentials of the Mekong River.

The world's largest dam, the Pa Mong on the Mekong, might in the future be capable of providing many people with protein resources.* However, the minute we look at that situation, we realize first of all that this is a big dam and that this Mekong River area is today already filled with 50 million people and will soon contain double that. Against the needs of that population, the needs of the people actually served by Pa Mong is really very limited. And this dam project has to be looked at against a background of all the complications that the Americans, the Chinese, the Russians, and the African biologists have found in developing these tropical reservoirs. The practical findings have shown how very difficult this undertaking is.

I think this overview also applies to our discussion of the Nile; when we add one million acres, this is a very impressive technical accomplishment, but in terms of the population situation of the Nile area, we should remind ourselves of the fact that this is a very small addition to the tremendous growth and resource needs of the population. I think it is very important in our discussions here that we relate these ecological facts to this fundamental fact of the already enormous and growing world needs.

WHITE: It should be remembered that a

* *Milton's note*: The proposed Pa Mong and other large Mekong dam projects may also contribute to serious fishery losses, especially in the Mekong mainstream fisheries and Cambodia's Great Lake, through interruption of spawning and other needs; the possibility of marine fishery losses off the Mekong Delta is also very real, due to loss of sediment and nutrients (as happened off the Nile Delta).

number of the relationships we have discussed here in the last few minutes concerning the Nile are still speculative. For example, we are not clear how much soil could be developed in the Nile Valley beyond that which is already under cultivation.

We also are not at all clear as to what the effect of a blanket of vegetation would be on evaporation from a lake surface. Total evapotranspiration from a saturated surface is primarily a function of energy input rather than the character of the surface. We are not at all clear what the full set of adjustments in channel conditions will be as the dam operates with its storage over a period of time.

There are a lot of question marks. But passing over these question marks, I think we can draw from the Nile several lessons that would be equally applicable to the Mekong or a good many other large river development schemes.

One lesson is that when a major project like the Sadd-el-Aali project gets under way, there comes a stage when the engineers and administrators turn to the ecologists and say, "What is going to happen?" At that stage they often respond, as Dr. Worthington quoted them as responding in his paper, by saying that prediction is hardly worth the paper it is written on because there will always be so many unknown factors. It often happens that the ecologist doesn't figure further in the project because he in effect has read himself out by indicating the very complexity of these systems with which he is dealing and his unwillingness to make the kind of intuitive judgments which Dr. Worthington was saying need to be made at some stage.

Second, when a proposal is made for improvement of an area, such as agriculture in the Delta of the Nile or agricultural production in the Mekong, public attention focuses on one alternative which seems to be promising. There then is a kind of closing of the ranks and a tendency to exclude consideration of any other alternatives.

This happened at one stage with respect to the Sadd-el-Aali. It is remarkable that today we do not have in the literature a careful analysis of what might be expected to be the full set of economic impacts of this project. Once the decision had been made to go ahead with it, consideration of the alternatives tended to be excluded.

We are seeing this happen again in the United States' current intervention on the Pa Mong Dam on the Mekong. Again there is a tendency to exclude consideration of any alternative ways of strengthening the economy. Somewhere along the line, it is particularly important to be sensitive to keeping the public consideration open to the other possibilities until there has been a chance for ecologists to explore the possible impacts in a broad fashion.

We may be a very long time finding out about the impacts of the Sadd-el-Aali. It has been possible to get government initiative with the United Nations Development Program to try to determine the immediate impacts of the reservoir in its fill area. However, there has been no comprehensive attempt to find out what the full effects will be downstream.

I think a major reason for this is that there was an early public commitment to one alternative and a reluctance now to investigate what the other possibilities might have been.

WORTHINGTON: I think this is a supremely important contribution by Professor White. It is reinforced by the fact that there was an alternative to the High Aswan Dam, namely the upper Nile project, the Jonglei Canal and the Lake Albert Dam, which had been thoroughly investigated. It was, in fact, an excellent ecological, economic, agricultural and sociological study and prediction of possible effects in the Sudan, published in several large volumes. This was, I suppose, one of the most thorough predictive studies ever

made for a major development project. But, it is all permanently on the shelf now because of the sudden decision to concentrate on the High Aswan Dam for which there is no such study.

COMMONER: Just a small question. Is there any functional connection between the choice of the alternative project and the fact that the project not chosen had been studied ecologically?

SCUDDER: Was the Aswan High Dam project worked out in connection with the knowledge known from the Jonglei Canal?

WORTHINGTON: No.

M. T. FARVAR: Dr. White's remarks precipitated two questions in my mind which are about the simplest questions one could ask about upstream and downstream effects.

Is it possible to assess at this point how much land has been lost upstream to the inundation of water, over the 500 kilometers from the Aswan Dam into the Sudan? Dr. Scudder has pointed out that this inundation caused the Nubian farmers to give up cultivation of the banks.

The second question is similar; how much land, if any, has been lost downstream since basin irrigation is no longer possible because the floods are not coming any more?

KASSAS: On the downstream part, we are not losing the 700,000 acres which is under basin irrigation. This area will be transformed into perennial irrigation—meaning an increase in the productivity. But this is all in Upper Egypt, between Aswan and Asyut.

SCUDDER: The upstream impact was very serious in 1903 when the first Aswan Dam was built and also serious during the first heightening in 1912 and the second heightening in 1933. In fact, the High Dam itself, because of the previous inundation, is now inundating under less than 10,000 feddans.

CONWAY: I want to turn to the Mekong. I visited the Nam Pong Dam about a month ago and studied it in some detail. It does provide a rather nice case history suggesting that there are going to be tremendous problems with the major dams along the mainstream Mekong.

This Nam Pong Dam was completed in 1966 at a cost of between $55 and $60 million and at present is yielding electricity at the rate of $1 million per year. The original estimate was that it would produce 8 million kilograms of fish per year. In the first two years, it produced 2 million kilograms per year and this year it has only produced about 1.3 million kilograms so far. The return from fish has only been half a million dollars per year.

So we have a return so far of $1.5 million per year on a $55 to $60 million investment.

The rest of the investment return is expected from irrigating the agricultural land below the dam. As I understand it, the assumption is that once the farmers receive the water, then they somehow will be able to use this and produce an estimated $3.5 million per year in crops. But there is no experiment station actually located there, and there is no real attempt at present to work out how this water can best be used.

Going back to the fisheries, there is a very dense algae cover on the surface of the water—large pieces of algae, perhaps a square inch or more. Not being an aquatic ecologist, I don't precisely know what this means. But it probably means there are no herbivorous fish to feed on the algae; if it all has to decompose, it is going to create anaerobic conditions.

Four thousand families were displaced from the area to be flooded. They were given money as compensation, and some of them have dispersed to goodness-knows-where in Thailand. Some others were given land—but not any of the new irrigated land —only upland land to one side of the dam which had no water brought to it at all. Only recently the New Zealand government has sent some volunteers into the area to build

pumps to bring up some water. Even then, there is less than an acre for each of these resettled farmers and the land they now have is much less productive.

The new irrigated land is planned to support 10,000 families. So 4,000 families above the dam have been displaced for the supposed benefit of the 10,000 down below. And even these benefits as yet are theoretical; they haven't come about.

I think this story brings out the relevance of ecology: not as some kind of side effect, but as a really central factor in the success of a development project. Hopefully, if ecologists are brought in at the beginning, they could say what would happen to the fish fauna of the river, how it should be managed, how the water should be used by agriculturalists, and how multiple-cropping could be inserted harmoniously into this system to bring about the highest yields.

SCUDDER: This is an interesting point. You can assess benefits at the national level and come to the conclusion that there are great net gains. On the other hand, if you assess benefits in terms of populations which are relocated and may very well not be involved in these gains (while other groups theoretically are), I think there are many kinds of trade-offs that should be looked into in terms of those people who may suffer as a result of the development project.

I think we were probably referring to this same problem in relation to the cost of fertilizer in the Egyptian fellaheen case.

DASMANN: There has been a great deal of talk about ecologists, and I do hope that we are all aware that there is no sort of superman called an ecologist who can be brought in at the start of a development project and who will foresee all the difficulties that may result from this project.

What we are really talking about is an ecological orientation among the various specialists who will be brought in to consult on a development project. I don't know who really can call himself an ecologist. Some of us do use that title, and yet when we hear the word used as it has been used in this conference, we are a little hesitant to apply it to ourselves. Obviously, I don't have the kind of abilities that are being discussed here. And I don't think any other ecologist does.

So I hope that we are thinking, not that we want to train this superman called an ecologist, but that we want to get an ecological orientation in the training of development experts, technicians of all kinds, who will be brought in to consult on these projects.

WHITE: There are two points that can be made in the case of the Nam Pong. With respect to its effect on aquatic biology, a person in the field of biology was asked during the planning whether or not he and his colleagues thought the dam would have a significant effect upon the fishery resources of the area. The judgment was it would be a very modest effect, so slight that they could go ahead and undertake the project and then see what could be done about sorting out fishery effects later on. That was one kind of judgment.

On the other hand, with respect to the dam's effects on farming in the area, it was pointed out clearly that, unless a whole set of auxiliary activities were undertaken at the same time the dam was being constructed, very few of the anticipated benefits could be captured from the concrete and steel construction activities.

For a variety of reasons these steps were not taken, although there were already a couple of dozen small projects constructed by the U.S. AID in the Khorat Plateau of Thailand which illustrate just what happens when dams are built and not all of the auxiliary activities are initiated.

Here we have an example of two sorts of difficulties—one a judgment that the effect would not be significant enough to work on at the time, and the other the judgment that analysis and action to solve other im-

pacts would be essential. The latter judgment was unpalatable to those who were proceeding with the construction.

BATISSE: I would like to emphasize one previous remark by Gilbert White which is a very important factor in all these important projects. It is the process of decision-making by governments and also by international agencies which implies that either you have a particular project or you have nothing.

I think this explains a lot of the mistakes which are made. The examples which have been given on the Nile and Mekong and many other places all seem to indicate a similar choice between a very big thing or nothing. There is a kind of convergence of interest in what I might call the ribbon-cutting complex where you want to have the president of the republic come with scissors and cut a red ribbon, issue a postal stamp and so on. It has to be a very big structure; otherwise, it is not interesting. All too often the engineers, the economists, the bankers and the politicians come together with converging interests to decide on huge projects which enhance their pride and which are not necessarily the projects best suited to meet the needs of the people.

This fact was discovered in Algeria a few years before its independence by the French engineers who had been building large dams. Belatedly, they discovered that these dams were not really useful for irrigation because the people were not accustomed to practicing large-scale irrigation; they then had to change to a "large program of small works" more suited to the actual needs of the people. Of course, for power production the dams have sometimes to be large. However, for irrigation, a series of small works often have greater benefits, are more flexible and adaptable to local needs, and better understood by the local population than grandiose structures. But nobody wants to do small things.

MILTON: In all the large dam-building

projects that we have been discussing here, there is an essential problem that runs through each one: the difficulty in pulling out of a major dam-building program once you have made large early commitments. Large dam construction projects involve a tremendous variety of private and institutional interests in the project which have a great deal to gain by going ahead quickly. Once they are involved, it then becomes extremely difficult to get more detailed environmental research supported to look into alternatives and costs if there is any indication that the results might be negative. For this reason we must apply our ecological research and criteria very early in the development process and insist that these criteria stick.

If we can effectively predict the various ecological impacts of these dams, we can avoid being inevitably tied into a massive project and can develop sounder alternatives when necessary. Perhaps, as Mr. Batisse has suggested, we need to emphasize series or systems of smaller projects, any one of which could be abandoned if at a later stage it was found not to be desirable or feasible. Because of small size, it would be easier to pull out of such an investment than a massive dam-building project which from an economic standpoint is virtually irreversible once it has proceeded far enough.

TALBOT: I have been concerned that perhaps we passed a little bit too quickly over the question of how much the Mekong program is taking ecology into account. I think we left it that fisheries and soils were being taken care of.

If we think about this massive program involving some 25 million people in the basin, the amount of money and the effort that has gone into the engineering feasibility is tremendous. By contrast, very little has been spent on basic environmental studies. We now have one full-time fisheries biologist and a few other people studying fishery resources for very short periods. The soil survey, which is very good, is, however, too large-scale for much regional usefulness, with the exception of a few pilot areas.

I have been involved with John Bardach in following Mekong development plans for several years through the Mekong seminar. The two of us have been extremely concerned that this was a classical situation of a massive development program with virtually no concern with ecology in the broader sense of the term.

When we first brought this up in the seminar, we were told that the biological-ecological considerations were the best-known part of the whole basin program. The United Nations Mekong Resources Atlas was cited as proof.

We then consulted the people who were making the Atlas, who have done a magnificent job. They pointed out that most of what they had done was to review the literature and bring together all available information. They felt that the greatest value of what they had done was to point out how little we really knew and how much more, therefore, must be known before anything can be safely initiated by way of a massive development scheme.

It seems to me this brings up the question that Dr. Batisse asked earlier. Is the object of this type of development the engineering of the project itself? If so, then our emphasis so far has been quite right. Or is the object the welfare of the people, these 25 million people that are involved? If so, then aren't the broader ecological considerations, which involve biology, hydrology, anthropology, ethnology, social studies, and so forth, the key parts of it?

From Dr. Bardach's paper, my own view of the Mekong situation, and the other comments that have been made, it seems to me that perhaps we should give more attention to the classical lack of ecological considerations in this great river development program.

MILTON: Development interests are now

talking about a series of future projects which are going to, if they come about, create massive changes that could make even the Mekong developments look small in scale. One such proposal, the North American Water and Power Alliance, would involve putting $100 billion into a program to redirect many of the rivers now flowing into the Mackenzie and much of the Canadian Arctic south into the United States to satisfy this country's burgeoning water demands. One estimate of the costs involved from the multiple side effects caused by this one proposed project indicated that the amount of money that would have to be spent to reverse the negative impacts might very well counterbalance all projected benefits from the project.

Another major project being talked about is the development of a series of hydropower dams in the Amazon Basin which would flood an area approximately the size of Montana. Again, very little consideration is being given to any of the great number of hazardous ecological side effects in this project. This Amazon proposal still is only in the talking stage, but my point is that the approach so far has only been one of engineering and narrowly-defined economic feasibility; concurrent with engineering studies, intensive environmental studies should be fostered to seek out the benefits and risks of the many ecological and social side effects involved.

At some point development specialists will have to come to grips with a basic question: How do we create effective institutional mechanisms that can take on responsibility for investigating all the significant environmental effects of particular development projects? If development interests are really to become concerned with human welfare, who is going to take on this responsibility?

15. THE IMPACT OF MODERN IRRIGATION TECHNOLOGY IN THE INDUS AND HELMAND BASINS OF SOUTHWEST ASIA

Aloys A. Michel

In 1849, when the British formally annexed the Punjab, the only significant canal irrigation between the 700-foot contour (which runs roughly from the Sutlej-Beas confluence through Lahore to Kalabagh on the Indus) and the Arabian Sea was provided by small inundation canals serving floodplain areas along the Sutlej and along the middle and lower Indus. Aside from wells in the floodplains or delta areas, the well-fed irrigation lay mainly between the 700-foot contour and the hills (Siwaliks, Salt Range, Suleiman and Kirthar Ranges) where the natural water table was within about 100 feet of the surface.

By 1949, modern canal irrigation, most of it perennial, had been extended to encompass an area of almost 40 million acres between the 700-foot contour and the sea, and all but one of the doabs, or interfluves, were laced with canals, distributaries, and watercourses. In many areas near these canals, water tables had risen to within a few feet of the surface; in some areas, the water table intersected the surface during the latter part of the summer (kharif) growing season. Historical data on the rise of the water table indicate average rates of from 0.6 to 1.0 feet per year since modern irrigation facilities were provided in a region underlain by thousands of feet of virtually unobstructed alluviums.

By 1959, of the 23 million acres annually canal-irrigated and sown to at least one crop in West Pakistan, about 5 million had been seriously damaged by waterlogging or salinity and between 50,000 and 100,000 additional acres were being affected each year, many of them passing out of crop production altogether.

In the Helmand Valley of Afghanistan, the situation in 1949 was comparable to that in the Indus Basin a century before: canal irrigation was limited to floodplain inundation canals supplemented by a few wells near the rivers or karez (tunnels) tapping the natural water tables at the foot of the hills. Ten years later, much of the middle Helmand region had been provided with modern perennial canal irrigation extending into the interfluves and onto the tablelands well away from the streams. But in this short space of time, waterlogging and salinity had seriously affected most of the new project areas away from the floodplains, forcing the curtailment of planned expansion, redesign of cropping patterns from grains and cotton to forage crops, and the summoning of experts from the U. S. Bureau of Reclamation to salvage this portion of the Helmand Valley Project by the introduction of drains and a shift to a new type of agricultural economy.

This paper analyzes natural and artificial factors which may have contributed to waterlogging and salinity, such as cyclical rainfall patterns, road and railroad embankments which follow the contours and thus impede surface drainage, and the contour link canal which both impedes the surface drainage and contributes, by seepage, to raising the local water table. The paper will also discuss some of the alternatives for restoring or simulating natural drainage conditions (e.g., surface or subsurface drains, reclamation tube wells, etc.). But the emphasis will remain on the fact that, in both the Indus and Helmand basins, man has applied modern technology without anticipating its impact on the ecology and now has to pay the price.

I.

A surface-water irrigation system may be viewed as a threefold (but four-dimensional) modification of the natural environment, increasing in both area and time the availability of water to the soil and, potentially, to any existing groundwater reservoir.

The distribution network of an irrigation system (canals, branches, laterals, and watercourses) represents a horizontal and essentially linear expansion of the number of channels through which water seeks its own level. In the process, this network produces a geometric expansion in the area over which this water is in contact with the soil. By far the greatest part of this geometric expansion occurs in the cropped fields themselves, whether the irrigation practiced is of the paddy or the row type. But the wetting of the fields is intermittent, even in rice cultivation where the paddies may be flooded for several weeks at a time. In row irrigation of cotton, the soil surface may be wet for only a few hours per week. By

contrast, the major distribution channels of a perennial irrigation system are designed to carry water for nine or ten months of the year and, being of much larger cross section than the watercourses and field channels, make up in volume and in time what they lack in area.[1]

If the first "artificial" effect of irrigation is to spread a given volume of water over more of the soil surface, its second effect is to lengthen the time which this volume of water spends in contact—or potential contact—with the soil surface.[2] This effect is obvious in any surface-water irrigation sys-

[1] Throughout this discussion, the interrelation of volume and time—summarized by the irrigation engineer in his terms "second-feet," "cusecs" (cubic feet per second), "cumecs" (cubic meters per second)—must be kept in mind, for irrigation means the movement of water over time from where it is not wanted to where it is wanted.

[2] As long as an unbroken hydraulic film is maintained, every drop of water above a given point, directly or diagonally, no matter how slight the gradient, may potentially reach that point, just as every drop of water in a bathtub is in potential contact with the drain.

tem which includes storage dams and reservoirs where one season's or one year's runoff may be largely postponed to the next. But brief reflection shows this to be true even of run-of-river systems which do not provide holdover storage. The essence of all gravity-flow irrigation systems lies in decreasing the gradient by diverting water from stream channels at a headworks and causing it to follow a longer and hence slower course to reach a given lower contour. For surface irrigation water to be of any value to crops, it must not only be carried away from the stream channels, but its flow must be slowed down as much as possible. Absorption is a function of time as well as of area, and what cannot be absorbed within the system must either be returned to the rivers or disposed of in some other, often costly, manner. Indeed, the worst nightmare of the superintending engineer is having admitted more water into his system than it can absorb over a given time.

The third modification is a direct result of the first two: by spreading surface water over a much larger area or "command" than it would naturally cover between two points on a stream channel, and by causing it to spend more time in the commanded area than it would spend in the stream channel, the irrigator induces a much greater downward movement into the soil than would naturally occur.[3] Part of this movement is beneficial, but once the water has passed both below the root zone of the crops and below the level (approximately ten feet in sandy loams) from which capillary action can raise it to the root zone,

it becomes useless. Indeed, it becomes a potential danger, for it decreases the amount of "freeboard" available before the groundwater table will rise to interfere with plant growth or before capillary rise combined with evaporation will increase salt accumulations in the upper soil horizons or on the surface.

Evaporation causes salts to come over the surface in another way. Where salts are present in the soil at very shallow depths, natural precipitation or insufficient applied irrigation water may penetrate to the level of the saline layer and dissolve it. On subsequent evaporation . . . the salts will appear on the surface. Salts are also present in irrigation water even though in small quantities (150–300 ppm). Continuous application of irrigation water in time may add salts in the soil profile. (Lateef and Shamsi, 1963, p. 9)[4]

Aside from the modifications in the area of channels, in the length of time that surface water remains in contact with the soil, and the resultant increase in the contribution of surface water to groundwater, a number of less obvious but equally significant ecological effects of irrigation should be noted. By expanding the surface area of the water in the system, total evaporation is increased. But from the irrigator's point of view, only the stored or diverted water which does not evaporate represents a gain. Efforts are made to reduce evaporation, but only where the cost is economically justifiable.

In irrigated areas the growth of noncultivated vegetation is unintentionally fostered

[3] For the purposes of this paper, such water will be termed "groundwater." The term "groundwater table" or simply "water table" will be used to designate the interface from which water rises by capillary action. This capillary rise takes place in the pore spaces or interstices among the aggregates of individual soil particles. These irregular particles consist of grains, held together by colloids, and the pore spaces among the particles, though essential for air and root penetration, are usually sufficiently small and continuous for capillary action to occur.

[4] Lining of main and branch canals will reduce seepage, but most of this occurs from the smaller channels which are hardly ever lined or from the fields which cannot yet be sealed on more than an experimental scale. In every lined surface-water distribution system known to the present author, sealing has been provided only where economic calculations indicated that the value of water lost by seepage, especially in crossing areas of more permeable soils, exceeded the cost of the lining. Canals, like rivers, will eventually, though incompletely and intermittently, seal their beds with silt and clay materials, and there is accordingly a great temptation to rely upon this fact.

along with that of crops. Where these "weeds" interfere with canal operation, impede cultivation, or consume an inordinate amount of water, efforts are made to remove them, but again only where economic returns outweigh costs. Some of this noncultivated vegetation may actually have economic value where it stabilizes canal banks, provides fuel or building material, or tran-

spires groundwater which would otherwise interfere with crop growth. Trees, of course, are especially useful in these respects and also provide welcome relief from heat and glare in villages, fields, and along the roads which often parallel the canals. In most cultures, aesthetic values are associated with the green landscape of irrigated areas, whether or not the plants have economic

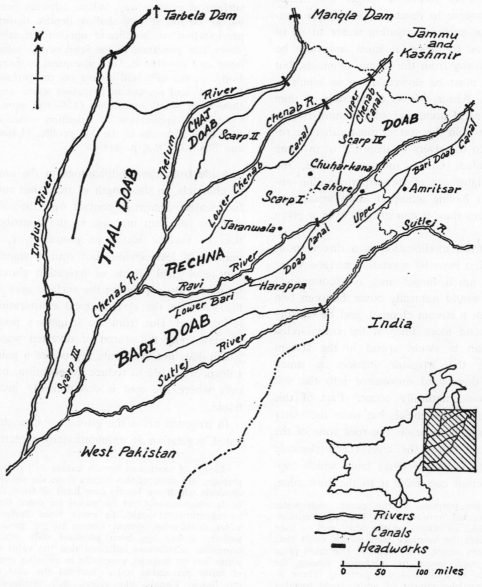

Figure 15–1 Middle Indus Basin irrigation system in West Pakistan (After A. A. Michel)

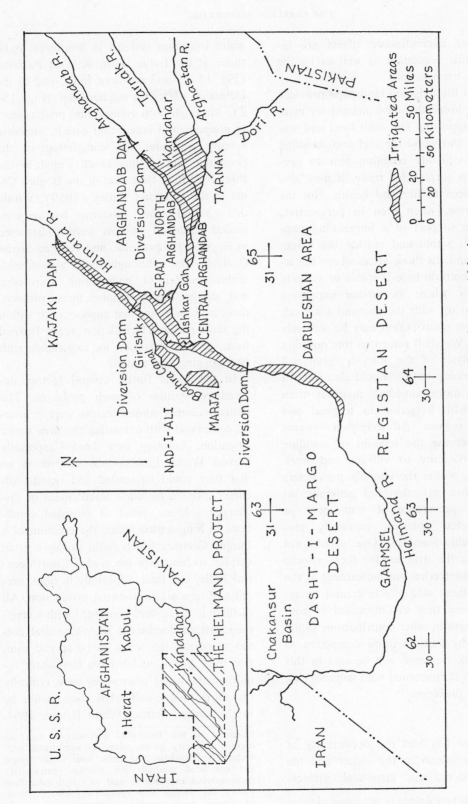

Figure 15-2 The Helmand Valley Project of Southwestern Afghanistan

value. Some microclimatic effects are induced by this vegetation as well as by the increase in evaporation.

Although the irrigated landscape provides a generally hospitable environment for man, not only supporting him with food and water, shade, and wood for fuel and building, but also frequently enabling him to produce a crop surplus for trade, it may also bring menaces to life and health. Not the least of these, when seen in perspective, may be the support of a burgeoning population both within and outside the irrigation command. In those areas where the irrigated agricultural base is stable or actually shrinking or where its further expansion cannot keep up with the demand for food, the long-term contribution may be seriously questioned. We shall return to this question in our analysis of the Punjab "granary," but before doing so we should also note in passing two more immediate menaces often associated with irrigation in tropical and subtropical regions. All irrigation systems serve to increase the amount of standing water in proximity to villages and work areas. Thus, within the climatic parameters of the vectors, irrigation has generally increased the prevalence of waterborne or water-supported diseases, especially malaria and schistosomiasis. One should not overly blame the irrigator for these effects, which are unintended and unwanted; at the same time, these side effects cannot be ignored. Because they are discussed at considerable length in other contributions to the Conference by authors more competent to analyze them, no more will be said in this paper, which is concerned with waterlogging and salinity problems.

II.

The author has had the opportunity of doing field research in the oldest and the newest of the modern,[5] large-scale surface-

water irrigation systems in Southwest Asia, those of the Indus Basin in West Pakistan (Fig. 15–1) and northern India, and of the Helmand Valley in Afghanistan (Fig. 15–2). Although both systems had predecessors in nonperennial inundation canals, almost a century separates the completion of the perennial Upper Bari Doab Canal in the Punjab (1859) from that of the Boghra Canal in the Helmand Valley (1950). Within this period the modern, barrage-controlled perennial systems were constructed in Egypt, Mesopotamia, and Russian-Soviet Central Asia. Although there was considerable transfer of engineering knowledge and design theory among these projects, there is no evidence that anyone, even within the same political jurisdiction, really learned from, or paid attention to, experience with waterlogging and salinity.

In the Indus Basin, several factors delayed recognition of such problems. The British colonial administrators were primarily concerned with extending the area under irrigation, bringing new lands—especially Crown Waste Lands—into cultivation so that they could be settled and taxed. Ancillary motives included resettlement of discharged soldiers, relief of crowded conditions in long-settled areas, the creation of a Punjab Granary which could supply a grain surplus to famine-prone areas of north-central India, and later, especially in Sind, creation of new areas of cotton production. All of these motives were combined with a cropping pattern dominated by wheat and cotton to permit the water to be spread thin. For these crops, which have low water requirements, water allowances were typically one-third to one-half what they would be in the United States (White House, 1964,

---

[5] "Modern" is here defined in technological terms to mean surface-water schemes employing the

advances of the Industrial Revolution: (a) cemented masonry giving place to reinforced concrete; (b) cast-iron and then steel sluice gates; (c) overhead controls for barrage gates; (d) earth-moving machinery; and (e) hydraulic flow theory on design and operation. All of these, of course, made possible operations on a scale not previously imaginable.

pp. 185 ff., and Appendix A.5), and although sugarcane was allowed on limited acreages, rice cultivation was generally discouraged in the doab irrigation commands until water tables had risen close to the surface.

Thus, although one can find references to waterlogging and salinity problems close to the Western Jumna Canal of the Ganges Basin as early as 1859 (Michel, 1967, p. 455), and although the irrigation channels were realigned and natural drainages cleared in that command between 1870 and 1880 with gratifying results (Montagu, 1946, pp. xii–xiii; cited in Michel, 1967, pp. 456–57), there was only scattered recognition of the general problem until 1925 when a Waterlogging Enquiry Committee was established. Even then, and despite the fact that the Lower Chenab Canal, opened in 1892, had produced serious waterlogging by 1908, there were those who maintained that irrigation per se was not to blame but rather that the canal, road, and railway embankments were interfering with surface runoff, or that the Punjab was in a "rainy cycle," or both. Although the Irrigation Branch of the Punjab Public Works Department was officially concerned with the problem by 1925, it included what may be termed an "anti-drainage lobby," a lobby which maintained that a high water table was actually an advantage because it facilitated the operation of hundreds of "Persian wheels" in shallow wells and produced some "regeneration" of water supplies by seepage during the dry seasons. The lure of adding new acreage was still strong, and few were interested in reclamation when lost acreage could be replaced elsewhere. Of course, the cost of bringing water to new acreage was increasing, and the new acres, whether in Sind or in the Thal Project between the Indus and the Jhelum-Chenab, had much coarser soils and lower initial fertility than those in the Punjab. In the desert areas to the west and south, both

seepage and evaporation rates were higher, and even the Indus Basin would eventually run out of new lands to replace the old in a gravity-fed surface-water irrigation system.

Despite these shortcomings it must be recognized that in 1947 the British left the Indus Basin with the most extensive and probably the least costly (on a per acre basis of commanded cultivable land) integrated irrigation system on earth. Partition destroyed the integration, but Pakistan did inherit the Sukkur and Thal Projects, both of which had (and still do have) a great deal of commanded cultivable area waiting to be settled. India inherited the Bhakra dam site on the Sutlej which would extend irrigation into Rajasthan.

The successor states of the subcontinent also were left with highly competent Public Works Departments, whose Irrigation Branches were skilled in the design, construction, and operation of modern irrigation systems. In Afghanistan, on the other hand, the years 1946–47 marked the transfer of the Helmand Valley Project from the Ministry of Public Works to an American firm which could more rapidly introduce modern design and technology in the form of heavy earth-moving equipment, rock-fill dams, and reinforced concrete barrages and canal structures. The need to employ the contractor, the designs, and the technology stemmed directly from a decision to extend irrigation from the Helmand floodplain areas—long irrigated with inundation canals—to the terraces west of the river which represented "virgin" lands (Michel, 1959, p. 149). The employment of this modern technology, at least as represented by a foreign, private contractor, led to a further increase in the scale of the project, for it soon developed that a storage dam would be necessary if the irrigation needs of the terrace areas were to be supplied without detracting from the uses of the floodplain areas and that there was an economic minimum level below which it would not pay the contractor to operate in Afghanistan (Michel, 1959, pp. 153–54). Also relevant to the decision to enlarge the scope of the Helmand Project to include the new lands west of the river was the Royal Afghan Government's desire (1) to provide areas for settlement of Pushtun nomads whose annual migrations to and from the Indus Plains began to be curtailed because of Pakistan's independence in August, 1947, and the ensuing dispute over "Pushtunistan," and (2) to obtain storage control of the Helmand and maximum use of its waters within the country in view of the dispute with Iran over allocation of flows in the river's inland delta region, the Chakansur Basin, which is transected by the border.

Thus, a variety of engineering, economic, and political reasons—to which may be added the usual considerations of professional optimism and personal-national prestige—led to the enlargement of the Helmand Project. This enlargement included two storage dams (Kajakai and Arghandab), a supposed potential of a quarter of a million acres of virgin or abandoned land on the terraces west of the river (Nad-i-Ali and Marja project areas) or on the interfluves between the Helmand and its Arghandab tributary (Seraj area) and between the Tarnak and Arghastan subtributaries (Tarnak project area), and additional areas on the floodplains (Shamalan, Darweshan, Garmsel, etc.).

It is essential to distinguish the Central Arghandab project area between the Arghandab and the Tarnak rivers from the rest of the Helmand Project. In this area for hundreds of years inundation canals had provided nonperennial irrigation to permeable soils with little evidence of waterlogging or salinity. The object of the Helmand Project was to make available an assured supply of water which would allow perennial irrigation of most of the acreage. The Central Arghandab area, focused on Kanda-

har, is one of Afghanistan's primary sources of winter wheat, vegetables, and deciduous fruit, with much of the latter exported, fresh or dried, to Pakistan and India. Here, the Helmand Project has been an undoubted success, doubling production and exports in good years and thus far producing little evidence of waterlogging or salinity though drains will eventually be required. The success in this area of "reinforced" agricultural production with good natural drainage is usually overlooked in assessments of the Helmand Project as a whole.

Also requiring separate treatment are the floodplain areas (Kajakai to Girishk, Shamalan, and Darweshan) where the project has brought increased supplies of water and an increase in annual cropped acreage to areas which had long been cultivated on a migrating inundation basis and which, due to the high natural water table, showed signs of waterlogging and intermittent salinity long before the advent of the project. Despite the construction of the two dams, control of runoff is far from complete. The storage provided can assure minimum flows but cannot prevent maximum flood runoff. And there is no control at all on the Arghastan and Tarnak rivers. Thus, the level of the water tables in the floodplains, especially in the active portions, depends primarily upon the fluctuations in the river levels. Though artificial irrigation certainly exacerbates waterlogging and salinity, restriction of surface-water supplies or even installation of gravity drains cannot, per se, reduce or eliminate the problem in flood years. Irrigation of these floodplains, as of most active and some inactive floodplains, has always been precarious. Where, as along the Helmand, the riverbanks ("natural levees") are generally the highest points on the floodplain, the danger of flood damage is extreme, as is the difficulty of building and operating any type of gravity drain. The Helmand Project, by providing fixed and regulable intake structures capable of withstanding most floods, and by providing gravity drains in those areas of the inactive floodplain where they will work when the water table is low, has decreased the cultivators' uncertainty and can be justified on the same grounds as the nonperennial canals built by the British and Pakistanis along the lower Indus and Sutlej. On the one hand, they are cheap to construct and guarantee a minimum supply of water, and, on the other, the effect of irrigation water seeping to the water table is minor in comparison with the natural fluctuations due to flooding or lateral seepage from the river itself.

This last factor does not hold true on the interfluves, and it was the extension of irrigation onto the terraces, notably in the Nad-i-Ali and Marja areas, that produced the serious and foreseeable problems which have given the Helmand Project its bad reputation in and outside Afghanistan. For here were conglomerate substratae through which irrigation water could not penetrate and which produced a 16-foot rise in the water table within three or four years of the opening of the Boghra Canal in the spring of 1949. The rapidity of the rise was due both to seepage from unlined reaches of the canal and to excessive application of water by settlers unaccustomed to such an abundance, but the fundamental cause was the substratum which created a local base level. The incredible part of this story is that the existence, though not the extent, of these conglomerate layers was known to the Afghans from their experience in constructing the predecessor of the Boghra Canal and to the contractors, from reconnaissance surveys (Michel, 1959, pp. 152–53).

But once again, optimism and shortsightedness precluded a detailed survey until the damage had been done. Afghanistan was left with over 40,000 acres of canal-commanded land on the terraces but no prospects for cultivating wheat or cotton, as had been originally planned, until drains had been installed and a long program of rec-

lamation, including the use of mechanical cultivation for salt-tolerant fodder crops and grasses, had been carried through. For reasons of policy and prestige, much of the burden of reclamation has been assumed by the U. S. Agency for International Development which has had Bureau of Reclamation teams working in the area for the past ten years, but it will be several more decades before the original promise of the Helmand Project in the terrace areas begins to be fulfilled.

What lessons have been learned from the Helmand experience? Unfortunately, none that could not have been learned without it! Irrigation experience in the adjoining Indus Basin, in Soviet Central Asia, and in the southwestern U.S.A. all had shown that drainage must go hand-in-hand with irrigation. The only remarkable points in the Helmand experience are that disaster struck so quickly and that the reasons for it were so obvious. Any engineer or planner should have seen them from the design stage, and some did (Michel, 1959). But instead of redesigning the project to exclude Nad-i-Ali and Marja, or substantially increasing the size of the individual holdings, or lowering the water allowances from the start, the project was implemented in defiance of reality. In view of what we have said about the usual time lag associated with waterlogging and salinity, there is ironic justice in the fact that nature struck back at those who ignored her before they could move on to other positions and to other projects. But the saddest thing about the Helmand experience is that it will probably be repeated, if not in Afghanistan, then in Iran or Iraq, though it may be difficult to find soils with drainage as poor as those of Nad-i-Ali and Marja. It is also unfortunate that the nature of the Helmand terrace soils, because of their very shallow depth above impermeable substrata and the consequent lack of both "freeboard" and underlying fresh groundwater supplies, would seem to preclude the type of tube well reclamation now being employed in the Indus Basin of West Pakistan.

III.

The Helmand experience is typical only in that it represents a microcosm of what has been going on in other surface-water irrigation projects over longer periods of time. For our purposes, the Indus experience is more typical and perhaps more hopeful. As we have seen, many of the British engineers and administrators recognized the problem forty or more years ago, and some of them tried to do something about it. Aside from the policy of spreading the water thin, which had always carried an economic rationale, canals were realigned. Some of them were lined in badly-leaking places, and surface drains were constructed. These policies, including the low water allocations, were continued by the Indians and Pakistanis after Independence. But the most promising attack on the problem was proposed as early as 1927. It was not approved until 1944 and not put into full operation until 1952, five years after Independence. This was the Rasul Scheme in the Rechna and Chaj Doabs of West Pakistan which employed 1257 tube wells ranged along badly-seeping canals in a dual effort to lower local water tables and also provide additional supplies of irrigation water. Because most of its wells were too close to the canals and actually accelerated seepage, the Rasul Scheme was not particularly successful (Michel, 1967, pp. 458–60), but its shortcomings led to further research and experiments and to the massive "Program for Waterlogging and Salinity Control in the Irrigated Areas of West Pakistan" initiated by the West Pakistan Water and Power Development Authority (WAPDA) in 1961.

In the meantime, some quantitative estimates of the extent of the damage were becoming available. An air photo survey made in 1954 under Colombo Plan auspices produced interpretations indicating that of the 51 million acres in West Pakistan, 11 million were poorly drained or waterlogged and another 16 million salinized, including 5 million acres severely salinized. These interpretations were later scaled down on the basis of field observations and laboratory tests. The estimates embodied in the White House–Interior Panel ("Revelle Panel") Report indicated that of the 23 million acres in West Pakistan annually canal-irrigated and sown to at least one crop, 5 million had been seriously damaged by waterlogging or salinity and between 50,000 and 100,000 additional acres were being affected each year, many of them passing out of crop production altogether. In the worst districts, located in Rechna Doab, 40 or 50 per cent of the cultivated land had been severely damaged. However, at least in the Pakistan Punjab, there was no indication that the rate of damage was increasing (Michel, 1967, pp. 464–65; White House, 1964, pp. 57, 62–63).[6]

Historical data on the rise of the water table showed average rates of from 0.6 to 1.0 feet per year since modern irrigation facilities had been provided in areas under-

[6] Unfortunately, there is no exact method of quantifying waterlogging and salinity damage because they will vary from season to season and from year to year, depending in part upon the strength of the monsoon and the areal and time distribution of rainfall and groundwater recharge. Evaporation will also vary according to temperature and ground cover. Crop damage varies according to the water and salt sensitivity of the particular plant. Almost like a skin rash, surface salinity appears in blotches which continually vary in intensity and extent. The White House–Interior Panel drew many of its estimates from a West Pakistan Department of Power, Irrigation and Development Report which defined salinity damage as "the areas in which white effervescence is apparent on the natural surface during the months of December, January, or February causing 1/8 or more damage to the crop of the area," and waterlogging damage as "the fields rendered unfit for cultivation to the extent of 1/8 or more of the area by their sub-soil moisture," but indicated that about 97 per cent of the damage was due to salinity.

lain by thousands of feet of virtually unobstructed alluviums.

In an area where the underground water
has a salinity of 1,000 parts per million (acceptable for virtually all crops) evaporation at
a rate of 2 feet per year (a typical value
where the water table is only a few feet deep)
will raise the salt content of the top 3 feet of
soil to about 1 percent in 20 years. This is
too high for even the hardiest crops (White
House, 1964, p. 56).

The farmer's response to the alarming increase in waterlogging and salinity in the
irrigated districts of the Pakistan Punjab has
been twofold. Where the water table is at
or very near the surface, he usually shifts
from wheat to rice cultivation. Although the
West Pakistani is traditionally a wheat consumer, rice is a fairly salt-tolerant crop
which thrives on a high water table. It
yields more calories per acre than wheat
and can be exported, either to East Pakistan
or abroad, and the money received can be
used to purchase Food for Peace wheat
which is sent almost exclusively to the West
Wing of Pakistan. Between 1949–50 and
1959–60, the acreage sown to rice in West
Pakistan increased over 30 per cent, from
2.3 to 3 million acres, and the yield per
acre increased from 773 to 823 pounds.
Over the same period, wheat acreage increased only from 10.3 million acres to 12.1
million, while the wheat yield per acre actually fell from 839 to 724 pounds (Government of Pakistan, 1964, pp. 78–79).

The usual response in irrigated areas affected by salinity rather than by waterlogging has been to try to delay the process by
sowing only one crop per year or to spread
the available irrigation water even more
thinly over the saline land. Although the
gross sown area in the Punjab districts with
major canal irrigation systems increased
about 1.5 per cent per year over the period
1949–50 to 1958–59, the White House–
Interior Panel reported: "In the older canal
systems, the increase in gross area almost

certainly means that the volume of irrigation water correspondingly decreased"
(White House, 1964, p. 45). Such a response will ultimately make the problem
worse as salts accumulate in soils that never
get enough water to leach the salt below
the capillary zone, or even below the root
zone. As we have seen, the combination of
capillary rise and evaporation will simply
return the salts to the surface where they
will accumulate until the land must be
abandoned.

Nor can new lands be brought into cultivation fast enough to offset the decline of
the old. The increase in gross sown area for
all of West Pakistan over the period 1949–
50 to 1958–59 was only 1.3 per cent per
annum, or less than that in the Punjab alone.
The overall population increase for West
Pakistan between the 1951 and 1961 cen-
suses amounted to 2.4 per cent per annum
(2.2 per cent per annum in the canal-irrigated districts of the Pakistan Punjab).
In summary, these figures mean that despite
the introduction of new irrigated lands, the
increase in gross sown area is not keeping
pace with population increase in West
Pakistan as a whole or in the old "Punjab
Granary." The sad historical fact is that,
due to population increase, by the time of
Partition the Punjab Granary had ceased
to provide any substantial grain exports,
and that although West Pakistan inherited
virtually all of the surplus-producing irrigated areas, population increase combined
with waterlogging and salinity damage
quickly overcame this initial advantage and
by the mid-1950's made the country a net
importer of wheat.

Even apart from per capita considerations, by the mid-1950's it was apparent
that a shortage of surface water for crop
and soil-leaching requirements was combining with loss of acreage and decreasing
yields due to waterlogging and salinity in
a vicious circle which somehow had to
be broken. So while the Pakistani nego-

tiators were working (1952–60) with their Indian counterparts and with the World Bank to devise surface-water replacement and enhancement possibilities, including storage dams, other technicians were looking below the surface. As we have seen, the Rasul Scheme indicated the possibility of using tube wells in a two-pronged attack on the problem: to lower water tables and at the same time to provide additional supplies for irrigation and leaching. In 1953 –54, a second Rasul-type scheme was inaugurated by Pakistani and F.A.O. technicians near Chuharkana in the Rechna Doab; and in 1957–58, a third pilot project was started near Jaranwala in Central Rechna. Under the U. S. Point Four Program, a team of U. S. Geological Survey experts arrived in 1954 to work on surveys and analysis with the Punjab Irrigation Department's Soil Reclamation Board (1952) and Ground Water Development Organisation (1954). When the West Pakistan WAPDA was established in 1958, it was specifically entrusted with "prevention of waterlogging and salinity and reclamation of waterlogged and saline lands" (Michel, 1967, pp. 463–67).[7]

From these antecedents developed WAPDA's Salinity Control and Reclamation Project Number One (SCARP I) including nearly 2,000 tube wells installed in the Rechna Doab and WAPDA's ongoing program to complete some 9,000 tube wells by 1972. But the key to the program, and the factor which differentiates it from its predecessors, lies in the concentration of these tube wells in fields (SCARPS I to IV) of from 1,500 to 3,000 tube wells, each of 3 or 4 cusecs capacity, and each serving approximately 600 acres. The capacity and spacing of the wells is designed to permit man to "dominate the drainage" within each project area. By 1975 the program may be

[7] An excellent description and analysis of the groundwater program in West Pakistan has been furnished by the former chief of party of the U.S.G.S. Ground Water Group. See Greenman, 1967, pp. 173–82.

extended to include some 20,000 wells and an area of 12 million acres, virtually all of which would lie within the existing commands of the surface-water system in the Punjab, Khairpur, and Sind regions of West Pakistan. Combined with supplies from an even greater number of privately-owned 1-cusec wells and the enhanced surface-water supplies made possible by the Mangla and Tarbela dams on the Jhelum and Indus rivers, the amount of water available for watercourse delivery in West Pakistan may reach 93.5 million acre-feet in 1975. Two-thirds of this supply would come from the surface-water storage and distribution system and almost one-fourth from the government-owned tube wells. The total supply represents a net addition of about 38 per cent of the 68 million acre-feet available in 1965 and thus will offer a substantial improvement over the traditional low supplies available to crops and an opportunity for leaching of salts from the topsoil.

But this increased amount of water spread on the surface would serve only to increase the waterlogging and salinity damage to soils and crops were it not that the massive concentrations of high-capacity tube wells offer the hope of controlling the level of the water table. Wherever the groundwater is of usable quality (roughly, 2,000 parts per million of total dissolved solids or less, depending upon the chemical composition of the salts), its use for crops should produce a net gain and, through consumptive use and evapotranspiration, result in a gradual lowering of the watertable. In other areas, saline groundwater will have to be mixed with surface water of good quality before being applied to crops. To accomplish this mixing, canal capacities in certain areas will have to be enlarged. In still other portions of the areas selected for initial development, the groundwater is too saline even for blending and will have to be exported either via the rivers or via new wasteways constructed for the purpose.

Thus the groundwater and reclamation program under way in West Pakistan represents an extremely complex and costly effort to offset the consequences of surface-water irrigation. For the periods of Pakistan's Third and Fourth Five-Year Plans (1965–75), the total cost of government-owned tube wells, canal remodeling, and drainage works (not including surface-water storage) will amount to 5.3 billion Pakistan rupees, or $1.1 billion at official exchange rates, slightly more than the cost of the Tarbela Dam, which itself represents roughly half of the total cost of the Indus Basin Project. The expectation is that the gains achieved in West Pakistan's agricultural sector, which has been growing at a healthy rate of 3 to 4 per cent per annum since 1960 (though most of the gain is due to nonfood crops), will eventually more than compensate for these investments. But these gains will depend not only upon increased surface-water and groundwater supplies but upon further inputs of fertilizers, improved seed varieties, insecticides and pesticides, and upon improved cultivation techniques. But this discussion is beyond the scope of the paper.[8]

IV.

Do man's experiences and expectations in the Indus Basin mean that he is about to achieve mastery over his environment in irrigation agriculture? Such a boast would smack of hubris, for nature undoubtedly holds unpleasant surprises for man. Some of these surprises turned up in the initial years of the tube-well program in the Punjab, where the obsolescence rates in portions of SCARP I were so alarming that by mid-1964 installation of wells in SCARP II was halted until the trouble could be diagnosed. The problem was found to be a combination of mechanical blocking and chemical

corrosion of the mild-steel strainers (filter screens used to exclude sand and gravel from the wells), abetted by the work of sulphate-reducing bacteria present in the groundwater or introduced in drilling the well. The remedy seems to be use of fiber-glass strainers (which by 1967 had become less expensive and easier to install than the mild-steel ones) combined with chemical solutions to initially sterilize and later occasionally clean the wells. But one would be foolish to conclude that similar problems will not arise in the future.

Indeed, two more problems are already emerging: First, what can ultimately be done with the salts which keep on accumulating down-doab and downstream? The completion of Tarbela Dam in 1975 or 1976 will raise the mean annual diversions of good-quality surface water in West Pakistan to the order of 92 million acre-feet. This supply can be supplemented for twenty or thirty years by "mining" the enormous reservoir of perhaps 2 billion acre-feet of good-quality groundwater underlying the Punjab. After the year 2000, mining would have to be tapered off, but use of perhaps 20 million acre-feet per year of groundwater recharge in the Punjab could continue. But sooner or later the concentration of salts, due to repeated capillary rise and evaporation followed by repeated irrigation and leaching, is bound to increase both down-doab and downstream. Sind is already alarmed both because the salt content of water in the lower Indus is slightly higher than in the upper Indus and in its Punjab tributaries and because the reservoir of good-quality groundwater in Sind appears to be far smaller than that underlying the Punjab (though it might yield as much as 12 million acre-feet per year). Actually, the principal justification for building Tarbela Dam, aside from its hydroelectric potential, is to assure Sind of firm supplies of good-quality surface water below the confluence of the Punjab tributaries. But in relation to the Punjab,

[8] The interested reader is referred to the White House–Interior Panel Report, 1964, and to Michel, 1967, Chaps. 8–10.

Sind is in much the same position as is Mexico to the United States on the Rio Grande or the Colorado, and it seems inescapable that the lower Indus must serve as the "sink" of the whole Indus system, whether in Afghanistan, West Pakistan, or India.[9] If anything is "natural" it is that water flows downhill and that it carries dissolved salts with it. Of course, it is feasible to "export" highly salinized water either directly to the ocean or into "sinks" along the desert margins, but the costs involved imply that the wasteways required are likely to be postponed while other elements are constructed.

The second problem is more human than "natural." It is the problem of operating and maintaining so vast and complex a system as that contemplated for the Indus Basin in Pakistan. It has been suggested that, because of the time factor, the large-scale irrigation systems of the last hundred years could not have been worked without the telegraph. It now appears that those of the next hundred years can be worked only with the computer. This will certainly be true in West Pakistan where man is attempting to control all four dimensions and to manipulate the groundwater reservoir as well as the surface flows. Fortunately, analog computers may easily be programmed to simulate groundwater pumping recharge and flows (Todd, 1967), and one can already imagine WAPDA House in Lahore being converted (over the protests of the Irrigation Department) into a command post flashing signals to hundreds of gate and pump tenders—or indeed to thousands

of automated valves, gates and pumps— to keep the system operating to maximize whatever goals are set. What is not so easy to imagine in a land where preventive maintenance is still only a slogan is an efficient and skilled army of mechanics and electricians repairing the breakdowns or, preferably, replacing valves, pumps, and well-screens upon signals of automated monitors given before the breakdowns occur. But this too will have to come. It is also hard to see, at this time, how Pakistan will get the money not only for the groundwater and reclamation program but for the overall agricultural development program needed to make it pay.

But a realistic awareness that problems are bound to arise should not prevent us from looking ahead to what the new irrigation technology might bring in the Indus Basin and in analogous irrigation systems elsewhere. Acceptance of the fact that irrigation and drainage are inseparable components of a single system has advantages once the tube well is employed as the instrument for controlling the water table. Wherever the groundwater is pure enough to be used, straight or mixed, for cropping, there is a windfall to be gained until the water table is below the economic reach of the pumps (and this economic reach will be lengthened as the efficiency of pump design increases, as power costs are lowered, particularly with nuclear-power plants, or as the relative value of crops rises). This windfall in groundwater irrigation may be compared to the initial advantage accruing to the cultivator of virgin lands who "draws down" the accumulated fertility for the first few years. When the cultivator has exhausted the initial fertility, he must find means of replacing it; so with the "miner" of the groundwater. In time, both will be helped by nature: the cultivator by fallowing or at least leaving stubble and roots to return nutrients to the soil; the groundwater irrigator by taking advantage of the

[9] It is not entirely clear from the Indus Water Treaty of 1960 that India cannot use the beds of the Eastern rivers as drains. The question hinges on the definition of "pollution." If discharge (whether surface or subsurface) of saline irrigation effluent constitutes "pollution" then the Treaty forbids it. If not, then West Pakistan and especially the Sind may just have to suffer the consequences. Failure to consider these consequences in detail in writing the treaty is another example of the optimism and procrastination noted in Section V of this paper. (See Michel, 1967, p. 338.)

The replacement of ancient techniques of irrigation by modern perennial irrigation systems in Egypt has created conditions where the snail hosts of diseases such as bilharziasis thrive. The problem is described by Henry van der Schalie in his paper **A CASE HISTORY OF A SCHISTO-SOMIASIS CONTROL PROJECT** (Page 116).

Bilharziasis is caused by a larva that emerges from snails in stagnant waters, penetrating human tissues and developing into worms that cause physical and mental deterioration. Before the introduction of perennial irrigation, the disease was unknown in many of these areas. As a result of the permanent supply of water and the exposure of great numbers of the population to natural and infested waters, well over one half of the population contracted the disease.

The Egyptian government, with the collaboration of WHO, works to control bilharziasis by controlling the snail population but has met with very limited success. In Photo 9-1 Dr. Henry van der Schalie (right) observes snail harvest. At the left of this picture, an Egyptian fellah is raising water from the canal to irrigate his fields. Since water pours over his knees into a gutter and since his feet are usually in the water, he is particularly likely to catch bilharziasis. Netting fish at the edge of a village (Photo 9-2) is another contact point. Bags of copper sulfate were hung in the canal to eliminate snails (Photo 9-3). Aquatic vegetation also disappeared.

The tremendous growth of lush aquatic vegetation is another side effect of perennial irrigation. Cattle and sheep put to pasture alongside vegetation-choked canals have contracted fascioliasis, another snail-borne disease. Its effects can be seen in the emaciated cattle shown in Photo 9-4.

9-1

9-2

9-3

9-4

In his report **THE ROLE OF THE ASWAN HIGH DAM IN CHANGING THE FISHERIES OF THE SOUTHEASTERN MEDITERRANEAN** (Page 159), Dr. George levels some criticism at the ecologists and engineers who have failed to anticipate some of the consequences of the construction of the Aswan High Dam. A project such as this will result in an alteration of the entire hydrological and sedimentary regimen of the Nile River, with notable influence on both the Delta and the sea. Such tremendous consequences will affect millions of people. The Dam impounds a body of water called Lake Nasser, ultimately to be five hundred kilometers long, and will hold the annual floodwaters and release them slowly for irrigation and navigation purposes. The impoundment of the rich floodwaters has all but eliminated the vital nutrients that used to support a sardine population of 18,000 metric tons annually. Egyptian fisheries are destabilized. The Delta lakes are shrunk, reducing the available fish protein there. Run-off insecticides, herbicides, and molluscides concentrate and produce massive fish kills. Shallow brackish waters are so over-fertilized that lakes become trophically rich and anaerobic water becomes a problem.

Photo 10-1 shows the Nile River at Aswan, looking northeastward from the western desert. Windblown sands drift eastward into the river near a number of granitic islands, forming the lower part of the first cataract. In Photo 10-2 feluccas rest at anchor at Baltim, a fishing village on the eastern shore of Lake Burullus. This village and the nearby village of El Burg have long depended on the catch of sardine, but the fish has failed to appear in commercial quantities following the closing of Sadd el Aali.

The salt marshes south of Lake Burullus (Photo 10-3) are a site of extensive land reclamation. Power lines, new canals, and roads now lace the area, formerly one of the most beautiful natural sectors of the Nile Delta.

The silty clay of the Nile is important in building. In Photo 10-4 handmade bricks dry in the sun alongside the canal that provided the material. The reduced silt supply following the construction of the Sadd el Aali may thus require an increased use of factory-made brick and concrete in domestic agriculture.

10-1

10-2

10-3

10-4

The Nile Delta is now in a process of active coastal retreat, described in Dr. Kassas' paper **IMPACT OF RIVER CONTROL SCHEMES ON THE SHORELINE OF THE NILE DELTA** (Page 179). The retreat is the sum of two opposite processes: (a) the natural process of building the Delta by the annual load of sediments brought to the shoreline by the river flood; and (b) the erosion action of waves and a westward shoreline current that prevails throughout the main part of the year. This erosion varies locally but its main effect is the distribution of bodies of coastal sand dunes, which are burying villages on one side and exposing the shoreline on the other side. Contrary to the earlier history of the area, this contemporary coastal retreat can be linked to river control schemes, such as the Delta Barrages (1881), the Aswan Dam (1902) and the Aswan High Dam (1967). The High Dam will bring the Nile under full control and will reduce the water discharged into the sea and its load of sediments to almost nil. Because of the Aswan High Dam, villages that depend on the sediments for fish propagation and land cultivation will be deprived of them. Photo 11-1 gives a close-up view of a sand dune overwhelming village houses, with the sea in background. The inlandward (lakeward) side of the dunes showing stages of sand-drowning of palms can be seen in Photo 11-2, and Photo 11-3 gives a general view from the Borg-el-Borollos village (on the eastern side of Lake Burullus exit) looking eastward. Note the sea wall, which is repaired yearly, the eroded coast in mid-ground and the body of sand dunes with date palms and dried-reed hedges that help restrain the dune movement. Photo 11-4 is another view of the dunes shown in Photo 11-1. Note the white mosque which is nearly engulfed by the moving dunes. Note also the dune encroaching on the village houses on the right-hand side. (Photos by Carl George.)

11-1

11-2

11-3

11-4

At the outfall of Lake Victoria itself, Her Majesty Queen Elizabeth pressed a button in April 1954 and thereby made the dream of a great British Colonial Secretary come true: "What fun to make the immemorial Nile begin its journey by driving through a turbine!" (Winston Churchill, 1908). The Owen Falls Dam, the first control work on the White Nile system, affects many of the local countries of the Upper Nile as well as Egypt. The dam's primary function is to supply hydro-electric power. The Owen Falls Dam is shown in Photo 12-1; besides its hydroelectric installation, this dam has flooded the Ripon Falls and, by controlling the level of Lake Victoria, converts it into the largest reservoir in the world (67,000 sq. km.). Ripon Falls (Photo 12-2), at the origin of the Nile from Lake Victoria, was discovered in 1865 by Speke. This photo was taken before the construction of Owen Falls Dam; the fish is *Barbus altianalis*, about ten pounds in weight. Murchison Falls on the Victoria Nile (Photo 12-3), the barrier between Victorian and Nilotic freshwater regions, is a Mecca for tourists and the site of a proposed hydroelectric project. Dr. E. Barton Worthington, in his paper **THE NILE CATCHMENT—TECHNOLOGICAL CHANGE AND AQUATIC BIOLOGY** (Page 189), discusses the technological changes initiated to meet the needs of the growing populations of the eight countries affected by the Nile catchment; in the paper, the five barrages of Egypt and the six Nile dams, only one of which is in Egypt, are sketched with reference to their purposes and influences on the aquatic ecosystems. Unlike other writers in this section, Dr. Worthington discusses the positive effects of technology, although he also stresses the need for more ecologists with the courage of their convictions. Throughout, he emphasizes the fact that each project usually has only one or two primary purposes, but numerous other effects also occur, particularly environmental impacts; he then notes that survey and project work in river basin development traditionally have tended to ignore the ecological implications. (Photos 12-1 and 12-3 courtesy of Uganda Ministry of Information.)

12-1

12-2

12-3

When it reached its maximum extent in 1963, Lake Kariba on the Zambesi River was the world's largest artificial reservoir, with a surface area of approximately 2,000 square miles and a storage capacity of over 120 million acre-feet. Over 50,000 people were displaced by the lake. To provide new occupations for these people, the government of northern Rhodesia made an ambitious attempt to develop a lake fishery while local extension officers in the resettlement areas tried to improve agriculture through intensification, cash cropping, and the expansion of cattle husbandry.

Because of insufficient land, the carrying capacity of the resettlement areas was exceeded after relocation. Dr. Scudder examines the inability of the planners to create ecologically acceptable systems of land use that are also culturally acceptable to the farmers in his report **ECOLOGICAL BOTTLENECKS AND THE DEVELOPMENT OF THE KARIBA LAKE BASIN** (Page 206). He points out that an ecological solution is worthless if it is unacceptable to the human beings involved. Problems of agricultural land use downstream, fisheries, and the spread of tsetse flies along the new reservoir's shoreline habitat are also discussed.

The danger of flash flooding has increased because of river bank cultivation (Photo 13-1). Here a flash flood in March 1963 is in the process of destroying the Lusitu pipeline that provides water to neighboring villages. The results of the flood are shown in Photo 13-2 (the disrupted pipeline) and in Photo 13-3 (severe erosion of maize gardens).

13-1

13-2

13-3

One example of modern technology's disastrous impact on ecology is discussed by Dr. Michel in **THE IMPACT OF MODERN IRRIGATION TECHNOLOGY IN THE INDUS AND HELMAND BASINS OF SOUTHWEST ASIA.** (Page 257) In both basins, where a modern surface water irrigation system was provided without the provision of adequate drainage, waterlogging and salinity problems negated much of the effort. Photo 15-1 shows an old canal in central Arghandab. In contrast to this traditional system, the new technique of irrigation led to overirrigated land and salinized soils within four years. Photo 15-2 shows salts along the Tarnak River, evidence of the poor drainage conditions that will soon result in agriculturally useless, abandoned land. Accumulations of salt in such archaeological sites as the ruins of Harappa (Photo 15-3) have led to a hypothesis that historically salinization was a cause of the downfall of such great civilizations.

15-1

15-2

15-3

natural recharge to the water table. And both can employ "artificial means" to recharge their elements: the cultivator with green manures and manufactured fertilizers; the groundwater irrigator by aiding nature through artificial recharge of the groundwater. The latter of course requires surface water to be infiltrated, but here again the factor of canal seepage can be turned to good use as the largest element in groundwater recharge, aided by the ponding which is necessary to reclaim saline soils or by excess ponding during fallow periods, or even by employing recharge wells. Such use of the groundwater reservoir eliminates the evaporation problem, converts stream-bed and canal and field seepage into advantages, and may even curtail the need for additional surface storage (with its accompanying disadvantages of evaporation from and sedimentation into the reservoirs). This last problem is particularly important in West Pakistan where good surface-storage sites are few and dam construction costs accordingly high.[10]

Once a groundwater reclamation and development program has been thoroughly integrated into a massive surface-water irrigation scheme, it may be hard to recognize the "natural system." The White House–Interior Panel envisages the day, circa 2000 A.D., when of the 136 million acre-feet entering West Pakistan in the Indus Basin in a mean year only 10 per cent or 13.8 million acre-feet will reach the sea, and 106 million acre-feet of surface and groundwater will be available for crops, permitting a water allowance of at least 4 acre-feet per acre of the 23 million now canal-irrigated (White House, 1964, pp. 283–88).[11] Whether this will be achieved

[10] For an excellent presentation of the advantages and the problems of such an integrated system in West Pakistan, see Greenman, 1967, pp. 177–82.

[11] This does not imply that the water should be so distributed. In fact the Panel cogently argues that it should be concentrated on a substantially smaller area.

depends on all the economic and physical factors enumerated in this paper, plus others which none of us has yet taken into consideration. But as far as we know, the technological means appear to be at hand in an impressive array. Man has already changed the natural system of the Indus Basin to the point where only 40 per cent of the natural flow reaches the sea. If, by the end of this century, he succeeds in reducing it to 7 per cent, he should at least be entitled to ask the question, "Does water really flow downhill?"

V.

With rare exceptions the surface-water irrigator has been rewarded with immediate and often spectacular results. These results stem from the fact that he is introducing a new element—water in large, assured, and more or less controlled quantities—into environments which are naturally arid or semiarid. In the vast majority of cases, he gains the initial advantages of plant nutrients built up over centuries or millennia, and, providing he is neither blind nor stupid, of a low groundwater table. But both of these initial assets are depletable, sometimes shockingly so. The nutrients, especially the nitrates, are quickly used by plants or carried beyond their reach by the water supplied to make the desert bloom. And the water which seeps into the subsoil usually accumulates until it becomes a menace to continued cropping either directly or by capillary rise and evaporation to the accumulation of salts in the topsoil.

There would seem to be a valid parallel between the efforts of the irrigator and those of the sodbuster. Both approach their environments with good will and earnest determination to improve their own lot and, indirectly, that of their fellow man. Both set out to improve nature and, initially, both usually succeed. But each is opening a Pandora's box and often derives results which he neither intends nor desires. The irrigator is eventually beset with declining fertility, waterlogging, and salinity; the sodbuster with gullying or soil blowing.

What amazes me about the history of agriculture is that the lessons of field cropping in the semiarid margins have to be learned again and again, from place to place and from time to time. The Soviets, in their famous Virgin and Idle Lands program, ignored not only the U.S. experience in the Dust Bowl but the experience of their own countrymen who abandoned the "idle" lands less than a century ago. We now have good reason to believe that the decline of the ancient irrigated civilizations of Mesopotamia and Central Asia was due not to climatic change or to Attila the Hun, but to soil depletion, waterlogging and salinity. The distribution system of the Lower Bari Doab Canal in the Punjab (see Fig. 15–1) encompasses the site of ancient Harappa, whose ruined granaries testify to the existence of an extensive irrigation-based civilization four thousand years ago. Although air-photo analysis now confirms earlier suggestions that the Ravi River has moved a few miles away from the Harappa site,[12] the unanswered question is, "Why did Harappa not move with it?" Nor is the downfall of Mohenjo Daro west of the lower Indus fully explained by alien invasions or migrations of the Indus.[13] In both cases, some additional factor must have made it unrewarding to rebuild the irrigation system.

[12] Herbert Wilhemy, Director of the Geographical Institute, University of Tübingen, Germany, has made a thorough study of the airphoto mosiacs of West Pakistan and has published a number of articles on the results.

[13] The *New York Times* of November 20, 1968 (p. 3), suggests that it was flooding from the Indus which caused the abandonment of Mohenjo Daro around 1500 B.C. But the article goes on to note that the river is again working close to the site, causing a rise in the water table and of salts, left behind by evaporation, in the ruins. The salts, by corroding the bricks, are threatening to destroy what is left of the ruins.

Knowing what we now know about the cumulative effects of irrigation in inducing high water tables and surface salinity, we must ask: are these same fields about to pass out of production a second time for reasons of declining fertility, waterlogging, and salinity? Is the irrigator still unable to cope with the consequences which his innovation inevitably introduces?

Many irrigation engineers have had the wisdom to recognize and the courage to state that provision of an artificial drainage system is an inescapable concomitant of providing an artificial irrigation system. But the time dimension of irrigation usually acts to ensure that only the storage and distribution components are initially provided. Since the irrigation-induced rise of the water table to a level where waterlogging and salinity seriously interfere with cropping normally requires years, there is a strong temptation to postpone drainage works, even though all concerned recognize that the ultimate cost will be higher because it will entail disruption of the irrigation system and of agricultural production while surface (opencut) or subsurface (tile) drains are installed. Reinforcing this temptation is the fact that the construction costs of the storage and distribution works almost always exceed the estimates, so that even where drainage works are included in the original plans they are the first elements to be dropped or postponed as construction proceeds.

Ingrained optimism and the tendency to procrastinate make yielding to this temptation all the easier, as does the fact that the system designers are often driven to underestimate costs or to include disposable items in order to obtain administrative, legislative, or voter approval for their schemes on the proven theory that once ground is broken the project will have to be completed. Furthermore, the engineer, planner, contractor, bureaucrat, or politician may be looking for a short-term personal or professional gain. By the time the omission of a drainage system begins to damage crops, he usually has moved on to another project or another constituency or has retired. These factors would seem to apply in all modern societies regardless of their ideological orientation. A recent article by I. P. Gerasimov, Director of the Institute of Geography in Moscow University, noted that

under the administrative pressure of the "anti-drainage lobby," no provision was made in the irrigation plans of the Golodnaya Steppe [southwest of Tashkent] for the construction of the required drainage structures, and calculations of water requirements and carrying capacity of the South Golodnaya Steppe Canal failed to provide for the additional water necessary to wash salt out of the soil. Water requirements for irrigation were based on minimal sprinkling norms. (Gerasimov, 1967)

A sober realization that waterlogging, or salinity, or both problems will inevitably arise in all but the truly exceptional surface-water irrigation systems and that, under all known political-administrative systems, there are strong temptations to overlook, minimize, or postpone the need for drainage works leads us to ask whether any safeguards can be suggested to prevent such ecological and economic damage. Because this conference is primarily concerned with ecological consequences of international development in the "developing" nations, we can direct our suggestions to those nations and to the governments and international agencies which have assumed the responsibility for evaluating the feasibility and underwriting the cost of large-scale irrigation schemes or projects analogous in their effects. Most of the "developed" nations have had experience with such schemes either in their own territory or in that of former colonial dependencies. In any event, they can be presumed to be either knowl-

edgeable enough to anticipate the well-documented consequences of irrigation without drainage or rich enough to bear unanticipated consequences. Such knowledge and money does not exist in the developing nations, and it is to them that our recommendations should be directed.

It has been suggested, and rightly so, that the first problem is one of knowledge —a problem which can be alleviated by bringing the case histories collected for this Conference to the attention of the international community and especially the nations and agencies giving technical and economic assistance and those receiving it. The inclusion of ecological evaluations along with the economic evaluations usually found in pre-audits of development projects has been suggested and is, of course, highly desirable wherever probable consequences can be predicted on the basis of analogous or near-analogous experience. The suggestions for post-project ecological evaluations or "post-audits" are also highly commendable, not the least because they will result in the compilation and dissemination of additional case studies from which lessons can be learned.

But knowledge, recommendations, and good-will have been insufficient in many development projects. Further provision in the form of sanctions is needed to ensure —or at least increase the probability— that all available analogous experience is actually taken into account before a project is begun. It has been suggested that the best mechanism for ensuring both pre-auditing and post-auditing of ecological as well as economic consequences is through the lending and technical assistance agencies. Provision of aid can be made contingent upon such surveys being carried out by the recipient nations or by foreign, preferably international, teams of ecologists, economists, engineers, planners, and other consultants with the full cooperation of the recipient nations.[14] It has also been suggested that such cooperation can be encouraged not only by making aid for new projects contingent upon monitoring those already completed (informally, at least, such is now usually the case) but by tying repayment terms (rates of interest, amortization, and requests for moratoria) to the monitoring performance. I would like to suggest an additional sanction that might ensure more pre-auditing attention to the ecological aspects of large-scale development projects including irrigation schemes. This

[14] With respect to development of the water, soil, and power resources of West Pakistan, such work has been going on for almost twenty years, starting with the F.A.O., Colombo Plan, and Point Four (U.S.G.S.) surveys mentioned in Part III of the text and continuing with the hiring of consultants by WAPDA and by the World Bank for the groundwater development and reclamation projects and the surface-water components of the Indus Basin Project. Regional planning consultants have also been hired for the Northern and Southern Zones of the Indus Basin in West Pakistan. In November, 1963, as a condition of further support from the World Bank and the Bank-organized group of aid-giving nations, Pakistan agreed to fully assist the Bank in carrying out a special study of the water and power resources of West Pakistan to serve as a basis for developmental planning and the wise use of outside and internal resources. The most interesting feature of the twenty-year series of surveys, from the standpoint of this Conference, is the growing emphasis on post-auditing project components and an increasing awareness—though still not as great as could be desired—of the need to include ecological factors in both the pre-audits and post-audits.

would consist of giving an international body such as the World Court jurisdiction over claims by recipient or donor governments or by lending agencies against contractors and consultants for losses sustained because of negligent oversight in the design and execution of projects. Such negligence should be defined to include disregard of ecological consequences which could, in the judgment of the Court, have been foreseen on the basis of the accumulated body of knowledge resulting from such case studies as those reported in this Conference.

My suggestion may appear extreme at first glance. But I would argue that in an age when such domestic nuisances as noise and air pollution are gaining recognition as justiciable injuries, when governments have already submitted, or even bound themselves in advance to submit, many of their international claims and disputes to international jurisdiction, and when billions upon billions of dollars are being spent upon international development projects which have the potential for untold harm as well as untold good, it would be no more than simple logic and common international justice to hold contractors and consultants responsible for environmental damage which can be foreseen and averted on the basis of the established record.

REFERENCES

Gerasimov, I. P. "Basic Problems of the Transformation of Nature in Central Asia," from *Problemy osvoyeniya pustyn'*, No. 5 (1967), pp. 3–17. In *Soviet Geography*, Vol. IX, No. 6 (June, 1968), pp. 444–58.

Government of Pakistan, Central Statistical Office. *Statistical Pocket-Book of Pakistan, 1964.* Karachi: Manager of Publications, 1964.

Greenman, David W. "Hydrology and Scientific Reclamation in the Punjab." In *The Challenge of Development,* Richard J. Ward, ed. Chicago: Aldine Press, 1967. Pp. 173–82.

Lateef, M. A., and Shamsi, R. A. "History and Magnitude of Waterlogging and Salinity Problems in former Punjab, West Pakistan." In *Symposium on Waterlogging and Salinity*. Lahore: West Pakistan

Engineering Congress, October, 1963. Pp. 1–14.

Michel, Aloys A. *The Kabul, Kunduz and Helmand Valleys and the National Economy of Afghanistan*. Washington, D.C.: National Academy of Sciences–National Research Council, 1959.

————. *The Indus Rivers*. New Haven: Yale University Press, 1967.

Montagu, A. M. R. "Presidential Address to the Punjab Engineering Congress, 33rd Session, 1946." *Proceedings of the Punjab Engineering Congress*, 33rd Session, Lahore (1946), pp. i–xvii.

Todd, David K. "Advances in Techniques of Ground Water Resources Development," in *The Challenge of Development*, Richard J. Ward, ed. Chicago: Aldine Press, 1967. Pp. 160–71.

White House–Department of the Interior Panel on Waterlogging and Salinity in West Pakistan. *Report on Land and Water Development in the Indus Plain*. Washington, D.C.: The White House, January, 1964.

16. SALINIZATION AND WATER PROBLEMS IN THE ALGERIAN NORTHEAST SAHARA*

Kamel Achi

The lower Algerian Sahara constitutes a zone with a relatively dense population where the only resources are provided by agriculture, particularly by the date palms which cover an area of approximately 11,000 hectares. This zone, which is subjected to an arid climate (50 millimeters of rain on the average per year in the Ouargla region), had never experienced intensive development activity until the discovery of important quantities of underground water. In the absence of surface water resources, these subterranean waters by themselves condition the life of Saharan populations. The known history of the exploitation of these natural resources goes back to slightly more than a century ago. In particular, the discovery of several artesian water tables, which yield gushing wells over a great part of their expanse, led to an anarchic multiplication of wells and bore holes, without taking account of their interdependence and their influence on the regime of the superficial water table that lies just below the surface. In the first ten years of exploitation the number of wells tapping the artesian water table closest to the soil was doubled from five hundred to over a thousand. There are presently nearly two thousand wells and bore holes of which a thousand already are either abandoned or technically defective. In particular, the wells of local make are filled with sand and the old tubings are corroded, causing leakage.

This abusive exploitation of the subterranean waters eventually had a disastrous effect on the superficial water table whose regime was seriously perturbed by the addition of water. The added water would not have had serious consequences by itself if the natural conditions of drainage were favorable. However, the lower Sahara is shaped like a saucer with a flat bottom where the subterranean

---

* Translated from the French by M. Taghi Farvar, who takes the sole responsibility for any inaccuracies of rendition.

out flow of water is not assured. Hence waterlogging is already observable in the lower parts, which are occupied by the palms that utilize the relative proximity of the superficial water table. The superficial water table in the zones of intensive exploitation is found at a depth of .50 meter to 1.50 meters. The root system of the palms thus becomes immersed in a zone saturated with water of high mineral content (up to 18 grams per liter of dry residue). At the present, one can observe many dead palm trees, particularly in zones where they are subject to these modifications in the environment.

Presently studies are being conducted on (1) the phenomena of secondary salinization of soils (due to irrigation), formation of salt crusts as a function of irrigation, and the fluctuation of the level of the superficial water table, and (2) characteristics required for efficient artificial drainage.

The Northeast Sahara in Algeria is bordered by the Aurès hills to the north, the Mzab massif to the west, and the 33rd parallel to the south. The eastern part is occupied by the great Eastern Erg (a region of dunes). The oueds[1] Mya and R'Hir cross this area from south to north toward a chain of Shotts[2] edging the foothills of the Aurès The Northeast Sahara is an important part of the vast Algerian Sahara. The only resource in the region is agriculture, particularly the date palms which cover an area of approximately 11,000 hectares. The palm trees planted along the valleys, particularly those of the Oued R'Hir, have supported a relatively large population, estimated at 120,000. The population had never experienced intensive development activity until the discovery of important quantities of underground water. In the absence of surface water resources, these subterranean waters are the controlling factor in the life of Saharan populations.

However, agriculture and related activities have created a difficult situation in which water is the basic problem. Beyond the technical and scientific aspects of these difficulties, one can verify the impact of man on an established system: an effect which results in the breakdown of a natural equilibrium.

BASIC WATER PROBLEMS

HYDROCLIMATOLOGY

The northeastern Sahara is arid. Average annual rainfall at Ouargla is 45 mm. Outside the flooding season of the oueds this rainfall is insignificant in the total balance of water resources of the region. Evapotranspiration varies from 1,600 to 2,000 mm/yr., depending on the method of calculation used. Evaporation of surface water amounts to more than 2,000 mm/yr. when measured under the same climatic conditions.

GEOLOGY AND HYDROGEOLOGY (See Cornet, 1952, 1961, 1964)

The Northeast Sahara has the shape of a synclinal basin. A schematic cross section passing through Fort Flatters (south) and Touggourt (north) would show the following stratification (Fig. 16–1):

[1] An oued or wadi (= arroyo) is a desert stream that has a seasonal flow.
[2] A shott is a shallow salt lagoon in the desert which dries up in the hot season.

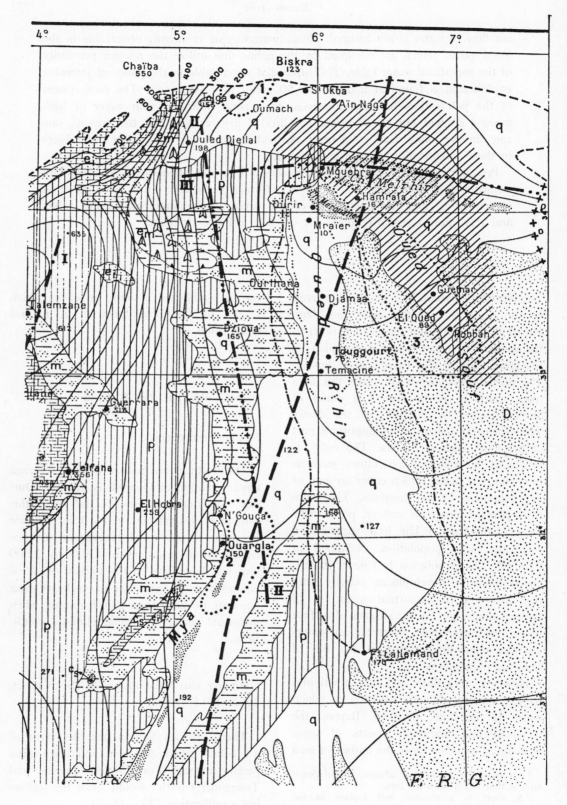

Figure 16–1

GEOLOGICAL SKETCH
OF N.E. ALGERIAN SAHARA

SCALE 1/2000000

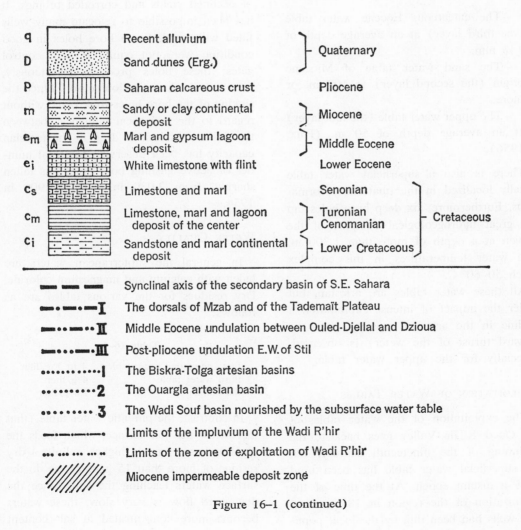

q	Recent alluvium	Quaternary
D	Sand dunes (Erg.)	
p	Saharan calcareous crust	Pliocene
m	Sandy or clay continental deposit	Miocene
e_m	Marl and gypsum lagoon deposit	Middle Eocene
e_i	White limestone with flint	Lower Eocene
c_s	Limestone and marl	Senonian
c_m	Limestone, marl and lagoon deposit of the center	Turonian Cenomanian
c_i	Sandstone and marl continental deposit	Lower Cretaceous

Cretaceous

— — — Synclinal axis of the secondary basin of S.E. Sahara

—·—·—I The dorsals of Mzab and of the Tademaït Plateau

—·—··—II Middle Eocene undulation between Ouled-Djellal and Dzioua

—·—··—III Post-pliocene undulation E.W.of Stil

·············I The Biskra-Tolga artesian basins

·········2 The Ouargla artesian basin

·········3 The Wadi Souf basin nourished by the subsurface water table

—·—·—· Limits of the impluvium of the Wadi R'hir

··· ··· ··· ··· ·· Limits of the zone of exploitation of Wadi R'hir

///////// Miocene impermeable deposit zone

Figure 16–1 (continued)

– The Albien, which rests on the Paleozoic "socle," levels off to the south of Fort Flatters.
   – The Cenomanian clay.
   – The Turonian limestone.
   – The Senonian clay.
   – The Eocene limestone, later marl.
   – The Continental Tertiary with clayey marl covered by a calcareous layer.

To the north of Touggourt these formations drop abruptly, forming the sub-Aurès pit.

Numerous wells and bore holes in the region have revealed three important water tables:

   – The calcareous Eocene water table (the third layer) at an average depth of 140 mm.
   – The sand water table of Miocène origin (the second layer) at 100 m. or more.
   – The upper water table (the first layer) at an average depth of 50 m. (Paix, 1956).

There is also a superficial water table usually localized in the quaternary formations. Furthermore, six deep bore holes tap the great hydrogeological complex of the Albien at a depth of more than 1,300 m. The water temperatures in this complex reach 50–60° C.

All these water tables are artesian, but under the impact of intense exploitation a decline in the artesian capacity (i.e., the upward thrust of the water) is observed, especially for the upper water table.

EXPLOITATION OF WATER TABLES

The exploitation of the water tables of the Oued R'Hir Valley goes back to the beginning of the nineteenth century, but the superficial water table has been used since a distant epoch. At the time of the colonization of the region in 1855, about 500 wells had been dug by the local population, tapping particularly the upper table.

Ever since the discovery of other water tables a few years later, large numbers of bore holes have been sunk chaotically. Between 1905 and 1915, the number of artesian bore holes tapping the first water table increased from 565 to 1,010. Concurrently the total output went from approximately 160,000 liters/min. to 257,000 liters/min. Presently there are about 2,000 watering points, nine-tenths of which draw from the first table.

There are many consequences of this intensive exploitation. Of the 2,000 wells, more than 1,000 present serious problems of declined yields and corroded tubings. It has been impossible to relocate many wells filled with sand. Some bore holes in good condition were not equipped with control gates; these holes produce continuously, even outside the irrigation season. Since the sinking of the bore holes took place without regard to the reciprocal influences between the wells, a noticeable drop in the artesian capacity has been observed; the total number of active gushing bore holes has fallen sharply, from 2,030 in 1915 to 900 in 1954.

WATER QUALITY

In general the subterranean waters are laden with calcium and magnesium chloride. Dry residues for the various tables are as follows:

Table 16–1

first and second water tables:	4 to 7 g/liter
third water table	4 g/liter
the Albien	1.8 g/liter

In contrast, the phreatic water table (that just below the soil surface, which feeds the plants) has a much higher salinity (dry residue of more than 15 g/liter), as do the surface waters leaching the soil. Since the downward flow is very slow, these waters become more concentrated in salt content due to the effect of irrigation and evaporation, and in the lower reaches they often form concentrated brine. Chemical analyses of the water tables show a "vertical zonality": the deeper water tables are of better quality than those closer to the surface. This is due to climatic factors, for arid climates tend to strongly concentrate the salts dissolved in water.

Hydrochemical studies also indicate a "geological zonality": the chemical composition of the water reflects the nature of the terrain in which it circulates. The water in the Albien has little dissolved salts for two main reasons. First, its great depth has protected it from "climatic contamination," and second, it circulates chiefly in sandstone which contains very little or none of the salts which generally increase water salinity (namely the chlorides and sulfates of sodium, calcium, and magnesium).

Another important salinizing factor is the speed of water circulation in a given terrain. The slower this speed, the more concentrated the water, because its contact with the rocks is more prolonged. How can this theory be reconciled with the fact that in the deep water tables the speed of flow is certainly less, yet the water is less mineralized? The answer lies in the fact that climatic rather than geological factors usually play the dominant role (Burgeap, 1964; Caponera, 1956). After the water filters through irrigated land it becomes more salt-laden because it passes through the first few meters of soil in which most salts are dissolved (Durand, n.d., 1956).

Thus the series of factors which contribute to salinizing a body of underground water can be put in the following categories. First, there are the natural factors (uninfluenced by humans): the nature of the terrain, the climatic conditions, the speed of flow, etc. Second, there are factors provoked by human intervention, such as intensive pumping which often causes infiltration of salty water into the deeper, less salty water tables; also, under certain conditions irrigation can lead salt-laden water to a water table. This second category can be considered ecological and results from the human occupation of the soil (Geopetrole, n.d.).

CAUSES OF THE PROBLEM

The Oued R'Hir Valley is suffering from a dangerous situation caused by the rise in the level of the subsurface water table. In roughly 60% of the area occupied by palm trees, the water table varies from a depth of 1.50 to 0.50 m. There are three basic causes for this waterlogging.

One is the increase in tapping of the water. Many bore holes continually draw from the subsurface water table and deposit water on the surface. Other circumstances, due to irrigation, which compound this problem are explained in the next section.

There are natural impediments which cause bad drainage. The outlet of this region is the shott Merouane, but the water flows so slowly that it results in waterlogging. The dynamics of the water system also have an effect. Since the water table is artesian, the vertical component of the flow is greater than the horizontal one. Therefore, the subsurface water table is fed through the entire semipermeable layer which separates it from the artesian water table below (Fig. 16–2). Again, this condition leads to an inflated subsurface water table.

Technical problems can also be the cause of waterlogging. In the Oued R'Hir Valley there is definitely an insufficient network of horizontal drainage. These artificial drains (Fig. 16–2, 16–3) consist of ditches dug by excavators. Many factors determine how deep and how far apart these ditches should be: e.g., the salinity of the irrigation water passing out of the soil, depth of the water table, permeability of the upper soil horizons. The drains are on the average 18 meters apart, which seemed satisfactory in

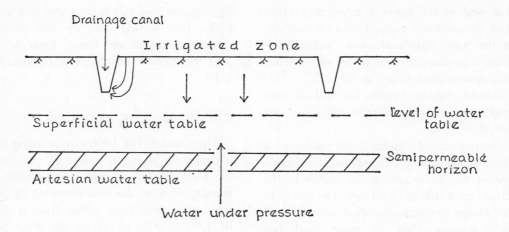

Figure 16–2 The principal geohydrological elements in the Lower Algerian Sahara—with adequate drainage conditions

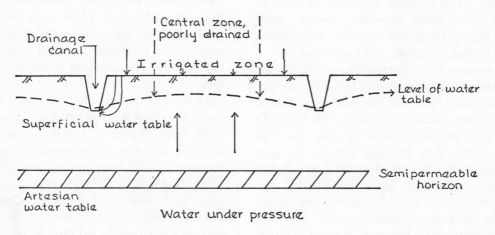

Figure 16–3 The principal geohydrological elements in the Lower Algerian Sahara, with impeded drainage leading to waterlogging and salinization

the past. To see why this is no longer true let us examine the mechanisms of the movement of irrigation waters in the soil.

Down to a certain "critical depth" (say 4 meters, depending on an external supply of water via irrigation), the existing system of drainage can be efficient. In this case, after percolation in the cultivated soil, the downward component of water flow predominates and the irrigation waters are largely tapped and carried away by the network of drains; the remainder percolates

down to a water table which continues to remain lower than the drains.

The problems occur when irrigation waters surpass a given volume. The network of drains carries off only a small amount of the water; the rest is added to the water table. A rise in the water table follows and the drains end up in the zone of excess water which is characterized by (1) a predominantly upward component of flow (caused by the charged water table) and (2) a weak horizontal component of the subsurface water table (slow drainage). The artesian regime of the deep water table makes itself felt at a much higher level. This influence causes a reduction in the downward flow of irrigation water to the level of the drainage ditches, which, in turn, results in a reduced lateral flow. In this case the depth of the drains is greater than the "critical depth" defined above. The percolating irrigation water stabilizes itself at a level which is no lower than that of the drainage canals (Fig. 16–3); the drainage network is now gravely insufficient.

Once this situation is established it is very difficult to combat even by bringing the drains closer together, a solution which presents great inconveniences and expense. Further research is needed on other possible solutions. For example, it may be possible to use horizontal and vertical drainage systems simultaneously and to control the flow of additional water to the table by means of irrigation.

WATER AND AGRICULTURE

In arid regions such as the Oued R'Hir Valley, much more than elsewhere, water and agriculture are intimately interdependent. No form of farming can exist here except irrigation agriculture. The near-total absence of surface water has forced agriculture to resort to subterranean waters.

AGRICULTURE

The region of Oued R'Hir comprises 11,-000 hectares of palm groves which constitute the main if not the only agricultural resource. These palm groves shelter mixed cultures of market-garden produce, whose modest output is used for subsistence consumption. About 1,300,000 palm trees are planted on these 11,000 hectares with an annual yield of 30,000 metric tons in the following categories: dates of superior quality (Deglet Nour), 20,000 tons; common dates, 10,000 tons.

Assuming that 1,000,000 palm trees produce the Deglet Nour variety, the productivity would be 20 kilograms per palm. Even this meager output does not tell the whole story. In fact in certain zones, particularly the low and peripheral zones of the palm groves, many palm trees have perished. In the case of annual subsistence crops growing between the rows of palms, salinization has meant reduced yields. Some of the causes of this deterioration are given below.

IRRIGATION

The water need of a palm tree is 50 liters/min./hectare; this means an irrigation norm of 25,000 cubic meters per year, and for the total of 11,000 hectares, a requirement of 550,000 liters per minute. However, the available supply is calculated to be 360,000 liters/min. In fact, this water deficit is distributed in various ways. Certain palm groves receive the needed supply, others do not. The basic deficiency is aggravated by incorrect irrigation techniques. Watering standards and hydromodules[3] are kept constant throughout the year. Given the water needs of the palms, this method of irrigation produces under-irrigation in the summer and over-irrigation in the winter. This misuse of water may be matched with the above-mentioned figures indicating a water deficit. The impact of this deficit might be lessened by a better utilization of the available supplies (Caponera, 1956; Ouvrard, 1961).

Another important factor affecting this water deficit is the parceling out of the palm groves. A great many lots have a surface of less than one hectare; such small lots mean an increase in the required number of supply canals. This subdivision of the land considerably increases loss by evap-

[3] A hydromodule is the amount of water a unit area receives per unit time.

oration and by percolation through the canals.

Evaporation certainly plays an essential role in areas where the water table is very near the surface, and hence there is a continuous supply of a capillary flow. Still another factor enters the equation, that of a low "coefficient of water utilization."[4]

THE CAUSES OF DETERIORATION

Various factors may be responsible for the observed deterioration of palms, but in this particular region water plays a paramount role, especially in low-lying, improperly drained zones and in the peripheral areas of the palm groves. A hydrogeological study has shown that the subsurface water table is just below the surface in the marginal regions, and for the palm groves located in improperly drained zones the depth of this water table varies between 0.50 meter and 1.50 meters. This fact becomes very important when it is considered in the light of the hydrodynamic regime of the water table (see Figs. 16–2 and 16–3). In fact the evolution of this water table cannot be considered to be cyclical. It takes place slowly and proceeds in a manner determined by the hydraulic balance sheet. The contribution made by irrigation to the "swelling" of the water table can be better understood if one considers that both evaporation and loss (natural as well as that through drainage) have definite boundaries of variation.

Since the roots of the palm tree are usually 1.40 meters deep, it follows that a great many of them have their root system continuously in the saturated zone. The first consequence is that the excess water, even if of good quality, reacts in an unfavorable way on the physiology of the plant. Agro-

[4] The coefficient of water utilization is the ratio of *amount of water effectively utilized for irrigation to total amount of water*. This ratio is always less than one, because a part of the water is inevitably lost by evaporation, percolation, and loss in the canals, etc.

nomic studies have shown a resistance of the palm tree to concentrations of salts as strong as 7 g/liter. In our present case, even if use

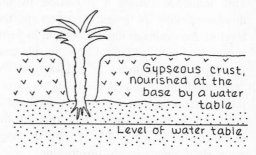

Figure 16–4 Schematic cross section of palm trees planted in "wedges"

were made of waters which had an original concentration equal to or less than 7 g/liter, one should not overlook that these waters are subsequently strongly concentrated by evaporation. The superficial water table has a salinity of 16 g/liter of dry residue; by the time the waters begin to leach, the concentration reaches 20 g/liter or even more. Here again irrigation plays an essential role in increasing salinity. In the valley of the Oued R'Hir, the capillary rise may amount to 1.50 to 2 meters. The salts deposited on the surface are recycled and returned to the water table by the irrigation water. By way of an example, studies carried out in the region of Ouargla have shown than the quantity of salts raised back to the surface was 50,000 to 75,000 tons per year.

In the valley of the Oued R'Hir, this phenomenon is accentuated by the regime of the water table. Since the horizontal component of the flow is weak, the salts are recycled due to irrigation-evaporation factors. The nature of deposited salts thus depends not only on geological and hydrogeological factors but also on solubility; the latter factor particularly affects the order of deposition. The first salts which are deposited in the region of the palm's growth are calcium and magnesium sulfates.

In the region further to the north (Biskra-Tolga), these salts form compact gypseous crusts 2 meters thick and obstruct the percolation of waters and the penetration of the roots to the point where the young palm trees are now planted in the wedges which cross the crust (Deicha, 1943; Durand, 1949, 1953). In the low-lying regions, especially in the outlets made up by the shotts, sodium chloride is usually deposited in the form of visible whitish scales. In certain regions (e.g. high plains of Constantinois) these salts are actually mined.

The salinity of the superficial water table certainly is important in the palm grove deterioration. Although the palm tree tolerates irrigation waters with a salinity of 7 g/liter of dry residue, it cannot do the same for waters with a mineral content on the order of 20 g/liter.

This brief exposé shows the disastrous role that irrigation plays when it is ill-managed, especially in the arid regions. The abusive exploitation of water for the purpose of irrigation can profoundly alter the regime of subterranean waters and create serious problems of drainage and secondary salinization of lands. These phenomena are inevitable when unfavorable natural drainage conditions and subterranean water regimes are present. The example just given shows that these situations may be created in just a few generations.

SOCIAL ASPECTS

The expert concerned with water problems in arid zones should not overlook the social and human aspects of his work. He may often face a great mistrust on the part of the population who dislike outside intervention. This attitude is readily understandable, for after all, water is *the* most precious commodity for these people.

The most common social attitude concerning irrigation is that of the peasant, who, whenever possible, prefers to have his private watering point, even for a small lot of less than one hectare. Land consolidation could have a favorable influence on this state of affairs. Furthermore, these small proprietors often do not have the proper tools; since their wells are built by hand, they are more subject to technical difficulties. In the Oued R'Hir Valley reclamation projects, technicians have envisaged a campaign to fill up the old wells. This campaign confronts serious social and human difficulties. It is very difficult to bring the peasants to understand that filling up the wells will ameliorate the condition of their palm groves. Since this campaign would cover some one thousand watering points, from an economic standpoint the operation will be costly. The average cost for filling up each well is 3,000 Algerian dinars (3,000 French francs). It is obvious that the small proprietors are not in a position to carry such a burden.

Right now another phenomenon is taking place in the Oued R'Hir Valley: a decrease in artesian capacity due to the intense exploitation of water tables. This process of diminishing capacity first affects the high zones of palm groves where the water lacks the force to reach. The cultivators then have a tendency to carry the palm culture to the lower-lying areas, i.e., those areas where the drainage problem is the most acute.

This points up a major social problem, which is the regulation of land use and water resources in the arid zone.

CONCLUSION

Experience in the Oued R'Hir Valley as well as throughout the world clarifies a problem neglected up to now, namely the geo-ecological aspects of development. Man's actions and their consequences follow the same rhythm as technical progress. Land reclamation, particularly in the vulnerable arid zones, should take into consideration all the possible ecological aspects in any development. The effect of irrigation technology must be carefully studied in particular. Hydrogeologic studies are especially essential. Among the unfavorable ecological conditions of arid lands being considered for irrigation are the following:

—A superficial water table of shallow depth.

—A morphology of the aquifers and of the soil which does not lend itself to an easy water flow.

—An artesian structure of the water table.

—Heavy soils not easy to drain.

—Climatic conditions of extreme aridity which concentrate the water and its salts.

Together, these basic conditions often unite with any anarchic exploitation of waters to bring about fatal waterlogging and secondary salinization of lands. The initial impact usually comes from the modification of the water table regime by irrigation waters. This aspect must be studied much more carefully in the future.

Geologic studies should include maps of isobaths showing the ceilings of various aquifer formations. A pedologic study should follow the geologic one. Heavy soils can create serious drainage problems even if the hydrodynamic characteristics are good to a considerable depth.

The regime of the regional water table must be surveyed regularly and recorded on hydrogeologic maps. In arid zones, underground waters are not subject to annual regulation. The modification of their regime is primarily due to irrigation. The effect of this contribution may be elucidated by determination of horizontal and vertical permeability of the upper horizons, by theoretical analysis of the rise in the water table under the influence of irrigation, and by research on experimental plots.

These studies naturally need support from other disciplines, in particular topography, geomorphology, hydraulics, and so on.

Also to be studied is an aspect of irrigation of no less importance: how to foster irrigation that contributes to only a minimal rise in the water table. The "critical depth" for the latter is determined by considering the penetration of the root system, the natural and artificial conditions of drainage, the importance of capillary rise, and the nature of the soil. All these studies must aim to define irrigation norms and, eventually, the leaching which should ideally equal the potential evapotranspiration. If this situation is not easy to achieve in practice, it can be approximated by acting on certain factors. Irrigation techniques also should minimize loss by percolation, especially in the canals.

This summary of the situation in the Oued R'Hir Valley shows the complexity of the problems of development considered from a geo-ecological angle. For the future, these experiences will hopefully serve to induce environmental studies to fill up the gap left by the technical and economic aspects of development.

REFERENCES

Burgeap. *Données sur les Ressources Hydrauliques des Départements Sahariens et Leur Utilisation Actuelle. Note Préliminaire.* Direction Générale du Plan Alger. Burgeap R352 Rueil Malmaison France, March, 1964.

——. *Etude du Continental Intercalaire Saharien.* 2 vols., 23 plates.

Caponera, D. A. *Le droit des Eaux dans les Pays Musulmans.* Collection F.A.O.; Progrès et mise en valeur. Agriculture. Cahier No. 43. Rome: F.A.O., 1956.

Cornet, A. "Les eaux du crétace inférieur continental dans le Sahara algérien (nappe dite "albienne")." *XIX Congrès Géologique International. La Géologie et les Problèmes de l'Eau en Algérie,* Vol. II. *Données sur l'Hydrogéologie Algérienne.* Algiers, 1952.

——. "Géologie de l'Oued R'Hir." *Terres et Eaux,* No. 37 (third and fourth quarters, 1961).

——. "Hydrogéologie saharienne." *Revue de Géogr. Physique et de Géol. Dynamique,* January–March, 1964.

Deicha, G. "Genèse et faciès du gypse." *Bull. Sté. Franç. de Minérologie,* Vol. XVI, Nos. 1–6 (1943), pp. 153–60.

Dervieux, I. "La nappe phréatique du Souf (Région d'El Oued). Algérie. Iᵉ Etude du renouvellement de la nappe. Contribution à l'étude des phénomènes capillaires dans un milieu pulvérulent." *Terres et Eaux,* No. 29.

——. "La nappe phréatique du Souf." *Terres et Eaux,* No. 31 (fourth quarter, 1957–first quarter, 1958).

Drouhin, G. "Expérience algérienne d'utilisation des eaux saumâtres pour l'irrigation, avec référence particulière aux sols salins." Arid Zone Research. *Salinity Problems in the Arid Zones. Proceedings of the Teheran Symposium.* UNESCO, 1961.

Durand, J. H. "Formation de la croûte gypseuse du Souf (Sahara)." *C. R. Somm. Sté. Géol. de France,* (1949), pp. 304–05.

——. Etude géologique, hydrogéologique et pédologique des croûtes en Algérie. Publications du Gouvernement Général de l'Algérie. Direction du S.C.H. Service des Etudes Scientifiques. Pédologie No. 1, Birmandreïs Alger. Thèse d'Ingénieur-Docteur, 1953.

——. "L'irrigation des cultures dans l'Oued R'Hir." *Travaux de l'Institut de Recherches Sahariennes Université d'Alger,* Vol. XIII (first & second half-year, 1955), pp. 75–130.

——. "Mouvement des sels dans le sol." *C.R. VIᵉ Congrès International de la Science du Sol,* D (1956), pp. 543–46.

——. "L'influence de l'eau d'irrigation sur le sol." Commission Internationale des Irrigations et du Drainage. 3e Congrès. R 12, Question 8. N.d.

Emberger, L. "Rapport sur les régions arides et semi-arides de l'Afrique du Nord." *Union Internationale des Sciences biologiques,* series B. (1951), pp. 50–61.

Geopetrole. *Etude des Forages du Continental Terminal.* 8 reports. Organisme de Coopération Industrielle, Rue Z. Roccas Alger. N.d.

Gouskov, N. "Le problème hydrogéologique du bassin artésien de l'Oued R'Hir." *XIX Congrés Géologique International. La Géologie et les Problèmes de l'Eau en Algérie,* Vol. II. *Données sur l'Hydrogéologie Algérienne.* Algiers, 1952.

Ouvrard, R. "La revivification des palmeraies de l'Oued R'Hir." *Terres et Eaux,* No. 37 (third and fourth quarters, 1961).

Paix, F. Les nappes artésiennes de l'Oued R'Hir. Université d'Alger, Faculté des Sciences. Thèse de Doctorat d'Université, 1956.

S.E.S. *Nombreux rapports et études.* Service des Etudes Scientifiques de l'Algérie. Clairbois. Birmandreïs, Algiers.

17. SALT CEDAR AND SALINITY ON THE UPPER RIO GRANDE

John Hay

Prehistoric peoples successfully used the water of the Upper Rio Grande for agriculture until the advent of the Spanish and the Americans. No ecological problems became obvious until the introduction of grazing animals which upset the delicate balance of vegetation on the desert. Soil erosion rapidly increased causing an increase of silt in the river valley and rapid silting of the man-made reservoirs. Introduction of salt cedars (tamarisk) to prevent this erosion resulted in an unanticipated and explosive growth of this plant which spread into thousands of acres of irrigable lands. Between 1935 and 1947, the plant took over about 10,000 hectares (24,500 acres) of irrigable farm land in the valley and consumed approximately 45 percent of the area's total available water. Building of dams to increase irrigable acreages caused more desert to be irrigated, with consequent leaching of salts into downstream river flows until the salt burden became more than the depleted river flow could handle. In the valley's Hudspeth County, for example, an irrigation well drilled in 1968 yielded over 16 grams of salt per liter (22 tons per acre-foot). The county is now in poor agricultural condition.

This complex of problems could have at least been anticipated if the processes of resource development in the valley had included relevant ecological studies in addition to the usual engineering ones.

This is a story of a river, a tree, a county and a country. The river is the Rio Grande, the Rio Bravo del Norte of the Mexicans. The tree is the tamarisk (*Tamarix pentandra*) or salt cedar, as it is called in the Southwest. The county is Hudspeth County, Texas, which lies downstream from the city and county of El Paso, Texas. I will discuss that part of Hudspeth County which lies in the irrigable portion of the Rio Grande between the El Paso County line and Fort Quitman, where mountains on both sides of the river close in to form a box canyon, terminating in what is referred to in the United States as the Upper Rio Grande. And the country is Mexico—that part of Mexico which lies below Ciudad Juárez and constitutes the irrigable valley lying between Ciudad Juárez and the mountains at Fort Quitman.

THE RIVER

The Rio Grande is a typical river of arid and semiarid regions. It rises in the snow-covered mountains of the state of Colorado and runs in a southerly direction through the central part of New Mexico until it reaches El Paso, Texas, where it swings southeasterly (Fig. 17–1).

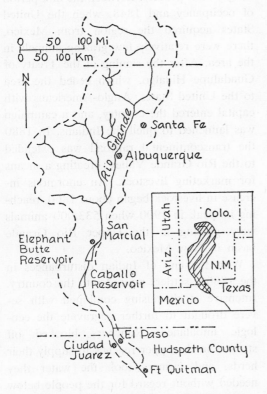

Figure 17–1 The Upper Rio Grande

Drainage area of the Upper Rio Grande is about 88,000 square kilometers, or 34,000 square miles (Hay, 1963). Over 99 percent of its water supply derives from snow melted in the high mountains of Colorado and New Mexico. Over a million people inhabit the area, most of them concentrated in the rapidly expanding urban centers of Albuquerque (New Mexico), El Paso (Texas), and Ciudad Juárez (Chihuahua, Mexico), the latter having the largest population (over 500,000). Arid lower reaches of this river basin have average annual rainfalls of only about 200 millimeters (eight inches).

The upper river is divided into three natural areas. That area in Colorado is known as the San Luis Valley. It is bounded on three sides by mountains and contains an irrigated area of approximately 260,000 hectares (650,000 acres). It is by far the largest irrigated area in the upper river. Its proximity to the mountains whose snow melt causes the birth of the river gives it first and least salty use of the river valley's water supply. Its sandy loam is excellent for raising potatoes, for which it is noted.

The middle reaches of the river, through the northern and central sections of New Mexico, are confined, to a large extent, in canyons and narrow valleys. Stream-bed slope is mild, and the accumulation of silt from eroding soils in ephemeral tributaries has caused an aggradation of the river bed, principally at and below Albuquerque, with a consequent waterlogging of adjoining valley lands.

The worst offender in silting is the Rio Puerco, which joins the Rio Grande approximately midway between Albuquerque and Elephant Butte Dam (Dortignac, 1963). The Rio Puerco watershed covers approximately 1.6 million hectares (3.9 million acres). It is a permanent stream only through the upper few miles of its channel; the remaining part and all of its tributaries have ephemeral or intermittent flow. From

1885 to 1963 an estimated 740 million to 987 million cubic meters (600,000 to 800,000 acre feet) of soils has washed from the Rio Puerco into the Rio Grande. The Rio Puerco, which comprises 23 percent of the contributing basin in the Upper Rio Grande above Elephant Butte Dam, produces 45 percent of the measured sediment in the main channel but only about 3 percent of the basin runoff.

The southern section of the Rio Grande extends from Elephant Butte Reservoir in south-central New Mexico to Fort Quitman, Texas, about 130 kilometers (80 miles) southeast of El Paso. This section is divided, physically, by a narrow canyon, or "pass," at El Paso, Texas, and by another engorgement to the north, at Rincon. Another division, caused by man, occurs at the El Paso–Hudspeth County line. This southern section, including the Mexican counterpart, the Juárez Valley, comprises approximately 70,000 hectares (175,000 acres). Its principal crops have been cotton and alfalfa.

Irrigation in the Rio Grande basin above Fort Quitman has been traced back to prehistoric times (Kirby, 1968). When the Spaniards, under Juan de Oñate, entered the valley in 1598, they found settlements of Pueblo Indians scattered up and down the basin and its adjoining valleys almost up to the Colorado state line. Archaeologists and dendrochronologists argue that these Indians were forced out of Mesa Verde in southwestern Colorado into the less severe conditions in northern New Mexico during an extended drought from 1276 to 1299 A.D. Indications have been found of relatively elaborate canal systems along the Rio Grande and the Rio Puerco. The earlier settlers of this region were the Anasazi, predecessors of the modern Pueblo Indians, who maintained small, settled communities and practiced a primitive form of agriculture.

The low brush and rock diversion dams and canals of the Indians did little to change the ecologic balance. In contrast, the arrival of the Spaniards with their grazing animals may have quickly upset the soil-vegetation equilibrium. For two hundred years Spanish colonists occupied these valleys in the central part of New Mexico. In the first part of the nineteenth century the Spanish were ordered to retire from the area following disturbances caused by roving bands of nomadic Indians, such as the Navajo. Since 10,000 head of cattle were removed from the Rio Puerco region alone, it may be conceivable that even at that early date overgrazing may have begun, and there are indications that the land resources had begun to disintegrate. Marauding Indians restricted grazing of sheep to the immediate vicinity of the Spanish communities, and the deterioration of vegetation in those locales may have started the cycle of accelerated erosion.

The deterioration of the land was a relatively slow process. Between the first period of occupancy and 1848, when the United States acquired the region from Mexico, there were relatively few grazing animals in the area. After the signing of the Treaty of Guadalupe Hidalgo, which ceded the area to the United States, Anglo-Americans with capital entered the country, and a campaign was launched to quell the Indians. In 1880 the transcontinental railroad was extended to the Rio Grande Valley, creating a means for marketing livestock. An enormous increase in livestock began about 1860, reaching its peak in 1900 when 533,000 animals were grazing in the Upper Rio Grande basin in New Mexico.

With the end of Indian disturbances in the 1880's, settlers poured into the country. Intensive stock raising combined with severe drought to further aggravate the ecologic imbalance. Ranchers blocked off streams in the upper reaches to supply their herds, and farmers took the water they needed without regard for the people below them on the river. The constant build-up of population added new demands on the already overtaxed water resources.

Continued expansion on the upper reaches of the river led to more and more serious disputes. Mexico was deprived of its rightful share of water and brought increasing pressure to bear on the United States. Finally, the more responsible parties of both countries met to discuss what might be done to alleviate the situation. After extensive investigations by the United States proved the feasibility of creating Elephant Butte Dam and Reservoir, representatives of both countries ratified an agreement in 1907 whereby Mexico, in exchange for dropping all previous claims to water from the Rio Grande, was allotted approximately 74,300,000 cu m (60,000 acre-feet or 2,613,600,000 cu ft) per year. The treaty further states: "In case, however, of extraordinary drought or serious accident to the irrigation system in the United States, the amount delivered to the Mexican Canal shall be diminished in the same proportion as the water delivered to lands under said irrigation system in the United States."

After an agreement had been reached on international problems of water allocation in the Rio Grande Valley between El Paso and Fort Quitman, studies on reservoir sites and canals were resumed. Construction was approved in 1910, and Elephant Butte Dam and Reservoir, with a system of diversion dams and canals, was completed in 1916. (Factual Data about the Rio Grande Project—Region 5, Bureau of Reclamation—Map No. 23–503–5059.)

When irrigation districts were organized following the completion of Elephant Butte Reservoir, contracts were negotiated for the construction of lateral distribution canals and drainage systems in addition to storage and drainage works. A critical seepage condition developed as a result of the rising ground-water table, and construction of the drainage system was expanded and expedited.

Caballo Dam and Reservoir were completed in 1938. Caballo Dam was included as a flood-control unit in the Rio Grande Rectification Project, and part of its cost was allocated for that purpose. It made year-round power generation at Elephant Butte Dam possible and also provided additional project storage. The Caballo Reservoir regulates the flow of water to the present canals. It was constructed 35 km (22 miles) below Elephant Butte. The dam is of earth-fill construction, and the reservoir has a capacity of approximately 424,000,000 cu m (344,000 acre-feet or 1,360,000,000 cu ft). This amount, with the Elephant Butte storage capacity of 3,260,000,000 cu m (2,369,000 acre-feet or 115,000,000,000 cu ft), gives a combined storage capacity for Elephant Butte–Caballo of 3,684,000,-000 cu m, as originally constructed.

Considerable silt was present in the river above Elephant Butte, much of which originates in the Rio Puerco. The rate of sedimentation in the two reservoirs caused some concern, and in 1957 a silt survey was made, finding the actual 1957 capacity of Elephant Butte Reservoir to be 2,706,000,-000 cu m (2,194,990 acre-feet), a loss of 547,000,000 cu m (444,010 acre-feet), and the 1957 capacity of Caballo Reservoir to be 424,700,000 cu m (343,990 acre-feet), a loss of 2,320,000 cu m (1,880 acre-feet).[1]

THE TREE

The tree is the tamarisk, or salt cedar, as it has become known in the Southwest. Salt cedar (*Tamarix pentandra*) is not a native of North America. *Tamarix pentandra* was not mentioned in the United States in early

---

[1] As of now, total construction costs of the Rio Grande Project are around $28,800,000 (Kirby, 1968). This includes the cost of main dams, diversion dams, canals, laterals, and drainage systems from Elephant Butte in New Mexico to the El Paso County–Hudspeth County line in Texas.

references, but many early specimens can be identified as this species (Horton, 1964). It may have been the plant introduced by nurserymen in the early 1800's and called "a handsome shrub, much admired." "French tamarisk, an ornamental shrub" was listed in a catalog of fruits and ornamental trees issued by Lawrence and Mills at the Old American Nursery, Flushing-Landing, near New York, in 1823.

Although it was introduced into this country over one hundred years ago, only in the last thirty years has it become a nuisance plant in the arid and semiarid regions of the western states. Indeed, in the northwest sector of New Mexico in 1935, salt cedars were being planted along eroding stream banks in an effort to control erosion. The salt cedar is highly water-consuming and salt-tolerant. It rapidly escaped cultivation and spread from one stream valley to another.

In 1936 the vegetation of the Rio Grande Valley was mapped by the Department of Agriculture during the Rio Grande Joint Investigation (Robinson, 1965). Although salt cedar was present and was mapped in field sheets, no separate classification was established for it, and it was included under the heading "trees-bosque." The rapidity with which it spread is dramatically emphasized by the Bureau of Reclamation survey indicating that in 1947, over a period of about ten years, some 24,500 hectares (60,640 acres) in the valley were taken over by "bosque growth."

In order to understand the enormous impact of this growth it is necessary to refer to the Rio Grande and its problems. Aggradation of the river bed was caused by the deposition of silt from tributaries, principally from the Rio Puerco. The subsequent waterlogging of valley lands, while forcing abandonment of agriculture, provided a perfect environment for the water-loving, salt-tolerant salt cedar (Forsling, 1950). The construction of Elephant Butte and Caballo dams caused a deposition of silt in the stream delta immediately above the reservoirs, since the reservoir was filled to capacity at only one period, 1941–1942. The extensive deltas below high-water level provide prime areas for the propagation of the plants. In a vicious cycle, the growth of the salt cedars retards the flow of the river, causing additional deposition of silt, accelerating aggradation of the river bed, waterlogging of adjacent soil, and increasing conditions favorable for the growth of more salt cedars.

The salt cedar is able to extract salt from saline ground waters and to exude salt crystals from specially developed salt glands within the plant itself (Decker, 1961). This phenomenon is well known in Pakistan, where certain peoples gather this salt, chiefly NaCl, for home consumption. The deleterious effect of the "salt whiskers" is the pollution of the soil surface with salt extracted from saline ground water. Any flow of fresh water over this soil thus picks up added salt dredged up from a depth harmless to plants with shallower roots.

The 24,500 hectares (60,640 acres) of salt cedars found in 1947 were consuming water at the rate of 12,200 cu m per hectare (4 acre-feet an acre), a total consumption of 294,000,000 cu m (238,700 acre-feet) a year. This amount of water is approximately 45 percent of the total consumption in the valley. For comparison with the 12,200 cu m per hectare (4 acre-feet an acre) used by the salt cedar, only 2,219 cu m per hectare (1.8 acre-feet an acre) of water are consumed each year in growing irrigated crops.

Eradication of the salt cedars above the reservoirs, whether by the use of chemicals to kill the plants or by mechanical means, which include mowing the tops or plowing the roots and rectifying the river channel to restore direct flow, will speed up the transportation of sediment into the reservoirs, thus threatening the future of the valley below them.

Phreatophyte[2] control projects on the Rio Grande were originally incidental to projects constructed for other purposes. As the phreatophyte problem became more evident and the water supply more critical, more consideration was given to water salvage. The first such project undertaken, completed in 1962, consisted of the rehabilitation of the irrigation and drainage systems above and below Albuquerque (Lowry, 1966). River channelization and levee improvements were carried out as part of this project and extended from a point some fifty miles above Albuquerque to Elephant Butte Reservoir, a distance of some two hundred miles. This channelization work was meant to control sedimentation and flooding by creating a floodway varying in width from about 200 meters (600 feet) in the upstream portion to 470 meters (1,400 feet) in the San Marcial area. This floodway, containing approximately 6,000 hectares (15,000 acres), must be maintained, and a principal item of maintenance is the control of phreatophyte reinfestation.

In 1957 an experimental program began to clear and maintain a tamarisk-infested area at the head of Caballo Reservoir. The fact that this area lay in a relatively short stretch of river channel, 35 km (some 22 miles), between Caballo and Elephant Butte made it suitable for a control study. The purpose of the project was the salvage of some 17,250,000 cu m (14,000 acre-feet) of water annually by clearing and controlling 2,500 hectares (6,200 acres). The program has been continued at an estimated

annual cost of $20,000. The removal of the salt cedars has not only reduced the water loss but has also improved the grazing capacity of the reservoir area.

Results of a study of water-salvage possibilities in the flood plains of the river and its tributaries above Caballo Reservoir made by the Bureau of Reclamation showed that approximately 21,500 hectares (53,000 acres) of the area were infested with phreatophytes and that it would be practical to clear some 20,000 hectares (48,000 acres). Since information on the consumption of water by phreatophytes was mostly theoretical, 2,600 hectares (6,400 acres) of phreatophytes were cleared on a prototype area about halfway between Albuquerque and Elephant Butte, and water data were recorded. This project is being continued to obtain a long-range projection of the amount of water recovery and its cost. Regrowth of phreatophytes is being prevented, and evapotranspiration tanks to measure the water used by the salt cedars are maintained at Bernardo, New Mexico, at the upper end of the experimental site.

In a similar study of salt-cedar eradication on the Pecos River (Robinson, 1959–1964), on about 16,000 hectares (40,000 acres) of heavily infested areas in the Pecos River Valley between Acme, New Mexico, and Mentone, Texas, an average annual water loss prevention over the next fifty years is predicted of about 185,000,000 cu m (150,000 acre-feet) at a cost of about $3.85 per cu m ($4.75 per acre-foot) for operation and maintenance. Assuming the water is used for irrigation, the benefits are estimated to vary from about $20.40 to $58.30 per 1233 cu m (acre foot), depending on where the water would be used. The studies presently being made on the Rio Grande will probably show quite similar results.

The time salt cedars have been present in the Rio Grande Valley in comparison to the time the area has known irrigated farm-

[2] A report by the Pacific Southwest Interagency Committee, entitled "Phreatophyte Symposium 66–3 meeting, dated August 30, 1966," defines a phreatophyte as "a plant that habitually obtains its water supply from the zone of saturation, either directly or through the capillary fringe." The phreatophyte problem in the arid and semi-arid regions of the western United States has become so serious that the United States Department of the Interior has established an interagency committee to research the problems. My paper attempts to summarize the findings of these various agencies, insofar as they refer to the Upper Rio Grande.

ing is indeed minuscule. For unknown hundreds of years the valley has known farming activities, and only during an extremely short period of that time, roughly thirty years, has the salt cedar been known as a troublemaker in the area. Concentrated efforts at control have been carried out for an even shorter period of time; long-range studies, taking into consideration the many complex problems involved, are only just beginning.

The U. S. Bureau of Reclamation began experimenting with chemical control of tamarisks in 1948, spraying 81 hectares (200 acres) of the plant with 2,4-D at the rate of one pound per acre.[3] Forty hectares (100 acres) of this area were again sprayed in 1949. Of the plants receiving the two applications, up to 85 percent were killed, and it was hoped that a relatively simple means had been found to control salt cedar. However, when 1,057 additional hectares (2,600 acres) of adult salt cedars were sprayed in 1961, using a similar formula with new herbicides added, the results did not duplicate the original success. Subsequent experiments have not proved that chemicals alone can solve the problem.

Since these earlier experiments, the Bureau of Reclamation has continued its exploration and evaluation of various methods of phreatophyte control. A combination of mechanical and chemical means is being used, with new chemicals proving to be more and more efficacious. Some of these, such as picloram, are materials used in Vietnam and have shown to have great resistance to degradation and breakdown. It is therefore conceivable that long after use, they will stay in the environment and cause agricultural and health hazards. More studies are needed to determine possible deleterious effects.[4]

A spray application of eight pounds of silvex ester per acre in diesel oil, reducing stands as much as 83 percent, is used immediately after mowing. Costs and methods of clearing salt cedar vary considerably, depending on density of plants and type of equipment used. The cost for clearing approximately 2,400 hectares (6,000 acres) in the Caballo Reservoir area mentioned above averaged approximately $45 per hectare ($20 per acre), but the cost of clearing 2,590 hectares (6,400 acres) midway between Elephant Butte and Albuquerque was $110 per hectare ($45 per acre). It must be pointed out, however, that the Caballo tract was cleared by Bureau of Reclamation personnel and equipment, while the middle reaches work was accomplished by a contractor. Also, the density of the stand of salt cedar and the texture and stability of the soil differed in the two areas, which must be taken into account when comparing costs.

Various methods of mechanical control of salt-cedar infestations have been tried. The most effective equipment for complete eradication is the root plow. The Bureau of Reclamation on the Rio Grande uses a 3.66 m (12 foot) root plow mounted on a crawler tractor. Other machines which have been used effectively for initial clearing are the rock rake, bulldozer, and rotary mower. Most of these cause secondary problems such as destroying the grass cover, which encourages soil erosion and reinvasion by trees.

[3] The root system of salt cedars is somewhat similar to that of Bermuda grass, in that a good part of the plant is below the ground level, and lateral roots near the surface may send up additional shoots. Plowing is necessary to eliminate these roots, and herbicides are necessary to control regrowth. Encouragement of a grass-type ground cover under these conditions is difficult.

[4] Eugene E. Hughes (1966), in his "Research in Chemical Control of Various Phreatophytes," states: "Whenever large areas of land are treated with herbicides, contamination of water resulting from surface runoff is always a hazard. This is especially true when floodways or river channels are treated. Herbicides having long persistence are especially a hazard in this respect." Hughes cites seventeen references in his article. The subject appears too complex to attempt to cover in one section of one short paper.

THE COUNTY

On the United States side of the Rio Grande, the channel of which forms the international boundary between Mexico and the United States, the Quitman Mountains reach the river, and the mountain range continues into Mexico. The river is confined to a narrow gorge or box canyon at this point. It is this gorge, sometimes called Fort Quitman after an early United States Army post at the upstream end of the gorge, that terminates geographically what is referred to as the Upper Rio Grande.

Geologically speaking, the river valley is a unit, from the box canyon of "the pass" at El Paso del Norte to the gorge at Fort Quitman. The valley has had a long history of occupation and irrigation development since the Spanish first reached the valley under Cabeza de Vaca in 1536 and under Coronado in 1540. (Factual Data about the Rio Grande Project—Region 5, Bureau of Reclamation, Map No. 23–503–5059.) The indigenous tribes occupying the valley when the Spanish arrived engaged in little or no agriculture. The agricultural history of the valley should probably be dated from 1598 with the journey of Juan de Oñate who continued up the river to colonize what is now New Mexico. A mission was established at Paso del Norte in 1659, and the Spanish used the settlement, which grew up around the mission as a way station on their travel route to and from Mexico, in their conquest and colonization of northern New Mexico during the seventeenth and eighteenth centuries (Kirby, 1968).

Slowly but steadily the colony grew. In 1680 revolting Pueblo Indians caused the retreat of the Spanish conquerors and their Indian converts from New Mexico to Paso del Norte. This resulted in the establishment of several settlements below Paso del Norte, of which Ysleta and Socorro still exist on the north (United States) side of the river.

The area now comprising the state of Texas was infiltrated by Americans in the early 1800's, causing friction between them and Mexicans already present in the area. Open hostilities eventually resulted in the treaty at Guadalupe Hidalgo (February 2, 1848), which divided the valley below El Paso del Norte into two sections, American and Mexican. Further political subdivisions occurred with the completion of Elephant Butte Dam; water improvement districts were delineated, and a new agricultural era began in the valley below the dam.

Original construction of this irrigation system was financed by a bond issue of $700,-000 (Wafer, 1956). From 1924 to 1956 additional sums increased total construction funds to $2,200,000.

These figures and the fact that the funds were raised by this district, acting independently, became significant when, with the completion of Caballo Dam and Reservoir, the area below the reservoir as far as the El Paso–Hudspeth County line became irrigation and improvement districts under the Bureau of Reclamation. The New Mexico portion of the project area consisted of 90,640 acres of water-right land with a total construction cost of $5,698,012. The El Paso County Water Improvement District consisted of 27,900 hectares (69,010 acres) of water-right land with a total construction cost of $6,746,111.

The Hudspeth County Conservation and Reclamation District No. 1 had a complete system of canals, check dams, laterals, and drains at this time. Perhaps the fact that the period 1941–1942 was a period of abundant flow in the river (including the fact that Elephant Butte Dam overflowed into its spillway for the only time in its history in 1942) gave confidence to the water-users in Hudspeth County. There was adequate water of an acceptable saline content, and the drains were carrying excess salts down the river. However, an extended period of dry, or subnormal, water flow in the river and many other factors subsequently caused drastic deterioration and disappointment for the area. A chart of Rio Grande discharge at San Marcial, New Mexico, at the head of Elephant Butte Reservoir, showed a gradual decrease in annual discharge from a high in 1925 of approximately 1,110,000,000 cu m (900,000 acre-feet) to approximately 838,-000,000 cu m (680,000 acre-feet) in 1967. As these figures are an indication of the progressive mean, including carry-over from excessive wet and dry cycles, it might be significant to point out that the discharge for the year 1967 totaled only about 481,-000,000 cu m (390,000 acre-feet).

The "Long-Range Program and Plan" (El Paso–Hudspeth Soil and Water Conservation District No. 205, State of Texas, prepared December 1966) shows water allotment for Hudspeth County District (Table 17–1). The report states: "Much of the land

in the Hudspeth County Conservation and Reclamation District has not been irrigated continuously since the beginning of the drought of the 1950's."

During a tour of the district the present manager (1968), Mac Guest, told me that "Caballo Dam ruined the Hudspeth County Conservation and Reclamation District." This seemed a startling and provocative statement until I learned more about the situation. A series of events, some unforeseen at the time, and some, such as droughts, phenomena of nature beyond human control at the present time, caused the present distress of the District. In general, the creation of Caballo Reservoir and the subsequent development of more stable irrigation conditions downstream allowed increased acreage to be brought under proper irrigation.

One fact was possibly overlooked or ignored. The Upper Rio Grande is considered to terminate at Fort Quitman, where the Quitman Mountains to the north form a box canyon with their extension into the south. The river, meandering across the alluvial valley downstream from El Paso, is throttled by the rocky barrier of the mountains, through which it has laboriously cut its course. From its earliest agricultural use to the present time, what is termed a normal (or mean) flow has allowed a constant discharge over the sill, or dike, closing off the lower end of the basin.

Increasing use of irrigation water above Fort Quitman and, indeed, throughout the entire Upper Rio Grande adds increasing amounts of salt to the river flow downstream. In periods of normal flow this salt burden is constantly shifted downstream through proper functioning of adequate drainage systems. Obviously, the farther downstream the water flows, the greater its salt burden. But in times of drought, drains fail and the small amount of available water is increasingly vulnerable to evapotranspiration. The upstream salts are left in down-

Table 17–1

HUDSPETH COUNTY WATER ALLOTMENT*
Hudspeth County Conservation and
Reclamation District No. 1

YEAR	ACRES IN CULTIVATION†	ACRE-FEET OF WATER AT HEADING	ACRE-FEET PER ACRE IRRIGATED
1950	17,329	42,771	2.47
1951	17,752	32,289	1.82
1952	18,207	38,125	2.10
1953	12,127	28,264	2.33
1954	12,127	3,381	0.28
1955	5,455	174	0.03
1956	4,477	none	none
1957	3,860	759	0.20
1958	4,023	18,215	4.53
1959	6,992	37,869	5.41
1960	8,907	57,823	6.49
1961	9,661	39,962	4.14
1962	11,404	68,326	5.99
1963	11,268	41,703	8.70
1964	8,421	2,213	0.26
1965	8,123	8,060	0.99

* Long-Range Program and Plan. Prepared December 1966. El Paso–Hudspeth Soil and Water Conservation District No. 205, State of Texas.
† Out of 18,432 total acres in the district.

stream ground water. And when ground-water flow is interrupted by a rock barrier, as is the case of the Fort Quitman engorgement, the salt content builds up at a continuous rate. As the surface flow decreases, water-users are forced to drill wells to meet their water needs. Wells become increasingly salty. I spoke to a farmer in Hudspeth County who had just completed the drilling of a new well. He told me that his new well showed a salt content of over 16 grams per liter (22 tons per acre-foot)—worthless!

The figures in Table 17–2 are from Research Report No. 106 of the U. S. Salinity Laboratory (1963). Tonnage of salt[5] crossing El Paso–Hudspeth County line is 79 per-

cent of tonnage below Caballo Dam. If output is corrected for tonnage of salt diverted into Mexico, the percentage becomes 93. There is no drainage from the Mexican side: this water is completely dissipated.

According to District reports prior to 1951 there was apparently an adequate supply of surface water. To be sure, the saline content of waste and drain water from upstream was quite high, but the Hudspeth drains were working and salinity in the soils could be kept at a level at which some of the more salt-tolerant crops could be raised successfully. Cotton, both long and short staple, was and is the predominant crop in the area; alfalfa ranks second. In the year 1950, 5,100 hectares (12,601 acres) were planted to cotton, 1,610 hectares (3,953 acres) to alfalfa, and 314 hectares (775 acres) planted to others.

As the dry cycle set in, less and less water was available, making less acreage available for cultivation. By 1955, cotton hectares were down to 1,317 (3,254 acres); alfalfa hectares dropped to 471 (1,163 acres), while 420 hectares (1,038 acres) were devoted to other crops.

The coming of the dry years forced the landowners to drill wells to augment the vanishing supply of surface water. Since 1951, 149 individually owned irrigation wells have been drilled. The 1955 figures indicate that the average depth of these wells was 30 meters (100 feet). Average discharge was 2,460 liters (650 gallons) per minute. Immediately, however, difficulties were encountered. The bottom of the barrel was collecting a tremendous amount of salt, and with the high cutoff sill at the Quitman Mountains, most of this exceedingly saline water was trapped, and the salt content was increasing. Some fifty of the wells drilled, at an average cost of $6,000 each, had been abandoned by 1955 due to poor quality of water. In that year the remaining wells were pumping an average of 5.54 grams of salt per liter of water (6.17

Table 17–2

VOLUME OF WATER AND TONNAGE OF SALT* CONSTITUENTS PASSING CONTROL STATIONS (1963)

	COUNTY LINE	FORT QUITMAN	COUNTY LINE TO FORT QUITMAN GAIN OR LOSS†
Discharge, acre feet	71,966	23,361	—48,605
Dissolved solids, tons	246,124	126,850	—119,274
Calcium, Ca, tons	18,791	9,945	—8,846
Magnesium, Mg, tons	4,451	2,685	—1,766
Sodium, Na, tons	56,952	29,009	—27,943
Bicarbonate, HCO_3, tons	8,988	4,701	—4,278
Sulfate, SO_4, tons	69,240	28,442	—40,798
Chloride, Cl, tons	73,632	44,176	—29,456
Nitrate, NO_3, tons	303	59	—244
Total ions, tons	232,357	119,026	—113,331

* Wilcox, L. V. *Discharge and Salt Burden of the Rio Grande above Fort Quitman, Texas, 1963.* U. S. Salinity Laboratory, Research Report No. 106 (final report of series of studies started in 1932). Agricultural Research Service, U. S. Department of Agriculture.

† The loss of salts indicated in the above table is the measured difference between salts entering and leaving the district. As brackish water is heavier than fresh, a reduction in the discharge of water would allow only the least brackish water to escape, causing a build-up of salts in the district.

[5] Salt tonnage as used in this context is the actual amount, by measurement, of dissolved salts in any given volume of water.

tons per acre-foot). This water could not be used over any extended period of time.

By the end of 1955 less than one-third of the irrigable land in the District was being cultivated. Most landowners moved their farming interests to other areas. Some of those who remained took jobs nearby and sold cotton allotment acreage in order to keep up land payments and taxes. Farm population of the District under what was called normal conditions in 1956 was estimated to be 4,500, but population in that year was estimated to be 1,000 (Wafer, 1956). The combined population of the four small communities in the District, Fort Hancock, Acala, McNary, and Esperanza, dropped from 700 to 400.

A farm of 80.2 hectares (198.1 acres) in the District, valued at $2,470 per hectare ($1,000 per acre) before the dry years and the salt problems occurred, was sold in 1967 by the Federal Land Bank for $10,000, or less than $125 per hectare ($50 per acre) (Bean, J. B., President, Hudspeth County Conservation and Reclamation District No. 1, personal interview). In order to hold his irrigation water rights on a farm in the District consisting of, for example, 400 hectares (1,000 acres) of irrigable land, the farmer must disc[6] the entire 405 hectares yearly, even though his water allotment, when he receives it, will only be sufficient to farm 100 hectares (250 acres), or one-quarter of his farm. If he fails to disc his entire irrigable acreage, it reverts to rangeland, and his water allotment is reduced to the actual acreage he has disked. This, of course, adds to his costs of farming per unit area.

In 1968 only enough water was available to successfully farm approximately 2,400

[6] A disc (plow) consists of a series of metal discs about 24 inches in diameter attached to an axle. This is pulled by a tractor and is used to break up surfaces of cultivated fields in preparation for planting. It is not so deep as a plow, serving mainly to "stir" the surface, as with a rake.

hectares (6,000 acres) of the District's irrigable land of 7,420 hectares (18,342 acres). Most wells and all drains at the bottom of the system are averaging approximately 6 grams of salt per liter (8 tons per acre-foot). With the present agricultural load on the river upstream, even a return to what is calculated as a normal flow in the Rio Grande will not solve the Hudspeth County District's water problems.

The only solutions even vaguely possible are the importing of water from another source or devising some means of desalinating the ground water.

THE COUNTRY[7]

Cabeza de Vaca and Coronado were the first Spanish explorers to reach the Juárez Valley. But it was not until sixty years later that agriculture really started in the valley. The Indian tribes these explorers encountered were primarily hunters and gatherers.

However, with the advent of Spanish colonizers, farming did spring up in the valley (Amaya Brondo; see References, The Country). The colonists found ample room for farming and an ample flow of water in the river. The mild climate, with a long growing season, was not unlike that of their native Spain. Brush and rock diversion dams were built, and the wild (unregulated) flow of the river was led through *acequias,* or canals, to the riparian lands. What if spring floods did destroy the crude dams? The colonists rebuilt them, repaired the canals, and soon were busily growing the next year's crops.

Slowly over the course of the centuries the farms grew in the valley. These were peaceful and prosperous times for the inhabitants, and the agricultural colony continued to expand until, at the beginning of the present century, there were approxi-

[7] Based on personal interview with Bustamante, Ing. Joaquin R., Engineer, International Boundary and Water Commission, Mexican Section.

mately 25,000 hectares (about 61,800 acres) under cultivation in the valley—the area lying south of the Rio Grande, across from the two districts to the north (El Paso County and Hudspeth County).

Rapid development of agriculture upstream from El Paso during the latter part of the nineteenth century created more and more demands on the resources of the river. The farmers of the Juárez Valley suffered acute water shortages, and strong disputes originated among the water-users on both banks of the stream in an effort to utilize the reduced flow which the Rio Grande was carrying. Mexico was deprived of a rightful share of this flow and brought increasing pressure to bear on the United States.

The situation became more and more serious until both countries met to resolve the difficulties. An agreement was ratified on January 16, 1907. (Treaties and Conventions Applicable to the International Boundary and Water Commission, United States and Mexico. El Paso, Texas, October 1964. Extracts.) It gave Mexico the right to divert water from the Rio Grande for agricultural purposes up to 74,000,000 cubic meters (60,000 acre-feet) per year, which would serve to irrigate the lands open to cultivation at that time. This set amount of water, allowed as a maximum amount of flow to be diverted in any one year, necessarily limited any future increase in irrigation from gravity flows.

The completion of Elephant Butte Reservoir in 1916 with its subsequent development of the Rio Grande Project on the United States side of the border did not seriously restrict water use in the Juárez Valley. In fact it was not until the completion of Caballo Dam and Reservoir and the formation of irrigation districts under the Bureau of Reclamation from 1938 to 1941 that curtailment of water was felt in the Mexican valley. At that time there were approximately 18,500 hectares under cultivation in the valley.

From that time the farmers in the valley drilled relatively shallow wells to withdraw ground water to supplement the irrigation of the area already under cultivation. Subsequently the Federal Government, through various interested agencies, assisted in this program.

From 1937 to date the volume of water delivered to the farmers of the Juárez Valley has varied between an annual minimum of 9,000,000 cubic meters to a maximum of 74,000,000, an average of approximately 35,000,000 cubic meters. Pumping ground water has varied in accordance with the volume of water delivered by the United States. It is considered that an average of 90,000,000 cubic meters of ground water per annum are being withdrawn to supplement the irrigation of approximately 11,000 hectares presently under cultivation.

Water used for irrigation in the Juárez Valley varies in quality in accordance with the total salt content. Surface water from the Rio Grande has a minimum salt content of 900 parts per million, while the ground water varies between 900 and 2,500, depending on the zone of extraction. Extreme salinity, such as in Hudspeth County, Texas, is not as noticeable in the Juárez Valley. It has been suggested that closer proximity of low mountains acting as a watershed on the Mexican side may add considerable quantities of water with relatively low saline content to the ground water available to the valley. It might be presumed that quantity rather than quality of water is the major factor in the future development of the valley. Nevertheless, the Juárez Valley has suffered seriously at times of shortage, when (by the 1906 agreement) its quota of 74,000,000 cubic meters (60,000 acre-feet) has been cut in proportion to the reduction in allotments on the United States side. In 1955 and 1956 it averaged less than 10,000,000 cubic meters (8,000 acre-feet); about half of its acreage, or about 10,000 hectares (25,000 acres), was abandoned or retired from production (Hay, 1963).

The reduction of the Rio Grande water available for agriculture after the construction of Elephant Butte and Caballo dams brought about a reduction in irrigated areas from 18,000 hectares to only 11,000 hectares, the present average. Light-textured soils with good vertical drainage have been preserved from salt saturation due to the excess water applied to satisfy the leaching requirements, but heavy-textured soils of difficult drainage have suffered a progressive salt saturation, mainly due to the lack of sufficient water and to the poor quality of the well water.

In this paper I have reconstructed the unfortunate story of the ill-fated and indiscriminate manipulation of a typical arid lands river in North America. The problems are typical of arid lands river development projects everywhere in the world. In his efforts to increase the yield from a river basin, modern man has virtually ruined it.

REFERENCES

The River

Dortignac, E. J. "Rio Puerco: Abused Basin." In *Aridity and Man,* C. Hodge and P. C. Duisberg, eds. Publication No. 74. Washington, D.C.: American Association for the Advancement of Science, 1963.

Hay, John. "Upper Rio Grande: Embattled River." In *Aridity and Man,* C. Hodge and P. C. Duisberg, eds. Publication No. 74. Washington, D.C.: American Association for the Advancement of Science, 1963.

Kirby, James Willis. *Water Resources—El Paso County, Texas, Present, Past, Future.* (PhD. Thesis, Univ. of Texas, El Paso, Texas, 1968.)

The Tree

Decker, John P. "Salt Secretion by *Tamarix pentandra* Pall." *Forest Science,* Vol. 7, No. 3 (September, 1961).

Forsling, C. L. "The Rio Grande Valley in New Mexico—Its Present and Future." *Journal of Forestry,* Vol. 48, No. 9 (September, 1950).

Horton, Jerome S. *Notes on the Introduction of Deciduous Tamarisk.* U. S. Forest Service Research Note RM-16. March, 1964.

Hughes, Eugene E. "Research in Chemical Control of Various Phreatophytes." Pacific Southwest Interagency Committee, Phreatophyte Symposium 66–3 Meeting, August 30, 1966.

Lowry, O. J. "Establishment, Operation, and Maintenance of Phreatophyte Control Projects." Pacific Southwest Interagency Committee, Phreatophyte Symposium 66–3 Meeting, August 30, 1966.

Robinson, T. W. "Introduction, Spread, and Areal Extent of Salt Cedar (*Tamarix*) in the Western States." *Geographical Survey Professional Paper 491–A.* 1965.

———. *Phreatophyte Research in the Western States, March 1959 to July 1964.* Geological Survey Circular 495.

The County

Kirby, James Willis. Water Resources—El Paso County, Texas, Present, Past, Future. 1968.

Wafer, A. J. Manager (1956), Hudspeth County Conservation and Reclamation District No. 1. Letter of information, 1956.

The Country

Amaya Brondo, Ing. Guillermo. Engineer, Jefe del Distrito, Secretaría de Recursos Hidráulicos, Distrito de Riego 09. Summary of Conditions in Mexican Section of El Paso Valley. Unpublished comments, in Spanish, translated by J. R. Bustamante.

18. CONSEQUENCES OF UNCONTROLLED HUMAN ACTIVITIES IN THE VALENCIA LAKE BASIN*

Alberto Böckh

Lake Valencia is located in the north central part of the Republic of Venezuela. This lake, of incomparable beauty, is suffering from the consequences of human activities carried out without planning or control. The water level is constantly declining, and the remaining water is being polluted at an alarming rate. During the past two and a half centuries the lake surface has dropped 21 meters, and its size has been reduced from 640 to 370 square kilometers.

Recent investigations have shown that less than three centuries ago the hydrological balance was positive. At this time the surplus water drained to the Orinoco River. But the increase in the uncontrolled agricultural and industrial activities drained more and more water from the tributaries and from the aquifers, until Lake Valencia was separated from the Orinoco Basin and established its own independent drainage system.

Equally alarming is the increasing salinity of the lake. In the year 1800 the German naturalist Alexander von Humboldt found the lake still clean. He wrote: "The Lake water is not salty, . . . it can be drunk without filtering. . . . it is surprising that an interior lake does not have a higher concentration of alkaline or earthy salts subtracted from the surrounding soils." One and a half centuries later sanitary engineer Octavio Jelambi found that the soluble salts which were 785 parts per million in 1920, rose to 1270 ppm in 1966.

Pollution levels are increasing alarmingly because of the lack of treatment plants for the sewage from the communities around the basin (one-half million inhabitants) and also because almost all the industries in the area do not have

* This work is dedicated to the memory of Antonio Manzano, who gave the first warning of the implications of uncontrolled human activities in the Lake Valencia Basin some 250 years ago.

any sewage treatment installations for their residual waters. All these wastes are draining into the tributary rivers and thus contributing to the progressive degradation of the lake.

Man has desiccated, salinized, and polluted this precious jewel of nature. The Valencia Lake Conservation Institute has already diagnosed the malady and elaborated projects to remedy the situation. Now is the time to act.

Lake Valencia, known in ancient times by the Indians as Lake Tacarigua, is located in the north central region of the Republic of Venezuela. It is the most important lake north of Titicaca. What has happened to this lake over the past few centuries?

It is readily apparent that Lake Valencia is drying up. If one stands on the highway

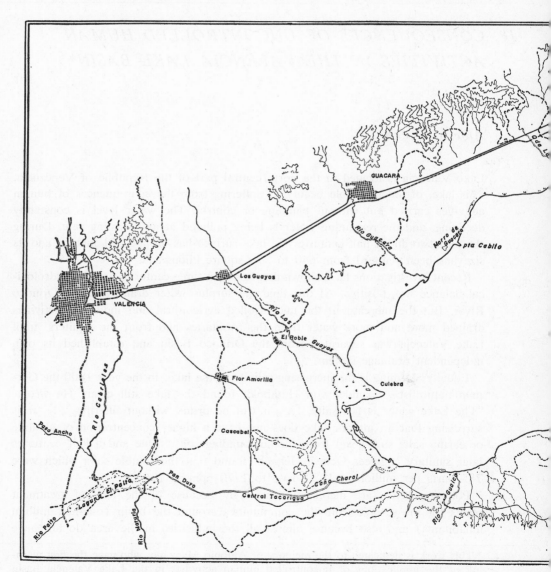

Figure 18–1 Map of Lake Valencia, 1955. Probable shoreline in 1727———; present shoreline———. Scale approximately 1:150,000

near Central Tacarigua and walks a short distance through the sugar-cane plantations, or approaches the shore from any point of the Maracay-Valencia highway, it is apparent that this body of water once extended over a much broader area. The fertile plains now surrounding it used to be part of the lake bottom. Myriad snail shells and other detritus of lake flora and fauna provide evidence of a larger body.[1]

In our investigations at the Institute for the Conservation of Lake Valencia we have sought answers to many questions: Why is the lake drying up? Is this a natural phenomenon or an artificial one caused by man? If artificial, when did it begin? What was the elevation of the surface of the lake prior to the drying process? How did this

[1] Among the various snails represented, the most abundant species is that of *Biomphalaria*

prona, of the Planorbidae family; its shells comprise almost all of these impressive layers. This mollusk is native to the area (Chrosciechowski. 1968).

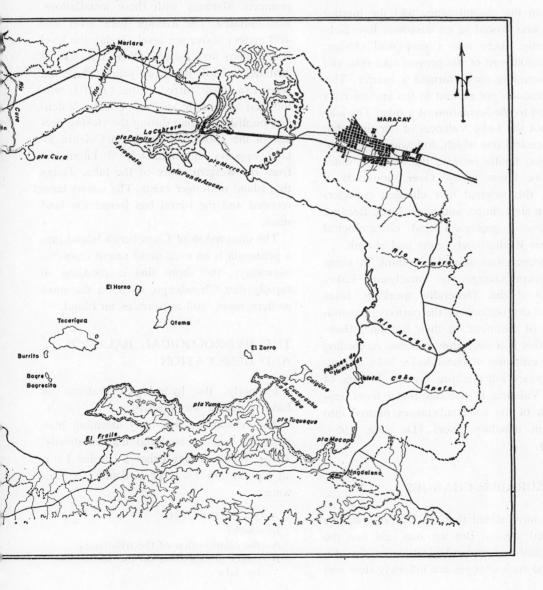

phenomenon take place? We will answer these questions one by one and examine three processes—desiccation, salinization, and pollution—that have contributed to the destruction of the lake.

GEOLOGICAL RESEARCH

The most recent geological research tells us that hundreds of thousands of years ago there was a mighty river in the area now occupied by Lake Valencia. It was funneled between the coastal range and the interior range and flowed in an east-west line. Subsequently, there was a geological change; the subsoil west of the present lake rose and the ascending rocks formed a barrier. This phenomenon put an end to the ancient river and led to the formation of a lake. The lake was not the Lake Valencia of our times but an ancestral one which, following a series of changes, finally became the body of water that we know today. Over thousands of years, this original lake changed considerably in size, shape, and water level. Because of several geological and climatological changes it alternately grew and shrank.

However, one should not think in terms of abrupt changes or cataclysms. Lakes form and die. Generally speaking, lakes tend to dry because of the periodic accumulation of sediment on their bottoms. However, this is a very slow process. According to the estimates of Oswaldo De Sola, a thousand years must elapse for the bottom of Lake Valencia to rise one meter from deposition of the solid substances poured into it from tributary rivers (De Sola, 1954, 1965).

MEASURABLE CHANGES

We have stated that the size of the lake changed greatly. But we also said that the geological and climatological factors that determine such changes are infinitely slow and consequently invisible to us. Why then do we witness very evident changes at present —phenomena that unfold over just a few years? For example, Club Náutico and the "Terminal del Lago" restaurant which are located south of Maracay were constructed barely ten years ago on the waters. Today they are in ruins and nobody thinks of rebuilding them because the lake has moved hundreds of meters away from its former location. In 1953, when the project for the construction of Avenida del Lago, which connects Maracay with these installations, was initiated, the average lake level was 408 meters above sea level. Today the level is less than 405 meters. Over 3 meters of altitude was lost in fifteen years! There are other examples. Alfredo Jahn (1940), who initiated systematic studies of Lake Valencia, published a map during the closing decade of the 1800's on which La Culebra Island appears approximately 3 kilometers from the western shore of the lake. Today that island no longer exists. The waters have receded and the island has joined the land mass.

The conversion of Chambergo Island into a peninsula is an even more recent example. Nowadays, the shore line is receding so rapidly that Chambergo, even on the most modern maps, still appears as an island.

THE HYDROLOGICAL BALANCE AND DESICCATION

Formerly, the hydrological balance of Lake Valencia was positive.

The reason for this truly alarming phenomenon can be analyzed mathematically. Three situations may exist: a surplus ($>$), an equilibrium ($=$), or a deficit ($<$) of water:

$$A+B+C-D-E \gtreqless 0$$

In which:
A = the contribution of the tributaries
B = direct precipitation on the surface of the lake

C=the contribution of subterranean waters

D=the evaporation from the surface of the lake

E=possible filtration outside of the basin

Where the volume of the positive components is greater than that of the negative ones, there is a *surplus*. In such circumstances, the watershed is not independent, and the surplus waters of the lake flow toward the sea.

When the loss equals the input, the system is said to be in a condition of *equilibrium*. The level of the lake remains stable. In this case there is no communication with the sea; the watershed is endoreic.

In the third instance, the input is not sufficient to offset the losses. The negative elements are predominant; there is a *deficit*. Consequently, the level of the lake begins to drop.

Formerly, the surplus waters drained away toward the Orinoco River. Today the opposite situation exists; the drop in the level of the lake now indicates that the equilibrium has been upset and that the balance is negative. Two questions arise: What caused the deficit? In which components have changes taken place?

Before answering these questions and analyzing the components one by one, we should make some general observations. First, there has been no major climatological change recently. A few decades ago when La Culebra Island was 3 kilometers from the shore, the values for evaporation and annual precipitation were practically identical with those of today. Thus, if the values of the elements comprised in the hydrological balance did change, the change was not due to climatological changes. Also, there have been no natural cataclysms from the time the region was first populated. Furthermore, modern geologists discard the hypothesis that fissures in the base of the basin may be a cause for the deficit. Consequently, the supposition that the present drying process of the lake is the result of natural causes may be discarded.

Let us also consider the two negative components of the balance—evaporation and possible filtration of subterranean waters. Research carried out by Tamers and Thielen (1966) about filtrations indicates that there is no leakage. In spite of the fact that the basin is open on its eastern and western sides, no water escapes. On the eastern side the subterranean waters flow slowly toward the lake. On the western side, according to age measurements by carbon 14, they have remained immobile for nearly 14,000 years. In the case of evaporation, the other negative element in the equation, the volume presently lost is less because the surface of the lake has decreased. If the balance is negative, there must be a great decrease in the input. Analysis of input components shows that the problem must be caused by reduced contributions of the tributaries. The precipitation value has not changed. If there has been a decrease in the surface on which rain falls, the decreased volume of evaporation is offsetting that loss. There is the possibility of a change in the volume of the subterranean waters that flow toward the lake. The general opinion among researchers is that this factor is secondary compared to the contribution of the tributary rivers and does not cause the imbalance.

THE BEGINNING OF THE DRYING PROCESS

Because the drying process is the result of artificial causes, we are no longer so bewildered in trying to determine when the process began. We need not go back to nebulous pre-Columbian times. Furthermore, various quotations from scientific works on the region provide helpful guidelines. For example, there is the monograph of E. W. Berry (1939) who studied the system of terraces and declivities molded by the waves of the descending lake on the La Cabrera Peninsula. On the basis of an analysis of human and animal remains found in the area, Berry concluded that the age of the soil here is no more than four centuries. Other more precise indicators can be found in the descriptions by Humboldt (1956) and Codazzi (1960). In spite of the fact that the valleys of Aragua are among the earliest populated areas of Venezuela, none of the ancient chroniclers mentions a drying process, and Humboldt wonders whether one should suppose that this was oversight. We doubt this, particularly if one considers the *History of the Province of Venezuela* by Oviedo y Baños (1940), which contains a rather detailed description of the lake. The withdrawal of the shore is so remarkable and has given rise to so many comments in recent historical times that it surely could not have escaped the attention of "the first historian of Venezuela," who spent almost his entire life in Venezuela.

The work of Agustín Codazzi, the noted geographer who explored the region between 1830 and 1840, has provided additional guidance. Confirming the observations of Humboldt, Codazzi stated: "The experience of nearly a century has demonstrated that the level of waters is not constant and that the equilibrium between evaporation and the waters that feed the lake no longer exists."

These and other references indicated the desirability of finding an author who had made observations on the lake during the first half of the eighteenth century. Fortunately, we found one—Antonio Manzano, an alderman in the city of Nueva Valencia del Rey. Manzano explored the regions around the lake and left a geographical description of them. Manzano compiled the first data relative to the depths of the lake, data praised by Humboldt for their accuracy.

In Manzano's description we find a clear reply to our question. According to Manzano, the decrease of the area of the lake began in 1727, "because I saw its waters still flow into the Maruria River (alias El Pao)." Elsewhere (1908) he states: ". . . prior to 1727 it drained off in the same place and it was possible to sail as far as that river (Pao)." Acceptance of this date is strengthened by Humboldt's observation that Oviedo had not referred to the drying process. Oviedo's history was written in 1723, that is, four years prior to the observations of Manzano.

It is remarkable that in Manzano's description we find a criticism of human activities that were to profoundly affect the ecology of the lake. This keen observer complained about the large number of irrigation ditches which deprived the lake of much water. He stated that the mountains were being sterilized by land-clearing operations and that during certain months of the year "the rivers suffer because of the lack of water."

THE LEVEL OF THE LAKE IN 1800

If we wish to know the level of the lake in 1800, we must consult Humboldt's work (1956). The data are of two types: absolute elevations originating in geographic descriptions and barometric measurements, and relative altitudes based on differences in elevation between the surface of the waters and certain points located on the shore or on the elevation of one of the islands above the level of the lake.

The barometric data and levels originating in geographic descriptions are extremely inaccurate and contradictory and consequently should be discarded. On the other hand, the data in the second group are absolutely reliable. Generally speaking, the measurements involved are small ones in which any error committed is of secondary importance. After having determined the absolute elevation of these points and subtracting from them the differences in elevation, we can determine the altitude of the lake on the corresponding dates. Consequently, if the points indicated by Humboldt were clearly defined and are identified accurately, we can determine correctly the levels that existed in 1800.

Of the points whose elevations were indicated by Humboldt with reference to the level of the lake, that of Las Piedras Island (also called Nuevos Peñones or Aparecidas) was the one that we found most noteworthy because of the accuracy of the absolute altitude that it provides. On the basis of Humboldt's description we know that these rocks emerged in 1796, east of the island of Caigüire, because of desiccation. In 1800 when Humboldt explored the region they had an average elevation of one foot above the water level. Inasmuch as the error that Humboldt may have committed is insignificant, the Peñones seem the most appropriate point for placing the level corresponding to 1796 and 1800.

With the help of Humboldt's work and with the description and map of Jahn (1940), we tried to identify these islands. We had some doubts because Humboldt referred to *three* islands and, in the place indicated by Jahn, we found only one. However, this might be explained because in 1800, when the top of the rocky island was barely level with the water, only three summits were visible. Today, with the further withdrawal of the waters, they form a single unit.

Some investigators, such as José Royo y Gómez and Octavio Jelambi, doubted the accuracy of the identification (which was verified in 1951). Intrigued by this uncertainty and now acquainted with other data submitted by Jelambi (1958), we again explored the region in 1967. On the eastern shore, we found three small rocky hills located on the line that connects the islands of Tacarigua, Otama, and Zorro. At present, these three small hills are on dry land, but on the map prepared by Antonio Muñoz Tébar and published in 1919 by Vicente Lecuna, the Peñones still appear as an island called "La Isleta."

Taking the average height of the three hills and subtracting the data indicated by Humboldt, we may state that, in 1800, the elevation of the lake was approximately 422 meters above sea level.

EL PAÍTO LAGOON—MAXIMUM ELEVATION

A study of the topography in the vicinity of the lake shows that the basin has an outlet to the west. The gap is located approximately 10 kilometers south of Valencia, at a place known as El Paíto (see Fig. 18–1). Absolute elevation at this point is 426 meters, the maximum level for the current geological era. It could never have been higher, because excess drained off through this natural spillway. Consequently, when the hydrological balance was positive and the lake was full, the water surface must have reached this point, and from this site the surplus must have flowed to the Orinoco River. Indeed, this is confirmed by the account of Manzano, who says that, to his knowledge, up to 1727 the lake drained at this point into the Pao River.

Up to 1727 the level of the lake did remain at the height of El Paíto Lagoon. Considerable evidence to substantiate this statement exists. Traces of the old shore line found around the lake are all at approximately the same elevation. They lie between 426 and 427 meters above sea level and coincide with the absolute elevation of the El Paíto opening.

At first glance, the El Paíto region appears to be a plain, but a topographic survey illustrates that the actual configuration of the terrain is that of a pass with gently sloping sides. In the center of this pass there is a lagoon known as El Paíto. Few bodies of water in the world are as strangely situated as this lagoon. The ground formation is such that, on a north-south line, the lagoon occupies the lowest point, but in an east-west direction it is the highest point of the terrain. As a result, water flows into the lagoon from the north and south and runs out east and west. Water flowing eastward reaches the lake, while the runoff to the west flows through the Paíto, Pao, Portuguesa, and Apure rivers to the Orinoco. Therefore, water from the Cabriales River flowing into this lagoon is divided between two hydrographic systems, that of the lake and that of the Orinoco. It may be incorrect to say that water from the Cabriales River *flows into* El Paíto Lagoon. It actually spreads out or disperses upon reaching it because the river lost its outlet when the shores of the lake receded from this point.

But it is not only the unique topographic situation of El Paíto Lagoon that attracts our attention. It has another outstanding, but very unfortunate, feature. Flying over in a helicopter, we realize that it is a swampy, unhealthy area with a stench that rises hundreds of meters above the ground. "Homo destructor" has transformed the Cabriales River into a conduit for the sewage from Valencia to El Paíto. This city of 250,000 inhabitants, in the midst of a population explosion (in 1948 it included only 50,000 inhabitants) still lacks a sewage treatment plant. As a result, El Paíto Lagoon is now a vast "hothouse of microbes."

THE TEMPERATURE OF THE LAKE

At the beginning of 1968 during the most recent limnological studies conducted by Professor Gessner, we became aware of a curious phenomenon. Gessner took temperature sections of the lake water at various sites. He found that the surface temperature averaged approximately 27° C. This is the normal value for an endoreic tropical lake. (Measurements by Octavio Jelambi recorded the following values for surface temperature: 1959, center of the lake, 27.1° C; 1964, average value of forty readings at various sites, 27.1° C.)

We recall that Humboldt gave a much lower temperature reading in his book. "The temperature of the lake surface," he wrote, "during my stay in the Aragua valleys, was a constant 23° to 23.7° in the month of February." In order to ascertain the authenticity of this sentence, we consulted the original French edition of Humboldt (1814) because we assumed that some error might have been made in the Spanish translation. But this consultation confirmed the fact: the figure is correct and given in centigrade, not Réaumur degrees. This was further confirmed by the geography of Codazzi (1960). Page 90 of Volume I contains a table showing the temperatures in centigrade for various lakes, lagoons, and rivers of Venezuela, with the following important note: "The observations have been made at many points and for weeks at a time during various navigations of the rivers and lagoons, all at different hours and times of year, taking care to reconcile them in order to obtain the most approximate knowledge of the average temperature." The figures for Lake Valencia in this table are 23° to 23.5° C. (In Codazzi's work the figures of Tacarigua lagoon in Miranda are 26.6° to 27° C and the figures for Lake Maracaibo are 25.5° to 26.6° C.)

According to these data, the temperature of the lake has risen about 4° C since the beginning of the last century. Further details would have to be known about the measurements to be sure of this fact. But the data are substantial enough to present questions and to prompt further investigation. It must be taken into account that these measurements are not haphazard results; on the contrary, they carry considerable weight. On the one hand, there is the temperature indicated by Humboldt and confirmed by Codazzi, two world-renowned observers. On the other hand, we have the results of Gessner's measurements, confirmed by Jelambi, two internationally recognized scientists. Furthermore, on both occasions, these measurements were not sporadic but averages derived from a great many readings.

This data could be additional evidence that the drying up of the lake is a comparatively recent phenomenon. At the time when the balance of the lake was positive and its water was constantly replenished, the mitigating influence of the tributaries must have been greater than today. (Unfortunately, we have been unable to compile data on the temperature of the tributaries to date.) It would, of course, also be necessary to take into consideration the possible effect of forest destruction in the basin on any change in temperature.

DIAGRAM OF LEVELS

The following chart shows the fluctuations in level from the beginning of desiccation to the present day (Table 18–1). In this diagram, the years are marked on the axis of abscissae and the levels (their absolute elevations) on the axis of ordinates. The points utilized for this diagram are shown in Table 18–1.

It must be stressed that this graph is no more than a sketch to broadly demonstrate the progressive ruin of the lake based on historical sources and direct measurements in the field. This graph answers the question posed in our introduction: Is it true that the lake is drying up?

As shown in the limnogram, up to 1727 the lake level held steady at an elevation of 426 meters, the height of the El Paíto gap. After that, the progressive decline of the

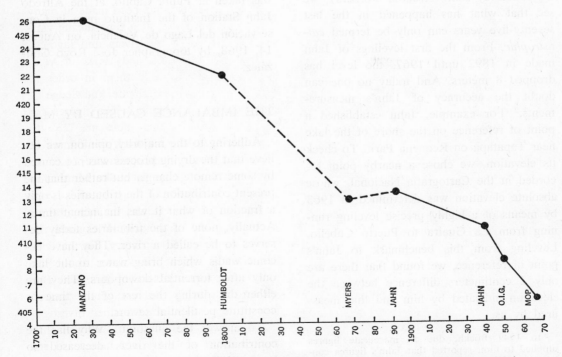

Figure 18–2 Variations of the level of Lake Valencia to 1968 (Alberto Böckh, 1968)

Table 18-1

YEAR	SPAN (YEARS)	HEIGHT ABOVE SEA LEVEL (ANNUAL AVERAGES IN METERS)	PARTIAL DROP (METERS)	RATE OF DESCENT (CM/YEAR)	NOTES
1727		426			Start of desiccation according to A. Manzano
1800	73	422	4.0	5.5	Journey of A. Humboldt
1867	67	413	9.0	13.5	Visit of Henry M. Myers
1892	25	413.5	−0.5	−2.0	First year recorded by Jahn
1939	47	410.9	2.6	5.5	Last year recorded by Jahn
1949	10	408.5	2.4	24.0	Observation by A. Böckh
1967	18	405.6	2.9	16.0	Data of Ministry of Public Works

Total years: 240
Total descent: 20.4
Average rate of descent.   8.5

lake began. Even omitting the data prior to 1892 (which continues to be a subject of discussion by some research workers), we see that what has happened in the last seventy-five years can only be termed *catastrophic*. From the first levelings of Jahn made in 1892 until 1967, the level has dropped 8 meters. And today no one can doubt the accuracy of Jahn's measurements.[2] For example, Jahn established a point of reference on the shore of the lake near Tapatapa on Requena Park. To check its elevation, we chose a nearby point recorded in the Cartografía Nacional, whose absolute elevation was determined in 1963 by means of a highly precise leveling running from La Guaira to Puerto Cabello. Leveling from this benchmark to Jahn's point of reference, we found that there are only 2 centimeters difference between the elevation indicated by him and that measured by us.

[2] In 1949 Böckh, due to inaccurate figures supplied to him, reported that Jahn's figures contained a constant error of 7 meters.

The trend is continuing. The most recent reading we have is 404.715 meters. This was taken at Punta Cabito, at the Alfredo Jahn Station of the Instituto para la Conservación del Lago de Valencia, on August 14, 1968, by topographer José Royo González.

THE IMBALANCE CAUSED BY MAN

Adhering to the majority opinion, we believe that the drying process was not caused by some remote change, but rather that the present contribution of the tributaries is only a fraction of what it was in ancient times. Actually, none of the tributaries today deserves to be called a river. They have become wadis which bring water to the lake only after torrential downpours. They are either dry during the rest of the time or constitute pestilential sewers.

To answer the question, "Why has the contribution of the rivers decreased so markedly?" we must accuse man. The deterioration of Lake Valencia is not of geological but of human origin. The accusation is explicitly addressed to the careless and irresponsible heirs of the discoverers and colonizers of the region. The shrinkage in the volume of the tributary rivers is a consequence of human activities carried out with neither planning nor control.

In 1800 Alexander von Humboldt, the distinguished naturalist, wrote:

Until the middle of the last century the mountains that surround the valleys of Aragua were covered by wild forests. Mighty trees of mimosa, ceiba, and fig cast their cool shadows over the shores of the lake. . . . With the growth of agriculture in the valleys of Aragua, the small rivers that feed Lake Valencia can no longer be considered as tributaries during the six months following the month of December. Downstream, their volume thins out because the planters of indigo, sugar cane and coffee have opened many irrigation ditches in order to water their lands.

It may be stated that the contribution of the tributaries has decreased because (a) the waters are used in an unplanned manner for farming and industries; and (b) indiscriminate deforestation has destroyed a considerable part of the lake's headwaters.

Irrigation is necessary. Consequently, it is inevitable that the lake will be deprived of some of the waters which used to reach it. However, much of the present waste can be avoided. Some irrigation systems operate with particularly great waste. These irrigated lands become swamps in which water lilies flourish instead of corn. Thus the lake is deprived of waters while these same waters usurp farmlands, converting them into unhealthy wastelands.

THE SALINITY OF THE LAKE

Formerly, when there was a positive hydrological balance, and the waters of the lake flowed off through the El Paíto gorge, they were constantly renewed and were fresh and limpid. Their saline content did not change and was equal to the average of the tributaries. However, following conversion of the lake into an endoreic system, the situation changed radically. The salts reach the lake in small quantities dissolved in the waters of the tributaries. In the lake the surface waters undergo the effects of evaporation. As the water evaporates, the salts remain. In a closed system in which the waters cannot be renewed, this results in continuous salt storage. Bonazzi's diagram is a dramatic warning of this accumulation (Bonazzi, 1962).

According to De Sola, the salinity of Lake Valencia increases each year at a rate of 3.4 parts per million (1954, 1965). By comparing total salinity and original salinity with this figure he concludes that the imbalance began approximately 250 years ago. Since that time, the salinity of the lake has increased *eightfold*.

A little over a century and a half ago, Humboldt found that the waters of the lake were still clean. He explored the region toward the end of February and the early part of March in 1800 and wrote: "The water of the lake is not as salty as they claim in Caracas. It can be drunk without being filtered. When evaporated, it leaves a very light residue of calcium carbonate and perhaps some potassium nitrate. Even then it is surprising that a lake in the interior of the country should not be richer in alkaline or clayey salts drawn from the surrounding soil" (1956). Humboldt's description is further evidence that the drying of the lake is a relatively *new* phenomenon; if the region had been endoreic for many thousands of years, the saline concentration of the lake would have been much greater by the time of Humboldt's visit.

It is difficult to fully appreciate the changes in the salinity of Lake Valencia over the one and a half centuries since Humboldt. Researcher Octavio Jelambi recently prepared the following table based on a study performed by Pérez Lecuña

(1966a and b) which shows a constant increase of salinity in the lake:

Table 18-2

CHANGES IN SALINITY AND SUSPENDED SOLIDS IN LAKE VALENCIA

YEAR	1920	1939	1950	1960	1966
Brackish solids (ppm.)	785	935	1,012	1,050	1,270
Sulfates (ppm.)		324	372	400	478

SUMMARY OF THE CAUSES AND CONSEQUENCES OF THE DESICCATION

In summarizing the results of the research, we have reached the following conclusions:

1. The progressive destruction of the lake is not caused by natural phenomena. It is the result of uncontrolled human activities.

2. In pre-Columbian times, the water budget of the basin was positive, i.e., there was a surplus.

3. In El Paíto, there was once a natural outlet for this surplus. Because of this outlet the basin of the lake belonged to the Orinoco River watershed.

4. The elevation of this spillway above sea level is approximately 426 meters. This is the maximum height which the level of the lake could have attained in the present geological era, and the lake remained at this altitude until the advent of historical, agricultural, and industrial operations.

5. These destructive activities drew off an ever increasing amount of water from the tributaries and aquifers, inverting the water budget.

6. Because of this inversion the level of the lake began to drop in 1727. The shore receded from the outlet, and the basin was transformed into an endoreic system.

7. At present, the surface of the lake is 405 meters above sea level. In less than two and one-half centuries the lake surface has dropped 21 meters, the equivalent of a seven-story building.

8. On the average, the lake level has dropped at a rate of 8.5 centimeters per year.

9. Once the watershed of Lake Valencia became separated from the Orinoco, salt began to concentrate in the lake. In the last two and one-half centuries, salinity has increased eightfold.

DECREASING DIMENSIONS

By tracing a contour line at an elevation of 426 meters above sea level, the ancient outlines of the lake are obtained. (See the boundary lines on the map.) As we determine the area covered by this contour, we discover that in the early part of the nineteenth century, the lake had a surface area of 643 square kilometers. Its present area is only half that size. In 1965, Roberto Alvarez (1967), who was preparing the isobath lines of the lake, calculated the surface area to be 369.8 square kilometers, and the maximum depth to be 40.84 meters.

De Sola thinks that in ancient times the lake contained approximately 16,650,000,-000 cubic meters of water (1965). Alvarez estimates that the figure for 1965 was 7,295,-600,000 cubic meters. With these data, and accepting 1727 as the year when desiccation began, we conclude that in the last 238 years the lake has lost 1,500 liters of water per second.

When we consult our map and compare the ancient shore with the one existing in 1955, we see that in some places, like the Yuma Peninsula with its rocky shore and its steep land slopes, the distance between the two shore lines is not very great. There are other places, however, such as the Central Tacarigua area, where land slope is almost nil. Consequently, for each meter of decrease in surface level, there is a corresponding strip of land half a kilometer wide, and the lake has receded nearly 10 kilometers from the shore.

Nowadays, the lake is nearly 30 kilometers long, with a maximum width of 18 kilometers. Its perimeter measures some 125 kilometers. According to our calculations, in Manzano's time these dimensions were approximately 40, 20, and 180 kilometers, respectively.

POLLUTION, A NEW CALAMITY

Besides the problems of the lowering of the surface level, reduced size, decreased volume, and increased salinity, a new calamity has recently been added. Pollution is rapidly increasing in the waters of the lake because of the lack of sewage plants for the communities located in the basin, and the lack of equipment to provide corrective treatment for industrial wastes. All of these effluents are dumped into the tributaries and contribute to the progressive degradation of the lake water.

It should be pointed out that Maracay and Valencia, two of the most important cities in Venezuela, are located close to Lake Valencia. Presently the total population of the basin, 500,000 inhabitants, is growing by leaps and bounds. The number of industries is also growing. In spite of such rapid development, there are no measures to check water pollution. Ciudad Alianza, a new population center in the area, is the only community which has a plant to treat its sewage. We have already mentioned El Paíto Lake. From altitudes of hundreds of meters one feels the stench of this swampy place. During one of our last reconnaissance flights we flew over the lower reaches of the Guacara river, and we understood the "progress" of the people in the city of Guacara. With population expansion and industrial development, the volume of disease-bearing and harmful liquids increased. These liquids require, but do not receive, treatment.

According to the July 1963 census of the Ministry of Development there were 465 industries in the basin (automobile, rubber, glass, tanning, paper, cardboard, textile, vegetable oil, beer, animal feed, electrical appliances, etc.). The number of new industries is increasing rapidly. This growth and its mounting effluents, together with the pollution caused by increased livestock-raising, produce great quantities of organic and inorganic residues which affect the tributaries, and thus the lake itself (Pérez Lecuña, 1966a and b, 1968). The following tables and the respective comments were taken from Pérez Lecuña's papers.

Pérez Lecuña states that "obviously the value of the biochemical demand for oxygen as an index of pollution has increased to an alarming extent in areas near the mouths of these highly affected rivers." With respect to these quantitatively small BOD factors, the volume of the body of water on which these samples have been taken should be considered. Moreover, we must not overlook the fact that the lake is located in a region which does not go through marked seasonal changes. The well-known thermocline phenomenon, which occurs in other latitudes, gives rise to the recovery of dissolved oxygen and thus increases the self-purifying power of the affected body of water. Of special interest is the study by F. Gessner entitled "The Eutrophication of Lake Valencia" (1964). Although we consider eutrophication a direct consequence of the constant inflow of highly degraded waters into the lake, we feel that it would be timely to obtain samples on a methodical and prolonged basis in order to confirm this phenomenon in a more exhaustive manner. Pérez Lecuña (1966a and b) commented on other problems:

The lack of adequate legal instruments at the present time makes it possible not only for the lake's surface layers to present conditions of obvious pollution and pathogenic contamination but also for such degradation to be present in the lower layers; the latter being affected by domestic and industrial discharges which are arbitrarily poured into sewers, taking advantage

Table 18-3

CHRONOLOGICAL COMPILATION FOR PHYSICAL-CHEMICAL ANALYSIS VALUES
OF THE WATER IN LAKE VALENCIA

AUTHOR	DATE	PLACE	DEPTH Meters	BOD^5* Mg/1	OD† Mg/1	SO‡ Mg/1	TEMP. °C	pH
Pearse	1918		0	—	7.00	—	27.6	
			15	—	6.87	—	27.2	
			25	—	6.29	—	26.9	
A. Bonazzi	1946	500 m de 0	3	—	5.18	—	—	
		300 m de 0	3	—	6.21	—	—	
		100 m de 0	7.60	—	6.89	—	—	
		300 m de 0	36	—	0	—	—	
F. Gessner Blohm	Sept. 1952		0		7.3			
			20		7			
			25		0			
O. Jelambi	1957 1958	Pta. Culebra 2 miles	surface	1.0	7.9			
		Idem	medium	0.7	7.8			
		Idem	bottom	0.4	7.4			
		Pta. Culebra 3 miles	surface	1.3	7.5			
		Idem	medium	0.8	7.3	—		
		Idem	bottom	0.3	7.1			
Study supply of water from Valencia (INOS)	Mar. 1959	East of Flor Amarillo	surface	0.9	7.4	—		8.96
F. Gessner	Oct. 1963	Station No.1 In front of Zorro Island	0	—	6.5	—	27.3	—
			15	—	6	—	27	
			20	—	0	—	24	
		Station No.2, halfway between Otama and La Cabrera	0	—	6.9	—	27.5	—
			18	—	6.8	—	27	—
			20	—	0.5	—	24.5	—
		Station No.3. In front of Chambergo	0	—	7	—	27.5	—
			10	—	6	—	27	—
			20	—	0	—	24	—
R. Pérez Lecuña DAP. C.A.	Aug. 1964	Maracay Wharves 150 meters	surface	4.23	6.02	226	30	8.7

*Biological Oxygen Demand at 5°C.
†
‡

of the natural permeability of the soil along the shore of the lake. These effects have caused regrettable situations, such as those which occurred in past years in the towns of Los Guayos and Naguanagua [in the state of Carabobo] where the number of children who were the victims of water-borne infections caused considerable consternation in the area. In both cases, it was determined that water drawn from deep wells was highly contaminated by seepage from sewers which did not seem to be too close to the wells.

Similarly, numerous cases are known of industries which have had to invest large sums of money to purify the water from their wells because it was highly contaminated.

Table 18-4

CHRONOLOGICAL COMPILATION FOR PHYSICAL-CHEMICAL ANALYSIS
VALUES OF THE WATER IN THE TRIBUTARIES OF LAKE VALENCIA

AUTHOR	DATE	PLACE	TEMP. °C	pH	VOLATILE SOLIDS	BOD[5] Mg/l	OD Mg/l
R. Pérez L.,	May 1959	Quebrada	28	6.8	950	146	7.1
I. Guevara and		Barrio Lourdes	28	6.8	950	125	3.3
S. Tebet. C.		ravine (gorge) of Maracay cemetery	30	6.9	—	160	2.0
		Güey River	28	7.8	520	83	6.5
		Maracay cross-roads	28	7.8	520	74	4.1
R. Pérez L. DAP.C.A.	July 1963	Aragua River at La Victoria	25	7.8	150	12	2.0
R. Pérez L. DAP.C.A.	Aug. 1964	Aragua River at Cagua highway	28	8.2	129	8.60	5.72
		Güey River across Ave. Boliv. Mcy.	27.5	7.8	131	8.3	4.39
		Cabriales River at Valencia highway	26	7.6	82	61	4.69
		Stream across route to Güigüe	25	8.2	68	4.79	5.00

Because of this intolerable situation, the Institute for the Conservation of Lake Valencia submitted to the municipal councils of Maracay and Valencia a proposed ordinance to end water contamination (Pérez Lecuña, 1967). In addition to containing precise, concrete proposals, this bill includes examples showing how the problem of water pollution has been dealt with and solved in other countries. We shall quote one of these examples:

As they flow through the most industrialized area in West Germany, the waters of the Ruhr river remain sufficiently clean to be used for water sports amidst the rows of smokestacks, thanks to the "Ruhrverband," a cooperative association of 250 municipalities and 2,200 industries located along the river. The success of the association is based on the following principle: *those who pollute the water will have to pay the expenses of having it purified.* Through the use of carefully calculated rates, the association has been able to build more than 100 treatment plants since 1948.

RECOMMENDATIONS

Now that we have indicated and analyzed the region's three major problems—desiccation, salinization, and pollution—we would like to recommend a few measures which together could effectively remedy the lake's problems.

1. Regulate irrigation so that no water is wasted. This reform would help to increase the volume which reaches the lake.

2. Irrigate during the night when there is less evaporation. In this manner, farming would consume less water, and the amount saved would feed into the lake. This procedure is followed in Israel, where water shortage is the country's number one problem.

3. Clean the beds of tributaries and canals so that there will be no stagnant water. This procedure was utilized in colonial times.

4. Improve the channel of the Cabri-

ales River and carry its water, which now spreads out to the south of Valencia, directly to the lake.

5. Drain swampy areas.

6. Reforest what was destroyed through exploitation and ignorance.

7. Protect the headwaters of the tributaries. For this purpose our institute proposed to the Venezuelan Ministry of Agriculture and Livestock that the Henri Pittier National Park be enlarged.

8. Put an end to forest fires and create an awareness of forestry resources, their values and proper management.

9. Avoid the unnecessary felling of trees; prevent arboricide.

10. Channel outside water into the basin. There are several interesting projects possible including those suggested by the Venezuelan engineer Lucio Baldó (1967).

11. Take measures to prevent water pollution; build sewage treatment plants; enact the ordinances recommended by Pérez Lecuña.

12. Study possible additional remedies for water-loss problems, including artificial rain-making and the reduction of evaporation (from the reservoirs located in the basin) through the use of chemical substances and other means.

The critical moment is approaching. Man is now given the last chance to remedy these environmental evils. We must heed John F. Kennedy's call "to re-establish a sound relationship between man and nature in order to protect our physical and mental health, and to pass on to future generations our ancestral heritage: a land full of life and beauty."

REFERENCES

Alvarez, Roberto J. "Levantamiento hidrográfico del Lago de Valencia." *El Lago* (Valencia), No. 2 (1967).

Avilán, Justo. "Nota preliminar sobre el Desecamiento del Lago de Valencia." *El Lago* (Valencia), No. 2 (1967).

Baldó, Lucio. "El Lago de Valencia—Posible solución del problema creado por la disminución de sus aguas." *El Lago* (Valencia), No. 3 (1967).

Berry, E. W. "Geology and Paleontology of Lake Tacarigua, Venezuela." *Proc. Amer. Philos. Soc.*, 81 (1939), 547–68.

Böckh, Alberto. *El Desecamiento del Lago de Valencia con prólogo de Mons. Gregorio Adam.* Caracas: Fundación Eugenio Mendoza, 1956. 4 maps, 64 illus.

———. *El Desecamiento del Lago de Valencia. Forum Pro-Conservación del Lago de Valencia, 1963.* Ediciones del Instituto para la Conservación del Lago de Valencia. París en América Valencia, 1966a.

———. *Bibliografía del Lago de Valencia.* Ediciones del Instituto para la Conservación del Lago de Valencia. París en América Valencia, 1966b.

———. El Lago de Valencia, víctima del hombre destructor. Report presented at the Conferencia Latinoamericana de Conservación de Recursos Naturales Renovables, San Carlos de Bariloche, Argentina, 1968.

Bonazzi, Augusto. "La Salinización de los suelos del Valle de Aragua." *El Farol* (Caracas), March–April, 1962, pp. 2–8.

Chardón, Carlos E. *Viajes y Naturaleza.* The chapters "Estudio sobre el Lago de Valencia," in collaboration with Raymond A. Crist, and "La Vegetación Acuática del Lago de Valencia y el origen de las tierras de Caracolillo." Caracas: Editorial Sucre, 1941. Pp. 352–75.

Chrosciechowski, Przemilaw. "Los Planorbídeos y otros gasterópodos del Lago de Valencia." *El Lago* (Valencia), No. 9 (1968).

Codazzi, Agustín. *Obras Escogidas.* 2 Vols. Caracas: Ediciones del Ministerio de Edución, 1960. Vol. I, pp. 90, 389, 392.

De Sola, Oswaldo. "El Lago de Valencia." Statement given in the Ateneo de Valencia on April 25, 1954, and published in the newspaper *El Carabobeño*, May 3, 1954.

———. El Lago de Valencia. Cycle of conferences organized by the Institute for the Conservation of Lake Valencia. Manuscript.

Gessner, Fritz. "La Eutroficación del Lago de Valencia. *Acta Científica Venezolana* (Caracas), 15 (5) (1964), 193–97.

———. "La zona de conchas de caracol en el Lago de Valencia." *El Lago* (Valencia), No. 3 (1967).

Humboldt, Alejandro. *Voyage aux Régions Equinoxiales du Nouveau Continent fait en 1799, 1800, 1801, 1802, 1803 et 1804.* Paris: Chez F. Schoell, Rue des Fossés, Montmartre, No. 14. 1814.

———. *Viaje a las Regiones Equinocciales del Nuevo Continente.* Translated by Lisandro Alvarado. 5 vols. Chap. XVI, Vol. III (Buenos Aires, Argentina: Imprenta López.) Caracas: Ediciones del Ministerio de Educación, 1956.

Instituto de Antropología e Historia del Estado Carabobo. Bulletin No. 2. Imprenta Nacional, Caracas: 1968.

Jahn, Alfredo. "Estudio sobre el Lago de Valencia." Boletín de la Academia Nacional de Historia, Vol. XXIII, No. 91 (July–September, 1940), pp. 488–508. Reprinted in *IV Centenario del Descubrimiento del Lago de Valencia*—1948. Caracas: Imprenta Nacional Publicaciones del Gobierno de Estado Carabobo.

Jelambi, Octavio. "Las Aparecidas." *Acta Científica Venezolana* (Caracas), Vol. 9, No. 5 (1958), pp. 99–101.

Kidder, Alfred. "Archaeology of Northwestern Venezuela." *Papers of the Peabody Museum of American Archeology and Ethnology.* Cambridge: Harvard University, 1944.

Manzano, Antonio. "Descripzion Geographica." Published by Angel de Altolaguirre y Duvale in *Relaciones Geográficas de la Gobernación de Venezuela 1767–1768.* Madrid, 1908. Pp. 33–49. Reprinted in *IV Centenario del Descubrimiento del Lago de Valencia*—1948. Caracas: Imprenta Nacional Publicaciones del Gobierno del Estado Carabobo, pp. 15–25.

Montesinos Barnola, Laura; García Valero, Julio Aníbal; Rotundo Liendo, Luis Alejandro; and Caldentey Luque, Lorenzo. Investigacíon Hidrológica del Lago de Valencia. Special work presented before the Ilustre Universidad Católica Andrés Bello to achieve the title of Civil Engineer. Caracas, 1966.

Myers, Henry Morris. *Life and Nature under the Tropics.* New York: D. Appleton and Co., 1871. Pp. 42, 43.

Oviedo y Baños, Jose de. *Historia de la Conquista y Poblacíon de la Provincia de Venezuela.* Facsimile edition by Paul Adams. New York, 1940. Pp. xx, 51, 137, 199–221, 223–24.

Peeters, Leo. *Origen y Evolución de la Cuenca del Lago de Valencia (Venezuela).* Caracas: Ediciones del Instituto para la Conservación del Lago de Valencia. Oficina de Divulgación Agrícola, Ministerio de Agricultura y Cría, 1968.

Pérez Lecuña, Roberto. *La Conservación Integral de las Aguas de la Cuenca del Lago de Valencia.* Caracas: ASOVAC 1966a.

———. *Conservación Integral de las aguas de la cuenca del Lago de Valencia.* XVI Convención ASOVAC. Caracas, 1966b.

———. "Proyecto de Ordenanza Municipal para el control de las descargas residuales industriales, elaborado para las ciudades de Maracay y Valencia." *El Lago* (Valencia), No. 6 (1967).

Proyectos y Construcciones DAPCA. *Proposition for the Execution of the Sanitary Study of the Valencia-Lake Area.* Report prepared by Roberto Pérez Lecuna for the UICN. Caracas, 1968.

Röhol, Eduardo. "Sobre la regularidad de las mareas atmosféricas en nuestras latitudes." *Revista Colegio de Ingenieros,* No. 148 (1943), pp. 85–87.

Schwarck Anglade, Armando. "Estudio de los factores que inciden sobre la Conservación de las zonas de captación de las hoyas del Lago de Valencia, Rio Tucutunemo y Cabeceras del Tuy." Prepared by Aeromapas Seravenca. (Known as the "Schwarck Report.") Caracas, 1962.

Tamers, M. A., and Thielen, C. "Radiocarbon Ages of Ground Water Flowing into a Desiccating Lake." *Acta Científica Venezolana* (Caracas), 17 (5) (1966), 150–57.

19. THE ANCHICAYA HYDROELECTRIC PROJECT IN COLOMBIA:
Design and Sedimentation Problems*

Robert N. Allen

The Anchicayá hydroelectric project in southwestern Colombia, with final installation of 64,000 kilowatts, was the first major power plant in the area and was destined to supply energy to the "power-starved," rapidly growing city of Cali.

Apparently too little reconnaissance was made in the nearly inaccessible, difficult, and jungle-covered terrain before the initial plans were prepared. Actual construction started in 1944, only to be stopped by financial problems in 1948 after the proposed conduction tunnel had been largely excavated, a 12,000 cubic meter portion of the thin arch dam had been constructed, and major equipment such as turbines, generators, penstocks, transformers, etc., had been ordered and partly delivered to the site. The original plans contained many questionable features, the major one being the thin arch dam, and, next in importance, the surge chamber. Unfortunately the designers completely failed to recognize the very serious sediment and debris problems which would arise from the construction of the highway and the deforestation of the watershed, which would cause landslides, heavy erosion, and rapid sedimentation of the small reservoir.

The difficulties with this project confirm several general ideas. First, careful and comprehensive preliminary planning of development projects must be done, and done with imagination so that significant ecological and technical considerations may guide the planning. This is the most important aspect of any engineering project, yet involves the least engineering per se.

Second, there is a great need for good descriptions of plans, changes, errors,

* Some of the highly technical design details have been abridged from the original paper presented at the Conference.

failures or near-failures, and other "skeletons in the closet" of apparently successful engineering projects. For example, consulting engineers at Anchicayá completely failed to recognize the sediment and debris problem by stating that "tropical rivers carry little sediment" and that "there would be no problem with sedimentation during the life of the project." Many hidden problems exist in such projects which will never be made public unless disaster strikes. Much could be learned from studying such failures and the perspective for future planning would be more realistic.

My efforts to revise many features of the design, to force recognition of the extremely severe sedimentation problem, to provide a better design of the outlet tower, to build debris barriers upstream of the reservoir, to secure a dredge to continually remove sediment from the reservoir, and to provide an excellent record of the progressive sedimentation of a small reservoir were largely successful.

This paper follows quite closely one of the aspects of the Conference, supplying a "post-construction analysis" considered advisable on major projects. The various changes of design features are analyzed after years of service.

The paper provides excerpts from many of my reports concerning Anchicayá; it also contains excerpts from two reports concerning these features by Dr. Lorenz G. Straub. Lastly it mentions my "pet project," the large Upper Anchicayá Hydroelectric Development, now under construction, which I first proposed in 1957. Also mentioned are certain proposals for future operation of the existing Anchicayá reservoir after the new power plant is completed. The details of the construction of Anchicayá dam which were included in the original conference papers have been shortened considerably here.

Fifty years of varied engineering and construction experience lead me to express several ideas confirmed by our many problems on the Anchicayá hydroelectric project in Colombia. Careful and complete preliminary reconnaissance is the most vital part of any engineering project, requiring comprehension, experience, and vision—in fact, inspiration, a quality acquired by few persons. Later design work becomes more a routine which can be performed by various specialists with less imagination. Nothing is more discouraging than to arrive on a project and find that the preliminary program was defective, too costly, or otherwise seriously questionable when it is too late to make desirable changes.

Unfortunately, engineering and construction literature and reports usually consist of success stories, whereas I sincerely believe that quite often more can be learned from "skeletons in the closet," if these are properly described, explained, and evaluated. Such major disasters as the failure of the Quebec bridge, the "galloping gertie" Tacoma Bridge, and the Viant dam disaster in Italy were quite well publicized and of great benefit to the engineering profession, but I know also that many successful projects have hidden "skeletons" about which nothing will ever be made public unless disaster strikes.

Lastly, I have been appalled by the lack of appreciation of biology and ecology. We have been rapidly spoiling our physical environment by man-made changes without realizing or understanding the long-term effects of such alterations. Modern technology has largely ignored the biological and ecological aspects of major development

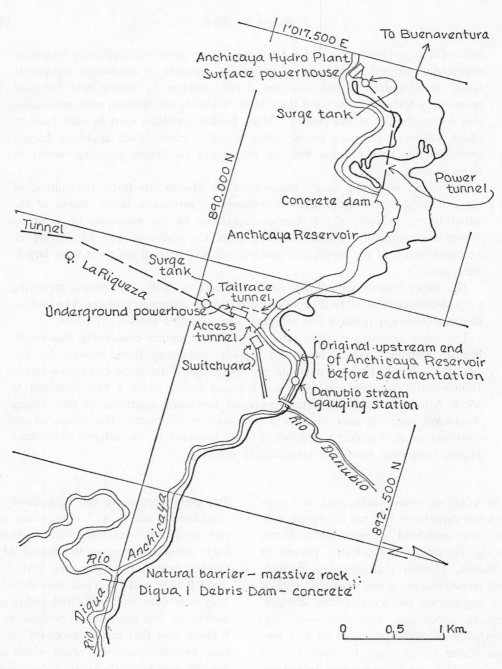

Figure 19–1 Anchicayá vicinity map

Labels in figure:
1'017,500 E
To Buenaventura
Anchicaya Hydro Plant
Surface powerhouse
Surge tank
Power tunnel
Concrete dam
Anchicaya Reservoir
890,000 N
Tunnel
Surge tank
Q. La Riqueza
Tailrace tunnel
Underground powerhouse
Access tunnel
Switchyard
Original upstream end of Anchicaya Reservoir before sedimentation
Danubio stream gauging station
Rio Danubio
892,500 N
Rio Anchicaya
Rio Digua
Natural barrier — massive rock
Digua. 1 Debris Dam — concrete
0   0.5   1 Km.

programs here and abroad. Conditions have now reached a critical stage, and an increasing awareness of the problems must be stimulated if humanity, now under the scourge of a "population explosion," is to survive.

In the Anchicayá project, several severe defects in the original planning can be briefly noted. The original reconnaissance was possibly at fault in not noting or using what appears to be a much superior damsite in a narrow gorge about 800 meters downstream from the present power plant (Fig. 19–1) where a dam over 150 meters high would have been possible. For some unknown reason this area was blocked out of the original topographic maps. The dam originally proposed at the present location was a thin arch, not suitable for the site. A 12,000 cubic meter portion of this original design previously constructed on the right bank was of poor quality on an improperly prepared base partly on soft rock. This block greatly complicated the design and construction of the gravity arch dam finally used.

The major error was that neither the originators of the project nor the later consulting engineers who reviewed the project made any mention whatsoever of the future sediment and debris problems or the deforestation already commencing. This unpardonable lack of foresight resulted in the

failure to recognize the hazard of the small reservoir filling rapidly with sediment, or the proposed outlet works becoming completely blocked by debris and sediment. Nothing could be done about the size of the reservoir at a later date since the dam height was fixed by the equipment already ordered, but entirely new plans were made for the outlet works, sluice gates, and trashracks. The surge chamber, previously designed for a hazardous site later covered by a landslide, was completely redesigned and placed in the mountain. Luckily, I was able to secure the modification of these items and many other objectionable features during the final design and construction of the project after joining the Anchicayá organization in April 1951 as technical advisor.

The Anchicayá power plant, dam, and

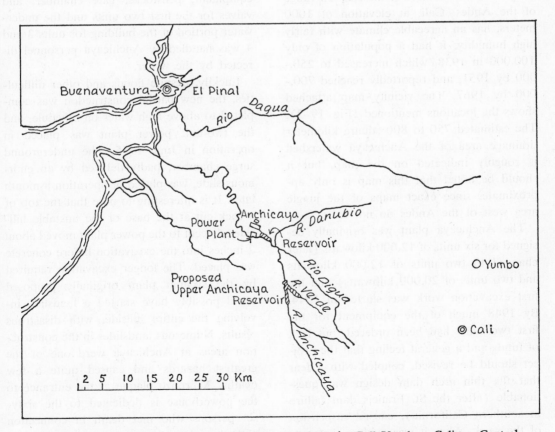

Figure 19–2 Vicinity map. Buenaventura—Anchicayá—Cali Yumbo—Calima. Central Hidroeléctrica de Anchicayá, Cali, Colombia

reservoir are all located in the steep-walled canyon of the Anchicayá River in south-western Colombia on the Pacific slope of the western range of the Andes Mountains. The terrestrial location is about 3°30' N latitude and 77° W longitude. The power plant is inland about 30 kilometers from the Pacific Ocean and 37 kilometers S 33° E from the Pacific port of Buenaventura. By the tortuous Simón Bolívar highway, the plant is 50 kilometers southeastward from Buenaventura and 90 kilometers northwestward from Cali. The very difficult Anchicayá section of this generally narrow, gravel-coated highway was not yet built when the first surveys were started for the project.

Cali, the principal load center for Anchicayá power, is a very rapidly growing city situated in the Cauca valley adjacent to the eastern foothills of the western range of the Andes. Cali, at elevation of 1000 meters, has an agreeable climate with fairly high humidity. It had a population of only 100,000 in 1938, which increased to 250,-000 by 1951, and reportedly reached 700,-000 by 1967. The vicinity map attached shows the locations mentioned (Fig. 19–2). The estimated 750 to 800 square kilometer drainage area of the Anchicayá watershed is roughly indicated on the map, but it should be noted that this map is only approximate, since exact maps of the jungle area west of the Andes do not exist.

The Anchicayá plant was originally designed for six units of 12,000 kilowatts (later changed to two units of 12,000 kilowatts and two units of 20,000 kilowatts) and the first excavation work was started in 1944. By 1948 much of the equipment for the first two units had been ordered, but lack of funds and a general feeling that the project should be revised, coupled with a fear that the thin arch dam design was questionable (after the St. Francis dam failure in southern California), caused suspension of the work. Also, it was evident that outside financing was necessary, and thus a

review of the project by competent engineers was a requisite for any IBRD (World Bank) financing. Following a review of the project by a U.S. firm who made quite a few major changes in the proposal design and definitely recommended changing to a gravity arch dam, financing was arranged, construction bids were advertised, and late in 1950 a design and construction contract was awarded to a Danish-Colombian firm. Work began early in 1951. This firm made fair progress on the powerhouse but accomplished very little on the dam and made numerous costly errors of judgment. The contract was finally canceled. After this, the contract was split up, the dam going to a French firm, the tunnel to one Colombian firm, and the powerhouse to another. Much of the work of completion, installation of equipment, penstocks, gate chamber, and valves for the first two units and the underwater portion of the building for units 3 and 4 was handled by Anchicayá personnel directed by the writer.

Luckily, despite floods and other difficulties, the new partial construction was completed to above high water on schedule, and the two-unit power plant was placed in operation in June 1955. The underground surge chamber, badly delayed by an enormous slide, was placed in operation a month later. It is interesting to note that the top of a rock cut at the base of the unstable hillside adjacent to the power plant moved about 2 inches into the excavation before concrete was placed. The longer excavation required by the six-unit plant originally proposed could possibly have started a landslide involving the entire hillside, with disastrous results. Numerous landslides in the construction areas at Anchicayá were one of the greatest hazards and caused quite a few deaths. A bronze plaque at the entrance to the powerhouse is dedicated to the sixty-six persons who met death in connection with the job.

The construction of the surge chamber,

part by contract but mostly by Anchicayá personnel, forms an odyssey too long to include herein. Numerous small slides resulted, and one major slide of about 25,000 cubic meters during a torrential rain (November 4, 1954) buried forever the entire working area on the original surge chamber site, covering office, concrete mixer, cement, aggregate, reinforcing steel, and miscellaneous equipment. This disaster, only eight months before the final operating date, luckily caused no injury to personnel. It did, however, add force to the continued newspaper clamor in Cali of "Anchicayá Nunca" ("Anchicayá—Never").

THE ANCHICAYA DAM

The proposed gravity arch dam followed more closely the consultants' recommendations, except for an entirely new concept of combined outlet tower attached to the dam with a higher conduction outlet in the upper portion and a sluiceway outlet below.

Nothing definite was known initially as to the depth or suitability of the river channel at the damsite but core drilling at a later date revealed sound quartz-diorite with few seams at around 10 meters depth of water. This was fully confirmed when the excavation was completed. This excellent foundation for the center blocks added much stability to the final structure, and a large number of large 1-inch and 1¼-inch reinforcement bars grouted in the rock on the sloping abutments added additional resistance against possible uplift and sliding.

The dam is of the overflow type with "ski-jump" features on the downstream slope to prevent downstream scour near the base of the dam. The central portions of the spillway have a total length of 111.0 meters at elevation 194.4 meters and 15 meters length of additional spillway adjacent to each abutment at 195.2 meters. The abutments are at elevation 201, with walls 1 meter higher. The total dam length is

206.5 meters, and the maximum height of dam from base rock to spillway crest is 53 meters. The calculated overflow capacity is 5700 cubic meters per second. One gallery leads from the right abutment to the outlet tower; the central gallery is further downward and passes horizontally through the dam rising to the left abutment. The lower gallery connects with the central gallery on each side and contains the mechanism for the two 5 feet by 6 feet hydraulically operated sluice gates.

Concrete aggregates were obtained from a new quarry about 5 kilometers upstream from the dam, where excellent diorite was exposed, but some sand and river gravel were needed to secure proper grading. All material had to be hauled to the primary crusher near the Anchicayá camp, then travel by a cableway to the secondary crusher above the damsite, then spill into bins, from which it was belt-transported to the mixing plant just above the dam. After mixing, the concrete was delivered by buckets from a cableway above the dam. These items generally worked satisfactorily, but slippage of splices on the continuous cableway between primary and secondary crushers caused many delays, a problem never solved by the British suppliers. I believe that this slippage, unknown elsewhere, was due to a rapid growth of algae common to the excessively humid tropics.

Another previously unencountered item was that the crushed rock became quickly coated with a greenish-gray coating resembling paint which could not be washed off. Testing of samples sent to the university in Medellín gave no remedy except slightly longer mixing time to partly abrade the coating, and, further, indicated that this coating could cause a decrease in strength of 10 to 15 percent in the concrete. It was presumed that the crusher dust from the diorite somehow combined to form the coating, but here again no positive cause was identified. These items are mentioned since they were primarily produced by the effects of a hot, humid, tropical climate with excessive rainfall. The transmission-line galvanized towers in the Anchicayá area also became quickly coated with a similar "paint," as did the top surfaces of the porcelain insulators. The skirts of the insulators rapidly accumulate algae and insect or wasp deposits, sometimes up to a centimeter in thickness. Use of silicone grease has ameliorated this condition somewhat but quickly creates a horrible appearance.

THE ANCHICAYA DIVERSION TUNNEL AND BOTTOM OUTLET

The consultants recommended use of the already excavated diversion tunnel, its entry already provided with guides for use of a large car-wheel gate for a future bottom outlet equipped with a Howell-Bunger valve inside the dam. When I first saw the site in 1951, the diversion tunnel entrance was about 95 percent blocked with tree trunks nearly a meter in diameter, along with debris and boulders, positive proof of what would happen to any bottom outlet with no means to keep out or remove large debris. No further consideration was given that plan, and a permanent tunnel plug was later installed downstream of the obstruction. Since this old diversion-tunnel entrance left no room for an upstream diversion dam, a new tunnel was branched off the old one and extended some 100 meters upstream, and a large gate was proposed by the contractor, for closure. Here again, slow and costly progress forced a new solution, a man-made slide to close the entrance.

THE ANCHICAYA COMBINED OUTLET TOWER

The consultants' revised design for the conduction tunnel intake consisted of a large vertical shaft descending from a bench well above high level and directly over the conduction tunnel. The major defect in this plan was that the long open end of the conduction tunnel included no provision whatsoever for removing large debris which could enter the tunnel. I proposed an exterior sloping trashrack structure built on the rock surface over the existing tunnel entrance, with grooves for trashrack units with small openings, including grooves for massive concrete beams to be placed below the movable trashracks as the sediment elevation continued to rise. This method would have provided perfect service for Anchicayá until the reservoir was practically filled with sediment and could readily have been supplemented later for full run-of-the-river operation. Unfortunately, the seriousness of the sedimentation and debris problems had not yet been recognized, and the consultants consistently maintained that "there would be no sedimentation problem." Thus, since the designer-contractor was also unfavorable to such new design, the idea was abandoned. Then, the idea of a combined outlet tower attached to the dam, my second choice, was finally approved by all concerned. The location of the proposed structure was practically fixed by a firm rock bench on the right bank of the river and several meters above normal river level requiring relatively little additional excavation, while at the same time providing perfect coordination with a block of the dam, and a correct angle so that the discharge of the proposed pair of 5-foot by 6-foot sluice gates would not hit the right bank below the dam.

The massive reinforced concrete outlet structure rises to an operating floor at elevation of 201 meters from a base at around 150 meters. The gate-operating mechanisms are in separate structures above the floor with pits to store the car-wheel gates below floor level. Gates are lowered by gravity in emergency, with normal lowering and raising by electric power. One gate serves the two sluice gates and is located on the dam proper, whereas the conduction tunnel gate and gatehouse are entirely on the outlet structure. The conduction tunnel is connected to the outlet tower by a massive circular reinforced concrete conduit supported on piers. The intake face of the tower, best shown on a drawing entitled "Sediment Profiles Upstream of Outlet Tower," has three equal vertical rows of trashracks, with sluiceway trashracks from elevation 154.5 to 165.0 meters, then a sealed section, followed by the conduction trashracks from 169.0 to 184 meters. The lower trashrack grooves are offset outward to permit separate operation and raising when necessary, and an electrically operated trashrack rake can be placed in any one of the three bays on either top or bottom trashracks. Also provided is an electrically operated crane, suitable for handling a special beam to hook and lift trashrack sections, or a large gang hook for removing tree trunks which lodge against the trashracks.

The main object of this combined outlet tower was to maintain the area in front of the conduction tunnel intake free of sediment for the longest possible time by opening the sluice gates in times of heavy floods and from time to time under normal conditions. The effectiveness of this method is very clearly indicated by the funnel-shaped depression existing around the outlet tower, even though the sediment deposit 30 meters upstream had been higher than the conduction tunnel intake for several years and was still rising. Only in 1967 was dredging started in the lower portion of the reservoir, and only in 1968 was dredging started adjacent to the tower.

THE SEDIMENTATION OF ANCHICAYA RESERVOIR

Many changes in the original design of the Anchicayá hydroelectric project described above were necessary because of an antici-

pated sediment and debris problem, completely ignored by the originators of the project and the consultants in their review of the project. I now want to describe the conditions leading up to this problem and the efforts made to ameliorate it, and to present what is probably the most authentic record of sedimentation of a small reservoir that has ever been made. Finally, I want to present the latest ideas on what has to be done in the future to extend the life of the reservoir.

When the Anchicayá project was initiated in 1944, the present Simón Bolívar highway which now passes the Anchicayá plant area was still under construction, and there were few settlers and very little deforestation in this generally steep-walled V canyon. Thus it is not too surprising that the originators of the project failed to realize that the major cuts of the highway on the very steep slopes would cause serious landslides and the influx of settlers would speed the destruction of the jungle cover, causing greatly increased sedimentation in the river and an enormous debris problem. However, these same planners did have in plain view the enormous *playas* (beaches) of the Digua River, the major tributary of the Anchicayá, which already contained enough sand and gravel to fill the small reservoir proposed for the plant in just one major flood. It can only be concluded that the originators lacked vision and full comprehension of what would happen in the future.

The first apprehension as to possible sedimentation apparently came shortly before the consultants' report when a major slide some 100 meters upstream of the damsite created a low dam, causing pondage which very rapidly filled with sediment. A letter from the manager to the consultants, noting the sedimentation and requesting information on possible sedimentation rates, brought the reply that tropical rivers carry little sediment and that there would be no sediment problem at Anchicayá.

After my arrival at Anchicayá in April 1951 I became alarmed by the visible evidence of the large gravel *playas* of the Digua River and the large quantity of tree trunks and debris left high and dry after each flood. I was certain that both sediment and debris would cause major problems at Anchicayá, and my first report thereon was dated May 1951. The following are essentially excerpted from that report:

1. Immediately upon starting work for Anchicayá, the silt problem in the proposed Anchicayá Reservoir assumed major importance in my studies of the project and proposed outlet works, since familiarity with streams in the western U.S. made the extremely small reservoir appear hazardous to future successful operation of the proposed development.

In considering the problem a letter was written to the consultants suggesting consideration of the problem and possible alteration of the proposed intake, with the result that the previously expressed idea that "there was no silt problem in tropical rivers" was repeated. I do not agree with this concept and will discuss the problem from a purely conjectural basis since no actual facts regarding the Anchicayá are available.

2. Records of other rivers are of major importance but vary widely depending upon the slope and stage of the river, and the type of terrain traversed.

The Mississippi River, for instance, with very flat slopes over the major portion of its length, is estimated to carry 1500 parts per million of silt or .0015, or about $\frac{1}{7}$ of 1 percent. Most rivers at flood stage carry an extremely high percentage of sediment. For example, at Obras Neusa, near Zipaquira, Colombia, a 0.35 to 0.70 cubic meter stream where 16 meters was the observed previous maximum, an abnormal 75 cubic meter per second flood moved about 200,-000 cubic meters of boulders, cobbles, and

gravel out of a narrow canyon in about forty-eight hours, depositing the debris at the mouth of the canyon, swamping and wrecking a power plant. In the Mojave desert of California I witnessed the results of a twenty-four-hour storm which stripped every vestige of vegetation from fifteen miles of canyon, depositing a delta one-third-mile long in Parker Reservoir and carrying floating debris down to Parker Dam which required many weeks of work with cranes and trucks to remove from the reservoir. Both of these caused erosion from single storms which under similar conditions would seriously endanger the Anchicayá project.

3. Assume that the Anchicayá carries one-tenth as much silt as the Mississippi. With an average flow of 90 cubic meters per second the annual volume carried by the Anchicayá is about 2,800,000,000 cubic meters, which at this factor would equal 420,000 cubic meters of sediment per year, or, with a reservoir capacity of 5,000,000 cubic meters, a reservoir life of twelve years. Assuming that only half this amount would settle in the reservoir, the balance being carried over the spillway or through the turbines, it would still leave a life of only twenty-five years.

4. The above figures are highly hypothetical. Nothing is known of the actual silt content of the Anchicayá or the percentage of the actual content, which is "bed load." The bed load is of great importance in heavy floods and will probably be the deciding factor in the life of the reservoir. A river like the Colorado, with about 1 percent silt content, would fill the reservoir in less than one hundred days! The reported silt content in the Yellow River in China would fill the reservoir *in less than twenty days* if all sediment was deposited.

Since sediment contents noted in my report were obtained from standard engineering works, it appears impossible that competent engineers failed to realize the seriousness of the Anchicayá sediment problem. With the reservoir capacity of 5,081,-000 cubic meters and an average flow in the Anchicayá of 90 cubic meters per second, the reservoir would fill one and a half times daily, and even the extremely low sedimentation rate of the Illinois River would produce about 110,000 cubic meters of sediment per year, allowing a reservoir life of at most forty-five years. Seeing the Anchicayá River in flood, a tumultuous torrent on a grade of over 1.5 percent, extremely muddy and carrying quantities of logs and debris, would quickly convince anyone that the Anchicayá was not a sediment-free stream.

Shortly after my report quoted above, I estimated a minimum reservoir life of about seven years and a probable average life of fifteen years for the Anchicayá Reservoir and proposed various changes in the design of the outlet works and certain other features. My correspondence with the designers in Copenhagen finally convinced them that sedimentation would be a very serious problem, and they finally estimated the life of the reservoir as about thirteen years, a figure somewhat more critical than my estimates. These various reports anticipating early loss of the reservoir were submitted to the consultants, who replied, "We do not believe that the estimates as to the possible rate of annual accumulation of deposits in the reservoir are justified"; and, "We are of the opinion that the Anchicayá watershed is such that the deposits will not accumulate to a serious extent within the economic life of the plant."

It is extremely unfortunate that such highly erroneous opinions were expressed, and luckily such opinions did not prevent me from making many changes in design to better cope with the many sediment and debris problems I anticipated. Even at this early date I had mentioned control of deforestation and construction of debris dams as partial answers to the still-unsolved sedimentation problems.

Between late 1951 and April 1955, design and construction were the primary occupations of everybody concerned, and only after closure of the dam could factual sedimentation be observed.

SEDIMENTATION RECORDING

Shortly before closure of the dam in April 1955, a sand bar appeared on the inside of the first curve at the upper end of the reservoir. It was probably due to waste materials from the rock quarry a short distance upstream, but it continued to build up rapidly after the quarry was shut down. Shortly thereafter new sand and gravel bars appeared further downstream, bringing the sediment deposition into full view. By the end of 1955, a year of heavy flow, it was evident that the reservoir was filling rapidly and that controls had to be established to measure the sediment input. Accordingly, sounding-section stations were placed in suitable locations about 100 meters apart along the reservoir. These locations were plotted on the fairly accurate topographic maps made by the originators of the project. Cross sections of each sounding section were prepared using topographic maps since practically the entire section was under water or already covered by sediment. This series of cross sections was used as a basis for all future soundings and for plotting each new sounding profile. A large tabulation (Fig. 19–3) showed the volume in each sounding section for 5-meter intervals vertically. The first complete set of soundings was not made until December 1956, some twenty-one months after closure of the dam. Calculations revealed that the total sedimentation in this period was 1,188,000 cubic meters, or 23.4 percent of the reservoir volume. This record for an average flow of 98.5 cubic meters per second, roughly 5 percent above normal at the time, clearly indicates what could have happened with the average flow of 123 cubic

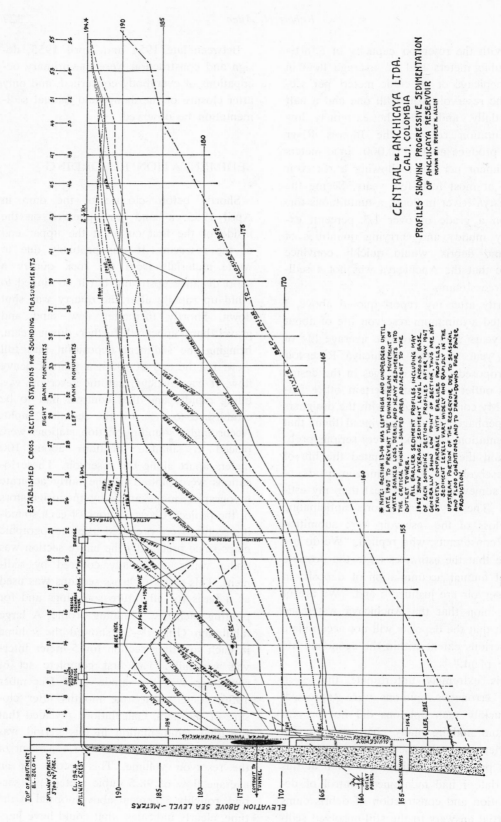

Figure 19-3 Anchicayá Reservoir, progressive sediment profiles

RECORD OF SEDIMENTATION IN ANCHICAYA RESERVOIR
ILLUSTRATED TABLES SHOW DATA RECORDED IN FIGURE 19-3

PERIOD BETWEEN SOUNDINGS	MONTHS	AVERAGE DAILY SEDIMENT DEPOSIT M³	AVERAGE FLOW ANCHICAYA RIVER M³/sec.	FLOW CONDITIONS
Mar. 1955-Dec. 1956	21	1880	98.5	Dr. Straub uses actual closure mid April for 20 mo: 1980-95.4. Above normal flow. Many large floods, one 1183 M³/sec.
Dec. 1956-Oct. 1957	10	560	60.0	Very low flow. Few small floods only
Oct. 1957-April 1958	6	1105	71.2	Low flow. No large floods
April 1958-Jan. 1959	9	1305	78.1	Low flow. Several minor, one major flood 1089 M³/sec.
Jan. 1959-Feb. 1960	13	1065	82.6	5 mo. low flow. Balance variable. Many small floods
Feb. 1960-Jan. 1961	11	1080	87.9	Near average flow. Many minor floods. One flood max. of record 1290 M³/sec.
Jan. 1961-Aug. 1962	19	647	77.0	Flow generally subnormal. Only few medium floods
Aug. 1962-Sept. 1963	13	652	77.8	Flow subnormal. Debris dams nearly full. One major flood 1146 M³/sec.
Sept. 1963-Oct. 1964	13	618	84.3	Flow near normal. Severe local floods. Rio Blanco flood 10/17/64
Oct. 1964-Dec. 1965	14	193	73.5	Below normal flow. Few floods. Max. flood 973 M³/sec. 11/9/65
Dec. 1965-May 1967	17		80.0	Below normal flow. No major floods. Max. 904 April 1966, 587 Aug. 1966

VOLUMETRIC ANALYSIS OF SEDIMENTATION

SOUND-ING DATE	DEAD STORAGE BELOW 185		ACTIVE STORAGE 185 TO 194.4		TOTAL STORAGE		PERCENTAGE OF STORAGE LOST		
	WATER VOLUME M³	SILT VOLUME	WATER VOLUME M³	SILT VOLUME	WATER VOLUME M³	SILT VOLUME	DEAD	AC-TIVE	TOTAL
At Closure 1955	2,695,200	0	2,385,816	0	5,081,016	0			
December 1956	1,853,458	841,742	2,039,772	346,044	3,893,230	1,187,786	31.4	14.5	23.4
October 1957	1,683,914	1,011,286	2,042,117	343,699	3,726,031	1,354,985	37.5	14.4	26.8
April 1958	1,554,719	1,140,481	1,972,724	413,092	3,527,443	1,553,573	42.3	17.3	30.6
January 1959	1,348,817	1,346,383	1,826,693	559,123	3,175,510	1,905,506	50.0	23.4	37.5
February 1960	1,038,737	1,656,463	1,720,873	664,943	2,759,610	2,321,406	61.4	27.9	45.7
January 1961	762,692	1,932,508	1,639,294	746,522	2,401,986	2,679,030	71.7	31.3	52.7
August 1962	481,180	2,214,020	1,552,827	832,989	2,034,007	3,047,009	82.1	34.9	60.0
September 1963	280,387	2,414,813	1,494,896	890,920	1,775,283	3,305,733	89.6	37.3	65.1
October 1964	200,936	2,494,264	1,329,547	1,056,269	1,530,483	3,550,533	92.6	44.3	69.9
December 1965	162,019	2,533,181	1,286,613	1,099,203	1,448,632	3,632,384	94.0	46.1	71.5
May 1967	Partial Survey Only. Total Water Volume to Sec. 25-26 848,000. Estimated Total Reservoir 1,000,000								80.±
January 1968	Partial Survey Only. Total Water Volume to Sec. 25-26 868,000.								

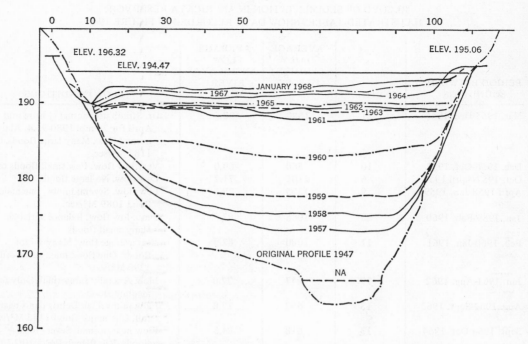

Figure 19–4 Progressive sediment cross section, Sounding Station 25–26, showing the gradual filling of the reservoir

meters per second in 1949–50. Since the increase in suspended load in most rivers varies at a rate somewhat greater than the square of the rate of discharge, the sediment volume could have been 70 percent higher or over 2,000,000 cubic meters, 40 percent of the reservoir capacity in twenty months. This theoretical calculation perfectly illustrates the hazard that exists at Anchicayá. Needless to say, the actual loss of 23.4 percent of the reservoir in about twenty-one months caused surprise and fully justified my previous estimates of the life of the reservoir (Fig. 19–4).

The second sediment sounding of October 1957 was received with some relief, since the new deposit was only 167,000 cubic meters in a ten-month period, with a very low average flow of only 60.0 cubic meters per second. However, in the intervening ten months aerial exploration on the proposed Upper Anchicayá project, new aerial photographs, a stadia survey in the

area, and a cost estimate all indicated that an upstream development on the Anchicayá would ultimately be constructed and help decrease sedimentation in the reservoir. Sites on the Digua River for future debris dams had been investigated. All of these were of vital interest to the future of Anchicayá Reservoir. Some excerpts and condensations from my 1957 report "Methods for Preventing Rapid Sedimentation of Anchicayá Reservoir" are of importance. Referring to the Anchicayá sedimentation records, I said, "Such conditions indicate the necessity of whatever measures can be taken to retard the sedimentation rate and prolong the life of the reservoir." I further described the general situation:

"Sediment deposited in reservoirs can be divided into two classes: first, the suspended sediment, normally only fine-grained to microscopic, which remains suspended in the flowing stream and slowly settles out as mud in relatively still water. This suspended sediment gives the water its muddy appearance, and settles out more or less uniformly over the entire still water portion of the reservoir. The second or bed load is that larger-grained material which is rolled along the bed of the stream and is deposited in sand or gravel bars wherever the flow velocity is decreased, and is immediately deposited when still water is reached. Such material immediately starts forming sand bars in the upstream end of a reservoir, the steeply inclined front of which advances downstream as more material is deposited. This bed load is the most serious in a reservoir since it deposits in the active storage section, thus immediately decreasing the regulatory storage available.

"There is no fixed dividing line between these two classes even in a single stream, since flood conditions with high velocity flow and great turbulence can readily carry sand and small gravel temporarily in suspension and will move immense boulders as bed load, whereas with normal stream flow the water may be clear with practically no suspended load except possibly colloidal matter and with bed load movement consisting only of small quantities of very fine sand. A major flood can thus deposit enormous quantities of heavy sediment in a reservoir in a short interval with a good percentage of the lighter suspended sediment passing on downstream, particularly in a small reservoir such as Anchicayá. Minor floods will carry less bed load but will deposit a larger percentage of the suspended sediment due to longer retention in the reservoir. Normal flow will deposit not only all the bed load, but practically all the suspended sediment, even in a relatively small reservoir.

"Silting of the reservoir is thus inevitable, but preventative measures can greatly increase the life thereof. The following quotations are taken from the *Handbook of Applied Hydraulics* by Davis, page 132, relative to the 'Control of Silt':

" 'Only in rare instances is the removal of silt from a reservoir by mechanical means justified economically. The removal of silt, once deposited, by reservoir sluices has never been particularly effective.'

" 'Usually though, watershed control is the only practical solution. In such cases, there may be economic justification for special check dams and debris barriers. Another solution is the construction of a silt barrier above the head of the reservoir. Owing to the tendency of debris to be deposited on a slope, there may develop large effective capacities.'

"Anchicayá Reservoir, with its extremely limited capacity and a mean stream flow sufficient to fill the reservoir 1.5 times a day, presents a particularly difficult problem in that even a very small percentage of silt in the flow will result in serious sedimentation in a relatively short period of time. The sharp V canyon surrounding the reservoir presents no possibility of removing sediment to adjacent areas. The known rapid sedimentation and the small reservoir capacity to be gained would probably never permit economical justification for raising the dam, although low flashboards could probably be used to advantage at some future time.

"There thus appear [to be] only the following solutions to the sedimentation problem: (1) Prevent as much of the sediment as possible from reaching the reservoir. (2) Utilize the sluice gates during periods of heavy flow, or of highly muddy inflow, to permit as much as possible of the suspended load to pass downstream. (3) Stop the continued deforestation which is taking place in the watershed, particularly that of the Digua, and prevent any future deforestation in the Upper Anchicayá basin. (4) Remove with a dredge as much of the sediment as is practical, discharging it downstream of the dam to be carried away by floods or water overflowing the dam.

"It appears that all of these methods will be required to retain the largest possible pondage for regulatory storage for the Anchicayá plant in the coming years."

The balance of the report elaborates on the methods outlined, suggests possible debris barrier sites in both the Digua and the Anchicayá, and the future major Upper Anchicayá project reservoir, and a possible upstream Digua hydro project called the Engaño, all these based on preventing sediment from reaching the reservoir.

The utilization of the sluice gates is also explained and justified. Prevention of deforestation is also given careful consideration and its benefits emphasized as the best, although to date the most neglected, method of prolonging the reservoir life. Lastly, reasons for obtaining a dredge immediately are outlined and recommended.

The report closes with the statement: "It is believed that the program of work outlined above will accomplish about all that can be expected, and about all that can possibly be economically justified in prolonging the life of Anchicayá Reservoir."

The reaction to the report was extremely favorable, and in another report dated December 11, 1957, I described the tentative bid of Ellicott Machine Corporation of Baltimore for a special 12-inch Dragon-type suction dredge and other accessories, and a tentative shore discharge line (later abandoned in favor of a discharge tunnel) economically justifying the purchase by preserving the peaking capacity of the plant.

Early in 1958 Dr. Lorenz G. Straub of Minneapolis, now deceased, a specialist in hydraulic problems, was retained to make a review of the sedimentation problems at Anchicayá. Dr. Straub reviewed the entire project with me. In October 1958, he submitted an extremely interesting report supplemented with photographs, drawings, and graphs. In his report, Dr. Straub had only three sounding records—the two already mentioned herein, and the third, of April 1958, covering only a six-month period with an average river flow of 72.5 cubic meters

per second, when an additional 192,600 cubic meters of sediment were deposited in the reservoir. The total sedimentation at the end of the thirty-six-month period after closure of the dam was 1,553,600 cubic meters, with an average river flow of 81.2 cubic meters per second, as compared with the long-term average flow of 92 cubic meters per second. Analyzing the existing data, Dr. Straub noted: "With all of these comparisons taken into account it must be accepted that the average annual rate of sedimentation in the reservoir is likely to be of the same order of magnitude as the three year average, or about 700,000 cubic meters annually. It must be further recognized by a review of earlier records that if the reservoir had been in operation during the hydrologic year October to September, 1949–50, a far greater sedimentation rate would have occurred, because for that year the runoff averaged 123 cubic meters per second, or about 135 percent of the long term average. Under such circumstances, the sedimentation in *one year* might well have been greater than occurred for the entire *three year period*."

Dr. Straub also noted that the three-year sedimentation period studied included part of the longest drought period in the Anchicayá records. This extremely dry period included March 1956 and terminated with May 1959, a thirty-nine-month period with an average flow of 69.5 cubic meters per second, and included the lowest twelve-month period of record, April 1957 through March 1958, in which the average flow was 62.8 cubic meters per second. Observations of the debris made on the Digua River during construction clearly showed that in periods of low flow, with the water clear, there was practically no movement of bed load and no deposition of sand or mud. A shallow pool some 20 meters long and 12 meters wide created in the river channel by an added lift in the dam showed nothing but organic debris, largely leaves, in two months' time. In contrast, every flood over the debris dams left immense deposits of sand and small gravel above the normal stream level above the dam, and these materials gradually washed downstream when the stream returned to normal.

Dr. Straub described the normal situation in the Digua River before the debris dams were constructed as follows:

A notable feature of the Digua is the so-called *playa* or beach area, which encompasses a stretch of about 6 kilometers upstream from a constricted section near the river mouth. Large quantities of gravel are deposited in the playa area; it has a relatively flat slope. During low flows, the river channel entrenches itself into the gravel bed. The conditions observed on the Digua are normal for a situation of this sort where there is a rigid constriction in the river channel which upstream has an erodible bed and a much wider channel. During high river flows the constriction produces backwater upstream in the much wider river channel. The wide channel in turn has much lower sediment transporting capacity for a given discharge than the normal breadth channel, resulting in a flattening of the slope and accumulation of sediment much the same as takes place at the head of the reservoir. The finer materials are, of course, carried entirely through the river length during all flows.

Dr. Straub's report analyzed the available data, using various formulae developed by him in his various previous studies. These analyses were supplemented by tests made in the hydraulic laboratory to duplicate Anchicayá conditions. He calculated the sizes of sediment, gravel, and small stones which can be moved into the reservoir with varying channel widths and flow velocities, and supplied a wealth of technical information, all closely confirming our known experience at Anchicayá. Of the various tables in Dr. Straub's report, the three included below are quite important and informative.

Table 19–1 shows that the river could transport 3″ material to the head of the reservoir 95 percent of the time during the initial sedimentation period, and 12-inch ma-

Table 19-1

ABILITY OF THE ANCHICAYA RIVER TO TRANSPORT BED LOAD MATERIALS OF VARIOUS SIZES DURING INTERVALS BETWEEN RESERVOIR SEDIMENTATION SURVEYS

INTERVAL BETWEEN SURVEYS	% OF TIME DURING WHICH FLOW OF RIVER WAS ADEQUATE TO TRANSPORT THE SPECIFIC SEDIMENT SIZES		
	3-inch Diameter	6-inch Diameter	12-inch Diameter
20 Months April 1955– December 1956	95	33	2.1
10 Months December 1956– October 1957	73	7.6	0
6 Months October 1957– April 1958	81	17.5	0

Sediment survey intervals were on mid-month basis.
River Breadth: 30 meters.
River Slope: S = 0.0158.

Table 19-2

FLOW AT WHICH BED LOAD TRANSPORTATION WILL START OVER AGGRADED BAR AT HEAD OF ANCHICAYA RESERVOIR

Estimated Bar Slope   S=0.0064
Breadth of Flow=B

SEDIMENT SIZE IN INCHES	B=25 METERS	B=50 METERS	B=75 METERS
3	87.8	176	264
6	245.5	490	736
12	691.0	1,382	2,073

Flows in cubic meters per second.

terial only 2.1 percent of the time. Table 19–3 indicates that 3-inch material could be transported across the bar at the head of the reservoir only 10.7 percent of the time during this same initial period. Table 19–2 clearly indicates that the larger bed load materials can only move across the bar during floods, and this explains the steep backwater curves of gravel and boulders above

Table 19–3

COMPUTED CAPACITY OF ANCHICAYA RIVER TO TRANSPORT MATERIAL OF
3-INCH SIZE OVER AGGRADED BAR AT HEAD OF ANCHICAYA RESERVOIR

PERIOD	DURATION OF PERIOD	% OF TIME WHEN BED LOAD TRANSPORTATION COULD OCCUR	ACCUMULATIVE TOTAL CUBIC METERS
April 1955– December 1956	20 months	10.7	211,000
December 1956– October 1957	10 months	0	0
October 1957– April 1958	6 months	2.9	6,150

Assumed Channel Breadth: 50 meters.
Assumed Bar Slope: S=0.0064.

the debris dams constructed later. Were it not for these backwater bars the quantity of bed load trapped behind the low debris dams would be relatively small. However, it must be remembered that these steep backwater bars could be washed down into the reservoir in a really major flood, unless the upstream destruction was so great that larger material would replace the existing material and actually increase the backwater bar slope; to date, there is very little backwater bar at the head of Anchicayá Reservoir except when the reservoir is drawn down. However, when the reservoir is low, large gravel bars are visible for some distance downstream, with the river confined to a narrow channel quite resembling the normal river channel above the reservoir and, until the reservoir level rises, quite capable of moving bed load similar to that listed in Table 19–1. This condition endangers the reservoir since the larger gravel continues to move downstream in the drawndown reservoir, covering finer materials capable of being removed by the dredge. Dr. Straub called special attention to this condition, mentioned previously in my reports, since it is one of the harmful results of drawing down the reservoir for the production of peak power.

Dr. Straub estimated that on the basis of the records then available, the sediment deposited in Anchicayá Reservoir would be about 700,000 cubic meters per year with normal flow, but stated specifically that the Anchicayá River was capable of transporting much more than this amount if it were available. He specifically recommended one or more hydraulic suction dredges to remove the 50,000 cubic meters per month deposit of sediment. To remove the gravel input, he estimated that two 12-inch dredges would be required. He also recommended the construction of low debris dams on the Digua River to prevent the bed load from reaching the reservoir, frankly stating, "One of the quite obvious steps to prolong the life of the reservoir is to prevent the gravel from escaping the Digua River as far as economically possible." His closing paragraph states: "In consideration of all aspects of the present situation, it would seem necessary to reconcile one's self to the fact that remedial measures to be taken in connection with the sedimentation of the Anchicayá Reservoir are a matter of expediency to take care of the peak load power requirements of the Cali area for as long a time as possible until the demands can be met by other means, including the possible construction of a proposed power development further upstream on the Anchicayá River. The measures that would be taken then would be in the nature of delaying action rather than permanent remedial measures. The present Anchicayá development would then eventually revert to a run-of-the-river plant without being obliged to furnish peak power."

THE DIGUA DEBRIS DAMS

My November 1957 report proposed construction of the first debris dam in the 300-meter restricted section of the Digua River, just above its junction with the Anchicayá, and below the last major *playa* section of the Digua. It was decided to build a dam bridging the deep canyon between hard abutments in a site where an immense quartzitic block existed in midstream. This site was considered satisfactory for a very unusual type of overflow dam slightly arched between abutments, the center resting on the big rock block, the right half on gravel at 3 meters below the water surface, and the left half part on solid rock and gravel. Both abutments against hard solid rock with a ski-jump on the downstream face 1.5 meters below water. When Dr. Straub visited the site in July 1958, construction was already under way using a method I had planned of switching the river through sluiceways to one side or the other of the center block as the dam progressed upward. Careful planning of every move permitted excellent progress despite numerous floods passing over the dam.

The dam stopped all downstream movement of sand and gravel as soon as construction rose above river level. As a result, existing sand bars downriver were rapidly scoured out, causing a surprising 30- to 50-centimeter lowering of the flow level, fully confirming my opinion that the Upper Anchicaya supplied only a small percentage of the total sediment reaching the reservoir. Our opinion was that the Digua watershed, already badly deforested, supplied only

about 30 percent of the river flow, but 75 percent of the sediment. We later increased this estimate to about 80 percent.

Digua No. 1, also called K-81, was planned as a massive dam, 12 meters wide at the base and 3 meters below water level with a wide ogee crest at 7 meters above water, to be built in stages to avoid trapping too much fine material instead of the heavier gravels. The initial stage was 4 meters. It was later raised to 8 meters with sluiceways at 7.2; then the right portion was raised to 9 meters in 1961 as it still exists today, not yet passing heavy bed load over the 7.2-meter-high spillways.

The instant success of this first debris dam, only partly completed, fully justified a second dam further upstream. The proposed design here was to construct the spillway, with temporary crest at 2.2 meters above the river level, then to use a riprap section between spillway and right bank with crest at 5 meters, ultimately to be covered with concrete on both upstream and downstream faces. This dam was practically completed in 1960 with final spillway at 4.0 meters, and after several floods safely passed over the dam, the largest flood on record, on December 12, 1960, created a flood crest of about 2.5 meters over the riprap crest, removing therefrom and depositing downstream blocks of riprap of over 10 tons in weight. Emergency measures had to be taken to return the flow to the sluiceways, bridge with a heavy concrete beam the gap caused by the loss of riprap, then replenish the riprap and the upstream gravel fill, and immediately place the concrete cover, all of which was completed by the middle of 1961. In this dam, the upstream gravel deposit practically kept pace with the construction, and the gravel-boulder upstream backwater curve was already well developed before final completion. The height of this dam, which raised the water level 4 meters, was controlled by the road elevation some 300 meters upstream, where the roadway had been covered with water during several floods. This dam could be raised several meters, but any increase in height would require raising several hundred meters of highway adjacent to a nearly vertical hillside.

The very rapid increase in slope of the backwater curve above both of these dams soon demonstrated that there was no vital need, except greater security, for placing dams at the two other sites originally planned, since these sites had somewhat less water level capacity, and the boulder backwater curve had quickly raised the river bed at these sites by more than 2 meters.

No exact measurements of the sediment trapped behind these two dams are possible but approximations from topographic maps indicate that probably over 500,000 cubic meters total sediment, mostly bed load, had been trapped by the end of 1967. Almost all bed load now passes the upper dam, but the downstream Digua No. 1 continues to trap the heavier bed load and will retain a large additional amount of heavy bed load when finally raised to full height.

THE ANCHICAYÁ DREDGE

Everyone finally admitted that the only way to retain the Anchicayá Reservoir was to remove the suspended load sediment deposit of around 50,000 cubic meters per month average with a dredge, although

mechanical devices were considered. Also, there was general agreement that the lighter sediments could readily be dumped over the dam to be carried away by floods, without any particular hazard until the size of the material dredged became too large. No money was available for purchase of a dredge, but IBRD representatives were convinced of the need and required a definite plan and cost estimate. Moreover, the success of the Digua debris dams had temporarily changed the sedimentation picture somewhat. Since I had presented the idea of a dredge discharge tunnel to greatly shorten the discharge line requirements and the power requirements of the proposed dredge, Dr. Straub was requested to review the new conditions and study the possible use of the proposed dredge tunnel to reduce the size and cost of the 14-inch oversize dredge then under consideration.

Dr. Straub released his second report on June 4, 1960, which included the two additional sediment reports.

Dr. Straub noted that the Digua dams apparently prevented about 10,000 cubic meters per month of heavy sediments from reaching the reservoir despite larger average river flows and reduced the estimated sediment to be removed by the dredge to around 40,000 cubic meters per month, but he did not mention any specific dredge size. (Luckily, we finally retained the 14-inch size.) He also made a very careful mathe-

Table 19–4

PERIOD	TIME (MONTHS)	ADDED DEPOSITION OF SEDIMENT (CUBIC METERS)	MONTHLY AVERAGE (CUBIC METERS)	DAILY FLOW (CUBIC METERS PER SECOND)
Mid-April 1958 to mid-January 1959	9	351,900	39,100	77.1
Mid-January 1959 to mid-February 1960	13	415,900	32,000	84.2

matical analysis to determine the best practical slope and shape of the proposed tunnel invert, if concreted, to handle the largest gravel expected, and recommended that the slope of the dredge tunnel should be greater than 5 percent and near 7 percent if possible.

Since his report fully recommended the use of the discharge tunnel, the revised plan was quickly approved by the Anchicayá Board, and we were authorized to proceed with the tunnel, the entrance tower, the wharf and roadway leading thereto, and the shore anchors, all to be constructed by Anchicayá crews. After some study of the dredge problem, somewhat complicated by special Anchicayá problems such as operation from shore anchors, a 25-meter dredging depth, and a constantly varying water level due to peak power demands, a more liberal plan of requesting informal bids was used. Bidders were invited to discuss their proposals and possible modifications thereof. As a result, a contract was finally awarded to the Ellicott Machine Corporation of Baltimore, for a specially designed Dragon-type 14-inch Hydraulic Dredge with underwater hydraulic motor driving the cutterhead and "outrigger" Sponson tanks as stabilizers with an A-frame support for the sheaves for lifting the ladder.

The dredge was shipped in factory-assembled pieces suitable for transport to the reservoir and was assembled on and adjacent to the small wharf, using a P & H dragline equipped as a crane. The main section consists of six tanks bolted together forming an assembly 17.68 meters long, 6.71 wide, and 1.83 high. The main pump is mounted centrally and low, with two diesel engine drive. Forward and at deck level is a comparable diesel engine driving an auxiliary water pump, degassing unit, oil pumps, etc. Further forward and also completely aft are the multiple winches for the operating cables at deck level. Further forward is the hinge joint for the 37-meter ladder and the rubber hose for the suction pipe, and at each side are large trusses connecting the dredge with the Sponson tanks. The ladder, suction pipe, and trusses all contain a 10-meter removable section to adjust the dredge for more shallow dredging, but this feature has not been used to date. The degassing unit is especially required to remove the gas released by the decaying organic matter which would otherwise seriously decrease the pump suction. In the reservoir, gas bubbles continually rise to the surface, and when the water level is being lowered rapidly, the water almost appears to be boiling. The gas is combustible, probably marsh gas, and at one time I wondered about its concentration as an explosion hazard; but the gas is so light it dissipates very rapidly with no hazard whatsoever, and the bubbling seems to have decreased in quantity.

The only operating difficulty not fully anticipated comes from battered pieces of trees, about 2 to 3 feet long and 4 to 7 inches in diameter, which enter the cutterhead, then lodge in the knife compartment just ahead of the pump impeller. Since these pieces are too large or strong to be cut or broken by the knife at the entrance to the pump impeller, they rapidly collect smaller debris requiring immediate stopping of the pump, the opening of the quick removable cover, and the manual extraction of the trapped material. This may happen a few or many times a day, depending upon what is encountered in dredging, and often causes lost time. In an effort to correct this condition, large bars were welded in the spaces between the cutters of the cutterhead, but they proved impractical since banana plants, branches, and vines quickly wrapped around the cutterhead. Lifting the ladder to clear the cutterhead was found to take more time than removing the small logs from the knife compartment. During floods, floating debris hangs up on the ladder, trusses, and cables to a dangerous degree and dredging must stop until such debris is removed. Usually the discharge line on the pontoons is quickly disconnected and anchored to shore for safety, but one small piece was carried away over the dam.

The problem of sunken logs and trees has been less than anticipated, but in portions of the reservoir near the discharge tunnel entrance, which has been dredged several times, the bottom of the excavation is almost "paved" with sunken logs. Contrary to conditions in temperate zones with large seasonal changes, the tropical jungle remains permanently green. It "feeds itself" with the continually falling leaves, debris and rotting trees. Almost all cut trees are heavier than water. Leaves falling into the water rarely remain on the surface. Largely because of turbulence, most of the battered tree trunks carried down the Anchicayá barely float; they usually sink upon reaching quiet water. We have always estimated that about 10 percent of the deposits in Anchicayá Reservoir are of organic origin, and Dr. Straub expressed the same opinion. Luckily, the smaller organic materials rapidly decompose in the relatively warm water (about 23° C).

Our original plan at Anchicayá was to mount a winch, boom, and some sort of orange-peel bucket or grapple on the dredge, but this proved completely impractical because of the operating cables attached to shore anchors. Then it was decided to mount the handling equipment on a barge, but only recently has this equipment been placed in operation due to the urgent need to remove sunken logs from in front of the sluiceway trashracks at the dam. A letter just received mentions removing tree trunks up to 2 feet in diameter and 14 feet in length from in front of the trashracks, with even larger trunks in view but not yet removed.

OPERATING PERIOD— AUGUST 1962–1967

Late 1962 was the end of the active construction period, with the dredge in operation and the two Digua debris dams constructed. The dams were already nearly full and the backwater curve of heavy gravel continually steepened with deposit of larger gravel and cobbles. This rapid buildup of the backwater deposits made any additional low debris dams almost useless. I proposed raising the Digua No. 3 dam as an alternative to constructing proposed Digua No. 4, but this would have required raising some 700 meters of highway. Another proposed site between Digua No. 1 and Digua No. 3 dams was suitable for a large rock-fill dam high enough to swamp Digua No. 3 if desired, but a long relocation for the highway would be required. Neither project materialized.

Sediment deposits in the reservoir continued to increase. Originally, the dredge was operated only on a single ten-hour shift, and its operation became a routine lacking any inspiration. Even the conduction tunnel trashracks were found to be nearly sealed on two occasions, and the funnel-shaped hole in front of the trashracks continued to become more hazardous. My recommendations for more operation of the dredge bore fruit but it was never employed full-time. We continued to lose reservoir capacity to sediment. The amount of sediment reaching the reservoir increased as the destruction of the jungle continued and rapidly spread into the Upper Anchicayá watershed.

In the October 1964 soundings, capacity of the reservoir had already been reduced to about 1,530,000 cubic meters. This survey was made just after the very disastrous flood in the Rio Blanco area, a tributary of the Digua River, which overnight placed an estimated 60,000 cubic meters of sediment in the reservoir and left in the river possibly an equal amount which ultimately reached the reservoir. The total flow reached a peak of 638 cubic meters per second at 5 A.M. on the Danubio gauging station, but apparently the maximum discharge of the Rio Blanco was around 400 cubic meters per second. A report was made on this highly unusual flood, since Anchicayá had for two previous years contracted for cloud seeding in an effort to obtain more flow in the river, and this Rio Blanco flood started just short of twenty-four hours after the smoke pots were shut down. During the contract period we had experienced several unusual and highly damaging floods in small areas, and an area just west of the Anchicayá basin had apparently received above-average precipitation. In checking these results we were informed that seeding could result in precipitation as much as twenty-four hours after seeding. The Rio Blanco flood was thus a borderline case, and as is usual, there was no way to prove what really happened. In any event, the cloud-seeding contract was not renewed.

Forty-three new landslides were reported in the area covered by the Rio Blanco flood, mostly of soft materials of an orange color readily identified. The regimen of the Rio Blanco was largely destroyed. Our wharf area at Anchicayá received a deposit of 20 to 25 centimeters of this orange mud and several mysterious mud balls where less than a meter of water had covered the wharf for something less than twenty-four hours. This quantity of deposit gives an idea of the enormous suspended-sediment content of this flood, since it was left by water, which had already passed through two kilometers of relatively quiet reservoir. The previous maximum deposit recorded was 15 centimeters during a larger flood of longer duration. The Rio Blanco flood carried an enormous amount of silt and debris, uprooted trees were left along the riverbanks, and the conduction trashracks were nearly blocked with debris. An inclined ¾-inch cable used for concrete chutes attached to the left abutment of Digua No. 1 dam accumulated so much debris that it snapped. My reports had repeatedly warned that a single flood could deposit more sediment in the reservoir in a day than normally is deposited in a month, and this flood did exactly that. I certainly hope that no major flood hits Anchicayá, since even a 2000-meter flood will probably flood the plant and possibly completely fill the reservoir.

I was somewhat irritated by this long operating period with worsening conditions. Time was running out on the reservoir, with no action leading to better conditions. In November 1965 I wrote a ten-page memorandum describing the increasing seriousness of the sediment and other problems and the approach of the run-of-the-river condition at Anchicayá. I once again urged consideration of my Upper Anchicayá project, first presented in 1956–57, and also suggested the possibilities of placing the proposed power plant below the Anchicayá Dam to lessen the difficult sediment problem, or just above the dam, with suitable works to utilize the existing plant.

Toward the end of 1965 I noted a revival of interest in both the Upper Anchicayá project and the Anchicayá Reservoir, probably stimulated by realization that the proposed intertie line to supply the Cali area with power from Bogotá was being seriously delayed and, even when its first stage was completed, would probably not supply the required power.

On January 17, 1966, and finally on February 15, 1966, I issued long memoranda covering various methods of preparing the Anchicayá plant for run-of-the-river conditions, for obtaining more power from Anchicayá by coordinating with the Calima plant which had been recently placed in operation, and again presenting my Upper Anchicayá project as the best way to solve the power problem. I do not know whether these last reports were instrumental in the sudden renaissance of my "pet project," but activity started early in 1966.

THE RENAISSANCE

Early in 1966, the CVC organization of which Anchicayá is a part was at long last interested in the Upper Anchicayá project which I had proposed, and former Anchicayá manager, Luis E. Palacios, had tried to promote some eight years previously. Trails were cut into the area rapidly, surveys and mapping were initiated, stream-gauging stations were established, preliminary geological investigations made, all existing data on weather, stream flow, and sediment records were assembled. The upper Anchicayá Preliminary Feasibility Report was issued on October 31, 1966. A large Feasibility Report jointly prepared by CVC and Acres International Limited of Niagara Falls, Canada, was issued in April 1968.

This project uses a damsite marked as alternate on my first preliminary 1957 plan which remained unstudied then despite a stadia survey carried in to near the damsite. The CVC power plant is on the exact location I proposed in 1957, on the upper end of Anchicayá Reservoir. The new plant will have a dam with normal pool elevation of 646 meters, an active storage of 30 million cubic meters, between 646 and 615 meters elevation, and a dead storage of 15 million cubic meters below 615 meters. The power tunnel will be 8.3 kilometers long, have a 5.5-meter inside diameter, and terminate in a 460-meter inclined shaft and 240 meters of steel lined tunnel. The underground power plant will have four 85-megawatt units for a total of 340 megawatts, an average continuous output of 201 megawatts, and an annual energy production of $1760 \times$ 10^6 kilowatt-hours, at an estimated cost of 4.1 U.S. mills per kilowatt-hour. The average flow is estimated at 56.0 cubic meters per second or about two-thirds of that at the Anchicayá Danubio gauging station. Full financing is imminent; initial construction work is already under way, and heavy construction will probably start early in 1969.

This intense activity has had a decidedly invigorating effect on Anchicayá personnel. A new station chief has taken intense interest in the dredge and sediment problems. The trashracks were found to be badly encrusted, apparently due to natural causes and unsatisfactory operation of the trashrack rake, and the area in front of the sluiceway trashrack was almost completely filled with tree trunks, timber, and debris. The funnel-shaped hole at the outlet tower was in a very hazardous condition, as I had previously mentioned. After soundings were used to map the sediment, and divers checked the conditions adjacent to the outlet tower, plans were made to remove by stages the generally small-grained light sediment between sounding section 13–14 and the dam. In previous years, when Anchicayá was the only major source of power, this section had been purposely left high to prevent trunks and major debris from moving downstream. The completion of the Calima plant permitted safe removal in this area and around the outlet tower. Three-shift operation of the dredge was approved, and an experienced dredge operator was obtained from Ellicott to again demonstrate efficient dredge operation. Additional dredge discharge pipe was obtained. Lastly, a barge with a special clamshell bucket was placed in operation to remove sunken logs from around the outlet tower. No report is yet available as to total gain in storage due to 1968 operations, but a recently received letter mentions that approximately 800,000 cubic meters of fine sediment has been easily removed from the downstream end of the reservoir.

RECOMMENDATIONS FOR FUTURE RESERVOIR MAINTENANCE

The proposed development of the Upper Anchicayá Project demands the maintenance of Anchicayá for as long as possible. Particular study was therefore given to the sediment problem, and six single-spaced pages cover the analysis and recommendations in the April 1968 Alto Anchicayá Project Feasibility Report, excerpts of which follow: "This power plant [Anchicayá] appears to be seriously endangered by the ever-increasing sedimentation of its reservoir, which within a period of 12 years has caused the almost complete loss of pondage, forcing the plant to change from peak load operation to a run-of-the-river plant. Continued sedimentation may cause an appreciable increase in the riverbed elevation at the tailrace outfall of the scheme of development for the Alto Anchicayá Project.

"The present [March 1968] water storage in the reservoir is estimated as about 1,000,-000 m³. At the rate of net deposition in the reservoir which has prevailed in recent years it can only be a short while before the existing power tunnel intake is blocked and the power plant is rendered useless. For a high flood of the same order of magnitude as the highest of record (1290 m³/sec.) a deposition of about 100,000 m³ of sediment has been estimated.

"Recommended measures: The existing 14-inch Ellicott suction dredge should continue to remove deposited materials from the reservoir. Information available on the existing dredge indicates that it should be possible to remove as much or even more material from the reservoir as there is flowing in.

"With the present equipment, material up to one inch in size may be handled effectively. All larger material cannot be handled and will deposit permanently in the reservoir. If it were possible to make the volume of the reservoir presently occupied by fines [fine sediment] available for storage of coarse sediments, then the complete siltation of the reservoir could be delayed by an estimated additional 25 years. Coarse materials are creeping in from the head of the reservoir, depositing on top of layers of previously deposited fines. When a sufficient volume of coarse materials exists over fine layers, inversion of the two materials may be carried out by injecting high-pressure water into the fines, causing the coarse sizes to sink and the fines to float to higher elevations where they will be picked up by the natural current in the reservoir and carried further downstream to then be removed by the suction dredge. When the deposition of coarse materials in the river begins to raise the water level at the location of the proposed Alto Anchicayá tailrace outfall, canalization of the river through the sediments downstream from this location is recommended. It has been estimated that all of the remedial measures described would postpone a possible interference with the full utilization of the presently available head by the Alto Anchicayá Plant for approximately 25 years.

"Suitable mechanical equipment would be installed for continuous removal of large-size deposited material in an area upstream from the present location of the suction dredge. Fine material would continue to be removed by the dredge and the area of the reservoir in front of the power tunnel intake would be kept free of sediments by the periodic opening of the bottom sluices of the dam; the coarse materials would be transported by an aerial ropeway into an adjacent valley."

Personally, I believe there is a good percentage of "wistful thinking" involved in this planning for a full flow through the existing Anchicayá plant, and I would have preferred that the new plant be constructed a short way below the existing dam, utilizing the total head and consigning the existing plant to a secondary role, or that the new plant be just above the dam, with discharge duct across the dam or reservoir to a specially-created small forebay to the existing plant, with skimming devices to utilize the remaining Digua flow only when reasonably clear.

I heartily approve the inversion plan for lowering the heavy sediments, but discount somewhat major movement downstream of the sand since the reservoir will normally be retained at near dam crest, with very low reservoir velocities initially or until the backwater rise of the gravel creates greater slopes. The heavy material cover over the fine sediment was almost entirely the result of drawing down the reservoir for peak power.

Moreover, I am thoroughly convinced that a major debris dam should be constructed in the Digua after the Buenaventura-Buga highway is completed and traffic can be diverted from the present Simón Bolívar highway.

Lastly, I do not believe that proper consideration has been given to the hazard of a major flood, since I consider that a 2000 cubic meters per second flood would swamp the Anchicayá plant, possibly even filling the existing reservoir with sediment, and might carry the dredge to destruction. Such a flood is a serious possibility.

Another feature is that the Feasibility Report barely mentions the extremely vital deforestation problem on the Digua. However, the following quotation indicates that, at long last, the importance of deforestation has been recognized: "At present the area surrounding the site [Alto Anchicayá] and upstream water courses is thickly vegetated (tropical jungle), and the CVC is taking strict measures to prevent settlement and clearing of forest in the watershed. Settlers have been relocated and all former agricultural clearings have reverted to jungle and will remain in that condition. The new reservoir will therefore not be subject to the severe sedimentation which occurred in the Anchicayá Reservoir." Another paragraph indicates that a periodic air patrol will check any future entry of settlers or destruction of the jungle.

This lengthy report is actually only a very brief summary of nearly seventeen years spent at Anchicayá, largely on transmission line and power plant and heavy construction work. The major concern, however, was concentrated on the ever present sedimentation problem, completely ignored and unmentioned by the originators of the project and the later consultants.

I hope that this report will be of assistance to those who may become involved in similar problems in the future.

DISCUSSION

BATISSE: I would like to say a few words on a particular case study in Tunisia. Much of the water in Tunisia has a salinity of more than 1,000 parts per million. This should mean according to U.S. standards that the water is unsuitable for irrigation. Of course, the Tunisians have been irrigating with this water for hundreds of years; they have no other water. With this starting point, we have developed with the UNDP, a project in Tunisia to discover the best possible method of irrigation with water of 1,000 ppm and up to 6,000 ppm. The results have been, I would say, quite successful.

The project has a central laboratory in Tunisia and three experiment stations: one in northern Tunisia where there is moderate rainfall, one in central Tunisia where there is less rainfall, and one in the desert where there is practically no rainfall. The answer, of course, has been devising adequate drainage in relation to the soil conditions in the various schemes. I think the interesting point about this experiment, which probably applies to countries other than Tunisia, is twofold:

First, that a systematic study of the physical and chemical conditions in the country led to results within a fairly short period of time. In the present case, such work has been going on for about five years.

The other relevant conclusion is that what is good for one country may not necessarily be good for another. And probably the *Riverside Handbook,* which says that water of more than 1,000 ppm salinity is no good for irrigation, applies to a particular economic and social situation—namely, that of California—which, of course, is very different from the social and economic situation of Tunisia. For Tunisia, the use of this water for irrigation helped by the drainage which has been developed brings results which are of real social and economic value. These results, where extended on a larger scale can raise agricultural production of the country.

M. T. FARVAR: Dr. Michel, what relative amount of the arable land in West Pakistan is affected by salinization and waterlogging, and how seriously?

MICHEL: The trouble with estimating relative amounts is that salinity, as you are undoubtedly aware, exists in differing percentages, in differing intensities. These change from season to season, from year to year. It will vary with the strength of the monsoon, and its effects on crops will vary.

One point that most people don't realize until they get into the arid zone is that not every field is cultivated every year even when water is available. In the Indus Basin, particularly, it is unusual for the same crop to be sown in the same field year after year or even for the same field to be cultivated season after season. This is a form of rotation, if you like, but it still includes fallowing in order to restore, principally, some of the nitrates to the soil.

When the Revelle panel was sent to West Pakistan by President Kennedy in 1962, it found estimates by Pakistanis that 100,000 acres were going out of cultivation each year in a net sown area of 23 million acres.

The Revelle panel very quickly had to revise those figures and said: "Between 50,-000 and 100,000 additional acres are being affected each year, some of which are passing out of crop production." They estimated that of the 23 million acres annually canal-irrigated and sown to at least one crop, about 5 million had been seriously damaged. But, again, you have to define what you mean by serious damage. Serious damage for a field that traditionally is sown to wheat is not serious damage for a field that is now being sown to rice. In fact, as I tried to point out in the paper, rice is a semi-salt-tolerant crop, and you actually get a better yield of calories from growing rice on a field that used to bear wheat. The problem in the Indus Basin, of course, is that the West Pakistanis are wheat eaters.

Aside from those estimates given in the Revelle report, I can't be exact about this figure. Yours is a highly relative question.

M. T. FARVAR: Well, you say that something like 5 million acres are affected, which varies according to different estimates. How are these acres affected by being waterlogged and salinized? What is the criterion used?

MICHEL: Yields of wheat or of cotton are reduced. How can you measure these problems in a given acre that one year is sown to wheat, the next year is fallow, in the third year has a good monsoon with a heavy leaching rain, and in the fourth year has a very dry spell when capillarity and evaporation raise a great deal of salts to the surface?

I know you like to be very specific in your case studies, but I don't think that this particular subject matter is susceptible to that type of specificity. Our knowledge is simply inadequate.

BATISSE: There have also been experiments made by Dr. Boyko in Israel with sea water and mixtures of sea water with fresh water. But these were very special conditions of very efficient drainage on sand dunes and very specific crops. Most were certain reeds which have limited economic value. The water used for this had a salt content in the order of 17,000 ppm. I don't think this can be of general application.

SCUDDER: Is there any plant-breeding program to develop more salt-tolerant crops?

TIMOTHY: There are a number of projects in which breeding programs are in progress for salt tolerance on certain grasses; one of these is on Bermuda grasses, and the others on grasses used in the mountain states. There is a program in California on selecting salt-resistant soybeans.

Another project, although not concerned primarily with food, is a salt spray and sand dune stabilization program in North Carolina for selecting different kinds of dune binding reeds and grasses. I don't know how well these varieties will resist concentrations of salt, but the recently released Hatteras beachgrass resulted from this program.

COMMONER: At the risk of being too general, I think some comments are in order here.

I am impressed with the fact that the discussion we have just been hearing deals with efforts to cope with a situation which is in disequilibrium. As far as I can tell, and I am no expert on this, what is happening in Pakistan cannot be allowed to go on indefinitely. In other words, the process is one which is inevitably deteriorating the quality of the soil.

I think it makes little difference at what point the salinity becomes economically disastrous. The real question that has to be asked is: Is the process of irrigation one which will conserve the equilibrium which is essential to the biological usefulness of the soil? In other words, you start with an equilibrium condition which is economically undesirable. Disequilibrium is introduced, for economic reasons, which then deteriorates the soil. And the question is: Will the system ever return to equilibrium given the process that is under way? The optimist says there may be an artificial technological fix which will restore equilibrium. However, it is very important for us to remember that the sodbuster approach ignores the need for equilibrium. This approach says: "Here is an equilibrium situation; I will grab what I can out of it and not worry about what happens next." We may say that this "aquifer buster" approach has been used in many areas.

The last comment I want to make stems from what Ray Dasmann said earlier. What is needed here is not an ecologist to say, "Don't do this"; what is needed is a very simple aspect of the ecological way of thinking which asks: "What happens next?" I think Dr. Michel put this very well in his paper when he noted that it was a novelty for engineers to ask: "How will the aquifer be restored?"

And I would suggest that ecology ought to be taught to engineers in order to make them worry about the consequences of what they do.

This is, I confess, a little propaganda, but I think it is worth bringing in.

MICHEL: I agree with everything Dr. Commoner has said. In the Indus Basin, the engineers started with surface water irrigation. About forty years ago, these surface water engineers realized what they were doing, realized that they were filling up the water table and that this surface water irrigation was a self-defeating system. Then some of them wondered: "Can we use the tube well designed for ground water irrigation as a means of drainage?" And this is the approach which was developed over the next twenty years or so.

Now our contemporary engineers in West Pakistan realize that they have a one-shot resource in the slowly-accumulated, fresh water layer at the top of the ground water reservoir. I think they understand that if they are going to mine this water it is going to be gone when they draw it down to 50 or 100 feet and that they have got to use that mined water, fossil water, to undo the effects of the surface water irrigation. At the end of this process, perhaps around the year 2000, they hope to start a new equilibrium.

But if I may just add this: There are still going to be some geographical and political sacrifices, because you still have to do something with the effluent. You are still going to have what I call the sink of the lower Indus or what John Hay calls the bottom of the bucket. The Revelle panel implied that Sind, which is at the bottom of the bucket, is going to have to forgo any expansion and perhaps even accept a reduction in acreage and allow their crops to be grown upstream, where the quality of the water will be better. In fact one can make a very good case that the main reason for the Tarbella Dam is a boon to Sind to keep water coming down the Indus to dilute the salt that comes down from the Punjab.

HAY: Dr. Michel has said you can mine water in the Indus Basin to a certain extent. But in talking about most arid countries, such as Arizona in our own Southwest, there is not enough surface flow and not enough drainage to take away your salts. When you irrigate with surface water in canals or anything else, you are leaching salt out of your land. And that salt has got to go somewhere. Salt water is heavier than fresh water; it goes underground, and it goes downstream.

It is all very well if you have got something like the Mississippi River or the Nile that has a regular flow into the ocean where it can dump salts. But in the Upper Rio Grande and many other rivers in arid countries, there are underground dikes in the river channel (for example where it hits a narrow mountain pass) which give you a closed basin underneath the ground. In the case of a river like the Rio Grande, where there is not enough water in the first place, the water that you get is used on your fields. Salt is being constantly added and goes underground or downriver until you hit the bottom of the barrel or a dike; then the saline water cannot go anywhere.

You can mine that water as much as you want, but you are still not getting rid of your salt no matter how many drains you have. This is a problem that has got to be faced politically, perhaps through getting fresh water from some other source, or giving up, because there isn't that kind of water in arid countries. There is not enough fresh water to wash the salt down and get it going into the ocean.

ALLEN: The Salton Sea is becoming so salty from the irrigation drain water that fish life is decreasing and may disappear entirely unless very costly remedial measures are taken. More and more miles of drains are being added to conserve the area presently irrigated with Colorado River water, but salinization problems are increasing. Already much land is unfit for cultivation. As salinity increases, yields of the less salt-resistant crops no longer provide profits, thus causing a change to a more salt-resistant crop, then a still more salt-resistant crop. But, the "end of the rope" is finally reached, causing abandonment of the land.

PHILLIPS: Mr. Chairman, there has been some discussion about equilibrium and disequilibrium. In the subdesert and arid sectors of South Africa, where the great Orange River project is to be concerned with a catchment of 328,000 square miles, equilibrium and disequilibrium in practice could be very significant.

Looking back 100 to 125 years, even 75 years in some sections of the Orange River Catchment, we see an arid area which earlier supported seminomadic men, a limited number of cattle, sheep, goats, and wild animals. There was a fair equilibrium among climate, soil, and the general ecosystem.

Then European man put an increasing pressure on the ecosystem. Today we see much disequilibrium. There is erosion and siltation in the valley of the Orange. Unquestionably, there will be siltation in the great dams which are being constructed, unless constant, effective control be exercised.

It is some consolation that several years ago the authorities commenced various ecological, pedological, economic, and other surveys of the existing situation and its meaning for the future. I believe that the disequilibrium that now exists in this area will not be readily readjusted. We shall not have a dynamic equilibrium on a sufficient scale in time to prevent much siltation and other deterioration.

Looking now to the Euphrates in Syria, one can also foresee a tremendous amount of prospective siltation. What has happened fairly rapidly in parts of the Orange Catchment has happened through millennia in the Middle East. These are very real problems. It will not be easy to reintroduce a dynamic equilibrium on a vast scale where man and his modern technology have been active for even a comparatively short time.

M. T. FARVAR: I would like to comment on an important problem mentioned in Achi's paper on Algeria. In that country the effect of salinization in the Sahara has been to create a monoculture of palm groves in large areas such as Touggourt, where, before these irrigation projects started, the people used to plant a large variety of crops and garden vegetables for subsistence between the palm rows. In the past, some 15 or 20 palms were enough to bring income supplementary to the people's subsistence.

Once this monoculture of palms is created it takes quite a number of palm trees, 80 to 90 palms at least, to support a family, because the yields of palm trees are constantly reduced. Often the government is the only one rich enough to run the monoculture.

The salinization of the soil is so high now that most of this land has been abandoned by the subsistence farmers who could no longer make a go of it. This leads into another question: What happens to the people who were driven off the land because their subsistence way of life was lost? In Algeria, by government's admission, unemployment rates are something on the order of 50 per cent or more in the cities. When one travels through Algeria, even the very arid parts of the country south of the Atlas Mountains, one is totally amazed by the extent to which such things as mechanization have been introduced. An immediate response to the introduction of machines is that many people simply must leave the land.

Salinization again has the same kind of effect. People must give up their land and they then flock into the cities. Similar problems exist all around the world. Perhaps Dr. Hardoy and you, Mr. Chairman, or other people can comment on this. But we have other cities swollen by the rural unemployed everywhere. In Cairo, there are close to 5 million people. Algiers is a sea of unemployed people. Tehran has at least 35 per cent unemployed.

What I am arguing for, in other words, is that attention be paid to the interdependence of causative factors; salinization does not end in itself; salinization is responsible for the destruction of an essential way of life in Algeria without its having been replaced with anything equally functional.

SCUDDER: This is a comment which relates to some of my own research. A majority of the Egyptian Nubian population, which has been influenced through time by the development of the Aswan system, now are urban residents. In fact, it is the first African population that we know of where well over 60 or 70 per cent of what was formerly a rural population is now resident in urban areas. Of course, this is in large part a result of the whole development of the Aswan Basin.

As you say, this urban immigration is occurring throughout Africa and many other parts of the world. It is not sufficient to have just an emphasis on increasing production; we must have a dual emphasis on production plus jobs. Many of these so-called solutions to the production problem, such as increasing mechanization, are often not really helpful because they are not providing jobs. Hence, of course, you have these fantastic, almost hidden unemployment rates; in cities like Nairobi, presumably well over 25 per cent of your manpower moving into the cities are then unemployed. There have been some studies showing that if the Kenya six-year development plan meets its goals, still 50 per cent of the manpower coming of age during that period will be unemployed because of the capital-intensive nature of many of these projects.

So we do have a two-pronged problem here—not just meeting the food needs of a growth in population, but also facing the problem of providing jobs to a rapidly increasing population, jobs that will meet their minimal needs and also their rising expectations. I think too little emphasis has been placed on this question.

CALDWELL: It seems to me in these discussions of large river basin projects, we have a picture of movement from essentially self-renewing natural systems to kinds of systems that have to be artificially managed. And I wonder if there is any way of calculating what the costs are of progressive movement from a self-renewing system to a system that cannot possibly renew itself without a considerably greater amount of human time, effort and attention being given to it.

We have a kind of paradox here in that on the one hand, many of these projects apparently remove people from their customary employment, either pastoral employment or agricultural employment, creating, then, the need to create jobs.

But on the other hand, we find governments and governmental departments and industrial activities engaged in doing the job that nature had hitherto done: maintaining a productive natural system which did support a population at a given level.

It seems to me that while it would be a very difficult and complex thing to do, perhaps consideration of how one could formulate a calculus for systems maintenance might be one profitable activity for ecologists or economist-ecologists to undertake.

COMMONER: There is a very good situation where I think this might be possible. Although I don't have the figures in my head, I think the qualitative picture is quite interesting. This is the problem of the San Joaquin master drain in California. The entire area which has been irrigated has had to be drained in order to take care of the salinization problem. But now the situation has gotten to the point where a master drain is required to collect the saline, insecti-

cide-laden water. And the big issue is where will the mouth of the drain go?

Now, in this case, I think it wouldn't be too difficult to take the total economic gain of the crop production in that area and then begin to calculate what it will cost to really do anything viable with this master drain. The last report I saw made this cost look so large that it probably will eat considerably into the economic gains of the entire project. (A subsequent engineering analysis indicates that at a cost of $100 million a year for at least 50 years, the drain can be directed from San Francisco Bay to the Pacific Ocean.)

In such situations there is an accumulated debt, a hidden cost, which doesn't appear in the account books of industry or agriculture.

20. ON IRRIGATION—INDUCED CHANGES IN INSECT POPULATIONS IN ISRAEL*

E. Rivnay

The introduction of irrigation in arid or semiarid countries may cause changes in the biocoenosis of the country; it may alter the microclimates in the stands, especially in overhead irrigation, and may induce physiological variations in the plants. Insect populations may be affected in the following ways:

Certain insects from remote areas may be attracted to crops which are introduced into an arid zone as a result of irrigation. This happened with the spiny cotton bollworm *Earias insulana* which attacked a small isolated experimental plot of cotton sown in the Negev Desert, fifty miles away from the nearest cotton-growing center.

Also local insects that already exist in the wild flora in the country may adopt a newly introduced crop, and increase beyond their previous numbers, as happened with *Chilo* sp. which attacked the introduced rice in the drained Hula area.

The activity period of some monophagous insects may be prolonged. They may raise more numerous generations as a result of the extended existence of their host plants due to irrigation. Thus *Atherigona varia*, a pest of *Sorghum*, and *Baris granulipennis,* a pest of melon, raise denser populations.

Due to the use of irrigation, there is an abundance of successive plants during the entire summer. This caused an increase in the population of the polyphagous Egyptian cotton worm *Spodoptera littoralis*.

The change in the microclimate of the soil due to irrigation may be favorable to

* The material in this paper was originally published in different form as "How to Provide a Nice Wet Place Where Insects You Don't Want Thrive," by E. Rivnay in *Natural History,* copyright © 1969, The American Museum of Natural History.

some insects and handicap others. Eggs of the melon beetle *Rhaphidopalpa foveicollis* require contact moisture for development; they will hatch in large numbers in overhead-irrigated fields. Hatching is far less numerous in furrow-irrigated fields.

The almond borer eggs (*Capnodis* spp.) will be killed because they are susceptible to a high degree of humidity.

Irrigation of fruit trees will enhance new growth and cause increased attack of aphids.

Changes in the cell sap of olive trees due to irrigation avert the diapause of the olive black scale *Saissetia oleae*.

The introduction of irrigation, especially overhead sprinkling, in arid or semi-arid countries presents us with an ecological dilemma. On the one hand, the artificial supplementation of water can be credited with improving productivity; on the other hand, the very changes brought about in the biocoenosis of the country have also caused invasions and an increase in many pests of agricultural importance. The destruction of entire fields of crops have followed. While many countries are engaged in adopting the techniques of modern irrigation, it is seldom realized that such innovations in practice constitute large-scale ecological experiments, and as such deserve careful studies to evaluate the consequences.

When discussing the changes in insect populations induced by irrigation, it is of interest to review changes in the extension and methods of irrigation and some of the agricultural developments that resulted from these changes. It should be borne in mind, that, small as Israel is, it has zones of aridity of all degrees, beginning with the extremely arid and arid (the desert in the southern Negev), to the semiarid (in the northern Negev), to the semihumid in the central and northern part of the country. In the northern zones irrigation is carried out in the summer only, while in the southern areas irrigation must be carried out in varying amounts even in the winter.

For centuries the sources for irrigation were springs, rivers and wells by which only the upper level of the water table was exploited. Distribution of water was by open canals, and irrigation occurred in lands lying lower than the pool of water. Often, water was raised by manual labor. From wells, the water was raised by a chain of buckets mounted over a large wheel. This water was collected into an elevated pool, from which open canals ran in all directions; the power behind the wheel was a horse. The areas that could be watered by these methods were limited. Eggplants, tomatoes, peppers, okra, cucumbers and squashes of various kinds were sown or planted on small tracts of land. These were watered in furrows. The fruit trees watered were mainly oranges, lemons and quinces, all of which were watered in basins around the trunks. The summer field-crops in dry farming were sorghum, sesame and watermelons.

Pumps driven by gasoline engines were introduced early in this century; these worked day and night to make up for their small output. In the 1920's deep drillings were made and improved pumps were introduced, making local collection pools unnecessary since the water was now pumped through closed pipes from long distances. These new sources of water facilitated the expansion of areas under irrigation. Later, permanent pipelines were laid in large fields in which summer field-crops were sown under irrigation. Corn, alfalfa and fodder beets were grown. The area of citrus groves increased, and stone fruit were grown under irrigation.

In the 1930's a large irrigation enterprise was accomplished. A pipeline was extended from the springs of the Yarkon River to the semiarid northwestern Negev; water was driven there by a pump, and the land under irrigation made possible the establishment, in 1939, of eleven new settlements in the midst of the desert.

After World War II, light portable irrigation pipes were introduced. At the beginning perforated pipes were employed for overhead irrigation; then sprinklers of all kinds took their place. The light portable pipes helped enlarge the areas under irrigation. Field crops, vegetables and trees now covered large tracts of land. Where sprinklers were not desirable, openings were cut in the pipes from which water in regulated streams ran into furrows, irrigating both trees and field crops. After the establishment of the state of Israel, cotton, peanut, and sugar beets occupied large areas, and commercial plantations of tropical fruits such as avocado and mango were planted. During that decade, another irrigation enterprise on a large scale was undertaken: the draining of Lake Huleh and its

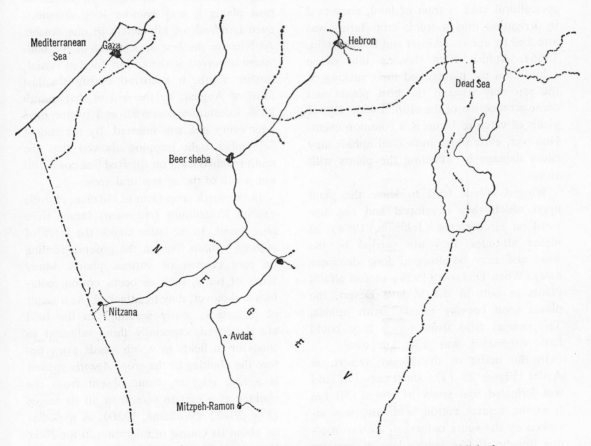

Figure 20–1 The Northern Negev, where oases have been established

swamps and the transfer through large tubes of some of the Jordan waters to parts of the country where water was needed.

The gradual development of irrigation in Israel, the increase in irrigated areas and, as a result, the introduction of crops hitherto not grown or grown sparingly brought changes in the environmental conditions. These changes affected the many organisms that functioned as an integral part of the ecosystems of agricultural communities. The effects of these changes on the pests of some crops of agricultural importance will be discussed in this paper.

CREATING AN OASIS IN THE DESERT

"When irrigation is introduced into a desert an oasis is made which will soon be invaded by pests specific to the crops raised" (Uvarov, 1964). Such a situation occurred in Israel.

At Nitzana, about 40 km from the nearest agricultural land, a tract of land, converted by irrigation into a truck crop farm, was attacked by aphids (Alpert and Loebenstein, 1966). Aphids often develop into dense colonies on the plants, and their sucking of the sap may weaken the host plants and cause a reduction of the crop; a 40% loss of yields of vetch or beans is a common event. However, even single individual aphids may cause damage by infecting the plants with virus.

Winged aphids tend to leave the plant upon which they developed and rise upward on air currents (Johnson, 1954); at higher altitudes, they are carried by the wind and may be dropped long distances away. When Dickson (1959) placed alfalfa plants in pots in the Mojave Desert, the plants soon became infested with aphids. The nearest field from which they could have originated was 130 km away.

In the midst of the Negev Desert, at Avdat (Figure 20–1), a small parcel of land was irrigated and sown to cotton, 50 km from the nearest cotton field, and was attacked by the spiny bollworm, *Earias insulana* Boisduval. The female lays its eggs on the fruiting bodies of cotton, the larvae bore into the cotton, and flowers and bolls drop. In Isarel, if no measures of control are practiced, the entire crop of a field may be destroyed; in 1956, when adequate control measures were not available, 80% of the fields in the upper Jordan valley were destroyed. Rivnay (1966) made a study of the flights of this moth in the Negev Desert in southern Israel. In its flights in search of host plants it may wander long distances, even hundreds of kilometers in one season. At Nitzana the first appearance of the bollworm occurred at the end of July; at Avdat, farther south, it occurred during the last third of August; by the end of that month 28% infestation occurred, and twelve days later every boll was infested. By the end of September light trapping showed that the moth reached Eilat on the Red Sea coast 180 km. south of the agricultural area.

In the truck crop farm at Nitzana, *Agrotis ypsilon* Rottenburg (cutworm) larvae were also found. In its latter stages the larva of *Agrotis ypsilon* lives in the ground, feeding on root crowns of various plants. Many kinds of hosts, such as beets, cotton, potatoes and clover, may be attacked. As a result of its attack, many seedlings in the field are destroyed, especially those adjacent to roads or in fields in which weeds grow before the planting of the crop. *Agrotis ypsilon* is a true migrant, being absent from the country at a certain season in all its stages (Fig. 20–2) (Williams, 1930). A hypothesis about its course of migration in the Near East was promulgated by Rivnay (1964),

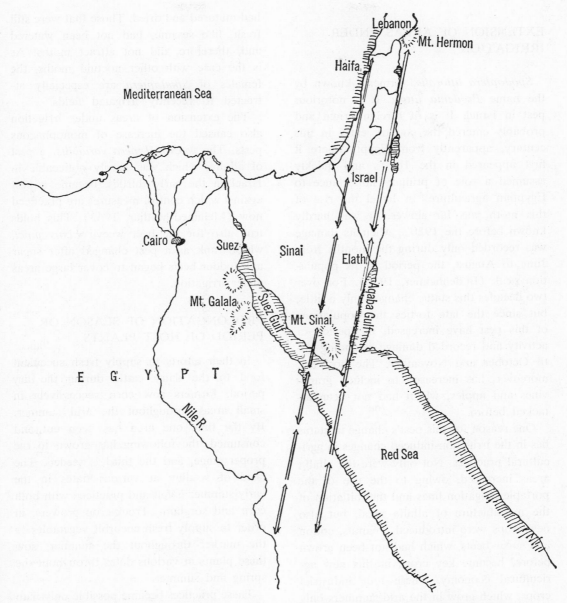

Figure 20–2 Southeastern Mediterranean countries and the migratory flight routes of *Agrotis ypsilon*

based on data of its occurrence in upper Egypt (Bishara, 1932), upon flight records (Williams, 1930) and upon light trapping in various sites in Israel (Rivnay, 1964). Moths migrate in the spring from upper Egypt northward, through the Sinai Peninsula and the Gulf of Aqaba, through Israel to the Lebanon and Mt. Hermon elevations.

A southward migration occurs in autumn. Along their routes of migration, moths will oviposit if vegetation is available. One of the routes of migration, according to eyewitness reports, is in the neighborhood of the Nitzana farm (the "White Canyon"—Rivnay, 1964). This migration pattern explains the presence of cutworms in this oasis.

EXTENSION OF AREAS UNDER IRRIGATION

Spodoptera littoralis, formerly known by the name *Prodenia litura,* is a notorious pest in Israel. It is of foreign origin and probably entered the country early in this century, apparently from Egypt, where it first appeared in the 1870's and quickly assumed a role of primary importance to Egyptian agriculture. In Israel the rise of this moth was far slower. It was hardly known before the 1920's, when its damage was recorded only during the months from June to August, the period of its population peak (Bodenheimer, 1930). For over two decades this status changed only a little, but since the late forties the populations of this pest have increased, the period of activity and recorded damage extending until October and November. The host list, moreover, has increased to include grape-vines and apples, which had not been attacked before.

One reason for this pest's change in status lies in the irrigation-induced changes in agricultural practices. Not only were the alfalfa areas increased, owing to the use of the portable irrigation lines and the initiation of the manufacture of alfalfa meal, but also new crops were introduced. Peanuts, cotton and sugar beets, which had not been grown before, became key crops in this new agricultural economy. These four industrial crops, which grow in the arid summers only because of irrigation, offered food to the polyphagous *Spodoptera* continuously from May until late in November; when one kind of crop dried out, another was still fresh a short distance away.

The lands upon which the irrigation crops now grow were covered, in the past, with dry-farming crops that did not attract *Spodoptera* moths. In June, when the population of the pest had become active, the wheat, chick-peas, lentils and other crops had matured and dried. Those that were still fresh, like sesame, had not been watered and, therefore, did not attract moths. As is the case with other noctuid moths, the females of *Spodoptera* are especially attracted to recently irrigated fields.

The extension of areas under irrigation also caused the increase of monophagous pests. The weevil *Hypera variabilis,* a pest of alfalfa, which was hardly noticeable in Israel in the early thirties, became a pest against which control measures are practiced now (Melamed-Madjar, 1963). This holds true also for the beet weevil *Lixus junci,* whose rank as a pest changed after sugar and fodder beets began to cover large areas under irrigation.

PROLONGATION OF SEASON OR PERIOD OF HOST PLANTS

In their efforts to supply fresh succulent food to the dairy cattle during the dry period, farmers sow corn successively in small areas throughout the arid summer. By the time one area has been cut and consumed, the following has grown to the proper stage, and the third is seeded. The need of seeding at various dates in the early summer is felt and practiced with both corn and sorghum. Truck-crop growers, in order to supply fresh cucurbit vegetables to the market throughout the summer, sow these plants at various dates throughout the spring and summer.

These practices became possible only with the improved method of irrigation. However, such improvements in farming also favor the development and increase of some insect pests.

THE ORIENTAL CORN BORER
Chilo agamemnon Bleszynski

The Oriental corn borer, *Chilo agamemnon,* can raise one generation in one summer month. The larva of this moth bores into the heart of the plant and, before pupating, girdles the stem from within. As a result the plant weakens; its growth is stunted and it becomes easily breakable. At Beer Tuvia, in the coastal plain, the standard yield of corn fodder was 4–5 tons per dunam (approximately one-quarter acre); after the invasion of this pest the yield dropped to ⅓–2 tons per dunam.

In view of its quick development and the presence of food all summer, the corn borer now raises six generations from May to early November (Rivnay, 1967). In the dry-farming system, only two or at most three generations of the moth could have been raised, because by August the stand has dried and become unsuitable for the larvae.

For an insect which spends half a year in dormancy and which is active only during the vegetative period of its host, the food supply is made continuous by sowing the host crop at the same time year after year in succession. An attempt was made to grow rice in the drained Hula area; with plenty of water in the area, rice was grown a few years in succession. In order to exploit an area so rich in water, it was planned to introduce this crop, which had not been cultivated before. But this same pest prevented it. At first the stand was beautiful, bearing fine yields. However, it was not long before an entomological factor brought an end to this enterprise. This *Chilo* species, which had not been known in the area before, attacked the rice. During the first year the percentage of infestation was 10–15%; the following year it rose to 33%. The infestation grew in subsequent years and reached a stage in which it was no longer worth cultivating rice, since no adequate cheap control measures were found.

THE SORGHUM SHOOT MAGGOT
Atherigona varia soccata RONDANI

The sorghum shoot maggot *Atherigona varia soccata* attacks only young sorghum plants. From sprouting until it is two to three weeks old, a plant may succumb to the attacks of this fly, then it becomes resistant. The neonate maggot works its way to the interior of the crown, where it scratches the surface and feeds upon the soft tissue of the innermost rolled leaves, and as a result, the central blade dries up and withers. Side tillers develop, the formation of grain is retarded, reduced, or fails altogether.

When sorghum was grown in dry farming, this fly was hardly known in Israel. Bodenheimer (1930), who made an inventory of all plant pests known to exist in the country at that time, does not mention it at all. If the fly existed in the country on wild sorghum plants, the cultivated sorghum probably escaped its attack, having grown to the resistant stage before the fly became active. With the cultivation of sorghum under irrigation the fly has become an important pest. *Atherigona varia soccata* may raise one generation every summer month, and as long as young plants are available, its population increases and remains high throughout the summer (Fig. 20–3).

Today, sorghum cannot be sown late in the spring or in the summer without suffering losses unless control measures are applied. Farmers as a rule sow early to escape the attack of the fly.

Usually no records are kept of damage by insects, which in this case is hard to estimate. From the practice of sowing early, now adopted in order to escape the damage, one may surmise the importance of the pest. In experimental plots sowing later in the season, infestation reached 40–70%.

THE CUCURBIT SNOUT BEETLE
Baris granulipennis TOURNIER

Availability of curcurbit fruit all summer encouraged the increase of the melon weevil, *Baris granulipennis*. It is still uncertain

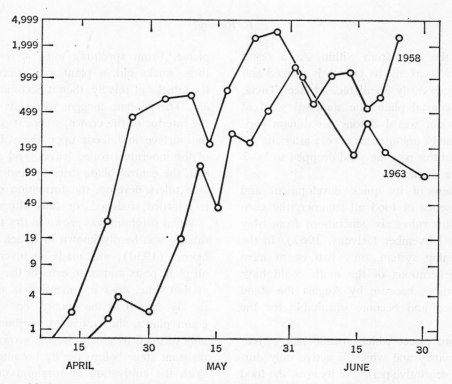

Figure 20-3 Trend of population of *Athergona varia soccata*, at Beit Dagan in a field where young sorghum plants were available till June (After Yathom, 1965. The lines show the continuous increase in the number of flies in the area until there were no more host plants of the proper age available)

whether this pest entered the country recently from Egypt where it had been first described or if it had been here before. But certainly in the late 1950's it increased so much that measures were taken against it, especially in fields where melon was grown for export.

The snout beetle oviposits in the young melon fruit. Its larvae develop within the fruit, feeding on the soft seed. After two or three weeks they mature and pupate within the peel, which has in the meantime become dry. The growth of the fruit is stunted due to the girdling of its stem by the female prior to oviposition. Quite often, "by mistake," the petiole of the adjacent leaf is girdled instead. Oviposition is then made in a fruit which continues to grow. An infested fruit may be recognized by the oviposition scars.

The natural host plant of this beetle is

Citrullus colocynthis. This plant and another host, the melon *Citrullus vulgaris,* cultivated without irrigation, yield young fruit until July or early August. After this, emerging beetles may not find suitable host fruit to oviposit. With the extension of the cucurbit season, due to irrigation, fruits, melon and cucumbers are available until late autumn, and two more generations of beetles can be raised.

The percentage of survival from the long hibernation depends upon the generation to which the beetle belongs and its age. The earlier the beetles enter hibernation the fewer the individuals that survive. Development of late generations has an important bearing upon the strength of the generations of the following years (Rivnay, 1960). Today, due to continuous and extensive insecticide applications against other pests, the beetle has become rare.

THE ONION FLY
Hylemyia antiqua MEIGEN

Before irrigation was extended in Israel, onions were grown in the winter by planting sets from previous years. Rains supplied the necessary moisture, and the bulbs matured and were harvested in June. Today, as a result of irrigation, seed is sown in September and October. The soft seedlings are replanted in the fields, but they are less resistant to fly maggots than the onion sets used in dry farming. The onion season is thus lengthened; onions are already in the fields by October or November.

Until two decades ago, the onion fly *Hylemyia antiqua* was considered a pest of little importance; no insecticides were necessary, as its damage was hardly felt (Bodenheimer, 1930). But with the new methods of cultivation resulting from irrigation, this fly has become conspicuous, thereby necessitating measures of control.

In Israel, as in colder European and North American countries, this fly raises two or three generations annually. According to Yathom (1963), the estivating generation of the fly emerges from diapause in November and December. The offspring of this—the autumn—generation matures in the middle of the winter and gives rise to the winter generation, which enters diapause in the pupal stage. The early individuals of this brood may continue to reproduce, and only their offspring will enter diapause. Records of appearance of the generations are given in detail because to explain the increase of the fly population due to irrigation we should point to the synchronization between availability of host plants and the awakening of the fly from diapause.

In the case of dry farming, there were no host plants upon which to oviposit when the flies of the estivating generation emerged from diapause; many, especially the earliest, perished before ovipositing. Only insects emerging in December and early January

could find host plants. In the case of farming under irrigation, the awakening flies in November find plenty of host plants; most of the flies lay eggs, thus giving rise to a strong generation to further attack the onion fields.

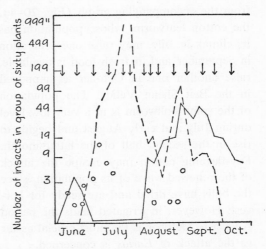

Figure 20–4 Fluctuations of population of *Spodoptera littoralis* (———), *Earias insulana* (— — —) and *Heliothis armigera* (circles) in an irrigated cotton field in the Coastal Plains of Israel (After Rivnay and Yathom, 1958)

THE SPINY BOLLWORM *Earias insulana* BOISDUVAL AND THE COTTON LEAFWORM *Spodoptera littoralis* BOISDUVAL

We have shown how insect populations increase due to the prolonged season of the host plant caused by repeated sowings. The period of a single stand may also be prolonged by irrigation as long as the temperature permits. Cotton, for instance, when grown without irrigation in Israel, is harvested during August; under irrigation this crop in the same locality is harvested during September and October. In the Beit Shean Valley (near the Jordan River) the vegetative period of the stand is extended until November. Here this prolongation is essential, because in the excessively warm days of July and early August there is a general blossom drop. The prolongation of the stand allows the fruiting of the late blossom to make up for the loss due to the drop in July.

These prolongations accentuate the infestations by the spiny bollworm *Earias insulana* Boisd. and the Egyptian cotton leafworm *Spodoptera littoralis* Boisd. As may be seen from the accompanying graph (Fig. 20–4), the cotton leafworm, whose population has its climax in July, may raise one generation in September and, if fresh food is available, raise another one in October as happened in the Beit Shean Valley. The population of the spiny bollworm is at a very low level during July and early August and begins to rise in the second half of the latter month. Dry-farming cotton may escape the attack of the renewed wave of its population, since the bolls have dried and are ready for harvest. However, in irrigated fields the period August to October is the most crucial as far as the attack of *Earias* is concerned.

IRRIGATION-INDUCED CHANGES IN MICROCLIMATES

THE SEED CORN MAGGOT
Hylemyia cilicrura RONDANI

The seed maggot, which belongs to the same genus as the onion fly, differs from it in being polyphagous. Yathom (1961), who studied this fly in Israel, states that until the early fifties this fly was hardly felt as a pest. Bodenheimer (1930) mentions it as a predator of locust eggs. Its first discovery as a seed pest in 1935 was recorded much later in a publication called *Rare Pests of Truck Crops* (Schweig, 1951). Today preventive measures must be taken against it when sowing cucurbits, peanuts, beans, cotton or corn.

In discussing the factors that have changed the status of the fly from an unknown insect to a pest of primary importance, Yathom shows that irrigated fields or those that have been plowed recently attract flies for oviposition. In her own work this author demonstrated that very few females of this species laid eggs on dry soil, whereas hundreds of eggs were laid on moist soil by the same number of females, which had been interchanged from time to time.

In dry farming the growth of summer crops is based on exploiting the moisture which has accumulated in the ground from rains during the winter. Some crops are watered afterward in their furrows. Such conditions do not encourage egg laying nor the development of the species as do the agricultural practices today, where the field is seeded and then watered by overhead irrigation. A small field experiment carried out near Rehovot demonstrates this. One plot was well irrigated and two days later seeded with beans. The other was first seeded and then irrigated. The latter was attacked by the seed corn maggot, whereas the first was hardly infested. In the first case the soil remained moist enough to cause germination of the beans but the surface became too dry to attract the ovipositing flies.

In our effort to explain how the population of *H. cilicrura* increased in Israel, we should consider the chances that in April the presence of many gravid adults is synchronous with ecologically favorable conditions for oviposition—namely, irrigated fields. Such fields were not available during dry farming when sesame, sorghum and melons were sown in moist soil without subsequent irrigation. Such fields are plentiful today when large areas of peanuts, cotton, corn and other crops are sown and subsequently watered by overhead systems. It is very often necessary to reseed the entire field once or twice due to the destruction caused by this pest.[1]

[1] The application of organo-phosphorous insecticides in granular form is often practiced on these fields. In fact one of the most serious problems in the adoption of overhead sprinkling is that, inevitably, this method has contributed immensely to the increased use of insecticides in Israel.

THE RED PUMPKIN BEETLE
Rhaphidopalpa foveicollis LUCCHESE

On emergence from diapause, *Rhaphido-palpa* beetles feed on the leaves of the young cucurbit seedlings. When they are numerous, they may inflict severe damage, necessitating reseeding of entire fields.[2] However, the more important injury is caused by the larvae which feed upon and bore into the roots. Bacterial rot develops, then the plant succumbs suddenly and entire fields may thus be destroyed. The damage is aggravated by its timing, often only a week or two before the fruit is picked for marketing.[3] Injury of a third type may be caused by the larvae when they emerge to the surface and feed upon the nearly mature fruit. In recent years this pest has become quite serious; the reason for this is the change from furrow to overhead irrigation (Rivnay, 1954).[4]

The eggs of *Rhaphidopalpa foveicollis* need contact moisture for development (Melamed-Madjar, 1960). Eggs deposited near plants growing under ditch irrigation may not have the necessary moisture, and thus many eggs perish. With overhead irrigation the entire area is uniformly watered, offering ideal conditions for the eggs to hatch. The larvae enter the soil and feed upon the roots. As they grow larger they penetrate the main root.

Unlike the eggs, mature larvae are susceptible to excessive moisture. When the field becomes saturated with water supplied by the sprinklers, the mature larvae leave the soil and seek shelter under the fruit upon which they also feed. In fields irrigated in furrows this does not happen, and in fields where overhead irrigation is not too copious the infestation may be limited to the lower sites of the field where more moisture is accumulated.

THE ALMOND BORERS *Capnodis* SPP.

Jewish settlers in Palestine, in their endeavor to improve their agricultural economy, planted almonds on large areas. This enterprise was financed by Baron Rothschild of France who sent a French horticulturist to supervise the plantations. Naturally, the methods of cultivation practiced in the western Mediterranean basin were followed. The trees developed nicely, and began to bear fruit; but after a few years, they began to deteriorate, and gradually the plantations were uprooted.

There were several causes for the failure of this tree, but the major one was *Capnodis* spp. Two species, *C. carbonaria* Klug. and *C. tenebrionis* L., attacked the trees.

The adults of these beetles usually feed on the bark of the soft twigs and upon the leaf petioles of various stone-fruit trees. The eggs are deposited in nooks and crevices near the root collar, and the neonate larvae work their way to the main roots into which they bore. When several such larvae feed on the cambium of the main roots, the tree weakens and finally succumbs.

A study of the ecology and physiology of these insects found that the eggs were quite resistant to desiccation and quite susceptible to a high degree of humidity (Rivnay, 1944). The egg shell is covered with hygroscopic salts which absorb moisture around the egg to render it resistant to dryness. Thus most eggs hatch even at a very low relative humidity. On the other hand, at high relative humidities, the percentage of mortality increased with the humidity and with the length of exposure to it.

---

[2] Farmers from Raanana, Ramle and other villages in the coastal plain complain every season about destruction of 20–50% of the seedlings in spite of dusting with insecticides. Only recently were more effective insecticides introduced. But it is not yet known for how long they will remain effective.

[3] At Ashdod, for instance, the writer witnessed the destruction of the entire crop of a 15-acre field of melons. About a year later, the owner appealed to the writer to testify about it in order to be exempted from income tax.

[4] It is a well-known fact that no such mishaps occur in dry farming, or in furrow-irrigated melon fields like those we find in the Arab villages.

When a tree is watered, the soil remains moist for several days; the upper layers may dry faster, but the air spaces in the soil and the spaces between the soil and trunk where the eggs are deposited remain humid for a longer period. Under such conditions the percentage of eggs hatching is reduced.

With the increase of water resources during the 1930's stone-fruit trees began to be watered in order to obtain more and better fruit. However, it was noticed that the major pest of the stone-fruit tree, *Capnodis,* began to diminish; fewer trees succumbed than before irrigation was introduced. Today almond plantations are not watered, or are watered with long intervals between the irrigations. Under such conditions *Capnodis* larvae may survive and become injurious. Farmers use preventive measures by dusting around the trunks with contact insecticides. As a result of the situation discussed above, it is more difficult to find *Capnodis* in Israel.

APHIDS

In Israel, the population of aphids reaches its peak in March. A sharp decline in the number of species and individuals takes place toward the end of April (Bodenheimer, 1940), but some species are active also during the summer. In a study of aphids on fruit trees in Israel, Swirski (1954) found that *Aphis pomi* De Geer remained longer and was more numerous on irrigated apple trees than on non-irrigated trees. Also *Aphis punicae* was more abundant on irrigated pomegranates than on non-irrigated trees.

This situation is due to the fact that irrigated trees continue to produce new growth and young leaves are available throughout the summer. That young leaves are attacked by aphids more than mature ones was pointed out by Kennedy *et al.* (1950), who noticed that young and senescent sugar-beet leaves were more infested

with *Aphis fabae* than mature leaves. Sokolov and Sokolov (1952) found that young leaves of apples are attacked more by *Aphis pomi* De Geer than mature ones, and that their infestation varied inversely with the osmotic pressure. Harpaz (1953) also explained various levels of infestation by the difference in osmotic pressure in leaves of different ages.

The aphid secretes saliva into the spaces between the cells. Since osmotic pressure of the cell sap is less than that of the saliva, the latter permeates into the spaces, and is sucked by the aphid. In the case of old leaves during the arid period, the osmotic pressure of the sap is greater than that of the saliva and it does not permeate into the spaces; no food can be obtained by the insect.

Another theory, advanced by Kessler *et al.* (1959), is that the proportion of soluble nitrogen in young and in senescent leaves is different. Since aphids usually prefer to feed upon young leaves, and assuming that the proportion of cytoplasm to the nucleus increases with the age of the leaf, they decided to induce these changes experimentally. Young apple leaves, of about one-fourth to one-third of their final size, were sprayed with 25, 50 and 100 ppm caffeine in water. Twenty days later they were analyzed for ribonucleic acid and deoxyribonucleic acid. Young, mature and senescent leaves were analyzed for comparison. When experimental leaves were infested with aphids and allowed to reproduce for about one month, the increase in aphid population was approximately inversely proportional to the caffeine concentration. Aphids increased to a much less extent equally on mature leaves and on leaves pretreated with caffeine.

The authors concluded that soluble nitrogen, which is greater in young than it is in mature leaves, and the ratio of RNA to DNA, which is smaller in young leaves than it is in mature ones, may be responsible for the increased infestation by aphids in young leaves. Irrigation in the summer stimulates the trees to produce young leaves throughout the summer, permitting the continuous reproduction of aphids.

The Olive Black Scale—
Saissetia oleae BERN.

In Israel, the olive black scale S. oleae, attacks olives and citrus, and usually raises one generation a year (Bodenheimer, 1951). Ovipositing females appear in April or May and crawlers settle mainly in May. The larvae, after developing a little, enter a state of diapause which lasts till the middle of November when they awaken and resume development. They mature in March or April.

In 1961–62, a survey on black scale infestation in various localities of the Esdraelon (Yizreel)* plain, on both citrus and olive trees, was carried out by Peleg (1965). From this survey it became apparent that in citrus and non-irrigated olive trees, the development of the scale insect follows the pattern described above. However, in irrigated olive trees the development of the pest follows a different pattern; a small percentage of the larvae follow the pattern described above, whereas the majority does not diapause but continues to develop. As a result, ovipositing females appear as early as November. The offspring also develop continuously and mature in the spring. Thus there are individuals of two broods on the same tree. In trees in which two broods develop, there is no uniformity in the hatching. A similar situation was reported also from the coastal areas in southern California where the lack of uniform hatching was termed "off hatch" in contrast to the normal hatch in the one-brood scale insects which is prevalent in the interior, more arid parts of California.

Naturally the population of the insect

* The newly adopted name for this plain.

should be denser in trees where two broods develop. This was demonstrated by our counts of the population of this insect in irrigated compared to adjacent non-irrigated trees in the Esdraelon valley. On ten twigs picked at random, in each of the sections of the grove, 115 insects were found on the irrigated trees and 16 were found on the non-irrigated trees.

When we try to find the cause for this phenomenon, we cannot help but think of the changes in the cell sap induced by irrigation. There are reports that changes in the food of some insects induced diapause. Thus a large percentage of larvae of the pink bollworms Platyedra gossypiella Sand entered diapause when fed on seeds containing a large percentage of fat and only 20% of water. When they were feeding on softer seeds containing a little fat and 70–80% of water, diapause was averted (Squire, 1939). A similar report was given by Urbahns (1920) on the alfalfa seed chalcid Bruchophagus gibbus Boh.

It is quite possible that in June (about three months after the rainy period) the olive-tree sap is too concentrated; this condition, in combination with the high prevailing temperature, induces diapause in the soft olive scale. In irrigated trees the sap may be very dilute and diapause is averted.

SUMMARY AND DISCUSSION

When land is irrigated in an arid zone an enclave of a different biocoenose,[5] an oasis, is created. Insects typical to this biocoenose and to the plants there will invade it. This invasion may be by drift as with the aphids; by dispersal as with Earias in the Negev; and by migration as with Agrotis ypsilon. It is quite natural that larger and more numerous fields of a certain crop will provide larger quantities of food for the insects that

[5] Biocoenose: the association of organisms (plants and animals) living together under the same determined conditions of existence.

depend upon this crop, and larger populations of these insects will develop; such a situation occurred with *Spodoptera littoralis* in Israel.

The prolongation of the vegetative period of a certain crop by repeated sowings will increase the insects depending upon it, provided biological habits permit it. This happened in Israel with *Chilo agamemnon* in corn, *Atherigona varia soccata* in sorghum and with *Baris grannulipennis* in cucurbit plants. Similarly, the prolongation of the vegetative period of the stand will increase the number of insects depending upon it. This was illustrated by *Spodoptera littoralis* and *Earias insulana* in cotton and by *Hylemyia antiqua* in onions.

In certain plants irrigation may cause changes in the composition of the cell sap. Such changes may cause the increase of aphids and prolong their activity period; such changes may also avert the diapause period in sucking insects, as in the olive black scale *Saissetia oleae.*

In Israel, the advantages of overhead sprinkling are: (1) saving expensive labor, (2) the possibility of employing labor unskilled in agriculture, and (3) the possibility of irrigating areas and slopes where furrow irrigation is impossible or difficult.

However, there are also some disadvantages to this kind of irrigation. In a comparative study between overhead sprinkling and furrow-irrigated plots in Israel, it was found that overhead-sprinkled tomatoes yielded less fruit than furrow-irrigated plots. Often the yield was one-third to one-half less than the yield in the furrow-irrigated plots (Rotem and Cohen, 1966; Yagev and Brush, 1965).

Also, some diseases develop more in overhead-sprinkled plots. It has been pointed out that overhead sprinkling created a microclimate over the stand that favors development of diseases. According to Rotem and Cohen (1966), the change of microclimate in the stand consists of a relative humidity 30–

40% above that of the surroundings and lowering of the temperature 2–8° C. However, these changes occur only during the sprinkling period and for an hour or two after this period; in addition, these changes occur only on extremely warm and dry days, and dry but windless nights. Only on organisms that are associated with excessive moisture could fungus, like *Stemphylum botryosparius* f. *lycopersici* on tomatoes, develop under the conditions created by sprinkling. Others, like *Oidiopsis taurica,* developed better in furrow-irrigated plots (Rotem and Cohen, 1966). As to differences regarding insect infestations, Yagev and Brush (1965) claim that sprinkled plots were slightly more infested with *Spodoptera* eggs than furrow-irrigated plots. Possibly the changes in the microclimate of the stand are of too short duration and at too long intervals to allow drastic changes in insect populations.

The situation is different with the changes in microclimatic conditions created in the soil by overhead sprinkling. The entire surface of the soil is moistened and the changes are of longer duration. Insects that need contact moisture for development will thrive better in overhead-sprinkled soil, as happened with the eggs of the red pumpkin beetle *Rhaphidopalpa foveicollis.* Insects that cannot stand too much moisture will leave the soil as will the larvae of the same pest. The moisture over the soil resulting from overhead sprinkling will attract moisture-loving insects like the seed corn maggot *Hylemyia cilicrura* in greater amounts. The development of the eggs and larvae in such soil will be more successful. Moisture in the soil, however, may be detrimental to some insects, as in the case of *Capnodis* eggs, or it may favor them, as with the eggs of the pumpkin beetle.

The introduction of irrigation, especially overhead sprinkling in arid or semiarid countries, presents us with an ecological dilemma. On the one hand, the artificial supplementation of water can be credited with improved productivity; on the other hand, the very changes brought about in the biocoenosis of the country will also cause invasions and an increase in many pests of agricultural importance. The destruction of entire fields of crops may follow. While many countries are engaged in adopting the techniques of modern irrigation, it is seldom realized that such innovations in practice constitute large-scale ecological changes, and as such deserve careful studies to evaluate the consequences.

REFERENCES

Alpert, Miriam, and Loebenstein, G. "Trapping of Flying Aphids in Several Areas of Israel, as a Guide to Growing Virus Free Potato and Iris Stocks." *Isr. J. Agr. Res.*, 16 (3) (1966), 143–46.

Bishara, Ibrahim. *The Greasy Cutworm (Agrotis ypsilon Rott.) in Egypt.* Tech. and Sci. Service, Ministry Agr. Egypt, Bull. 114. 1932. 55 pp.

———. "The Cotton Worm *Prodenia litura* F. in Egypt." *Bull. Soc. Ent. Egypte*, 18 (1934), 288–415.

Bodenheimer, F. S. *Die Schädlings fauna Palästinas.* Monogr. ang. Ent. 10 Paul Parey. 1930.

———. "The Ecology of Aphids in a Subtropical Climate." Sixth International Congress of Ent., Madrid, 1935, 2 (1940), 49–58.

———. *Citrus Entomology.* The Hague: Dr. W. Junk, 1951.

Dickson, R. C. "Aphid Dispersal over Southern California Deserts." *Ann. Ent. Soc. Amer.*, 52 (1959), 368–73.

Harpaz, I. *Aphids on Graminaceous Plants in Israel.* Ph.D. thesis submitted to the Hebrew University, 1953. 141 pp. (In Hebrew with English summ.)

Johnson, C. G. "Aphid Migration in Relation to Weather." *Biological Reviews*, 29 (1954), 87–118.

Kennedy, J. S.; Ibbotson, A.; and Booth, C. O. "The Distribution of Aphid Infestation in Relation to Leaf Age. I. *Myzus persicae* (Sulz) and *Aphis fabae* Scop. on Spindle Trees and Sugar Beet Plants." *Ann. App. Biol.*, 37 (1950), 651–79.

Kessler, B.; Swirski, E.; and Tahori, A. S. "Effects of Pourines upon Nucleic Acids and Nitrogen Metabolism of Leaves and Their Sensitivity to Aphids." *Ktavim*, 9 (3–4) (1959), 265–74.

Melamed-Madjar, V. "Studies on the Red Pumpkin Beetle in Israel." *Ktavim*, 10 (3–4) (1960), 139–45.

———. "The Biology of the Alfalfa Weevil *Hypera variabilis* in Israel." *Ktavim*, 13 (1) (1963), 41–49.

Peleg. B. A. "Observations on the Life Cycle of the Soft Olive Scale *Saissitia oleae* Bern. on Citrus and Olive Trees." *Ktavim* (Hebrew series), 15 (2) (1965), 95–100.

Rivnay, E. "Physiological and Ecological Studies on the Species of *Capnodis* in Palestine. I. Studies on the Egg." *Bull. Ent. Res.*, 35 (1944), 235–42.

———. "A New Type of Damage by the Pumpkin Beetle in Israel." *Hassadeh*, 34 (1) (1954), 53–54. In Hebrew.

Rivnay, E., and Yathom, S. "Field Trials against the Spiny Boll Worm *Earias insulana* Boisd. in Cotton in 1957." *Ktavim*, 9 (1–2) (1958), 3–17.

———. "The Life History of the Melon Weevil *Baris granulipennis* Tour. in Israel." *Bull. Ent. Res.*, 51 (1) (1960), 115–22.

———. "A Contribution to the Biology and Phenology of *Agrotis Ypsilon* Roft. in Israel." *Z. Ang. Entomologie*, 53 (3) (1964), 295–309.

———. "The Flights of *Earias insulana* Boisd. in the Arid South (Negev) of Israel." *Isr. J. Ent.*, 1 (1966), 49–54.

———. "A contribution to the Biology of the Maize Borer *Chilo agamemnon* Blesz." *Isr. J. Ent.*, 2 (1967), 15–27.

Rivnay, E., and Melamed, V. "Studies on

the Ecology and Phenology of *Lixus Junci* Boh. in Israel." *Ktavim*, 7 (1956), 63–82.

Rotem, I., and Cohen, Y. "The Relationship between Mode of Irrigation and Severity of the Tomato Foliage Diseases in Israel." *Plant Disease Reporter*, 50 (9) (1966), 635–39.

Schweig, K. *Rare Insect Pests of Truck-crops.* Tel-Aviv: Hassadeh Publ. Co., 1951. In Hebrew.

Sokolov, A. M., and Sokolov, R. A. "The Role of the Osmotic Pressure of the Cell Sap in the Resistance of Apple to the Green Apple Aphid *Aphis ponii* Deg." *Dokl. vsesoyus Akad sel Khoz Nauk Lenina*, 17 (1952), 12–18.

Squire, F. A. "Observations on the Larval Diapause of the Pink Boll Worm *Platyedra gassypiella* Saund." *Bull. Ent. Res.*, 30 (1939), 475–81.

Swirski, E. "Fruit Tree Aphids." *Bull. Ent. Res.*, 45 (1954), 623–38.

Urbahns, T. D. *The Clover and Alfalfa Seed Chalcis Fly.* U. S. D. A. Bull. 812. 1920. 20 pp.

Uvarov, B. P. "Problems of Insect Ecology in Developing Countries," *J. Appl. Ecol.*, 1 (1964), 159–68.

Williams, C. B. *Migration of Butterflies.* Edinburgh: Oliver & Boyd, 1930.

Yagev, S., and Brush, S. "Observations on Furrow Irrigated and Overhead Sprinkled Tomatoes." *Hassadeh*, 45 (1965), 1275–78. In Hebrew.

Yathom, S. "Laboratory Studies on the Bionomics of *Hylemyia cilicrura* Rond. in Israel." *Isr. J. Agr. Res.* (*Ktavim*), 1 (1) (1961), 51–56.

———. "The Sorghum Shoot Maggot and Its Control." *Hassadeh*, 45 (8) (1965). In Hebrew.

———. "Bionomics and Phenology of the Onion Fly *Hylemyia antiqua* Meig. in Israel." *Isr. J. Agr. Res.*, 13 (2) (1963), 93–105.

DISCUSSION

M. T. FARVAR: I would like to mention a related motivational problem from my survey of the Middle East in 1968; it seemed to me that many countries were emulating each other—trying to introduce new techniques that their neighbor or somebody else had thought about.

One example of this is the new system of irrigation, overhead sprinkling, which is now widespread in Israel. In Algeria it is now being adopted as one of the prevalent methods of irrigation, even though the climate of Algeria generally is far hotter than most of Israel. Much of the water immediately evaporates when it is sprinkled, even before reaching the ground. So you already have an increase in salinity of the water by the time it hits earth; then the rest of it evaporates and salinizes the soil. This is a geohydrological problem that is quite well known.

I specifically questioned the Algerian scientists: "Does anybody know what happens to the insect populations when you convert to overhead sprinkling techniques?" The truth is that most people haven't even thought about the possibility that such changes can have profound impact on the ecology of insects or insect pests living in the steppes of Algeria, the Sahara, or in any other arid lands.

SMITH: A number of entomologists have run experiments on this problem in the U.S. Usually overhead sprinkling comes into an agricultural area for other overriding reasons such as soil so shallow they cannot level it for other types of irrigation. Economically the entomological aspects are pretty well ignored in practice even though we do have some indication that there are negative changes under this system of irrigation. We have seen this on cotton in California and to some extent on alfalfa and other crops.

RIVNAY: A comment about the difference in overhead irrigation and furrow irrigation: perhaps those of you who read my paper recall the case history of the Red Pumpkin beetle pest that reproduces at a much faster rate in overhead-irrigated soil than under furrow irrigation. This is because the eggs are hatched at a better rate when they contact moisture. However, this moisture contact is not usually available if the soil is furrow-irrigated. Thus, overhead irrigation may have important negative effects other than raising salinity.

I would like to ask Mr. Farvar if they use overhead irrigation during the night in Algeria. This is quite a common practice in Israel. One of the reasons is to prevent excessive evaporation on the soils.

M. T. FARVAR: Much of the time in Algeria it might not make much difference, since the night is very often quite hot, particularly when the sirocco blows.

KASSAS: I would like to refer to a case in Sudan. During the Second World War, a large-scale experiment in mechanized agriculture was carried out in the savannah area, involving savannah-type crops and open forest sorghum agriculture.

In the first year of the experiment, the crop yield was high. In the second year it was about 20 per cent less. Nobody worried much about it.

In the third year, the crop loss was over 40 per cent. Then people started to worry about it.

In the following year, the drop was more than 60 per cent of the crop, and the project was abandoned.

When the entomologists finally were asked to come and advise, they discovered that four insect pests were causing all this trouble. Two of these insects were new to science, a third one had been recorded before as a very rare insect in the area, and the fourth was recorded as a common insect, but not as an agricultural pest.

This case shows the effect of opening new ground for agriculture and its impact on pest populations.

In later years people came back and reopened these areas to agriculture, and eventually reached an equilibrium between the insects and the cultivation.

The earlier project, I believe, started under the auspices of the British Army, who required a higher output from the ground. To them, a drop of 50 per cent meant that the project was not economic. But in a subsistence situation in extensive agriculture, a loss of 50 per cent to insects is quite bearable.

HASKELL: I would like to follow this up because I think it is an important point. The relationship between insects and host plants is, I think, very subtle. We are beginning to realize only now—and there is a hint of this in Professor Rivnay's paper—just what are the physical effects of irrigation on *Aphis* populations, for example.

I want to take up Professor Kassas's point about development of new areas. A few years ago the Botswana government began to plant cotton in an area which had never been used before for agriculture. The crop was immediately attacked by an insect species new to science, a new species; however, related species found all around the continent of South Africa had *never* attacked cotton before.

They were extremely alarmed about this. But after a year or so, the incidence of damage went right down, almost to nothing, although the pest is still there. This seems to have something to do with the offering of food on a plate to begin with; but it has not kept up, because, in this case, an acceptable equilibrium was reached.

Locusts are another example of a species that always takes immediate advantage of a change in ecological conditions. When the Shire Valley sugar estates were extended some two or three years ago, there was a tremendous outburst of *Locusta migratoria;* we all rushed down there thinking there might be another plague developing. In fact, however, the population fell off naturally.

There were some local control operations mounted, but they only creamed off a certain amount of the worst population. The population itself went down to almost nil again after a short time.

These relationships are very subtle, and we ought not to rush into conclusions about the necessity of chemical control until we have studied the situation at least for a year or two.

FRASER DARLING: Dr. Scudder, I was wondering while you were speaking of the Kariba Dam whether there were any really large acreages of drawdown in this dam and whether there was sufficient time in the drawdown to establish vegetation which would be ideal for locusts. In several areas in Central Africa, such as Lake Mweru and Antipa, you get a variable shoreline. These are the great natural locust breeding areas.

SCUDDER: This is a fascinating question and demonstrates one more unpredictable aspect of this project. I don't know of any specific studies that would give us an indication of the answer, however.

HASKELL: The Volta Dam scheme is worrying us considerably more than the Kariba situation in this regard. There is a real possibility of locusts because it is in an area which is open to *Schistocerca* as well as severe local grasshopper infestations.

There are other development schemes of this sort which produce conditions that locusts like. I have mentioned some of these in my paper which is in the next section. I think this ought to be looked into. In fact, at the beginning of the Volta scheme many years ago, we did suggest that unanticipated fostering of locust increases was a possibility that ought to be studied.

The University of Ghana was asked to take up some of these problems. We put somebody there to start looking, but unfortunately the money ran out halfway through —before the study was even properly off the ground.

But now there is some evidence that things are moving again. And the results with respect to locusts are rather worrying in this respect. But I don't think Kariba will be worrying because it is outside the general area of locust infestation. There is an odd little thing about *Salvinia* because there is a grasshopper called *Paulinia* which eats *Salvinia* preferentially. This has been suggested as a possible biological releaser if you could breed *Paulinia* so it would eat the *Salvinia* to make it release its nutrients into the stream again which, in turn, might help the fish population.

SCUDDER: I hope that it is done under carefully controlled conditions.

HASKELL: Well, this is being worked on in the university a little bit.

SCUDDER: I am going to sum up this session in part by noting two things which have come out of our discussions. Regardless of whether or not we educate everybody in terms of an ecological perspective, in terms of a historical perspective, or in terms of natural systems, we still have a very great problem of developing some means to integrate all these various concerns each of us has in our own discipline, for a better understanding of the problems. *There is still no effective mechanism or "calculus" whereby we can:*

(1) escape from the single alternative syndrome that Dr. White mentioned, and,

(2) evaluate various alternatives and present the implications of these alternatives for policy planners to choose between, and actually work out a methodology for measuring benefit-cost. I think it is highly unlikely that this can be done the way economists are doing it, because in most cases we cannot apply a dollar evaluation to these problems.

Finally, although we still need research to fill the critical information gaps, there is still the problem of repetition of mistakes. There is obviously a lot of knowledge around. There are a lot of people in each country that have this knowledge. Nevertheless, the same mistakes are still made time and time again, even within the same country which should have learned from a similar project some five or ten years earlier.

But here we have got to realize that we are dealing with complex social organizations and with complex individuals in these organizations, just as ecologically we are dealing with complex biological systems. An analysis is useless unless it is related to the nature of the societies that we are dealing with. Human societies have to be a part of the ecosystem that we are analyzing. Otherwise, it will be impossible to communicate these alternatives to the very politicians and local populations that we are trying to reach.

III ECOLOGICAL CONSEQUENCES OF INTENSIFICATION OF PLANT PRODUCTIVITY

Ray F. Smith and E. W. Russell, Co-Chairmen

21. Effects of Manipulation of Cotton Agro-Ecosystems on Insect Pest Populations
Ray F. Smith and Harold T. Reynolds   373

22. The Relationship between Insect Pests and Cotton Production in Central Africa
F. E. M. Gillham   407

23. Ecological Consequences of Pesticides Used for the Control of Cotton Insects in Cañete Valley, Peru   *Teodoro Boza Barducci*   423

24. Some Ecological Implications of Two Decades of Use of Synthetic Organic Insecticides for Control of Agricultural Pests in Louisiana   *L. D. Newsom*   439

DISCUSSION   460

25. Ecological Aspects of Pest Control in Malaysia   *Gordon R. Conway*   467

26. Toxicity of Insecticides Used for Asiatic Rice Borer Control to Tropical Fish in Rice Paddies   *L. T. Kok*   489

27. Locust Control: Ecological Problems and International Pests   *P. T. Haskell*   499

28. Ecological Effects of Chemical Control of Rodents and Jackals in Israel
H. Mendelssohn   527

DISCUSSION   545

29. Problems in the Use of Chemical Fertilizers   *John Phillips*   549

30. The Impact of Technological Developments on Soils in East Africa *E. W. Russell*   567

31. Nitrate Problems and Nitrite Hazards as Influenced by Ecological Conditions and by Fertilization of Plants   *W. Schuphan*   577

32. Lateritic Soils in Distinct Tropical Environments: Southern Sudan and Brazil
Mary McNeil   591

33. Problems of Tropical Settlement—Experiences in Colombia and Bolivia
Harold T. Jorgenson   609

34. Plant Germ Plasm Resources and Utilization   *David H. Timothy*   631

DISCUSSION   657

A BALLAD OF ECOLOGICAL AWARENESS (continued)

By undiscriminating use of strong insecticide
Our temporary gain is lost when all our friends have died.
With strip planting of alfalfa something new is making sense:
Spend the millions now on tribute—not a penny for defense!

The locust as an insect is extremely international,
It runs a downwind airline, it's adaptable and rational.
For biological controls the beast is far too mobile;
It seems a shame to persecute an animal so noble.
But though the locust is a most engaging little rascal,
I think I'd put my money on Ecology and Haskell.

One principle that is an ecological upsetter
Is that if anything is good, then more of it is better,
And this misunderstanding sets us very, very wrong,
For no relation in the world is linear for long.

Pursuit of agriculture on a lateritic soil
Is a classical example of an Unrewarding Toil,
For the unsuspecting settler gets a very nasty shock
When the lateritic soil turns into lateritic rock.

The poisoned mouse eliminates the useful owl and vulture,
But the growing world economy insists on monoculture.
O! Science may be phony but the social system's phonier,
And so spread on, insecticide, and sulphate of ammonia.

A developed Agriculture is a fabulous polluter;
As development gets faster, then the problem gets acuter.
We are loading up the planet with a lot of nitric trash,
And if nitrogen falls off its cycle—wow! is that a crash.

Development is fatal to the local and specific;
A single culture spreads from the Atlantic to Pacific.
So preserving every specimen of life is quite essential
If we're not to break the bank of evolutionary potential.

Too many governments, alas, in tropic parts today
Say, "Let us group the little farms," and then say, "Let us spray."
Pests and Pollutions prosper then, and what is more the pity,
It drives the people off the land to fester in the city.
So how do we inculcate in a heterogeneous nation
The sober sense of ignorance that leads to conservation?

—K. E. BOULDING

21. EFFECTS OF MANIPULATION OF COTTON AGRO-ECOSYSTEMS ON INSECT PEST POPULATIONS

Ray F. Smith and Harold T. Reynolds

The cotton agro-ecosystem is composed of the total complex of organisms in a crop-producing area together with the over-all conditioning environment and is further modified by the various agricultural, industrial, recreational, and social activities of man. The determination of insect pest population levels is broadly under the influence of the agro-ecosystem and a knowledge of how this influence operates is essential to an ecological approach to pest control. (The major components of the cotton agro-ecosystem and their complex interrelationships are discussed.)

Case histories of major cotton-growing areas in Central and South America, the United States, the Middle East, and Australia illustrate vividly the impact of the use of pesticides in a cotton agro-ecosystem and demonstrate the world-wide crisis which is rapidly intensifying because pest control has been developed in isolation. Use of pesticides must be considered and applied in the context of the agro-ecosystem in which the pest populations exist and in which control actions are taken. (The case histories with reports of the accelerated pest control problems and analyses of the violent disruptions of the ecosystems in each case are given.) The use of chemical pesticides without regard to the complexities of cotton agro-ecosystems, especially the fundamental aspects of the population dynamics of pest species, has been the basic cause of the dramatic exacerbation of cotton pest problems over the last ten to fifteen years.

There is now strong evidence that the integrated control approach with its strong ecological inputs has proved to be a markedly better way to solve a wide variety of pest problems than has a total reliance on pesticides. Integrated control attempts to use a combination of suitable control techniques in as compatible a manner as possible to maintain the pest populations below defined economic injury levels. Integrated control derives its uniqueness of approach from its emphasis on the fullest practical utilization of the existing mortality and suppressive factors in the environment.

The cotton pest control crisis is not unique and similar crises must be faced now or in the near future with a wide variety of other pests, such as mosquitoes, house flies, ticks on cattle, and many other situations where pesticides have been used extensively. This crisis presents a challenge that we believe can be met with an imaginative approach to the management of agro-ecosystems if we act now. In this way, pests can be controlled without continued magnification of the problem and we can preserve some of the richness of the environment.

The term "agro-ecosystem" is derived from the well-known ecological term "ecosystem" and emphasizes the special characteristics of agricultural ecosystems. These agro-ecosystems are a part of what Marston Bates (1962) has called the "man-altered landscape." The agro-ecosystem is a unit composed of the total complex of organisms in a crop-producing area together with the over-all conditioning environment and further modified by the various agricultural, industrial, recreational, and social activities of man. In any case, the cotton agro-ecosystem should be considered more as a man-manipulated system than as a natural one (Doutt, 1964). An attempt is made here to analyze the components of cotton agro-ecosystems and to illustrate how changes in these systems can aggravate pest problems on the one hand and, on the other, can be used for more effective management of pest populations.

In the practical analysis of an agro-ecosystem for pest management, emphasis is placed on the populations of the pest species, their competitors, the organisms that prey on them, their main and alternative food supplies, and the manner in which the other elements of the environment modify all of these. The determination of insect pest population levels is broadly influenced by the agro-ecosystem, and a knowledge of how this influence operates is essential to an eco-logical approach to pest control. This ecological approach to the control of insects is now commonly referred to as integrated control (FAO, 1966; Smith and van den Bosch, 1967). A thorough understanding of the agro-ecosystem is also necessary to harmonize control practices for different pests in such a manner as to prevent unacceptable disruptive effects. In the same way, a knowledge of the agro-ecosystem permits assessment of the mortality factors operating on a pest or potential pest population and will suggest subsequent manipulations to reinforce and enhance their action. Finally, the information developed must be incorporated in a harmonious and acceptable manner into the prevailing agronomic practices for cotton production.

The cotton agro-ecosystem is a very ancient one. Cotton fabrics dating back to 3000 B.C. have been found in the Indus River Valley and cotton specimens dating to 2500 B.C. in Peru (Lewis and Richmond, 1968). Recently, in the Oaxaca Valley of Mexico, a boll weevil was found associated with a cotton boll at least one thousand years old (Warner and Smith, 1968).

Approximately 31 million hectares of cotton are grown in the world each year (see Table 21–1). This is about 2.5% of all cultivated land. In the United States, cotton is the most important cultivated crop in large agricultural states such as California

Table 21-1

COTTON PRODUCTION IN MAJOR
PRODUCING COUNTRIES
(1967-68 Season)

COUNTRY	WORLD RANK	1,000 BALES	1,000 HECTARES	KILOS PER HECTARE
U.S.S.R.	1	9,460	2,442	840
U.S.A.	2	7,215	3,236	501
China	3	7,000	5,059	300
India	4	5,330	8,215	141
Brazil	5	2,750	2,266	263
Pakistan	6	2,400	1,732	300
U.A.R.	7	2,014	683	639
Mexico	8	2,000	689	630
Turkey	9	1,825	718	551
Sudan	10	900	486	401
Syria	11	585	240	530
Iran	12	545	291	406
Nicaragua	13	470	146	696
Colombia	14	465	174	578
Greece	15	443	138	699
Peru	16	390	155	643
Guatemala	17	360	89	876
Argentina	18	335	293	248
Tanzania	19	325	263	268
Spain	20	300	149	438
Uganda	21	285	868	72
Mozambique	22	195	316	135
Chad	23	175	297	128
El Salvador	24	160	45	764
Australia	25	150	29	1,128
Israel	26	131	30	970
Thailand	27	125	87	312
Nigeria	28	125	–	–
Afghanistan	29	90	121	160
WORLD TOTAL*		47,817	31,005	336

* Note: Totals include other countries.

and Texas. In some countries, e.g., Nicaragua, Egypt, and Syria, it makes up 40% or more of the value of all export earnings. In nearly all cotton-growing areas, insects are a serious hazard to the production of cotton and large amounts of insecticides are widely used for insect control.

COMPONENTS OF THE COTTON AGRO-ECOSYSTEM

In spite of its superficial simplicity, the cotton agro-ecosystem is a complex biologi-cal system. This system is dominated by a rather uniform, dense population of a highly selected strain of plants. The major components of a cotton agro-ecosystem include the population of cotton plants, the soil substrate and its essential biota, the enveloping chemical and physical environment, an energy input from the sun, and the varied additional inputs of man. In certain situations or at particular times, additional elements such as weedy plant species, plant pathogens, or phytophagous arthropods may become critical or dominant components in the system. The physical limits of a cotton agro-ecosystem are rarely precise. Very few, if any, agro-ecosystems are self-contained. For the practical purposes of pest control, rather arbitrary limits are determined. However, the area included must be large enough so that the more significant populations can complete most of their major biological activities within its limits. Thus crudely delimited, the cotton agro-ecosystem will usually include a group of agricultural fields (cotton as well as other associated crops) together with their marginal areas, and often certain other intermixed areas as woods, streams, and weedy or uncultivated areas. As agricultural practice creates a large amount of disturbance, there is typically much movement of species within, into, and out of the system (Smith and Reynolds, 1966). The cotton-growing valleys of Peru (see Chapter 23, by Boza Barducci, this volume) are an unusual example of relatively closed agro-ecosystems. The cotton agro-ecosystems in Central Africa are also discussed by Gillham in Chapter 22 of this volume.

THE COTTON PLANTS

The species and varieties of cotton. Over thirty species of cotton exist, but only four are cultivated commercially. The cultivated species native to the Old World are *Gossypium arboreum* and *G. herbaceum*. The

New World cultivated species are *G. hir-sutum* and *G. barbadense*. The famous long staple cottons of Egypt, Tanguis cotton of Peru, the Sea Island cotton of the West Indies, and the Pima cottons of southwestern United States are derived in large part from *G. barbadense*. The bulk of the other commercial cottons of the world are highly selected strains of *G. hirsutum*.

In many areas, commercial cotton varieties also grow the year round as escaped plants. Although most of the modern cottons are grown as annual shrubs, in some climates they may retain the perennial characteristics of their ancestors. In some cotton agro-ecosystems, this perennial characteristic is utilized when the cut-off cotton plants are permitted to send out new shoots in the second or third growing season (known in various areas as stub cotton, ratoon cotton, or *socas*). See Pearson and Maxwell-Darling (1958), and Lewis and Richmond (1968).

Special strains of cotton have been developed to provide desirable fiber quality, time of fruiting, high fiber yield, and other characteristics of interest to man. Most of these agronomic developments have occurred with little consideration of their relationship to pest problems. This was first dramatically demonstrated by the devastating impact of the boll weevil on susceptible cotton plantings as it spread across the U. S. Cotton Belt in the early part of this century. The early cottonseed entrepreneurs in the United States selected special strains of cotton on the basis of boll size, plant appearance, apparent local adaptation, and yielding ability, and with no consideration of insect pests. When the cotton boll weevil struck near the turn of the century, these early cotton varieties were devastated. This was described dramatically by Loftin (1945):

As the boll weevil moved in its relentless march across the Cotton Belt, the damage it caused threatened to ruin the cotton industry. To appreciate the chaos caused by the weevil,

it must be remembered that southern agriculture and industry depended almost entirely on the one crop—cotton—and that loss of from one-third to one-half of the yield occurred for the first few years in each newly invaded area. Farmers, merchants, and bankers were bankrupted; farms and homes in whole communities were deserted; labourers and tenants were demoralized and moved to other sections; and a general feeling of panic and fear followed the boll weevil, as it moved into locality after locality. . . .

Plant breeding for resistance. In some cotton-producing areas, considerable attention has been given to incorporating some insect resistance into commercial cotton varieties. Success in the breeding of cotton varieties for resistance to *Empoasca* leafhoppers has been achieved in Africa, India, and Australia (Painter, 1951). The results of plant breeding in Central Africa are discussed by F. E. M. Gillham in this volume (Chapter 22). With this exception, the great potential of plant resistance as a means of controlling cotton pests has been largely ignored (Newsom and Brazzel, 1968). There have been reports of various levels of resistance to thrips, fleahoppers, cotton stainers, whiteflies, boll weevils, spider mites, and several lepidopterous pests. Recently, there has been renewed interest in the United States to develop varieties resistant to the cotton fleahopper and the bollworm.

The pigment gossypol is present in small lysigenous glands in all parts of the plant (except the roots) of nearly all cottons. Because gossypol is toxic to nonruminant animals and has other disadvantages in processing cottonseed, considerable effort has been devoted to developing commercial cotton varieties with low gossypol content. Although desirable for these reasons, low gossypol cotton has proved to be highly attractive and susceptible to several cotton insects (Lukefahr and Martin, 1966; Bottger *et al.,* 1964; Murray *et al.,* 1965). In fact such cottons are attacked by insects not previously recorded as cotton pests. The chrysomelids, *Maecolaspis flavida* and *Gastro-*

physa cyanea, and the blister beetle *Epicauta vittata,* none of which attack glanded cotton, do attack the glandless cotton severely. The cotton leafworm *Alabama argillacea* prefers glandless cotton to glanded cotton (Jenkins *et al.,* 1966). Gillham (1965) suggests that gossypol glands have evolved in cotton as a protective mechanism against the attacks of pests. And Lukefahr and Martin (1966) suggest increasing the gossypol content of cultivated varieties of cotton to make them resistant to bollworm and other lepidopterous pests.

Fruiting characteristics and compensation. The cotton plant is characterized by having two forms of branches (vegetative and reproductive), indeterminate growth, and by its shedding of small floral buds (squares) and young bolls (Eaton, 1955). These characteristics are of great importance to insect pest management. Flowering is progressive and for a time it becomes more rapid as the plant grows. Normal shedding is slight early in the growing season but gradually increases. For a time, boll retention is considerably greater than shedding; but later in the season the situation usually reverses. Even when there are no insects to bother fruiting forms, over a season nearly two-thirds of the pre-boll fruiting forms fail to produce mature bolls. In a sense, the cotton plant has a limited capacity to set and mature bolls depending upon its present fruit load, general physiology, and growing conditions. Those cotton squares and small bolls in excess of this level will drop from the plant even if no insects are present. It matters not at all whether a square drops because of insect feeding or because of limited fruit-carrying capacity of the plant. Insect-caused injury affecting fruiting forms in excess of the carrying capacity does not result in crop loss (Eaton, 1955; Flint *et al.,* 1963; Newsom and Brazzel, 1968; Pearson and Maxwell-Darling, 1958). The ability of the cotton plant to compensate and respond to the environment is also shown by the fact that within the range of 25,000 to 75,000 plants per acre, cotton will, under comparable conditions, produce about the same yield (Adkisson, Hanna, and Bailey, 1964).

The occurrence of larval populations of bollworms broadly parallels the flowering cycle of the cotton plant. Greatest numbers of larvae are present during the period when the plants have the greatest number of flowers. As the cotton approaches maturity, the larval population declines rapidly (Adkisson, Hanna, and Bailey, 1964). In a similar way, the cotton boll weevil is timed to and by the appearance of squares (Walker, 1966).

The seasonal distribution of flowering and boll-set in relation to insect infestations is also important. Some varieties of cotton, at least under some growing conditions, will set most of the cotton crop within a period of a few weeks. Hence, protection of the plant from the ravages of insects throughout the entire growing season is less critical than in the case of indeterminate varieties which set cotton over most of the season.

Continuous and well-marked changes in composition occur during the development of the cotton boll. The changes are related to changes in susceptibility to pests and diseases. In the first two weeks of boll development when most physiological shedding occurs, growth is extremely rapid, the dry weight doubling every two days. In the second and third weeks, reducing sugars and moisture content are highest. Bolls at this stage are extremely attractive to lepidopterous larvae. The lint, oil, and protein of the ripe seed are mainly laid down after the boll reaches full size (about four to five weeks). The ripe seed is essential for the development of the pink bollworm and certain bugs (Rainey, 1948).

THE INSECT COMPLEX

Insects and related arthropods are a problem nearly everywhere that cotton is grown.

In the United States, over a hundred species of insects and spider mites are known to attack cotton (Newsom and Brazzel, 1968; Watson *et al.,* 1965). In most cotton agro-ecosystems, there is a variable group of lepidopterous larvae attacking the roots, leaves, squares, and bolls. The complex varies from area to area, and at different times and places, appears to preclude economically-sound production of cotton lint. In certain parts of the Western Hemisphere, weevils are the most important pests. From a world viewpoint, the widespread pink bollworm *Pectinophora gossypiella* is considered to be the most destructive cotton insect but locally other insects often cause more damage. A large array of other pests, including stem weevils, plant bugs, aphids, thrips, and spider mites, attack in varying degrees all parts of the plant at all times in the growing season (see Pearson and Maxwell-Darling, 1958). There were 1,326 species of arthropods from cotton listed in 1948 (Hargreaves, 1948). Only about 15% of them can be considered significant pests, and less than half of these are of major importance. With the exception of the pink bollworm, the major cotton pests are indigenous to the continents where they cause damage. Appropriate manipulation of the agro-ecosystem by man can aid in preventing economic damage by insect pests.

Associated with the insect pests of cotton is a complex of beneficial organisms (parasites, predators, pathogens). A large number of insects are also attracted to the cotton plant to feed at nectaries located on leaves and fruiting forms. The common cotton varieties are partly self-pollinated and partly cross-pollinated, and insect pollinators are not critical for commercial production of the *G. hirsutum* varieties. Additional species in the cotton agro-ecosystem insect fauna are associated with weeds and other plants.

Key pests. There are usually one or two key pests in any cotton agro-ecosystem. Key pests are serious, perennially occurring, and persistent species that dominate control practices, because in the absence of deliberate control by man, the pest population often exceeds the economic-injury levels. In the cotton agro-ecosystems of the San Joaquin Valley of California, the key pests are the bollworm and the lygus bugs. The Egyptian cotton leafworm *Spodoptera littoralis* and the pink bollworm are the key pests in the United Arab Republic (Hosny and Iss-hak, 1967). In the Cotton South, the boll weevil is the sole key pest over much of the area (see Newsom, this volume, Chapter 24). Although the *Heliothis* bollworm complex may be more destructive than the boll weevil in many areas of the South, many entomologists consider it to be less than a key pest in the absence of ecosystem disruption such as often follows insecticidal application, particularly repeated applications for weevil control.

Evolutionary changes in cotton pests. The cotton pests are subject to many evolutionary pressures in addition to those resulting from the application of pesticides. Changes in the agro-ecosystem can eliminate a pest population or reduce it to insignificance. Or with some species, individuals in the surviving population of insects may be well adapted to the new conditions and assume greater importance as pests. In a similar way, pest populations may evolve, developing new characteristics so that they can expand their geographical distribution, host range, or even host preference.

For many years, the cotton boll weevil *Anthonomus grandis* in the United States was confined to the more humid regions of the South with significant summer rainfall. It was assumed that it could not survive in the hot, arid regions of the Southwest. Then in the early fifties it gradually moved westward into some of these formerly unoccupied areas. In 1953 an outbreak occurred at Presidio, Texas, and started to spread up the Rio Grande. It reached the lower end of the El Paso Valley in 1961 and although not well established, the boll weevil has been found several times at El Paso. About this same time, the boll weevil crossed another barrier and moved above the Caprock in Texas and now occurs over much of the High Plains (Newsom and Brazzel, 1968).

In the past, *Empoasca solana,* a phloem-feeding leafhopper species, developed enormous populations in the Imperial Valley of California, but only on sugar beets. After many years of virtual host specificity, this leafhopper moved to cotton fields in vast numbers, but only when the sugar beets were harvested or when the sugar-beet plants became unattractive to the pest just prior to harvest. A few years later the leafhopper began to reproduce on cotton early in the growing season when sugar-beet plantings were still attractive to the species. Although sugar beets are still considered to be the preferred host and also provide the major overwintering site, this leafhopper provides an elegant example of adaptation to a new host plant and a significant pest relationship between crops (Reynolds and Deal, 1956; Reynolds, unpublished data).

In the Near East, the Egyptian cotton leafworm *Spodoptera littoralis* seems to have changed its habits. Formerly, the larvae fed almost entirely on the leaves, but now in the middle and late instars, larvae often enter the bolls. Also, this insect has now become the worst pest of apples in Israel, while prior to 1950 it had never been recorded on that crop (see also Rivnay, this volume, Chapter 20).

Natural mortality. The actions of parasites, predators, and pathogens are important causes of pest mortality in many cotton agro-ecosystems. In other areas, especially where heavy use of pesticides has eliminated the natural controls, such biotic mortality may be minimal. The importance of parasites and predators in cotton agro-ecosystems has been most clearly demonstrated by the unleashing of secondary pests through the use of broad-spectrum organic insecti-cides. Also, in many instances, there have been tremendous resurgences of "primary target" pest species following the use of pesticides. These pest resurgences and secondary outbreaks are largely the result of the elimination of parasites and predators. There are many examples of such pesticide-induced outbreaks including those of bollworm, tobacco budworm, cotton aphids, and spider mites in the Cotton South of the United States. Jassid control with DDT, Sevin, or Zectran results in increased incidence of whitefly in the Sudan. However, this resurgence is not necessarily the effect of elimination of natural enemies. Examples from other countries are given in later sections of this paper. It should be emphasized that it would not long be possible to produce most crops, including cotton, economically or at all without the regulatory impact of beneficial species upon the pest complex.

Direct action on natural enemies is only one of the ways insecticides can disrupt natural control. Disruption of food chains can also be important. For example, if aphids, spider mites, and thrips (the usual prey of abundant, omnivorous predators such as *Chrysopa, Nabis, Geocoris,* and *Orius*) are eliminated from the cotton agro-ecosystem early in the season by chemical treatments which in themselves are not significantly harmful to the predators, the latter will starve, emigrate, or cease reproducing. Later in the season, when such strong-flying species as *Lygus* and *Heliothis* invade the same fields, they are essentially free from predator attack and an explosive outbreak of these pests often occurs. These alternative food sources for the predators thus can maintain critical mortality factors (Smith and van den Bosch, 1967).

In some circumstances the value of partial control (e.g., 80% kill with an insecticide) in preference to full control of the pests (98–100%) can also be demonstrated. Each situation, including economic implications, must be carefully evaluated with full consideration of all implications to the population dynamics of the pest species.

SOILS, FERTILIZERS, AND WATER

"How much water cotton needs depends on many factors, such as weather, climate, length of growing season, variety, depth and texture of soil, fertility, leaching requirements, quality of water, and the efficiency of scheduling and applying irrigation water" (Longenecker and Erie, 1965). Optimum use of water is rarely achieved, and in most cotton agro-ecosystems the timing, quantity, and quality of water is less than ideal.

In India, only 12% of the cotton is under irrigation. Where irrigation can be provided, the yields of lint are 200 to 400 lb per acre. Where there are no irrigation facilities, production is only 90 to 110 lb per acre, and in unfavorable weather the yields are even lower. The average yield last year in India was only 126 lb per acre (the highest on record for that country).

The highest yields of cotton are attained in agricultural areas with bright sunshine and adequate supplies of irrigation water. The highest yields come from Australia (969 lb of lint per acre in 1967–68), Israel (865 lb per acre in 1967–68), California (1,072 lb per acre in 1968), and Arizona (1,151 lb per acre in 1968). These are average yields for the total area. In individual commercial fields, 2,000 lb per acre is not rare, and in experimental plantings even higher yields have been achieved.

In the Sudan, much of the success of the cotton crop depends on early and adequate pre-sowing rains (Ripper and George, 1965). Sixty percent of the considerable differences in yield from season to season are correlated with the amount of pre-sowing rains and with insect pests (Jackson, 1963). In years of light pre-sowing rains, more insecticidal treatments are needed over a longer period than when there are adequate rains. Poor pre-sowing rains allow nitrate to accumulate in the top part of the soil and the young cotton plant is able to take up more nitrogen. In these years of poor rain, the plant does not use as much nitrogen for growth. The nitrogen in the leaf tissue is therefore available for the cotton jassid. When the nitrogen content is above 3%, the jassid fecundity is greatly increased. If the application of fertilizer is combined with poor pre-sowing rain, the increase in jassid populations is still higher. Thus more treatments are needed because of the heavier infestations and also because the growing season is extended (Ripper and George, 1965; Joyce, 1961).

The significant impact of water in shaping and maintaining agricultural ecosystems is well demonstrated by the coastal valleys of Peru. There are some fifty short mountain streams or rivers traversing the coastal desert of Peru. The amount and seasonal occurrence of water in these streams largely determines the extent of the local agricultural development. The valleys differ in size, climate, soils, water supply and quality, crops, and pests. Each of these valleys is thus a small self-contained micro-agro-ecosystem isolated from the others by harsh desert stretches. Some of the streams extend far up into the Andes and have a permanent flow throughout the year. The shorter rivers that have their source in the lower hills flow only during the rainy season (December through April). In some of the valleys, irrigation water from wells has been developed to supplement and extend the supply from the rivers. In each of these valleys, a different pattern of pest control has been developed to fit the special characteristics of the local agro-ecosystem.

In the Manabí area of Ecuador, the rainy period is normally from January to April during planting time. The rainfall for this period ranges from 40 to 110 cm. During the 1967–68 growing season there was only one rain. As a result of the severe drought, there was a crop failure. In the affected provinces of Manabí, Guayas, and Los Ríos, there were 19,650 hectares planted to cotton, but only 3,910 hectares were harvested, and in these the yields were about half of normal (i.e., 127 lb of lint per acre).

In Texas, under dry, nonirrigated conditions, the pink bollworm tends to affect fiber quality more than yield. Damaged bolls, unless almost completely destroyed, are harvested. The stained and cut lint resulting from feeding of the pink bollworm larvae is thus ginned. This stained lint contributes to lower cotton grades and hence, low prices. In areas with high humidity and particularly when these areas are irrigated, the plant microenvironment is conducive to boll rots. Under such a condition, bolls damaged by the pink bollworm often rot so much that they are not harvested. In one dry-land situation, up to 50% of the bolls could be infested with one or two larva before significant losses in yield occurred; but under irrigated conditions, a 40% infestation resulted in severe losses (Adkisson, Brazzel, and Gaines, 1963).

Irrigation and fertilizer practices may affect the qualities of the cotton plant and influence the insect through the plant. Little information on this point is available for cotton, but it is a common observation that *Heliothis* and the other lepidopterous species oviposit more heavily on plants with succulent growth (Adkisson, 1958). In contrast, the cotton leaf perforator *Bucculatrix thurberiella* and a whitefly, *Trialeurodes abutilonea,* prefer field margins or areas of weak, new growth within the field in the desert areas of California (Reynolds, unpublished data). Likewise there is abundant evidence that lygus bug populations prefer rank cotton, often concentrating in such areas within a field with irregular growth.

In some of the irrigated western states, "skip-row" plantings are common. Various combinations of skips are utilized—two rows in and one row out, two in and two out, four in and two out, etc. Such plantings interspersed with skip rows change the environment enough so that pests such as the perforator and whitefly prefer the open areas. Although cotton rows next to the skipped areas produce more cotton, airplane applications of insecticides are more costly because the entire area must be treated as if it were a solid planting.

Irrigation may also influence directly the insect pest population by modifying the prevailing physical environment. For example, Andres (1957) calculated a net reproduction rate of 131 for the spider mite *Tetranychus pacificus* under hot, dry conditions and only 63 under humid conditions.

WEATHER AND CLIMATE

Although we are limited in what can be done to manage the physical environment of a cotton agro-ecosystem, an understanding of the influence of physical factors on the physiology of the cotton plant and the insect pests is useful. The cotton plant originated as a desert shrub and although extremely variable, it is basically adapted to hot and dry conditions.

Both excessively low and high temperatures cause the plant to shed squares, the sensitivity varying somewhat with the variety. In some areas, such as Israel, the excessively high temperatures of midsummer cause the cotton plants to stop setting bolls. Hence, there are two periods of boll set (about July 1 and September 1), which extends the growing season and aggravates pest problems. A similar situation exists in the hot, arid desert valleys of southeastern California (Imperial and neighboring valleys). The variety, Acala 44–2, shed squares and small bolls during the hottest period of summer, resulting in an early boll set and a second period of set starting usually early in September. When the cotton plants begin to shed rather than set fruit, the plants become vegetative, growing tall and rank—a situation attractive to bollworms, lygus bugs, and certain other pests. In September the tall plants begin to set heavily on the top, soon becoming top-heavy and falling over or lodging, creating excessive problems with boll rots, harvesting, etc. This situation has now been circumvented in the desert areas by switching to another cotton variety which sets cotton reasonably well during the hottest period of weather. It should be noted that improper production practices, particularly excessive fertilizer and irrigation, can also cause rank, excessively vegetative plant growth with similar problems.

Among the wild cottons, there are species representing both long-day and short-day photoperiodic types. However, most of the commercial cotton varieties are day-neutral or only slightly photoperiodic (Carns and Mauney, 1968). In contrast, many of the cotton insects are strongly affected by day length. For example, growth and reproduction of the pink bollworm are confined to the seasons of the year in which the daylight period is somewhat longer than 12.5 hours. When days become shorter, diapause intervenes although this reaction is modified somewhat by nutrition (Adkisson, 1966). The pupal diapause in the bollworm is also under photoperiodic control (Phillips and Newsom, 1966), but this response is modified by temperature (Wellso and Adkisson, 1966). The conditions prevailing for the adult and eggs also modify the later larval response to day length. The prevailing temperature and day-length regime in the fall also determine if another generation of boll weevils will be produced, but the precise form of the regulatory mechanism is not clear (Earle and Newsom, 1964; Sterling and Adkisson, 1966).

Some pests, e.g., pink bollworm, through gradual population accumulation during the summer and early fall, are a most serious problem late in the season. In areas where the pink bollworm is a serious pest, it is often necessary to curtail the growing season even though the plant condition and weather are favorable for continued boll set. In this way large numbers of diapausing larvae do not accumulate and problems early in the succeeding crop are reduced.

Climate is, of course, very important in determining the geographic distribution and seasonal incidence of insect pests. For example, the severity of the 1967 outbreak of *Spodoptera littoralis* in Israel has been blamed on the abnormally low temperature in July and August of that year. In Peru, *Anthonomus vestitus* and *Mescinia peruella* develop outbreak numbers in the spring when there are fewer hours of sun than normal (Beingolea, 1962a).

WEEDS AND OTHER PLANTS

The cotton agro-ecosystem contains a large variety of plants that find its special conditions of cultivation suitable for their growth and survival. Not only do these undesirable plants compete with the cotton plants for water, nutrients, and light, but they harbor and maintain insects and diseases. Some, e.g., *Sida,* are hosts for cotton viruses. Others maintain insect pest populations. For example, the cotton fleahopper *Psallus seriatus* in Texas and Oklahoma is dependent upon a sequential series of host plants. In the spring it lives on horsemint and other weeds, and then migrates to cotton. When cotton has matured, the fleahopper transfers to croton and other weeds. Weeds also interfere with cultural practices and harvesting, and when abundant, lower the grade of the mechanically harvested fiber. In some special situations, certain plants (weeds) may be useful in helping to maintain beneficial insects. For example, in Peru the weed *Ambrosia artemisioides* as well as *Rumex crispus* help to maintain populations of *Rhinacloa* and other important predators of *Heliothis* in cotton (Beingolea, 1959). It is also common to find hymenopterous parasites and other beneficial insects obtaining nectar from weeds in and near cotton fields.

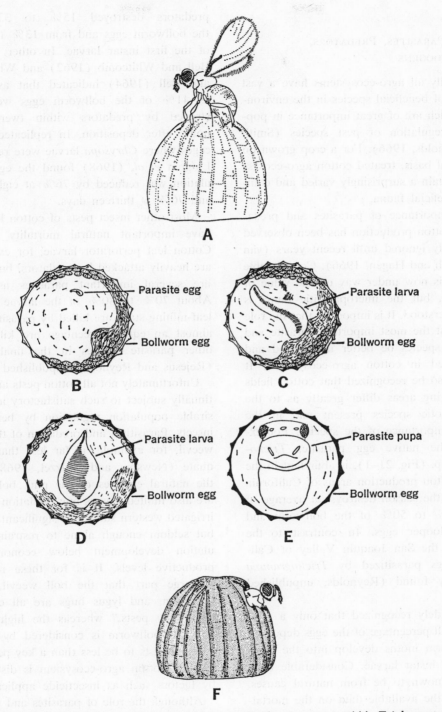

Figure 21-1 Life history of a parasitic wasp, *Trichogramma* sp. (A) *Trichogramma* female ovipositing in a bollworm egg. (B) *Trichogramma* egg within a bollworm egg (dorsal view). (C and D) Stages of larval development of *Trichogramma* sp. (dorsal view). (E) Pupa of *Trichogramma* sp. (dorsal view). (F) *Trichogramma* adult emerging from a bollworm egg through hole chewed in the eggshell. Drawings by C. F. Lagace, after Marshal (1936), Peterson (1930), and Sweetman (1958)

Insect Parasites, Predators, and Pathogens

Virtually all agro-ecosystems have a vast number of beneficial species in the environment which are of great importance in population regulation of pest species (Smith and Reynolds, 1966). For a crop grown on an annual basis, treated cotton agro-ecosystems contain a surprisingly varied and complex beneficial fauna.

The importance of parasites and predators to cotton production has been observed but largely ignored until recent years (van den Bosch and Hagen, 1966). Considerable research is now under way on the value of predators, but the microparasitic fauna is little understood. It is important that the role of at least the most important parasite and predator species be better understood and appreciated in cotton agro-ecosystems. It should also be recognized that cotton fields and growing areas differ greatly as to the native biotic species present and in the relative importance of the species. For example, the native egg parasite, *Trichogramma* sp. (Fig. 21–1), is abundant in the desert cotton production areas of California and over the season destroys an average of from 40% to 50% of the bollworm and cabbage looper eggs. In contrast to the north, in the San Joaquin Valley of California eggs parasitized by *Trichogramma* are rarely found (Reynolds, unpublished data).

It is widely recognized that only a relatively small percentage of the eggs deposited by bollworm moths develop into the damaging late instar larvae. Considerable mortality is known to be from natural causes. Although the available data on the mortality of the eggs and small larvae is more suggestive than conclusive, it is apparent that a large proportion of the deaths are the result of the action of insect predators. Fletcher and Thomas (1943) found that predators destroyed 15% to 33% of the bollworm eggs and from 13% to 60% of the first instar larvae. In other studies, Bell and Whitcomb (1962) and Whitcomb and Bell (1964) indicated that as much as 41% of the bollworm eggs were destroyed by predators within twenty-four hours after deposition. In replicated study cages where *Chrysopa* larvae were released, Lingren *et al.* (1968) found the egg population was reduced by 76% at eight days and 96% at thirteen days.

Most other insect pests of cotton likewise have important natural mortality agents. Cotton leaf perforator larvae, for example, are heavily attacked by predators, but there are several important parasites as well. About 70% to 80% of the larvae in the leaf-mining stage are killed by parasites and almost an equal percentage are killed by other parasite species in the final stage (Rejesus and Reynolds, unpublished data).

Unfortunately not all cotton pests are continually subject to such satisfactory and desirable population regulation by beneficial insects. Parasitism and predation of the boll weevil, for example, is far less than adequate (Newsom and Brazzel, 1968) and the natural enemies of the pink bollworm are also limited. Lygus bug predation in the irrigated western states is a significant factor but seldom enough alone to restrain population development below economically productive levels. It is for these reasons in large part that the boll weevil, pink bollworm, and lygus bugs are all considered "key pests," whereas the highly destructive bollworm is considered by many entomologists to be less than a key pest unless the cotton agro-ecosystem is disturbed by factors such as insecticide applications.

Although the role of parasites and predators is not fully understood, their importance has been repeatedly demonstrated when beneficial populations of natural enemies have been destroyed by the use of insecticides. Frequently, tremendous resurgences of target pests have followed insecticide application and the status of species of secondary importance changed to the point that they became important pests (Newsom and Brazzel, 1968).

It is now widely recognized that predators and parasites have a substantial effect in cotton agro-ecosystems and often satisfactorily regulate most pest species to populations below economically productive levels. In situations where beneficial insect populations are inadequate, some cotton entomologists have suggested augmentation of the natural enemies by periodic release of mass-produced individuals (Ridgeway and Jones, 1968; Lingren *et al.,* 1968); others have attempted supplemental feeding in the field to stimulate rapid beneficial insect increase (Hagen, unpublished data).

While it is important to recognize the significance of natural biotic forces in the cotton agro-ecosystem, it is unrealistic to expect these natural forces to take care of all the insect pest problems. In fact, experience in most cotton-growing regions has shown that the natural control must be supplemented with other control measures. But when supplemental controls, e.g., insecticides, are necessary, it is evident that so far as possible, beneficial insect populations should be protected.

Because of selectivity and pesticide resistance, there is great interest in the use of insect pathogens. Preparations of *Bacillus thuringiensis* are selective and recommended for control of pests that feed on cotton foliage. There is equal interest in the potential value of insect virus diseases for control of several pests, particularly for bollworm and cabbage looper. There is a great deal of research necessary before the true potential of these insect pathogens as man-manipulated controls is realized.

In addition to the natural enemies of the insect pests, there are many other insects in the cotton agro-ecosystem. Some of these are attracted to flowers for nectar and pol-

len. Another large group feed at the abundant extrafloral nectaries on the cotton plant. Finally, there are many scavengers and decomposers. At present, we have only the vaguest concept of how these numerous species operate in the cotton agro-ecosystem and of their importance.

PLANT PATHOGENS

A great variety of pathogens, including viruses, bacteria, and fungi, occur wherever cotton is grown. From the time the seed is planted in the ground until harvest, the cotton plant is subject to serious diseases (Presley and Bird, 1968). Plants infected with disease are sometimes more attractive to other pests and the weakened plants frequently are more susceptible to attack by insects. Some of the virus diseases of cotton are transmitted by insects, e.g., leaf-crumple by *Bemisia* whiteflies.

VERTEBRATE WILDLIFE

Although cotton agro-ecosystems have been designed and developed for cotton production, they do have other values for society and other uses. As in the case of our utilization of forested lands, the multiple-use concept should be considered in determining the best use of cotton lands and the protection of values beyond those directly related to cotton production. In many agricultural areas often far more is at stake, particularly in the long-run view of things, than the personal interests of the individual farming the land at a particular moment in time. For example, the cotton field and its margins are important habitats for quail, doves, pheasants, rabbits, fish, toads, frogs, and other vertebrates. By and large, these animals do not have any significant influence on the production of cotton in the area (for details on the impact of cotton pesticides on wildlife, see Newsom, Chapter 24, this volume). Where decisions in pest control are made only from the viewpoint of short-run increased cotton production, they may have disastrous impact on other values important to society.

INFLUENCE OF AGRONOMIC PRACTICES IN COTTON AGRO-ECOSYSTEMS

Any modification of cotton agro-ecosystems has the potential to change the characteristics of the crop plant and the crop environment and, hence, the attractiveness and suitability of the plant or environment to pests. On the one hand, changes in agronomic practice have been introduced without regard to their influence on pest populations and often have aggravated the pest problems. These changes have involved cultivation practices, plant spacing, new varieties, and modified fertilizer rates among many other agronomic changes. On the other hand, these same cultural practices can be utilized to man's advantage in the total effort to manage cotton pests. Over the decades, a series of traditional cultural controls have been developed that have aided cotton pest control. These include production of an early cotton crop, a uniform planting date, a cotton-free period, early harvest, destruction of infested bolls, destruction of alternate hosts, early stalk destruction, and use of trap crops (Newsom and Brazzel, 1968). The introduction of a new cultural practice or the modification of an old one may not have an immediate impact on the pest complex, but only after a period of several years of adjustment by the pest populations and the other elements of the agro-ecosystem are the full effects revealed.

The planting time of the cotton crop is a factor which can have profound effects on insect problems. In most areas, the planting is timed to harvest during a relatively dry season. With pink bollworm, the planting can be delayed to take advantage of a "suicidal" emergence of the adults before fruiting forms are available on the cotton. The cotton planting is also timed to have optimum soil temperature for rapid germination of the seed and growth of the seedling plants. Any factor that extends the growing season tends to expose the crop to a greater risk of damage from inspect pests. It is also desirable to plant the entire crop in any one area in as short a time as possible so that the plants all develop and mature at approximately the same time. Defoliation, rapid harvesting, and destruction of crop residue also offer great potential for reduction of crop pests.

In central Texas, the pink bollworm is successfully managed almost entirely by cultural controls. This program is dependent on the additive effects of the partial controls resulting from community-wide stalk destruction, legally timed plowing-under of the shredded crop residues, suicidal emergence of the pink bollworm moths, preharvest defoliation, modern ginning operations, and sanitation around the cotton gins (Adkisson and Gaines, 1960).

In Colombia the Neiva is a small cotton-growing district in the upper reaches of the Magdalena River in the state of Huila. Normally, cotton is planted in mid-January in the river bottom and is harvested in May or June prior to river flooding. There is abundant wild cotton in this area, but apparently because of the short growing season, its presence does not seem to aggravate the pest problems significantly. Similarly, in all the "inland" cotton-growing districts of Colombia, cotton is grown only in the first half of the year. In 1961 it was decided in the Neiva district that cotton production, and hence profits, could be greatly increased by double-cropping cotton, i.e., growing another crop in the second half of the year. This led to an economic catastrophe because of the severe pest problems that developed. In the first half of the year, 5,236 hectares of cotton were planted and production was about normal, averaging 956 kg of lint per hectare. In the second half of the year, 3,100 hectares were replanted to cotton. Severe insect outbreaks occurred, and in spite of a heavy and costly regimen of insecticides, the yield dropped to 773 kg per hectare, an economic disaster for the cotton farmers because of the very high costs of crop protection. The next year, only 480 hectares of cotton was grown in the Nevia district. In a separate paper in this volume, Chapter 23, Boza Barducci has detailed the importance of cultural practices in the control of pests in the Cañete Valley of Peru.

HETEROGENEITY IN COTTON AGRO-ECOSYSTEMS

The fact that crop monocultures are often severely damaged by pests whereas the diverse climax vegetation of many natural environments is apparently little harmed, has led to the assumption by many non-agriculturists that maximum diversity is desirable in agricultural areas. It is thought that this will preserve or enhance the stability inherent in natural environments; however, careful analysis of pest problems in agricultural areas of varying diversity does not support this. Hedgerows and other "semi-natural" vegetation that adjoin crops often serve as alternate host plants of many crop pests and as disease reservoirs. Hence, the diversity can aggravate rather than stabilize pest problems. Such vegetation may also at times benefit natural enemies of cotton pests if it supports their alternative hosts or prey, but this fact will not automatically favor biological control, since much depends on whether this temporary advantage for the natural enemies counteracts benefits to the pest population. Once the delicate stability of the climax vegetation has been disturbed by man, if only slightly, the vegetation, although still complex, may never-

theless have been sufficiently altered so that pests are benefited relative to their natural enemies.

In the present state of knowledge, it is difficult to generalize. Sometimes any form of diversity of plant species and age structure decreases pest damage, but other examples show that damage may also decrease with increasing simplification. The best examples of the latter are where essential alternate hosts for the pests are removed at least for critical times of the year.

Man has tended to organize and simplify the cotton agro-ecosystem to maximize the yield of cotton fiber. The simplified cotton agro-ecosystem is advantageous for efficient production and harvesting of cotton fiber. Many agronomic practices such as cultivation, irrigation, fertilization, and harvesting are greatly simplified when cotton plants are grown in uniformly spaced conditions and competition from other plants is eliminated. Control of weeds has eliminated or reduced their competition with the cotton plant for water, light, and nutrients. Efficient utilization of these same resources has been achieved by spacing the plants, proper timing of planting, fertilization, and irrigation (Kennedy, 1968). Pest control is also facilitated by the simplifying procedures such as uniform planting date, plow-up regulations, and a cotton-free period. On the other hand, the homogeneity thus introduced can create problems. When the cotton farmer turned to chemicals to eliminate pests, he unwittingly brought another type of simplification. This use of insecticides often destroyed or greatly reduced populations of beneficial forms such as parasites and predators.

Kinds of diversity. Diversity within the cotton-field environment should be considered separately from diversity in the "semi-natural" uncultivated environments often found adjacent to it and from that in the total area cropped locally. Within the cropped area, diversity can often be readily established and manipulated in terms of numbers of plant and animal species, plant age, and cultural practices. This practice is already important in integrated control systems in some cotton-growing areas (e.g., strip-cutting of alfalfa and interplanting of alfalfa in cotton fields). In any case, the kind and amount of diversity must be considered. Futhermore, the same kind of diversity can be harmful in one place and beneficial in another. For example, in parts of Tanzania and elsewhere growing maize with cotton apparently increases *Heliothis* damage to cotton, whereas in Peru, this same kind of diversity is reported as an aid in management of *Heliothis* populations. The full explanation for these differences is not known but it is associated with differences in the cotton varieties grown and differences in the species or strains making up the *Heliothis* complex of each area. In some circumstances, the maize is the source and cause of damaging *Heliothis* attacks but in others, conditions favor continuity of natural enemies and the establishment of a stable equilibrium between the pest and its enemies which keep the pest scarce.

In the cotton-growing areas of the Sudan, one of the main factors which influences the extent of *Heliothis* bollworm infestation is timing of planting and size of acreage of alternate hosts. Large plantings of durra (grain sorghum) and peanuts support populations of *Heliothis* before cotton. Lubia, *Dolychos lablab,* which has a distinctive scent even when not flowering and has a strong attraction for the moths, will often divert the moths away from cotton (Ripper and George, 1965).

Recent studies in the San Joaquin Valley of California have resulted in the introduction of an unusual type of heterogeneity which is useful in reducing problems with lygus bugs and other pests (Stern 1969b; Stern and van den Bosch, 1969). For example, alfalfa has been planted in 20-foot strips after every 128 rows of cotton or

approximately 400 feet across a 160-acre cotton field. In the field, this practice adds up to 10 acres of alfalfa. Only half of each alfalfa strip is mowed at one time, so some succulent, attractive alfalfa is always present. When lygus bugs move into the cotton from adjacent fields of freshly-cut alfalfa, safflower, or other sources, they concentrate in the alfalfa strips. Hence, it is not necessary to treat the cotton for lygus bugs. The insect predators so important in natural control of bollworms are not destroyed by insecticides. In addition, the alfalfa strips produce significant numbers of other beneficial parasites and predators early in the season; these move back and forth between the alfalfa and the cotton. In some field experiments to date, no insecticide treatment of the cotton for either lepidopterous larvae or lygus bugs was necessary.

Adjacent uncultivated areas. The effects and value of the diversity in uncultivated areas adjacent to crops are very difficult to assess, especially in complex areas (van Emden, 1965). Very small changes in the complexity may be all that is needed to aid biological control agents. Often these alterations can provide food or shelter for parasite and predator adults or alternate hosts for their larvae during times in the seasonal history of the population (Beingolea, 1959). The emphasis should be on the selective use of the right kind of diversity (Kennedy, 1968).

Dirty-field technique. Another aspect of heterogeneity is related to maintaining low but significant levels of the pest species. The local populations of natural enemies which depend on the abundance of the pest will invariably be more harmed than the pest if the pest is locally exterminated or if the pest becomes scarce at a critical time. This damage to predators and parasites is a cause of many pest resurgences which will occur in these circumstances even if selective pesticides in favor of the parasite or predator are used (Smith and van den

Bosch, 1967). Resurgence of treated populations has become an increasingly common phenomenon among cotton pests (Newsom and Brazzel, 1968). After treatment, the pest population often attains its original or even a higher level in a very short time. Treatments of parathion for cotton aphid give control but cause rapid resurgences. Another example is bollworm following treatment with Azodrin®. The preservation of the minimum but finite pest numbers necessary to maintain an effective local population of the natural enemies can be important. In California, this is the main basis for recommendations against early season chemical control and avoidance of any treatment of cotton until economic damage is threatened. Under some circumstances, it may even be advisable to release populations of the pest at critical times of the year to maintain the continuity of the pest population for the regulatory species. This concept has been tested experimentally in strawberry fields in California, but to our knowledge has not been utilized for cotton pests.

Interactions with other crops. The sequence of crops in a given area also affects the type and extent of pest infestation. In central Texas, where alfalfa and maize are often grown in the same river valley as cotton, the bollworm is greatly favored. The overwintering population of bollworm attacks alfalfa in the early spring. This does not damage the alfalfa significantly but it allows this pest to bridge the period between spring emergence and the appearance of the favored host, maize. The second generation of bollworms then may increase to large numbers on corn. During the summer, cotton is the main host for the bollworm with alfalfa becoming important again in the fall. In contrast, the tobacco budworm has no important hosts in this area, other than cotton, and is not able to maintain as large a population as is the bollworm (Henry and Adkisson, 1965).

In the Cauca Valley of Colombia in recent years there has been an increasing diversity of agricultural production. Acreages of sorghum, maize, and tomatoes (all hosts for the bollworm) have been increased greatly, and the bollworm problem on cotton has increased correspondingly.

Size of plantings. Differences in size of cotton plantings between Costa Rica and Guatemala (Table 21–2) may explain in part the respective magnitude of cotton pest problems in each country. In Costa Rica, the fields are scattered and often surrounded by pasture land or uncultivated areas. In Guatemala, the cotton plantings are often grouped into nearly solid, large blocks containing 30,000 manzanas (1 manzana = 1.7 acres) or more. The problem is complicated by many other factors, but Costa Rican cotton growers have far less of a cotton pest problem than do the Guatemalan growers. Gillham (this volume, Chapter 22) also discusses the relationship of size of plantings to *Diparopsis* infestations in cotton in Central Africa, and Timothy (this volume, Chapter 34) mentions the general aspects of size of plantings on infestations.

Table 21–2

SIZE OF PLANTING PER GROWER (MANZANAS[1])	NO. OF GROWERS	TOTAL AREA (MANZANAS)
Costa Rica		
Less than 50	40	1,063
50–99	29	2,025
100–199	17	2,081
Over 200	11	2,975
	97	8,144
Guatemala		
Less than 500	36	9,130
500–1,000	30	20,200
Over 1,000	34	74,400
	100	103,730

[1] 1 manzana = 1.7 acres

ECONOMICS OF CROP PROTECTION

It is essential for the rational development of a pest control system in an agro-ecosystem to determine for the several pest populations a threshold level below which any inputs for control operations would be economically unwarranted or perhaps harmful. From the broad view of human society, all crop losses (diminished supply of food and fiber) are to be considered real losses; however, the costs of achieving the full crop potential may exceed the value of the potential benefit. Systems analysis can help decision-making on measures to maximize the return to both society in general and the individual crop producer. The latter may consider only a portion of the reduction in yield or quality as a loss to him. His determination, however made—consciously, or intuitively or on good or bad advice—will be influenced by such elements as the technology available for crop protection, the cost of avoiding the potential loss, marketing conditions, the ultimate use of the crop, and other benefit-related factors for the producer than can be achieved by avoiding the loss. Furthermore, and importantly, the exogenous economic matrix must be understood by the crop protection specialist and fully meshed with an understanding of the ecology of the pest species and their natural enemies (Smith, 1969b).

In developing decision-making procedures for crop protection actions, it is essential to understand the relationship between pest infestation level and potential crop loss. Although the relationship between pest numbers and crop is complex (Smith, 1967a, 1969a; Pearson and Maxwell-Darling, 1958; Johnson, 1965), some guidelines are needed for efficient crop protection. It is now a common goal in entomological research to determine "economic injury thresholds," that is, the maximum pest population that can be tolerated without a resultant economic crop loss. With the economic injury levels defined, it is possible to design the management system to keep the pest population below these levels rather than attempt total elimination of the pest.

Cotton entomologists in recent years have made numerous studies to establish economic levels. Most of these investigations have involved insecticidal manipulation of the pest populations with insecticides or evaluating artificial infestations on caged plants (Smith, 1967a). For example, in Texas significant yield losses from *Heliothis* did not occur until the damaged squares or bolls exceeded 3% (Adkisson, Bailey, and Hanna, 1964). Their studies also showed that yield was affected more than quality.

Initially, tentative economic injury thresholds can be determined on empirical evidence, e.g., by deducing from experiences with the pest in the past. However, these levels should be reviewed constantly and readjusted in accordance with changes in farming practice and with additional information obtained from continuing observations and from experiments specially designed for the purpose.

THE ROLE OF CHEMICAL CONTROL

In 1964 alone, 143,184,000 pounds of insecticides were used on agricultural crops in the United States. Over half of this amount (78,000,000 pounds) was applied to cotton fields, corresponding roughly to 6 pounds of active ingredient per acre (Eichers *et al.,* 1968). In 1967, 3,295,835 "treatment-acres" were applied by commercial operators to the 590,000 acres of cotton in California (Anonymous, 1968). Cotton accounts for nearly 30% of the total crop acreage treated commercially in California. Considering the additional treatments by the farmers themselves, the average number of treatments per acre for cotton in California was six. This meant a production cost (insecticidal treatments) amounting on the average to about $35 per acre, but some cotton farmers spent nearly $100 per acre for pesticides. In Nicaragua during the 1966–67 season, 15,-381,389 liters of liquid insecticides and 2,897,579 kg of dusts were applied on 155,000 hectares (i.e., 99.2 liters plus 18.7 kg per hectare). It is clear that large amounts of insecticides are applied to cotton.

Although in some cases, insecticides are used excessively in cotton agro-ecosystems, it is also clear that the maintenance of these agro-ecosystems with profitable and high yields of lint has been dependent on pesticides (Smith, 1967b). While the integrated control approach attempts to employ non-chemical control procedures and to utilize environmental suppressive elements to their fullest, it should be understood that chemicals are, and probably will remain, a critical and important tool in the management of cotton pest populations, especially at times when the pests approach or exceed economic infestation levels. It is vitally important to integrated control programs that an adequate array of pesticides be available and that they be used in such a manner as to reduce threatening populations with minimum disruption to the agro-ecosystem.

While discussing the importance of chemicals in integrated control programs, it is essential to give special consideration to selectivity. If chemicals are to be used in a harmonious manner in the agro-ecosystem, we must have materials that are biochemically selective or which can be used selectively. All pesticides have some selectivity, but the range in degree of selectivity is substantial (Reynolds et al., 1960). For many years, much effort has been expended in seeking materials with relatively high toxicity to invertebrates and low toxicity to

mammals. This is, of course, necessary for safety of human health; but we must also seek differential toxicity to groups within the phylum Arthropoda. We do not need that ultimate in specificity which would permit us to prescribe a specific and unique chemical for each pest species. However, we do need effective materials that are specific for *groups of pests* such as aphids, locusts, caterpillars, weevils, and muscoid flies. There are now some indications that the chemical industry can produce such materials on an economically feasible basis (Metcalf, 1966). New so-called "third-generation" pesticides such as juvenile hormone analogs show considerable selectivity for the important cotton stainers *Dysdercus* spp. (Suchy, Sláma, and Šorm, 1968).

Under integrated control systems, often the population dynamics of the pests or the pest abundance–crop damage relationship is such that we do not need to have a high level of pest mortality. Instead of seeking 95% mortality or higher, we may be satisfied with or even much prefer a kill of 75% or even much lower. Under these circumstances, the low dosage of pesticide needed for the lower percentage mortality may permit the desired selective action between pest and beneficial forms.

The development of new highly specific pesticides will undoubtedly come very slowly and we should expect them to be more costly than many widely-used pesticides available today. In the meantime, we shall have to make the best use of those chemicals now available. This must be accomplished through the modification of dosages, formulations, times of applications, methods of application, and other techniques. Over the years, economic entomologists have developed a wide array of procedures to increase the percent mortality to the target pest species. These same techniques should now be explored to provide a differential mortality between the target pest and the non-target organisms.

We do not need "perfect selectivity"; rather, it is more desirable to have a differential kill that leaves the balance in favor of the beneficial forms. There is abundant evidence that in many cases this can be achieved even with the present chemical tools.

Pesticides, in addition to their impact on arthropod populations, may also affect the growth and physiology of the cotton plant and other organisms in the agro-ecosystem. The effect on the cotton plant may be evidenced by accelerated or delayed maturity or survival percentage of fruiting buds (Ripper and George, 1965).

Some of the obvious unwanted effects of the use of pesticides have encouraged a major effort to find alternative control measures. These efforts have met with some success, e.g., sterile male technique, genetic control, repellents, attractants, microbial control, and chemical control. Whatever the new technologies developed for the control or management of pest insects in the future, they must be applied with a knowledge of the pertinent agro-ecosystem and fitted to that situation. For example, investigators developing applications of the "sterile-male technique" have continually encountered serious deficiencies in our knowledge of the agro-ecosystem involved and of the bionomics, behavior, and ecology of the target pest insects. Among the critical missing data for such applications are details of absolute population size and dispersion, flight range and other aspects of vagility; seasonal abundance, especially at those times of the year when populations are lowest; and mating behavior and the factors which modify it.

INSECT RESISTANCE TO PESTICIDES

The development of pest resistance to insecticides has played an exceedingly im-portant role in the increasing difficulties encountered in pest control in cotton agro-ecosystems. The appearance of such resistance in a particular pest population and its rate of development will depend on whether genes for resistance are present in the population, the degree and kind of selective pressure, the genetic mechanism controlling the resistance, the genetic plasticity of the species, the rate of gene flow in the population, characteristics of the species and population such as dispersal behavior, generation time, and reproductive rates, and the degree of isolation of the population. In an integrated control system, there is reduced risk or better chance for delay in the development of resistance than where there is heavy selection presure associated with the intense use of pesticides. An integrated system entails a lowered level of selection pressure because pesticides are no longer responsible for the bulk of the mortality. This relates to the fact that the selective action of the pesticide is directed against only relatively small portions of the population scattered in time and space. In the intervals between pesticide treatments, different selective pressures from other control procedures and from other elements of the environment will modify the large remaining population and may reduce any trend toward resistance. The use of selective pesticides enhances this pattern and avoids the development of resistance in other pest species associated with the target species (Kennedy, 1968).

United States Cotton Belt. The cotton leafworm (*Alabama argillacea*) and the cotton aphid (*Aphis gossypii*) were the first cotton pests in the U. S. Cotton Belt reported to develop resistance to chlorinated hydrocarbons. As these insects were relatively unimportant pests, crop protection practices for cotton were not affected seriously. However, by 1955, the boll weevil had also become resistant to the chlorinated hydrocarbons. Thereafter resistance developed rapidly in all the other major cotton pests in some part or all of their areas of distribution. For the control of the boll weevil and the other resistant pests, a change was made to the organophosphorus insecticides. These chemicals have been fairly successful, but in 1965 a population of *Heliothis zea* was found to show appreciable resistance to organophosphorus insecticides in Oklahoma. More recently, the same was shown for populations of *H. virescens* in central Texas. Spider mites have also developed such resistance (Newsom and Brazzel, 1968). Additional details on the development of insecticide resistance in cotton pests in Louisiana are given by Newsom (this volume, Chapter 24).

Peru. In the development of the cotton crisis in the Cañete Valley (see Boza Barducci, this volume, Chapter 23), insecticide resistance was a critical factor. In late 1952, BHC was no longer effective against aphids. In the summer of 1957, toxaphene failed to control the leafworm *Anomis.* In the 1955–56 season, *Anthonomus* reached high levels of abundance in spite of insecticide treatments. Next a very heavy infestation of *Heliothis virescens* developed and the pest showed a high degree of resistance to DDT. The result was a dramatic crop failure (Herrera, 1958; Beingolea, 1962a).

Egypt. Annually Egypt produces about a million bales of extra-long staple cotton (1⅜ inches and over) and another million bales of long staple cotton (1⅛–1⅜ inches), which represent about one-half and one-third respectively of the world supply of these special cottons. These cottons are derived largely from *Gossypium barbadense* and have evolved in Egypt over a period of more than 150 years. The isolation of this closed cotton agro-ecosystem and the widespread and intensive use of insecticides for control of the Egyptian cotton leafworm (*Spodoptera littoralis*) have combined to facilitate the rapid development of insecticide resistance in that pest. As a result,

a severe drop in yield and total production occurred in 1961. In the 1960–61 season, 2,205,000 bales were produced on 1,945,-000 acres with an average yield of 542 lb of lint per acre. The following year production dropped to 1,548,000 bales on 2,062,000 acres (average yield of 359 lb per acre). This decrease was largely attributed to *Spodoptera* which had developed resistance to toxaphene and flourished despite heavy treatments and because there had been relaxation in the intensity of hand collection of its egg masses. In 1966, a similar loss occurred and costs of attempted control with insecticides were very high. The *Spodoptera* population is now also resistant to endrin and parathion. More potent insecticides such as Azodrin® and Cyolane® have been introduced, but their cost is considerably higher, and the probability that resistance to them will develop clouds the outlook for the future (Zeid *et al.,* 1968). In the Sudan, in contrast, the cotton agro-ecosystems are surrounded by grasslands, savannah, and fallow lands. Only a portion of the pest populations are subject to the selective pressure of the insecticide treatments. An attempt has been made to restrict treatments only to fields in which economic infestations have developed. As a result, no significant levels of pest resistance to insecticides developed in the Sudan (Ripper and George, 1965). The contrast in the use of insecticides in these two countries and major differences in the value of their cotton agro-ecosystems have created different cotton pest problems both in specifics and in magnitude.

Iraq and Syria. The situation in Iraq is quite similar to that in Egypt except that the spiny bollworm (*Earias insulana*) is the main pest rather than *Spodoptera.* In some years the spiny bollworm is reported to destroy 80% to 90% of the crop. In 1953, endrin was introduced for its control. By 1964, it was useless because of resistance, and spider mites had also become a serious problem (Stern, 1969). In nearby Syria, no insecticides have been used for the past two years on cotton. A number of pests (aphids, leafhoppers, cutworms, and thrips) are reported to cause minor damage and *Heliothis* occasions sporadic local damage. *Spodoptera* has not been reported in recent years. *Earias* and *Pectinophora* both appear regularly at the end of the season but the damage they cause is light (Schmitz, 1969). Thus although production of cotton in Syria leaves something to be desired from the standpoint of efficiency, farmers at least do not have the severe pest problems brought on by the misuse of pesticides.

A LESSON UNLEARNED

The story of cotton pest control in the Cañete Valley of Peru (see Boza Barducci, Chapter 23, this volume; and Beingolea, 1954, 1955, 1958, 1959, 1962a, 1962b; Beingolea and Gamero, 1956; Garcia, 1959; Herrera, 1958, 1961; Lamas, 1958; Lamas, 1967; Lobaton, 1959; Marie, 1939; Mercado, 1957; Simon, 1956, 1957; Wille, 1951, 1952, 1956; Wille and Beingolea, 1957; Wille *et al.,* 1959) stands as a classic example of the impact of use of pesticides in a cotton agro-ecosystem. The experiences in Peru in the early fifties strikingly illustrate that pest control cannot be analyzed or developed in isolation; rather, it must be considered and applied in the context of the agro-ecosystem in which the pest populations exist and in which control actions are taken. But this important lesson has not been learned in spite of other relevant examples in cotton agro-ecosystems around the world. This is illustrated in the following brief sketches of the cotton pest control situation in several other cotton-producing areas of the world. The parallels to the Cañete Valley of Peru are obvious.

CENTRAL AMERICA

The growth of the Central American cotton industry has been phenomenal. As late as 1950–51, there were less than 100,000 acres of cotton in Central America and a total production of 55,000 bales. By the late fifties the crop was grown on about 300,000 acres with a production of 340,000 bales. The great increase in cotton acreage is the result of land reform, opening of new areas to agriculture through malaria control and new roads, and government-supported cotton prices (Mobley, 1955). In the peak season of 1964–65, the acreage was 928,-000 with production reported at 1,335,000 bales. At least 90% of this cotton is exported; thus cotton is an important and often critical source of export earnings for these countries. Cotton production has not remained as high in recent years because of low rainfall in some areas and significantly increasing pest problems. For example, in Nicaragua the yield per acre dropped from 821 lb of lint in 1964–65 to 621 lb in 1967–68.

With the exception of the cotton-producing districts in Honduras, almost all of the cotton in Central America is grown in the fertile Pacific plain extending from Tapachula, Mexico, to the Guanacaste Province in Costa Rica (Mobley, 1955). In general, pest problems are very similar in all parts of the area. In El Salvador and in Guatemala, there seem to be more problems with rank cotton and boll rots. In Costa Rica, where the somewhat isolated fields are surrounded by pastures and undeveloped land, cotton production has fewer insect problems. The average number of insecticide treatments is only about ten per season in Costa Rica as compared to thirty or more in the other countries. In general, cotton is planted at the beginning of the rainy season and harvested in the dry season.

There has been a significant change in

the composition of the insect pest complex on cotton during the past ten years and a major increase in magnitude of the problem. About ten years ago, the Colombian or false pink bollworm (*Scadodes pyralis*) and the cotton boll weevil (*Anthonomus grandis*) were the most important pests. The cotton bollworm (*Heliothis zea*) was an occasional pest as were the cotton aphid (*Aphis gossypii*) and the cotton leafworm (*Alabama argillacea*) (Miner, 1960). With increasing cotton production, there has also been a great increase in insecticide usage. In spite of increasing dosages and numbers of applications of pesticides, control effectiveness has declined in recent years. The organochlorine insecticides have largely gone out of use, probably because of the development of resistance; but this is not well documented (George D. Peterson, unpublished data; Smith, 1969c).

Currently the Colombian pink bollworm is seldom found, and the cotton boll weevil is of secondary status, while cotton bollworms (principally *Heliothis zea* but including *Heliothis virescens* and *H. subflexa*) are the most important pests. On the other hand, an array of formerly minor pests has risen to major status. For example, in the last two years a complex of lepidopterous larvae belonging to the genus *Spodoptera* (= *Prodenia*) has assumed major importance. There are at least five species involved (*sunia, ornithogalli, eridania, dolichos,* and *latifascia*) but not all are of major importance for cotton. Their relative importance, habits, and control are not known adequately. The cabbage looper (*Trichoplusia ni*) and a species of *Pseudoplusia* have reached outbreak status in many fields. In all areas, the cotton whitefly (*Bemisia tabaci*) (and its associated cotton viruses) has appeared as a major pest and is now very difficult to control. This pest appeared in El Salvador in the 1961–62 season, in Honduras in 1964, and in Nicaragua and Guatemala in 1965 (Kraemer, 1966). Pre-

sumably, these secondary pests have risen to severe pest status because of their release from their natural controls (Bareket and Brito, 1968).

In several areas, the number of insecticide applications average more than thirty per year, and some farmers apply over fifty treatments to a given field in a single season, relying heavily on the use of methyl and ethyl parathion to control these cotton pests. There is considerable evidence of serious and increasing insect resistance to the chemicals. As this resistance continues to develop and crop protection costs go up, the possibilities of a complete crop failure are very great.

During the 1966–67 and 1967–68 growing seasons, serious residue problems developed in some districts, particularly when the cotton insecticides drifted to beef and dairy cattle pasture areas and livestock were allowed to graze in cotton fields after the harvest. An increased hazard to man also resulted. There were hundreds of cases of insecticide poisoning in man with many deaths reported (George D. Peterson, unpublished data).

The situation in Central America is not a simple causal relationship between the misuse of pesticides and severe pest outbreaks. Other factors are involved, including below-normal rainfall; poor agricultural practices, especially those relating to cultural control; increasing incidence of cotton diseases; and in some areas, inadequate soil fertility. During the 1966–67 and 1967–68 seasons, rainfall was deficient and, in many growing areas, this had a severe adverse effect on the cotton crop. But more importantly, there has been a general neglect of good cultural practices by many farmers. Abandoned cotton fields are often allowed to stand until the next growing season, producing flowers, fruits, and insects. In the fields where the cotton plants are cut off and burned, the plants ratoon and provide survival sites for insects and a major source of virus diseases. Many fields are not plowed until it is time to prepare the land for the next growing season. In most Central American countries government regulations prescribe a cotton-free period and other important cultural control practices, but these regulations are inadequately enforced. Nevertheless, the misuse of pesticides and the resulting aggravated insect infestations have been the major cause of the declining yields in Central America.

TURKEY

At present Turkey is the sixth largest exporter of cotton lint and the ninth largest world producer of cotton fiber. The yield per hectare has more than doubled since 1950 (264 kg to 551 kg) as the result of better varieties, use of fertilizers, irrigation, insecticides, and better soil management. The Kaban Dam on the Upper Euphrates River will bring about a half-million hectares of land under irrigation, and most of this will be planted to cotton. On the surface the outlook is bright but the familiar danger signals are present. Pest problems have been gradually increasing in recent years. The Egyptian cotton leafworm has become resistant to methyl parathion. The spiny bollworm is resistant to endrin. Spider mites, which were not important pests prior to 1965, now require treatments regularly at least in the Adana area. Mostly because of lack of rotation (cotton crops may be grown successively ten years or more in the same field), verticillium wilt is serious in some areas. For these reasons, the cost of production has been rising, mainly because of the increasing use of pesticides, but there has not as yet been a serious crop failure (Stern, 1969).

COLOMBIA

Although cotton pest control is under a rigidly enforced supervised control program, some new pest problems are appearing and some of the now familiar patterns of trouble are indicated for the future. Authorization to purchase and apply organic pesticides to cotton can only be made by a licensed *Ingeniero Agrónomo*. A serious attempt is made to avoid unnecessary treatments with parathion as happened in 1964. In that year, early treatments with parathion for *Alabama* greatly aggravated problems with *Heliothis* later in the year. The growers now try to control *Alabama* and other early-season lepidopterous pests with arsenicals. However, when *Heliothis* appears, methyl parathion is used. The *Heliothis* problem has been increasing because of increased production of maize and other crops. The use of methyl parathion also augments the problems with *Tetranychus telarius, Eotetranychus planki, Liriomyza* sp., *Bemisia tabaci,* and probably *Spodoptera* and *Prorachia daria.* These unleashed pests and the impending resistance to parathion in *Heliothis* present a grim outlook for the future of cotton pest control in Colombia (Smith, 1969c).

SOUTH TEXAS

The bollworm (*Heliothis zea*) has become an increasingly important pest of cotton over the past twenty years or more. The tobacco budworm (*Heliothis virescens*) has more recently become important as a cotton pest. In recent years, its importance has paralleled or exceeded that of the bollworm. Destruction of predators and parasites appears to be the major factor in the changing pest status of these *Heliothis* species. The problem has been further aggravated by the development of resistance in the bollworms to all of the chlorinated hydrocarbons and to the carbamate insecticides. In recent years, chemical control of these pests has depended on use of methyl parathion. During the 1968 growing season, populations of the tobacco budworm in the lower

Rio Grande Valley were found to be moderately resistant to methyl parathion. The level of resistance is already sufficient in the valley to interfere with chemical control and to add to its cost. There is every reason to believe that very shortly methyl parathion will be ineffective against the tobacco budworm. The development of resistance in the cotton bollworm can be expected to closely follow the pattern of the tobacco budworm. No adequate substitute chemicals are available at this time. Opinion varies as to how much time is available before the current chemical control procedures fail completely. In any case, time is short (Adkisson, 1969).

Imperial Valley

The Imperial Valley of California has been transformed from absolute desert to a highly productive agricultural area through use of abundant water, fertilizer, and modern, mechanized crop production practices. Cotton is an important crop with average yields sometimes exceeding three bales (1,500 lb of lint) per acre. It presents an interesting case as pest control practices have gone through a full cycle of change from bad to good and back again. These changes clearly illustrate many of the basic principles of integrated control.

The situation is closely analogous to that which occurred in the Cañete Valley of Peru. In the early fifties following the development of the organic insecticides, broad-spectrum, persistent insecticides, e.g., DDT, toxaphene, endrin, alone and in combination, were repeatedly and successfully applied. For several years the results were spectacular. Gradually, however, resistance and residue problems forced a change to other types of pesticides. In the case of several pests, more frequent applications were needed with the new compounds and importantly they were often broad-spectrum, short-lived materials. Production costs in-

creased significantly and, simultaneously, beneficial insect populations were gradually depleted in these cotton agro-ecosystems. As a result, key pest populations increased at alarming rates soon after pesticide treatments. Furthermore, a number of secondary pest species appeared and their populations surpassed economic levels repeatedly. Obviously, drastic changes in the approach to pest control were necessary, and several years of intensive research provided some relief to the cotton producers. The changes were dramatic and were based primarily on careful evaluation within each field as to the need for treatment and the use of insecticides which, depending upon the pest, ranged from highly to moderately selective in favor of beneficial insects (including honeybees). The former repetitive treatments became almost unnecessary. Gradually the native parasite and predator populations regained their former effective levels. The secondary pests (primarily cotton leaf perforator, cabbage, looper, beet army worm, salt-marsh caterpillar, omnivorous leaf roller and spider mite) seldom reached economically injurious population levels. Some pests virtually disappeared from the cotton fields, and the primary pests, such as bollworm, rarely attained economically significant populations.

In 1965, a new key pest, the pink bollworm, invaded the Imperial and neighboring valleys. Populations of this new pest literally exploded. Applications of broad-spectrum insecticides were made at frequent intervals. Pest control costs increased sharply from a relatively few dollars per acre to $30 to $40 and in some cases to as much as $90 per acre. At the same time beneficial insects were quickly reduced to completely ineffectual population levels. New research programs under way may provide information in the near future which should largely alleviate depredations by the pink bollworm, but in the meantime, secondary pest problems have become so serious as to threaten continued cotton production. The cotton leaf perforator, for example, already resistant to several chlorinated hydrocarbon insecticides, developed resistance in almost one and one-half years of heavy selection pressure from the broad-spectrum organophosphorus insecticides used for pink bollworm control. In addition to resistance, the perforator problem was greatly aggravated as highly effective parasites and predators were eliminated by the pink bollworm insecticide treatments. Without this natural control, total reliance had to be placed on insecticides to control this explosive insect pest. An effective alternative insecticide (Perthane®) was found, but resistance to this compound has already been reported in Peru, and the pattern will undoubtedly recur in California.

It has been noted that at the end of the season many of the secondary pests listed above rapidly increase to high populations in cotton fields as soon as insecticide pressure is relaxed. Furthermore, it is anticipated that resistance will occur rapidly in some species. In fact, low levels of resistance are already known to occur in some populations. It is also obvious, although largely based upon circumstantial evidence, that an area-wide impact of the heavy treatment schedules on cotton for pink bollworm has been severe. Fall and winter production of vegetable crops and sugar beets has had the most severe pest infestations ever known in these crops; in fact, the stand in some entire fields was destroyed and had to be replanted. Even if the pink bollworm can be reduced to non-pest status, as it must be, it may take several seasons to regain population levels of beneficial species so that integrated control programs can be reinstituted in other crops as well as cotton.

San Joaquin Valley of California

Cotton production in the San Joaquin Valley of California has reached a high level of agronomic efficiency and in many respects is very sophisticated. In recent years, insect pest control has become increasingly complicated and very costly in this area. Among the several reasons are: (a) the development of insecticide resistance in several pests; (b) restrictions on the use of highly effective chlorinated hydrocarbon insecticides; (c) pest resurgences and secondary pest outbreaks resulting from imbalances created in the agro-ecosystems by the broad-spectrum, short-residual materials which have replaced the chlorinated hydrocarbons, and (d) a general rise in cotton production costs which has narrowed the dollar margin available for pest control expenditures (Falcon et. al., 1968). The key insect pests in the San Joaquin Valley are the lygus bug (*Lygus hesperus*) and the bollworm (*Heliothis zea*). Early-season control for lygus bugs aggravates the bollworm problem and unleashes secondary pests such as the cabbage looper and spider mite. Recent research indicates that higher levels of lygus bugs than formerly believed can be tolerated in cotton fields without loss of yield or quality. This knowledge in combination with interplantings of alfalfa in the cotton (mentioned elsewhere in this paper) offers a means of revolutionizing pest control in cotton in the San Joaquin Valley. If early-season control for lygus bugs can be minimized or eliminated, then the bollworm problem will be greatly reduced. Unfortunately, the majority of cotton farmers are still using broad-spectrum, short-residual insecticides early in the growing season and thus eliminating the effectiveness of natural control.

Australia

Cotton has been grown for over one hundred years in several parts of Australia. Almost all of the early cotton grown was dependent on rainfall. The area planted was small and the yields extremely variable.

In recent years, large new areas of irrigated cotton have been developed, largely in Queensland, New South Wales, and the Ord district of Western Australia through the development of new irrigation districts. Under very favorable growing conditions and using modern cultural and harvesting techniques, the yields have increased spectacularly to equal the highest commercial yield per acre for any country. In each of the growing areas, local insects have found the cotton agro-ecosystems most suitable and have become serious pests. For example, in New South Wales *Heliothis punctigera* and *Earias huegeli* are the key pests. The growers have been using rather heavy and frequent applications of DDT for the former and endrin for the latter. Thus far, no resistance has been reported in these pests, but in 1968 well-developed resistance to parathion has been found in some populations of *Tetranychus ludeni* (G. Pasfield, unpublished information). Spider mites, *Aphis gossypii,* and *Plusia argentifera* infestations have been aggravated, probably by the heavy use of DDT and endrin. The low-yielding nonirrigated cotton grown ten years ago received not more than two or three applications of insecticide per season. Now, eight to ten applications are regarded as the minimum and many cotton growers apply fifteen or more.

DISCUSSION AND CONCLUSIONS

The cotton agro-ecosystem is more than the relationships among the cotton plants and their conditioning environment. The agro-ecosystem also includes the associated agricultural, industrial, recreational, governmental, and social activities of man. Crop pest control, as part of this, must conform to the long-range viewpoint of general society. Furthermore, the habits, customs, and traditions ingrained in a culture must be accommodated. The structure of land tenure, religious beliefs, pricing and marketing systems, political organization, and educational institutions can all help or hinder a technological change or modify the magnitude of a pest problem. Furthermore, an action that brings about a new technology or a change in technology may have significant social and political consequences. These extralimital aspects of the agro-ecosystem pose serious questions for the pest management specialist as well as for the ecologist (Smith, 1969b).

Governmental regulations involving price supports and acreage allotments for cotton are examples of extralimital factors that can greatly influence the cotton agro-ecosystem. Reduction of acreage allotments force individual farmers to make adjustments in cropland and other farm resource use. Adjustments made by the individual may not be profitable if a large group of farmers make the same adjustment. Hence, adjustments in use of resources is a continuous and often circular process. Other governmental controls involving such items as housing for labor, wages, and transportation may have similar external effects on the cotton agro-ecosystem (Amick *et al.,* 1968).

Another extralimital factor seriously affecting the cotton agro-ecosystem is the development of the synthetic fiber industry. In recent years, the cotton industry has produced a smaller and smaller percentage of the total world demand for fiber. The future trends in the struggle for this world fiber market, particularly as influenced by development of new synthetic fibers for specialized uses, will have significant impact on cotton agro-ecosystems. Whole regions may be forced to stop producing cotton for economic reasons and other areas may have to modify production practices greatly.

In some situations new or modified techniques for pest control are developed and certain advantages to be derived from their use are clear, but there is no motivation for the cotton farmer to change his current practices. This is particularly so in those areas where subsistence or peasant agriculture is the way of life. The modifications needed to introduce a more productive agriculture (with better pest control as a part of it) may require a shift in human values, patterns of ownership of the land, long-established customs, or other difficult changes. Greatly increased efficiency in the production of cotton may not be worthwhile if, for example, it can only be achieved with the destruction of local cultures or other human values of great importance. The significance of land ownership and social structures are exemplified by the "self-sufficient" hacienda or fazenda system of Latin America with its isolating and conservative influences (Tannenbaum, 1960).

Another consequence of pest control actions that has received considerable attention lately, at least in certain quarters, is the broad implications of pest control decisions to the interests of general society. This is especially clear in pest control actions in forests where multiple use of the land is a clearly established principle. An ill-considered action may control the target pest attacking the forest stand but at the same time seriously erode recreational potential, fishery and hunting resources, or other valuable resources. The same may apply to pest control actions taken in agricultural areas. The problems of possible pollution, destruction of wildlife, soil depletion, and other deterioration of resources can be just as great in agricultural lands as in forested or other wild lands.

The possibilities of a cotton crop failure in Central America, brought on largely by the misuse of insecticides, are very great in the next year or two. The possible social and political implications are many, especially when one considers that over 30% of the export dollars for countries like Guatemala and Nicaragua come from the sale of cotton fiber. It is no exaggeration to say that pest control advice which leads to an economic calamity may topple a government. The further complications are many and foreboding.

Scientific pest control has always required a knowledge of ecological principles and especially of the natural factors regulating pest populations (FAO, 1968; Smith, 1969b). With the introduction of new and more sophisticated pest control technologies, it will be more necessary than ever before to take into consideration the ecological aspects of agricultural production.

The use of chemical pesticides without regard to the complexities of cotton agro-ecosystems, especially the fundamental aspects of the population dynamics of pest species, has been the basic cause of the exacerbation of cotton pest problems over the past ten to fifteen years. A review of these problems in many cotton-growing regions of the world shows a common pattern. Typically, the initial introduction of the widespread use of modern pesticides to cotton agro-ecosystems results in significant increased yields of seed and lint. But then more frequent applications are needed; the dosages must be increased to achieve control, and the treatment season is extended. It is noted that the pest populations soon resurge rapidly to new, higher levels after treatment. The pest populations gradually become so tolerant of the pesticides that the latter become useless. Other insecticides are substituted and the pest populations become tolerant to them too, but this happens more rapidly than with the chemicals that were first used. At the same time, pests that had previously never, or only occasionally, caused damage become serious and regular ravagers of the cotton fields. This combination of pesticide resistance, pest resurgence, and unleashed secondary pests causes greatly increased production costs and often brings on an economic disaster.

Modern holistic approaches in ecology

have now reached the stage where they can be used to understand and analyze insect pest problems. In many situations, alternative control procedures may be selected, or a choice made between the positive and negative values of an action or group of actions. Modern computer systems analysis theoretically offers opportunities to obtain the best decision (Watt, 1968). It is, of course, critical that in the use of these techniques we pose relevant and incisive questions to the computer. However, the ability of computers to store and transmit information and to arrive at conclusions based upon the information by high-speed logical processes offers us a powerful tool for pest population management and resource management.

It becomes clearer each day that resources of all categories are limited and decisions as to the allocation of the resources are extremely difficult. The difficulty lies in the complexity of our environment, the subtle, varied, and multiple implications of specific actions, and the conflicts in interest and opinion about what is important and desirable. In many situations, the short-run view indicates that resources should be allocated to create higher productivity so that people may be fed; but in the long run other values, such as the quality of human existence and the stability of production, should be considered. Again, systems analysis offers a tool to help us optimize the allocation and utilization of resources (Watt, 1968).

The integrated control approach attempts to avoid the pitfalls of pest control detailed in this chapter and in other chapters on crop protection in this volume. There is now ample evidence that the integrated control approach with its strong ecological inputs has proved to be a better approach than has a total reliance on pesticides (Smith, 1969c; Smith and van den Bosch, 1967; FAO, 1966, 1969). Integrated control attempts to use a combination of suitable control techniques, in as compatible a manner as possible, to maintain the pest populations below defined economic injury levels. Integrated control derives its uniqueness of approach from its emphasis on the fullest practical utilization of the existing mortality and suppressive factors in the environment.

The cotton pest control situation described in this chapter is not unique. Similar crises are upon us or are soon to be faced in the control of mosquitoes, fruit pests, spider mites on many crops, house flies, cabbage loopers on vegetables, ticks on cattle, and in many other situations where pesticides have been used intensively. In many of these situations, time is running out. The world population is facing a most critical food shortage. This is a crisis shared by crop protection specialists all over the world. We believe that with an imaginative approach to the management of agro-eco-systems this challenge can be met, that pests can be controlled without continued exacerbation of the magnitude of the problem, that our food supply need not be shared unreasonably with the insects and their allies, and, at the same time, that we can preserve some of the higher qualities of life on this planet and a richness of the environment.

REFERENCES

Adkisson, P. L. "The Influence of Fertilizer Application on Populations of Heliothis zea (Boddie) and Certain Insect Predators." Jour. Econ. Ento. 51: (1958), 757–59.

———. "Internal Clocks and Insect Diapause." Science, 154 (3746): (1966), 234–41.

———. "How Insects Damage Crops." In How Crops Grow. Conn. Agric. Exp. Sta. (in press), 1969.

Adkisson, P. L.; Bailey, C. F.; and Hanna, R. L. "Effect of the Bollworm, Heliothis zea, on Yield and Quality of Cotton." Jour. Econ. Ento. 57 (4) (1964), 448–50.

Adkisson, P. L.; Brazzel, J. R.; and Gaines, J. C., "Yield and Quality Losses Resulting from Pink Bollworm Damage to Cotton." Texas Agric. Exp. Sta., MP-632. 1963. 8 pp.

Adkisson, P. L., and Gaines, J. C., "Pink Bollworm Control as Related to the Total Cotton Insect Control Program of Central Texas." Texas Agric. Exp. Sta., MP-444. 1960. 7 pp.

Adkisson, P. L.; Hanna, R. L.; and Bailey, C. F. "Estimates of the Numbers of Heliothis Larvae per Acre in Cotton and Their Relation to the Fruiting Cycle and Yield of the Host." Jour. Econ. Ento. 57 (5) 1964, 657–63.

Amick, R. J. et al. "Cotton. The Effects of Allotments on Supply and Farm Resource Use." Southern Coop. Ser. Bull. No. 128. 1964. 81 pp.

Andres, L. A. An Ecological Study of Three Species of Tetranychus and Their Response to Temperature and Humidity. Unpublished Ph.D. dissertation. University of California at Berkeley, 1957.

Anonymous. Acreages Treated for Agricultural Pest Control by Counties, 1967. Calif. Dept. Agric. Mimeo. 1968.

Bareket, G., and Brito, L. M. Control de plagas del Algodonero. Minist. Agric. Gand., Dir. Gen. Invest. y Ext. Agric. Publ. Esp. No. 1–68, 1968. 99 pp.

Bates, Marston. The Human Environment. The Horace M. Albright Conservation Lectureship, II. Berkeley: University of California, School of Forestry. 1962. 22 pp.

Beingolea, O. "Contribución al conocimiento del complejo parasitario de Heliothis virescens F., perforador grande de la bellota del algodonero y la influencia de los insecticidas orgánicos sobre el." Bol. Dir. Gral. Agric., Nos. 8–9. Min. Agric., Lima, Peru, 1954.

———. "Contribución al conocimiento del complejo parasitario de Heliothis virescens F., perforador grande de la bellota del algondonero. Evaluación de la importancia relativa de sus enemigos biológicos." Bol. No. 4, Divulgación e Informes. Min. Agric., Lima, Peru, 1955.

———. Evidencia de un processo regulador en la declinación de las poblaciones estacionales de Anomis taxana Riley." Inf. No. 107. Est. Exp. Agric. La Molina, Lima, Peru, 1958.

———. "Notas sobre la bionómica de arañas e insectos benéficos que occuren en el cultivo de algodón." Rev. Peruana Entomol. Agric., 2 (1) (1959), 36–44.

———. "Empleo de insecticidas orgánicos en el Perú y posibilidades de reducirlo por medio del control integrado." Rev. Peruana de Entomol. Agric., 5 (1) (1962a), 31–38.

———. "Factores ecológicos y poblaciones del gusano de la oja del algodonero Anomis texana Riley." Rev. Peruana de entomol. Agric., 5 (1) (1962b), 39–78.

Beingolea, O., and Gamero, O. Control natural y químico del picudo peruano Anthonomus vestitus Bohm. Inf. No. 101, Est. Exp. Agr. La Molina, Lima, Peru, 1956.

Bell, K. O., and Whitcomb, W. H., "Efficiency of Egg Predators of the Bollworm." Arkansas Farm Res., 11 (1962), 9.

Bottger, G. T.; Sheehan, E. T.; and Lukefahr, M. J. "Relation of Gossypol Content of Cotton Plants to Insect Resistance." Jour. Econ. Ento. 57 (2) (1964), 283–85.

Carns, H. R., and Mauney, J. R. "Physiology of the Cotton Plant." In Advances in Production and Utilization of Quality Cotton: Principles and Practices, F. C. Elliott, M. Hoover, and W. K. Porter, eds. Ames, Iowa: Iowa State University Press, 1968, pp. 41–73.

Cole, Lamont C. "The Complexity of Pest Control in the Environment." In Scien-

tific Aspects of Pest Control. Washington, D.C.: National Acad. Sci.–Nat. Res. Council, 1966, pp. 13–25.

Doutt, R. L. "Ecological Considerations in Chemical Control. Implications to Non-Target Invertebrates." *Bull. Ento. Soc. Amer.* 10 (2) (1964), 67–88.

Earle, N. W., and Newsom, L. D. "Initiation of Diapause in the Boll Weevil." *J. Ins. Physiol.* 10 (1964), 131–39.

Eaton, Frank M. "Physiology of the Cotton Plant." *Ann. Rev. of Plant Physiology,* 6 (1955), 299–328.

Eichers, T.; Andrilenas, P.; Jenkins, R.; and Fox, A. "Quantities of Pesticides Used by Farmers in 1964." U. S. Dept. Agric., Economic Research Service. *Agric. Econ. Rept.* No. 131. 1968. 37 pp.

Falcon, L. A.; van den Bosch, R.; Ferris, C. A.; Stromberg, L. K.; Etzel, L. K.; Stinner, R. E.; and Leigh, T. F. "A Comparison of Season-Long Cotton Pest Control Programs in California during 1966." *Jour. Econ. Ento.,* 61 (3) (1968), 633–42.

FAO. *Proceedings of the FAO Symposium on Integrated Pest Control.* Food and Agriculture Organization of the United Nations, Rome, Italy. October 1965. 3 vols. 1966.

————. *Report of the Second Session of FAO Panel of Experts on Integrated Pest Control.* FAO, Rome, Italy. 1969.

Fletcher, R. K., and Thomas, F. L. "Natural Control of Eggs and First Instar Larvae of *Heliothis armigera.*" *Jour. Econ. Ento.* 36 (1943), 557–60.

Flint, R. N.; Sloane, L. W.; and Clover, D. F. "Effect of Deflorating Cotton on Yield, St. Joseph, Louisiana, 1956–1963 Inclusive." *Ann. Rep. N.E. Louisiana Agric. Exp. Sta.,* 1963.

Garcia B., Godofredo. "Contribución al estudio de la resistencia del arrebiatado, *Dysdercus peruvianus* Guerin, al hexaclorino de benceno." *Revista Peruana Entomol. Agric.,* 2 (1) (1959), 91–101.

Gillham, F. E. M. "Evolutionary Significance of Glands and Their Importance in Cultivated Cotton." *Empire Cotton Growers Rev.,* 42 (1965), 101–03.

Hagen, K. S. Unpublished data on file, University of California, Berkeley, California.

Hargreaves, H. *List of Recorded Cotton Insects of the World.* London. Commonwealth Institute of Entomology, 1948, 50 pp.

Henry, P., and Adkisson, P. L. *Seasonal Abundance of Bollworms and Tobacco Budworms on a Typical Cotton Plantation.* Texas Agric. Exp. Sta., MP-767. 1965. 6 pp.

Herrera, J. M. "Resistencia de ciertas plagas de algodonero a insecticidas orgánicos en el Valle de Cañete." *Rev. Peruana de Entomol. Agrícola,* 1 (1) (1958), 47–51.

————. "Problemas entomológicos en el cultivo de los algodones Tanguis y Pina en el Perú. Medidas de Control y su organización." *Rev. Peruana de Entomol. Agric.,* 4 (1) 1961, 58–66.

Hosny, M. M., and Iss-hak, R. R. "Factors Stimulating the Outbreaks of the Cotton Leaf-Worm in U.A.R. and the Principles of Its Prediction." *U.A.R. Ministry of Agric. Tech. Bull.* No. 1. 1967. Pp. 1–36.

Jackson, J. E. "Seasonal Variation and Quality of Cotton." *Ann. Appl. Biol.,* 51 (1963), 519.

Jenkins, J. N.; Maxwell, F. G.; and Lafever, H. N. "The Comparative Preference of Insects for Glanded and Glandless Cottons." *Jour. Econ. Ento.* 59 (2) (1966), 352–56.

Johnson, C. G. *Entomology Department, Rothamsted Exp. Sta. Rep.* (1964) (1), 77–194.

Joyce, R. J. V. "Some Factors Affecting Numbers of *Empoasca lybica* (de Berg) Infesting Cotton in the Sudan." *Gezira. Bull. Entomol. Res.,* 52 (1) (1961), 191–232.

Kennedy, J. S. "The Motivation of Integrated Control." *Jour. Appl. Ecol.,* 4 (1968), 492–99.

Kraemer, P. "Serious Increase of Cotton Whitefly and Virus Transmission in Central America." *Jour. Econ. Ento.,* 5 (6) (1966), 1531.

Lamas, C. J. M. "Control del picudo peruano, *Anthonomus vestitus* Boh., con arsenato de plomo, sólo y en mescla con melaza de caña." *Rev. Peruana de Entomol. Agric.* 1 (1) (1958).

————. "Aplicación de plaguicidas dentro de un programa de control integrado." Caracas: Reunión Latinoamericana de Fitotécnia, 1967.

Lewis, C. F., and Richmond, T. R. "Cotton as a Crop." In *Advances in Production and Utilization of Quality Cotton: Principles and Practices.* F. C. Elliot, M.

Hoover, and W. K. Porter, eds. Ames, Iowa: Iowa State Univ. Press, 1968, pp. 1–21.

Lingren, P. D.; Ridgway, R. L.; and Jones, S. L. "Consumption by Several Common Arthropod Predators of Eggs and Larvae of Two *Heliothis* Species that Attack Cotton." *Jour. Econ. Ento.*, 61 (3) (1968), 613–18.

Lobaton, Manuel. "Equilibro biológico de *Mescinia peruella* Schaus., en la zona baja del Valle de Pisco. Campaña algodonero 1958–59." *Rev. Peruana de Entomol. Agric.* 2 (1) (1959), 113–15.

Loftin, V. C. "Living with the Bollweevil for Fifty Years." *Smithsonian Report for 1945.* (1945), 273–92.

Longenecker, D. E., and Erie, L. J. "Irrigation Water Management." In *Advances in Production and Utilization of Quality Cotton: Principle and Practices,* F. C. Elliot, M. Hoover, and W. K. Porter, eds. Ames, Iowa: Iowa State Univ. Press, 1968. 321–45.

Lukefahr, M. J., and Martin, D. F. "Cotton-Plant Pigments as a Source of Resistance to the Bollworm and Tobacco Budworm." *Jour. Econ. Ento.* 59 (1966), 176–79.

Maher, A. A.; Bishara, R. H.; Elsawy, M. S.; Hussein, M. M.; Abdel Salam, F. A.; and Isak, I. "On the Resistance of the Egyptian Cotton Leaf-Worm, *Prodenia litura,* to Insecticides." *Agric. Res. Rev.* 40 (1962), 51.

Marie, Victor. *El cultivo del algodonero en el Valle de Cañete, en relación con las plagas entomológicas.* Minist. de Fomento: Dir. de Agr. y Ganaderia Informe No. 51. Est. Exp. Agric. La Molina, 1939.

Mercado, Oscar. "Preferencias de *Heliothis virescens* y *H. zea* en relación a los cultivos de algodon y maiz." *Ing. Mens.* April, 1957. Vol. 31, No. 357. Est. Exp. Agric. La Molina. Lima, Peru, 1957.

Metcalf, R. L. "Requirements for Insecticides of the Future." In *Proceedings of the FAO Symposium on Integrated Pest Control,* Rome, FAO, 2 (1966), 115–33.

Miner, F. D. "Cotton Insects in Nicaragua." *Jour. Econ. Ento.* 53 (2) (1960), 291–96.

Mobley, L. A. *Cotton in Central America.* Memphis, Tenn.: National Cotton Council of America, 1955. 35 pp.

Murray, J. C.; Verhalen, L. M.; and Bryan,

D. E. "Observations on the Feeding Preference of the Striped Blister Beetle, *Epicauta vittata* (Fabricius), to Glanded and Glandless Cottons." *Crop Science,* 5 (1965), 189.

Newsom, L. D., and Brazzel, J. R. "Pests and Their Control." In *Advances in Production and Utilization of Quality Cotton: Principles and Practices,* F. C. Elliot, M. Hoover, and W. K. Porter, eds. Ames, Iowa: Iowa State Univ. Press, 1968, pp. 367–405.

Painter, R. H. *Insect Resistance in Crop Plants.* New York: Macmillan Co., 1951. 520 pp.

Pearson, E. O., and Maxwell-Darling, R. C. *The Insect Pests of Cotton in Tropical Africa.* London: Commonwealth Institute of Entomology, 1958. 355 pp.

Peterson, George D. *The Quiet Crisis in Nicaragua.* Unpublished manuscript.

Phillips, J. R., and Newsom, L. D. "Diapause in *Heliothis zea* and *Heliothis virescens.*" *Ann. Entomol. Soc. Amer.,* 59 (1966), 154–59.

Presley, J. T., and Bird, L. S. "Diseases and Their Control." In *Advances in Production and Utilization of Quality Cotton: Principles and Practices.* F. C. Elliot, M. Hoover, and W. K. Porter, eds. Ames, Iowa: Iowa State University Press, 1968, pp. 347–66.

Rainey, R. C. "Observations on the Development of the Cotton Boll, with Particular Reference to Changes in Susceptibility to Pests and Diseases." *Ann. Appl. Biol.,* 35 (1948), 64–83.

Rejesus, Romeo S., and Reynolds, H. T. Unpublished data on file at University of California, Riverside. (Based upon Ph.D. thesis and one or more manuscripts in preparation.)

Reynolds, H. T. Unpublished data on file, University of California, Riverside.

Reynolds, H. T., and Deal, A. S. "Control of the Southern Garden Leafhopper, a New Pest of Cotton in Southern California." *Jour. Econ. Ento.,* 49 (1956), 356–58.

Reynolds, H. T.; Stern, V. M.; Fukuto, T. R.; and Peterson, G. D. "Potential Use of Dylox and Other Insecticides in a Control Program for Field Crop Pests in California." *Jour. Econ. Ento.,* 53 (1) (1960), 72–78.

Ridgway, R. L., and Jones, S. L. "Field-Cage Releases of *Chrysopa cornea* for Suppression of Populations of the Bollworm and the Tobacco Budworm on Cotton." *Jour. Econ. Ento.*, 61 (4) (1968), 892–98.

Ridgway, R. L.; Lingren, P. D.; Cowan, C. B.; and Davis, J. W. "Populations of Arthropod Predators and *Heliothis* Spp. after Applications of Systemic Insecticides to Cotton." *Jour. Econ. Ento.*, 60 (4) (1967), 1012–16.

Ripper, W. E., and George, L. *Cotton Pests of the Sudan, Their Habits and Control.* Oxford: Blackwell Scientific Publications, 1965. P. 345.

Schmitz, G. "Cotton Pest Problems in Iran, Syria, and Greece." In *Rept. of the Second Session of FAO Panel of Experts on Integrated Pest Control.* Rome, FAO, 1969.

Simon, F. J. "Nuevas experiencias con insecticidas sistémicos en el algodonero, 1955–56." *Bol.* No. 65, Est. Exp. Agr. de La Molina. Lima, Peru, 1956.

———. "Insecticidas sistémicos e insectos del algodonero." *Bol.* No. 68. Est. Exp. Agric. La Molina. Lima, Peru, 1957.

Smith, Ray F. "Principles of Measurements of Crop Losses Caused by Insects." *FAO Symposium on Crop Losses.* Rome, FAO, 2–6 Oct., 1967. 1967a, pp. 205–24.

———. "Recent Developments in Integrated Control." *IVth British Insecticide and Fungicide Conference, Brighton, Nov., 1967.* 1967b.

———. "The Importance of Economic Injury Levels in the Development of Integrated Pest Control Programs." *Qualitas Plantarum et Materiae Vegetabile* 1969a.

———. "The New and the Old in Pest Control." *Acad. de Lincei*, 1969b.

———. "Summary Report on Cotton Pests in Central America and Northern South America." In *Rept. of Second Session of FAO Panel of Experts on Integrated Pest Control.* Rome, FAO, 1969.

Smith, Ray F., and Reynolds, H. T. "Principles, Definitions and Scope of Integrated Pest Control." *Proceedings of the FAO Symposium on Integrated Pest Control,* vol. 1, Rome, FAO, (1966), 11–17.

Smith, Ray F., and van den Bosch, Robert. "Integrated Control." In *Pest Control. Bi-ological, Physical and Selected Chemical Methods,*" W. W. Kilgore and R. L. Doutt, eds. New York and London: Academic Press, 1967. Pp. 295–340.

Sterling, W. L., and Adkisson, P. L. "Differences in the Diapause Response of Boll Weevils from the High Plains and Central Texas and the Significance of This Phenomenon in Revising Present Fall Insecticidal Control Programs." *Texas Agric. Exp. Sta. Bull.* 1047. 1966.

Stern, V. M. "Cotton Pest Problems in Turkey, Israel, and Iraq." In *Rept. of Second Session of FAO Panel of Experts on Integrated Pest Control.* Rome, FAO, 1969.

———. "Interplanting Alfalfa in Cotton to Control Lygus Bugs and Other Insect Pests." In *Proceed. Tall Timbers Conference on Ecological Animal Control by Habitat Management.* Pub. Tall Timbers Res. Stat., Tallahassee, Florida, No. 1 (1969), 55–69.

Suchý, M.; Sláma, K.; and Šorm, F. "Insect Hormone Activity of p-(1, 5-dimethylhexyl) Benzoic Acid Derivatives in *Dysdercus* Species." *Science,* 162 (1968), 582–83.

Tannenbaum, F. *Ten Keys to Latin America.* New York: Alfred A. Knopf, 1960. 237 pp.

van den Bosch, R., and Hagen, K. S. "Predaceous and Parasitic Arthropods in California Cotton Fields." *Calif. Agric. Exp. Sta. Bull.* 820, 1966. 32 pp.

van den Bosch, R., and Stern, V. M. "The Effect of Harvesting Practices on Insect Populations in Alfalfa." In *Proceed. Tall Timbers Conference on Ecological Animal Control by Habitat Management.* Pub. Tall Timbers Res. Stat., Tallahassee, Florida, No. 1 (1969) 47–54.

van Emden, H. F. *Sci. Hort.,* 17 (1965), 126.

Walker, J. K. "The Relationship of the Fruiting of the Cotton Plant and Overwintered Boll Weevils to the F. Generation." *Jour. Econ. Ento.,* 59 (2) (1966), 323–26.

Warner, R. E., and Smith, C. Earle. "Boll Weevil Found in Pre-Columbian Cotton from Mexico." *Science,* 162 (1968), 911–12.

Watson, J., *et al. Cotton Insects.* A report of a panel of the President's Science Advisory Committee. Washington, D.C.: The White House, 1965. 19 pp.

Watt, K. E. F. *Ecology and Resource Management, a Quantitative Approach.* New York: McGraw-Hill Co., 1968. 450 pp.

Wellso, S. G., and Adkisson, P. L. "A Long-Day, Short-Day Effect in the Photoperiodic Control of the Pupal Diapause of the Bollworm, *Heliothis zea* (Boddie)." *Jour. Insect Physiol.,* 12 (1966), 1455–65.

Whitcomb, W. H., and Bell, K. "Predaceous Insects, Spiders and Mites of Arkansas Cotton Fields." *Univ. Arkansas Agric. Exp. Sta. Bull.* 690. 1964. 84 pp.

Wille, J. E. "Biological Control of Certain Cotton Insects and the Application of New Organic Insecticides in Peru." *Jour. Econ. Ento.,* 44 (1) (1951), 13–18.

————. *Entomología Agrícola del Perú.* Direc. General de Agric., Minist. de Agric., Lima, Peru. 2nd ed., 1952.

————. *Insectos e Insecticidas en la Campaña Algodonera 1955–56.* Est. Exp. Agr. La Molina. Lima, Peru, 1956.

Wille, Juan E., and Beingolea, O. *Insectos e Insecticidas en la Campaña Algodonera 1956–57.* Est. Exp. Agr. La Molina. Lima, Peru, 1957.

Wille, E.; Beingolea, O.; and Gonzalez, J. E. *Insectos e Insecticidas en la Campaña Algodonera 1958–59.* Est. Exp. Agr. La Molina. Lima, Peru, 1959. 24 pp.

Zeid, M.; Saad, A. A.; Tantawi, G.; and Eldefrawi, M. E. "Laboratory and Field Evaluation of Insecticides against the Egyptian Cotton Leafworm." *Jour. Econ. Ento.,* 61 (5) (1968), 1183–86.

22. THE RELATIONSHIP BETWEEN INSECT PESTS AND COTTON PRODUCTION IN CENTRAL AFRICA

F. E. M. Gillham

The relationship between an insect pest and its host is one of dynamic equilibrium in which each is under the influence of a number of environmental factors. In the natural condition, the population density of the insect is kept in check by climatic factors, by limitations of food and by pathogens, parasites and predators. These checks lead to a situation of relative population stability. However, when a plant species is grown as a crop over an extensive area, available food for insect pests is capable of supporting a much larger population and a state of relative instability is introduced in which the pest can increase and disperse rapidly unless checked by other controls. The use of insecticides accentuates this instability by removing many parasites and predators, permitting an almost unrestricted increase of those pests which are not controlled by the insecticide. Eventually other checks will often come into play, limiting further increase in the population, but by this stage, the pest may have done a considerable amount of economic damage.

Cotton production in Central Africa has been erratic since the crop was first introduced in the early 1920's. The level of production was regulated by yields and price levels. However, in the first few years after the introduction of cotton to a new area, yield levels were usually relatively good and the red bollworm *Diparopsis castanea* was not observed. After a few years, this pest made its appearance, increasing steadily over the years and leading to reduced yields and eventually to reduced production. The jassid *Empoasca* spp., the bollworm *Heliothis armigera* and the cotton stainer *Dysdercus* spp. also emerged as major pests during the early years of production. During this period, cotton was a major crop in Malawi, production was at a low, erratic level in Rhodesia and, at times, nonexistent in Zambia.

An insect control program was introduced in Central Africa by the Cotton Pest Research Team in 1959. This team was established by the Government of the Federation of Central Africa and its member countries and the Government of Great Britain. The program was based on scouting to determine what pests were present in the crop, the choice of the most effective insecticide to control these pests and efficient application of the insecticides. Insect control has resulted in a general improvement in plant growth, increasing its attractiveness to certain pests. In addition, the incidence of certain parasites and predators has been reduced. These two factors, in combination, have led to an increase in oviposition by *Heliothis* moths, although these pests are being controlled by insecticides. Following the use of organic insecticides, red spider mites *Tetranychus* spp. have begun to make their appearance in the crop earlier in the season. This pest can do very serious damage to cotton.

Prior to the establishment of the Cotton Pest Research Team, the main means of limiting insect damage was through plant breeding. For many years, the main emphasis in the breeding program was on resistance to *Empoasca*. In addition, prolific varieties with large numbers of small bolls were bred in an effort to minimize the depredations of bollworms. Breeding for host plant resistance requires, first, a knowledge of the characteristics of the plant which will affect the behavioral pattern of the pest and, secondly, the ability to transfer these characteristics to a commercially acceptable variety. The first requirement can be met through a study of insect responses to specific phenotypes of cotton and through a study of the effect of various chemical constituents of the plant on the insect pest under consideration. The second requirement is complicated by the fact that in many cases, resistance to one pest leads to susceptibility to another and that the requirement for resistance is often overruled by other economic considerations.

The world-wide extent of the destruction of agriculture products attributable to pests is difficult to estimate but could amount to as much as one-third of all products. The economic importance of pest damage is directly related to the crop under consideration. Horticultural crops may be rendered unmarketable by a small amount of damage while a similar amount of damage in a field crop will be of little consequence, apart from reducing the yield. Similarly, determinate plant types are subject to pest attacks over a far shorter period than plants with an indeterminate flowering habit. Thus the period of insect attack on a crop like coffee or cotton is far more prolonged than on a grain crop.

With the exception of the Soviet Union where cotton production extends to 47° N, the major cotton-producing areas of the world are between 35° S and 37° N latitude. A wide range of cotton insect pests are found in this area. Hargreaves (1948) lists 1,326 insect species of the world which have been found on cotton, of which 482 are recorded from Africa, south of the Sahara. Many of these species are not important. However, a considerable number of species are found in any cotton-producing area, presenting a very complex pattern which varies considerably from season to season and from location to location.

The relationship between the insect and its host plant involves the feeding preferences of the adult and its oviposition preferences which, in turn, are related to the feeding preferences of the juvenile forms. This relationship is, necessarily, a complex one (Gillham, 1964). Dethier (1952) describes the whole drama of changing feeding preferences as a dynamic equilibrium between the two changing systems, the plant and the insect. By its very nature, any agricultural endeavor has a profound influence on this equilibrium. In the first place, a single host plant species is planted without competition over a considerable area, thus providing an abundant and readily available host for its particular pest complex. The natural enemies may be able to regulate the population increase of the insect pest species and so protect the crop plant from excessive damage. However, when natural controls are not sufficient to keep the population density of the pest species at a low level, serious economic damage may result. In these circumstances, therefore, an increase in production becomes a primary factor in the development of plant pests and parasites.

As soon as insecticides are introduced for the control of any overabundant insect species, the parasites and predators of this and other species may be destroyed, facilitating the development of high population densities of any species not controlled by the insecticide being used. Such a situation has frequently been reported in the case of the red spider mite *Tetranychus* spp., a cotton pest, where spraying for the control of other species of insect has destroyed its natural controls (Husseine, 1958; McKinlay, 1959; Hassan *et al.,* 1961). This permits the mite population to increase to economically serious proportions at a time in the season when they can do serious damage.

The population levels of certain insect pest species have been influenced by the level of production of cotton in Central Africa and these pests, in turn, have affected further expansion in production. This paper will demonstrate the difficulties of developing an effective program for the control of all the major pests in the insect complex on cotton. Continued research to maintain the effectiveness of the program has been required by the changed ecological situation produced by the program's activities.

FACTORS WHICH INFLUENCE THE PREVALENCE OF INSECTS

All animal populations have an innate capacity to increase, the expression of which is regulated by climatic factors, the availability of suitable food, by competition within and between species and by natural enemies. The climate directly affects the speed of development, fecundity and longevity of the animal and indirectly affects the animal by controlling the availability of food. Temperature, moisture and light are the most important climatic factors, while wind may play a major role in the dispersion of certain insects (Andrewartha and Birch, 1954; Cacheme, 1961).

All animals have a favorable temperature and moisture range within which they live and multiply. Most animals can survive in the extremes of light and darkness found in nature, but they are influenced by illuminance, direction, photoperiod, wavelength and degree of polarization of light. These factors provide the necessary stimuli to those mechanisms which regulate the life cycle and keep it in step with the season (Andrewartha and Birch, 1954). Many insects spend at least part of their life cycle within the structure of a host plant or animal where the temperature, humidity, light intensity and wind velocity may differ markedly from the surroundings. Thus the relative importance of microclimate and macroclimate must be borne in mind (Gillham, 1968).

Where a limitation to population growth is not imposed by climatic factors, other factors, such as the availability of suitable food, competition for the same ecological niche or the prevalence of specific and non-specific predators and parasites, may regulate the abundance of a given species. However, even under favorable climatic conditions, in the presence of abundant food and the absence of predators, an upper limit to numbers will be imposed by the influence of density on birth rate and death rate (Andrewartha and Birch, 1954).

Insects can be grouped into those which feed on living plant matter, those which feed on dead or decaying plant matter, those which live on live animal matter, those which live on dead animal matter and those which live on both animal and plant matter. A few species have omnivorous feeding habits, but most insects have specialized to some extent and phytophagous or plant-eating insects may be divided into polyphagous, oligophagous and monophagous groups. The first group has a wide range of host plants, the second a relatively restricted range while members of the third group are highly specialized, restricting their activities to one or two closely related hosts (Gillham, 1968). Gause (1934) stated that two or more forms of animal with the same ecological requirements cannot coexist indefinitely in the same ecological niche because one of them will, in all likelihood, be more efficient than the other and will out-breed and supplant it. This principle is demonstrated by the evolution of increasing specialization from polyphagous to oligophagous to monophagous feeding habits, providing new species with spatial isolation.

The factors regulating the abundance of insects can be well demonstrated on cotton, Gossypium hirsutum (L.). Cotton is a perennial plant but it is generally cultivated as an annual. The plant is characterized by a main stem with a dominant apical bud. This bud is extremely attractive to a number of insect pests, particularly in the early stages of development of the plant. The aerial portions of all species of the genus Gossypium are characterized by the presence of pigment glands which vary in size, number, distribution and pigmentation in different species. They secrete a volatile oil which is probably responsible for the characteristic odor of the cotton plant (Stanford and Viehover, 1918). The pigment gossypol, one of the constituents of the glands, is toxic to a number of pests and pathogens in its free form. I suggested (Gillham, 1965) that the glands may have evolved in this genus as a protective mechanism against the ravages of pests. With the exception of Gossypium tomentosum which is found in Hawaii, all species of the genus are also characterized by the presence of extra-floral nectaries on the underside of the leaf and at the base of the bracts.

Cotton is normally planted from seed during the spring. It takes from six to eight weeks to start flowering. The plant has an indeterminate flowering habit, lasting about twelve weeks. Since it takes about eight weeks for the boll to develop from pollination to maturity, the plant normally carries buds and bolls in various stages of development for most of its flowering period. Rainey (1948) demonstrated the influence of the development stage of the cotton plant on its susceptibility to various pests and diseases. Since the plant carries bolls for a fairly prolonged period in all stages of development, it is subject to attack by a range of insect pests over a long period.

A wide range of insect pest species, falling into the polyphagous, oligophagous and monophagous groups, inhabit the temperate and tropical regions of the world where cotton is normally grown as a crop plant. The species attacking cotton will obviously vary considerably from season to season and from one location to another, but a fairly typical pattern of attack will consist of those species which attack the apical bud early in the development of the plant and which may continue for a prolonged period, followed by leaf-sucking and leaf-eating

The lower Algerian Sahara constitutes a zone with a relatively dense population where the only resources are provided by agriculture, particularly by the date palms that cover the area. This zone had never experienced intensive development until the discovery of important quantities of underground water, which led to an exploitation of that resource through wells and bore holes. This exploitation is traced in **SALINIZATION AND WATER PROBLEMS IN THE ALGERIAN NORTHEAST SAHARA** by Kamel Achi (Page 276).

Inadequate drainage, combined with the abusive utilization of the subterranean waters, has had a disastrous impact on the superficial water table, seriously disturbing its regime.

Photo 16-1 shows hand irrigation works. Photo 16-2 illustrates how young palm trees are planted in wedges that cut across the crust of gypseous rock in the lower Algerian Sahara.

16-1

16-2

The use of irrigation in the region of the Upper Rio Grande has been traced to prehistoric times. In the late nineteenth century the introduction of intensive stock raising combined with severe drought to aggravate ecologic imbalance. In addition, constant population growth made increasing demands upon already overtaxed water resources. A new system of dams built to relieve the resulting water shortage caused considerable silting problems as reported by John Hay in his paper **SALT CEDAR AND SALINITY ON THE UPPER RIO GRANDE** (Page 288).

Dr. Hay describes how salt cedar trees were planted along stream banks in an effort to stop erosion, but the salt cedar, highly water consuming and salt tolerant, quickly escaped cultivation and spread from one valley stream to another (Photo 17-1). The tree extracts salt from saline ground waters and exudes salt crystals from specially developed salt glands within the plant itself, quickly polluting the soil surface with "salt whiskers" (Photo 17-2). Photo 17-3 shows a damaged cotton crop that resulted from this pollution. Thus in man's efforts to increase the yield from a river basin he has virtually destroyed it.

17-1

(USDA-SCS Photo by J. H. Barksdale.)   17-2

(USDA-SCS Photo by J. H. Pogue.)   17-3

Lake Valencia, once a lake of exceptional beauty in the north central part of Venezuela, has been desiccated, salinized, and polluted. Alberto Böckh, in his paper **CONSEQUENCES OF UNCONTROLLED HUMAN ACTIVITIES IN THE VALENCIA LAKE BASIN** (Page 301), describes how careless and irresponsible use of its tributary waters for farming and industry and indiscriminate deforestation have eroded and destroyed a considerable part of the lake's headwaters. The dramatic retreat of the lake's shoreline can be seen in the photo. The restaurant (left of the Plaza) and the Maracay Nautical Club (right) stood over the lake when they were built. Because of the desiccation caused by man, the shoreline has retreated several hundred meters in the past decade alone. (Photo courtesy of Guillermo Zuloaga.)

18-1

THE ANCHICAYA HYDROELECTRIC PROJECT IN COLOMBIA, described by Robert N. Allen on Page 318, was the first major plant in the area and was constructed to supply energy to the power-starved, rapidly growing city of Cali. Too little ecological reconnaissance was made in the nearly inaccessible, difficult, and jungle-covered terrain and, after the dam was built, little active concern was given to protecting the reservoir's watershed. As a result, very serious sediment and debris problems arose, caused by nearby highway construction and the deforestation of the watershed.

The Anchicaya dam, power plant, and reservoir are shown in Photo 19-1. The Rio Neusa flood of April 1950 washed out an estimated 200,000 cubic meters of material from the canyon, depositing it in the canyon entrance, swamping the powerhouse, washing out the highway, and isolating the workers' camp (Photo 19-2). The hydro plant was severely damaged; the crescent-shaped objects in the center of Photo 19-3 are the tops of the generator and turbine.

19-1

19-2

19-3

Irrigation is an attempt to improve artificially the productivity of an agricultural ecosystem by supplementing the supply of water, the most basic life-sustaining substance. As a result of this changed provision of water the environmental components of the system change, leading in turn to biological change. One of the most dramatic achievements of man in arid regions is the creation of oases in the desert. In his paper **ON IRRIGATION INDUCED CHANGES IN INSECT POPULATIONS IN ISRAEL** (Page 349) Professor Rivnay describes several cases in which crops introduced into the desert were infested by pests that had migrated to the site of new plantings from as much as hundreds of kilometers away.

In ancient times water was pumped by mechanical action; in one method a camel walked continuously around a well, turning a device that operated a pump—simply a series of buckets that raised the water to ground level. This system is still prevalent in many parts of the Near East, but in Israel it has given way to modern techniques such as the sprinkler (Photo 20-1). One side effect of vastly more efficient irrigation techniques has been new pest infestations; for example, watermelon was infested with larvae of *Baris granulipennis* (Photo 20-2). (Photos courtesy of Comm. Inst. Ent.)

20-1

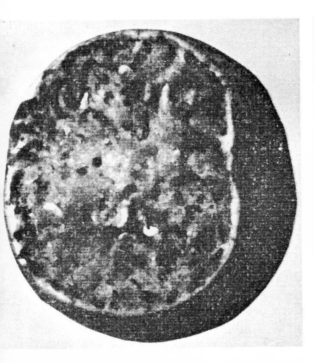

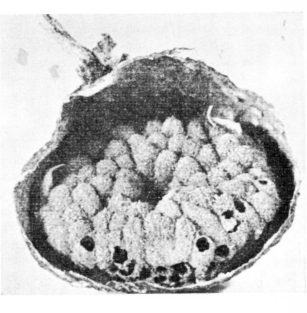

From an ecological point of view the concept of the "agro-ecosystem" is essential to understanding the population dynamics of cotton pests and to devising systems for their management or control. Major cotton-growing areas in Central and South America, the United States, the Middle East, and Australia have one factor in common: intensive use of chemical pesticides. Ray F. Smith and Harold T. Reynolds discuss the need for integrated control approach to cotton pests in their paper **EFFECTS OF MANIPULATION OF COTTON AGRO-ECOSYSTEMS ON INSECT PEST POPULATIONS** (Page 373). Through various case histories, the authors demonstrate how indiscriminate spraying of pesticides can do more harm than good and even promote pest outbreaks. Photo 21-1 shows cotton bolls completely destroyed by the pink bollworm, *Pectinophora gossypiella*, which from a world viewpoint is considered to be the most destructive cotton insect, although locally other insects often cause more damage. An important predator on cotton aphids is the adult of convergent lady beetle, *Hippodamia convergens* (Photo 21-2). One of the most important beneficial insects in cotton fields is the adult of green lacewing, *Chrysopa carnea* (Photo 21-3). Airplane application of insecticides to cotton (Photo 21-4), although at times needed for crop protection, can cause widespread damage to other living things in the environment and may result in a complete disruption of natural biological controls. Insect fauna in a cotton field are sampled with a vacuum sampler (Photo 21-5).

21-1

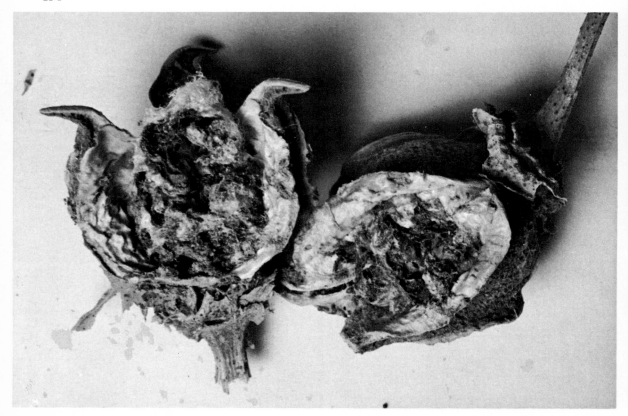

21-4

21-5

In his report (Page 423) Teodoro Boza Barducci describes the **ECOLOGICAL CONSEQUENCES OF PESTICIDES USED FOR THE CONTROL OF COTTON INSECTS IN CAÑETE VALLEY, PERU.** The Cañete Valley in Peru suffered greatly from the use of synthetic-organic pesticides during the period 1949 to 1956. Synthetic-organic pesticides were developed shortly after World War II to facilitate peacetime conversions of big industries while improving many operations of agriculture. The result of their widespread use was disastrous. Costs of cotton production rose due to excessive use of the insecticides. It was also discovered that pests kept appearing in the fields, because the natural predators and parasites of these pests had been largely wiped out and because the pests themselves had developed resistance to the chemicals used. The proposals of the agricultural Experimental Station and the Cañete Farmer's Association were then accepted by the farmers of the valley. Synthetic-organic insecticides were prohibited; mineral ("natural") insecticides were used when chemical control was needed; natural enemies of the cotton pests were reintroduced into the fields; and cotton culture practices were developed and regulated to best boost the natural ecological processes destructive or inhibiting to pests. This integrated control proved very effective. Photo 23-1. A field of Tanguis cotton ready for picking. Photo 23-2. Eggs of *Hippodamia convergens* collected for breeding purposes. Photo 23-3. Larvae of *Hippodamia convergens* feeding on liver preparations. Photo 23-4. Daily collection of *Sitotroga* eggs from the cabinets.

23-1

23-2

23-3

23-4

species and followed, in turn, by those species which attack the fruiting bodies. There will obviously be a considerable overlap between the various groups, but all are directly and indirectly influenced by climatic factors and all enjoy a certain amount of both spatial and temporal isolation resulting from the part of the plant actually attacked and the timing of the attack. An apparent exception may exist in the case of bollworm species; but generally, in areas which have more than one species, the pattern of attack is typified by the predominance of one species at any one time during the season.

THE INSECT PESTS OF COTTON IN CENTRAL AFRICA

Pearson and Maxwell-Darling (1958) confined their attention to about 150 species of the 482 cotton insects recorded by Hargreaves from Africa south of the Sahara. They indicated that most of the others have little or no economic importance. The major pests which are of concern for cotton in Central Africa are listed in Table 22–1.[1]

The pattern of insect attack on cotton in

Central Africa, as in other parts of the world, varies considerably from season to season and from location to location. However, taken in sequence in a fairly typical season, some lygus damage can be expected in the seedling stage. *Empoasca* makes its appearance fairly early and can be present on the crop for a considerable part of the season. Where alternative food sources are not available, *Diparopsis* and *Earias* may eat their way into the growing tip and act as stem borers. These two species can be present more or less throughout the season, feeding on the growing tip prior to the onset of flowering and attacking the bolls once these have started to develop. *Heliothis* feeds mainly on buds and bolls moving into the cotton crop during the course of flowering. *Dysdercus* spp. feed on the developing seed, attacking the cotton plant as the bolls start to ripen, and thus tend to be late-season pests. Aphids may attack cotton virtually at any time during the plant's development, while under natural conditions, *Tetranychus* is a late-season pest if it makes its appearance at all. In certain areas, leaf-eating caterpillars *Cosmophila flava* (F.), and the Elegant grasshopper, *Zonocerus elegans* Thub., may cause severe damage

---

[1] Cultivated cottons of the world belong to four species, two of which, *Gossypium arboreum* and *Gossypium herbaceum*, are known as Old World species while the other two, *Gossypium hirsutum* and *Gossypium barbadense*, are commonly known as New World species. The American upland varieties belong to the species *Gossypium hirsutum* and are by far the most commonly grown throughout the world. All cultivated Central African varieties belong to this species.

The red bollworm, *Diparopsis castanea* Hmps., confines its activity to the genus *Gossypium* and its close relative *Cienfugosia* and is the single representative of the monophagous group. McKinley (personal communication) has expressed doubt as to the ability of this pest to feed and breed on *Cienfugosia*. The oligophagous group, which has a number of Malvaceous host species, is represented by the cotton stainer *Dysdercus* spp., the spiny bollworm *Earias* spp., the dusky stainer *Oxycarenus* spp., and the leaf eaters *Cosmophila* spp. and *Xanthodes graelsii*. The pink bollworm, *Pectinophora gossypiella* Saund., is regarded as being oligophagous, having been recorded as feed-

ing and breeding on *Hibicus dongolensis* as well as *Gossypium hirsutum* in Rhodesia (Matthews *et al.*, 1965) and on several host plants elsewhere (Shiller *et al.*, 1962). However, outbreaks have been recorded in Malawi without any alternative host plants being found (Matthews *et al.*, 1965). The polyphagous group has a wide range of alternative host plants and forms by far the largest group of cotton pests. The bollworm, *Heliothis armigera* Hbn., is probably the most destructive of the pests falling within this group. The larvae of various species of this genus function as bollworms in all the major cotton-producing areas of the world. They feed on the fruit of a wide range of plants, among which maize, *Zea mays,* is a preferred host. The wide distribution of the species of this genus makes it one of the most destructive of all cotton pests. The aphids *Aphis gossypii* Glov. and jassids *Empoasca* spp. are also major polyphagous pests on cotton in Central Africa. The Acarina spider mites, *Tetranychus* spp., have a wide range of host plants and under certain conditions can cause serious damage to the cotton crop.

Table 22-1

THE MAJOR PESTS OF COTTON IN CENTRAL AFRICA

ORDER	GENUS	SPECIES	COMMON NAME	PLANT PART ATTACKED
Lepidoptera	Xanthodes	graelsii		leaf
	Anomis	sabulifera		leaf
	Cosmophila	flava	semilooper	leaf
	Spodoptera	littoralis	Egyptian cotton	leaf
	Prodenia	litura	leafworm	leaf
	Diparopsis	castanea	red bollworm	boll
	Earias	spp.	spiny bollworm	boll
	Heliothis	armigera	American bollworm	boll
	Pectinophora	gossypiella	pink bollworm	boll
Hemiptera	Dysderous	spp.	stainer	seed
	Empoasca	facialis	jassid	leaf
	Empoasca	lybica	jassid	leaf
	Helopeltis	schoutedeni	helopeltis	leaf, stem and boll
	Helopeltis	bergroth	helopeltis	leaf, stem and boll
	Lygus	vosseleri	lygus	terminal bud
	Oxycarenus	spp.	dusky stainer	seed
Aphidae	Aphis	gossypii	aphid	leaf
Acarina Tetranychidae	Tetranychus	telarius lombardinii ludeni neccaledonicus	red spider mite	leaf

to young plants (Tunstall and Matthews, 1965).

THE INFLUENCE OF COTTON PRODUCTION ON THE RED BOLLWORM Diparopsis castanea

Cotton was grown on a limited scale in Malawi from 1905 and in Rhodesia from the early 1920's. By the mid-1920's, Empoasea spp. had emerged as a major pest. By reducing the efficiency of the foliage of the plant and causing actual defoliation, yields were being reduced and the quality adversely affected to such an extent that future production appeared doubtful.[2]

[2] Despite this, Cameron (1927) considered that Dysdercus spp. were to be feared far more than Empoasca. Hamilton and Peat (1927) observed that Empoasca would definitely come within the

However, during the 1926–27 season, the bollworm attack was extremely small and consisted almost entirely of Earias. In that year there was virtually no Heliothis damage throughout the country, possibly due to the late arrival of the first rains, and there was no Diparopsis activity (Peat, 1928).

The following season, shedding due to bollworms at the Research Station at Gatooma was once again slight and mainly due to Earias. A few Heliothis were observed on the crop, but once again, no Diparopsis were recorded although they were reported

control of the plant breeder, but that Heliothis was undoubtedly the most serious pest. They went on to record that Earias spp. did some slight damage while Diparopsis did not appear to be present. The breeding program for the development of Empoasca-resistant varieties will be discussed in a later section of this paper. In this section consideration will be given to the developing importance of Diparopsis with increased production.

to be present in cotton in the Bulawayo and Mazoe Valley areas. At the time, a comparison between the flora in the different areas was considered, as this might have given an indication of the reason for the presence of *Diparopsis* on cotton in one area and not in another. This investigation was not followed up because by the following year, this pest was recorded on cotton at the Research Station as well (Peat, 1928).

A small plot of ratooned cotton was established at the Research Station for the study of bollworm and stainer attacks (Peat, 1929). This was done to provide a source of food for these pests throughout the year. In the 1928–29 season, a very severe attack of *Heliothis* occurred. However, on the ratooned trap crop, the ratio of *Diparopsis* to *Earias* to *Heliothis* was 46 to 13 to 1 in a collection of 180 bollworms.[3] In a later collection, 22 *Diparopsis* were found, 10 *Earias* and 1 *Heliothis*. Thus *Diparopsis* formed 76% of the total bollworms collected from the ratoon trap crop in that year—the first time this species had been recorded on cotton on the Research Station. In contrast, although *Diparopsis* were recorded on the annual crop, they formed only 0.001% of the recorded bollworm population in the annual observation plot. In this plot, 3.1% of the bollworms collected were *Earias* while 96% were *Heliothis* (Peat, 1930).

By 1930, *Heliothis* was considered to be the most serious problem and Cameron (1931) considered that it was imperative that every effort should be made to counter

[3] The red bollworm, *Diparopsis castanea* Hmps., is distributed through the main cotton-producing areas of South and Central Africa. It is monophagous, confining its activities to the genus *Gossypium* and its close relative *Cienfugosia*. The former is found wild in Rhodesia while the latter is not. The larvae of this pest tend to move into a boll and remain there until it is eaten out. By contrast, the larvae of *Heliothis* are very active, attacking buds, flowers and bolls and are capable of destroying a considerable proportion of the potential crop in a relatively short time.

the activities of this pest. The 1929–30 season was completely dominated by an attack of *Heliothis* from the beginning of March into May. However, by comparison with the figures for the previous year, the proportion of *Heliothis* collected between February and the end of May fell to 72% while *Diparopsis* rose to 9% and *Earias* to 19%. For March the percentages were 83% *Heliothis*, 2% *Diparopsis* and 15% *Earias;* and for April, 75%, 12.5% and 12.5% respectively. The lateness of the *Heliothis* attacks suggested that it may be possible to escape serious damage by forcing an early crop through breeding and through agronomic practices. The same could not be said of *Diparopsis* (Peat, 1931).

The 1930–31 season was characterized by severe drought, and losses due to insect attacks were secondary to those caused by climatic conditions. However, in contrast to previous years, *Diparopsis* became a major pest on annual cotton at the Research Station. This was considered to be serious and disturbing, but despite this, *Diparopsis* was not feared so much as *Heliothis* because of the differences of the proportion of damage done by individuals of each species (Peat, 1932).

The following season was considered the best during the first seven years of the station's establishment. *Heliothis* made its appearance early and was the principal pest. However, the incidence of *Diparopsis* was prolonged and moderately severe from the beginning of January to the end of the season. *Earias* was not at any time as severe as in previous seasons but it was present throughout the whole season (Peat, 1933).

The 1932–33 season was described by Cameron (1934) as being lopsided, with too much rain at the beginning and not enough later on. The *Heliothis* attack in the 1933–34 season was fairly similar to that experienced in previous years. The period of attack varied according to the earliness or lateness of the crop and, generally speaking, late-planted cotton suffered most. Serious *Diparopsis* damage was experienced in the latter part of the season. On top of the *Heliothis* attack, this damage led to serious losses of the remaining mature bolls. It was believed that the attacks had increased largely by a buildup from year to year of an endemic *Diparopsis* moth population. The knowledge gained concerning this species indicated that ratooning would be a highly inadvisable practice in infested areas since the population would breed on the ratoon crop and would then make devastating attacks on annual cotton later on in the season (Peat, 1934).

These reports indicate that between 1928, when *Diparopsis* was not observed on cotton on the Research Station, and 1933, this species had become a major cotton pest. The history of cotton production in Rhodesia from 1920 to 1959 was one of fluctuating production. The precise reasons for this cannot be ascribed to any particular cause. Nevertheless, over a period of years, increased seed cotton prices led to acreage expansion until price recessions or reduced yields resulting from a buildup of insect pests caused a reduction in acreage. The pattern of increasing importance of *Diparopsis* was repeated on many occasions. For various reasons, a district would go out of cotton production for several years. When it came back to cotton, *Diparopsis* would not be found on the crop for the first year or two and yields would be reasonably good. In succeeding years, *Diparopsis* would increase steadily and yield levels would decline. The most recent occurrence of this type was in the Mazoe Valley where interest in cotton increased rapidly following the introduction of the insect control program in 1959. For the first two or three years, no *Diparopsis* were found on cotton crops in the area, but in succeeding years they spread steadily. Their importance has, in this location, been kept in check by effective application of chemical insect con-

trol practices. These practices called for regular scouting to determine what pests were actually present, followed by the application of the insecticide most effective against the prevalent pests. In the case of *Diparopsis,* control was aimed at the larvae and was continued as long as heavy oviposition was recorded.

There are many similar patterns of a steady increase in the prevalence of pests with a limited host range following an increase in production of a host plant. In the United States, for example, there was the steady spread of the boll weevil *Anthonomus grandis* Boh. through the cotton-producing areas of the southeastern United States during the present century. Following its spread into Texas from Mexico in 1894, this pest advanced by 40 to 160 miles per year, and by 1922 had invaded more than 85% of the U.S. cotton belt (Gaines, 1952). In Rhodesia, the pink bollworm, *Pectinophora gossypiella,* was probably present on its wild host, *Hibiscus dongolensis,* in the southeastern part of the country for many years. Cotton was introduced to the area as a commercial crop in 1957, and by 1959 *Pectinophora* was an established pest on this crop (Whellan, 1960; Matthews *et al.,* 1965). Stringent quarantine measures calling for timely crop residue destruction, the destruction of alternative host plants in the vicinity of cotton fields and fumigation of all seed cotton leaving the area, kept further expansion in check for a number of years. However, an increase in cotton production in the area could very well lead to this pest becoming established once again. In Malawi, a severe outbreak of *Pectinophora* occurred in 1959, but the pest was not found on any wild host plants. It was believed that this outbreak was the result of a steady increase in population density during a period of two years when the closed season for cotton was not adequately observed (Matthews *et al.,* 1965). In a similar situation in the Sudan the increase in *Pectinophora* attack was related to a steady increase in standover (ratoon) cotton (Rose, Low, and Hamdan, 1957). The relationship between the prevalence of an insect pest with a limited host range and the increase in production of a host plant is far easier to trace than similar relationships of a pest with a wide host range, since in the latter, the population density of the pest is influenced by a number of factors relating to the whole of its host range. Thus the increases in *Diparopsis* population densities described can be directly related to cotton production whereas population densities of *Heliothis,* which has a wide host range, can seldom be related to any particular host.

The influence of increased productivity of a host plant on the incidence of an insect pest can take several forms. *Diparopsis* and *Pectinophora* were probably present in wild host plants in Rhodesia when the cotton crop plant was introduced. In time, the pest transferred onto the cultivated plant, where the population density steadily increased with increased production. The converse occurs when a crop is already established and a new pest is introduced to the area, often without its predators and parasites. The introduction of the European corn borer, *Pyrsusta nubilalis,* to the United States and its subsequent spread onto new hosts through vast areas is an example of this type of situation. This pest feeds mainly on *Artemesia vulgare* L. in its native habitat in Europe. It was first observed on sweet corn near Boston, Massachusetts, in 1917. It spread rapidly and by 1952 was present in thirty-seven states east of the Rocky Mountains, becoming a major pest of maize, *Zea mays,* in the U.S. corn belt (Bradley, 1952). A third situation occurs when a new crop plant is introduced into a rotation, closing a gap in the food cycle of a pest which is already in the area, and while not economically damaged itself, enabling the pest to reach epidemic proportions on other crops. A good example is provided by the lygus, *Lygus hesperus* Knight, in California which overwinters on lucerne (alfalfa), doing very little damage to this crop, but migrating onto neighboring annual crops such as cotton where it may do very serious damage (Stern *et al.,* 1964). Finally, the practices employed to control one pest may destroy the natural controls of another, permitting it to establish itself as a major pest. The establishment of red spider mite, *Tetranychus* spp., following the use of insecticides for the control of other pests has been mentioned (Hassan *et al.,* 1961; Husseine, 1958; McKinlay, 1959).

THE DEVELOPMENT OF THE INSECT CONTROL PROGRAM IN CENTRAL AFRICA

Pfadt (1962) defined integrated insect control as control of pests which combines and integrates chemical methods with natural and biological control. Chemical control is applied only as necessary and in a manner which is least disruptive to natural and biological control. This is the ideal aimed at by economic entomologists. However, the attainment of the ideal is difficult in a crop like cotton because of the complex pattern of insect attack in which the control practices necessary for one insect species directly influence other species in the complex. Nonetheless, every effort must be made to minimize the disruptive effects of the insect control program on the overall insect ecosystem.

The Cotton Pest Research team was established in Central Africa in 1956 by the Governments of the Central African Federation, the Federal Territories and Great Britain, with the prime objective of developing control measures for *Diparopsis.* By this time, despite the ravages of the *Heliothis, Diparopsis* was recognized as the major pest limiting further development of cotton production in the area. The research program developed by this team covered a complete study of *Diparopsis,* including the thorough study of the biology of the pest with particular reference to the mechanisms involved in initiating and breaking the diapause of overwintering pupae, a study of the sex attractants of the female moth, a study of the possible utilization of chemosterilants for the control of the pest and finally, a study of chemical means of control. Efforts were also made to study the parasites and predators of this and the related species, *Diparopsis watersi* (Roths.) in North Africa, *Diparopsis tephragramma* B.-B. in Angola and *Sacadodes pyralis* Dyar. in South America.

Because of the incidence of other insect pests on cotton, the main emphasis was placed on the development of effective chemical control measures to cover the whole of the insect complex. The initial program covered the screening of insecticides against the major pests in the laboratory, the field-testing of the most promising insecticides and finally, extension trials throughout the territory to study the effectiveness of the insect control recommendations under a wide range of environmental conditions (Matthews, 1966a, 1966b, 1966c; Tunstall and Matthews, 1965).

The results of the initial screening program indicated that no single insecticide was sufficient in itself to control all the insects in the complex attacking cotton. It also indicated that the effective control of *Diparopsis* depended on the newly hatched larvae coming into contact with the insecticide between hatching and entrance into the boll. Similarly, effective control of *Heliothis* also depended on control of the newly hatched larvae since the larvae are not exposed to the insecticide once they enter the boll and older larvae become increasingly difficult to kill. The effectiveness of the insect control program, therefore, depended not only on finding suitable insecticides but also on ensuring a thorough coverage of the plant. The first practical development was the modified knapsack sprayer which has proved extremely effective, particularly under present agricultural conditions (Tunstall *et al.,* 1961). This was followed by the adaptation of the tail boom for ox-drawn and tractor-mounted ground-spraying equipment for more extensive acreages (Tunstall *et al.,* 1965). Finally, comparisons were made between the ground-spraying equipment and aerial applications of insecticide since the latter has advantages under certain conditions (Johnstone and Matthews, 1965; Matthews and Tunstall, 1965). Finally a system of scouting had to be developed so that the incidence of the various pests in the crop could be assessed to form the basis for the choice of insecticide and the timing of spraying (Matthews and Tunstall, 1968).

Large-scale trials tested the effectiveness of the spray program developed under field conditions in the three Central African territories. The overall mean yields in sprayed and unsprayed trial plots in the three territories in 1960 and 1961 were 1,480 and 585 pounds of seed cotton per acre, respectively.

There was an increase in *Heliothis* oviposition on sprayed cotton in trials throughout the area. While reduced mortality as a result of fewer parasites and predators was one of the main causes of this, increased attractiveness of the plant was also an important factor. Once spraying had commenced, the importance of scouting was accentuated since increased oviposition on unprotected plants could lead to very serious crop losses (Matthews and Tunstall, 1968).

The Cotton Pest Research Team studied all aspects of insect control. Prior to the introduction of chemical control, host plant resistance was the only means used to control *Empoasca.* In view of the complex pattern of insect attack on cotton, the development of varieties which are resistant to the full range of pests is unlikely. However, continued research in this field was considered to be important since even a low level of resistance to one of the major pests could have a profound influence on the overall pattern of insect control.

BREEDING FOR HOST PLANT RESISTANCE

Host plant resistance is the ideal method of pest control. Insect resistance is defined as the ability of a certain variety to produce a larger crop of good quality than do ordinary varieties at the same level of insect populations (Painter, 1951). Even a low level of resistance can result in a significant reduction in the population of *Empoasca* spp. in cotton (Pannell *et al.,* 1949).

Host plant resistance may be due to any one or any combination of three interrelated mechanisms. The first is preference or non-preference, which is the group of plant characteristics and insect responses which lead to or away from the use of a particular plant for oviposition, food or shelter; the second is antibiosis, which is the tendency to prevent, injure or destroy insect life; and the third is tolerance, which is the ability of a plant to reduce or repair injury to a marked degree in spite of supporting an insect population approximately equal to that damaging a susceptible host (Painter, 1951).

In Rhodesia, cotton was first produced in the early 1920's, but by the middle of that decade *Empoasca* spp. threatened to put an end to future production (Peat, 1928). The situation in Malawi was not so clear-cut, but nonetheless this pest was a problem (Ducker, 1930). The relationship between leaf hairiness and the incidence of *Empoasca* was demonstrated in South Africa (Pannell *et al.,* 1949). The development of hirsute *Empoasca*-resistant varieties became the sole method of control through-

out southern Africa and made continued cotton production possible over thousands of acres for some thirty years, until the introduction of other methods of control.

Investigations were initiated in 1960 into possible sources of resistance to the bollworm *Heliothis zea* in North Carolina and *Heliothis armigera* in Rhodesia. The objective was to determine the influence of specific plant characteristics of cotton on the behavioral pattern of *Heliothis* (Stephens, 1957). This was strictly a study of insect preference. The characteristics under study were red and green leaf color, the presence and absence of glands, the presence and absence of extrafloral nectaries and the presence and absence of leaf hairs. The glandless, red leaf and plant hairiness phenotypes were chosen as variants from normal which could influence the sensory perception of *Heliothis,* while the nectariless variant was chosen for its possible adverse effect on the longevity of the *Heliothis* imago through the removal of a food source.

The results of these investigations indicated that the *Heliothis* imago prefers a hairy plant to a smooth plant for oviposition. Survival rates on the glandless variant appeared to be higher than on normal cotton. Apart from the influence on *Heliothis,* the glandless variant was attacked by a wider range of pests than the normal plant. The different characteristics studied are being combined on a common background for continued investigations.

In laboratory and field cage trials on similar genetic strains, it was demonstrated that the glabrous and nectary-free cotton plants had lower populations of bollworm *Heliothis zea* (Boddie); the tobacco budworm, *Heliothis virescens* (F); the pink bollworm, *Pectinophora gossypiella* (Saunders); the cabbage looper, *Trichoplusia ni* (Hübner); and the cotton leafworm, *Alabama argillacea* (Hübner) (Lukefahr *et al.,* 1965). In follow-up field experiments, significantly fewer larvae of the bollworm and the cotton fleahopper, *Psallus seriatus* (Reuter), were found on a glabrous and nectary-free strain than on normal cotton (Lukefahr *et al.,* 1966). These investigations require integration with other pest control practices before they can be applied in practice. The expression of the nectary-free character in reducing insect populations is very sensitive to plot size and is, therefore, difficult to test under field conditions.

In developing a breeding program for host plant resistance, the breeder requires a thorough knowledge of the life history of the insect and the nature of the, damage caused. This knowledge forms the basis for selecting possible sources of resistance for further study among related varieties and species of the host plant. The nature of any resistance must be identified and it must be shown that it is transmitted to the progeny (Gillham, 1963). In the absence of a thorough knowledge of the nature of the resistance, the breeder has a difficult task because of the small number of plants in a segregating population which possess the correct gene combination to confer resistance and because of the difficulty in identifying resistant plants (Stephens, 1957). This was demonstrated in population mixtures between pilose plants which had some resistance to the boll weevil and susceptible plants. The incidence of weevil on pilose plants was higher when they were grown in mixtures than when they were grown in pure stands (Wessling, 1958). Similarly, the nectariless character of cotton only influences insect population density when nectary-free plants are grown over a large area.

Research on host plant resistance is necessarily of a long-term nature. Planning must take this into account since success can lead to maintained or increased yields at lower cost. This is essentially an ecological approach to pest control.

*

The relationship between the host plant and its pests is one of dynamic equilibrium in which each influences the other and is, in turn, influenced by a number of environmental factors. In natural conditions, this equilibrium reaches a status of relative stability in which the population density of the pest is kept in check. The introduction of agriculture may introduce instability by removing the check imposed on the insect population growth by limitations of available food. If equilibrium is restored at a low pest population density as a result of an increase in natural and biological controls, little economic damage will result. Numerous cases of successful biological control have been reported (Lounsburg, 1900; Steinhaus, 1947; Sweetman, 1936; Wigglesworth, 1965). However, equilibrium may only be reached when the pest population density has reached a level where there is serious economic damage, in which case some means of control other than natural and biological control may be necessary.

The pattern of biological control in cotton varies considerably from location to location. Overwhelming evidence was found in Arkansas that predators frequently prevent outbreaks of bollworms, aphids and spider mites (Whitcomb and Bell, 1964), while in the Sale Valley area of Arizona, the predator complex was unable to bring the *Lygus* infestation below the destructive level and a high predatory insect complex did not prevent a severe outbreak of either salt-marsh caterpillars, *Estigmene acrea,* or the cotton leaf perforator, *Buccalatrix thurberiella* (Wene and Skeets, 1962). In Central Africa, biological control of cotton pests has not, as yet, been sufficient to keep the major pests, *Heliothis, Diparopsis* and *Dysdercus,* in check. In the absence of insecticides, it has checked *Aphis* and *Tetranychus.*

When biological control is unable to prevent insect populations from reaching economically damaging proportions, other methods have to be resorted to. The more specific these measures are to the particular pest doing the damage, the less will be the disruption of the insect ecosystem. Chemosterilants have been successfully used for the control of screwworm, *Cochliomyia hominivorax* (Coq.), in Forida (Knipling, 1962a, 1962b). This approach is highly specific but requires an ability to produce large numbers of insects for sterilization and release, sterilization techniques which will not impair the mating ability of sterilized individuals, and is aided in species where the female mates only once. The plant itself may provide a means for specific control. Thus the cotton plant contains a feeding arrestant and oviposition stimulant (Dethier *et al.*, 1960) to the boll weevil (Keller *et al.*, 1962; Maxwell *et al.*, 1963) in addition to an attractant (Keller *et al.*, 1962) and a repellent (Maxwell *et al.*, 1963). A dynamic balance probably exists between these chemicals which determine the pattern of insect responses through the season (Maxwell *et al.*, 1963). The population density may possibly be regulated by changing this balance. Many insects are subject to this form of olfactory stimulus for finding feeding or oviposition sites. Many are also subject to olfactory stimuli in finding a mate. Many of these attractants are species-specific and can be used in traps or to cause confusion and so prevent mating or successful oviposition (Jacobson and Beroza, 1964).

Host plant resistance is the ideal method of pest control. However, it is often complicated by undesirable correlations in which the characteristics which provide resistance to one pest increase susceptibility to another or are unacceptable commercially. Thus leaf hairiness provides resistance to *Empoasca* but may be correlated to low lint quality (Rose, Hughes, and Low, 1957), increased susceptibility to *Aphis* and white fly, *Bemisia tabaoi* (Dark and Saunders, 1958), and to *Heliothis* (Gillham, 1963). Successful host plant resistance breeding depends on a basic knowledge of the biological and biochemical relationship between the insect and its host (Beck, 1965; Jenkins and Maxwell, 1965).

The problems associated with the development of these species-specific control measures have resulted in increasing reliance being placed on chemical control. The disruptive effect of insecticides imposes a limitation on their use but an additional limitation is imposed by the patience and financial ability of the farmer to carry an insecticide program through to its conclusion. A poorly executed program may be more harmful than no program at all (Stephens, 1957). Effective chemical control calls for the use of the most suitable insecticide at a time when the pest is most sensitive. Thus scouting is essential to form a basis for selecting the insecticide to provide an index of effectiveness and to determine the most suitable time for treatment. The importance of timing cannot be overstressed (Lincoln and Leigh, 1957; Matthews and Tunstall, 1968; Mistric, 1964). Many cases of insecticide resistance have been reported (Brazzel, 1963, 1964; Chapman and Coffin, 1964; Eldefrawi *et al.*, 1964; Lowry and Berger, 1965), but frequently the apparent failure of an insecticide is due to incorrect timing and poor application.

The need for scouting and the necessity to use different insecticides for different pest species opens the way to abuse through the temptation to use mixtures of insecticides on a routine basis. This is condemned both on economic and on biological grounds but it has considerable appeal and can only be counteracted by an effective extension service which is free of commercial ties.

The case histories of *Diparopsis* and *Pectinophora* have been used to demonstrate how an increase in the production of a crop can lead to a buildup of insect pests. Various avenues of research are outlined which can ultimately lead to the development of measures which will prevent this

happening without causing a severe disruption of the ecosystem. However, for the immediate future, insecticides will remain an essential part of agricultural production. Thus there does not appear to be any immediate relief in sight for insecticide-induced problems.

ACKNOWLEDGMENT

The author wishes to acknowledge the advice and assistance given by Mr. A. H. McKinstry, Mr. J. P. Tunstall, Mr. D. J. McKinlay and Dr. S. W. Broodryk in the preparation of this paper and the permission of the Ministry of Agriculture of Rhodesia to have it published.

REFERENCES

Andrewartha, H. C., and Birch, L. C. *The Abundance and Distribution of Animals.* Chicago: University of Chicago Press, 1954.

Beck, S. D. "Resistance of Plants to Pests." *Ann. Rev. Ent.* 10 (1965), 207–32.

Bradley, W. G. "The European Corn Borer." U.S.D.A. *Yearbook of Agriculture,* 1952. Pp. 614–21.

Brazzel, J. R. "Resistance to DDT in *Heliothis virescens.*" *J. Econ. Ent.* 56 (1963), 571.

———. "DDT Resistance in *Heliothis zea.*" *J. Econ. Ent.* 57 (1964), 455–57.

Cacheme, J. "Wind Opportunity for Locust Transport and Concentration in India and West Pakistan." U.N. Development Program: *Desert Locust Project Progress Report* No. UNSF/DL/RFS/6, 1961.

Cameron, G. S. *Prog. Rep. Exp. Sta. 1925–26: Southern Rhodesia.* London: Emp. Cott. Gr. Corp., 1927.

———. *Prog. Rep. Exp. Sta. 1929–30: Southern Rhodesia.* London: Emp. Cott. Gr. Corp., 1931.

———. *Prog. Rep. Exp. Sta. 1932–33: Southern Rhodesia.* London: Emp. Cott. Gr. Corp., 1934.

Chapman, A. J., and Coffin, L. B. "Pink Bollworm Resistance to DDT in the Laguna Area of Mexico." *J. Econ. Ent.* 57 (1964), 148.

Dark, S. O. S., and Saunders, J. H. *Prog. Rept. Expt. Stn. 1957–58: Sudan.* London: Emp. Cott. Gr. Corp., 1958.

Davich, T. B.; Keller, J. C.; Mitchell, E. B.; Hiddleston, P.; Hill, R.; Lindquist, D. A.; McKibben, G.; and Cross, W. H. "Preliminary Field Experiments with Sterile Males for Eradication of the Boll Weevil." *J. Econ. Ent.* 58 (1965), 127–31.

Dethier, V. G. "Evolution of Feeding Preferences in Phytophagous Insects." *Evolution* 8 (1952), 33–51.

Dethier, V. G.; Brown, L. B.; and Smith, C. N. "The Designation of Chemicals in Terms of Responses They Elicit from Insects." *J. Econ. Ent.* 53 (1960), 134–36.

Ducker, H. C. *Prog. Rep. Expt. Sta. 1928–29: Nyasaland.* London: Emp. Cott. Gr. Corp., 1930.

Eldefrawi, M. E.; Toppozada, A.; Salama, A.; and Elkishen, S. A. "Reversion of Toxaphene Resistance in the Egyptian Cotton Leafworm." *J. Econ. Ent.* 57 (1964), 593–95.

Gaines, R. C. "The Boll Weevil." U.S.D.A. *Yearbook of Agriculture,* 1952. Pp. 501–04.

Gause, G. T. *The Struggle for Existence.* Baltimore: Williams and Wilkins, 1934.

Gillham, F. E. M. "The Response of Bollworm, *Heliothis zea* (Boddie) to Certain Genotypes of Upland Cotton." Unpublished Ph.D. thesis, North Carolina State University, Raleigh, N.C., 1963.

———. "Resistance to Insect Pests in Upland Cotton." *S. Afr. J. of Sci.,* 60 (1964), 218–21.

———. "Evolutionary Significance of Glands and Their Importance in Cultivated Cotton." *Emp. Cott. Gr. Rev.,* 42 (1965), 101–03.

———. "Climate, Pests and Agriculture." *Agroclimatology Methods.* NESCO, 1968. Pp. 131–39.

Hamilton, I. G., and Peat, J. E. *Prog. Rep. Expt. Stn. 1925–26: Southern Rhodesia.* London: Emp. Cott. Gr. Corp., 1927.

Hargreaves, H. *List of Recorded Cotton Insects of the World.* London: Commonw. Ent. Inst., 1948. 50 pp.

Hassan, A. S.; El Nahal, A. K. M.; and El Badry, E. A. "Infestations of Cotton with Spider Mite (Acarina)." *Bull. Soc. Ent. Egypt* 42 (1961), 357–400. (From *Rev. Appl. Ent.,* 49, Ser. A, 8:431.)

Husseine, K. K. "Effect of Insecticides on Outbreaks of Spider Mite on Cotton in the Jordan Valley." *FAO Pla. Prot. Bull.,* 6 (1958), 155.

Jacobson, M., and Beroza, M. "Insect Attractants." *Sci. Amer.* 211 (1964), 20–27.

Jenkins, J. N., and Maxwell, F. G. "Research Developments and Needs in Host Plant Resistance." *Proc. 24th Plen. Meeting of the Int. Cott. Adv. Comm.,* Washington, D.C., 1965.

Johnstone, D. R., and Matthews, G. A. "Comparative Assessment of Dosage Distributions in Cotton Resulting from Helicopter and Ground Spray Treatments." *Ann. Appl. Biol.,* 55 (1965), 431–38.

Keller, J. C.; Maxwell, F. G.; and Jenkins, J. N. "Cotton Extracts as Arrestants and Feeding Stimulants for the Boll Weevil." *J. Econ. Ent.* 55 (1962), 800–01.

Knipling, E. T. "Potentialities and Progress in the Development of Chemosterilants for Insect Control." *J. Econ. Ent.* 55 (1962a), 782–86.

———. "The Sterility Principle of Insect Population Control." *PANS* 10 (1962b), 587–603.

Lincoln, C., and Leigh, T. F. "Timing Insecticide Applications for Cotton Insect Control." Agric. Expt. Stn. Fayetteville, Ark., *Bull.* 588. 1957. 46 pp.

Lounsburg, C. P. *Rep. Govt. Ent. Cape of Good Hope.* Cape Town: W. A. Richards & Sons, 1900.

Lowry, W. L., and Berger, R. S. "Investigations of Pink Bollworm Resistance to DDT in Mexico and the United States." *J. Econ. Ent.* 58 (1965), 590–91.

Lukefahr, M. J.; Cowan, C. B.; Pfrimmer, T. R.; and Noble, L. W. "Resistance of Experimental Cotton Strain 1514 to the Bollworm and Cotton Fleahopper." *J. Econ. Ent.* 59 (1966), 393–95.

Lukefahr, M. J.; Martin, D. F.; and Meyer, J. R. "Plant Resistance to Five Lepidoptera Attacking Cotton." *J. Econ. Ent.* 58 (1965), 516–18.

McKinlay, K. S. "Toxicities of Various Acaricides to Mites of the *Tetranychus* Complex in East Africa." Col. Pest. Res. Unit. Arusha, Tanganyika, Misc. Rep. No. 219 1959.

Matthews, G. A. "Investigations of the Chemical Control of Insect Pests of Cotton in Central Africa. I. Laboratory Rearing Methods and Tests of Insecticides by Application to Bollworm Eggs." *Bull. Ent. Res.,* 57 (1966a), 69–76.

———. "Investigations of the Chemical Control of Insect Pests of Cotton in Central Africa. II. Tests of Insecticides with Larvae and Adults." *Bull. Ent. Res.,* 57 (1966b), 77–91.

———. "Investigations of the Chemical Control of Insect Pests in Cotton in Central Africa. III. Field Trials." *Bull. Ent. Res.,* 57 (1966c), 193–97.

Matthews, G. A., and Tunstall, J. P. "Aerial and Ground Spraying for Cotton Insect Control in Rhodesia." *Emp. Cott. Gr. Rev.,* 42 (1965), 180–92.

———. "Scouting for Pests and the Timing of Spray Applications." *Cott. Gr. Rev.,* 45 (1968), 115–27.

Matthews, G. A.; Tunstall, J. P.; and McKinley, D. J. "Outbreaks of Pink Bollworm (*Pectinophora gossypiella* Saund.) in Rhodesia and Malawi." *Emp. Cott. Gr. Rev.,* 42 (1965), 197–208.

Maxwell, F. G.; Jenkins, J. N.; and Keller,

J. C. "A Boll Weevil Repellant from the Volatile Substances of Cotton." *J. Econ. Ent.*, 56 (1963), 894–95.

Mistric, W. J. "Early Detection of *Heliothis* on Cotton." *J. Econ. Ent.*, 57 (1964), 858–59.

Painter, R. H. *Insect Resistance in Crop Plants*. New York: Macmillan Co., 1951.

Pannell, F. R.; King, H. E.; and Ruston, D. F. "Jassid Resistance and Hairiness of the Cotton Plant." *Bull. Ent. Res.*, 39 (1949), 539–75.

Pearson, E. O., and Maxwell-Darling, R. C. *The Insect Pests of Cotton in Tropical Africa*. London: Emp. Cott. Gr. Corp. and Commonwealth Inst., 1958.

Peat, J. E. *Prog. Rep. Ext. Stn. 1926–27: Southern Rhodesia*. London: Emp. Cott. Gr. Corp., 1928.

———. *Prog. Rep. Exp. Stn. 1927–28: Southern Rhodesia*. London: Emp. Cott. Gr. Corp., 1929.

———. *Prog. Rep. Exp. Stn. 1928–29: Southern Rhodesia*. London: Emp. Cott. Gr. Corp., 1930.

———. *Prog. Rep. Exp. Stn. 1929–30: Southern Rhodesia*. London: Emp. Cott. Gr. Corp., 1931.

———. *Prog. Rep. Exp. Stn. 1930–31: Southern Rhodesia*. London: Emp. Cott. Gr. Corp., 1932.

———. *Prog. Rep. Exp. Stn. 1931–32: Southern Rhodesia*. London: Emp. Cott. Gr. Corp., 1933.

———. *Prog. Rep. Exp. Stn. 1932–33: Southern Rhodesia*. London: Emp. Cott. Gr. Corp., 1934.

Pfadt, R. E. *Fundamentals of Applied Entomology*. New York: Macmillan Co., 1962.

Rainey, R. C. "Observations on the Development of the Cotton Boll with Particular Reference to Changes in Susceptibility to Insects and Diseases." *Ann. Appl. Biol.*, 35 (1948), 64–83.

Rose, M. F.; Hughes, L. C.; and Low, A. *Prog. Rep. Exp. Stn. 1956–57: Sudan*. London: Emp. Cott. Gro. Corp., 1957.

Rose, M. F.; Low, A.; and Hamdan, Eff Hannay. *Prog. Rep. Exp. Stn. 1956–57: Sudan*. London: Emp. Cott. Gr. Corp., 1957.

Shiller, I.; Noble, L. W.; and Fife, L. C. "Host Plants of the Pink Bollworm." *J. Econ. Ent.*, 55 (1962), 67–70.

Stanford, E. E., and Viehover, A. "Chemistry and Histology of the Glands of the Cotton Plant with Notes on the Occurrence of Similar Glands in Related Plants." *Jour. Agr. Res.*, 13 (1918), 419–35.

Steinhaus, E. A. *Insect Microbiology*. London: Constable and Co. Ltd., 1947.

Stephens, S. G. "Sources of Resistance of Cotton Strains to the Boll Weevil and Their Possible Utilization." *J. Econ. Ent.*, 50 (1957), 415–18.

Stern, V. M.; van den Bosch, R.; and Leigh, T. F. "Strip Cutting of Alfalfa for *Lygus* Bug Control." *Calif. Agric.*, 18 (1964), 4–6.

Sweetman, H. L. *The Biological Control of Insects*. New York: Comstock Publishing Co., 1936.

Tunstall, J. P., and Matthews, G. A. "Recent Advances in the Control of Cotton Insect Pests in the Rhodesias and Nyasaland." *Proc. Cent. Afr. Sci. and Med. Congress*. Elmsford, N.Y.: Pergamon Press, 1965. Pp. 519–28.

———. "Large Scale Spraying Trials for the Control of Cotton Insect Pests in Central Africa." *Emp. Cott. Gr. Rev.*, 43 (1966), 121–39.

Tunstall, J. P.; Matthews, G. A.; and Rhodes, A. A. K. "A Modified Knapsack Sprayer for the Application of Insecticides to Cotton. *Emp. Cott. Gr. Rev.*, 38 (1961), 22–26.

———. "Development of Cotton Spraying Equipment in Central Africa." *Emp. Cott. Gr. Rev.*, 42 (1965), 131–45.

Wene, G. P., and Skeets, L. W. "Relationship of Predatory and Injurious Insects in Cotton Fields in the Sale River Valley Area of Arizona." *J. Econ. Ent.*, 55 (1962), 395–402.

Wessling, W. H. "Resistance to Boll Weevil in Mixed Populations of Resistant and Susceptible Cotton Plants." *J. Econ. Ent.*, 51 (1958), 502–06.

Whellan, J. A. "Pink Bollworm, (*Platyedra gossypiella*) in the Federation of Rhodesia and Nyasaland." *FAO Pla. Prot. Bull.*, 8 (1960), 113.

Whitcomb, W. H., and Bell, K. "Predaceous Insects, Spiders and Mites of Arkansas Cotton Fields." Agric. Expt. Stn. Fayetteville, Ark., Bull. 690. 1964.

Wigglesworth, V. B. "Biological Control of Pests." *Sci. J.*, 1 (1965), 40–45.

23. ECOLOGICAL CONSEQUENCES OF PESTICIDES USED FOR THE CONTROL OF COTTON INSECTS IN CAÑETE VALLEY, PERU

Teodoro Boza Barducci

The development, experimental testing, and marketing of synthetic organic pesticides began in earnest after the Second World War. At that time there was an urgent need for peacetime conversion of the big industries which had been created specifically to produce war explosives and toxic gases. Efforts were made to modernize and make more efficient many of the operations of agriculture, so that the food supply of the world could be increased. The development and deployment of agricultural chemicals were a natural result of this overall process.

Spectacular successes were obtained when pesticides were used on small experimental plots, and good results were obtained during the initial applications of pesticides over larger areas. This in turn encouraged wide and rapid use of these pesticides, which was a methodological mistake of serious proportions; subsequent long-term use of the pesticides over large and typical agricultural areas proved in many cases to be a disaster.

The Cañete Valley in Peru is one area studied closely by the author where extremely serious problems occurred for cotton farmers using the synthetic organic pesticides from the period 1949 to 1956. Farmers found they had to greatly increase the amount of pesticide used to achieve any significant control over pests, which added prohibitively to costs of cotton production. They also discovered that pests kept appearing in the fields, because the natural predators and parasites of these pests had been largely wiped out and because the pests themselves had developed resistance to the chemicals used.

The farmers in the Cañete Valley area therefore stopped using pesticides as the exclusive control measure and from 1957 to 1963 organized themselves to implement a control program based on an understanding of the ecology of the cotton field. Synthetic organic pesticides were completely prohibited; mineral ("natural") insecticides were used when chemical control was needed; natural enemies of the cotton pests were reintroduced into the fields; and cotton culture practices were developed and regulated to best boost the natural ecological processes destructive or inhibiting to pests. (A detailed list of methods used in the integrated approach is given; a long list of helpful insects and spiders is also provided.)

The new integrated ecological program was considered a clear success by farmers and scientists in the area. This experience in Peru strongly refutes the claims of "theoretical efficiency" made by the producers of organic pesticides.

From our experience in the Cañete Valley of Peru it is now possible to say that industrialists, technologists, entomologists, extension people, and farmers have expected too much from pesticides, even the most efficient ones, in controlling insects that attack crops. When such pesticides were used on a small scale on demonstration plots, the spectacular results raised expectations. Good results were also furnished by large-scale tests and field applications at the beginning of pesticide development. However, such results were not projected to long-term use of pesticides and were not analyzed in the light of knowledge about the ecology, biology, and evolution of living organisms.

In practice, the use of synthetic organic pesticides of various chemical groups (chlorinated and phosphate compounds and others) in the Cañete Valley on very large areas (15,000 to 17,000 hectares) during the period 1949 to 1956 proved to be disastrous.

First, the farmers' expenditures continually increased because of the many applications of pesticides recommended (eight or nine applications, on the average) and the high cost of mixtures of insecticides used to better control the pests. Second, the cotton yields were progressively reduced by the increased damage inflicted by the old pests and the new ones that developed in treated fields after two or three years of pesticide applications. The final result at the end of

that seven-year period was a total loss equivalent to 50% of the 1956 crop.

In 1956, the year of crisis in Cañete Valley, we concluded that it was nearly impossible, in practice, to obtain successful control of cotton pests by chemical methods, including the most efficient pesticides presently known. These substances, when applied over large areas, particularly with airplanes, break down the original stability of the insect population, which is in natural equilibrium within ecosystems. The useful insects existing in those fields are totally destroyed. This rupture favors one or another of the components of the original population and produces advantages for pests. The latter then develop without restrictions, increasing in numbers to the point of producing tremendous damages to the crops and consequently to the farmer's economy and to the country. Such drastic losses as in the Cañete Valley disprove the worldwide belief in the theoretical efficiency of chemical products, an illusion created by the chemical industry.

The ecological approach to the problem of insect control in the irrigated valleys of the central section of Peru is of special significance. Each of these arid valleys represents an ecosystem potentially in equilibrium because each valley is isolated from the others but also more or less connected with the Inter-Andean humid valleys. In the Inter-Andean areas a permanent vegetation

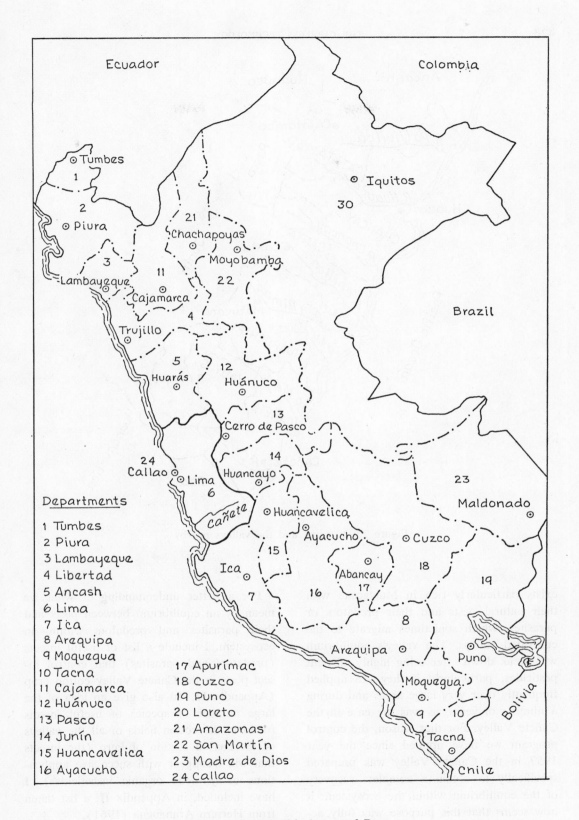

Figure 23-1 Political map of Peru

Figure 23–2 Lima and the valleys nearby

exists particularly rich in Malvaceae with their natural pests and their predators or parasites, which sometimes migrate to the cultivated valleys. The valley's equilibrium will break down after using highly efficient pesticides, particularly if they are applied frequently over very large areas and during a number of years, as was the case in the Cañete Valley. For that reason, the control program we have applied since the year 1957 in the Cañete Valley was prepared specifically to obtain a complete recovery of the equilibrium within the ecosystem; it now seems that this purpose was fully accomplished.

For a better understanding of what we mean by an equilibrium between pests and their parasites and predators within an ecosystem, I include a list of useful insects (predators and parasites) that control insect pests in the Cañete Valley cotton crop (Appendix I). To also give an idea of the large number of species of useful insects found in the cotton fields of all the valleys of the coastal section of Peru (the insects that will disappear with successive applications of synthetic organic insecticides), I have included, in Appendix II, a list taken from Herrera Aranguena (1961).

The Cañete Valley in the central coastal

section of Peru has a total cultivated area of 22,000 hectares of fertile soils. The Cañete River provides good year-round irrigation. The valley has always attracted the attention of farmers from the various coastal valleys of the country not so much for its climate or its soil but rather for the spirit of progress and collective organization that the established farmers have shown in the past. This spirit of progress has translated itself into the Farmer's Association of Cañete, comprising 88% of the area of the valley, and the Cañete Agricultural Experiment Station, created in 1926 and subsidized by the Association with a voluntary tax paid by its members according to the amount of marketable cotton produced. The Association has at various times also contracted foreign experts to study cotton improvement, entomological problems, mechanization of farms, fruit culture, and citrus growing.

Until the end of the First World War the Cañete Valley was an important sugar-cane producer for the country; later it was devoted almost exclusively to cotton monoculture (35% to 90% of its cultivated area). The valley is today undergoing an evolution increasingly oriented to the diversification of agriculture. In the year 1958 cotton occupied 56.8% of the cultivated area of the valley, followed by maize (13.6%), potatoes (10%), sweet potatoes, horticultural plants (such as tomato, pumpkin, cabbage, cauliflower, lettuce, onion, and garlic), and forests (each 4.5%), fruits, mainly citrus, apples, and grapes, (3.6%), wheat (1.4%), and all others (0.9%).

This evolution of agriculture in the valley is a consequence (a happy one, if you will!) of the serious cotton crisis experienced in the valley between 1953 and 1956 as a result of the buildup of insect pests. Attempts to control these insects necessitated major deficit expenditures for insecticides each year, which in turn damaged the usefulness of the crops, and finally resulted in considerable losses of the harvest, particularly in 1955 and 1956. The catastrophe occurred even though an average of fifteen applications of insecticides were finally used in the valley (twenty-five on some large plantations). No control whatsoever was achieved, because of resistance acquired by the insect pests to these organic insecticides. In addition, new insects harmful to cotton appeared because their natural control agents were destroyed by the same insecticides. These events led to the valley's finally accepting the regulation of cotton-growing in the Cañete Valley, first proposed in August of 1949 by the author.

From this disastrous experience in so large an area, we may conclude that in practice it is impossible to obtain over a period of years a good control of cotton pests using chemical methods. Attempts to use even the most efficient insecticides tested in laboratory conditions or in small experimental plots are doomed in large cotton fields.

Before the use of synthetic organic insecticides on cotton crops, the early insect problems of the valley were caused by the following pests: leafworm (*Anomis texana*, Riley), bud weevil or *picudo* (*Anthonomus vestitus*, Bohm.), aphis or *melaza* (*Aphis gossypii*, Glov.), minor bollworm (*Mescinea peruella*, Schaus.), white scale (*Hemichionaspis minor*, Mark.), and cotton stainer (*Dysdercus peruvianus*, Guen.). Many of these insects were controlled with mineral insecticides. For example, arsenic was used in the case of leafworms and bud weevils, and nicotine sulphate was used for other pests such as aphids. Mechanical methods such as the collection of insects by hand and the collection of damaged cotton squares (the small floral buds) were also useful (see Table 23-1).

Biological control at that time was possible without limitations, depending only on the efficiency of the biological equilibrium existing between populations of damaging insects and useful insects, as these populations were

Table 23–1

COTTON PEST COMPLEX IN THE CAÑETE VALLEY, PERU,
DURING THREE PEST CONTROL REGIMES
(From R. F. Smith and R. van den Bosch, 1967, with data from T. Boza Barducci, 1965)

PEST COMPLEX

HEAVY METAL AND BOTANICAL INSECTICIDES 1943–1949	SYNTHETIC ORGANIC CHEMICAL INSECTICIDES 1949–1956	INTEGRATED CONTROL 1956–1963
Anthonomus vestitus	A. vestitus	A. vestitus
Anomis texana	A. texana	A. texana
Aphis gossypii	A. gossypii	A. gossypii
Heliothis virescens	H. virescens	H. virescens
Mescinea peruella	M. peruella	M. peruella
Hemichionaspis minor	H. minor	H. minor
Dysdercus peruvianus	D. peruvianus	D. peruvianus
—	Argyrothaenia sphaleropa	—
—	Platynota spp.	—
—	Pseudoplusia rogationis	—
—	Pococera atramentalis	P. atramentalis
—	Planococcus citri	—
—	Bucculatrix thurberiella	—

influenced each year by ecological factors.

Later on, in the year 1939, the bollworm (*Heliothis virescens,* F.) appeared in a northern section of the valley and produced damages. The use of mineral insecticides (like calcium and lead arsenate, London purple, and Paris green) and some other insecticides (such as Criolite) complicated the problem by producing a rapid buildup of aphids which also attacked the crop. The bollworm problem increased every year. It caused a very bad crop in 1949. In that year the average production was 366.16 kilograms of lint per hectare. (See Table 23–2 for yearly production figures from 1943 to 1963.) Because of this situation, the Cañete Farmers Association decided to reorganize the Experiment Station to obtain more help to solve the insect problem and to increase cotton yields.

After studying the problem in the valley, we at the Experiment Station proposed "the initiation of a new program for growing cotton in the Cañete Valley" based on the following key points:

1. Ratoon cotton will be prohibited. (Ratoon cotton is cotton propagated by allowing cut-off cotton plants to send out new shoots in a second or third growing season. This practice prevents proper clearing of the field to control pests.)

2. The use of "early maturing" strains of Tanguis cotton will be convenient for the valley and help the crop escape insect attack; by this means the amount of insecticide will be reduced. Moreover, it will be easier to renew the cotton crop each year.

3. The proper control of insects with the proper insecticides if needed.

4. Good techniques for cotton growing, especially good irrigation methods, will help to control insects naturally.

5. The use of crop rotation instead of "cotton after cotton" will also help reduce insect problems.

6. The adoption of some of the provisions in "Regulations for cotton growing in the Cañete Valley" such as fixed dates for sowing cotton and for destroy-

Table 23-2

PRODUCTION OF LINT COTTON IN THE CAÑETE VALLEY DURING THE YEARS 1943 TO 1963
(Boza Barducci, 1965)

PERIOD	YEAR	AREA/Ha	PRODUCTION In Metric Tons	PRODUCTION Quintal (100 lbs)	YIELDS Quintals/Ha	Kg/Ha	%
I	1943	13,080	6,469	140,627	10.75	494.5	135.2
	1944	14,929	7,276	158,171	10.59	487.1	133.2
	1945	15,980	9,499	205,417	12.85	591.1	161.6
	1946	19,155	9,156	199,049	10.39	477.9	130.7
	1947	17,911	8,346	181,441	10.13	465.9	127.4
	1948	16,547	8,239	179,102	10.82	497.7	136.1
	1949*	18,417	10,728	146,518	7.95	365.7	100.0
II	1950	17,289	6,740	185,600	10.73	493.6	134.9
	1951	17,320	8,538	233,212	13.46	619.1	169.1
	1952	18,607	11,471	249,378	13.40	616.4	168.5
	1953	17,284	11,258	244,739	14.16	651.3	178.1
	1954	17,970	13,083	284,410	15.83	728.2	199.1
	1955	19,095	9,826	213,599	11.18	514.3	142.2
	1956*	19,618	6,514	141,614	7.22	332.1	90.8
III	1957	13,920	7,327	159,284	11.44	526.2	143.9
	1958	13,556	9,814	213,345	15.74	724.0	197.9
	1959	14,728	12,626	274,485	18.63	856.9	234.3
	1960	15,230	15,789	343,242	22.53	1,036.3	283.3
	1961	18,000	13,096	284,699	15.81	727.2	198.8
	1962	14,900	12,712	276,345	18.54	852.8	233.2
	1963	15,715	12,582	273,516	17.40	800.4	218.8

*Years of crisis.

Table prepared by the author based on data published by the Camara Algodonera del Perú. Annual Report 1963. Lima, Peru.

ing cotton stalks from the previous crop should be helpful when combined with a short period of clean field and the prohibition of ratoon cotton.

Economic considerations like the lower cost of ratoon cotton cultivation in comparison with new plantings, prevented the adoption of this plan in full. An intermediate plan based on growing ratoon for a one-year period and on using chemical methods for the control of cotton pests along with some of the cultural methods previously used was finally approved.

From the season 1949–1950 on, chemical methods were used to control cotton pests, because of the good control obtained with the new insecticides in small tests carried on by state extension people in the Cañete

Valley. Synthetic organic insecticides like DDT 5%, BHC 3%, mixtures of both with sulphur in a 3–5–40 formula, and Toxaphene 20% were used in large amounts to control bollworms, aphids, and other pests.

To carry out these insecticide operations, the Experiment Station organized an Entomological Extension Service and prepared personnel to help the farmers in the field. Books for pest control recording were prepared, printed, and put into the hands of the farmers to record insect counts and the insecticides used in various fields. Duplicates of these sheets were collected by the Experiment Station weekly and the data they contained were tabulated to graph the evolution of the cotton pest in the four geographical sections of the Cañete Valley. The official recommendations made in the annual meetings of the Southern States Cotton Entomologists in the U.S.A. were followed in the applications of insecticides.

During the first five years of chemical methods the results were very good, and a definite increase in yield was obtained by controlling bollworms, aphids, leafworms and bud weevils. The yield increased until in 1954 it reached 199% of the yield of the bad crop in 1949.

However, after the third year of using chemical methods for the control of cotton pests, a new problem was observed. A repeated decrease in the lethal effect of the insecticides was noted. Many explanations were given, but finally analysis of the problem led to the discovery of "a natural increased resistance of the insects to the insecticides used to control them."

In order to correct the situation, the doses of insecticides recommended by the Experiment Station were raised and new chemicals were tested. Those chemicals which were found to give good control were recommended again. They included aldrin, dieldrin, endrin, and mixtures. A reduction in the time between applications was also suggested. All these measures not only proved costly but in most cases were shown to be useless.

A new group of insecticides with high toxicity, the phosphorus compounds, like parathion and Folidol, were also tested with success. However, after these insecticides were tried for a few years, new cotton pests appeared which caused great losses and proved very difficult to control.

To the previous list of cotton pests, we now had to add the leaf rollers (*Argyrothaenia sphaleropa*, Meyrick, and *Platynota* sp.), the major leafworm (*Pseudoplusia rogationis*, Guen.), the apex bollworm (*Popocera atramentalis*, Led.), the mealy bug (*Pseudococcus citri*, Risso), and the leaf perforator (*Bucculatrix thurberiella*,

Busck.). Of these the most damaging were the leaf rollers and the major leafworms (see Table 1).

Resistance of many of these important damaging insects to insecticides in the Cañete Valley was suggested by Price Gaviria in 1952 (1951–1954) and was proved by Herrera Aranguena in 1956 (1958). *Aphis gossypii* was resistant to BHC, *Anomis texana* to Toxaphene, and *Heliothis virescens* to DDT and mixtures of BHC and DDT. In the United States in 1957 (cases cited by Herrera Aranguena) resistance of insects to insecticides used for their control was also found. *Anthonomus grandis*, *Bucculatrix thurberiella*, and *Trichoplusia ni* were proved resistant to chlorinated compounds; *Thrips* spp. were proved resistant to DDT; *Empoasca solana* was suspected resistant to DDT; and *Aphis gossypii* was suspected resistant to BHC.

In 1956 when all insecticides failed to control the cotton pests, we produced the worst crop in the history of cotton production in the Cañete Valley. Even with an average of fifteen applications of insecticides, we lost nearly 50% of the crop.

By the end of the period 1950 to 1955, the destruction of useful insects in the valley was so complete that even many useful Arachnidae also disappeared. Reptiles and all kinds of birds were also exterminated, and thus the situation so well described by Rachel Carson (1962) in *Silent Spring* came to pass.

Faced with a crop of only 332.1 kilograms of lint per hectare, the farmers decided to fully accept the original recommendations of the Experiment Station that were proposed in 1949. Very good results were obtained in the Cañete Valley during the period 1957 to 1963 with (1) the prohibition of synthetic organic pesticides, (2) the return to mineral or natural organic insecticides like calcium or lead arsenate and nicotine sulphate, (3) the utilization of biological control methods for cotton pests, and (4) the official approval of "Regulations for the management of the cotton crop in the Cañete Valley." A project incorporating the regulations was approved by the farmers and by the Ministry of Agriculture in July 1956 and initiated in the season 1956–1957. This project was based on the following points:

a. The cotton area in the Cañete Valley will be reduced to 70% of the area cultivated with that crop the previous year, eliminating marginal lands.

b. Only *plantadas* (new plantings) will be permitted in the old section of the valley (75% of its area) each year.

c. *Plantadas* or one year of ratoon cotton will be permitted in the new section of the valley (Irrigación Pampas de Imperial) because of the lack of water for the renewal of cotton in a larger area.

d. Farmers will have to prepare soil in dry conditions without pre-irrigation to increase the destruction of pupae of *Heliothis virescens* F. (cotton bollworm) in soils.

e. The use of synthetic organic insecticides will be prohibited. In only very special cases, a permit may be granted to farmers for application to small areas and for low concentrations of pesticides (25–50% of the doses recommended by the manufacturers of the pesticides).

f. The valley will be repopulated with the useful insects destroyed by the previous applications of insecticides during the period 1949 to 1956. (To accomplish this part of the project, in 1956–1957 we imported from California approximately 130,000,000 of the microwasp *Trichogramma minutum* Riley (North American races), and also about 20 gallons of lady beetles, the Coccinelid *Hippodamia convergens,* Guer., to be liberated in cotton fields for the control of leaf rollers, bollworms, and aphids. From the western part of the Andes, our entomologists also collected more than 15,000 specimens of

the Coleoptera (Carabidae) *Calosoma abreviatum* Chaud., black beetle, a very active predator of leafworm or bollworm larvae. Moreover, in 1956 the author visited some private insectaria in California, the universities at Berkeley, Davis, Riverside, and Albany, and Dr. S. E. Flanders, the well-known entomologist who developed the use of the microwasp for biological control. After I returned to Peru, our Department of Entomology established a pilot laboratory to breed *Trichogramma* spp. artificially in the Experiment Station. We produced the host *Sitotroga cerealella* Oliv. (Indian wheat moth), and collected his eggs in order to produce the *Trichogramma* inside them. We released the microwasp at a rate of 12,000 to 17,000 or more per hectare. Since 1957 this microwasp has played an important role in controlling the worst cotton pests, such as *Heliothis, Argyrothaenia,* and *Pseudoplusia.* (The possibility of such biological control in the Cañete Valley was demonstrated for *Heliothis virescens* F. during the years 1939–1941 by Dr. Edson J. Hambleton, who found *Anthocoridae* bugs preying on eggs of *Heliothis* in corn silk. He suggested planting corn in alternate rows with cotton to increase natural control of bollworms. This method has been used for many years by planting one row of corn for every 12 or 18 rows of cotton.)

g. Fixed dates were set for finishing the most important cultural practices of cotton cultivation in order to obtain some period of clean fields without cotton.

h. Farmers must observe the following technical recommendations for a better management of the crop:

(1) The utilization of the proper strains of Tanguis cotton in each location, according to the recommendations of the Agricultural Experiment Station.

(2) A good preparation of land before sowing cotton.

(3) Seed disinfection to prevent losses and the reduction of plant populations in the fields.

(4) Optimal crop density for each location, following recommendations by the Agricultural Experiment Station based on previous experimental work.

(5) Proper depth for seed planting, in accordance with soil characteristics.

(6) Early thinning of plants where convenient.

(7) Optimal fertilization of soils, including the kind of fertilizers applied, the quantity to be applied, and the proper time of application to soils or plants for the seven series of soils determined for the Cañete Valley.

(8) The volume, frequency, and duration of irrigation must be suited to the characteristics of the particular soil.

(9) Good control of cotton pests, using *chemical methods* with mineral or natural organic insecticides only; *mechanical methods* including collecting by hand the squares or small fruits damaged by bud weevils or the dry flowers at the tip of unopened bolls, most of them containing larvae of the apex bollworm *Pococera atramentalis* Led.; and *biological methods* including periodic liberation in cotton fields of *Trichogramma* spp. or *Coccinelidae* to aid in the control of pests.

(10) Cut field irrigation in accordance with the fruiting period of plants in order to help the opening of capsules and to obtain a greater volume of mature cotton at the first picking, the cheapest and most economical of the three pickings during which the crop is collected.

(11) Cotton must be picked at the proper time, and with care in order to keep and preserve fiber qualities.

This plan, followed in all details since the 1956–1957 season, has been highly successful. According to the statistical studies of our Department of Entomology, in the campaign of 1957–1958, the average number of insecticide applications in the valley was 2.35 (using only mineral and natural insecticides), compared to an average of 16 in 1954–1955 and 15 in 1955–1956. This reduction in insecticide use represents for the Cañete Valley an annual savings of 18,000,000 Peruvian soles (U.S. $671,140, at an exchange rate of 26.82 Peruvian soles per dollar). To this economic advantage, one must add the greater harvest and the better grade of cotton obtained because of the absence of insect pests. At the actual price of cotton this increase can be estimated at about 10,000,000 Peruvian soles (U.S. $372,856).

After seven years of this program, the Cañete Valley insect problem has disappeared in practice. The useful insects (see Appendix I) have increased, and the natural balance between detrimental and useful insects seems to be re-established. The useful insects now play an important role in controlling cotton pests. The resulting increase in the production of cotton may be seen in the table which gives the "Production of Lint Cotton in the Cañete Valley during the years 1943 to 1963." These figures give a very clear idea of the practical importance of the integrated method for pest control. Reduction of insect damages in cotton will permit the full expression of the genetic potential for yield of the strains of Peruvian Tanguis cotton developed by breeders and will, with good cultural cultivation practices, permit an increased production of cotton per hectare.

From Dr. Smith's publication on "Integrated Control of Pests" (1967), I have reproduced the table which was constructed with data furnished by us and which shows the significance of the success of the program developed in the Cañete Valley. Such results "invariably have been products of crises" (Smith and van den Bosch, 1967) as was the case of programs like those of Pickett and McPhee (1965) in Nova Scotia for the control of apple and pear pest and Stern *et al.* (1959) in California for the control of the spotted alfalfa aphid. A wide field has thus been opened for more complete entomological techniques which take advantage of the ecological approach.

Problems similar to those described in this paper still occur in many parts of the world. In some Central American countries (El Salvador, Nicaragua, etc.) cotton production is now obtained with twenty-six to thirty or more applications of insecticides during a period of ninety days, or an average of an application once every three days. Production of cotton in such a manner and at so high a cost would seem impossible for countries whose yields are not as high as those of Central America and where support prices or intense subsidies to cotton production do not exist. I have also seen similar problems in cotton-growing areas of Colombia and Venezuela while I was providing technical assistance at the request of officials or private institutions.

Until this year pest control in the Cañete Valley has continued to be fairly good, in spite of a few errors committed recently by farmers who voted in favor of increasing the area of *socas* (ratoon cotton) in the 1967–1968 and 1968–1969 seasons. Naturally the attacks on cotton fields by the bud weevil were greater, and in a few cases entomologists authorized the use of synthetic organic insecticides (chlorinated ones) on a small scale to control the insect. Certainly as time passes and new management controls the farms, a few people forget the history of Cañete Valley's cotton insect problems and the way they were solved.

Many cotton valleys in Peru other than the Cañete Valley have adopted programs similar to the original one described in this paper. Such programs have proved satisfactory in producing high yields and reducing the cost of production. This has been of great importance to us because, in spite of the decrease of cotton prices in the international market, we have been able to tolerate the fall in the price and still compete in many cotton fiber markets. This same situation in the period 1949 to 1956 probably would have forced us to replace cotton with another crop of higher revenue.

In conclusion, because of the facts explained in this paper, it seems imperative that all programs concerning the production, testing, and use of insecticides for protecting crops against pests be revised, and that in the development and application of programs for the control of pests an ecological approach be taken to obtain beneficial results.

REFERENCES

Boza Barducci, T. "Informe sobre la producción algodonera de Colombia y Recomendaciones para fomentar este cultivo en el país." Instituto de Fomento Algodonero, Medellín, April 1948. Mimeographed. 70 pp.

——. "La Estación Experimental Agrícola de Cañete y el control de las plagas del algodonero en la campaña 1949–50. Algunas recomendaciones para los cultivadores de algodón." Est. Exp. Agríc. de Cañete, Circular 5, August 1949. Mimeographed.

——. "Sobre la conveniencia de adoptar modelos 'standard' de libros para llevar las anotaciones sobre las contadas de insectos y las aplicaciones de insecticidas en los cultivos de algodonero en el valle de Cañete." Est. Exp. Agríc. de Cañete, Circular 8, October 1949. Mimeographed.

——. "Memorandum. Bases técnicas para un proyecto de reglamentación del cultivo del algodonero en el valle de Cañete." Est. Exp. Agríc. de Cañete. January 1955. Mimeographed.

――――. "Problemas de la agricultura del valle de Cañete." Primera Convención Regional del Sur Chico. Ica, May 1959. Reprinted by *La Vida Agrícola*, Lima, September 1959.

――――. "Observaciones sobre la producción del algodón en Venezuela y recomendaciones técnicas para su mejoramiento." Ministerio de Agricultura y Cría (MAC), Biblioteca Rural No. 9, Caracas, October 1959. 104 pp.

――――. "Observaciones sobre el desarrollo del Programa de Investigaciones y Experimentación Algodonera que realiza el C.I.A. en Maracay y sobre el Plan Nacional de Fomento de la producción del algodón en Venezuela." Maracay, December 10, 1960.

――――. "Experiencias sobre el empleo del control biológico y de los métodos de control integrado de las plagas del algodonero en el valle de Cañete—Perú. (S.A.)." Paper presented to the Seminar organized by the Cotton Production Investigation Committee under the auspices of International Cotton Advisory Committee, Washington, D.C., May 18–19, 1965. 25 pp.

Boza Barducci, T.; del Carpio Burga, R.; Herrara Aranguena, J.; and Urbina Cevallo, J. "Recomendaciones para el cultivo del algodón en el valle de Cañete, Campaña 1957–58." Est. Exp. Agríc. de Cañete. Circular 13, July 1957. Mimeographed.

Boza Barducci, T., and Herrera Aranguena, J. "Informe sobre la situación del cultivo del algodón en Colombia y Recomendaciones técnicas para su mejoramiento." Bogotá: Federación Nacional de Algodoneros de Colombia, December 1963. Mimeographed. 45 pp.

Carson, Rachel. *Silent Spring*. Boston: Houghton Mifflin, 1962.

Herrera Aranguena, J. "Resistencia de ciertas plagas del algodonero a los insecticidas orgánicos en el valle de Cañete." *Rev. Peruana de Entomología Agrícola* (Lima), I (June 1958), 47–51.

――――. "Problemas entomológicos en el cultivo de los algodones Tangüis y Pima en el Perú. Medidas de control y su organización." *Rev. Peruana de Entomología Agrícola* (Lima), Vol. 4, No. 1 (December 1961).

Ordish, George. *Biological Methods in Crop Pest Control*. London: Constable, 1967. P. 220.

Price Gaviria, C. *Boletines Entomológicos*. Est. Exp. Agríc. de Cañete, 1951–1954.

Smith, R. F., and van den Bosch, R. "Integrated Control. Practical Application of the Integrated Control." In *Pest Control. Biological, Physical and Selected Chemical Methods*. W. W. Kilgore and R. L. Doutt, eds. New York and London: Academic Press, 1967. Chap. 9.

APPENDIX I

List of Useful Insects (Predators and Parasites) That Control Insect Pests in the Cañete Valley Cotton Crop (Boza Barducci, 1965). (Spanish common names given in parentheses)

1. *Anthonomus vestitus* Bohm. Bud weevil (or *picudo peruano*).
   Chalcididae: wasp of the genus *Catolaccus* spp. and Braconidae: *Microbracon* spp. (predator).
2. *Anomis texana* Riley. Minor leafworm (or *gusano menor de la hoja*).
   Braconidae: wasp *Rogas* spp. (parasite), low parasitism on larvae.
   wasp *Meteorus* spp. (parasite).
   Miridae: *Hyalochloria denticornis* Tsai Yu Hsiao (predator), bug.
   Aphelinidae: *Prospaltella* spp. (parasite), wasp.
   Tachinidae: *Eucelatoria australis* T.T. (parasite), fly.
   Reduviidae: *Zelus* spp. (predator), bug.
   Nabidae: *Nabis punctipennis* Blanch. (predator).

Aracnidae: Lycosidae, *Lycosa* spp. (predator), spider.

Salticidae, *Attus* spp. (predator), spider.

Thomasidae, *Misumena* spp. (predator), spider.

3. *Aphis gossypii* Glov. Aphid or (*pulgón de la melaza*).

Coccinelidae: a few species: *Scymnus* spp., *Cycloneda sanguinea* L., *Eriopis connexa* Germ., *Hippodamia convergens* Guer., *Coleomegilla maculata* D.G. (all predators).

Chrysopidae: *Chrysopa* spp. (two), (predator).

Syrphidae: *Syrphus* spp. (predator). *Baccha* spp. (predator).

Braconidae: *Aphidius phorodontis* Ashm. (parasite), wasp.

4. *Argyrotaenia sphaleropa* Meyrich. Leaf rollers (or *enrolladores de la hoja*) and *Platynota* spp.

Trichogrammatidae: *Trichogramma minutum* Riley (parasite), wasp.

Tachinidae: *Nomorilla angustipennis* (parasite).

5. *Heliothis virescens* F. Bollworm (or *perforador grande de la bellota*).

Miridae: *Rhinacloa forticornis* Reuter, *R. subpallidicornis, R. aricana* Carvalho (all predators), bugs.

Nabidae: *Nabis punctipennis* Bluch., (predator), bug.

Anthocoridae: *Orius tristicolor* (predator), bug.

Paratriphleps laeviusculus Champ. (predator), bug.

Trichogrammatidae: *Trichogramma minutum* Riley (parasite), wasp.

Aphelinidae: *Prospaltella* spp. (two) (parasite), wasp.

Chrysopidae: *Chrysopa* spp. (two), (predator).

Coccinelidae: a few genera and species.

Coleoptera (predators). (See *Anomis texana*.)

6. *Mescinea peruella* Schaus. Minor bollworm (or *perforador pequeño de la bellota*).

Trichogrammatidae: *Trichogramma minutum* Riley (parasite), wasp.

APPENDIX II

List of the Beneficial Species of Insects (Predators or Parasites) Frequently Present in Cotton Fields in Peru
(from J. Herrera Aranguena, 1961)

ORDER	FAMILY	SPECIES	PRED-ATOR	PAR-ASITE	PREY OR HOST INSECTS
Neuroptera	Hemerobiidae	*Sympherobius californicus* Banks	+		*Pseudococcus* spp.
	Chrysopidae	*Chrysopa* supp. (two species)	+		*Aphis gossypii,* Glov. *Pseudococcus* spp. Lepidoptera, (eggs and larvae)
Hemiptera	Miridae	*Rhinacloa aricana*	+		*Heliothis virescens* F. (eggs and small larvae)
		R. forticornis Reuter	+		*Heliothis virescens* F. (eggs and small larvae)
		Hyalochloria denticornis Tsai Yu Hsiao	+		*Heliothis virescens* F. (eggs and small larvae) plus *Anomis texana* Riley (eggs)

ORDER	FAMILY	SPECIES	PRED-ATOR	PAR-ASITE	PREY OR HOST INSECTS
	Anthocoridae	*Paratriphleps laeviusculus* Champ.	+		*H. virescens* (eggs and small larvae)
		Orius insidiosus Say.	+		*H. virescens* (eggs and small larvae)
	Nabidae	*Nabis punctipennis* Blanch.	+		Lepidoptera (larvae), *Heliothis* and *Anomis*
	Reduviidae	*Zelus* spp.	+		*Heliothis, Anomis* and other Lepidoptera (larvae)
		Rasahus hamatus	+		*Heliothis, Anomis* and other Lepidoptera (larvae)
	Lygaeidae	*Geocoris punctipes* Say.	+		*Heliothis* and other Lepidoptera (larvae)
		G. borealis	+		*Heliothis* and other Lepidoptera (larvae)
	Neididae	*Parajalysus spinosus*	+		*Heliothis* and other Lepidoptera (larvae) Also *Bucculatrix thurberiella* Busck (larvae)
	Pentatomidae	*Euchistus convergens* H.S.	+		Various Lepidoptera (larvae)
		Podissus spp.	+		Various Lepidoptera (larvae)
		Edessa spp.	+		Various Lepidoptera (larvae)
		Piezodorus guildini Westw.	+		Various Lepidoptera (larvae)
Coleoptera	Cicindellidae	Cicindella peruviana Lap.	+		Lepidoptera (larvae)
		Tetracha chilensis Cast.	+		Lepidoptera (larvae)
	Carabidae	Colosoma abbreviatum Chand.	+		Lepidoptera (larvae)
	Coccinellidae	*Microweisia* spp.	+		*Tetranychus peruvianus, Aphis gossypii* (specially *Pseudococcus* spp.)
		Scymnus spp.	+		*Aphis gossypii*
		Cycloneda sanguinea L.	+		*Aphis gossypii*
		Eriopis connexa Germ.	+		*Aphis gossypii*
		Hippodamia convergens Guer.	+		*Aphis gossypii*
		Coleomegilla maculata D.G.	+		*Aphis gossypii*
Diptera	Cecidom-yüdae	*Diadiplosis* spp.	+		*Pseudococcus* spp.
	Asilidae	*Erax* spp.	+		*Anomis texana* and *Alabama argillacea*

ORDER	FAMILY	SPECIES	PRED- ATOR	PAR- ASITE	PREY OR HOST INSECTS
		Mallophora spp.	+		*Anomis texana* and *Alabama argillacea*
	Syrphidae	*Syrphus* spp.	+		*Aphis gossypii*
		Baccha spp.	+		*Aphis gossypii*
	Tachinidae	*Eucelatoria australis* T.T.		+	*Anomis texana* and *Alabama argillacea*
		Euravinia spp.		+	*Alabama argillacea*
		Rileyella spp.		+	*Alabama argillacea*
		Reaumuria pacifica		+	Earthworm (larvae of Noctuids)
		Archytas spp.		+	*Heliothis virescens*
		Plagiotachina peruviana		+	*Heliothis virescens*
		Nemorilla angustipennis		+	*Argyrothaenia sphaleropa, Platynota* spp.
		Schizactia spp.		+	*Gelechidae franjeado*
		Acaulona peruviana T.T.		+	*Dysdercus peruvianus*
		Paraphoronta peruviana T.T.		+	*Dysdercus peruvianus*
Hymenoptera	Braconidae	*Microbracon vestiticida*		+	*Anthonomus vestitus*
		Heterosphilus hambletoni		+	*Eutinobothrus gossypii*
		Aphidius phorodontis		+	*Aphis gossypii*
		Lysiphlebus spp.		+	*Aphis gossypii*
		Apanteles spp.		+	*Pococera atramentalis, Platynota* spp., and *Mescinea peruella*
		Meteorus spp.		+	*Anomis texana, Alabama argillacea* (larvae)
		Rogas spp.		+	*Anomis texana, Alabama argillacea* (larvae)
	Ichneumo- nidae	*Idechtis peruviana* Crawf.		+	*Mescinea peruella*
		Pimpla spp.		+	*Platynota* sp., *Argyro- thaenia sphaleropa*
		Itoplectis spp.		+	*Platynota* sp., *Argyro- thaenia sphaleropa*
		Sagaritis spp.		+	*Heliothis virescens*
		Ophion spp.		+	Larvae of noctuids
	Chalcididae	*Catolaccus townsendia* Crawf.		+	*Anthonomus vestitus*
		Aspidiotiphagus citrinus		+	*Hemichionaspis minor*
	Encyrtidae	*Aenasius massi* Dom.		+	*Pseudococcus* spp.
		Grandoriella lamasi Dom.		+	*Pseudococcus* spp.
		Achrysopophagus spp.		+	*Pseudococcus* spp.
		Anagyrus sp.		+	*Pseudococcus* spp.
	Aphelinidae	*Prospaltella* spp. (two species)		+	*Anomis texana* and *Heliothis virescens*

ORDER	FAMILY	SPECIES	PRED-ATOR	PAR-ASITE	PREY OR HOST INSECTS
Hymenoptera	Trichogram-matidae	Trichogramma minutum Riley		+	H. virescens, Alabama argillacea. Anomis texana
		Trichogramma spp.		+	Mescinea peruella
	Sphecidae	Sphex chilensis (Reed)	+		A. texana, A. argillacea, and others. Noctuids
		Bembix spp.	+		A. texana, A. argillacea, and others. Noctuids
		Podium spp.	+		A. texana, A. argillacea, and others. Noctuids
	Vespidae	Polistes canadiensis L.	+		A. texana, A. argillacea, and others. Noctuids
		P. versicolor L.	+		A. texana, A. argillacea, and others. Noctuids
		Eumenes spp.	+		A. texana, A. argillacea, and others. Noctuids

Arachnidae

Araneida	Lycosidae	Lucosa spp.	+		A. texana, A. argillacea, and others. Noctuids
	Salticidae	Attus spp.	+		A. texana, A. argillacea, and others. Noctuids
	Thomisidae	Misumena spp.	+		A. texana, A. argillacea, and others. Noctuids

24. SOME ECOLOGICAL IMPLICATIONS OF TWO DECADES OF USE OF SYNTHETIC ORGANIC INSECTICIDES FOR CONTROL OF AGRICULTURAL PESTS IN LOUISIANA

L. D. Newsom

Louisiana's climate, geography, major crops and pest complexes are similar to those of many of the developing nations where intensification of agriculture is now taking place. Twenty years of intensive use of synthetic organic pesticides has helped increase crop production but has also caused some unanticipated problems. Pesticide use in cotton production has contributed most heavily to the adverse effects on the environment, the development of insecticide-resistant pests and the changing status of pest populations. Louisiana's cotton pest control program was developed around the control of the boll weevil, the most seriously damaging pest of cotton. In 1955 boll weevil populations became resistant to chlorinated hydrocarbons, requiring a shift to the use of organophosphate compounds. With each shift to a new class of insecticides a change has occurred in the status of some relatively innocuous pest species. In most cases the change has been from that of little or no importance to major importance, but the reverse has also been true in a few cases. The major factor in the change is attributed to the destruction of predators and parasites which had kept these formerly unimportant species in check. Resurgence of pest populations has also become a regularly occurring phenomenon. The rapid increase of pest populations to injurious levels following treatment with the relatively short residual organophosphate pesticides is shortening the time between treatments and adding to the growers' pesticide bill.

Louisiana's agricultural areas harbor an abundance of wildlife. Streams, ponds and estuaries produce thousands of pounds of fish and shellfish annually and are an important wintering area for a substantial portion of the migratory waterfowl of the North American continent. Although the intensive use of synthetic pesticides has had a severe short-term impact on wildlife populations, especially fish and shellfish, there is little evidence or information from which we can ascertain lasting effects. The most disturbing effect of pesticides from the point of view of agriculture has been the development of resistance in some pest species (such as the cabbage looper and the two-spotted spider mite and several others), which cannot be controlled by any pesticide now available.

The need is universally recognized for drastic increases in production of food and fiber to feed and clothe a rapidly expanding population, a large percentage of which is now undernourished and poorly clothed. It is also recognized that much of the increase required must come from the intensification of agricultural production in the developing nations. Not so well understood is the necessity for more effective control of many species of pests if the required increases are to be realized. The impact of pests on agricultural production is poorly understood and much disagreement exists on the question of how best to control them. There is controversy over the wisdom of continuing to employ the techniques of pest control based on repetitive applications of synthetic organic insecticides that currently occupy such a prominent position in the agriculture of many of the developed nations. That the use of these materials has created many serious problems as well as great good is hardly a matter for argument among reasonable men. Controversy develops when an attempt is made to weigh the good against the bad that has resulted from their use.

The most enthusiastic advocates of the use of synthetic organic insecticides will agree that serious mistakes have been made in their use. It seems reasonable to believe that the developing nations can avoid some of these mistakes as their agriculture is intensified. The two decades of experience gained in the use of these controversial chemicals in agriculture should allow for a reasonable assessment of some of the ecological implications of their widespread use. The purpose of this paper is to attempt such an evaluation.

Louisiana appears to be especially well suited for such an evaluation as it relates to the developing nations. Its climate, geography, major crops, and pest complexes are similar to those of many of the nations where intensification of crop production must be achieved. Cotton, rice, sugarcane and soybean are planted on more than 90 percent of the cropland in the state (Table 24–1). Soybean provides an example of a relatively new crop that has undergone a drastic intensification of production in a short period of time. In Louisiana acreage planted to this crop has increased from 197,000 acres in 1961 to 1,345,000 acres in 1968 (Table 24–2).

Louisiana's climate, bordering on the subtropical, favors the development of large populations of a complex of pest species, many of which are present throughout a relatively long growing season. A high percentage of the acreage planted to cotton, sugarcane and rice has been treated with one or more of the chlorinated hydrocarbon and organophosphorus insecticides during a substantial part of the last two decades. Cotton has been treated with an estimated average of eight applications per acre per year since 1949; sugarcane with three applications per acre per year since 1959; and rice with one application per acre per year

Table 24-1

TRENDS IN YIELDS AND ACREAGE PLANTED TO THE THREE MAJOR
CROPS GROWN IN LOUISIANA DURING 1939-1968[1]

	COTTON		RICE		SUGAR CANE	
PERIOD	AV. NO. ACRES HARVESTED (1,000)	YIELD, Lb Lint/A	AV. NO. ACRES HARVESTED (1,000)	YIELD, Lb/A	AV. NO. ACRES HARVESTED (1,000)	YIELD, Tons/A
1939-43	1,049.4	262	543.2	1760	239.8	18.22
1944-48	792.0	305	595.6	1724	253.6	18.84
1949-53	880.0	367	586.0	1975	272.9	19.17
1954-58	533.8	424	492.6	2635	225.6	22.99
1959-63	523.8	494	477.0	3000	266.3	23.55
1964-68[2]	421.4	586	535.6	3690	299.3	24.74

[1] Data from Louisiana Crop and Livestock Reporting Service, U.S. Department of Agriculture, Stat. Rept. Service and La. State Univ. Dept. Agri. Econ.

[2] Preliminary estimates.

Table 24–2

TRENDS IN YIELDS AND ACREAGE
PLANTED TO SOYBEANS IN LOUISIANA
DURING 1959–68[1]

	ACRES HARVESTED (1,000)	YIELD, Bu/A
1959	193	23.5
1960	216	24.0
1961	187	24.0
1962	219	22.0
1963	270	22.0
1964	423	19.0
1965	622	21.5
1966	871	25.0
1967	1,306	23.0
1968[2]	1,345	26.0

[1] Data from Louisiana Crop and Livestock Reporting Service, U. S. Department of Agriculture, Stat. Rept. Service and La. State Univ. Dept. of Agri. Econ.

[2] Preliminary estimates.

since 1960. Less than one-fifth of the soybean acreage has received any insecticide application and usually no more than two applications have been made to any of the acreage planted to this crop in one growing season.

Louisiana's geography, like that of many of the developing nations, is such that problems arising from the use of insecticides are likely to be accentuated. Agricultural production is concentrated along the floodplains of three major rivers, the terrace soils adjoining them, and the coastal prairies in the southwestern areas of the state (Fig. 24–1). These areas produce tremendous populations of upland game species, fish and shellfish. In addition to the wildlife produced within the borders of Louisiana, the state also serves as a major wintering ground for substantial portions of the migratory waterfowl of the North American continent—ducks, geese, and woodcock especially. Estuarine areas bordering the Gulf of Mexico are highly productive of shellfish and fish. Not only do the insecticide residues from agricultural operations within the state cause problems, but materials carried in the water and sediments from other areas drained by the Mississippi, Ouachita and Red rivers also contribute to these problems.

CONSEQUENCES OF COTTON PEST CONTROL

Perhaps no other crop has contributed as much to the problems associated with the use of synthetic organic insecticides for the control of agricultural pests as has cotton. Control of the boll weevil *Anthonomus*

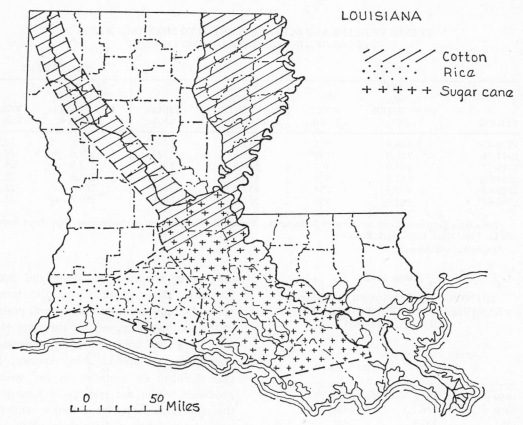

Figure 24–1 Areas devoted to the production of cotton, rice, and sugarcane in Louisiana

grandis, a key cotton pest throughout the southern United States, has required the application of large amounts of insecticide on an annual basis throughout the cotton-producing areas of Louisiana. Infestations by this pest are heavier and longer-lasting in the alluvial areas of the lower reaches of the Mississippi River and its tributaries than anywhere in the country. Consequently, more insecticide has been used in this area than anywhere in the United States with the possible exception of relatively small acreages of fruit orchards in some sections of the country.

Almost all of the acreage devoted to cotton production in Louisiana is located in the floodplains of the Mississippi, Ouachita and Red rivers and the adjacent terrace soils. Streams, lakes and ponds are numerous in the area. The acreage planted to cotton on most farms is considerably less than half of the total. Other crops, such as corn, small grains and soybeans, and pastures and woodlands, compose the remainder. Such an agricultural ecosystem furnishes favorable habitats for many species of mammals, birds, reptiles, amphibians, fish, crustaceans and insects. The comparatively large ratio of uncultivated to cultivated area is especially important as reservoirs for populations of predatory and parasitic insects as well as other species of wildlife.

There has been an estimated average of eight applications of insecticides per acre per year for all the acreage planted to cotton in Louisiana since 1949. During the period 1949 to 1956, substantial amounts of calcium arsenate were used for cotton pest control but it was replaced by the synthetic organic insecticides in less than ten years after their introduction. Commonly used mixtures have been BHC-DDT-sulfur applied at the rate of approximately 0.3 plus 0.5 plus 4.0 pounds per acre; dieldrin, aldrin or heptachlor at 0.25 plus DDT at 0.5 pound per acre; toxaphene at 2.0 pounds plus DDT at 1.0 pound per acre; and endrin at 0.2 pound per acre per application. The average estimated amount of insecticide applied per acre during each season of this period ranged from 1.6 pounds of endrin to 24 pounds of the toxaphene-DDT mixture.

Beginning in 1956, aldrin, BHC, dieldrin, endrin and heptachlor were rapidly eliminated from use on cotton and there was a great increase in use of the toxaphene-DDT mixture and mixtures containing 0.25 pound methyl parathion or azinphosmethyl (guthion) plus 1.0 pound of DDT. Since 1963 there has been an increasing trend toward the use of even more complex mixtures; the most popular has been 2 pounds of toxaphene plus 1 pound of DDT plus 0.25 pound of methyl parathion per acre.

Applications of such large amounts of highly toxic insecticides to about 500,000 acres containing many lakes, ponds, bayous and rivers has had the following ecological consequences:

1. Development of insecticide resistant populations
2. Change in status of pest species and resurgence of treated populations
3. Adverse effects on non-target organisms
4. Pollution of the environment with persisting residues of toxic chemicals

RESISTANCE TO INSECTICIDES

Data in Table 24–3 show that all the important cotton pests in the United States now have populations resistant to one or more of the chlorinated hydrocarbon, organophosphate or carbamate insecticides. It is now obvious that cotton pests are becoming resistant faster than the chemists can develop satisfactory alternative insecticides. Populations of *Heliothis* spp., *Tetranychus* spp. and *Trialeurodes abutilonea* that can no longer be controlled satisfactorily by any currently available insecticide now exist in the Cotton Belt. The situation has reached the critical stage.

Resistant populations of the cotton aphid, *Aphis gossypii,* and the cotton leafworm, *Alabama argillacea,* developed within five years after the chlorinated hydrocarbon insecticides were first used. However, little attention was paid to these important developments, and it was not until populations of the boll weevil, *A. grandis,* were recognized in 1955 as resistant to the chlorinated hydrocarbon insecticides that the importance of the phenomenon was fully appreciated. The impact upon the cotton industry and the insecticide industry was tremendous, requiring a drastic shift from the chlorinated hydrocarbon to the organophosphorus insecticides for control of the boll weevil. This shift had both good and bad effects. Use of methyl parathion instead of such persistent materials as aldrin, dieldrin, endrin and heptachlor reduced the potential hazard to men of chronic toxicity from exposure to these persistent materials but substituted the hazard of acute toxicity from exposure to methyl parathion. Serious problems were encountered during late 1955 and 1956 among aircraft pilots, spray flagmen, and spray-mixing crews. A number of cases of acute intoxication from exposure to methyl parathion occurred and some fatalities were recorded.

CHANGE IN STATUS OF PEST SPECIES

The entire program of cotton pest control in Louisiana has been developed around the

Table 24–3

COTTON PESTS THAT HAVE DEVELOPED RESISTANCE TO INSECTICIDES IN
THE UNITED STATES[1]

CHLORINATED HYDROCARBONS	ORGANOPHOSPHATES	CARBAMATES	ARSENICALS
Alabama argillacea			
Anthonomus grandis			
Aphis gossypii	A. gossypii		
Bucculatrix thurberiella	B. thurberiella		
Empoasca solani			
Estigmene acrea			
Euschistus conspersus			
Frankliniella fusca			
F. occidentalis			
Heliothis virescens	H. virescens	H. virescens	
Heliothis zea	H. zea	H. zea	none
Lygus hesperus			
Pectinophora gossypiella			
Psallus seriatus			
Spodoptera exigua	Tetranychus cinnabarinus		
Tetranychus pacificus	T. pacificus		
T. urticae	T. turkestani		
Thrips tabaci	T. urticae		
	Trialeurodes abutilonea[2]		

[1] Data from twenty-second Annual Conference Report on Cotton Insect Research and Control, New Orleans, Louisiana, January 7–8, 1969.

[2] Unpublished data, Department of Entomology, Louisiana State University.

boll weevil since it has been the only regularly occurring, seriously damaging pest of the crop. Prior to the introduction of the chlorinated hydrocarbon insecticides, calcium arsenate was the only material effective for its control. Use of this material destroyed aphid predators to the extent that the cotton aphid, Aphis gossypii, became a regularly occurring serious pest. The bollworm, Heliothis zea, was an occasionally occurring serious pest capable of causing severe damage during outbreak years. Another species, the tobacco budworm, Heliothis virescens, was virtually unknown as a pest of cotton, although the difficulty of distinguishing it from the bollworm in its immature stages may have somewhat masked its importance. The cotton leafworm, Alabama argillacea, was an occasionally occurring serious pest. The plant bugs, Lygus lineolaris, and the cotton fleahopper, Psallus seriatus, were occasionally occurring pests

of relatively minor importance. Spider mites, Tetranychus spp., and the banded-wing whitefly, Trialeurodes abutilonea, were virtually unknown.

Drastic changes in status of some species of pests have occurred after two decades of use of the synthetic insecticides. The boll weevil remains the key pest although the more or less regular outbreaks that occurred prior to 1956 no longer occur. The two species of Heliothis have increased in importance to the extent that many entomologists are now convinced that they are more important than the boll weevil. Both the cotton leafworm and the cotton aphid have become insignificant as cotton pests. Spider mites, Tetranychus spp., are now regularly occurring, serious pests. The status of the plant bugs is unchanged.

An interesting and potentially important development is the case of the banded-wing whitefly, Trialeurodes abutilonea. This whitefly was unknown as a pest of cotton in Louisiana prior to 1964. It had been observed in various localities of the state during 1947 and succeeding years, in large enough numbers to attract attention, but not enough to cause concern, especially in fields that had been treated with toxaphene or BHC-DDT mixtures. During 1964 in the Red River Valley of northwestern Louisiana populations developed to such levels that some premature defoliation occurred in a few fields. The intensity of infestation and extent of area has increased steadily. During 1968 many fields suffered serious defoliation and discoloration of lint from fungus growth developing on honeydew which was secreted by the insect. It has now become a serious pest in Northwest Louisiana.

The major factor involved in the increasing importance of some species as cotton pests is undoubtedly the disruption of natural control agents, especially destruction of the predators and parasites, by the use of insecticides (Newsom and Brazzel, 1968). This has been particularly apparent in the case of *Heliothis* spp., *Tetranychus* spp. and *Trialeurodes abutilonea*. On the other hand, the cotton leafworm and the cotton aphid have declined in importance in spite of the fact that their predators and parasites have been affected in the same manner as those of the species which have increased in importance. This is apparently due to the fact that both species are extremely sensitive to the organophosphorus insecticides and thus far have not developed populations that are effectively resistant to these materials.

Resurgence of treated populations of cotton pests has become a common phenomenon. The abnormally rapid increase to economically injurious levels following pesticide treatment is typical of populations that are usually controlled adequately, but not completely, by natural enemies which are destroyed by the pesticide. Resurgence of a population of low density is a basic biological principle since its own density is a major factor influencing the reproductive capacity of an organism. At low population levels competition is at a minimum and reproduction at maximum levels. Populations, especially spider mites, driven to low levels by pressure of insecticide applications often resume production at maximum levels when control pressures are relaxed and rebound to even higher levels than before application. Especially in the case of the spider mites, it has been observed that populations often attain higher levels than the original in a very short time after cessation of insecticide treatments.

Repetitive applications of broad-spectrum insecticides for control of cotton pests exert extreme pressure on populations of predators and parasites. Gaines (1954) showed that populations of lady beetles, flower bugs, big-eyed bugs, and spiders were virtually eliminated from fields which had received three applications of chlorinated hydrocarbon insecticides. Newsom and Brazzel (1968) presented data showing that populations of a predator complex consisting of *Hippodamia convergens, Coleomegilla maculata, Scymnus* spp., *Orius insidiosus, Geocoris punctipes* and *Chrysopa* spp. were reduced by about 97 percent by one application of 2 pounds of toxaphene plus 1 pound of DDT per acre.

In spite of the severely depressing effects of cotton pesticides on populations of predators and parasites, all available evidence indicates that no permanent damage has occurred. Populations of these beneficial species decline sharply when exposed to treatment but when pesticide applications are discontinued, they rebound to their original level of abundance. There is no reason why the response to pesticides by "pest" and "beneficial" species should differ. Some of the most convincing evidence that populations of parasites have not been permanently damaged by use of the synthetic organic pesticides is furnished by Chesnut (1966). He compared the abundance of five species of parasites of the boll weevil during 1965 with that reported for the same areas in 1935 and found that there was no change.

ADVERSE EFFECTS ON NON-TARGET ORGANISMS

The effects of cotton pesticides on populations of crustaceans, amphibians, reptiles and fish in cotton field ecosystems in Louisiana have been similar to those on insects. Most birds and mammals have not been so drastically affected because they are more mobile than other species of wildlife and thus likely to spend less time in treated cotton fields. Some species of non-target organisms are extremely sensitive to most of the pesticides used on cotton while others are relatively resistant to these toxicants. Fish are almost unbelievably sensitive to some of the pesticides that have been widely used for control of cotton pests. For example, several species are killed by exposure to endrin in

concentrations less than 1 part per thousand million.

Fish kills of enormous magnitude have been observed frequently in streams, lakes and ponds of cotton-producing areas following applications of synthetic organic insecticides but little definitive work has been reported on the long-term effects of these kills upon populations. Apparently fish are like insects in their ability to recover from the effects of heavy mortality. Data summarized in Tables 24–4 and 24–5 show annual catches of fish, crawfish and frogs from the Atchafalaya and Red rivers in Louisiana and from the estuarine and coastal waters of the Louisiana Gulf Coast. Although such data may reflect many influences in addition to those of agricultural pesticides, and thus are of limited value, trends exhibited do not suggest that there have been any catastrophic effects from the use of insecticides on populations of these animals in Louisiana.

Only limited information is available on the effects of exposure to acutely toxic concentrations of pesticides for many species comprising the fauna of cotton field ecosys-

Table 24–4

TRENDS IN YIELDS OF FISHERIES PRODUCTS PRODUCED FROM THE ATCHAFALAYA AND RED RIVERS AND THEIR TRIBUTARIES IN LOUISIANA DURING 1950–1966[1]

YIELD, 1,000 POUNDS

PERIOD	BUFFALOFISH, *Ictiobus* spp.	CATFISH, *Ictalurus* spp.	FRESHWATER CRAWFISH, *Procambarus* spp.	FROGS, *Rana catesbeiana*
		Atchafalaya River		
1950	786	1,833	1,010	27
1954–58	720	1,342	620	20
1959–63	839	1,645	1,134	22
1964–66	729	839	3,488	20
		Red River		
1950	4,945	1,122	—	49
1954–58	882	343	—	9
1959–63	837	419	—	19
1964–66	1,068	372	—	13

[1] Data from Fishery Statistics of the United States, Statistical Digests, Bur. Sports, Fisheries and Wildlife, U. S. Department of Interior.

Table 24–5

TRENDS IN YIELDS OF FISHERIES PRODUCTS DELIVERED TO GULF COAST
PORTS IN LOUISIANA DURING 1949–1966[1]

YIELD, 1,000 POUNDS

PERIOD	BUFFALOFISH, *Ictiobus* spp.	CATFISH, *Ictalurus* spp.	FRESHWATER CRAWFISH, *Procambarus* spp.	FROGS, *Rana catesbeiana*	SHRIMP *Penaeus* spp.
1949–53	672	4,738	86	25	83,861
1954–58	687	3,049	417	10	58,301
1959–63	679	5,807	748	7	54,906
1964–66	711	5,105	1,482	13	61,353

[1] Data from Fishery Statistics of the United States, Statistical Digests, Bur. Sports, Fisheries and Wildlife, U. S. Department of Interior.

tems. Even less information is available on the effects of exposure to concentrations that are chronically toxic. For example, fish that are killed by exposure for twenty-four hours to endrin at 1 part per thousand million concentration can tolerate indefinite exposure to one-fourth this amount. In this manner residues may concentrate in their tissues amounting to many parts per million! This is an intriguing question for which no satisfactory explanation is available.

The solubility and storage of chlorinated hydrocarbon insecticides in animal fats is a well-known objectionable property of these chemicals. It is this property that makes possible their concentration in food chains which many believe may be the most hazardous aspect of their use. Data in Table 24–6 show that residues of the chlorinated hydrocarbon insecticides are found in a wide variety of animal species, often in substantially large amounts.

Like insects, some species of fish and frogs have become resistant to both the chlorinated hydrocarbon and the organophosphorus insecticides. Ferguson (1967) has reported levels of resistance in *Ictalurus* spp., *Notemigonus crysoleucas*, *Gambusia affinis* and *Lepomis* spp. ranging from twofold or threefold to fifteen hundredfold. These fish were collected from natural populations in streams of cotton-producing areas of the Mississippi Delta which have been subjected to heavy insecticide applications for twenty years. The occurrence of resistance at such high levels provides the strongest kind of circumstantial evidence for high mortality rates in such populations. Such high levels of resistance could not have occurred without stringent selection pressure having been applied.

One of the most serious features of the development of populations resistant to insecticides is that individuals of such populations can store much higher levels of residues than those of susceptible populations. Rosato and Ferguson (1968) have demonstrated experimentally that this phenomenon is a potential hazard. By exposing a population of resistant mosquito fish, *Gambusia affinis,* to endrin in water at 2 parts per million (ppm) they found that about half of the population survived after seven days and that the survivors of the treatment had accumulated endrin residues of more than 800 ppm of whole body weight. When single specimens of these mosquito fish were fed to eleven species of vertebrates, including birds, snakes, turtles and fish, approximately 95 percent of these animals died. Ferguson *et al.* (1966) also reported that resistant mosquito fish tolerated exposure to 0.5 ppm

Table 24-6

LEVEL OF RESIDUES OF CHLORINATED HYDROCARBON INSECTICIDES IN SAMPLES OF VARIOUS ANIMAL SPECIES IN LOUISIANA[1]

SPECIES	SAMPLE ANALYZED	RESIDUES, ppm		
		DDT AND METABOLITES	ALDRIN + DIELDRIN	HEPTACHLOR + HEPTACHLOR EPOXIDE
Human, New Orleans	Fat	10.30	0.29	0.24
Cottontail, *Sylvilagus floridanus*	Whole body	0.22	–	–
Beef Cattle	Fat	1.07	0.12	
Swine	Fat	2.84	0.07	
Quail, *Colinus virginianus*	Whole body	1.09	–	
Yellow-Crowned Night Heron, *Nyctanassa violacea*	Fat	31.70	–	0.20
Cattle Egret, *Bubulcus ibis*	Fat	12.10	0.20	0.40
Blue-Winged Teal, *Anas discors*	Preening gland		0.11	
Fulvous Tree Duck, *Dendrocygna bicolor*	Preening gland		0.22	
Common Grackle, *Quiscalus quiscala*	Fat	54.02	–	
House Sparrow, *Passer domesticus*	Fat	170.00	–	
Hummingbird, *Archilochus colubris*	Whole body	0.44	0.43	
Meadow Lark, *Sturnella magna*	Whole body	0.10		
Common Gallinule, *Gallinula chloropus*	Eggs	3.25	12.46	0.04
	Eggs	–	0.36	
Red Crawfish, *Procambarus clarkii*	Whole body	–	0.06	
	Viscera	–	1.50	
Freshwater Mussel, *Quadrula quadrula*	Whole body	0.09	–	
Cabbage Looper, *Trichoplusia ni*	Whole body	2.85	–	
Ground Beetle, *Harpalus pennsylvanicus*	Whole body	12.89	–	
Water Scavenger Beetle, *Tropisternus lateralis*	Whole body	2.48	–	
Predaceous Diving Beetle, *Thermonectes basilaris*	Whole body	2.58	–	
May Fly, *Hexagenia* sp.	Whole body	0.38	0.21	0.02
Lady Beetle, *Coleomegilla maculata*	Whole body	90.11	–	
	Eggs	24.64	–	

[1] Data from Hayes et al. (1965), Causey et al. (1968), ElSayed, et al. (1967), Hendrick et al. (1966), and Atallah and Nettles (1966); and unpublished data on file, Department of Entomology, Louisiana State University.

endrin for two weeks and accumulated residues as high as 214 ppm, more than 400-fold concentration. Individual fish were capable of excreting enough endrin into 10 liters of tapwater to kill five susceptible mosquito fish. Although these experiments were done under laboratory conditions of pesticide concentrations more than twenty times higher than any that could result from agricultural operations, they demonstrate the possibility of potential hazards that may arise from the concentration of residues in individuals from resistant populations.

CONSEQUENCES OF SUGARCANE PEST CONTROL

Most of the sugarcane-producing areas of Louisiana are located in the lower sections of the floodplains of the Red, Atchafalaya and Mississippi rivers, and along Bayou Teche and Bayou La Fourche. These areas are thickly interspersed with smaller streams, lakes, bayous, ponds, drainage canals and hardwood swamp that form excellent habitat for both terrestrial and aquatic wildlife unequaled in numbers and diversity of species by any other agricultural ecosystem in the state. The ratio of cultivated to uncultivated land in the area is relatively small.

Prior to 1959, little insecticide was used to control the only major pest of this crop, the sugarcane borer, *Diatarea saccharalis*. These insecticides were cryolite, ryania, and a small amount of chlordane. Endrin was first recommended for control of sugarcane borer in 1958. This recommendation was enthusiastically accepted by sugarcane growers because for the first time they had a material which would give excellent control of sugarcane borer. Unfortunately, endrin is one of the most toxic materials known to many species of fish. In 1959, tremendous fish kills were observed in the streams and bayous of the area, usually following heavy rains during July and August when the treatment period was at its peak. These kills occurred each season thereafter until endrin use was drastically reduced in 1966 and virtually discontinued in 1967.

Five years after it was first recommended, but only four years after it was used generally, endrin failed to control the sugarcane borer in areas near Port Allen, Louisiana (Yadav *et al.*, 1965). Laboratory studies showed that this population had developed approximately a tenfold resistance to endrin. Populations exhibiting lower levels of resistance were identified from several other areas. Resistance spread through the population rapidly and made it necessary to change to azinphosmethyl. The change occurred quickly. About 50 percent of the acreage was treated with azinphosmethyl in 1966, 90 percent in 1967, and virtually 100 percent during 1968.

From the standpoint of its overall effect on wildlife, the advantage of using the new material is tremendous. Considering that it is applied at 0.75 pound per acre compared to 0.33 pound per acre for endrin, its acute toxicity to bluegill is still less than one-fifth that of endrin. Its relative lack of persistence makes it even less hazardous. However, its toxicity to two species of cladocerans, *Simocephalus serrulatus* and *Daphnia pulex* (Sanders and Cope, 1966), is more than ten times that of endrin. This fact illustrates the importance of species-specificity in response to agricultural pesticides and suggests the difficulty of evaluating the relative importance of different pesticides on food chains.

Almost all of the endrin applied to sugarcane was in the form of granules. Less than 20 percent of the amount applied adhered to the plants, leaving about 80 percent lying on the soil surface to be transported in runoff water into drainage systems. This aspect of the problem has been alleviated to some extent by the use of emulsion concentrate sprays of azinphosmethyl. Davis (1965) found that about twenty-five times more insecticide was retained on sugarcane foliage when azinphosmethyl was sprayed than when the same amount was applied in granular formulations. This sharply reduces the amount available for transport by runoff waters. Conversely, it increases the amount available on foliage of plants for herbivores such as rabbits and deer which browse on many of the common weeds found in sugarcane fields in Louisiana. No studies have been reported of attempts to evaluate the difference in potential hazard of the two methods of application to vertebrate species. However, Davis (1965) showed that there was no difference in effects on the predatory arthropod fauna when the two formulations were compared at equal rates of application.

CONSEQUENCES OF RICE PEST CONTROL

Rice in Louisiana is grown in an aquatic environment during much of the growing season and thus is comprised in a unique agricultural ecosystem. Several species of wildlife spend substantial portions of each year in rice fields. Among the more important are the purple gallinule, *Porphyrula martinica,* the common gallinule, *Gallinula chloropus,* the fulvous tree duck, *Dendrocygna bicolor,* the red crawfish, *Procambarus clarkii,* and mosquito fish, *Gambusia affinis.* Both species of gallinules and the fulvous tree duck nest in rice fields and feed extensively on rice. Crawfish farming is an important industry in the rice-producing area and the acreage devoted to it is increasing rapidly.

Such an agricultural ecosystem is extremely sensitive to the effects of pesticide application. Fortunately, rice has only two major pests, the rice stinkbug, *Oebalus pugnax,* and the rice water weevil, *Lissorhoptrus oryzophilus.* The amount of insecticides required for their control has been relatively small. The stinkbug never infests more than a relatively small percentage of the approximately half-million acres of rice planted each year, and one application of an effective insecticide is usually all that is required for its control.

During the decade beginning with 1950 the rice stinkbug was commonly controlled by the application of toxaphene, dieldrin, DDT, or mixtures of these materials. The most common mixture contained 2 pounds of toxaphene plus 0.25 pound of dieldrin per acre. Applications of insecticide for rice stinkbug control are usually made when rice is in the milk or early dough stages, when fields are flooded to a depth of four to six inches. Probably no more than 10 percent of the insecticide applied is retained on the plant and most of the remainder goes directly into the water. Assuming that 1.8 pounds of toxaphene and 0.22 pound of dieldrin is deposited in the water and that the crop is flooded to a depth of six inches at the time of application, the initial concentration would be 1.08 ppm of toxaphene and 0.13 ppm of dieldrin. According to Edson

(1958) dieldrin at this concentration would be about 12 times the maximum safe upper limit for fish-bearing waters, and toxaphene about 200 times. As might be expected, fish kills were often spectacular in both intensity and magnitude in rice fields treated with these materials and in the canals and streams composing irrigation and drainage systems.

Both toxaphene and dieldrin are toxic to birds. In their survey of the toxicology of aldrin and dieldrin, Hodge *et al.* (1967) reported that mortality occurred from repeated short-term or chronic doses of 0.5 ppm aldrin and 1 ppm dieldrin for quail; 12.5 ppm aldrin for turkey; and less than 100 ppm for pheasants. Toxaphene was less toxic, but it was considered to be among the highly toxic insecticides to many species of birds.

Probably no more than 5 percent of the total amount of insecticide applied to rice is retained on the seed heads. Average yields of rice obtained during the early part of the 1950's were about 2,000 pounds per acre (Table 24–1). This would mean that the initial concentration on rice treated with 2 pounds of toxaphene plus 0.25 pound of dieldrin per acre would be about 95 ppm for toxaphene and 12 ppm for dieldrin. Birds whose diets consist of large quantities of rice could conceivably be subjected to considerable hazard from feeding in treated fields.

As soon as the hazard to fish and wildlife from the application of chlorinated hydrocarbon insecticides to flooded rice fields was recognized, substitute materials were sought. Malathion at 0.5 pound, methyl parathion at 0.25, phosphamidon at 0.25, and carbaryl at 0.8 pound per acre were found to be effective substitutes. These materials have been used exclusively in rice since 1960 for control of rice stinkbug. Not only are they much less hazardous to wildlife and fish, they are also considerably more economical than the chlorinated hydrocarbons previously used. Assuming that all of the material was deposited in the water, the initial concentrations of these pesticides applied at recommended rates to rice fields flooded to a depth of six inches would be: malathion, 0.30 ppm; methyl parathion, 0.15 ppm; phosphamidon, 0.15 ppm; and carbaryl, 0.48 ppm. These amounts are up to three times the maximum safe upper limits listed by Edson (1958) for fish-bearing waters. However, when their toxicities to crawfish are considered, an example is provided of the difficulty of finding pesticides that are equally safe for all species that it is desirable to protect. Data in Table 24–7 show the comparative toxicity to red crawfish of materials representing the three major classes of synthetic organic insecticides. Methyl parathion was the most toxic compound to crawfish, about eight times more toxic to these animals than endrin. The initial concentration in water of methyl parathion ap-

plied for stinkbug control would be only one and one-half times the maximum safe upper concentration for fish but it would be about four times the maximum safe upper concentration for crawfish. Under field conditions, however, Hendrick *et al.* (1966) reported that the yield of crawfish was not adversely affected in rice paddies treated with aldrin, methyl parathion, and carbaryl, or any of their combinations, used for control of rice pests in Louisiana. Rapid adsorption of these chemicals by soil particles and organic material probably accounts for their lack of toxicity to crawfish when they are applied to rice fields at such relatively low rates.*

For the first time the chlorinated hydrocarbon insecticides provided a means for

* See Chapter 26 by L. T. Kok for an account of toxicity to fish of pesticides used in rice paddies in Southeast Asia (eds.).

Table 24-7

RELATIVE TOXICITIES OF SOME COMMONLY USED PESTICIDES TO SOME SPECIES OF WILDLIFE AND ZOOPLANKTON[1]

TOXICANT	*Simocephalus serrulatus* 48-HR LC$_{50}$[2] (mg/l)	*Daphnia pulex* (mg/l)	*Procambarus clarkii* 48-HR TLm[3] (ppm)	*Lepomis Macrochirus* 48-HR LC$_{50}$ (mg/l)	RATS ORAL LD$_{50}$[4] (mg/kg)
DDT	0.003	0.004	0.60	0.0160	113
TDE	0.005	0.003	–	–	3,400
Toxaphene	0.019	0.015	–	0.0035	90
Endrin	0.026	0.020	0.30	0.0006	25
Aldrin	0.023	0.028	–	0.0130	35
Heptachlor	0.047	0.042	–	0.0190	90
Dieldrin	0.024	0.250	–	0.0079	60
Lindane	0.520	0.460	–	0.0770	125
Ethyl parathion	0.001	0.006	–	–	3
Malathion	0.004	0.002	–	0.0900	1,400
Methyl parathion	–	–	0.04	1.9000	15
Azinphosmethyl (Guthion)	0.004	0.003	–	0.0050	12
Sevin	0.008	0.006	3.00	5.3000	600
Trifluralin	0.450	0.240	–	0.1000	5,000

[1] Data from Sanders and Cope (1966), Muncy and Oliver (1963), Henderson et al. (1960), Pickering et al. (1962), Hughes and Davis (1967), and Gaines (1960).

[2] LC$_{50}$ = Lethal concentration for 50% of the test population after 48 hours of exposure.

[3] TLm = Median tolerance limit.

[4] LD$_{50}$ = Dosage necessary to kill 50% of the test population in a given period of time.

effectively controlling the rice water weevil, *Lissorhoptrus oryzophilus*. This root-infesting coleopteran had long been recognized as one of the most important rice pests in Louisiana. Attempts to control it were based on withholding water and drying the soil. This practice was only moderately successful at best, and it depressed growth of rice to some extent. When it was found that application of aldrin to rice seed at the rate of 0.25 pound per 100 pounds of seed gave excellent control of the rice water weevil and improved yields by an average of about 300 pounds per acre, growers adopted the practice in 1961, and it has been used on virtually all of the half-million acres planted to rice since that time.

Problems with wildlife soon developed. Growers reported occasionally finding dead ducks and gallinules around fields during the planting season. This was not surprising since rice treated at 0.25 pound of aldrin has an initial concentration on the seed of 2,500 ppm. Causey *et al.* (1968) found that food in the gizzard of common and purple gallinules collected from rice fields in early September 1966 was composed of 71 and 90 percent rice, respectively. The average dry weight of rice per bird was 0.90 gram for the purple and 0.88 gram for the common gallinule. They pointed out that purple gallinules feeding on rice treated at this rate would have to consume only 1.76 grams to equal an oral dose of 20 ppm and the common gallinule would have to consume about 3.0 grams to get a dose of 20 ppm. Both birds might easily consume this much rice in one day since birds of both species collected at night were found to have an average of about 0.9 gram of rice remaining in the digestive tract. Birds arriving on their breeding grounds before or during the rice planting season would have ample opportunity to feed on this highly contaminated rice. Sowing rice by airplane is becoming an increasingly common practice in Louisiana. Where this is practiced, seeds are readily available in the fields, on headlands, levees, and in the drainage ditches and irrigation canals.

A study was begun in 1965 of the effect of this practice on gallinules (Causey *et al.*, 1968). Results obtained were similar for both species and are summarized in Table 24–8 for the common gallinule. Eggs for

Table 24–8

THE EFFECTS ON GALLINULES OF RICE SEED TREATMENT WITH ALDRIN IN LOUISIANA[1]

	RICE FIELD POPULATION	ROCKFELLER REFUGE POPULATION
Clutch Size	8.94	8.26
Hatchability, Percent	84.2	86.50
Dieldrin residues, ppm		
Eggs	9.37	ND[2]
Edible Portion of Flesh	0.13	0.06
Preening Glands	1.48	ND[3]
Gizzard Contents of Birds Collected in September	ND[3]	ND[3]

[1] Data from Causey et al. (1968).
[2] Not detected at 0.1 ppm.
[3] Not detected at 0.025 ppm.

study were collected during or immediately after the planting season in the spring. Birds were collected in late summer. Since no insecticide residues were detected in rice from the gizzards of birds taken during September and growing rice is no longer treated with aldrin or dieldrin, the dieldrin residues detected in eggs in edible flesh must have come from treated rice seed ingested by the birds during, or soon after, the planting season. The amount of residue in edible flesh and preening glands of the birds collected in September was undoubtedly much less than the amount that was present during the laying period. It is not likely that 9 ppm of dieldrin could accumulate in eggs produced by birds having less than 1.50 ppm in the preening glands.

The LD_{50} (dosage required to kill 50 percent of the treated population within a specified period of time) of dieldrin to bob-white quail and mourning dove is 12–14 and 44–46 mg/kg respectively (Dahlen and Haugen, 1954). If the acute toxicity of dieldrin to gallinules is within this range, in one day either species could easily consume enough rice seed treated at 2,500 ppm to equal or exceed the amount equivalent to the LD_{50} of quail or mourning dove. However, Causey *et al.* (1968) indicate that the gallinules can tolerate much greater amounts of dieldrin than this. The two populations they studied did not differ significantly in size of clutch or in hatchability.

The problem of dieldrin residues in gallinules and its potential adverse effect on populations of these birds in Louisiana has now been solved. The rice water weevil has become so highly resistant to aldrin that seed treatment is no longer effective for control of this pest and the recommendation for use of aldrin on rice seed has been withdrawn. The development of resistance to aldrin in populations of the rice water weevil to levels making it virtually useless for control of this pest required only five growing seasons (Graves *et al.*, 1967).

ENVIRONMENTAL POLLUTION

It is literally true that insecticide residues are ubiquitous in Louisiana. This should not be surprising when the following are considered: amount of insecticides used in agriculture and related pest control operations; residues in the air from dusting and spraying operations; volatilization by co-distillation with water vapor escaping from the soil; and the small amounts carried into the upper atmosphere with dust particles and pollen. Even with analytical methods sensitive only to 0.01 ppm, residues have been detected in most samples that have been analyzed in connection with a pesticide-monitoring program conducted in Louisiana (Epps *et al.*, 1967).

The relatively large percentage of total area covered by lakes, streams and ponds in the agricultural ecosystems of Louisiana make the pollution of water an especially serious problem. Residues of various insecticides find their way into these waters principally through runoff but also in drift from spraying and dusting operations and by direct contamination from carelessness on the part of applicators. Five monitoring sites were chosen during 1964 for studying pesticide residues resulting from agricultural operations. They were: (1) Six-Mile Bayou, which drains a forested area almost totally devoid of agricultural operations; (2) Tensas River, which drains a large cotton- and soybean-producing area of the Mississippi River floodplain; (3) Mermentau River, which drains a large area devoted almost exclusively to rice production; (4) Bayou Chevreuil, which drains an area producing sugarcane; and (5) Bayou Courtebleau, which drains an intensively farmed area producing cotton, soybeans, sweet potatoes, corn, sugarcane and rice. Three species of fish chosen as test animals for monitoring pesticide residues in streams showed a remarkable ability to concentrate insecticides according to the kinds and amounts used in a particular area. Twenty-two samples of bluegills, *Lepomis macrochirus,* seventeen samples of gizzard shad, *Dorsoma cepedianum,* and twenty-seven samples of catfish, *Ictalurus punctatus,* were analyzed during the preliminary stages of this program. Data in Table 24–9 show the levels of residues in fish from the various areas. Quite obviously residue levels were related to kinds and amounts of pesticides used in the drainage basins of various streams. The data also suggest that populations of all three species have become resistant to the chlorinated hydrocarbon insecticides in the four streams that drain agricultural areas. The data in Table 24–9 show average values; about one-third equal or exceed the 9.65 ppm of DDT in the highly resistant mosquito fish used by Rosato and Ferguson (1968).

Table 24-9

PESTICIDE RESIDUES (ppm) IN EDIBLE PORTIONS OF FRESHWATER FISH
FROM FIVE STREAMS IN LOUISIANA[1]

	BAYOU CHEVREUIL	BAYOU COURTEBLEAU	MERMENTAU RIVER	SIX-MILE BAYOU	TENSAS RIVER
DDT and Metabolites					
Bluegill	0.96	5.88	0.35	0.03	2.68
Shad	0.05	9.47	0.48	0.13	4.14
Catfish	0.14	10.06	0.48	0.24	6.28
Toxaphene					
Bluegill	N[2]	P	0.35	N	2.06
Shad	N	4.75	1.00	N	3.17
Catfish	N	6.60	0.40	N	5.05
Dieldrin					
Bluegill	N	0.33	0.05	N	0.03
Shad	P[3]	0.50	0.08	0.01	0.02
Catfish	N	0.14	0.04	N	0.08
Endrin					
Bluegill	P	0.03	N	N	P
Shad	0.87	0.04	N	N	P
Catfish	0.31	0.06	N	N	0.01
Total Residues					
Bluegill	0.96	6.24	0.75	0.03	4.77
Shad	0.92	14.76	1.56	0.14	7.33
Catfish	0.45	16.86	0.92	0.24	11.42

[1] Data from Epps et al. (1967).
[2] Not detected.
[3] Detected at minimum level of detection.

Fish from all streams except Six-Mile Bayou contained pesticide residues in excess of legal tolerances that have been established for meat by the federal Food and Drug Administration. The potential hazard for animals at higher trophic levels, including humans, whose diet might contain significant amounts of these contaminated food fish, remains unexplored.

Water samples from these streams, taken when the fish were collected, never showed the presence of any insecticide residues at detection levels sensitive to 0.001 ppm. This common finding in water analysis emphasizes the rapidity and degree of adsorption of pesticides by soil particles and organic matter. Bailey and White (1964) have pointed out the significance of the partitioning of organic insecticides from water to bottom sediments and suspended silt.

Lauer et al. (1966) made an intensive study during 1961 and 1964 of endrin contamination of surface waters in the Bayou Yokely basin which drains about 3,300 acres of sugarcane. During the period 1959 to 1964 an average of about .5 pound of endrin per acre per year was applied to the 3,300 acres on which sugarcane was grown. In the area endrin was never detected in the streams at levels higher than a few parts per trillion but it was detected in bottom sediments in parts per thousand million. As much as 1.7 ppm were detected in the soil during November of 1964, approximately two months after the last application for the season. Endrin residues persisted in the soil from one season to the next. Also, water pumped from Bayou Yokely during the latter half of August 1964 killed fish in the Franklin Canal and measurable quantities

Table 24–10

AMOUNTS OF CHLORINATED HYDROCARBON INSECTICIDE RESIDUES IN 85 SAMPLES OF AGRICULTURAL SOILS AND 46 SAMPLES OF SOYBEANS FROM LOUISIANA, 1966[1]

DDT			TOXAPHENE			ALDRIN + DIELDRIN			ENDRIN		
NO. WITH RESIDUES	RANGE	MEAN	NO. WITH RESIDUES	RANGE	MEAN	NO. WITH RESIDUES	RANGE	MEAN	NO. WITH RESIDUES	RANGE	MEAN
Residues (ppm) in Soils											
84	0.01–14.83	2.37	33	0.08–12.80	3.08	11	0.01–1.00	0.13	18	0.02–0.42	0.09
Residues (ppm) in Soybeans											
26	0.01–0.24	0.03	0	—	—	0	—	—	13	0.01–0.09	0.03

[1] Unpublished data on file, Department of Entomology, Louisiana State University.

of endrin were present in water processed through treatment plants for use by cities in the area.

Soils collected from cotton-producing areas of Louisiana in the fall of 1966 and winter and spring of 1967 were contaminated by substantial amounts of chlorinated hydrocarbon insecticides (Table 24–10). The significance of these residues is not understood except that soybeans grown on soils containing residues of such materials as dieldrin, aldrin, heptachlor and endrin may be expected to absorb and translocate to the seed residues at about one-tenth the level present in the soil (Bruce *et al.,* 1966). Since tolerance for these materials in soybeans is zero, their presence in soils presents a potentially serious problem.

SUMMARY

The results of two decades of use of synthetic organic insecticides for control of agricultural pests in Louisiana may be summarized as follows:

I. Control of important crop and livestock pests has been unprecedentedly effective. Many pests have been controlled effectively for the first time and some, for example, the cotton aphid, *Aphis gossypii,* and the cotton

leafworm, *Alabama argillacea,* have been controlled so well that they are no longer important pests. The improved efficiency of pest control has contributed significantly to the increased efficiency of crop production. Per acre yields of cotton, rice and sugarcane have increased during the period by 124, 100 and 36 percent, respectively (Table 24–1). Yield increases of this magnitude could not have occurred, and cannot be sustained, without the proper use of conventional insecticides.

II. Development of resistance to insecticides has occurred in fifteen major pest species, including the key pests of cotton, rice and sugarcane. The time required for populations of these species to overcome susceptibility to the various insecticides involved has ranged from four to fourteen years. The situation has now reached the critical stage in populations of a few pests where no satisfactory insecticides are available to substitute for those rendered ineffective by the development of resistant populations. Populations that are no longer effectively controlled with any insecticide available for commercial use include the rice water weevil, *Lissorhoptrus oryzophilus,* the cabbage looper, *Trichoplusia ni,* the "soybean" looper, *Pseudoplusia includens,* the banded cucumber beetle, *Diabrotica balte-*

ata, the two-spotted spider mite, *Tetranychus urticae* and the banded-wing whitefly, *Trialeurodes abutilonea.*

The rapidity with which resistant populations have developed and the number of species involved attest to the effectiveness of the synthetic organic insecticides for their control. In fact, the more effective an insecticide is in killing susceptible individuals of an insect population, the faster will be the evolution of resistance. The amount of pressure required to select resistant strains at the rate observed must meet two criteria. (1) The selecting agent must be toxic enough to kill a high percentage of the population to which it is applied. (2) A relatively large percentage of the total population within the treated area must be exposed to the toxicant. Recognition of the importance of these criteria for the development of resistance in populations of pest species can be used to prevent or delay its occurrence. For example, pests of seedling corn in Louisiana have been controlled effectively by seed dressings with dieldrin applied at the rate of 2 ounces per bushel with an appropriate fungicide. Corn is seeded at the rate of 10 pounds per acre or less; thus only a few grams of insecticide per acre are added to the environment. Since an extremely small percentage of the total pest population, consisting only of those individuals that attack seedling corn, are affected by the insecticide, resistant populations have not occurred. In the Midwest, however, where control of pests of seedling corn has required broadcast or banded applications of aldrin, dieldrin, or heptachlor at rates of 2 pounds per acre, resistant populations have occurred to the extent that the chlorinated hydrocarbon insecticides are no longer effective in many areas.

III. The short-term effect of the use of synthetic organic insecticides on population of non-target organisms has been severe. The most obviously and seriously affected of these have been insect predators and parasites, honeybees and other pollinating species, and fish. Rapid change from little or no importance to that of major pest status has become commonplace among insects and spider mites of agricultural ecosystems in which insecticides have been used extensively. This phenomenon has been observed more in cotton than other crops. Previously innocuous species, such as *Tetranychus* spp. and the tobacco budworm, *Heliothis virescens,* have become major cotton pests in Louisiana after having been released from the pressure of natural control through the destruction of their predators and parasites by insecticides. The bollworm, *H. zea,* has also changed from an occasional secondary pest to an annually occurring, major cotton pest during the last two decades.

Heavy mortality from insecticide intoxication has been observed among fishes in the major agricultural areas of Louisiana. Huge fish kills have been observed in many areas following the application of endrin, dieldrin, aldrin, heptachlor, toxaphene, strobane, and DDT to various crops. Indirect evidence of mortality of much greater magnitude than that directly observed is provided by the fact that large residues of one or more of these materials are common in fishes throughout the agricultural areas of the state. Only highly resistant populations can tolerate residues of the magnitude commonly found in these populations. In order for resistant populations of fishes to have developed, heavy selection pressure must have been applied involving mortality of a high percentage of the exposed population.

The possibility of long-term effects on animal populations of Louisiana agricultural ecosystems poses a question for which no answer is presently available. Suitable data on populations in these areas and population trends prior to the introduction of modern insecticides to agriculture do not exist. It is difficult to separate the effects on the animal populations of pesticides used in agriculture from the effects of other environmental hazards. It is known that the effects of industrial pollution on wildlife species can be at least as great as the effects of pesticides. It is also known that clearing land for agricultural use has drastic, long-term effects on animal populations. Techniques for separating the short-term and long-term effects of the various environmental hazards to which animal populations are exposed have not been refined sufficiently to provide reliable data. Long-term, fundamental studies to assess the relative importance of these environmental hazards on wildlife population are badly needed.

IV. Agricultural ecosystems have been grossly polluted with insecticide residues, especially the chlorinated hydrocarbon insecticides, throughout the state. Data in Tables 24–6, 24–8, 24–9, and 24–10 show the extent to which this has occurred. These data also indicate that the residue concentration at the higher trophic levels may pose a potentially serious problem. Studies are urgently needed to establish the effects of concentration of pesticide residues in food webs.

When it became obvious that soybean production was destined to grow into a major agricultural enterprise in Louisiana (Table 24–2), the decision was made by personnel of the Department of Entomology, Louisiana Agricultural Experiment Station, to develop a program of insect pest control for this crop that would not have as many of the undesirable features listed above. The following principles for the intelligent use of insecticides for control of agricultural pests of a relatively new, rapidly expanding crop, such as the soybean in Louisiana, were adopted.

1. Determine the economic injury thresholds for potentially important species and withhold recommendations for their control until the apparent injury they cause is determined to be real.

2. Establish the importance of natural control agents—predators, parasites, and microbial pathogens—in suppressing populations of the various species of potential pests.

3. Use the smallest possible amounts per acre and the fewest number of applications of insecticides necessary to prevent economic damage by the various pests.

4. Avoid using broad-spectrum, persistent pesticides as much as possible. Take full advantage of specificity that exists among species in response to chemicals (Table 24–7).

5. Base recommendations for all insecticide applications upon the results of thorough, accurate, and continuing assessment of pests and their natural control agents and treat only when pest populations reach economic injury thresholds.

6. Conserve and augment the populations of natural control agents by all feasible means.

By observing these principles the following results should be possible: to reduce or prevent the accumulation of persistent, toxic chemical residues in the environment; take full advantage of natural control agents; delay or prevent the development of insecticide-resistant pest populations; impose minimal hazards upon populations of non-target organisms; and hold down production costs.

Until a completely integrated system of pest management can be developed, the short-term approach to pest control for a rapidly expanding new crop in a new area should help to avoid, or at least to minimize, the occurrence of serious difficulties from the use of insecticides. It is recommended for consideration by the scientists whose responsibility it will be to control agricultural pests in nations where agricultural production must be greatly intensified during the next few decades.

REFERENCES

Atallah, Y. H., and Nettles, C. W., Jr. "DDT-Metabolism and Excretion in *Coleomegilla maculata* DeGeer." *J. Econ. Entomol.*, 59 (1966), 560–64.

Bailey, G. W., and White, J. L. "Soil Particle Relationships: Review of Adsorption and Desorption of Organic Pesticides by Soil Colloids, with Implications Concerning Pesticide Bioactivity." *Agr. Food Chem.*, 12 (1964), 324–33.

Bruce, W. N.; Decker, G. C.; and Wilson, Jean G. "Relationship of the Levels of Insecticide Contamination of Crop Seeds to Their Fat Content and Soil Contamination of Aldrin, Heptachlor, and Their Epoxides." *J. Econ. Entomol.*, 59 (1966), 179–81.

Causey, M. K.; Bonner, F. L.; and Graves, J. B. "Dieldrin Residues in the Gallinules *Porphyrula martinica* L. and *Gallinula chloropus* L. and Its Effect on Clutch Size and Hatchability." *Bull. Environ. Cont. and Toxicol.*, 3 (1968), 274–83.

Chesnut, T. L. Survey of Arthropod Parasites of the Boll Weevil, *Anthonomus grandis* Boheman. M.S. thesis, Mississippi State University, 1966.

Dahlen, James H., and Haugen, Arnold D. "Acute Toxicity of Certain Insecticides to Bobwhite Quail and Mourning Doves." *J. Wildl. Mgmt.*, 18 (1954), 477–81.

Davis, Leland A. Some Effects of Spraying Low Volume Concentrate Insecticides for Control of the Sugarcane Borer, *Diatraea saccharalis* (F.). M.S. thesis, Louisiana State University, 1965.

Edson, E. F. "The Risk of Pesticides to Fish." In D. H. Grist, *Rice*. London: Longmans, 1958. Pp. 402–06.

ElSayed, E. J.; Graves, J. B.; and Bonner, F. L. "Chlorinated Hydrocarbon Insecticides Residues in Selected Insects and Birds Found in Association with Cotton Fields." *Agr. Food Chem.*, 15 (1967), 1014–17.

Epps, E. A.; Bonner, F. L.; Newsom, L. D.; Carlton, Richard; and Smitherman, R. O. "Preliminary Report on a Pesticide Monitoring Study in Louisiana." *Bull. Environ. Contam. Toxicol.*, 2 (1967), 333–39.

Ferguson, Denzel E. "The Ecological Consequences of Pesticides Resistance of Fishes." *Trans. Thirty-second North Amer. Wild. Mgmt. Inst.*, 1967. Pp. 103–07

Ferguson, D. E.; Ludke, J. L.; and Murphy, G. G. "Dynamics of Endrin Uptake and Release by Resistant and Susceptible Strains of Mosquitofish." *Trans. Amer. Fish. Soc.*, 95 (1966), 335–36.

Gaines, R. C. "Effect on Beneficial Insects of Several Insecticides Applied for Cotton Insect Control." *J. Econ. Entomol.*, 47 (1954), 543–44.

Gaines, T. B. "The Acute Toxicity of Pesticides to Rats." *Toxicol. Appl. Pharmacol.*, 2 (1960), 88–99.

Graves, J. B.; Everett, T. R.; and Hendrick, R. D. "Resistance to Aldrin in the Rice Water Weevil in Louisiana." *J. Econ. Entomol.*, 60 (1967), 1155–57.

Hayes, W. J., Jr.; Dale, W. E.; and Birse, V. W. "Chlorinated Hydrocarbon Pesticides." *Life Sci.*, 4 (1965), 1611–15.

Henderson, C.; Pickering, Q. H.; and Tarzwell, C. M. "The Toxicity of Organic Phosphorus and Chlorinated Hydrocarbon Insecticides to Fish." In *Seminar on Biological Problems in Water Pollution*. Cincinnati: Taft Engr. Center, 2 (1960), 76–88.

Hendrick, R. D.; Bonner, F. L.; Everett, T. R.; and Fahey, J. E. "Residue Studies on Aldrin and Dieldrin in Soils, Water, and Crawfish from Rice Fields Having Insecticide Contamination." *J. Econ. Entomol.*, 59 (1966), 1388–91.

Hendrick, R. D.; Everett, T. R.; and Caffey, H. R. "Effects of Some Insecticides on the Survival, Reproduction, and Growth of the Louisiana Red Crawfish." *J. Econ. Entomol.*, 59 (1966), 188–92.

Hodge, Harold C.; Boyce, Alfred M.; Deichmann, William B.; and Kraybill, Herman

F. "Toxicology and No Effect Levels of Aldrin and Dieldrin." *Toxicol. Appl. Pharmacol.,* 10 (1967), 613–73.

Hughes, J. S., and Davis, J. T. *Toxicity of Pesticides to Bluegill and Sunfish Tested during 1961–1966.* Monroe, La.: Louisiana Wildlife and Fisheries Commission, 1967. Mimeo. report 8 pp.

Lauer, Gerald J.; Nicholson, H. P.; Cox, W. S.; and Teasley, J. I. "Pesticide Contamination of Surface Waters by Sugarcane Farming in Louisiana." *Trans. Amer. Fish. Soc.,* 96 (1966), 310–16.

Muncy, Robert J., and Oliver, Abe D., Jr. "Toxicity of Ten Insecticides to the Red Crawfish, *Procambarus clarkii* (Girard)." *Trans. Amer. Fish. Soc.,* 92 (1963), 428–31.

Newsom, L. D., and Brazzel, J. R. "Pests and Their Control." *Advances in Production and Utilization of Quality Cotton: Principles and Practices.* Fred C. Eliot, Marvin Hoover, and Walter K. Porter, Jr., eds. Ames, Iowa: Iowa State University Press, 1968. Pp. 365–405.

Pickering, Q. H.; Henderson, C.; and Lemke, A. E. "The Toxicity of Organic phosphorus Insecticides to Different Species of Warmwater Fish." *Trans. Amer. Fish. Soc.,* 91 (1962), 175–84.

Rosato, Peter, and Ferguson, Denzel E. "The Toxicity of Aldrin-Resistant Mosquitofish to Eleven Species of Vertebrates." *BioScience,* 18 (1968), 783–84.

Sanders, H. O., and Cope, O. B. "Toxicities of Several Pesticides to Two Species of Cladocerans." *Trans. Amer. Fish. Soc.,* 95 (1966), 165–69.

Yadav, R. P.; Anderson, H. L.; and Long, W. H. "Sugarcane Borer Resistance to Insecticides." *J. Econ. Entomol.,* 58 (1965), 1122–24.

DISCUSSION

RIVNAY: The cotton problem in Israel deserves special attention. Every other country started with production of cotton and then the pest problem developed. Israel first encountered the pest problem and then began to raise cotton.

The first experimental lots were heavily attacked. The stands were beautiful; they were so high that a man could not be seen when he entered them. But when we began to look for bolls, there were none.

We soon learned that our problem was the spiny bollworm, which is probably native to the country, but was never known to us because we had never raised cotton. We now understand that the reason cotton wasn't raised in Israel all these years, even though the climate and soil were suitable, was probably this pest. Some travelers of the fourteenth century related that cotton was grown in the Bet-Sheau Valley; but, it has not been there for centuries because of the spiny bollworm.

Then, reports reached us of a new insecticide, endrin. Remember, that was about 1954. We began to use endrin, and the results were favorable. A year later, the area in commercial cotton grew to a considerable extent. The insecticide applications were usually preventive: It was decided to use the insecticides every ten days or so in order to prevent a buildup of the pest.

In 1967, nevertheless, there was a severe outbreak of the spiny bollworm, *Earias insulana*. It was so bad that in the upper Jordan Valley, the Musone Valley and part of Galilee the entire crop of many fields was completely wiped out.

Then another insecticide appeared on the market, and that was *gusathion*. [Here they pronounce it "guthion," I believe.] This was also used as a preventive measure; fourteen to fifteen applications were made in some areas. And we succeeded in raising cotton in spite of this pest.

In the meantime, I had completed some studies on the phenology of the pest, and I realized that the pest population drops in the middle of the summer, practically to zero. My recommendation was then to reduce the number of applications, but the farmers were against it. They said, "We must be sure, we must prevent any buildup of the pest."

A year or two later, another factor appeared which made continuous application necessary, *Spodoptera littoralis,* the Egyptian cotton leafworm.

Little by little, the question of the cotton leafworm became more serious, and it became more injurious than the bollworm. The insecticides now were used against this pest rather than against the other one.

The situation reached such a stage that the Minister of Agriculture questioned: "Is the gain from cotton worthwhile after we have to spend so much money for insecticides?" Indeed, income and expenditures were almost equal.

And then the idea was brought forth that we must restrain ourselves from lavish application of insecticides. It was decided to apply the insecticides only when the level of injury reached a certain stage. It became apparent that the threshold of application is when the percentage of injury is about 2 or 3 per cent. Accordingly, the practice brought about a reduction in the number of applications, and we can get along now in raising cotton profitably.

CAIRNS: I would like to comment on a point raised in Ferguson's study (see bibliography, 1967) about the resistance of certain fishes to insecticides. He notes that *Gambusia* (mosquito-eating fish) acquire resistance rather rapidly to insecticides. Once this resistance has been established, these fish then carry sufficient quantities of insecticides to be lethal if the predator ingests enough.

We exposed guppies for twenty-six months to sublethal concentrations of the insecticide dieldrin and found that the initial response was an increase in the number of individuals in the population, though the biomass remained the same. After about eight months, there was a restoration of the balance which suggested that the initial disequilibrium and overproduction of small individuals was due to a cessation of predation of the adults on the young. Thus one of the consequences of exposure of fishes to sublethal concentrations of insecticides may be overproduction of stunted or smallish fish, which may not be desirable.

We have also found that parathion in sublethal concentrations will affect the visual acuity of sunfish to the point where they probably can't function very well. This apparently is the result of interference with cholinesterase production.

One final point: We found that certain algae, particularly diatoms, will tolerate enormous quantities of chlorinated hydrocarbon insecticides, which may accumulate on the surface or inside the diatom. If these diatoms were to wash from sprayed swamps into streams and then be consumed by fish, they might actually increase the biological

magnification possibilities far in excess of those predicted.

COMMONER: I would like to ask a question of the group. I was struck by the fact that the situation in Peru's Cañete Valley arose out of a very careful following of the prescribed procedures developed by the Entomological Society. Now, clearly, this society has certain responsibilities. It should understand what problems may arise from its actions—ecological failures.

I want to ask the question: What are the reasons for this failure?

SMITH: First, may I interject, I do not believe that it was really the Entomological Society of America's procedures. I believe they were from a so-called Memphis Conference. This is actually The Annual Conference Report on Cotton Insect Research and Control.

COMMONER: All right.

BOZA BARDUCCI: Perhaps I can help with a little more background information on the case history. All these isolated valleys in Peru form one agro-ecological region with a sound balance. By repeated applications of insecticide you destroy all the useful insects. In that case, new races of the pest which are resistant to the insecticide will develop and new pests will appear.

That result doesn't necessarily occur in all other parts of the world because a very important factor is the isolation of the valley, which means that the effect of insecticides will be tremendous. For instance, in the San Joaquin Valley in California, they also used insecticides a few times, but the effect was not the same because the area is so big. They also rotate the crop which is not the case in Peru because we have a very long vegetative period of cotton; the cotton grows for practically nine months. We make a fall rotation with some other crop like corn, for instance, which is attacked by some other kind of pest common to the cotton, too. Also, we grow cotton that is a second-year crop from the same old plant. We cut and then let it sprout again. That makes a bridge between the insect generations, and there are at least three generations.

Our entomologists made a very careful study, picking up some insects from other valleys and then testing them in the laboratory. The insects from Cañete are either not killed at all or just around 10 percent are killed; but insects imported from another valley and tested with the same insecticide under the same conditions were killed at a rate of 80 to 90 per cent. The only explanation was that this is a new race resistant to the pesticide.

COMMONER: I hate to persist, but let me propose a hypothesis regarding the reason for the difficulties that you have all reported.

The hypothesis would be this: that the difficulty with the kind of scientific work which has been done on insect control, at least in relation to your problem, is that it is concerned directly, and narrowly, with the artificial control of insects directly rather than leading from an analysis of the interaction between insects and plants in nature, and deriving from that analysis a view of how man could best control a given insect pest.

BOZA BARDUCCI: You are right.

SMITH: I think he is wrong. (Laughter.)

COMMONER: Let me try to spell out what I mean. I notice that the invention of the alfalfa strip is regarded as a discovery. You say this is a new thing. It is *not* a new thing. After all, plants grew in a mixed way in nature long before man. Alfalfa and cotton and other things were all intermingled. What has been rediscovered here in a crude way, I would assert, is the impact of the complexity of the distribution of plants on the control of any given insect population—through the harboring of predators, the nursery effect, and so on.

What impressed me is that this group of scientists had to turn to a natural phenomenon only after they had been beaten over the head by the failure of the chemical in-

secticides. What is there about the system of science that failed to teach students of entomology the way in which insects and plants have lived together in nature?

SMITH: The warnings are all there. Entomologists have been making these warnings for one hundred years.

COMMONER: They have?

SMITH: And in the Cañete Valley in 1949, the warning was there: Don't use these pesticides.

COMMONER: So why were they used?

SMITH: The farmers insisted on using them. They insisted on trying them: they went ahead and used them: they had to go into a crisis before a change came about.

BOZA BARDUCCI: I would like to explain that. When we came to the Cañete Valley in the year 1949, the first problem was the aphid, and then came the leafworm.

We tried to induce the farmer to use insecticides to do the controlling and then also to use some crop regulation to prevent the spread of this insect.

They didn't like that, first because of the publicity all over the world about the good results obtained with new insecticides.

Second, the local big publicity given by the big companies who produce insecticides was most effective. They released pamphlets which on one side showed a field without application of the new insecticide. Like Professor Rivnay described, these showed no bolls at all, and no fruit.

On the other side, they told of successful crops treated with so-and-so insecticide. This was the modern way to push people into using their material!

The people saw these promotional materials and said, "Well, Professor, why do you want to change this modern method, since we can easily use more insecticide without complicating our lives." Meanwhile, a company to market pesticides, and another to spray from planes, were established in the valley. Even more pressure was applied to use them.

I insisted on our program; but these men insisted on using the pesticides. So we used them. But certainly, after seven years of use, they came back to the same proposition that I gave them originally.

SMITH: I had the pleasant opportunity to visit Cañete Valley last spring. Many of the growers there now do not remember the crisis of 1956. They are new farmers. As a result, the cultural controls and the careful use of pesticides Boza Barducci has described have lost their impetus.

So there is this continued evolution of a system even in that one valley. And, remember, the Cañete Valley is one system. What worked out there does not apply except to a couple of adjacent valleys in Peru. There is a different system when you go to other valleys.

GEORGE: I would like, in a most friendly manner, to challenge your use of the term agro-ecology, Dr. Smith. I think what we are seeing, really, is the idea that perhaps the agriculturalist is not viewing crop production in a fully ecological manner. For example, they are participating in a much larger ecosystem. The insecticides are influencing far more than just your crops. What happens to stream life and the life of marine bays nearby?

I like to think that maybe the agriculturalist is going to have to be increasingly aware of the influence of his crop practice on the surrounding environmental situation.

SMITH: By all means. This is exactly my viewpoint, that there should be an increasingly ecological viewpoint of how crops are grown and managed, including how pest control is carried out. My term was "agro-ecosystem," and I use the prefix "agro" to emphasize the features which are different or unique in agricultural ecosystems. The forester now talks about multiple use of the forest, and that concept could be in our agro-ecosystem, too.

GILLHAM: Mr. Chairman, I would like to come back for a moment to what Dr. Commoner was saying, and comment on our own situation in Central Africa.

Between 1920 and 1959, the average cotton yield in Rhodesia was about 250 pounds of seed cotton to the acre. During that period, we were relying entirely on jassid-resistant varieties because without the jassid resistance, the jassid was so severe that we couldn't produce anything. This practice, as I mentioned, was probably increasing the susceptibility of the crop to *Heliothis*. But there was nothing we could do about that.

Since introducing an insect control program based on controlled use of insecticides, using the correct insecticides for the insects that are actually present, the average yield for the country has been increased to about 1,100 pounds of seed cotton to the acre, even though we have had a whole string of drought years; irrigated areas in some cases have grown in excess of 5,000 pounds to the acre. Without the use of insecticides at the present time, these irrigated areas would not be able to produce anything because of the severe attack both of the *Empoasca* and the cotton stainer.

Our recommendations are based on using the correct insecticide for the particular species that is there. However, this opens the way for abuse because the farmer has to get in there and scout and know what is in his field. It is very tempting for the commercial people to come along and sell a program based on routine spraying of a cocktail of insecticides. And this is being done. And this is where the danger lies.

The scouting is also effective in giving an early warning of any buildup of insect resistance. So far we have had suggestions of resistance in red spider mites, *Tetranychus,* which has been coming in earlier as a result of the use of insecticides like DDT. But in all cases investigated so far, the supposed resistance has been more a question of incorrect timing or incorrect technique in applying insecticide which has led to its failure.

In one case during the past season, effective control of the red spider mite was obtained in an area where resistance had previously been suspected, by doing all the spraying before eight o'clock in the morning, before the temperature got too high. This question of timing and correct methods is just as important as using the correct insecticide for the particular pest that is there.

SCUDDER: I would like to follow up on Dr. Commoner's line of reasoning from a slightly different angle.

If you look at the archaeological record, there is extensive evidence of the growing of cotton in the past. To deal with the area I know best, Central Africa, Fagan's evidence from the Middle Zambezi Valley, a site called Ingombe Llede in Zambia, indicates that cotton was grown there in the seventeenth century and apparently had been grown there through a fairly extended period of time. I think that if the system of agriculture today is anything like the system of agriculture in that area used to be, there may be quite a bit to learn from this old, extensive cultivation of cotton.

Of course, there was no pure cropping of cotton. There would have been a heavy weed population. There would have been intentional interplanting with leguminous crops, with cucurbits and with grains in an area which we know has a heavy density and variety of malvaceous plants and also is populated by a very large proportion of the insect pests which have been reported from Central Africa.

Yet apparently, judging from the archaeological records, cotton was grown through extended periods of time in such areas prior, of course, to the use of pesticides. I am wondering whether entomologists have looked into the archaeological records and thought about their implications in terms of devising more natural agricultural systems for the present.

SMITH: In Ecuador today we have the two systems of cotton culture existing side by side. Cotton is grown by Indians on hillsides right next to bottom lands growing modern cottons; one system using essentially no insecticides and the other system using too much insecticide.

SCUDDER: Is there evidence on what yields are maintained?

SMITH: Very low yields of low quality cotton in most cases in the hill area, but with very low cost of production.

SCUDDER: On the other hand, some of these societies have very heavy population densities, especially where cotton was perhaps grown under irrigation. And it presumably was meeting a large proportion of the fiber needs. Perhaps they were getting very heavy yields in the past.

COMMONER: Dr. Smith, the point I would like to make is not that one should go back to this interplanted, scattered type of agriculture because, obviously, you wouldn't get the interest on your investment back, so to speak. It is simply uneconomical.

Rather, what I am saying is that research aiming toward a truly economical agricultural system might start from these natural systems and devise ways to achieve natural insect regulation, such as by interpenetration of crops, and yet organize the planting physically in such a way as to make economical harvesting and treatment feasible.

One obvious thing is strip planting, interlayered agriculture. I should think it wouldn't make too much economic difference if the farmer, instead of working three successive plots of different types of crops, had the three of them interpenetrated and simply went over the same plot three times with different machines.

SMITH: There are some management problems in this type of plan too. Many of these ideal things you can do only in a highly developed agriculture where you have irrigation water piped into the field in such a way that you can move in and out of all the plots easily.

With alfalfa, for example, this approach

works if you do the stripping of the alfalfa next door to cotton and have alfalfa in two height levels. But even though this is a proven thing, we have not been able to sell it extensively to the farmers. The man that grows the alfalfa is not always the man who is growing the cotton next door.

MILTON: Dr. Smith, could you enlarge on how we might develop more effective institutional responsibility for your broader concept of the agro-ecosystem? For example, if the farmer and the local agricultural industry are mostly interested in cotton and perhaps some other related crop production problems, who is looking into the environmental responsibility for impact on fisheries, river systems and human health which also may be related to the insecticides sprayed in these cotton-producing areas?

SMITH: I think cotton entomologists have a responsibility in this, but there are other people concerned. And somebody else here in this room perhaps can speak better to that.

MILTON: Let me enlarge on my question. I am wondering who has the responsibility to investigate, integrate, and communicate to the decision-makers and public all the necessary information relevant to the ecosystems being affected by spraying or other agricultural technologies. You may be spraying for the purpose of controlling cotton pests. Yet the spraying will have an impact on a much broader ecosystem than the cotton agricultural system alone. Who takes on the responsibility for looking into these other impacts? If no one does, then how do we develop such ecologically-concerned institutions in the less-developed regions of the world?

HEDGPETH: Even in the state of California, nobody has done this. (Laughter.)

MARSHALL: Along the lines of John Milton's comments, one wonders about the effect of interaction between certain types of vector-borne diseases, primarily malaria, and the use of insecticides for the control of cotton pests. You may be selecting for resistant mosquitoes by the wide use of pesticides against cotton pests.

SMITH: Well, mosquito abatement people are doing this well enough all by themselves. They have been rapidly producing resistant mosquitoes due to mosquito abatement control activities. This bothers me and I will challenge you, Joel Hedgpeth, that nobody is worrying about it in California.

HEDGPETH: I didn't mean nobody is worried about ecosystem pollution; I said there is no central organization or person responsible. The people worried about the rivers are neither agriculturalists nor very good ecologists. They have been improperly manned and funded.

BOULDING: I think what you are worrying about is something very hairy, indeed, and that is the corruption of science which is a very real danger now. It is sometimes called a Constantinization of science. That is, science now is in about the position that Christianity was at the time of Constantine. (Laughter.)

Science, as an ideology, is in grave danger of being taken over. On the other hand, we have a counter-ideology here, an ecological ideology which you might call the defense ideology. That is, the attitude of our ecological papers analyzing insecticides is almost exactly like that of the Air Force toward Communism. (Laughter.)

I have a little rhyme on it here if you don't mind:

By undiscriminating use of strong insecticide
Our temporary gain is lost when all our
  friends have died.
With strip planting of alfalfa something new
  is making sense:
Spend the millions now on tribute—not a
  penny for defense!

(Laughter.)

There is something in this: the ecological point of view is profoundly antithetical toward war on anything, whether this is insects or poverty. You see, the War on Poverty means eliminating the poor. (Laughter.)

This is a very general philosophical principle.

M. T. FARVAR: I want to go back, if I may, for a moment to the problems in the Cañete Valley. And the reason is this: To me as a member of the educated class in the underdeveloped countries, the story of the Cañete Valley seems to be a microcosm of a very, very widespread problem which extends far beyond cotton in an isolated valley. In effect, it is a mental problem.

It seems to me that we, the educated people (including the agricultural engineers and all the way down the line) are virtually raped by some of the techniques used in the introduction of technology: for example, the very effective marketing pictures showing on the one side the enemy (an insect doing damage), and on the other side the field after victory has been achieved by means of the Knight in Armor— the insecticide produced by company X, coming to the rescue on a white horse. We take this, we begin to believe it ourselves. Then we become agents trying to convince everybody else in our countries; we become

Constantinized and become the apostles of truth and all of a sudden believe that everything that the peasants, our peasant brethren, let us say, have been doing for thousands of years is wrong and we have got to change that, *and now*.

In the Middle East, at least, we find that the peasants are at first resistant to the technology, and then we do our best to sweep them off their feet, and they finally fall for the public relations pictures, *et cetera*. And they then say: "All right, it really looks good. So let's do it and, furthermore, profit from it!" The education we receive abroad also serves to reinforce these values. We take the recommendations of the Memphis Conference or the agricultural textbooks too seriously. We transplant this alien technology on our soils. Some say the problem is that there is little adaptive research. But it is more fundamental than that, because in the "advanced" countries, too, the technology (e.g., pest control) is based on the wrong foundation, i.e., the use of pesticides. As a result one has the situation in South Texas where the end of the rope has been reached in that there is no insecticide available to economically control *Heliothis* populations on cotton.

25. ECOLOGICAL ASPECTS OF PEST CONTROL IN MALAYSIA*

Gordon R. Conway

The use of broad-spectrum contact-acting insecticides has increased considerably in Malaysia over the past fifteen years. This has brought considerable benefits, notably in the control of rice pests, locusts, and mosquitoes. However, the experience of entomologists working with the pest problems of cocoa and oil palms has shown that under certain conditions such insecticides may aggravate existing problems or create new ones. Both these crops have been planted on an extensive scale only since the Second World War. At first, the damage they suffered from pests was relatively minor, but when growers embarked on programs of heavy applications of various contact-acting insecticides, major outbreaks of a number of pests, notably bagworms, ensued. All the pests involved were indigenous to Malaysia, and it would seem that under the conditions of the local environment, they are normally kept under control by their natural enemies. Use of the contact-acting insecticides appears to have resulted in a heavy mortality of these enemy species, which allowed the pests to break out. The serious situations which developed on both crops were corrected in many cases by stopping the use of these insecticides, and thus natural control of the pests was re-established. In other cases more selective insecticides were found which gave good control of the pest species without interfering with their enemies or those of other pests.

In retrospect it can be seen that selective control measures should have been employed at the outset. On a third crop, rubber, this has been the case. An

* The material in this paper was originally published in different form as "Pests Follow the Chemicals in the Cocoa of Malaysia" by Gordon R. Conway in *Natural History*. Copyright © 1969, The American Museum of Natural History.

integrated control program has been devised against the grubs of cockchafer beetles which cause serious damage to rubber in certain localities. The program relies on restricted application of insecticide and careful timing of light trapping so that there is little likelihood of mortality of natural enemy species while producing effective control of the pests.

In addition to producing pest problems directly, use of broad-spectrum contact-acting insecticides can also result in far-reaching side effects, as experience with the mosquito control campaign in the Borneo states has shown. The campaigns have been extremely effective in their primary objective, and the incidence of malaria has been greatly reduced, but the reliance on spraying with DDT has resulted in at least two unwanted side effects. First, there have been outbreaks of a larva which feeds on the thatch roofs of the houses. Second, the spraying has induced a chain reaction whereby the DDT has been picked up by other house-dwelling insects such as cockroaches and passed on either directly or via lizards to domestic cats. Such accumulations frequently have been lethal, and the consequent loss of the cat population in many villages has resulted in outbreaks of rats with the attendant hazard of spreading serious disease.

Malaysia, comprising mainland Malaya and the Borneo states of Sabah and Sarawak, lies just north of the equator (Fig. 25–1). It has a hot, humid climate with average daily temperatures varying from 70° to 90° F and, in most areas, an annual rainfall of over 100 inches without any very marked dry season. Tropical rain forest is the predominant natural climax vegetation, and it still covers over 70% of the land area. The

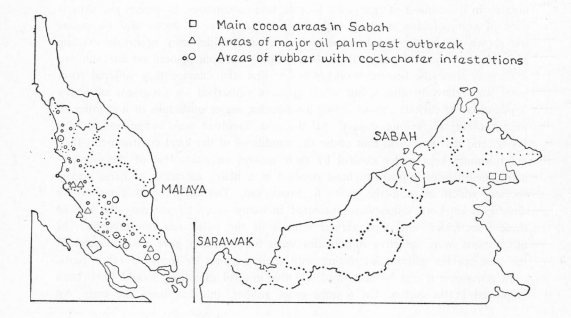

Figure 25–1   Malaysia, showing the agricultural regions and some of the pest outbreaks discussed

main crops are wet rice, rubber, oil palms, and coconuts, and in certain localities there are also fairly large acreages of cocoa, manila hemp (abaca), sago, and pepper. Vegetables and fruit are widely grown but usually on a small scale. Shifting cultivation based on dry rice, tapioca, vegetables, and bananas is still commonly practiced, particularly in the Borneo states; in consequence, secondary forest is widespread, and in some areas, where the land has deteriorated seriously, extensive stands of lalang grass (*Imperata cylindrica*) are present.

Crop pests and their control have been the subjects of research in Malaysia for the past fifty years. Before the Second World War attention was focused mainly on the pest problems of rice, coconuts, vegetables, and fruit. The entomologists working on these problems, like their colleagues working in the then Dutch East Indies, employed an approach which was dominated by ecological considerations. See, for example, the papers of Corbett (1930, 1932), Miller (1940), and Pagden (1930), and the books of Dammerman (1929) and Kalshoven (1950–51). They made a considerable effort to understand the habits and life histories both of the pests and their natural enemies and how these were affected by the weather and the cropping pattern. The control programs they devised relied heavily on sound cultural practices, such as the careful timing of planting and the destruction of crop residues, and the encouragement of natural enemies wherever possible. Often quite elaborate steps were taken to ensure the presence of particular parasites or predators in a crop. These measures were supplemented by light trapping or by collecting insects with simple mechanical devices or even by hand. Pesticides when used were in the form of arsenicals, derris, or various soap and kerosene mixtures. It is difficult to judge, now, just how successful these control measures were. Un-

doubtedly, many outbreaks were prevented and others which did develop probably were brought to an end much sooner than would have occurred naturally. But for chronic pest problems such as those on rice, the control measures seem to have been only marginally effective. The best results were obtained on mostly small-holder vegetable and fruit crops, but in these cases the patience and intensive care of the grower and his family were the decisive factors.

After the war, the new synthetic insecticides, DDT, BHC, dieldrin, endrin, malathion, and others, became available. Their use in Malaysia grew slowly at first but has accelerated in the last fifteen years with the establishment of several vigorous concerns specializing in the sale of agricultural chemicals. BHC, DDT, and dieldrin have been particularly effective against rice pests (Lever, 1966–67); in Sabah dieldrin has provided a cheap and effective means of combating the locust outbreaks which had previously been so serious; DDT and dieldrin have also been the main instruments of the successful malaria control campaigns. However, my experiences and those of other entomologists in Malaysia suggest that the increasing reliance on these pesticides has not been wholly beneficial. Used indiscriminantly and without regard to the ecological factors of the situation, they may aggravate existing pest problems or create new ones, and they can produce unwanted and far-reaching side effects.

In the following I attempt to summarize some of these experiences. Inevitably, much remains open to conjecture. Entomologists confronted with immediate pest problems have often not the time or resources to unravel all the complex relationships which might seem relevant or to obtain firm proof of deductions based on cursory observations. Frequently, the only proof lies in the success of control measures based on these deductions.

COCOA PESTS IN SABAH

Cocoa is a new crop in Sabah; the first commercial plantings were made in 1956. Ten years later there were some 6,000 acres under cultivation, mostly in the southeast corner of the state at Quoin Hill and Tiger where there are large areas of volcanic soils. In 1958 a Cocoa Research Station was set up by the Department of Agriculture at Quoin Hill, and as entomologist in the department from 1961 to 1966, I was concerned with cocoa pest problems there and throughout the country. Brief references to this work have appeared in a number of previous papers (Conway, 1964, 1968; Conway and Tay, 1969; Conway and Wood, 1964) and a fully detailed account is to be published shortly (Conway, 1969).

The soils which were chosen for cocoa planting naturally support rich stands of primary dipterocarp forest. In the areas to be planted the forest species yielding commercial timber were first felled and extracted by levering on runways to prevent soil damage. Some second-story trees and regenerating dominants were left as top shade for the cocoa, and the remainder were felled, partially cut, and left to decompose. Secondary forest trees such as *Macaranga, Mellotus,* and *Acanthocephala* were then allowed controlled growth to provide the main shade.

As the cocoa acreage has grown, the primary forest has been pushed back, but the cocoa remains essentially an island within it. Much of the cocoa is thus physically close to primary forest. In some parts, at the forest edge, along roads, and at uncultivated clearings, it also borders on uncontrolled secondary scrub or forest.

EARLY PESTS, 1958–1960

The first serious insect pests at the Cocoa Research Station were borers—a ring bark borer, *Endoclita hosei,* which is the larva of a hepialid or swift moth, and two branch borers, *Zeuzera* spp., the larvae of cossid moths. The former bores into the young cocoa tree, either at ground level or at the fork, and from the shelter of the tunnel feeds on the bark, girdling the trunk and often causing the death of the tree. The branch borers, as their name implies, tunnel along the upper branches and shoots. Attacked branches usually die above the boring site. Neither pest was initially present in large numbers, but the extensive damage caused by individual ring bark borer larvae immediately made them serious pests. During the first two years of growth, when the cocoa is at its most susceptible, deaths often amounted to 20% or more per field. The earliest attempts at control were by hand; laborers were employed to seek out fresh borings and destroy the larvae inside by inserting a wire or by introducing paradichlorbenzene crystals or a dieldrin mixture. The labor involved in this method soon became too costly, and in 1959 spraying with high concentrations of insecticides was adopted. Dieldrin or DDT was applied as high-volume spray to the branches, fork, and trunk (dieldrin at 15 to 25 ounces and DDT at 12 to 15 ounces active ingredient per acre). This did give some degree of control, but the inaccessibility of the borer larvae precluded very high kills.

In 1959 several other pests, including various leaf-eating caterpillars, aphids, and mealy bugs became noticeable. Again, these were present in very low numbers, but they were felt to be a potential danger and in early 1960, in addition to the spraying for borer control, further general spraying was carried out as a prophylactic measure. Dieldrin, endrin, DDT, BHC, lead arsenate, and a white oil (Albolineum) were variously used, either in combination or alone. Applications were irregular but often frequent so that during 1960 and 1961 the cocoa received a very heavy insecticide coverage (Table 25–1).

Table 25-1

SPRAYING PROGRAM OF A REPRESENTATIVE FIELD AT THE COCOA RESEARCH STATION,
QUOIN HILL, 1960-1965*

	1960 **ND	1961 JFMAMJJASOND	1962 JFMAMJJASOND	1963 JFMAMJJASOND	1964 JFMAMJJASOND	1965 JFMAMJJASOND
Endrin	(+)	++				
Dieldrin	(+)+	+	+			
DDT	+	+ + +	++			
BHC (Technical)	+	+ + + +			+	
Lindane					+ +	+ +
Lead Arsenate		+ ++ +	+	+		
Trichlorphon			+++ ++++	+++		
Albolineum	+	+				

+ = one application, (+) = two applications.

* Letters in columns refer to months of the year.

**Detailed records are not available before November 1960, but the heavy spraying began some ten months earlier.

Major Pest Outbreaks, 1961

The situation, however, gradually became worse (Fig. 25–2). First, the branch borers increased. By the beginning of 1961, the incidence of attack rose to one new boring per six trees per month. Then outbreaks occurred of three other pests. Two were leaf-eating caterpillars—one a looper or geometrid, *Hyposidra talaca;* the other a nettle caterpillar or limacodid, *Setora nitens,* which was hitherto known in Sabah only as a major, periodic pest of coconuts. The third outbreak was of a flatid or plant hopper, *Colobesthes falcata.* All of these became very abundant. The leaf-eating caterpillars caused considerable damage to the young green pods, although the damage this caused was of lesser consequence.

In July of 1961 a fourth outbreak occurred which proved the most serious of all. This outbreak involved several species of bagworms (Psychidae), the principal ones being two species of *Clania* and an unidentified species of *Mahasena.* Bagworms are unusual insects with a number of characteristics which make them particularly troublesome pests. As the name implies, the larval bagworm lives in a bag of silk which is covered with pieces of leaf or short lengths of twig. When moving or feeding, only the head, thorax, and legs are exposed, and when disturbed, the whole larva quickly retracts into the bag, closing up the open end. The bag is retained throughout the larval and pupal periods; as the larva grows, it is extended and new leaves or twigs are added. The adult male is a typical winged moth, but the female is wingless and "degenerate," being little more than a large, egg-producing sac which stays within the pupal case inside the bag. Numerous eggs are produced (from 3,000 to 4,000 in the case of the related *Mahasena corbetti*), and they too are retained in the bag. On hatching, the young larvae make their way onto the surface where they quickly spin their own bags,

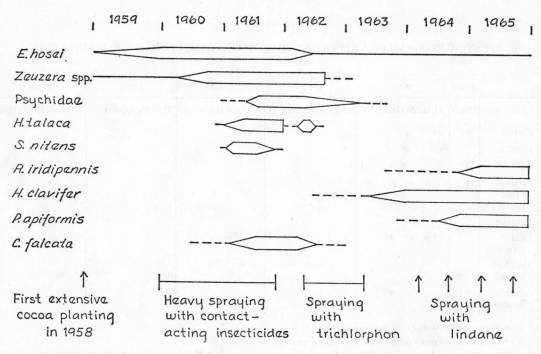

Figure 25–2 The sequence of pest outbreaks at the Cocoa Research Station, Quoin Hill, Sabah (Note that this is very schematic; the bars do not directly indicate the size of the population, only the periods during which the species was of economic importance as a pest.)

covering them with material from their parents' bag. They also produce copious silk threads and, with the help of these, are blown away, often over a long distance.

The bags give the insect protection throughout its lifetime, not only from the weather but also, apparently, from insecticides. In a series of replicated trials with bagworms on sprayed cocoa seedlings, they showed almost complete resistance to DDT, BHC, dieldrin, diazinon, and dimethoate, all applied to run off at 0.25% active ingredient or more. Some feeding occurred in the trials, but apparently the amount of insecticide ingested was not sufficient to cause mortality. The bags prevented the insecticides from acting through contact. Removing the larvae from their bags and dipping them in the same insecticides, at the previous concentrations, gave rapid and complete

kills as compared with control larvae dipped in water.

The damage caused by bagworms is very serious. Not only are they voracious feeders, but they also chew off large areas of leaf surface to make their bags. As defoliation progresses, extensive dieback of the branches occurs and the trees respond by proliferation of shoots from unaffected buds which are, in turn, eaten. With extreme defoliation, the bagworms turn to feeding on the bark. Because of the reproductive and dispersal characteristics, outbreaks occur in the form of explosions which radiate out from a central focus. The outbreak of 1961 began in one field at the Cocoa Research Station and rapidly spread in this fashion. By late 1961 some 70 acres were affected, and repeated defoliation had produced large numbers of bare and dying trees.

Spraying with DDT, dieldrin, and the other insecticides continued throughout 1961, but the bagworm outbreak persisted unaffected. Some attempt at hand collection was made, but this proved ineffective and very costly. With the exception of the nettle caterpillar, *S. nitens,* which died out in September, the other outbreaks also continued.

CESSATION OF SPRAYING, END OF 1961

In October of 1961, with the pest situation extremely serious, a decision was made to stop the spraying. Although some pests had been present since the beginning of cocoa planting, it was only after the introduction of the heavy spraying program that the major outbreaks had occurred. Further, nearly all the insecticides used had been of the broad-spectrum, contact-acting type: that is, they killed most insects which came in contact with them. Since parasitic and predatory insects tend to explore widely, they are more likely to contact insecticide deposits than are pest insects, particularly when these are relatively stationary, leaf-eating caterpillars. Differential mortality then occurs and the pest species are able to escape from the control imposed by their natural enemies. By stopping the spraying, it was felt that there would then be a chance for the re-establishment of some degree of natural control.

NATURAL CONTROL RE-ESTABLISHED, 1962

The level of spraying was reduced in October and November and finally stopped in December, except for two fields which had exceptionally severe bagworm infestations and were sprayed twice more, in January and February. Almost immediately a braconid parasite, a species of *Apanteles,* appeared in large numbers and attacked the looper, *H. talaca.* Twenty or more parasites developed in each larva. The looper popu-lation dropped suddenly and remained low until May when it flared back, only to be followed by another parasite buildup. Within three to four weeks, the population had again declined, this time to a level at which damage was negligible. In April and May it became evident that the plant hopper, *C. falcata,* also was declining rapidly. Although there was some evidence of predation and an entomophagous fungus was present, the cause for the decline was not obvious. It continued and by August the hoppers were present in only very small numbers.

The next pests to come under control were the branch borers. These had persisted in abundance through the first half of 1962, continuing to inflict severe damage. But in August a decline in new borings became noticeable, and when a sample of borings were opened and examined, it was found that over 50% of the branch borer larvae were parasitized by braconid wasps, belonging mostly to the genus *Iphiaulax.* The population continued to decrease rapidly so that at the end of September, few new borings were to be found and by the end of the year, the damage was infrequent.

SELECTIVE CONTROL MEASURES, 1962

Following the cessation of spraying, it was felt that the damage caused by the looper and plant hopper and to a lesser extent by the branch borer could be tolerated without taking any action other than waiting and hoping that natural control would be re-established. However, the damage caused by the ring bark borer and by the bagworms was too severe to be ignored for any length of time, and attention was turned to finding selective means of control which would not interfere with any natural control being re-established over the other species.

As mentioned above, although the ring bark borer damage was severe, the population present was not very high. Thus it was decided to revert to inspection and eradication of individual borers. More labor was available for this form of control because the general spraying program was being stopped. Small teams were organized to inspect the cocoa and treat new borings with a jet of 1% dieldrin from a hand sprayer. Since the life cycle of the ring bark borer is very long, probably up to a year in duration, it was thought that an initial blitz of two inspections a month followed by others at monthly intervals would bring the population down to tolerable levels which could then be maintained by much more infrequent inspections. By applying the insecticide in this extremely localized fashion, there was also little possibility of affecting the natural enemies of the other pests. A second control measure resulted from the discovery that an important alternative host of the borer was a secondary forest tree, *Trema cannabina*. This tree was not only common in the cocoa fields but was also present in nearly pure stands along roadsides and in other areas. Individual trees were often found supporting several borer larvae at once, living in a complex of tunnels. In the cocoa fields such trees were acting as foci for the borer infestations and, therefore, steps were taken to eradicate *Trema* from the fields and from much of the surrounding areas. Combining these two measures proved immediately effective, and borer damage dropped off rapidly. In most fields from 1962 onward, mortality in new plantings during the first two years was well below 0.5%.

In the case of the bagworms an intensive search was carried out in the hope of finding a selective insecticide which would give control. Finally, in March of 1962, samples of trichlorphon (Dipterex) and of a preparation of the bacterium *Bacillus thuringiensis* (Thuricide) were obtained and in a series of trials with sprayed cocoa seedlings were found to give rapid and complete mortality. Elsewhere, trichlorphon had been shown to

have considerable selective properties (Bartlett, 1963); it is only of moderate toxicity to such insects as the parasitic wasps, and it is a persistent stomach-acting insecticide with only short-lived contact action. *Bacillus thuringiensis* similarly is selective, causing mortality mostly to larvae of lepidopterous pests, such as the bagworms. Of the two, trichlorphon was the more readily available, and a high volume test spraying of an infested field with 0.25% spray appeared to give a very high kill. Regular monthly spraying of the infested 45 acres at the Cocoa Research Station was thus begun in May. The trichlorphon was applied at about .75 pound active ingredient per acre. The treatment brought about an immediate effect; the bagworm population dropped rapidly and the trees began to recover, putting out new flushes of leaves which were able to survive. Later it became evident that kills were not as high as they had first appeared and the hope of obtaining complete control with two or three applications was not realized. Spraying at monthly intervals was continued, though, and gradually control was obtained. The population dropped lower each month with occasional mild resurgences. By April of 1963 the population was very low and the damage insignificant; the sprayings were stopped.

Thus, during 1962, most of the pests which had been important in 1960 and 1961 had succumbed to natural control or, as in the case of the ring bark borer and the bagworms, were under effective and selective artificial control. In 1963 trichlorphon spraying of the bagworms was no longer needed, and the high incidence of tachinid flies in the remaining individuals suggested that these parasites were now responsible for keeping them in check. Significantly, in the subsequent five years, none of these pests have built up again.

The commercial cocoa estates near Quoin Hill were urged to follow the example of the Cocoa Research Station, and in early 1962 most of them abandoned the use of contact-acting insecticides. Their experience was the same: most of the major pests numerically declined in 1962 and have remained at low, insignificant levels ever since. The control measures devised against bagworms and the ring bark borer were also widely adopted with similar success. The situation has been different on only one estate which persisted in the use of contact-acting insecticides; it has continued to be plagued by branch borer damage and by periodic outbreaks of bagworms and other leaf-eating caterpillars.

LATER PROBLEMS, 1963 TO THE PRESENT

The story is not quite complete because other pest problems have arisen subsequently. In 1963 two mirid species, the mosquito bug, *Helopeltis clavifer,* and the bee bug, *Platyngomirioides apiformis,* appeared in the cocoa at the research station and on other cocoa estates in the area. Both species slowly, but not uniformly, spread through the cocoa, and were mostly present in small pockets. Their numbers have never been high but the damage caused can be severe. The developing and the maturing pods are attacked primarily, the bugs feeding through their needle-like mouthparts and producing lesions which subsequently provide a ready entry point for pathogenic fungi. It has been estimated for a related mirid species that a single individual can produce ten to fifty lesions a day (De Silva, 1960), so that the potential damage of even a small population is great. In West Africa where the damage has been particularly severe, control has centered on the use of lindane (gamma BHC) sprays. When the mirids first appeared in Sabah, no action was taken, but as the level of damage increased, lindane was sprayed; the West African recommendation of applying 4 ounces of active ingredient per acre by low-volume mist blower was followed. Lindane was not an ideal choice. It is a contact-acting insecticide, and

there is some evidence that in West Africa it has upset control by natural enemies (Entwistle *et al.,* 1959). However, at the time a better alternative was not available. In an endeavor to keep such possible effects to a minimum, spraying was restricted to twice a year prior to the fruiting seasons; and where the infestation was localized, only spot spraying was carried out.

Lindane spraying in this manner has continued to the time of this writing, and the mirids have been kept economically under control. With the exception of one pest, an eumolpid beetle, *Rhyparida iridipennis,* no other pest problems of any severity have arisen. The beetle was first noticed in a small pocket in 1963, and toward the end of 1964 it began to spread through the cocoa, pockets appearing mostly at the edges of fields. It has never become very abundant, but the damage caused by the adult beetles feeding along the veins of the young flush leaves has been important. The beetle is partially susceptible to trichlorphon and lead arsenate (a selective stomach-poison pesticide). Some spot-spraying with these insecticides has been carried out, but a really effective form of control is still being sought. Possibly, if a more selective replacement for lindane such as a systemic insecticide were found, then some degree of natural control for the beetle might be re-established.

There have been a few minor pest problems. The young cocoa in its first year is particularly susceptible to leaf damage caused by crickets and caterpillars and to mealy bugs attacking the growing points. Often this can be ignored, but, if necessary, it can be effectively curtailed by limited applications of trichlorphon or lead arsenate against the leaf-eating pests or a white oil against the mealy bugs. The cocoa remains rich in fauna with many potential pests present including a number of species such as the noctuids *Spodoptera litura* and *Heliothis armigera,* which are notorious for their damage to tropical crops. But it would seem that a stable faunal balance has arisen over the past five or more years which generally keeps the pest potential well in check.

SUMMARY

All the insects on cocoa in Sabah, including the pest species, are indigenous. At first, it was thought that they had come from the primary forest. But the discovery that the ring bark borer was present and tolerated in large numbers in *Trema* strongly suggested that this secondary forest tree was a primary and original host and raised the possibility that other cocoa pests had a similar origin. On further examination several secondary forest trees, such as *Macaranga* and *Acanthocephala,* were found to be common hosts of the ring bark borer and the plant hopper and occasionally several other pests. A search of the literature showed that in other countries where these cocoa pests also occur their recorded wild hosts are predominantly or exclusively secondary forest, or in some cases riverine, plants. None of this is very strong evidence. Secondary forest growth is widespread and easily inspected, which may account for the predominance of records. Until more is known of the fauna of the primary forest and particularly of the canopy foliage, the question cannot definitely be resolved. However, this rather circumstantial evidence is also backed by certain theoretical considerations.

Most of the plants of the secondary forest and of riverbanks and roadsides are essentially fugitive species. They have well-developed powers of dispersal, reproduction, and growth which enable them to rapidly colonize suitable sites as they become available. These plants are also hosts to many insects and, as Southwood has argued (1962), the insects must be adapted in the same way to this special situation. An example of an insect which shows these fugitive characteristics to an extreme is the plague caterpillar of Southeast Asia, a noc-tuid *Tiracola plagiata*. This species has an enormous reproductive potential; the eggs are laid in batches of up to 1,200 each. The caterpillars feed on a wide variety of plants, and both moths and caterpillars are very mobile (Catley, 1963b). An outbreak of the caterpillar occurred in the east of Sabah in 1965, in an area of primary forest about .75 mile long by .25 mile wide which had been cleared and allowed to develop into low secondary forest, mostly consisting of *Trema* sp. The outbreak consisted of a vast army of the caterpillars, all approximately of the same age, which moved slowly along the strip of secondary forest and finally pupated. This was in every sense a pest outbreak, except that no crop was involved. Fortunately, in Sabah very few adult moths emerged from the pupae, and the outbreak died out as suddenly as it had arisen. But in New Guinea, following such outbreaks on secondary vegetation, the caterpillar has frequently moved onto nearby crops, such as cocoa, and has become an extremely serious pest (Catley, 1963a, 1963b). Clearly, as in the case of the plague caterpillar, possession of these fugitive characteristics preadapts an insect to the role of crop pest. Many of the cocoa pests in Sabah show these characteristics to some degree, and this alone is good reason to accept that they have come from the secondary forest habitat.

But the secondary forest should not be seen only as a source of potential pests. Undoubtedly, it also supports their natural enemies and similarly their adaptation to this habitat must show characteristic fugitive features (i.e., well-developed powers of dispersal and habitat [host] finding, a high reproductive rate, and probably some degree of polyphagy).

In nature, destruction of part of the primary forest may result from earthquake, lightning, whirlwinds, flood, or perhaps more commonly from the natural death of an emergent, which in falling brings down its neighbors. Whatever the cause, this destruction creates a habitat for fugitive species and initiates a secondary forest succession. This succession begins with the colonization of the bare area by herbaceous and spreading plants. Herbivorous insects then invade the area, and as they increase in numbers, they are in turn found by parasitic and predatory insects. The latter multiply and cause the herbivorous insects to decline. But the first plant colonizers do not remain for long; they are replaced by other plants more shrubby in form. Some of the first insects can move onto these, but the newly created microhabitats bring about a second wave of herbivorous insects. In the hot, humid climate of Malaysia conditions are almost continuously favorable for growth and reproduction of both plants and insects. And so the succession goes on with new waves of colonizing plants, herbivorous insects, and their enemies, each exploding briefly and dying down.

Apparently, the clearing of the primary forest for cocoa growing in Sabah has resulted in a somewhat similar chain of events. Following the clearing, the bare areas have become colonized by secondary forest plants and by the transplanted cocoa seedlings. These plants have attracted a number of fugitive insect species. Because of the severity of the damage they cause, some of these insects have become cocoa pests. But at this point the sequence has been complicated by the intrusion of heavy applications of broad-spectrum contact-acting insecticides. In effect these seem to have either prevented the expected natural enemies from entering the crop or destroyed those which were already present and exercising some degree of control. Many of the pests, therefore, instead of exploding briefly and dying out, continued to multiply, producing major and prolonged outbreaks. It is significant that in the cocoa-growing area at Tiger, where this type of insecticide was used much less, the major pest outbreaks did not occur, and harm has been largely due to pests causing damage at low densities. At Quoin Hill cessation of the spraying at the end of 1961 appears to have corrected the situation. Most of the major outbreaks came under natural control. Only a few, mostly low density, pests were left, and these could be controlled by selective, artificial measures. As the cocoa has aged and the microhabitats have changed, other pests—as was to be expected—invaded the crop. But the absence of contact-acting insecticides has meant, for the most part, that these pests have come quickly under effective natural control, again leaving only the low density pests in need of attention.

Of course, this is a hypothetical and simplified explanation of what occurred. Undoubtedly other factors enter the picture. For example, in 1961 when the major outbreaks occurred, the rainfall was lower, and this could have been a contributing cause although similar dry periods have occurred without subsequent outbreaks. It should also be noted that the outbreak of the nettle caterpillar, *S. nitens,* died out while the heavy contact-acting insecticide spraying was still being carried on, and this could also possibly be said of the looper, *H. talaca.* This explanation does, however, appear to fit the facts better than any other; more importantly, by acting on it, effective economic control of the pest problems on cocoa has been achieved in Sabah.

OIL PALM PESTS IN MALAYA

Perhaps more convincing evidence of the role of contact-acting insecticides in causing or aggravating pest problems can be derived from experience with oil palms in Malaya. B. J. Wood, entomologist at the Chemara Research Station in Johore, has described many instances of pest outbreaks on oil palms which can be traced to the use of such insecticides. Furthermore he has been able to demonstrate this effect experimentally. Wood's findings have been referred to already in a number of publications (Conway and Wood, 1964; Wood, 1965, 1966, 1967), including a comprehensive oil palm pest handbook published recently (Wood, 1968).

Oil palms, like cocoa, are a relatively new crop in Malaysia. Although some commercial planting was carried out before the Second World War, this has only been extensive in the last twenty years (there are now some 250,000 acres). Most plantings are on a large scale, from several hundred to 20,000 acres or more. In some areas oil palms have been placed in cleared primary forest, but large plantings have also been made on old rubber land—the rubber trees being felled and burned prior to planting. Oil palm plantings, unlike cocoa, are almost pure monocultures; they do not require shade so that the only other vegetation present consists of various legumes which are planted as ground cover crops.

The crop originated in West Africa and damage by pests there has never been a major problem. At first this was also true of the Malaysian plantings. There was some minor damage attributable to cockchafers, bagworms, or nettle caterpillars, but apart from the attacks of the rhinoceros beetle, *Oryctes rhinoceros,* there was no serious damage.

BAGWORM OUTBREAKS

From 1956 onward, however, a number of severe outbreaks of bagworms and other pests have occurred. In examining these outbreaks Wood found that many had occurred following the use of contact-acting insecticides such as DDT, dieldrin, and endrin. These insecticides had begun to be used on a large scale at about that time, either as a general prophylactic measure or as a preventative for minor damage caused by cockchafers or bagworms. On one estate, for example, a contact-acting insecticide was applied in combination with a fungicide, purely as a general prophylactic measure, and a serious increase in bagworm numbers occurred. On a second estate a severe outbreak of bagworms affecting several hundred acres began around an area which had been sprayed a number of times with DDT to control cockchafers. The bagworms were in turn sprayed with DDT, but it was found that as each field was sprayed, successive bagworm outbreaks occurred in adjacent areas. Apparently, the drift of DDT from the sprayed area resulted in the destruction of natural enemies in these areas. Gradually, as the outbreaks recurred, a very wide area was sprayed and resprayed. Finally, however, spraying was stopped and despite new outbreaks occurring around the most recently sprayed fields, these too were left untreated. Soon a high degree of parasitization was noted, mainly by ichneumon wasps, and the infestation declined.

On other estates which began spraying against minor outbreaks of bagworms or the nettle caterpillar, *S. nitens,* these pests only increased and became permanently important. Thus, on one estate in Perak which began applications of contact-acting insecticides in 1956, in nearly every subsequent year they found it necessary to treat between 1,000 and 2,500 acres with endrin to control bagworms. Spraying in this fashion was still being continued in 1964. As Wood points out, all these outbreaks occurred on estates in quite different localities in Malaya, and they began at different times; but, in each case, the sequence of events was very similar.

Damage by bagworms to oil palms is as severe as to cocoa. The larvae feed on the leaves, and there is a progressive necrosis of leaf tissue with eventual skeletonization. In the first year after attack crop losses of up to 40% over hundreds of acres have been recorded following such defoliation (Wood, 1968).

Where bagworms were initially present as minor pests, they were usually of the species *Cremastopsyche pendula,* but in the major outbreaks which followed insecticide spraying, a different species, *Metisa plana,* was the more important. Prior to 1956 *M. plana* had not been recorded from oil palms at all. Wood has made a study of the biology of these bagworms and has identified a number of parasites and predators which are important in their natural control.

THE EXPERIMENTAL EVIDENCE

To test the hypothesis that the use of contact-acting insecticides was causing the bagworm outbreaks, Wood carried out a small-scale trial based on De Bach's insecticidal check technique. In an oil palm stand with a small population of bagworms of the species *M. plana,* an area of about 2 acres was given a number of very light mist sprays with an insecticide often recommended to control the pest. As he had expected, an explosive bagworm increase resulted in the sprayed and surrounding areas. Counts across the sprayed plot and for up to half a mile away in six different directions clearly showed that the sprayed central area was the point of heaviest buildup, with a gradual decline away from the center in all directions.

SELECTIVE CONTROL

While it was perhaps possible to find alternative explanations for these bagworm outbreaks and for the results of the experiment, Wood was personally convinced that the hypothesis was correct and began a search for more selective forms of control which would allow the oil palm growers to abandon the use of contact-acting insecticides. Lead arsenate had been used against bagworms before the war, and it was known to have little effect on natural enemies. Applied at about 4 pounds per acre, it proved fairly effective, but the kill was not very rapid. In order to obtain a better kill, Wood turned to trichlorphon (Dipterex). Ground trials soon showed that it was more rapidly effective than lead arsenate and, in fact, was comparable to endrin in this respect.

Trichlorphon has been subsequently adopted on a large scale in Malaysia for bagworm control. Wood has developed an effective census technique which allows for the correct placing and timing of application which, like the contact-acting insecticides, is usually carried out from the air. The results have been very encouraging. Widespread outbreaks of *M. plana,* affecting areas of up to 3,000 acres, have been dealt with remarkably effectively. After a single application of trichlorphon, populations averaging up to fifty bagworm larvae per frond have been virtually eliminated. At the most only mild resurgences have occurred. In general, where these selective measures of control have been used, the importance of bagworms as pests is declining.

SUMMARY

In his recent book (1968), Wood discusses the various possible causes of oil palm pest outbreaks in Malaysia. As with the cocoa pests in Sabah, the oil palm pests all appear to be indigenous. Many have come to the oil palm from coconuts or other cultivated palms; others have come from wild palms or other plants of the natural vegetation. The direct environmental changes brought about by oil palm cultivation have thus been one such set of causes. For example, the presence of rotting logs and stumps of wild palms or previously cultivated oil palms or rubber provide breeding sites for rhinoceros beetles. Similarly, the opening of the previously shaded area before planting and the consequent changes in ground vegetation contribute to the buildup of such pests as grasshoppers and cockchafers.

However, Wood considers, as do I, that the key to understanding the causes of most of these outbreaks lies in the recognition of the importance of natural enemies in regulating potential pest species. Perennial tree crops in Malaysia, such as oil palms and cocoa, mostly support a rich herbivorous insect fauna. When mature, they provide a relatively stable habitat with almost continuously favorable climatic conditions and an abundance of potential food; yet these insects rarely become abundant. The only obvious explanation is that they are kept in check by their natural enemies. Casual observation of many pests on such crops suggests that high levels of parasitism and predation are the normal rule. A graphic example is furnished by the outbreaks of the leaf-roller caterpillar, *Erionota thrax,* on manila hemp (abaca) in Sabah (Conway and Tay, 1969). For half of the year this caterpillar is heavily attacked by two species of parasitic wasps. In August, however, the population begins to increase, reaching a peak at the beginning of the following year. During the growth of the outbreak the parasites are seldom in evidence; but in February and March they suddenly reappear in huge swarms, and the leaf-roller outbreak comes to a sudden end.

Thus, in looking for the cause of most outbreaks, we have to consider factors which could upset regulation by natural enemies. One such factor is the weather which, despite the lack of extremes, at certain times may favor pest species rather than their enemies. Some evidence is that the numbers of leaf-eating caterpillars in Malaysia tend to be higher at the beginning of the year (Wood, 1968). Life cycles of enemy species may also grow out of phase with those of their hosts. Possibly a combination of this and the weather was responsible for the leaf-roller outbreaks. There are also other, less natural factors. For example, Wood draws attention to the importance of road dust on oil palm estates.

It has been observed that outbreaks of various caterpillars often begin at the side of busy roads, especially after a dry spell. Road dust can kill insects by abrasion, cutting through the cuticle which acts as a waterproof covering. This dust affects the natural enemies more than the pest species because they are usually more active and have smaller, more delicate bodies. Nevertheless, whatever other factors may cause the breakdown of natural control, it seems evident from Wood's experiences that one major factor is the use of residual contact-acting insecticides.

RUBBER PESTS IN MALAYA

The severe pest problems which arose on cocoa and oil palms, apparently as a result of the use of contact-acting insecticides, led to hurried and piecemeal attempts to obtain better control through more selective measures. Ideally, pest problems should be countered at the outset with measures of this kind, designed and executed with a thorough understanding of the biology of the pest and the ecology of the pest situation. Such an approach is now referred to as integrated pest control. As a concept, it draws much of its inspiration from the work of various California entomologists, in particular from Dr. R. F. Smith who has written widely on the subject (Smith, 1968; Smith and van den Bosch, 1967). In Malaya an integrated control program on rubber has been devised for the control of the grubs of cockchafer beetles by B. S. Rao of the Rubber Research Institute at Kuala Lumpur (1964, 1966).

As a crop, rubber is unusual; it is relatively free from pest attack. However, increasingly there are a number of pest problems which have become important economically because of the high levels of efficiency that the commercial exploitation of this crop has attained. Further, in young rubber, the ground between the trees is planted to a cover crop, and this is prone to damage, particularly by leaf-eating caterpillars. There has been some suggestion that outbreaks on these cover crops could be attributed to the use of contact-acting insecticides. Therefore, when control measures were being sought for the cockchafer damage, an attempt was made to keep such insecticide use to a minimum.

THE COCKCHAFERS AND THEIR DAMAGE

Rao (1966) lists seven species of cockchafer (Melolonthidae) known to be pests of rubber plantations in Malaya. They were almost unknown until 1930, when their numbers started building up, in particular those of the species *Psilopholis vestita*. Each year more areas were attacked, and by 1938 about 3,400 acres were infested. The outbreaks diminished from then on, but apparently not because of any applied control measures. Following the war, attacks continued on a small scale, but after 1955 there was a sudden increase in activity which had continued up to 1965 when Rao wrote his account. The outbreaks are not widespread through Malaya but are confined to isolated centers on the western side of the peninsula, in particular to two areas: one area overlapping the states of Johore, Malacca, and Negri Sembilan and the other in Kedah and central Perak. Although *P. vestita* is still an important cockchafer, the species responsible for most of the recent outbreaks has been *Lachnosterna bidentata*.

The cockchafers have an annual life cycle. The eggs are laid during March and April, and, on hatching, the young grubs feed in the soil, first on dead vegetable matter and then on roots. Pupation occurs deep in the soil and is usually completed by January or February. These, though, are dry months, and the adult beetles remain in the soil until wet weather occurs. Then they emerge in large numbers and take to flight; they do not feed on rubber or on the cover crops but rather fly to primary or secondary forest or occasionally to grassland, to feed and mate.

The damage caused can be quite severe. Many plants are quickly killed when rubber nurseries or field plantings are established on land in which the grubs have persisted from an old stand. In plantings on clean land, infestations begin in the second year as the leguminous cover crop becomes established in the inter-rows. *Lachnosterna bidentata* in particular seems to be attracted to oviposit under the cover-crop plants. The grubs begin by destroying the cover in extending patches and then proceed to feed on the rubber roots, killing many young trees. Mature rubber has an extensive root system, and at first, infestations at this age have little effect; but successive reinfestations produce extensive damage. On rubber in hilly terrain, destruction of the cover and loosening of the soil by grub movements can lead to soil erosion and the collapse of contour terraces.

DEVELOPMENT OF SELECTIVE CONTROL

Before the Second World War, hand digging was the only form of grub control. It was laborious, only partially effective, and added to soil erosion. After the war several effective insecticides became available. In particular, it was found that control lasting for at least three years could be achieved with heptachlor applied as a 0.1% emulsion. Poured into holes placed eighteen inches apart through the area, it will, for example, easily protect nurseries; when applied to the soil immediately around the root system, it will similarly protect the trees in first-year plantings. But to obtain control in older plantings, the insecticide would have to be injected both beside the trees and under the cover crop. This would mean the wide dispersal of a residual contact-acting insecticide, and it would be prohibitively expensive.

Rao has found, however, that the adult beetles—at least in immature plantations—can be effectively controlled by light-trapping. Before the war, light-traps (usually built around kerosene lamps) were commonly used for pest control. Although large catches of insects were obtained, light-traps have generally been regarded as a very inefficient means of control. The catches, though large, were often only a small proportion of the total population, and they tended to include mostly males, or females that had already laid their eggs. Often traps acted as a focus of subsequent infestation, attracting pests from all the neighboring areas. They also tended to catch a large number of beneficial insects. However, in the case of the rubber cockchafers there is a well-defined swarming period. This occurs with the first rains, during the second half of February or the first half of March, and is further confined to mass flights for about an hour just after dusk so that a large proportion of the population can be easily trapped. The most effective trap Rao found was one with a 15-watt, black-light, fluorescent tube suspended over a funnel. The traps are operated for one hour a day, after dusk, during the six-week swarming period. A high proportion of the catch consists of females which have not yet laid their eggs; only a small number of natural enemies are caught. If larger species, such as the scoliid wasps, are trapped, they can easily be set free. In a trial conducted in an area heavily infested with *L. bidentata,* light-trapping resulted in a reinfestation in the following season of an average of 9 grubs per square yard as compared with 46 grubs per square yard in the control plots.

Unfortunately, neither light-trapping of the adults nor chemical control of the grubs gives adequate protection to mature rubber. Rao has found that good control can be achieved in this situation by applying heptachlor to the soil surface, directed not at the grubs, but at the emerging beetles.

In the trial referred to above, this control method resulted in a reinfestation of only 2 grubs per square yard in the next season. The potential drawback to the method is that the widespread insecticide application could adversely affect natural enemies. The cockchafer grubs are mostly parasitized by scoliid wasps and by tachinid flies, but fortunately both of these natural enemies complete their life cycle and emerge from the soil before the cockchafer grubs pupate. Rao was thus able to obtain selective control by delaying the treatment until just a month before the flighting season of the beetles.

THE INTEGRATED PROGRAM: A SUMMARY

Rao has devised three methods of control against the cockchafers. Depending on the pest situation and the condition of the plantation, these can be variously combined to give effective integrated control. In very young rubber localized application of insecticide against the grubs gives cheap, efficient control with only a limited possibility of interfering with the natural enemies. In older, but still immature plantations, the same insecticide application can be combined with light-trapping of the adults, again with little effect on natural enemies. Finally, in mature rubber, overall chemical application against the beetles has to be used, but, if timed correctly, the enemy species are again only slightly affected.

Obviously, there is still room for improvement in this control program because it can probably be made yet more selective. Rao is, for example, considering the use of the "Green muscardine" fungus (*Metarrhizium anisopliae*) which is often encountered in the field. Nevertheless, this case history does show that, given the right approach, effective economic pest control can be achieved without the hazard of further problems. It also illustrates that when the older traditional methods of pest control are applied with correct insight into the biology of the pest, they can compete efficiently and economically with modern pesticides.

MALARIA CONTROL IN THE BORNEO STATES

So far I have only been concerned with the direct effects of the use of contact-acting insecticides in causing or aggravating pest problems. This final case history illustrates the kind of side effects which can result.

In the Borneo states of Sabah, Sarawak, and Brunei, malaria used to be an important disease; in some areas over 90% of the population had enlarged spleens. In 1955 the World Health Organization (WHO), in cooperation with the local medical departments, embarked on a program of malaria control (Colbourne, 1962; Colbourne *et al.*, 1960). The program was aimed at chemical control of the mosquito vectors (*Anopheles balabanensis* in Sabah and *A. leucosphyrus* in Sarawak), together with treatment and administration of prophylactic drugs. DDT and dieldrin have been used (DDT at 2 grams and dieldrin at 0.6 gram per square meter, applied to the inside of dwellings) and, apart from some mosquito resistance to dieldrin, they have been extremely effective in their primary objective. As a whole the campaign has been regarded as a model one, and has been used in training for later campaigns in other countries. In 1957 the original aim of control was changed to one of eradication, and today this has been all but achieved. But there have been some undesirable side effects of the mosquito control spraying, and these are worth considering.

THATCH-EATING LARVAE

Dr. F. Y. Cheng, the WHO entomologist in Borneo, referred to one of the side effects in a note published in 1963. About this time a number of complaints were received from villagers who believed that the DDT spraying was causing the thatch (*attap*) roofs of their houses to rot. On examination, it was found that the damage was being caused by heavy infestations of the larvae of a pyralid moth, *Herculia nigrivitta*. A survey carried out in sample unsprayed and sprayed areas revealed that the number of live thatch-eating larvae per square foot of infested roof was 4.2 in the unsprayed area, 6.6 in the DDT-sprayed area, and 0.2 in the dieldrin-sprayed area.

In a test on the susceptibility to DDT of these larvae, Cheng found that the larvae have the ability to distinguish the presence of the insecticide and will refuse to feed on DDT-sprayed thatch, even if they have been starved for twenty-four hours. In the case of dieldrin, though, they are very susceptible and produce a mortality rate of up to 92%.

A sample of full-grown larvae was collected and bred out, and from a number of the pupae, small chalcid parasites, *Antrocephalus* sp., appeared. Sixteen percent of the pupae were parasitized in this way. In a preliminary test with the parasites, Cheng discovered that enclosing them in a piece of DDT-sprayed thatch caused a complete knockdown. The high incidence of thatch destruction in the DDT-sprayed areas could thus be attributed to the avoidance reaction of the thatch larvae and the susceptibility of their natural enemies to the insecticides.

The problem that was created was insignificant compared to the benefits in malaria control which were attained from the continuation of DDT spraying. Furthermore there was a high density of larvae and of rotten thatched roofs in the unsprayed area, and it has been suggested that part of the problem was due to the poor preparation of *attap* before thatching. However, the second side effect, although it produced an equally minor problem, carried the potential of something much more serious.

RAT OUTBREAKS

In Sarawak following the spraying of the houses, the insecticide deposits were not only picked up by the mosquitoes but also by the many other insects normally present, including the frequently large populations of cockroaches (Harrisson, 1965). During the actual spray operation, domestic animals such as cats were kept outside; afterward, they returned, and while feeding on the dead or affected cockroaches the cats picked up the insecticide. The accumulation of the insecticide was frequently lethal, and many areas, particularly in the uplands, no longer had their cats. The result was an explosion in rat populations in the treated villages. In Sabah the story was the same except that the probable route for the chain reaction was through the house lizards, small geckos known locally as "chi-chaks." Normally, a score or more of these lizards live in each house and are commonly seen running on the roofs and walls and feeding on all kinds of insects. Like the cockroaches, they too are frequently eaten by cats and thus can pass on the accumulated DDT.

There are many species of rats in the Borneo states, but only a few can live in houses (Harrison, 1964; Medway, 1963). In the port areas and large coastal settlements, the brown rat (*Rattus norvegicus*) and the black rat (*R. rattus diardii*) are the common species; but inland, they are replaced by the little rat (*R. exulans*) and the Malaysian field rat (*R. tiomanicus sabae*). This latter species is equally at home in plantations, scrub, and secondary forest, and thus there is a permanent reservoir for house infestations. More important,

though, is the fact that many of these rats are potential carriers of plague, leptospirosis, and various rickettsial diseases, such as typhus. When attention was drawn to the extensive death of cats and consequent rat explosions, attempts were made by the authorities to replace the cat population. In Sabah cat owners in the towns were encouraged to donate surplus cats and litters of young kittens, and these were transported to the upland areas. In Sarawak, where the interior is much more inaccessible, a quite remarkable operation known as "Operation Cat Drop" was undertaken by WHO in cooperation with the Royal Air Force in Singapore (Harrisson, 1965). The donated cats were packed in special containers and dropped by parachute over the upland villages.

Luckily, these rat outbreaks did not produce any outbreaks of disease. The major consequence was the villagers' resistance to having their houses resprayed at a later date. Nevertheless, the case history is important because it graphically illustrates the far-reaching effects of such contact-acting insecticides as DDT.

DISCUSSION

The basic ecological problem in natural resource development can be described fairly concisely. In a natural climax ecosystem the energy received from the sun and the available minerals, gases, and water are converted into a maximal production of living materials. Because of the way the system has evolved and is structured, this productivity is stable and long-lasting. But because only a part of the material produced is directly useful to man, the natural ecosystem is soon replaced by an artificial one in which the productivity, measured as yield, comes in a more utilizable form. However, experience has shown that artificial ecosystems tend to be unstable, with long-term or short-term deterioration. The ecological problem thus becomes: How can the stable characteristics of the natural ecosystem be combined with the high-yielding qualities of the artificial one?

Pest control is but a special case. In attempting to obtain a high crop yield or a healthy human population, we create artificial ecosystems. Nevertheless, elements (pests) from the remaining natural ecosystems continue to intrude. These can in turn be controlled by additional artificial measures, such as the use of contact-acting insecticides; but as we are finding out, such control tends to create further instability either in the target pest or in other features of the ecosystem. The ecological answer lies in inserting the features of natural ecosystems into the artificial ecosystems which will allow efficient but more stable levels of pest control to be attained.

In practice, this simply stated solution is complex and difficult to attain, largely because of the insufficiency of our knowledge. We urgently require much more fundamental research, for example, on the structure and functioning of natural ecosystems. We need to know precisely why they are frequently so stable. To what extent and under what conditions do factors such as variety of habitat, complexity of food chain, or climate contribute to stability? We have to understand more clearly why some elements of natural ecosystems (such as certain secondary forest herbivores) rather than others are more likely to invade and disrupt artificial ecosystems. Above all, we need to learn how the characteristics of stability can be infused into artificial ecosystems without depressing their yields. Does the complexity and organization of the natural ecosystem have to be reproduced in detail or can stability be achieved by the addition of only a few very carefully selected features, and if so, which ones? Action on these questions becomes even more urgent when we realize that much of the world's remaining areas of natural ecosystems is fast disappearing. If we lose these, the solutions will become even more difficult and in many cases impossible.

Research of this kind must inevitably be long-term, and in the meantime, we have to take the utmost advantage of available information. Much work has already been done by ecologists on the problem of stability in natural ecosystems. Studies in some depth have been carried out on the influence on pest situations of natural or semi-natural vegetation, such as hedgerows in temperate countries. Moreover, a great many pests have been the subjects of research for a long time. The information, though, is scattered and often disconnected. More attention needs to be devoted to gathering this information together in order to uncover common principles.

We need to use the information more formally to build theoretical constructs which can contribute to a sounder basis for pest control decisions. The complexity of such a task may seem daunting, but in recent years, electronic computing and developments in applied mathematics under the general heading of systems analysis, have provided powerful tools for analyzing natural phenomena. Ecosystems can be mimicked by models built in mathematical or computer language, and depending on the information available and the skill and discipline of the model builder, these models can yield great insights (Watt, 1967). As yet this approach has been rarely used in pest control, but the potential benefits are very great. For example, well-developed models of pest populations and their interactions would be invaluable in training applied entomologists.

Finally, throughout the world there are the immediate day-to-day practical pest problems which have to be acted upon. All too frequently, there is little detailed information for the field entomologist to go on, and decisions have to be based on a wide variety of economic, social, and ecological considerations. Each entomologist will have to continue to develop his own strategy based on how he sees the workings of pest situations in the particular country, climate, and general environment with which he is concerned.

From what has been said in this paper, it is evident that I feel that in countries with conditions similar to those of Malaysia, the overall pest strategy must place prime importance on the utilization of natural enemies as regulatory mechanisms and must recognize the hazards to such control which can arise from the use of contact-acting insecticides. As a general rule, it would seem desirable to attain at the outset the highest possible degree of natural control through cultural and other measures. This means taking into account the environment of the crop and that of nearby natural vegetation, considering the latter not only as a possible source of many of the pests present in the crop but also as a potential reservoir of regulating natural enemies. I have suggested previously that this may call for a policy of preserving such natural vegetation, leaving intact blocks of forest or keeping elements of the natural vegetation within the crop itself. Probably the amount of such vegetation that remains and its ratio to that of the crop area is a critical one; with our present lack of knowledge only trial and error in each case will tell what needs to be done. This strategy undoubtedly provides the greatest chance of success against

problems of perennial tree crops which in many respects come closer to re-creating natural forest conditions. At the other end of the scale, quick-maturing, high-value vegetable crops which are grown under largely artificial conditions would seem to provide much less opportunity for the establishment of a stable form of natural control. Nevertheless, by careful rotation and a mosaic form of cropping, perhaps some success can be achieved.

In some cases the re-creation of natural control may provide all that is necessary, but for the most part pest problems, particularly from low density pests, will remain, and these will require further artificial control measures. The strategy then must be to concentrate on choosing selective measures. They may be biological, cultural, mechanical, or insecticidal in form. Many pesticides are available, e.g., lead arsenate, trichlorphon, Thuricide, which have been shown to be highly selective. If there is no alternative and residual contact-acting insecticides have to be used, then they must be applied to ensure a minimum of interference with natural control (cf. the control program devised by Rao). In practice this means a conscious and energetic effort on the part of applied entomologists to avoid the use of these insecticides and on the part of the manufacturers and distributors of pest control material to concentrate on producing and providing the kind of selective materials that are required.

ACKNOWLEDGMENTS

I am indebted to Brian J. Wood and B. Sripathi Rao for their comments and permission to quote from their writings.

REFERENCES

Bartlett, B. R. "The Contact Toxicity of Some Pesticide Residues to Hymenopterous Parasites and Coccinellid Predators." *J. Econ. Ent.*, 56 (1963), 684–98.

Catley, A. *"Tiracola plagiata Walk.* (Lepidoptera: *Noctuidae.*) A Serious Pest of Cacao in Papua." *Papua New Guinea Agr. J.*, 15 (1963a), 15–22.

———. "Observations on the Biology and Control of the Army Worm *Tiracola plagiata Walk.* (Lepidoptera: *Noctuidae*)." *Papua New Guinea Agr. J.*, 15 (1963b), 105–09.

Cheng, F. Y. "Deterioration of Thatch Roofs by Moth Larvae after House Spraying in the Course of a Malaria Eradication Programme in North Borneo." *Bull. WHO*, 28 (1963), 136–37.

Colbourne, M. J. "A Review of Malaria-Eradication Campaigns in the Western Pacific." *Ann. Trop. Med. and Parasit.*, 56 (1962), 33–43.

Colbourne, M. J.; Huehne, W. M.; and Lachance, F. de S. "The Sarawak Anti-Malaria Project." *Sarawak Mus. J.*, 9 (13–14) (1960), 215–48.

Conway, G. R. "A Note on Mirid Bugs (Hemiptera: Miridae) and Some Other Insect Pests of Cocoa in Sabah, Malaysia." *Proc. Conf. Mirids and Other Pests of Cocoa*, 1964 (Ibadan, Nigeria). West African Cocoa Res. Inst. (Nigeria), Ibadan. 1964. Pp. 80–84.

———. "Crop Pest Control and Resource Conservation in Tropical South East Asia." In *Conservation in Tropical South East Asia*, L. M. and M. H. Talbot, eds. Morges: Intern. Union Conserv. Nature and Natural Resources, 1968. Pp. 159–63.

———. "The Pests of Cocoa in Sabah, Malaysia, and Their Control, with a List of the Cocoa Fauna." *Dept. Agr. Malay. Bull.*, 1969. (In preparation.)

Conway, G. R., and Tay, E. B. "Crop Pests and Their Control in Sabah, Malaysia." *Dept. Agr. Malay. Bull.*, 1969. (In press.)

Conway, G. R., and Wood, B. J. "Pesticide Chemicals—Help or Hindrance in Malaysian Agriculture?" *Malay. Nat. J.*, 18 (1964), 111–19.

Corbett, G. H. "The Bionomics and Control of *Leptocorisa acuta* Thunb. with Notes on Other *Leptocorisa* Spp." *Malay. Dept. Agr. S.S. and F.M.S. Sci. Ser. Bull.* No. 4. 1930. 39 pp.

———. "Insects of Coconuts in Malaya." *Dept. Agr. S.S. and F.M.S. Gen. Ser. Bull.* No. 10. 1932. 106 pp.

Dammerman, K. W. *The Agricultural Zoology of the Malay Archipelago.* Amsterdam: J. H. de Bussy, 1929. 473 pp.

De Silva, M. D. "Biology of *Helopeltis ceylonensis* De Silva (Heteroptera: Miridae), a Major Pest of Cacao in Ceylon." *Trop. Agriculturist*, 117 (1960), 149–56.

Entwistle, P. F.; Johnson, C. G.; and Dun, E. "New Pests of Cocoa (*Theobroma cacao* L.) in Ghana Following Applications of Insecticides." *Nature* (London), 184 (1959), 2040.

Harrison, J. L. *An Introduction to the Mammals of Sabah.* Jesselton: Sabah Soc., 1964. 244 pp.

Harrisson, T. "Operation Cat-Drop." *Animals*, 5 (1965), 512–13.

Kalshoven, L. G. E. *De plagen van de cul-*

tuurgewassen in Indonesie. Vols. I, II. The Hague and Bandung: N. V. Uitgererij W. van Hoeve, 1950–51. 1,065 pp.

Lever, R. J. A. W. Discussion in "Insecticides: Boon or Bane?" *Proc. Roy. Ent. Soc.* (London) (C), 31 (1966–67), 28.

Medway, Lord. "Mammals of Borneo." *J. Malay. Br. Roy. Asiatic Soc.,* Vol. 36, No. 3. 1963. 193 pp.

Miller, N. C. E. "Fruit Flies." *Malay. Agr. J.,* 28 (1940), 112–21.

Pagden, H. T. "A Preliminary Account of Three Rice Stem Borers." *Dept. Agr. S.S. and F.M.S. Sci. Ser. Bull.* No. 1. 1930. 30 pp.

Rao, B. S. "The Use of Light Traps to Control the Cockchafer *Lachnosterna bidentata* Burm. in Malayan Rubber Plantations." *J. Rubber Res. Inst. Malaya,* 18 (1964), 243–52.

———. "Cockchafer Attacks in Malayan Rubber Plantations and Integrated Control." *Proc. 11th Pac. Sci. Congr.* (Tokyo) (1966), pp. 54–62.

Smith, R. F. "Recent Developments in Integrated Control." *Pest Art. and News Summ.* (A), 14 (1968), 201–06.

Smith, R. F., and van den Bosch, R. "Integrated Control." In *Pest Control,* W. W. Kilgore and R. L. Doutt, eds. New York: Academic Press, 1967. Pp. 295–340.

Southwood, T. R. E. "Migration—an Evolutionary Necessity for Denizens of Temporary Habitats." *Proc. 11th Int. Congr. Ent.* (Vienna), 3 (1962), 54–58.

State of Sabah. *Annual Report 1963.* Jesselton: Government Printing Office, 1964. 267 pp.

Watt, K. E. F. *Ecology and Resource Management.* New York: McGraw-Hill, 1967. 450 pp.

Wood, B. J. "Severe Outbreaks of Caterpillars on Oil Palm Estates in Malaya Induced by the Use of Residual Contact Insecticides." In *Proc. 12th Int. Congr. Ent.* (London, 1964). 1965, pp. 574–75.

———. "Insect Pests of Oil Palms in Malaya." *Planter, Kuala Lumpur,* 42 (1966), 311–15.

———. "Aerial Spray Campaigns against Bagworm Caterpillars (Lepidoptera: Psychidae) on Oil Palms in Malaysia." Mimeo. 1967. 24 pp.

———. *Pests of Oil Palms in Malaysia and Their Control.* Incorporated Society of Planters, Box 262, Kuala Lumpur. 1968. 250 pp.

26. TOXICITY OF INSECTICIDES USED FOR ASIATIC RICE BORER CONTROL TO TROPICAL FISH IN RICE PADDIES

L. T. Kok

Application of insecticides into the water to control lepidopterous rice borers has become common in Asia. The resulting contamination of the aquatic environment necessitates evaluation of the effects of such insecticides on fish. Evaluation is essential because of the importance of fish culture in the rice paddies of Asia, especially in Indonesia, Malaysia and Pakistan. Hence, the toxicity of the two most popularly used insecticides for rice borer control, γ-BHC and diazinon, was investigated.

In initial tests conducted in aquaria containing water alone, carp (*Cyprinus carpio* Linnaeus), tawes (*Puntius javanicus* Bleeker) and tilapia (*Tilapia mossambica* Peters) suffered high mortalities even at 1.0 ppm γ-BHC. Remarkable reductions in mortality were obtained when soil was introduced into the aquaria, and in field fishponds with a water level of 10 cm deep, the test species could tolerate up to 2 kilograms per hectare (kg/ha) active ingredient of a single application of γ-BHC. Further tests conducted on tilapia in rice fields revealed that multiple applications of γ-BHC were lethal to fish, and differences in field water level had little effect on the mortality rate for single applications of 2 kg/ha of γ-BHC. Mortality per application, however, was slightly lower in fields with greater water depth for double applications. This reduction was small compared to the large increase in mortality rate as a result of multiple applications. These results indicate that plant absorption, soil adsorption, degradation of γ-BHC and the lowering of the insecticidal concentration due to increased water depth are not sufficient to reduce the lethal effects of multiple applications of γ-BHC to fish. Compared to γ-BHC, diazinon was far less lethal to tilapia. Even with three applications of 2.5 kg/ha, fish mortality was negligibly low, suggesting that diazinon is either of very low lethality to fish or that it is degraded rapidly in rice paddies. At these rates, it is almost equal to γ-BHC in effectiveness for the control of the rice borers.

IMPORTANCE OF FISH CULTURE IN RICE PADDIES OF ASIA

Rice and fish are staple foods in the Southeast Asian countries, and farmers often raise fish in rice fields to supplement their income. The combination of fish and rice culture is particularly important in rural areas because fish is a cheap source of protein and is acceptable to different ethnic groups. Besides the additional income obtainable with comparatively little extra effort, the excreta of fish fertilize the rice plants; fish eat many caterpillars of insect pests; and the rat problem is reduced because the greater water depth prevents rats from digging holes in the bunds.

Countries in the Asian region with fish culture in the rice paddies include Indo-nesia, Malaysia, Pakistan, Japan, Taiwan, India and Vietnam, with substantial acreages in the first three. The most common fish species are the common carp (*Cyprinus carpio* Linnaeus), tilapia (*Tilapia mossambica* Peters), tawes (*Puntius javanicus* Bleeker) and sepat siam (*Trichogaster pectoralis* Regan) (Table 26–1). Stocking the rice fields with fish fry is common in Indonesia (Simizu, 1943), Japan (Hiyama, 1949), Taiwan (Chen, 1953) and in more recent years also in Malaysia. Stocking rate depends on the productivity of water, size of fish introduced, and species and duration of culture, and is in the range of 1,000 to 2,000 fingerlings per hectare for a mixture of common carp, tilapia and tawes. Yield is greatly increased when food is provided for the fish. Over a two-month period, yield averages 30 to 50 kg/ha in Indonesia and

Table 26–1

SPECIES OF FISH COMMON IN THE RICE PADDIES OF ASIA

NAME	DISTRIBUTION	COUNTRY OF MAJOR IMPORTANCE
Common carp (*Cyprinus carpio*)	China, Japan, Vietnam, Thailand, Ceylon, India, Philippines, Malaysia, Indonesia	Indonesia, Japan, Vietnam
Tilapia (*Tilapia mossambica*)	Africa, Indonesia, Malaysia, Philippines, Thailand, Ceylon, Pakistan, India	Indonesia, Malaysia, Taiwan, Thailand
Tawes (*Puntius javanicus*)	Indonesia, Thailand, Vietnam, Malaysia, Philippines, Ceylon	Indonesia
Sepat siam (*Trichogaster pectoralis*)	Thailand, Cambodia, Vietnam, Malaysia, Indonesia, East Pakistan, Ceylon	Malaysia
Catla (*Catla catla*)	West Pakistan, India, East Pakistan, Burma, Ceylon	India, Pakistan
Cat fish (*Clarias batrachus*)	India, Ceylon, East Pakistan, Burma, Malaysia, Thailand, Cambodia, Vietnam, Indonesia, Philippines	Malaysia
Aruan (*Ophiocephalus striatus*)	India, Ceylon, China, Indonesia, Malaysia, Philippines	Malaysia

10 to 20 kg/ha in Indo-China. Average yield in Japan is 145 kg/ha and 2,250 kg/ha per annum without and with artificial feeding, respectively (FAO, 1962). In Malaysia, the natural fish population of sepat siam (*T. pectoralis*), aruan (*Ophiocephalus striatus* Bloch) and sometimes catfish (*Clarias batrachus* Linnaeus) is large (Soong, 1948, 1949, 1950). Yield ranges from 20 to 135 kg/ha per crop, but as much as 1,000 kg/ha has been recorded (Heath, 1934). As protein deficiency is prevalent among the rural population in the region, fish constitutes a major protein source.

Rice culture in Southeast Asia had been relatively free of chemicals up to the Second World War. Use of chemicals greatly increased with the introduction of the chlorinated hydrocarbon insecticides in the post-war period. Intensified cropping resulted in frequent pest outbreaks and greater reliance on chemical control. The present trend indicates a distinct increase in pesticide use to control the major insect pests, the most important being the lepidopterous rice stem borers. Some of the popular insecticides used in rice borer control are the chlorinated hydrocarbons endrin, dieldrin and γ-BHC, and the organophosphorus compounds EPN, methyl parathion, dipterex and diazinon (Table 26–2).

These chemicals were first applied as foliar dusts or sprays, but recently direct application into the rice field water has significantly increased (Table 26–3). The extent of their use in areas with fish culture is determined greatly by pest outbreaks and the economics of application. Substantial yield increases accompanying their use has made their application more feasible. When applied as sprays or dusts on the leaves, only some of the insecticide comes into direct contact with the fish in the rice paddies. But the addition of insecticides directly to the paddy water is fast becoming popular because this method of insecticide application gives efficient rice borer control (Koshihara and Okamoto, 1957; Okamoto,

Table 26-2

INSECTICIDES COMMONLY USED FOR RICE BORER CONTROL IN COUNTRIES
WITH FISH CULTURE IN RICE PADDIES

(WET RICE FIELDS IN HECTARES)*

COUNTRY	WITHOUT FISH CULTURE	WITH FISH CULTURE	% AREA WITH FISH CULTURE	INSECTICIDES COMMONLY USED AGAINST BORERS
Indonesia	4,500,000	67,000	1.5	Endrin, methyl parathion
Malaysia	314,500	45,500	14.5	Dieldrin, γ-BHC dipterex, diazinon
Pakistan	43,400	12,000	27.6	Methyl parathion, diazinon, endrin, γ-BHC, EPN
Japan	2,991,100	8,500	0.3	Methyl parathion, dipterex, diazinon
Taiwan	520,000	8,000	1.5	Endrin, parathion
India	5,762,792	1,619	0.03	γ-BHC, EPN, (Methyl parathion)
Vietnam	4,067,990	1,550	0.04	Endrin, diazinon, dipterex

*F.A.O. Fisheries Biology Technical Paper No. 14, 1962.

Table 26–3

METHOD AND RATE OF APPLICATION OF INSECTICIDES COMMONLY USED IN RICE BORER CONTROL

INSECTICIDE	CONCENTRATION (% or kg./ha. a.i.)	METHOD OF APPLICATION
Chlorinated hydrocarbons		
Dieldrin	0.04%	Spray—foliar
Endrin	0.03 to 0.05%	Spray—foliar
γ-BHC	2 to 3 kg./ha.	Water directly
"	3% to 5%	Dust—foliar
Organophosphorus compounds		
Diazinon	0.04%	Spray—foliar
"	3 kg./ha.	Water directly
Dipterex	0.03 to 0.05%	Spray—foliar
EPN	0.05%	Spray—foliar
Methyl parathion	0.03 to 0.05%	Spray—foliar
"	1.5%	Dust—foliar

1963; Kok and Pathak, 1967; Okamoto *et al.,* 1963; Pathak, 1967). The resulting contamination of the aquatic medium, therefore, raises a serious problem to fish in the rice fields as they are directly exposed to the toxicants. It is imperative that the lethal effects of insecticides on fish be carefully evaluated before such insecticides be advocated for wide use.

EFFECTS OF PESTICIDES ON FISH IN RICE PADDIES

Although pesticide effects on temperate fish species have received much attention, such studies in the tropics are very recent. In particular, information on pesticide toxicity to fish in rice paddies is scarce because investigations have been somewhat neglected.

In Japan, dieldrin and endrin were found to be extremely lethal to young carp fish compared to the organophosphorus compounds sumithion, parathion and methyl parathion in aquaria tests (Iyatomi and Tamura, 1963).

In Malaysia, this problem first received attention in 1957 when Wyatt studied the

effects on aruan (*Ophiocephalus striatus*) of several chlorinated hydrocarbon insecticides mixed with water in aquaria. These insecticides were lethal to fish at less than 0.5 ppm, endrin and dieldrin being more lethal than DDT and γ-BHC. The wettable powders of these compounds were significantly less lethal than the emulsifiable concentrates (Wyatt, 1957). No field investigations were carried out up to 1957, but in 1962 I was informed of fish dying in the Tanjong Karang rice fields of West Malaysia within 24 hours of a 0.1% dieldrin spray. Subsequent personal observations in the rice fields of Malaysia and the Philippines of fish mortality after the application of chemicals emphasized the importance of studying insecticidal lethality to fish. The high toxicity of γ-BHC in water was confirmed in aquaria tests but field tests conducted in the rice paddies revealed that tilapia, carp and tawes fishes can tolerate up to 2 kg/ha active ingredient of a single application of γ-BHC (Kok and Pathak, 1966).

In the rice paddies of Bengal, the weedicides Brestan-60, copper sulphate and copper oxychloride gave good control of algal weeds and were not lethal to fish at the recommended dosages (Mukherji, 1968). Results of tests carried out by workers in temperate countries showed that in general, chlorinated hydrocarbon insecticides are much more lethal than organophosphorus compounds and that herbicides 2,4-D (2,4-dichlorophenoxyacetic acid), MCPA (4-chloro-2-methyl phenoxyacetic acid), Simazine (2-chloro-4,6-bis-ethylamino-s-triazine) and Monorun (3-p-chlorophenyl-1,1-dimethylurea) at equivalent rates of 1 to 2 kg/ha are nonlethal to fish (Jones, 1964). Dalapon (2,2-dichloropropionic acid), diquat (1,1'-ethylene-2,2'-dipuridylium dibromide) and paraquat (1,1'-dimethyl-4,4'-bipyridinium salt) are non-toxic to fish at concentrations recommended for aquatic weed control in rice fields (FAO, 1968). However, a number of promising herbicides like PCP (pentachlorophenol), DCPA (dimethyl 2,3,5,6-tetrachloroterephthalate) and Propanil (3'4'-dichloropropionanilide) are used at relatively much higher concentrations of 4.0 to 8.0 kg/ha (IRRI, 1968). These may adversely affect fish at the applied dosages.

In view of the scarce information on pesticide effects on fish in rice paddies and the increasing use of insecticides in Southeast Asia, we investigated the effects on fish in the rice paddies of γ-BHC and diazinon, currently the most promising insecticides for rice borer control. Tests were first conducted with γ-BHC in water alone, then water plus soil in glass aquaria and later in field fishponds, to the three most common tropical freshwater species of fish in the rice fields (Kok and Pathak, 1966). The effects of multiple applications of γ-BHC and diazinon on the mortality of tilapia fish, the most sensitive of the three species in the initial series, were subsequently determined in field studies.

Laboratory tests were conducted in glass aquaria of $24'' \times 10'' \times 12''$ fitted with tubings connected to compressed-air outlets for aeration. Twenty fish were placed in each aquarium tank for at least 24 hours before insecticide application. Fish mortality was very high in aquaria containing γ-BHC dissolved in water, with tilapia and tawes suffering 95 percent mortality at 1.0 ppm. Carp was the most tolerant, with less than 12 percent mortality at this dosage. When a 3-inch layer of soil was placed at the bottom of each aquarium before treatment, mortality at rates below 1.0 ppm was low (Table 26–4). This significant reduction in mortality indicated that the soil has a buffering effect on γ-BHC, possibly due to ad-

Table 26–4

TOXICITY OF γ-BHC TO FRESHWATER FISH IN AQUARIUM AND FIELD EXPERIMENTS
(Average % mortality, 4 replications)

DOSAGE (ppm)	WATER ALONE			WATER AND SOIL			FIELD FISHPONDS		
	TAWES	TILAPIA	CARP	TAWES	TILAPIA	CARP	TAWES	TILAPIA	CARP
0.25	8	34	1						
0.50	30	57	2	3	0				
0.75	88	78	5						
1.00	96	97	11	27	3	7	1	0	0
1.50					13	27			
2.00	100	100	78	60	100	30	4	2	0.5
3.00							48	52	0.5
4.00			99	100		47	56	84	8
Control	0	0	1	0	0	0	0	0	0

sorption and degradation of the chemical. Subsequent field tests confirmed this lowered mortality rate.

FIELD TESTS

The first experiment tested the effect of a single application of γ-BHC to fish in ponds of 10 cm depth. Using one-meter-square tanks of corrugated metal sheets 30 cm wide, water was maintained at a depth of 10 cm. Fifty fish fingerlings were released in each tank one week before application of the chemical. Fish mortality was less than 5 percent up to 2 kg/ha γ-BHC, but at 3 kg/ha, significantly increased mortality was found in the test fishes, except for carp (Table 26–4). In terms of mortality, the fishes showed a 9, 7 and 5-fold increase in tolerance to γ-BHC for tilapia, tawes, and carp respectively. Biodegradation and volatilization of γ-BHC could have decreased the toxicity of the insecticide in the presence of soil. Raghu and MacRae (1966) showed that γ-BHC persisted for about 55 days in flooded soils and that a large proportion of it was degraded by microorganisms within the first 30 days. The resulting microbial population could degrade a subsequent application at a much faster rate.

Recent reports confirmed the amount of γ-BHC persisting in the soil and irrigation water after 30 days to be very small (IRRI,

1967). This would imply that if the insecticide is not degraded rapidly enough, the recommended rates of γ-BHC for rice borer control at 2 and 3 kg/ha active ingredient within 30 days (total of 5 kg/ha) would be highly lethal to fish.

The next experiment examined the effect of double applications of γ-BHC to fish in similar tanks also containing rice plants maintained at 10 cm depth; tilapia were released in the tanks four weeks after transplanting the rice seedlings. The first application of 1, 2 and 3 kg/ha of γ-BHC made one week after the introduction of fish showed low mortality except in the 3 kg/ha treatment. A second application 30 days later at rates of 3, 2 and 1 kg/ha (total of 4 kg/ha per treatment) resulted in significantly increased mortalities in all treatments (Table 26–5). This clearly confirms that single applications of up to 2 kg/ha did not kill tilapia, but single applications of 3 kg/ha and double applications totaling 4 kg/ha or more were highly lethal. Plant absorption of γ-BHC did not appear to significantly affect the mortality.

As the concentration of toxicant is affected by depth of water in the rice fields, tests were also conducted to study the effect of differences in water level on fish mortality. Rice plants were grown in field fishponds maintained at the usual range of field water level of 5 to 20 cm. Tilapia were released in ponds of 5–10 cm, 10–15 cm, and 15–

Table 26–5

EFFECT OF DOUBLE APPLICATIONS OF γ-BHC TO TILAPIA IN FIELD
FISHPONDS OF 10 CM DEPTH

TREATMENT:	kg/ha	TOTAL INSECTICIDE kg/ha	% MORTALITY (AVERAGE OF 4 REPLICATIONS)	
	1st:2nd Appl.		1st Appl.	2nd Appl.
γ-BHC:	3.0:1.0	4.0	83	83
γ-BHC:	2.0:2.0	4.0	7	70
γ-BHC:	1.0:3.0	4.0	0	85
Control:	0 :0	0	0	0

20 cm depths one week before the first application of γ-BHC. Control was maintained between 5 and 20 cm.

Fish mortality was less than 10 percent in all treatments after the first application of 2 kg/ha. Thirty days later, γ-BHC was applied again, making the total insecticide application 4.5 and 5.0 kg/ha. Mortality was slightly lower in the ponds with greatest water depth (15–20 cm) because of the reduced concentration, but this difference was small when compared to the large increase in mortality caused by the additional application of γ-BHC (Table 26–6).

Next, because of the high toxicity of

γ-BHC to tilapia at concentrations of more than 2 kg/ha, three applications of 1.5 kg/ha or less of γ-BHC were applied at 20-day intervals and compared to triple applications of diazinon. Treatments were made 50, 70 and 90 days after transplanting. Two applications of 1.5 kg/ha of γ-BHC caused less than 25 percent mortality, but mortality was doubled when the third application was made. Applications totaling more than 5.0 kg/ha resulted in more than 65 percent mortality (Table 26–7).

These results show that plant absorption, soil adsorption, degradation of γ-BHC and the lowering of insecticide concentration due

Table 26–6

EFFECT OF DOUBLE APPLICATIONS OF γ-BHC TO TILAPIA IN FIELD FISHPONDS OF VARYING DEPTHS

TREATMENT: kg/ha		DEPTH OF POND (cm)	TOTAL INSECTICIDE kg/ha	% MORTALITY (AVERAGE OF 4 REPLICATIONS)	
	1st:2nd Appl.			1st Appl.	2nd Appl.
γ-BHC:	2.0:2.5	5–10	4.5	10	68
γ-BHC:	2.0:3.0	5–10	5.0	1	84
γ-BHC:	2.0:2.5	10–15	4.5	4	78
γ-BHC:	2.0:3.0	10–15	5.0	0	91
γ-BHC:	2.0:2.5	15–20	4.5	6	51
γ-BHC:	2.0:3.0	15–20	5.0	1	68
Control:	0 :0	5–10	0	0	0
Control:	0 :0	10–20	0	0	0

Table 26–7

EFFECT OF TRIPLE APPLICATIONS OF γ-BHC AND DIAZINON TO TILAPIA IN FIELD FISHPONDS OF 10 CM DEPTH

TREATMENT: kg/ha		TOTAL INSECTICIDE kg/ha	% MORTALITY (AVERAGE OF 4 REPLICATIONS) AFTER		
	1st:2nd:3rd Appl.		1st	2nd	3rd Appl.
γ-BHC:	1.0:1.5:1.5	4.0	1	1	37
γ-BHC:	1.5:1.5:1.5	4.5	16	21	49
γ-BHC:	1.5:1.5:2.0	5.0	18	24	65
γ-BHC:	2.0:2.0:2.0	6.0	19	58	85
Diazinon:	1.5:1.5:1.5	4.5	1	1	1
Diazinon:	2.0:2.0:2.0	6.0	1	1	1
Diazinon:	2.5:2.5:2.5	7.5	0	0	0
Control:	0 :0 :0	0	2	2	2

to increased water depth are not sufficient to reduce the lethal effects of multiple applications of γ-BHC to tilapia. Hence, multiple applications of this insecticide at rates essential for efficient control of rice borers are lethal to fish.

Diazinon, on the other hand, was apparently harmless to fish. Even three applications of 2.5 kg/ha, totaling 7.5 kg/ha, did not cause any mortality (Table 26–7). This shows that diazinon is either of very low toxicity to fish or that it is rapidly degraded in the rice paddies. At these rates, it gives almost as good control of the rice borers as γ-BHC; compared to the latter, diazinon is more satisfactory for use in areas where fish culture is common.

The foregoing series of tests reveals that fish mortality is greatest within 72 hours after chemical application and few deaths occur 7 days after treatment. This enables easy assessment of immediate lethal effects to fish. However, accumulation of sub-lethal doses of insecticides by fish can occur with less apparent results. The planktonic biota, filamentous algae, weeds, organic manure, larvae and adult insects absorb chemicals present in the water and fish feed on them. This may result not in death but in reduction in fertility and possible degradation of fish quality. In this respect, the objectionable smell and peculiar taste accompanied by the burning sensation of γ-BHC on contact makes it rather unpalatable and acts as a warning against consumption of dangerous amounts, reducing the risk of γ-BHC to fish, wildlife and man. Although diazinon is much less persistent than γ-BHC, it does not have the unpalatability of the latter. Hence further bioassays to examine the cumulative effects of regular applications of the chemical to fish as well as to the whole food chain of the ecosystem of the rice paddies are necessary. Such studies have been neglected and there is urgent need for detailed studies on the bioaccumulation of pesticides in fish growing in rice paddies.

IMPLICATIONS OF FISH TOXICITY TO PRESENT AND FUTURE DEVELOPMENT PROGRAMS OF RICE PRODUCTION IN ASIA

In Asia the increase in food production is emphasized to meet the demands of the rapid population growth. Increase in rice production must come from the existing land devoted to rice, as significant increase in acreages does not appear likely. Hence in areas where irrigation and adequate supplies of water can be maintained throughout the year, double or triple-cropping of rice is being introduced. The successful development of non-photosensitive, short-term varieties have made this possible and more land is being brought under continuous cropping. However, such cropping may create conditions suitable for the propagation of pests and diseases to the rice plant. For example, better irrigation means better growth conditions for weeds, many of which harbor harmful insects. Use of short maturation or new high-yielding varieties may produce crops which are more susceptible to pest and disease infestation. Also, intensification of crop production increases the food supply for pests, enhancing their biotic potential. The implementation of intensified cropping therefore creates an ever more artificial and monotypic system, forcing us to rely more and more on artificial controls.

Dependence on chemicals is increasing. Unfortunately, in most of the developing countries where rice production is greatest, the shortage of suitably trained personnel often leads to indiscriminate use of chemicals. Often initial successes in pest and disease control measures lead to "insurance" applications and increased use of chemicals. The remarkable success of γ-BHC applied in the irrigation water for rice stem borer control is a good example of increased use of chemicals in the production of rice. In many of the rice-producing countries in Southeast Asia, γ-BHC is now applied into irrigation water to protect the plants from the ravages of the stem borers. These applications result in continuous contamination of the aquatic environment, effecting ecological changes. This technique of insecticide application has been gaining popularity and more chemicals are being tried as alternatives to γ-BHC in the search for a chemical efficient for both stem borer and leaf hopper control. The former, but not the latter, is effectively controlled by γ-BHC. The hoppers are sap suckers and vectors of virus diseases, ranking next in importance as pests. Hence there is the need for effective control of these two major insect pest problems of rice, preferably by a single insecticide.

Diazinon appears to control both the borers and the hoppers, but the vast array of insect pests and diseases of rice ensures the continued use of a wide range of pesticides. Such programs would be a constant threat to one of the cheapest protein sources of the rural people. Fishing is part of a way of life for many of the farmers; they derive nourishment and pleasure from it. As protein shortage is widespread and often critical, an alternative source of protein, equally cheap and acceptable, has to be ensured if fish are eliminated or harmed.

Fish can be affected in three major ways. The most apparent is death by contact with the toxicants. They may also accumulate a high level of toxicant, much greater than that of the initial application, by feeding on plants and organisms which are exposed to the same aquatic environment. Fish suffer also as a result of organic depletion of oxygen level in the water caused by decomposing vegetation. Vegetation affected by pesticides utilizes oxygen in decomposition, decreasing the oxygen level in water which is often limiting for fish survival. Fish survival alone, however, does not justify usage of any chemical. Although chemicals may be accumulated in the fish without causing their death, there are many possible effects on fish quality and fertility. Humans feeding on such contaminated fish may in turn be adversely affected.

Much can also be learned by detailed studies of the characteristics of the chemicals themselves—their persistency, whether they are readily metabolized or degraded by physical or biological processes, their dispersal mechanisms and the form of their accumulation in the tissues of plants and animals. Careful evaluation of chemical use cannot therefore be overemphasized and the success of any such programs may well depend on the acceptance of the changes which accompany them.

REFERENCES

Chen, T. P. "The Culture of Tilapia in Rice Paddies in Taiwan." Fish Ser. Chinese-American Joint Commission on Rural Reconstruction, Vol. 2 (1953). 29 pp.

FAO. *Handbook on Fish Culture in the Indo-Pacific Region.* FAO Fisheries Biology Technical Paper No. 14 (1962). 204 pp.

FAO Fisheries Reports *44* (5). Proceedings of the World Symposium on Warm-water Pond Fish Culture. Rome, Italy, May 1966, 1968. 411 pp.

Heath, R. G. "Fish Production in the Krian Irrigation Area." *Malayan Agric. J.,* 22 (4) (1934), 186–89.

Hiyama, Y. "Rice-Paddy Carp Culture in Japan." *Proc. U.N. Sci. Conf. Cons. Util. Res.,* 1 (1949), 124–26.

IRRI. *The International Rice Research Institute Annual Report 1966*. Los Baños (Philippines), IRRI, 1967. 302 pp.

IRRI. *The International Rice Research Institute Annual Report 1967*. Los Baños (Philippines), IRRI, 1968. 308 pp.

Iyatomi, K., and Tamura, T. "TLM of pesticides for fish," in *Sumithion Technical Manual*. Sumitomo Chemical Co. Osaka, Japan, 1963. 9 pp.

Jones, J. R. E. *Fish and River Pollution*, 1964. 203 pp.

Kok, L. T., and Pathak, M. D. "Toxicity of Lindane Used for Asiatic Rice Borer Control to Three Species of Fish." *J. Econ. Ent.*, 59 (3) (1966), 659–63.

———. "Bioassay Determination of γ-BHC Absorbed from Soil and Translocated in Potted Rice Plants." *Inter. Rice Comm. Newsl.*, XVI (2) (1967), 27–34.

Koshihara, T., and Okamoto, D. "Control of the Rice Stem Borer by Application of BHC Dust in the Paddy Soil." *Jap. J. Appl. Entom. Zoo.*, 1 (1957), 32–35. (In Japanese; English summary.)

Mukherji, S. K. "Chemical Control of Algae in West Bengal Paddy Fields." *World Crops*, 20 (1) (1968), 54–55.

Okamoto, D. "Insecticide Application in the Paddy Field." *Plant Protect.* 17 (4) (1963), 131–34.

Okamoto, D.; Koshihara, T.; and Abe, Y. "Control of the Rice Stem Borer by the Application of Some Synthetic Organic Insecticides in the Paddy Fields." *Chugoku Agr. Res.*, 25 (1963), 35–37. (In Japanese.)

Pathak, M. D. "Significant Developments in Rice Stem Borer and Leaf Hopper Control." *PANS A* (13) (1967), 45–60.

Raghu, K., and MacRae, I. C. "Biodegradation of the Gamma Isomer of Benzene Hexachloride in Submerged Soils." *Science*, 1954 (1966), 263–64.

Simizu, S. *Perkanan Disawah (Balai Pustaka)*. Djakarta, 1943. 35 pp.

Soong, M. K. "Fishes of the Malayan Padi Fields. 1. Sepat Siam." *Malayan Nat. J.*, 3 (2) (1948), 1–3.

———. "Fishes of the Malayan Padi Fields. II. Aruan: Serpent-head Fishes." *Malayan Nat. J.* 4 (1) (1949), 29–31.

———. "Fishes of the Malayan Padi Fields, III. Keli-Catfishes." *Malayan Nat. J.*, 5 (2) (1950), 88–91.

Wyatt, I. J. "Field Investigations of Padi Stem Borers 1955–1956." *Dept. of Agric., Malaya Bull.*, 102 (1957), 41–42.

27. LOCUST CONTROL: ECOLOGICAL PROBLEMS AND INTERNATIONAL PESTS

P. T. Haskell

The organization, strategy and tactics of locust control have developed directly from a knowledge of the peculiar ecology of the locusts. At present, the most widespread and effective method to kill locusts in an infested area is through the use of chemical agents, although experiments have been undertaken to interrupt breeding or egg-laying patterns. Chemical control methods have seldom exhibited untoward biological effects in the surrounding environment, since the concentration of toxic materials used on locusts is much lower than for many other pests and the areas are seldom resprayed because of the migrations of the swarms. However, there is some danger of damaging effects and the possibility of locusts developing resistance to the chemicals presently used.

The most serious problem connected with locust control is the effect of development projects, particularly agricultural schemes. The incidence of locusts and similar pests is often directly related to particular ecological disruptions made by such projects. Such development-related locust problems have occurred in Thailand, Rhodesia, Australia and the United States (detailed case history from Thailand given). Indeed, locust swarms are sometimes a man-induced scourge. All too frequently, insufficient ecological knowledge is available or utilized when development is being planned or carried out. Extensive surveys of the ecological situation should be made before development begins, whenever possible and feasible. Often, however, this cannot be done; it would seem preferable under these circumstances to foster continuing research programs which could elucidate general guidelines, information and past experience, using the ecological principles which underlie processes of change and development of certain types. Tackled in this way, a body of data and experience could be assembled which could be either directly or by extrapolation applicable to wide fields of development with, it is hoped, avoidance of at least the worst blunders of the past.

Organizations do exist that are working on international locust control and research. In the organizations considered in this paper, the interplay of politics, finance and science has been successfully mediated by a clear statement of the ecology of the pest organism, and such a perspective is applicable to efforts made to control all international pests. An attempt to set up control organizations, whatever the pest, whatever the area, will be successful only if based on as detailed a picture as possible of the overall biology and ecology of the pest and its environment.

For the purposes of this paper, the term "international pest" will refer to an animal species which is migrant across national borders and capable of causing economically significant damage to agriculture. This definition does not consider species which, while causing economic damage in many countries and thus being international in distribution, nevertheless arise independently in these countries, are not normally migrant across national borders and can be controlled by measures mounted on a national basis. This definition involves three major factors—science, politics and finance; the principal objective of this paper is to show that only a broad ecological approach can permit useful interplay of these factors.

One of the earliest recognized, the best-known, and potentially the most dangerous genus of international pest is the swarming locust. Man's struggle against this insect probably began with the dawn of agriculture some eight or nine thousand years ago; the desert locust is depicted in carvings at Saqqara in the U.A.R. dated about 2400 B.C., and there are records of the Oriental migratory locust in Shantung Province, China, in 707 B.C. Every major land mass in the world contains at least one species of swarming locust, each distributed over several countries; all staple food crops of man and fodder for his animals are open to attack.

This paper is concerned with case histories of the attempts of man to deal on an international basis with two species of swarming locust; these cases are of particular relevance because they are concerned with international organizations specially set up to deal with these problems. The paper will seek to illustrate the interplay of the prime factors mentioned above —science, politics and finance—and thus derive information relating to the principles of international development in this field.

Before embarking on detailed case histories, it is relevant to outline certain aspects of locust biology. It should first be emphasized that the term "locust," so universally employed, covers a number of species of the Orthoptera family, Acrididae, which display to a greater or lesser degree the phenomenon of phase polymorphism established by Uvarov (1921) and by Faure (1932). The individuals of such species, when at high density, differ in behavior, physiology, color and body form from low-density individuals; moreover the one phase, or morph, can change into the other. Thus, when individuals of these species exist at low densities, the so-called "solitary phase," they behave like grasshoppers; they are mostly sedentary by day, fly at night, take no notice of other individuals of the species and in fact tend to avoid them. However, should the density of such individuals be increased, they undergo physiological changes which can lead quite rapidly to changes in behavior which cause them to associate with their fellows; this results in the so-called "gregarious phase," when the insects maintain communication with one another. Thus,

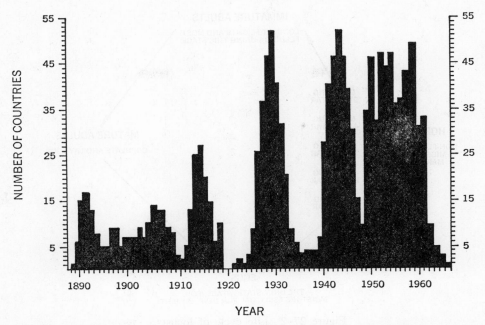

Figure 27–1 Fluctuations in the number of countries invaded by the desert locust: 1890–1966

in the young hopper stage, they march together in close formation, forming hopper bands which may vary in size, according both to absolute numbers and to the stage of development, from a few square feet to many square miles in area (Ellis and Ashall, 1957). When they become adults and take to the wing, this gregarious cohesion produces the flying swarms, the typical and dangerous manifestation of locust species; such swarms, which contain millions of individuals and can cover several hundred miles, move with the wind as coherent entities losing relatively few of their numbers during weeks of migration when they may cover hundreds or even thousands of miles (Waloff, 1946; Rainey, 1963a).

The solitary and gregarious phases differ markedly in behavior and physiology and to a lesser extent in color and body form. Under appropriate conditions, one form can change into another in the lifetime of an individual, although in nature the change is generally spread over more than one generation (Ellis, 1959).

Among the species of Acridids that are called locusts, it is a reasonable generalization that the most dangerous economically are those in which the most intense phase and swarming activity is found. The very qualities of aggregation of large numbers and the mobility associated with it during both ground and aerial stages place locusts among the most dangerous of agricultural pests.

An appreciation of the phase polymorphism of locusts is fundamental to investigation of their ecology and control. It had been recognized early that the incidence of locust species was subject to large fluctuations (Fig. 27–1). Periods characterized by the presence of many populations in the swarming phase, such as the 1930's and 1944, are said to be "plague" periods, while those characterized by low overall numbers of locusts in low-density popu-

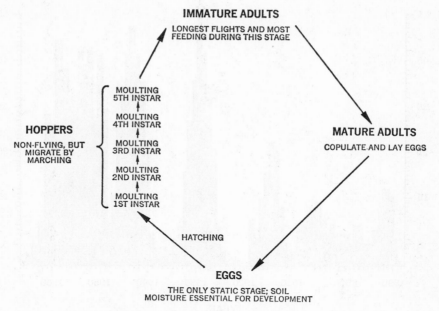

Figure 27–2 Life cycle of locusts

lations, such as 1920 and 1965, are called "recession" periods. One of the major problems of locust ecology concerns the mechanisms and conditions required for a change from plague to recession and vice versa. The phase theory provided the basis for an answer, suggesting that locusts did not disappear during recession periods but changed into the solitary phase and were different in behavior, color and shape from the large number of insects found in plague periods. In fact, Uvarov based his phase theory on a study of what had until then been described as two distinct species, *Locusta migratoria* and *Locusta danica,* which he showed to be two extreme morphs of the same species (Uvarov, 1921).

The life cycle of locusts is relatively simple (Fig. 27–2). It is useful to indicate certain important ecological aspects of each stage. The eggs, the only static stage, are laid up to 10-cm deep in bare soil; locusts will not lay under vegetation and thus a necessary feature of the oviposition environment is the presence of patches of bare

soil, ranging from gravel to fine alluvium. Most important are moisture content and salinity—locusts will not lay in soil containing less than about 3% by weight of water or more than about 1.5% salt content, nor can eggs develop without available water.

The incubation period varies greatly in relation to temperature, ranging from less than 10 days in hot climates to more than 100 days in cold ones.

The hopper stage comprises a number of instars (larval stages); growth is by molting, and the presence of vegetation is important both for feeding and for molting, best accomplished hanging head down from a twig. Diurnal activity is characteristic of the hopper, and marching bands formed by large populations move throughout the day and can cover up to twelve miles during the duration of the hopper instars (Ellis and Ashall, 1957).

The adult stage can be considered in two parts. The first, a period of sexual immaturity, is also the time of greatest flight and feeding activity and thus the most dan-

gerous from the point of view of agricultural damage. Locusts are poikilotherms
(cold-blooded) and can only fly when their
thoracic muscle temperature is about 25° C
or above; as a rule swarms move only after
sunrise when this temperature is reached
and generally continue either until dusk or
until their thoracic temperature falls below
the required minimum. Night flight of
swarms is unusual but can occur if air
temperature is high enough. Thus temperature requirements for flight are a limiting factor to geographical distribution of
swarms. (See Waloff and Rainey, 1951,
for discussion.)

Since the sexes migrate together, no elaborate mate-finding mechanisms (as in grasshoppers) have developed in gregarious locusts, but it is necessary for the sexes to
mature at the same time, and a complex
system of maturation accelerating and inhibiting pheromones (chemicals that provide
biological signals) exists to synchronize maturation (Norris, 1964; Carlisle and Ellis,
1967). When this occurs, swarms pause in
their flight for copulation and oviposition,
afterward resuming flight until the second
ovarial cycle is complete, when mating and
oviposition occur again. Few locust females
survive to lay more than three times. Life
spans of locusts vary with the species, and,
in any one species, with the environment,
but most have only one generation a year.

The mobility of swarms is one of the
most important features of locust behavior
and also one of the factors making control
difficult. Cartographical analysis of the
movements of swarms and tracking of
swarms by light aircraft has confirmed their
amazing mobility; in 1952, for example,
swarms of the desert locust produced in
Ethiopia and Somaliland moved 2000 miles
to breed in a belt extending from Jordan
to Pakistan, while in 1950 breeding on the
Red Sea coast of Saudi Arabia in the early
months of the year produced swarms which
reached Atbara in the Nile Valley in May

and then reached Darfur, 700 miles away,
fifteen days later.

Since laboratory and field experiments
show that the maximum air speed of locusts in still air is on the order of 12 mph
(5.5 meters per second), flights such as
those mentioned above could only be undertaken in the absence of wind, in very
light winds, or downwind; moreover, field
observations showed that locusts do not fly
with consistent orientation for long periods
(Waloff, 1958; Rainey, 1963a). But cartographic analysis of swarm movements
showed a reasonably consistent pattern of
regular major swarm movements, and this,
together with a comparison of swarm movements and current weather data for the
areas concerned, led to the hypothesis, suggested by R. C. Rainey (1951), that all
major swarm displacements take place
downwind. Further experience and experiment has confirmed this hypothesis. Figures
27–3 and 27–4 show some aspects of the
detailed evidence given in Rainey (1963a).

This theory of movement has important
implications for locust ecology. As mentioned above, locust eggs require soil moisture for development, but cartographical
analysis shows that locusts inhabit areas
characterized by generally low and erratic
rainfall; thus, to ensure successful breeding,
eggs have to be laid in synchronization
with rainfall. Detailed consideration of the
meteorological significance of downwind
swarm movement provided at least part
of the answer; in general, winds within a
few thousand feet of the earth's surface
tend to blow into zones of convergence, and
the swarms displaced by such winds would
tend to move into those zones and collect
there (Rainey, 1963a). Areas of marked
low-level convergence are areas where rainfall is likely, so that moving with the winds
ensures that a significant proportion of a
population will move into areas which receive rainfall. This ensures that soil moisture is available for oviposition and sub-

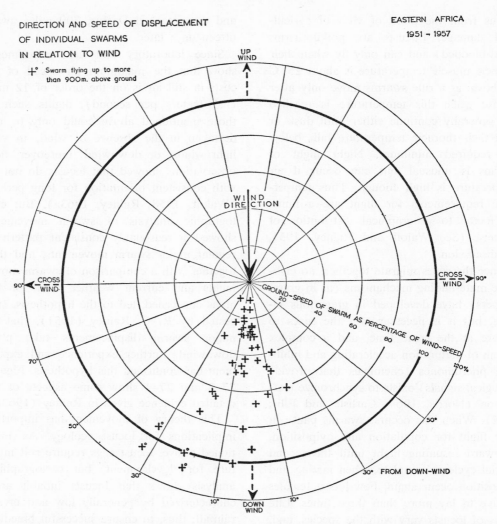

Figure 27–3 Direction and speed of displacement of individual swarms in relation
to wind (After Rainey, 1963)

sequent egg development and also provides food for emergent hoppers in the form of the vegetation flush resulting from the rain. Recent experiments have shown the possibility of elaborate hormonal feed-back mechanisms between locusts and certain desert plants, which could help to synchronize locust maturation with rainfall (Carlisle *et al.*, 1963, 1965; Carlisle and Ellis, 1967). These adaptive ecological mechanisms are of primary importance both for the continued survival of the locusts and also for the development of a scientific basis of both the strategy and tactics of locust control.

In terms of general ecological significance, it is clear that locusts require two different sets of environmental conditions to complete development: eggs must be laid in bare ground, a major element of the "oviposition habitat"; on the other hand, hoppers and adults need vegetation for molting, food and shelter, the so-called "food-shelter habitat." This dual requirement can best

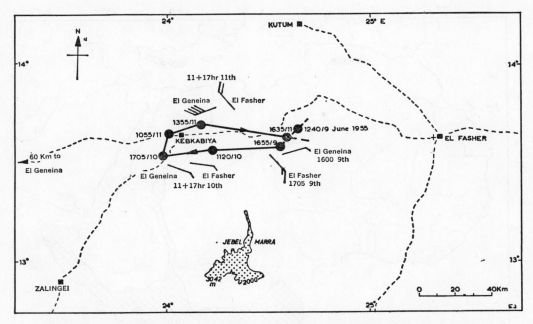

Figure 27–4   Movement of a swarm with reversal of wind direction in the vicinity of the inter-tropical convergence in the Sudan. (After Rainey, 1963). Solid black line shows track of swarm; circles show nightly roost sites, and the figures beside them show time and date of observation of swarm position. Wind speed and direction are shown by the feathered arrows; each full feather = 10 km/hr. The wind readings were made at the stations of El Fasher and El Geneina, and this and the hour and date of reading are shown beside each arrow. All dates refer to the month of June 1955

be provided in areas of mosaic vegetation. Locusts need moisture for egg incubation and food, but live in areas of low and erratic rainfall; hence fluctuations of locust populations are to some degree weather-regulated. The degree and subtlety of this regulation depend both on synoptic and medium-scale weather and medium-scale and small-scale climatic changes. Within this general ecological framework, there is wide variation, as the following case histories show.

A further corollary of this ecological balance is that alterations of the ecology of an area by man can provide the stimulus for a population upsurge of endemic locust or grasshopper species. Thus development projects such as deforestation to provide agricultural land, or irrigation schemes, can trigger such outbreaks.

CASE HISTORIES OF LOCUST CONTROL

The two species of locust selected for detailed consideration are the red locust, *Nomadacris septemfasciata* Serville, and the desert locust, *Schistocerca gregaria* Forskål. These two species have been chosen because they have different ecological backgrounds. As a result, the strategies and organizations adopted to control them have been different.

THE RED LOCUST, NOMADACRIS SEPTEMFASCIATA SERVILLE

A cartographical analysis (Morant, 1947) provided a clear picture of the chronological and geographical develop-

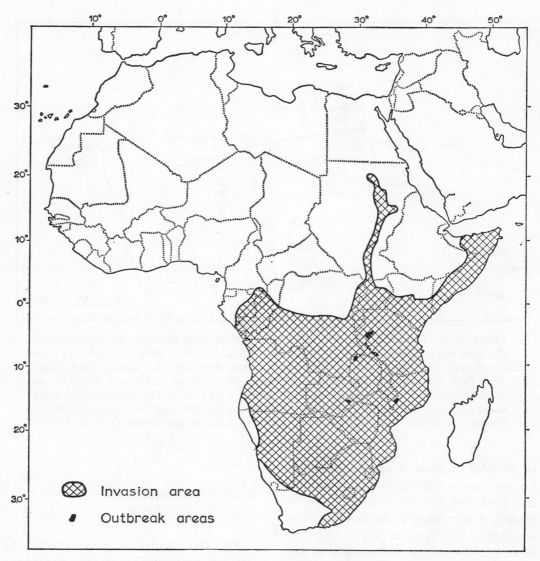

Figure 27–5(a)   Red locust plague and the maximum area invaded by swarms during the last outbreak (1930–1944)

ment of the red locust which began in 1927 in the Mweru wa Ntipa marshes of Zambia; a series of field investigations by British, Belgian and South African entomologists had implicated further areas, or "outbreak areas," as they are now called (Fig. 27–5a). It was suspected that such areas always harbored populations of the locust, which under certain conditions multiplied, aggregated, formed swarms and

moved outward beyond the fringes of the "outbreak area" into the "invasion area" (Fig. 27–5b). Field investigations substantiated this idea and led to the suggestion that permanent supervision in the outbreak areas could lead to the control of swarming populations at their sources. In 1936 the British delegation to the Fourth International Locust Conference in Cairo proposed a plan for such permanent supervision in

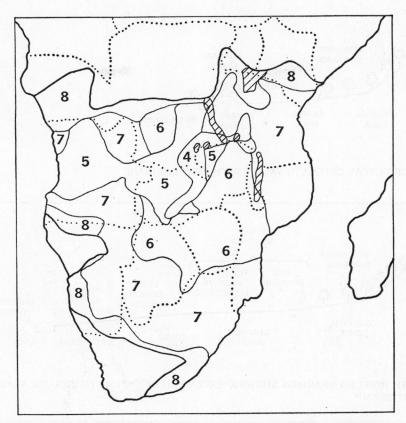

Figure 27–5(b)   Red locusts. Two known outbreak areas in 1927–1929
(After these three years, the numbers from four onwards show the annual expansion of
the invaded area for the period 1930–1934. Dotted lines are national borders.) (After
Morant, 1947)

two red locust outbreak areas (the Mweru wa Ntipa and Rukwa) by an internationally financed organization, and this scheme was again discussed in Brussels in the 1938 Conference. Political difficulties and the outbreak of war delayed agreement, but by then the plague was at its height and in 1940 the British and Belgian governments decided to set up an organization for red locust control. Abercorn (now Mbala) in Zambia was chosen as the most convenient base and operations began in 1941 (see Uvarov, 1951; and Gunn, 1960).

The principal functions of the International Red Locust Control Service were to organize control in the known outbreak areas, to organize an information service and to study the ecology of the red locust and methods for its control. The general principle of operation, based on the ecological concept of the function of outbreak areas, was to patrol the area and to initiate control measures where large populations were discovered.

Although the application of the "outbreak area" principle had reduced the area of operations from almost the whole of Africa south of the Sahara to a region of less than 2000 square miles, even this represented a formidable area of varying ecology. All the red locust outbreak areas are in the Rift Valley system of East Africa and are areas of closed or impeded drain-

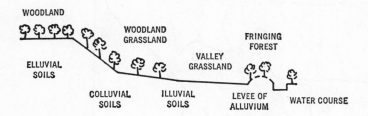

A. DIAGRAM OF TYPICAL CATENA IN VALLEY WITH FREE DRAINAGE

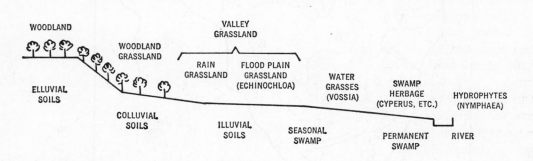

B. VALLEY WITH IMPEDED DRAINAGE SHOWING EXTENSION OF CATENA TO INCLUDE SEASONAL AND PERMANENT SWAMP

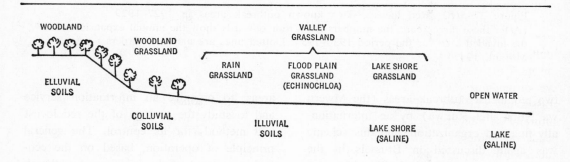

C. VALLEY WITH CLOSED DRAINAGE, SHOWING CATENA MODIFIED BY INCIDENCE OF LAKE SHORE GRASSLANDS SURROUNDING SHALLOW SALINE LAKE

Figure 27-6 Diagrams of vegetation in valleys with different types of drainage (After Vesey-Fitzgerald, 1955)

age; Fig. 27–6 is a diagram summarizing the type of vegetation complex which typically occurs in these areas. Both the Rukwa Valley and Mweru wa Ntipa outbreak areas are regions of closed drainage and each has a shallow brackish lake, fed by small rivers, subject to great variations in water level. There are three major hydrological factors operating—rainfall, river flooding, and saline back-floods from the lakes; the interplay of these factors, which varies between and during wet seasons in relation to absolute rainfall, relative drainage and other factors, causes variability in the resultant vegetation, producing alterations in the size of the areas inhabited by various grasses.

This ecological instability has important effects on the biology of the red locust. The locust has a single generation per year; breeding, perhaps in relation to an associated fall in maximum daily temperatures, starts during the rainy season, which lasts from November to March; hoppers hatch from January to March and consequently the new generation of adults begins to appear in February. As the rains end, the adults then diapause through the dry season until the next rains; since they have to live throughout the dry period, when the grasses dry out and are burned off either naturally or deliberately, their survival depends on finding an adequate food-shelter habitat. Movement of adults to such habitats, which are restricted in area during the dry season, may cause concentration, a factor favoring aggregation and hence swarm production. When the rains begin, the adults mature and need bare ground—the "oviposition habitat." This is apparently found by flight, and the adults return to the "food-shelter" habitat. Owing to the instability of the overall habitat, wet years in which bare soil areas are restricted could result in concentration of laying adults; alternatively, in dry years when there is plenty of bare soil, dispersion of adults may occur.

It was realized early that a study of the numbers of locusts and their fluctuations in an outbreak area was of the greatest importance for both control techniques and logistics. There seemed to be two mechanisms by which swarms could arise: if egg-laying was concentrated, dense hopper bands could produce swarms; but also, if there were sufficient adults, these could progressively concentrate in the dry season and finally produce swarms. A great deal of research by many scientists (see, e.g., Scheepers and Gunn, 1958; Symmons, 1959, 1963) finally showed that the latter process was probably of the greater importance. This research also enabled a dangerous population to be quantified; thus Scheepers and Gunn concluded that in the North Rukwa outbreak area a small migrant swarm could contain some 5–10 million locusts. If the total population of the area was of the order of 20 million, a swarm was unlikely to be produced, whereas populations of 50 million could produce swarms.

Population dynamics was thus of the utmost importance in relation to control, the objective of which was to prevent the escape of migrant swarms. It was thus desirable to evolve methods relating these variables to some measurable parameter of the outbreak area, but the complexity of the ecological situation, described above, was such that straightforward correlation of population with measurable environmental factors was most difficult. An example of this complexity is the work of Symmons (1959) on the effect of rainfall on locust numbers. One obvious relationship depends on the lake size; from 1937 to 1942 the level of Lake Rukwa was very high and locust populations very low, because the area of suitable ground for adult survival and oviposition was small. But more surprisingly, a negative correlation existed between multiplication in one wet season and the total rainfall in the previous wet season. Symmons produced an equation:

$$y = 6.518 - 0.160 \; x_1 + 0.425 \; x_2 + 0.092 \; x_3$$

where

y = adult locust population in mid dry season,

x_1 = mean rainfall, in inches, in the Rukwa Valley and its drainage basin in the last but one wet season,

x_2 = the level of the parental population,

x_3 = rainfall in the Rukwa Valley in the preceding October–December.

The total regression is highly significant ($R=0.93$, $P<0.01$) and the standard error of estimate was 0.55 unit in the scale of five units of infestation levels utilized. This equation enabled the size of the adult locust population to be estimated so that the scale of hopper control measures could be appropriately modified. This forecasting method worked well until 1961 when the lake flooded.

Locust control at source was the raison d'être of the Service, and the methods used had progressed from beating locusts to death with sticks, to the broadcasting of poisonous dusts such as sodium arsenate, to the use of BHC from large power dusters. At first only hoppers could be attacked because suitable insecticides and techniques to deal with mobile adults had not been developed, but in 1947, trials with 20% di-nitro-ortho-cresol from medium aircraft were made on desert locust swarms in Kenya and showed great promise; however, it was concluded at that time that powerful ground sprayers would probably be more economical for red locusts (see Gunn, 1960, for details).

Both the research and the control techniques, which had developed interdependently, were costly; both demanded all-weather access to outbreak areas, requiring roads, bridges, dams and many specialized vehicles with adequate maintenance facilities. Both used much manpower, requiring the recruitment, training, accommodation and servicing of large scouting and control labor forces. The scientific requirements

also grew, so that the budget rose from £76,000 in 1948 to some £259,000 in 1956.

Such increases are bound to be queried and by 1952 the economic value of the Service was questioned. The plague had ceased in 1944, but many swarms had escaped from the outbreak areas without giving rise to a new one, although the reasons for this are not known. Furthermore, since it was impossible to estimate what damage might have occurred, no fundamental economic yardstick was available to assess the value of the large expenditure. Since swarm escapes continued to occur, both scouting and control were clearly inadequate; indeed, it was obvious that the control potential then available to the Service was insufficient to deal with the possible peak locust populations in the outbreak areas. Thus, better and more economical control methods had to be found, and from 1952 to 1957 the highest priority was given to operational research on control methods; at the same time, control by toxic chemicals was recognized as only one method and a search for ecological methods was instituted.

Insecticide research was carried out and has been fully described by Lloyd (1959). The success of this work can be judged from the fact that by 1957 all the control methods used in 1952 had been superseded. The major technique became aerial spraying by light aircraft, using 20% DNC in oil against adults, both settled and flying, and dieldrin emulsion against hoppers in a lattice spraying technique. The economy and efficiency of aerial spraying, even with hired aircraft, was so impressive that in 1956 the Service bought two Piper Super Cubs and set up its own aerial control unit.

Side by side with the research into chemical techniques had gone investigations on ecological control, of particular interest because they represent the most detailed study ever made of these methods for locusts; the techniques investigated were fire control, water control, afforestation and ranching.

Fire control depended on the locust's ovipositional requirement of bare ground. In the dry season in the Rukwa, the grasses are fired both naturally and deliberately by the local inhabitants, producing areas of bare soil of varying size and of random distribution. The purpose of fire control was to limit indiscriminate grass-burning by deliberately burning control strips to make large firebreaks, and thus to leave areas for oviposition easily accessible for control. An alternative to fire control was total fire prevention to reduce the bare ground available and hence interfere with oviposition. But both these techniques were costly and difficult to operate because of the habits of the indigenous human population.

Water control, restraining flooding and stabilizing the environment, was impracticable because of the impeded drainage, but flooding to produce permanent lakes over the outbreak areas was more attractive, since such lakes might then be used as fish farms. Such a scheme was proposed for the Mweru wa Ntipa and was investigated in detail, but was dropped mainly because of the high capital cost.

Red locusts are insects of grasslands and are not found in forests; schemes to plant trees in various areas of the Rukwa were therefore investigated, but plantations proved difficult to establish because of ecological instability, and there was no evidence as to the efficacy of the method. Ranching was attempted in Rukwa to see if cattle could eat the grasses preferred by locusts, but after some years of investigation it was concluded that the method was impracticable.

A great deal of money and research effort was put into these investigations on ecological control and it is unfortunate that they could not be pursued further. Today there is increased pressure to look for and utilize ecological methods, if possible; however, such pressure could result in the premature employment of methods which in the long run might prove to be less efficient, more costly and even ultimately as deleterious as toxic chemicals. This last possibility rarely seems to be considered but it is just as important to ensure that the long-term changes which might follow ecological control methods are not harmful to man or his agriculture as it is to minimize the danger from toxic residues resulting from chemical control. This requirement brings us up against one of the main scientific difficulties: it is often impossible to forecast in detail the long-term changes which certain operations may cause. The proposals to stabilize the water level of the Mweru wa Ntipa, and hence effectively eliminate it as an outbreak area while at the same time providing an increased source of fish, foundered partly because of cost and partly because of uncertainty that the biological objectives would be achieved. (See Gunn, 1957, for further details of all this work.)

By 1959 the increasing efficiency of aerial survey and control led to the proposal that all operations could be carried out by aircraft alone, thus eliminating the expensive ground transport and its associated maintenance, road-building and labor costs. After preliminary trials, this policy was adopted in the early 1960's and has been increasingly pursued. The initial difficulties with an all-aerial service were mainly in accurate survey of populations in the outbreak areas; this is necessary both to pinpoint populations for control attack and also to formulate logistic requirements. Early attempts at aerial survey, even with specially adapted light aircraft, emphasized the difficulties if not the impossibility of such methods (Symmons *et al.*, 1963). But in 1964 the Service acquired a helicopter, and in further work in 1964 and 1965 Symmons was able to show (1966) that because the helicopter was flown at an altitude of 10 feet and a speed of 10 mph, it caused adult locusts to flush completely. Because these could be counted by the observer, aerial estimation of a complete outbreak area population was possible. This powerful support for all-aerial operation was important and timely because both research and events had shown the existence of further outbreak areas of the red locust; thus the Wembere Steppe in Tanzania, the Kafue Flats in Zambia and the Lake Chilwa swamps in Malawi were known to be capable of producing swarms, and survey and control of these areas, distant from the main service base, would have been costly and cumbersome without aircraft.

Today, after more than two decades, the Service probably constitutes one of the most efficient international pest control bodies in existence; its annual budget is economical, and its techniques and resources are adequate to deal with reasonably large-scale infestations in several outbreak areas. Furthermore, it is becoming increasingly probable year after year that the absence of a plague for a quarter of a century is due to the work of the Service; and while it would be foolish to aver that there will never be another plague, at least it can be claimed that outbreaks that might give rise to a plague will occur less frequently in the future.

These apparently satisfactory results of the Service conceal some weaknesses. First, the Service has never, since adopting the all-aerial policy, had to deal with large-scale outbreaks in widely separated outbreak areas; this could cause severe logistic and operational difficulties. Second, as part of the economy and streamlining measures, the research side of the organization was disbanded and the only locust scientist on the staff is the director. The Service has a research contract with the Anti-Locust Research Centre whereby certain research, mostly operational research on new insecticides and spray gear, is carried out. But the reduction of scientific staff means

that all experience of locust control, survey and operational techniques resides now with two or three men. Finally, and paradoxically, because of the success of the present arrangements, little or no research is going on about the long-term prospects of controlling the red locust by means other than toxic chemicals. The possible long-term effects of continual spraying of toxic chemicals, even in the very low dosages now used, and the possibility of the development of resistance to insecticides, have already been demonstrated in locusts (MacCuaig, 1958, 1960).[1]

What then does the future hold? It would be foolish to expect permanent ecological solutions; the ecological complexity of the problem, the vast areas involved and the cost of even the smallest scheme make such solutions impractical within the foreseeable future. Permanent biological solutions, such as the artificial production of a locust genotype with non-swarming characteristics which could be introduced into all outbreak areas in sufficient numbers to change the population character, are perhaps, even taking into account the progress of molecular biology, equally difficult to envisage and certainly could not be accomplished without a complex and expensive research program. But the facts of red locust biology and ecology, indicating that plagues originate in finite although large areas, and that they can be avoided by action against the locust populations in those areas, suggest that something on these lines might provide an acceptable solution.

Investigations into the natural enemies of the red locust have shown that although many exist, including Asilid flies and certain Odonata, they seem to operate at a low level, subsidiary to the other ecological factors (Stortenbeker, 1967). Thus classical biological control is almost impossible.

[1] A large variation in the LD_{50} minimum toxic dose is found in laboratory-reared cultures and, clearly, by selecting the most resistant individuals, a resistant strain could probably be built up.

What of the newer methods? The sterile male technique must obviously be considered, but classical objections apply; the locust is a multiple-mating insect, and it is the last injection of sperm which fertilizes the eggs. Even low populations, by locust standards, contain many millions of insects and it would be extremely difficult and very costly to rear, sterilize and release sufficient numbers at the right time and place, particularly as the locust is migrant even in its outbreak areas. Many of these difficulties could be avoided by application of chemosterilant chemicals in situ; it is therefore disappointing that trials of the presently available insect chemosterilants have shown little promise with locusts, the sterilizing dose of these very toxic compounds being near the lethal dose and in all cases higher than that of the most toxic insecticides. But this does not preclude the discovery of better compounds in the future. Furthermore, the use of attractive sterilizing traps is a possibility, since recent research has shown the existence of plant chemicals attractive to locusts (Haskell *et al.,* 1962). However, these may not be sufficiently active in heavy vegetation, and in any case the requirement of placing them and checking the population in all outbreak areas might be more costly than the present chemical control, although this could be overcome by designing traps which could be dropped from the air.

The difficulties inherent in all these methods suggest that new lines of attack are needed, and work carried out in the Anti-Locust Research Centre over the last five years has indicated a fruitful area for research; broadly speaking, the objective of this research is to find chemicals, active on locusts but not on man or other animals, which interfere with aspects of the reproductive physiology of the insect. This work arose from studies on the hormonal and pheromonal mechanisms involved in locust reproduction, which together produce an adaptive mechanism to synchronize matura-

tion between the sexes, and to relate this maturation to the onset of rainfall, so that eggs are laid in conditions ensuring their development and the presence of food supplies for the emergent hoppers. Furthermore, as mentioned above, evidence is now available, at least for the desert locust, of a feed-back mechanism between chemical constituents of certain plants of the locust habitat and the reproductive mechanism of the insect, which seems to represent a further factor in the fine adaptation of the locust to its environment. (For details, see Carlisle *et al.,* 1963; Carlisle and Ellis, 1967; Carlisle *et al.,* 1965; Norris, 1964.) The field is a large one, ranging from chemicals which may inhibit aggregation to chemicals which advance or retard maturation; it requires a great deal of basic research before anything practical can appear. But already this work has discovered relatively simple, nontoxic chemicals, which when applied externally to the locust, can induce early maturation, disrupting the relationship between the insect and its environment and presumably thus inducing heavy mortality both in the egg and hopper stages. This work is just beginning and practical application is a long way off since it has to be preceded by adequate trials to ensure both that the method is efficient and economic and also that it has no deleterious long-term effects. However, it seems to offer a possible line of approach to new methods of locust control, which do not suffer from some of the drawbacks attendant on present techniques.

The Desert Locust, schistocerca gregaria (Forskål)

Figure 27–7 shows the extent of desert locust invasion and recession areas.[2] Figure 27–8 summarizes the seasonal migration pattern of the species. The figures show that

[2] For further information see Waloff, 1946, 1966; Donnelly, 1947; Davies, 1952; Fortescue-Foulkes, 1953; Rainey, 1963a.

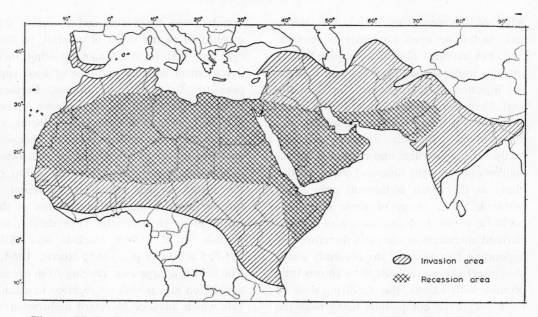

Invasion area

Recession area

Figure 27–7 Desert locust's maximum distribution area liable to invasion during plagues and the smaller locust area during recessions

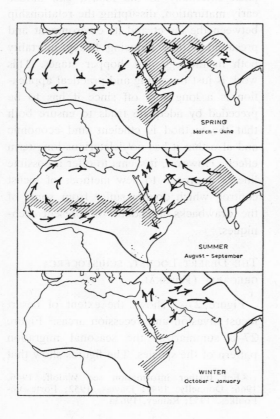

SPRING
March – June

SUMMER
August – September

WINTER
October – January

Figure 27–8(a) Seasonal breeding areas and major movements of desert locust swarms. Spring (March–June) breeding areas and movements of swarms produced in them

Figure 27–8(b) Summer (August–September) breeding areas and the movements of swarms produced in them

Figure 27–8(c) Winter (October–January) breeding areas and the movements of swarms produced in them

over most of the area there is in general a two-generation annual cycle of breeding; in western Africa locusts breed from about July to September and their progeny migrate northward, typically arriving in Morocco and nearby countries in October through November. These adults breed from March to June, the so-called "spring breeding," and the resultant swarms, appearing from April onward, recross the Sahara southward to the summer belt and a new cycle begins in the monsoon rains.

Such a system of transfer to northern areas in the spring is characteristic of the other regions of the invasion area, but in the central region it is modified by the influence of the more complicated wind systems of the Red Sea basin and East Africa so that a third breeding period, the "winter season," occurs from about October to April. Although much migration of swarms occurs within each region, migration is frequent between the regions and thus the mobility of populations follows the seasonal whole vast area constitutes the "invasion area" of the desert locust.

The mechanism and significance of these migrations have been outlined above. During plague periods, the invasion area is characterized by the widespread presence of numbers of high-density, gregarious populations which in general beget similar populations; but in any one area or season, dispersion of these populations can occur, so that there is always a spectrum of phase types in existence, but with the great majority of locusts present in swarms. Periods of recession are characterized both by low overall populations and a reduction in the area containing most of the locusts to about 50% of the invasion area; both solitary and swarming populations occur, but the latter are much reduced compared to plague years and may be completely absent for several successive generations in any one region. Within the reduced "recession area" (Fig. 27–7), which roughly coincides with the east-west arid belt of the invasion area, the mobility of populations follows the seasonal plague pattern. Waloff (1966) has made a detailed study of the upsurges and recessions of the desert locust from 1920 to the present time and should be consulted for details.

The biogeographical and ecological research carried out on the desert locust has verified that no permanent breeding areas exist for this species and moreover has emphasized the extreme ecological adaptability of the insect (see Popov, 1965; Uvarov, 1957). It is impossible to characterize "the habitat" of this species, which has developed an opportunistic biology characterized by seasonal breeding in areas of differing vegetation and climate. The only unifying features are represented by the environmental requirements at breeding, related to the water necessary for oviposition and egg development and the bare soil of the oviposition habitat. The locust lives in very unstable environmental conditions and depends upon its migratory behavior mechanism, which seems to be partly initiated and controlled by the weather, to take it to areas with suitable environmental conditions for breeding. Bearing in mind the small-scale and medium-scale variations in weather, even in regions in which the synoptic pattern is relatively stable, this mechanism is clearly hazardous, and subsidiary mechanisms have evolved to refine the basic adaptation. These are the complicated physiological mechanisms, referred to above, for synchronizing maturation between the sexes and with rainfall, which together ensure that individuals can take advantage of suitable breeding areas when they reach them.

In theory, control of the desert locust should be subject to economic considerations and should not be undertaken if damage is likely to be light or if the expense of control exceeds potential damage. But, because of its ecology, the desert locust is a political insect both nationally and internationally. Internationally, countries are under pressure from their neighbors to prevent escapes over their borders, and nationally they will come under pressure from agricultural interests. Ministers of agriculture are thus forced to consider issues ranging from the danger of large-scale damage, with perhaps the need to import food to avert famine, to local cases of districts or individuals whose livelihood has literally been eaten up by locusts. These facts have ensured the continuation of pressure for action, both national and international, against the desert locust, and for this reason, taking a long-term view, reasonable if not always adequate financial support has been available; the problem is how to spend it most efficiently. As Gunn (1960b) points out, four locust control strategies are available: (a) outbreak area control, (b) frontier defense, (c) overall attack, (d) local defense of crops. The ecological argument is dominant here, since it shows clearly that for the desert locust (a) is inapplicable, (d) will have little effect on overall plague control and (b) is too difficult to operate since the locust frontiers are ecological and cut across national boundaries. Thus overall attack is the only possible strategy; the problem is how to execute it.

The seasonal ecology of desert locust movements serves as a general indication for areas and seasons of attack, but regional strategy and tactics demand further knowledge of locust biology. In the early days of locust control only the hopper stage or swarms at night could be attacked; however, with the advent of aircraft spraying, first developed scientifically against the desert locust, the control mobility more nearly matched the locust mobility, and control of flying swarms became possible. The behavior of locusts, both in swarms and in hopper bands, in relation to their density at various times of day and their speed of movement, the use of new and more concentrated insecticides and the develop-

ment of both ground and air ultra-low-volume application methods (for details see Sayer, 1959; Courshee, 1959, 1964) have produced cheap and effective methods of control, so that given a suitable administrative, logistic and financial basis, a modern locust control organization has the technical means to kill such large numbers of desert locusts that a plague might be stopped.

But so far this has not proved possible, as the recent upsurge in 1967–68 dramatically demonstrated. This was partly due to political and financial factors which have prevented the adequate functioning of the necessary organization, but mainly due to the great perennial difficulty of control organizations—that of finding the locusts. Before considering this latter aspect a word must be said about possible future methods of control. Clearly there is some room for improvement in the present techniques and doubtless they will be improved; but it is rather unlikely that in the foreseeable future, or during the course of the new plague which has just started, they will improve dramatically. As regards the development of new methods of control, all the arguments considered above in relation to the red locust apply to the desert locust, most of them a fortiori. There is clearly no possibility of general ecological control, and local attempts, which might perhaps be possible by water control or afforestation, would be very costly and moreover pointless from the point of view of plague prevention. All work on the parasites and predators of the desert locust (see Greathead, 1963, for a review) has demonstrated the impossibility of classical biological control, mainly because the mobility of the locust populations impedes build-up of the parasite-predator population and also because expenditure might not be significantly less than present control costs. It is salutary in this context to realize that the number of locusts in even a small swarm is vast enough to swamp all available predator potential in the locality;

thus, while locust swarms in eastern Africa are often attended by great flocks of birds, even those of very high capacity such as storks which can eat over one thousand locusts at a sitting, hardly make any difference to the size of a single swarm. The newer methods of biological control which, as stated above, could perhaps be considered in some form for red locust outbreak area control, are inapplicable to the desert locust and the search for new control methods by biologically active chemicals is in its infancy.

Thus it is difficult to see at present how any form of permanent biological control could be applied to the desert locust in a plague period, owing to the vast number of insects and their mobility through the invasion area; if an efficient method were to be found, it might be used during a recession, but even then the difficulty of finding the important populations to which to apply it would still be paramount. Indeed it is clear that this difficulty applies to any control method for the desert locust and it must be concluded that this is the central problem. It arises because of the ecological lability of the locust, and the migrant drive related to it. There is no simple answer to the problem of finding in good time dangerous populations of the desert locust; the method presently advocated and used with reasonable success by several organizations is a combination of aerial and ground survey. Aerial survey is necessary for swarm reconnaissance; and since dense hopper bands can sometimes be detected from the air, it can often produce a bonus by indicating the areas containing them. The range of visibility of swarms from aircraft depends on factors related to locust behavior and to meteorological conditions (see Rainey, 1963a, for discussion) and varies from 1 to 50 km; this range might be extended by the use of radar, which can detect swarms, and research on its use is under way.

Ground reconnaissance is still essential in most regions but the area covered is necessarily limited and the sample size correspondingly small; it has advantages in that identification is certain and accurate information on the size, density and state of the populations is obtainable, and that in some areas the best distributed source of information, the local people, can be tapped. More precise knowledge of the ecology of the species throughout the invasion area would clearly help to delimit seasons and areas of search, and research on this should have a high priority; this in turn could lead to a more exact appreciation of the danger potential of populations in various areas. This varies in relation to seasonal and meteorological factors, since under certain conditions it is known that breeding, oviposition or hatching would be unsuccessful and such populations need not be controlled. Information of this sort requires a better knowledge of the meteorology of certain areas and improved weather forecasting is of great importance. Satellite data have already proved of value, but this method does not provide very precise data, which are essential.

As Uvarov (1957) has pointed out, no simple correlation can be found between locust population dynamics and any index of weather, such as mean temperature or precipitation, or any combination of such factors; but given adequate ecological data, correlations might be found locally which would simplify and render more accurate the present forecasting methods. The latter are most important because in addition to their main function of indicating survey areas they determine both the level and the timing of the administrative and logistic operations which necessarily precede control; an excellent example of this is the warning, formulated by the Desert Locust Information Service and issued by FAO in December 1967, of an impending upsurge of the desert locust. At a subsequent international meeting member countries ex-

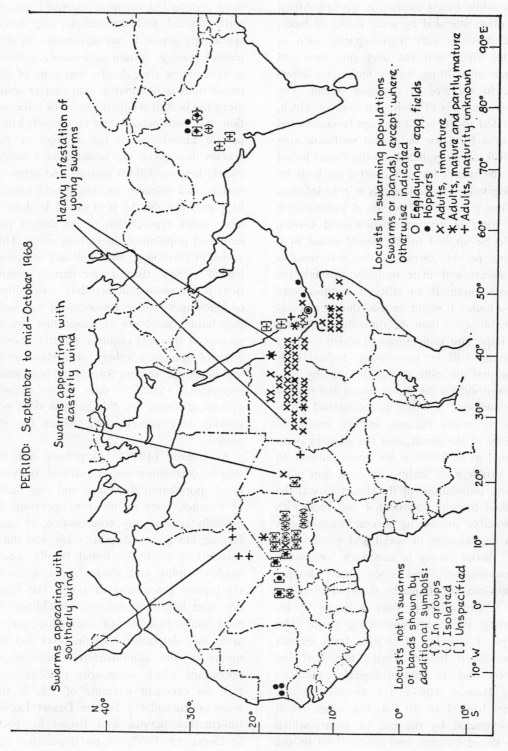

PERIOD: September to mid—October 1968

Heavy infestation of
young swarms

Swarms appearing with
easterly wind

Swarms appearing with
southerly wind

Locusts in swarming populations
(swarms or bands), *except where*
otherwise indicated

○ Egglaying or *egg fields*
● Hoppars
✕ Adults, immature
✱ Adults, mature and partly *mature*
+ Adults, maturity unknown

Locusts not in swarms
or bands shown by
additional symbols:
{} In groups
() Isolated
[] Unspecified

Figure 27–9 The map sent out with the Desert Locust Monthly Summary by the
Desert Locust Information Service, London

pressed their appreciation of the value of this warning which had given them four or five months to prepare their organizations and to order insecticides before the infestation became heavy (for an example of such information see Fig. 27–9). But improvement of forecasting is badly needed and can result from the amassing and analysis of further ecological and meteorological data and the pursuit of investigations into new methods such as computer-based techniques. The above brief analysis of the central problem of desert locust control suggests that at present the best approach is further ecological research on the distribution, movements and the reproductive and survival capacity of locust populations, with particular reference to weather.

Finally we have to consider the form of international cooperation which could best facilitate both this research requirement and also the chemical control which must continue through the foreseeable future. The present administrative basis consists of a mixture of regional organizations and regional commissions, the former being independent bodies with executive powers, the latter only responsible for coordination and cooperation between members; research, survey and control are conducted by these bodies in their own areas and the only truly international operation is that of the information service. It is clear from what is known of the present upsurge of the desert locust, which began about November 1967 and produced the current plague, that this came about because survey coverage was insufficient and control potential inadequate in many areas. This was partly due to the lowered morale and hence inefficiency of survey organizations produced by the recession and partly because in the absence of locusts other internal pressures on departments of agriculture produced cuts in anti-locust budgets or the diversion of resources for other, more urgent purposes. However, in many countries agricultural development

proceeded apace; now the locust is back and these countries have more at risk; this will undoubtedly produce budgetary increases for anti-locust operations, at least to begin with, and has already resulted in heavy requests for capital aid and technical assistance from the United Nations Development Programme (U.N.D.P.), FAO and donor countries, such as U.S.A., U.K., Canada and France, who have responded with a total of more than one million U.S. dollars. But this aid is mainly to repair initial capital deficiencies and represents a fraction of the total cost of survey and control.

Clearly, if the nations affected have reached the upper limit in provision of locust finance, and the effort this money provides has not prevented the return of the locust plague, the situation is serious, and since it is doubtful whether the nations concerned can bear a large permanent increase in their locust budgets, it may appear irredeemable. There is, however, one constructive approach left; because of the research which has been carried out in many countries over the past ten to fifteen years, it is now possible to produce a regionally based strategic plan for the control of the desert locust throughout its invasion area which would give details of the survey and control potential required, all relevant details of the times and areas of effort and the likely logistic requirements and an estimate of the cost. Preliminary consideration suggests that the total financial requirements of the plan might fall within the financial provision now available and this alone suggests that this proposal is worth considering.

For reasons given above, it is still not feasible to propose a single centralized control agency for the desert locust, but the adoption by all existing regional organizations of a single agreed strategic plan could revolutionize the whole approach to the problem. The plan would set both the pattern and the limit of resources to be provided, could be used as a yardstick to measure effort and inaction and would enable international bodies like U.N.D.P. and FAO and likely donor countries to measure and provide assistance to those areas where it would do most overall good.

PROBLEMS AND POSSIBILITIES

The foregoing consideration of the national and international efforts directed to the control of the red and desert locusts over several decades emphasizes that the considerable degree of success obtained has been based on extensive ecological research, using the term in its broadest sense; but great problems remain and may well be intensified in the future because of the need for continued rapid development of agriculture in relation to world food requirements. These problems can be considered under two headings—scientific, and political and financial. It is also relevant at this point to discuss international pests, as defined at the beginning of this paper, other than locusts, and consider how the lessons derived from intensive and long-term studies of the latter can help to formulate efficient and safe control techniques for the former. As examples of international pests one could consider some of the migratory species of Lepidoptera such as the African army worm *Spodoptera exempta*, the lesser army worm *Spodoptera exigua*, and the cotton leaf worm *Spodoptera littoralis;* these are serious agricultural pests of world significance, as the paper in this volume by Rivnay (Chapter 20) and the review by Brown (1962) show. In the same category come many bird pests, such as the weaver birds (*Quelea* spp.) widespread in Africa and causing tremendous damage to cereal crops. The major scientific problems relating to control of all such pests are first, the investigation of their distribution, movements,

population fluctuations and damage potential, which is necessary as a basis for the strategy and tactics of control; second, the problems of control themselves, such as pest resistance to chemicals and the problems of toxic residues and environmental contamination; and third, the problems of the extension or intensification of pest problems due to developmental processes initiated by man himself.

As regards the first problem, distribution and movements of populations, the methods of locust research are more or less directly applicable to many other pests, in both practical and theoretical considerations. An excellent illustration of this is the joint research on the African army worm, *Spodoptera exempta,* carried out during the last few years in East Africa on an international basis by the Army Worm Division of the East African Agriculture and Forest Research Organization and the Anti-Locust Research Centre, with cooperation from the relevant ministries in Tanzania, Kenya, Uganda, Ethiopia and the Somali Republic as well as the Desert Locust Control Organization for Eastern Africa. The research has not only clarified the migratory behavior of the moth and cast light on its seasonal movements and their relation to weather systems, but also shows promise of providing a basis for a forecasting system which will be invaluable for control (for details see Brown *et al.,* 1969).[3]

Pest resistance to chemical control, which is a major problem with static pests when insecticides are applied with no basic ecological considerations (see the papers in this

---

[3] At the end of 1968, the Anti-Locust Research Centre, at the request of the East African Community of Kenya, Tanzania and Uganda, put a team into East Africa to study the ecology of the weaver bird, *Quelea* spp.; this team will work for at least three years on the basic biology and distribution of the birds, and a determination of their damage potential to agriculture, as a basis for the formulation of rational control methods. Some of the research techniques used will be based on methods developed for locust work.

volume by Smith, Conway and Boza Bar-ducci), seems unlikely to become as difficult with migratory locust pests; because of the mobility of populations and their consequent mixing, it is improbable that any one population will be sprayed to the level where only resistant survivors remain and for these resistant survivors to meet and breed with similar survivors from other operations. But clearly with outbreak area locusts, like the red locust, such a possibility does exist, and since, as mentioned above, the potential for resistance does seem to be present in locusts (MacCuaig, 1958, 1960), a careful check on the appearance of this phenomenon is necessary; so far no manifestations have been recorded. The dangers of toxic residues and environmental contamination are also to some extent minimized in this class of pest because the area of operations varies from season to season and year to year. Even in areas such as the Sousse Valley in Morocco, where because of topographical and meteorological factors combined with the siting of vulnerable crop areas, spraying is carried out in substantially the same area during each locust infestation, on-the-spot checks have shown no untoward build-up of residues in the soil or alteration of ecological balance. This is related to the fact that the special ultra-low-volume spraying techniques developed for locust work deposit perhaps only a hundredth of the dose of active toxic ingredient on vegetation as compared with normal agricultural spray practice. Even direct contamination of rivers or lakes is unlikely to cause biological damage unless it occurs repeatedly, which is improbable because of the shifting target areas. However, the existence of this danger is known and work is already in progress on the use of nonpersistent insecticides for locust control in certain areas where there is a danger of build-up. For the future, work of a long-term nature on entirely new methods of control is already under way to obviate the use of toxic chemicals.

A more serious problem is the effect of development projects, notably agricultural schemes, on the incidence of locusts and other similar pests. Uvarov (1957) has already warned that locusts are to a large extent man-made pests, and the opportunistic ecology of these insects can result in a rapid upsurge of population when suitable opportunities present themselves. Thus extensions of the Shire valley sugar estates in Rhodesia in 1964–65 resulted in an immediate upsurge of *Locusta,* the African migratory locust, and it seems likely that the extension of the range of the Australian plague locust *Chortoicetes terminifera* in recent years is connected with overgrazing by sheep and cattle, also a factor in the range grasshoppers problem in the U.S.A. (for more examples, see Uvarov, 1962).

A particularly interesting and revealing example of ecological malpractice which has directly induced a locust outbreak is to be found in Thailand where recent outbreaks of the Bombay locust *Patanga succincta* have occurred (Roffey, 1965). Two traditional agriculture methods have been used in Thailand; one is the permanent clearing of lowland forest for rice and the other is shifting cultivation in which small areas of upland forest are cleared, planted for a few years with such crops as tobacco and yams and then abandoned. Recently upland crops such as maize, sorghum and sugar have been grown in such clearings, the areas increasing from some 710,000 hectares in 1950 to 3,970,000 hectares in 1963. Within the past six years much of the forest area has been declared a reserve area to conserve natural resources. While this has not stopped the tree-felling and snatch-cropping, it has deterred the intensive cultivation of the land, which is marked by fallen logs, unremoved tree stumps and numerous termite mounds. Such ground rapidly becomes infested with grasses such as *Imperata cylindrica* and the composite *Eupatorium odoratum;* and since these grasses are ideal for locust breeding, the increase in such areas has recently led to serious outbreaks of *Patanga*. When such areas are intensively cultivated, however, and tree stumps and termite mounds removed, *Imperata* and *Eupatorium* rapidly disappear and with this change in ecology the locust populations fall to an economically insignificant level. Thus we have the paradox of a conservation measure resulting in changes which induce pest outbreaks! The long-term solution, as Roffey points out, is a change in policy which allows for ecological control, either by reafforestation or encouragement of intensive cultivation.

These examples pinpoint the dilemma facing much agricultural development; because of the world food problem, the need for development and expansion is urgent, but all too frequently insufficient ecological knowledge is available to predict their consequences. It is clear from many of the papers in this Symposium that just such problems occur in all fields, including the building of dams and man-made lakes and irrigation development.

Frequently the suggestion is made that prior to any development schemes, extensive surveys of land use, flora and fauna be made in order to predict the possible results of the development. But such ecological surveys always take time, generally several years, and the urgency of the problem, related as they often are to a predicted population increase which cannot by definition be stemmed in under a generation, does not permit this. Then again, where such intensive surveys have been made, they have never covered all problems; a good example is the Volta River scheme, which was held up many years to allow for wide-ranging surveys to be made and yet is now the subject of a "salvage" operation in respect to certain unpredicted developments (for more detail see White's paper, Chapter 49 in this volume). It is quite unrealistic to imagine that adequate survey operations could be carried out in relation to all development schemes; it would seem preferable therefore to arrange continuing ecological research programs with a view to elucidating the ecological principles which underlie the processes of change and development in relation to certain specified types of development projects. Tackled in this way, a body of data and experience could be assembled which would be either directly or by extrapolation applicable to wide fields of development, with, it is to be hoped, consequent avoidance of at least the worst of the blunders which have hitherto been made, some of which are reported in the present volume.

The control of international pests brings us to the last of our problems for the future —politics and finance. Continuing ecological programs are relatively expensive and in developing countries make heavy demands on the generally limited resources of skilled manpower; furthermore, and perhaps above all, they rarely provide immediate tangible returns. Developing countries therefore are not normally inclined to invest heavily in such work which must thus be covered by aid programs or technical assistance: such programs are often set up piecemeal and need capital expenditure for such basic facilities as housing, laboratories, transport and scientific equipment. However, all these things are to be found in the international locust research and control organizations that already exist in several countries, and it would seem perfectly reasonable to expand their role to cover other aspects of agricultural pest control research on a long-term basis. Precedents for this exist; the O.C.LA.-LAV organization in West Africa is already a combined locust, grasshopper and *Quelea* (weaver) bird organization, and in eastern Africa the Desert Locust Control Organization has undertaken, at the request of member governments, work on cotton pests, water weed eradication, tsetse fly and *Quelea* bird control. Also, in the case of DLCOEA, important links have been forged with the universities of some contracting governments, which carry out research projects on locusts and which provide a source of recruits for scientific posts in the organization.

Judicious strengthening of these existing facilities could thus produce organizations which could play a major role in the agricultural development processes of their member governments; these organizations have the advantage of being known politically and scientifically and have already demonstrated in a practical way their work in locust research and control to the contributing countries.

It has already been pointed out above that the sound scientific basis on which locust control has been built has withstood political tensions, and the locust threat has resulted in continuing financial support. But as development proceeds and the locust problem perhaps becomes amenable to less costly and continuing treatments than at present, the potential of these international scientific bodies for other work should not be overlooked. We ignore ecology in relation to international development at our peril; this can only be corrected by further ecological research and application of that research. I suggest that in the important sphere of agricultural pest control research we have to provide through actual international organizations and the policies on which they were founded, instruments both to carry out the research necessary for the future and to apply it to practical effect.

SOME CONCLUSIONS

The history of efforts to control the red and desert locusts has demonstrably involved the interplay of politics, finance and science. The scientific understanding, acquired over the years, of the international ecology of these locusts has been a powerful inducement to political cooperation, and their damage potential has likewise resulted in a readiness to finance projects. The form of organization and the strategy and tactics of control have developed directly from a knowledge of the ecology of the locusts, and the demonstration that this is a correct basis has imparted political stability to anti-locust organizations even in times of tension.

Research on biology and ecology has produced reasonably efficient and economical chemical control measures, without untoward biological side effects, and may in time produce an acceptable permanent solution, although this is not yet foreseeable. Control by toxic chemicals will remain for many years, although long-term research on new selective methods has begun.

In the organizations considered, the interplay of politics, finance and science has been successfully mediated by a clear statement of the ecology of the pest organism, and it is suggested that this is a conclusion applicable to all international pests; any attempt to set up control organizations, whatever the pest, whatever the area, will only be successful if based on as detailed a picture as possible of the overall biology and ecology of the pest and its environment.

ACKNOWLEDGMENTS

I am grateful to several of my colleagues for permission to reproduce illustrations from their papers, acknowledgment being made on the figures, and also to Dr. P. Symmons, Mr. C. Ashall, and Dr. T. H. C. Taylor for their critical comments and suggestions on the text and to Mr. R. C. H. Greig and Miss J. Grant for their help in preparation of the paper.

REFERENCES

Brown, E. S. *The African Army Worm* Spodoptera exempta (*Walker*) (Lepidoptera, Noctuidae): *a Review of the Literature.* London: Commonwealth Institute of Entomology, 1962. 69 pp.

Brown, E. S.; Betts, E.; and Rainey, R. C. "Seasonal Changes in Distribution of the African Army Worm, *Spodoptera exempta* (Walk.) (*Lepidoptera, Noctuidae*): with Special Reference to Eastern Africa." *Bull. Ent. Res.,* 1969 (in press).

Carlisle, D. B., and Ellis, P. E. "Synchronisation of Sexual Maturation in Desert Locust Swarms." *5th Congr. Un. Int. Etude Insectes Soc.* (Toulouse) (1965), pp. 63–67.

Carlisle, D. B.; Ellis, P. E.; and Betts, E. "The Influence of Aromatic Shrubs on Sexual Maturation in the Desert Locust, *Schistocerca gregaria.*" *J. Insect. Physiol.,* 11 (1965), 1541–58.

Carlisle, D. B.; Osborne, D. J.; Ellis, P. E.; and Moorhouse, J. E. "Reciprocal Effects of Insect and Plant Growth Substances." *Nature* (London), 200 (1963), 1230.

Courshee, R. J. "Drift Spraying for Vegetation Baiting." *Bull. Ent. Res.,* 50 (1959), 355–70.

———. "Control of Desert Locust Hoppers from the Air." *Agric. Aviat.,* 6 (1964), 22–24.

Davies, D. E. "Seasonal Breeding and Migrations of the Desert Locust (*Schistocerca gregaria* Forskål) in North-Eastern Africa and the Middle East." *Anti-Locust Mem.,* No. 4. 1952. 56 pp.

Donnelly, U. "Seasonal Breeding and Migrations of the Desert Locust (*Schistocerca gregaria* Forskål) in Western and North-Western Africa." *Anti-Locust Mem.,* No. 3. 1947. 42 pp.

Ellis, P. E. "Learning and Social Aggregation in Locust Hoppers." *Anim. Behav.,* 7 (1959), 91–106.

Ellis, P. E., and Ashall, C. "Field Studies in Diurnal Behaviour, Movement and Aggregation in the Desert Locust (*Schistocerca gregaria* Forskål)." *Anti-Locust Bull.,* No. 25. 1957. 94 pp.

Faure, J. C. "The Phases of Locusts in South Africa." *Bull. Ent. Res.,* 23 (1932), 293–405.

Fortescue-Foulkes, J. "Seasonal Breeding and Migrations of the Desert Locust (*Schistocerca gregaria* Forskål) in South-Western Asia." *Anti-Locust Mem.,* No. 5. 1953. 35 pp.

Greathead, D. J. "A Review of the Insect Enemies of Acridoidea (Orthoptera)." *Trans. R. Ent. Soc. Lond.,* 114 (1963), 437–517.

Gunn, D. L. "The Story of the International Red Locust Control Service." *Rhod. Agric. J.,* 54 (1957), 8–24.

———. "Nomad Encompassed. The Development of Preventive Control of the Red Locust, *Nomadacris septemfasciata* Serville, by the International Red Locust Control Services." *J. Ent. Soc. S. Afr.,* 23 (1960a), 65–125.

———. "The Biological Background of Locust

Control." *Ann. Rev. Ent.*, 5 (1960b), 279–300.

Haskell, P. T. "The Fight against the Locust. The Rôle of the Anti-Locust Research Centre." *Trop. Sci.* (London), 6 (1964), 122–30.

Haskell, P. T.; Paskin, M. W. J.; and Moorhouse, J. E. "Laboratory Observations on Factors Affecting the Movements of Hoppers of the Desert Locust." *J. Insect. Physiol.*, 8 (1962), 53–78.

[First] International Locust Conference (Rome, 1931). Rapport de la Réunion Internationale Convoquée par le Ministère pes Colonies d'Italie pour l'étude du Problème des Acridiens migrateur. Rome, 1931. 8 pp.

[Second] International Locust Conference (Paris, 1932). Procès-Verbal des Séances de la Deuxième Conférence International pour les Recherches Antiacridiennes. Paris, July 15–23, 1932. Soc. Ent. France. 1932. 29 pp.

[Third] International Locust Conference (London, 1934). Proceedings of the Third International Locust Conference in London. September 1934. London (H.M.S.O., Cmd. 4725), 1934. 184 pp. (including 24 appendices), 4 plates, 2 maps.

[Fourth] International Locust Conference (Cairo, 1936). Proceedings of the Fourth International Locust Conference in Cairo. April 1936. Cairo: Govt. Press, 1937. 105 pp. plus 51 separately paged appendices.

[Fifth] International Locust Conference (Brussels, 1938). Comptes Rendu de la Vme Conférence Internationale pour les Recherches Antiacridiennes. Brussels, 1938. Brussels: Minist. Colon., 1938. 445 pp. (including 49 reports), 5 plates, 13 maps, 1 fldg. table.

Lloyd, Hadyn, J. "Operational Research on Preventive Control of the Red Locust (*Nomadacris septemfasciata*, Serville) by Insecticides." *Anti-Locust Bull.*, No. 35. 1959. 65 pp.

MacCuaig, R. D. "The Toxicity of Insecticides to Adult Locusts." *J. Sci. Fd. Agric.*, 9 (1958), 330–42.

———. "The Toxicity of Some Insecticides to Fifth-Instar Nymphs of the Desert Locust." *Ann. Appl. Biol.*, 48 (1960), 323–35.

Morant, V. "Migrations and Breeding of the Red Locust (*Nomadacris septemfasciata* Serville) in Africa 1927–1945." *Anti-Locust Mem.*, No. 2. 1947. 59 pp.

Norris, M. J. "Accelerating and Inhibiting Effects of Crowding on Sexual Maturation in Two Species of Locusts." *Nature* (London), 203:(4946) (1964), 784–85.

Popov, G. B. "Desert Locust Ecological Survey: Review of the Work, June 1958–March 1964." FAO Report UNSF/DL/E8/8. 1965.

Rainey, R. C. "Weather and the Movements of Locust Swarms: a New Hypothesis." *Nature* (London), 168 (1951), 1057–60.

———. "Meteorology and the Migration of Desert Locusts. Applications of Synoptic Meteorology in Locust Control." *Anti-Locust Mem.*, No. 7. 1963a. 115 pp.

———. "Aircraft reconnaissance and assessment of locust populations." *2nd Int. Agric. Aviat. Congr.* Grignon, 1962. 1963b. Pp. 228–33.

Riley, C. V.; Packard, A. S. Jr.; and Thomas, C. *First and Second Annual Reports of the United States Entomological Commission Relating to the Rocky Mountain Locust.* Washington, D.C., 1878. 773 pp., 403 pp.

Roffey, J. "Report to the Government of Thailand on Locust and Grasshopper Control." FAO Report No. 2109. Rome, 1965. 60 pp.

Sayer, H. J. "An Ultra-Low Volume Spraying Technique for the Control of the Desert Locust, *Schistocerca gregaria* (Forsk.)." *Bull. Ent. Res.*, 50 (1959), 371–86.

Scheepers, C. C., and Gunn, D. L. "Enumerating Populations of Adults of the Red Locust, *Nomadacris septemfasciata*, (Serville) in Its Outbreak Areas in East and Central Africa." *Bull. Ent. Res.*, 49 (1958), 273–85.

Stortenbeker, C. W. "Observations on the Population Dynamics of the Red Locust, *Nomadacris septemfasciata* (Serville) in Its Outbreak Areas." *Pudoc. Agric. Res. Rep.*, No. 694. 1967. 118 pp.

Symmons, P. M. "The Effect of Climate and Weather on the Numbers of the Red Locust, *Nomadacris septemfasciata* (Serv.). in the Rukwa Valley Outbreak Area." *Bull. Ent. Res.*, 50 (1959), 507–21.

————. "The Patterns of Distributions of Adults of the Red Locust (*Nomadacris septemfasciata* Serville) in an Outbreak Area." *Ent. Exp. and Appl.* (Amsterdam), 6 (1963), 123–32.

————. "Assessing the Size of Populations of Adults of the Red Locust, *Nomadacris septemfasciata* (Serv.) in Their Outbreak Areas by Means of a Helicopter." *Bull. Ent. Res.*, 56 (1966), 715–23.

Symmons, P. M.; Dean, G. J. W.; and Stortenbeker, C. W. "The Assessment of the Size of Populations of Adults of the Red Locust, *Nomadacris septemfasciata* (Serville), in an Outbreak Area." *Bull. Ent. Res.*, 54 (1963), 549–69.

Uvarov, B. P. "A Revision of the genus *Locusta*, L. (-*Pachytylus*, Fieb), with a New Theory as to Periodicity and Migrations of Locusts." *Bull. Ent. Res.*, 12 (1921), 135–63.

————. "Locust Research and Control, 1929–1950." *Colon. Res. Publ.*, No. 10. 1951. 67 pp.

————. "The Aridity Factor in the Ecology of Locusts and Grasshoppers of the Old World." In *Arid Zone Research: VIII. Human and Animal Ecology, Reviews of Research.* Paris; UNESCO, 1957. Pp. 164–98.

————. "Development of Arid Lands and Its Ecological Effects on Their Insect Fauna." *Arid Zone Research: XVIII. The Problems of the Arid Zone.* Proceedings of the Paris (1960) Symposium. Paris: UNESCO, 1962. Pp. 235–248.

Vesey-Fitzgerald, D. F. "The Vegetation of the Outbreak Areas of the Red Locust, *Nomadacris septemfasciata* Serville, in Tanganyika and Northern Rhodesia." *Anti-Locust Bull.*, No. 20. 1955. 31 pp.

Waloff, Z. "Seasonal Breeding and Migrations of the Desert Locust (*Schistocerca gregaria* Forskål) in Eastern Africa." *Anti-Locust Mem.*, No. 1. 1946. 74 pp.

————. "The Behaviour of Locusts in Migrating Swarms." *10th Int. Congr. Ent., Montreal, 1956*, 2 (1958), 567–69.

————. "The Upsurges and Recessions of the Desert Locust Plague: an Historical Survey." *Anti-Locust Mem.*, No. 8. 1956. 111 pp.

Waloff, Z., and Rainey, R. C. "Field Studies on Factors Affecting the Displacements of Desert Locust Swarms in Eastern Africa." *Anti-Locust Bull.*, No. 9. 1951. Pp. 1–50.

28. ECOLOGICAL EFFECTS OF CHEMICAL CONTROL OF RODENTS AND JACKALS IN ISRAEL

H. Mendelssohn

Israel, situated where several zoogeographical regions overlap, has a relatively rich fauna, notwithstanding its small area of approximately 20,000 square kilometers. The impact of modern development on the fauna has been conspicuous, influencing many species adversely by changing the environment by pollution and by pesticides, and by favoring other, adaptable species, some of which have become pests. The present paper will mainly consider the northern and central parts of Israel which have a Mediterranean climate, becoming arid toward the south. They have been much more influenced and changed by development than has the southern desert.

Among the twenty-eight species of rodents occurring in Israel, three species of field mice showed cyclic population changes in the past. In certain areas, mass populations of these rodents occasionally caused heavy damage to agricultural crops.

Prior to 1950, thirty-six species of diurnal birds of prey occurred regularly in Israel. Field mice were the main food for twelve species, most of which could be considered as common or very common. The population density of birds of prey was especially high in winter and spring, coinciding with the main reproductive season of the field mice.

As agricultural development opens hitherto uncultivated regions and intensifies the use of the other farm areas, the control of pests becomes a major concern. Thallium sulfate-coated wheat, for example, has been used in Israel for rodent control and has had a heavy impact on the populations of diurnal birds of prey. Predation by these birds of prey on rodent populations is discussed. A jackal-eradication campaign, impinging on other predators and on prey species, is also discussed.

Wheat coated with thallium sulfate, which had been used on a small scale for field mice control before 1950, was applied in large quantities over large areas several times during the winter of 1950–51, when a mass reproduction of field mice occurred. This large-scale application of poisoned grain was continued during the following years until recently, even when no increase of field mice populations was apparent.

After every application of thallium-wheat, dead and paralyzed birds of prey were found in the fields. All specimens checked for thallium contained large amounts of this metal. Birds of prey killed as a result of other causes, even in areas where thallium had not been used, were also found to contain thallium.

Captive birds of prey, fed experimentally on mice poisoned with thallium sulfate wheat, displayed the same form of paralysis as birds found in the field.

By 1955–56, breeding, as well as wintering populations of those species of birds of prey which fed mainly on rodents, had been almost entirely exterminated. Other species, which feed only occasionally on rodents or on grain-eating birds, were slower to disappear. Only one species, *Circaetus gallicus,* which feeds exclusively on reptiles, was not affected at all, and its population density did not decrease. Populations of mammal predators of field mice were also affected by secondary poisoning by thallium, but to a lesser degree.

After the continuous application of poison and the disappearance of the predators, regular cyclic population changes of field mice were no longer observed. Mass increase of field mice and sometimes also of other species of rodents occurred irregularly and took place also in areas in which this phenomenon had not been observed previously.

During the years 1964 to 1965, campaigns were carried out to exterminate jackals. Chicks poisoned with fluoracetamide were used as bait and widely distributed in large amounts. Populations of jackals as well as of other mammal predators, especially mongooses, were drastically reduced. Two consequences were conspicuous: a mass increase of hares, which began in 1966 and is still continuing, and a slower, but steady, increase of vipers and of snake-bite cases.

The influence of thallium and fluoracetamide on other forms of wildlife, as well as the general influence of other pesticides, is also conspicuous.

FIELD MICE, THALLIUM AND BIRDS OF PREY

Among the 28 species of rodents in Israel, one species, the levant vole (*Microtus guentheri guentheri* Dunford and Alston, 1880)[1] has displayed regular cycles of mass reproduction. Two other species,

Tristram's jird (*Meriones tristrami* Thomas, 1892) and the house mouse (*Mus musculus praetextus* Brants, 1827), also participate to a certain degree in these cycles (Bodenheimer, 1949). It was probably *Microtus guentheri* whose mass reproduction was mentioned in the Bible. The same species was the object of ecological studies carried out by Bodenheimer (1949, 1953, 1957) and by Bodenheimer and Dvoretzky (1952). Bodenheimer stated that *Microtus guentheri* displayed ten-year cycles of mass

[1] *Microtus guentheri philistinus* Thomas, 1917, does not seem to be different morphologically from *Microtus g. guentheri,* if variability in size and color in populations from northern and southern Israel is considered.

reproduction and three-year to five-year cycles in between.[2]

In order to estimate the possible role of predators and their influence on the populations of field mice in Israel, the biology of *Microtus guentheri* should first be considered. *Microtus guentheri* inhabits open country on heavy alluvial soils in plains and valleys, which in winter absorb large amounts of rainwater and in summer dry on top, forming large surface cracks, but retaining a certain amount of humidity in the deeper layers. *Microtus guentheri* prefers humid soils and is able to dig its burrows even in soil which the winter rains have turned to mud. It prefers to feed on green food, but takes also a certain amount of grain. It may reproduce all year round, but its main reproductive season is from November to April, and population density is generally highest in spring. Its fertility is greatly reduced and even interrupted for six to eight months during the summer in dry areas (Bodenheimer, 1953). In spring, when the winter grain crops are being harvested, most of the annual vegetation has dried up and the voles rely to a large extent on grain, which they collect and store in their burrows. As the food intake of each specimen is small, the damage caused by this species is, therefore, generally restricted to years of mass populations and to areas of heavy alluvial soil,

[2] Bodenheimer discusses the development of mass reproduction and the crash with which these mass reproduction cycles generally end, in Israel as well as elsewhere (Elton, 1942; Lack, 1954). He discusses also the role of predation in regulating populations of this vole and of the two other species of field mice participating in the cycles and arrives at the conclusion that the role of predation is negligible. Elton (1942) and Lack (1954), summarizing other authors, maintain as well that predation is generally not an important factor regulating populations of small rodents. Other authors (Chitty and Phipps, 1966; Errington, 1943; Golley, 1960; Kalabukhov and Raevskii, 1933; Klimov, 1931; Pearson, 1964, 1966; Pitelka *et al.*, 1955) found that predation may, under certain circumstances, and generally in combination with other factors, have an influence on rodent populations. Bodenheimer and Dvoretzky (1952) arrive at a similar conclusion.

which is at the same time the best agricultural soil. Some damage may also be caused to alfalfa, vegetables and occasionally to fruit trees by gnawing their roots.

The other two species of rodents which participate in the mass increase together with *Microtus guentheri,* generally at the same time, but to a lesser degree, inhabit lighter and drier soil and also hilly areas, whereas the vole is restricted to level ground. *Meriones tristrami* is the more important of these two species, causing damage sometimes also in the south-central part of Israel, where *Microtus guentheri* is rare.

In Israel, the larger part of the grain crops is grown in wide open plains, which are cultivated mechanically. The density of field-mice populations in these fields is generally low in normal years, amounting to about one to five specimens per 1000 square meters (Bodenheimer, 1949). The method used by Bodenheimer (1949) for estimating populations of field mice was to plug the burrow openings and check the reopened burrows. The number of reopened burrows was used as an indication of the number of voles present. As one burrow of *Microtus* may have several openings, this method cannot be considered as accurate. According to personal observations, an average population of 1 vole per 1000 square meters in grain fields appears to be closer to reality in normal years. During years of mass reproduction, the population density may reach up to 25 specimens per 1000 square meters in spring or even more; according to Bodenheimer (1949), even 500 per 1000 square meters in some cases. Only under these circumstances is real damage caused by these field mice.

The question arises how much predation would be able to influence the population density of field mice in Israel and in this way prevent the development of damage. Bodenheimer (1949) took the barn owl as a model of predation, the composition of whose food in Palestine has been studied by Dor (1947). Bodenheimer came to the conclusion that the influence of the barn owl on rodent populations is negligible, even though the food of the barn owl contains about 70 per cent voles and other mice. This conclusion is correct for several reasons. The barn owl nests and roosts in buildings and generally does not forage at a distance of more than 1 km from its nest or roost. It feeds mostly in and around settlements, where it preys on house mice, young rats, sparrows and shrews; voles, which may represent 50% of its food, are collected only in the surroundings of the villages. Therefore, the barn owl makes little use of the open fields, where *Microtus* are common.

Bodenheimer mentioned only incidentally the mammalian predators, whose food intake is much larger than that of the barn owl, but which also do not generally feed much in the open fields, where no hiding or resting places are available. Bodenheimer, however, did not mention at all the possible influence of diurnal birds of prey, many species of which feed in open country. The relation between diurnal birds of prey and another subspecies of *Microtus guentheri* has been mentioned by Harting (1893) for *M. g. hartingi* Barrett-Hamilton, 1903, in Thessaly, Greece.

It would have been worthwhile, however, to study this influence because Israel had a very rich fauna of diurnal birds of prey. The list comprised thirty-eight species, part of which were winter visitors, part summer breeders. A third group could be called residents, even though with some species apparently the breeding populations were at least partly different from the wintering populations. Some of the winter visitors were very common and occurred in high population densities.

From the point of view of a possible biological control of field mice, the important species of birds of prey which live in open country and feed mainly on small rodents, especially the most common eight species of winter visitors and four species of summer breeders. By examinations of crop and stomach contents it was found that mice were the staple food of these eight winter visitors which are also very common in spring migration, until May. During summer, however, mice were represented to a lesser extent in the food of the four common species of mice-feeding summer breeders, as reptiles and insects were now included in the diet of the diurnal birds of prey. Availability of prey species was generally reflected in the crop and stomach contents.

The availability of mice as food is apparently an important factor in the predator-prey relation. After fields are sown in autumn, rodents living in these fields have no cover and are vulnerable to predation. This situation continues when the grain starts to germinate after the first winter rains and until the plants have developed sufficiently to provide the rodents with cover, which is not before February. Thus, mice were generally the prominent food of birds of prey, living in the open fields until the end of February or even until the first half of March, depending on precipitation. During March and April, mice were in many cases less conspicuous in the food of the birds of prey which were collected in the fields, and more reptiles and insects appeared in the food with the onset of activity in heliothermic reptiles and the increasing populations of larger insects. In May and June, after the harvest, rodents are again deprived of cover and appear to a larger extent in the food of the birds of prey, which now feed their young also on rodents. An important difference between winter and summer is that the population density of the breeding birds of prey is lower than that of the wintering species.

The mainly, but not exclusively, nocturnal activity of the field mice does not prevent their being preyed upon by diurnal birds of prey. Even the mole rat (*Spalax ehrenbergi* Nehring, 1898), a subterranean rodent of much lower density than voles and other field mice, appeared surprisingly often in the food of diurnal birds of prey, especially the Egyptian vulture and the black kite. These victims were mostly sub-adult specimens which, prior to establishing territories of their own, appear more on the surface than do territory owners.

Among the diurnal birds of prey occurring in winter, eight species have been common enough to have affected field-mice populations. These species include the eagles *Aquila clanga* and *Aquila pomarina,* which in the present paper will be considered as one species, as it is difficult to distinguish between them in the field. The wintering populations of the somewhat rarer *Aquila heliaca* also subsisted mainly on mice. The buzzards *Buteo b. buteo* and *Buteo v. vulpinus,* the black kite *Milvus m. migrans,* the harrier *Circus macrourus,* and the kestrel *Falco tinnunculus* were the other important predators. Other species were less common, but for instance a *Buteo rufinus* could take the place of an *Aquila pomarina,* or a *Circus cyaneus* that of a *Circus macrourus.*

On the basis of fifteen counts conducted during the years 1933 to 1945 it may be supposed that the average population of wintering mice-feeding diurnal birds of prey per 10 square kilometers of grain-field area was two eagles, ten buzzards, four kites, four harriers and twelve kestrels. The counts were made in the vicinity of the town of Afula in northern Israel, about 35 kilometers southeast of Haifa. Afula is situated in a vast plain, typical *Microtus guentheri* country. In this uniform, open country, counting the birds was not very difficult. Counts were made on three consecutive days along transects 300 meters broad.

In order to ascertain the average daily food consumption of these birds when feeding on small rodents, captive birds of these species were fed on mice and rats of 20–90 grams weight. It was found that the average daily food intake for birds which kept their normal weight for ten to fourteen days was: for eagles, 200 grams; for buzzards and kites, 90 grams; for harriers, 60 grams; and for kestrels, 40 grams. According to these observations, the total food consumption of the diurnal birds of prey living on an area of 10 square kilometers would be 2380 grams of food per day. Because it is based on birds kept in captivity, this food consumption must be considered as minimal; birds in nature are more active and probably have a larger food consumption. On the other hand, even though these birds feed mainly on mice, they take a certain amount of other food as well.

The average weight of the Levant vole in nature may be taken as 30 grams, as few of them reach an age of one hundred days and a weight of 40 grams (Bodenheimer, 1949). The thirty-two birds of prey living on an area of 10 square kilometers would therefore consume 79 voles per diem or 2370 voles per month. As during an average year the vole population per 1000 square meters was about 1, and on 10 square kilometers therefore, 10,000, the removal of 2370 voles per month by birds of prey constitutes an influence on the vole population which, together with predation by other predators and other mortality factors, may participate in regulating the population in winter and prevent or decelerate increase. Nothing is known about the reproduction rate of the Levant vole in nature, either in normal or cycle years. Bodenheimer (1949) and Bodenheimer and Dvoretzky (1952) assumed that even a slight change in reproduction rate may cause increase or decrease of vole populations. Predation such as that described here can be important only if the rate of increase of the rodent population is not too high.

Thus, the regulatory influence of predation on field-mice populations is likely to be effective only during normal years. As soon as the reproduction rate of the mice rises and a mass increase develops, the role of predation decreases relatively. Even though areas of a mass outbreak of field mice attract all kinds of predators, and the increase in diurnal birds of prey is very conspicuous, still the increase in their population density is much less than the increase in mice populations. During the height of the ten-year cycle of *Microtus guentheri,* vole populations may increase twenty-five times their normal density or more whereas the increase in population density of birds of prey was found to be not more than three to four times the average density. The influence of predation on field-mice populations is, therefore, relatively negligible during a mass outbreak. Bodenheimer and Dvoretzky (1952) and Pearson (1966) state that predation is relatively more important during times of low population density and negligible during times of high density.

A mass outbreak of the Levant vole occurs generally over large areas and may even extend over the whole of the Near East (Bodenheimer, 1949). The populations of the wintering diurnal birds of prey were more or less constant and did not change much from year to year. Their populations could, therefore, shift to areas of denser mice populations, but no larger concentrations of these predators could be expected. The situation may be different if a local increase of voles takes place, while their density remains low in surrounding areas. This occurred in alfalfa fields, which offer especially favorable conditions to *Microtus guentheri.* So, for instance, in March, 1952, an alfalfa field of 100 acres was found to be heavily infested with *Microtus,* with an estimated density of 200–300 per acre. Around each burrow the plants were grazed down to the ground on several square meters, exposing the voles to predation. Eight eagles, 11 buzzards, 13 kites, 3 har-

riers, and 7 kestrels were counted on these 100 acres. Some of these birds, however, may have been migrants which stopped during migration at this ample source of food.

The influence of mass outbreaks of voles and other field mice on the reproduction rate of predators may be considerable. During the 1949–50 outbreak it was found that mongoose (*Herpestes i. ichneumon* Linnaeus, 1758) and wild cat (*Felis lybica tristrami* Pocock, 1944) had not only one litter in spring, as usual, but also a second one in summer. Barn owls were found to nest almost the year round, rearing larger broods than usual, and, probably because of lack of proper nesting sites, were found to nest in unconventional places such as on the ground in dense thickets. Up to nine nestlings were found in a family, whereas generally barn owls in Israel rear only four to five nestlings. Long-eared owls (*Asio otus*) and short-eared owls (*Asio flammens*), which generally do not breed in Israel, do so almost regularly during mass outbreaks of field mice. All these predators, reproducing in Israel, had much less influence, because of their local distribution, than the wintering birds of prey with their high density.[3]

The connection between populations of field mice and diurnal birds of prey has been well demonstrated by the influence of field-mice poisoning on these birds (Mendelssohn, 1962). Thallium sulfate-coated wheat was recommended by Bodenheimer (1949) for field-mice control, and different concentrations were tried, containing between 1.2 to 1.7 per cent thallium sulfate in the wheat bait. Bodenheimer eventually recommended a preparation containing 2 per cent thallium sulfate, and this was used until 1964. This preparation was prepared

[3] The influence of the increase of rodent populations on the reproduction rate of predators has been summarized by Elton (1942) and by Lack (1954). Dawaa (1961) reports on the increase of *Aquila rapax, Buteo hemilasius* and *Vulpes corsac* in relation with the increase of *Microtus brandti* populations.

locally and used for the first time during the vole outbreak in 1930–31. It was also used during the outbreak in 1939–40 but still on relatively restricted areas and only during the outbreak. Another large outbreak occurred in 1949–50, when field-mice control using thallium sulfate-coated wheat was recommended by the Plant Protection Department of the Ministry of Agriculture and carried out on a large scale. The poison baits were distributed repeatedly over large areas. The original instructions were to put up to twelve poisoned grains in every occupied burrow, whereas actually one or two poisoned grains alone contained the lethal dose. Soon the poison bait was, however, distributed wholesale over the fields, at first manually and later on mechanically or by planes. Whereas, according to the directions, not more than 1600 grams of bait per acre should be distributed, equivalent to about 15 poison grains per square meter, evidence showed that generally much larger quantities were used. This very dense distribution of the thallium sulfate-coated grain made it possible for the mice to ingest much larger amounts than the minimum lethal dose.

Thallium is a poison which is only slowly excreted by the body. It works slowly, causing paralysis and finally killing the mice after several hours and up to two days. As the poisoned mice move slowly on the surface of the ground, and have difficulty in reaching their burrows, they are easy victims of birds of prey and other predators.

The field-mice-control actions actually attracted larger than ordinary concentrations of diurnal birds of prey to the fields on which the poison had been distributed, as larger numbers of mice were to be seen on the ground and were easily caught. Beginning from the fifth day after the distribution of thallium bait, paralyzed and dead birds of prey were found in the fields. The development of the thallium paralysis in birds of prey presents a very typical picture. First the flight of the birds is labored and unsteady, and then they are unable to fly but still are able to stand. Later they are unable to keep their wings in the normal posture and the wings droop. Then the leg muscles become paralyzed; the bird is unable to stand; it squats on the tarso-metatarsus, leaning on the drooping wings and the tail. Soon it is unable to lift its head and eventually it lies prostrate on the ground and soon dies. Full development from the first external signs of poisoning to death will take between three to ten days depending on the amount of poison ingested. Partially paralyzed birds, which are already unable to stand, may still recover if artificially fed. In the field, however, probably all birds which start to develop paralysis eventually succumb because even partly paralyzed birds are unable to feed or to adopt the proper posture if it rains; they become soaked, are unable to keep up thermoregulation and die of exposure.

Birds found paralyzed or dead in the fields after distribution of thallium sulfate were examined and found to contain large amounts of thallium. Even birds of prey which did not display external signs of thallium poisoning and were tested for thallium were also found to contain certain amounts of it.

Captive birds of prey, fed experimentally on thallium-poisoned mice, developed the same form of paralysis as observed in the field and eventually died. Experimental birds fed continually on thallium-poisoned mice took more time to develop paralysis than the time interval between thallium application and appearance of paralysis in birds in the field. Buzzards and kites used in these experiments generally refused food on the eighth day of the experiment and displayed the first signs of paralysis the next day. There may be two reasons for this difference; the food consumption of birds in the field may be larger than in the laboratory, and they will therefore ingest larger amounts of thallium in less time. They may not ingest lethal amounts of thallium after one control action, but accumulate increasing amounts of this slowly excreted poison during successive control actions, until the lethal level is reached.

Before 1949–50, poison bait was distributed only during an actual field-mice outbreak; but after the outbreak of 1949–50, poisoning was repeated several times every year in most areas. The reason for this activity may not have been real need, but rather that during the outbreak of 1949–50 a department for field-mice control was established and continued active even when no subsequent damage was caused.

Whereas prior to 1949–50 the influence of the thallium sulfate on populations of diurnal birds of prey had not been conspicuous, afterward this influence was felt increasingly. The larger part of the wintering populations of birds of prey was eliminated by secondary poisoning during the years 1950 to 1955–56. Several years later the most common species of mice-feeding birds of prey had disappeared almost entirely, because field-mice control by repeated intensive application of highly concentrated thallium bait was selectively destructive to field-mice predators.

As most of the field-mice control actions were carried out during the winter, wintering birds of prey, whose staple food was small rodents, were most severely affected. During the summer, fewer actions against field mice were carried out, and therefore the breeding birds of prey were less affected and were slower to disappear.

In Table 28–1 an attempt is made to compare the populations of birds of prey prior to the extensive field-mice-control campaigns and after them. When considering the table it should be kept in mind that in Israel there is almost none of the animosity toward birds of prey which is such a strong tradition in many other countries. Shooting of birds of prey has, therefore, no influence on their population. Besides, all birds of

prey, like most other wild birds, are strictly protected by law in Israel and trespassers are fined.

Besides the already mentioned connection between the application of thallium-poisoned wheat and the occurrence of thallium poisoning among birds of prey, some unusual cases should be mentioned. During the autumn migration of 1961, a cinereous vulture (*Aegypius monachus*) was found with typical signs of thallium paralysis in Eilat on the shore of the Gulf of Aqaba. This case was considered to be strange, as no agriculture existed then in these desert surroundings. Upon investigation, it was found, however, that in the agricultural settlement of Yotvata, 35 kilometers to the north, thallium bait had been applied a week earlier. This case well demonstrated the slow action of the thallium and its consequently wide spatial influence. Another unusual case concerns a population of lappet-faced vultures (*Torgos tracheliotus*). A small resident population of this species exists in the Arava valley in southern Israel, entirely isolated from the main distribution area in Africa. This small resident population, which was estimated at about twenty-five pairs and about thirty to forty immature specimens, displayed a steady decline after 1950. It was found that part of the population was feeding on poisoned field mice in the area north and west of Beersheba, 90 to 150 kilometers to the west and northwest of the main distribution area of this population; poisoned birds were found there in the fields. Large vultures are supposed to feed on carcasses of large mammals. Feeding on poisoned, small rodents has, however, been reported also for the California condor (Koford, 1953).

Other birds, which occasionally also feed on mice, were also found to be poisoned by thallium, for instance cattle egrets (*Bubulcus ibis*) and purple herons (*Ardea purpurea*). Of the latter species, a considerable part of the breeding population of the Hula

Table 28-1

LIST OF FALCONIFORMES FOUND IN ISRAEL AND THEIR POPULATION STATUS

SPECIES	PRIOR TO 1950				RECENT SITUATION			
	RESIDENT	SUMMER BREEDER	WINTER VISITOR	MIGRANT	RESIDENT	SUMMER BREEDER	WINTER VISITOR	MIGRANT
Pernis apivorus				Very common				Very common
Milvus migrans	Common and increasing		Extremely common	Extremely common	No recent observations		Very rare	Extremely common
Milvus milvus			Very rare				No recent observations	
Accipiter gentilis			Very rare				No recent observations	
Accipiter brevipes			Rare				No recent observations	
Accipiter nisus			Very common	Common			Very rare	Common
Buteo rufinus		Common	Common	Common		Extremely rare	Extremely rare	Common
Buteo vulpinus			Very common	Very common			Very rare	Very common
Buteo buteo			Common				Very rare	
Hieraëtus fasciatus	Common				Very rare (only in southern desert)			
Hieraëtus pennatus			Rare	Not Rare			Very rare	Not Rare
Aquila heliaca	Very rare (only in southern desert)		Very common	Common	Very rare (only in southern desert)		Extremely rare	Common

Table 28-1 (continued)

SPECIES	PRIOR TO 1950				RECENT SITUATION			
	RESIDENT	SUMMER BREEDER	WINTER VISITOR	MIGRANT	RESIDENT	SUMMER BREEDER	WINTER VISITOR	MIGRANT
Aquila nipalensis			Fairly common	Common			No recent observations	Common
Aquila clanga	Rare		Very common	Common	No recent observations		Extremely rare	Common
Aquila pomarina			Very common	Common			Extremely rare	Common
Aquila verreauxei	Occasional				Occasional			
Haliaëtus albicilla	Very rare				No recent observations			
Torgos tracheliotus	Not rare in southern desert				Rare			
Aegypius monachus			Not rare	Rare			No recent observations	Rare
Gyps fulvus	Common			Not rare	Quite rare			Not rare
Neophron percnopterus		Very common		Not rare		Extremely rare		Not rare
Gypaëtus barbatus	Very rare				Very rare			
Circus cyaneous			Not common				Extremely rare	
Circus macrourus			Very common				Extremely rare	
Circus pygargus			Rare				Extremely rare	

Table 28-1 (continued)

SPECIES	PRIOR TO 1950				RECENT SITUATION			
	RESIDENT	SUMMER BREEDER	WINTER VISITOR	MIGRANT	RESIDENT	SUMMER BREEDER	WINTER VISITOR	MIGRANT
Circus aeruginosus	Not rare (local)		Very common		No recent observations		Rare	
Circaëtus gallicus		Common		Not rare		Common		Not rare
Pandion haliaëtus			Fairly common				Very rare	
Falco biarmicus feldeggi		Not rare				No recent observations		
Falco biarmicus tanypterus	Fairly common				Rare (only in southern desert)			
Falco cherrug			Fairly common				No recent observations	
Falco peregrinus		Very rare	Common			No recent observations	Very rare.	
Falco subbuteo		Fairly common				Not rare		
Falco eleonorae				Occasional			Occasional	
Falco concolor		Very rare				Very rare		
Falco columbarius			Fairly common					
Falco vespertinus				Rare				No recent observations
Falco naumanni		Extremely common	Fairly common	Common		No recent observations	No recent observations	Common
Falco tinnunculus	Extremely common		Common		Quite rare, lately increasing		Rare	

Nature Reserve was exterminated in June, 1960, and it was found that prior to this mass mortality of adult birds and nestlings, thallium had been distributed in the fields of the Hula Valley.

The decline of populations concerns all species of birds of prey in Israel except one. This one species, which succeeded in keeping its numbers at about the same level, is the short-toed eagle (*Circaetus gallicus*), who feeds exclusively on reptiles, mostly snakes. Reptiles are apparently little influenced and contaminated by pesticides. It would, of course, be possible for snakes to feed on thallium-poisoned mice after field-mice-control action during the summer. The food intake of snakes is, however, much lower than that of endothermic animals and seems, therefore, to effectively prevent any considerable accumulation of thallium in their bodies. The short-toed eagle seems even to have increased in some areas. This might perhaps be explained by lack of competition for nesting sites after other birds of prey disappeared. Another reason could be the disappearance of the long-legged buzzard (*Buteo rufinus*), who perhaps competed formerly with the short-toed eagle for food, as it feeds partly on reptiles.

The changed status of birds of prey in Israel, before and after the widespread application of thallium, is summarized in Table 28–1. In the column "migrant," only those species are mentioned which are conspicuous during migration. Breeding species which survived in reduced numbers after introduction of thallium did so mainly in mountainous areas or in the southern desert, where thallium was not used much.

The influence of other pesticides, especially the persistent organochlorine compounds, cannot of course be ruled out, as these pesticides have been used extensively in agriculture in Israel since about 1950. The exaggerated use of pesticides in Israel is corroborated by the high amount of residues in human tissues (Wassermann, 1967). The influence of insecticides is probable in birds like the lesser kestrel (*Falco naumanni*), which feeds mostly on insects, and has disappeared entirely as a breeding bird. This bird was the most common of birds of prey breeding in Israel prior to 1949–50. Other birds of prey may also have been influenced by persistent pesticides other than thallium, but there was then no possibility in Israel to examine carcasses for other pesticide residues besides thallium. The influence of thallium is, however, proved not only by the results of post-mortem examinations and by feeding experiments, but also by the temporal relation between the application of thallium in the field and mortality of birds of prey. The influence of persistent organochlorine insecticides on birds of prey, causing mortality as well as lowering fertility, is well known by now (Ames, 1966; Lockie and Ratcliffe, 1964; Moore, 1964; Moore and Walker, 1964; Prestt, 1965, 1966; Ratcliffe, 1965, 1967). Fertility may also be influenced adversely already in mice, the second link in the food chain leading to birds of prey (Bernhard and Gaertner, 1964).

After the large vole outbreak of 1949–50, the tendency for cyclic mass reproduction was obscured by the large-scale application of poison baits in all agricultural areas. However, field-mice populations obviously tended to build up large populations at irregular intervals and irregularly in different areas, in which favorable conditions prevailed. This accords with Elton's (1942, p. 59) assumption that "partial reduction of the population may prolong the plague at a lower, though still formidable, level." It seems that the almost complete elimination of one extermination factor, that of predation, upset the balance existing between the mice population and its extermination factors.

In the semiarid areas of the western

Negev, other species of mice, especially Tristram's jird (*Meriones tristrami*), were increasing periodically and occasionally causing damage to grain crops. Here the formerly mentioned wintering birds of prey occurred in less dense populations, but three other species were common predators of field mice in winter: *Aquila rapax orientalic, Buteo rufinus* and *Falco cherrug*. Thallium was applied and birds of prey were exterminated by secondary poisoning in this area, too. Because of the irregular precipitation, growing of grain crops without irrigation has been discontinued in recent years in the more arid parts of this area and, therefore, field-mice control was discontinued as well. In 1965–66 there occurred an unprecedented mass increase of all the gerbil species inhabiting the area: *Meriones tristrami, Meriones sacramenti, Gerbillus pyramidum* and in parts of the area also *Gerbillus allenbyi*. This mass increase was probably made possible by the absence of the birds of prey which previously had wintered here and by the discontinuation of poison bait. The dense populations of mice, vulnerable to predation because of the thin plant cover, attracted large concentrations of migrant birds of prey, mostly black kites (*Milvus migrans*) but also long-legged buzzards (*Buteo rufinus*) and Egyptian vultures (*Neophron percnopterus*). Whereas in former years few birds of prey occurred in this area in summer, many immature birds of the mentioned species, especially kites, did not migrate and remained. In July, 1966, it was found that a relatively large number of burrows were deserted. Lack of food may have been one reason for the decline of these mice populations, as in many places actually all the plants were collected near the burrow entrances and deprived of all their seeds. Predation, however, was also conspicuous, as remnants of these jirds and gerbils were found in the pellets regurgitated by these birds, proving that they actually fed on these rodents.

INFLUENCE OF THALLIUM AND OTHER PESTICIDES ON BIRDS

The wholesale use of thallium bait had, of course, also affected the grain-eating birds. The collared dove (*Streptopelia decaocto*), for instance, which in Israel is not anthropophilous as it is in Europe but lives in open fields, was most conspicuously injured. The populations of this bird increased considerably after reduction of hunting pressure, but later the population decreased again in direct correlation with the increasing application of thallium. In contrast a related bird, the palm dove (*Streptopelia senegalensis*), which in Israel lives only in towns and villages and does almost no feeding in fields, increased continuously and is still doing so. Other birds were harmed as well; for instance, in January, 1960, in the Hula Nature Reserve, hundreds of starlings and dozens of mallards were found dead after application of thallium in the fields surrounding the nature reserve. Both starlings and mallards were found to contain large amounts of thallium. Chukar partridges (*Alectoris graeca*), which are very common in Israel, were not much affected by thallium, as they live mainly in hilly areas and do little feeding in the plains where thallium is mostly applied. However, some partridges which were found dead contained large, probably lethal, amounts of thallium. Other specimens which were shot during the open season were found to contain small amounts of thallium. In Israel the Chukar partridge is the main food of the Bonelli's eagle (*Hieraëtus fasciatus*), which has been the only common resident eagle. The disappearance of this eagle between 1955 and 1965 is probably due to slow thallium poisoning via the Chukar partridge. As relatively little thallium is found in Chukar populations, its influence on

Bonelli's eagles may have developed very slowly. No dead eagles of this species were found, and therefore no examination for thallium could be made on carcasses. However, a bird with typical first-stage signs of thallium poisoning was observed in spring 1955, and thereafter the populations began slowly to disappear. One nesting site after another became deserted; even earlier only one chick was reared instead of the ordinary two, or no young were reared at all. Small flocks of the European crane (*Megalornis grus*) which were wintering in plains inhabited by *Microtus guentheri* were also almost entirely exterminated by thallium during 1956–1959. They displayed the typical form of paralysis; thallium was found in one bird examined after its death. As cranes may feed on grain as well as on mice, it is not known if the cranes were killed by direct or by secondary poisoning. The same uncertainty holds for the wintering populations of rooks (*Corvus frugilegus*) and jackdaws (*Corvus monedula*), which might feed on poisoned grain as well as on poisoned mice. Wintering rooks disappeared entirely from Israel, and jackdaw populations were reduced to a small percentage of the huge flocks wintering here in former years.

As already mentioned, it is very possible that pesticides other than thallium, especially the persistent organochlorine insecticides, played a certain role in the disappearance of birds of prey. The long-lived, late-maturing birds of prey are apparently more vulnerable to the influence of these pesticides, as they may accumulate high concentrations of residues even before they mature. Some other earlier-maturing birds did not display the same influence of pesticides on their populations; or perhaps they may be able to withstand higher concentrations in their tissues.

Another case concerns the cattle egret (*Bubulcus ibis*), which established breeding colonies in Israel in highly contaminated agricultural areas after 1950 and thereafter increased, notwithstanding its living and feeding in areas in which pesticides are constantly applied. Cattle egrets, which feed on small vertebrates, including rodents, as well as on insects, were occasionally found to have been poisoned by thallium; specimens affected with tremors and convulsions were also found, indicating acute poisoning by DDT or related compounds. Still the size of their populations was not affected. One important factor may be that cattle egrets mature when one year old, not like most birds of prey, which mature at the age of two or more. It should also be noted that notwithstanding their continual exposure to pesticide contamination, the fertility of cattle egrets has not been adversely influenced; three nestlings still are generally reared from each clutch, and breeding continues from March to August and in some colonies even in winter.

Two other species of birds which apparently are not affected by pesticides, even though they live in agricultural areas, are the white-breasted kingfisher (*Halcyon smyrnensis*) and the hoopoe (*Upupa epops*). Both species feed extensively on mole crickets (*Gryllotalpa*), which build up dense populations in irrigated areas. Mole crickets are a bad pest to agriculture and are controlled more or less successfully in Israel by dieldrin application. Even though the kingfisher and the hoopoe feed in many cases on dieldrin-poisoned mole crickets, their populations are still not affected; no poisoned birds have been found and the populations of the hoopoe have increased considerably in recent years. Another case concerns the bulbul (*Pycnonotus capensis*), which lives in orchards and feeds on fruit that is constantly sprayed with pesticides. But still populations are not affected; on the contrary, the bulbul has increased to such a degree that it has become an important pest.

JACKAL CONTROL

Among the mammals, one species which adapted excellently to the conditions existing in agricultural areas and near dense human populations is the jackal (*Canis aureus*). Jackals built up large populations, especially in the densely populated coastal plain of Israel. In many areas they reached a density of several specimens per square kilometer. Jackals are omnivorous, mainly scavengers, but they also prey on many kinds of animals up to the size of hares or lambs. Their influence on populations of other animals is especially prominent when their own populations are dense. Around the settlements on the north end of the Dead Sea, jackals built up a population which grew from a few specimens in 1933 to several hundred in 1946. This jackal population fed mainly on the garbage of the settlements, but had by 1945 almost completely exterminated the formerly very common sand rat (*Psammomys obesus*), whose populations decreased in proportion to the increase of jackals. As jackals fed also on a variety of fruits and vegetables, they caused damage to agriculture. They were also supposed to play a role in the epidemiology of rabies, although the main source of rabies in Israel is feral dogs. For almost fifty years attempts were made to control jackal populations by application of poisoned baits, mainly strychnine. Success was only moderate and jackal populations continued to increase. The use of strychnine was more conspicuous in the decrease of the numbers of griffon vultures (*Gyps fulvus*). Both species fed on strychnine-poisoned bait, but griffon vulture populations were much more affected because of their low reproduction rate and late maturation. Griffons lay their first egg when five or six years old and rear one chick; jackals have their first litter when one or two years old and rear four to eight cubs. Jackal populations are therefore much better able to withstand losses.

In 1964 and in 1955 the Plant Protection Department undertook an extensive campaign to eradicate jackals by distributing bait in which a 15 per cent fluoroacetamide solution was injected. These poison baits were distributed wholesale; uneaten baits were not collected, and no care whatsoever was taken to prevent poisoning of animals other than jackals. The influence of this action was extremely disastrous, as small chicks were used as bait and proved to be attractive for many animals. Jackals disappeared almost entirely, but so did other small mammal predators as well: mongooses, wild cats, and foxes. Some birds also decreased conspicuously, especially the hooded crow (*Corvus corone*), which had been very common in the same areas as the jackal. Along with the crows, the crested cuckoo (*Clamator glandarius*), which parasitizes the hooded crow in Israel, became very rare.

The most conspicuous result of the disappearance of the jackal was, however, an enormous increase of hares (*Lepus europaeus*) which in 1967–68 reached a density of one or even more per acre in some areas, a density unprecedented prior to jackal extermination. The damage done by the hares to agriculture in many cases was greater than that done earlier by jackals.

The results of the jackal extermination campaign were felt also in the increase of the populations of a reptile, the Palestine viper (*Vipera xanthina palaestinae*). This venomous snake takes well to agricultural settlements, where it finds more moisture in summer than in natural surroundings, where moisture is apparently suboptimal for this snake. An ample supply of food in the form of mice and rats is also available to the snakes in agricultural settlements. Therefore, vipers had developed well-established populations in and near agricultural settlements. Viper populations seemed to increase considerably after the jackal extermination campaign, and this is probably connected with the concomitant disappearance of the mongoose (*Herpestes ichneumon*), which preyed to a large extent on reptiles, including vipers. Possibly, mongooses kept the viper populations in check, as mongooses had been also common near settlements.

DISCUSSION

The disastrous influence of pesticides on birds of prey is apparent in many countries. There are two obvious reasons for the vulnerability of these predators: they are located at the end of food chains and they mature late, especially the larger species. The latter have a low reproduction rate as well. Generally the chlorinated hydrocarbon pesticides are supposed to be the cause of the decline in the populations of birds of prey. In this paper, secondary poisoning by thallium has been demonstrated. It is highly possible that a more sparse application of thallium in lower concentrations could effectively control field mice and prevent damage without causing secondary poisoning and thus selectively destroying biological control. The intense application of thallium, as described in this paper, was favored by the Plant Protection Department "in order to eradicate field mice entirely all over Israel" (Y. Naftali, personal communication). This aim has not been reached. So far, mice populations still increase and decrease; increase has to be stopped by application of poison.

If they are compared to some other birds which are also on the end of food chains, it is somewhat difficult to understand the vulnerability of birds of prey to secondary poisoning. In North America, gulls were found to carry very high amounts of pesticide residues (Stickel, 1968). In England, popula-

tions of the heron (*Ardea cinerea*) were less affected than birds of prey (Prestt, 1966), and this was also found to be the case in Israel with the cattle egret, the hoopoe and the white-breasted kingfisher. Besides, these last three species live in highly contaminated surroundings, whereas some birds of prey lived in little-contaminated areas and still were reached by pesticides. Possibly, the actual physiological vulnerability toward pesticides is different in different families of birds.

Biological control of pests among vertebrates seems to be rare. Apparently such a relation existed between field mice and wintering birds of prey in Israel. It is highly probable that the birds of prey which wintered in Israel depended for long periods mainly on the rodent species living in open fields for their staple diet. It is now impossible to study this relation thoroughly, and the situation can only be considered retrospectively. This case, however, demonstrates how easily a relatively well balanced situation may be upset by a single individual, if ecological considerations are not taken into account. Quite recently a similar case occurred when, in an attempt to eradicate the jackal populations, all species of mammalian predators were heavily decimated, causing an increase of prey species which became pests.

From 1964 on, thallium sulfate was replaced by fluoracetamide as field-mice poison. Wheat soaked in a 0.2 per cent solution is now being used as poison bait, being applied and distributed according to the same regulations laid down for thallium sulfate. In laboratory experiments it was found that fluoracetamide, in the same concentration as that used for field-mice control, did not cause secondary poisoning to birds of prey, but proved to be dangerous to mammals fed on fluoracetamide-poisoned mice. It is, however, not known if there are any long-term effects on birds of prey.

Recently experiments were performed in

order to test whether effective field-mice control could be obtained by applying smaller amounts of poison per area than those recommended by the Plant Protection Department. The experiments were carried out by Z. Zook-Rimon of the Nature Protection Research Institute of Tel-Aviv University. The test animal was the jird, *Meriones tristrami,* and the populations were checked by trapping, marking and retrapping. It was found that one wheat grain, soaked in a 0.2 per cent fluoracetamide solution and containing 0.08–0.1 milligram of the poison, was sufficient to kill a jird.

For control experiments in the field, the same poisoned wheat was used. On three experimental plots of twelve acres each with 10 grains per square meter, the following different mixtures were used: only poisoned grains, poisoned grains mixed with unpoisoned ones in ratios of 1 to 5 and of 1 to 10. In all three cases, the same measure of control was obtained, proving that 1 poisoned grain per square meter is as effective as the 15 poisoned grains per square meter recommended by the Plant Protection Department. Secondary poisoning of predators is, however, less probable if the field mice ingest only the minimum lethal dose by feeding on one poisoned grain among a number of unpoisoned ones than by feeding on poisoned grains only and ingesting several times the lethal dose. The disastrous effects of thallium and the destruction of the biological control of field mice in Israel could probably have been avoided by a more careful application of the poisoned bait.

ACKNOWLEDGMENTS

At the Institute for Forensic Medicine, Tel-Aviv (Prof. H. Karplus, director), bird carcasses were examined for thallium under the supervision of Prof. I. Fischer and Dr. W. Hirsch. My sincere thanks are due to all three of them for their kind help in this nonroutine work. Mr. A. Zahavi of the Institute for Nature Protection Research, Tel-Aviv University, has read the manuscript, and his most useful criticism is gratefully acknowledged. Mr. U. Marder, Mr. Z. Zook-Rimon and Mr. Y. Braverman of the Department of Zoology, Tel-Aviv University, were helpful with the poisoning experiments. Dr. Dafni of the Veterinary Institute, Ministry of Agriculture; Mr. Y. Naftali and Mr. Wolf of the Plant Protection Department, Ministry of Agriculture, supplied useful information. Mrs. L. Schaefer and Mrs. R. Manneberg of the Department of Zoology, Tel-Aviv University, arranged and typed the manuscript. My sincere thanks are due to all.

REFERENCES

Ames, P. L. "DDT Residues in the Eggs of the Osprey in the North-Eastern United States and Their Relation to Nesting Success." In "Pesticides in the Environment and Their Effects on Wildlife." *J. Appl. Ecol.*, 3 (Suppl.) (1966), 87–97.

Ames, P. L., and Mersereau, G. S. "Some Factors in the Decline of the Osprey in Connecticut." *Auk*, 81 (1964), 173–85.

Bernhard, F. B., and Gaertner, R. A. "Some Effects of DDT on Reproduction in Mice." *J. of Mammal.*, 45 (1964), 272–76.

Bodenheimer, F. S. *Problems of Vole Popu-*

lations in the Middle East. Jerusalem: The Research Council of Israel, 1949. Pp. 4–77.

——. "Problems of Animal Ecology and Physiology in Deserts." Publications of the Research Council of Israel, 2 (1953), 205–29.

——. "Experimental Vole Populations in 2 Sq. M. Cages with Various Initial Population Densities." Studies in Biology, 1 (1957), 24–40.

Bodenheimer, F. S., and Dvoretzky, A. "A Dynamic Model for the Fluctuation of Populations of the Levante Vole (Microtus guentheri D. a A.)." Bulletin of the Research Council of Israel, 1 (4) (1954), 62–80.

Chitty, D., and Phipps, E. "Seasonal Changes in Survival in Mixed Populations of Two Species of Vole." J. of Animal Ecology, 35 (1966), 313–31.

Dawaa, N. "Beobachtungen an Brandt's Steppenwühlmaus (Microtus brandti Radde) in der Mongolischen Volksrepublik." Zeitschr. f. Säugetierkunde, 26 (1961), 176–83.

Dor, M. "Examinations of the Food of the Barn Owl in Israel." Hateva ve Haaretz, 7 (1947), 337–44; 414–19. In Hebrew.

Elton, Ch. Voles, Mice and Lemmings. Oxford, 1942.

Errington, P. L. "An Analysis of Mink Predation upon Muskrats in North-Central United States." Agricultur. Experiment. Sta. Iowa State College Res. Bull., 320 (1943), 797–924.

Golley, F. B. "Energy Dynamics of a Food Chain of an Old-Field Community." Ecolog. Monogr., 30 (1960), 187–206.

Harting, J. E. "Observations on the Common Field Vole of Thessaly." Zoologist, 17 (1893), 139–45. (Quoted by Bodenheimer, 1949.)

Kalabukhov, N. I., and Raevskii, V. V. "Methods for the Study of Certain Problems in the Ecology of Mouse-like Rodents." Rev. Microbiol. (Saratov), 12 (1933), 47–64. (Quoted by Elton, 1942.)

Klimov, I. N. "On the Biology of Microtus (Stenocranius) gregalis and the Method of Its Control." Bull. Plant Prot. (Siberia), 1 (1931), 100–25. (Quoted by Elton, 1942.)

Koford, C. B. The California Condor. Research Report No. 4. New York: National Audubon Society, 1953.

Lack, D. The Natural Regulation of Animal Numbers. Oxford, 1954.

Lockie, J. E., and Ratcliffe, E. A. "Insecticides and Scottish Golden Eagles." British Birds: 57 (3) (1964), 89–102.

Mendelssohn, H. "Mass Destruction of Bird Life Owing to Secondary Poisoning from Insecticides and Rodenticides." Atlantic Naturalist: 17 (4) (1962), 247–48.

Moore, N. W. "Man, Pesticides and the Conservation of Wildlife." Biology and Human Affairs, 29 (2) (1964), 1–7.

Moore, N. W., and Walker, C. H. "Organic Chlorine Insecticide Residues in Wild Birds." Nature (London), 201 (4924) (1964), 1072–73.

Pearson, O. P. "Carnivore-Mouse Predation: An Example of Its Intensity and Bioenergetics." J. of Mammal., 45 (1964), 177–88.

——. "The Prey of Carnivores during One Cycle of Mouse Abundance." J. of Animal Ecology, 35 (1966), 217–33.

Pitelka, F. A.; Tomich, P. Q.; and Treichel, G. W. "Ecological Relations of Jaegers and Owls as Lemming Predators near Barrow, Alaska." Ecolog. Monogr., 25 (1955), 85–117.

Prestt, I. "An Enquiry into the Recent Status of Some of the Smaller Birds of Prey and Crows in Britain." Bird Study, 12 (1965), 196–221.

——. "Studies of Recent Changes in the Status of some Birds of Prey and Fish-Breeding Birds in Britain. Pesticides in the Environment and Their Effects on Wildlife." J. Appl. Ecol., 3 (Suppl.) (1966), 107–12.

Ratcliffe, E. A. "Organochlorine Residues in Some Raptor and Corvid Eggs from Northern Britain." British Birds, 58 (3) (1965), 65–87.

——. "Decrease in Eggshell Weight in Certain Birds of Prey." Nature 215, (5097) (1967), 208–10.

Stickel, Lucille F. "Organochlorine Pesticides in the Environment." U. S. A. Department of the Interior, Bureau of Fisheries and Wildlife, Special Scientific Report, Wildlife No. 119, Washington, D.C. 1968.

Wassermann, M.; Wassermann, Dora; Zellermayer, L.; and Gon, M. "Pesticides in People." Pesticides Monitoring Journal, 1 (2) (1967), 15–20.

DISCUSSION

GEORGE: The emergence of the biological control idea is very clear, but I would like to challenge it with the idea that we may be in danger of accepting this particular idea—as we accepted the chemical control method—as a panacea.

I think that Mother Nature abhors monoculture. She doesn't practice it anywhere herself. In fact, she attempts to avoid it to produce a complex ecosystem.

I would like any member of the panel to carry the idea further that biological control may not ultimately be the answer that we think it is.

SMITH: I will take a start.

The protagonists of biological control of insects are divided into two camps—one saying that we can handle any pest problem, given time, money and people, with biological control. That group is getting smaller and is being replaced by people with an integrated control approach, which uses this natural biological control and supplements it with other forms of control.

Now, you must be sure of how you use the term biological control. Classical biological control is collecting the parasite or predator from some foreign country and dumping it into a pest population that was introduced. Other people would broaden the definition to say it is the impact of all parasites and predators on depressed populations. Still others would broaden the meaning of biological control to mean the use of any biological method as a control procedure or technique.

HASKELL: I think it really depends solely on whether you look at it philosophically or realistically. If you are going to be realistic, you have to accept that many societies in the world virtually depend on monoculture agriculture. Look at the Sudan, for example, with the Gezira scheme on which they depend entirely.

You can argue whether this is the right thing to do, but they are stuck with it. And now you have got to make it operate somehow. If you are going to make it operate within the foreseeable future, all the papers here today show that we are walking down the wrong street with more and more applications of persistent insecticides. We have got to have some alternative. Biological control might not be the best or the only alternative, but it is something that ought to be worked on. But certainly, it is not a panacea.

However, in doing the work that is required on biological control systems, to explore how to use them properly, we may turn up something even better in the future. For example, I would mention those chemicals in plants which affect insect maturation and metabolism and so on. We may be able to grow plants with a genetic or chemical treatment which will have these chemicals in such concentration that insects will not attack them.

There are thousands of possibilities. But realistically, we are stuck with monoculture agriculture; and also, I think, we are stuck with the use of toxic chemicals in some measure or other for the next ten to fifteen years, because progress in biological research will not be fast enough to release us from chemicals sooner.

CARLOZZI: I think we have here a kind of real, lasting problem, because we will have a real, lasting need to create circumstances with agriculture which are bound to produce pests. The very concept of agriculture implies creation of an optimal substrate for some forms of life. And whether a pest is there when we create this habitat or whether the pest evolves like a new variety of wheat stem rust or whether it is an insect which modifies its behavior, no matter what controls we have for a field of one kind of energy-producing plant, we are simply creating and maintaining an optimal substrate that is very attractive to pests.

The question that I pose for people who are concerned with insect or pest control is: How well can we adjust this situation so that we aren't always striving for a total annihilation of those organisms other than man which find our agricultural crop an optimal substrate?

It seems to me the kind of supposition lying back of massive use of chemical, traditional, or old-fashioned biological means is, "Let's get after that pest or parasite and wipe it all out." I don't think we have come around to the point of understanding just where our limits are.

I am concerned, like Dr. George, by the costs of this kind of control on other elements of the environment; these elements may not be part of agriculture but they lie adjacent to it. Somehow chemical materials or introduced organisms are transmitted to other parts of environmental systems through the agricultural scheme.

SMITH: This is true, in the integrated control approach, the so-called dirty field technique, which involves leaving some of the harmless bugs there. It is very critical.

RIVNAY: With your permission, I want to tell you a small case history which relates also to the papers of Conway and Marshall.

North of the Red Sea a small oasis was created with planted date palms and other plants. And along with the palms, Parlatoria, a scale insect, developed. The control of this pest was carried out by limited spraying with oil.

Then, a mishap occurred when locusts came and did considerable damage to the palms. In order to prevent extermination of the entire foliage synthetic insecticides were applied. But the infestation by the scale insect became aggravated due to this activity, so much so that the original method of control—namely, spraying with oil—did not help the situation.

A survey of the biological situation was made, and it was discovered that there are two predacious beetles, of the genus *Pharoseymnus*, and two parasites, one a species of *Aphytis* and the other a species of *Casca* which destroyed the pest to some extent. These useful insects have apparently been exterminated by the application of the contact insecticides. An attempt was then made to rear these beetles, and they were liberated in the infested area. The situation was improved to some extent, but not entirely.

However, relief was achieved later by another method. For other reasons, the members of the kibbutz decided to exploit the soil between the palm trees. The distance between the rows was quite large, and they decided to grow alfalfa and other crops. This cultivation needed irrigation, since there was little rainfall there.

As a result, the dust which usually accumulates on the leaves was eliminated. Elimination of this dust had made it possible for the two scale insect parasites to be active. It is a known fact that where there is dust on the foliage of citrus, scale insects abound more than in places where there is no dust. Now the situation has improved thoroughly to the satisfaction of everyone.

BATISSE: I would like to come back to Haskell's locust story. It happens that I was associated with the beginning of this desert locust ecological survey which later gave birth to the big FAO project. I think it is interesting to note the difficulties we ran into.

The first difficulty was to try to implement the idea of an ecological study of the desert locust to understand how this animal behaved and bred.

We found a lot of resistance to the idea, not from the politicians but from the people who were concerned with locust control in the various countries. These people are supposed to be scientists, but I would say they are administrators, administrators of agriculture and so on. Instead of a new scientific approach to the problem, what they really were asking for was more insecticides and more aircraft.

The second difficulty referred to international cooperation on a problem like this. The difficulty did not come so much from the politicians as it did from the same scientists who were responsible for the administration of desert locust control in the countries. These people were gathered together, and they were sitting behind tables like this where their names were not mentioned, but their country. Maybe this was the source of the trouble. They had to fight: they had the flag of their country in their hands. But perhaps they were frightened, when returning home, to have done something wrong to their country.

I want to stress that the difficulty came from people with a scientific background who first didn't want to accept a new approach to the problem and second, perhaps wanted everything that happened in their own country to be centralized in their own country rather than to depend on cooperation with some multinational organization or project abroad.

COMMONER: I have begun to see very close parallels between the experience reported here and experience which some of us who are not entomologists have had in an analogous situation.

First let me say how I see the situation described here. It runs something like this: there is a scientific discipline concerned with the single-valued goal of coping with insects. This is entomology, insect control and so on. It exists. Entomologists have been trained to move toward that goal. One writes papers on this subject, one's efficiency is measured by the degree to which insects are successfully controlled.

The next thing I see is that certain rigidities of ideas develop. And I also note a reluctance to engage in scientific interchange of different ideas. I think Dr. Newsom's paper said controversy arises when an attempt is made to weigh the good against the bad. When there is a conflict of ideas, people seem to duck away from it.

The farmer and the politician therefore get a one-sided view of how to handle their problems. Whichever answer is the stronger at the moment will impress the farmer. Then, when catastrophes develop because these one-sided views don't work, there hasn't been a history of argumentation, so that those who were right, but lost the fight, say, "Now, you see, we were right and you should learn this lesson." This is what happened in Peru.

Now, there is in recent history an episode which also deals with exactly these factors, the fallout controversy. Let me just say a word about it.

The fallout controversy arose because of the reductionist construction of science in the United States. The physicists exploded bombs and thought that they were conducting an experiment in physics and engineering, whereas actually they were conducting the largest ecological experiment in the history of the earth. What they were doing was disseminating radioactive material right through the earth's ecosystems.

They were unaware of it partly because of a special condition which affects chemical control companies, too: Secrecy. There were secret committee meetings and restriction of basic data. For example, there was a secret committee that met on the hydrogen bomb in Santa Monica which failed to understand that nutrients are absorbed through the leaves of grass; the committee therefore miscalculated the ecological consequences of hydrogen bombs. If they had gone outside that locked room, and asked a competent rose gardener how nutrients are brought into plants, he would have said, "Well, I spray it on the leaves," and they might have learned something. But, of course, the rose gardener didn't have security clearance. (Laughter.)

The point I am making is that here is another case of a single-valued approach. Those responsible didn't see all of the ecological consequences.

Now, what happened was, fortunately, that the scientific community began to learn about it, and a most bitter controversy arose among scientists first between physicists and biologists, then among biologists, and others. The controversy really arose between those scientists who were responsible for the development of the nuclear program and those who were on the outside, who did not have a vested interest in it.

In the early days of the fallout problem, there were forceful government statements saying, "There is no problem here at all." A minority of scientists said, "Yes, there is a problem." The fact that any controversy took place at all was the most important thing. As it happened, it turned out that the government had to admit there was much more damage involved than it had said at first. The test-ban treaty was enacted because, essentially, the government realized something was wrong.

The fact that there was a controversy meant that people remembered the early arguments and realized that those scientists who talked about the ecological consequences were right. You can now see the effects of this realization on the nuclear reactor problem. The public is now unwilling to accept the kind of reassurances they have got about radioactive risk from nuclear reactors because they remember strontium 90.

These problems are due to some basic weaknesses in the scientific enterprise. Our scientific establishment has the very serious weakness of being governed largely by a reductionist approach. Scientific truth is isolated into segments.

The second weakness is that we are afraid of controversy. Yet, this is the way science gets at the truth. We get at the truth not because we don't make mistakes, but because we make our mistakes in public so that they can be corrected. And this is why controversy is essential.

Third, there is a reluctance to go to the social milieu, the politicians, the public, who need to make the decisions, and to tell them that a controversy exists. The result is that we don't learn from our mistakes.

In summary, I think there is a sharp analogy between what has been going on in the pest control problem and in the fallout problem. I think that the lesson we learned from the fallout problem ought now to be applied to the insecticide problems. Controversy should be encouraged.

29. PROBLEMS IN THE USE OF CHEMICAL FERTILIZERS

John Phillips

The ecological effects of the widespread use of chemical fertilizers are sometimes good, sometimes bad, but almost always complex. Manifold combinations and permutations of these effects occur depending on the local climate, soil characteristics, indigenous vegetation, kind of crop, the domestic animal factor, soil husbandry, and other factors. (A detailed review is given of specific cases of fertilizer use in particular ecologies and the effects of the fertilizer on the crops, the soil and other elements in the agricultural environment.)

Fertilizer use on such a scale raises complex and basic ecological questions which require answers as rapidly and as fully as possible. Among these are: What kind, amount and timing of fertilizer for a specific purpose in a particular ecosystem is most beneficial and at the same time least damaging to the crop, the soil or other aspects of the ecosystem? What are the interactions of the prime elements in mixed fertilizers? Will the application of a particular element or combination of elements be likely to induce an imbalance of nutrients in the soil? What amount of acidification is likely to be produced by, say, ammonium sulphate, under particular bioclimatic and cropping conditions, and how could this be counteracted effectively and economically? What fertilizers produce toxic effects in the crops grown, such as cyanosis, which is harmful to children? What is the nature of the fixation of phosphorus or of the rapid leaching of nitrogen and phosphorus from the soils in certain ecosystems?

Several approaches seem justified in light of the evidence already presented. Research should be conducted more intensively into those effects of the use of certain fertilizers which might prove detrimental to the soils and to the crops within the developing countries, so that the nature and the degree of harm may be determined and steps may be taken to reduce such harm. In addition, specific study should be made of the effect of fertilizers upon the ecology of soils and of communities within the ecosystems, both natural and man-made, that is, upon the agricultural ecosystem on both arable and pastoral land. Should the results of these researches warrant any special action, they should include the guidance of the agricultural extension staff in accordance with a suitably prepared list of points of importance. This might also involve the preparation of fertilizers to reduce to a minimum the presently harmful features.

The extensive program of fertilizer trials being conducted by the Food and Agriculture Organization should be supported by those in a position to cooperate and otherwise assist. This field service should, however, be checked against a more intensive and more widely distributed program of scientific research into problems which are either known to exist or which are suspected to show themselves in due course.

As fertilizers are almost everywhere produced by notable and financially strong organizations with some sense of public service, it is urged that approaches be made to these firms to institute research into the toxic effects of fertilizers. Collaboration among producers, research soil scientists, agriculturists and students of public health is urgently needed if we are to help maintain in good condition those remaining nonrenewable basic elements of the environment on which agriculture depends.

Particular interest has been expressed by the organizers of this Conference about the ecological consequences of the use of chemical fertilizers in tropical soils. The subject is sufficiently significant to stimulate a wide-ranging discussion of both scientific and applied nature. I confess I am neither a chemist nor a pedologist, but merely an ecologist who has worked on aspects of the fertility of some African soils and has taken an interest in the economic prospects of certain countries in Asia and Latin America. I attempt, however, to present the matter as I see it and trust this will stimulate those who know more about the physical, chemical and biochemical details to challenge my views.

Ecological effects, good and bad, are indeed complex, with manifold combinations and permutations of variation according to the local climate, soil characteristics,[1] indigenous vegetation, kind of crop, interplay of the animal factor and the method and the

efficiency of preparation and husbandry of the soil and other factors. It is therefore imperative to review—if only in a cursory manner—both the encouraging and the puzzling aspects of the subject.

It is evident that forest, although much reduced in area and vigor through the activities of man, is still well represented in portions of West, Equatorial and portions of East Africa (Phillips, 1959). However, the replacement of forest by wooded savanna and grassland usually is accompanied by a deterioration in fertility.

This is an involved subject, the details depending on the circumstances of the bioclimatic subregion (kind of vegetation, humidity, rainfall, length of the ecologically dry season and temperature), the particular soil *series,* the degree and dimensions of the clearing of forest and the associated introduction of insolation and direct rainfall, soil and crop husbandry and the duration of continuous cultivation. Available nitrogen and phosphorus decrease as the savanna

[1] See the Appendix regarding features in Trans-Saharan Africa.

replaces the forest[2]; water relations alter, either becoming wetter or drier; and the microbiota are accordingly influenced.

THE NUTRIENT CYCLE

The concept that deeper-rooted trees and larger woody shrubs absorb nutrients from the whole of the *solum* and concentrate these in the upper horizon, through the normal processes of cast and decomposition of organic matter, has not yet been given sufficent attention.[3]

The phenomenon is worthy of much detailed investigation because it might teach us more about the intimate actions and reactions characteristic of the interrelations of the habitat and the vegetation. This should in turn teach us more about how best to maintain the fertility of land deprived of deeper-rooted woody growth. Here fertilizers are probably the only practicable substitute for the natural renewal of fertility, once deeper-rooted vegetation is permanently removed, either wholly or for the greater part, as it always is prior to any form of crop production other than that known as *shifting cultivation*. The natural renewing of nutrients from below is impossible because of the absence of deep-rooted plants. Their application from above is the only alternative.

RECENT AND PROSPECTIVE USAGE OF PLANT NUTRIENTS IN AFRICA

To view this matter in perspective it is imperative to examine the recent and the prospective use of fertilizers, in approximate amounts, in Africa, Asia, the Far East and Latin America. For present purposes Australasia may be omitted.

According to the Food and Agriculture Organization (1965), the total plant nutrients, largely in the form of nitrogen, phosphorus, and potassium (NPK) applied in the developing countries of the tropics and subtropics in 1959–1960, were[4]:

CONTINENT	MILLIONS OF METRIC TONS
Africa	0.40
Asia and the Far East	2.53
Latin America	0.83
	3.76

The comparable world consumption was 28 million tons.

Clearly, the total use in these continents was relatively small in relation to the vast terrain, even if land unsuitable climatically, physiographically and edaphically be omitted.

By 1963–64 the total nutrients used in Africa had risen to 0.85 million tons, still only 4.3 per cent of the world total. Of this a fair proportion (0.3 per million tons) was used in the mainly European-owned farming areas in South Africa, the proportion currently used by the Bantu still being much smaller.

Looking at the prospective usage (FAO, 1965; Parker, 1960) in Africa and the other two largely tropical and subtropical continents by 1980, we note that, while an appreciable increase is estimated as imperative to meet the anticipated food and other requirements for populations which will probably have doubled, at least, in relation to their dimensions in 1960, the ton-

---

[2] See Nye and Stephens (1960); also the experience of other investigators in West and Central Africa.

[3] Kellogg and Davol, 1956, in the Congo; Greenland, Kowal and Nye working in my department in Ghana, 1957–1959, gave some detailed attention to this (see Phillips, 1959; Nye and Greenland, 1960, 1964).

[4] The details of consumption of nitrogen, phosphorus, and potassium fertilizers in the various states in Africa and elsewhere are recorded by FAO in its production yearbooks. For various administrative and other reasons these often cannot be more than approximations, error usually being on the side of overestimation rather than underestimation.

nages even then would not really be very great:

CONTINENT	MILLIONS OF METRIC TONS
Africa	8.6
Asia and the Far East, including Mainland China	20.0
Latin America	7.3
	35.9

This is not to belittle the vast amount of agricultural extension, community development or "self-investment," organization, planning and financing demanded to translate these estimates into fact, but I wish to emphasize the still modest amount of prime nutrients which would be applied in Africa in comparison with the 70 million tons estimated to be the world need. The FAO (1965) considers that while there will be a leveling of the consumption curves in Europe and the United States, consumption in the developing countries will rise rapidly due to the demands for increased food production. According to the figure cited above, the most striking increase by 1980 should be in Africa: about twenty-one times that in 1960!

For practical purposes, and merely as an example of what is being attempted and achieved, mention should be made of the recent accomplishments of the Food and Agriculture Organization (FAO, 1965) through its Fertilizer Programme in the tropics and subtropics in West Africa. This program achieved the following broad results by 1965 (Hauck, 1965):

For all crops and seasons in all the countries concerned, from 13,000 simple trials and demonstrations during 1961–62, 1962–63 and 1963–64, mean increase in yield was 73 per cent. Regional means were West Africa (Nigeria, Senegal, Ghana), 71 per cent; Near East and North Africa, 56 per cent (due to the limiting factor of adequate moisture); and Latin America, 95 per cent. Most important is the fact that the value-cost ratio (VCR), that is, the value of the increase in yield divided by the cost of the fertilizer used, generally increased. The results in West Africa for the best fertilizer treatments were:

NIGERIA

Maize: The combination of nutrients did not prove economic on local varieties, but paid on improved ones. NPK at 22.5 kg/ha gave an average increase of 30% and a VCR of 1.8–3.4.

Rice: PK at 22.5 kg/ha gave an increase of 31% and a VCR of 3.6, whereas NPK at 22.5 kg/ha gave an increase of 28% and a VCR of 2.1. Obviously the response to N was negligible and the cost involved not justified.

Yams: NP at 22.5 kg/ha gave an increase of 38% and a VCR of 7.5, whereas NPK at 22.5 kg/ha gave an increase of 33% and a VCR of 4.5 only. Again, the addition of K was not justified by either yield or value-cost ratio.

SENEGAL

Rice: N at 22.5 kg/ha gave an increase of 35% and a VCR of 5.2. N at 45 kg/ha gave an increase of 61% and a VCR of 4.5 NPK at 45 kg/ha each per element gave an increase of 82% but was only just economic.

Millet: N at 22.5 kg/ha gave an increase of 65% and a VCR of 4.4.

NP at 22.5 kg/ha gave an increase of 79% and a VCR of 2.4.

NPK at 22.5 kg/ha gave an increase of 87% and a VCR of 2.3.

Groundnuts:

NPK (6–20–10) at 135 kg/ha gave an increase of 27% and a VCR of 2.8. NPK (8.3–8.3–8.3) at 135 kg/ha gave an increase of 30% and a VCR of 3.0. There was, however, a problem with "pops" or empty shells with the use of fertilizers; see section on *Nutrient Imbalance* under Some Detrimental Effects Producible by Fertilizers.

GHANA

Maize: NPK at 22.5–25.2–22.5 kg/ha for each element gave a 62% increase and a VCR of 2.3.

Rice: NPK at 22.5–22.5–22.5 kg/ha for each element gave a 82% increase and a VCR of 7.5.

Yams: NPK at 22.5–22.5–22.5 kg/ha for each element gave a 51% increase and and a VCR of 4.0.

Groundnuts:

P at 45 kg/ha gave a 59% increase and a VCR of 4.7.

The few years' experience summarized for West Africa indicates several features which earlier work by the local Departments of Agriculture and other investigators foreshadowed. It must be noted that the data presented above are for the best treatments, made under expert supervision. In practice, therefore, we should expect less ambitious results.

In the Humid to Humid-Subhumid Forests the main increase in yield is produced by N, but this is increased economically by the addition of P. By contrast, the boost by P is greatest in the wooded savanna (both Derived Savanna and also the Subhumid Wooded Savanna), but this is augmented by the addition of N. Addition of K to NP in a high proportion of trials increases yields in both forest and savanna.

The largest economic increment in yield following increased rates of application of NPK appears to be produced by the first 20 kilograms per hectare (kg/ha) of each of the three nutrients. While there is a further appreciable and often economic increment between 20 and 40 kg, the resultant increment curve is much less marked when 40 and 60 kg are applied. Applications above 60 kg produce no better responses. This is partly due to the local varieties of the specific crops grown and the standard of the soil and crop husbandry; when more suitable seed is used and these practices are improved, the larger amounts of fertilizer might well produce economic returns.

Deficiency symptoms such as reduced vigor, stunted growth, abnormal coloration of foliage, low yield of grain or other "seed" or fruit, observed in crops after unbalanced fertilizer treatments, demonstrate how low the available nutrient reserves are in some soils. They also demonstrate the precariousness of fertilizer use unless great care is taken to avoid imbalances. Obviously, further trials in both West and East Africa are required to provide more reliable data.

It is admitted, of course, that FAO's function is extension and not research. It is furthermore clear that many of the local varieties of maize, sorghum, millet, legumes and cassava return disappointing responses to even balanced and adequately applied fertilizer. Hybrid maize and selected varieties of other crops usually return more encouraging results economically.

SOME DETRIMENTAL EFFECTS OF FERTILIZERS

It would be unscientific to assume that the application of fertilizers could be considered without deterimental effect under all bioclimatic and edaphic conditions, and irrespective of the knowledge and experience of the user. As experience in progressive farming circles in Britain, Europe, the United States, Canada, Australia, New Zealand, South Africa and elsewhere testify, mistakes in the application of fertilizers, in kind and amount, do produce detrimental effects. Thus it is obvious that even more serious errors might be committed in the developing countries, where by comparison scientific, technical and practical experience is so slight.

1. EFFECT UPON GERMINATION

It is well-known among agriculturists that various commonly applied fertilizers may reduce the per cent of germination of maize, wheat, sorghum, millets and other cereals, groundnut, other legumes and the seeds of a number of other crops.

In some instances, the reduction in germination or in vigor of growth of the young seedling is produced through osmosis (for example, in urea), or through a *toxic* effect (by ammonium salts and notably, in decreasing order, by anhydrous ammonia, ammonium nitrate, and ammonium sulphate). Urea, sodium nitrate, potassium chloride, ammonium nitrate, ammonium sulphate, potassium sulphate, triple superphosphate and "straight" or "ordinary" superphosphate may decrease germination for one reason or another. It is also clear that protection of the seed from direct contact with the fertilizer and avoidance of applying fertilizer during dry periods greatly reduce the risk.[5] My own experience supports the view that contact of fertilizer and seed is often responsible for reduced germination.

2. RETARDATION OF GROWTH OF SEEDLINGS

Retarding of the rate of growth of young roots and stems is linked with the above noted fertilizers and also with others when these are in contact with or very near the plant. This is evident for the most common annual crops grown in tropical and subtropical Africa but notably so for groundnut. Among perennials, cocoa, coffee and tea show the same responses: a curtailment of development of fine roots (observations by Phillips in East and West Africa for the perennials and widely in Africa for the annuals).

[5] Cooke (1967, p. 316) provides a useful review of this subject, citing works by Rader *et al.* (1943), Prianishnikov (1922), Gasser (1961), and Davies *et al.* (1964) upon cereals, sugar beet and other crops under temperate conditions —European, Russian and American. See also McVickar *et al.* (1963); rework by Allred (1962) on diammonium phosphate.

3. "SCORCHING" of YOUNG GROWTH

The top dressing of stands of cereals and of young or reshooting pasturage with ammonium salts, notably ammonium sulphate and ammonium nitrate, induces "scorch" or "burn" of the foliage.

Careless application of ammonium sulphate to the roots of young coffee, tea, cocoa, oil palm, rubber and other plants also may produce "scorching" of the foliage and, indeed, result in death of part or all of the plant.

Boron, excessively applied as a trace element where deficiency is suspected, may induce toxicity, reflected by a progressive necrosis commencing at the tip or margins of the leaves, which later appear as if "scorched."

4. INCREASE IN SOIL ACIDITY

The continuous application of ammonium sulphate, the most common carrier of nitrogen used in the tropics and subtropics, may in time greatly reduce the pH of the soil solution: even the relatively low rate of application at 24 lb per acre per annum (27 kg/ha) under an annual rainfall of 40 inches (1000 mm) considerably lowered the pH in Ghana (Ofori and Potakey, 1965).[6]

Where soils are originally acidic, repeated use of this fertilizer could in time make liming necessary—a provision almost impossible on a large scale because of the complex problems associated with the transport of this bulky material.[7]

[6] Examples are given by Omar Touré (1964) in his survey of fertilizer studies in the Sudan Zone of West Africa (twelfth to sixteenth parallels, North latitude: rainfall 450 mm (16 inches) to 1000 mm (40 inches), June–October, in ferruginous soils, in northern Nigeria, Senegal, Chad and Mali. [Equivalent to the Arid Wooded Savanna and the Subarid Wooded Savanna (Phillips, 1959).] The phenomenon is also well-known in East and southern Africa.

[7] See Haylett and Theron, 1955; Weinmann, 1950; Saunder, 1959. Russell (1969, this volume) also stresses the problem created by excessive and continuous use of ammonium sulphate in the tropics of East Africa.

5. NUTRIENT IMBALANCE

Excessive or other unsound application of certain fertilizers may induce nutrient imbalance. On weakly buffered soils, common in the tropics and subtropics, the fixation of nutrient elements may be caused by excessive applications of the otherwise widely efficacious mixed fertilizer of nitrogen, phosphorus and potassium; this could render zinc unassimilable and thus induce a zinc deficiency.[8]

An excessive application of nitrogen will produce marked vegetative response accompanied by a reduced yield of fruit or seed. A common example is the large groundnut devoid of kernels or with very small kernels known as "pops."

It is noteworthy that ammonium sulphate decreases the total exchangeable bases, especially calcium and potassium and accordingly, *inter alia,* increases the acidity, as

noted above. This is recorded from Puerto Rico, West and southern Africa and elsewhere (Abrûna *et al.,* 1958; Henzell, 1962). Ammonium nitrate is also reported to exert a marked reducing effect upon exchangeable potassium in the lower horizons of red-yellow podzolic soils in Georgia, U.S.A., the possible explanation being the accelerated uptake of potassium by the vigorous grass and an increased leaching (Abrûna *et al.,* 1961; Hentzel, 1964).

Potash applied alone in moderate quantity might reduce organic carbon excessively, whereas a balanced application with either nitrogen and phosphorus or with phosphorus alone would increase organic carbon.

Heavy dressings of phosphate, continued for some time, are reported to "fix" phosphorus in very insoluble form, in soils rich in free iron and aluminium oxides. Although examples of this "fixation" are reported from Hawaii, Australia and Africa, we know too little about this and thus cannot assess meaningfully the implications for the subregions where "fixation" occurs.

If "fixation" of phosphorus is a problem in some soils, the leaching of nutrients applied in bioclimatic regions of higher rainfall is another. Leaching occurs more often from light, sandy, acid soils with little structure, when excessive amounts of phosphorus are applied. This is particularly marked when superphosphate is used, the loss of phosphate from mineral rock phosphate being much less. Applying superphosphate to acid hydromorphic soils (sometimes wrongly termed "peaty" soils) also induces loss of soluble phosphorus through leaching.

Leaching of nitrate also occurs in light, structureless soils, the degree depending upon the form in which nitrogen is applied and the amount, distribution and intensity of the rainfall. It is accordingly more marked in Humid Forests and Subhumid Wooded Savanna than in the drier bioclimatic regions but is also experienced where irrigation is conducted in the arid, subdesert

---

[8] It is noteworthy that Martens (1968) states that as soil fertility increases, zinc deficiencies may become more marked. High *p*H also contributes, although zinc deficiencies have been noted recently in Virginia (U.S.A.) soils with *p*H levels as mild as 6.2 to 7.4. Zinc may be present but becomes unavailable to crops under certain conditions, among these being the phenomena induced by high fertility. Crops vary greatly in their zinc requirements; maize, for example, has a high zinc requirement but many other common field crops appear to have little need for this element. In the course of the Conference, Schuphan (1969) discussed the nitrate problems and the nitrate hazards influences by ecological conditions and by the fertilizing of crops. He pointed out that a high nitrate accumulation due to excessive application of nitrogenous fertilizer (greater than 80–90 kg/ha) may be a hazard for man and beast and cited various references. This is true of countries where nitrogen is applied heavily. I have encountered an increase in nitrogenous, phosphatic and potassic elements in drinking water on sites adjacent to veld experimentally fertilized with nitrogen, phosphorus, and potassium (Frankenwald, Transvaal, 1935–1948). It is noteworthy that McHarg *et al.* (1968) have recently discussed the role of nitrites in drinking water in the vicinity of St. Paul and Minneapolis in the United States, with reference to the incidence of the condition known in "blue babies," cyanosis (McHarg, 1969). The subject of fertilizing of soil, the accumulation of nitrate in vegetables and other crops and the effect of this upon livestock, are discussed for claypan (McGredie), Missouri, by Brown and Smith (1966).

and desert regions in Africa and the Middle East.

Removal of the phosphate and the nitrate in itself might induce other chemical changes in the upper soil and where there is a semipermeable or impermeable pan of iron sesquioxide. The accumulation of nitrate and phosphate might also generate chemical reactions unfavorable to indigenous vegetation. The subject is involved and has not been sufficiently studied.[9]

INFLUENCE OF FERTILIZERS UPON VEGETATION IN THE HIGHVELD OF THE TRANSVAAL, SOUTH AFRICA

There is little literature on this subject. In the early thirties my colleagues, Hall, Meredith, Murray and Glover and some other of my senior students established a series of fertilizer and grazing trials on the higher stages of the grassland succession leading ultimately to *Acacia-Other Species Scrub.* Where regulated grazing was practiced, the purple veld (*Trachypogon-Tristachya-Other Species*) responded nobly in vigor, volume and enhanced palatability to a balanced nitrogen-phosphorus-potassium fertilizer. Where further nitrogen, in the form of ammonium sulphate, was added and the resultant lush growth in the vicinity of gates, drinking points, salt licks and other sites on which cattle concentrated was taken with avidity, the higher-stage grasses gradually gave way to those lower in the primary succession. These were principally *Eragrostis* spp. and *Cynodon dactylon,* which in their younger stages are palatable and nutritious. Control camps showed, by contrast, growth of much less vigorous purple veld, whereas that heavily grazed but not well supplied with fertilizer (notably not

[9] Some interesting work has been done upon the leaching of phosphate from sandy soils in West Australia (Ozanne *et al.,* 1961). See also work by Martens and Mattingly (1965) and Sutton and Larsen (1963) in the temperate regions, on sandy soils and peat soils respectively.

with additional nitrogen), did not show reversion to the lower successional grasses.

Much later, Hall *et al.* (1955) described this work and at the same time Roux (1954, 1969) and Jong and Roux (1955) expressed the view that ammonium sulphate, sodium nitrate and sodium sulphate tend to repress the growth of the higher-stage grasses perhaps because these are very sensitive to even very low salt concentrations; it is argued that so-called "climax" species could not thrive until low concentrations of soil solutions are induced. There was the further thought that these species were also active in retarding, if not preventing, high concentrations through their checking of nitrification.

Whatever the precise biochemical explanation may prove to be, my working view is that the heavy grazing, trampling and manuring by cattle of the lush "climax" grass communities, induced by the fertilizers, play a major role in this conversion on purple veld to intermediate-pioneer stages. There has been a tendency in the literature to miss this practical point. The "throwing backward" of the ecological status of the grass communities is a matter of some interest to the specialist; but this is clearly more than compensated in *practical* terms by the increased volume and weight, more luscious growth and much greater palatability to livestock of the *Eragrostis* communities favored at the expense of the less vigorous, less tasty communities of the higher stages of the *Trachypogon-Tristachya* or "purple" veld.

SOME OTHER EFFECTS OF FERTILIZER UPON VEGETATION

Our knowledge is still limited, but the following points are of some interest:

(a) Excessive distribution of ammonium sulphate on veld and established pasturage—particularly during the drier periods in the warmer season in southern

Africa—causes a "scorching," temporary or more lasting. Where the "scorch" is more severe, bare patches are formed and these in time are colonized by pioneer grasses such as *Cynodon* and *Eragrostis* and even more by weedy forbs.

(b) No study of either incidental or experimental fertilizing of secondary "bush" (forest or wooded savanna secondary wooded stages), of which I know, has recorded the effect of fertilizers upon the indigenous sub-shrub, large shrub and other woody growth. Incidental observations I made in Tanganyika, Rhodesia, South Africa and Ghana suggest, however, that apart from encouraging a lusher growth, no particularly significant responses have been shown. I do not suggest that a detailed quantitative ecological study would not show such responses, for instance the encouragement of certain species and the retardation and subsequent disappearance of others through competition with species of more assertive natures.

(c) Where wooded savanna carries lush grass, there is often a very marked response in vigor, height and volume, especially if nitrogen and phosphorus are added but little visible result if phosphorus and potassium, either alone or together, are applied in the absence of nitrogen.

(d) It is feasible that in forest soils the application of nitrogen-phosphorus-potassium and other fertilizers could affect the microflora and the microfauna. Incidental observations supported by experimental grazing studies have shown that domesticated animals as well as antelope and buffalo are attracted to areas where fertilizer has been distributed—attracted probably by the bases. When sodium chlorate was used extensively in scrub control trials in South Africa about thirty years ago, my students were unpopular with the owners of cattle, sheep and goats because these animals were attracted by

the sodium and accordingly suffered from severely blistered mouths, tongues and noses!

CONCLUSION

The use of fertilizers on a grand scale raises some basic ecological questions which require answering as rapidly and as fully as possible. Among these are questions concerning the following:

a) The kind, amount and timing of fertilizer for a specific purpose in a particular ecosystem,

b) the interactions of the prime elements in mixed fertilizers and whether the application of a particular element or combination of elements is likely to induce an imbalance of nutrients in the soil,

c) the amount of acidification likely to be produced by, say, ammonium sulphate, under particular bioclimatic and cropping conditions, and how this could be counteracted effectively and economically,

d) the toxicity associated with some fertilizers, such as cyanosis in children,

e) the fixation of phosphorus in the soils in certain ecosystems,

f) the rapid leaching of nitrogen and phosphorus from the soils in certain ecosystems.

The following would seem to be justified in the light of this paper:

(1) Research should be conducted more intensively into those effects of the use of certain fertilizers which might prove detrimental to the soils and to the crops within the developing countries, so that the nature and the degree of harm may be determined and steps may be taken to reduce such harm.

(2) Specific study should be made of the effect of fertilizers upon the ecology of soils and of communities within the ecosystems, both natural and man-made, that is, upon

the agricultural ecosystem on both arable and pastoral land.

(3) Should the results of these researches warrant any special action, this should include the guidance of the agricultural extension staff in accordance with a suitably prepared list of points of importance. This might also involve the preparation of fertilizers to reduce to a minimum the features presently causing harm.

(4) The extensive program of fertilizer trials being conducted by FAO should be supported, wherever desirable, by those in a position to cooperate and otherwise assist. This field service should, however, be checked against a more intensive and more widely distributed program of scientific research into problems which are either known to exist or which are suspected to show themselves in due course. To this end, FAO, the Food and Agriculture Organization, should be supported by research conducted by other appropriate bodies. As fertilizers are almost everywhere produced by notable and financially strong organizations with some sense of public service, it is urged that approaches be made to these firms to institute research into the toxic effects of fertilizers. Collaboration among producers, research soil scientists, agriculturists and students of public health is urgently required.

APPENDIX

The Soils of Trans-Saharan Africa—
A Brief Review of Some of Their Prime
Characteristics in Relation to the
Role of Chemical Fertilizers

The 15 million square kilometers (9 million square miles) of Trans-Saharan Africa could not be described satisfactorily in a short note, but I record several features which bear directly upon the role of fertilizers in the present and the prospective development of the utilizable portions of this vast terrain, for crop, livestock, forestry and wild game production. Relevant literature is growing apace but the nonspecialist could obtain a good background—in English—to the nature and distribution of the soils by consulting, *inter alia,* D'Hoore (1964), who compiled the soil map of Africa and prepared the explanatory monograph, under the auspices of C.C.T.A. (Commission for Technical Co-operation in Africa); the journal published earlier by B.I.S. (the Inter-African Bureau of Soils) an agency of C.C.T.A.[10]; in regard to the role of shifting cultivation in the husbandry and the deterioration of soils, the monograph by Nye and

[10] African Soils.

Greenland (1960); and the less-specialized references contained in these publications.

1. CERTAIN GREAT SOIL UNITS ACCORDING TO THE BIOCLIMATES OF TRANS-SAHARAN AFRICA

It should be borne in mind that the soils of the highly humid to humid to humid-sub-humid tropical and subtropical *forest bioclimates,* those of the subhumid, subarid and arid *wooded savanna* (Phillips, 1959, 1961–1966, 1964; Aubréville, 1949) and those of the *sub-desert* are markedly different pedogenically, in physical, chemical and biological nature, resistance to disturbance and to exposure to insolation, and also in actual and potential productivity according to crop and soil husbandry. It is impossible to discuss these here, but reference to D'Hoore (1964), Nye and Greenland (1960) and Phillips (1959, 1961–1966, 1964) would help.

As it is imperative to study the soils as portions of the *ecosystem:* climate, physiography, geology, vegetation, animal life and man, I assemble some relevant information in the following table:

Table 29–1

GROUPS OF BIOCLIMATIC REGIONS (Phillips: 1959, 1961–1966, 1964)	GREAT SOIL UNITS (D'Hoore: 1964)	SELECTED PRIME AGRICULTURAL FEATURES
Highly Humid Forest, Humid Forest, Humid/Subhumid Forest—all at low and medium elevation, tropics and subtropics, but including the comparatively small, scattered Montane Forests in East, Northeast, Central and West Africa. (An extensive group of bioclimatic regions: West and Equatorial Africa, with outliers in East Africa, Ethiopia and elsewhere: say 2.5–3 million square km); appreciable portions now converted to *Derived Wooded Savanna* by shifting cultivation and other man-induced processes.	A. Ferrallitic soils B. Ferrisols C. Alluvium D. Hydromorphic soils	A. Strongly leached, low in nutrients, readily erodible on exposure; B. less leached; C. moderate to good in nutrients, moderate to great depth, highly erodible; D. nutrients variable, texture and drainage poor, but amenable to management; responses to wise application of fertilizers: 1. fair to good, 2. good to moderate to poor, 3. moderate to excellent, 4. moderate to good, depending on drainage; removal of forest canopy and exposure of the soils to insolation and frequent, heavy, rain deteriorates the physical characteristics through erosion, short period "baking" and induration of the surface
Derived Wooded Savanna of the above bioclimates (Forest converted to Wooded Savanna, tall to short, with scrub and grass)	Soils as above	In many parts soils are deteriorated by 2–3 years of shifting cultivation with resting periods 3–6 years; where rest is 10–15 years some rehabilitation of soils occurs; responses to fertilizer much as in above bioclimatic group, N, NP and NPK according to soil and crop; while short-period cropping alternating with long-period "bush fallow" permits a short period of re-use, steady physical and other deterioration occurs where cropping periods are more frequent and longer.

Table 29–1 (continued)

GROUPS OF BIOCLIMATIC REGIONS (Phillips: 1959, 1961–1966, 1964)	GREAT SOIL UNITS (D'Hoore: 1964)	SELECTED PRIME AGRICULTURAL FEATURES
Subhumid Wooded Savanna and Mild Subarid Wooded Savanna. The most extensive group of bioclimatic regions, about three-fold that of the Forest; extensive north and south of the forests, with great arms in West Africa and large but interrupted extensions into Angola, Zambia, Tanganyika, Mozambique—say 6 million sq km	A. Chiefly Ferrallitic soils B. Ferrisols, but also C. Fersiallitic (Ferruginous tropical soils) and D. Vertisols locally	A. Ferrallitic soils much leached, B. Ferrisols somewhat less leached, C. Fersiallitic soils slightly to moderately leached; nutrients low in A and somewhat higher in B and C; D. Vertisols, depending on origin, nutrients fair; excellent to good to fair for agriculture; responses to wise application of fertilizer; 1. fair to good, 2. moderate to good, 3. good, depending on drainage, 4. good to excellent, according to origin and topography (drainage)
Subarid to Arid Wooded Savanna north and south of the foregoing, with outliers in East and Southern Africa	A. Fersiallitic soils B. Lithosols C. Vertisols D. Alluvium E. Halomorphic soils	A. Much leached, B. generally shallow, poor to fair, C. nutrients fair, D. moderate to good in nutrients, E. saline. Where rainfall is inadequate in amount and distribution, no crop production should be attempted other than incidental "catch" subsistence crops: fertilizing is always hazardous and returns usually very poor; where rainfall is more satisfactory, fair to moderate crops, except on halomorphic soils but moderate to good crops on alluvium; where supplementary irrigation is possible, careful fertilizing, according to soil

Table 29–1 (continued)

GROUPS OF BIOCLIMATIC REGIONS (Phillips: 1959, 1961–1966, 1964)	GREAT SOIL UNITS (D'Hoore: 1964)	SELECTED PRIME AGRICULTURAL FEATURES
		(other than halomorphic) and crop may render application of N, NP and NPK economic; halomorphic soils require special treatment which cannot be discussed here; poor irrigation and unwise application of fertilizers produce brack conditions in soils near-neutral to alkaline in reaction; climatic and soil characteristics call for special care in the use of fertilizers
Arid Wooded Savanna (also transition Arid Wooded Savanna to Subdesert Wooded Savanna); 2.5–3 million sq km; extensive north of the above bioclimatic group and also extensive in Northeast Africa with large outliers in Southwest Africa and Botswana		Generally too arid for cultivation, except on the occasional alluvial soils after rain; where irrigation has been developed, as on a small scale in West Africa, Sudan, East Africa, Horn of Africa, Southwest Africa, good management produces fair to good yields of cereals and cotton;
	A. Brown soils of arid and subarid tropics and subtropics	A. brown soils, better suited to extensive pastoral usage, but under irrigation produce sorghum, millet and cotton, but structure deteriorates with other than short usage; response to fertilizer fair to good
	B. Vertisols	B. Vertisols, well drained, fertilized and otherwise managed, produce good yields under irrigation;
	C. Halomorphic soils and, on sandy parent material, some fersiallitic soils	C. fersiallitic soils, in their better types, are also amenable to the same kind of management; the halomorphic soils are difficult to ameliorate, unless much water can be used for leaching salts;
	D. Lithosols	D. the lithosols are commonly too shallow for irrigation

Table 29–1 (continued)

GROUPS OF BIOCLIMATIC REGIONS (Phillips: 1959, 1961–1966, 1964)	GREAT SOIL UNITS (D'Hoore: 1964)	SELECTED PRIME AGRICULTURAL FEATURES
Subdesert Wooded Savanna—an extensive strip north of the above group of regions, with smaller outliers in Kenya, Horn of Africa, Southwest Africa and South Africa	Variable desert and subdesert soils (sands, clays pavements and others, with halomorphic soils)	Usable under careful irrigation only; require the most skillful application of water and fertilizer
Highveld pseudopodsolic soils: South Africa, parts of Angola, Kenya: Subhumid to Subarid Wooded Savanna, in which open grassland is common, either through human agency or because of intensely fierce fires in the dry season	High pseudopodsolic soils (mainly subtropics, higher elevations, 1000–8000 m)	Extensively and, locally, intensively grazed; liable to erode under heavy pressure by livestock and also when cultivated carelessly; where rainfall is 30 and more inches (750 mm), maize, sorghum, millet and other annuals—yield well when suitably fertilized
Ferruginous cuirasses, crusts and hardpan ("ouklip" in South Africa); main sector 5–20 degrees N. to 10–15 degrees W.; but also scattered in Forest and Wooded Savanna of various types in East, Central and Southern Africa; exceptionally well developed in Ivory Coast, Dahomey, Guinea, Upper Volta, Liberia, Mali, Niger, Senegal and Sierra Leone	Developed from rocks of various kinds, in various bioclimatic regions, but mainly where warm and humid; much ancient, so-called "fossil" laterite, pea-ironstone, "ouklip," exists in various parts of the subcontinent; soils with ironstone hardpan drain poorly: a perched water table in the wet season but, in the dry, deficient in moisture; currently produced wherever forest and denser canopied Wooded Savanna is subjected to insolation	Where this material occurs under forest it is gradually softened and broken, the soil then exposed being suitable for tree planting and small-scale subsistence cropping; in Wooded Savanna it is not much broken even under closer canopy; when broken by hand, the soil exposed supports hardy trees

2. Some Features of Forest and Wooded Savanna Soils in Trans-Saharan Africa Bearing Upon the Prospective Role of Chemical Fertilizers

I summarize that the soils of Trans-Saharan Africa, whether bearing closed canopy forest or wooded savanna of varying degrees of crown density and stocking are, for the greater part, only moderately to poorly supplied with the prime nutrients required by annual subsistence and cash crops. For the needs of the indigenous vegetation—the mighty forest trees to the savanna grassland and petty herbs—more than enough organic and mineral nutrients exists to supply the needs of these relatively closely stocked plant communities.

Based on my review of the knowledge available some years ago (Phillips, 1959, 1961–1966, 1964), I summarize some of the relevant points, bearing in mind that there is wider variation according to the particular *forest*—bioclimatic region, whether highly humid or humid-subhumid and the particular wooded savanna region, whether subhumid, subarid or arid.

Table 29–1 (continued)

FOREST SOILS

SOILS OF THE WOODED SAVANNA

RAW AND DECOMPOSING ORGANIC MATTER

Relatively abundant to moderate to slight, according to the bioclimatic subregion and type, usually more abundant than in wooded savanna; readily decomposes and disperses on canopy being removed from clearings more than a hectare; provides a good biochemical and physical setting for nitrogen, nitrogen-phosphorus and nitrogen-phosphorus-potassium fertilizers.

Except in denser Subhumid Wooded Savanna and on locally moist soils, moderate to sparse to very sparse to absent—depending upon bioclimate, frequency and intensity of fire; where grass and shrub growth are fertilized, heavy vegetation growth produces more organic matter but this is readily lost where insolation and intensity of rain are high and mild subarid to arid conditions pertain; only locally and temporarily sufficient to provide a satisfactory setting for fertilizers.

NITROGEN

Usually fair but becoming deficient after a year's exposure to insolation—as in shifting cultivation and complete clearing for mechanized or other "progressive" cultivation; Carbon:nitrogen ratio 10:12, W. Africa, much as for temperate farm soil.

Relatively slight compared with forest soils under similar climates (i.e. in *Derived Savanna*) except where canopy and stocking are dense and fire has been long excluded; the more arid the bioclimatic type (from Subhumid, through Subarid to Arid Wooded Savanna), the lower the total and available nitrogen.

Return of nitrogen on recovery of canopy and stocking fair to moderate: e.g. Ghana, say, 160 lb per acre per annum. (Nye and Greenland, 1964).

Carbon:nitrogen ratio 13:18 in Subhumid Wooded Savanna: West Africa.

Adequate for annual subsistence crops for 3–8 years after exposure, but, for economic production, addition of nitrogen imperative; increase of 50 to more than 100 per cent readily shown: such yields much higher than in savanna.

Return of nitrogen in *Derived Savanna* and Subhumid Wooded Savanna much less: 30 lb per acre per annum only (Nye and Greenland, 1964).

Usually adequate for subsistence crops at low yield but, for economic yield, nitrogen must be added; such yields may be economic in variable degree, depending upon bioclimate, crop and amount of fertilizer.

PHOSPHORUS

Always adequate for forest needs—indigenous and exotic trees—in primary and secondary communities even on light soils, much leached; inadequate for annual crops where bioclimate is highly humid to humid and intensity of rain is heavy; where less humid and rain less intense and soils of heavier texture, leaching much less; phosphorus readily lost in shifting cultivation, where exposure is severe and is even more readily lost under "progressive" mechanized farming, where exposure to insolation and

Deficiency is common and widespread—much less phosphorus than in forest in total and available forms (de Endredy and Quagraine: 1952; Nye and Bertheaux, 1957a, 1957b, 1957c; Vine, 1953); particularly limited where organic matter is lacking; much less accumulated phosphorus in upper soil horizon than in forest; much leached from lighter soils, due to "scavenging" action of iron oxides; addition of phosphorus and nitrogen-phosphorus fertilizer essential where economic production is required; subsistence

Table 29–1 (continued)

FOREST SOILS	SOILS OF THE WOODED SAVANNA
heavy rain is severe; secondary forest growth restores phosphorus, total and available; (Nye: 1951, 1953, 1954; Nye and Bertheaux, 1957a, 1957b); as organic phosphorus is related to organic carbon, the higher organic matter of the forests provides more phosphorus than in the wooded savanna; the addition of phosphorus and preferably of nitrogen-phosphorus to forest soil under shifting and "progressive" mechanized cultivation is essential for continuing satisfactory yield.	production much enhanced where phosphorus and nitrogen-phosphorus are applied.

POTASSIUM

Status of total and exchangeable potassium fair in all but the highly humid bioclimates (*vide* map in Phillips, 1959, 1961–1966, 1964), (Reed: 1951, reports for Liberia—primary and secondary forest) that exchangeable potassium is relatively high; Kellogg and Davol (1949) report for the Congo a slightly lower exchangeable potassium in old *Derived Wooded Savanna* than in heavy forest; deficiencies reported in Nigeria (Benin), Ivory Coast and Dahomey, for oil palm by various workers; but Stephens (1953) and Nye (1954) report no response to potassium by maize under moderate rain in Ghana; application of potassium cannot be prescribed generally—detail depending upon the local conditions and the crop (oil palm, maize, cassava, yam, rubber, lemon and coffees reflect some deficiency—depending on the soil and the rainfall).	Total and exchangeable potassium status higher in *Derived Wooded Savanna* and secondary forest than in primary forest (Nye, 1958; Nye and Stephens, 1960); this refers to Subhumid, Subarid, Arid and Subdesert Wooded Savanna; although potassium deficiency is local and infrequent, it is reflected in Subhumid to Mild Subarid Wooded Savanna by sisal, cassava, banana, sweet potato, potato, tomato, pineapple and citrus; groundnut responds to potassium in some circumstances, for instance in Senegal; application is not a matter of rote but should be guided by local conditions and the crop—and obviously by the adequacy of rain and soil moisture.

LIME

Where the *p*H is greater than 5.5, no responses are shown by maize to lime (Nye, 1951, 1954; and other workers), but on highly leached acid soils (*p*H 4.5) in southeast Nigeria maize and yam respond (Vine, 1953); the addition of lime probably renders conditions more conducive to the development of nitrate; in the Knysna forests, South Africa, lack of lime (*p*H 4–4.5) produces small-boned livestock and induces decay in human teeth where no countermeasures are taken; application of fertilizer must be guided by local study, the crops concerned and, economically, by the transport costs for this bulky material.	Sometimes lacking in Subhumid Wooded Savanna but more often adequate in the Subarid, the Arid and the Subdesert bioclimates; infrequently an important limiting factor in the higher rainfall areas of the Subhumid Wooded Savanna—but sisal may make heavy demands, continuous cropping inducing acidification; application of fertilizer must be guided as noted for the forest.

Table 29–1 (continued)

FOREST SOIL	SOILS OF THE WOODED SAVANNA

TRACE ELEMENTS

In West Africa, the Congo and elsewhere the detailed study of oil palm, coconut, coffee, citrus and rubber has thrown some light on the local significance of boron, copper, molybdenum, manganese and zinc, sometimes in association with phosphorus, calcium, potassium and magnesium; more detailed study continues.

Little is known about the role of these elements; only small responses (below 10 per cent) have been recorded in preliminary trials with copper, magnesium and molybdenum in Subhumid Wooded Savanna in West Africa (I.R.H.O., 1952), manganese and boron having no effect; work continues.

REFERENCES

Abrûna, F.; Pearson, R. W.; and Elkins, C. B. *Proc. Soil. Sci. Soc. Amer.*, 22 (1958), 539.

Allred, S. E. Ph.D. Thesis, Purdue University, Lafayette, Indiana, 1962.

Aubréville, A. *Climats, Forêts et Désertification de L'Afrique Tropicale.* Paris, 1949.

Brown, J. R., and Smith, G. E. "Soil Fertilization and Nitrate Accumulation in Vegetables." *Agron. J.* 58 (1966), 209–12.

Cooke, G. W. *The Control of Soil Fertility.* London: Crosby Lockwood, 1967.

Davies, E. B.; Giovanelli, J.; and AP Rees, T. In *Plant Biochemistry*, 1964. P. 365.

de Endredy, A. S., and Quargraine, K. A. 5th International Soil Congress, Paris, 1957.

D'Hoore, J. D. "L'accumulation des sesquioxides libre dans les sols tropicaux." INEAC, Brussels, *Série Scientif.*, No. 62. 1954.

———. "Soil Map of Africa; Explanatory Monograph." Joint Project 11, C.C.T.A., Lagos, Nigeria, 1964.

Dumont, R. "African Agricultural Development." FAO/ECA: ref: E/CN. 14/342, 1966.

Food and Agriculture Organization. *The FAO Fertilizer Programme* (by F. V. Hauck: in OAU/STRC: pub. 98, 427–39, 1965).

Gasser, J. K. R. *J. Sci. Food Agric.*, 12 (1961), 562–73.

Hall, T. D.; Meredith, D.; and Altona, R. E. *The Grasses and Pastures of South Africa*, 1st ed. Johannesburg: CNA, 1955. Pp. 637–52.

Hauck, F. V. Food and Agriculture Organization (1965) above.

Haylett, D. G., and Theron, J. J. "Studies in verband met die bemesting van in grasher stelgewan," *Sci. Bull.* 351. Dept. Agric., S. Afr., 1955.

Henzell, E. F. "The Use of Nitrogen Fertilizers on Pastures in the Sub-Tropics and Tropics." In *C. A. B. Bull.* 46. Harpenden, 1962.

I.R.H.O. (Inst. de Rech. Huile et Oleagineaux, Paris): Sundry reports on oil palm studies in former French West Africa: Togo, Dahomey, Guinea, 1952.

I.U.C.N. *The Ecology of Man in the Tropical Environment.* Report of I.U.C.N., U.N.E.S.C.O. and FAO conf., Arusha, Tanganyika, 1964.

Jong, K., and Roux, E. R. "A Further Investigation of the Nitrogen Sensitivity of Veld Grasses," *S. Afr. J. Sci.*, 52 (1955), 27.

Kellogg, E. C., and Davol, F. D. INEAC, Brussels. *Série Scientif.*, No. 46. 1949.

McHarg, I. L. *Design with Nature.* Garden City, New York: The Natural History Press, 1969.

———. et al. *A Plan for Nature in Man's World.* Univ. of Pa., Philadelphia, Pa., mimeo, 1968.

McVickar, M. H.; Bridger, G. L.; and Nelson, L. B. "Fertilizer Technology and Usage." *Soil Sci. Amer.* (1963).

Martens, D. "High Fertility Might Lead to Zinc Deficiencies." *Extension Service News,* Virginia Polytechnic Institute, Blacksburg, Va. 1968.

————, and Mattingly, G. E. G. "Residual Effects of Phosphatic Fertilizer." *Rep. Rothamstead Exp. Sta.,* 1964. 1965.

Nye, P. H. "Studies of the Fertility of Gold Coast Soils," *Emp. J. Expt. Agric.* 19 (1951) 275–83.

————. "A Survey of the Value of Fertilizers to the Food Farming Areas of the Gold Coast," *Emp. J. Expt. Agric.* 21 (1953) 176–83.

————. "Fertilizer Responses in the Gold Coast," *Emp. J. Expt. Agric.* 22 (1954) 101–11.

————. *J. West African Sci.* 4 (1) 1958, 31–49.

————, and Bertheux, M. "The Distribution of Phosphorus in Forest and Savannah Soils of the Gold Coast," *J. Agric. Sci.,* 49 (1957a).

Nye, P. H., and Greenland, D. G. *The Soil under Shifting Cultivation.* Harpenden (England): C.A.B., 1960.

————. "Changes in the Soil after Clearing Tropical Forest." *Plant and Soil,* XXI (1) (1964).

Nye, P. H., and Stephens, D. "Soil Fertility," *Agriculture and Land-use in Ghana.*

————. *Ibid.* Chapter 71.

Ofori, C. S., and Potakey. "Effects of Fertilizers on Yield of Crop under Mechanical Cultivation," *Symposium on Maintenance and Improvement of Fertility.* OAU/STRC, pub. 98. 1965. Pp. 113–19.

Omar Touré, El Hadj. In "Sols Africains." *CCTA,* IX (2) (1964), 221–46.

Ozanne, P. G.; Kirton, D. J.; and Shaw, T. C. "The Loss of Phosphorus from Sandy Soils." *Austral. J. Agric. Res.,* 12 (1961), 409–23.

Parker, F. W. "Does the World Need More Fertilizer." *I.M.C. World,* 1 (4) (1960).

Phillips, John. *Agriculture and Ecology in Africa: A Study of Actual and Potential Development South of the Sahara.* London: Faber, and New York: Praeger, 1959.

————. *The Development of Agriculture and Forestry in the Tropics: Patterns, Problems and Promise.* London: Faber, 1961; New York: Praeger, 1966. 2nd ed.

————. "Irrigation in Trans-Saharan Africa: The Basis and the Challenge." In *Africa and Irrigation,* C. S. Wright. London: Wright Rain, 1962.

————. "Shifting Cultivation." *The Ecology of Man in the Tropical Environment,* International Union for the Conservation of Nature, pub. 4. 1964. Pp. 210–19.

Prianishnikov, D. N. (1922). Cited by Bonner in *Plant Biochemistry.* New York: Academic Press, 1951; and by Cooke, G. W., *The Control of Soil Fertility.* London: Crosby Lockwood, 1967.

Rader, L. F.; White, L. M.; and Whittaker, C. W. *Soil Sci.,* 55 (1943), 201–18.

Reed, W. E. *U. S. Dept. of Agric. Inf. Bull.,* No. 66. 1951.

Rosevear, R. D. "Soil Changes in Enugu Plantation (Nigeria)." *Farm and Forest,* 5 (1) (1942).

Roux, E. R. "The Nitrogen Sensitivity of *Eragrostis curvula* and *Trachypogon spicatus* in Relation to Grassland Succession," *S. Afr. J. Sci.,* 50 (1954), 173–76.

————. *Grass: A Story of Franken Wald,* O.U.P., 1969.

Russell, E. W. "The Impact of Technological Developments on Soils in East Africa." (In this volume.)

Saunder, D. H. *Rhodesian Agric. J.,* 56 (1959), 47.

Schuphan, W. "Nitrate Problems and Nitrite Hazards as Influenced by Ecological Conditions and by Fertilization of Plants." (In this volume.)

Stephens, D. Report by Agricultural Chemist, Gold Coast, MS. 1953.

Sutton, C. D., and Larsen, S. "The Residual Value of Fertilizer Phosphate Applied in Two Field Experiments." *Pl. Soil,* 18 (1963), 267–72.

U. S. Plant, Soil and Nutrition Laboratory Staff. *U. S. Dept. of Agric. Inf. Bull.,* No. 299. 1965.

Vine, H. *Notes on the Main Types of Nigerian Soils.* Lagos: Govt. Press, 1953.

Weinmann, H. "Productivity and Nutritive Value of Star Grass Pastures." *Rhodesian Agric. J.,* 47 (1950), 435.

Wright, C. S. *Africa and Irrigation.* London: Wright Rain, 1962.

30. THE IMPACT OF TECHNOLOGICAL DEVELOPMENTS ON SOILS IN EAST AFRICA

E. W. Russell

The impact of technology on agriculture in East Africa has been recent. The best known of the postwar "development" schemes was the ill-fated Groundnut Scheme which as a major agricultural project was a financial disaster due to poor ecological planning. Aside from such ambitious schemes, the destructive aspects of modernized agriculture have been minimized in some instances because ecological considerations played a large part in planning and implementation of agricultural innovations. Some crops were introduced only after local farmers had access to extension and veterinary services which taught them proper management techniques; as a result yields have been high and erosion and other soil problems have often been prevented. Introduction of certain crops was tailored for the ecological character of the different regions, which has helped avoid problems.

However, the new cash-crop agriculture has also brought troubles. For example, the misuse of chemical fertilizers has resulted in widespread acidification of the soil. Pesticide problems have also occurred. Another difficulty is that many traditional farmers cannot at present afford to properly plant and manage cash crops. Research has been started into the particular problems the farmer and the land face with a view to whether means can be worked out eventually to make it possible for the farmer to successfully plant a cash crop without jeopardizing his subsistence crop or significantly damaging his land. Also, technological development in the grazing lands has led to very severe degradation of the environment. Another widespread problem is the great difficulty in maintaining the humus content of the soil, and the problems of humus loss will increase as land use becomes more intense with the introduction of modern agriculture. There are also crucial ecological and social problems to be solved before future wide use of tractors may be justified.

The problems which the present expansion of modern cash-crop agriculture will bring to East Africa must be faced soon if we wish to aid the farmer instead of leading him to farming practices which will ultimately destroy his land.

East Africa is a region in which large areas have inadequate rainfall for sedentary agriculture. Even in much of the agricultural areas, rainfall is sufficiently erratic to cause very large fluctuations in yield from season to season. Crop yields are therefore dependent on the availability of water. Further, the length of the growing season is dependent on seasonal rainfall and in really wet seasons, which can give potentially high yields, the rains may extend over the whole of the harvesting period, giving a harvested crop that will be too moist to store well, or even a crop containing toxins, such as aflotoxin found in groundnuts (peanuts) when harvested in wet conditions. This erratic rainfall means that in many years the crop grows under water stress during part of its development, and that perennial crops, such as grass, coffee and forest, may be under stress for considerable periods of the year. Furthermore, many of the East African soils are so deep that perennial crops may dry out the soil to 15 ft (5 m) or more, and the deep subsoil may remain dry for a number of consecutive years during periods of low rainfall. Short-season crops, such as cereals and grain legumes, differ from perennial crops in having much shallower root systems, rarely going deeper than about 6 ft (2 m). Therefore, if much of the rain falls in the early part of the growing season, a part of the water will percolate below the rooting depth of the annual crops, although it will remain in the zone tapped by the roots of perennial crops (Dagg, 1965).

Except for certain large-scale development projects, most notably the Groundnut Scheme, the impact of technological development on East African agriculture has not yet been very striking. In many countries this impact has, in the past, first been seen in greatly increased soil erosion and flash flooding, but this has not been a feature of development in East Africa because precautions have been taken from the beginning to reduce these consequences to a minimum. This is not to say that there is no soil erosion in East Africa, for in fact severe erosion occurs in several areas. This erosion, however, is due to a greatly increased population trying to live off the land by using traditional farming methods. It is very fortunate that some of these densely populated areas are in regions whose soil is derived from basalts and other rocks fairly high in iron, so the soil itself is high in iron oxides, hydrated oxides and aluminum hydroxide. In well-drained soils, these materials are deposited as thin films over the surface of clay particles and this gives the soil an excellent and very stable structure which is resistant to soil erosion.

In West Africa there are some soils under old rain forests whose subsoils are high in these hydrated iron oxides. If these subsoils lose their surface soil by erosion after the forest has been cut down and the land cultivated to annual crops, the soil material will become exposed to the sun and will set into a hard bricklike material which becomes quite unsuitable to cultivation. (It can possibly be softened again only by putting it under rain forest for a number of years—which is very difficult to do.) It is similar to the material which F. Buchanan in 1807 first called laterite.[1] I am not aware that such material exists in East Africa, but I believe that some of the Senegal and Ivory Coast forests were on these soils, for the French have given examples of this

[1] For a review on laterites see Haignen, 1966.

laterization occurring on some of the areas where groundnuts have been grown for a number of years.[2]

Most technological development in East Africa has occurred recently. We have been very fortunate because many of the men responsible for planning these developments have been first-class ecologists. In Kenya, for example, the country has been divided into ecological regions, based on rapid surveys which incorporated available ancillary material, and developments appropriate to each region were planned (Brown, 1962). In addition, a much more detailed ecological survey is in progress in that part of Kenya with a rainfall high enough for agriculture.

The basic idea behind agricultural development in East Africa has been that it must increase the cash income from the land. Development has usually meant the introduction of a cash crop, such as cotton, pyrethrum, milk, coffee or tea, into a subsistence economy, and the new system is expected to increase farmers' incomes fivefold or more. It is also introducing new varieties of crops, such as hybrid corn, which require a higher level of management and of cash expenditure than was customary. These varieties have to be tailored to the ecological characteristics of the regions into which they are to be introduced.

SOIL CONDITIONS NECESSARY FOR HIGH YIELDS

The objective of most technological developments is the creation of systems of farming that will allow much higher cash incomes, which often means much higher crop yields, than were previously obtained. High crop yields are possible only if, from the moment of germination, the soil is a suitable environment for the growth of the crop roots. The soil must contain a well-

[2] See, for example, Aubert, 1954.

distributed system of pores into which the young roots can grow; it must be reasonably well aerated, except for a few crops such as rice; there must be an adequate supply of water available to the roots, particularly at certain periods in the development of the crop; and there must be an adequate but not excessive supply of all the essential plant nutrients accessible to the roots.

A number of these conditions are not independent of each other. A soil that allows the development of a well-ramified root system must also be well aerated when the soil is wet, provided that the soil is drained and its water table is below, or at the bottom of, the natural root range of the crop. Such soil will also allow rain water to percolate into it rapidly, provided the soil surface is protected, so crops will be less likely to suffer from drought than they do in soils with a less well distributed system of coarse pores. Further, the well-ramifying root system will be able to tap a larger volume of soil for water and nutrients than a restricted system.

The farmer has only a limited ability to improve his soil. In general, the distribution of the pores just large enough for young rootlets to enter easily, that is pores between 50–200 mu (μ) in size, is very largely inherent in the soil itself. Clay soils tend to have relatively few of their pores in this range, and those pores are usually cracks or old root channels, while coarse sandy soils can have a large number of pores in this range. The better structured the soil, the more fine cracks there will be between the crumbs forming the structure; and soils with a large proportion of their crumbs in the size range of 2–5 mm usually have as good a structure as a soil can possess.

The structure of the actual surface soil is much more under the direct control of the farmer. Almost any bare soil will have its surface structure completely destroyed by even a few minutes of a heavy rainstorm, for the wet crumbs are not strong enough to withstand the impact of fast-falling raindrops. The soil particles constituting the crumb are broken off and dispersed in the raindrops and block all the coarser pores in the surface. This reduces the speed with which water can penetrate into the soil and increases the proportion that runs off and is lost to the crop. This runoff is also very likely to carry soil particles with it and to cause erosion. This surface structure can be created by appropriate cultivation practices, and it is usually easier to create the correct structure if the soil contains an adequate level of humus. Soil can be protected against rainstorms by covering it with a surface mulch of dried vegetation, such as stover or cut grass, and it is naturally protected once the leaves of the crop have developed sufficiently to intercept most of the raindrops before they hit the soil surface.

The ability of a soil to supply nutrients to the crop is now very largely under the farmer's control through the use of fertilizers. I do not need to discuss this aspect of development because Dr. Phillips has described this in detail in his paper. There is, however, one point mentioned by Dr. Phillips that I want to emphasize—the harm that can be done by the misuse of fertilizers or the wrong choice of fertilizer. The continued use of a fertilizer may have very undesirable consequences on the soil, the most common being the acidification produced by the use of ammonium sulphate as a nitrogen fertilizer. An acid soil is characterized by a low content of exchangeable calcium and often a high level of exchangeable aluminum and manganese, and the levels can easily be sufficiently high to prevent root growth or to kill the roots. Soil acidity can be corrected by applying an appropriate quantity of a liming material, such as calcium carbonate in the form of crushed limestone; and the acidity produced by 100 kg of ammonium sulphate can be neutralized by 110–120 kg of calcium carbonate.

Most African soils contain only a small amount of exchangeable calcium, the exceptions mainly being some cracking black clays or vertisols. The commonest nitrogen fertilizer used in all field experiments has been ammonium sulphate, which has been both the cheapest and the best conditioned. On the other hand, limestones are very scarce in most of Africa, except near some of the coasts where coral limestones occur. Thus, because of cost, experimenters have not been neutralizing the acidity produced by ammonium sulphate and in fact have ignored this cost in their work (Russell, 1968). It is most unfortunate that the large series of fertilizer experiments being run by FAO under the Freedom from Hunger Campaign in West Africa use ammonium sulphate as the nitrogen fertilizer, and in the reports giving the financial benefits derived from its use, the cost of neutralizing the acidity has been ignored, so its profitability has been seriously overestimated. Unfortunately, every long-term fertilizer experiment I am aware of in tropical Africa has been based on the use of ammonium sulphate and has been harmful because no action was taken to neutralize the acidity it produced. Thus we have no adequate experiments to test how far soil fertility can be maintained through the proper use of fertilizers and good management. I believe there are a few long-term experiments now being designed in which the nitrogen fertilizer will be a mixture of ammonium nitrate and calcium carbonate which has no effect on soil acidity.

SOME EXAMPLES OF AGRICULTURAL DEVELOPMENTS IN EAST AFRICA

Agricultural development in the African areas of East Africa has followed two different courses: the introduction of crops developed in the European farming areas and the improvement and extension of crops originally grown in the African areas. Tea, coffee and milk from dairy cows are three examples of the former group of crops, although coffee has been grown in African areas of Uganda and Tanzania; cotton is a good example of the latter. For a number of years, Africans in Kenya were not allowed to grow tea or coffee nor could they keep dairy breeds of cattle because of disease and quality control and also because of the great shortage of extension and veterinary officers. But these industries had their own research stations, and when the African started to develop them he did so under restrictions which ensured that he knew how to look after his bushes, pastures and cattle properly. Thus his crop yields and the quality of his products are comparable to those of the research stations. On the other hand, yields of cotton both in the areas where it has been grown for a long time and in areas where the crop is new are usually far below those of the research stations set up to serve the cotton growers. The growers have either continued to use practices developed several decades ago or they have simply copied their neighbors who have been using these older practices. Technology has therefore had minimal impact on cotton growing or cotton yields, although cotton production has developed very considerably in the last thirty to forty years due to a greatly increased acreage. On the other hand, technology has had a major impact on the first group of crops.

The Groundnut Scheme, originally planned for large areas in Kenya, Zambia (formerly Northern Rhodesia) and Tanzania (formerly Tanganyika), received strong financial support from Britain's House of Commons. Following a series of brief surveys that began in 1946, £37 million had been authorized for the project by 1951. Production of fats and oils, which were urgently needed by Britain, provided the initial motive for the development, and a number of related benefits for African development were postulated.

Due to the haste with which the project was promoted, there was very limited time for study of the soils, hydrology, climate, labor sources, and communication problems. Virtually no ecological study preceded the selection of sites for the development. Much of the area to be cleared was covered with a tough, woody vegetation; when mechanized and manual clearing of stumps, roots and rhizomes began, it proved to be much more costly and difficult than was anticipated. Then the cleared areas developed unanticipated problems of erosion, soil waterlogging, abrasion and compaction. Other problems also developed: poor germination, drought in some areas, low agricultural yields, viral (rosette) disease, and rapid growth of weeds where heavy rains caused delays in mechanized cultivation. Several areas, particularly at Urambo and Nachingwea, proved to be of mediocre to low fertility, requiring expensive nitrogenous and phosphatic fertilizers to spur agricultural yields (Phillips, 1959).

By 1951 it was clear that the original bold plan, under which the British Government had decided to develop 3,210,000 acres for an ultimate annual production of 800,000 tons of groundnuts (Matheson and Bovill, 1950), was a failure. At that point, the government lessened the scheme to a small pilot project. The production of groundnuts, *Arachis hypogaea,* by large-scale mechanized farming methods has never been revived in East Africa.

The development of tea-growing in East Africa and of coffee and milk production in Kenya illustrates the kind of precautions that must be taken if a conservative system of farming, based on high yields, is to be feasible. The most important soil problem in growing tea and coffee is the great care that must be taken to suppress all weeds between the bushes, because these lead to reduced yields. The local rhizomatous grass *Digitaria scalarum,* if not controlled, will almost kill the bushes. If weed control is done by continuously hoeing the soil, it will become very loose and dusty during dry weather but may likely seal up completely once the rains come, causing runoff or even soil erosion. Furthermore, coffee is grown in areas where the rainfall is usually inadequate to allow the trees to grow throughout the year, so water conservation is an extremely important factor. The method developed to meet the requirements of weed control and water conservation is to apply a thick mulch of coarse grass on the soil between the trees; but because of the expense and the shortage of grass, it has been best to apply the mulch annually to alternate rows of soil between the bushes, so that the whole area receives mulch once in two years (Pereira and Jones, 1954). The mulch reduces evaporation from the soil during the dry season; it reduces runoff by allowing the surface soil to remain more open; it suppresses weeds for about a year after it has been applied; and in the following year when the soil must be cultivated to control the weeds, the soil is still in a very friable and crumbly condition.

In tea cultivation, the bushes are much closer together; weed control is usually through a suitable herbicide; and the surface soil is protected by the prunings of the tea bush left on the soil surface. Methods are therefore available and in regular use for maintaining the permeability and surface tilth of these soils, and the nutrient status is maintained through the use of fertilizers. It is interesting to note that the grass mulch carries a large amount of plant nutrients on to the coffee areas, so that it is often necessary to apply fertilizers to the areas growing the grass mulch rather than to the coffee itself.

The problems of milk production are: growing a supply of high-quality fodder available throughout the year and the management of dairy cows capable of giving a high yield of milk. Unfortunately the indigenous herds of cattle, although resistant to the local diseases, are all very poor milkers, since they have evolved under conditions of frequent shortages of high-protein fodders. Therefore the dairy industry must be based either on purebred temperate milking breeds or their crosses with indigenous cattle. These are much more susceptible to local diseases, so the industry requires an adequate supply of veterinarians and veterinary assistants. The Kenya milk schemes in the high-production areas are based on the temperate dairy breeds, largely Jersey and Guernsey, with high-quality sown or planted grass-legume pastures which are properly fenced and watered and which receive whatever fertilizers are profitable. This is a system which can build up the soil structure very well; when the pasture is plowed out and cropped to maize and other short-season crops, the soil condition remains good for several years. Unfortunately the soil improvement brought about by the pasture often does not last as long as expected because of the rhizomatous grass weeds in the pasture which are difficult to kill by cultivation. The amount of cultivation necessary could probably be considerably reduced if suitable herbicides were introduced into these areas (Pereira *et al.,* 1954).

Over most of tropical Africa the indigenous system of agriculture is the so-called shifting cultivation, in which patches of land, usually unfenced, are cultivated for a few years and then abandoned and allowed to revert to natural vegetation (Allan, 1965; Nye and Greenland, 1960). The essential requirements for higher yields are the use of fertilizers and better systems of management. Here we come up against a very great difficulty; in much of Africa, in many but not all seasons, crop yield is dependent on sowing date, and a short delay from the optimum date can result in a severe loss of yield (Turner, 1966; Akehurst and Sreedharan, 1965). In normal indigenous agriculture both cash crops and subsistence crops are grown, and the subsistence crops take priority over the cash crop; consequently the cash crop is sown late and therefore gives a poor yield (Manning, 1949). This is one of the reasons why the yield of the cash crop is so low and why it receives little fertilizer; for late-sown crops give a smaller response to fertilizer than those sown at the optimum time; and the additional yield produced by the fertilizer may hardly cover its cost. Further, most of the subsistence crops are consumed by the farmer and his family, so they bring in little money and the farmer feels he cannot afford to spend money on fertilizers for these crops. This means that the soil fertility and the crop yields remain low.

The methods being developed on the experiment and research stations for increasing the yields of these annual crops include finding out the conditions under which planting date is important, so that methods can be developed for extending the period of planting without serious loss of yield; the development of systems of cultivation or management that will allow all the rain to percolate into the soil if the subsoil is dry, but to lead off unwanted water from the land during wet periods when the subsoil is wet; and the development of crop rotations and systems of fertilizer use that will maintain high yields without building up too high a pest or disease problem or without damaging the soil condition too badly. It is also increasingly being recognized that the problem of raising the level of production of crops which have been grown by the African small farmer is not solely one for the agronomist and agriculture scientist to solve; its solution will involve the development of much more sophisticated systems of marketing and farm credit as well as a much clearer understanding of the motivation of the farmers, their day-to-day problems of living and their whole social structure.

SOME PROBLEMS IN FUTURE DEVELOPMENTS

There are two further groups of problems that are worth commenting on in the context of this paper: the need to maintain the humus content of the soil and the consequence of introducing tractors into areas previously cultivated by the land hoe.

It is a sad reflection on the soil research that has been done in tropical Africa that we still have very little good experimental data on the importance of the humus content of the soil. It is quite true that added organic matter tends to decompose quickly in tropical soils, so that it is difficult to maintain a high humus content, and it is also true that if the humus content falls too low, many difficult problems of management arise. It is known that even quite small dressings of farmyard manure can give appreciable increases in crop yields (Hartley and Greenwood, 1933; Hartley, 1937). In some soils this is due to the plant nutrients, but in others the experimental data is inadequate to prove if the effect is through the inorganic nutrients it contributes or if there is some additional effect due to the organic matter itself. However, it is usually easier to persuade farmers to use fertilizers than manure because most have no carts and no easy means of transporting it from the yard to the field.

A second way of maintaining the organic matter content of the soil is through the use of temporary grass or grass-legume pastures. One already-mentioned difficulty is that rhizomatous weed grasses tend to develop and these are very difficult to kill before the next crop is planted. But another very serious problem is to make a profitable financial use of these planted pastures, for the local animals are relatively unproductive and normally find their fodder in the areas not immediately under cultivation. Experimental work in selected areas where conditions are unsuitable for a dairy industry shows that by using the correct grass-legume mixture, the correct fertilizer, which is usually a phosphate or a phosphate-sulphate fertilizer, fencing to allow control of the grazing, and an improved beef animal which may have to be a cross between the local and a temperate beef breed, it is possible to get a high yield of meat from these pastures. Unfortunately the economics of this system are not always good because of the low price of meat in East Africa. It is interesting to note that at Serere in Uganda it is possible to increase meat production from 100 lb to 700 lb liveweight gain per acre annually but even this is barely profitable (Russell, 1966).

The technological problem of changing cultivation from men and women working with hoes to something more modern is still very difficult. In areas where oxen can be kept, ox plows are coming in and there is some interest in developing other ox-drawn equipment. But tsetse fly and ticks carrying East Coast fever prevent the use of heavy oxen in many areas. Therefore interest in tractors has developed. Furthermore, the tractor has a great psychological attraction over oxen, because it implies a more modern system of agriculture. But most African agricultural systems are based on the cultivation of small isolated plots quite unsuited to tractor cultivation. Tractor cultivation is likely to be restricted to the larger holdings on level or gently rolling land. Provided adequate soil conservation practices are used, only rarely have unforeseen harmful effects been found. One of the most striking of these occurred in Central Tanzania in a semiarid region where the sand particles had sharp edges and corners. When the soil lost structure, these sand particles slumped down into a solid mass and were extremely abrasive to plows and cultivators, particu-

larly when the soil was dry.[3] But often the problems of mechanical cultivation are more social than technical; namely, problems of servicing, organization of work and supplies, credit, and the development of a system of cropping with an associated marketing system so the farmer can earn enough money to pay the full costs of the tractor and its associated equipment.

PROBLEMS OF THE GRAZING LANDS

So far only development in crop husbandry has been discussed, but very large areas of East Africa are too dry for reliable arable cropping and can only be used as grazing grounds for domestic stock or wild animals. There are also other areas with adequate or marginally adequate rainfall inhabited by pastoralist tribes, who also use them as grazing grounds for their domestic livestock, mainly cattle, sheep and goats. The livestock population is usually so high that most of the palatable grasses and often browse plants have been killed under the heavy grazing pressure, leaving large areas of bare soil having a compacted surface, covered with an often sparse vegetation of unpalatable bush and dwarf short-season grasses. This surface can accept rainfall only slowly; much of every rainstorm runs off as a flash flood (Heady, 1960; Pereira et al., 1962).

On the whole, technological development in these areas has led to very severe degradation of the environment. Disease control keeps more animals alive; the supply of more watering points allows the animals to degrade a larger area during the dry season; and the elimination or reduction of tsetse fly and trypanosomiasis has opened up more land for domestic stock, which then becomes degraded. In all these developments it has been administratively impossible to

[3] For a description of some of these soils, see Anderson, 1957.

enforce a strict control of the number of animals which are kept. It is proving extremely difficult to undo the damage to the environment that this uncontrolled grazing pressure has brought about, but a small beginning is being made in parts of Kenya by using contour bunds to spread the flash floods over a much wider area of the valley floors, increasing very considerably the area receiving sufficient water for reasonable herbage production. But any new methods will be of little importance until the fundamental problem of the control of livestock numbers has been solved.

CONCLUSIONS:

1. With such major exceptions as the Groundnut Scheme, technological development has not yet had a widespread influence on the agriculture of East Africa. Most of the agricultural practices used are still based on traditional lines. Technological developments can only be successful if they are based on sound ecological planning. The Groundnut Scheme in Tanganyika was an example of a scheme that was a financial disaster because no proper account was taken of the soil or climatic conditions for the economic production of this crop.

2. Technological development so far has largely been an extension of crop production practices developed in the European farming areas and based on the results obtained in research and experiment stations. In Kenya, which has the largest area of such development, the general policy of development has been based on plans produced by senior ecologists in the Department of Agriculture.

3. In some cases, technological development has been economically successful where a completely new cash crop, giving a high monetary return, has been introduced into African agriculture. More attention, however, should be given to related ecological, social and nutritional disorders, the last two being outside the scope of this paper.

4. Most technological developments in the grazing lands have resulted in a marked deterioration of the habitat, due to an inability to control the number of domestic animals being pastured on the land.

REFERENCES

Akehurst, B. C., and Sreedharan, A. "Time of Planting—a Brief Review of Experimental Work in Tanganyika 1956–62." *E. Afr. Agric. For. J.*, 30 (1965), 189–220.

Allan, W. *The African Husbandman.* Edinburgh: Oliver & Boyd, 1965.

Anderson, B. "A Survey of Soils in the Kongwa and Nachingwea Districts of Tanganyika." Reading University, 1957.

Aubert, G. "Lateritic Soils." *Trans. 5th Int. Congr. Soil Sci.* (Leopoldville), 1 (1954), 103–18.

Brown, L. H. *A National Cash Crops Policy for Kenya.* Nairobi: Govt. of Kenya, 1962.

Dagg, M. "A Rational Approach to the Selection of Crops in Areas of Marginal Rainfall in East Africa." *E. Afr. Agric. For. J.*, 30 (1965), 296–300.

Haignen, R. "Reviews of Research on Laterites." UNESCO Natural Resources Series IV. 1966.

Hartley, K. T. "An Explanation of the Effect of Farmyard Manure in Northern Nigeria." *Emp. J. Expr. Agric.*, 5 (1937), 254–63.

Hartley, K. T., and Greenwood, M. "The Effect of Small Applications of Farmyard Manure on the Yields of Cereals in Nigeria." *Emp. J. Expr. Agric.*, 1 (1933), 113–21.

Heady, H. F. *Range Management in East Africa.* Nairobi: Govt. Printer, 1960.

Manning, H. L. "Planting Date and Cotton Production in the Buganda Province of Uganda." *Emp. J. Expr. Agric.*, 17 (1949), 245.

Matheson, J. K., and Bovill, E. W. *East African Agriculture.* London: Oxford University Press, 1950.

Nye, P. H., and Greenland, D. J. "The Soil under Shifting Cultivation." *Tech. Comm.* 51. Commonw. Bur. Soil Sci., 1960.

Pereira, H. C. "Grazing Control in Semi-Arid Ranchlands." *E. Afr. Agric. For. J.*, 27 (1962), Special Issue 42–75.

Pereira, H. C.; Chenery, E. M.; and Mills, W. R. "The Transient Effects of Grasses on the Structure of Tropical Soils." *Emp. J. Expr. Agric.*, 22 (1954), 148–60.

Pereira, H. C., and Jones, P. A. "Field Responses by Kenya Coffee to Fertilizers, Manures and Mulches." *Emp. J. Expr. Agric.*, 22 (1954), 23–36.

Phillips, John. *Agriculture and Ecology in Africa.* New York: Praeger, 1959.

Russell, E. W. In *Soils and Soil Fertility in Tropical Pastures.* W. Davies and C. D. Skidmore, eds. London: Faber and Faber, 1966.

———. "The Place of Fertilizers in Food Crop Economy of Tropical Africa." *Fertiliser Soc. Proc.* 101 (1968).

Turner, D. J. "An Investigation into the Causes of Low Yield in Late Planted Maize." *E. Afr. Agric. For. J.*, 31 (1966), 249–60.

31. NITRATE PROBLEMS AND NITRITE HAZARDS AS INFLUENCED BY ECOLOGICAL CONDITIONS AND BY FERTILIZATION OF PLANTS

W. Schuphan

Our research on nitrate problems is closely related to agricultural and climatic conditions prevailing in Central Europe. The results, therefore, may be transferred only if similar conditions prevail. Four questions make up the background of our research work:

1. The role of nitrogen fertilization—especially in excess—as actually used in Central Europe in order to increase yield in spinach and to facilitate the technique of crop harvesting with special machines.

2. The response to this procedure in plant metabolism, especially in leafy food and fodder crops concerning protein contents and its biological value, nitrate accumulation, vitamins and mineral contents. Field experiments in sites different in ecological conditions, in concrete-framed plots in open air and in phytotrons under controlled conditions have been the basis for these investigations.

3. The response in the soil and in the groundwater.

4. Hazards of nitrate accumulation in food plants, e.g., in spinach to infants (described in detail).

The results of seven years' trial with spinach in concrete plots of 10 square meters each are given in graphs and tables.

Fertilizers and pesticides—increasing in use every year—give rise to worldwide interest, but also to harsh criticism. The problem is complex. The application and effect of fertilizers and pesticides more or less depend upon the interacting influence of climate, soil and soil management. The failure of agricultural projects in developing countries

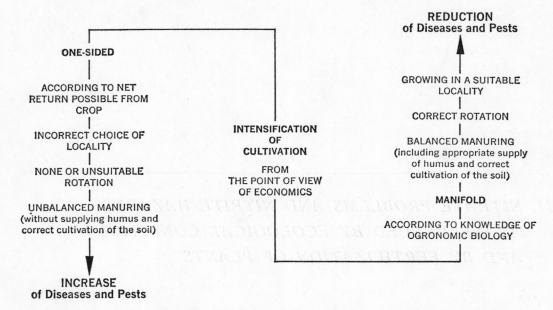

Figure 31–1   Schematic representation of two approaches to crop management and their consequences

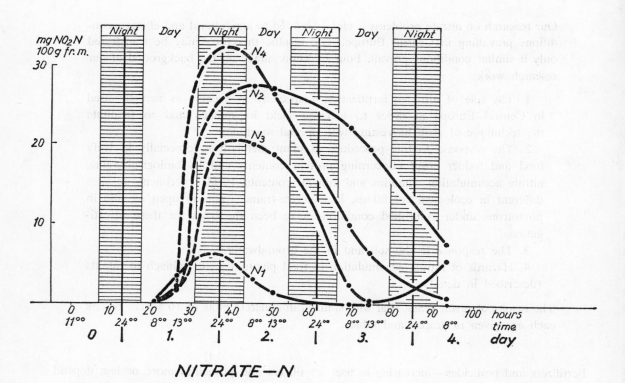

NITRATE—N

Figure 31–2   Formation of nitrite in deep-frozen spinach after allowing to thaw and to store at room temperature (about 20° C) in Geisenheim/Rh. (Koepf, 1969)

is often the result of neglecting the effect of these ecological interactions, the long work of experience, and the proved excellence of biological rules (Schuphan, 1965a).

Intensification of cultivation according to a one-sided view of economics will increase plant diseases and pests, making necessary an increased use of pesticides, which may result in higher pesticidal residues in food and fodder plants. The causal associations are demonstrated in Fig. 31–1. It is well known (Schuphan *et al.*, 1967) that plant diseases increase as a result of high nitrogen supply; and in the absence of suitable measures for maintaining and promoting soil fertility (humus), the army of pests increases. Consequently, chemical methods of large-scale control become necessary in order to ensure the profitability of the crops.

A fertilizer problem is dealt with in this paper. Special attention has been given to the effects of an excessive nitrogen supply to plants. This excess leads to alterations of the biological value of plant protein (Schuphan, 1961), to more plant diseases and pests, by weakening the plant constitution and by reducing the firmness of cell walls and plant tissues, and even to hazards for infants by rising contents of nitrate-nitrite in plants.

Infants in West German cities Berlin, Hamburg and Kiel (West Germany), age 2 to 10 months, showed more or less severe symptoms of methemoglobinemia after eating spinach. The spinach had been eaten chiefly as a cooked fresh vegetable, but also as a deep-frozen product which was heated, and after a refrigerated storage of 24 to 48 hours, was reheated and eaten by the infants. It was concluded that nitrate was not the toxic principle but, rather, that nitrite had been formed during storage or in the intestines of infants by the action of bacteria during dysentery. Our findings proved that only large amounts of nitrate in spinach exceeding about 50 mg NO_3 were conducive

to conversion to nitrite to make spinach a hazard as toxic food. Figure 31–2 gives evidence that a normal supply of nitrogen to spinach ($N_1 = 80$ kg N/ha) does not lead to high amounts of nitrites dangerous for infants, while N_2 (160 kg N/ha), N_3 (240 kg N/ha) and N_4 (320 kg N/ha) give rise to remarkable amounts of nitrite after storage of thawed processed spinach (deep-frozen) at room temperature of 20° C.

The next two figures, Figs. 31–3 and 31–4, show nitrate levels of spinach at each level of fertilization in every year (1960 until 1966). The abscissa is divided up, not according to high yields, but according to the amounts of applied nitrogen. Here, too, the nitrate levels increase more or less clearly with increased levels of nitrogen.

For the evaluation from a medical point of view of the nitrate-nitrite problem in both drinking-water and plant products, interest has almost exclusively been confined to symptoms of its influence on circulation and methemoglobinemia. Experts in animal nutrition and physiology are also discussing hazards, such as those in fodder plants. According to the literature, effects have been found in animal trials on the thyroid metabolism, the fermentative system, and on the status of carotene, vitamin A, and vitamin E, even using a fodder having a relatively small nitrate-nitrite accumulation (Becker, 1967).

Besides the ecological conditions, cultural methods play a role which can decisively alter the findings. Ecological factors are climate and soil. Climate is important because of the long-term influence of weather fluctuation, especially sunshine, temperature, and rainfall, on sowing time, germination of seed, and the correlation of cultural methods with both ecological factors and fertilization.

According to the world literature and to our own experiments since 1953, we can summarize the situation as follows (Schup-

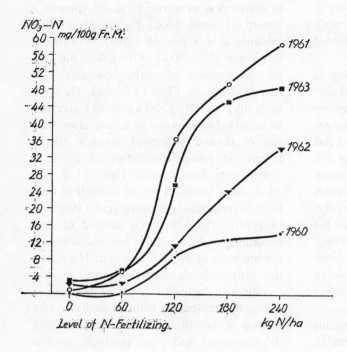

Figure 31–3 Spinach. Mean of 4 years' experiments (1960–1963) with N-fertilizers

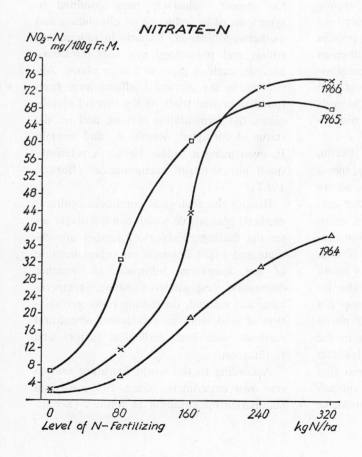

Figure 31–4 Spinach. Mean of 3 years' experiments (1964–1966) with N-fertilizers

han, 1961, 1965a–f; Becker, 1967; Boek and Schuphan, 1959):

1. Depending on its physiological constitution, the plant takes up nitrogen as NO_3^- or NH_4^+ ion in order to build up amino acids and high molecular protein.

2. This process takes place without remarkable residual amounts of nitrate-N only if all factors influencing growth are optimal. Decisive growth factors are water supply, insolation and, to a certain extent, temperature.

3. Drought, causing continuous dryness in the soil, leads to a high concentration of nitrite in the plant, even at normal nitrogen supply. Due to high nitrite contents caused by drought in fodder plants, quite a number of cattle died in the state of Missouri in 1950, of asphyxia due to methemoglobinemia (Brown and Smith, 1966).

4. High insolation and suitable growth conditions, especially water supply, favor photosynthesis and the resulting formation of protein. These factors also cause a decrease of the nitrate level in the plant even when a higher nitrogen supply is available from soil storage and applied fertilizers.

5. In addition to ecological factors such as light and water, cultural methods are responsible for the amount of nitrate-N accumulated in the plant. High levels in applied nitrogen result in high nitrate accumulation. Additional application of trace elements (copper, zinc, boron, molybdenum and cobalt) does not influence the amount of nitrate accumulation in plants (Brown and Smith, 1966). After an application of the herbicide 2,4-D the content of nitrate increases in plants to the same extent as after high nitrogen application.

6. A high nitrate accumulation caused by high nitrogen levels in the soil or by excessive nitrogen fertilization (more than 80–90 kilograms nitrogen per hectare) may be a hazard for man and animal. Long transport or storage of harvested spinach of a high nitrate content before cooking and processing might give rise to bacterial reduction of nitrate to toxic amounts of nitrite. According to J. Borneff (Wagner and Borneff, 1967) bacterial nitrate reduction is possible in frozen spinach with high nitrate contents, when it is cooked, stored and then rewarmed.

7. Relatively large amounts of nitrate-N are stored by ruderal plants belonging to the family of Chenopodiaceae (spinach and beets), by cultivated plants of the Cruciferae, especially by those of the genus *Brassica* (white and red cabbage), in cauliflower, in green and fodder kale, and in tubers of the genus *Raphanus*, especially in small and big radishes. Nitrate accumulation in carrots is surprisingly low, and even after a high application of nitrogen cannot cause any nitrate-nitrite troubles (Schuphan, 1965a, p. 50; Brown and Smith, 1966).

Because of the great importance of this problem we have carried out trials since 1953 with a "model plant," the Chenopodiaceae spinach (*Spinacia oleracea* L.), closely related to beet root, and the sugar and fodder beet (*Beta vulgaris*). In field trials, in special experiments in concrete plots and in phytotrons, the latter under controlled conditions of all factors including light and temperature, the mechanism of formation of protein, amino acids, nitrate, and nitrite was investigated in food and feed plants under varying ecological conditions.

For a convincing account of the problem, experimental results are here demonstrated in tables and graphs derived from long-term trials with our model spinach. Table 31–1 shows findings of 1954, gained from trials in phytotrons at Geisenheim (Boek and Schuphan, 1959). Plants grown under a

Table 31-1

N-FERTILIZING TRIALS IN MITSCHERLICH–POTS.
SPINACH (CULTIVAR: "UNIVERSAL"). EXPERIMENTS IN A PHYTOTRON.

INTENSITY OF LIGHT IN LUX	LIQUID MANURE Mg NO₃ in %		N₀ Mg NO₃ in %		N₁ Mg NO₃ in %		N₂ Mg NO₃ in %		N₃ Mg NO₃ in %	
	FR.*	DR.†	FR.	DR.	FR.	DR.	FR.	DR.	FR.	DR.
5,000-6,000	410	3,460	270	3,170	280	3,120	260	2,920	400	3,820
6,000-7,000	280	2,430	180	2,040	180	2,090	200	2,090	200	2,050

*Basis: fresh matter.
†Basis: dry matter.

Table 31-2

SPINACH TRIALS ON TWO DIFFERENT SITES
(KIEL, NORTH GERMANY; GEISENHEIM/RHINE, SOUTH WEST GERMANY)

N-FERTILIZING	LEVEL OF NITROGEN IN Kg/Ha	Mg NO₃ IN 100G DRY MATTER	
		SITE KIEL	SITE GEISENHEIM
O	—	Traces	56
N₀	—	Traces	10
Ca-Ammonium-nitrate			
N₁	60	390	280
N₂	120	570	480
N₃	180	760	—
N₄	240	—	760

light intensity of 5000–6000 lux clearly showed higher nitrate accumulation compared with those under 6000–7000 lux. At lower light intensity the accumulation of nitrate increased by 60–85%. Liquid manure (column 1) also increased nitrate contents in spinach. The values found are roughly the same as those of a mineral nitrogen supply of N₃ (column 5). Similar results of the influence of light on accumulation of nitrate in fodder plants were reported by Scharrer and Seibel in 1956 (Scharrer and Seibel, 1966). In 1955 there were trials with spinach (Table 31–2) grown at various levels of nitrogen supply at two different sites, in Kiel (North Germany) and in Geisenheim (Southwest Germany). The nitrate accumulation in spinach from Kiel

grown under a relatively low light intensity was found to be much higher than in Geisenheim with its higher light intensity.

In 1960 we started seven years of long-term nitrogen-fertilizing experiments in concrete-framed plots of 10 square meters with four replications. Every year from 1960 to 1963 each of the trials received one of the following amounts of nitrogen: 0, 60, 120, 180 and 240 kg/ha. In 1964 the trials were changed to the following levels of N: 0, 80 kg/ha (normal nitrogen level recommended for spinach in vegetable textbooks), 160, 240 and 320 kg/ha. Thus comparable findings on the same site were obtained over a period of seven years, producing significant results.

Figures 31–5 and 31–6 show the average

amounts of important nutrients found in each of the periods in the test spinach. The results of the two periods correspond very well. As a result of an increasing nitrogen supply, dry matter contents in spinach

decrease regularly; total N increases as well as protein-N, the latter not to the same extent. The nitrate levels increase rather steeply.

Figure 31–7 shows negative correlations

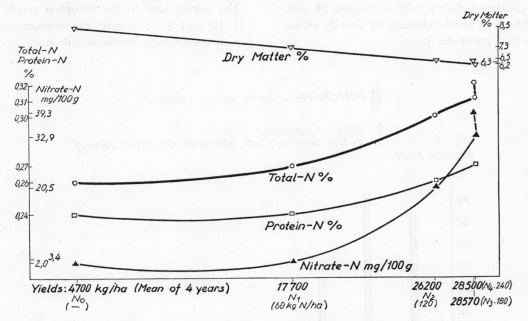

Figure 31–5 Spinach. Mean of 4 years' experiments (1960–1963) with N-fertilizers

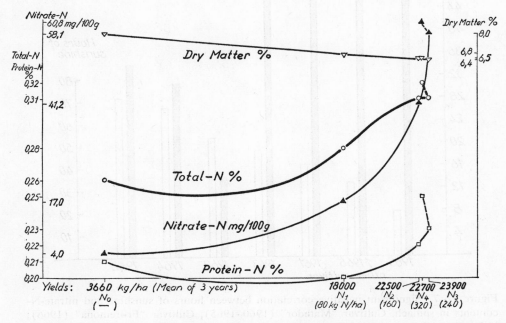

Figure 31–6 Spinach. Mean of 3 years' experiments (1964–1966) with N-fertilizers

between hours of sunshine from the eleventh to the twentieth day after sowing and the nitrate-N contents in the harvested crop. Only in 1960 were there unexpected results, showing a relatively low value of nitrate-N. However, this spinach was harvested about eight days before it fully developed, because of fears of greater damage by beet-fly attack in that particular year.

According to Figs. 31–8 and 31–9, increased amounts of N-fertilizers had a negative influence on the sugar and ascorbic acid contents of spinach in both test groups. On the other hand, the mean measure of the carotene contents hardly changed.

The curves seen in the following graphs (31–10 and 31–11) give the amount or percentage of each chemical substance ac-

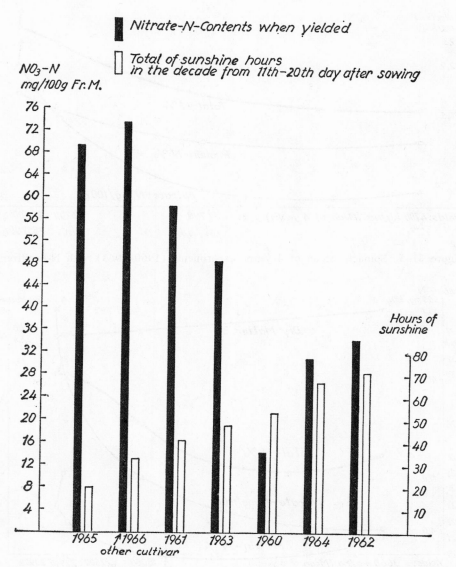

Figure 31–7 Significant negative correlation between hours of sunshine and nitrate-N-contents in spinach. Cultivar "Matador" (1960–1965), Cultivar "Früremona" (1966); N-Fertilizer Experiment (240 kg N/ha)

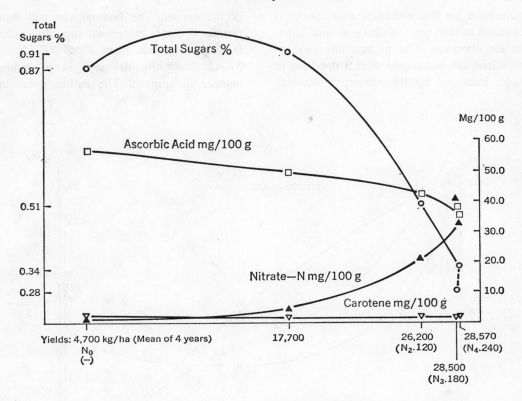

Figure 31–8   Spinach. Mean of 4 years' experiments (1960–1963) with N-fertilizers

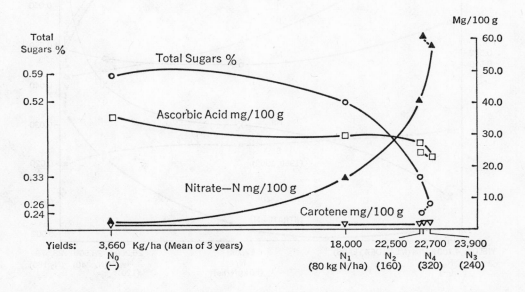

Figure 31–9   Spinach. Mean of 3 years' experiments (1960–1963) with N-fertilizers: effect of increasing fertilization on plant content of nitrate, ascorbic acid, total sugars, and carotene

cumulated on the ordinates and the yield
obtained at each level of nitrogen application
on the abscissae. The highest nitrogen applications are associated with a decrease in
yield, indicated by the recurrent tendency

of the curves. The findings are still more
distinct if plants are grown strongly shaded.
It may be taken from Figs. 31–10 and
31–11 that minerals react in a peculiar
manner in spinach. The cation potassium

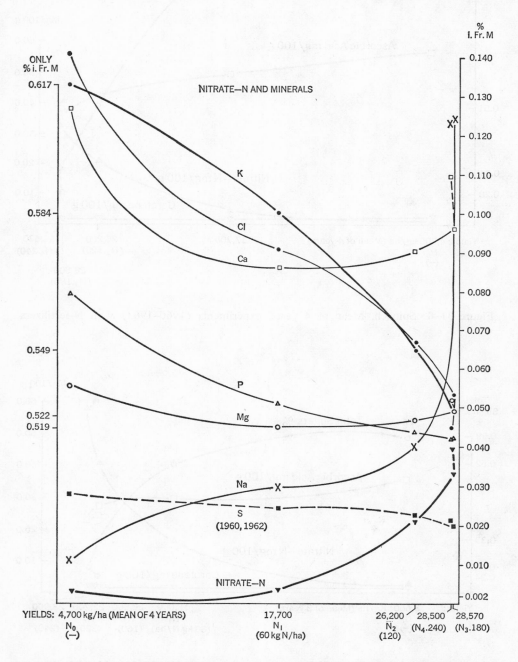

Figure 31–10 Spinach. Mean of 4 years' experiments (1960–1963) with N-fertilizers:
effect of increased fertilization on various minerals in the plant

occurring in spinach in relatively large amounts decreases strongly when influenced by higher amounts of supplied nitrogen. Calcium behaves to potassium in an antagonistic sense according to the Ca-K law of Ehrenberg (Schuphan, 1940). The curve of chlorine seems to be similar to that of potassium. This contrasts to nitrate-N and sodium, which increase considerably with increased nitrogen fertilization. Elevation of

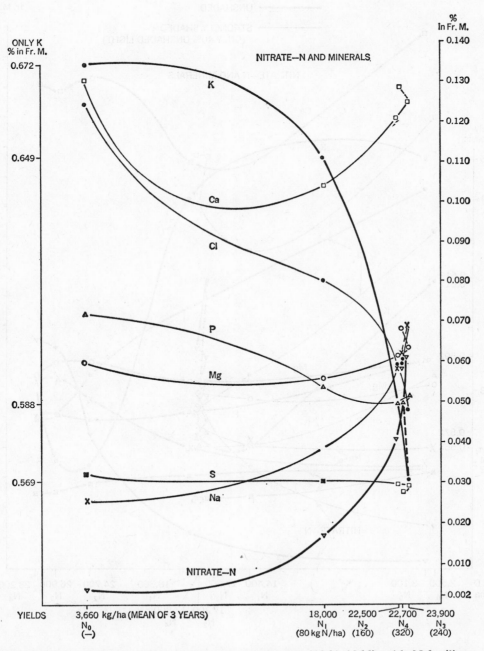

Figure 31–11 Spinach. Mean of 4 years' experiments (1964–1966) with N-fertilizers

chlorides in fertilizing suppresses the formation of nitrate, as reported by K. Schmalfuss
(1953) for sugar beets.

Experiments with spinach in 1966 on the
same plots, now in partial shade, led to the
following results (Fig. 31–12): Shading was

remarkably associated with a loss in yield
and a decline in content of total sugars,
ascorbic acid, and all minerals.

From the viewpoint of human health it
seems to be noteworthy that high nitrogen
supply is leading to a remarkable increase

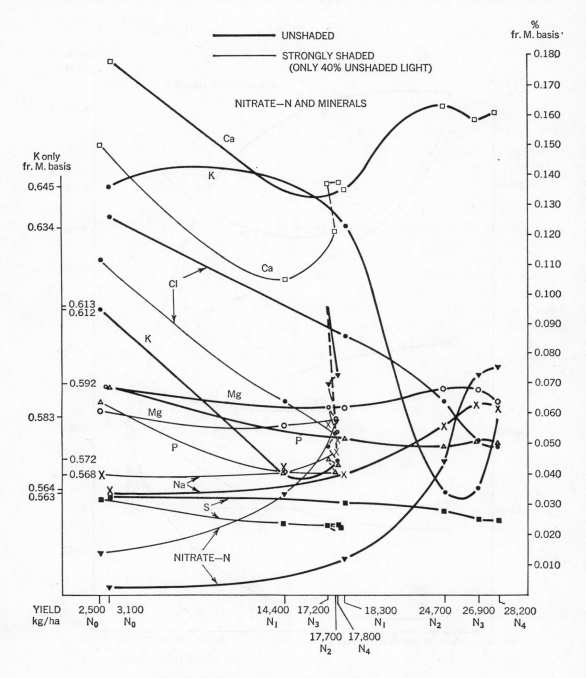

Figure 31–12 Spinach. N-Trial. Spring 1966

Table 31-3

N-TRIAL WITH SPINACH (CULTIVAR: "MATADOR")
(PLOTS 10m², CONCRETE FRAMES, GEISENHEIM. YIELD: 16.5. 1960)

N-SUPPLY	METHIONINE* %		SIGNIFICANCE		EAA-INDEX	
	FR.†	DR.‡	t	p	8 EAA	7 EAA (METHIONINE = 0)
N_0	0.017	0.24			72	47
			3.83	< 0.05		
N_1	0.019	0.30			71	47
			2.26	> 0.05		
N_2	0.018	0.33			71	47
			27.08	< 0.001		
N_3	0.007	0.13			60	45
			9.44	< 0.001		
N_4	0.003	0.06			54	44

*An essential amino acid in rat nutrition.
†Basis: fresh matter.
‡Basis: dry matter.

of sodium and to a sharp decrease of potassium. Meneely and coworkers (Meneely *et al.*, 1960; Meneely, 1966) found in nine life-span experiments in 945 rats that increasing amounts of sodium chloride per ounce was associated with elevation in systolic blood pressure, serum cholesterol, total exchangeable body sodium and the incidence of electrocardiographic abnormalities. Bringing the potassium to sodium ratio toward one dramatically lengthened the mean duration of life.

A decreasing tendency of the curves is distinct for the phosphate; for sulfur it is only slight. The curve for magnesium is similar to that of calcium but less declined. To summarize, the curves of the minerals suggest that they tend to diverge without nitrogen supply but to converge significantly with increasing amounts of nitrogen fertilizers.

In other words, amounts of 80 to 90 kg

N/ha—supposed to be normal levels from an empirical point of view—are leading to mineral contents divergently distributed in plants, while higher amounts of N-fertilizers seem to converge the minerals considerably, with the exception of calcium and, to a limited extent, sodium.

To be complete, we must note that a decrease in the biological value of protein, influenced by a significant decrease of methionine content in spinach, is the result of increasing N-supply by fertilizers (Schuphan, 1961) (Table 31–3).

Finally it should be said that harvesting methods yielding chiefly leaf blades by removing stems and petioles can lower nitrate contents to an average of about 57% (Schuphan, 1967). Thus a real chance seems to have been given to improve the biological value and to avoid detrimental effects in infants, especially if nitrogen fertilization is kept within reasonable limits.

REFERENCES

Becker, M. "Nitrat/Nitrit in der Tierernährung." *Qual. Plant. et Mater. Veg.*, 15 (1967), 48–64.

Boek, K., and Schuphan, W. "Der Nitratgehalt von Gemüsen in Abhängigkeit von Pflanzenart und einigen Umweltfaktoren." *Qual. Plant. et Mater. Veg.*, 5 (1959), 199–208.

Brown, J. R., and Smith, G. E. "Soil Fertilization and Nitrate Accumulation in Vegetables." *J. Agron.*, 58 (1966), 209–12.

Koepf, H. H. "Relations between Soil Management and the Quality of Surface- and Groundwater Supplies." *Qual. Plant. et Mater. Veg.*, 17 (1969), 45–65.

Meneely, G. R. *Toxicants Occurring Naturally in Foods.* Publication 1354, Nat. Acad. Sci.–Nat. Res. Council. Washington, D.C., 1966. Pp. 267–79 (Toxic effects of dietary sodium chloride and the protective effect of potassium).

Meneely, G. R.; Darby, W. J.; Tucker, R. G.; Ball, C. O. T.; and Youmans, J. B. "Cardio-Vascular and Biochemical Changes Observed in Life-Span Increased Dietary Sodium Chloride: The Protective Effect of Potassium Chloride on Hypertension and Median Duration of Life." 5th Intern. Congr. Nutrit. *Abstracts,* No. 30. Washington, D.C., 1960.

Scharrer, K., and Seibel, W. "Über den Einfluss der Ernährung und Belichtung auf den Nitratgehalt von Futterpflanzen." *Landwirtsch. Forsch.*, 9 (1956), 168–78.

Schmalfuss, K. *Pflanzenernährung und Bodenkunde.* Leipzig: Hirzel, 1953.

Schuphan, W. "Über den Einfluss der Chlorid- und Sulfatdüngung auf Ertrag, Marktgängigkeit und biologischen Wert verschiedener Gemüse unter Berücksichtigung edaphischer und klimatischer Faktoren." *Bodenk. u. Pflanzenern.*, 19 (1940), 265–315.

————. "Methioningehalt und Eiweissqualität von Blattpflanzen in Abhängigkeit von der Stickstoffdüngung." *Qual. Plant. et Mater. Veg.*, 8 (1961), 261–83.

————. *Nutritional Values in Crops and Plants, Problems for Producers and Consumers.* London: Faber & Faber, 1965a.

————. "Ertragsbildung und Erzeugung wertgebender Inhalts- und Schadstoffe in Abhängigkeit von der N- und P- Düngung." *Landwirtsch. Forsch.*, 19 (Special number) (1965b), 195–205.

————. "Der Nitratgehalt von Spinat (Spinacia oleracea L.) in Beziehung zur Methämoglobinämie der Säuglinge." *Z. Ernährungsw.*, 6 (1965d), 207–09.

————. "Die Beeinflussung des biologischen Stoffkreislaufs durch körperfremde chemische Substanzen." *Informationsblatt der Förderation Europäischer Gewässerschutz* (FEG), Nr. 13. Zurich, 1965f.

————, and Harnisch, S. "Über die Ursache einer Anreicherung von Spinat (Spinacia oleracea L.) mit Nitrat und Nitrit in Beziehung zur Methämoglobinämie bei Ratten." *Z. Kinderheilk.*, 93 (1965c), 142–47.

————, and Schloffmann, H. "N-Überdüngung als Ursache hoher Nitrat- und Nitritgehalte des Spinats (Spinacia oleracea L.) in ihrer Beziehung zur Säuglings-Methämoglobinämie. (Untersuchungen an frischem, transportiertem, gelagertem und tiefgefrorenem Spinat.) *Z. Lebensmitt. Unters.*, 128 (1965e), 71–75.

Schuphan, W.; Bengtsson, B.; Bosund, J.; and Hylmö, B. "Nitrate Accumulation in Spinach." *Qual. Plant. et Mater. Veg.*, 14 (1967), 317–30.

Wagner, M., and Borneff, J. "Hygienisch-bakteriologische Untersuchungen an Tiefkühlgemüse." 1., 2. und 3. Mitt. *Arch. f. Hygiene,* 151 (1967), 64–90.

32. LATERITIC SOILS IN DISTINCT TROPICAL ENVIRONMENTS:
Southern Sudan and Brazil

Mary McNeil

The myth of fertility of tropical soils is giving way before abundant evidence to the contrary. Many areas of the tropics have soils which are in a more or less advanced stage of natural laterization, which occurs when the soil is leached of silica, leaving residual minerals such as iron, aluminum, manganese and nickel. These widespread laterite-prone soils are usually covered by rain-forests or savannas. Most available organic matter is quickly reused by the living plants on such soils instead of forming a layer of humus. Thus, the soils are quickly impoverished when forest or other plant cover is gone.

The southern Sudan and parts of Brazil have such laterite-tending soils, and the history of development projects in these areas exposes an almost complete disregard for the limits and conditions which such areas impose for productive development. In the Sudan, the peoples living on laterite soils had developed their agriculture in harmony with the requirements of the land and practiced a shifting agriculture which allowed a long fallow period for rejuvenating and preventing the loss of soils. Development projects have restructured traditional agricultural styles, often forcibly, resulting in overuse of the land, with consequent social and agricultural disasters. Other areas are threatened by a proposed canal to regulate the flow of the White Nile and conserve its waters. Studies indicate that the intimate and delicate relationship of the surrounding lands to the annual flooding would be disrupted, with consequent permanent destruction of much of the grazing and farming land and possible serious problems for fishing.

In Brazil, many thousands of hopeful pioneers have been lured into rain-forest areas of the Amazon basin and have cleared the forest for agriculture. Little thought had been given to adapting the type of agricultural practices and crops to the nature of the soil. As a result, the soils have quickly become exhausted as the closed tree-soil-tree cycle has been destroyed. In addition, the minerals in the soil have tended to cake, producing a hard semidesert over much of the colonized areas. The colonizers have moved yet deeper into the forest trying to make a go of agriculture, but with the same results. A small group of Japanese colonists had the insight to plant useful trees; their example offers some hope for a nondestructive and realistic development of the area.

These case studies show how crucial it is for man to recognize all the many forces operating when he tries to permanently modify the environment. The price paid in terms of an altered ecosystem must be worth what man gets in return. Survival of a small segment of humanity or a whole nation often depends upon how well we can distinguish between the real costs and real benefits of our development programs. With knowledge of the entire ecosystem involved, these costs and benefits can be better defined.

The myth of fertility of tropical soils which has been around since the days of Alexander von Humboldt is slowly giving way. The lushness of the tropical rain-forest has proven to be more apparent than real. Close examination of large portions of these forests in Africa and South America has shown them to be relics of a former climatic regime: the so-called rain-forests in many cases are subject to periods of little or no rainfall. Through clearing, construction and cultivation, man has disturbed the delicate balances of relief and biology. In many instances these interferences have led to a rapid acceleration of the process of laterization.

We shall consider two widely separated areas of the tropics, both ranging in vegetation from savanna to rain forest. The climate in these rain-forested areas is closer to the savanna type than to the true rain-forest. The selected regions are in northern South America and southern Sudan. The South American area comprises three different locations within the vast Amazon region. Included are the savannas of Roraima which stretch from the province of Rio Branco, Brazil, into Guyana. Within these savannas are the laterite uplands. The second loca-

tion is the Bragantina region of the state of Pará in what was formerly true rain-forested terrain; the final one is on the Amazon plains in the territory of Guaporé, Brazil. Whereas the South American area is subdivided, the region in southern Sudan is contiguous, with separate belts ranging from the Ironstone (laterite) Plateau in the south to the savannas along the Bahr el Ghazal River (see Fig. 32–1).

The case histories in this study show many parallels. Although geomorphologists have often found comparisons of land forms valuable to their interpretation, it is not usual for these comparisons to include the man-land relationships in any great detail, nor is it usual to compare very widely separated areas.

In both northern South America and southern Sudan, the slopes tend to be more fertile than the plateau surfaces, and indigenous populations have long relied on them and the seasonally flooded lowland areas for food production. These slopes are easily eroded and must be skillfully worked.

The weathering process in these widely separated regions is one of *laterization* and is represented by many different stages. Laterization is the wearing down of the

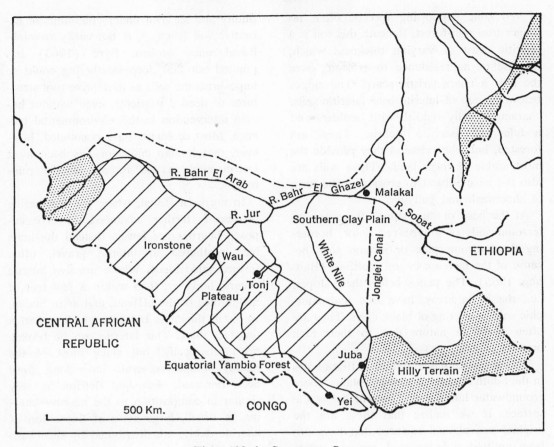

Figure 32–1   SOUTHERN SUDAN

earth's surface which results in the removal of silica and other solubles from the soils and the accumulation of residual minerals such as iron, aluminum, manganese and nickel. The process in its mature stage, has resulted in some of the major mineral deposits of the world and great expanses of infertile soils.

Similar facets of topography often carry the same type of vegetation, an ecosystem of land-forms, soil types, and plant communities, now usually referred to as a "catena" (Eyre *et al.,* 1953). Milne defined the catena as a regular repetition of soil profiles and vegetative cover in association with a certain topography, relief, and soil climate. His purpose was to simplify general areal mapping. His concept may be ex-

tended for our use. The existence of one member of the laterite catena, i.e., the laterite crust or laterite nodules, should lead us to suspect the presence of complementary members. We may assume general characteristics for large areas of the tropics and more readily predict the types and productivities of the soils by relating the vegetation and topography to the catenary sequence. This "catena concept" serves as a basis for evaluating the possible long-term effects of modern agricultural technology on the soils of northern South America and southern Sudan.

In the laterite catena, soils are related to relief and moisture levels in the drainage basins. In the areas dissected by erosion the crestal surfaces are covered by a thin veneer of red soils supporting forests, often no longer true rain-forest. Beneath this soil is a lateritic crust of varying thickness which, because of its resistance to erosion, gives the hills a characteristic scarp. The slopes below the cap of laterite bear lateritic soils, characteristically reddish with boulders and nodules of lateritic debris. They are forested, but when cleared they provide the most arable of these lands. These soils are also the most subject to erosion in the form of sheetwash and gullying.

At the base or "toe slope" there are interzonal soils of grayish-red color, bordering the hydromorphic or swamp soils because of the increase in soil moisture (Bunting, 1965). The plains below these slopes, i.e., the basin areas, have true hydromorphic soils consisting of black clays. They are often peaty in nature due to their high organic content.

This sequence has a variant in those areas in the South American forested plains where groundwater laterites are present below the surface. If we realize that these are the original peneplained surfaces that have not been uplifted and dissected, we may relate these laterites to the crestal laterite crusts. It must be kept in mind that neither the lateritic crusts nor the soils are end products, though the former are more durable. Both are stages in the geomorphic process itself.

The environment of this weathering process of laterization is an important variable. Climate is critical, especially the microclimate of the mass being weathered. The amount and regime of precipitation and runoff are important in laterization since this process is one of leaching, though this is an oversimplification. The natural environment includes the biota within and upon the physical mass. This organic complex is extremely important to the establishment of equilibrium through time.

The closed "plant-soil-plant" cycle of the rain-forest, which is responsible for its continuity and survival under conditions of excessive soil leaching, is not easily re-established once broken. Eyre (1963) has pointed out that deep weathering could so impoverish the soils as to deprive root structures of needed nutrients, even without human intervention in this environmental balance. Most ecologists have concluded, however, that human endeavor has been most instrumental in the retreat of the rain-forests.

In northern Brazil, where the weathering process is farther advanced, massive exposed laterites are fewer. Instead the mass has weathered to laterite gravel, often formed into ridges. Where massive laterite occurs, however, it is within a few feet of the surface of the plateau, and as in Sudan, varies in thickness but is rarely less than a few feet thick. This laterite can be broken up mechanically, but since most of the readily soluble minerals have long since been removed, deposited detritus is very similar in composition to the massive laterite. In Brazil, large areas of deposition of lateritic debris are distributed by sheetwash on the lower slopes and onto the plains. Many of the plains are literally paved with aggregations of this material, locally termed "canga."

Both of the subject regions are characterized by laterite uplands which are, however, at different stages in the weathering cycle: those of northern South America are far more dissected and broken by erosion than those of southern Sudan. There are hill remnants or Inselberge found on the plains of Rio Branco Province, Brazil, but the greatest expression of these is located across the frontiers in Guyana (Sinha, 1968). The uplands of Roraima Province, Brazil, are similar in many respects to the Ironstone Plateau of southern Sudan. The presence of shale beds below the laterite in the Brazilian profiles, however, makes for a striking difference in detail.

Southern Sudan and northern South

America have many differences as well as similarities. One of the major differences is the length of the dry season. It is more humid in northern South America; however, wholesale clearing of areas has led to a lengthening of the dry season, with a lessening of the rates of precipitation (Ackermann, 1962).

THE SOUTHERN SUDAN

The southern Sudan is a vast, little known portion of Africa between 4° and 10° north latitude. The landscape is a very diverse one, sparsely inhabited by many tribes. Ardrey (1967) states in *African Genesis* that "timid people tend to live at unfashionable addresses," and this is certainly true of the tribes scattered through the many inhospitable environments of the southern Sudan. The possible single exception has been the Azande, who suffer the trauma of the conquered conqueror. To survive, all these tribes have developed traditional methods of agriculture, hunting and fishing, which are adaptive responses to the environment.

The whole area is only sparsely inhabited by Nilotic and Central African tribes, essentially agriculturalists who have been competing among themselves for the rare arable lands. Basinski (1957) speaks of the equilibrium with the environment which has been established by these people through trial and error. "Any revolution in these methods, unless well thought out and tested, may lead to deterioration rather than improvement of agricultural output."

The key words here are "well thought out." We shall explore some of the instances where there has been either consideration or lack of it regarding ecological implications of development programs. In the cases where ecological studies were made, we will note whether the information was included in the implementation phases and what the results are to date. We will also consider some of the programs still envisioned for the area.

THE JUR RIVER DISTRICT OF SOUTHERN SUDAN

In 1863, Dr. Theodore Kotschy described the country we know today as the Jur River District around Wau as the "best of all those in the Bahr-El-Ghazal." The country offered "great advantages to the inhabitants by its soil being somewhat elevated, ferruginous and very fertile" (Tothill, 1947, p. 35). Dr. Kotschy was describing what we now call the Ironstone Plateau, the hills of which are flat-topped and of massive laterite, which outcrops throughout the area. The ridge of this plateau now supports the all-weather road from Wau to Tonj.

On closer inspection these "very fertile" soils show evidence of widespread erosion of the thin veneer of lateritic loams which have been extensively worked by the Jur tribes in a traditional system of shifting cultivation.

All this region and more of the Ironstone Plateau is covered by savanna-type vegetation composed of a largely fire climax genre. Of the some 28% of the Ironstone Plateau country considered to be "middle level" in terms of slope, a sizable amount is not cultivatable due to distances from water supplies, shallowness of soils, outcrops of ironstone laterite, presence of stumps and tribal conflicts of ownership. Thus, we have people widely scattered on the "good sites," which have been carefully selected and distributed in an equally careful manner by the tribes. An estimate of 10% of the plateau as suitable for cultivation may well be high.

The system of cultivation used by the Jur limited agriculture to the gentlest slopes, thus limiting the man-made erosion in the area (Eyre *et al.,* 1953). In order to have ready access to water, these people settled in the areas of the permanent streams. The Jur River district has many broad stream valleys which frequently become water-logged in the flood season. Therefore, the Jur selected the middle-level slopes for their fields. They usually cropped their lands for five to eight years and then let them lie fallow for twenty to thirty years. For its rotation, this traditional system required some 17 hectares per family to permit subsistence.

In 1953, Eyre *et al.* recommended an elaborate ecological survey of the Jur River district, since the evidence at that time indicated that there was little agricultural land in the area which was not already incorporated in the clan system of the Jur and cultivated. Such a survey has not yet been made, in part due to the conditions of civil war which have prevailed in the region since 1956.

Resettlement programs sponsored by the government have brought havoc to the traditional systems of rotation. Instead of receiving recognition for the enormous adjustments they have made to subsist, the Jur have been summarily uprooted and forced into strip settlements, primarily to make problems of civic administration easier. This has inevitably resulted in a reduction of the productivity of the area, and an additional burden has been placed on the carrying capacity of the land.

The opening of the Jur River district by the extension of Sudan Railways, which now terminates in Wau, has served to further increase the pressures on the land. The total pressure exerted on the Jur is such that unless some re-evaluation is made, the 1980's will find a population which will be unable to sustain itself.

THE ZANDE[1] SCHEME OF
SOUTHERN SUDAN

The Azande[2] occupy a district of the Sudan along the Nile-Congo Divide in an estimated area of 54,000 square kilometers.

[1] Zande—term used for nation.
[2] Azande—term used for people.

This Zande country is largely a tropical forested area. Zandeland is composed of the higher portions of the Ironstone Plateau, which receives a greater annual precipitation than the Jur River district to the north. It is more densely covered with bush and forest. A greater percentage of the area is covered by woodlands recently derived from rain-forest but there are still patches of true rain-forest vegetation.

McCall and Wilson (1954) summarize the region: "Zandeland is therefore not a land of milk and honey where an easy livelihood can be gained without real effort. The soils are not particularly fertile and can speedily become unproductive if great care in their cultivation is not exercised. Food or cash crop production is not easy and is limited by the difficulties of cultivating in thick bush country with poor implements, poor health and a lack of any real desire to produce more than the bare necessities of life."

The Azande people in the Sudan represent only a portion of the entire Zande nation which crosses into the Congo and the Central African Republic. The latest population figures for the Azande give an estimate of over 180,000 people in the Sudan. As is common in Africa, the arbitrarily established boundaries have greatly disturbed the nation. Until the time of the European invasions, the power of conquest and assimilation was in the hands of the Azande. The Zande nation was then the dominant cultural influence in this part of Africa.

The freedom of the Azande has been greatly curtailed and they have been "compelled to give up their traditional mode of territorial distribution and live herded together in settlements which they abominate" (Evans-Pritchard, 1931b, p. 146). This "herding" began as far back as 1922 when the colonial administration forced them into settlements along the roads in efforts to control sleeping sickness among them. The roads were built along the ridges which are relatively free from the tsetse flies which abound in the valley bottoms. The Azande have been moved three times since that first resettlement, always as a result of governmental orders. One of the main difficulties with the Zande Scheme for agricultural development has been this disregard for the residential preferences of the Azande (Wanji, personal communication).

As part of an attempt to introduce cash-cropping to the district, the Zande Scheme opened in the 1940's with the commissioner resettling five thousand homesteads in the Yambio area. The theory was that the cotton-producing scheme would be more successful if the supervision were easier. Although the rationale for this effort was supervision of the cash crop, ultimately fifty thousand familes were resettled, almost the entire population. An examination of the evidence surrounding this wholesale redistribution of people seems to show that there have been a number of misplaced good intentions involved and very little real knowledge of the ecology of the Azande.

Professor Reining (1966) found that the "Azande regarded themselves as good and industrious agriculturalists, able to choose the best land and knowing the various requirements for their various crops. They practiced what is usually referred to as shifting cultivation, involving the clearing of forests for small fields that were useful only for two to four years after which they had to be allowed to regenerate the natural vegetation."

Reining (1966) set out to discover why the Azande became disenchanted when they had originally been enthusiastic about the development program. The scheme, which began shortly after World War II, had been evolved from the original proposals of Dr. Tothill, who surveyed the Equatorial Region in the thirties. He suggested that there might be development of agriculture, transport and internal trade and that cotton would be suitable and profitable.

Dr. Tothill followed up his original proposal to the Ministry of Agriculture with some more specific recommendations. His plans were to bring the Azande from subsistence to a state of community self-sufficiency in view of the remoteness of the area (Tothill, 1948). The enterprise called for a vertically integrated operation of cotton production with the finished cloth to be sold on the Khartoum market. Export from the region was to consist of cotton, palm oil, jute and coffee. There was to be concomitant industry for sugar, charcoal, timber and iron, all for local consumption. This scheme was very quickly emasculated by the various committees charged with its feasibility, the end result being one crop for cash—cotton. The evils of monoculture were not considered.

The cotton crop was a success for the first few years and the yields were high, but after three years of operation the production dropped off markedly. Force was then applied to attain the desired production levels and the Azande became plantation "peons" instead of the prime actors in a great drama of the advance out of the Neolithic Age. From this point on, the scheme deteriorated in terms of its original objective of self-sufficiency.

What is of special importance is what happened to man's relationship to the land and its capability to provide for him. The cotton crop reached over eight million pounds by 1950. With cotton prices high, planting expanded well into land which ecologists had declared unsuitable. Since settlement expanded with the expanding acreages, there were homesteads on marginal lands, and these homesteads were soon without their promised cash crop. The executors of the Zande Scheme chose to ignore the information which had been provided to them by an ecological survey made prior to the institution of the Zande Scheme. Ferguson (1954), in reviewing the available information, described Zandeland as a "problem region" lying between the equatorial forest and the savanna, with a limited potential for the production of plantation crops.

The present family holding is roughly 14 hectares, allowing for a fixed grass rotation system to develop, a form of bush fallow thought by the designers of the scheme to be sufficient for the infertile soils. Strip cropping was introduced to control erosion to which these lateritic soils are susceptible. But strip cropping was not carried out properly. The "close supervision" which was made so much of as a part of the Zande Scheme broke down and the cultivators did not maintain the ten years' fallow required by the system. The length of the fallow period was selected as a minimum requirement. We have seen earlier that traditional systems of rotation gave twenty to thirty years for fallow, a figure arrived at empirically.

The capability of the soils to replenish themselves varies widely with the grass length and time of fallow. Ferguson (1954) notes that the soil "might not adequately maintain fertility *in perpetuo* or [for agriculture to] be possible at all if the population were to increase." To regenerate soil fertility, "bush fallow must be sufficiently long to permit the growth of deep rooted species which mine the nutrients from deeper soil levels and deposit them in the form of litter on the soil surface" (Basinski, 1957).

Besides the length of fallow, there are other problems besetting production in the Zande Scheme. The increase of the cotton pests with expansion of cotton production has been difficult to deal with. Perhaps the greatest problem of all, however, is the control of bush fires. These frequently become so hot that they destroy the surface layers of the soils as well as the vegetative cover. These fires have been steadily increasing in number and extent with population growth in the area.

Changes in climate are occurring as clearings of the bush by fire and cultivation continue, resulting in a lengthening of the dry season and an increase of the "derived" savanna with permanent destruction of the forested areas. Morrison *et al.* (1948) describe a profile from the Yei area taken halfway downslope on a typical hill of this Ironstone Plateau, the crest of which had the usual ironstone cap. They found a thick horizon of pea iron with intermixtures of blocks of iron. The area was channeled by termites, and the channels in turn had iron oxide around them due to fluctuations in the water table; the iron apparently precipitated in the dry season. These authors theorize that the "ironstone sheet" was once part of the subsoil and hardened when exposed by erosion. The subsequent drying out of the mass resulted in the irreversible separation of the iron.

THE AWEIL RICE PROJECT AND THE TOICHLANDS OF SOUTHERN SUDAN

Where drainage becomes seriously impeded by changes in slope and contour, the fringing and gallery forests are replaced by open grassland known as toich (Smith, n.d., p. 19). Along the frontier where the Ironstone Plateau is in abrupt contact with the Clay Plains or the "toe slope" of the catena, we find extensive toichlands. These toichlands join the Ironstone Plateau at about the 418 meter contour above sea level. Other toichlands are found along the White Nile. Morrison *et al.* (1948) made an ecological study of the tropical lateritic clays and vegetation of these seasonally flooded areas.

The distinguishing feature of these toichlands is that they are flooded by the overspill of the rivers and remain under water many months of the year. They are not the result of flooding from runoff in the rainy season, which would result only in intermittent water-logging. Because of their higher organic content, the toichlands are among the more fertile soils of the southern Sudan. The usual use of the toichlands in the dry period is for cattle grazing. Cultivation of these lands is very sporadic due to the natural reluctance on the part of the population to accept the role of farmer and the difficulties, especially drainage problems.

Sudan is an importer of rice and, as changes in custom have been occurring, rice consumption in the country has been increasing. After many trials, the natural conditions around Aweil, Bahr el Ghazal Province, appeared to the Ministry of Agriculture to be the best in Sudan for the production of rice. The Ministry decided on a series of pilot projects in the Aweil area which confirmed the earlier trials. Increases in world prices of rice became an additional spur and the Aweil Toich Rice Project was initiated in 1954 (Hakim, 1963).

The Aweil Toich parallels the river Lol and is about 35,000 hectares in size. By 1963, about 500 hectares were under rice cultivation. The project has been considered successful by the Government and there have been plans to bring the acreage up to 4,000 hectares, sufficient to supply the Sudanese demand for rice.

There seems to be little doubt that the area is suited for rice production, but some of the cultural practices used on the Aweil Toich bear careful scrutiny. Mechanization has been introduced to the scheme, and as yet its effect on soil structure is unknown. Dikes have been constructed, and more will be, to control the water in the additional acreages. This practice tends to limit new silting of the soils which is one of the ways in which the soils are enriched by a natural regeneration in necessary nutrients.

According to Hakim (1963), no land is to be left fallow nor is there to be another crop in rotation with the rice. The Senior Inspector of the Aweil Rice Project feels that the heavy weed growth that would result on fallow land would make the project uneconomic. No fertilizers whatever are used. Declining yields are blamed on excessive flooding, which may or may not be the critical factor. It seems logical to assume that cultural practices such as these will inevitably lead to a decline in yields. Since there will be no regenerative silting and constant flooding will cause a transition to swamp soils, these lands will become unproductive.

If the purpose of the project is to improve the standard of living of the Dinka of the area, it has its drawbacks in that the Dinka are traditionally cattle people, and these toichlands have been their grazing lands. Few Dinka wish to be farmers, and few will work for wages. Therefore, the scheme is plagued with labor problems, and rice is a labor-intensive crop. Meanwhile, the people must search out new grazing areas.

The Aweil Rice Project is neither an economic nor a social success. The savings in foreign exchange are a mirage in view of costs of production and the capital investment, which might have been better employed elsewhere. The costs of cultivation presently not included, such as rotation, weeding and fertilizers, should be added. This accounting would show the domestic rice to be much more expensive than the imported article. Under the present cultivation plan, the life of the project will be limited, and it will be years before these lands will again be usable for grains, forage crops and grazing, unless the changes brought about by diking can be reversed.

THE JONGLEI CANAL PROJECT, SOUTHERN SUDAN

Sir William Garstin in 1904 conceived the idea of conserving the waters lost through evaporation and transpiration in the Sudd of southern Sudan. The Equatorial Nile Project, which is the name given to the Victoria-Albert-Jonglei Scheme, was designed not only to save part of the water now lost but to regulate completely the flow of the Nile.

The proposed Jonglei Canal would be a series of cuts through the Sudd to a point near Malakal at the mouth of the Sobat River, a distance of 280 kilometers. Their purpose would be to increase the average flow of the White Nile while reducing the variability of the flow.

The Sudd is one of the largest and most important swamps in Africa. It is built on an inland delta with its apex at Mongalla and its base from Lake No to the Sobat River (Glennie, 1957). This is an area of about 8,000 square kilometers, which the Jonglei would delimit (Debenham, 1954). Some estimates have been made that the total area which would remain as swamp would be 1,000 square kilometers. This swamp has served for thousands of years as a natural relief valve for the lower Nile and saved Sudan and Egypt from many a disastrous flood. It is also a spawning ground for fish and affords the toichlands a natural flood irrigation, making agriculture possible.

The seasonality of the Nile in this region is its most distinguishing characteristic and is of primary importance to both man and animals between Mongalla and Malakal. The banks of the Nile are above the surrounding countryside north of Jonglei, and when the river is in flood, its waters overspill these banks and spread out over the almost flat plain. Of the 27 billion cubic meters entering at Mongalla, it has been estimated that 14 billion, more than half, are lost in the Sudd.

The Colonial Sudanese Government in 1946 was aware of the potential disruption which the project might create and, therefore, set about to determine the magnitude of the problem. They established the Jonglei Investigation Team which reported on their findings in 1954. The team was charged with determining the effects on the regime of the Nile on agriculture, grazing, fisheries,

people and other problems related to engineering alternatives (Howell, 1954).

The area to be surveyed by the team stretched from Nimule on the Uganda border to Kosti, a distance of 1,625 kilometers on the Nile. The directly affected area is estimated at 300,000 square kilometers. No estimates, much less studies, have been made of the indirectly affected areas.

The team found that the first need was for further research, or that the effects of this proposed Jonglei Canal were still somewhat unknown (Barbour, 1961). They recognized the need for the "nutritive pasture" provided by the Nile and that changes in the "ecological characteristics of the floodplains" would result. In their report they carefully discuss potential changes in the Nile, reach by reach. In terms of actual pasture lost, estimates were given at 35% as best guesses. No real estimates could be given of fisheries lost, although an assumption was tacitly made that the fish would adapt to the complete reversal of the regime of the river in some of its reaches. On the effects on spawning, which is intimately related to flood cycles in the toich, no real prognosis could be given. An assumption was made, however, that introduced commercial fisheries could make acceptable substitution for the losses.

The Nilotic tribes of the region are "minutely related to the existing regime of the Bahr-El-Jebel and other rivers of the region" (Barbour, 1961). These people rely completely on the pasture formed in these toiches in the dry season, since the pasture away from the swamp areas which they use during the flood period becomes valueless as fodder once the rains subside. The existence of the Sudd pastures is also dependent upon the floods. Barbour (1961) again states the situation well: "If no remedial steps were taken . . . the effect of the Jonglei Canal would be to destroy the livelihood of many of the Nilotes and completely alter their way of life which is intimately related to the keeping of cattle."

These people, numbering some 700,000 in 1954, have developed a rhythm of life in tune with the floods on the Nile. They move to high ground in the rainy period of April to December and return to the riverain lands in the dry period to graze their cattle, grow a few crops, fish and hunt. The five months spent on the floodlands provide for their cattle when natural forage on the uplands becomes inedible.

The Jonglei Canal Scheme would destroy this rhythm of life by making these floodlands unavailable at just those times of year when they are most necessary. The seasonality of the river itself would be altered. The floods would cease to invade their former areas in part of the Sudd, and soil and vegetation changes would be inevitable. In other parts of the Sudd, the area would be permanently flooded and valuable lands permanently lost.

Morrice and Winder of the Investigation Team stated:

"It would be an exaggeration to say that all peoples in this area rely exclusively on animal husbandry as a source of livelihood, for rain grown crops are of great importance in their subsistence economy. Yet the production of grain crops is on the whole a precarious undertaking. In this region the mean annual rainfall is usually adequate, but its monthly distribution is extremely variable. Moreover in most parts the soil is heavy and impermeable, the slope is exceptionally small, and the drainage system often inadequate to carry away the accumulations of rainfall. In the early months of the wet season there is sometimes so little rain that the newly planted crops perish from drought, whereas later in the year they may be damaged by torrential storms or drowned by heavy flooding. The very laborious processes of crop production for these reasons are cut to a minimum and the peo-

ple rarely attempt to grow more grain than would be sufficient to meet their own needs were they successful. Cattle and other animal stock are therefore of paramount importance because they provide the only reliable alternative to crop husbandry. Peoples in all parts of this area also rely on fish to supplement their diet and fish are usually available in large quantities in the pools and lagoons on the flood plain of the Nile." (Howell, 1954).

The assumed effects on topography and climate were considered negligible in general but effective on the microscale. The cessation of seasonal inundation and, hence, seasonal anaerobic conditions will result in the oxidation of a considerable proportion of the organic matter in the soils (Howell, 1954). The investigation team therefore expected a loss of fertility in the toich soils. In all probability the actual soil type would in very few years be so altered that the toich would be obliterated in some areas and greatly reduced in others. It would be possible to predict the probable extent of this destruction by careful mapping of the present toichlands in relation to the proposed engineering design.

Soil mosaics, such as found in southern Sudan and described by Morrison *et al.* (1948), are related to the stage of relief and dissection of the topography. The soils may vary somewhat with the lithology but, certainly in the case of the lateritic soils, the parent rock is not the decisive factor. We can expect, therefore, to find the catenary sequences; such sequences have been described by Morrison and by the Jonglei Investigation Team. Although non-catenary sequences of soils will be found in the area, the concept will highlight the edaphic changes which will result with the implementation of the Canal Project. It should be realized that individual soil profiles will react individually.

Figure 32–2A shows a generalized picture

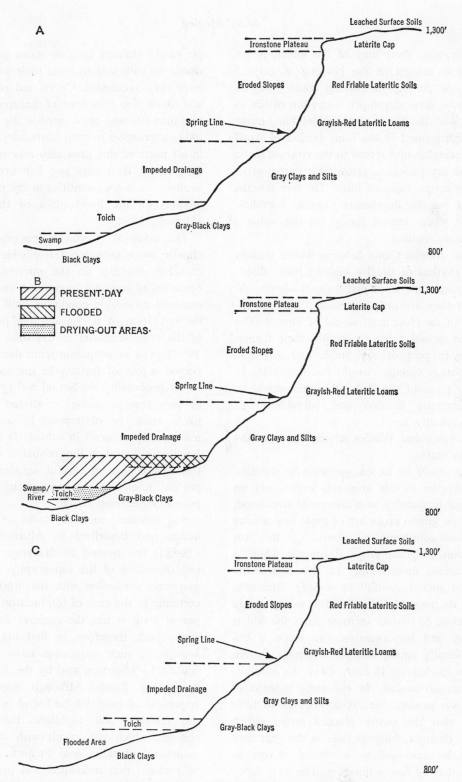

Figure 32–2 A. Present-day laterite catena from Southern Sudan; B. Projected laterite catena with drying-out of parts of the Sudd area in the Sudan; C. Projected laterite catena in flooded areas in Southern Sudan

of the catena to be found where Ironstone Plateau meets the flood plains. If we vary topography in relation to flood levels by completely inundating certain areas and leaving others to permanently dry out, we must expect an alteration toward the "type" environment newly created. Thus, if we slide up or down the profiles as indicated, we will be able to predict the new soil type which will be developed and make some predictions as to the type of vegetation, if any, it will support. The most interesting result is that the valuable toichlands tend to become greatly diminished whether we move the water level up or down (Fig. 32–2).

Earlier it was pointed out that these lands, which are so very important to the local economies, are the result of seasonal flooding, not natural runoff. If these soils are permanently submerged they will become lake or swamp sediments. From an interzonal soil they will be transformed into true hydromorphs. Permanently dried out, they will tend to move toward the type classification "impeded drainage," such as is usually found at the base (toe slope) of these catenae. Either possibility makes them unavailable for cultivation, forage, hunting or fishing. We are perhaps able to estimate the loss in all these activities with the exception of the fisheries. Whether the lost spawning grounds or the reversal of the time of flood will result in permanent damage is as yet unknown; but it is an eventuality which must be recognized.

THE PROPOSED BOA VISTA DEVELOPMENT PROJECT, BRAZIL

Boa Vista is located on the Rio Branco River which drains the territory of Roraima, Brazil. The Rio Branco flows south to join the Rio Negro, which is a major arm of the Amazon. The region is part of a vast savanna of 54,000 square kilometers extending from Brazil into Guyana.

Laterite in this savanna is in a belt parallel to the Kanuku Mountains located across the frontier in Guyana (Sinha, 1968). These mountains have a foothill region composed of laterite uplands which trend northeast to southwest and which are strikingly similar to those described for the Ironstone Plateau of southern Sudan. These uplands are primarily on the Guyana side of the border. The "Baixadas" or toichlands equivalents are to be found along the many stream courses. The dunes and swamps occupy an intermediate position between the laterite uplands and the plains (Sinha, 1968).

Guerra (1957) found extensive areas of laterite on the peneplain of Rio Branco. This laterite is absent only in the northeastern part of the territory of Roraima where there is a large structural depression from which the laterite has been removed. The laterites of the savanna-land surface are largely detrital, but massive laterite has been found extensively ranging from a few inches to many feet. The profile at Boa Vista shows the lateritic gravel to be 33 feet thick.

Sinha (1968) found that the laterite on the Guyana side was even more widespread. Until further explorations of the soils of the Rio Branco savanna are made, its true extent in Brazil will not be known.

Throughout the region we have laterite catenae, related to topography, bearing a distinctive vegetative cover. The repetitive pattern differs in detail from that of southern Sudan. These differences appear directly related to their different geomorphic histories. "It is clear that once a laterite deposit is exposed, it may be broken down mechanically and transported mechanically and in solution, but the minerals are likely to reappear elsewhere in the same area as secondary laterites" (Sinha, 1968). The exact origin of the laterite is an academic question for a farmer in these areas. He cares little whether they are *in situ* or transported in the geologic sense. In all probability these laterites of the savanna of Rio Branco are both, the detrital portion originating in the Kanaku Mountains and their foothills, the laterite uplands.

The Indian farmer has carefully selected his small cultivated areas to take maximum advantage of recent alluviums along the riverbanks. He has drainage problems but on the whole has managed to utilize well the available arable land. His system of moving his plot after a year or two of production and allowing a fallow period has made it possible for him to continue marginal agriculture. The limited area which would be suitable for agriculture makes the further opening up of the plains to agricultural development hazardous. Yet the "pioneer" is encouraged, though the lessons of colonial agriculture in laterite zones have been hard indeed.

THE BRAGANTINA COLONIES

If you take the railroad from Belém in the state of Pará, Brazil, and travel the 228 kilometers eastward along the Amazon mouth, you pass through a region which is being progressively transformed into a semi-desert by man. The process began in 1883 with the penetration of the railroad into what was then true Amazon rain-forest (Ackermann, 1962). In the first thirty years thirty thousand colonists settled this region, using slash-and-burn techniques of land preparation.

People moved in from southern Europe and northeast Brazil to farm what they thought were fertile soils. Disheartened by their inability to sustain themselves, these settlers moved farther and farther north and south away from the railway line, clearing more and more land.

This part of Brazil is a lowland, presumably an ancient peneplain (Ackermann,

1962). The region is dissected by many rivers and streams draining east and north. The landscape today will do nothing to excite the naturalist. The Amazon rainforest has been replaced by scrub, mute "testimony to the destructive activity of man under the pretext of colonization" (Gourou, 1961). Everywhere, gullying has transformed the even plain into an undulating one. The whole regime of the rivers has been altered, and many streams have been reduced to trickles in the dry season.

"Progress" has come with the building of towns and cities in the region populated by people deserting the deteriorating farms. Here urban areas with all the attendant difficulties have resulted, due primarily to the shortsightedness of planners.

The Government established many colonies in Bragantina. No studies were made, but colonists were encouraged to move in. The forest was destroyed and subsistence farms were established, to be later abandoned due to the infertility of the soils; in place of the forest the brushland grew. "With successive clearing and burning, the land was exhausted up to the actual point where the Region is being transformed into a semi-desert forming stony pavements" (Ackermann, 1962).

Extensive areas are now covered by the "Pará gres," as it is called in the region. This material is none other than lateritic nodules of limonite. The desiccation of the area which has a pronounced dry season has carried iron and aluminum by means of capillarity to the surface, where they have been precipitated. Although lateritization in the Bragantina region has not yet reached that of the states of Maranhão and Amapá where it is mined as ore, it has progressed greatly. These areas are more useful for road construction than for agriculture.

Today this region with one of the largest populations in the state of Pará is unable to feed itself. The only crops which are still being grown are native plants utilized for fibers. Yields are diminishing yearly, and some of the lands devoted to this culture have ceased to produce.

The laterization process here has taken about fifty to seventy years to produce a semidesert. No records have been kept for us to actually pinpoint the time, which for a given acreage is surely shorter.

THE PRESIDENT DUTRA (IATA) COLONY, BRAZIL

In Guaporé uplands capped with laterite again are part of a peneplain which was uplifted and dissected. Geologists still dispute the extent of the peneplain. The landscape is dotted by eroded uplands cut by the Guaporé, Madeira, and Mamoré rivers and a multiplicity of tributaries. The region stretches from these foothills of the Plateaus, or "Chapadas" as they are called in Guaporé, to the confluence of the Madeira and Mamoré rivers at Porto Velho (see Fig. 32–3). The area was opened up originally

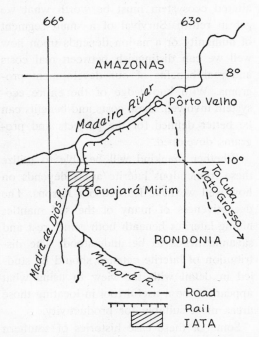

Figure 32–3 THE PRESIDENT DUTRA (IATA) COLONY, BRAZIL

in the early part of the twentieth century by the famous Amazon rubber boom. A railroad was constructed in the dense Amazon Forest between the present-day towns of Porto Velho and Guajará-Mirim, a distance of 366 kilometers. When the railroad, which "cost a life a tie," was completed, the boom was over, but for better or for worse this inhospitable area was opened up.

The city of Porto Velho differs in elevations with the upper part capped in laterite up to 17 feet thick (Guerra Teixera, 1953). We have again a series of laterite catenae and the complications of transported and *in situ* laterites.

At the confluence of the Madeira and Madre de Dios rivers (see map in Fig. 32–3) an agricultural colony was established in the late 1940's. President Dutra Colony was to be the new homeland for some of those forced off the land in Bragantina, Pará.

Here the forest is also true Amazon rain forest. The climate in this region is true humid tropical. "Laterization is in an advanced state, in some areas almost in the final stage" (Guerra Teixera, 1953). The terminology "final stage" may be deceptive but is extremely apt from the colonist's point of view. Guerra Teixera is referring to the drying out and hardening of the mineral residues into a rock formation of aggregated laterite.

The colonists found the story of Bragantina repeated. Traditional agriculture did not provide them with even a subsistence living. The fertility of the so-called soils was exhausted within three years and had to be left to the bush. The life of an individual *roca* or individual cultivation was even less than the colonist was used to in Pará. The toil to survive was unbelievable. Fields were cultivated among blocks of laterite. The laterite was aggregated on the surface or just below it, and the farmer had simply exposed it. The soils he worked compacted to rock in five years. They were really not soils at all but residual minerals mixed with the organic materials of the forest. When these were exhausted or leached by the heavy rains, the settler was left with only the residue.

THE JAPANESE COLONY AT TOMÉ AÇU

A small ray of hope for man's adaptation to the laterite zones can be found in the successful Japanese colony at Tomé Açu on the River Acará-Mirim south of Bragantina. These people replaced the forest species with tree crops, particularly the black pepper. Their success both in productivity and soil conservation is beginning to have a salutary effect on the Bragantina region itself, where their example is being emulated today. Some efforts to produce other tree crops in the region, among them rubber trees, are beginning to prosper. Much of the region has been ruined, however, and must wait until structural rejuvenation for the surface laterites to be eroded off or until technology finds a way to remove them mechanically.

CONCLUSION

We note that there are areas which are more fertile than others. We can generally relate these to relief as we could in southern Sudan. In the vicinity of Iata and the city of Porto Velho at the confluence of the Madeira-Mamoré the soil mantle is thicker on the slope sides. When profiles are cut, we find, as we did at Yei in Sudan, that the laterites are exposed beneath the mantle; thus these highly erodiable slope sides require great care for their preservation. The excessive leaching in Guaporé makes their usefulness limited since the nutrients were mere remnants of the forest which was removed and these are quickly carried off in solution.

Camargo (1942) called the "great error"

of colonizing these lands an action which could only result in their devastation and the loss of valuable forests which took centuries to develop.

When we consider the speed with which modern technology and population pressures can institute enormous changes in the environment, it is necessary to consider the consequences of these changes. Adjustments in the balance of nature made necessary through man-made intrusions in the environment have in the past been rendered possible by the allotment of much time. Thus, the impact of these changes has been spread over time and the curve covering the positive and negative effects smoothed out. Today, we make these changes rapidly and we compound them. We look with pride to the positive aspects and consider man's industry rewarded, but too often we ignore the negative ones.

Man will continue to modify his environment, but if these modifications are to have lasting value, he must recognize the forces operating. The price paid in terms of an altered ecosystem must be worth what we get in return. Survival of a small segment of humanity or a nation depends upon how well we can distinguish between real costs and real benefits of our development programs. With knowledge of the entire ecosystem involved, these costs and benefits can be better defined for the projects and programs developed.

Whether mankind will be able to utilize these tremendous laterite areas depends on how well we have learned our lessons. The deceptiveness of many of the soil mantles hiding laterites beneath both rain-forest and savanna needs to be understood. The distribution of laterite catenae should be studied in detail with the view to using what appears to be a useful tool in locating those areas most suitable for productivity.

Some of these case histories of southern Sudan and northern South America indicate a recognition of the role of ecology in planning, insufficient though it is. In the case of the Jonglei Canal Scheme, the investigation team actually performed a Herculean task when we consider the vastness of the affected area, the costs involved, the

limited time, and the bureaucratic difficulties. Other case histories show ignorance of ecological implications. Still others sadden us when we consider the almost criminal negligence.

REFERENCES

Ackermann, F. L. *Geologia e Fisiografia da Regiao Bragantina, Estado do Para*, Belém, 1962a. 66 pp.

———. "Laterito e Laterizacao." *Engenharia* (Rio de Janeiro), 36 (1962b), 301–06.

Ardrey, R. *African Genesis*. New York: Atheneum Press, 1967. 334 pp.

Barbour, K. M. "The Waters of the Nile and Their Control." In *The Republic of the Sudan, a Regional Geography*. London: University of London Press, 1961. Pp. 109–27.

Basinski, J. J. "Some Problems of Agricultural Development in the Southern Provinces of the Sudan." *Sudan Notes and Records* (Khartoum), 34 (1957), 21–46.

Bunting, B. T. *The Geography of the Soil*. Chicago: Aldine Press, 1965. 213 pp.

Camargo, F. *Terra e Colonização no Antigo e Novo Quaternário da Zona da Estrada de Ferro de Braganca*. Paper presented at the Interamerican Conservation of Natural Resources Conference. Denver, Colorado, 1942.

Debenham, Prof. F. "The Water Resources of Africa." *Sudan Notes and Records* (Khartoum), Vol. 35, Pt. 2 (1954), pp. 69–75.

Egyptian Ministry of Public Works. *The Nile Basin*, Vol. VII. Cairo: Ministry of Public Works Press, 1946.

Evans-Pritchard, E. E. "Mani, A Zande Secret Society." *Sudan Notes and Records* (Khartoum), Vol. 14, Pt. 2 (1931a), pp. 105–48.

———. "The Mberidi (Shilluk Group) and Mbegumba (Basiri Group) of the Bahr-El-Ghazal." *Sudan Notes and Records* (Khartoum), Vol. 14, Pt. 1 (1931b), pp. 15–48.

Eyre, S. R. (1963) *Vegetation and Soils, a World Picture*. Chicago: Aldine Publishing Company, 1963.

Eyre, V. E. F.; Ramsey, D. M.; and Jewett,

T. N. *Agriculture, Forests, and Soils of the Jur Ironstone Country of the Bahr-El-Ghazal Province, Sudan*, Ministry of Agriculture, Khartoum, Bulletin No. 9. 1953. 40 pp.

Farran, D. C. O. "The Nile Waters Question in International Law." *Sudan Notes and Records* (Khartoum), 41 (1960), 88–100.

Ferguson, H. *The Zande Scheme*. Ministry of Agriculture, Khartoum, Bulletin No. 11. 1954. 33 pp.

Glennie, J. F. "The Equatorial Nile Project." *Sudan Notes and Records* (Khartoum), Vol. 37, Pt. 2 (1957), pp. 67–73.

Gourou, P. *Tropical World*. London: Longmans, 1961.

Greene, H., and Cox, H. F. "Some Soils of the Anglo-Egyptian Sudan," *Soil Research*, 6 (1939), 325–38.

Guerra, A. Teixera. *Estudo Geografico do Território do Rio Branco*. Rio de Janeiro-National Geographic Council, 1957.

Guerra Teixera, A. "Formação de Lateritos sob a Floresta Equatorial no Território Federal do Guaporé." *Revista Brasileira de Geografia*, Rio de Janeiro, Year XIV, No. 4 (1953).

Hakim, Osman A. *Economic Appraisal of Bahr-El-Ghazal Rice Project*, Agricultural Economics Division, Department of Agriculture, Khartoum. 1963. 75 pp.

Howell, P. P. (Chairman). *The Equatorial Nile Project and Its Effects in the Anglo-Egyptian Sudan*. A report of the Jonglei Investigation Team. Introduction, Summary and 4 vols. 1954.

Lebon, J. H. G. "Some Concepts of Modern Geography Applied to Sudan." *Sudan Notes and Records* (Khartoum), 42 (1961), 3–28.

McCall, A. G., and Wilson, K. L. "Some Notes on Zandeland." A paper presented at the 1953 Conference on Food and Society in the Sudan. Khartoum: Philosophical Society of the Sudan, 1954. 16 pp.

Morrison, C. G. T.; Hoyle, A. C.; and Hope-Simpson, J. R. "Tropical Soil-Vegetation Catenas and Mosaics." *Journal of Ecology,* 36 (1948), 1–84.

Oliveira, A. I. "Bacia do Rio Branco, Estado do Amazonas." *Boletim Serv. Geol. e Min. do Brasil* (Rio de Janeiro), No. 17 (1929), pp. 1–69.

Reining, C. C. *The Zande Scheme, An Anthropological Case Study of Economic Development in Africa.* Evanston, Ill.: Northwestern University Press, 1966. 255 pp.

Sandon, H., ed. "The Problems of Fisheries in the Area Affected by the Equatorial Nile Project." *Sudan Notes and Records* (Khartoum), 32 (1951), 6–36.

Sinha, N. K. A. (1968) *Geomorphic Evolution of the Northern Rupununi Basin, Guyana.* Montreal: McGill University, 1968. 131 pp.

Smith, J. *Distribution of Tree Species in the Sudan in Relation to Rainfall and Soil Texture.* Ministry of Agriculture, Khartoum, Bulletin No. 4, n.d.

Tothill, Beatrice H. "An Expedition in Central Africa by Three Dutch Ladies," *Sudan Notes and Records* (Khartoum), 28 (1947), 25–44.

Tothill, J. D., ed. *Agriculture in the Sudan.* London: Oxford University Press, 1948.

Weck, J. *Report on a Study Tour through the Sudan Made in Spring 1957.* Forestry Section, Federal Research Institute for Forestry and Timber Industries, Rumbek, 1958.

Whitehead, G. O. "Crops and Cattle among the Bari and Bari-speaking Tribes." *Sudan Notes and Records* (Khartoum), 43 (1962), 131–42.

Wright, J. W. "White Nile Flood Plain and Proposed Schemes." *Geographical Journal* (London), 114 (1949), 4–6.

———. "The White Nile and the Sobat." *Sudan Notes and Records* (Khartoum), 32 (1951), 113–30.

33. PROBLEMS OF TROPICAL SETTLEMENT— EXPERIENCES IN COLOMBIA AND BOLIVIA

Harold T. Jorgenson

Large-scale migration of poor farmers to frontier areas in many Latin American countries is occurring whether or not it is in the national interest. Stimulated by the population growth and search for employment and income opportunity, these pioneers generally locate on marginal lands. In Latin America, most frontier lands are widely dispersed over the one billion hectares of humid tropical lowlands of uncertain agricultural utility. Much of wet tropical Latin America is now haphazardly occupied by man. The fact that most of this land is unsuitable for settlement is slowly becoming better known.

The most extensive system of pioneering the new, and in many areas untried, lands of Latin America is by spontaneous occupancy of vacant land. Such settlement is characterized by primitive housing, subsistence agriculture, problems of soil erosion or leaching, ill health due to malnutrition and poor sanitation, isolation from markets, unstable land-tenure, and an underdeveloped infrastructure. This situation seems to demand more social control of land settlement, including determination of location, size and type of farming units, and various forms of assistance to facilitate production.

There are many pioneer settlements which are government-sponsored and government-directed with management procedures designed to ensure a high degree of control in their development. Such projects unless well planned and executed, however, are sometimes even less successful than spontaneous settlements, according to recent project studies by the Inter-American Development Bank. Many projects involving government assistance to already established spontaneous settlements, especially if rather well adapted to physical and economic limitations, appear from IDB's study to be less beset by problems of human maladjustment and environmental deterioration. Review of semidirected and volunteer settlement projects in Colombia and Bolivia serve to illustrate this belief.

Inaccurate yield estimates, unknown soil recuperation cycles, and other questions concerning tropical farming systems remain, hampering widely dispersed attempts to solve the problems of land use in the humid lowlands of Latin America.

Land settlement is occurring at an accelerating rate as population pressure mounts in Latin America. Such settlement is increasingly venturing into marginal areas by reclaiming arid or swampy land or by pioneering in many virgin and untried humid tropical areas. Old as the settlement process is in human experience and familiar as the costs may be to man and land of haphazard occupation of unsuitable ecosystems and to the public purse if widely scattered along the pioneer fringe, most of it still goes on almost wholly unmanaged by the agencies of society. For a long time there has been clear empirical evidence of the urgent need to subject land settlement to greater social and economic order over extensive areas of Latin America, especially since over one billion hectares of its land area lies in humid tropical lowlands which in many places still have quite uncertain utility. The consequences of increasing natural and human resource damage which attends this process cannot be tolerated any longer.

This is not to suggest that fully directed settlement is the ideal answer. A recent review of the results of the Inter-American Development Bank's (IDB) 1962–1968 programs of loan assistance in tropical land settlement as well as other internationally aided land development endeavors strongly indicates that government-sponsored and government-directed projects (which imply a high degree of control through selection of areas, determination of size and type of farms, management of production as well as assistance in land clearing, extension of credit, and provision of technical services) are hardly the right approach.

The administration of directed land settlement has been inefficient, with a few notable exceptions such as the Bank-aided La Chontalpa project in Mexico and the Tingo Maria Project in Peru; and, in the case of some USAID-assisted projects, such as the Alto Beni I in Bolivia and the Santo Domingo Project in Ecuador, the results have been almost disastrous. On all projects it has proven very difficult to harmonize the various physical development processes and the manifold human ambitions, capacities, and frailties into successful development of pioneer colonization schemes. In some cases, even the selection of areas for settlement was unfortunate, either because natural resource information was inadequate or unrealistically appraised, or because factors such as availability of public land or desire to occupy vacant borderland were overriding considerations. Much has been learned, however, from such projects, and there is now a much clearer understanding of the elements which make for "success" or "failure" in colonization.

A number of private endeavors in directed pioneer settlement were also studied in connection with the IDB appraisal of tropical land settlement, involving land subdivision and infrastructure development; their performance ranges from almost total failure to total success, depending on degree of "know-how," managerial ability, financial resources, and dedication of settlers. In the most successful projects such as that of the Paraná Land Company and the Ivenhema in Brazil very dynamic forms of area development have occurred.

Semidirected colonization projects tend to

be more successful than fully directed colonization projects. They generally involve
assistance to already established spontaneous settlements in order to consolidate
and expand their development and to induce
more people to settle in the area. Usually
they are characterized by rather recent
settlement, limited land clearing, random
and unregularized land claims, some low-
grade roads, inadequate infrastructure and
public services, poor housing conditions,
mainly subsistence farming but some commercial production, and limited access to
national markets. A number of factors tend
to help a more successful outcome with the
advent of governmental assistance, the most
important seeming to be self-reliance of settlers, their tropical agricultural experience,
product commercialization opportunities,
and conditions for a simpler form of administration. Most serious drawbacks may
be unfavorable land conditions and an ir-
rational pattern of landholdings. The semidirected projects evaluated by IDB at Santo
Domingo in the western lowlands and in the
Rio Upano Valley in the eastern lowlands
of Ecuador and at Puerto Presidente Stroes-
ner in Paraguay were all dynamic and
making social progress.

By far the most extensive form of land
settlement is the spontaneous occupancy of
vacant land in frontier areas of Latin
America. Its occurrence is normally related
to development of a penetration road, river
transportation, airfield installation, or forest
or other resource based industry in an isolated section of a country. Generally it is
characterized, at least in its initial stages,
by recent and continuing settlement, random and sometimes unwise selection of
land, unregularized landholdings, limited
slash-and-burn clearing, unstable land tenure, deficient local road development, primitive housing conditions, subsistence agriculture, high incidence of ill health due to
malnutrition or inadequate sanitation, predominance of poverty, inadequate infrastructure and public service, isolation from
markets, little social organization, and scant
urban growth. On the whole it is a dis-
ordered and discouraging setting for rural
development.

Looking at the magnitude of the settlement process in the tropics or subtropics in
a few countries and the requirements for
new land to accommodate even current
needs, affords some perspective as to the
significance of arranging proper land settlement.

In these countries, about 200,000 newly
settled farmers are striving to gain a livelihood in agriculture in the tropical lowlands.
Including family members, over a million
people are involved in such frontier settlement.

The future for all these people and the
great numbers yet to come is deeply dependent on the success or failure to better
understand and properly utilize the tropical
environment, the locale of the last remaining extensive land frontiers still available.
And beyond these needs are certain subsidiary requirements which deserve special
mention in connection with future settlement: (1) Improved and less costly
methods for orderly and economical settle-

	COLOMBIA	ECUADOR	PERU	BOLIVIA	COSTA RICA
Present settlement farmers[1]	80,000–100,000	20,000	25,000–30,000	40,000	30,000
Settlement farms needed[1]	250,000	100,000	225,000	110,000	N.A.

[1] Exclusive of traditional colonial and generally subsistence settlements in the tropical lowland such as in the Tarapoto area of the Central Huallaga Valley of eastern Peru or the Upano River Valley of eastern Ecuador. For sources and bases for estimates, see explanatory notes at conclusion of chapter.

ment and development of land are needed.
(2) Improved control, guidance, and assistance in voluntary land settlement in most
national development programs are necessary. (Planned and directed colonization
is but a trickle compared to the random
and unsupported voluntary settlement occurring in most countries.) (3) Also required is a greater regard for the large-
scale ecologic interventions that are occurring in the settlement process and the need
to minimize their damages.

The need to mitigate the human and
ecologic damage being wrought by overcrowding in the highland *minifundio* (small
subsistence farm) areas is overriding. Poverty and hunger stalk the inhabitants; soil
depletion and erosion injure the land. Without the withdrawal of people and relief of
land pressure, man and land both in the
highlands and in the vicinal lowlands will
be the losers. The spillover of injury in the
form of social tensions and land abuse has
already been witnessed in some areas of

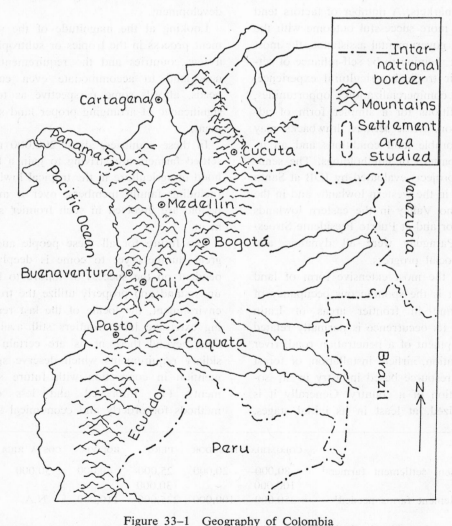

Figure 33–1 Geography of Colombia
Source: Adapted from map in *Economics of Improving Marketing Organizations and
Facilities to Accelerate Agricultural Development and Land Settlement Projects,* Latin
American Agricultural Marketing Institute, Bogotá, 1967

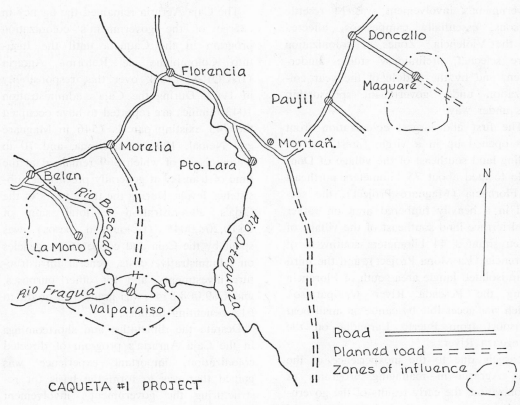

Figure 33–2 Caqueta #1 project
Source: Ibid. Figure 33–2

Colombia, Ecuador, Bolivia, and other countries of Latin America.

Against this backdrop of experience, especially in view of the dubious results of directed colonization schemes and the urgent need to find workable and low-cost alternative models of settlement, it may be very instructive to examine in some detail both a fairly representative semidirected colonization system and a spontaneous colonization experience.

In connection with both semidirected and spontaneous forms of settlements, it is clear from the IDB review of land settlement projects that, even in rather marginal ecosystems for agricultural development in the humid tropics, family settlement farming may be made economically viable and socially satisfactory, if it is carried on in ac-

cord with the natural aptitudes of the ecosystem. This is especially so if aided by infrastructure developments, provision of agricultural production and farm improvement loans, and effective technical assistance as in the case of semidirected settlements.

CAQUETA SETTLEMENT EXPERIENCE

The first significant involvement of the Colombian government in programs of colonization in the region of Caquetá (Figs. 33–1, 33–2) began in 1959 with a program of directed colonization administered by the Caja de Crédito Agraria (Agricultural Credit Bank). The rationale behind the government's involvement was to resettle persons, essentially campesinos, affected by the Violencia.[2] Zones of colonization were selected, preliminary studies undertaken, and by the middle of the year colonization under government sponsorship was under way.

The first and largest colonization front was opened up in a virgin forest area of rolling land southeast of the village of Doncello located about 75 kilometers northeast of Florencia (Maguaré Project), the second in a heavily timbered area on rather level terrace land southeast of the village of Belen situated 44 kilometers southwest of Florencia (La Mona Project), and the third in an isolated jungle area south of Florencia along the Pescada River (Valparaiso) which was accessible by canoe or small boat transport from Puerto Larandia on the Orteguaza River.

Largely due to the inexperience of the Caja Agraria in managing programs of colonization, the early results of the government's program, particularly in terms of economic returns and agriculture productivity, were well below the expectations envisioned by the planners. In adequate preliminary studies and development planning, lack of roads and other means of communications, and a variety of technical and administrative problems all tended to frustrate the establishment of economically viable and market-oriented agriculture in the region by means of the colonization program. In the hurry to get started farm units were laid out almost without regard to terrain conditions and project technicians were not adequately prepared. Perhaps the greatest handicap, however, was the inadequacy of the credit program, since so much of it went into providing subsistence or consumption needs of the colonists.

[2] *Violencia* is the popular term for the widespread civil disorder, mainly rural, that erupted in central Colombia, principally from 1948 to 1953, as a consequence of social wants, including agrarian reform, and which resulted in deaths variously estimated between 200,000 and 300,000.

The Caja Agraria remained the agency in charge of the government's colonization program in the Caquetá until the Instituto Colombiano de Reforma Agraria (INCORA)[3] took over that responsibility in 1962. During the Caja's administration 1043 families are reported to have occupied the 745 existing parcels (546 in Maguaré and Nemal, 129 in La Mona, and 70 in Valparaiso), of which 569 remained at the time of transfer at generally precarious subsistence levels. During the three years of the Caja's administration a total sum of C$10,208,004* (Colombian pesos) was spent by the Caja and cooperating agencies on administrative costs, general infrastructure investments, and for other purposes, and C$9,008,814* was granted in credit to 612 benefiting families.

Despite the difficulties and shortcomings in the Caja Agraria's program of directed colonization, important experience was gained that was to form the basis for restructuring the government's involvement under INCORA. The program directed by the Caja had served to further the opening up of the Caquetá region, and had to some degree indirectly encouraged the settlement of over ten thousand other colonists. The experience of the Caja also had demon-

[3] INCORA is an autonomous agency organized under Agrarian Reform Law 135 of 1961. Its objectives as established under the Law 135 of 1961 (December 13) as amended of 1 a of 1968 (January 26) are (a) to reorganize the agrarian social structure of Colombia by eliminating both the inequitable concentration of land in large holdings and uneconomic fractionization of land into small holdings, (b) to encourage the economic development and exploitation of uncultivated or inadequately used land in private holdings, (c) to increase the national crop and livestock production and increase productivity on agricultural land, (d) to improve contractual arrangements and other conditions for small tenant farmers and sharecroppers, (e) to raise the level of living of the rural population, and (f) to facilitate the conservation, improvement, and adequate utilization of natural resources.

* The free rate exchange for Colombian pesos per U.S. dollar for period was as follows: 1959—7.01; 1960—7.23, 1961—8.82; 1962—9.00 (figures taken from end of each year).

strated the inadequacy of paternalistic directed projects and credit programs poorly conceived and insufficiently supervised.

Beginning in 1962 and fortified by increased funding from both domestic and international sources, INCORA embarked on a new program of government involvement in colonization in the Caquetá, a program that was to steer away from the concept of directed colonization development to assistance for voluntary settlement, mainly through infrastructure building and provision of credit based on the concept of investment rather than consumption.

Soon after the transfer of responsibility for administration of directed colonization on the Caquetá area from the Caja de Crédito Agraria to the Colombia Institute of Agrarian Reform, an evaluative comparison was made by the Land Tenure Center, University of Wisconsin, of directed and spontaneous land settlement in the region.[4] Its purpose was to ascertain if there were significant differences between the two forms of settlement in terms of economic or social results. It was carried out by interviewing almost one hundred directed and one hundred spontaneous settlers. The evaluation involved a comparison of various factors indicating the background and experience, farm management results, and social and economic benefits of the directed and spontaneous settlers. Especially noteworthy in this system of comparison of directed and spontaneous forms of settlement were the findings of farm management results. The spontaneous colonists did better in terms of acquiring, clearing, and cultivating their land, developing pastures and stocking of cattle, and making more efficient use of their labor.[5] Larger percentages of

[4] Ronald L. Tinnermeier, *New Land Settlement in the Eastern Lowlands of Colombia,* Research Paper Number 13, Land Tenure Center, University of Wisconsin, December 1964.

[5] Unfortunately, in considering these matters, the element of time expended in the respective development of their farms is not well known, and this could make less of a difference in favor of the directed settlers.

the spontaneous settlers also thought that they had equal or better homes and equal or better earnings than before becoming settlers in Caquetá. Curiously, despite their seemingly better performance and greater belief in an improved living standard, a smaller percentage of spontaneous settlers than of the directed settlers wanted to stay in Caquetá. It is thought this viewpoint is most fundamentally related to the fact that in general the spontaneous settlers came from areas of less violence than did the directed settlers and therefore were less appreciative of the relative peace and tranquility of life in the Caquetá region.

The principal conclusions of the study more broadly summarized were as follows:

(1) The government assistance program for the directed colonists in Caquetá has not been effective; (2) Land was not the real limiting factor of production (as the size of farm increases, the percent of land cultivated decreases—family labor can handle only a given amount of land and hiring of labor usually does not pay—farmers with less land cleared farmed more intensively by crop production and those with more land cleared farmed more extensively by livestock production); (3) Insecurity of land ownership is found in Caquetá even though there is an abundance of land; (4) Farm labor productivity is extremely low and seriously limits production (mainly hand labor—lack of equipment—little field use of animals); (5) There is a great need for more effort in the field of technical assistance; and (6) A road is one of the necessary social services needed in any new settlement area (a road acts as a catalyst in generating farm incomes). (Tinnermeier, 1964)

Aware of much of this through empirical observation and research findings of its own, INCORA adopted the strategy of working with all settlers in the region to the extent permitted by its personnel and financial resources, and temporarily, at least, made no new plans for opening up other directed colonization projects. It placed emphasis on guiding settlement to the better lands, entitlement of land, provision of supervised agricultural credit (operations linked with technical assistance), development of infrastructure (including community development participation), organization and capitalization of cooperatives, and introduction of new forms and methods of agriculture. The latter included introduction of tree product culture such as African palm and rubber and fertilization and spraying practices.

By 1962, there were an estimated 10,000 colonists in the Caquetá Project Area, with the large majority being spontaneous or voluntary. The area in which all this land settlement and development was taking place by now roughly comprised the northern half of the extensive Amazonian piedmont east of the Andes of Colombia. It extended from the Caquetá River on the southwest to the divide between the Amazon and Orinoco drainage systems on the northeast.

The area consists of an irregular pioneer fringe which stretches along the eastern foothills of the Cordillera Oriental for about 210 kilometers and varies in width from a few kilometers to more than 50 kilometers. It encompasses over a million hectares (1,050,000) as shown in Table 33–1.

The general aspect of the terrain in the area is level to rolling, with the general elevation being about 500 meters near the base of the Andes and falling off gradually from there to the east where the piedmont merges into the broad plains of the Amazon Basin. In general, the underlying sedimentary formations have derived from eroded metamorphosed igneous material washed down from the Andes to the west. At least the newer soils formed from this parent material have the benefit of mineral elements from such material.

The sandy loam to dry loam alluvial soils of the nearby level river floodplains and lower terraces are moderately fertile (Classes II and III of a six-class rating system of land for agricultural purposes in Colombia). Some of this land is occasionally flooded, however, and some is imperfectly drained. The next best are the medium-textured soils on the higher and more uneven terraces and eroded interstream sedimentary areas which spread over large areas between some of the major drainages (Class IV). The older residual and most intensively leached soils derived from Tertiary sediments are the most extensive and generally the least fertile in the area (Classes V and VI). A general physical land capability classification of the area by the Instituto Geográfico Agustín Godazzi broadly summarizes the area's land resources in Table 33–1.

Table 33–1

PHYSICAL LAND CAPABILITY
CLASSIFICATION OF CAQUETÁ AREA

LAND CLASS	LAND USE ADAPTABILITY	APPROXIMATE AREA IN HECTARES	APPROXIMATE PERCENT OF AREA
Class II	Sustained crop production and cultivated pastures	199,500	19.0
Class III	Periodic crop production and cultivated pastures	63,000	6.0
Class IV	Cultivated pastures and permanent crops	315,000	30.0
Class V	Extensive livestock grazing with some permanent cropping	446,250	42.5
Class VI	Mainly non-agricultural	26,250	2.5
Totals		1,050,000	100.0

The Caquetá settlement area has a tropical rain-forest climate. At Florencia the mean annual temperature is 26.5° C. Rainfall is both heavy and distributed almost throughout the year, with an annual mean of 3975 millimeters. According to the Leslie R. Holdridge system of classification of natural plant or natural life zones, the area is on the border between Tropical Moist Forest and Tropical Wet Forest. No doubt most of it is Tropical Wet Forest.

By 1968, the area had become occupied by about 22,000 settler farming units comprising about 950,000 hectares. Of this large number nearly one-fourth, or 4870 units with 248,335 hectares, had been adjudicated for entitlement by June 1968.

Over two-thirds of the settlement farming units in Caquetá Project are in the size range 20 to 100 hectares, or what may be regarded as family farm size units. Only one-fifth of the farms are less than twenty hectares in size, and only one-seventh are over 100 hectares. Average-size farm units tend to increase in the settlement belt with distance north and south of Florencia which is the regional center—San Vicente Zone at the north has 188 hectares, Florencia Zone in about the middle has 57 hectares, and Valparaiso at the south end has 108 hectares.

The basic crops for the Caquetá settlement area are rice and corn. The major part of the average colono's cash income results from these crops. Main subsistence crops are yucca, sugar cane, and plantains, but in some zones, especially those nearest Florencia, a part of this production is brought to the market also. This basic production was enlarged in recent years by the introduction by INCORA of new crops such as the African oil palm and rubber, principally where technical and financial assistance were available. In the future, the large cattle program which INCORA has started will become increasingly important. In Table 33–2 the average land use of set-

Table 33–2

AVERAGE USE OF FARM LAND IN CAQUETÁ BY COLONOS RECEIVING INCORA ASSISTANCE IN AUGUST 1968

CULTIVATED AREAS	HECTARES
Rice	4.7
Corn	2.4
Plantains	1.2
Yucca	.7
Sugar Cane	.4
African oil palm	.1
Other	.1
Total cultivated area	9.6
Farmsteads	1.8
Pastures	25.0
Forested	27.3
Fallow/bush/jungle	9.5
Waste Land	.9
Total Farm Land	74.1

Source: Average of 1991 farms involved in the INCORA supervised credit program for 1 year or longer.

tlers assisted by INCORA in Caquetá is shown.

It is important to note that only 13 percent of the total farm land is cultivated, and that almost 40 percent is unused land, available for long-term rotation farming mainly because little farming is mechanized. Of the cultivated area, however, less than one-fifth is in permanent crops, indicating a still heavy reliance on soil-depleting annual crops.

The distribution of farm-land usage changes considerably if one goes to a remote area not under the assistance of INCORA (Table 33–3).

In this case, the cultivated area is about 11 percent of total farm land, but the total cultivated area is only 4.5 hectares as compared with 9.6 hectares for those under the INCORA program. Pasture land is also less, being only one-third that of farms assisted by INCORA.

The major features of the rural economy of the Caquetá settlement area for 1967–1968 can be ascertained through examina-

Table 33–3

ESTIMATED AVERAGE USE OF FARM
LAND ON MORE REMOTE SETTLEMENT
FARMS IN CAQUETÁ INVOLVED ONLY
RECENTLY OR NOT AT ALL IN
INCORA CREDIT PROGRAM

CULTIVATED AREAS	HECTARES
Rice	1.3
Corn	1.0
Plantains	1.1
Yucca	.7
Sugar Cane	.3
Other	.1
Total cultivated area	4.5
Farmsteads	1.0
Pastures	8.6
Forest	26.0
Total Farm Land	40.1

NOTE: All land holdings larger than 200 hectares
were excluded as settlement farms in making this
estimate.

tion of the farm-land use, production, and
income data derived from current supervised farm credit reports for the eight different credit zones of the Caquetá Project.
These reports summarize this information
and a great deal of data, concerning a total
of 1991 farmers involved for one year or
more in the INCORA supervised credit and
technical assistance program. The nearly
two thousand farms thus reported upon in
detail provide a comprehensive representation of the more developed farm economy
of the region.

Data abstracted from the reports are
ordered for the eight credit zones north to
south in Table 33–4, which places the
Florencia Zone, the most developed section
of the region, at about the middle. The figures given for each zone for various aspects
of farm-land use, production, and farm unit
incomes are zonal averages for the farms
reported on in the supervised farm credit
program.

The gross and net average incomes per
farmer of the nearly two thousand involved
in the INCORA supervised credit program
are, respectively, C$33,136 and C$12,710.

The distribution of gross incomes for 1824
farms is shown in Table 33–5.

Table 33–5

INCOME GAINS (c$)*	NO. OF FARMS
0– 5,000	508
5,001–10,000	559
10,001–15,000	257
15,001–20,000	181
20,001–30,000	58
30,001–or more	34
LOSSES	
0– 5,000	194
5,000–or more	83

The average debt per farm was C$24,-
657 owed to the supervised credit program
and to the Caja Agraria for cattle, annual
or perennial crop production, and farm improvement loans. The estimated average
farm-land value is C$33,310.

The average net income per capita of the
families involved in the INCORA supervised credit program is C$1816; the average
net income per hectare of improved farm
land (cultivation and pasture) is C$367.

In considering the change in land settlement policy which was initiated by
INCORA and which subsequent development certainly seems to have justified, it
is well to recall that when directed colonization was begun in 1959 by the Caja Agraria,
the major concern was the resettlement of
as many victims of violence as possible at
minimum cost. For a great many of these
colonists, especially for those without
farm experience and resources for farm development, the almost inevitable result was
a form of subsistence farming or eventual
project abandonment because of hardships,
inadequate incomes, marketing difficulties,
and health problems. By the time INCORA
took over, the violence problem had receded
and the stress was more on development of

* The free rate exchange for Colombian pesos
per U.S. dollar for period was as follows: 1967—
3rd qtr. 15.36; 1967—4th qtr. 15.82; 1968—1st
qtr. 16.04; 1968—2nd qtr. 16.32; the average was
15.88.

Table 33-4

COMPARISON OF GENERAL FARM LAND USE, CROP AND LIVESTOCK DEVELOPMENT,
AND FARM INCOMES BY SECTORS IN THE CAQUETA REGION

ZONE	AV. SIZE OF FINCA	AV. HA CUL-TIV.	AV. HA PAS-TURE	AV. HA IM-PROVED	PER-CENT CULTI-VATION OF AV. FINCA	PER-CENT PAS-TURE AV. FINCA	PER-CENT IM-PROVED AV. FINCA	AV. NO. CAT-TLE ALL TYPES PER. AV. HA PAST	AV. HA RICE/ FINCA	AV. NO. CAT-TLE PER FINCA	AV. NO. PIGS PER FINCA	AV. NO MILK COWS PER FINCA	AV. GROSS INCOME	AV. NET INCOME
San Vicente	188	9.4	58.5	67.9	.050	.311	.361	.92	.77	53.6	23.1	2.8	33,000	16,460
Puerto Rico	93.8	18.4	24.9	43.3	.197	.266	.462	.74	11.10	18.5	7.3	N.A.	17,358	6,874
Maguare.	64.4	9.7	27.5	37.2	.150	.427	.577	.80	5.17	22.1	2.8	3.2	25,190	16,700
Paujil	74.7	10.5	27.0	37.5	.141	.361	.502	.81	4.55	21.8	3.3	2.6	11,165	5,901
Florencia	57	4.5	29.1	33.6	.079	.511	.590	.94	.35	23.9	3.8	1.9	61,887	32,251
Morelia	73	10.0	31.1	41.1	.137	.426	.563	.53	6.19	16.5	2.7	2.8	12,282	6,853
La Mona	54	7.8	19.7	27.5	.144	.365	.509	.84	3.17	16.6	4.5	N.A.	15,568	10,438
Val-paraiso	108.3	11.2	27.7	38.9	.103	.256	.359	.95	6.71	26.0	4.7	N.A.	8,646	6,201

viable family farms in accordance with the precepts of the Agrarian Reform Law of 1961, including the development of commercial farming and provision of more adequate infrastructure and agricultural services in the area.

Beyond this, the soil and climatic limitations of the Caquetá region were not adequately considered when colonization was begun. Long-run successful farming in the moderately fertile to rather infertile soils and in the humid tropical climate of the area in major part must be based on livestock and tree crops, which minimize soil depletion, erosion, and flooding, and the rapid shifting of cultivation with attendant cutting and burning of forest cover. Credit made available to the settlers was insufficient for such farming; cattle were not made available in sufficient number; technical assistance in pasture and cattle and tree crop development was inadequate; and settler farming experience in tropical agriculture was generally lacking.

Settlement experience in the area had indicated that the settlers who came entirely on their own worked hard in clearing and cultivating to gain possession of the land they occupied and, with some money in their pockets to survive the time until they harvested their first crops, were most successful. This voluntary settlement seemed to provide a natural screening of settlers which was better than any other system for selection.

Accordingly, INCORA shaped a program to assist both the established settlers and the newer frontiersmen which would enable them to convert to farming more suitable to the humid tropics—by providing greater farm credit and technical assistance needed for cattle, African palm, rubber, bananas, pigs, and other suitable production, and to become commercial producers. It also provided for the more adequate service facilities such as access roads, schools, and health services, and some resources and skills for

settler self-help through cooperatives and communal action groups.

The strategy is apparently proving successful. The agricultural frontier is expanding rapidly in ecologically suitable directions; farmer incomes are rising substantially, and the percentage of farm credit repayments is commendable. Settler satisfaction now seems quite general, and development responsibility is being shared between the settlers and public service agencies. Since substantial settlement and development began in the area, an *ex post facto* crude calculation of the internal rate of return on investments in relation to agricultural production is in the range of 12 to 15 percent.

The flow of settlers into the area, more than two thousand a year, however, has been more than INCORA can adequately handle with its limited resources of staff and funds. Adequate funds for the road construction so needed to reduce farm-to-market costs have been especially lacking, and so in some areas the settlers are out in front of penetration roads as much as 30 kilometers or more. This in turn reduces the effectiveness of the technical assistance staff and increases the costs of administration.

Against this backdrop of experience in the typical directed and semidirected settlement schemes we shall now examine a spontaneous colonization process in Bolivia.

CARANAVI SETTLEMENT EXPERIENCE

The Caranavi area embraces land on both sides of the lower Coroico Valley in the eastern subtropical foothills and valleys of the Andes, which in Bolivia is referred to as the Yungas, a regional designation derived from an Aymara word meaning valleys. The small town of Caranavi, which is the principal urban center of the area, lies approximately 172 kilometers northeast of La Paz.

It may be reached from La Paz by a rather narrow gravel road that descends the long and steep eastern front of the Andean Mountains.

Settlement of the area is relatively recent (Fig. 33–3). There were, no doubt, many scattered settlers along the Coroico River, even before the 90 kilometer road from La Paz to Coroico was completed in 1944, but the first settlement in the lower valley was established in 1945 at Santa Ana, which is 70 kilometers below Coroico in the vicinity of Caranavi. In 1945, construction of the road from Coroico to Caranavi began and with it settlement down the valley increased. When it was completed in 1953, there were 500 colonists, by 1958 an estimated 2000, and by 1967, 6300. Colonists in the area and settlement had spread out over the hills of the valley as much as 20 kilometers in places. Thus the maturity of the project might be regarded as about fifteen years.

The rate of settlement in the area has been rapid, with colonization averaging 600 settlers per year. Total population, rural and

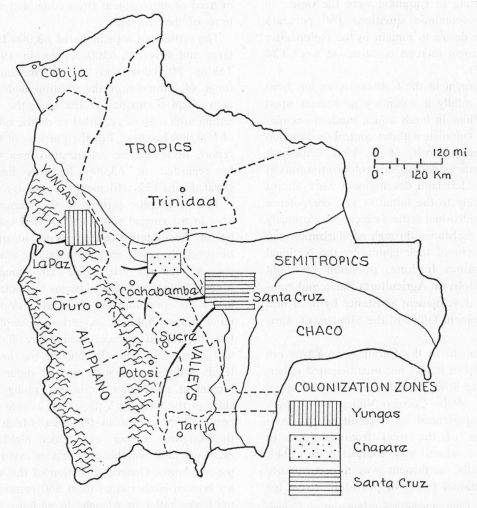

Figure 33–3   Bolivia. Internal migration patterns during recent decades, Bolivia, 1968
Source: Kelso Lee Nessel, "An Economic Assessment of Pioneer Settlement in the Bolivian Lowlands" (unpublished thesis, Cornell University, 1968)

urban, was approximately 36,000 in 1967. There are about 3600 people living in towns, villages, or lesser urban nuclei, with Caranavi having about 2000.

Practically all the settlers of the Caranavi area are nationals of Bolivia from rural background. About 86 percent of them have come from the department of La Paz. About 10 percent have originated from the department of Oruro and minor percentages have come from the departments of Potosí, Cochabamba, and El Beni. Approximately 2 percent have moved in from the Puno section of Peru.[6] Principal reasons expressed for settling in Caranavi were the desire to change economic situations (66 percent) and the desire to remain in the region after employment in road construction work (24 percent).[6]

Settlement in the Caranavi area has been almost totally a voluntary movement upon public domain lands and a random occupation by colonists without control or direction from any authority of any kind. Settlement represents a spontaneous colonization model that has left land development work almost completely to the initiative and competence of the individual settlers except for extremely limited assistance through regularization and entitlement of their claims by the National Colonization Institute, provision of credit by the Bolivian Agricultural Bank, and community development assistance by the Rural Development Office of the Ministry of Agriculture.

Settlement in the Caranavi area was not planned but it was not unanticipated either, since the flow of settlement into the upper reaches of the Coroico Valley had already been experienced as a result of the construction of the road from La Paz to Coroico, which was completed in 1944. Principally, settlement was a consequence of a national policy of providing access for

the occupation and development of the tropical lowlands of eastern Bolivia for reasons of security and economic growth. The whole stretch of road from La Paz to Caranavi and beyond, started in 1931, was part of this objective.

The highway builders no doubt rationalized some of the expenditures for the development of the various segments of the highway down to and through the Caranavi area by expectations of en-route national benefits accruing from expansion on suitable land of agricultural settlement and subtropical production and resettlement of people in need of employment from congested sections of the altiplano.

The settlement area included 63,000 hectares and involved 6300 settlers in 1967. Taking 20 kilometers as the maximum range of influence of the existing highway network in occupancy of the area, the potential area may be regarded as on the order of 500,000 hectares. For the purpose of this report, however, the colonization area will be regarded as 63,000 hectares incorporated into 132 settlements (colonias).

The geographic setting of the Caranavi area in the rugged valley and foothill country of the eastern Andean piedmont must be generally considered marginal for extensive agricultural settlement. The country ranges from very limited areas of bottom lands to predominantly steeply sloping mountainous uplands. A series of steplike but interrupted terraces, which are flatter and of more recent alluvium at the lower levels and more irregular and of older alluvium at the higher levels, run along the sides of the Coroico Valley and provide the best cultivable land in the area. Much of the rougher, steeper, or stonier highland areas are most suitable as forest or eventual pasture lands. General elevation of the valley bottom lands ranges from 560 meters in the lower valley at Alcoche to perhaps 500 meters in the upper valley near Coroico, while the surrounding uplands reach over

[6] Data from unpublished manuscript on Colonización Espontánea en Caranavi—Estudio Socio-Económico, information on social aspects by Tomás Lenz, Instituto Indigenista Boliviano, 1967.

1400 meters. Original vegetation of the area was an evergreen seasonal forest, but a considerable area has been cleared or cut for timber.

Rainfall is generally convectional in origin and sufficient throughout most of the year, with an annual mean of 1669 millimeters at Alcoche. The period of most rainfall is from September to March, when northeasterly rain-bearing trade winds predominate. The rainiest months are from December to March, when mean monthly precipitation at Alcoche exceeds 200 mm. The driest period is from May through August and coincides with the cooler months of the year. Driest months are June (23.8 mm) and July (40.1 mm). According to a moisture regime classification that has been applied to the central piedmont of Bolivia, the Caranavi area, with a weak dry season of four months and two months (July and August) when evapotranspiration tends to exceed precipitation plus available soil-stored moisture, would nevertheless be regarded as humid and suitable for tree crops such as bananas, cacao, and coffee; grasses such as capingordura, guinea, and pangola; and legumes such as tropical kudzu.[7]

The climate of the Caranavi area is tropical to subtropical because of variations in elevation. At Alcoche in the lower valley, where mean annual temperature is 24.8° C the climate is tropical. According to the Leslie R. Holdridge system of ecologic mapping, the lower valley area, where temperatures are highest and rainfall probably lowest, is tropical dry forest environment. The more elevated and therefore somewhat cooler sections may be assumed to be subtropical moist forest lands.

The soils of the Caranavi Valley that have developed on the flood plains, recent

[7] T. T. Cochrane, "Land Systems Map of Central Tropical Bolivia," p. 9, and "An Initial Assessment of the Land Use Potential of the Central Piedmont and the Santa Cruz Regions of Tropical Bolivia," p. 7, published, respectively, in 1967 and 1968 jointly by the Ministry of Agriculture and the British Agricultural Mission in Bolivia.

alluvium of the more youthful and extensive lower terraces, and the older alluvium of the higher and more limited terrace remnants are moderately fertile yellowish-brown sandy loam to clay loam which in places may be quite stony. The residual soils formed on little consolidated sandstones and shales of the uplands are reddish-yellow loams to clays with more intensive leaching.

In general, the topsoils vary from medium texture and moderate permeability to clay soils with little permeability. The subsoils, which usually occur from 0.50 to 1.50 meters in depth, tend to be of heavy clay texture.

The area has been classified mainly on the basis of slope condition into physical capability classes as in Table 33–6.

Table 33–6

SLOPE PERCENT (100 = 45°)	SURFACE AREA PERCENT	CLASS	USE SUITABILITY
0–20	15	II	Cultivation
20–40	10	VI	Forest and pasture
40–100	30	VII	Forest
100–150	40	VIII	(Natural areas
150–more	5	VIII	and recreation)

SOURCE: Colonización Espontánea en Caranavi—Estudio Socio-Económico, 1967, the chapter on Consideraciones sobre Suelos by Ing. Javier Flores, Departamento de Suelos, Ministerio de Agricultura, p. 73, unpublished manuscript.

According to this classification, only 15 percent of the land is capable of cultivation and 10 percent is suitable for pasture and forest (presumably also tree cropping). Seventy-five percent of the land has slopes in excess of 40 percent and so is considered usable only for natural forest and eventually recreation purposes. In general, soils also have fertility limitations, especially with regard to phosphorus, calcium, and nitrogen. Some sheet and gully erosion has occurred in hilly cultivated areas and occasionally even some topsoil slippage on steep cleared land where moisture has accumulated over clayey subsoils.

Under the capability classification used, only 9450 hectares is regarded as suitable for agricultural use. Much hilly land is, in fact, under rather noninjurious tree cropping. Presently about 19,500 hectares of the land is in cultivation under permanent crops and about 7560 hectares under annual crops, some of which is intertilled with permanent crops.

Major land-use concerns are the effects of further rapid and largely uncontrolled settlement and of the extensive deforestation of the uplands on erosion and flooding in the valley. At the present time, only 36 percent of the area has been cleared of forest, however, and of this, most is in so-called permanent crops. Other deterrents to erosion and runoff are the checkered pattern of cultivated areas with brush and virgin forest land, negligible practice of clean cultivation, very limited annual cropping (the average farm only has about 1 hectare), and the rapid growth of weeds, grasses, and brush cover on open fields. Nevertheless, the importance of controlling settlement and forest exploitation in order to minimize soil erosion and rapid runoff from the soft sandstone and shale hills of the area, the injurious effects of which might, unless inhibited, not only be felt in the valley itself but be carried on downstream to increase the already serious annual flooding problem in the Beni lowlands, has been noted by land management technicians in Bolivia.[8]

All soils under continuous crop use without beneficial crop rotation, opportunity for natural recuperation by fallowing, or fertilizer enrichment, suffer rather rapid declines of fertility, especially from annual field cropping which hastens losses of organic material and leaching of soluble elements. In a way, this serves to promote tree cropping, however, which tends to minimize erosion and flood hazards and restore organic material.

During the comparatively short duration of voluntary colonization of the Caranavi area, widespread progress has been made at least along the main road system, much of it through mutual assistance efforts of settlers in developing the infrastructure needed for some integration and promotion of community living. But much more needs to be done everywhere, especially in the more isolated back country.

The uncontrolled settlement has limited the opportunity to formulate a rural development pattern most suitable to terrain, soil, and moisture conditions and most economical in relation to the provision of access, services, and marketing facilities. On the whole, local technicians of the Ministry of Agriculture and the National Colonization Institute, however, believe the rural settlement pattern is satisfactory considering the random occupancy that occurred and the generally unfavorable terrain conditions in the area.

Most of the settlers have access to about as much land as they wish to plant, considering the labor needs of the farming techniques commonly used in the area. Family farming dominates rural life and the economy, and farm sizes tend to be quite small.

The approximate size distribution of landholdings is as shown in Table 33–7.

Table 33–7

SIZE CLASS (in hectares)	APPROXIMATE NUMBER	PERCENT TOTAL
0– 5	630	10
6–10	4,725	75
11–15	630	10
15 or more	315	5

Cooperativism is by now almost commonplace in the backlands of Caranavi. Some of the settlement colonies even bear the name

[8] General concern about this has been expressed in "Land Systems Map of Central Tropical Bolivia," by T. T. Cochrane, Ministry of Agriculture and British Agricultural Mission, p. 2, 1967, and in the unpublished manuscript on Colonización Espontánea en Caranavi—Estudio Socio-Económico in the chapter on Consideraciones sobre Suelos, by Ing. Javier Flores, Departamento de Suelos, Ministerio de Agricultura.

of the cooperatives. But cooperative association has been much more important in assisting in the founding of new communities and constructing necessary communal facilities, than in establishing cooperative economic services, such as consumer, farm supply, credit, or marketing organizations.

The attitudes and characteristics of the settlers appear to be generally favorable for stability and continued progress—77 percent of the settlers have indicated an intent to reside permanently on their holdings; 53 percent of their family members have six years or more of schooling; 80 percent indicate some knowledge of the Spanish language; 70 percent of the colonos have a formal or informal marital association, and about 52 percent of the total settlement population is in an economically active age range.[9] The average size of families is about five members. Data on economic welfare of the settlers prior to their immigration are not available, but their limited possessions —houses, tools or implements, and livestock —indicates it was generally quite low.

Total gross value of agricultural production in 1967 has been estimated at $b. 36,000,000* (Bolivian pesos) using sale prices in Caranavi and total value of farm product exports from the region at approximately $b. 27,000,000.*[10]

Bananas are the main commercial crop of the area. Over one-third of the colonists grow them, with about 30 percent growing enough to sell at least some of the production. Growers average about 1.9 hectares in cultivation. According to a survey of banana marketing in the Caranavi area in 1967, the average grower produced 212 *chipas*[11] in the preceding year, from which he grossed $b. 15,700 if he sold them in La Paz at prices reported in May and June.[12] The dominant variety grown is the dwarf Cavendish.

The town of Caranavi has organized a cooperative for the marketing of bananas and the producers utilize it to a great extent. The co-op pays the farmers the regular wholesale price, which means it is earning the profit formerly gained by the wholesale country assemblers.

There are practically no pastures or cattle in the Caranavi area. This situation is attributed to the rugged relief and natural vegetation of the area. Yet in many parts of the world, Puerto Rico and Antioquia in Colombia being outstanding tropical examples, cattle do well on slopes.of 50 percent or more.

Most of the orange, tangerine, coffee, and avocado produced are sold outside the area, and about 50 percent of the rice (10 percent of rice sold in La Paz comes from Alto Beni and Caranavi areas) and 40 percent of the corn crops as well. Nearly all of the yuca, vegetables, walusa, and papaya is consumed on the farms or sold locally at the fair.

It is evident that substantial progress is being made by most farmers of the Caranavi area along the continuum of subsistence to commercial in the development of their landholdings. This is desirable since commercial farming brings in money for farm and home improvements. According to local agricultural informants the evolution in general has proceeded as follows:

1ST YEAR: 1 to 2 hectares cleared with about ½ ha of rice or corn or both, and ¼ ha of yuca and other subsistence crops.
2ND YEAR: 2 to 3 hectares cleared with about ½ ha of rice or corn or both, ½ ha

[9] Data from unpublished manuscript on Colonización Espontánea en Caranavi—Estudio Socio-Económico, information on social aspects by Tomás Lenz, Instituto Indigenista Boliviano, 1967.

* The exchange rate for Bolivian pesos per U.S. dollar at the end of 1967 was 11.88.

[10] Michael Nelson, An Economic Evaluation of Programs for Development of New Lands in the Humid Tropics of Bolivia, p. 21, Resources for the Future, Inc., unpublished manuscript, 1968.

[11] A bundle of 1200 bananas wrapped in banana leaves and tied with rawhide.

[12] Michigan State University study of Marketing of Agricultural Products in Bolivia, preliminary review report, 1968.

of citrus, ¼ ha of coffee, and ¼ ha of banana or avocado planted and yuca and other subsistence crops intertilled.

3RD YEAR: 3 to 4 hectares cleared with about 1 ha of rice or corn or both, ½ ha of citrus, ½ ha of coffee, and ½ ha of banana or avocado planted and yuca and other subsistence crops intertilled.

4TH YEAR: 4 to 5 hectares cleared with about 1 ha with rice or corn or both, 1 ha of citrus, ½ ha of coffee, 1 ha of bananas or avocado, and yuca and other subsistence crops intertilled.

5TH YEAR: about 5 hectares cleared with about 1 ha of rice or corn or both, 1 ha of citrus, ½ ha of coffee, 1 ha of banana or avocado, ½ ha of other permanent crops with yuca and other subsistence crops intertilled.

At present, almost one-third of the colonists grow enough bananas to sell a significant amount. Similarly, about one-half grow sufficient coffee, 10 to 15 percent adequate citrus, a small percent enough avocado, and a large percent enough rice or corn or both to enable some sales disposal in local or national markets. The marketable surplus produced goes to obtain cash for the necessities of life such as nonfarm produce required for better nutrition and the clothing, utensils, tools, improved seeds, medicines, sewing machines, and radios desired on every farm. With present farming methods, the area of cultivation that an average farm family can handle seems to be 4 to 5 hectares.

Except for clearing operations when axes and saws are used (and fire does much of the work), man's labor generally is not aided by any implement more effective than a machete. Because of fertility limitations, it seems that the age-old system of slash-and-burn agriculture (whereby a new field is cleared and burned every few years during the dry season and a permanently cropped area is abandoned for recu-

peration) is destined to prevail over much of the area.

The principal ecological factors governing past and future production, noted especially by Michael Nelson in "An Economic Evaluation of Progress for Development of New Lands in the Humid Tropics of Bolivia" are: The exhaustion of the soil and consequent need to either abandon the lands, lengthen the bush-fallow period, use capital and/or labor-intensive practices such as terracing and fertilizers, or change the management practice to mainly tree crops or pasture and livestock. There are a number of issues associated with such land-use decisions: the rate of yield decline, the break-even point for abandoning land, the output response to added capital and labor, the short-run and long-run returns from various combinations of soil-depleting and soil-conserving practices, and the access to additional land. There is a great need for additional knowledge about some of these issues.

With respect to soil exhaustion, some erosion and loss of soil nutrients are inevitable with regular cropping, especially under annual cropping in absence of fertilizer use or conservation practices, on lands where only 15 percent are classified as suitable for agriculture and 75 percent have slopes in excess of 40 percent. At the present time, however, only 36 percent of the area subdivided has been cleared of forest.

The general practice that has been followed to date has been to sow annual crops (rice, corn, or yuca) for the first two to three years after clearing the forest. At the same time, permanent crops such as bananas, coffee, or citrus have been intersown in the second and third years. This has resulted in an intensive use of land and a slow rate of forest clearing after the third year. Thus, over a period of ten to fifteen years, the colonists have on an average cleared 1 to 2 hectares per year, up to 4 to 7 hectares each. The average property has 1 hectare of annual crops and about 3 hectares in permanent crops. There is no widespread application of bush-fallow, although, if fertilization practices, more concentration on tree cropping, and livestock farming do not develop, this would appear to be the next step in the evolution of agriculture in the area in order to restore soil nutrients and take advantage of richer lands elsewhere.

The questions of yield declines, adoption of bush-fallow or shifting agricultural practices, and the actual or potential rate of abandonment of lands, all remain uncertain. There are insufficient experimental and experiential data to properly quantify these important matters. It has been estimated that up to 30 percent of the land now in cultivation may have to be abandoned or shifted within the next three to five years unless use is made of artificial fertilizers or essentially tree cropping or pasturing of livestock, but without any indication of whether the ensuing bush-fallow should last five, ten, or more years.

There are indications of the yield level trends that become unacceptable to producers under present cost-price relationships: rice and corn—a decline from 2500 to 1000 kg/ha over a period of three–five years of consecutive cropping; yuca—50,000 kg to 10,000 kg/ha over a period of five years; and bananas—a decline from 1200 racimos/ha in the third year to 400 in the seventh year. In the case of citrus, many of the orchards are essentially neglected within five to ten years due to disease or lack of markets. However, there is no firm basis for projecting the rate at which land may be abandoned, the length of the bush-fallow period, or the technical steps (within the constraints of economics, management ability, and availability of capital and labor) which may be taken to avoid or reduce such abandonment. Furthermore, products that do currently have a good market, such as rice and corn, are not well suited to the re-

gion and furthermore are severely damaging to the soil, except on the limited alluvial lowlands.

The general implication of the foregoing is that cultivated land may be abandoned at an accelerating rate of between 500 and 2500 hectares annually over the next five years. This may also signify abandonment of many smaller farm units where shifting cultivation cannot be accommodated. At the same time, it is estimated that the clearing of virgin forest is proceeding at a rate of 3000 to 4000 hectares per year. Of this area, about 2000 hectares are being cleared by established colonists.

Settlement in the Caranavi area has developed significant employment opportunities, which are badly needed in Bolivia. Foremost is the gainful employment of the operators of the 6300 small family farms in the area, 95 percent of whom work only on their own property or locally in exchange of labor. The other major primary sources of employment are in the forest and mining industries in which about 350 men are employed full-time and about 100 part-time in logging, saw-milling, mining, and other work. Generation of secondary employment in commercial and service activities, mainly in the smaller towns and villages of the area, is estimated at over 900. Public services employment, including military personnel, totals about 200. The average annual income of unskilled workers is about $b. 3000* and average annual gross income of family farms is about $b. 5700.*

Social welfare conditions on the pioneer fringe are generally low anywhere, and those in the Caranavi area are no exception. There are solid indications of future improvement, however, when more time and income may be devoted to bettering the quality of life. Settler satisfaction can perhaps best be gauged by the high percentage (77 percent) who have expressed an

* The exchange rate for Bolivian pesos per U.S. dollar at the end of 1967 was 11.88.

intention to stay permanently on their land-holdings. Including the full cost of highways below Coroico and assuming a zero alternative marginal opportunity cost of labor, the internal rate of return on development of the Caranavi area has been estimated at 16 percent.

The development sequence of the region appears to be intimately related to the highway construction program. Prior to the decision to extend the road below Coroico, economic activity in the lower valley was negligible apart from the operations of *quineros* (cinchona bark harvesters). Without the highway, the flow of human and capital resources into the region would not have taken place. Further, it would appear that other government programs such as extension, credit, research, and education were not established until after 1960 when the population had already reached 15,000 and substantial private investment had taken place. Thus they cannot be considered as truly development promotion activities but merely as servicing an already established demand. While government expenditures (other than roads) in the region after 1962 undoubtedly stimulated capital formation in the region by creating amenities for permanent settlement, the highways continued to be the prime force for development through opening up new lands for agricultural and forestry exploitation.

Huge sums have been spent in Latin America on studies of proposed colonization projects, and very little on appraisals of what has been gained or lost as a result. The Inter-American Development Bank has undertaken a searching evaluation of the social and economic consequences of selected directed and semidirected projects, in spontaneous settlement areas, and on private land settlement and development projects with the view of formulating operational guidelines to respond to future member-country applications for loans for land settlement endeavors. From this review may come a clearer idea of where, when, how, and under what development strategy and administrative procedure colonization should be undertaken.

There are many unknowns in tropical farming systems, even such fundamentals in many places as the degree of accuracy of yield estimates under complex intercropping systems and large rounded unit reporting, the length of bush or forest fallow fertility recuperation periods needed, length of economical grazing on most common pastures, and degree to which weed control rather than soil fertility governs intensity of land use and choice of crops. Fortunately, a study of the comparative productivity of food-crop cultivation systems in tropical environments by the Associated Colleges of the Midwest intends comprehensive work on these matters with support from the National Science Foundation.

Large-scale spontaneous and scattered tropical settlement is occurring in many countries, whether or not desirable and economical, which if properly directed and developed usually could be made into a positive national asset, but if left unordered and ignored might well represent little gain to a nation and possibly a serious social and economic loss, and in some areas an ecological disaster as well.

EXPLANATORY NOTES

The sources and bases for estimates of numbers of settlement farmers and number of settlement farms needed in various countries are as follows:

COLOMBIA

Estimates of present future farmers from Thomas Lynn Smith, *Social Structure and the Process of Development*, University of Florida, 1967.

Estimates of settlement farms needed: A rough approximation of the additional family farms needed in Colombia, if a reasonably equitable distribution of land resources could be effected for all farm families, is on the order of 500,000. This is arrived at by assuming that if the 765,000 sub-family farms could be reconstituted into viable small farms, about 382,500 families would need to be located elsewhere, and that farming opportunities are desirable for the 75,000 renters, sharecroppers, and squatters occupying family-sized farms and nearly one-half of the 118,000 landless farm workers. Rough estimates indicate half might be provided through agrarian reform, and the other half met through colonization.

ECUADOR

Estimate of present settlement farmers: *Plan General de Desarrollo Económico y Social* of the National Planning Board of Ecuador, published in 1963, Volume 6, *Colonización,* estimates there were 18,000 families on lands of the public domain or lands subject to reversion to public ownership in 1962. Since then many have been issued titles and many additional families have moved onto the public domain. It is believed the net change is about 2000 additional settlement farmers.

Estimate of settlement farms needed: *Plan General de Desarrollo Económico y Social* of the National Planning Board of Ecuador, published in 1963, Volume 6, *Colonización,* estimates new farming opportunities must be found for almost 80,000 families by means of colonization. This estimate has been raised to 100,000 to provide for added rural family formation needing land through colonization since the original estimate in 1962.

BOLIVIA

Estimate of present settlement farmers from Kelso Lee Wessel, "An Economic Assessment of Pioneer Settlement in the Boliva Lowlands," Ph.D. thesis at Cornell University, June 1968.

Estimate of settlement farms needed: *Plan General de Desarrollo Económico y Social,* 1962–1971, Secretaria Nacional de Planificación y Coordinación, Republica de Bolivia, 1961.

COSTA RICA

Estimate of present settlement farmers based on estimates of Gerhard Sander, "Agrarkolonisation in Costa Rica, Siedlung, Wirtschaft and Sozialefuge an der Pioniergrenze," *Schriften Geografiske Inst.* der Univ. Kiel, Volume 19, Number 3, 1961, as modified and updated in accordance with past trends.

Estimate of settlement farms needed: Not available.

PERU

Estimate of present settlement farms compiled from *La Carretera Marginal de la Selva,* Tippetts-Abbett-McCarthy-Shatton, Lima and New York, 1965; *Evaluación del Potencial Económica y Social de la Zona Tingo-Maria-Tocache,* Huallaga Central, Servicio Cooperativo Inter-Americano de Fomento, Lima, 1962; and Wolfram U. Drewes, *The Economic Development of the Western Montana of Central Peru as Related to Transportation,* Peruvian Times, 1958.

Estimate of settlement farms needed: A rough approximation of the additional family farms needed in Peru, if a reasonably equitable distribution of land resources could be effected through an agrarian grant reform, is on the order of 550,000. This is arrived at by assuming that if the 694,000 sub-family farms could be reconstituted into viable small farms, about half or 350,000 families would need to be located elsewhere, and that farm opportunities are desirable for at least one-third or 100,000 of the 300,000 landless farm workers (data from Inter-America Committee on Agricultural Development reports). Crude estimation indicates that about half of these farm needs might be provided for if a fairly drastic redistribution of land resources on the 10,000 largest-sized holdings were carried out, leaving the other half or 225,000 to be met through colonization.

34. PLANT GERM PLASM RESOURCES AND UTILIZATION[1]

David H. Timothy

From the day man first began to domesticate plants, he has made use of genetic variability. For continued improvement, even today, we still depend upon the variability of those species and their wild relatives. Successful plant breeding programs, accompanied by increased production and new agricultural technology, cause great changes in local farming systems and hence, the landscape and biota. In many cases, the release of outstanding varieties or hybrids has been so successful that local biotypes can no longer be found. By our success, then, we can destroy future sources of as yet unknown but perhaps very useful genes. The conditions under which cultivated plants are grown have continually changed, and there is little reason to suspect that they will not continue to do so. Germ plasm unnecessary today may be vitally important tomorrow and germ plasm necessary today may be less important in the future. Comprehensive collections of germ plasm must be made and properly maintained before this irreplaceable material is forever lost through the destructive onslaught of increasing population and agricultural pressures.

Most of our governmental agricultural development programs have been failures, planning for only two-year or three-year terms. The successful programs have been long-range in philosophy, objectives, funding, and staffing. They have also applied a regional or ecological approach to increasing food production through continuous team effort among related disciplines. Several examples are cited which illustrate how regional efforts have solved disease problems, produced

[1] Paper No. 2765 of the Journal Series of the North Carolina State University Agricultural Experiment Station, Raleigh, North Carolina 27607.

outstanding crop varieties and hybrids, and led to the adoption of entirely new agricultural technologies. Innovative use of germ plasm and modification of the germ plasm and the microenvironment to utilize the genotype-environment interaction has been stressed in these accomplishments.

Most agricultural research programs with the objective of increased utilization of plant and soil resources are long-range. A few political and historical points have influenced our thinking in establishing and operating plant improvement programs in underdeveloped areas. The philosophy under which such programs have been established has, in most cases, determined a restricted biological concept of what should be done and how it might be accomplished.

The rediscovery of Mendel's laws of heredity in 1900 and the statistical design of experiments put plant breeding on a scientific basis in which the results often followed a predictable pattern. Associated sciences in biology and concomitant advances in agricultural and industrial technology led to enormous increases in U.S. agricultural production, beginning in the 1930's and reaching staggering proportions in the following years. Our subsequent technical assistance programs were based largely upon this experience and upon the educational training and philosophic system of a highly industrialized and successful country in a temperate zone.

In this context, we have repeatedly tried to introduce our technology and varieties into other countries as crash programs of relatively short-term duration, often meeting with failure. In some instances, we tried our own varieties even where the plant had originated or in the center of genetic diversity, as in the introduction of U.S. potatoes and corn hybrids into the American tropics. That this would not work was readily apparent, but the organizational system was not conducive to many alternatives.

International development is a nebulous term, and its meaning seems to reflect the opinion, interest, and profession of the beholder. The literature is of such prodigious nature that an authority can be found to substantiate almost any viewpoint. This being the case, I call forth the brothers Paddock (1964), Theodore W. Schultz (1965), and W. David Hopper (1968). If a synthesis of their writings can be formulated, it is this: *Agricultural potential is a prime resource and as such must be transformed from a traditional way of life into a dynamic conglomerate of agribusiness, beginning now with quick payoff items of improved seeds and cultural practices based on research. Other things can come later.* This seems to be realistic. The infrastructure in other sectors can come later, since their usefulness and economic return are incongruous in the midst of prolonged and widespread famines. The President's Science Advisory Committee Report on "The World Food Problem" (1967), probably the most comprehensive study made, concluded:

"1. The scale, severity, and duration of the world food problem are so great that a massive, long-range, innovative effort unprecedented in human history will be required to master it.

"2. The solution of the problem that will exist after about 1985 *demands* that programs of population control be initiated now. For the immediate future, the food supply is critical.

"3. Food supply is directly related to agricultural development and, in turn, agricultural development and overall economic development are critically interdependent in the hungry countries.

"4. A strategy for attacking the world food problem will, of necessity, encompass the entire foreign economic assistance effort of the United States in concert with other developed countries, voluntary institutions, and international organizations."

The changing currents of emphasis in development programs over the past twenty years have illustrated many errors of policy, judgment, and execution. From these and a host of other ills, we have learned, hopefully, that success is difficult, perhaps unattainable, under the tenets of any one particular profession, and probably doomed with a policy of one-year to two-year personnel and funding in any or all sectors. However, there has been, over this same twenty-year period, an outstanding example of continuous and concentrated effort—that of the cooperative agricultural programs of the Rockefeller Foundation. Many of the examples and data from these programs will be used in this presentation.

Substantial increases in food supply are possible in the near future and over the long term. In discussing germ plasm resources and utilization, some distinction is needed between germ plasm utilization in the broadest sense; i.e., the policy of a government for total development which might require several generations, and that use which must stave off the impending famines during the last quarter of this century. Procedures for the two courses of action would be different but would both be based upon demonstrated biological principles. In the end, progress will depend upon a thorough knowledge of each agricultural species, its variability and evolution, environmental conditions under which the plants will or will not grow, and the manipulation of any or all of these factors.

FROM NEOLITHIC MAN TO THE IRISH FAMINE

Mangelsdorf (1966) has estimated that man has used 3,000 or more plant species

for food and cultivated at least 150 species to the extent that they have entered into commerce. This same authority states that of these, about fifteen species of plants actually feed the world. "These include five cereals: rice, wheat, corn, sorghum, and barley; two sugar plants: sugar cane and sugar beets; three 'root' crops: potato, sweet potato, and cassava; three legumes: the common bean, soybean, and peanut; and the two so-called tree crops: the coconut and banana."

These crops and others have long been associated with man. The earliest records, from about nine thousand years ago at Jarmo in the Iraqi Kurdistan, indicate the reaping and grinding of two-row barley and two forms of wheat by the villagers (Braidwood, 1960). Plant domestication was advanced, although plant selection had not been carried far. The paleo-ethnobotanical studies of Helbaek (1959) have shown the effect of man's early migrations on distribution of useful plants and animals. While field peas, lentils, and vetch types were found at Jarmo, it is not certain that they were domesticated at that early date. However, by 5000 B.C., flax was grown in the foothills of the Kurdish mountains and the plains of Mesopotamia and Egypt. Between the third and fourth millennium B.C., lentils were in Egypt and Hungary, and Swiss deposits have yielded pea and vetchling remains. The horse bean was in the Mediterranean area between 3000 and 2000 B.C. and had arrived in Britain by the first millennium B.C. Thus, with the domestication, selection, and transport of plants and animals, Stone Age man began the Agricultural Revolution. By continuing this process, moving to more fertile areas, increasing productivity, and accumulating surpluses, the people of southern Mesopotamia had begun to support an urban civilization. We still return to this fertile crescent for collecting germ plasm. Many of the wheats and their wild relatives are endemic there. The remarkable accomplishments of late Stone Age man in domesticating plants may never be equaled. Their agriculture built a civilization. Now, oddly, our civilization must build an agriculture.

With the possible exceptions of the bread wheats and some of the leguminous pulses, the major crop plants listed in Table 34-1 were domesticated by Neolithic man (Harlan, 1956). Furthermore, with the probable exception of the pumpkin, *none* of these crops is indigenous to the United States. The agriculture of the United States, the most productive in the world, is based on introduced plants. Not one of the commercially important crops is native to this country. Peanuts and soybeans are recent introductions, and in many areas of the country the soybean is now pushing corn from its foremost position.

Man, in his migrations and travels, has introduced food plants into new areas ever since he became an agriculturist. Many of his plantings were complete failures or, at best, limited successes; but over many hundreds of years natural selection, coupled

with mass selections for desired types, has resulted in the widespread cultivation of several kinds of plants. Thus, rice and millets spread throughout Asia and Africa. The small grains were taken from the fertile crescent of the Middle East to many areas of the Old World. In the New World, corn, potato, and bean culture expanded throughout the hemisphere. The exploitation of the Americas and the circumnavigation of the globe led to a flurry of plant interchange which is still going on.

Introductions from the New World to the Old have had many successes and often unexpected results. The importation of the white potato from South America to Europe contributed indirectly to the large number of Irish immigrants to this country. The spectacular growth of the potato in Ireland led to its becoming a staple; people had more to eat than ever; and the population increased. Then a fungus, for which the introduced potato had no resistance, struck and wiped out the potato plants. The Irish Potato Famine drove many people to American shores.

Table 34–1

A LIST OF SOME MAJOR CROP PLANTS
(After Harlan, 1956)

Gramineae	Solanaceae
Wheats, bread wheat, emmer, einkorn	Potato
Rice	Tobacco
Corn	Tomato, pepper, eggplant
Sugar cane	Cucurbitaceae
Sorghum	Pumpkins, melons, etc.
Barley	Euphorbiaceae
Millets, eleusine, teff, other grains	Cassava
Forages, thatch bamboo	Convolvulaceae
Leguminosae	Sweet potato
Soybeans	Malvaceae
Beans, common, mung, lima, etc.	Cotton
Chick-pea	Palmaceae
Cowpea	Coconut
Garden pea	Date
Lentil	Musaceae
Peanut	Banana
Alfalfa, clover, others	Plantain

PLANT IMPROVEMENT, VARIABILITY, AND DISAPPEARING GERM PLASM

That man was able to introduce crops to new areas and make selections of more desirable types was due to variability. To succeed, a breeding program must be based upon variability. Without variation, there would be nothing to select for except new mutations—every plant would be the same. A breeder, therefore, must be concerned about the natural variation of a crop, its geographic origin, and its entry route—either by related species or direct transport. He must know of the primary centers of diversity and origin, as well as secondary centers of diversity. These centers are the fountainhead of genetic material from which plant improvement will succeed or fail.

Plant improvement, per se, is generally based on the inherent variation of genetic or inherited traits within a species and its relatives. Plant production is based on the genetic potential within a strain or variety, the environment in which that plant is grown, and the interaction of that genetic potential with various environmental factors. In other words, the performance of a plant is a function of its genetic make-up and the environment.

Plant improvement or genetic progress is limited by the genetic variability of the species and its relatives and further limited by the methods employed to manipulate the variability at our disposal. To increase variability, collections have usually been obtained by sporadic and insufficient expeditions and by correspondence with collaborators around the world. From such collections, which represent a fraction of the species variability *in toto,* only a few introductions which superficially have the best characteristics are selected and incor-

porated into breeding programs. If the introduced material does not flower because of poor response to photoperiod, or if it is attacked by one of the prevalent diseases or pests, or if it just doesn't look good, it is often discarded. If interest in a particular entry is not high, the collection is also often lost by poor shelf life of the seed. For cross-pollinated plants, the proof of the parent is its progeny, and yet, a great deal of material has been discarded on the basis of parental appearance.

Harlan (1956) gives an excellent example of the value of collections and what happens when they are not maintained. The melon industry was seriously threatened by attacks of mildew. At the growers' insistence that something be done, a project was established for the exploration and assemblage of a world collection. Mildew-resistant sources were found and the susceptible types were discarded. "After a period of breeding to introduce resistance into types that produced, shipped, and marketed well and which received good public acceptance, the problem was, in fact, rather satisfactorily solved. No sooner had the bulk of the susceptible material been thrown away than attacks of a virus began to threaten the industry. Much of the material had to be assembled a second time, and the entire procedure repeated to solve this problem. If, in the process of breeding for virus resistance the second collection is largely discarded, then still a third collection will no doubt be required to solve the next problem that comes up." Many difficulties are encountered in maintaining a world collection. Individual plants may require a lot of space, and controlled pollination may be necessary to maintain the integrity of the varieties.

Harlan (1956) continues, "Plant exploration is relatively inexpensive, and it may be that the procedure just mentioned is really the most economical and efficient. Unfortunately, the geographic centers of diversity upon which we have depended so much in the past for our sources of germ plasm are in great danger of extinction. Modern agriculture and modern technology are spreading rapidly around the world. . . ." New fertilizer-responsive and high-yielding varieties are replacing old mixed or unresponsive populations that have been grown. in some countries, for two thousand to five thousand years. Harlan (1956) says of his exploration in southern Turkey during 1958: ". . . I found great acreages of flax planted to a single variety. It was a selection of Argentine origin resistant to rust. From one end of Cilicia to the other I could not find a single indigenous variety, although this very area had at one time been a center of diversity for flax."

Another illustration is from Colombia's Cauca Valley—roughly the size of Puerto Rico. In its deep, rich, level soil, a corn race called Común had been grown for many, many years. Yet in 1960, only ten years after the Rockefeller Foundation and the Colombian Ministry of Agriculture initiated their agricultural program in that country, we could find only three small plantings of this variety. I have recently been told that the variety is presently not planted by any farmers; it has been replaced completely by improved varieties and hybrids (Climaco Cassalett D., personal communication). In this case, however, the germ plasm had been collected and preserved, as one of the first steps in developing the Colombian corn program.

When the Rockefeller Foundation began its cooperative corn program with the Mexican and Colombian governments, it was readily apparent that a survey of the indigenous maize varieties was needed to serve as an inventory of available material for breeding. Out of this work and the interest of the National Academy of Sciences–National Research Council, funds were made available for the collection and preservation of as many native varieties of

corn as possible (Clark, 1956). These are now preserved in germ plasm banks in Brazil, Colombia, Mexico, and the United States, and total more than twelve thousand collections. They represent what was deemed best to serve the indigenous needs of a traditional agriculture from sea level to 3,810 meters elevation near Lake Titicaca in Bolivia and Peru, from the dry tropics to those areas having rainfall up to 11,000 mm (Patiño, 1956) along the west coast of Colombia, and from lat. 45° S. near Chiloé Island in Chile to almost lat. 50° N. on the Gaspé Peninsula of New Brunswick, Canada.

The value of these collections is readily apparent in the simple fact that they are already irreplaceable. Land reform, social changes, and new agricultural technology have altered the land-use patterns so radically in the fifteen or twenty years since the collections were made, that they could not be duplicated. For example, an improved variety of the Mexican corn Tuxpeño was released in northern Honduras in 1963, and by the end of 1964 the native varieties had almost disappeared (Rockefeller Foundation, 1964–1965). Thus, the germ plasm banks in which the collections are stored and maintained are already serving their purpose, as a repository of readily available living material. From this source of material, exceptionally high resistance to the type of destructive corn rust prevalent in Kenya was found in a Colombian variety (Grant et al., 1963). Other areas where Latin American corns have been useful include Algeria, India, the Philippines, and Thailand. In addition to preserving genes for disease and insect resistance, the germ plasm banks contain varieties capable of producing vastly increased yields as shown in Table 34–2. Here, crosses of an Ecuadorian and Colombian variety produced yield increases of 51 and 44 percent, respectively over the recommended and generally grown corn variety. In Kenya, the

Kitale II and Ecuador 573 material is now being used in a sophisticated breeding scheme to utilize the genetic diversity of the two varieties and additional improvement in yield has been made (M. M. Harrison, unpublished material).

Table 34–2

GRAIN YIELD OF LOCAL AND EXOTIC (LATIN AMERICAN) CORN VARIETIES AND CROSSES

	kg/ha.	YIELD IN % OF LOCAL VARIETY
Kenya (22)		
Kitale II	3900	100
Ecuador 573	2780	71
Kitale II x Ecu. 573	5900	151
Indonesia (38)		
Indian variety x		
Colombian variety	6528	144
Recommended variety	4519	100

When the collections were begun in Mexico and compared for productivity, disease resistance, and other agronomic characteristics, the need was apparent to bring taxonomic order out of a bewildering array of diversity. With additional study it became possible to delineate similarities and relationships among these varieties and to group them into definable and recognizable natural races. This outstanding work was published as "Races of Maize in Mexico" (Wellhausen *et al.*, 1952). From that experience, similar collections were deemed necessary throughout the Western Hemisphere. This effort led to a series of monographs which, taken together, attempt to define and reduce to workable levels a cultivated crop upon which several civilizations had been built (see References, Races of Maize in Latin America).

LEAVES OF GRASS

Maize and the other cereal grasses produced over 1 billion tons of grain in 1965. The forage grasses supported over 2.75 billion animals (FAO, 1966). The grass family truly replenishes the world's feedbag.

It has been estimated that grasslands compose 24 percent of the earth's vegetative cover (Shantz, 1954). However, the grasses are geographically ubiquitous. In addition to their dominance in prairies and steppes, they are also found in forests, swamps, and deserts. As a group, they are noteworthy in their ability to adapt themselves to diverse ecological conditions.

". . . It is a far cry indeed from tropical forests where grasses constitute less than 0.5% of the ground cover—and this mainly where some natural or artificial breakage has occurred in the tree canopy—to the prairies and pampas where grasses may make up 99.5% of the ground cover. In the former, the grasses appear to have little obvious ecological significance; in the latter, they are dominant and determine both the aspect and the economics of the vegetation" (Hartley, 1964).

The ecological factors determining the occurrence of natural grasslands are still debated, and apparently vary among regions and types of grassland. Whether grasslands develop within very broad climatic limits ". . . is determined by many other factors, including microclimate (especially as affected by local topography), soil differences, and the effects of fire and grazing. Since these factors operate differently from place to place, and indeed from time to time, it is hardly surprising that no very satisfactory general relationship has been determined between climate and grassland development, and it is questionable whether tropical grasslands, at least, can be regarded as climatically controlled . . ." (Hartley, 1964).

One of the problems in plant introduction is in deciding which regions are most likely to contain useful material. Several schemes based on agroclimatic homologues have been devised and suggested as guides for introduction (Nuttonson, 1948; Prescott *et al.,* 1952). These have generally been derived from temperature and rainfall patterns, day-degrees, length of growing season, and day length. An agrostological index has also been formulated based on relative frequencies of grass species to determine the climatic and ecological conditions of a given region (Hartley, 1954). From this, agroclimatic or bioclimatic homologues have been used for purposes of plant introduction. At the tribe level and in early phases of an intro-duction program they have been useful, e.g., in Australia. There are weaknesses in the system, and at the generic and spe-cific levels these schemes are not highly successful. The large amounts of genetic diversity within a genus or species, respond-ing to various climatic and ecological con-ditions, negates the generalities of the above approaches. For example, 360 species of grasses have been found in North Carolina (Blomquist, 1948). They represent 13 of the 14 tribes of grasses of the world. How-ever, there are 97 species of *Panicum* and 22 species of *Paspalum* (33 percent of the grasses in the state) from one tribe which is tropical in its origin and affinities. Yet one of the most promising experimental forage introductions in the state, *Pennise-tum flaccidum,* originates from the Hima-layan foothills at elevations from 1,600 to 4,300 meters. To my knowledge, it has never been used anywhere as a seeded pas-ture, and only one accession has been in-troduced to the United States (Chatterji and Timothy, 1969). *Pennisetum* is a trop-ical genus, and except for the above collec-tion, we have found only one other species in the genus that can survive the winters of North Carolina and is suitable for animals. Other examples illustrate that ecological and environmental generalizations, while helpful, are not sufficiently reliable to be used with any degree of confidence in agri-cultural development programs, except in very preliminary stages. *Dactylis,* orchard

grass, is usually thought of as a widely dispersed temperate grass used in Europe and the northeastern United States, flowering once early in the growing season and grow-ing from basal tillers. Yet there is a sub-species from the Canary Islands which has branched stems, initiates flowers from axil-lary buds, and has truly biennial or peren-nial stems. It flowers almost continuously during the growing season and is killed by frost.

No predictive process or index will serve in lieu of on-site or adaptive research. In some cases, successful introduction appears to be a hit-or-miss situation, as in the pre-vious example. One reason for this is the enormous plasticity within a genus and a species, readily apparent when the adaptive range of a cultivated species is considered. This range is due to genetic variability, which may be considerable within many locally adapted populations. Additional variation as a consequence of genotype-environment interactions is expressed when rooted cuttings are placed under various environmental conditions (Cooper, 1954; McMillan, 1965).

THE WILD SEED

The seed-sown cultivated food plants may sometimes be seen as escapes in weed patches and disturbed sites for a few sea-sons, but they cannot persist outside the artificial environment that man has created for them and for which they have been selected and bred. They cannot persist with-out man's aid even in the areas where the crop has supposedly originated. It appears, in fact, that "degree of domesticity" might be expressed as a gradient of the inability to escape cultivation and form a part of the vegetative succession. It also follows that the number of life cycles that a crop is associated with man is related to domestic-ity. Thus, some of the tuber and root crops such as the potato and *manihot* are not as many generations removed from the wild state as corn; the forage grasses perhaps are even less removed.

The forage grasses, as a group, escape to adjacent sites, subsequently disperse to wider areas, and establish themselves as an integral part of the natural system, persisting in favorable niches in one or more of the vegetational levels of succession. Examples of this in the United States are Kentucky bluegrass, *Poa* sp.; orchard grass, *Dactylis;* tall fescue grass, *Festuca;* Johnson grass, *Sorghum;* Bermuda grass, *Cynodon;* and in South America, Kikuyu grass, *Pennisetum;* and guinea grass, *Panicum.* Some of these introduced grasses have become so successful and ubiquitous as to be declared noxious weeds. However, cultigens of these same species form a major part of the beef and dairy industries of many of those same areas.

From the ecological point of view, flowering and seed production are a response to any one or a combination of factors, such as photoperiod, temperature, or rainfall. In any given locality, ecotypes which best conform to local conditions have been selected for years or centuries. The ecology of such natural populations is entirely different from that of a cultivated monoculture of a food plant. Yet while most of the pasture grasses have not been completely domesticated, we attempt to impose upon them a set of biological conditions which have been used in growing our highly domesticated and cultivated food plants. In spite of this, a few highly productive grasses do well as cultigens. A common feature of these grasses is that there has been a mechanism for feral escape. Some are closely related to cultivated cereals, and gene exchange between the forage grass and the domesticated food plant is evident. Others are asexually propagated. By using such grasses, we take advantage of ecological and physiological processes favoring intensive monoculture and

man's needs, rather than be thwarted by a natural system favoring species perpetuation.

FORAGES FOR FEED

Cultivated grasses are found well outside the climatic limits of their natural distribution. The cultivation process alters the genetic composition of the population and the environment, and the plants are not as dependent on the natural environment for growth and survival. Of perhaps 10,000 grass species, only about 40 are important as cultivated pasture grasses, and these are widely used outside their limits of natural distribution. Many consistent grasses of the world have not been successful domesticates. They have evolved along with grazing animals. Their environment, at least when compared to cultivated grasses, is relatively stable. The grasses most successful as domesticates have been those occurring naturally in and around forest margins and woodlands. These areas are often sites disturbed by flooding and washing, fire, uprooted trees, etc., and can be considered as floristic and ecological transition zones. The grasses forming part of such subclimax zones are opportunistic and aggressive, a highly desirable trait for any pasture grass.

The use of intensely managed pastures is a relatively new innovation of man and has been going on for only a few hundred years, but the advances made with the grasses of temperate climates have been notable. Many of the *Phleum, Festuca, Dactylis, Bromus,* and *Poa* have been developed under the rigors of intensive agriculture, notably in Europe. Intensive grassland agriculture in tropical or subtropical areas has been nonexistent until the last fifty to one hundred years. Are we so naive to conclude that we have been as efficient in a century or so of selecting, domesticating, and improving wild forage grasses as our forebears who, since the dawn of man, selected, domesticated, and improved our food crops? I believe not. The exploitation of natural ranges on an extensive basis is another matter. But, assuming that we have not exhausted the possibilities of finding new domesticates of forage grasses for intensive management, how do we go about it? It is impossible to collect and preserve everything, yet every year that we delay, more of the marginal and transitional ecological areas in which many of the subclimax grasses can be found are disappearing under increased agricultural pressures.

It is interesting to speculate what we might be able to obtain from forages if they were as developed in the "cultivated" sense as are our food crops. The latter are cultivated in an ecosystem of harmony between the genotype and environment. Elephant grass (or Napier grass), *Pennisetum purpureum,* is not highly domesticated. However, under excellent growing conditions it will yield over 270 tons of green fodder per hectare (Vicente-Chandler *et al.,* 1964; Whyte *et al.,* 1959). Unfortunately, tonnage alone is not of paramount importance. An important criterion of feeding value is total digestible nutrients (TDN). Using a TDN value of 15 percent of the green weight (Morrisson, 1940), elephant grass yielded 40.5 tons of TDN per hectare in the above example. The percentage of TDN for flint corn with ripe kernels, 28.5 percent is appreciably higher than that for elephant grass (Morrisson, 1940) but total TDN per hectare is less because of lower corn yields. For example, two crops of corn yielding 60 tons of silage per harvest would yield 34.2 tons of TDN. In terms of grain, such a yield would approximate 600 bushels of grain per acre, truly phenomenal. Yields of this quantity are not yet possible. Presently, 30 tons of silage per harvest are attainable and 40 tons might be anticipated in the future. These calculations are subject to serious criticism; they do, however, illustrate that forages are usually overlooked in develop-

ment planning and are also mismanaged at the production level.

Dairy production is usually limited to some degree of intensive management. Beef production is relegated to areas of marginal land or land which can be put to no other use, and it is managed in an extensive fashion. This does not necessarily have to be so. On steep clay hillsides in the humid mountain area of Puerto Rico, an average gain of over one ton of beef per hectare was produced experimentally on elephant grass (Vicente-Chandler *et al.,* 1964) to which about one ton per hectare of 14–8–4 fertilizer was applied, with grazing on a three-week rotation. Similar intensively managed grass pastures in this area are being used in commercial operations. "On one farm . . . heavily fertilized, intensively managed guineagrass, pangolagrass, and napiergrass pastures are carrying two steers per acre in the winter and three steers throughout the remainder of the year, and producing close to 1,000 pounds of gain in weight per acre yearly" (Vicente-Chandler *et al.,* 1964).

The key here is intensive management based on adaptive concurrent research with forages and animals. It is expensive research in terms of land, animals, and personnel. Cattlemen are notoriously poor agronomists, and agronomists are equally poor animal scientists, so the requirements for team research are essentially doubled in terms of personnel inputs. The philosophic differences of the agronomist and animal scientists, as ancient as the conflict between nomad and agriculturist, are not breached in most plans for development. Most of the research is on animals or on forages, but very little is on animals and forages. Just as plant breeders select varieties for response to fertilizers, it seems logical that animals might be selected which respond better to forages than to concentrates. Too much animal selection has been practiced using diets of high-energy concentrates. One hopes that, when the concentrates are needed to feed people, the animals will perform equally well on a roughage diet. The present situation has been promulgated in the United States by surplus grain, with prices such that grain can be fed economically. What the future holds is unknown, but on land not amenable for intensive and repetitive cultivation, forages and cattle can be used. It is a matter of determining how to use them best in any particular region.

BORLAUG AND THE SEMI-DWARFS

Food needs over the next several decades will not wait the fifteen to twenty-five years required to develop a corps of trained scientists in sufficient numbers to solve the problem. However, while personnel are being trained, interim programs of adaptive research can be initiated with experienced scientists and available germ plasm. Of the several outstanding examples of this approach, the most noteworthy is that involving Dr. Norman E. Borlaug of the Rockefeller Foundation, the International Maize and Wheat Improvement Center (CIMMYT), and Pakistani scientists and officials. Borlaug's account (1968) of this program with the twenty years' work in Mexico which preceded it, and subsequent programs in other countries is required reading for anyone interested or involved in producing more food. I have drawn freely from his presentation.

In 1961 and 1962, several young Pakistani wheat scientists who had received practical training in Mexico returned to their country with many small samples of dwarf wheats from the Mexican program. Some of these were released varieties and others were still in the experimental stages. The best adapted germ plasm was selected for further research and seed increase. "Perhaps 75 to 80% of the research done in Mexico on cultural practices and fertilizers was valid in Pakistan. Research done in Pakistan while the imported seed was being mutiplied provided the necessary information to cover those gaps where the Mexican data were not valid" (Borlaug, 1968). In addition to improved germ plasm capable of responding to 120 kilos of nitrogen per hectare (the older varieties showed no response above 50 kilos of nitrogen because of lodging), an entire new technology was introduced as a package to the farmer. Within the package were included proper land preparation, date of seeding, depth of seeding, time and rate of fertilizer application, herbicide and pesticide use, etc. Perhaps just as important was that the scientists and extension people could and would do these things because they had been trained to do so. During the 1964–1965 season, 10 hectares were planted with the Mexican wheats, 11,000 in 1966–1967, and 3,000,000 in 1967–1968. But what has happened to wheat production during this time? It rose from a previous high of 4.6 million tons in 1965 to an estimated 7 million tons in 1968 (Borlaug, 1968). Borlaug estimates that 43 percent of this harvest was due to the dwarf varieties and new technology, which were used on only 20 percent of the acreage sown to wheat. National average yields rose in the last year from 802 kilos per hectare to 1,167 kilos per hectare.

"Pakistan has achieved self sufficiency in three years after launching its accelerated wheat production programme, whereas it took Mexico 13 years to achieve this result. . . . Moreover, it has the thrust, scientific knowhow, and technology to maintain self sufficiency for the next decade if aggressive leadership and sound fiscal policies are followed. . . . Experience gained in Mexico permitted bolder action in Pakistan, and many of the pitfalls encountered in Mexico were avoided" (Borlaug, 1968). Similar efforts are now being exerted in India, Turkey, and Afghanistan.

It was previously stated that varieties, technique, research, etc., could not be directly transported, and yet the above examples would seem to refute that statement. They do not, however, for several reasons: (1) The programs were directed by experienced, competent, mature scientists who intimately knew the technology needed and the genetic material at their disposal. (2) On-site research was done correctly as a screening procedure. (3) Additional on-site research was done to fill gaps where "transplanted" procedures or technique were not applicable.

Behind all this was twenty years of research in the Mexican wheat program. Many of the wheats in that program are now insensitive to photoperiod. In addition, they are widely adapted to other environmental conditions. To speed up the breeding procedure for improved varieties, two generations of selection are practiced in Mexico. The winter nurseries are in Sonora at lat. 28° N., a few meters above sea level, and grown in the winter. The second generation is seeded in May near Toluca at 2600 m. elevation and lat. 18° N. (Borlaug, 1968). At the winter nurseries, day length is about 10.4 hours on November 21 and then decreases to 10.2 on December 21. It begins to *increase* in succeeding months to 10.4, 11.1, and 12.0 hours. Near Toluca, day length is 13 hours on May 21, increasing to 13.2 hours on June 21, then decreasing each succeeding month to 13.0, 12.6, and 12.0 hours.

DISEASES AND PESTS

There are two growing seasons each year in many areas of the tropics and two generations in a breeding program are possible. Differences between the two seasons are often consistent because of day length, temperature, rainfall distribution, etc. In spite of this, continuous and serial selection for yield and other characteristics, without regard to seasonal differences, will broaden the range of adaptability of the selectants surviving the screening process. There is increasing evidence that homeostasis (a kind of physiological buffering system enabling the organism to perform equally well under reasonable environmental differences) occurs in plants. The opposite viewpoint advocates two separate selection programs each year, one for the first season and another during the second. This might increase yields at the research farms because the selectants would be more environment-specific, but their adaptation would be appreciably reduced. Furthermore, since it is impossible to breed varieties for the multitudinous environments which exist, it is foolish not to take advantage of a system which will halve the time lag until a variety release is possible. In addition, the life of a variety is relatively short and will vary from three to five years. Perfection in a variety is impossible, so the plant breeder selects and releases the best line or lines available under the circumstances.

The wide-scale use of a newly released variety does not call for the cessation of research for still more varieties. This is especially so with the use of modern cultural methods. Thicker plantings, denser stands, increased rates of fertilization, with or without irrigation, weed-free fields, all combine to create a new ecosystem. The micro-environments within this system may now be more favorable to a new array of disease organisms and insect pests. If the organisms are able to establish and increase to what might be called a critical mass, a crop failure and perhaps famine are just around the corner. This phenomenon will become more important when a single variety or a group of closely related varieties is planted over a wide area. The researchers breeding new lines of corn, rice, or wheat at the international or regional centers are well aware of the danger, and they are continually recording insect and disease damage on breeding material. They are often able to forecast which diseases might become pandemic and then, given time, they change the genetic composition of the variety or release a new one. In some cases, a variety may be on the shelf for just such an event. In others, it may be necessary to screen the collections in the germ-plasm banks to find the necessary tolerance or resistance and then to incorporate the resistance into an acceptable agronomic variety.

Just as man is stricken by different strains of influenza or encephalitis, so, too, are plants infected by different strains or races of disease. The causal organism of wheat stem rust has many different physiological races, expressed by their degree of pathogenicity on a set of differential host varieties. Once a race becomes established, its prevalence is determined by favorable environmental conditions and the varieties being grown. Changes in race structure of the rust population can be very rapid. However, the devastating attacks of rust are not as capricious as they appear to be, once the underlying causes are known.

The wheat rust epidemic in 1916 destroyed about 300 million bushels of wheat in the United States and Canada (Stakman and Harrar, 1957). Rust-resistant durum wheats were substituted for the susceptible hard red spring wheats. New rust races soon appeared, and the durums were then vulnerable. In 1926 a new wheat was released, and in 1928 rust race 56 began to appear. It caused the rust epidemic of 1935. Beginning in 1934, a series of wheats resistant to the major rust races was released, and except for 1935 and 1937 there was no serious outbreak of rust for many years. "These new varieties were highly resistant to all the North American races of rust. During this period the number of prevalent races decreased to three or four, and no major epiphytotics occurred" (Allard, 1960). But during this time small quantities

of several rust races had been observed on or near the pathogen's alternate host, barberry. One of these races, 15 B, observed since 1938 in the northern United States, ". . . suddenly exploded in the United States and Canada in the summer of 1950 and ruined late fields of varieties that had been immune for almost a decade. High winds carried race 15 B into Mexico in the fall of 1950; it survived the winter on fall-sown wheat in a few places, then multiplied fast on spring-sown wheat in the exceptionally wet summer of 1951. . . . Race 15 B had smashed the Hope and Newthatch types of resistance" (Stakman *et al.,* 1967).

The necessity of having diverse samples of germ plasm available in a breeding program was readily apparent in 1951. "Some 60,000 varieties and lines from the Mexican program and another 6,000 from the World Wheat Collection of the United States Department of Agriculture were grown and evaluated" at four locations in Mexico. "In this vast test, only four varieties grown commercially in North America were resistant to stem rust, and all were Mexican made . . . and they all have Kenya-type resistance" (Stakman *et al.,* 1967).

Unexpectedly, race 139, known for twenty years, struck these varieties in 1953. This race had been rare and ". . . unimportant practically, although it had excited curiosity because of its exceptionally weak parasitism and its persistence in minute quantities in northern Mexico. But it now demonstrated far more strength than it had shown previously; it knocked out varieties that the generally stronger race 15 B could not hurt. Race 139 (and possibly the closely related 49) had the weapons for breaking through the Kenya-type resistance, just as 15 B had the weapons for breaking through the Hope and Newthatch resistance.

"But stem rust was not yet finished. Races 29 and 48, long known in certain areas of the United States but not in Mexico, made threatening gestures in 1953, provoking Borlaug to write in 1954: 'The varieties now being grown commercially must be replaced by newer varieties with different types of stem rust resistance. This is necessitated by three major changes in rust races which have occurred since 1950. . . . Varieties resistant to some or all of these races, as well as to the races formerly prevalent, have been developed by the cooperative program. . . . The constant shifting in population of stem rust races illustrates the necessity of a continuous breeding program to combat this parasite which is constantly a threat to the wheat crop' " (Stakman *et al.*, 1967).

THE REGIONAL APPROACH

Another dramatic illustration of the need to preserve diversity and to use it wisely is available from rice (Chandler, 1968). In 1962 the average rice yield in Southeast Asia was about 1,500 kilograms per hectare, while Japan was producing about 5,000 kilograms per hectare. Research was obviously needed, and the International Rice Research Institute began collecting germ plasm and crossing types which had various desirable attributes. From among the hundreds of segregants of the eighth cross, they selected the now famous IR-8. One of its parents was a semi-dwarf variety from Taiwan and the other was a tall variety developed in Indonesia. IR-8 was semi-dwarf and fertilizer-responsive, enabling it to utilize fertilizer without lodging. It was highly tillered and had upright leaves which permitted more heads per plant and more efficient light interception. Equally important, it was insensitive to photoperiod and could be planted at low elevations within the tropics around the world. The wide adaptability of IR-8 and the versatility of some of the improved varieties from Taiwan have been demonstrated in Africa, Asia, and Latin America.

Yields of 4,000 to 6,000 kilograms per hectare are not uncommon, and yields over 10,000 kilograms per hectare have been obtained (Chang, 1967).

The success of the rice program has been due primarily to the isolation and use of two genetic systems. Genetic studies indicate the semi-dwarf character is controlled by a single major recessive gene and modified slightly by minor genes. By putting the gene in a homozygous condition and selecting progenies with appropriate modifiers, a range of short-statured plants can be obtained. The shortest types could then be used where water control and cultural management were very precise. The taller forms of the semi-dwarfs might be recommended in other areas where water control was less precise or erratic and cultural practices less refined (Aquino and Jennings, 1966). Photoperiod insensitivity is the other genetic system, and it contributes immeasurably to the adaptability of the varieties. Sensitivity to photoperiod is apparently controlled by one or two dominant genes (Chang, 1967).

Varieties containing these two genetic systems can be used as a base for further improvement and environment-specificity within a country. In Colombia, for example, rice is grown from near sea level in the Sinu Valley along the northern coast to over 1,000 meters elevation in the Cauca Valley. Climatic factors, while similar, are sufficiently different to affect most crops. Mean annual temperature differs by only 2° C; at the lower altitude the mean is 28° C; and the humidity is oppressively high to many people. By contrast, the Cauca Valley has a comparatively salubrious and invigorating climate. Both areas have a bimodal rainfall distribution. By contrast, the grassland plains of the Llanos, extending eastward from the foothills of the Eastern Cordillera into Venezuela, have one rainfall period per year.

Biotic differences among these three areas are great indeed. Fertility deficiencies can be ameliorated largely by fertilizers. Climatic differences in the environment are vast. For practical purposes, field beans cannot be grown in the Sinu. Also, the complex of disease organisms on corn is distinct in that area. From this, and all past experience in plant breeding, it is almost a foregone conclusion that different varieties of rice eventually will be grown in these three areas. The varieties might differ in reaction to a range of insect or disease organisms. They might also differ in maturity or response to heat by having different rates of respiration. In any case, better-performing varieties than the widely adapted IR-8 type can be created for more environment specificity or ecological specificity. With proper cultural procedures, three crops a year may be possible.

From these examples we might conclude that science can be transported. The technology or applied science, however, cannot be transported per se, but must be adapted to fit the myriad conditions in which it will be used. This has been the key to success with the rice and wheat varieties emanating from the research centers in Mexico and the Philippines, where the variety remained constant and cultural conditions were modified. In corn, photoperiod insensitivity has not yet been found. So, in addition to localized cultural modifications, germ plasm from the large research centers is usually modified at the local level by hybridization. Occasionally a synthetic variety with a broad genetic base can be used without modification in areas not greatly dissimilar to that in which the variety originated. In this case, the heterozygous state of a broad genetic base permits good performance under slightly different environmental conditions. Results with corn have not yet been as spectacular as those with rice and wheat, but as new germ plasm resources are identified and new broad-base gene pools are formed, corn yields will continue to increase.

The agricultural advancements associated with hybrid corn in the United States have been remarkable. Yet, the success of hybrid corn has done a great deal of philosophic harm. It created a condition of hybridomania throughout the world. It is true that hybrids can and should be produced in numerous areas of undeveloped nations. It is equally true that there are other regions where they are unsuitable, such as many of the isolated mountainous zones or lowland fringe areas, or both. Farmers with small landholdings often replant seed from their harvest or sell it to neighboring farmers for planting. This practice greatly reduces yields in the case of hybrid corn. For such areas and conditions, there is a real need for improved varieties or synthetics. These possess a broad genetic base, enabling them to perform well over more varied environmental conditions than can double-cross hybrids. The use of synthetics does not require as sophisticated and elaborate a seed industry for producing and distributing seed as does the use of hybrids. In addition to commercial use, synthetics may also be used as source material for inbreds whenever hybrids are feasible.

Some recent studies have indicated surprisingly high yields of synthetics. In one case, after four cycles of selection, the synthetic yielded 3 percent less than the highest-yielding hybrid developed for the area (Johnson, 1963). In another, the fourth-cycle synthetic yielded only 5 percent less than the hybrid check (Wellhausen, 1965). In both studies, gains in yield were about 10 to 12 percent for each selection cycle. Similar advances are being obtained in Kenya, Ecuador, and Colombia (CIMMYT Report, 1966–1967). The synthetic populations still contain variability, and further advances should be possible.

The heart of these corn programs is the maize germ plasm collection, twenty years of experience, dedicated personnel, and innovation in breeding methods. Varietal crosses have been released as hybrids. Occasionally, when the advanced generation of the cross did not have the usual drastically reduced yields, it was released as a synthetic. Hybrids have been made with lines inbred only one generation—heresy to a classicist, but resulting in improved local yields. Visual selection for multiple ears has resulted in a released variety 20 percent better than the original source. Varietal and racial crosses are widely used, often as a basis for compositing germ plasm for regional programs throughout the world. Experience with these germ plasm pools is such that it will soon be possible to prescribe which pools should be used as an initial base for improvement in specific parts of the world (CIMMYT Report, 1966–1967).

The success of the regional corn programs is notable. Yields have increased slowly and steadily, but without the benefit of the major genes such as stiff straw and photoperiod insensitivity which led to the breakthroughs with wheat and rice. A comparable event or break-through in corn, superimposed on yields already attainable, would be astounding.

These accounts illustrate several important features necessary for successful utilization of germ plasm: First, while a problem may be local, the underlying short-term causes or solutions may be of regional or international interest. Second, the collection of germ plasm available must be sufficiently large to contain a broad base of diversity, thereby giving a reasonably good chance of isolating the desired plant characteristics for incorporation into an acceptable variety. Third, the desired characters are often contained in exotic material. Fourth, success was a result of continuous team effort. A breeder or pathologist or agronomist or soils man alone could not have been successful within the time allotted. Nor could the team effort have been successful in a stop-start series of short-term effort and funding.

Crop yields already attained indicate, to some at least, that we can produce sufficient food over the next quarter century to feed the predicted six or seven billion people. Others believe that associated inputs, such as fertilizers, pesticides, herbicides, etc., cannot be economically produced in the required quantities to make use of known technology and germ plasm. Whatever the outcome, we must depend upon agricultural resources as prime food needs for some time. Short-term prospects for staving off the impending famine over the next several decades must depend upon regional centers such as CIMMYT (International Maize and Wheat Improvement Center) and IRRI (International Rice Research Institute). Others now in operation or contemplated could be listed, but these two are probably the most widely known and serve as excellent examples.

Much of the technology and germ plasm that will determine the fate of millions will originate from these centers. Hopefully, many individual nations will be able, with proper assistance and encouragement, to improve on these techniques and germ plasm. To date, most national programs have demonstrated their inadequacies to solve their food problem. Our foremost hope is that the regional concept is successful. If not, famine appears certain to strike. If successful, we have only bought time until population control can reduce food demands to supply capabilities. Either way, food demands will be increased in the future.

ACALA COTTON AND CUBA CORN

Among biologists, collecting and maintaining germ plasm of cultivated plants is easily understood, appreciated, and justified although justification before budget committees, planners, and legislatures is somewhat more difficult. However, when the uncultivated wild relatives are mentioned, resistance to the program is often impenetrable, unless, of course, a disease or pest is threatening to wipe out the crop and its associated industries.

It is true that we usually don't know the genetic characteristics of wild species or their value for unforeseen circumstances in the future. However, since many of them are in danger of disappearing, it behooves us to collect and preserve them before it is too late. Wild relatives have not been used often, but a few instances of use have resulted in sufficient economic benefit to justify a vigorous program of collection. Several wild diploid (two sets of chromosomes) relatives have been used for bringing disease resistance into commercial tobacco (four sets of chromosomes), *N. longiflora* and *N. plumbaginafolia* for black shank resistance, *N. glutinosa* for mosaic virus resistance and *N. debneyi* for wildfire resistance. Crown rust resistance in oats has been transferred from the 14 chromosome species of wild oats to the commercial 42 chromosome varieties (Sadanaga and Simons, 1960). The commercial tetraploid cotton, TH-149, has increased lint strength which came from a wild diploid, *Gossypium thurberi*. A large portion of the U.S. acreage now is planted with this or similar varieties (L. L. Phillips, personal communication). Yet the increased lint strength came from a wild relative which has no lint, only seed fibers a few millimeters long. There are other examples in sugar cane, melons, potatoes, and forage grasses. The value of collections, as insurance for the future, is difficult to assess. The time when any particular one may be useful is equally obscure. But "a crop worker made a small collection of cottons in Acala, Mexico, in 1906. No one thought much of the collection at the time, and it was only through luck that it was preserved. A single selection . . . developed from this same collection was worth 300 million dollars to California farmers in 1952" (Robertson, 1955).

Preservation of germ plasm, including wild relatives, is too complex to be handled by any single nation. One country might be able to maintain viable material of a portion of the variability, but the ecological requirements of an entire widely spread genus or species are such that many types would be lost through natural selection. The maize germ plasm banks in Brazil, Colombia, Mexico, and the U.S. were organized so that each center was responsible for germ plasm collected within a specified geographical area. Even here, there are serious difficulties. Many of the maize races were highly artificial in that they had been selected by man for specific purposes, e.g. dyes, fermented drink, religious ceremonies, etc. However, that they also were confined to certain environmental limits is undeniable. Some races are restricted in their adaptation to altitude, which is a function of temperature, light intensity, and photoperiod, while others are more flexible (Wellhausen *et al.,* 1952). In Colombia, a race usually grown above 1,800 meters will not produce seed below 1,000 meters. Likewise a race from 0 to 800 meters shows extreme lack of adaptation above 1,800 meters (Roberts *et al.,* 1957). A compensatory effect of latitude and altitude is apparent in that maize from 1,500 meters at 6° N. in Colombia can be moved to 25°–30° N. or S. if used at lower altitudes (Grant *et al.,* 1963). Some, such as Cuba Yellow Flint (Hatheway, 1957), can be used in breeding programs around the world below 1,500 feet and at latitudes 30° or less (Grant *et al.,* 1963). The interrelationships of altitude and latitude are not simple and not clear.

Maize from Chile is stored in the Colombian or Andean Center. Because of photoperiod response, most of the Chilean material cannot be grown and replenished in Colombia, so it must be sent to other areas. The lowland races were grown occasionally in Iowa and Mexico for seed increase and maintenance of germination level. High-altitude Chilean races were grown in the mountains of Mexico. The FAO has recently initiated programs for germ plasm maintenance, in which cognizance is given to the biological requirements of the plant. Early indications with some of the forage grasses are encouraging.

GERM PLASM MAINTENANCE

While it is in the national interest of many governments to maintain broad collections of their most important crops, it is not possible or reasonable for every country to attempt to maintain complete collections of every crop and its relatives. A regional or ecological approach is called for.

Many of the problems associated with germ plasm conservation were discussed at a 1967 Food and Agricultural Organization of the United Nations technical conference on "Exploration, Utilization and Conservation of Plant Gene Resources" in Rome (in press). The conference was in cooperation with the International Biological Program (IBP) subcommittee for Plant Gene Pools on the Use and Management of Biological Resources Section. These organizations and UNESCO have expressed interest and concern and, in some cases, have initiated or aided programs of germ plasm collection and preservation.

The way in which individual lines or samples of germ plasm are maintained is extremely important. Asexually propagated plants (many of the tubers, fruit trees, grapes, sugar canes) have usually been maintained as vegetative stock, although the danger of a virus being spread by cutting is high. Means and feasibility of perpetuating vegetative stocks in national repositories are being discussed (Larson, 1961). It is presently necessary for the interested researcher to maintain his own collection or arrange for new material through correspondence with associates. The efficiency of

such systems is very low and limited by the inability of individuals to collect and maintain sufficient collections.

The seed-sown crops are of two principal categories, based on mode of reproduction: (1) Cross fertilizers, in which the female is pollinated by male gametes from other plants. This system insures that natural populations are in a continual state of hybridization and heterozygosity. (2) Self-fertilizers, where females are pollinated by male gametes from the female parent. Plants in these populations may be genetically identical or a mixture of pure lines. In either case, the genes are generally all in the homozygous condition. However, if a cross has occurred, about 97 percent of all the genes in the population are returned to homozygosity in five generations.

The integrity of the self-fertilized strains is easily maintained by planting each sample in a row and harvesting the seed. Since no crossing has occurred, there will be no recombination. All progeny will resemble the parent.

Cross-pollinators maintained without pollen control beget progeny with half their genes from the female and the other half from various strains throughout the plantings. Half the parentage is unknown. Unfortunately, many of the collections have been maintained in this fashion, especially forages. Pollination control in some species, such as corn, is relatively easy because of flower structure, and those collections have been maintained with a greater degree of integrity.

Ideally, every collection would be maintained as a separate entity, with measures taken to insure its genetic integrity whenever it was planted for increase or maintenance purposes. The expense, facilities, and personnel required for sizable collections of cross-pollinators often preclude exercising the ideal. Furthermore, controlled-pollination progenies are the best indication of a parent's worth. Any decent-sized collection then becomes unmanageable, and complete evaluations are beyond the realm of imagination. The number of possible crosses among n objects is equal to

$$\frac{n(n-1)}{2},$$

or 499,500 crosses for a collection of 1,000 strains. Almost 5 million crosses would be required for 10,000 strains. There are about 12,000 entries in the maize collection, over 3,000 in the cotton collections (S. G. Stephens, personal communication), about 2,000 soybeans (C. A. Brim, personal communication), 18,000 wheats, including released varieties, lines, and collections (C. F. Murphy, personal communication), and 15,000 peanuts (D. A. Emery, personal communication). Although many of these are cross-pollinated, Herculean effort is required to hand-cross the self-pollinators, in order to obtain new genetic recombinations.

Compromise of the ideal with practicality has usually been exercised in germ plasm maintenance. The Andean Maize Germ Plasm Bank in Medellín, Colombia, had, by 1961, received 5,482 indigenous strains from Colombia, Bolivia, Chile, Ecuador, Peru, and Venezuela. A severe strain was placed on facilities, budget, and personnel by maintaining the collections in viable condition and simultaneously carrying on a high-caliber corn improvement program for the entire country. Furthermore, it is not possible to evaluate collections of this size in all environments against all the plagues and vagaries of nature. To facilitate maintenance, evaluation, and use of the germ plasm bank, a biologically systematic compositing of material was begun. The indigenous strains of maize from each Andean country had been classified into races (see References, Races of Maize in Latin America). From an almost unmanageable collection of over 5,000 indigenous strains, 191 races have been described for the Andean zone. Ear and grain character measurements were taken from the original ears grown in their native environment. Physiological, morphological, and chromosome data were obtained in Colombia, Mexico, or Iowa from nurseries at suitable altitudes. Some strains, usually three to five, were chosen as "type" or "typical" examples of a race, and these were individually maintained and increased. Other collections which were equally as representative of the race, were classified as "others." Briefly, the compositing system consisted of mixing together equal numbers of viable seeds (as determined by germination tests) of all collections classified as race "A." Race "A" composite included the "typical" strains as well as the "others." A second mixture was made of those classified as race "B," and so on. Some races contain subgroups differing, for example, in grain color or kernel characteristics. Therefore, if race "C" had both yellow and white grain types, and also flour and flint starch texture, there may have been five different composites made for this race: white flint, yellow flint, white flour, yellow flour, mixed or segregating for starch and color. Likewise, the collections intermediate between races "A" and "B" were composited to form one population of "A-B" germ plasm. The intermediates of "E" and "F" were composited into an "E-F" complex.

This system, which still maintains typical individual collections, permits maintenance of large seed supplies of composite races. Numerous requests from all parts of the world are more easily filled. It also allows more thorough study and evaluation of native races to determine the sources of genes for yield, insect resistance, disease resistance, and other economic characteristics.

Certain races have no immediately apparent economic characteristics but may prove valuable in the future. Other races which look highly desirable do not contribute appreciably to increased yields, while others, extremely undesirable on aesthetic grounds and low yield, exhibit considerable amounts of hybrid vigor when crossed. All these types of corns make up the collections which are the world's only real source of material for the development of superior corns. By growing the races, alone and in crosses, patterns of adaptability and good combining ability emerge. Certain races then become identified by their outstanding performance as varieties. Some are exceptional sources of inbred lines or new variability and diversity at the local and international level. The long-range problem is determining how the really superior corns were made or evolved, then being able to make further improvements.

Understanding more of the evolutionary history of the species and varieties we work with would certainly contribute to more judicious use of exotic germ plasm than the often wasteful and haphazard usage practiced in the past.

APPEARANCE, UNIFORMITY, AND DIVERSITY

There is evidence that good material has complex and diverse origins, although diversity per se is not the answer. The evolutionary histories of truly outstanding germ plasm have similarities which cannot be ignored (Timothy, 1966). There are several examples in maize: the Corn Belt Dents of the United States; the Tuxpeño race from Mexico; Eto from Colombia, the Cuban Yellow Flints. A good example in self-pollinated crops is Composite Cross II in barley. There is even an example from an undomesticated apomictic polyploid perennial forage grass, *Bothriochloa ischaemum*. The essential feature in the formation of these superior gene sources is that after diverse germ plasm had been brought together, no stringent selection for "desirable" types was practiced by man. Natural se-

lection undoubtedly occurred among the various genotypes in the population, but it is a slower process than that exercised by man. There was time for genetic linkages to break up and recombination of genes to occur; time for the different genotypes in the population to reach a state of dynamic equilibrium in which their frequencies fluctuate within certain limits according to environmental conditions. Periodic infusions of new germ plasm may amplify the genetic base, and the process is repeated. Most of the failures in the use of exotic germ plasm are probably due to premature attempts at selection in newly created populations. Another reason for failure in the use of local-exotic crosses is that they have been prematurely discarded on the basis of appearance.

One wonders at the irreparable genetic damage or loss perpetuated over the years for appearance's sake. The old corn shows were marvelous examples of much-ado-about-nothing. Prizes were given for the best-appearing and most uniform corn ears. The prize really went to those who spent the most time sorting through mounds of corn. There was no regard for performance or yield. Many farmers soon realized they could often get better yields from non-show-type corn; and the corn shows, as sources for seed, were soon discontinued. Vestiges of this outmoded, refuted, and useless custom still continue to this day. Walk through the exhibit halls at state fairs. Look in the arenas or show rings where beef, dairy, and swine are judged. The custom has unfortunately been accepted by many underdeveloped countries. Many a show animal, often with unknown prepotency as a sire or performance as a dam, has been imported at a cost of thousands. The animal may win many ribbons, yet be completely unsuited for the environment—and worse, contribute nothing of real value to the herd or country.

When I was director of the Colombian-

Rockefeller Corn Program, our corn was often criticized by visiting U.S. colleagues for being "shaggy" or "lousy" looking. The leaves didn't arch prettily, and the plants were tall with ears high on the plant. Many of the varieties and hybrids had a few diseased leaf spots or pustules, the plants weren't as uniform as those in the States, and so forth. Given an acceptable industrial or comestible quality, the only important matter is really yield—nothing else. It would take five generations to incorporate resistance into a line used for hybrids. In the same five years, an entirely new hybrid with new lines could also be released. Therefore, minor disease and insect reaction were not stressed, especially when the new hybrids would yield more than their predecessors by 15 to 40 percent (unpublished annual reports, Instituto Colombiano Agropecuario, Maize Section). In corn, a hybrid or varietal population is not homozygous, such as is the case with wheat. The implications of disease and insect problems were less important in corn because they were not critical or limiting. The heterozygous state and diverse parental germ plasm of the maize populations were apparently sufficient to prevent the explosive epidemics so common with self-pollinated crops such as wheat.

To many, uniformity is a necessary requirement for appearance, and the way to phenotypic uniformity is through genetic uniformity. This is an erroneous conception leading to restricted germ plasm and the discarding of many genes. Uniformity of phenotype is needed for grain or fruit quality or machine harvesting, and used in varietal identification or seed laws. There also appears to be uniformity for uniformity's sake, perhaps unconsciously from the influence of genetics. Studies of Mendelian genetics require genotypic and phenotypic uniformity. In plant breeding, the more genotypically homogenous the variety becomes, the more it is restricted in its eco-logical tolerances. Performance is also restricted since microenvironment, edaphic, and climatic differences exist within the areas in which a variety is planted. Phenotypically homogeneous populations with genotypic heterogeneity will probably be used more in the future.

The use of double-cross hybrids, three-way hybrids, varietal crosses, and synthetics of cross-pollinated plants also utilize genotypic heterogeneity, although those breeding methods were not developed with that in mind and the point is usually overlooked. Ample evidence favoring genotypic heterogeneity within phenotypic homogeneous populations of cross-pollinators is available in the Colombian corn improvement program. Isolation of inbred lines in open-pollinated varieties begins with a self-pollination. Some of the resulting seed were planted in special crossing blocks to determine the worth of the line. The remaining seed of the line would ordinarily be kept in storage for two planting seasons until the worth of the line was determined by yield tests. Without facilities in the humid tropics, seed storage is difficult, and in some cases, almost impossible. However, we were able to obtain reasonable germination if the seed were not stored for more than one growing season. So my predecessors figured that the only way to maintain the line was to plant it before its worth was known. They developed the following system: In a plot of some sixty plants of the S_1 or first generation inbred line, five of the best-appearing plants were self-pollinated for the S_2 or second inbred generation. Ten to fifteen other plants in the same plot were sib-mated. After harvesting the controlled pollination seed, the five S_2 lines and the S_1-sib_1 line were planted and individually crossed onto a tester to determine the worth of each of the six lines. The process was then repeated. Much of this was lost effort if the original S_1 line was discarded, but there was no alternative, as time was important for the release of improved corn. If, however, the line was selected on the basis of yield trials, we had several different advanced generations on hand to continue. The upshot was that most all lines, perhaps more than 95 percent of those in released or experimental hybrids, did not have many generations of self-pollination in their pedigrees. Furthermore, the self-pollinated generations were usually interspersed and separated by several generations of sib-mating. I have not studied the pedigrees lately, but such was the situation up to 1961.

The most obvious explanation is that self-fertilization and accompanying selection is a very drastic procedure. In each generation one-half of the remaining heterozygous genes are fixed in equal proportions, 25 percent as homozygous recessives and 25 percent as homozygous dominants. Selection of a plant for continued selfing, with a gene in the homozygous recessive state, permanently eliminates the possibility of obtaining the dominant gene in later generations and vice versa. With continued selfing, many genes are essentially eliminated before they can be evaluated. Sib-mating offers a slower approach to homozygosity, and by the system used, there was selection for major genes effecting easily recognized characters. Sib-mating among such plants would tend to delay the fixation and random discarding of many genes effecting quantitative characters. The lines developed by the self-sib system were phenotypically homogeneous but genotypically heterogeneous and in some cases heterozygous. Although these lines did appear to be very uniform, it was possible to select for and fix genes for certain characters in late generations, e.g., grain color, disease and insect reaction, fertility restorers for cytoplasmic sterility. The system also delays the chance discarding of new genetic recombinations which occur as a result of crossing over between linked genes.

Even with self-fertilized crops, considerable evidence indicates that genotypic heterogeneous populations will be widely used in the future (Allard and Jain, 1962; Harlan, 1956; Jensen, 1965; Schutz et al., 1968), although the concept has often been maligned and overlooked. There have been a number of reports where multiline or composite varieties have yielded more than the average of the lines making up the composite. There are also cases where heterogeneous populations yielded more than the highest yielding individual entry (Jensen, 1965; Schutz et al., 1968).

The most striking evidence of the above is from populations composited by bulking F_1 lines, and then seeding and harvesting year after year without rigorous selection. The most notable population, Composite Cross II, of barley, has slowly increased in yield from about 74 percent to 104 percent of a commercially grown variety (Harlan, 1956). This has been over a period of twenty-eight generations, but after the initial crosses were made, no special methods or skills were used. These kinds of populations are extremely variable, even in late generations (Allard and Jain, 1962; Harlan, 1956). At any time they can be sampled for extraction of commercial types. In fact, a significant number of commercial barleys can be traced to such populations, and some selections from the F_{24} generation yielded 56 percent more than the commercial variety, Atlas (Harlan, 1956).

Such populations have enormous adaptability, variability, and potential, but limited by the numbers of crosses which can be made. This problem has recently been circumvented. The "American collection of spring barleys gleaned from all parts of the world . . ." was crossed onto male sterile females to form Composite Cross XXI (Suneson and Weibe, 1962). A tremendous array of variability has been combined. The male sterile gene will insure many generations of additional hybridization and genetic recombination. The diversity of segregations and types which might be selected from this composite stagger the imagination. But, based on experience with earlier composites, this one should be a splendid future source of new material for many parts of the world.

CONCLUSION

Certain items of this presentation have been stressed, perhaps too much, while others have been glossed over. I do not advocate one breeding scheme over another, but do wish to emphasize a philosophy which usually seems to escape many of those responsible for planning, financing, and executing programs of development. To others who may become involved in development programs, I recommend reading the various annual reports, symposia proceedings, and publications of the Ford and Rockefeller Foundations, in addition to reports from the International Maize and Wheat Improvement Center (CIMMYT) and the International Rice Research Institute (IRRI). In these, the philosophy, accomplishments, and hopes for man and his nations are stated more eloquently and completely than I am capable of doing here.

The world's immediate and short-term needs can be met only by a system similar to the regional approaches mentioned. The great mass of germ plasm and technology must come from these centers. With the centers as a base, competent local effort of other individual governments should contribute additional increments of benefits, if adequately supported.

Each nation cannot be efficiently self-sufficient in all foodstuffs. Certain foods can be produced more economically in some areas than others and they could serve as a source of foreign exchange. Other countries could best concentrate on production of different crops. We don't need a world economy based on the systems and policies of the present-day markets in coffee, cocoa, sugar, and the like—even though the future commodities may be corn, wheat, *manihot,* millet, and rice.

Individual national commitment will be needed to develop and promote new commodities. Perhaps specialized markets could be developed by promoting cultivation of plants presently used in an indigenous or dooryard agriculture. Examples might be tubers or relatives of the cultivated potato, *Solanum* sp.; *Oxalis* sp.; *Ulloca* sp.; quinoa, *Chenopodium quinoa;* teff, *Eragrostis abyssinica;* amaranths, *Amaranthus* sp.; taro, *Colocasia* sp.; arracacha, *Arracacia* sp. The list could go on and on. Some of these have never really been investigated for commercial agricultural potential, but they are all already domesticated, at least partially. Medicinal and industrial crops may also serve as foreign exchange items. There are several excellent examples of research payoffs that resulted from changing plants to fit the requirements of commercial and industrial operations: soybeans, castor beans, safflower, and sorghum. Other possibilities have certainly not been exhausted.

With this gazing into the crystal ball, I am very much concerned about germ plasm preservation. Premature or indiscriminate bulking and compositing of individual collections must be avoided. Compositing should be done only after a systematic study of the material has been completed. All individual collections should be maintained separately, if possible. The composites could be used for preliminary adaptive studies or source material for established breeding programs. This would meet most requirements. Individual collections could be reserved for special cases of highly refined and sophisticated studies. The composites and germ plasm complexes will be the base upon which we will modify and build to satisfy our future food needs.

Only four crops—wheat, barley, maize, and rice—represent over 80 percent of the world's cereal production. If we include potatoes, sweet potatoes, yams, pulses, and consider one-third of the oil seeds as edible, then those same four cereals represent almost 70 percent of the crop production of the world (FAO, 1966). This percentage will undoubtedly increase to avert famine. But, then what—is man to exist on these few plants? Physically he can exist, but by his very humanity, he desires and perhaps deserves more.

A collection of germ plasm is extremely valuable stuff. The myriad differences are "each due to a particular DNA sequence, taking eons to arrive at, each a unique thing, perhaps a 'rare gene,' and arrived at under the harshest conditions. A germ plasm collection, then, preserves the unimaginable combinations of these sequences —sequences which may never be arrived at again, at least until we control DNA synthesis in its entirety" (W. C. Gregory, personal communication). Comprehensive collections of germ plasm must be preserved —before the material is lost forever. Some effort in this direction has been made, but not enough. It is a formidable task, but it must be done on a broad scale. We would benefit from such an effort, but more important, our obligation to the welfare of succeeding generations of mankind demands such a legacy.

REFERENCES

Allard, R. W. *Principles of Plant Breeding.* New York: John Wiley & Sons, 1960. 485 pp. P. 364.

Allard, R. W., and Jain, S. K. "Population Studies in Predominantly Self-Pollinated Species. II. Analysis of Quantitative Genetic Changes in Bulk-Hybrid Population of Barley." *Evolution,* 16 (1962), 90–101.

Aquino, R. C., and Jennings, P. R. "Inheritance and Significance of Dwarfism in an Indica Rice Variety." *Crop Sci.,* 6 (1966), 551–54.

Blomquist, H. L. *The Grasses of North Carolina.* Durham, N.C.: Duke University Press, 1948. 276 pp.

Borlaug, Norman E. "Wheat Breeding and Its Impact on World Food Supply." *Proc. Third Internat'l. Wheat Genetics Symposium.* Canberra, Australia, 1968. Australian Academy of Sciences, Canberra (1956), 1–36.

Braidwood, Robert J. "The agricultural revolution." *Scientific American,* 203 (1960), 130–48.

Chandler, R. F., Jr. "The Case for Research." In *Strategy for the Conquest of Hunger.* New York: The Rockefeller Foundation Symp., 1968. Pp. 92–97.

Chang, T. T. "The Genetic Basis of Wide Adaptability and Yielding Ability of Rice Varieties in the Tropics." *Internat'l. Rice Commission Newsletter,* 16 (1967), 4–12.

Chatterji, A. K., and Timothy, D. H. "Microsporogenesis and Embryogenesis in *Pennisetum flaccidum* Griseb." *Crop Sci.* 9 (1969), 219–22.

Clark, J. Allen. "Collection, Preservation and Utilization of Indigenous Strains of Maize." *Economic Botany,* 10 (1956), 194–200.

Cooper, J. P. "Studies on Growth and Development in *Lolium. IV.* Genetic Control of Heading Response in Local Populations." *J. Ecol.,* 42 (1954), 521–66.

Food and Agricultural Organization of the United Nations. *Production Yearbook,* Vol. 20, Rome, 1966.

Harlan, Jack R. "Distribution and Utilization of Natural Variability in Cultivated Plants." *Genetics in Plant Breeding.* Brookhaven Symposia in Plant Breeding, No. 9, 1956. Pp. 191–208.

Hartley, W. "The Agrostological Index. A Phytogeographical Approach to the Problems of Pasture Plant Introduction." *Austral. J. Bot.,* 2 (1954), 1–21.

——. "The Distribution of the Grasses." In *Grasses and Grasslands,* C. Barnard, ed. London: Macmillan and Co., 1964. Pp. 29–46.

Helbaek, Hans. "Domestication of Food Plants in the Old World." *Science,* 130 (3372) (1959), 365–72.

Hopper, W. David. "Investment in Agriculture: The Essentials for Payoff." In *Strategy for the Conquest of Hunger Symp. Proc.* New York: Rockefeller Foundation, 1968. Pp. 102–13.

International Maize and Wheat Improvement Center (CIMMYT) Report. Mexico, D.F. 1966–1967. 103 pp.

Jensen, N. F. "Multiline Superiority in Cereals." *Crop Sci.,* 5 (1965), 566–68.

Johnson, E. C. *Agronomy Abstracts.* Amer. Soc. of Agron., 1963.

Larson, R. E. "Perpetuation and Protection of Germ Plasm as Vegetative Stock." In *Germ Plasm Resources.* Publ. No. 66, AAAS, Washington, D.C., 1961. Pp. 327–36.

McMillan, C. "Grassland Community Fractions from Central North America under Simulated Climates." *Amer. Jour. Bot.,* 52 (1965), 109–16.

Maize Research Section. *Annual Report.* National Agricultural Research Station, Kitale, Kenya, 1967.

Mangelsdorf, P. C. "Genetic Potentials for Increasing Yields of Food Crops and Animals." *Proc. Nat'l. Acad. Sci. Symposium "Prospects of World Food Supply."* 56 (2) (1966), 370–75.

Morrisson, F. B. *Feeds and Feeding,* 20th ed. Ithaca, N.Y.: Morrisson Pub. Co., 1940.

Nuttonson, M. Y. "Preliminary Observations of Phenological Data as a Tool in the Study of Photoperiodic and Thermal Requirements of Various Plant Material." In A. E. Murneek and R. O. Whyte, eds. *Vernalisation and Photoperiodism,* Chronica Botanica, 1948. Pp. 129–43.

Paddock, William, and Paddock, Paul. *Hungry Nations.* Boston: Little, Brown & Co., 1964. 344 pp.

Patiño, Victor Manuel. "El Maíz Chococito. Noticia sobre su cultivo en América Ecuatorial." *América Indígena.* 16 (1956), 309–46.

Prescott, J. A.; Collins, J. A.; and Shirmurkar, G. R. "The Comparative Climatology of Australia and Argentina." *Geog. Rev.,* 42 (1952), 118–33.

President's Science Advisory Committee. Report of the Panel on World Food Supply. "The World Food Problem." Vols. I, II, III. The White House. U. S. Gov't. Printing Office, May, 1967.

Robertson, D. W. Testimony at hearing of Agricultural Appropriations Subcommittee. House of Representatives. May 10, 1955.

Rockefeller Foundation. Program in the Agricultural Sciences. New York: Rockefeller Foundation, 1964–1965.

Sadanaga, K., and Simons, M. D. "Transfer of Crown Rust Resistance of Diploid and Tetraploid Species to Hexaploid Oats." *Agron. J.,* 52 (1960), 285–88.

Schultz, Theodore W. *Economic Crises in World Agriculture.* Ann Arbor: University of Michigan Press, 1965. 114 pp.

Schutz, W. M.; Brim, C. A.; and Usanis, S. A. "Inter-Genotypic Competition in Plant Populations. I. Feedback Systems with Stable Equilibria in Populations of Autogamous Homozygous Lines." *Crop Sci.,* 8 (1968), 61–66.

Shantz, H. L. "The Place of Grasslands in the Earth's Cover of Vegetation." *Ecology,* 35 (1954), 143–51.

Sprague, E. W. "Research to Improve Production of Corn in Asia." In *Agricultural Science for the Developing Nations,* A. H. Moseman, ed. Amer. Assoc. Adv. Science Publ. No. 76, 1964. Pp. 53–68.

Stakman, E. C.; Bradfield, Richard; and Mangelsdorf, Paul C. *Campaigns against Hunger.* Cambridge, Mass.: Belknap Press. 1967.

Stakman, E. C., and Harrar, J. G. *Principles of Plant Pathology.* New York: Ronald Press Co., 1957. 581 pp. P. 25.

Suneson, C. A., and Weibe, G. A. "A 'Paul Bunyan' Plant Breeding Enterprise with Barley." *Crop Sci.,* 2 (1962), 347–48.

Timothy, D. H. "Considerations on the Use of Exotic Germplasm, Genetic Recombination and Natural Selection." *Proc. IX Internat'l. Grassl. Congress.* 1966. Pp. 175–77.

Vicente-Chandler, J.; Caro-Costas, R.; Pearson, R. W.; Abruña, F.; Figarella, J.; and Selva, S. *The Intensive Management of Tropical Forages in Puerto Rico.* Univ.

Puerto Rico Agric. Exp. Sta. Bull., No. 187, 1964. 152 pp.

Wellhausen, E. J. "Exotic Germ Plasm for Improvement of Corn Belt Maize." *Proc. 20th Hybrid Corn Industry-Research Conference.* 1965. Pp. 31–45.

Whyte, R. O.; Moir, T. R. G.; and Cooper, J. P. *Grasses in Agriculture.* FAO Agricultural Studies, No. 42. Rome: FAO, 1959. 417 pp.

RACES OF MAIZE IN LATIN AMERICA

Brieger, F. G.; Gurgel, J. T. A.; Paterniani, E.; Blumenschein, A.; and Alleoni, M. R. "Races of Maize in Brazil and Other Eastern South American Countries." Nat. Acad. Sci.–Nat. Res. Council, No. 593. 1958.

Brown, W. L. "Races of Maize in the West Indies." Nat. Acad. Sci.–Nat. Res. Council, No. 792. 1960.

Grant, U. J.; Hatheway, W. H.; Timothy, D. H.; Cassalett, D. C.; and Roberts, L. M. "Races of Maize in Venezuela." Nat. Acad. Sci.–Nat. Res. Council, No. 1136. 1963.

Grobman, A.; Salhuana, W.; and Sevilla, R.; in collaboration with Mangelsdorf, P. C. "Races of Maize in Peru, Their Origins, Evolution and Classification." Nat. Acad. Sci.–Nat. Res. Council, No. 915. 1961.

Hatheway, W. H. "Races of Maize in Cuba." Nat. Acad. Sci.–Nat. Res. Council, No. 453. 1957.

Ramirez, E. R.; Timothy, D. H.; Diaz, B. E.; and Grant, U. J.; in collaboration with Nicholson, G. E.; Anderson, E.; and Brown, W. L. "Races of Maize in Bolivia." Nat. Acad. Sci.–Nat. Res. Council, No. 747. 1960.

Roberts, L. M.; Grant, U. J.; Ramirez, E. R.; Hatheway, W. H.; and Smith, D. L.; in collaboration with Mangelsdorf, P. C. "Races of Maize in Colombia." Nat. Acad. Sci.–Nat. Res. Council, No. 510. 1957.

Timothy, D. H.; Hatheway, W. H.; Grant, U. J.; and Torregroza, C. M.; Sarria, V. D.; and Varela, A. D. "Races of Maize in Ecuador." Nat. Acad. Sci.–Nat. Res. Council, No. 975. 1963.

Timothy, D. H.; Peña, V. B.; and Ramirez, R. E.; in collaboration with Brown, W. L.; and Anderson, E. "Races of Maize in Chile." Nat. Acad. Sci.–Nat. Res. Council, No. 847. 1961.

Wellhausen, E. J.; Fuentes, A.; Hernandez Corzo, O. and A.; in collaboration with Mangelsdorf, P. C. "Races of Maize in Central America." Nat. Acad. Sci.–Nat. Res. Council, No. 511. 1957.

Wellhausen, E. J.; Roberts, L. M.; and Hernandez, X. E.; in collaboration with Mangelsdorf, P. C. "Races of Maize in Mexico." The Bussey Institution, Harvard Univ., 1952. Pp. 1–223.

DISCUSSION

CAIRNS: The agriculture industry has probably been responsible for more pollution than any other single industry. This is so primarily because regulatory agencies are mostly looking at point sources of pollution and not particularly at dispersed and intermittent pollution.

It seems to me that the agriculture industry has not developed even the primitive pollution abatement programs that other industries have developed. I wonder if any member of the panel has seen any concern about this generally, and whether it is possible that even a primitive pollution abatement program will develop in the agriculture industry.

PHILLIPS: I have worked in Natal and Zululand in an area of 30,000 square miles where we have a very good system of water analysis conducted by a fine water research institute. A careful tab is being kept upon the influence of pesticides and fertilizers to see what chemicals find their way to the streams and ultimately to the sea. Africa is, in most parts, still a comparatively lightly populated continent. Not much fertilizer is used yet, nor much pesticide and insecticide. But the indications are that there are detectable traces of chemicals in the local ground water. And this makes one pause.

COMMONER: I would like to present a few data on this problem as it exists in the Midwest. I think perhaps the area that is best understood is Illinois. The Illinois State Water Resources Board has been doing a very careful analysis of the chemical composition of surface water and ground water, in relation to agricultural practice. And I can give you from memory the situation as they are about to report it in their next annual report.

Every river system in Illinois apart from one small river in a nonagricultural corner of the state is now eutrophic. This means that the amount of plant nutrient in the water is sufficient to overwhelm the oxygen-carrying capacity of the water. The addition of nutrients stimulates the growth of aquatic plants such as algae. The algae die and decompose—an oxygen-consuming process—hence oxygen depletion and water pollution.

The question is: Where does the nutrient come from? The best data indicate nitrate as an important agent. Data now show that during the spring, when most of the nitrate is being carried down the rivers, 99 per cent of it cannot be accounted for by sewage. There is a very clear monthly pattern. Present data indicate a rising delivery of nitrate in the spring, falling off to a minimum in the late summer; then it begins to rise again in the fall and the winter.

In the last ten or fifteen years in Illinois, the maximum nitrate concentration in the spring has been rising in parallel with the intensified use of fertilizer. Since 1945 in the United States, the amount of nitrogen used as chemical fertilizer has gone up about twelvefold on the average. This rise in use certainly contributes to the springtime nitrate level in the rivers. Experiments have been conducted in which tile drains have been inserted under certain fields to measure the nitrate content of the drainage water. This has shown that the nitrate concentration in drainage water, month by month, parallels what is found in the rivers.

The conclusion that one must reach is that the vast bulk of the nitrate carried in Illinois rivers comes from drainage of agricultural fertilizer.

The public health aspect of this is very important. The town of Decatur, located in the Illinois corn belt, like many other towns gets its drinking water from a surface stream. This one happens to be the Sangamon River, which is dammed up to form a lake.

The Public Health Department in the town conducts nitrate analyses of drinking water from farm wells because of the problem that Dr. Schuphan mentioned. Methemoglobinemia, particularly of children, occurs if the well water has too much nitrate and is used in the infant formula. Two years ago, a water sample was brought into the Public Health Department, analyzed for nitrate, and found to be over the Public Health Service limits. When the man came back for the report, he was told, "You must not use this water." To which he replied, "But it came from the Decatur tap!"

The Sangamon River and the reservoir used for Decatur tap water had gone over the Public Health Service limits for nitrate. We have here another classic case of a system in disequilibrium. The humus content decreases; the efficiency of nutrient uptake declines. We make up for this, more than make up for it, by pouring nitrogen on the soil, but the soil in its recalcitrant wisdom forces much of the excess nitrate out of the system into drainage and rainfall. (Rainfall all over the United States now carries considerable nitrate.)

In a number of places, this process is exacerbated by the fact that an additional amount of nitrogen, equal to one-third the total nitrogen input to the U.S. soil, comes from nitrogen oxides produced by automobiles in the United States.

The turnover of nitrogen in the United States is about 7 million tons a year. In other words, that's what we eat. We put on the soil about 7 million tons of nitrogen a year as fertilizer. Also we produce as sewage probably about .8 million tons of nitrogen. We inject into the air 2.5 million tons by means of automobiles and trucks.

As a result of all this we have seriously unbalanced the nitrogen cycle in the United States.

RUSSELL: I wish to make some comments on problems of agriculture in East Africa.

We have examples of crops such as sisal, introduced into Africa by Europeans, which have the very undesirable characteristic of taking large amounts of nutrients from the subsoil, so causing its very appreciable impoverishment. It is technically difficult to return these nutrients directly to the subsoil: they can only easily be returned to the surface soil. But most nutrients are strongly adsorbed by the surface soil, so it takes a long period of years and frequent fairly heavy surface applications before enough has washed down to make good the loss due to the earlier cropping.

We have also had troubles with the wrong use of fertilizers. As John Phillips has pointed out, one of the main troubles has been the acidification produced by sulfate ammonia. Sulfate of ammonia is, I suppose, the most dangerous fertilizer used in Africa, because it makes such large demands on the calcium supplies of the soil, and in most of Africa the calcium supplies are very low.

We have also been interested in the problems of maintaining soil structure and, in particular, in the importance of the level of soil organic matter for its maintenance. In general the more productive systems of agriculture coming into use are likely to give lower soil humus levels than the old indigenous systems of farming, which were low-yielding systems but were also systems in which the soil suffered little disturbance.

There are methods available for minimizing the harmful effects of a partial loss of soil structure. One of these was developed in America but, I believe, has never been popular with you, although it can be used with success in both East and West Africa. This system, which you call basin listing, works extremely well if the soil is reasonably permeable and the rains not too prolonged. However, the system is liable to cause waterlogging of the soil, with consequent killing of the crop in periods of prolonged rain, as the surplus water cannot be run off the land.

Another method we have been working with is keeping the soil surface covered with litter or a mulch and killing weeds with herbicides. But this method of surface litter has given us trouble because of insect pests. If you use plant residues to protect the soil surface, you are nearly always giving some insects almost exactly the conditions they want for their own comfort, and they will normally repay you by attacking the next crop.

Not a single well-designed experiment on the possibility of maintaining the fertility of soils using fertilizers has run for any length of time in tropical Africa. I believe all those intended to test this have failed because the nitrogen fertilizer used was sulfate of ammonia, and it has always acidified the soil sufficiently to prevent good crop growth. It is unfortunately now a by-product of nylon manufacture, and the manufacturers have to get rid of the stuff, so it is cheap. As I have said it is well conditioned and easy to handle, so it is difficult to persuade African Governments not to use it.

ZONNEVELD: The lateritic process is still a controversial subject. We only know that it may lead under certain conditions to the formation of soil layers that may harden after removal of protection against desiccation. We know that there is an increased danger when soil erosion comes in. We need more research in order to see under what conditions the chemical process of weathering will deteriorate tropical soils when we exchange the natural vegetation for various cultivated crops. Generalizations are dangerous, especially in this matter. There are still too many adversaries of "conservation" eager to undermine our action if we are proven wrong.

I fully agree with you that for each agricultural development project, a soil survey, carried out by good soils specialists, should be done. The lack of such surveys has led too often to the kind of disasters you have mentioned.

MCNEIL: I also would like to say that the general term "laterization" has been very much misinterpreted. I have tried to be very careful to use the word "laterite" only for those hard crusts which you usually find on the uplifted peneplains of tertiary horizons. I have tried to show that this process of weathering pretty well prevails throughout the tropical rain forest and monsoon forest and in the intermittent rainfall area of the edge of the savannah. These areas of the globe are subject to high leaching and a desilicification which apparently has led to a present-day process of the building up of something called ground water laterites.

There are certain places where agriculture intercepts these soils in the process of becoming laterite. Man's land uses accelerate the process; he is not the primary cause of it. The process is going on all the time, but man's influence affects the rates.

I think that we have to be very careful when we talk about laterization. Are we referring to an ironstone cap or are we simply referring to erosional slope soils, some of which have been excellent homes for people through the ages? I think we can use Milne's approach to laterization and the laterite catena which he described in Africa and which has been described again and again by ecologists as guides to map the tropical areas. We can pick out those areas of the tropical lateritic catenae which can be utilized, but they are first going to require some kind of wholesale mapping.

We now have planners and politicians who just say that some particular hunk of ground would make a lovely spot for a colony and then dump people in. And immediately they cut the forest, exposing the lateritic soils beneath, and the leaching process is rapidly accelerated. I think there is considerable evidence to show that this process is going on today.

MILTON: I would like to mention several problems closely related to road building; in particular, I am concerned about the spontaneous and planned colonization that inevitably follows new roads in the wet tropical regions.

In years of experience living and traveling through tropical rain-forest areas in Latin America, I have noticed a serious disregard in many ambitious road-building schemes of their implications for colonization. Typically, many roads are built on a single-purpose basis, usually to support large-scale industrial, mining and agricultural programs. Or they are built with no plan at all. But roads usually are built where it is cheapest to build them. This often means they pass through areas of high susceptibility to erosion or to rapid loss of soil nutrients when spontaneous colonization exposes the land to high rainfall and temperature. As a general rule, people follow to colonize wherever new roads are located in the Latin American tropics. If thought is not given to whether the land through which roads pass is suitable for colonization, these same roads become focal points for tomorrow's rural slums: ecological disaster areas of degraded, unproductive soil and a miserable level of human life.

Closely linked to this problem of spontaneous colonization following roads is the nutritional impact of the process. In Bolivia, for example, a number of roads have been built from the high, dry Altiplano into the low, moist Yungas. Most people who have followed the roads and moved down into this zone are either Aymara or Quechua families from the Altiplano. Coca (*Erythroxylon coca*), a popular local Andean drug that is chewed to relieve hunger, grows well in the moist valleys of Yungas. The local people also have found that coca, which is planted in well-terraced fields on steep mountainsides, finds a ready export market available to other areas. However, the subsistence crops available to them in Yungas are not the same as those which were once grown in the Altiplano. A series of high carbohydrate crops such as banana, yucca, hualusa and racacha are grown instead; all of them are seriously deficient in plant protein. By contrast, many of the crops grown in the Altiplano, such as quinoa, karahua and haba, provide a good balance of protein and carbohydrates. One result of the migration down into the Yungas has been protein malnutrition.

The implications of road technology-induced protein deficiency in such areas as the Yungas are serious, particularly now that we know that severe damage to the human nervous system and brain regularly occurs under such conditions. From mid-pregnancy (in the mother's womb) until the child is five years of age is a particularly dangerous period, when most of the harm is done. This damage is essentially irreversible and it can condemn a whole generation to a downward spiral of health. Indeed, if people's intelligence has been nutritionally impaired, how can we expect them to have the ability to improve *their* children's situation? The whole culture affected may face a long-term process of degradation covering generations.

There have been other adverse consequences of faulty colonization as well. Because of the steep slopes, many areas planted to subsistence crops are subject to erosion. Vertical planting, a practice prevalent in the dry Altiplano, has had drastic erosional effect in the steep, wet Yungas. Similarly, the old highland custom of building houses with small windows to conserve heat continues in the humid valleys, creating an environment that promotes new problems of disease.

All these are classical problems of a culture moving from an old environment where there is a high degree of cultural adaptation to ecological conditions—to a new environment where there is little or no such adaptation. Wherever a new road is built in the developing countries, the various social and ecological implications of the road must be studied, and programs undertaken to solve anticipated problems *before* road construction begins. Otherwise we cannot consider such development humane or sound.

BORGSTROM: I would like to address myself to the question of the nutritional implications of the increase in plant productivity we have been discussing in this session. I think that we have been far too obsessed with quantity and have overlooked the quality—particularly in nutritional terms— of the products that have been produced.

I have three points.

One refers to the production of plants largely through the enormous increase in fertilizers which we have been analyzing. I might say that I was very worried, to say the least, when I discovered that we have been forcing tremendous quantities of fertilizers on countries like Taiwan and South Korea. More than 60 per cent of the protein they are eating today actually originates from industrially produced nitrogen. I think we have underrated the losses in nutritional terms. Some losses, particularly due to leaching of nitrates, may be behind much of the pollution issue. I have seen statements that the leaching has been measured up to 60 per cent loss of what has been applied to a particular field.

The second point is that undoubtedly the increased quantity that we have been getting not only has pushed the C/N (carbon-nitrogen) ratio upwards, meaning that we are getting less protein and more carbohydrates; also often we are getting a product which is less adapted to human use. Nitrogen-forced agricultural products fit the human aminogram less well, and we are getting far fewer amino acids. This whole subject has only been studied now and then, and I think we need a much broader insight into this whole area. Are we gaining nutritionally what we are gaining in quantity? How does this approach compare to the natural nitrogen increase taking place through biological channels?

The third point occurs if we look at our agricultural production at large and at the history of colonization and see that we are moving into less suitable ecological conditions.

The further we get down from meat protein diets, the more carbohydrates we have; we finally end up with "chubbyism." On the basis of modern nutrition we can say that you can supplement cereals with bean protein but it is not possible to really supplement chubbyism. The only cure which is really feasible is to resort to animal protein.

I would submit to this group that we enter into a very important ecological issue here, because we talk even now in terms of the increased yields of the new rice varieties and the new wheat varieties. I am rather surprised that nutritional quality hasn't been discussed more. These new varieties are a very impressive accomplishment in terms of quantity. The minute we look at the qualitative aspects it becomes very questionable in my view, because I think the protein content has dropped between 10 and 25 per cent. This loss has to be compensated.

Many countries operate very close to protein deficiency now. You could very well foresee a tremendous increase in protein deficiency symptoms as a consequence of increased production of nutritionally poorer plants when you are that close, as we are in India. Also, we don't know how these new varieties will adjust to new ecological conditions. The only public statement I have seen about this is Pathak's review in *Annual Review of Entomology*. I think he brought out this very point.

I would like to add that having traveled in India and knowing Indian universities, I think it is a tragic mistake that India is paying far more attention to nuclear physicists than to cytopathologists and entomologists. I think the latter fields might be the key to the future of India.

WORTHINGTON: I would like to put a question to Dr. Timothy concerning plant gene pools. He estimated that man has used 3,000 or more plant species for food and has cultivated at least 150 species, but that only some 15 species of plants feed the majority of the world.

If one considers this ratio in terms of animals, the number of animal species used for food or for other products is a great deal more than 3,000. The number domesticated is a great deal less then 150 species. And the number of animal species that actually feed the world is less than 15.

I want to address my question about plants but the animal comparison is important: What practical steps does Dr. Timothy envisage toward better conservation of plant gene pools for future generations of plant breeders?

We have to remember that of the total primary biological productivity in the world, by far the greatest part has nothing to do with these food species. Species which aren't even casually used as food produce the bulk of the primary productivity. But, many of them may serve a useful purpose; for example, nobody can tell what particular species may turn out to be important as nitrogen fixers.

Does Dr. Timothy envisage that the problem is best dealt with through experimental farms, one devoted to potatoes, another to wheats, another to rices, places where you can keep many species which are already known by a great expansion of living collections and collections of seed; or could the need be met by a major operation which is currently being undertaken by the International Biological Programme and the International Union for the Conservation of Nature. These organizations are involved in the analysis and identification of all the major world ecosystems and the earmarking of representative samples of each of these ecosystems for permanent conservation in managed reserves.

TIMOTHY: Ideally I would like to see a combination of approaches. I have seen a number of these preserves, not necessarily created only for germ plasm but largely for ecological preserves of both plant and animal communities. I was in one designated natural area last spring in Colombia and half of it was completely destroyed. The trees were down, the animals were gone. You need armed guards really to keep people from destroying these preserves. However, preserves alone are not sufficient. There are too many sites and too many plants that would need to be preserved, and too many already endangered or obliterated. Preserves, however, are valuable and I certainly agree that they are needed. As you say, we don't know what we will need twenty-five years or fifty years from now. We cannot yet put together DNA in the proper sequences to do the things we would like a plant or an animal to do. Until that time arrives, if it ever does, or until we are able to feed ourselves with algae in a palatable manner, we have to depend upon plant and animal resources.

So it seems to me that we have got to preserve some of these plant and animal resources; but I speak particularly of plant resources, the species which are now being used, their relatives, and those species which look as if they might have some future potential.

The experimental farm approach, each devoted to certain crops containing the extant species, strains, etc., is the most appealing. This is a tremendous undertaking, but it's feasible now, and already begun, in one or two instances. The scope of the undertaking requires multi- or international participation. The organizations you mentioned, in addition to others, should become involved in several fashions, e.g., actively collecting and storing material, operating as a clearing house, coordinating whenever possible, etc.

The most important consideration, regardless of whatever scheme is used to preserve germ plasm, is that the collection be duplicated as a safeguard against physical disaster or political policy. A collection would be too valuable to be in any one place.

We have also had problems keeping intact our collections of plant germ plasm. Collections have been made, and often have been discarded. Recently many thousand samples of an indigenous corn collection were sent to the Federal Seed Laboratory at Fort Collins. I recently heard, I have not been able to verify this personally, that these were being disposed of simply because no one yet had requested them. The primary purpose for constructing this seed storage facility was to create a place where this germ plasm would be preserved. It would not be a repository for people that wanted it for everyday usage.

Now this is the kind of thing we are up against, and I don't know what to do about it. Several of my colleagues are in the same position, and I guess we are like many ecologists. We are voices crying in the wilderness.

KASSAS: I would like to make a couple of general remarks. First, I think the people in the Anti-Locust Research Center, because they were very much ecologically minded in their locust work, have made very valuable botanical surveys in areas like the Arabian Peninsula and parts of Africa. This botanical knowledge has come out as a by-product of the work, but it is a most valuable product.

Second, we may talk about ecological systems, but all over the world people are agriculture-minded, crop production-minded. Just as crop *protection* people are chemical-minded, the crop *production* people are agriculture-minded, thinking that agriculture is the only means of land use. Because this idea dominates the thinking of people, they would always go, as Miss McNeil and others have been telling us, and clear out forests and grow cotton there. Doing so we are upsetting the ecosystem which is the natural forest type.

Two systems are operating within the ecosystem of the forest. The vegetation is developing into a state of dynamic equilibrium; also involved is the climax type of soil which likewise is in a state of dynamic equilibrium. If we clear the forest and put our cotton there, then we are upsetting both systems. If we would understand the climax type of vegetation and the climax type of soil, however, we could try to replace the climax type of vegetation rather than to change it.

When I say "replace" I am thinking of the very successful development of the corn and wheat belt in the United States. This crop pattern was successful because it replaced a grassland type of climax vegetation by vegetation similar to it. If we are to develop rice fields in some areas where the natural climax vegetation is open marshy vegetation, then we are doing the right thing. But if we are destroying forests and replacing them with a crop culture, then we are making a mistake and we should expect lots of trouble.

SMITH: A point of personal privilege. The statement was just made that crop protection people are chemical-minded. That is like saying all birds are blue. I think the proper statement is *too many* crop protection people are chemical-minded!

(Laughter.)

SCUDDER: I would like to generalize briefly on a point which was hinted at earlier. It is a point that relates to controversy, which is why I want to bring it up. When I mentioned cotton in the archaeological and the local indigenous context, I was very interested in the quick reaction, "Yes, that is interesting, but it is not economic today." This strikes me as a bias which is based on consideration of a limited set of alternatives. It does not take into account any possible intensification of small holdings, which is my bias.

Let me give a brief example. Cotton is once again being grown in the middle Zambezi Valley by small holders on plots of about one to five acres. These plots are highly dispersed in fields of maize, sorghum, and other crops. The yields are good, 600 to 1,000 pounds per acre. These results meet the expectations of the small-holder farmers. In fact the revival of small-holder farming appears to be cutting down labor migration rates. Fewer people are moving into the cities, more local jobs are being provided, more people are being held on the land.

The reaction of the government to this success is an interesting one: "This looks like a going thing, so let's group these small holders." (Laughter.) The first group farm has been introduced just this last year. Aerial spraying of insecticides is now being considered. (Laughter.)

The government is considering tremendous intensification of cotton holdings, but in a way which is more amenable, through mechanization, to capital intensive procedures. I am willing to predict that within five years, if this intensification occurs, cotton as a major cash crop will not be produced in the middle Zambezi Valley; that the present buildup, having gone in this one direction, will have died down; and that labor migration rates will have gone back up again. I am suggesting that an alternative is to encourage this mixed form of cropping which makes a lot more sense ecologically. Instead of having three cotton growers in each village I think we can get ten, fifteen or twenty, cutting down labor migration rates even more by encouraging greater labor opportunities locally for picking.

We could avoid getting up to these large holdings where you run into the insecticide problem and the picking problem.

RUSSELL: Of course the mixed form does work in some areas. In other areas such as Tanzania it can be fatal because the same pests attack cotton and maize and sorghum, and the best way of killing your cotton is by growing it next to maize or sorghum.

SCUDDER: You have had cultivation there for years and years. Isn't much of this a problem of soil degradation?

RUSSELL: Put on fertilizer and it is easy to get a high yield, but you still get your pests.

SCUDDER: The peasants have to pay for the fertilizer. That is part of the syndrome I am criticizing. In the middle Zambezi Valley if you combine cotton with a fairly simple rotation rather than a four-crop rotation you might, to a large extent, be able to get rid of the fertilizer.

RUSSELL: It depends on the yields you want.

SCUDDER: The peasant should determine that because *he* is the one we want to keep on the land. That should be determined by the peasant rather than by the demonstrator.

CONWAY: You know, it is false to make an antithesis between the ecologist who says everything will be all right if you just have some heterogeneity and the agriculturalist who may be moving another way. The point is that the ecologist doesn't know much more than that bald statement you made just there.

SCUDDER: I am talking about an actual system of farming which is viable at the moment, which is keeping people on the land, and which is meeting their expectations as they define them.

CONWAY: In other words, you are saying it is a trial-and-error process. It is not always true that heterogeneity is a good thing.

SCUDDER: I am not convinced it is a trial-and-error process. It is a continuation of an indigenous system of agriculture which has been effective in this area for at least one thousand years.

SMITH: I will continue the heterogeneity comment. Costa Rica is a country in Central America that produces cotton that does not have the severe pest problem that has been described for Guatemala, Nicaragua, and El Salvador. Cotton in Costa Rica is grown in small holdings surrounded by either pasture land or undeveloped land. They do some treating, but there is a much simpler pest problem.

In Cauca Valley of Colombia there is great heterogeneity of environment, a great variety of crops grown, and that heterogeneity aggravates the pest problem. A similar aggravated pest problem, because of the heterogeneity, is characteristic of the Brazos Valley in Texas.

I tend to side with Gordon that we should not say we must have heterogeneity, that heterogeneity is in all cases a good thing for the environment. I think we must have the right kind of heterogeneity, must know what we are doing when we plan the system.

SCUDDER: I don't think my point quite got across. I am not looking at it only as an ecologist. I am also looking at it as an anthropologist, which means I am looking at it from the point of view of the peasant who is growing the crops. I think this viewpoint, the perspective of the peasant, is a viewpoint which has to be stressed much more. In this case it leads to hetero-geneity, which seems to be an ecologically viable solution. In other cases heterogeneity may create problems.

But I think, granted the demographic problem and the tremendous increase in numbers of people, we have to think not only of intensification of agriculture and production but also of increasing the number of jobs; this puts more emphasis on small holders and the kinds of systems which make sense for small holders, which may not be capital-intensive systems with insecticides, fertilizers and the like. We have to work out ecologically viable solutions so that they don't put much capital into their gardens, but get enough capital out, and at the same time the economy gets some export.

COMMONER: One brief comment should be made about heterogeneity. That is—and this is not being facetious—it is more complicated than homogeneity: we are much more likely to be ignorant about a heterogeneous system than we are about a homogeneous system. I think that a good deal of what Dr. Timothy has been saying is a warning that where there is a heterogeneous system which is more successful, and so complex that we don't understand it, it may be very wise for us to cherish it because there may be within it something that we later need to know which will be totally lost.

What is at issue here is a kind of scientific hubris which asserts that that which we understand is important, but that which is complex, heterogeneous, and poorly understood lies outside the realm of science because we don't understand it. But what lies outside the realm of science in our case lies within the realm of nature; it seems to me that the kind of issue that Dr. Timothy has raised is extraordinarily important. He represents a conservationist approach which takes into account the probability of our ignorance about the importance of the complexity of the world. I only want to add one caution: the notion that we will ever be able to reproduce a DNA sequence which represents the information content of a species is extraordinarily dangerous. There is no evidence in the present data of molecular biology to show that the theories can even explain speciation. The DNA theory relates to the data of genetics, which are derived from mating groups, but the difference between a wheat plant and a rose is not accountable in these terms because they don't mate.

CONWAY: I agree with what you said just now. In fact, it is in the discussion that I wrote for my paper. My point is that I think in addition to preserving natural ecosystems which are heterogeneous, there is an obligation on the part of the ecologist to understand the nature of those ecosystems and how it is that they achieve stability and productivity, so that entomologists can use this information.

There is a tendency for ecologists to blame entomologists for not being ecological; but in fact there is also a paucity of information for entomologists, and an entomologist is day-to-day faced with a decision-making process. He may walk into an oil-palm field of 7,000 or 8,000 acres in which the decision to destroy the heterogeneity has already been made. The oil palms are there, and he must make a decision about what he will do and must make it on the basis of the facts known to him. If more theories and facts are presented by ecologists to show why an ecosystem is stable and why

it is also productive, and he can use these, then he will be a much better entomologist.

SMITH: Yesterday in discussing many of these development projects the term "multiple cropping" was used. Some such projects would permit year-around operations. This practice takes us right back into the question of heterogeneity again.

Double or triple cropping of the same plant is a very aggravated example of homogeneity and may lead to all sorts of complicated pest control problems in the future. The burden on the crop protection specialist will be even greater under those conditions.

RUSSELL: I wish to add just a couple of comments to the discussion to reflect something of what we have learned. One concerns fertilizers. If you add a nitrogen fertilizer to a soil, you naturally increase its nitrogen content and you usually get a bigger crop of higher nitrogen content. But is the extra nitrogen in the crop doing you any good or not? This question of the *quality* of the nitrogen compounds produced by nitrogen fertilizers in the crops is one that we agricultural scientists have rather ignored. This question should receive much more attention than it has in the past.

Finally, I am not certain whether I ought to be coming here in sackcloth and ashes or as a proud man. I am an experimental agriculturalist whose job was, I thought, to try to increase production per acre. Now I am unsure whether I have been shouted down as being a very wicked person or not.

IV INTENSIFICATION OF ANIMAL PRODUCTIVITY

F. Fraser Darling, Chairman

35. Ecological Consequences of Sedentarization of Nomads
                        F. Fraser Darling and Mary A. Farvar   671

36. Ecological Consequences of Bedouin Settlement in Saudi Arabia
                                        Harold F. Heady   683

37. Ecological Consequences of Rangeland Development in Masailand, East Africa
                                        Lee M. Talbot   694

38. The Ecological Impact of the Introduction of Domestic Cattle into Wild Life and Tsetse Areas of Rhodesia   *Oliver West*   712

39. The Tsetse Fly: A Blessing or a Curse?   *Frank L. Lambrecht*   726

40. The Sheep and the Saltbush: The Utilization of Australia's Arid Lands
                                        Peter Crowcroft   742

41. Ecological Aspects of Protein Feeding—the Case of Peru   *Georg Borgstrom*   753

DISCUSSION   775

A BALLAD OF ECOLOGICAL AWARENESS (continued)

The oceans we have mobilized to feed the too-well-fed;
The rain is red in Adelaide from deserts newly bred;
We nibble at the nomads, though oil-rich and water-poor;
Displaced Masai, domesticated, have a drought in store.

The tsetse fly can guard the wild, as long as it survives;
As men and cattle press the land, the game no longer thrives;
The tourist business is a trap, it is a tainted honey;
Man clearly should have stayed in bed, and not invented money.

—KENNETH E. BOULDING

The increased use of broad-spectrum contact-acting insecticides has yielded considerable benefits in the control of rice pests, locusts, and mosquitoes. However, as Gordon Conway reports in his paper **ECOLOGICAL ASPECTS OF PEST CONTROL IN MALAYSIA** (Page 467), entomologists working with the pest problems of cocoa and oil palms have learned that such insecticides may also aggravate existing problems or cause new ones.

In Malaysia major outbreaks of pests, notably bagworms, followed heavy applications of contact-acting insecticides. All the pests involved were indigenous to Malaysia and normally were kept under control by their natural enemies. Unfortunately, use of contact-acting insecticides resulted in heavy mortality of these enemy species, allowing the pests to proliferate rapidly.

Bagworms (Psychidae) damaged cocoa at Quoin Hill, Sabah, in 1961 (Photo 25-1); a bagworm larva *(Cremastopsyche pendula)* feeding on a cocoa leaf in Sabah is shown in Photo 25-2. Oil palms in Malaya (Photo 25-3) were heavily damaged by the bagworm *Metisa plana* in recurrent outbreaks during a period when there was extensive use of endrin. Photo 25-4 shows a predatory bug, *Sycanus dichotomus* (Reduviidae), feeding on a bagworm on an oil palm in Malaya. A light trap (Photo 25-5) is used for catching cockchafer beetles in rubber plantations in Malaya. (Photos 25-3 and 25-4 courtesy of B. J. Wood, Chemara Research Station; Photo 25-5 courtesy of B. L. Rao, Rubber Research Institute.)

25-1

25-2

25-3

25-4

25-5

Diurnal birds of prey were common in Israel prior to 1950. Their main food was field mice. In his paper **ECOLOGICAL EFFECTS OF CHEMICAL CONTROL OF RODENTS AND JACKALS IN ISRAEL** (Page 527), Dr. Mendelssohn explains the widespread effects of the use of thallium sulfate-coated wheat to control field mice. The application of large quantities of thallium sulfate was repeated every year until recently, even though there was no apparent increase of field mice population. One unanticipated result of this application was the death and paralysis of birds of prey in the fields. Even in areas where thallium was not used, the dead birds of prey were found to contain thallium. The photos show two lappet-faced vultures *(Torgos tracheliotus)*—one dying, one dead—found in 1957 after distribution of thallium bait in Bet Qama, about 20 kilometers north of Be'er Sheva.

28-1

28-2

The myth of the fertility of tropical soils is giving way to vast evidence to the contrary. Many areas of the tropics have soils that are in a more or less advanced stage of natural laterization, the wearing down of the earth's surface, which results in the removal of silica and other solubles from the soil and the accumulation of residual minerals such as iron, aluminum, manganese, and nickel. This process has resulted in some of the major mineral deposits of the world.

These widespread laterite-prone soils are usually covered by rain forests or savannas. Due to continuously high temperatures and often heavy rainfall, most available organic matter on such soils is quickly reused by living plants instead of forming a layer of humus. Thus, soils are quickly impoverished when forest or other plant cover is replaced by cash cropping "development."

In her paper **LATERITIC SOILS IN DISTINCT TROPICAL ENVIRONMENTS** (Page 591), Mary McNeil illustrates the dangers of altering tropical ecosystems, citing case histories from the southern Sudan and Brazil. The photographs show laterite formations in Brazil. Photo 32-1: A laterite formation over a possible pre-Cambrian horizon found along the Maranhao road, Brazil. The elongated blocks of laterite were apparently formed by precipitation of the iron hydroxides from ascending waters. Photo 32-2: A laterite formation overlying pre-Cambrian filites on the Para Maranhao road. Photo 32-3: This cut on the Para side of the Belem-Brasilia road shows the undulating topography of the area. Laterite may be observed in the upper strata overlying the Barreiras clays, which here appear without their characteristic grooves. The surface laterite resulted from infiltration of iron oxides and surface phenomena. (Photographs courtesy of Dr. Fritz Ackermann.)

32-1

32-2

32-3

Nomadic peoples generally have a way of life and organization that is deemed incompatible with civilization by sedentary populations and centralized national governments. In 1925, entire towns were built to settle nomads in Persia while their grazing lands were confiscated.

Since nomadic pastoralism is the only possible way of life in many areas where rainfall is inadequate for crop growing, Iran was deprived of many useful commodities such as milk, meat, wool, hides, and draft animals. Not surprisingly, the nomads, used to perceiving the world from their open, mobile tents, were unhappy at the prospect of giving up their freedom for the drabness of enclosures (Photo 35-1).

The paper **ECOLOGICAL CONSEQUENCES OF SEDENTARIZATION OF NOMADS** (Page 671) describes how crowded human and animal space, lack of water, overgrazed pastures, and extreme temperatures exposed man and livestock to malnutrition, infection, and disease. Epidemics wiped out large numbers of people. Mud houses were virtually washed away with the first rain (Photo 35-2). Today, only a few donkeys and their owners can be seen around the ruins of settlement towns.

35-1

35-2

Water is as important as oil to Saudi Arabia. No elevation of living standards or true social progress is possible until problems of water supply are solved. But the ecological consequences of haphazard water development and manipulation are great. The report **ECOLOGICAL CONSE-QUENCES OF BEDOUIN SETTLEMENT IN SAUDI ARABIA** (Page 683) explores the unforeseen side effects of water supply and oil development when many Bedouins were permanently settled. The effects of heavy grazing on the fragile arid grasslands around such settlements were particularly serious.

Panicum turgidum (Photo 36-1) dominates a little grazed grassland in northeastern Saudi Arabia. This shrub-like grass with perennial stems is common on deep sands, particularly after heavy rains. Wadi channels (Photo 36-2) are the most favorable habitats for range forage production. These broad, flat valleys receive runoff water, which permits increased density and growth of both shrubs and herbaceous plants. Haloxylon is shown here. Where permanent water supplies are established, animal concentration often leads to overgrazing. At Wadi Ruthiyah, overgrazing and drought resulted in the dead Salsola plants shown in Photo 36-3.

Saudi Arabia has no watercourse flowing continuously to the sea. Water flows in the wadis for a short time, but it soon disappears into the sands and is stored in the wadi fill at depths of two to twenty meters. It is within reach of hand digging and promotes more vegetative growth than could be supported by rainfall alone. The long, winding wadi strips furnish water and forage that have supported wild animals, domestic animals, and human populations for centuries. They are the lifelines of the desert. Much of the recent effort at water control, however, was ill conceived, and its negative consequences are widespread. Major problems are excess water, high salinity, and poor drainage. Sand encroachment into irrigated areas also is common. Often all these problems occur in the same area. In Photo 36-4, taken at the edge of the Hofuf oasis, crop land has been covered, irrigation canals plugged, and drainage reduced by moving dunes.

36-1

36-2

36-3

36-4

35. ECOLOGICAL CONSEQUENCES OF SEDENTARIZATION OF NOMADS

F. Fraser Darling and Mary A. Farvar

The greatest arid regions in the world and those regions in which nomadism is prevalent are the interior Asian steppes, Southwest Asia and the Arab Near East. Nomadic pastoralism in these areas ranges over a continuum from the migratory nomad with no permanent settlement or agricultural pursuits to the settled pastoralists raising livestock in a circumscribed area and perhaps also farming the land. Surveys in the Sahara and elsewhere indicate that living standards of nomads are higher than those of the sedentary population. Nomadic strains of sheep, such as those in the Iranian province of Fars, tend to be larger and more productive than sedentary village strains.

For many countries striving to achieve a progressive role among modern nations, it has not been acceptable to have "backward" nomads around. Forcible attempts to settle nomads have led to drastic stock losses, particularly in the case of nomads with long migratory routes. This occurs because, in the inhospitable arid environment to which nomadism is an adaptive response, animals of differing tolerance and habits are found: when those nomads are settled whose animals are not able to adapt to extremes in temperature, large numbers of these animals die. In Iran, sheep mortality of 70 to 80 percent has been reported after forced sedentarization in 1925. After the Kazakh nomads were settled in Russia the numbers of horses, cattle and sheep fell drastically. In the early forties, the nomads' flocks had to be built up again, and experienced shepherds and stock raisers were imported to make up for losses resulting from sedentarization.

Overgrazing has resulted when nomads have settled in an area around permanent water holes in the Sahel. This continuous overgrazing has changed the composition of the pasturage and is reflected in a decline in the quality of the beasts.

Nomads and their animals are well adapted to their environment and way of life. When they are settled they may be subject to many diseases and a poorer diet. Around family wells in the Sahel, where livestock has not yet exceeded the capacity of the land, poor conformation plus a rise in deficiency diseases and parasitic infections are apparent. In the Sahara, settled nomads lose their energy and resistance to endemic diseases. Among the Somali, coronary disease incidence is virtually nil despite diets high in dairy fat. When the Somali are settled, the balance achieved by centuries of adaptation to nomadism will be adversely affected and higher incidence of coronary diseases will undoubtedly appear.

Development schemes are conceived by economists and agricultural scientists rather than ecologists and nomads. Nomadic pastoralism can be a complex and efficient form of land use. Yet, in the determination to change a way of life, countries have not realized the complex relationship between ecological, cultural and economic factors.

Nomadism is the pastoralism of domesticated animals across the great steppe regions of the world; it is pastoralism on the extensive scale, following the grass and the water, mingling with the wholeness of the environment in closer fashion than most sedentary cultures can achieve with their buffered home places.

Paul Shepard, a poet among ecologists, calls the pastoral nomad a destroyer and near parasite (Shepard, 1967). Yet he also says that "the pastoralists' watch over and breeding of a stock is a continuing lesson in the relationship between authority and lineage, a confirmation of the extension of paternity, of a creative patriarchate." Assessment of the place of the nomad in land use is a much more subtle exercise in human ecology than most administrators are ready to give time to consider.

Absolute nomadism exerts its own discipline in an environment of subsistence where no permanent positive improvement can be effected. The outside world has exaggerated notions of the distances covered by the nomad and no understanding of their design. All too often nomads are dismissed as wanderers, which they are certainly not; rather, they are close observers of seasonal home ranges. Grazing routes and territories are well understood and observed. Extreme distances between summer and winter grounds are not more than 150–200 miles and the temptation is always to halt and enjoy for as long as possible, but scarce resources demand movement. This absolute necessity of movement is what literate civilization has not understood: education, politics, and medical attention are always attempting to halt the nomad, whether he is a Lapp reindeer herder or a Kurd or a Turcoman, or a Masai.

Nomadism varies enormously in character in various parts of the world. There is a continuum of patterns of pastoralism ranging from the migratory nomad with no permanent settlement or agricultural pursuits to the settled pastoralists raising their livestock within a circumscribed area and perhaps also farming the land. The role of the migratory nomad and its ecological significance for human society is little understood and consequently much interfered with, especially in recent years, by governments anxious to modernize their peoples.

At one extreme, migratory nomadism is distinguished by complete mobility: it admits little or no dependence on agriculture, no fixed settlements, no provision for stabling or fodder for its animals other than that to be found in the fields throughout the year. Nomadism is based on the traditional knowledge of the appearance of fresh pastures in the intimately known route of migration. Among some nomads such as those in southwest Iran, the routes between summer and winter pastures are long. However, the Central Asian pattern is different. Groups such as the Mongols have a circular migration pattern covering smaller mileages. However, where rainfall is sporadic, the pattern of migration may vary from year to year.

Nomads know their animals well and adapt themselves to their various needs. Among some nomad peoples, animals are separated according to kind in order that each may be placed on the pasture most suited to it. This may mean splitting up the tribe to take different species to the most suited pastures.

In various localities of Southwest Asia, pastures are utilized by one species or another belonging to different groups of nomads throughout most of the year. There tends to be a succession of occupants, and their flocks utilize pastures in different stages of development. In the Zagros foothills of South Kurdistan, sheep-raising nomads pasture during the winter season. As these nomads vacate the area in the spring, camel-keeping Arab nomads draw in from the adjoining desert to escape the summer heat and drought. Since the camels have a much greater tolerance of parched food and poor water, they thrive under conditions which are too severe for the Kurdish nomads' sheep. They use what there is of summer pasture in the foothill areas and vacate them in favor of the desert when the winter rains come (Barth, 1960).

Thus, in each locality there are likely to be several different niches, each of which can be filled by a group of nomads during some part of the year. This possibility for regular succession of nomadic groups through the seasons in an area is increased by the fact that strains of animals of differing tolerance and habits are found in the Middle East. These strains tend to develop in response to differing but regular patterns of migration imposed by the herders and owners—in effect a slightly biased natural selection.[1]

EXTENT OF NOMADISM AND POPULATION ESTIMATES

Nomadism is an adaptive response to an inhospitable arid environment. The greatest arid regions in the world are composed of the interior Asian steppes, Southwest Asia (Iran Afghanistan, Pakistan), the Arab Near East and the Saharan belt of Africa.

Table 35–1 represents the variation in the nomadic population by country of the Sahara compared with the total population within the Sahara regions of each country. Similar figures for the inhabitants of other desert regions in North Africa and the Middle East are not available, but in terms of the overall population of certain countries, we can say the following:

Table 35–1

TOTAL & NOMADIC POPULATION IN THE SAHARA BY COUNTRY
(After Capot-Rey, 1962)

TERRITORY	TOTAL POPULATION WITHIN THE SAHARA REGION	NOMADS
French Sahara	539,000	202,000
Morocco	500,000	100,000
Mauritania	600,000	150,000
Spanish Sahara	50,000	30,000
Mali	100,000	30,000
Niger	250,000	150,000
Chad	50,000	45,000
Tunisia	400,000	30,000
Libya	1,091,000	255,000
Egypt	150,000	23,000
Sudan	1,000,000	200,000

[1] For a useful discussion of the ecological concepts of niche, etc., in nomadism, see Barth, 1956.

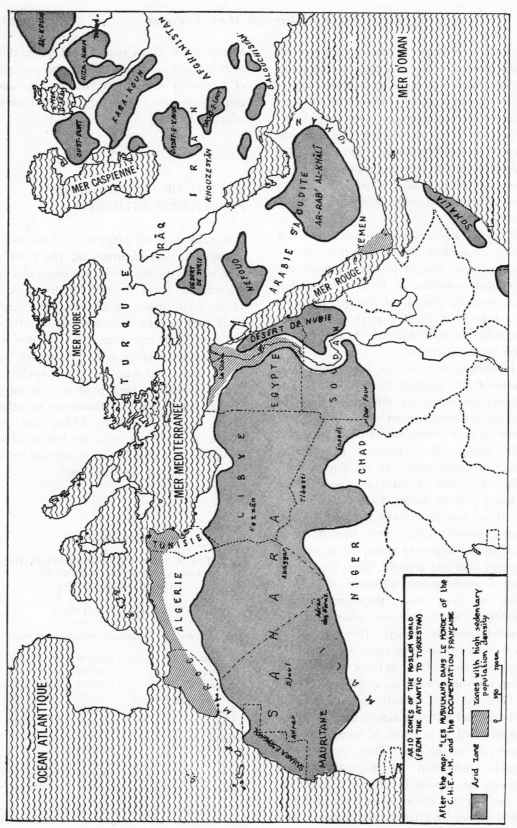

Figure 35-1

In Southwest Asia there are about 5 million nomads, approximately 10 percent of the population in mountain and plateau areas (Barth, 1960). Somalia is over 70 percent nomadic (Silberman, 1959a). Recent estimates in Turkey of the nomads of western Anatolia range around 50,000, while nomad bands in the east total larger numbers (de Planhol, 1959). In Saudi Arabia, the Bedouin nomads represent 50 to 60 percent of the total population of the kingdom (Helaissi, 1959). The Bedouin of Israel number less than 22,000 and are becoming more and more sedentarized (Muhsam, 1959).

THE NOMADS' ANIMALS

Of course, conditions of life for nomads vary from region to region. A spectrum of animals suited to these conditions is available to the nomads: horses, cattle, sheep, goats, camels of two species, asses and mules and yaks. All these animals have been bred selectively to fill certain niches or habitats, and therefore in our time represent a valuable stock of adapted genetic material from which to choose for establishing stock adapted to various habitats. However, in animal breeding and stock improvement projects it must be realized that any attempt to breed desert livestock away from the prevailing levels of fodder reserves should be avoided unless there is a clear possibility of providing stable supplies of grazing and fodder of a superior quality to meet the demands of improved livestock (Whyte, 1957; FAO, 1962). Indeed, the desert animals are characterized by their adaptation to environments of not only great extremes in temperature, but also of low availability of food and water. Thus the ability and the need in desert animals to migrate in search of fresh pastures imply the necessity of freedom of movement for the nomad.

The stratification of Asian nomadism at its best is as exquisite and precise as the stratification of sheep breeds and crosses in Britain, a country of many habitats, many sheep breeds and differing markets. The farmers there may be sedentary but the sheep are moved—in trucks now, but one remembers the old ten-day staged treks through the Highlands of Scotland to wintering grounds for the young stock.

Goats appear to have the widest ecological range and toleration of any domesticated animals but are most commonly found in the drier tropical and subtropical zones. One of the values of the goat in nomadic communities is its intelligence and capacity to lead sheep. Its meat is considered inferior to that of the sheep, but its soft, fine leather is superior. Goatskins make good storage containers for cheese and water. Goats are considered the most efficient of any domesticated animal in converting the meager resources of the desert into milk and meat.

The sheep kept in southeastern Europe and some parts of the Near East are mostly triple-purpose breeds which furnish milk, mutton and some wool. Many hardy breeds of sheep in the nomadic areas are especially adapted to the steppe and semidesert climates. Their wool is coarse, has little grease and is very suitable for carpet manufacture. Many breeds are able to store surplus fat, and are referred to as fat-tailed or fat-rumped. The fat is used by the body not only as stored energy in the less clement season, but also as a source of physiological water.

Cattle seem to have the smallest ecological range, but within the species there are wide differences. The Caucasian humped cattle which undoubtedly accompanied Indo-European migrations across Asia and into India were well adapted to long movements in search of water. In so far as this was reflected in skeletal structure, it also fitted in with the domestic function of speedier draft. Humped cattle which we now call *Bos indicus* have larger and more numerous sweat glands than *Bos taurus* types (European) and the muzzle glands differ in their rates of secretion. Kidney function varies in cattle types, and there are also breed differences in fecal water content. The physiology of environmental tolerances in such domesticated animals in hot climates and the particular adaptations of different types are well summarized by W. V. Macfarlane in Hafez (1968). We would suggest that nomadism has contributed markedly to the range of behavioral, physiological and anatomical adaptation which the world has at its disposal in cattle stocks.

The camel, of course, is the animal par excellence of the open desert and disappears with mountains and wet country. Camels have an advantage over other domestic animals in that they can go a long time without drinking even in the hot season, making it possible to disperse them over a wider area and make maximum use of desert vegetation when there are no nearby watering points. Every second year female camels provide five to nine pints of milk per day, on which nomads can subsist during desert treks. The camel is valuable not only for its milk and milk products, but also for its meat. Today camel nomadism is the most characteristic way of life of pastoral peoples inhabiting the Syrian and Arabian deserts and the Sahara. In Egypt, camel-herding nomads exist only in small groups, whereas a majority of the Somali are nomadic camel herders. The value of the camel as a transport animal for the desert nomad is such that poor nomads who lack enough camels to transport their tents often must settle by an oasis and lose their independence. The two-humped camel of Central Asia could reach into colder dry areas and was the basis of the caravan trade between China and the Caspian.

Nomadic pastoralism postdates either agriculture or domestication of animals. It is a highly specialized form of land use which arose in the steppe regions of the Old World and has continued there until the present. The horse was a natural denizen of this region and became a prominent member of the pastoral nomadic group of animals. It yielded milk and heavy leather, it was capable of subsisting on very little water, and it could move farther in the day than any other pastoral species. The art of riding allowed more differentiation of nomad activities. The mounted nomad could reach the potential mobility of the horse, but the rest of the stock could move only at its own rate—cattle slowest, sheep and goats much faster. Livestock protection was easier altogether once riding had been achieved.

Most significantly, riding produced the nomadic cavalry as a military force. Krader (1963) in his *Peoples of Central Asia* says, "The Mongol empire was the product of the breakdown of the relations between farmers and herders on the Asiatic steppes. The weaknesses of the farming regions, political as well as economic, created the era of the nomadic conquests." The empirical balance between the cultures of oasis and steppe was broken down by the mobility of equestrianism, which enabled, for example, the distant Mongol to descend on the oasis of Merv. The oasis of Merv is fifty or sixty miles across and until the descent of the Mongols was a city of no mean order.

Turcoman nomads had grazed the steppes around Merv in ecological tolerance long before the descent of Genghis Khan. But this local balance of oasis and nomadic populations meant nothing to the newly mobile Mongols, who may have been nomad pastoralists back home but were only mounted raiding bands in their devastating western movements. We suggest that the memory of that time has produced the warped civilized judgment that nomadism is a practice to be discouraged or stamped out.

Yet an examination of nomadism will show that the nomads have realized the value of oases and the sedentary populations around them. Nomads live on animals, but they like cereal grain and the fruits which can be grown around the oasis. So long as access to water is assured, the nomad as an empirical ecologist sees quite clearly that the sedentary oasis dweller is a functional entity in society.

Settled occupiers of land fear the myriad mouths of the nomads' stock passing through their land. Hatred can build up, and law, belonging to the settled, seems to favor a title to land rather than age-old custom. As settled populations increase, they are reaching out and nibbling at the nomads' winter or dry-season grazing, raising the tension. Nomads, being the strong and self-reliant people they are, dealt drastically with this situation in the past and relieved the tension. Now they are in retreat everywhere.

COMPARISON OF STANDARDS OF LIVING

While many speak of the inferior or backward life of the nomad, it is apparent in most areas that nomads have a better standard of living than their sedentary neighbors. In the Sahara region, two surveys in the northern and southern Sahara indicated that the nomads' living standards in both places were higher than those of the sedentary population, even though the traditional way of the nomad had been already deeply affected.

Similarly, in 1955, Borkou nomads (see Figure 35–1) had 500 grams of dates, 180 grams of millet and 4 liters of milk a day plus enough money for taxes, some clothing and tea. The settlers had only 400 grams of dates, 400 grams of millet, little milk and 12 francs a day in cash (Capot-Rey, 1962; see Table 35–2).

Furthermore, the negative effects of sedentary pastoralism must be included in any such comparison. Pastoralism can cause

Table 35–2

1955 STUDY OF THE REGION OF LAGHOUAT
(After Merlet, 1957)

	INCOME PER DAY	CALORIES PER DAY	ANNUAL INCOME
Nomad	53–54 francs	1,776–1,797	115,323 francs
Sedentary	24–46 francs	1,349–1,776	106,754 francs

extensive damage to habitat if overgrazing is allowed. In analyzing cases of such damage from around the world, one can see that too many animals are kept too long at one spot because the populations are sedentary. As governmental actions are impinging on the range and style of the traditional nomad, the lessons of the recent past should be remembered.

What might be called the nomad period of extensive pastoralism in North America is idealized in the persistent "western" of the cinema. But it was only a half-baked nomadism, mixed up with European "home-place" heritage. "Home-place" admixture implies overuse of neighboring land, thus destroying the advantage of nomadism. So extensive grazing in western America did destroy immense areas; and the lesson has not been learned even yet in the Southwest, where cattle are being trucked around to where a shower has brought a bite of grass. The Mormons of Utah are intensely aware of home-place, and their outer watersheds, away from those neat little towns, are in a bad way. History shows how Utah's grass has deteriorated in a hundred years (Cottam, 1948).

In the past hundred years or more, nomadic pastorialists have had to face increasing pressure from the sedentary world. As the central power of governments is extended, modern legislators and rulers may take the side of the settled tribes. Nomadic tribes do not often feel allegiance to the central government but to themselves as a tribe, and this is a threat to nationalist design. Conflicts often develop between tribal values and loyalties and the demands of the bureaucratic state administration. In the military field, there has been mutual suspicion and occasional battles between state armies and some large nomadic groups (Barth, 1962).

Nomadism is anathema to the politician, for the nomad cannot be organized the politician's way; instead of being at the polling booth on election day, he is miles away where the grass is. For many countries striving to achieve a progressive role among modern nations, it has not been acceptable to have "backward" nomads around.

ECOLOGICAL CONSEQUENCES OF SEDENTARIZATION

The ecology of nomadic pastoralism is an adaptation to an environment in which the availability of water and grass are critical factors. Whereas agencies like the FAO encourage steps to maintain and improve the productive capacity of the land through projects like artificial reseeding, there are areas in Iran, for example, where not more than 10 percent of grazing ranges are even susceptible to reseeding (FAO, 1962, p. 359).

In the Iranian province of Fars there is a clear contrast between the sheep of the nomads and those of the sedentary villagers. The nomadic strains tend to be larger and more productive. However, their resistance to extremes of temperature is less than that of the strains in the mountain villages, and their tolerance of heat, drought and parched fodder is less than that of the strains kept in the hotter southern villages.

A dramatic consequence of these ecological adaptations is seen when these nomads become sedentary. Barth (1962) has described the results of sedentarization in the case of the Basseri tribe of Fars. Here during the reign of Reza Shah a government program to settle the nomads was instituted in the 1920's. Nomadism in Iran was then seen as an obstacle to modernization, a mili-

tary threat, and therefore politically undesirable. It was argued then that in order to pacify, modernize and educate these people, it is necessary to settle them in village-like schemes. Barth (1962) reports a sheep mortality of 70 to 80 percent when the nomads were settled and kept through the year, along with their sheep, in either lowlands or mountainous areas. Hardy though the nomadic strains may be, they cannot withstand the heat of the lowlands in summer or the cold of the mountains in winter. Some nomads, luckier than others, were able to pay a young relative or bribe officials to keep their sheep on the move. This helped keep alive the valuable stocks later used by the nomads to resume their herds when they were able to go back to nomadic pastoralism upon the outbreak of the Second World War and the abdication of Reza Shah.

In 1925, entire tribes were forcibly resettled elsewhere and forced to live in stone houses while their grazing lands were confiscated; though forced resettlement may have had political justification, the other results were disastrous. When nomad families were compelled to remain in one place, various diseases developed, and large numbers of Iranian tribesmen were wiped out by epidemics. Since pastoralism is the only possible way of life in many districts of Iran where rainfall is inadequate for crop-growing, Iran was deprived of many useful commodities such as milk, meat, wool, hides and draft animals. Between 1920 and 1940 the nomads who were not used to the life of cultivation, much less to being settled in a very difficult semiarid region, were unable to feed themselves due to disease and lack of food (Fisher, 1950). Since these failures, nomadic pastoralism has increased and is providing a major source of the Iranian meat supply.

Another country which dramatically attempted to settle the nomads was the Soviet Union (see Bacon, 1966), which in 1921 passed a resolution to eradicate the "political, economic and cultural backwardness of the nomads" (Tursunbayev and Potapov, 1959). It is felt by non-Russian writers that the settling of Kazakh nomads under compulsion had disastrous effects:

Between 1929 and 1933, according to the official statistics the number of horses fell from four million to 460,000, the number of cattle from 7 million to 1,600,000 and the number of sheep from 25 million to 2,700,000. In 1942 the nomads' flocks had to be built up again, and in 1944 experienced shepherds and stock raisers had to be found. Nearly a million Kazakhs had moved away towards the industrial centers of Siberia, and the geographer P. George wrote in 1947, that nomadism is almost dead. (Monteil, 1959)

The horse nomads of Kazakhstan were an integral part of the ecosystem. Their horses utilized the natural vegetation of the semi-arid wilderness. Today these nomads have been settled and integrated into the urban-industrial life of the Soviet Union. The biocoenoses of which they formed a part have been transformed, under Khrushchev's Virgin Lands program, into plowed lands for growing crops. The result is a repetition of history, a lesson unlearned. According to *Prostor,* the Kazakhstan literary magazine, Kazakhstan is today becoming a dust bowl with parts of the Virgin Lands a sandy desert due to hasty plowing and clearing methods and severe Asian climate. The Kazakh horse nomads of this area used to provide essential meat and dairy products. Now livestock fall ill and dust storms affect people's health with dust-caused throat infections, pneumonia, silicosis and eye diseases (*Washington Post,* December 26, 1968).

Not all countries are forcing sedentarization to the extent carried out by the Russians or by Reza Shah in Iran. Sedentarization can also originate with the nomads themselves, sometimes by choice, as when they buy land, sometimes unwillingly, or sometimes when drought forces them to be sedentary temporarily. Many countries have proj-

ects aiming at settling the nomads bit by bit. Whether the programs are crash programs or long-term, the important fact remains that in most of these countries the complete disappearance of nomadism would not only leave certain humans without employment or subsistence but would leave the steppes unused since they cannot be utilized in any other way. The end of nomadism would mean a definite loss of protein food and, at a time when a significant portion of mankind is suffering from hunger, we must question the wisdom of letting a region such as the French Sahara, which feeds one million people, return to the desert. This is Capot-Rey's question (1962), though the larger ecological question remains of how to rehabilitate the still-spreading Sahara.

The Sahel is that region of southern Sahara that extends from the Atlantic southeastward to the Sudan. Here settlement has been around government settlement posts or around family-owned wells. Agriculture north of the 300 millimeters per year rainfall line is uncertain and the land is low in productivity. Thus families must combine crop farming with the raising of livestock retained from nomadic days. There has been continuous overgrazing around government posts which were established at watering points in the nomad zone. This continuous overgrazing has changed the composition of pasturage and is reflected in a decline in the quality of the beasts; after just a few years of experience by the FAO and local governments, settled herds are seen to be undernourished and the pastures deteriorated. The sacrifice of mobility becomes especially painful when rains are late and sufficient feed cannot be produced (Bremaud and Pagot, 1962).

Around family wells, where the livestock has not exceeded the capacity of the land, other effects of sedentarization have become apparent after some time, in poorer conformation and a rise in deficiency diseases and parasitic infection. Other effects of sedentarization have become apparent around family wells even when carrying capacity of the land has been studied; conformation suffers and there is a rise in incidence of deficiency diseases and parasitic infections.

The cost of settling nomads is high. The settled life is considered a "social scourge" as the nomads then "lose their energy and resistance to endemic diseases" (Monteil, 1959). The Somali nomads, for example, live almost exclusively on camel milk. Their daily intake is up to 6,200 calories. However, their blood cholesterol level is low, and the incidence of heart disease is virtually nil. Given the diet of these tribesmen and the composition of camel's milk, this was most unexpected! There are good grounds here for postulating an adaptive process that over the centuries has achieved a real homeostasis in these people. Researchers among these tribesmen consider that factors favoring the onset of some degree of coronary disease in highly developed countries are compensated among these tribesmen. These people are not subject to innumerable psychosomatic disturbances to which people living in urban environments are prey. Later, when these people migrate to town, dietetic changes and nervous tensions need to be considered when coronary disease appears in all its diverse forms (Lapiccirella *et al.*, 1962).[2]

There has been no rapid settlement of the 1,200,000 nomadic inhabitants of the Sahara (Capot-Rey, 1962). They are spread through regions where artesian wells could not be sunk as has been done in other regions (for example, in the case of the Palestinian nomads). Agriculture and sedentary stock raising have therefore not been practicable on a large scale. The oil and mining companies cannot absorb that much labor. It may be repeated that if the steppes are left unused, there will be a loss of high-quality food supplies.

Most projects in the Egyptian desert have encouraged sedentarization at the expense of animal husbandry, which has depleted the animal wealth of the nation (Abou-Zeid, 1959). Meat rations are now quite common in Cairo, even for the first-class hotels, restricting purchase of each kind of meat to certain days of the week. So far it seems that the African government whose policy is most in line with the ecological principles of pastoral nomadism is that of Somalia. The Somali government's three planning bodies have agreed that the development of livestock in Somalia is the most important goal in development. The government is in fact concerned with keeping the nomads mobile to avoid overgrazing (Silberman, 1959).

Somaliland and the Sudan are more enlightened than many other African countries. They realize that some parts of their terrain would be uninhabitable if they were not under nomadic pastoralism. Lee Talbot has written in this volume (Chapter 37) of the Masai, a Nilotic people that have come out of their well-watered homeland into the dry steppe of Kenya and Tanzania. The Nilotics in the upper Nile and Bahr-el-Ghazal are partial nomads, moving their quite glorious cattle between bush and plain (toich), as inundation directs. Movement may be only a few miles, with young folk managing the cattle camps. It should be emphasized that in this region there is a body of people with immense expertise in cattle management.

The Black Arab tribes of the sub-Saharan dry belt are necessarily nomadic, and their cattle are different in character from those of the Bahr-el-Ghazal. The people live on the products of animals and to a lesser extent on the animals themselves. Their diet is adequate in protein. It is impossible for ecologically apical species to increase vastly in numbers, but if an apical species is pre-

[2] Similarly, serum cholestrol is lower in the Negev Bedouin than in Western populations. See Groen, *et al.* (1964) for a discussion of Bedouin nutrition.

pared to descend a stage in the ecological pyramid, ousting the species that formerly occupied that niche, then increase is possible. Man has indeed done this by descending from his apical, mainly proteinous, diet to being a herbivore, a starch eater. The prairies of the United States and the plains of the Ukraine and the Kuban have produced the starch that has bred the seething populations of Europe. If rice is to become the crop of the Bahr-el-Ghazal and wheat the produce of the Kafue and Chambeshi Flats, then Africa will seethe with people also.

Political assessment of the influences of nomadism has been colored by what is finally a deleterious interference with a social anthropological situation. Obviously, the nomad measures wealth by numbers of stock, but he knows that some of that stock must be "spent" in loss from various causes. Veterinary departments of governments have prevented much of that traditional loss without any attempt at socio-anthropological amelioration or modification of culture. The result has been chronic destruction of habitat, a result not attributable to nomadic pastoralism per se, but to badly considered notions of "improvement" by foreign administrations.

The nomadic adaptation has made it possible to utilize lands unsuitable to most agriculture and to provide surplus animal products for sedentary populations. Nomadic peoples generally have a way of life and social organization which is often deemed incompatible with civilization by the sedentary population. Yet in their determination to change a way of life, countries have not realized the complex relationship between ecological, cultural and economic factors.

Development schemes are conceived by economists and agricultural scientists rather than by ecologists and nomads. Our desire in this paper is to emphasize that nomadic pastoralism in its proper place, which is in the steppe countries of the world, can be a complex and efficient form of land use. If nomadism is extended into forested and cultivable lands, it will probably lead to degradation of environment as, for example, in the watersheds of the Ngoro Ngoro Crater in Tanzania. Curtailment of nomadism and change of husbandry to carbohydrate production may have deleterious effects on both the nomads and their environment. Ecological assessment may help determine whether change of land use would be environment-building or destroying, and socially enhancing or degrading.

REFERENCES

Abou-Zeid, A. M. "The Sedentarization of Nomads in the Western Desert of Egypt." *International Social Science Journal,* 10 (1959), 550–58.

Awad, Mohammed. "The Assimilation of Nomads in Egypt." *The Geographical Review,* 44 (1954), 240–52.

———. "Nomadism in the Arab Lands of the Middle East." *The Problems of the Arid Zone.* Paris: UNESCO, 1962.

Bacon, E. E. "Types of Pastoral Nomadism in Central and Southwest Asia." *Southwestern Journal of Anthropology,* 10 (1954), 44–68.

———. *Central Asians under Russian Rule; a Study in Culture Change.* Ithaca: Cornell University Press, 1966.

Barth, Fredrick. "Ecologic Relationships of Ethnic Groups in Swat, North Pakistan." *American Anthropologist,* 58 (1956), 1079–89.

———. *Nomads of South Persia: The Basseri Tribe.* Oslo: Oslo University Press, 1961.

———. "Nomadism in the Mountain and Plateau Areas of South West Asia." *The Problems of the Arid Zone.* Paris: UNESCO, 1962.

Bataillon, C. "Résistance ou Décadence du Nomadisme." *Nomades et Nomadisme au Sahara.* UNESCO, 1963.

Berque, J. "Introduction to Symposium on Nomads and Nomadism in the Arid Zone." *International Social Science Journal,* 11 (1959), 481–98.

Bremaud, O., and Pagot, J. "Grazing Lands, Nomadism and Transhumance in the Sahel." *The Problems of the Arid Zone.* Paris: UNESCO, 1962.

Capot-Rey, R. "The Present State of Nomadism in the Sahara." *The Problems of the Arid Zone.* Paris: UNESCO, 1962.

Cottam, Walter P. "The Role of Ecology in the Conservation of Renewable Resources." In *Proceedings of the Inter-American Conference on Conservation of Renewable Natural Resources.* U. S. Dept. of State Publication, No. 3382. Denver, Sept. 7–20, 1948.

de Planhol, Xavier. "Geography, Politics, and Nomadism in Anatolia." *International Social Science Journal,* 11 (1959), 525–31.

FAO. "Nomadic Pastoralism as a Method of Land Use." *The Problems of the Arid Zone.* Paris: UNESCO, 1962.

Fisher, W. B. *The Middle East: A Physical, Social, and Regional Geography.* New York: E. P. Dutton, 1950.

Forde, C. Daryll. "The Kazakh: Horse and Sheep Herders of Central Asia." *Man in Adaptation—The Cultural Present.* Chicago: Aldine, 1968.

Goldschmidt, Walter. "Theory and Strategy in the Study of Cultural Adaptability." *Man in Adaptation—The Cultural Present.* Chicago: Aldine, 1968.

Groen, J. J., et al. "Nutrition of the Bedouins in the Negev Desert." *American Journal of Clinical Nutrition,* 14 (1964), 37–46.

Hafez, E. S. E., ed. *Adaptation of Domestic Animals.* Philadelphia: Lea & Febiger, 1968.

Helaissi, A. S. "The Bedouins and Tribal Life in Saudi Arabia." *International Social Science Journal,* 11 (1959), 532–37.

Kolars, John. "Locational Aspects of Cultural Ecology: The Case of the Goat in Non-Western Agriculture." *Geographical Review,* 56 (1966), 577–84.

Krader, Lawrence. "Ecology of Central Asian Pastoralism." *Southwestern Journal of Anthropology,* 11 (1955), 301–26.

———. "Culture and Environment in Interior Asia." *Studies in Human Ecology.* Pan American Union Social Science Monographs No. 3. 1957.

———. "The Ecology of Pastoral Nomadism." *International Social Science Journal,* 11 (1959), 499–510.

———. *Peoples of Central Asia.* Bloomington, Ind.: Indiana University Press, 1963.

Lapiccirella, V.; Lapiccirella, R.; Abboni, F.; and Liotta, S. *Bulletin of the World Health Organization,* 27 (1962), 681.

Lattimore, Owen. "The Steppes of Mongolia and the Characteristics of Steppe Nomadism." *Inner Asian Frontiers of China.* Boston: Beacon, 1962.

Merlet, H. "Enquêts sur le revenu de la population de la commune mixte de Laghouat." *Trav. I.R.S.,* Vol. 15, first half-year, 1957 (ref. in Capot-Rey, 1962).

Monteil, Vincent. "The Evolution and Settling of the Nomads of the Sahara." *International Social Science Journal,* 11 (1959), 572–84.

———. *Les Tribus du Fârs et la Sédentarisation des Nomades.* Paris: Mouton and Co., 1966.

Muhsam, H. V. "Sedentarization of the Bedouins in Israel." *International Social Science Journal,* 11 (1959), 539–49.

Nelson, Lars-Erik. "Dust Scours Kazakhstan." *Washington Post,* Dec. 26, 1968 (C11).

Silberman, Leo. "Somali Nomads." *International Social Science Journal,* 11 (1959), 559–71.

Symposium on Nomads and Nomadism in the Arid Zone. *International Social Science Journal,* 11 (1959), 481–585.

Shepard, Paul. *Man in the Landscape.* New York: Knopf, 1967.

Tursunbayev, A., and Potapov, A. "Some Aspects of the Socio-Economic and Cultural Development of Nomads in the U.S.S.R." *International Social Science Journal,* 11 (1959), 511–24.

UNESCO. *The Problems of the Arid Zone.* Paris: Imprémieries Oberthur, 1960.

———. *Nomades et Nomadisme au Sahara.* Munich: Graphische Betriebe GmbH., 1963.

Van Royen, William. *The Agricultural Resources of the World.* New York: Prentice-Hall, 1954.

Whyte, R. O. "Animal Husbandry." In *Guidebook to Research Data for Arid Zone Development,* B. T. Dickson, ed. Paris: UNESCO, 1957.

36. ECOLOGICAL CONSEQUENCES OF BEDOUIN SETTLEMENT IN SAUDI ARABIA

Harold F. Heady

One unplanned and unforeseen side effect of the oil industry in Saudi Arabia has been settlement of many Bedouins. In numerous instances, but not all, the new way of life has been both satisfying to the people and productive for the country. However, permanent domestic watering points in the oil fields and along the Trans-Arabian Pipeline have fostered yearlong grazing of sensitive desert vegetation. Areas of vegetational destruction as much as 60 to 75 kilometers in radius around the watering points commonly occur. Well drilling, which results in uncontrolled artesian water, in turn results in problems of salty water and impeded drainage. Controlled, promoted, and improved pastoral nomadism is necessary for maintenance of productive desert resources where forage supplies are irregularly fluctuating and the scattered water supplies ephemeral.

The primary purpose of this paper is to trace the recent development of water and grazing for domestic animals in the Arabian desert. Ecological effects of modernizing the Bedouin and changing their pastoral nomadism to sedentary living were not planned nor widely realized. Largely, they have been the unforeseen side effects from the oil industry.

The Saudi Arabian case history is likely to be unique for three reasons. First, oil resources have kept the kingdom from the beggar's position in obtaining funds for develop-ment. Scanty information and entrenched social custom limit development more than lack of funds. Second, the climatic harshness is extreme. More humid parts of the world have been the sites of nearly all development projects. Third, most changes to date in use of the Arabian desert are directly attributable to outside influences, such as the development of motor vehicles and the accompanying growth of the oil industry in Arabia. Therefore, this paper examines a history of normal and slow changes by local peoples in response to materials and ideas brought to them through unpremeditated effort from a modern world.

Saudi Arabia's economy is based on revenues from the oil industry, which are paid through royalties, salaries and local purchases. These monies are used to develop other industries and to improve standards of living. Money has been used at a rapidly increasing rate for construction of schools, hospitals, roads, airports and laboratories, and for the establishment of services in security, education, agriculture, health and communications. Interacting and unpredicted

results from these developments have caused the Government of Saudi Arabia to embark on inventory, planning and feasibility studies during the last decade.

To develop its water and agricultural resources, the Government has contracted with international consulting firms for natural resource inventories (Klemme, 1965). These studies, extending over three years and costing several million dollars, are feasibility studies from which programs for land and water improvement will develop.

This paper is based on my reconnaissance of grazing resources in Saudi Arabia

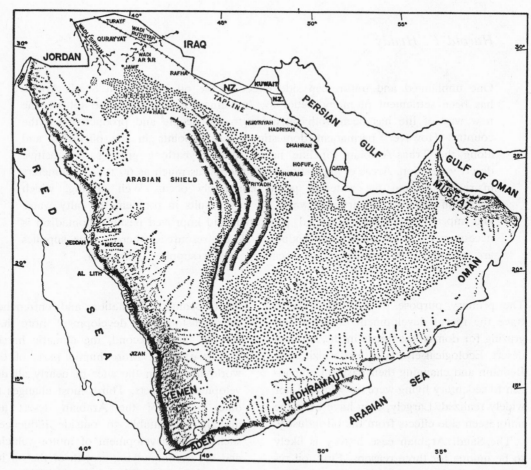

Figure 36–1 The Arabian Peninsula, showing geographic regions and names. Generalized from U. S. Geol. Survey Misc. Geol. Investigations, Map 1-270 B-1

(Heady, 1963) and later studies in the country amounting to eight months, nine weeks of which were used in desert safari.

THE BASIC RESOURCE

Saudi Arabia includes nearly four-fifths of the Arabian Peninsula, covering slightly more than 1.5 million square kilometers (Fig. 36–1). It is bounded on the north by Jordan and Iraq; on the west by the Red Sea; on the east by Kuwait and the Persian Gulf. Several sheikdoms or small states occupy coastal positions along the southeast and south from Qatar to Yemen. Accurate topographical, geographical and geological maps and aerial photographs of Saudi Arabia have been prepared through joint effort by the U. S. Geological Survey, Arabian-American Oil Company and the kingdom of Saudi Arabia. The high quality of these maps suggests that reliable inventory and census data of people, livestock, soils, vegetation, climate, land use and water resources are also available. They are not. Statements about the quantity and location of these resources must be considered as estimates based on scarce data and informed guesses.

The topographic or physical appearance of Saudi Arabia is best described as a series of north-south belts that one crosses during west-east travel. The narrow (50 kilometers) coastal plain along the Red Sea merges abruptly into the Asir Mountain chain composed of crystalline and metamorphic basement materials and volcanic rocks. Steep escarpments face the Red Sea with gradual slopes toward the east. The peaks seldom rise above 2,200 meters north of Mecca. Southward, they are increasingly higher, attaining 3,760 meters in central Yemen.

Eastward of the western mountains lies the Arabian Shield. It is relatively narrow at either end but extends nearly 800 kilo-

meters into north central Arabia. The elevation is 1,000 to 1,300 meters, and the rocks are pre-Cambrian crystalline basement with igneous intrusions toward the north. The shield gives way to an escarpment region, formed by six distinctive ridges with steep westward-facing escarpments and gentle eastern slopes. The most prominent of these escarpments is known as the Tuwaiq Mountains, which are about 800 kilometers long, 900 meters in elevation, and rise 300 meters above the plains. Sedimentary deposits from the Paleozoic (outcropped in the escarpments) to the Quaternary period have covered the basement with increasing thickness from west to east.

In the northern part of the escarpment region is the Great Nefud, a sand desert approximating 57,000 square kilometers. The reddish sand is variously sculptured into crescent dunes, parallel ridges, and cones 100 to 300 meters high. A narrow belt of sand connects the Nefud in the north with the Rub' Al Khali or Empty Quarter in the south, an area of 650,000 square kilometers, at least 80 percent covered with sand dunes. Eastward from the sands is a gentle coastal plain which decreases to sea level at the average rate of approximately 1 meter per kilometer. Beneath this coastal plain are most of the country's oil resources, some of the richest oil deposits in the world.

Large areas of gravelly and rocky plains and lava beds without significant soil development occur in Saudi Arabia. There are agricultural soils in the wadis, near oases, and places where silts have been deposited, but agricultural crops in Arabia require irrigation with few exceptions. Soils studies and inventories are just now beginning with reconnaissance surveys and laboratory analyses based on standards used in the United States. Soil maps and the results of laboratory analyses are not yet available in quantity as the first laboratory for study of Arabian soils was planned in early 1965.

Where irrigation and rainfall are inadequate for crops, soils are destined to remain useful for range forage production. Such land constitutes 98 to 99 percent of the kingdom, as no more than 1 percent is likely to be cultivated. The better range soils include the sands, which have little profile development, and the wadis, which are usually mixtures of sand, silt and clay. Large, flat plains with extremely high clay and salt content are numerous. These are barren but may be flooded occasionally. Exposed clay banks often show layering of salts and various textures of alluvium. In the escarpment region, limestone is the principal parent material. Large areas of bare and sloping outcrops of both sandstone and limestone have little soil and are nearly devoid of vegetation.

Few weather stations have been established in Saudi Arabia. Data are scarce and unreliable. Weather data are being collected systematically in conjunction with airline operations, but these records began too recently to produce reasonable averages and measures of variation (Meteorological Services, 1959–1965).

The whole of the peninsula is arid except the mountains in the southwest. It is estimated that over 90 percent of the country has less than 100 millimeters average annual rainfall. Dhahran, over a twenty-three-year period, averaged 89 mm of rain, with a range between 17 and 176 mm. At Jawf, over a five-year period (1957–1961) the average annual precipitation was 56 mm and the average number of days with rain per year was five. Ten days during the five years had over 10 mm of rain. Similar data for Hail were 91 mm, ten days of rain each year and thirteen days with over 10 mm. Local people in both areas considered these five years (1957–1961) a drought period. The high mountains in the southern Asir receive 300 mm or more average rainfall. Rainfall occurs mainly during winter in the north and during summer in the south.

However, it is irregular and often comes as downpours of high intensity.

Temperatures are extremely high during the summer months. Temperatures over 38° C occur for weeks, with frequent days over 45° C and occasionally over 50° C. The winters are characterized by a few nights below freezing and daytime temperatures as high as 25° C. Humidity is very high on coasts of the Red Sea and the Persian Gulf and very low inland, with zero relative humidity frequently recorded.

Many problems and uncertainties exist concerning the relation of rainfall to the total water resources of Saudi Arabia. Ecological consequences of haphazard water development and manipulation will be examined in later sections. Water is or can be as important as oil to Saudi Arabia. No elevation of living standard nor true social progress is possible until problems of water supply are solved.

Full description of the vegetation in Saudi Arabia must await detailed study. Broad vegetational types have been mapped and described by Vesey-Fitzgerald (1955, 1957a, 1957b) and by Tothill (1952). These authors have generalized, but it is difficult to do otherwise in brief tours of areas long without rain and lacking a published flora. All areas I visited in 1962 had vegetation, with the exception of the occasionally flooded mud flats. The gravel plains support a thin cover of annual grasses and herbs following rains, even though they appear bare of vegetation most of the time. The major vegetational types upon which grazing animals depend are as follows:

Areas of deep sand occur along the Persian Gulf and the Red Sea; in the Great Nefud, Dahna, and Rub' Al Khali; and in smaller areas throughout Saudi Arabia. The principal grass is Thuman (*Panicum turgidum*). Following rains, vast green carpets of annual grasses and herbs cover the sands.

With exceptionally heavy rains, the annuals form a dense cover as tall as half a meter. The common shrubs *Calligonum* and *Artemisia* are productive and are grazed extensively. These sands have an extremely high infiltration capacity and a very low water-holding capacity. Since much of the rain comes in high-intensity storms, these two soil characteristics prevent runoff and promote deep penetration of water. Thus, the sands store all the rainfall and support more vegetation than might be expected with such light rainfall. The *Panicum* grass type is best developed on the plains of the Red Sea south of Jeddah, where the soil is so covered with vegetation that it disappears from view at a distance of 10 to 15 meters from the observer.

The wadi channels are the most favorable habitats for range forage production throughout Saudi Arabia. These broad, flat valleys receive runoff water, which brings silt and manure along with additional moisture. Shrubs and grasses form a more dense cover than on surrounding uplands. In the north, the only plants available were found in the wadis. Practices that might prevent the accumulation of water or its infiltration into the wadi fills could be damaging to this range type. The major wadi forage plants are species of *Salsola, Artemisia, Atriplex,* and *Achillea.* Annuals are abundant in the wet season. Some of the wadis are salty, in which case *Haloxylon* is the most common species.

On the limestone plateaus outcrops of limestone have plants scattered in the pockets where soil has accumulated. If a sand layer covers the limestone, *Rantherium* forms a dominant cover, and *Stipa tortillis* is a common associate along with many other grasses. This type, found principally in the north central region, is grazed extensively.

In the western mountains, juniper (*Juniperus procera*) forest occurs high on the slopes. Below are various combinations of species in the genera *Olea, Acacia, Commiphora, Euphorbia* and many others. The mountains have been very heavily grazed for many centuries so the vegetation which remains is largely unpalatable. The species of grasses surviving in protected spots indicate that many palatable grasses were formerly abundant and have not completely disappeared.

One cannot travel far in this large and varied region without being impressed with the repetition of vegetational types as the various habitat conditions repeat. Vegetation is closely correlated with stratigraphy, sand, topography, drainage and salt. Except for the high mountains, the overall climate is much the same throughout Saudi Arabia, so the vegetational types are more closely related to soil conditions than to climate. Major variations are associated with the Mediterranean climatic influence in the north and the monsoonal effects in the south.

GRAZING HISTORY

The Arabian Peninsula has been grazed by domestic animals for several thousand years. By piecing together the records of early travelers (Krader, 1959) and by observing the deserts today, one may reach two conclusions. Many settlements and irrigated areas have existed which are now abandoned, suggesting times of crises throughout history. Relic areas of ungrazed vegetation suggest that vegetative cover in the past few decades was more dense than it is today. If one accepts these propositions, then it is interesting to examine the reasons for change.

When the late Ibn Saud unified the Arab tribes in the first quarter of this century, numerous changes occurred in the use of the grazing land (Aramco, 1960). Tribal warfare was reduced. As this warfare usually centered on raids for livestock, it is surmised that animal populations began to increase. Government policy to control the Bedouin, although not widely enforced, resulted in concentration of people and animals where permanent water occurred. These areas were already occupied by cultivators who also owned livestock. Bedouin settlement crowded more animals onto the local grazing resources, accentuating overgrazing near water. Extensive development of new areas for settlement awaited and has been a consequence of the oil industry. Nearly two hundred attempts to develop new communities before oil was discovered were failures. Many Bedouins were employed directly by the oil industry and have successfully exchanged desert living for an urban environment. Others were attracted to the newly developed water within the oil fields and along the Trans-Arabian Pipeline (commonly called Tapline).

Serious droughts between 1955 and 1963 in northern Arabia intensified these movements toward settlement on fewer and fewer permanent water locations. There was no other place to go. Ninety percent of some herds were lost in 1958–1961, not only from the scanty feed but from increased disease. Camel scab was serious during the drought and spread rapidly among the congregated herds. This crisis added urgency to discussions and proposals for development of Saudi Arabia's water, grazing, and agricultural resources. The first scheme in Wadi Sirhan in 1961 settled many Bedouins on small acreages. Wells were dug and pumps installed to produce irrigation water. For various reasons including little understanding of cultivation principles and the mechanics of pumping water, this scheme has had little success; certainly the herds were not saved.

There is no doubt that forage production has been and is sufficient to support many thousands of sheep, goats, camels and don-

keys. As no reliable census data on numbers of animals were available in 1962, I attempted a field survey of animal numbers so that an appraisal of landscape effects caused by grazing could be made. Counts and locations were recorded of all camels, sheep and goats, donkeys and Bedouin tents during the course of 5,758 kilometers of desert automobile travel. Measurements of visibility along the roads indicated that the livestock were seen with reasonable completeness on a strip of land averaging about 2 kilometers wide. The findings indicate the average densities for the particular regions and particular season of travel to be:

	NUMBER PER SQ. KM.	NUMBER PER SQ. MILE
Bedouin tents	0.13	0.34
Camels	0.59	1.52
Sheep and goats	2.43	6.29
Donkeys	0.04	0.11

If one considers that 5 sheep and goats or 2 donkeys are equivalent to 1 camel in the amount of forage consumed, the area visited averages 1.0 camel unit of grazing per square kilometer or 2.8 camel units per square mile. This figure may be taken as an estimate of the stocking rate over much of Saudi Arabia. A later and more sophisticated aerial survey by one of the contractors in the Great Nefud in 1966 indicated 2.7 camel units per square mile, a heavier grazing pressure than exists in much of the desert areas of the southwestern United States.

These data also suggest that livestock numbers in Saudi Arabia as a whole are as follows (the calculated totals have been reduced by 20 percent to correct for low densities in the great sand desert, which was not visited):

Bedouin tents	227,000
Camels	1,004,000
Sheep and goats	4,158,000
Donkeys	75,000

Regions in which large numbers of animals were found include those near Nuayriyah, Ar'ar, Dahna sands in a 50 kilometer strip about 250 kilometers south of Rafha, and the coastal plains south of Jeddah. These should not be considered areas of permanently high concentrations because all animals are migratory, except those maintained in or near villages. For example, counts for the first 100 kilometers southeast from Ar'ar along the Tapline road on two dates were as follows:

	OCTOBER 31	NOVEMBER 14
Bedouin tents	26	109
Camels	61	106
Sheep and goats	200	1,683
Donkeys	4	14

Showers occurred between the two dates and migrations into the area were in progress on November 14. Another point of interest is that the only area where the number of tents equaled or exceeded the number of livestock was along Wadi Sirhan in northern Arabia. Three recent years of drought had caused severe livestock losses in the region.

The effects of livestock use on the vegetation is of special interest. Many areas were in reasonably good condition. For example, the region halfway between Turayf and Qurayyat had excellent stands of *Salsola* and *Poa sinaica,* both highly palatable species. A 50-kilometer-wide area of *Panicum turgidum* near Hadriyah along the Tapline road was in excellent condition, as were similar stands near Al Lith', south of Jeddah. The *Rantherium* type appeared generally to be in good condition. The headlands of many wadis were also producing forage in considerable quantity.

On the other hand, some locations had been overgrazed so severely that all plants had been destroyed. Wadi Ar'ar and its tributary, Wadi Ruthiyah, were lacking forage species. The damage in Wadi Ruthiyah was so recent that the dead *Salsola* plants were still present. Yet 75 kilometers toward the headwaters of Wadi Ar'ar, there were abundant palatable species. Similar

areas of complete forage destruction around permanent water were seen at Khurais and Nuayriyah. Wadi Sirhan had recently been used very heavily during three consecutive drought years. The most severe destruction occurred around permanent water established by the oil industry. Palatable forage species were dead and shrubs not normally grazed had been very heavily used. Locally and commonly along the route traveled, areas of poor range condition were found. More land was producing below its potential than was in satisfactory condition. Overgrazing was gradually destroying much vegetation.

HYDROLOGY

Saudi Arabia has no watercourse which continuously flows to the sea. Floods of a few hours or at most a few days reach the ocean but these are only from the Asir Mountains and short coastal streams. Water may flow in the wadis for a short time, but it soon disappears into the sands and is stored in the wadi fill. Water which flows onto the salt or mud flats is lost by evaporation.

Runoff from large areas of impermeable outcrops and clay pans which concentrates in the sandy wadis is a fortunate natural phenomenon. Much of this water is stored in alluvium at depths of 2 to 20 meters or more. It is within reach of hand digging and promotes more vegetative growth than could be supported by the rainfall alone. The long, winding wadi strips are too narrow to show on most maps and may be ignored by the newcomer. However, they furnish water and forage which has supported wild animals, domestic animals and human populations for centuries. They are the lifelines of the desert.

The Asir Mountains and Arabian Shield, composed of pre-Cambrian crystalline rocks, do not contain large bodies of deep groundwater. Numerous aquifers and large groundwater reservoirs occur in the sedimentary basin which includes the eastern two-thirds of Saudi Arabia. They outcrop in the escarpment region and may be recharged from water in the wadis. As the sedimentary strata dip slightly to the eastward, water occurs as large flowing springs along the Persian Gulf. Many wells in the eastern region are artesian.

As a consequence of drilling for oil in eastern Arabia, flowing water-wells were developed and a drilling boom was under way by 1940 (Aramco, 1960). Many wells were improperly completed, wasting much water. One common mistake was failure to cap the wells, resulting in continuous flow and loss of control over artesian water. The second was improper casings which allowed mixing of waters from different aquifers with differing salt contents. Some aquifers produce high quality water, but others have as much as 2,000–4,000 parts per million of dissolved salts (Aramco, 1961).

As drilling for water expanded across Arabia, water control was not obtained; the consequences are widespread and affect all the land resources. Major problems are excess water, high salinity and poor drainage. Sand encroachment into irrigated areas is common. Often all of these problems occur in the same area. The oasis at Hofuf, for example, since 1940 has developed a drainage problem which concentrates salts upon evaporation of impounded waters. Similar situations exist at Al Jawf and Buraydah. Clearly, any irrigation or water development scheme in Saudi Arabia must provide for drainage.

Improved water use is beginning through the plugging of some wells, control of flow, better conveyance of water and better irrigation practices. A survey of over 3,500 wells in northern Saudi Arabia during 1966–1968 provided the basic information needed for this water management.

Large bodies of water undoubtedly exist in the sedimentary basin of Arabia and abundant water will be available for many years. However, it is certain that these water resources have limits. Pressure within aquifers and the water level in nonflowing wells have dropped. Recharge water may be entering the deeper aquifers, but it is not keeping pace with discharge. More and more wells will need pumps. Evidently, water accumulated in these aquifers over recent geological time and is susceptible to mining and depletion.

Many water developments that are now used for livestock and domestic purposes have occurred as a consequence of the oil industry and have unintentionally changed the patterns of nomadic grazing, as illustrated by the small community of Khurais, east of Riyadh, and the pumping stations along the Trans-Arabian Pipeline at Ar'ar and Nuayriyah. These water sources are recent, too far from others to permit ready movement between water points, and they are permanent, yearlong supplies. Grazing has changed near them from occasional nomadic use to yearlong grazing by livestock permanently based at these villages. Destruction of vegetation has resulted in bare soil near water and little vegetation closer than 50 kilometers to the three centers.

In attempts to improve water supplies, dikes or low dams have been used to spread water laterally across wadis, to slow the runoff flow, and to promote infiltration in desert area. Commonly, the dams are spaced 100 meters or so apart, depending upon the wadi gradient. They are open at alternate ends so that the water flows slowly in a zigzag fashion from one side of the wadi to the other.

This practice is of doubtful value in Saudi Arabia except where it can be used as an irrigation system to raise planted crops, such as the schemes employed in the Wadi Jizan and others of the southern Tihama coast. For several reasons the value of water spreading is questionable. (1) There are almost no waters that flow from Saudi Arabia to the sea; therefore, the water infiltrates into the wadi sands or evaporates. Since little water is lost, increased infiltration is not needed. Holding the water in one place would reduce the water in the wadi further along, where someone else needs it. (2) Dams or dikes which slow the velocity of flow allow the silt and clay fractions to settle. These tend to seal the soil, preventing infiltration and increasing evaporation of the water held above ground. This effect has already been demonstrated in Saudi Arabia in the dam at Riyadh and at other places. Dikes in Wadi Khulays north of Jeddah are used for a few years to trap the silt. Plowing breaks the sealed surface and crops are raised on the improved land by irrigation from wells. (3) Water-spreading dikes are expensive to build and are likely to be destroyed by the large floods, in which case there is so much water that a spreading system is not needed, especially one which allows silt and clay to seal the sandy surface. When water is needed in times of drought, there is too little water to spread. (4) Water-spreading systems must be protected from livestock grazing at the beginning and carefully managed later. Indiscriminate livestock use will destroy them by trampling. With careful engineering and continuous care, water-spreading systems will improve forage production, but these conditions are not available under nomadic grazing in Saudi Arabia.

WILDLIFE

Many species of animals and birds are natural components of desert ecosystems. Saudi Arabia was no exception, but now many species are rare or extinct. As recently as World War II great herds of gazelle roamed the deserts of Arabia. The Arabian oryx was certainly more numerous than at present. The ostrich is recently extinct. Not only have larger species suffered severe reductions but smaller animals and birds are diminishing.

Much of Arabia is easily traveled cross-country by motor vehicle. The advent of four-wheel drive plus other fittings for desert travel has given new facility to the Bedouins, hunters, and others. The gazelles, for example, have little means of winning a chase with these vehicles, especially from the hunter who also uses spotter aircraft and high firepower in his arms. These modern tools in the hands of people who live off the land and traditionally carry guns have spelled the demise of wild animals, large and small. The historic balance between wildlife and nomadic peoples in Saudi Arabia has been upset, largely because the pickup truck is replacing the camel and providing a rapid means of chase. Facility for hauling of water and provisions is opening areas for grazing during times when they were not formerly available, resulting in detrimental habitat changes for wild species.

NOMADISM VS. PERMANENT SETTLEMENT

Pastoral nomadism is a way of living dictated by arid climate, irregularly fluctuating forage resources and widely scattered ephemeral water supplies. Nomadic tribes have their own customs, social structure, agreements on the use of land and other respected traditions. Like other people, they resist change in their way of life. However, forces to change that way of life have become stronger in recent years. Besides the official policy of many governments including Saudi Arabia to settle the nomads, several factors of an economic and sociological nature are at work. These include the development of irrigation on the best lands; employment in expanding industries such as the oil industry; water developments; rapid transport by auto on new roads; improved communications; extension of mechanized agriculture with incentives such as low rents, credit, technical aid, and veterinary services; localized health facilities; schools; and transfer of authority from the tribal chief to the central government. There is little doubt that tribal life holds back economic development and in the words of Helaissi (1959) "the nomads must catch up with the caravan of modern civilization." Present evidence is abundant that the Bedouins respond in modern society and many have forsaken their tents for permanent dwellings.

With more individuals selecting a sedentary way of life, nomadic grazing may be greatly reduced or eliminated and the vast areas that can only be used for grazing may be lost as a basis for livestock production. Perhaps the best approach is to let these people choose their own way of life and at the same time to improve livestock production and living conditions in the range areas. Such steps could include development of additional water, traveling schools, frequent communication of forage conditions and news, traveling stores, extension training in range management, veterinary services, improved marketing facilities, and livestock fattening operations in the irrigated areas.

To argue for not modifying the nomadic way of life is a futile exercise. But modernization should be taken to the Bedouin. He should not be forced to move to a new habitat. The arid climate cannot be changed and irrigation is possible on only a tiny fraction of the arid lands. Why waste the grazing resource of the vast areas? This is not to suggest that traditional migratory grazing should not be changed. It suggests that modernization of Bedouin life *in situ* with all the services available from technical agriculture and other aspects of modern society should be brought to bear on the problems of livestock production in arid regions. The philosophy of "the desert is a wasteland" should be replaced by one of "production at the full potential," however low or high it may be. Nomadism is necessary for the use of desert grazing resources, but this philosophy can prevail only if Bedouin life is allowed to flourish. Intentional settlement of all Bedouins should be questioned. The unplanned, unintentional and often unrealized ecological influences which have invaded the deserts in Saudi Arabia because of Bedouin settlement need to be studied and controlled before these fragile ecosystems are upset beyond repair.

REFERENCES

Aramco. *Aramco Handbook*. Dhahran, Saudi Arabia: Arabian-American Oil Company, 1960. 343 pp.

———. *Properties and Criteria of Arabian Ground Waters*. Report No. 21 to Kingdom of Saudi Arabia, August 26, 1961. 1961.

Heady, H. F. *Report to the Government of Saudi Arabia on Grazing Resources and Problems*. FAO, ETAP Report No. 1614. Rome, 1963. 30 pp.

Helaissi, A. S. "The Bedouins and Tribal Life in Saudi Arabia." *International Social Science Journal*, 11 (4) (1959), 532–38.

Klemme, M. *Pasture Development and Range Management: Report to the Government of Saudi Arabia.* FAO, ETAP Report No. 1993. 1965. 27 pp.

Krader, L. "The Ecology of Nomadic Pastoralism." *International Social Science Journal,* 11 (4) (1959), 499–510.

Meterological Services. Annual climatological reports, Saudi Arabia. 1959–1965.

Tothill, J. D. *Report to the Government of Saudi Arabia on Agricultural Develop-ment.* Report No. 76. Rome: FAO, 1952. 88 pp.

Vesey-Fitzgerald, D. F. "Vegetation of the Red Sea Coast South of Jedda, Saudi Arabia." *J. Ecol.,* 45 (1955), 477–89.

———. "The Vegetation of the Sea Coast North of Jedda, Saudi Arabia." *J. Ecol.,* 45 (1957a), 547–62.

———. "The Vegetation of Central and Eastern Arabia." *J. Ecol.,* (1957b), 779–98.

Management, A study of the Conservation

37. ECOLOGICAL CONSEQUENCES OF RANGELAND DEVELOPMENT IN MASAILAND, EAST AFRICA

Lee M. Talbot

The Masai are a conservative East African people whose culture and survival in their largely arid lands is based on seminomadic pastoralism. Much effort has been expended to assist the Masai through rangeland improvement and development, but in large measure the results have contributed to long-term deterioration of the range resources, culminating in a catastrophic famine in which most Masai livestock and many Masai died. The history of attempts to develop Masailand provides a classical example of the consequences of rangeland development when basic ecological principles are overlooked or ineffectively applied. It illustrates well the following principles:

Any form of development should be part of a comprehensive resource use program which takes into account the ecology of the people and the area.

Development actions which remove environmental limitations on livestock numbers (i.e. veterinary activities, predator control, and above all, water development) should be undertaken only when effective substitute controls are assured.

Without adequate, effective grazing control no range management activities can succeed in the long run.

Stocking rates should be determined on the basis of range conditions and trend.

Arid land use should be based on knowledge of the uncertainty and irregularity of precipitation and the likelihood of periodic droughts.

Development requires adequate ecological knowledge; appropriate research (which recognizes the periodic wet-dry climatic swings) should be part of any major development project. It is misleading to apply to Masailand ecological knowledge and methodology based on experience and conditions in other areas, particularly in Europe or America.

Any development must take into account the culture of the people involved. It is not safe to assume that any pastoralists, particularly nomadic pastoralists, are living or have lived in equilibrium with their environment.

Some form of nomadic or rotational grazing is the only way to graze much of Masailand, but this use depends on the availability of the few water points, which should not be usurped by other forms of development. Tourism based on wildlife viewing is Masailand's most stable source of income (and East Africa's second largest foreign currency earning industry) and wildlife is more productive (in terms of meat production and long-term range productivity) than domestic livestock. In East African rangelands, wildlife represents far greater economic value to the countries and their people than livestock, and any comprehensive development plan should take this factor into consideration.

This paper describes some of the ecological consequences of the various attempts to assist the Masai people, largely through improvement of grazing and development of their rangeland resources. The Masai are a proud, conservative people whose culture and survival in their largely arid lands is based on pastoralism. Improvement of this pastoralism has been the focus of most development work in Masailand, but in large measure the results have contributed to long-term deterioration of the range resources, culminating in a catastrophic famine in which most Masai livestock and many Masai died.

These adverse ecological consequences of the developments were not intentional. They were, however, anticipated, predicted and documented by some range managers, wildlife ecologists and other biologists who knew the area. The basic problem has been that improvements of water supplies and other forms of development have been carried out separately, not as a part of a comprehensive resource management program that took into account the ecology of the whole area.

The ecological principles involved—and often overlooked—in the development of Masailand are not new. Those involving range management, for example, were summarized by Jardine and Anderson in 1919. They should be all too familiar to ecologists and others concerned with research and management of arid land resources. But in spite of this knowledge, resource-degrading development activities have occurred and, in some cases, are still occurring in Masailand. More significantly, they are a basic part of much current development activity in the world's arid lands, particularly in Africa and Asia. Consequently, the Masailand case history has broad significance in the context of ecological aspects of international development.

MASAILAND[1]

The area now known as Masailand covers some 93,000 square kilometers—roughly 33,000 in southern Kenya, and about 60,000 in northern Tanzania. It is an irregularly-shaped area, extending from roughly latitude 1 to 6 degrees south, between longitude 35 and 38 degrees east (Fig. 37–1).

The topography of Masailand is extremely

[1] This paper is based on an aggregate of over five years of field research and survey in Masailand, carried out between 1956 and 1967.

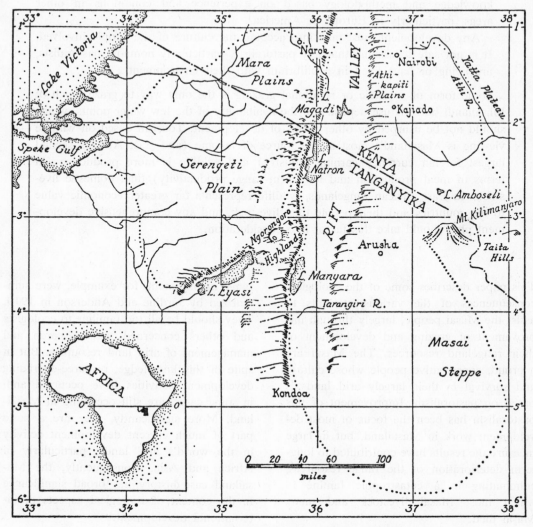

Figure 37–1   Ecological regions of Masailand
(The west wall of the Rift Valley divides eastern from western Masailand. The limits
of the ecological regions are shown by dotted lines which correspond fairly closely
with the political boundaries of Masailand)

varied. Generally it consists of level or undulating plainsland or plateau, between 900
and 1,800 meters elevation, split from north
to south by the Great Rift Valley and interrupted sporadically by scattered hills and
occasional isolated volcanic mountains or
mountain ranges rising to 2,400 meters or
more (Fig. 37–2).

There are very few permanent watercourses in Masailand, and the eastern and

southern areas are particularly poorly supplied. Most surface water is seasonal temporary rain-fed streams and pools.

Forests or mountain moorland are found
on most of the main mountain masses, and
strips of river-line forest follow some of the
main watercourses (Fig. 37-3). The more
level areas are grass or bushlands of two
main vegetation types: scattered tree grassland or open grassland, and desert grass-

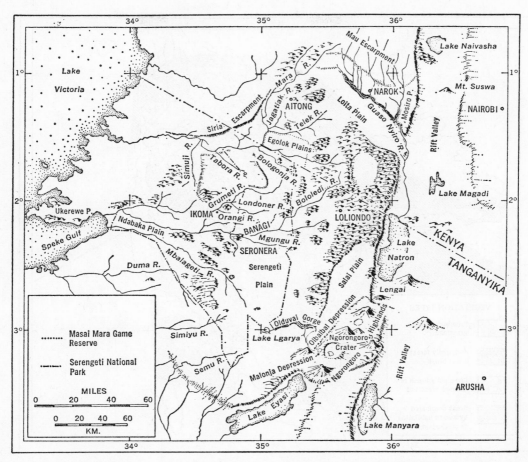

Figure 37–2 Physical map of western Masailand and environs showing the main topographic features and reserved areas

bushland (Edwards and Bogdan, 1951; Edwards, 1951).

The first type, which falls within the *Themeda Hyparrhenia* Zone (Heady, 1960), consists of perennial grassland, either open or with scattered trees or bushes, predominantly species of *Acacia*. It is usually found at elevations between about 1,200 and 2,000 meters.

The *desert grass-bush land,* or Heady's *Chrysopogon-Chloris-Aristida* Zone, is a more arid, poorer vegetation type; the bush assemblages characterized by species of *Acacia* and *Commiphora,* but with occasional taller trees. This vegetation is usually found at elevations below 1,200 meters.

The species composition and density of the grass and woody vegetation are largely determined by land use, grazing animals and fire. The savanna or grassland is largely maintained by periodic fires. The Masai set fires to encourage grazing for their cattle and to discourage the tsetse fly and ticks. Some fires are set by Wanderobo honey hunters while they are burning out bee trees to extract the honey; other fires are set by poachers. Where fire has been excluded through overgrazing (which removes the fuel) or protection, woody vegetation (often initially the whistling thorn acacia *Acacia drepanolobium*) quickly takes over much of the grassland. In time this veg-

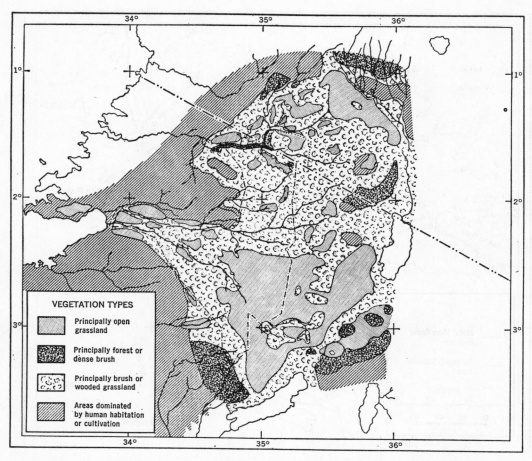

Figure 37–3 Vegetation of western Masailand. Forests or mountain moorland are found on most of the main mountain masses, and strips of riverine forest follow some of the main watercourses. The more level areas are grass or bushlands of two main vegetation types: scattered tree grassland or open grassland, and desert grass-bushland

etation may grow to a height of 6 meters or more, forming a dense but thin-stemmed forest through which other woodland trees may slowly grow (Heady, 1960, 1966; Talbot, 1960, 1964).

Climatic data from Masailand are very sparse. The lowest rainfall occurs in the Rift Valley and extreme eastern Masailand, averaging between 250 and 500 mm (10 and 20 inches). Elsewhere, except for the mountains, most of Masailand receives an average of somewhat over 500 mm (20 inches) annually, and in the west and northwest this rises to over 750 mm (30 inches).

Most rain falls in two seasons, the "short rains" in November and December, and the "long rains" from February to May. However, the rainfall in the region is characterized by extreme irregularity both in terms of time and distribution. There is frequently great variation in precipitation from one year to the next, and the region as a whole is likely to receive less than 500 mm (20 inches) per year. Characteristically, periods of one or more relatively "wet years" alternate with periods of drier ones. Relatively severe drought conditions are to be expected periodically. The des-

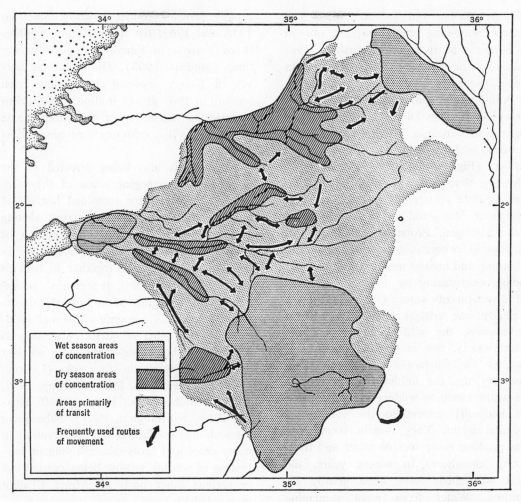

Figure 37–4 Seasonal distribution and movements of the most common wild ungulates of western Masailand. (Comparison with Figs. 37–2 and 37–3 will show the relationship between the seasonal distribution and movements of the animals, vegetation, topography, and water)

iccating factors—high temperature, low humidity, and constant dry winds—are very pronounced. Because of these factors, the effective precipitation is often far less than the average total rainfall would indicate. The vegetation exists in a relatively precarious balance with the moisture, and the area is particularly vulnerable to desiccation induced by overgrazing, cutting or burning of the vegetation cover.

Masailand probably contains the greatest concentration of mixed species of plains

wildlife left in the world. There are over thirty species of wild ungulates ranging from the 4.5 kilograms dikdik to the 5-ton elephant. From ten to thirty species of ungulate may feed in the same area. Predators and scavengers, ranging from lions to small wildcats, are also common. During their irregular "migratory" movements across the Serengeti Plains in search of food and water, wildebeests and other plains animals occasionally aggregate into vast herds, numbering tens of thousands of individuals (Talbot and Talbot, 1963). The greatest remaining concentrations are in the Serengeti-Mara area, in northern Tanzania and the adjacent Narok District in Kenya. There are smaller concentrations on the Athi-Kapiti Plains and in the Amboseli Reserve in Kajiado District, and near Lake Manyara in Tanzania. Wildlife is still found elsewhere in Masailand, but in much lower numbers (Fig. 37–4).

At the time of early European settlement, wildlife apparently was as abundant throughout Masailand as it is at present in the Serengeti. Probably the subsequent reduction elsewhere is due to a combination of hunting and habitat modification, through fencing, overgrazing by domestic livestock and diversion of water. Dry-season water is clearly one critical factor. During the wet seasons, the wild ungulates are dispersed widely, but as the dry season approaches and surface-water supplies and grass dry up, the animals which require free water (such as wildebeest, zebra, topi, and kongoni) retreat to the vicinity of perennial water. They remain there until rains produce more surface water and fresh grazing elsewhere. In recent years, the forest watersheds have been greatly diminished. Water from most remaining watersheds has been diverted for agriculture or piped to water troughs for the Masai. Of the seven or eight major dry-season water supplies that existed within the past twenty years in the Masai Steppe of northern Tanzania, only two remain available to wildlife (Lamprey, 1963; Simon, 1962; Talbot et al., 1961).

Starting in 1945 a series of park and reserve areas have been established in and adjacent to Masailand. These include the Nairobi, Lake Manyara, and Serengeti National Parks, the Masai Mara and the Masai Amboseli Game Reserves, and the Ngorongoro Conservation Unit. In general, these areas protect the wildlife and its habitat, and they attract an important part of the rapidly growing tourist industry. Between 1948 and 1963, the income from wildlife-based tourism in Kenya multiplied twenty times (Stewart, 1963). The Economic Survey of Kenya reported the income from tourism in 1967 at $42 million, and tourism is now the second most important single source of foreign currency throughout East Africa.

Attention is also being directed to the possibility of managing some of the wildlife of Masailand for sustained harvest of animal products. For some years visiting ecologists noted that the phenomenon of twenty to thirty species of ungulates in large numbers, feeding together in balance with their environment, represented an extremely high degree of ecological adaptation, and that as a source of animal products in many parts of Africa, wild animals appeared to be considerably more efficient than exotic domestic livestock (Lebrun, 1947; Petrides, 1956; Fraser Darling, 1958, 1960a, 1960b, 1960c; Heady, 1960; Huxley, 1961; Worthington, 1961). Subsequent research has confirmed this observation in many cases and economic cropping or harvesting of wildlife is now being carried out in various other parts of Africa (Talbot et al., 1965).

MASAI HISTORY

The early history of the Masai has been discussed by a number of writers (Fosbrooke, 1948, 1956; Gower, 1948; Grant, 1954, 1957; Hollis, 1905; Leakey, 1930; Peters, 1891; Sanford, 1919; Simon, 1962; and Thomson, 1887). The Masai are considered to be of Nilo-Hamitic stock, traditionally seminomadic pastoralists and warriors. It is believed that they occupied lowland country in northwest Kenya about four hundred years ago. They subsequently moved southward and by about 1640 they arrived in the center of the present Kenya Masailand (Fosbrooke, 1948). During the next 150 years they moved over 500 kilometers southward, and by 1800 a few Masai made what proved to be the tribe's maximum penetration into Tanzania. Thus in a period of roughly 250 years the Masai moved over 1,100 kilometers.

By about 1880 the tribe reached their maximum landholdings, cattle numbers and power. They occupied an area estimated at 200,000 square kilometers on the central highlands of Kenya and Tanzania, and the raids of their warriors reached from Lake Victoria to the Indian Ocean.

Their new lands were basically grassland. However, the Masai considerably expanded the grassland at the expense of forests and other woody vegetation. It appears that at least in parts of Masailand, the combination of overgrazing and burning, coinciding with a period of dry years (about the 1880's) created widespread denudation of rangelands and an impact on the forests that was not equaled until about 1960 (Talbot, 1960, and unpublished data).

A combination of disasters struck the Masai around 1890. The rinderpest epizootic, which in a few years traversed virtually the whole of Africa, killed most of the Masai cattle along with many of the wild bovids. This coincided with a smallpox epidemic, a severe drought and famine. Warfare within the tribe further weakened its structure and dispersed some of its members. Some surrounding tribes took advantage of the situation and raided the remaining Masai, partly in revenge for what they had suffered at Masai hands in the past. Part of the Masai sought refuge with largely agricultural tribes in surrounding areas, and some still maintain an agricultural way of life. By the end of the nineteenth century, the remaining people and livestock were greatly reduced in numbers and widely scattered. Consequently, the rangeland had several decades of reduced grazing pressure in which to recover.

When German East Africa was established as a colony in the late 1880's, the Germans found relatively few Masai in the north, and until they lost Tanganyika in 1918, they restricted most of the Tanganyika Masai to the Masai Steppe, south of Arusha and Moshi. As a result, much of Tanganyika north of Arusha had relative freedom from grazing by domestic livestock for twenty to thirty years.

Although relatively few in numbers, the Kenya Masai were widely distributed in the early 1900's. Because of actual or potential conflict with the increasing numbers of European settlers, the British Government of the new colony negotiated with the Masai to create a Masai reserve. The present boundaries of Masailand (with the exception of an additional 2,600 square kilometers they received subsequently) were established by the treaty between the government and the Masai signed in 1911.

Following the First World War, the British took over Tanganyika as a Trust Territory. They relaxed the German restrictions on the lands between the Kenya boundary and the Arusha-Moshi line and actively encouraged the Masai to move back into this area, partly by provision of water supplies. Parts of the area were quickly occupied by Masai from both sides of the border.

During the next two and a half decades, there was a steady increase in the population of the Masai and their livestock. The governments provided veterinary services, some water development, some protection against predation, and they discouraged cattle raiding and warfare. At the peak of Masai power in the 1800's, the population was estimated at around 45,000 (Simon, 1962). By the mid-1920's they had recovered from their series of disasters and their numbers were estimated at about 50,000 (Joelson, 1928). In 1948 they numbered 107,309 (Fosbrooke, 1948) and by 1961 there were about 117,000. The increasing herds were probably still within the carrying capacity of the rangeland at least into the 1930's, and in many places, into the 1940's.

MASAI RESOURCE USE

There are dangers in generalizing about "the Masai." In Masailand there are a series of political, administrative, cultural and ecological divisions and subdivisions of the Masai. A frequent and valid criticism of the work of anthropologists and sociologists studying the Masai, and of ecologists and others concerned with the impact of Masai on their environment, is that conclusions are usually based on acquaintance with only one (possibly atypical) group of Masai; results may not hold for the Masai as a whole. Therefore, what follows is a very generalized description, acknowledging that there are a number of variations in detail from area to area. The emphasis here is on resource use and impact on their ecosystem.

The Masai exert a major influence on their ecosystem through grazing of domestic livestock and burning; other influences stem from cutting woody vegetation, their exclusion of most agricultural and hunting peoples from their lands, and from their indirect protection of wildlife.

The traditional Masai life has been semi-nomadism or transhumance based on the requirements and movements of the livestock and modified by the requirements for defense or warfare. Livestock, and particularly cattle, are the basis of the Masai economy. Although the relationship is complex, in large measure the more cattle a Masai has, the greater is his wealth, prestige and security. Cattle provide milk but are not generally raised for meat or for sale, and the major emphasis of cattle husbandry is on quantity rather than quality.

The Masai live in temporary villages, popularly called *bomas* or *manyattas*. The boma consists of a circular fence made of thorn bushes, surrounding a series of low, mud, dung and wattle huts. The livestock are driven inside the boma fence each evening and herded out to graze each day. The thorn fence keeps the livestock from straying, and at least in the past, provided protection against raiding Africans and wild predators.

The location of the village is determined primarily by availability of water. Movement normally occurs twice a year. When the rains start, the Masai move to the wet-season grazing grounds, and in the dry season they return to their permanent water. Bomas may be reused for many years. When they are abandoned, a new one is usually built nearby. Although in the past there were no fences, each group of Masai had a recognized area in which they grazed their livestock and an established dry-season water source.

At present tribal territories appear fairly permanent because of the fixed boundaries of Masailand. In the past the Masai must have abandoned territories and moved on to new areas fairly frequently, considering the rate at which they moved south and occupied what is now Masailand.

The Masai livestock, cattle, goats and sheep are herded in tightly packed groups. This method facilitates protection from predators and raiders, and makes herding easier. However, it maximizes impact on the range both from the animals' hooves and from grazing pressure.

The Masai burn regularly to make new grass available to their livestock, to clear an area of pests and often to remove woody vegetation. There may have been tribal rules to control burning in times past, but during the period of the present study in East Africa, the Masai were observed to light fires whenever there was any fuel available. The same area was frequently burned twice a year, and one study plot was burned four times during one year. This regime of burning clearly influences the vegetation patterns.

Grazing and burning are intimately interrelated, since heavy grazing removes fuel, preventing fires and allowing growth of ungrazed woody vegetation. Under certain conditions periodic fires promote grazing by maintaining open grassland. Fires also can create grassland by destroying woodland or forest. Annual fires in Masailand remove a significant amount of woody vegetation even in relatively "normal" or "wet" years. In very dry years, however, fires can cut deeply into remaining forests and woodland. In a similar fashion, the impact of grazing on vegetation is most pronounced in a period of climatic stress. Although very few in numbers, the Masai have had a profound influence on changing the face of the earth in the areas they have occupied, and this influence is most clearly marked in the occasional severe drought.

Overgrazing is apparently built into the Masai pastoral system because of a variety of factors, including close herding in tight groups, use of few watering points by very large concentrations of livestock, and most significantly, the emphasis on increasing livestock numbers. These factors were necessary; they represented adaptations which helped enable the Masai to maintain their way of life in a difficult environment. But under this system the Masai never achieved a stable balance with the resources of their environment in any one area. After an area became denuded and overgrazed, they presumably moved on. At least, from what little we know of their history, it appears that for the past several hundred years they have been slowly but constantly moving southward.

The emphasis on numbers appears to have been the major factor in this process. A Masai family requires a certain minimum number of cattle and other livestock to provide their requirements for milk and meat. More are required for ceremonies and necessary trade, as in the case of bride prices. In pre-European times, the limiting factors in the environment were so severe that a constant effort was required just to maintain minimal livestock numbers. The resultant pastoral methodology and customs apparently are strongly directed toward increase of livestock numbers. We have seen no evidence of voluntary practices aimed at any limitation of numbers of cattle or other livestock.

Consequently, when the environmental limiting factors were reduced or removed, there was no cultural mechanism to replace them, and the livestock numbers increased until they far exceeded the carrying capacity of the rangelands. Starvation became the new limiting factor.

LIVESTOCK LIMITING FACTORS AND RANGELAND DEVELOPMENT ACTIVITIES

Reduction or elimination of limiting factors was the objective of the rangeland development efforts of the governments of Kenya and Tanganyika. Following the Second World War, these efforts were intensified and the resultant programs involved demonstration ranches, grazing schemes, tsetse clearance projects, intensified veterinary services, and provision of water.

Disease was a major limiting factor to livestock numbers. Foot and mouth disease, pleuropneumonia, East Coast fever, trypanosomiasis, and more recently, rinderpest, have all caused significant losses to Masai livestock. Government Veterinary Services have greatly reduced losses from these and other diseases.

Predation from lions and other animals was a constant threat. Government Game Departments now dispose of troublesome predators, and through hunting and control work, the overall population levels of most predators have been drastically reduced.

Raiding and warfare involving both other tribes and other Masai were another potent limiting factor. Since the late 1880's governments have discouraged these practices, and though cattle raiding is not extinct, where it does exist it now increases stock, since most raiding is done by the Masai, resulting in movement of additional cattle into Masailand.

The above limiting factors not only affect adult animals, but most of them influence the rate of reproduction and survival of the young animals. At best, the rate of reproduction of livestock kept under nomadic conditions is much lower than similar livestock kept under optimum ranch management. Brown (1963) cites the then-current average calving rate of 90 per cent for well-managed ranch cattle in East Africa as compared to 70 per cent for nomadic herds, and he cites an overall (adults and young) loss of 4 per cent in managed cattle against 20 per cent losses (in calves alone) in nomadic herds. In pre-European times when the limiting factors had not yet been counteracted, the nomadic herds probably would have had a much lower reproductive rate and much higher death rate.

The presence of tsetse flies, carriers of trypanosomiasis, denied the Masai cattle access to considerable areas of Masailand. Various projects have been carried out involving bush clearance and spraying, and in some cases, extermination of the wild animals suspected of carrying the disease. These are expensive and frequently destructive operations, and where the areas have been successfully cleared, the result has frequently been to open additional lands to destructive overgrazing.

Water was perhaps the greatest single limiting factor to Masai herds. The size of the herds kept by any Masai family was effectively limited by the amount of available dry-season water. If the water failed, the herds died or the Masai were forced to move elsewhere in search of more water. In an effort to help the Masai, the governments provided additional and more reliable water supplies through boreholes, dams, and pipelines. The objectives of this development activity were admirable. Better water distribution was intended to spread the grazing pressure more evenly throughout the range, enabling the Masai to fully utilize areas previously unused because of lack of water. This was to have reduced the number of animals at each water hole, thus reducing overgrazing on overused water points. Reliable water would reduce the chance of water failure during droughts, lessening hardships on both humans and animals and promoting better health for all.

The results were generally the opposite. Instead of spreading the existing herds more evenly throughout the range, the herds increased to the limits of the new waters and spread the existing overgrazing throughout the range in aggravated form.

THE EXAMPLE OF TWO GRAZING DEVELOPMENT PROJECTS

The above principles are well illustrated by the history of the grazing development projects in Kajiado District. Between 1946 and 1961, the Government of Kenya had spent over $2,240,000 on grazing schemes and range demonstrations in an effort to bring about proper management and development of the range resources throughout the colony (Fallon, 1962). During this period over $120,400 was spent on grazing development schemes in the Kajiado District, much of that raised by the Masai through self-tax levies (Fallon, 1962). By 1959 most of Kajiado District was severely overgrazed and the range resources were badly degraded. The foci of the worst devastation were the water points, grazing schemes and demonstration ranches. Two of the larger projects illustrate what happened.

Konza Demonstration Ranch. In 1946,

the Konza Demonstration Ranch was established. Its objectives were:

1. To demonstrate the results of grazing management in improving the carrying capacity of the land and the productivity of the cattle.
2. To demonstrate improvement of stock by breeding and selection.
3. To conduct experiments in pasture improvements.

Over $364,000 was spent to develop the ranch. The developments included an exterior perimeter fence consisting of a wire fence inside a triple fence line of sisal plants, interior fences to create four paddocks, three boreholes for water, and a chemical dip for disease protection. A manager was in residence most of the time until 1958. Ten families (approximately ninety persons) were chosen by the local Masai authorities to settle the ranch in January, 1949. They owned 1,400 cattle. Their settlement on the ranch was subject to the agreement that they: (1) dip livestock weekly and give prophylactic inoculations, (2) follow a rotational plan of grazing, and (3) restrict livestock to the prescribed numbers.

The Range Management Advisor to the Government of Kenya described the failure of the ranch as follows (Fallon, 1962, p. 24):

The Konza ranch should have been a success, but it wasn't. . . . The wire fences did not stop the game animals and soon were in a poor state of repair. By 1955 the wire and posts had all been removed. The residents through the years refused to honor their commitments particularly as to the restrictions placed on numbers of livestock.

The cattle population, by 1954, had increased from the original 1,400 to 2,300. Attempts to impose reductions led to 4 families leaving with 666 cattle. The remainder agreed that they would not exceed a maximum of 1,700 but by 1958 the number of cattle had increased to 2,441. This time an agreed limit of 2,000 was set. Then came the drought

and by mid 1961 the ground was bare and all the residents left. . . .

The Ilkisongo Grazing Scheme. Sectional grazing schemes were another form of range development attempted by the Government of Kenya during this period. These schemes involved dividing a range area into several grazing blocks, instituting a relatively simple rotation system (based on the traditional movement of Masai livestock between wet-season and dry-season areas), providing water supplies and disease control, and attempting to provide for destocking by creating special markets. Livestock officers administered and supervised each scheme. These officers acted under special ordinances and by-laws, which empowered them to: (1) approve which Masai were allowed to graze livestock in the scheme, (2) determine the number of animals each was allowed to graze, and (3) select the area to be grazed.

The first such grazing plan was the Ilkisongo Grazing Scheme, established in 1954. It covered some 526,000 hectares, and prior to the drought the estimated numbers of cattle in the scheme area were 110,000 to 120,000 head.

This scheme, like the others, was a disastrous failure. By 1956 the area was severely overgrazed. In 1959 the destruction was so bad that where the scheme used to be, a jagged, bare, red earth scar in the savanna landscape was visible from a high-flying airliner whenever the ground was visible through the blowing dust.

The Range Management Advisor summarized the process at Ilkisongo, and the lessons learned from the failure of these development schemes in general, as follows (Fallon, 1962, pp. 25–26):

Politically it was not possible to enforce the stringent regulations. The range was overstocked at the time the Ilkisongo scheme was established. Direct destocking was not acceptable to the people of the Ilkisongo Section and had destocking been insisted upon, it would have meant no scheme at all. It was hoped that through improved management practices there would be sufficient increase in forage production to absorb part of the excess cattle and destocking could be accomplished over a period of years.

A special stock market was established for the Ilkisongo Scheme to provide a destocking outlet. Approximately 750 herd of cattle passed through the market monthly. Records, however, indicate that during the operation of the scheme the livestock numbers actually increased rather than decreased.

The drought accomplished what administration was unable to do—it destocked the range although disastrously and wastefully.

In establishing the schemes every consideration was given to features that would conform as nearly as possible to traditional grazing use. An aggressive water development program was initiated, which unfortunately contributed to the depletion of the range resources, because the livestock population was not controlled. During the drought the schemes ceased to function and to date have not been re-activated.

In their failure the grazing schemes clearly demonstrate the futility of water development and management measures without control of the livestock population. The danger of water development and range improvement projects in general without adequate management provisions can not be too strongly stressed for almost invariably the result is the deterioration or destruction of the range resource involved.

The Consequences of Development

The direct effect of the rangeland development activities discussed above was to remove certain limiting factors on Masai livestock numbers without supplying any alternate limitation.

In the absence of any effective management or control, the numbers of the livestock of the Masai increased greatly, reaching a peak about 1960. At the same time, the overgrazing brought about widespread critical range deterioration throughout Masailand.

In Narok District, for example, in April, 1956, the cattle population was about 330,000 head (Dept. Vet. Services, 1958). By April, 1958, the population had risen to about 378,000 head (Dept. Vet. Services, 1958), and in May of 1960 it was reported at 450,000 head (Mann, 1960). This represented an increase of over 36 per cent in four years (partly achieved through reproduction and part from stock movements into the area).

Assuming that about 25 per cent of Masailand is not available for grazing because of factors such as topography, and taking five goats or sheep to equal one cow, the overall stocking rate for Kenya Masailand in 1961 would have been roughly 2.3 hectares per cow (Brown, 1963). This constitutes gross overstocking for this type of rangeland under the best climatic conditions.

Nomadic herds will always suffer to some degree from drought, but when the range is in good condition the impact of drought will be much less severe (Heady, 1960). A series of dry years culminating in 1961 constituted the most severe drought on record in Masailand. This was followed by heavy floods. The effect upon the Masai was broadly proportional to the condition of their rangelands; this condition, in turn, varied inversely with the amount of development they had suffered. Kajiado District had the greatest concentration of attempts at range improvement and had accordingly suffered the most severe range deterioration the previous years. Consequently, the losses there in 1961 were catastrophic. Around three-quarters of the total livestock died, and the surviving animals were generally in extremely weakened condition. In spite of massive famine relief efforts by national and international agencies, the Kajiado Masai starved in considerable numbers. There were also heavy losses in the most abused parts of Tanganyika Masailand and Narok District, but the overall impact was heaviest on the Kajiado Masai.

Famine relief was continued in some areas throughout 1962. During 1961 and 1962, the only income of the Kenya Masai came from the revenue from tourist visits to Amboseli Reserve in Kajiado and the Masai Mara Game Reserve in Narok District. These two magnificent wildlife areas had been developed as local parks operated by the Masai of the district concerned.

In general, the weather in Masailand since 1961 has been relatively "wet." This condition, coupled with considerably reduced grazing pressure (because of the mortality among domestic and wild grazing animals), produced a considerable recovery of the range. Following the famine, and partly because of the attention it directed to the Masai, a series of rehabilitation and development projects have been instituted. Some Masai turned, at least in part, to agriculture. Others started individual ranches. The governments have turned their attention to comprehensive Masailand development programs. The Agency for International Development projects, other bilateral programs, and a large-scale FAO-UNDP (Special Fund) range development project which involves part of Masailand, have been established.

In 1961 Tanganyika (later Tanzania) became independent, and Kenya followed in 1963. The new political status, plus the famine, appears to have convinced many of the Masai that change in their way of life is necessary. Perhaps equally important, it has shown the administrators and advisors that change is possible and that the Masai are a much more adaptable people than was formerly believed.

At least prior to independence, the Masai held a special status in East Africa. They were the only tribe with a separate treaty with the British Government. To many Western visitors and administrators their picturesque, independent, nomadic way of life and rejection of westernization were admirable characteristics. Two beliefs grew:

first, that they *could* not be changed, and second, that they *should* not be changed.

One of the most potent factors inducing change was development assistance provided to help maintain their traditional way of life. Where these efforts involved rangeland developments, the efforts themselves caused drastic change by removing the limiting factors on which Masai pastoralism was based. Yet when the need to limit cattle numbers has been pointed out to some administrators, they have responded that "to enforce limitations on livestock would be to interfere with the culture of the Masai and our policy is to leave it unchanged."

The idea that the Masai should not change their way of life stemmed from the belief that they were—and always had been—living in balance with their environment. As described above, this premise appears incorrect. The sixty or seventy years they have occupied their present reserve appears to be the longest continuous period of occupancy of a single area in their history. This relative stability has been aided by the facts that at the start of this period (1) both cattle and human populations were low, drastically reduced from former levels, (2) traditional political and social patterns had been disrupted by the series of disasters, plus the advent of Europeans, and (3) the rangeland was in excellent condition; the population of all grazing animals, wild and domestic, were very low because of the epizootic, and the rangeland had benefited from several decades of reduced grazing pressure.

Those who held that the Masai were in a constant "balance" with their environment also failed to take into account the density of human population and the carrying capacity of the area for humans under a nomadic pastoral way of life. At the time of their greatest population prior to European settlement, there were an estimated 45,000 Masai in 205,000 square kilometers, a density of 0.22 Masai per square kilometer. In 1961 there were about 117,000 Masai in 92,000 square kilometers, a density of 1.3 Masai per square kilometer. The twentieth-century Masai have to live in an area with fixed boundaries, at a population density about six times greater than the estimated maximum density of the nineteenth-century Masai who were constantly changing or expanding the area they occupied. The two situations are profoundly different.

Further, as Brown (1963) has pointed out, under a nomadic pastoral life, human subsistence requires a certain minimum number of domestic animals per person. Therefore the human-carrying capacity of nomadic pastoral lands is determined by its livestock-carrying capacity, which will vary from time to time with environmental conditions (Heady, 1960). This factor enforces a limit on the number of humans that can survive in a given fixed area in a given time under a nomadic pastoral culture. If this number is exceeded, the way of life necessarily changes.

CONCLUSIONS

The history of the attempts to develop Masailand provides a classical example of the consequences of rangeland development when basic ecological principles are overlooked or ineffectively applied. The development activities cited were carried out in good faith and with what were considered to be the best interests of the Masai in mind.

However, the immediate results were overgrazing and widespread severe degradation of the rangeland. Among the longer-term consequences was the castastrophic impact of the long drought. Periodic droughts are a characteristic of Masailand. Severe drought will always cause hardship, and sometimes loss, to nomadic pastoralists, but the severity of the impact of the drought will be determined by the prior condition of

the rangeland. The severe 1961 drought cannot be attributed to development activities, but the severity of the impact of the drought on the Masai and their livestock was a clear result of the development-induced range deterioration.

The Masailand case history illustrates well the following principles:

1. No form of development is likely to succeed unless it is part of a comprehensive resource use program which takes into account the ecology of the people and the area.

2. Forms of development which remove environmental limitations on stock numbers, such as veterinary activities, predator control, and above all, water development, should not be undertaken when effective substitute controls on animal numbers are not assured. Without grazing control no range management activities can succeed in the long run.

3. Stocking rates should be determined on the basis of range condition and trend and should bear in mind the likelihood of drought.

4. Range development activities and other aspects of land use should be based on knowledge of the uncertainty of precipitation and the likelihood that periods of severe drought may follow periods of above average rainfall. Development activities that assume that periods of abundant, regular rainfall are "normal," are almost certain to fail during the subsequent drier years. This principle involves settlement, various types of grazing schemes and cultivation. For example, during the past several "wet" years, increasing acreages of wheat have been planted at the northern end of the Loita Plains in Narok District. Although during these wet years good harvests have been obtained and the cultivated acreage has consequently expanded, the area is considered submarginal for agriculture (Talbot, 1960) and a "dust bowl" situation is anticipated with the next drought period.

5. Development should be based on adequate knowledge. Short-term visiting experts and short-term researchers (one to two years) often will base their results on nontypical conditions (e.g., either the wet or the dry end of the cycles). For this reason, hasty development, based on the need to meet short-term budget cycles or political expediency, is likely to fail in the long run.

6. Ecological conditions vary from area to area, and it is extremely misleading to judge conditions in Masailand or to base recommendations on experience and conditions in other areas, particularly in the northern temperate zones. There is inadequate knowledge for many aspects of development in Masailand, and appropriate research should be a major part of any development program.

7. Cultural conditions in Masailand vary considerably from those in many other lands. Management techniques based on the assumption that meat production is the objective of cattle raising are not appropriate to a people who raise cattle for prestige, milk and security. Ultimately any development must take into account the culture of the people involved.

8. It is not safe to assume that any pastoral people, particularly nomadic pastoralists, are living, or have lived, in a static equilibrium with their environment.

9. The carrying capacity of the rangeland for livestock determines its carrying capacity for pastoral nomads, and when this point is passed some change in their way of life will necessarily follow.

10. In a large part of Masailand, because of the climate and other ecological conditions, permanent sedentary grazing is not possible. Some form of seminomadic grazing by domestic or wild animals is the only way to use these lands, but this use is often dependent upon the availability of scarce water supplies or watered areas which are used as dry-season watering or holding areas. These limited areas may well support sedentary or agricultural development, but such development may be uneconomical since it denies the dry-season water and grazing to a much larger area, rendering it unproductive.

11. Tourism based on the wildlife of Masailand has proved the most stable economic resource of the Masai. It is also of great economic value to the country as a whole, providing the second largest single source of foreign currency. Development projects should take this into account, but most do not. The Nairobi National Park is a good example. It is a small—110 square kilometers—area adjacent to Nairobi. Its easy access and abundant wildlife have made it the show window of East African wildlife. The park has proven itself of very great economic value to Kenya. The park, however, is not viable as it stands. It has the only yearlong available water in that area and the wildlife that use it rely on much of the Athi-Kapiti Plains to the south for grazing land. Current ranch development plans call for settled ranches and fencing adjacent to the park, which would deny the park animals access to the plains to the south, outside the park. If this were done the small park could only support a few animals and the present spectacle and consequent economic resource would be lost.

12. Wildlife makes more productive use of parts of Masailand than domestic livestock and the economic potential of wildlife harvest is worthy of serious examination. Most development projects have not taken this potential, as well as the proven tourist value, into account or have argued that the needs of Masai livestock must come first (Pratt, 1968). However, according to the Director of Agriculture of Kenya, in the range areas of Kenya, wildlife represents far greater economic value to the country than livestock (Brown, 1963). Any comprehensive development plan should take this factor into consideration.

REFERENCES

Brown, L. H. *The Development of the Semi-Arid Areas of Kenya.* Nairobi: Ministry of Agriculture, 1963. 48 pp. Mimeo.

Department of Veterinary Services, Kenya. Memo. Livestock Marketing in Southern Province, Ngong, Provisional Administration, Kenya. 1958. 3 pp. (typed).

Edwards, D. C. "The Vegetation in Relation to Soil and Water Conservation in East Africa." *Commonwealth Bureau Pastures and Field Crops Bull.,* 41 (1951), 28–43.

Edwards, D. C., and Bogdan, A. V. *Important Grassland Plants of Kenya.* Nairobi: Pitman and Sons, Ltd., 1951. 124 pp.

Fallon, Leland E. *Masai Range Resources, Kajiado Dist.* Nairobi: U.S.A.I.D., 1962. 48 pp.

Fosbrooke, H. A. "An Administrative Survey of the Masai Social System." *Tanganyika Notes and Records* (Nairobi), 26 (1948), 1–50.

———. "The Masai Age-groups Systems as a Guide to Tribal Chronology." *Afri. Stud.,* 15 (4) (1956), 188–206.

Fraser Darling, F. "Conservation and the Ungulates." *Mammalia,* 22 (1958), 317–22.

———. *Wildlife in an African Territory.* London: Oxford University Press, 1960a. 160 pp.

———. "An Ecological Reconnaissance of the Mara Plains in Kenya Colony." *Wildlife Monogr.,* No. 5 (1960b). 41 pp.

———. "Wildlife Husbandry in Africa." *Sci. Amer.,* 203 (1960c), 123–28.

Glover, P. E., and Gwynne, M. D. "The Destruction of Masailand." *New Scientist,* 11 (249) (1961), 450–53.

Gower, R. H. "Two Views on the Masai." *Tanganyika Notes and Records* (Nairobi), 26 (1948), 60–67.

Grant, H. St. J. "Human Habitation in the Serengeti National Park." Provisional Administration Northern Province, Arusha, Tanganyika. 1954. 34 pp. (typescript).

———. "Masai History and Mode of Life." Report compiled for the Serengeti Committee of Enquiry. 1957. 21 pp. (typescript).

Heady, H. F. *Range Management in East Africa.* Nairobi: Government Printer, 1960. 125 pp.

———. "Influence of Grazing on the Composition of *Themeda triandra* Grassland, East Africa." *J. Ecol.,* 54 (1966), 705–27.

Hollis, A. C. *The Masai: Their Language and Folklore.* Oxford: Clarendon Press, 1905. 359 pp.

Huxley, J. *The Conservation of Wildlife and Natural Habitats in Central and East Africa.* Paris: UNESCO, 1961. 113 pp.

Jardine, J. T., and Anderson, Mark. "Range Management on the National Forests." *U. S. Dept. of Agr. Bull.* 790. 1919. 98 pp.

Joelson, F. S., ed. *Eastern Africa Today.* London: East Africa Ltd., 1928. 420 pp.

Lamprey, H. F. "Ecological Separation of the Large Mammal Species in The Tarangire Game Reserve, Tanganyika." *E. Africa Wildlife J.,* 1 (1963), 63–92.

Leakey, L. S. B. "Some Notes of the Masai of Kenya Colony." *J. Royal Anthrop. Inst.,* 60 (1930), 185–209.

Lebrun, J. *La Vegetation de la Plaine Alluviale au sud du Lac Edouard.* 2 vols. Brussels, 1947.

Mann, I. "The Conversion of Unproductive Animals from Overstocked Areas into High Protein Human Food." *E. Afr. Med. J.,* 37 (5) (1960).

Peters, K. *New Light on Dark Africa.* English ed., New York, 1891, cited by Gower, 1948.

Petrides, G. A. "Big Game Densities and Range Carrying Capacity in East Africa." *Trans. N. Amer. Wild. Conf.,* 21 (1956), 525–37.

Pratt, D. F. "Rangeland Development in Kenya." Report presented to the Rockefeller Foundation East African Rangelands Workshop. 1968. 29 pp. Mimeographed.

Sanford, C. R. *An Administrative and Political History of the Masai Reserve.* London: Waterlow and Sons, 1919.

Simon, N. M. *Between the Sunlight and the*

Thunder; The Wild Life of Kenya. London: Collins, 1962. 384 pp.

Stewart, D. R. M. "Development of Wildlife as an Economic Asset." *Bull. Epiz. Dis. Afr.*, 11 (1963), 167–71.

Talbot, Lee M. "Land Use Survey of Narok District, Kenya." Off. of Dist. Admin., Narok, Kenya. 1960. 68 pp. Mimeographed.

———. "The Biological Productivity of the Tropical Savanna Ecosystem." In *The Ecology of Man in the Tropical Environment.* Morges, Switzerland: IUCN, 1964. IUCN New Series No. 4. 355 pp. Pp. 88–97.

Talbot, Lee M.; Payne, W. J. A.; Ledger, H. P.; Verdcourt, L.; and Talbot, M. H. Review: "The Meat Production Potential of Wild Animals in Africa; a Review of Biological Knowledge." Commonwealth Bur. of Animal Breeding and Genetics, Edinburgh. Tech. Communication No. 16. 1965. 42 pp.

Talbot, Lee M., and Talbot, Martha H. "The Wildebeest in Western Masailand, East Africa." *Wildf. Monog.* No. 12. 1963. Pp. 8–88.

Talbot, Lee M.; Talbot, Martha H.; and Lamprey, H. F. "An Introduction to the Landscape; Wildlife and Land Use Ecology in Masailand and Other Areas of Southern Kenya and Northern Tanganyika." Nairobi, Kenya: Govt. Printer, 1961. 38 pp.

Thomson, J. 1887. *Through Masailand.* 4th ed. Boston. Houghton, Mifflin Co., 1887. 583 pp.

Worthington, E. B. "The Wild Resources of East and Central Africa." Colonial, No. 352. London: H.M.S.O., 1961. 26 pp.

38. THE ECOLOGICAL IMPACT OF THE INTRODUCTION OF DOMESTIC CATTLE INTO WILD LIFE AND TSETSE AREAS OF RHODESIA

Oliver West

Cattle were first introduced into Rhodesia more than 1,200 years ago with the migrations of cattle-owning and cultivating Iron Age peoples who in successive waves made their way south into country already occupied by hunter-gatherer, Stone Age people.

The first cattlemen took advantage of the grasslands and wooded-savanna vegetation, produced and maintained by fire during the Stone Age, and kept their cattle on the high-lying, watershed country out of contact with tsetse fly. Their shifting, slash-and-burn methods of cultivation accelerated the trend toward open grassland and wooded-savanna, while extensive denudation of the surface cover was avoided because the population was small and occupied the country on a shifting basis.

The most important consequence of the changes which accompanied recent European settlement was an explosive increase in both human and cattle populations. Population growth accompanied by land enclosure restricted freedom of movement. Thus the damage done to the habitat by settlement could no longer be mended by the rest which formerly followed the shifting of the population.

This damage has resulted in a general thickening of the woody vegetation accompanied by a reduction in the amount of grass and in extensive denudation of the surface cover in drier areas.

Endeavors are being made to counter these effects by enlarging the cultivated area and making it more productive. There is an effort to improve cultural practices, develop irrigation and encourage the use of fertilizers in order to reduce dependence on the grazing areas. These areas are being improved by selective bush clearing followed by methods of management designed to encourage grass and prevent bush encroachment, and by the encouragement of stocking rates sufficiently low to allow the recovery of denuded country. The use of irrigated pastures to supplement dry veld grazing and to increase the cattle-carrying capacity of the dry country is being investigated. The gradual reduction of the area of tsetse-infested land by improved techniques for fly control have made more land available for settlement. This will assist in relieving the pressure of overpopulation in the drier areas.

Population growth together with agricultural development has exercised a very depressive effect on the game animal population. It is pointed out that the future for large game animals is secure only on national land, in game reserves and national parks, which fortunately cover a large proportion of the country.

The presence of domesticated cattle in Central Africa has been a feature of the environment for so long that the history of their introduction is lost and the impact made by their introduction is difficult to assess. In Rhodesia there have been two distinct periods of cattle introduction, the first beginning more than 1200 years ago with the migrations of Iron Age cattle owners, and the second with the beginning of European settlement at about the turn of the present century.

In this paper an attempt is made to recognize the effects of the impact of the entry of these two distinct cattle-owning cultures on the ecosystems and to outline the measures required to repair the harm to the habitat producted by some of these effects.

HISTORY OF CATTLE INTRODUCTION

In Rhodesia the first introduction of domesticated cattle coincided with the close of the Later Stone Age and the beginning of the Early Iron Age between about 90 A.D. (Clark, 1959) and 700 A.D. (Oliver, 1966). Cattle entered Rhodesia with the migrations of the Iron Age, cattle-owning and cultivating Bantu peoples who in successive waves made their southward passage through Africa. Because they owned cattle, the country they could inhabit was

confined by the availability of water, the presence of grass and the absence of tsetse flies.

A glance at the map of Africa will show that the high-lying, tsetse-free, watershed country which forms the backbone of Rhodesia provided a natural southward route by which cattle-herding peoples were able to bypass the low-lying tsetse-ridden country to the east. This route also avoided the arid western country where watering points are scarce.

The cattle population of Rhodesia must have been continually refreshed by the arrival of new migrations from the north and later by the northward movement of cattle-owning people displaced in the south. Between 1820 and 1870, waves of southern Bantu, displaced by the rise of the Zulu power in Natal, made their way north, and of these the Ndebele, who brought many cattle, settled in Rhodesia.

The arrival of the Pioneer Column in 1890 heralded the beginning of European settlement and marked a new era of cattle introduction and a tremendous growth in the population of both humans and cattle.

IMPACT ON THE ECOSYSTEM BEFORE EUROPEAN SETTLEMENT

Man affects his environment by various means; in primitive times the most important ones appear to have been by fire, the ax and hoe and the use and management of domestic animals.

Studies of the plant succession show that grasslands in Rhodesia, whether they be open or savanna types, are subclimax communities produced and maintained by fire. These grasslands thicken up into densely wooded communities containing very little grass when fire is excluded (West, 1954, 1965). For this reason the importance of fire in producing suitable habitat for grazing animals and domestic cattle in Rhodesia is overriding.

Carbon datings from the Kalambo site on the borders of Zambia and Tanzania provide positive evidence that Stone Age man in Central Africa used fire more than 53,000 years ago (Clark, 1959), that is, more than 50,000 years before cattle-owning men appeared. Primitive man used fire to further his hunting activities (Burchell, 1822), and it is certain that the hunting fires of Stone Age man must have played a very important role in producing the grassy habitat required by the wild grazing animals and later occupied by cattle-owning Bantu people.

This trend toward open grassland or savanna grasslands was greatly accelerated when the territory of Stone Age man was occupied by immigrant Iron Age man, who brought cattle and who practiced a shifting, slash-and-burn agriculture.

Bartlett (1955, 1957) has shown the universality of the primitive systems of shifting agriculture, by which forest was slashed or felled and burned for crops grown in the ashes. Gardens or fields produced in this way were cultivated for only a few years, until the fertility of the soil was exhausted, and then abandoned in favor of new gardens slashed from virgin areas where the accumulated fertility of the soil could again be exploited. In the abandoned fields perennial grasses following annual pioneers in the natural course of the plant succession, provided areas where fire could take hold and eat into the surrounding forest. Presumably these cleared areas were also burned by cattle owners to get rid of old grass and to encourage new growth for their grazing animals, and so the clearings were maintained while the destruction of the forest proceeded. Because of the shifting nature of their cultivation a comparatively small population living in close-knit communities and occupying relatively small areas for short periods was able to produce profound changes over very extensive areas.

The inroads made on the forest in this way by the cultivators produced the grasslands and savannas required by the stock-owning graziers, and the use of fire as a means of producing and maintaining grazing land became established custom among the primitive inhabitants of the tropics and subtropics (West, 1965).

Iron Age man, bringing cultivation and cattle, entered Rhodesia early in the Christian era, during a period when the climate was much the same as at present and the rainfall considerably less than it had been in the previous pluvial period (Summers, 1960). This means that the rainfall was marginal for forest then existing over large areas of Rhodesia. Because of this, forest was destroyed much more easily.

Aubreville (1937, 1947, 1949a, 1949b, 1950) presents a most depressing picture of forest destruction and its replacement by savanna vegetation over most of tropical and southern Africa. He maintains that while changes in climate may have induced a state of physiological disequilibrium which made forests in some parts easier to destroy, the major cause of destruction was man's activities assisted by fire. Fire upset the delicate balance that had been established between forest and the drier climate.

Thus before the beginning of European settlement, spectacular changes in Rhodesian vegetation were brought about. The tropical and montane forests of the high-rainfall eastern districts were almost completely cleared, and over enormous areas hillsides formerly covered by evergreen forest were terraced and cultivated (Swynnerton, 1917; Summers, 1960). In spite of the fact that the rainfall of this eastern area is and as far as can be ascertained has always been sufficient for the development of forest, only relic patches of these ancient forests remain. The swamp forests, which existing relics show must have covered much of the presently open vlei areas, were almost entirely destroyed by the activities of prehistoric, Iron Age man, who, because of the wetness of the vlei soils, was able to grow crops in these areas during the dry season. There is also much evidence to show that the Brachystegia woodlands as well as the stretches of grassland which cover areas of the higher-rainfall watershed country have resulted from the effects of man's activities in ancient times. Everywhere a trend toward the reduction of forest and development of grassland and savanna was initiated.

The great changes in the habitat brought about by Stone Age and Iron Age occupation must have produced correspondingly great changes in animal life, affecting profoundly the abundance and distribution of most species, including tsetse fly. It is probable that the level of human and animal predation maintained the game population, including the larger mammals such as elephant and hippopotamus, at levels which enabled both the game and the habitat to exist in a healthy condition.

IMPACT ON THE ECOSYSTEM AFTER EUROPEAN SETTLEMENT

The most important consequence of the changes which followed the arrival of European settlers was the beginning of an explosive increase in both the human and the cattle populations.

Before this last settlement, the human and domestic livestock populations were low and could move over vast areas of unoccupied land. They were kept low by intertribal raiding, warfare, drought, famine, disease and other biological controls. Stock losses caused by rinderpest[1] shortly after the settlement illustrate how effective the control by disease could be. A cattle population estimated at approximately 500,000 in 1890 was reduced to about 25,000 by the end of the epidemic in 1898 (Nobbs, 1927).

Droughts, in addition to causing human and stock losses by starvation, forced cattle owners into tsetse areas where their cattle died of nagana.[2] The effect of raiding and intertribal warfare on both the human and animal populations is well illustrated by the disturbance set in motion by the Zulu rise to power, which spread devastation over thousands of miles, from the Natal Coast and the Eastern Cape northward to Malawi and Tanzania (Wills, 1964).

The advent of European settlers in 1890 ended this epoch. Tribal warfare and raiding were suppressed; famine relief and medical aid for both man and beast were provided. The controls which had operated in past ages were removed and populations began to soar.

HUMAN POPULATION

The rise in the human population is illustrated by the following figures. It was estimated in 1901, eleven years after the beginning of European colonization, that the indigenous African population amounted to 500,000; by 1920 it had increased to 850,000; by 1940 to 1,390,000; by 1960

[1] Rinderpest or cattle plague is a disease of ruminants which first appeared in Africa in Somaliland in 1889. It swept through Africa, crossing the Zambesi in 1896. Although endemic in the north it is now successfully controlled by preventive inoculation.

[2] Nagana, or trypanosomiasis, is the cattle disease transmitted by tsetse flies.

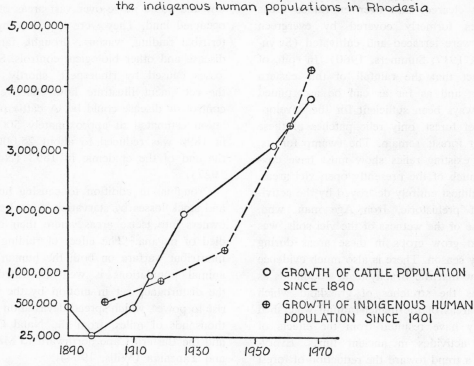

Figure 38–1   Trends since 1890 in the growth of cattle and the indigenous human population in Rhodesia

a census revealed 3,400,000, and by 1967, 4,330,000 (Fig. 38–1). The population of people of European origin is increasing much less rapidly and numbered only 232,-000 in 1967.

The effects of the population explosion have been dramatic. An ecosystem that for ages had been in balance with a small and shifting human population, that left nature to repair the disturbance created by cultivation and grazing, was abruptly saddled with a population so large that the old shifting life was no longer possible. The population was fixed by the demarcation of tribal and farming areas and the fencing of the boundaries of individual holdings. The people were forced to cultivate the same fields and to graze the same areas, while the area available for individual use was constantly reduced by population growth.

CATTLE POPULATION

The rise in the cattle population has been equally spectacular. According to Nobbs (1927), official estimates at the time of the 1890 settlement put the total number of cattle in Rhodesia at about 500,000 head. This population was reduced to about 25,000 by the rinderpest epizootic between 1896 and 1898. Fourteen years later, in 1911, the number was still under 500,000 although there had been considerable importations of breeding stock. By 1917, the figure had risen to more than 1,000,000. In 1927, there were well over 2,000,000 head in Rhodesia. At the end of 1967 the cattle population totalled 3,939,534 (Central Statistical Office, 1968), considerably more

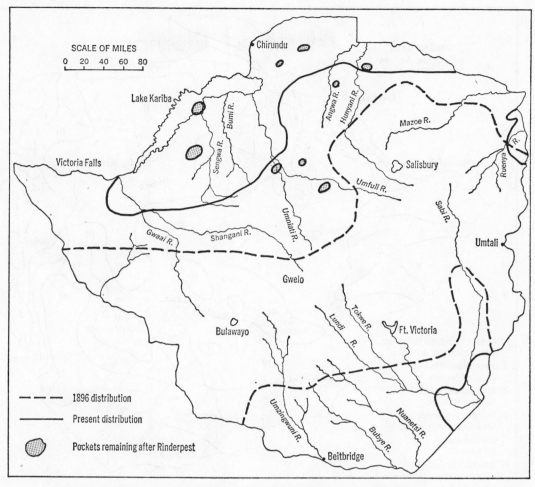

Figure 38–2 Distribution of the tsetse fly in Rhodesia, 1896 and present

than half of which are owned by the native population (Figs. 38–2 and 38–3).

BUSH ENCROACHMENT

Over the country as a whole, both human and animal populations rapidly grew to levels approaching "subsistence densities" which Dasmann (1966) has described as essentially a disaster level but a level at which man has kept his domesticated animals in many parts of the world. In Rhodesia, this growth formerly occurred only in isolated areas and for short periods of time.

Now this level was being approached over most of the occupied area. Because of increased grazing pressure and because grass that formerly was burned was now eaten, fire could no longer exercise its role in producing and maintaining grassland, and so the bush thickened while the grass decreased. Thus, developed the paradoxical situation that as the number of cattle increased, the grass available for grazing was reduced, not only relatively to the increasing numbers of cattle but actually in total amount of dry matter available for consumption. The effect of the thickening of the bush reflected by the reciprocal increases

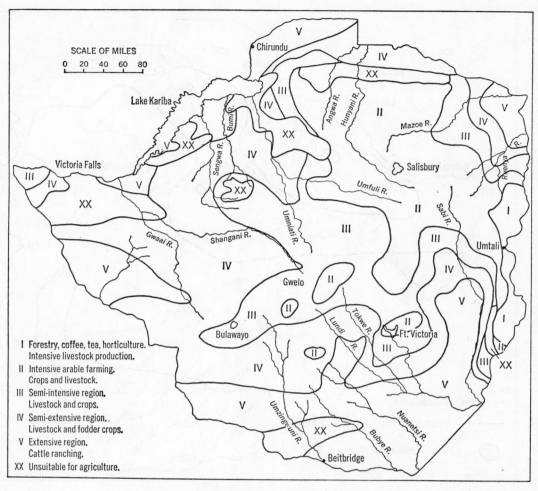

SCALE OF MILES
0   20 40 60 80

I Forestry, coffee, tea, horticulture.
   Intensive livestock production.
II Intensive arable farming.
   Crops and livestock.
III Semi-intensive region.
   Livestock and crops.
IV Semi-extensive region.
   Livestock and fodder crops.
V Extensive region.
   Cattle ranching.
XX Unsuitable for agriculture.

Figure 38–3 Natural regions in Rhodesia

in yield of grass obtained from plots cleared of bush, is illustrated by the following figures from cleared and uncleared plots in various parts of the country (Table 38–1).

The attack on the problems posed by bush encroachment falls into two parts, firstly the thinning or eradication of existing bush and tree growth and secondly the prevention of encroachment, by which existing bush or tree veld is thickened and open areas are invaded by woody species.

The cheapest, most widely used and probably most effective method is ringbarking. In suitable circumstances, however, arboricides, principally 2,4,5–T and Tordon, are effective. Mechanical clearing using chain, bulldozer blade or root plow is expensive, but is used to a limited extent.

In the higher-rainfall regions where intensive agriculture is practiced, the problems posed by bush encroachment are temporary because this land is gradually being cleared for crop production and the cost of clearing is usually met by the profit from the first crop.

Encroachment in the region of medium rainfall is a serious problem but is effectively countered by systems of management which make provision for the rotation of

Table 38-1

THE EFFECT OF CLEARING THE TREES ON YIELDS OF GRASS HERBAGE

HARVEST DATE	SEASONAL RAINFALL UP TO TIME OF HARVEST (inches)	HERBAGE YIELDS (lb DRY MATTER/ACRE)	
		TREES NOT CLEARED	TREES CLEARED
Tuli Experiment Station (on paragneiss)			
April 6, 1964	7	280	520
April 1, 1965	11	220	760
May 5, 1966	12	160	1,450
June 15, 1967	28	601	2,851
Nyamandhlovu Experiment Station (on red Kalahari sand)			
May 1, 1964	16	1,220	2,620
April 1, 1965	15	1,320	2,080
May 4, 1966	21	1,040	2,000
Matopos Research Station (on basement schist)			
May 21, 1963	22	1,370	2,900
March 17, 1964	13	1,020	2,060
April 7, 1965	12	580	1,150
June 14, 1966	19	720	1,070
Matopos Research Station (on granite)			
May 20, 1963	29	1,260	1,350
March 17, 1964	13	1,040	1,430
May 25, 1965	15	940	1,280
June 22, 1966	24	780	1,460
Makoholi Experiment Station (on granite)*			
1961	24	310	1,070
1962	27	390	1,350
1963	33	460	1,430
1964	18	110	1,350

*Yields of herbage for this site in air-dry herbage per acre.

(N.B. It should be noted that the increase on cleared plots is often relatively greater in dry years. Thus bush clearing provides an insurance against drought.)

growing-season rests, followed by controlled burning of the rested area in the late dry season.

Denudation in dry areas. Bush encroachment resulting from overgrazing and poor management is most marked in the regions of medium to higher rainfall. It proceeds at a slower pace in the drier regions, but in dry areas the perennial grasses are extremely sensitive to overutilization, especially during the growing season, and are rapidly eliminated as a result of overstocking.

In the drier areas particularly, increasing grazing pressure has led to the denudation of millions of acres of grazing land (Cleghorn, 1966). Over much of this area perennial grasses have been virtually eliminated; the country now supports a cover of annuals when sufficient rain falls. These are rapidly consumed when drought prevails, leaving the ground bare and forcing the livestock to subsist almost entirely on browse and fallen leaves. Conditions in some areas are growing worse, and this decline is reflected in the changing balance of the livestock population in certain tribal areas where the numbers of small stock, goats and

Table 38-2

LIVESTOCK POPULATION FIGURES FOR AFRICAN LAND IN THE
DISTRICTS OF BEIT BRIDGE AND NUANETSI

	BEIT BRIDGE			NUANETSI		
	Cattle	Sheep	Goats	Cattle	Sheep	Goats
1959	46,545	8,739	24,262	51,486	2,396	17,996
1967	52,111	17,393	55,406	77,940	10,735	59,058

sheep, are increasing in relation to the cattle population (Table 38–2).

It is considered that the changes shown in the numbers of the various species of livestock are a result of the increasing degradation of the environment. Such degradation is now imposing a severe limitation on the growth of the cattle population but not on the goat and sheep populations. The great danger in this trend is that the degradation which was initiated by cattle will be continued to the ultimate (uninhabitable desert) by the more versatile goats and sheep, which are known to be able to continue to exist in environments degraded below the level cattle are capable of tolerating.

Degradation due to overstocking can only be cured by reducing the grazing pressure during the growing season when the grasses are vulnerable to overgrazing. The most obvious means of reducing grazing pressure is by reducing the number of animals in the overstocked area. In some cases all that is necessary is a redistribution of the existing livestock population. Such redistribution can be brought about by fencing and the development of watering points to ensure that specially favored areas are not overstocked and to make areas available for grazing which are presently inaccessible because of the absence of watering points. Where an actual reduction in stock numbers is required, some progress is being made, especially among the more enlightened stock owners, by education in which demonstration of the results obtained in controlled grazing management trials plays

an important part. Other approaches include the encouragement of regular sales of stock by providing the necessary facilities for auction sales and for the transport of cattle out of the area.

Sweet veld possesses the very special advantage that cattle will do well on it during the dry season with minimal supplementary protein feeding; it is, however, intolerant of and easily damaged by grazing during the growing season. Recognizing this fact, West (1968) has shown that in the southern lowveld the problem could be solved by using the very great, but still largely undeveloped, irrigation potential of the region to provide growing-season grazing at high stocking rates on fertilized, irrigated pastures. This would make it possible to provide a growing-season rest for very large acreages of dry veld each year.

Experimental results show that fertilized, irrigated pastures in this area can be stocked at a rate of five beasts to the acre for the six months from November to March. This means that where the carrying capacity of the dry veld is one beast to 40 acres, each acre of irrigated pasture would enable 200 acres of dry veld to be rested throughout the growing season. In southern Matabeleland alone, the driest and most arid part of the lowveld region, the explored irrigation potential amounts to 36,189 acres, which is sufficient to depasture 180,945 head and to provide a six months growing-season rest for 36,189,000 acres.

It is calculated that over most of the southern lowveld the existing cattle population could live on fertilized, irrigated pastures at a stocking rate of five head to the acre for the six months from the beginning of November to the end of March. This would provide a growing-season rest each year for most of the dry veld and would have the effect of immediately doubling the carrying capacity of the rested area, as dry-veld grazing would be required for only six months of the year instead of twelve months.

It is known from experimental results that if this type of utilization could be brought about, the resting during the growing season, assisted where necessary by conservation works, bush clearing and harvester termite eradication, would enable the veld to recover very rapidly. The carrying capacity of the dry-season grazing would undoubtedly improve, where sufficient irrigation is available, and the country would eventually be able to carry easily a stocking greater than the present cattle population which is reducing the land to desert.

CATTLE AND TSETSE FLY

Tsetse flies live mainly on the blood of wild animals and cattle. They harbor trypanosomes which they transmit to their hosts. Most wild animals are resistant to the trypanosomes, but cattle are not immune and when bitten by an infected fly develop a fatal disease called trypanosomiasis or nagana. For this reason cattlemen always used to avoid fly areas and were careful to keep their animals out of contact with the fly. Some species of trypanosomes transmitted by tsetse flies give rise to sleeping sickness, a fatal human disease responsible for much misery in Africa and an ever present danger to the northern parts of Rhodesia. By far the most important tsetse fly in Rhodesia is *Glossina morsitans*. In the middle of the nineteenth century, *G. morsitans* occupied approximately half of the area of Rhodesia. The insect was confined

to altitudes below 4000 feet and the infested portions of the country were separated into two main areas, northern and southern, by the watershed, a great belt of high-lying country which was fly-free.

In 1896, a rinderpest epizootic swept through Rhodesia from the north, destroying vast numbers of cattle and game animals, the hosts of the fly. It is estimated that the rinderpest killed 95% of the cattle and decimated most of the game population. Of the game animals, it is said that buffalo, eland and kudu suffered the greatest numerical reduction, but the majority of the antelopes as well as giraffe and wart hog fought the disease readily and perished. Only hartebeest, wildebeest and waterbuck appeared to be immune.

Following the rinderpest, which decimated the game animals on which the fly was dependent, the tsetse areas were greatly reduced in size. In the south, the fly disappeared completely while the northern fly area was reduced to a few isolated foci.

Thus the great barrier to the spread of cattle in Rhodesia was removed and cattle began to move into areas from which they were formerly excluded by disease. However, the retreat of the fly was not permanent, and as early as 1900 there were signs of increase of both game and fly in the still unoccupied northern area.

Eventually and inevitably, contact between fly and cattle was re-established in 1918 and the government, in order to protect the human inhabitants largely dependent on cattle, was forced to attempt to control the advance of the fly, which was re-occupying land at the rate of 1000 square miles a year.

At first, as an experiment, and from 1933, as an established policy, the government used what then appeared to be the only means at its disposal, the elimination of the host game animals by shooting. In this first campaign, the aim was the total elimination of game animals in areas threatened by invasion. It was successful, and by 1945 the advance had been stopped, and some 10,000 square miles of country had been cleared of fly and was ready for agricultural development. This was undoubtedly the greatest tsetse reclamation effort ever made in Africa.

In 1960, the shooting of game was suspended in favor of discriminative bush clearing because it was believed that the flies were dependent during the dry season on riverine forest and certain other vegetation types. In addition to bush clearing, close settlement was encouraged in certain strategic areas to make the habitat unsuitable for fly.

These measures, however, proved ineffective and a resurgence of fly began which led to the reinvasion of great areas of country. Contrary to what had been believed, new research findings indicated that discriminative bush clearing was largely a waste of effort; the fly showed little preference for any specific woody vegetation type at any time of the year (Pilson and Pilson, 1967). In addition, a new technique for identifying the source of the blood meals of recently fed tsetse flies showed that the fly did not feed indiscriminately on all game animals, but almost exclusively on certain favored species.

On the basis of these findings, a new approach involving the selective elimination of the most favored host species together with the use of insecticides was tried. This approach, promising in preliminary experiments, became official policy and has been in full operation since January, 1965. The most favored hosts, determined by blood meal examination, are kudu, bushbuck, bush pig, and wart hog. Usually elephant and buffalo are also removed, either by shooting or, in the case of elephant, by driving them out of the area. The removal of the most favored hosts is accompanied by the use of contact insecticides. The insecticides, formerly dieldrin

and now DDT, are applied very selectively by hand-spraying to the sites on which flies rest by day: tree trunks, overhanging branches, dead wood, knot holes, etc.

The area sprayed amounts to a minute fraction of the habitat, but the operation is very effective because the area used by the fly for resting during the day is extremely restricted. Discriminative bush clearing, the great hope during the period 1960–1965, is used sparingly and only where necessary; bush is cleared either by mechanical means or by ring-barking.

It is encouraging that in the face of what was an expanding fly population these operations are achieving very marked success; as time goes on, continuing advances in technique will undoubtedly make them more successful.

At present, the first priority is given to stabilizing the fly fronts. When this has been achieved, the next step is the attrition of the fly belt in areas where the land reclaimed can be fully utilized. Prophylactic drugs are being used at present to maintain cattle populations in a healthy condition in tsetse country where the challenge is light but where formerly cattle could not have survived.

THE FUTURE FOR GAME ANIMALS

Selous (1893) and other early hunters and travelers tell how numerous, varied, and widespread was the game population of Mashonaland and Matabeleland at the time of the colonization. During the seventy-eight years since that date, this game population has been drastically reduced except in some tsetse areas and on national land, in forest reserves, game reserves and national parks. There are still numbers of game animals on private land and in tribal areas if one knows where to find them, but the spectacle that game used to provide for the casual traveler in Rhodesia no longer exists except in the national parks. The reasons for the disappearance of game animals from farming areas in Rhodesia are basically and historically similar to those which led to the disappearance of the buffalo from the North American prairies.

The natural prairie produced buffalo and prairie chickens which people could eat, but when the prairie was ploughed and planted to corn . . . the sparse population which could have been supported by the native grasses and animal life became a dense population fed by agricultural produce. The prairie became a bread basket for the world. (Dasmann, 1966)

In less than eighty years, the population of Rhodesia has increased tenfold. Agriculture has become a large and important industry which in addition to feeding the rapidly growing population exports beef, maize, cotton, tobacco, sugar, citrus and other produce.

A study of the present trends in this developing and largely agricultural country leaves little doubt that in most categories of land the future for representative populations of large game is a bleak one. In farming and ranching areas including the tribal lands, as development proceeds, the trend is toward the elimination of game, and over much of the developed area large game has already disappeared. (It is encouraging, however, that despite this, there is a compensatory trend, as farmers become prosperous, to encourage those game species which can be tolerated in developed farming areas. Small game such as reedbuck, oribi, steenbok and duiker, and game birds such as guinea fowl and francolin as well as water fowl are valued and encouraged on the majority of developed farms, and there is a growing demand for the supply of species suitable for restocking.)

It is evident that large game will not abound in tsetse areas if these areas are rendered habitable for cattle, and the indications are that this will be brought about in the not too distant future. For representative populations of game we are left then with national land which in Rhodesia includes forest areas, forest reserves, game reserves, and national parks. National land at present totals 10,524,000 acres or slightly more than one-ninth of the area of Rhodesia. Of this total, game reserves and national parks together account for 7,839,087 acres (national parks, 4,074,639 acres; game reserves, 3,764,448 acres).

Some of the forest land contains considerable game populations. At present, this game is valued and preserved, but it must be remembered that the chief consideration in forest land is the welfare of the timber. Only in game reserves, and most of all in the national parks, is the preservation of the game and their habitats paramount.

National Parks are a key factor in the conservation of wildlife. . . . They give some guarantee of permanence. . . . They are a source of prestige and actual or potential profit to the territories in which they lie. . . . If properly managed they constitute the best means of preserving a representative sample of Africa's large wild animals for the enjoyment and interest of future generations. (Huxley, 1961)

In Rhodesia, the permanence of the national parks is guaranteed to some extent by the lucrative nature of the presently large and rapidly growing tourist industry. It is certain, however, that population growth and increasing demand for land for human settlement will begin eventually to infringe upon the area of the parks. It is vital that this tendency be foreseen so that it can be resisted. Perhaps the best means of ensuring effective resistance would be by educating all people to appreciate the importance of conserving wildlife in typical natural habitats, not merely because of its economic importance, but more importantly because of the obligation of providing living room for all forms of life and of the aesthetic importance of wildlife and its value for scientific and recreational purposes.

ACKNOWLEDGEMENTS

I would like to thank Mr. Desmond Lovemore and Mr. Roelf Attwell for reading this manuscript, Mr. A. J. Beeson for his help in the preparation of the maps and figures and Miss J. Skinner for the trouble she took in producing the typescript. I am very grateful to them all.

REFERENCES

Aubreville, A. "Dix années d'expériences sylvicoles en Côte d'Ivoire." *Rev. Eaux For.*, Vol. 75, No. 4 (1937), 289–302; Vol. 75, No. 5 (1937), 385–400.

———. "The Disappearance of the Tropical Forests of Africa." *Unasylva,* 1 (1947), 5–11.

———. "Climats, forêts et desertification de l'Afrique tropicale." *Soc. d'Édit. Geogr., Marit. et Colon.* Paris, 1949a.

———. "Contribution à la paléohistoire des forêts de l'Afrique Tropicale." *Soc. d'Édit. Geogr., Marit. et Colon.* Paris, 1949b.

———. "Flore Forestière Soudano—Guinéenne, A.O.F.—Cameroun—A.E.F." *Soc. d'Édit. Geogr., Marit. et Colon.* Paris, 1950.

Bartlett, H. H. "Fire in Relation to Primitive Agriculture and Grazing in the Tropics. Annotated Bibliography." In *Int. Symposium, Man's Role in Changing the Face of the Earth.* Ann Arbor: University of Michigan Botanical Gardens, 1955.

———. "Fire in Relation to Primitive Agriculture and Grazing in the Tropics. Annotated Bibliography." Vol. II. Ann Arbor; University of Michigan Botanical Gardens, 1957.

Burchell, W. J. "Travels in the Interior of Southern Africa." 1822–24. Reprinted 1953, Batchworth Press, London.

Clark, J. D. *The Prehistory of Southern Africa.* Pelican Books, London: Penguin Books, 1959.

Cleghorn, W. B. "Report on the Conditions of Grazing in Tribal Trust Land." *Rhodesia Agric. J.,* 63 (3) (1966), 57–67.

Cockbill, G. F. "A Second Review of the Tsetse and Trypanosomiasis Position in Southern Rhodesia, 1964." Department of Veterinary Services, Ministry of Agriculture, Salisbury, 1964.

Condy, J. B. "The Status of Disease in Rhodesian Wild Life." *Rhodesia Science News,* 2 (6) (1968), 96–98.

Dasmann, R. F. *Wildlife Biology.* 2d ed. New York: John Wiley & Sons, 1966.

Harris, T. M. "Forest Fire in the Mesozoic." *J. Ecol.,* Vol. 46, No. 2 (1958), 447–53.

Huxley, J. *The Conservation of Wild Life and Natural Habitats in Central and East Africa.* Paris: UNESCO, 1961.

Moodie, D. F. C. *The History of the Battles and Adventures of the British, the Boers and the Zulus, etc., in Southern Africa.* Cape Town: Murray & St. Leger, 1888.

Nobbs, E. A. "The Native Cattle of Southern Rhodesia." *S. Afr. J. Sci.,* 24 (1927), 328–42.

Oliver, J. "The Origin, Environment and Description of the Mashona Cattle of Rhodesia." *Expl. Agric.,* 2 (1966), 81–88.

Pilson, R. D., and Pilson, B. M. "Behavior Studies of *Glossina morsitans* Western in the Field." *Bull. Entomological Research,* Vol. 57, Pt. 2 (Feb. 1967), pp. 227–57.

Selous, F. C. *Travel and Adventure in South-East Africa.* London: Rowland Ward & Co., 1893.

Summers, R. "Environment and Culture in

Southern Rhodesia: A Study in the "Personality of a Land-Locked Country." *Proc. American Phil. Soc.,* 104 (3) (1960), 266–92.

Swynnerton, C. F. M. "Some Factors in the Replacement of the Ancient East African Forest by Wooded Pasture Land." *S. Afr. J. Sci.,* 14 (1917), 493–518.

Vincent, V., and Thomas, R. G. "An Agricultural Survey of Southern Rhodesia. Part 1. Agro-Ecological Survey." Salisbury: Government Printer, 1961.

Vorster, T. H. "The Production of Beef in the Native Reserves of Southern Rhodesia as Compared with Different Systems of Stock Rearing on European Farms." *Rhod. Agric. J.,* 57 (6) (1960), 429–35.

West, O. "Plant Secession and Veld Burning Considered Particularly in Relation to the Management of Bushveld Grazing." *Veld Gold.* Proceedings of Southern African Grass Conference, Pretoria, 1952. Pretoria: National Veld Trust, 1954.

———. "Fire in Vegetation and Its Use in Pasture Management with Special Reference to Tropical and Sub-Tropical Africa." *Mimeographed Publication* No. 1/1965. Commonwealth Bureau of Pastures and Field Crops, Hurley, Berkshire, England, 1965.

———. "The Vegetation of Southern Matabeleland: A Study of the Reasons for Its Present Degradation and Possible Means of Rehabilitation." In *Symposium on Drought and Development,* 1st Rhodesian Science Congress, 1967. Salisbury: Collins, 1968. Pp. 85–103.

Wills, A. J. *An Introduction to the History of Central Africa.* London: Oxford University Press, 1964.

39. THE TSETSE FLY: A BLESSING OR A CURSE?

Frank L. Lambrecht

The life expectancy of man at birth has doubled from about thirty-five years only three centuries ago to the present average of about seventy years (Deevey, 1960) through his ever increasing knowledge, some of which is used as a defense against eliminating factors of natural selection such as disease, predators and famine. However, the tremendous advances in technology since the years of the industrial revolution have also resulted in grave social and physical consequences; mankind is facing a crisis as acute as any during his long evolution.

Until recently, man in tropical Africa lived in equilibrium with his environment, as a hunter-gatherer or a seminomadic agriculturist. Presently with the introduction of cash crops and modern means of farming and husbandry, the precarious energy cycles of the shallow African soils are in danger of rapid degradation. The biological equilibrium is further upset by the depletion of game due to hunting or the destruction of game biotopes.

In the past, the spread of man and cattle in tropical Africa over some four million square miles was largely checked by the presence of tsetse flies (*Glossina*) and their trypanosomal parasite which causes the fatal sleeping sickness disease in man and a similar disease, nagana, in domestic stock. Tsetse flies have thus been responsible for the preservation of the original fauna, immune to the disease, and of the flora. But progress and human encroachment can no longer be stopped except in areas which, through timely intervention, have been declared national parks or reserves.

Areas are being liberated from the tsetse fly by vegetation clearings, game control and the use of insecticides. Such methods have not always been used with the full knowledge of what the environmental consequences might be.

The maintenance of an animal population in a given environment depends upon the equilibrium between the energy required by the former and supplied by the latter. This principle also applies to human populations of the past when primitive bands of hunter-gatherers had to live on the natural products of the land. With the arrival of the first agriculturalists and pastoralists, man was liberated from his daily chores as a hunter-gatherer. Since then he has made a number of stepwise technical advances but each of them has added, in one way or another, to the precariousness of his position within his own environment.

In tropical Africa the abuse of the environment is due not so much to industrialization as to the misuse of agricultural land and the overgrazing of grassland by domestic stock. In addition to land misuse, the destruction of wild animal biotopes and hunting have been responsible for drastic changes in faunal composition and numbers.

In the stage of hunter-gatherers or shifting cultivation by sparsely distributed inhabitants, Africa presented a picture of balanced climax biotopes. The equilibrium of a climax biotope occurs under natural conditions through the methodical use of the available energy cycling through the climax components. The destruction of one or more of the components may rupture the cycle, perhaps irreversibly, and cause the complete collapse of the system or reduce it to a secondary, low-grade community (Lambrecht, 1966). The introduction around 5000 B.C. of cattle and the later rapid increase of the human and cattle population, especially after the introduction of modern medicine, hygiene and cash crops, have changed the picture to a point of complete degradation in many areas.

The greater part of tropical Africa lies within tsetse fly belts. Some twenty-four species of tsetse (genus *Glossina*) are known. Both male and female flies feed on vertebrate blood. If the blood meal derives from a trypanosome-infected animal, the protozoan flagellate becomes established in the fly, which then remains infective to each subsequent animal on which it feeds. Two trypanosome species infective to man cause sleeping sickness, while other trypanosome species affect domestic animals by inducing a disease called nagana. African game animals harbor both human and cattle trypanosomes but are themselves tolerant to the parasites circulating in their bloodstream. This tolerance has been acquired from eons of contact with tsetse and trypanosomes, resulting in the natural selection of those that were resistant. Man and cattle, however, are of relatively recent evolution, and immunity mechanisms have not developed, nor has natural selection had the chance to operate. Man and cattle are thus forced to live outside the fly belt or die.

In the past, the migration routes of people and cattle in Africa were very much influenced by the presence or absence of tsetse (Lambrecht, 1964). It can be assumed that early human populations avoided areas of high tsetse density, if only because of fly annoyance (Summers, 1960). The early pastoralists were even more affected by the presence of tsetse. They suffered heavy losses in their livestock whenever cattle were kept in contact with fly or traveled through a fly belt.

Migrations southward from the Nile Valley occurred along the high ridge country on both sides of the Central Rift Valley. The route followed by the first migrants has played an important part in the diffusion of culture and subsequent occupations. These migration patterns became important in later economic development as the fly-free migration corridors fused into connecting links between trading posts and other permanent settlements. The presence of tsetse, especially the savannah flies, curtailed the full occupation of vast areas otherwise suit-

able for cattle and agriculture, thus preserving original biotopes and their related
fauna. This natural protection affected travel
of the first western explorers and settlers,
who were dependent upon oxen and horses
for drawing their supply wagons. Many expeditions had to turn back after they had
set out from coastal and other fly-free
areas. Andersson (1857) tells of one party
of Englishmen with many horses, accompanied by natives and their cattle, jour-
neying to the north of Lake N'gami, and
how they had to turn back after they had
lost most of their horses and also sustained
heavy losses in cattle, all victims of the tsetse
flies.

When motorized transport became available, the full impact of Western technology
and occupation on the interior of the African continent was felt. Penetration and
permanent settlements also increased after
the establishment of adequate medical services and better knowledge of the causative
agents of tropical diseases and vectors. Human and animal trypanosomes and their
transmission by flies of the genus *Glossina*
were discovered and described between the
years 1895 and 1912. A great epidemic
raged north of Lake Victoria between
1902–05; 200,000 people died out of a
population of 300,000. The reasons of this
big upflare are not certain. Later outbreaks
are better documented. A brief account of
them is given below.

A reorganization, which at first seemed
wise, changed the destiny of a whole human population in the Semliki Valley area
after the start of the Belgian administration
in that part of the Congo. The valley was
grassland and supported a flourishing agricultural population living on the western
slopes of Mount Ruwenzori. Wing cattle
grazed in the valley. Belgian administrators,
impressed by the fertile soil of the valley
floor, moved the native population from the
slopes to the banks of the river. This move
permanently established contact between

man and *Glossina palpalis* which infested
the forest gallery lining the river. By 1920
most of the human population was either
dead, had fled or had been hospitalized.

The Gambian sleeping sickness spread to
the shores of Lakes Edward and George,
where the Uganda Government was forced
to evacuate many thousands of people and
their cattle from areas that had been occupied for three hundred to four hundred
years. The abandonment of the grassland
resulted in the growth of thickets, allowing
G. pallidipes to reach and occupy these
valleys from higher-level forests, where they
had been confined previously through agricultural activities. From this area, *G. pallidipes* spread eastward and was finally
halted fifty years later about one hundred
miles further east. In 1921 some Uganda
cattle owners returned to their old pasture
land with about 120 head of cattle. Three
years later all the cattle were dead, presumably because of trypanosomiasis transmitted by *G. pallidipes* (Ford, 1960).

The development of *Acacia* savannah
after the abandonment of grassland seems
to be a general rule, at least in East Africa.
Should this occur adjacent to established fly
belts, the fly will probably advance into the
newly created habitats as soon as sufficient
tree cover and hosts are available. This
type of fly advance occurred in the Karagwe region of the Bukoba District in the
northwestern corner of Tanzania (Ford and
Hall, 1947). The excellent grazing lands
in this area were occupied by cattle owned
by a pastoralist tribe. Tribal wars during
the latter part of the last century disrupted
the cultural structure, resulting in the
abandonment of the grazing lands by the
pastoralists. Soon the grassland reverted to
Acacia and other pyrophitic tree species
savannah which allowed later invasion by
G. morsitans. The fly continued to advance
and by 1950 had reduced the three-hun-
dred-mile gap between the northern and
eastern belts to about fifty miles.

The abandonment of pasture land is often caused by the degradation of the grassland through overstocking, the tendency among tropical pastoralists being to keep more cattle than the land can support, for herdsmen take pride in the number of animals they own.

In the Bugesera region of Rwanda, good grassland developed into suitable tsetse *Acacia* woodland after the inhabitants had left following an outbreak of rinderpest in their herds. The spreading *Acacia* vegetation joined the Tanzania *G. morsitans* fly belt, resulting in westward advance of the fly into unoccupied habitats. Watutsi (Watusi) pastoralists later reoccupied the Bugesera but close contact with *G. morsitans,* which by now had spread over large areas in the wake of vast numbers of game, resulted in heavy cattle losses and an outbreak of human sleeping sickness.

A recent example of the creation of manmade tsetse habitats is the Alego District of Kenya, a hilly country of high rainfall east of Lake Victoria. The area is densely settled because of fertile lands, a network of permanent rivers and the proximity of a number of important towns. *Glossina fuscipes* and *G. pallidipes* were confined to the lake's shores and the adjacent bush and woodland. Sleeping sickness was found mainly among the fishermen. No tsetse had been reported from the higher plateaus before 1960, but a sudden increase in cases of sleeping sickness, this time among the inhabitants of the inland villages, indicated the presence of flies and the occurrence of local transmission. An entomological survey revealed that *G. fuscipes* had invaded the plateau land and bred in dense patches of neglected *Euphorbia tirucalli* and *Lantana camara* (the latter an ornamental hedge plant introduced by white settlers) planted for paddocking groups of huts and fields. Under the circumstances, contact between man and fly became very intimate and resulted in intense transmission of sleeping sickness, producing some seventy cases per month by the end of 1964.

CONTROL OF TSETSE FLIES

The first ideas about the control of sleeping sickness through control of its *Glossina* vector came in the early 1920's with the basic studies of the ecological requirements of the fly. Methods for control were for many years a matter of trial and error. At present, practical large-scale anti-tsetse measures fall into three categories: (1) vegetation clearing, (2) game control, and (3) the application of insecticides.

The feasibility of tsetse control by bush clearing was realized when early studies showed that the flies were dependent upon microclimatic conditions within certain vegetation communities. No tsetse habitat was ever found in open grassland and it was obvious that none of the tsetse species could survive in a completely denuded area. But ruthless bush clearing is expensive, and its effect on the soils thus exposed to weathering and erosion was unclear. Some thought that erosion after bush clearing would wash away fertile topsoil; others thought that removal of tree cover would promote grass growth which would hold soil better, especially in dense upper canopy where grass cover was often poor and erosion *did* occur.

Cost and other considerations led to refinements in bush-clearing methods, such as "selective or discriminative clearing" in which only enough shade trees are felled to make the habitat unsuitable for the fly. These methods met with varying degrees of success. Failures were often due to the application of a certain degree of clearing that had proved successful in another area, disregarding the fact that ecological requirements are not always the same in all areas, even for the same tsetse species. Indeed, requirements not only depend on the vegetation but also include local climate, length of dry and rainy seasons, altitude and the availability of vertebrate hosts on which the fly feed. Regeneration is a major problem which necessitates recurrent expenditure, unless the cleared area happens to be an isolated block that has no contact with other fly belts.

The other method of tsetse control is the elimination of its food supply by shooting game animals. This method has been successful and relatively cheap in certain areas of Uganda, Rhodesia and Zululand. Game control has been fiercely criticized; rightly so, being brutal and distasteful. Its organization may be very difficult and expenses increase rapidly with game density, difficulties of terrain and the need of close supervision. Its success is dependent, among other things, on how well the treated area can be protected from reinvasion of game from the surrounding areas. The danger also exists that after the shooting of game the fly will still be able to survive in small foci where it can feed on domestic animals and man. This, in turn, might result in increased man-fly contact or domestic animal-fly contact and bring about increased trypanosome transmission.

Large-scale tsetse control by insecticides has been done (a) by "contact" insecticides from the air, or (b) by "residual" insecticides on the ground.

The first method is expensive and presents many technical problems. Its main advantage is the speed with which large areas can be treated. It has been successfully applied in Zululand and during experimental trials by the Tropical Pesticides Research Institute in Tanzania. If cost and certain technical problems can be reduced, aerial spray could be used in many instances.

Ground spraying has been applied against several tsetse species in many areas of Africa, usually with great success. Its advantage over aerial spraying is that ground-spraying can be done in restricted areas of principal key habitats, if known, with resulting lower cost and greater efficiency. A good example of selective spraying based on the precise knowledge of fly behavior was against *G. fuscipes* in Kenya. The application of insecticide was restricted to the edge vegetation facing the riverbanks after it had been observed that the fly used the inside edge during its travel along and across the watercourse. This very selective spraying was completely successful in eradicating the fly from a vast river system.

The effect of insecticide spraying on wildlife has been the object of studies and publications. *Silent Spring* typifies the outcry of the American naturalist (Carson, 1962). In regard to the application of insecticides in the control of tsetse flies, the noxious effect upon wildlife is not as serious as one might believe. With ground application the insecticide is sprayed only on the boles and lower branches of trees, not on the foliage. Bird life is thus affected very little. In addition the insecticide is applied to a relatively small part of the total area to be liberated and to a very small proportion of the vegetation. Application on only the bark of trees eliminates the risk of the chemical being ingested by browsing and grazing animals. No resistance to the pesticide has so far been observed in tsetse fly populations.

Biological control as a possible method of tsetse eradication has been investigated over the last few years. The "sterile male technique" has shown possibilities. The difficulties of its application in the field is a matter of breeding and releasing sufficient numbers of treated males.

GAME HUSBANDRY VERSUS DOMESTIC STOCK

The commercial development of the cattle industry in Africa is directly related to the presence of tsetse flies. The industry's survival is only possible in the rare fly-free regions, areas which have been made fly-free by control measures or by keeping the cattle under anti-trypanosomal drugs. Over the last few years the possibilities of exploiting the natural ungulate fauna have been explored. In the African environment wild animals are far superior to domestic stock. They are less susceptible to diseases (including trypanosomiasis), make use of almost all African grass species, need smaller ranges, require far less water, reproduce faster and have a faster gain in liveweight and maturity. Because of these overwhelming advantages, the possibilities of utilizing this vast source of animal protein should be investigated. Possible methods include the culling of animals from "natural" herds or from "ranched" wild an-

imals and the breeding and selection of certain wild species.

In a previous paper (Lambrecht, 1966) I concluded from analyses of publications by Dasmann and other authors that on comparable land, other factors being equal, the harvest of meat from wild animals should be greater than that from domestic livestock under the prevailing conditions in most of Africa. Added to the direct gain of game-ranching are all the advantages of long-term conservation principles, e.g. the maintenance of natural vegetation cover and the preservation of fauna adapted to their natural environment.

The domestication of selected wild animal species, to which game farming could eventually lead, opens up another fascinat-

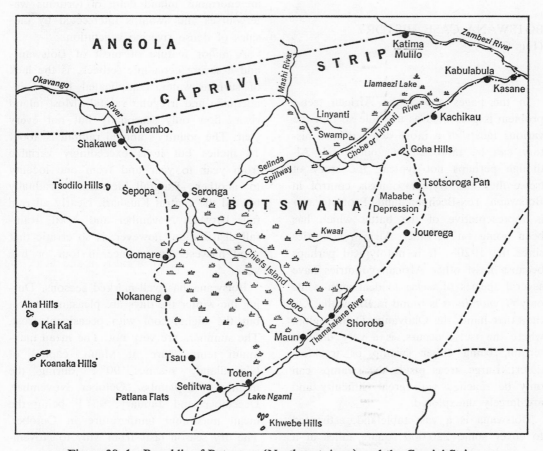

Figure 39–1 Republic of Botswana (Northwest Area) and the Caprivi Strip

ing and profitable field with practical application. Larger animals such as the eland would obviously be the first choice, if only for its size and gentle nature. Domesticated eland are already herded in certain parts of the Transvaal and Rhodesia, and in Zambia domesticated herds of goats, eland and lechwe have been kept successfully for years.

The large-scale utilization of natural fauna would eliminate the need of tsetse control over vast areas, and efforts and expenditure for control could be restricted to the protection of the immediate vicinity —villages, fields and important roads and river crossings.

BOTSWANA CASE HISTORY
(Fig. 39-1)

In the pages above, the African tsetse problem is presented as a whole so that the various facets of a more detailed case history can be more easily understood. Although perhaps not typical, the story of tsetse flies and trypanosomiasis control in Botswana (ex-Bechuanaland Protectorate) is representative of the battle which has been going on in other African countries since the 1920's. It is not typical perhaps because most other African countries have several species of tsetse to deal with while only *G. morsitans* is found in Botswana. On the other hand, the Okovango Delta region, where the tsetse occurs, is a very difficult terrain, being either swamp or trackless desert. Large areas inside the swamps can only be reached with great difficulty and are largely unexplored.

Botswana is a vast tableland, estimated to cover some 220,000 square miles at a mean altitude of 3,300 feet. The country

is bounded on the east by the Republic of South Africa, on the northeast by Rhodesia, on the north by the Caprivi Strip, on the northwest by South-West Africa and on the south by the Cape Province of the Republic of South Africa. It lies between latitudes 18 and 26° S., longitudes 21 and 29° E.

Three broad natural regions characterize the country: the Kalahari Desert and its marginal shrub and bushveld cover the vast southwest; in the east the harsh desert environment is relieved by the high elevations of some pleasant hill country with better rainfall and relatively more luxuriant vegetation; in the northwest the Kalahari is conquered by the waters of the great Okovango River draining the high rainfall plateaus of southern Angola. These waters enter N'gamiland at Mohembo and form an enormous inland delta of tortuous watercourses and swamps intersected by mosaics of dense riverine vegetation.

A major feature of most of Botswana, and a severe economic setback, is the lack of surface water, complicated by the inadequate and irregular rainfall. Most inland rivers flow only seasonally but not every year. The country's annual rainfall is about 18 inches but it is exceedingly variable from year to year and from one locality to another. Rainfall decreases gradually toward the central Kalahari. Nearly all rain falls between November and April. Rainfall distribution, however, is so erratic that good harvests occur once in four or five years.

Botswana has well-marked seasons. During the winter the days are pleasantly warm but the nights cool with occasional frost. The summers are very hot. The mean maximum temperature at Maun, capital of N'gamiland, reaches 90° F during the months of September, October, November, December and January, 95° F being the mean maximum temperature in October. The dry season lasts from May to November, when no rain falls except on unusual occasions. In some years the dry season may continue for nine months.

Glossina morsitans is found only in the northwest. There the large Okovango River is trapped and diffused in the hot sands of the Kalahari where most of the inflow evaporates or is soaked up into foamy soils and swamp vegetation. In years of good flow some water emerges to run southward into Lake N'gami and eastward, via the Botletle River and Lake Dow, into the Makarikari, a salt pan of some seventy square miles, where final evaporation occurs.

The Okovango Delta covers some 6,500 square miles. It is the home of large herds of game. Most of the area is infested by the tsetse fly, *G. morsitans*. The combination of suitable vegetation and large amounts of game compensate for the rather severe climatic conditions covering long periods of the year. The presence of permanent and seasonal water makes this area attractive to man and his domestic stock, resulting in contact with the tsetse fly and the trypanosomes carried by both the vector and the game. The Chobe River area in the northeast presents a similar situation of good watering points, relatively fertile soils and the concentration of settlements, game and tsetse, although in a much smaller area.

The 1964 Census Report lists a population of 45,000 in the Okovango and Chobe Districts. The (Ba)Tawana are the ruling tribe in N'gamiland. This cattle-raising tribe is an offshoot of the (Ba)Mangwato who moved north around 1800 and first settled near Lake N'gami and the Khwebe Hills. They then spread to other areas around the swamps, replacing or absorbing in the west the (Ba)Yei, themselves invaders who migrated from the north around 1700 to the lower reaches of the Okovango River, displacing the Masarwa (Bushmen) of the swamps and the western fringes and the Makalahari settlements around sections of the (Ma)Mbukush tribe, infiltrating from

the upper Chobe at the beginning of the nineteenth century.[1]

The true cattle breeders of N'gamiland are the Herero; they do not engage in agriculture. Their scattered groups form small communities within the Tawana settlements along the western and southwestern Okovango reaches. Their migration dates only from the beginning of this century when they fled their traditional areas in South-West Africa as a result of their wars with the German occupational forces. Because they take good care of their cattle by keeping them away from the tsetse belt, they do not have much contact with the fly. Sleeping sickness does not appear in the tribe.

The way of life of the Tawana and the Yei is somewhat unusual when compared with other African populations in that they group themselves in large communities of several hundred huts. This concentration of people, in combination with the dispersion of arable land, pasture and water, has resulted in a system of seasonal nomadism that revolves around three areas of activities: the fields, the cattle post and the village of residence. People spend four or five months of the year at their permanent residence in the main village, usually after the harvest has been collected in June or July until the start of the new crop during the rains in October or November. Shifting cultivation is practiced, a new field being tilled on the average of once every three years. Crops include red and white sorghum, millet, maize, beans, pumpkins, groundnuts and tobacco. Periods on the "lands," at the "cattle post" and in the village are usually shared by the whole family. There are some important exceptions: the children of school age often stay in the main village, usually with an older

---

[1] According to a 1958 stock census made in connection with a foot-and-mouth disease campaign, there were in N'gamiland 133,437 cattle, 35,135 goats, 4,022 sheep, 1,595 horses and 4,293 donkeys.

female member of the family, often the grandmother, in order to attend school. During the weekends they travel to the family on the lands, or preferably to the cattle post.

Hunting is an important winter activity after the harvest. Only the men hunt, but occasionally the women, and even the older children, go out to fetch the spoils. Such activities, together with the collection of wild honey, wild fruits and berries and grasses for basket weaving, are of great epidemiological significance because during these activities people are exposed more than anywhere else to the bites of trypanosome-carrying tsetse.

Most of the human population of N'gamiland lives in a narrow strip of country varying in width from less than four miles to about ten miles at the most, between the fringing swampland and the dry shrub of the desert along the four-hundred-mile-long perimeter of the Okovango Delta. They are confined to this strip of land because of the tsetse infestation in the central part of the Okovango Delta and the waterless expanses extending beyond the fringing area. Fly advances constitute a serious threat to the people and the occupied land on which they raise their crops and graze their cattle. Several villages with good local wells have been abandoned. The movement of additional herds of cattle into fly-free areas is aggravating the overgrazing and water shortage so evident in these parts during the long dry season.

In 1903 an epidemic due to trypanosome infection transmitted by the tsetse *G. palpalis* erupted on the shores of Lake Victoria, causing a high mortality rate. For the next few years it appeared that trypanosomiasis in humans was confined to the riverine habitats of this fly, for the disease seemed to be absent from areas where only the game tsetse, *G. morsitans,* was found. In Botswana, however, a disease called

kotsela ("drowsiness" in Sechuana) resembling sleeping sickness was known from the Okovango swamps well before this date. In 1909 two medical doctors, Dr. Moffat and Dr. James, were posted in N'gamiland to look for the disease, but they discovered no cases. Because only *G. morsitans* had been identified in this region it can hardly be surprising that the medical authorities were not impressed by the possibility of trypanosomiasis occurring, the human disease believed at that time to occur only in *G. palpalis* areas. In the same year, however, a mineral prospector developed an infection after a visit to the Luanga Valley in Zambia, an area free of *G. palpalis* but infested with flies of the *G. morsitans* group. The trypanosome in his blood had characteristics quite distinct from *Trypanosoma gambiense* of West and Central Africa and was named *Trypanosoma rhodesiense*.

In Botswana the talks of *kotsela* died away until 1930 when it was rumored that the disease affected people eating wild honey. (It is interesting that in Tanzania today about one-third of the five hundred cases of sleeping sickness occurring annually are probably acquired on expeditions to gather wild honey.) In 1934 the disease was finally diagnosed in two constables who fell sick after a patrol in an area between the Okovango Delta and the Chobe River. No more cases were reported for four years, until in 1938, four cases of *T. rhodesiense* infections were found in widely separated areas at the periphery of the Okovango Delta. This triggered a full-scale investigation by Dr. Mackichan who examined twenty thousand people between June 1939 and July 1940, finding nine infected people, a prevalence of 0.05 per cent. Most cases were widely dispersed but four were from the Maun area, the capital of N'gamiland. Two additional cases from the same area were diagnosed in Johannesburg. Mackichan's report probably gave a fair indication of the state of the disease at that time. It was widespread in N'gamiland but only at low levels.

A very serious epidemic occurred between the years 1940 and 1942 on the western side of the swamps. Its history, strangely enough, is very obscure. It is said that 828 cases of sleeping sickness were admitted to the Maun hospital during the epidemic, with 223 reported deaths (Buxton, 1955). By the time the government medical officer came to Maun at the end of 1945 the epidemic on the western side of the swamps had died away.

During the next thirteen years only 146 cases were treated at the Maun hospital, an average of 11 per annum. A Tsetse Fly Control Organization had been established and during its early years, until 1951, over 90 per cent of the cases were among its staff. As T.F.C. personnel were examined at least once a month and few surveys were made among other people, it could be argued that the number of cases was not comparable with previous years when only very occasional surveys were made. This may be so. However, the fly which had been almost completely driven out, except in a few small foci, following the epizootic of rinderpest in the game animals at the end of last century, had by 1945 recovered most of its previous habitats and had reached certain peripheral areas of the swamps close to human habitations and fields. From 1958 on there was a sharp increase of sleeping sickness cases, both in N'gamiland and Chobe District. This increase gave rise to some concern but it was not sufficient to cause alarm. It soon became evident, however, that the encroachment of fly into the fertile and well-watered fringing areas was inevitable unless large-scale drastic measures were taken. Clearings, which undoubtedly contributed to the control of the disease, were made to protect the larger villages of N'gamiland—Maun,

Tsau, Nokaneng, Gomare and Shorobe. The main efforts of T.F.C. were directed, however, toward the control of trypanosomiasis in domestic stock which was so important to the economy of the country, and more specifically to protect valuable grazing areas in the face of the fly advance. From about 1962 a small number of safari companies began to operate in northern Botswana, partly within the endemic sleeping sickness areas of N'gamiland and Chobe District. There was a fear that the risk of infection to staff and clients might damage the prospects for this new source of revenue, but no infections occurred. In the latter half of 1965 there were a number of cases, but this was part of a general increase in the prevalence, and by and large the safari companies have not fared badly.

There were 65 human cases in 1958 and a peak of 100 cases in 1960. Since then the number of cases per year has remained between 60 and 80, with another peak of 105 in 1966. In 1967 the number dropped to 40, the lowest since 1958. The infection rate over the years 1957–65 in the total population of N'gamiland, calculated at around 40,000, is 0.13 per cent. This rate is based on the whole population of N'gamiland, whereas, in fact, probably less than half are threatened. It is worthwhile mentioning that the infection rates are different for each of the eight main ethnic groups of N'gamiland. This seems to reflect their different ways of life. For instance, not a single case was ever found among the pastoralist Herero, who number just over 7,000, while there were 348 cases in only a slightly larger Yei population.

Let us now examine the history of sleeping sickness in Botswana from the entomological side. The presence of tsetse flies in southern Africa was recorded as early as 1836. Some of the reports already mentioned the damage caused by this fly to cattle. Probably the earliest record of fly in

N'gamiland is the one of C. J. Andersson (1857) who visited the country during his extensive travels from 1850 to 1854. He reported tsetse as far south as the junction of the Taoghe River with Lake N'gami. Several other travelers—Livingstone, Selous and Oswell (1900)—reported that tsetse existed in N'gamiland and that the flies were recognized by the inhabitants as a menace to stock. It was Gordon Cummings who started the use of the Sechuana word *tsetse* to indicate flies of this genus, during his travels along the Limpopo River. The diaries of Oswell and Cummings indicate that there was little or no penetration of fly westward from the Limpopo Valley into Bechuanaland until the latitude of the Macloutsie River was reached. Baines (1877) reported the same observation. The latter was among the first to produce maps indicating the presence of flies. At the close of the nineteenth century a general retreat of tsetse from large areas in Africa occurred. This retreat has been related to the great rinderpest epizootics that decimated large herds of game in central and southern Africa. The records of the well-known travelers Andersson (1857), Livingstone (1857) and Passarge (1943) clearly indicate that before the rinderpest, tsetse fly in N'gamiland occupied all available habitats within the Okovango and Chobe River systems, including extreme peripheral areas such as Lake N'gami, the Botletle River and areas south of Andara along the Okovango River in the Caprivi Strip. After the rinderpest epizootic the paucity or even complete absence of fly from these areas was noted by such travelers as Gibbons (1904) and Hodson (1912). The contraction was such that around 1900 the fly was said to occupy only three small foci: one near the center of the swamps (Chief's Island), one in the Chobe District (Dyei), and one at the eastern edge of the swamps (Zankuio). After the effect of the rinderpest had worn off, the game population slowly recovered and started to reoccupy its previous territories.

This recovery was followed by a similar movement of tsetse from their residual foci. In N'gamiland the rate of recovery of the fly, once it started, was very fast. It is estimated that between 1922 and 1942 the fly reoccupied some 3,000 square miles. By 1962 the fly had almost filled the entire territory (about 6,500 square miles) it had been forced to abandon as a result of the depletion of the game population. Awareness of the advance of fly is reflected in the notations of fly belt limits produced around 1923 by Captain A. G. Stigand, Resident Magistrate for N'gamiland at that time. Tsetse fly research and control was still in its infancy everywhere, and no further attention was attached to the fly situation in N'gamiland. The threat was pointed out again in a report by G. D. Hale-Carpenter in 1931, calling attention to the danger of widespread nagana to the cattle trade. In 1940 the Colonial Development Fund provided money for a general tsetse fly and trypanosomiasis survey of the country. This was carried out by J. W. Macaulay (1942) from 1940 until 1942. His reports constitute the first detailed study of fly distribution in N'gamiland and the Chobe area. As a result of Macaulay's recommendations, a Tsetse Fly Control Unit was formed in 1943, supported by a grant from the Colonial Development and Welfare Fund. General policies were later decided by a Central Policy Committee consisting of senior officials of the Administration, Heads of Departments, Representatives of the public, the Tsetse Fly Control Officer and Consultants.

One of the major problems facing tsetse control in the Okovango Delta is that fly dispersing from the center is constantly available to replenish suitable habitats at the periphery and that the eradication of fly from the 6,000 square miles of swamps is economically and even technically a near impossibility with the present methods of control. Under the circumstances, tsetse fly control in N'gamiland had been defensive, an effort to stop the fly's advance and to protect threatened settlements. Game control, together with selective clearing in certain areas, formed the basic principle of tsetse control.

At that time the Maun area was seriously threatened and had been vacated by cattle. It was decided that Maun, an area of relative high population density and the administrative capital of the Tawana, should have priority in game control. A start was made by erecting an eight-strand fence, running from Toteng to Shorobe, a distance of eighty miles, the flanks of which were protected by two ten-mile-long fences at right angles to the main fence on either side of Maun. Intensified game hunting was carried out within this area. By the end of 1945 the game had been reduced to a very low density, resulting in a very marked reduction of tsetse fly densities around Maun and a noticeable decrease in nagana cases in stock. In the west, riverine vegetation was cleared to a depth of one mile on the west bank of the Taoghe River between Tsau and Tubu Island. In 1946 the Colonial Development and Welfare Fund approved a sum of £78,548 to be used by T.F.C. over the next ten years. Work on the fence and game control continued on the Maun front. It was also necessary to cut regrowth along the Taoghe River in previously cleared areas. Near the end of 1946 the work on the Maun fence was completed and a second fence started, roughly parallel to the first and about ten miles north of it. The year 1950 saw increased difficulties with personnel. By September of that year the T.F.C. Officer became infected for the second time, as did seven subordinates. These and other difficulties resulted in a certain deterioration of the situation on the Maun front. At this time fly started to extend westward more rapidly from the Taoghe River between

Tsau and Nokaneng. From the end of 1950 until 1954 there was no Chief T.F.C. Officer and the District Commissioner was in charge of the unit. In May 1955 a Colonial Development and Welfare Scheme for £56,000 was approved to cover the cost of field investigations and experimental clearings for the next two years. The information derived from this was expected to form a basis to the preparation of larger schemes, Maun and Tsau-Nokaneng having again first priority.

The advance of fly in the west resulted in the mass withdrawal of cattle north toward Gomare and west to Xangwa Springs. In the Tsau area the stock was taken south to the Lake N'gami areas. At about this time the situation in the Chobe District caused concern following rumors of fly in places thought to be fly-free. A 1949 stock census had put the number of cattle in the Chobe area at 26,000. It was shortly after the stock census that people began complaining of heavy losses. The situation deteriorated very rapidly in the wake of advancing fly; cattle died in great numbers and others were moved away so that by 1960 only about 1,000 remained. The threat of trypanosomiasis had dramatically changed the previous even distribution of cattle around the swamps; by 1962 about 52 per cent were concentrated south of Makakun in the Lake N'gami areas, 20 per cent along the Okovango River north of Sepopa and 11 per cent along the Botletle River. This has resulted in permanent damage of pastures in those overstocked areas, complicated by subsequent years of drought.

The advance of fly in the Chobe District was not only of local concern but was also viewed with justifiable apprehension in the adjacent territories of the Rhodesias. On the Chobe River "flats" man-fly contact had become very close and eventually caused a sharp sleeping sickness outbreak in 1962. Because the advance of fly was on a narrow front, a barrier clearing was used to hold it.

Started in 1959 and completed in 1963, the clearings consisted of the removal of all fly habitat over a front of one to two miles between the village of Kachikau and Ngoma, a distance of some twenty-four miles. This action was completely successful in stopping the fly's advance and the threat of invading the territories to the east, while liberating many settlements from fly contact. Surveys had indicated that a similar threat was in progress by flies dispersing from certain foci in the Mababe Depression and advancing eastward in suitable fly habitats in the Ngwezumba Valley. This advance was foiled by ring-barking all *Acacia* in the valley over a distance of more than forty miles.

The Botswana Government had applied for advice from the World Health Organization and WHO consultants paid several visits over a number of years. In 1961 they initiated two experiments using a residual insecticide in small areas near Shorobe. The main objective of these trials was to assess the feasibility and the effectiveness of control methods, spraying regimes and sites within the fly's habitat. In 1963 WHO consultants made a detailed study of the resting sites of the local fly population so that eventual insecticide applications would be more economical and more efficient. From 1966 to 1968 a WHO team was stationed at Maun to investigate the epidemiology of human trypanosomiasis and to work in close collaboration with the T.F.C. Unit to study the possibilities of more efficient and aggressive methods of control which would permit reclaiming areas invaded by the fly.

In 1966 the results of many years of anti-tsetse measures could be summarized as follows. The methods of control were game shooting, the discriminative vegetation clearings around threatened settlements and ruthless barrier clearings in the line of advance of the fly. On the Maun front game control had been used for almost twenty-

five years. The system of game fences had prevented the invasion of larger animals and reduced shooting operations, but of course did not keep out the smaller animals such as the wart hog (the main *G. morsitans* host), the steenbuck and the duiker. A certain amount of clearing in river systems leading from the swamps to the Maun area had proved effective. It was realized that game control under the circumstances experienced in N'gamiland would never be of permanent value in spite of the fences.

Selective clearing was based on the fact that the majority of favorable fly habitats were to be found in *Acacia giraffae* woodland and that the removal of these trees would make the rest of the woodland unsuitable for fly populations. Although the method resulted in a marked reduction in fly density in most of the treated areas, it did not prevent fly invasion from bordering untreated habitats. The only partial success is also explainable by the way selective clearing was carried out. Usually clearing is done by felling the trees thought to be of primary importance in the fly's habitat. *A. giraffae* is a big tree with hard wood; it was killed by "ring-barking." In other parts of Africa the trees which have been cut dry out quickly and deteriorate after a short while from termite action and bush fires. By the method used in N'gamiland the trees were left standing and withering and weathering were very slow processes in spite of yearly bush fires. The drastic change in the vegetation community which should be achieved as quickly as possible in order to upset the fly's habitat requirements was not reached until the dead trees finally tumbled down, more than seven years later. Moreover, the principle of the selective clearing was the destruction of *A. giraffae* only. Where the vegetation consisted largely of this tree species, the method was moderately effective. However, in mixed tree communities, the ring-barking of only *A. giraffae* was proportionally less effective.

Sheer clearing (complete removal of vegetation) was carried out in the villages and the immediate perimeter. Although some flies managed to infiltrate from the low-density ring-barked areas, there was little doubt that these control measures, in spite of their shortcomings, were effective in preventing serious outbreaks of human trypanosomiasis within the settled perimeter. To protect the large cattle population in the Lake N'gami areas sheer barrier clearings had been made south of Tsau.

Fly movement along communication routes from infested to non-infested areas was minimized by checking stations (fly pickets) at strategic points on roads and main footpaths. Two deflying chambers were operating, one at Tsau, the other at Nokaneng.

In 1966 an uneasy truce existed. The fly was contained on all fronts, although a bit gingerly in the west at Sepopa where a breakthrough and advance of fly was expected, in spite of clearings, which would bring the fly to the last remaining fly-free habitats along the Okovango River. With 105 sleeping sickness cases in N'gamiland and 22 in the Chobe area, 1960 was a record year. From epidemiological studies and investigations it was concluded that this peak year was the result of previous years of drought during which many fields had to be planted further inside the floodplains and in many cases closer to the main fly belt and well within regular contact with fly.

In 1967, large-scale insecticide campaigns were carried out in two different areas: one in the Chobe "flats" (floodplains) in the northeast, another south of Sepopa along the northwestern Okovango fringes. There were various motivations for the choice of these two areas. In the Chobe District the area to be treated was small enough so that it could be handled in a single campaign and still, if successful, would eradicate the fly from the inhabited parts of the flats; on the western Okovango the elimination of fly south of Sepopa would cut off its advance and prevent the invasion and subsequent occupation of fly in the still fly-free but suitable habitats stretching all the way into the Caprivi Strip. At the same time the Sepopa area would be safer for man and cattle, which were being moved out following losses by nagana.

The basic principle of the insecticide campaigns was the application of dieldrin emulsion to vegetation in those parts of the fly's habitat which pupae searches had indicated as major breeding sites. Near the end of the dry season fly and pupae sites are mostly concentrated in specific vegetation communities and thus occupy a proportionally small area of the general habitat. Both campaigns, therefore, were carried out between August and November. The insecticide was applied selectively in the breeding sites which were located in the following communities: riverine vegetation, lower slopes of ridges, edge vegetation bordering higher ground on floodplains, edges of drainage lines and pans, edges of ecotones. The insecticide was sprayed to the boles and the lower branches of trees to a height of about ten feet. The undersides of fallen logs were also treated as they are a favorite breeding site of *G. morsitans*. The residual effect of the insecticide was estimated to last about three months.

The insecticide campaigns were successful; they resulted in the complete collapse of the fly population in both areas treated. It is estimated that the liberated areas will allow the increase of cattle from a few thousand to about ten thousand. Both areas should be safe for human occupation and will be kept so by continuous patrolling for stray flies and, if necessary, by small-scale mopping-up operations. Although its immediate value has been to halt the fly's advance toward the north, the western campaign in the Sepopa-Gomare areas is only a first step toward the more ambitious goal of driving the fly back all the way to Tsau and thus liberating all of the western Okovango hinterland.

These two large-scale experiments have shown the feasibility of tsetse control by ground spraying of residual insecticides in carefully selected areas of the fly's habitat under the local conditions in N'gamiland. About 450 square miles were liberated from fly in the Chobe District at a cost of about $80 per square mile. In the west the cost per square mile was even less, $60. The speed and relative low cost, compared with previous methods of control, will make insecticide spraying the choice in the years to come. It should be stressed, however, that whereas the future insecticide campaigns will liberate more land from fly, the transmission of human sleeping sickness cannot be expected to cease. Rhodesian sleeping sickness, a zoonosis infection, should be expected to turn up in hunters and travelers penetrating into the fly belts of the interior of the swamps where game and fly will continue harboring *T. rhodesiense*.

Meanwhile the Okovango swamps, one of the last remaining wild areas of Africa, known well only by a few scattered bands of "river Bushmen" and a crocodile hunter, and visited by an occasional anthropologist, have come under the scrutinizing eyes of economists and hydrologists. Presently surveys are being made and water potentials measured. Plans are on the drawing board showing how the flow of water could be guided and controlled through permanent canals. This would prevent the enormous evaporation which now takes place and the resulting vastly superior volume of surface water could be used to fill up Lake N'gami, in the process of desiccation, with still enough water for many other areas now completely waterless or which at the present are only watered by seasonal floods. Irrigation would vastly increase agricultural potentials. The canalization into proper channels would no doubt desiccate large swamp areas. This in turn would perhaps reduce the amount of suitable tsetse vegetation. At least navigation on the open canals would allow easier access to trouble spots.

It is an ambitious plan which, no doubt, would bring prosperity to this quite underdeveloped part of Africa. But it would also mean the end of vast herds of game, including the beautiful, swamp-adapted sitatunga (*Tragelaphus spekei*) and the disappearance of one of the most extraordinary regions in the world.

CONCLUSION

Tsetse flies have acted for a long time as a buffer against man's encroachment of African biotopes. The presence of trypanosome-carrying tsetse flies in Africa is one of the most remarkable examples of the implication of a single group of insects upon the ecology of a continent. Its decisive role in African prehistory can be postulated (Lambrecht, 1964, 1966, 1968) and its influence on human history can be traced from Late Stone Age sites (Summers, 1960). Today we witness the big efforts and vast amounts of money spent to keep settlements and grazing lands free from its destructive effects. The story of the battle against tsetse as a whole can be considered a case history and a typical example of man's desire to develop and extend his hold on virgin land and the deterioration that might result from upsetting ecological systems.

With the increase of the indigenous population, the urge for economic development, superior agricultural machinery and modern means of tsetse control, the tsetse fly's role as the guardian of natural environments in Africa is coming to its end. Tsetse eradication schemes should be based on land-use programs and conservation projects. We must ask ourselves if we really need the liberated land. Is it suitable for human settlement? Vast areas occupied by savannah flies are marginal lands with poor soil; they are often nothing more than wastelands. It would be unwise to spend large amounts of money to eradicate the fly from those areas should it be proven that the land cannot support a permanent human population or provide sufficient grazing for cattle. Such marginal areas are not "lost" if they can be used wisely. They could be organized into national parks and become a permanent source of tourist income, providing better monetary returns than when converted to farming or grazing lands on poor soil. Some of these areas could serve as local sources of animal protein through judicious methods of culling and still preserve all the elements of the natural environment.

REFERENCES

Andersson, C. J. *Lake N'gami: Four Years Wanderings in the Wilds of South West Africa (1850–54)*. London: Hurst & Blackett, 1857.

Baines, T. *The Gold Regions of South-Eastern Africa*. London and Port Elisabeth, 1877.

Buxton, P. A. *The Natural History of Tsetse Flies*. London School of Tropical Medicine & Hygiene, Mem. No. 10. London: H. K. Lewis, 1955.

Carson, R. L. *Silent Spring*. Boston: Houghton Mifflin, 1962.

Cummings, R. G. *Five Years of a Hunter's Life in the Far Interior of South Africa*. Vols. I and II. London, 1850.

Dasmann, R. F., and Mossman, A. S. "Commercial Utilization of Game Animals on a Rhodesian Ranch." *Wildlife*, 3 (3) (1961), 6–14.

Dasmann, R. F. "Conservation by Slaughter." *Pacific Discovery*, 15 (2) 1962), 3–9.

Deevey, E. S. "The Human Population." *Scientific American*, 203 (3) (1960), 194–204.

Ford, J. and Hall, R. de Z. "The History of the Karagwe, Bukoba District." *Tanganyika Notes and Records*, 24 (1947), 3–27.

Ford, J. "Distribution of African Cattle." *Proc. 1st Sci. Congr.* Salisbury. 1960. 357–65.

Gibbons, St. Hill A. *Africa from South to North, through Marotse Land*. London, 1904.

Hale-Carpenter, G. D. "Report on the Investigations into the Cattle Trade of N'gamiland." Report to the Bechuanaland Protection Administration. 1931.

Hodson, A. W. *Trekking the Great Thirst*. New York: Scribner, 1912.

Lambrecht, F. L. "Aspects of Evolution and Ecology of Tsetse Flies and Trypanosomiasis in Prehistoric African Environment." *J. Afri. Hist.*, 5 (1) (1964), 1–24.

———. "Some Principles of Tsetse Control and Land-Use with Emphasis on Wildlife Husbandry." *East African Wildlife J.*, 4 (1966), 89–98.

———. "Notions concerning the Evolution of Communicable Diseases in Man." *S. Afr. J. of Sci.*, 64 (2) (1968), 64–71.

Livingstone, D. *Missionary Travels and Research in South Africa*. London: Ward, Lock, 1857.

Macaulay, J. W. A. *A Tsetse Fly and Trypanosomiasis Survey in Bechuanaland, 1940–42*. B. P. Govt. Vet. Dept., 1942.

Oswell, W. E. *William Cotton Oswell, Hunter and Explorer. The Story of His Life*. Vols. I and II. London, 1900.

Passarge, S. "Das Okovangosumpfland und Seine Bewohner." *Z. Ethn.*, 37 (1943), 649–716.

Stigand, A. G. "N'gamiland." *Geo. J.*, 62 (6) (1923), 401.

Summers, R. "Environment and Culture in Southern Rhodesia: A Study in the 'Personality' of a Land-Locked Country." *Proc. Amer. Phil. Soc.*, 104 (1960), 266–92.

40. THE SHEEP AND THE SALTBUSH:
The Utilization of Australia's Arid Lands

Peter Crowcroft

The state of South Australia is largely an arid territory, with many regions receiving 10 inches of rain or less a year. Periodic dry spells occur, extending over many months or several years. The chief natural plant cover of such dry areas is saltbush and bluebush, augmented by grasses when there is enough rain.

For well over a hundred years many of these arid areas have been severely overgrazed by the Merino sheep introduced by settlers for wool production. Many areas will now support no sheep as the plant cover is entirely gone; experiments at letting the land lie fallow indicate great difficulties in re-establishing the saltbush or other cover on the altered and unproductive soil.

The early settlers and governments encouraged such destruction because they were ignorant of the different conditions and weather cycles in Australia, and by accident had surveyed the arid lands during a wet period. However, for some time there has been evidence given by sheep owners and by botanists and other scientists which makes clear what overgrazing does permanently to the land and to the sheep owner. (Detailed anecdotes and scientific evidence are given.)

Unfortunately, the pastoral industry continues to prosper in the patchily denuded country because of low rentals, low capital investment, low labor costs and high wool prices. The development of surface-laid water reticulation has moved the sheep into formerly inaccessible regions. This is, of course, a further "mining operation," the digging of subsidiary shafts after the main lode has been exhausted. Wool production thus continues to receive a subsidy through the depletion of the natural capital of vegetation and topsoil.

Proposals to remove sheep from the arid lands will not receive serious attention, even though Australian wool production could continue to prosper if other, wetter areas, now undergrazed, were properly utilized. There appears to be no possibility that damage to the arid country will be stopped until it is so severe that sheep cannot be economically supported there, or unless artificial fibers can compete successfully with wool in the near future.

Ultimately much of the problem is that of attitudes and beliefs of the local landowners and Pastoral Board inspectors, who do not look beyond their own personal roles at what is happening to their land. How are we to deal with such attitudes before the remaining resources of the arid areas, which could be permanently productive if used differently, are wiped out?

The area of Australia is about the same as that of the United States, and it extends through a wider range of latitudes. One-third of the area receives less than 10 inches (250 mm) of rain annually and is useless for present agricultural purposes. There is very great pressure to uphold and extend the well-known and remarkable Australian pastoral industry, which utilizes much of this arid land for Merino wool production.

This paper deals with conditions and developments within the state of South Australia, where I resided from 1962 until 1968. Five-sixths of this state (317,600 square miles out of the total area of 380,070 square miles) receives less than 10 inches (250 mm) of rainfall annually. This leads South Australians to refer to their home, with wry affection, as "the driest state in the driest country on earth." Grave conse-

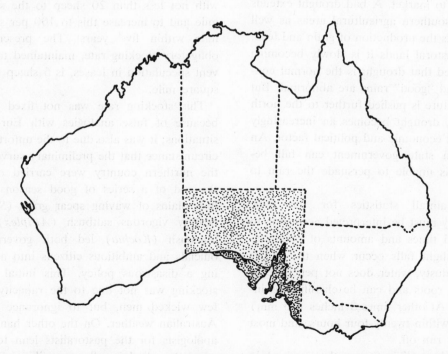

Figure 40–1 Outline of Australia indicating rainfall within South Australia (Broken lines show state boundaries. Light dotted area shows the part of S.A. with less than 10 inches of annual rainfall)

quences have resulted from introducing sheep into these dry regions.

Figure 40–1 shows the political boundaries of South Australia and the position of the 10-inch (250-mm) isohyet, which marks the approximate northern boundary of the lands fit for agricultural use. Above this boundary, pastoral leases have been issued for about 190,000 square miles. The portion of this area protected by the Dog Fence contains about 2 million sheep. It contains no permanent rivers, and the annual rainfall is unreliable.

It is necessary, at this point, to define the Australian concept of "drought." In Europe, a drought is a period, usually measured in weeks, during which no rain falls. In Australia, it has come to mean a period of months *or years,* during which the rainfall is inadequate and ineffective. During a prolonged drought, all surface water disappears; much of the native vegetation dies, and the value of sheep falls below the cost of sending them to market. A bad drought extends into the southern agricultural areas as well and affects the production of grain and feed. In the pastoral lands it is slowly becoming appreciated that drought is the normal condition, and "good" rains are abnormal. But as agriculture is pushed further to the north and west, drought becomes an increasingly important economic and political factor. An Australian state government can fall because it is unable to persuade the rain to fall.

The rainfall statistics for this type of country must be interpreted according to the actual times and amounts of precipitation. If slight falls occur when the soil is dry and dusty, water does not penetrate to the plant roots and can be classified as ineffective. At other times 3 inches (75 mm) may fall within twenty-four hours, and most of it will run off.

South Australia's first settlers arrived in 1836. Preliminary land sales had been conducted in London, and others were con-

ducted in Adelaide in the following year. All of these dealt with land near the coast, for the most part under dense mallee or sclerophyl forest, two plant communities dominated by various species of *Eucalyptus.* This coastal strip receives between 15 and 30 inches of rainfall annually.

In order to encourage rapid colonization of the huge tracts of shrub-steppe country to the north, large holdings were offered for lease at public auctions, under the provisions of the first Pastoral Act. The Merino sheep had already demonstrated their remarkable suitability for arid Australian conditions in New South Wales, so settlers were encouraged to acquire large flocks from that colony.

From the start of colonization, policy decisions were made which were to ensure the destruction of the shrub-steppe plant communities. The first lessees were required, upon pain of forfeiture, to stock their runs within three months of allotment with not less than 20 sheep to the square mile and to increase this to 100 per square mile within five years! The present-day obligatory stocking rate, maintained to prevent speculation in leases, is 5 sheep to the square mile.

This stocking rate was not fixed solely because of false analogies with European situations; it was also due to the unfortunate circumstance that the preliminary surveys of the northern country were carried out at the end of a series of good seasons. The lush plains of waving spear grass (*Stipa*), healthy vigorous saltbush (*Atriplex*) and bluebush (*Kochia*) led both government officials and ambitious citizens into accepting a disastrous policy. This initial overstocking was not due to the rapacity of a few wicked men, but to ignorance about Australian weather. On the other hand, the apologists for the pastoralists lean too far when they disclaim all responsibility for the damage which has been done in the past hundred years.

The Surveyor-general, Goyder, reported in 1865 that the combination of drought and sheep had wrought great destruction less than thirty years after settlement:

> The change from the country suffering from excessive drought to that where its effect has only been slightly experienced is palpable to the eye from the nature of the country itself, and may be described as bare ground, destitute of grass and herbage, the surface soil dried by the intense heat, in places broken and pulverized by the passage of stock, and forced by the action of the wind into miniature hummocks, surrounding the closely cropped stumps of salt, blue and other dwarf bushes, whilst those of greater elevation are denuded of their leaves and smaller branches as far as the stock can reach.

Evidence about habitat destruction is available from two little-known sources. First, there are the descriptive accounts of the country soon after settlement. As usual, these are of no value for making quantitative comparisons, but considered in the mass, they convey a convincing picture of better times. Even when the historic accounts are in general terms, certain localities and stations can be positively identified. The complete absence of vegetation where it is known to have been present can be connected with the introduction of stock which is known to eat and trample it. Evidence of this kind can be found in the reports of the two Royal Commissions (1898, 1927) which have investigated the pastoral industry in South Australia, as well as in the diaries of the early explorers.

Second, there is a comprehensive series of observations upon the regeneration of shrub-steppe plants and the effects of grazing upon them carried out by the Botany Department of Adelaide University. These studies have produced such a wealth of detailed information that ignorance of the facts can no longer serve as an excuse for not taking a stand against the continuing habitat destruction.

THE EVIDENCE OF THE ROYAL COMMISSIONS

During the past hundred years, Australia has suffered at least seven major droughts over areas extending across most of the southern part of the continent. The most disastrous was the drought of 1895–1903, which reduced sheep numbers from over 100 million to about 50 million. Prior to that drought there had been a series of good seasons, and the growing numbers of sheep were well distributed. As the surface waters disappeared and the sheep congregated about the wells, the density of sheep close to water reached plague numbers. Many graziers were forced to walk off their holdings, losing their capital improvements as there were no buyers for their leases. The pastoral industry in South Australia seemed about to collapse, and the Royal Commission of 1898 was appointed to inquire into and report upon action to be taken "to induce the occupation and development of the pastoral lands of the province." The men giving evidence were the prominent graziers of the state. They or their fathers had opened up virgin country and attempted to maintain the stocking rates prescribed by the crown.

The following examples are representative of the evidence put before the commissioners: Mr. Thompson of Talia Station had 33 square miles of country. Last year he could only muster 3,700 of the 8,500 sheep he had shorn the year before. This year he had only 2,800. Mr. Dearlove of Ketchowla had 50 square miles and had tried to carry 8,000 head. He realized after years of trouble that the most he should have carried was "80 to the mile . . . to do justice to the country." The saltbush had been killed, he said, by the rabbits, but during his evidence he mentioned that the bush had got a "tremendous dressing" from his stock in the bad seasons.

Mr. Young of Netley Head Station had 150 miles. He stated that the bush was completely eaten out by overstocking before he went there. He had attempted to run 15,000 to 16,000, but now felt that the country would only carry 70 to the mile. The bush was now destroyed within a four-mile radius of the waters.

Mr. Scott of Port Lincoln had taken up 150 miles of country in the Gawler Ranges, and had suffered four bad seasons. The 10,000 to 11,000 sheep of the previous year had been reduced to 5,200, the rest having died or been killed. He thought the country would carry 70 per mile in a good season, but only 40–45 in a bad season.

The most articulate witness was Mr. Wooldridge, a retired grazier of vast experience. He gave evidence of his disenchantment with the pastoral industry:

. . . In 1876 I took up a large tract of country north-west of Port Augusta, which I named and is now known as Arcoona and Parakylia. I sent in 11,800 wethers across . . . and in 1878 and 1879 I sent 7,000 more. . . . I went into New South Wales, bought 25,000 there, and took them across. . . . I put 100,000 sheep on the run from the time I went on it to 1884, and I sold 40,000 to 50,000 sheep. I lost through drought about 50,000 sheep.

(Commissioner: *Were you able to sell at a profit?*) "No; the Queensland Mortgage Company took away the station from me because I had a covenant in the mortgage to keep 50,000 sheep on the run. They foreclosed, thinking I had mismanaged the run, and were going to show me how to manage it. They have done it since to the tune of losing about £70,000–£80,000."

(Commissioner: *From your experience, do you think that run can be successfully occupied?*) "I think so. When I first saw it I thought I had the finest run in Australia. . . . in all my travels I had never seen a finer looking tract of country. There were lakes, lagoons, waterholes, and canegrass swamps, with pelicans, swans, and ducks in millions. That was in 1876. I sent across my stock in 1878. At that time one could not walk five

miles without coming across one of those beautiful lagoons or canegrass swamps. . . ."

(Commissioner: *Have you ever known the country to look so well since then?*) "No. There were three lakes on the country. The best tracts were known as the Elizabeth, Phillips Ponds, and Lake Campbell, and I stripped off one bleak day, swam out 100 yards, and sang out to my man, 'You look out for me when I go down.' I went down and could not touch bottom. At the head station there were 15 feet of water. . . . I stocked it with 50,000 sheep, 2,000 cattle, and 800 horses. . . . I had to put down any amount of wells, build a new woolshed, etc., and then I sent up a boat to put on the lake, but soon afterwards there was no water there. . . . in 1883 I filled 750 bales of wool at Arcoona and 210 in the West Coast. I had 960 bales that year. I had a boast that if I could fill 1,000 bales, I would take my wife for a tour; but I am sorry I had not, for if I had had forty bales more I should have cleared off half my stock. Next year I had 230 odd bales at Arcoona."

(Commissioner: *Do you think there is any vitality in that country?*) "If they got a few seasons again, like they had on the Elizabeth when I saw it first, there would be very great encouragement."

(Commissioner: *What would you suggest as a means of tempting people to occupy it with advantage?*) "The country just now really wants a rest. It has been eaten out. The rabbits have put the finishing touch on it, by ring-barking and killing all the edible bush."

(Commissioner: *The pastoral country generally?*) "Yes. Perhaps the squatters are to blame for stocking it too much."

The Commission concluded that the industry was, and had been for many years, in an extremely depressed and unsatisfactory condition . . . this condition we attribute mainly to the following causes:

(a) The want of length and security of tenure under the Pastoral Acts previous to 1893, which prevented the proper development of the country.

(b) The excessive rents promised at auctions by lessees.

(c) The sub-division of many runs into small blocks carrying heavy charges for improvements.

(d) The deterioration of pastoral country caused by the abnormal increase in rabbits, and the great loss of sheep consequent upon the ravages of wild dogs.

(e) The decline in the prices of wool and stock.

(f) The frequently occurring droughts and the unusually protracted one of the last four years.

Commissioner Downer expressed a dissenting opinion, that the disaster did not apply where a large capital had been available for development, and where the lessees "had held large tracts of country, and have thus been enabled to rest portions of their country, and lessen the effects of drought on parts of their runs by shifting stock to parts less seriously affected."

The Surveyor-general gave his views at length about the desirability of dividing the huge paddocks into smaller units in order that some control could be exercised over the movements of stock. He stated that he "knew of numerous instances where country had been destroyed by overstocking around the waters. . . . No provision could be made in leases to prevent country around the waters from being eaten out."

The Royal Commission of 1927 was requested by "a deputation of persons prominently interested in the pastoral industry and representing the Stockowners' Association of South Australia." There was still a strong body of opinion in the community and within the State Public Service, that the big leasehold properties, with their low fixed rentals, which had resulted from the Royal Commission of 1898, should be subdivided. The "big" graziers maintained, as had Commissioner Downer in 1898, that only they had the resources to endure a series of bad seasons and to rest sections of the country as required.

The witnesses were men of a later generation, but they were predominantly members of the same families. They were now sufficiently removed from the pioneer days to be able to admit to the destruction wrought by their fathers and grandfathers, and a recurring phrase in the evidence was,

"I do not believe in overstocking." They had more modest ideas about the carrying capacity of saltbush. The new tenant of Arcoona, for example, where 100 head to the mile was formerly considered a permissible stocking rate, now replied that he carried "about 18 to 19. That is what we have averaged since we went there. The highest number we have shorn is 34,000, the lowest 16,000."

(*Do you know of any of our country which will carry 100 sheep per mile when properly improved?*) "No, I do not, not below an 8 inch rainfall."

(*When country is eaten out will not the bush come back?*) "In the majority of country once it is eaten out it will never return."

(*How long does it take to kill the bush?*) "One bad year will do it."

Chief spokesman for the large companies was Mr. Brooks, in charge of Clifton Hills Station on the Diamantina (5,100 square miles) and of Kanowna on the Cooper (5,333 miles), the two properties adjoining.

"Some of these large holdings are of great benefit to the State; they produce an enormous amount of wealth, and employ a large number of people directly and indirectly, which would be curtailed if they were subdivided. I have Ned's Corner Station in mind. It was producing an enormous amount of wealth under one management. It was cut up, and the result was chaos. When things reached a climax they held a meeting, and decided to throw the whole lot into one concern, and appoint a general manager, since when the station has gone ahead as it did before. . . ."

(*You said that the bush had disappeared on these small holdings. Is it not your experience that the bush disappears while it is in big holdings?*) "In some cases, pests, like caterpillars, have killed the bush."

(*Do you not think that in some cases the bush was killed through having big waters?*) "Yes; before they knew that underground water existed. They put 10,000 sheep on one well, and naturally all that country was killed out."

(*There has been no inducement to sacrifice the sheep to save the bush?*) "Yes, the sheep were the main factor, not the country."

(*You suggest that the country was eaten out intentionally?*) "No, through ignorance."

(*Even in these days, if it was freehold, do you think they have sufficient knowledge of the country not to eat it out?*) "No, I would not say so, but they would think twice before knocking the country out."

(*It seems hard to understand that after 10 or 15 years' occupation that a man would not know something about the carrying capacity of the country.*) "He should, but the seasons are a great factor. He might carry his sheep for five, six or eight years, but as soon as a dry season sets in he is in trouble. . . ."

The big leases were not subdivided, and longer terms of tenure were granted. A Pastoral Board was set up within the State Department of Lands, one member of which was to be a person with experience in the pastoral industry. This board was to inspect the leasehold properties regularly, report upon the state of the country and recommend reductions in sheep numbers if thought desirable.

Before we consider the practicality of those control measures and the present state of affairs, let us examine the studies of the Adelaide University Botany Department. They provide the corroborative details to support the observations of the graziers themselves.

THE BOTANICAL EVIDENCE

The difficulty of getting reliable information about the effects of stock on native vegetation at a time when no systematic observations were possible, leads us to rely "on inferences from changes which are occurring now under the changed conditions" (Griffiths, 1910). The effects of grazing upon the South Australian shrub-steppe plant community have been exceptionally well documented. Very little of the evidence has been published, but a massive photographic record and detailed documentation of the regeneration of an overstocked range is available in the records of the Botany Department of Adelaide University.

When the second Royal Commission (1927) was sitting, Professor T. G. B. Osborn, then Professor of Botany at Adelaide University, gave evidence before the commissioners, in the form of an illustrated lecture. He informed them of the commencement of long-term studies in regeneration upon one of the eaten-out properties. Professor Osborn's lecture provides a succinct summary of the problem.

Dense mallee is the type of vegetation that will develop on a 15 inch to 18 inch rainfall. The undergrowth consists of many hard-leaved shrubs, and after suitable rains, grasses. . . . With diminishing rainfall we notice a radical change in the undergrowth. It changes to various soft-leaved hairy shrubs, the salt bushes and blue bushes. The change occurs somewhere about the 10 inch rainfall line. Beneath the mallees the ground cover consists of salt or blue bushes. . . . Going further north the density of the mallees lessen, until they are finally lost altogether. . . . There may be such trees as mulgas, black oak or sandalwood, but tree growth is limited and usually scrubby. . . . Going still further north, the salt and blue bushes, which we first noticed as undergrowth beneath trees, are the only really important ground covering over huge areas.

In a "good season" there may be an abundance of grass and herbage . . . , but in the same place during a bad season there will be none. . . . Annuals have no value as permanent ground covering. . . . But in the salt bushes we have a perennial ground covering . . . that is marvellously suited to the peculiar droughty conditions. . . .

The work of Professors Wood and Osborn and their coworkers was carried out on Koonamore Station in north-eastern South Australia. In the main experimental paddock the saltbush (*Atriplex*) had been eaten out, but there were a few bluebush plants (*Kochia*). The main ground cover was the "bindyi" (*Bassia*) which usually replaces the saltbush and is not liked by stock. There were some scattered trees of the genera *Acacia, Casuarina,* and *Myoporum* and some lower shrubs, including a little mallee (*Eucalyptus* spp.).

The relationships between the saltbush and the bluebush have been investigated (Carrodus and Specht, 1965). In many places they appear to be in a dynamic "balance" with major changes in dominance occurring over long periods, depending upon the soil and the weather. The bluebush is deeper rooted and its presence is usually correlated with the depth to which the soil is wetted by the "normal" rainfall; it is usually on soils which can be wetted to two inches or more. The saltbush is very shallow rooted, but seeds better when a drought breaks. Both plants defoliate under drought to the same extent, but the saltbush can reduce the soil moisture to a significantly lower level under drought. Its ability to absorb moisture from air containing more than 85% humidity appears to account for its success, for there are usually times at night, even during a drought, when the air humidity exceeds that proportion.

After six years' exclusion of sheep from the Koonamore Reserve, the bare areas, especially the sheep pads, sunken a centimeter or two below the surface, still remained devoid of any vegetation even after good rains (Osborn *et al.,* 1935). Few new saltbush plants appeared. The bluebush, which at enclosure had been broken down to woody stumps, had recovered in part, in spite of a drought during 1929. There had been no flowering, and no reseeding had been possible from outside, because trampling and wind erosion had removed the surface soil. The most alarming evidence, at this stage, was of the destructive effects of the rabbits upon tree regrowth. In one hectare quadrat, it was known that 18 one-year-old mulgas (*Acacia aneura*) were destroyed in one night by one rabbit.

The large saltbush paddocks on other parts of Koonamore provided an opportunity to observe the progressive effects of grazing upon the saltbush. The paddocks were so large and the waters so few that some areas, many miles from water, remained free from sheep, while other regions, especially those around the waters and along the fences which crossed the prevailing winds, were heavily overgrazed and trampled. Osborn and his coworkers (1932) were thus able to deduce by observations and plant counts at selected points and quadrats, how the degeneration of the plant community would progress in any one overgrazed locality.

The long-term quadrat observations revealed that *even in the absence of sheep,* drought produces a high proportion of dead and defoliated plants. Light grazing, one or two miles from water, produced a significant increase in the mean number of bushes and in the mean number of wilting bushes. In the zone of moderate grazing, which was defined as the main feeding grounds up to a mile from water, there was a significant increase in the number of dead and defoliated plants, and *also in the number of plants classified as healthy and vigorous.* This was an unexpected result. In the region of heavy grazing around the waters, there was, of course, severe damage; all living saltbush were removed, followed by the removal of the dead plants through trampling. In these regions the debris and topsoil blew away, leaving a sterile waste.

The apparently beneficial results of light grazing were explained as follows: "The first effects of grazing . . . consist in the mechanical removal of dead bushes. The second effect . . . is in the marked improvement in the vigor of the bush . . . due to pruning; the constant removal of the terminal buds stimulates development of lateral shoots so that more compact vigorous bushes result. These bushes stand in marked contrast to those of the ungrazed country which are sparse and twiggy" (Osborn *et al.,* 1932). The spasmodic activities of stock may also be beneficial in assisting in the mechanical planting of seed, *if this seed has time to germinate and form established plants before the next stocking period*. There was also some indication that heavy stocking *for short periods* might have a beneficial effect, in pruning bushes, trampling out weak ones, and mechanically planting seed, which then has time to germinate and take hold before the next stocking period.

A study of one of the main fodder grasses (*Stipa nitida*) clearly showed the advantages of "spelling" the country for one or two years. In most years the spear grass germinates in March–April and is killed off by the December heat. However, if it should become established by late rains just before the hot season starts in September, it may last through two years and form substantial tussocks. This is a palatable grass which is soon eaten out, but because it readily dies in the absence of sheep, the detrimental effects of grazing relate to the potential for regrowth in the following season. The Koonamore observations show that *Stipa* disappears from an area mainly because of the mechanical effects of eating and trampling the *dead* plants, which provide the seed beds.

When the dead tussocks are broken up and blown away, the accumulated little piles of sand and detritus blow away as well, leaving a hard soil and limestone nodules, swept free of awns by the wind (Osborn *et al.*, 1931). The loss of spear grass is also correlated with the loss of the saltbush, as it too provides loci for accumulations of dust and detritus in which the awns can become entangled and can germinate with the first summer rains.

THE FUTURE OF THE ARID LANDS

The pastoral industry continues to prosper in the patchily denuded country, because of low rentals, low capital investment, low labor costs and high wool prices. The development of surface-laid water reticulation has moved the sheep into formerly inaccessible regions. This is, of course, a further "mining operation." It is analogous to digging subsidiary shafts after the main lode has been exhausted. Wool production thus continues to receive a subsidy through the depletion of the national capital of vegetation and topsoil.

In theory, we now know enough about the ecology of the arid lands and about the unpredictability of the weather to be able to exploit the saltbush country without damaging it. We can even accept that light grazing can be beneficial, providing it is followed by an adequate resting period. This is the most powerful argument for the retention of large holdings. Unfortunately, events have proved that large landholders are not necessarily less hungry for profits or better informed than small ones. Numerous large holdings continue to be damaged by overstocking.

In practice, stock is almost always moved in as soon as there is evidence of recovery. Stock is quickly moved into any paddock which takes on a green bloom after a thunderstorm, regardless of the composition of the vegetation. I know of stock being purchased and trucked hundreds of miles, in order to utilize the herbage resulting from a single thunderstorm; there was no question of waiting for the new growth to take hold and set seed. In time of drought, no man will kill his animals to save other people's plants. In 1968, no less than in 1868, "the sheep were the first consideration, not the country." This leads us to wonder whether a man might kill his animals to save his own plants.

Some conservationists believe that abolition of the present leasehold system and sale of the land would remove the old attitudes and lead to husbandry of natural resources. This proposed solution is unlikely to succeed for at least two reasons.

First, the present leasehold system does amount to virtual ownership, for leases can be handed down in the family with ministerial permission, which could not be withheld without a political furore, which assures tenure for the best part of a century. Second, the social effects on the offspring of affluent parents tend to produce absentee landlords. The son of a grazier, after attending Geelong Grammar School and Oxford University, and making a successful marriage, is not inclined to bury himself in the outback for more than a few weeks each year. The manager he employs on a salary plus commission has his eye more on the size of the wool check than on the state of the saltbush. Neither man can be condemned for his choice; his attitudes reflect the generally low cultural level of the Australian population in relation to conservation.

The alternative solution, that sheep should be banned altogether from the arid country, seems startling, until one appreciates the relative unimportance of the pastoral industry. There are ten times as many sheep, and one hundred times as many human dependents upon them in the narrow belt of country receiving more than ten inches of rain. Further, this area, with greater development efforts, could support many more sheep than it does at present. This drastic solution cannot come about in the present political climate, and most people cherish the erroneous belief that the pastoral industry in the outback is the economic mainstay of the state. The pastoralists control very few votes, but they have them in the right places.

The Australian pastoral industry, in general, has expanded in recent years, stimulated by capital from Britain and the U.S.A. In South Australia, however, expansion is held up by lack of water. The southern region of the enormous Nullarbor Plain has rich reserves of sheep country, but there is no stock water. A study conducted by one-time owners of Nullarbor Station, which at that time carried 1,500 sheep on 450 of its 900 square miles, showed that stock water could be distilled from the underground waters, but that the factor preventing the expansion of the flocks was the cost of transporting the fuel for the distillation plant. This narrow margin might be closed in the near future by the development of cheaper distillation plants or of cheaper sources of energy.

The Pastoral Board has prepared plans for opening up a further 50,000 square miles as soon as water becomes available. The land will be offered on the leasehold system. A proposal from the National Parks Commission to set aside 3,000 square miles of this country for recreational use was opposed by the chairman of the Pastoral Board on the grounds that it would "emasculate" his scheme for expanding the industry.

There appears to be no possibility whatsoever that damage to the arid country will be stopped until the damage is so severe that sheep cannot be economically supported there. This has already happened in parts of New South Wales and has led to some of the denuded land being offered to the National Parks authority. If funds become available, it might be possible to reconstitute samples of the original plant communities. In certain regions natural regeneration might occur if the country were kept free of rabbits for several decades. An unpredictable factor is the speed with which the growth of the artificial fiber industry can match the growth of the world demand for fabric fibers. The demand for Merino wool is constantly expanding because of an active advertising program.

The power of the State Pastoral Board to prevent overstocking is made impotent by social factors which, as in other contexts, often frustrate the best intentions of legislators who are not in intimate touch with the practical situation. In theory, the inspector regularly visits the leasehold properties, pronounces upon the state of the country and sets the stocking rates. Even if we assume that it is physically possible to inspect thousands of square miles of vegetation from an automobile, we cannot expect the man to behave officiously as if he had come from City Hall to inspect the drains. For the inspector probably attended Scotch College with the man who manages the property, and as the homestead is some hundreds of miles from the nearest town, he comes as an overnight guest. After dinner, he broaches the subject of overgrazing thus:

"Don't you think, Jim . . ." He pauses

to take a sip from his third free Scotch and water.

"Don't you think they are a bit too thick in the southwest Paddock?"

His host, who has been telling him about the performance of his race horse, replies: "Yeah. Still a bit of green pick in the watercourses, though."

He pauses, and then continues enthusiastically, "Gawd! You should have seen how that little filly headed for home!"

The moment has passed. And after all, it *may* rain tomorrow or next week. The inspector hopes that it will not rain tonight, for he has to drive to another station tomorrow.

REFERENCES

Carrodus, B. B., and Specht, R. L. "Some Aspects of the Ecology of Arid South Australia: The Relative Distribution of *Atriplex vesicarium*, and *Kochia sedifolia*." *Aust. Jour. Bot.*, 13 (1965), 419–33.

Griffiths, D. "A Protected Stock Range in Arizona." *U.S. Dept. Agr. Bur. Plant Ind. Bull.* 177 (1910), 1–28.

Hall, E. A. A.; Specht, R. L.; and Eardley, C. M. "Regeneration of the Vegetation on Koonamore Vegetation Reserve, 1926–1962." *Aust. Jour. Bot.*, 12 (1964), 205–64.

Osborn, T. G. B.; Wood, J. G.; and Paltridge, T. B. "On the Antecology of *Stipa nitida*, a Study of a Fodder Grass in Arid Australia." *Proc. Linn. Soc. N.S.W.*, 56 (1931), 299–324.

——. "On the Growth and Reaction to Grazing of the Perennial Salt Bush, *Atriplex vesicarium*, an Ecological Study of the Biotic Factor." *Proc. Linn. Soc. N.S.W.*, 57 (1932), 377–402.

——. "On the Climate and Vegetation of the Koonamore Vegetation Reserve to 1931." *Proc. Linn. Soc. N.S.W.*, 60 (1935), 392–427.

Report of the Pastoral Lands Commission. Adelaide: Government Printer, 1898.

Report of the Royal Commission on the Pastoral Industry. Adelaide: Government Printer, 1927.

Report of the Surveyor-General. Adelaide: Government Printer, 1865.

41. ECOLOGICAL ASPECTS OF PROTEIN FEEDING— THE CASE OF PERU

Georg Borgstrom

Regional food resources, natural or man-created, were a limiting feature in man's history well into the nineteenth century. But major innovations in transportation and food-preserving techniques have made food resources everywhere available for exploitation by countries with the necessary power and technology. This comparatively new situation has blurred and obscured the basic awareness of dependence on distant resources. The beneficiaries of this new technological power to harvest far-distant food have been a minor portion of the world's population, largely white. Generations have grown up thinking they were feeding themselves when actually distant prairies, pampas, grasslands, and seas of other areas of the world made substantial contributions. Ecological awareness is nowadays almost completely lost, particularly among the urbanized millions. Yet many examples and statistics can be given to show the degree to which some major countries have found themselves detached from their geographical as well as ecological framework. (Tables illustrating this situation are given.)

The marshaling of the world's grasslands to provide for the Western well-fed world is almost reaching its finale. But an almost parallel undertaking is beginning in the oceans, tapping the major plankton pastures. This paper is addressed to this particular issue with special emphasis on the use of the anchoveta riches of the Peruvian Current.

The fantastic amount of fish in the Peruvian Current has been heavily exploited in recent years, mainly by nonlocal companies and by means of massive "aid" programs of fishing equipment and know-how. However, the limits of the ocean and the dangers to the ecological patterns have become apparent. Overfishing has contributed to the starvation of great numbers of sea birds who normally live on the fish; this has cut down the production of guano which is an important natural fertilizer resource for the area. In addition, the Peruvian-Chilean export of fish meal in the period 1966–1968 was enough to provide 413 million people a minimum (7.5 kilograms per year) protein diet for a year; yet this vast amount of protein went to distant places in the well-fed world outside South America. The continent was thereby deprived of 50 percent more animal protein than its total meat production. The major portion of the Peruvian-Chilean protein aids the highly developed countries of the world, not the local populations whose need is much greater.

If the degree of profit-making is to determine what we do and if short-range losses and gains are never weighed against long-range costs and benefits, both in terms of the ecological balances and the needs and interests of the countries directly involved, the world is bound to become enmeshed in increasingly dangerous environmental predicaments.

Regional food resources, natural or man-created, were a limiting feature in man's history almost up to the second half of the nineteenth century. Notable examples are the massive cereal deliveries to the Roman Empire from the trans-Mediterranean granaries of Egypt and Carthage, as well as the large-scale trade in salted and marinated fish from as far east as the Black Sea and as far west as Spain to Greece and Rome. A second telling example is the medieval trade in salted herring and dried fish (Cutting, 1955; Borgstrom, 1962). This constituted the protein backbone of the urban and rural dwellers of major portions of northern and continental Europe, including Russia.

Another key story in this context is the

Table 41-1

FISH PROTEIN USE (1964-66)

POP. (millions)		ANNUAL FISH PROTEIN INTAKE 1,000 TONS	FISH MEAL PROTEIN USED 1,000 TONS	RATIO	PER CAPITA PROTEIN Kg/Yr	
					FOOD	FEED
	Western Europe	457.9	1,089.4	2.8		
12.7	Netherlands	9.0	132.6	14.7	0.735	10.4
6.2	Switzerland	4.7	28.3	6.0	0.76	4.6
9.7	Belgium	9.5	46.9	4.9	0.982	4.8
60.3	West Germany	70.7	335.8	4.8	1.16	5.7
55.8	U.K.	81.4	312.5	3.8	1.46	5.7
32.4	Spain	72.5	76.6	1.01	2.24	2.36
50.4	France	88.5	80.2	0.9	1.75	1.59
52.8	Italy	62.0	60.5	0.9	1.18	1.15
20.8	*Scandinavia*	58.6	103.7	1.8	2.82	5.6
91.8	*Eastern Europe*	72.3	145.9	2.0	0.79	1.59
201.3	*U.S.A.*	172.5	478.7	2.8	0.86	2.37
239	*U.S.S.R.*	486	104	0.2	2.04	0.44
20.7	Canada	25.6	22.9	0.9	1.235	1.11
12.8	Peru	15.5	22.4	1.4	1.21	1.74
101	Japan	464.0	306.5	0.7	4.58	3.03
47.3	Mexico	15.8	28.3	1.8	0.334	0.60
2.8	Israel	2.5	8.5	3.4	0.893	3.01
4.7	South Rhodesia	3.3	3.6	1.1	0.703	0.77

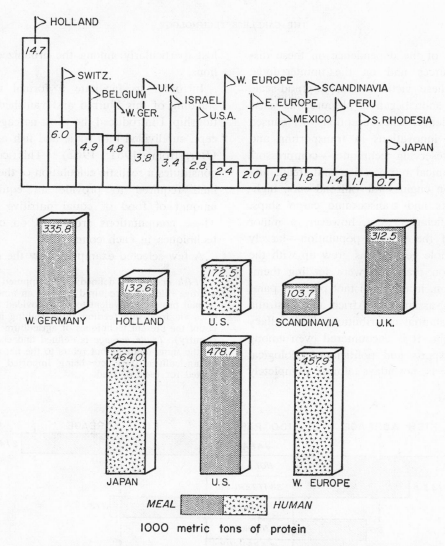

Figure 41–1 Fish consumption for feed and food in selected countries. Top figures show ratio of feed to food protein from Table 41–1

tapping of the Lofoten banks off Norway and subsequently the Grand Banks of Newfoundland (de Loture, 1949). The major cod resources of these banks were thus mobilized as a protein basis for subsistence. The Norwegian endeavor goes back to the Middle Ages (Konow, 1945). The deliveries reached out to the Mediterranean and tropical Africa and later also to Latin America. The Portuguese and Spanish forays to the Grand Banks were the basis of protein subsistence not only of the homelands, but also of other Mediterranean countries. Later in the sixteenth century

Great Britain, France, and others joined this first human undertaking in processing (salting) at sea (Ducèré, 1893; Bellet, 1902; de la Morandière, 1962). The wavering beachhead of the New England Puritans laid the foundation for what later was to be the big flow of indispensable protein to the plantation workers of the southern states and of the Caribbean. This flow was later re-enforced and superseded by the Canadian cod fisheries. (See Table 41–1 and Fig. 41–1 for fish protein use for a number of countries.)

In all these instances, there was a basic

awareness of the dependence on these distant resources and on the uninterrupted flow of these victuals. But a grand-scale deception soon began to obscure this sense of dependence. The deception was caused by major innovations in transporting and in food-preserving techniques—compressors for mechanical refrigeration and steam and combustion engines for railroad cars, highway trucks and transoceanic cargo ships. The beneficiaries were, however, a minor portion of the world's population—largely white. Whole generations grew up with the false notion that they were feeding themselves when, in effect, distant prairies, pampas, and grasslands of Africa and Australia made substantial contributions. This fallacy still prevails. It is encountered even among leading experts and politicians. Ecological awareness is nowadays almost completely

lost, particularly among the urbanized millions.

In order to facilitate a formal understanding of this blurred and vanished relationship, I introduced the ghost acreage concept, subdivided into trade and fish acreage (Borgstrom, 1961, 1962).[1] This concept constitutes a realistic calculation of the tilled land required to provide an equivalent amount of food of equal nutritive value. These computations are based on current techniques in each country.

A few selected examples show the degree

[1] *Fish acreage* is defined and computed as the average tilled land required to raise an amount of animal protein equivalent to that provided by fisheries via food and feeding stuffs (taking into account the present techniques of agriculture in each country). *Trade acreage* is defined and computed by the same methods but refers to the net amount of agricultural products being imported or exported for food or feed.

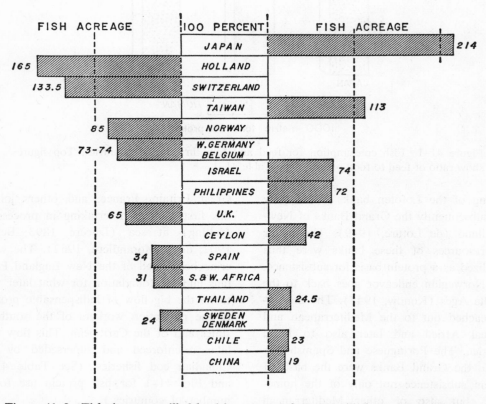

Figure 41–2   Fish Acreage—tilled land in percent of present tilled acreage required to raise an equivalent amount of animal protein

to which some major countries have found themselves detached from their geographical as well as ecological framework (see Table 41–2 and Fig. 41–2). It is evident that this kind of freewheeling life cannot be copied by many more nations. Nor is it likely, given the present population explosion, that many, if any, of these countries can in the long run sustain their present patterns of survival.

Table 41–2

GHOST ACREAGE OF SELECTED
COUNTRIES (1963–1965) AS A
PERCENTAGE OF TILLED LAND

	FISH ACREAGE	TRADE ACREAGE	GHOST ACREAGE
Japan	214%	120%	334%
U.K.	65	240	305
Netherlands	165	105	270
West Indies	120	110	230
Israel	74	140	214
West Germany	73	135	208
Italy	19.5	29	48.5

The world-wide grab for food and feed resources by earmarking transoceanic soil and water resources, works to the overwhelming advantage of the well-fed, rich world. This is the case in spite of the political independence that has come to major portions of the poor and hungry world since World War II. This profound change has not yet manifested itself in the political and economic field. Only in food grain has the flow been reversed. It now moves in the opposite but more reasonable direction—to the needy.

The marshaling of the world's grasslands to provide for the western well-fed world deserves to be written as the history of not only a grand-scale deception but also as a study in global ecology. It reveals how the overdimensioned ecosystems of Western man were maintained. The most dismal aspect of this study, however, is the failure of our education to provide the recognition of this colossal imbalance in protein and energy input.

THE FISHERIES MIRACLE IN PERU

This large-scale mobilization of the globe's grasslands to the exclusive benefit of a minority is almost reaching its finale. But now we seem to be witnessing an almost parallel undertaking in the oceans—marshaling the major plankton pastures. This paper is addressed to this particular issue with special emphasis on the tapping of the anchoveta riches of the Peruvian Current. This tapping is on an ecological scale far overshadowing anything that ever took place in (1) the meat and cattle deliveries from the prairies to Western Europe, (2) the beef, mutton, and bonemeal exports from the pampas to the eastern U.S.A., U.K., Scandinavia, and other European destinations, or (3) the eggs, butter, and meat dispatches from Australia and New Zealand mainly to the U.K.

The Peruvian fishing industry began a spectacular growth in 1959, with the fishing anchoveta on a large scale for reduction purposes (making of meal and oil) (Schaefer, 1967). The catch volume of Peru surpassed that of the United States in 1960, the U.S.S.R. in 1960, China presumably in 1962, and Japan in 1962 to become the top-ranking fishing nation of the world (Table 41–3 and Fig. 41–3). (Total world aquatic catches are seen in Figure 41–4.) Around 96 percent of the catch was anchoveta *Engraulis ringens* L., the abundant raw material for fish meal production.

This anchoveta catch in the Peruvian Current (sometimes called the Humboldt Current) has become the world's largest ocean harvest of a single species. In the brief time span since 1945, it has shown a two-hundredfold increase, and a tenfold one since 1955. This development has led to the almost unbelievable fact that two Peruvian ports (Callao and Chimbote) hold the world record in received amount of fish. The total catch tops the combined marine catch of both Japan and the U.S.S.R., which have far-flung world-wide fisheries!

THE PERUVIAN CURRENT

The submarine continental shelf of western South America is jagged, as is the land which rises abruptly into the Andes. There are many deep canyons in the shelf extending all the way to the ocean floor. With the aid of a counterclockwise current (Fig. 41–5), this formation creates a strong upwelling of deep ocean waters heavily charged with organic matter (carbon, nitro-

gen, phosphorus, sulfur, ammonium, and manganese) (Wyrtki, 1963). This upwelling is sustained by a persistent off-land wind and is strongest between the latitudes 8° to 12° S. The shelf that actually produces most of the fish is narrow and largely inshore, where the shelf slopes rapidly downward. Shoal banks are seldom encountered out at sea (Popovici, 1962–1963).

Down to a depth of 100 feet near the coast, plankton bloom in the dim light of the cool, rich waters. This is the layer with abundant sea life (Popovici, 1961–1962). Anchoveta feed primarily on diatoms but to some degree on zooplankton. The Peruvian Current, with its abundant fish and its cold water in relation to latitude, was well-known to the Incas (Gunther, 1936).

Table 41-3

BASIC STATISTICAL DATA*

A. *World Fisheries for Food and Feed* (million metric tons)

	1958	1959	1960	1964	1965	1966	1967	1968
World marine								
fish catch	24.1	26.8	29.2	40.9	40.8	43.9	46.0	49.6
Food fish	18.8	19.5	20.6	24.3	24.5	25.2	25.8	26.0
Feed fish	5.3	7.3	8.6	16.5	16.3	·18.7	20.2	23.6
Feed fish as % of								
total catch	22	27	29.5	40.5	40	42.5	44	47.6
Anchoveta catch								
Peru	0.9	1.91	3.1	8.9	7.2	8.5	11.5	12.4
Chile	0.03	0.04	0.08	0.93	0.44	1.15	1.20	1.49

·B. *Fish Meal Production* (million metric tons)

	1963	1964	1965	1966	1967	1968
World	2.96	3.68	3.60	3.81	3.34	3.84
Peru	1.13	1.55	1.28	1.39	1.69	1.91

C. *Fish Meal Exports* (million metric tons)

	1961	1962	1963	1964	1965	1966	1967	1968
World	1.36	1.72	1.78	2.43	2.44	2.46	2.66	3.58
Protein content	1.02	1.28	1.33	1.81	1.82	1.84	1.98	2.67
Peru	1.71	1.06	1.04	1.43	1.41	1.30	1.50	2.02
Protein content	1.27	0.79	0.76	1.07	1.05	0.97	1.12	1.51
Chile	0.04	0.07	0.09	0.15	0.07	0.19	0.47	0.59
Protein content	0.03	0.05	0.07	0.11	0.05	0.14	0.35	0.44

*Computed by the author on the basis of (1) F.A.O. Fisheries Statistics, (2) official data provided by Peruvian and Chilean governments, and (3) the Peruvian monthly *La Pesca*.

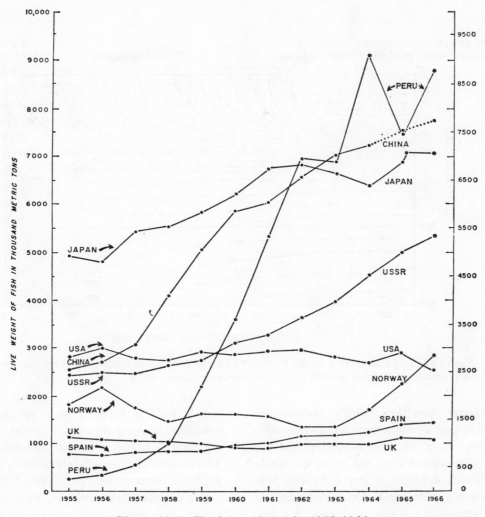

Figure 41–3   Total Aquatic catch, 1955–1966

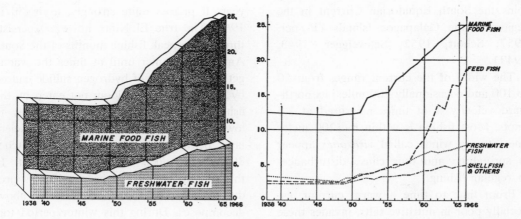

Figure 41–4   Catches of food fish, 1938–1966 (Note feed fish in the right-hand section) in 1000 metric tons

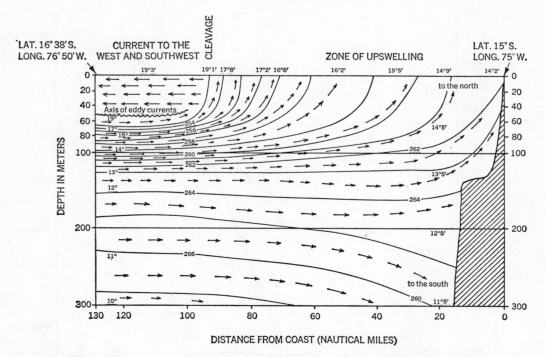

Figure 41–5   Cross section of the Peruvian Current—from San Juan toward the Southwest with lines of equal specific gravity of sea water (June 1931)

Alexander von Humboldt's observations were at best a rediscovery and a reassertion of these facts. He also introudced the notion of a current along the coast, the northern limits of which he traced through temperature measurements along the coast. At the latitude of the seaport Talara, this cold current deviates to the northeast and finally joins the South Equatorian Current in the region of the Galapagos Islands (Posner, 1957; Schott, 1952; Schweigger, 1943, 1949).

The width of the current ranges from 50 to 100 and occasionally 200 miles; its northward velocity is at times measured at 2.5 knots. Most fishing is within the 200 meter line. Stormy winds called *virazones* appear in springtime and thus cause disturbances in regular fishing.

From time to time a warm current, especially poor in nutritive salts, invades these waters off Peru and Chile (Wooster, 1961; Bjerknes, 1961). It moves southward and presses itself in between the coast and the northward-moving Peruvian Current, causing mass flight and killing of the anchoveta. This equatorial current is bittersweetly called El Niño because, like the Christ Child, it comes around Christmas time. To a certain extent, this warm current regularly forces its way southward, but every two or three years it presses quite strongly, as it did in 1965. The true El Niño, however, persists through the peak fishing months of the South American summer until at times the waters get a strong odor of hydrogen sulfide caused by the excess water bloom not eaten by the fish. The excess dies and precipitates to lower layers. There is an oxygen-deficient layer below 30 to 40 meters that stretches 800 meters deep and 100 miles out. In this bottom region hydrogen sulfide is produced when the organic matter from above decomposes. During this winter period torrential rains and northwest winds may lash the normally placid, rainless coast.

ANCHOVETA BIOLOGY

The anchoveta prefer cold waters (13–17° C). They congregate in big schools at spawning time for several months in spring and early summer. Then they begin a migratory period searching for feeding grounds of massive phytoplankton production (Jordan *et al.,* 1965). The schools furthermore evade enemies such as bonito, yellowfin, albacore, corvina, robalo. A second standstill period of spawning follows the migratory period in the winter season. When first spawning, the fish reach a length of six inches.

Major changes in water temperature greatly affect the anchoveta movements. Fifteen nautical miles from the coast of northern Chile the surface temperature mounts to 19–20° C. Far less plankton is available here than in the waters closer to the coast.

In the Peruvian section of the coast, this plankton-eating anchoveta is abundantly spread from Punta Aguja (lat. 5° 50′ S.) to Lota (37° 4′ S.) in the south. Most schools are concentrated within fifty miles of the coast. According to IMARPE (Instituto del Mar de Perú) the potentials of the three subdivisions of the coastal area of Peru are: (1) Northern Region (Chicama–Casma), 2.85 million metric tons; (2) Central Region (Casma–Lomas), 4.59 million metric tons; and, (3) Southern Region (Lomas–Ilo), 0.74 million metric tons (Anon., 1965b; Saetersdal *et al.,* 1965). The anchoveta zone actually runs from Talcahuano in Chile to Chimbote in Peru and still further north to Talara.

THE BIRD-MAN-FISH RELATIONSHIP

In addition to man there are guano birds that depend on the anchoveta riches of the Peruvian current. Guano-producing birds appear on a key sector of the coast between Pisco Bay and the Lobos (Seal) islands. They provide a revealing analogy to man because they, too, catch fish (Jordan *et al.,* 1966). Throughout the year, but especially during the summer months of December to February, cormorants, gannets (guanayes), and pelicans appear like storm clouds in the sky looking for schools of anchoveta, on which they feed voraciously. In normal years they consume at least 2.5 to 3 million metric tons of fish a year, worth more than $50 million at 1965 prices. But periodically, because the fish disappear due to El Niño, millions of these birds fall into the sea and are washed up on the beaches. They die of starvation because they live almost exclusively on the anchoveta (Avila, 1953; Vogt, 1940; Marmer, 1951).

Although such mass mortality of sea birds is known elsewhere (e.g., off the western coast of southern Africa), its effects are particularly dramatic off the coast of Peru. Great crises for the sea birds occurred in 1957–1958 and 1964–1965. The latter crisis occurred after the fish meal factories moved into high gear and produced a reckless overdrive which increased fish landings in western South America. In Peru the increase was more than tenfold in late 1964. Nearly 20 million out of a total population of 27 million birds died in 1957–1958 for lack of food. Similar disasters were recorded in 1941, 1925–1926, and 1891, with minor crises interspersed in between.

The industry weathered El Niño in 1957–1958. The profits earned by each boat remained comfortably high. The consequences for birds, however, were much more grave in 1964–1965 when the industry had increased tenfold.

GUANO

Pro-guano sentiment has always been very strong in Peru. These islands with the guano-producing birds have been protected since the days of the Incas. Carved wooden Inca spades are still occasionally dug up during guano harvests and the ever present birds are a visible link with the nation's past. Furthermore, for a long time guano was used by the Peruvian government as a means of subsidizing the country's agriculture. Shares in the company were used as favors.

It was naturally assumed that the more fish were caught the less guano there would be because, in ecological terms, guano is one link further along on the food chain. In the early days both products sold for about the same amount per ton. The birds are at a disadvantage because even under favorable conditions they only produce 1 ton of guano to 16 tons of fish. Half the excrement is lost to the sea by inadvertent dripping or by runoff from the islands. The ratio of fish meal to fish is an ominously competitive 1:5.5, or occasionally 1:8; 1:6 is used as a fair average ratio in estimates.

Average fish intake of guano birds is 0.3–0.4 kg per day or 110–150 kg per year. Currently 150,000 tons of guano are deposited per year. This would require a fish consumption by the birds of 2.4 million tons. Guano is important to agriculture because it is an indispensable source of organic and inorganic material. It has a nitrogen content of 14 percent and phosphate (P_2O_5) content of 12 to 26 percent. These percentages mirror the fertilizer value of guano. The annual deposit of 150,000 tons is modest compared to what was mined in the latter part of the nineteenth century. This digging, which reached into deposits covering many years, exceeded 1 million tons.

FISHING METHODS

The catching of anchoveta is an inshore process and carried out by small vessels (13 to 26 meters). The fish are caught by large (long and deep) fine-mesh seines. All handling of the fish is by hydraulic pumps. Incoming loads are discharged in port at the rate of 120 tons per hour.

Some fleets are served by helicopters. This is normally not required because the location of the schools is revealed by clouds of seabirds servicing the guano islands. Low-flying pelicans move out to the fish banquets and constitute another readily observable lead to the shoals.

TRADE

Fish meal exports constitute the bulk (82–86 percent) of Peru's shipments of fish products (FAO, 1959–1967). Fish oil is a by-product of the fish meal reduction process. Peru surpassed the United States as the leading world supplier of fish oil in 1961 (see Table 41–4). In magnitude this fish meal transaction overshadows anything ever done in foreign-aid programs involving protein. It is the biggest single transaction in world protein trade, surpassed only by

Table 41-4

FISH OIL EXPORT
(1,000 metric tons)

YEAR	WORLD TOTAL	U.S.	PERU	FISH OIL EXPORT OF PERU AS % OF WORLD TOTAL
1958	139	42.7	1.6	1.2
1959	205	65.5	17.2	8.6
1960	251	65.2	35.0	13.9
1961	301	55.6	102.3	34.1
1962	366	55.8	128.0	35.0
1963	422	119.0	125.5	29.6
1964	383	68.7	110.6	28.9
1965	446	47.1	137.5	30.8
1966	457*	35.0	87.4	19.3*
1967	617*	34.8	192.7	31.4*

*For comparison of this world total, Norway provided 19.9 percent and 28.6 percent in 1966 and 1967, respectively.

the protein involved in the total dispatch of all food cereals to the hungry and starving world (around 3.6 million metric tons).

The decisive moment in the growth of the fish meal industry in Peru came in 1952, when the pilchard fisheries in California collapsed, probably due to overfishing. There fish meal manufacturers noted that the guano birds consumed five or six times as many fish per year in the Peru Current as had ever been found in the California Current. Later, U.N. experts were to point out that resources of fish cannot be judged in the same way as mine resources might be. Up to a certain level, at least, the more fish taken out of highly feed-rich waters the more room there would be for new fish. The only change to be expected in the marine environment is a somewhat greater drain on the vast plankton resources.

After 1952, entire factories were shipped down piece by piece from California. When a government decree tried to limit the size of the industry in Peru, attorneys for the fish meal manufacturers attacked the decree on the grounds that an article of the constitution guaranteed freedom of enterprise. Then the Japanese began offering nylon nets at up to $12,000 with eighteen months to pay. Norwegians raised their credit to two years. As a result, by the end of 1964, anchoveta landings in Peru were close to 9 million metric tons (8.86) and fish meal production topped 1.5 million metric tons. Because of oceanic disturbances (*El Niño*), landings in 1965 did not reach 7 million metric tons, but by 1967 they had surpassed 11 million metric tons, reaching 12 million metric tons in 1968. Peru's offshore waters are now worth more than much of its land (*La Pesca,* 1965–1968).

The peak of the grand expansion was reached in 1963. Forty-five shipyards were then building new anchoveta catchers (*bolicheras*) full-blast. No less than 1,200 such vessels were then built. In 1962 alone the Callao shipyards built 300 new catchers, or close to one each working day (*La Pesca,* 1965–1968).

The ocean was glowingly described in those days as the big new eldorado—the scene of the great adventure of our days. The boom affected a number of subsidiary activities: shipyards, gear manufacturing, imports, harbor installations, processing plants, water needs, etc.

At the peak of the expansion, Peru had more than 150 plants servicing 1,800 seiners. Facilities were created for the manufacture of nets in the country. Many shipyards, one large mill, and factories for miscellaneous plant equipment were started. Engines, electronic gear, processing equipment, and pumps were imported (*La Pesca,* 1964–1965).

THE DECLINE IN CATCHES

The abundance of fish was greatest in 1959. In 1963 and the first quarter of 1964 the availability of fish dropped considerably. From 1962 to 1963 a decline in average catches per vessel as well as per trip of 30–40 percent took place. 1963 was actually the lowest of the recent years. The catch in 1963 was 2 percent above that of 1962 but the number of catchers had grown, due to the boom, by no less than 67 percent, i.e., by 473 new vessels (Anonymous, 1965, 1966, 1967, 1968).

The cause of the catch decline can be attributed to one of several of the following factors: (1) movements of schools into other waters than those regularly fished; (2) less abundant year classes: i.e., the crops from these years are smaller than those from other (or normal) years; (3) reduced total stocks as shown by biological inventories.

High bird mortality was noted by IMARPE in the fall and winter of 1963. Compared to 1961 the water blooming areas were reduced. Water of low mineral content intruded both vertically and horizontally.

Low fish abundance was noted in the whole region from Antofagasta (Chile) in the south to north of Chibote in Peru. The persistence of low availability in 1964 pointed to reduced stocks (Anonymous, 1965–1967).

Peruvians complain that their restrictions do not apply to Chilean catchers. The Chileans fish freely and tap south Peruvian resources in spite of catch restrictions. This may be an additional factor in the declining fisheries of Peru.

In 1964 in Callao five shipyards were closed, twelve were paralyzed, twenty-two functioned sporadically, and only six produced normally. In 1966 only five shipyards were still in business, with a total production of 480 boats per year. The 1967 yard capacity was 300 ships per year, and the trend was toward 200-ton ships built of steel instead of wood. Larger boats with increased carrying capacity and higher speed have been the trend ever since the boom faded (*La Pesca,* 1965, 1966, 1967, 1968).

Twenty-one fish meal plants closed down in 1965. In May 1966, 149 plants were still operating but one year later there were only 94. In 1968, fish meal was produced by fifty manufacturers in 84 plants. In 1967 six foreign countries owned 29 plants in Peru. This constituted ownership of 36.8 percent of the plants compared to 12.6 percent in 1963. The following table shows the decline at Arica (in the Taltal province) comparing 1966 with 1967 (*La Pesca,* 1968):

Table 41–5

DECLINE OF FISHERIES AT ARICA FOR 1966–1967

	1966	1967
Fish meal plants (No.)	38	17
Tons of fish per hour (plant capacity)	1,320	690
Anchoveta vessels (No.)	224	120
Average catch load carried (1000 tons)	30	17.2

Even though in the beginning there seemed to be no limit to Nature's abundance, it is now clear that the limit of man's ability to exploit the anchovy profitably in the form of fish meal and fish oil has been nearly reached. In 1958–1959, a fishing vessel out of Callao with a holding capacity of no more than 50 or 60 tons could seine 15,000 tons of anchoveta a year. Now a vessel with almost three times that capacity is lucky to fish 6,000 tons a year and generally brings in about half that volume. The holding capacity of Peru's fishing vessels increased by more than 90 percent between 1962 and 1964, while the total landings went up only about 40 percent (Lora, 1965; *La Pesca,* 1963–1969).

Until the peak boom the catch per trip increased considerably (cf. later figures above). The catch in 1953 was 32.0 tons per trip; in 1960, 37.6 tons per trip; and in 1961, 41.2 tons per trip. Overfishing has further resulted in declining size of captured fish, implying a higher percentage of younger specimens. In December 1965, 60 percent of the landings (1.1 million metric tons) were immature anchoveta—*peladillas.* Naturally this reduced the yield per fishing effort. Traditionally rich areas are suffering from poor landings. Too many plants are concentrated in one area. Transfer to new and better-yielding zones has taken place, but there is clear evidence of overextension in certain areas. Only by such indiscriminate fishing was it possible to exceed the 7 million mark in the crisis of 1965.

Instituto del Mar de Perú (IMARPE) has established 9.5–10 million metric tons as the maximum take of anchoveta in the Peruvian waters to sustain the stock and avoid the risk of its reduction. This maximum includes what is taken by man for the meal industry as well as what the birds prey on. The catch in 1968 exceeded 12 million metric tons. As a regular catch quota for the fish meal industry IMARPE proposed 7–7.5 million metric tons, acknowledging that the eighteen million guano birds would consume an additional 3 million tons. In 1966 after mass mortality of birds, their number dropped drastically to three million, which needed only 0.5 million tons of anchoveta. An excess of 2.5 million metric tons thus became available for meal manufacture, and the total permissible harvest reached 9.5–10 million metric tons.

At the start of the sixties the total anchoveta stock along the coast of Peru was appraised at 25 million metric tons. This appraisal would allow an annual catch of 7.5 million metric tons. However, due to excessive exploitation, by 1965–1966 the total stock was reduced to 12–13 million metric tons. Recuperation is therefore needed. *Drecreto Superior No. 5,* February 17, 1965, fixed the limit for small-size, young specimens of no more than 12 centimeters length to no more than 30 percent of the catch (Anon., 1965a, 1965b, 1966, 1967, 1968; Boerema *et al.,* 1967; Gulland, 1968).

The potential Chilean resources of anchoveta have been determined by IMARPE to be 0.8–1.2 million metric tons. There is a sharp southern limit to the productive zone; only the northern section of the Chilean coast carries this prolific fish (Brandhorst, 1965; Brandhorst *et al.,* 1966, 1967; for other references see bibliography on Chile). Current catches consequently exceed sustainable resources.

BIOLOGY AND TECHNOLOGY

Annual demand for replacement and renewal of catching vessels is currently estimated at 200 vessels per year. In 1967 only eight shipyards were in operation in Peru with an annual capacity of 300 vessels. Furthermore, there is an excess of no less than 600 *bolicheras* (anchoveta catch-

ers). They could, however, be employed for the catching of white food fish.

The annual catching capacity of the fleet at this time (1968) has been estimated at 23.3 million metric tons. A five-day fishing week and a six-week summer shutdown have been introduced. Nonetheless, there is a glaring lack of adjustment between biology and technology. Many prerequisites need to be fulfilled if these waters are to accomplish what promotion articles describe and promise: "This, the richest fishery in the world, will continue to produce millions of tons of vital protein assisted by U.S. rope-makers and equipment suppliers."

The ocean is definitely not without obvious limits and limitations. To gain a sense of proportion in appraising the role of the oceans, one could point to the sobering fact that the entire catch of the oceans is not providing the world with as much animal protein as the United States consumes annually in the form of meat. Contrast this with the fact that close to 1.5 billion people are receiving their fill-in between malnutrition and survival through fish protein.

Fish meal has become Peru's biggest earner of foreign exchange, exceeding $200 million a year. Any serious threat to the anchovy affects the national economy.

Foreign investment in Peru's fish meal plants has grown to replace the smaller domestic plants which have sold out. The percentage of all foreign investment in fish meal endeavors has grown from 12.6 percent in 1963 to 28.7 percent in 1965, and 36.8 percent in 1966 (*La Pesca,* 1965–1967). The foreign capital, also in part invested in the national enterprises, originates in Western Europe (West Germany, Holland, Norway, U.K., and France), the U.S., and Japan. In 1967, 129 fish meal plants, 29 of which are foreign-owned, constituted joint ventures, but the latter were dominated by large-volume enterprises. The 1964–1965 overexpansion resulted in extensive bankruptcies and other payment difficulties, shutdowns, mergers, and a great deal of reorganization, primarily in the smaller, "national" companies.

The full price of fish meal in Peru started out at $250–300 per ton in 1960, dropped to around $110 in 1962, and recovered slightly to $124 in 1968. In Chile the price in 1968 was only $110 compared to $160 in 1966 and $115 in 1967 (*La Pesca,* price lists, 1960–1968). Profit margins in the start were exorbitant—more than 100 percent.

Both the government and concerned nationals have tried through parliamentary moves to channel some of the fish riches to the highly protein deficient population of Peru (Doucet, 1965) and expand the fishing of other species such as tuna, bonito, robalo, etc. In 1965–1966 there were, however, only five refrigerated warehouses along the entire Peruvian coast, mostly in the Paíta region, two of which were closed. Greater Lima then had no such warehouse. The fish terminal was outmoded and lacked refrigeration. The absence of an effective infrastructure was notable: no refrigerated warehouses, no ice plants, no adequate fish terminals, etc.

A great deal of fish other than anchoveta were, when canned, bypassing the Peruvian market, as in 1967 when four-fifths of the canned bonito was shipped abroad—two-fifths to the U.S. and three-fifths to Argentina. Exports also dominate the tuna packs.

Italian high-sea trawlers were permitted to catch in Peruvian waters and keep 60 percent of the catch although there was no lack of demand for fresh fish in Peru. This was strongly criticized in Peru both by fishing organizations, mass media, newspapers, and by political groupings.

The most telling appraisal of the significance of the Peruvian-Chilean fish meal protein delivery is seen when its total amount is placed within the context of the closely involved continent of South America. Through this single operation South America is deprived of 50 percent (1965–1967) more animal protein than it is producing as meat, including what is delivered from Argentina to Europe and North America. This operation deprives South America of no less than almost three times the milk protein of the continent (see Table 41–6). When nutrition is appraised in biological terms, these facts throw an interesting light on the relative significance of agriculture compared to fisheries.

Table 41-6

SOUTH AMERICAN EXPORT OF FISH MEAL RELATED TO TOTAL ANIMAL PRODUCTION
(1,000 metric tons protein)

TOTAL SOUTH AMERICAN PRODUCTION 1965-67 (average)		EXPORT OF FISH MEAL PROTEIN (Peru and Chile)	
Meat	960	1966	1,250
Milk	522	1967	1,550
		1968	1,730

Computed by the author on the basis of official Peruvian data and F.A.O. statistics.

In terms of cattle this corresponds to a slaughter of 50 million head and requires a sustaining stock of at least 200 million, which is more than the total cattle population of North America (U.S. and Canada) and 30 percent more than that of Europe. Temperate-region fish cultivation ponds, rendering 150 kilograms of fish per hectare or 13.5 kilograms protein per hectare would be needed to cover no less than 110 million hectares to provide the same amount of protein.

From the point of view of nutrition and ecology it might be more useful to relate this high quantity of animal protein to the actual intake of animal protein in Peru and Chile as well as in South America (Table 41–7).

In agricultural terms Peru would need 35.7 million hectares (ha) of tilled land to

Table 41-7

ANIMAL PROTEIN INTAKE COMPARED WITH FISH MEAL EXPORTS OF PERU (1966-1968)

| | POPULA-TION (millions) | ANIMAL PROTEIN INTAKE PER PERSON | | | % OF THE PROTEIN IN PERUVIAN-CHILEAN MEAL EXPORT (1.5 million tons) |
		G/Day	Kg/Year	TOTAL X 1,000 tons	
South America (excl. Argentina and Uruguay)	155.1	20.0	7.3	1,103.9	76.0
Peru	12.4	18.2	6.6	82.5	5.5
Chile	8.9	28.9	10.5	105.8	7.0.

Computed by the author on the basis of F.A.O. data.

produce the amount of animal protein contained in the anchoveta catches. The average yield or protein via milk is around 42 kg/ha. This big acreage is almost half the total tilled land of South America. Peru currently has 2.6 million ha, allowing 0.44 acre per capita. Approximately only half of this land is actually available for feeding the Peruvian population which grows annually (1968) by 400,000 people, i.e., 3.1 percent per year; this means a doubling of the population every twenty-three years. The remaining land is devoted to cash crops, such as sugar, cotton, etc. This means that there is only 0.2 acre per person to support a meager subsistence. Compared to India, this is only one-third of the amount of land available, per person, for subsistence (see Table 41–8).

This staggering flow of animal protein can be illustrated in different ways (see Table 41–9). Based on the average Peruvian nutritional standard, a quarter of a billion (250 million) people could be provided with their entire animal protein intake. On the average level of the hungry world this number would exceed half a billion. Even on the standard of the satisfied world 100 million people could derive their entire protein intake from this massive loss.

EUROPEAN PARASITISM

Sooner or later the parasitic nature of European agriculture will need to be recognized by economists and nutritionists. The lack of awareness about these relationships is simply a question of faulty and inadequate teaching on all levels: universities,

Table 41-8

LAND AND SEA RESOURCES AND POPULATION IN PERU AND CHILE

| | TILLED LAND (million ha) | POPULATION | | FISH MEAL ACREAGE | |
		(millions)	% Net Growth	(million ha)	TIMES PRESENT TILLED ACREAGE
Peru	2.6	12.8	3.1	35.7	13.7
Chile	4.5	9.1	2.2	3.7	0.82
Total	7.1	21.9	—	39.4	5.6

Computed by the author on the basis of F.A.O. data.

Table 41-9

THE PERUVIAN-CHILEAN EXPORT OF FISH MEAL (1966-1968)
1.50 Million Metric Tons of Protein
(All world 2,70 million metric tons)

A. *In Terms of Agriculture*

Kg PROTEIN/HECTARE	MILLION HECTARES	Kg PROTEIN/HECTARE	MILLION HECTARES
15	100	40	37.5
20	75	50	30
25	60	60	25
30	50	80	18.8

B. *In Terms of Fish Pond Cultivation*

	YIELD Kg/HECTARE	PROTEIN Kg/HECTARE	MILLION HECTARES
Temperate region	150	13.5	111.0
Tropical region	1,500	135.0	11.1

C. *In Terms of Nutrition*

	ANIMAL PROTEIN G/Day	POTENTIAL NUMBER OF PEOPLE FED; MILLION		ANIMAL PROTEIN G/Day	POTENTIAL NUMBER OF PEOPLE FED; MILLION
I. – Hungry World	8	513	II. – Satisfied World	44	94
Peruvian standard (Brazil)	18.3	224	Italy	33	125
Mexican standard (Colombia, Venezuela)	23.8	172	U.S.A.	66	62.5

Potential number of people that could be fed on minimum nutritional standard of 7.5 kg/year (20 g/day) of animal protein: 413 millions.

D. *In Terms of Fisheries*

World average catch of food fish (in protein): 3.1 million metric tons (3,500 million people): 0.89 kg/year.

E. *In Terms of Trade*

The dominance of the fish meal protein in terms of world trade brings more sharply into focus the pivotal nature of this protein transfer.

WORLD TRADE (1966-1968)
(million metric tons protein)

Fish meal:	2.70	*Meat:*	0.63
Peruvian-Chilean part:	1.50	Raw:	0.50
Other parts:	1.20	Bacon, ham:	0.13
Food fish products:	0.48	*Milk:*	0.63
		Dried	0.38
		Cheese	0.20
		Evaporated	0.05
		Eggs:	0.056
		Raw	0.05
		Dried	0.006
Total protein:	3.18	*Total protein:*	1.32

Table 41-9 (continued)

F. *In Terms of Animal Production*

ANIMAL PRODUCTION, FISH MEAL BASED
(calculated)

	AGRICULTURAL ANIMAL PROTEIN %	PROTEIN IN POULTRY AND EGGS %
Japan	82	210
Holland	61	–
West Germany	35	397 (eggs)
Western Europe	20	222 (eggs)
U.S.A.	–	125 (eggs)
(See also Fig. 5)	–	118 (poultry meat)

This is total fish meal and *actual amount*, without taking into account conversion losses.

colleges, high schools, and grade schools.

In terms of ghost acreage (Borgstrom, 1965), which is computed as percent of tilled land, the Peruvian contribution is overwhelming. The Netherlands is certainly not aware of the fact that this influx of animal protein would need 1.18 times its present tilled acreage (Fig. 41–2). West Germany would correspondingly need additional tilled land which would amount to

more than one-third (38 percent) its present tilled acreage. Indeed the protein crutches of Europe are no minor matter. They amount to nothing less than a resurrected colonialism in the marine context. Table 41–10 further illustrates the Peruvian purchases (Chile not included).

These figures speak for themselves but may nevertheless need some amplification. For Japan (Fig. 41–6) they indicate the

Table 41-10

THE "PERUVIAN FISH MEAL COLONY" OF EUROPE (1966-1967)

	"FISH MEAL" ACREAGE MILLION Ha	% TILLED LAND	FISH MEAL OF OTHER SOURCES	
			% OF TILLED LAND	MILLION Ha
Spain	3.4	16.5	0.5	0.13
West Germany	3.1	38.0	18.5	1.51
Poland	1.6	5.0	3.0	0.96
Italy	1.5	9.5	0.5	0.08
Yugoslavia	1.17	14.5	0.5	0.04
Netherlands	1.13	118.0	21.0	0.20
Greece	0.95	26.0	80.0	2.92
East Germany	0.81	16.0	6.0	0.31
Hungary	0.66	4.0	8.0	1.32
Czechoslovakia	0.43	8.0	11.0	0.59
Finland	0.36	13.0	21.0	0.58
France	0.35	2.0	6.0	1.05
Belgium	0.32	29.0	105.0	1.15
Bulgaria	0.18	4.0	3.0	0.13
Sweden	0.12	4.0	12.0	0.36
U.K.	0.12	1.5	41.5	3.32
Total Europe	16.20	–		13.70
Japan	0.86	14.5	93.5	5.53

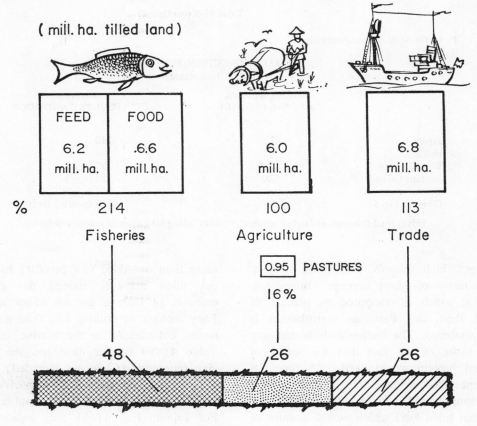

Figure 41–6   Feeding basis of Japan (in protein terms) 1963–1965

degree to which these islands depend on a constant ferrying of food from North America, South America, and Oceania. The figures also gauge in similar terms the role of fisheries in all the oceans. The postwar boom in Japanese livestock and poultry production is based on receiving, in terms of fish protein, 110 percent of what man is getting as fish. As hinted earlier this animal-producing drive is incompatible with the land resource base of Japan. This explains why the floating fish meal factories initiated in 1958–1959, for acquiring feed protein, are now being step by step re-equipped for the manufacture of minced meat instead of fish meal. This ground meat is used as human food in the manufacture of *kamaboko* (fish jellies) and fish sausages, thus circumventing the conversion losses via animal-based production of meat, milk, eggs, etc.

It is little recognized that, to a great extent, the dairy production of Europe depends on transoceanic sources of feed grain, oilseeds, etc. Besides the prairie and the pampas, tropical Africa is absurdly enough an indispensable artificial leg to the postwar animal production of Europe. Equally essential is the influx of 1.6 million metric tons of fish meal protein (half the world's total intake of aquatic protein in human food). The protein crutches of Europe are sizable. They testify to the lack of awareness of the true ecological realities of that continent. Table 41–12 shows the protein dependence of the U.S.

Table 41-11

FISH MEAL BASIS OF EUROPEAN AGRICULTURE*

Import: South America	1.0
S. and SW. Africa, Angola	0.8
Export within Europe:	
Norway	0.1
Denmark	0.2
	2.1

* Computed by author on the basis of FAO data.

Table 41-12

U.S. FISH PROTEIN BALANCE, 1967
(1,000 metric tons)

	DOMESTIC		PURCHASED FROM WORLD MARKET		TOTAL
		%		%	
Food	158	49	160	51	318
Feed	195	31	443	69	638
Total	353	37	603	63	956

Imported Fish Meal:

	PERU	OTHERS	TOTAL	YEAR
Fish meal	300	143	443	1967
	414	142	556	1968
% U.S. total				
catch	85.5	40.5	126	1967
	111.5	42.0	153.5	1968
% U.S. fish				
meal prod.	154	73.4	227.4	1967

U.S. Fish Acreage: (million ha)

	1967	1968
Food fish	7.95	8.25
—domestic	3.95	4.00
—imported	4.00	4.25
Feed fish (meal and solubles)	15.38	17.25
—domestic	4.33	3.35
—imported	11.05	13.9
Peru:	7.60	10.6

Comparisons:

	million ha
U.S. soybean acreage (1967)	14.0
U.S. wheat acreage (1967)	20.1

* Table 41–12 specifically relates the Peruvian fish meal to U.S. ocean catches and to domestic fish meal production. In addition the fish acreage is computed for 1967 in terms of million hectares with reference to totally imported fish meal but particularly to that from Peru. The acreages for wheat and soybean are given as a comparison to visualize the relative magnitude of this major protein influx.

This Peruvian-Chilean protein aid to the satisfied world overshadows, both in absolute and relative terms, anything done in the postwar period to alleviate the shortages of the Hungry World. It is further noteworthy that a foreign-aid program focused on the mobilizing of this invaluable source of high-grade protein, would have surpassed both in dimension and in significance anything aid programs have ever contributed to any country through all sources. A similar tapping of invaluable protein resources but on a much more modest scale (approximately 100,000 tons) is taking place along the Atlantic coast of South Africa. This protein also bypasses the protein-short continent of Africa in order to support largely European animal production. On the whole, close to one-half of the marine fish catches is channeled via fish meal and oil into the hopper of the satisfied world (Fig. 41–7).

It is frequently said that fish and fish products are not acceptable to Latin Americans. To anyone who, like this author, has traveled through the Central and South American Andean region, this argument carries little weight. Several fish are eagerly consumed; they are frequently dried and used as a "spicing" ingredient in casseroles and soups. They are also commonly encountered in rural marketplaces but in entirely inadequate quantities. In fact, the Inca empire successfully tapped the anchoveta riches of the Humboldt Current and distributed them throughout the huge Andean empire. The fish was dried along the sun-bathed beaches, immediately after landing. This item was also a staple in their famed granaries.

If the degree of profitability is to determine what we do, and if short-range gains are never weighed against long-range benefits, mankind is bound to lose its bearings. As long as these vital matters are not appraised from the vantage point of the needs and national interests of the countries di-

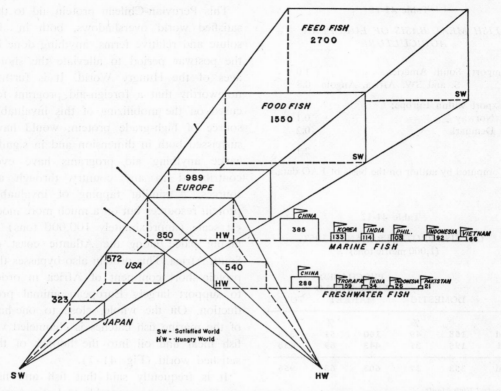

Figure 41–7   Marine fish catches (one thousand metric tons of protein) 1964–1966

rectly involved, we are bound to wander astray.

Irrespective of all economic considerations, this Peruvian-Chilean example is a glaring indication of my introductory observation: that modern technology and transportation, allowing distant provisions in time and space, have blurred all ecological awareness of man's dependence on Nature's basic endowments. This fundamental relationship prevails, however, in spite of all technology and verbal veiling.

REFERENCES

A. GENERAL

Avila, E. " 'El Niño' en 1953 y su relación con las aves guaneras. Problemas básicos referentes a la anchoveta." *Bol. Cía. Adm. del Guano*, 29 (5) (1953), 13–19.

Bellet, A. *La grande pêche à Terre-Neuve depuis la découverte du Nouveau Monde par les Basques au 14e siècle*. Paris, 1902.

Bjerknes, Y. " 'El Niño': Studio Based on Anal-

ysis of Ocean Surface Temperatures 1935–1957." *LATTC Bull.*, 5 (3) (1961), 219–303.

Borgstrom, G. "New Methods of Appraising the Rôle of Fisheries in World Nutrition. *Fishing News Intern.*, 1 (1) (1961), 33–38. Revised edition in Dohrs, F. E., and Sommers, L. M. *Economic Geography: Selected Readings*. New York: Thomas Y. Crowell Co., 1970. Pp. 152–65.

————, ed. "Fish in World Nutrition." In *Fish as Food*, Vol. II. New York: Academic Press, 1962. 777 pp. Pp. 267–300.

————, ed. "Utilization of Fish and Shellfish." In *Fish as Food*, Vol. II. New York: Academic Press, 1962. 777 pp. Pp. 637–725.

————. *The Hungry Planet—The Modern World at the Edge of Famine*. New York: Macmillan, 1965. 487 pp. (Revised paperback edition, 1967. New York: Collier-Macmillan. 507 pp.)

————. "Food from the Sea." In *Technology in Western Civilization*, M. Kranzberg and C. W. Pursell Jr. Vol. II. New York: Oxford University Press, 1967. 722 pp. Pp. 402–13.

————. "The Rôle of Fish Protein in World Feeding." *Proc. Intern. Wennergren Symposium on Novel Protein Products*, Stockholm, Sept. 1968, 1969. 110 pp.

Cutting, C. L. *Fish Saving. A History of Fish Processing from Ancient to Modern Times*. London: Leonard Hill (Books) Ltd., 1955. 372 pp.

de la Morandière, Ch. *Histoire de la pêche française de la morue dans l'Amérique septentrionale (des origines à 1789)*, Vol. I. Paris: G.-P. Maisonneuve et Larose, 1962. 506 pp.

de Loture. *Histoire de la pêche à Terre-Neuve*. Paris, 1949.

Ducèré. *Recherches historiques sur la pêche de la morue par les Basques et les Bayonnais*. Bayonne, 1893.

FAO Fisheries Yearbook. 1959–67. Section commodities.

Gunther, E. R. "Variations in the Behaviour of the Peru Coastal Current with an Historical Introduction." *Geogr. J.*, 88 (1936), 37–65.

Jordan, R., et al. "La anchoveta (*Engraulis ringens* L.). Conocimiento actual sobre su biología, ecología y pesquería." *Publcs. IMARPE, Info. No. 6*. 1965.

Konow, C. *Tørrfiskhandel*. En faglig utredning om Tørrfiskhandel fra 1914 til 1945 med saerlig henblikk på omsetningsformene i mellomkrigstiden. Bergen: A. S. John Griegs Boktrykkeri, 1945. 238 pp.

Marmer, H. A. "The Peru- and Niño-Currents." *Geogr. Review* (New York), 1951. Pp. 337–38.

Popovici, Z. "Corrientes oceánicas y la pesca peruana." *Anuario de Pesca* (Lima), 1961–1962. Pp. 162–72.

————. "Horizontes oceánicos de Sudamérica. Bases naturales de sus pesquerías." *Anuario de Pesca* (Lima), 1962–1963. Pp. 22–76.

Posner, G. S. "The Peru Current." *Bull. Bingham Oceanogr. Col.*, 16 (2) (1957), 106–55.

Schott, G. "La corriente Peruana." *Bol. Soc. Geogr. de Lima*, 69 (1952), 3–13.

Wooster, W. S. "El Niño." *Univ. of Calif. Scripps Inst. of Oceanogr. Contributions 1960*. 1961a.

Wooster, W. S., and Gilmartin, M. "The Peru-Chile Undercurrent." *J. Mar. Res.* (New Haven), 19 (3) (1961b), 97–122.

Wyrtki, K. "The Horizontal and Vertical Field of Motion in the Peru Current." *Bull. Scripps Inst. of Oceanogr.* (Los Angeles), 8 (4) (1963), 313–46.

B. PERU

Anonymous. "La pesquería de la anchoveta." *Publcs. IMARPE, Info. No. 1*. 1965a.

————. "Efectos de la pesca en el stock de anchoveta." *Publcs. IMARPE, Info. No. 7*. 1965b.

————. "La pesquería de la anchoveta." *Publcs. IMARPE, Info. No. 14*. 1966.

————. "Informe complementario sobre la pesquería de la anchoveta." *Publcs. IMARPE, Info. No. 15*. 1967.

————. "La pesquería de la anchoveta y recomendaciones para la temporada 1967–68." *Publcs. IMARPE, Info. No. 20*. 1968.

Barandiaran P., J. F. "Investigaciones oceanográficas en la costa norte del Perú." *Rev. Marina*, 89 (3), (1954), 255–52.

Boerema, L. K., et al. "Informe sobre los efectos de la pesca en el recurso peruano de anchoveta." *Publcs. IMARPE, Bol. No. 4*. 1967.

Doucet, F. W. "Mercado de peces marinos de consumo en el Perú." *Publcs. IMARPE, Info. No. 5*. 1965.

Fiedler, R. H.; Jarvis, N. D.; and Lobell, M. J. *La pesca y las industrias pesqueras en el Peru*. Con recomendaciones para su futuro desarrollo. Lima: Companía Administradora del Guano, 1943. 371 pp.

Gulland, J. A. "Informe sobre la dinámica de la población de anchoveta peruana." *Publcs. IMARPE, Bol. No. 6.* 1968.

Jordan, R., *et al.* "Las problaciones de aves guaneras y su situación actual." *Publcs. IMARPE, Info. No. 10.* 1966.

Lam C., R. "Estudio sobre la variación del contenido de grasa en la anchoveta peruana (*Engraulis ringens* L.)." *Publcs. IMARPE, Info. No. 24.* 1968.

La Pesca. Lima: Ediciones Sudamericanas; 1963–1969.

Lora, J. "Crecimiento de la flota pesquera industrial al 31 de Diciembre de 1963." *Publcs. IMARPE, Info. No. 2.* 1965.

Saetersdal, G., *et al.* "Fluctuaciones en la abundancia aparente del stock de anchoveta 1959–1962." *Publcs. IMARPE, Bol. No. 2.* 1965.

Schaefer, M. B. "Dinámica de la pesquería de la anchoveta *Engraulis ringens* en Perú." *Publcs. IMARPE, Bol. No. 5.* 1967.

Schweigger, E. *Pesquería y oceanografía del Perú y proposiciones para su desarrollo futuro.* Lima: Compañía Administrador del Guano, 1943. 356 pp.

———. "Der Perustrom nach zwölfjährigen Beobachtungen." *Erdkunde, 3* (2/3) (1949), 121–32, 229–40.

Vogt, Wm. "Una depresión ecológica en la costa peruana." (Proceedings of the 8th Conference of the *Scientific American,* May 1940, Washington, D.C., EE. UU.) *Bol. Comp. Adm. del Guano,* 16 (10) (1940), 307–29.

C. Chile

Brandhorst, W. "Die Chilenische Fischerei und ihre weiteren Entwicklungsaussichten." *Ber. über Landw.* (Bonn), 43 (1) (1965), 148–87.

———. "Upwelling and the Anchoveta Fishery in Chile." *2nd Intern. Oceanogr. Congr., Upwelling Symposium* (Moscow). MS, 1966.

Brandhorst, W., and Canon, J. R. "Resultados de estudios oceanográfico-pesqueros aereos en el norte de Chile," with English summary. *Inst. Fom. Pesq.* (Santiago, Chile) *Publ. No. 29,* 1967. 44 pp.

Brandhorst, W., and Rojas, O. "Distribución geográfica de la pesca de la anchoveta en el norte de Chile y su composición del tamaño, de marzo de 1961 a julio de 1963." *Inst. Fom. Pesq.* (Santiago, Chile) *Publ. No. 24.* 1967a.

———. "Investigaciones sobre los recursos de la anchoveta (*Engraulis ringens* J.) y sus relaciones con las condiciones oceanográficas en agosto-septiembre de 1963 y marzo–junio de 1964," with English summary. *Inst. Fom. Pesq.* (Santiago, Chile) *Publ. No. 31.* 1967b. 38 pp.

Brandhorst, W., *et al.* "Observaciones oceanográfico-biológicas sobre los recursos de la anchoveta (*Engraulis ringens* Jenyns) en la zona norte de Chile." Part 1. *Inst. Fom. Pesq.* (Santiago, Chile) *Publ. No. 22.* 1966.

DISCUSSION

WEST: I would like to emphasize that the real hope for game in Rhodesia lies in the national parks. The idea that the utilization of game by game farming would assist in the preservation of game gave all of us a lot of hope some years ago. This, on European land, was taken up fairly widely.

But I would say that game farming over much of Rhodesia has had a disastrous effect on the game population rather than an encouraging one.

One of the most important reasons is that the complexity of farming the multiple species game population is much greater than people anticipated. Farming with one, two or three types of domesticated livestock is comparatively simple; and yet, judging by the effect livestock are having on the country, it is beyond the capacity of most farmers. But managing a multiple species game population, which theoretically should be a much more productive type of husbandry because it uses a much wider spectrum of the available food supply is beyond the ordinary farmer.

The idea was to make game compete with beef, goat flesh and mutton. This really degraded the status of game, and it put an impossible pressure on the game population. People were unable to count game. We knew too little about reproductive rates and population growth, and there were practical difficulties. One of the most important of these practical difficulties is the cropping itself.

The disturbance caused by cropping presents an almost insuperable difficulty, and most game farming as a money-making occupation on private land doesn't appear to have a rosy future.

In the national parks where game culling has been employed to reduce overly large populations of elephants, buffalo and other animals, it has been done very successfully because it has been handled by people who are sympathetic and whose aim is to produce an effect on the habitat which is desirable and not to make money out of the meat and the products of the culling exercise.

DASMANN: I guess I have to come in at this point. Since I was partly responsible for this game ranching effort in Rhodesia, I would like to make some comments about it.

I am glad that Dr. West made the distinction between game farming, as he called it, and game culling in the national parks. I think that a number of distinctions need to be made. I would say that the term, game farming, should be restricted to the kind of activity successfully practiced in South Africa where one or two formerly wild species of game are kept in paddocks and essentially managed much like a domestic animal. Game ranching is the deliberate management and cropping of large mixed populations of wild game in open range situations.

Game culling, which is often confused with game ranching, particularly in East

Africa, is simply a method of thinning down surplus populations.

Game ranching has the capacity in Africa, in many areas, of producing more meat per acre than can be obtained from the traditional domestic animals on the same land. The reasons are the advantages of diversity that we have talked about in the last session. You have a diverse vegetation on this land, and a great number of species of wild animals can make use of the many different layers and the many different species involved in that vegetation.

We ran a pilot project in Rhodesia at the Henderson Ranch in which over a couple of years we showed that you could not only produce more meat, but you also could harvest and market the meat. The landowner could bring in a higher dollar income than he could have obtained from his domestic cattle. We didn't pretend it was easy. We didn't pretend that this process could be turned over to inexpert ranch owners, farmers, or cattlemen who knew little about wild game.

After the first year of very intensive cropping under carefully controlled conditions, the game were tamer than they were at the start of that year. Cropping need not be a disturbing influence, but cropping handled inexpertly is inevitably disturbing and once the disturbance sets in, the game move away. It becomes increasingly difficult to census them, to know what crop one should take next year, and the whole thing begins to break down.

This development scheme has been of only limited success because it didn't capture the imagination of the government. The government was unwilling to properly finance a game department to take on the technical work that needed to be done if this scheme was to be successful. If left to the farmers and the ranchers to whom it may sound like a good idea but who lack the experience to carry it through successfully—I think it inevitably must fail. You must first build the corps of technical people who can oversee, guide, and direct this type of operation if it is to succeed.

WEST: I would like to pay tribute to Ray Dasmann, and Archy Mossman, Thane Riney and the American biologists who worked in Rhodesia. They may not be aware of it, but the time they spent in Rhodesia was the most productive period in game research that the country ever entered into. They started something which has gone on, and it looks as if it may go very much further.

Our game department now has a strong team of biologists. We have a chief biologist and about five assistants who are working not only in national parks but in game ranching projects all over the country.

The growth of this work is entirely due to Dasmann, Mossman, and Riney. I don't think that the fact that game ranching on farms hasn't proved as successful as we once hoped it would is due to discouragement by the government. I think it is due to the innate profit-seeking of the individual farmer, to the fact that some farmers didn't believe in game ranching and used the opportunity provided by their game ranching license to get rid of animals that competed with their domestic stock.

I don't think that Ray Dasmann can say that he proved that game animals could be more profitable than stock. I think a lot more than two years' work would be needed to prove that. I think this cropping difficulty is one of the most serious snags; there is also the lack of knowledge of reproduction rate and growth rate and this kind of information about which a lot more work needs to be done.

I know that people have been told they have fifty sable on their property and they can crop so many of them; but this fifty sable uses their property only as part of its home range, and the neighbor who also has a part of the home range also has a permit to crop so many of a herd of sable that graze and browse on his farm. These kinds of snags have arisen because of inadequate knowledge of the ecology and behavior of the new animals being used for production. But I think if we could value wildlife higher than just to make it compete economically with domestic stock, we would be much nearer achieving the objective we want. If you could use this game for sport hunting or for expensive meat, we would have a much better hope. People are doing this now, and I think this will be a development in game ranching on private properties that will be more successful than the idea of using sable as ration meat to be sold on the cheapest market.

FRASER DARLING: We really ought to be changing this subject a little. As one who early was advising cropping wild game, I think I should say that I never had the profit motive in mind. What I saw in a place like Zambia was a lot of protein that could be fed to a protein-deficient human community. I think most game cropping in Africa should lead toward feeding the African native a bigger share of protein.

I don't like the idea at all of canned eland, etc., coming to the European or American market. It is not a profit matter at all. It is a way of land use, a way of economically tapping the natural resources in Africa for the good of the African native. That is how I saw it.

GEORGE: I have a question I would like to direct to Dr. Fraser Darling. In Lebanon there has been great friction between the nomad and the resident Lebanese peasant. The upland, particularly above 6,000 feet, is in serious trouble now. The cedar forests, of course, are nearly gone, with only some fifteen or sixteen groves left, perhaps a total of 500,000 trees. The fir is also well on its way out. Much of this loss is due to the constant pressure of goat and sheep flocks.

Now, does your concept of the value of the nomad apply to a situation like these more forested uplands that are not really a part of the savannah desert?

FRASER DARLING: Any forested uplands should be outside any nomadic activity whatsoever, wherever it is. This is not nomad country. Nomadism is a pursuit of the steppe country, wherever it is found.

M. T. FARVAR: I thought we Turks were responsible for removing the cedars of Lebanon. (Laughter.)

FRASER DARLING: No. I think if you read ancient Egyptian manuscripts you find there was a great trade by sea of cedar logs many thousands of years ago.

CROWCROFT: I thought the Romans cut them down to make crosses. (Laughter.)

CARLOZZI: In relation to the presently recognized potential of much of the African game country for tourism, having studied for six years an area whose real economic life is coming to depend more and more on tourism, I have some rather strong thoughts on this.

Despite the kind of bad range management which evolves out of a culture which is not quite tuned to the range, as in the Masai, or an interruption of certain range procedures which has not produced desirable ecological effects, the people there at least derive some direct energy from the land that they occupy. Whatever may be said about the production of that land, it does accrue to those who live on it, badly or well, however that may be.

When you introduce tourism, you capitalize those self-same resources, and I am quite sure it can be demonstrated that the money derived out of this exceeds the value of that productivity which is currently coming from the land.

All my experience with tourist areas, however, indicates that the greatest bulk of that new economic accrual doesn't go to the people that live on the land. It goes to the people who have invested in tourism. For the people who live on that land, it provides jobs. And these jobs in themselves, I am convinced, cut people off from the reality of their existence on the land.

They become objects which provide service, which when seen from the viewpoint of the person who provides the service, is a kind of euphemism for servitude. The end result, which is the same everywhere I have been, is a growing ambivalence on the part of the people toward what their economy is based on.

If this type of development grows too large, if it becomes too compelling, it has a dehumanizing effect and an isolating, alienating effect between the person and the land from which he was derived.

As a result of Carribean experience, I view it myself with great ambivalence. I feel that Dr. Darling's comments about the importance of this productivity and protein as it relates to the nutritional needs of the people in Africa is really on the right track, because this to me is the proper flow of productivity for people in that circumstance.

HEADY: At least three of us in the room spent about a week in June examining these game livestock problems, in a group of twenty or so people; this very point came in for a great deal of discussion.

Briefly, we didn't argue with one man who said that the production of income, foreign exchange, was greater per acre with some of the tourism and wildlife products than it was from livestock. Although we didn't go into detail here, I think at least some of us in that group had the feeling that the people who were on that land were doing two things. First, they weren't getting this return. It didn't accrue to them. Second, there was a tendency to put them into the museum that the tourists were there to see. Both of these things are bad. But we didn't come up with any solutions.

TALBOT: It is a little more complex than you make it, Carl. The Masai, as far as we know, had a relatively exploitive economy before European times. Their present situation is untenable. The damage that has accrued has basically been due to attempts by both government and outside agencies to help them. But the point is they are not in balance now. They can't survive under this situation, and the drought and die-off has brought this into sharp focus.

There is another factor and that is political. Since the African countries have become independent, the Masai occupy these arid lands at the rate of about three people per square mile. From sixty up to a hundred people per square mile live in the agricultural land nearby. Masailand will not support that kind of dense occupancy. Nonetheless there is a strong political push to take over the Masai lands. The national parks and reserves have been one of the strongest political factors in enabling the Masai to keep their land. However, the argument of some of the other tribes has been that these people provide nothing to the country, and in fact they are a drain. Therefore, why should we maintain them, as the colonial power maintained them, as a privileged people. Let's put them to work.

As it happens, wildlife-based tourism is the single largest money-earning industry in Kenya as of 1968. This factor looms large in the minds of the government of Kenya. It also looms large in the minds of the Masai politicians. Therefore, the park aspect, the tourist aspect, may be one of the only ways to help them maintain some semblance of their former culture.

The tourist money doesn't go to the Masai, except in the two Masai district parks. The Masai run these parks, and the revenue goes into the Masai district treasury, providing the only income that the Masai received during 1961 and 1962. These district parks are still the major single income source for the Masai.

In the case of one of these two reserves, because of good training of staff to run it, the reserve has been quite successful. The last time I was there, less than a year ago, the Masai district council was in the process of expanding the reserve. The other one, because of poorer training and some of the factors that Dr. West has talked about, has not been anywhere near that sort of a success, and the whole stability of the situation is questionable.

But the point is that our tourism is not a clear-cut cultural good or evil. From what appears to be the standpoint of the Masai, and certainly from the standpoint of the Kenya treasury, it is an important and desirable resource. From the standpoint of wildlife conservation it is probably the most important single positive factor, since an aesthetic appreciation of wildlife is something not necessarily shared by the peoples there.

MILTON: Both Lee and Carl have brought up extremely important points. In much of my own work on national parks in Latin America, the dilemma of whether or not to introduce tourism as an economic prop to sustain local cultures and wild areas has been very real. On the one hand, tourism can provide an important stimulus to retain diverse environmental and cultural values that people from elsewhere are willing to pay to see. Without such interest, many areas, and the cultures inhabiting them, would be swallowed up by the sorts of massive, poorly regulated, narrow-minded economic development projects that have been identified at this conference.

On the other hand, I am concerned, not only that the bulk of the income generated by tourism does not go into enhancing the local cultures and their environment, but that also tourism itself usually tends to destroy the very cultural and natural diversity that first attracted the outside world. Studies in the U. S. National Parks have clearly shown how intensive tourist use without regard for park carrying capacities can lead to ecosystem deterioration, logging, reser-

voirs, misplaced construction of highways, gas stations, hotels, restaurants, trailer camps, administrative buildings and a host of other uses that reduce the unique natural qualities for which the parks were established. If we are to retain some semblance of the world's natural diversity through creation of an earth-wide system of national parks supported by tourism, then tourism developments must be much more rigorously controlled than they have been in North America. Our reserve management must be designed to adequately protect and retain natural ecosystem diversity; to realize this will require limiting both the quality and quantity of man's use of natural areas.

Similarly, the impact of global tourism on unique cultures often leads to destruction of those very qualities that made these cultures unique. Cultural variety, at least in part, has evolved through periods of long group isolation and a relatively slow rate of introduction of new technological elements. With modern tourism comes cultural contact with new life-styles and value systems, high-speed jets, airport construction, road building, homogenized styles of resort and hotel architecture, monetary pressures to export local works of art, and an economic structure no longer independent, but subservient to the whims of the rich international tourist industry. On a global scale, the trend toward absorbing small-group cultural variety into a more uniform national (and even world) culture is proceeding at an amazing pace. In part, this is due to the spread of tourism, but it is much more a function of the rapid spread of new communications and transport technologies, along with large-scale economic development programs. The political surge away from local communities to nationalism also has contributed to loss of social diversity.

If our future development is not to diminish the world's immense natural and cultural variety, these fundamental problems must be realized, and new solutions must be found and acted upon. Developmental change must allow a dynamic evolution from within a broad series of differing value systems. And we must respect that, in many cases, the imposition of little or no outside change may be the most desirable goal.

CAIRNS: I want to mention a problem in this country that is beginning to assume enormous proportions, pollution from beef cattle in the Midwest. At a time when the government is encouraging municipalities to develop sewage treatment plants, the farmers of Kansas and other Midwestern states are building feed lots where cattle are concentrated in a very limited area, usually on rather hilly, rocky ground. The animals' wastes accumulate on this ground and are flushed into the stream during heavy rains, and the effect is very startling, to say the least.

The pollution equivalent of one head is that of about twenty-five to thirty-five people, so the amount of organic waste going into the streams of Kansas from this source exceeds the amount of waste from the human population by several orders of magnitude.

This pollution is, for the first time, turning the state water pollution control boards toward the regulation of agricultural wastes, but not rapidly enough.

FRASER DARLING: You are pinpointing, if I may say so, a tendency in all development of natural resources. To a farmer of the past, organic manure was the basis of his farming; now you don't know what to do with it. You run it down into the nearest river, which is crazy, when we still need that organic manure, but we haven't arrived at a socioeconomic system which could prevent waste. This matter should interest this conference as a whole, that developmental technology is so imperfect that we have worldwide waste, which we can't afford.

HEADY: At our home ranch in southern Idaho, if you will pardon a personal experience here, it is now much cheaper to apply chemical fertilizers than it is to haul the manure from the barnyard and put it on the land. Which are you going to do?

COMMONER: It is cheaper in your annual income, but what is the status of the land ten years from now?

HEADY: We have to live from year to year. (Laughter.)

COMMONER: I want to ask Dr. Borgstrom if he would go into what he regards as the reasons for the topsy-turvydom of the fish meal situation in which a vast protein resource is being shipped to exactly where it is not needed—to lower the price of broilers in the U.S. I would like to ask him if he sees any parallel to the situation in the feed lots in which the economic motivation is that the farmer must make a quick profit out of the use of his capital, his land. He simply can't afford to preserve the land, which is what he would do if he used the manure. In other words, it is a question of eating up capital.

BORGSTROM: Of course the immediate and easiest answer here is the very simple one that it pays off better. There is a greater profit margin in selling feed to the rich Western world than in selling food to impoverished Latin America.

In short-range terms of course, this is also economically acceptable, but it becomes almost a scandal that the international organizations have not entered into this to try to inculcate long-range perspective.

Having said this, I would like to bring out two more factors. One is the fact that if you go into the history of this Peruvian fishery, there is no question in my mind that it was initiated by the collapse of the California sardine industry. The California sardine industry was faced with overfishing, only some biologist, perhaps would not accept that. He said, perhaps, that there were other factors involved. But there was no doubt that it was too great an out-take and there was no basis for a sustained yield of the stock. All of a sudden the sardine disappeared. With this change went the tremendous boom in animal products production in the Western world, which started in the middle fifties. Until then, these sardines meant that we had constantly improved our nutritional situation in terms of eggs, poultry and meat.

Our American poultry meat is cheap, but this is basically due to the ocean. Besides what we are buying from the Peruvian catch, we are overusing our menhaden fish resources as well; in addition, we are buying still more fish meal protein, which all goes to explain the very low price of poultry meat.

This increased animal production in the rich Western world is due basically to two factors. One was the fish meal expansion of Peru and Chile and South Africa.

The other factor was the mobilization of oilseeds, which has led to the very surprising situation that the milk production of Europe today actually depends on two things. One is the fish meal influx and the other is the influx of oilseed from Africa. The European milk production could not be maintained without tropical Africa, another absurdity in today's terrible protein shortage.

I might furthermore add that I would call the Peruvian fishery easygoing capital market, because if you start looking at the investment which is taking place here, it is not only American. I am anxious to stress that it is really more West European, due to the circumstances which initiated it. It was first West German capital, Dutch capital, Norwegian capital, British capital and later also French capital. Then the U.S. moved in. We have been very instrumental, I think, in taking over bankrupt companies and putting in our capital and producing bigger units.

The boom, I will say, was so impressive to these capital markets that the degree of lending which was allowed was extremely high. This rate was also partly explained by the very reasonable urge of the Peruvian

government to try to get itself into this in order to channel some of this fish into the fish markets of Peru and into the fish markets of South America. That meant, of course, that they gave support to some national industries there, which perhaps has not really held up under this competitive pressure of the overinvestment.

COMMONER: You are saying this case is a form of nutritional colonialism?

BORGSTROM: Of course it is. I think it is even more extreme than any other case we have had here earlier.

HEDGPETH: It is a form of ecological plunder also. We shouldn't forget that 25 million tons is half the total ocean fisheries production and that from just one species. Now, some other fish have also had a bad history. The herring disappeared, nobody knows why, in the Middle Ages, and never returned.

This compares in a way to what has been said about the small numbers of species of animals used as food. The sea doesn't have the great diversity of land. Only about 20 per cent of all living species are marine; and while we may be using more fishes, I think we are depending, nevertheless, on comparatively few species.

I think Borgstrom's sermon is very well taken, but we don't seem to be learning very well from the history of our fisheries. Now, there has been developed another system of fishing, in Oregon, for instance. They come in with massive boats and clean out a large area. It may be five years before there is enough there to fish again. They also may be selecting the school members of the species, and leaving us with the scatterbroil. We don't know.

It is estimated that now that we have gotten rid of the blue whale, we have something like 50 to 200 million metric tons per year of what it fed upon to harvest if we can do it as efficiently as a whale could. This, however, is highly debatable.

But again, this would be a fish meal type

of fishery. As Chapman says, this would not be fishing for fish, it would be fishing for chickens! (Laughter.)

But there is another question that occurred to me. Now that the guano birds have had a decline (and you are cutting into them by taking that many more anchovies) maybe they, also, won't be able to come back; we just heard a gentleman from Peru yesterday say that the Peruvians would like some of the guano back, but we are going to unbalance that too.

BOULDING: I want to say I think many of you are doing a nice bit of preaching this afternoon, but as I look around I observe at least half the members of this conference are overweight. (Laughter.)

I wouldn't really say I feel that the preaching was very effective. I haven't heard a single practical suggestion as to what to do. This perhaps illustrates the weakness of those ecologists who can see problems but who don't have the remotest idea what the solutions are.

The plain fact is that the stuff you are talking about this afternoon has no solution whatever in the present stage of human organization. You don't have any world government. There is no world method of redistributing income, and there is not going to be for a long time. As long as there isn't, the people who have the income will enjoy it, as you have also enjoyed it, if I might say so.

So, I have a feeling that the sermon ought to be a little muted.

The whole concept of human need is practically worthless as an operational concept. That is the trouble. The only thing that is operational is demand: either economic or political. You don't solve this by going to socialism either, because that is an illusion, too. You don't solve it by planning either, because planning is 90 per cent ritual. (Laughter.) In any society whatever, planning is ritual, and will continue

to be so for a very long time to come, I suppose.

I am a good preacher myself, but I think one ought to recognize when you are preaching.

BATISSE: What I wanted to say is very much in line with what has just been said by Dr. Boulding.

It seems to me most of the papers this afternoon are going further than anything which has been said before in this conference: they are almost questioning the whole basic concept of development.

This applies to nomadism, if we want to conserve the nomads. This also applies to the tsetse fly. It may be desirable sometime to stop development, but I think we have to accept the fact that if we have development, this means control. It means control of the tsetse fly, and it also means control of the nomads.

All central governments will tell you this about the nomads. In fact, one of the main problems of development is that it not only means control over the environment but also means control over all the people everywhere. Perhaps this is the price we have to pay for development. Maybe we don't want development.

FRASER DARLING: Development is an effort to use something more productively than it had been, presumably; and I think the burden of this afternoon has been that there are areas which will not withstand the kind of development which the developer likes to manage.

I think that we could do much better in many cases by leaving things alone, which has nothing whatever to do with preserving nomads or preserving anything else, but it just happens to be the best way of land use pro tem.

DAVIS: I think I disagree with Dr. Boulding who just said demand is the only operational concept, not human need. Demand is made by advertising and also by creating public acceptance. You can't just put in high-protein food and tell the under-developed people that the high-protein nature of the food is why you should eat it. You have to dress the package up. A good example of that is the cereals we all have for breakfast. Very little nutrient value at all—and look at the vast amounts of money spent on persuading us to eat these cereals in the morning.

BORGSTROM: The whole question of human need and human demand is one of the key questions; I constantly find in discussing with my economist colleagues that they always seem to construct this world of demand or effective demands, whichever they call it. They bring out their models to fit this kind of world with its particular concepts, while as a biologist I like to start from the other end and look at man's biological requirements and need. I think it is very easy to formulate the minimum needs of protein today. We have all the knowledge that is required. When I then come to the conclusion that more than half of the world's population lacks the means required to fill these minimum needs, I say something is fundamentally wrong somewhere. Furthermore, you recognize we have a growing backlog of such malnourished people; we have not taken care of the 2.5 billion which we added in this century, and we are faced with 1 billion more people in the next ten years.

This increase in need will require a completely new approach, and the fact that I didn't mention programs doesn't mean I don't have programs. I will put it this way: If the Secretary of State in this country had been advised by a food scientist on foreign aid, he could have developed the most successful and cheapest foreign-aid program this country ever had. For example, we might have gone in and developed the Peruvian anchoveta industry as a foreign-aid program for food, not feed. I travel regularly through all the countries of the Andean area; and I have been to their markets and seen women literally tear each other's hair for only one little piece of dried fish from the adjacent lake. They know the value of this food, and they know the value everywhere man is hungry.

We might learn something from history. The Incas organized, as I already hinted, the whole distribution of this fish protein. Proper use now really would mean a big gain to Peru and to the Latin American continent. There is no question that we could remove all protein deficiency, and we also have the technical methods to do this without interfering with what I would call the dietary patterns of the area.

We don't need to go into fish protein concentrate, although I think that it is a very good possibility for the cities. I would like to remind you we have not faced this issue, either. We have a tremendous urban influx and we are getting slums, which in Latin America are overwhelming. I would like to submit another concrete suggestion. I think the General Assembly of the U.N. should make a general declaration that the oceans are the common property of mankind—and I really think that proposal would be supported. As far as I know the Russian situation, I think it would be supported by the U.S.S.R.

I have a book just in print on the Soviet fishing revolution. Their whole thinking has been very conservation-minded in terms of operation. With all due reverence to what was said here, I think they have been much more conservation-minded than the Japanese. I think they all realize, even the Japanese, that there is some need for international agreement. The minute we take this step we will also get the opportunity to develop completely new types of foreign aid.

RUSSELL: I want to comment on the problems of increasing animal productivity in Africa. One can do a great deal to increase productivity by putting money in areas where the rainfall is over 35 inches. In East Africa, there is a good example of a successful scheme where low-grade beef production has been converted to intensive milk production over quite large areas. Rainfall is over 35 inches in this particular case, the altitude over 7,000 feet. This conversion of what was once fairly poor land into high-production dairy land was made by the use of phosphate, fencing, water, dipping, housing, and the complete replacement of local stock by high-yielding dairy breeds.

There are other examples, still experimental, at altitudes of 4,000 to 5,000 feet, where we have been able to increase the annual liveweight gain of stock from 100 to 700 lbs. per acre. Here the rainfall is about 45 inches. Again the responsible factors were phosphate, plowing out the old vegetation and reseeding with suitable types of grass and legumes which will maintain palatability and digestibility over a good many months, and using production breeds of cattle.

If one puts one's sights on those areas where there is enough rainfall to grow a certain amount of fodder reliably, there appears to be no difficulty in having much more intensive animal production.

As long as one thinks in terms of areas where the rainfall is too erratic for reliable food production, you obviously can't have any great fodder production. I think we want to distinguish between those areas where production is possible with adequate water and those areas where we have to do something with the land but there is not enough rainfall to give reliable cropping.

Now it does happen in a great deal of East Africa—in fact it happened in a great deal of Kenya and Uganda—that because of scandalous overgrazing we have land that can't be cropped any longer at 35-inch rainfall. All the perennial grass has gone. The runoff is about 40 per cent of the rainfall. The soil never gets wet below about 18 inches, in spite of a 35-inch rainfall. We are in fact trying to grow plants on the equivalent of about 10 to 12 inches, which can't be done properly.

It is economical to try to farm land at a 35-inch rainfall for animal production. Economical farming of land for animal production below 25-inch rainfall in the tropics is I think very questionable.

FRASER DARLING: This is a needed corrective, but it happens that this group of papers were all dealing with the land outside your rainfall criteria, which is a pity. It would be so much better if development really went in on the land that would take it, but this is not the way in which governments have often seemed to act.

DAVIS: It is well known that in parts of Africa, if the people haven't had milk, they are nutritionally intolerant of it. You might bring in the best milk cows in the world and make the natives ill. It has been proven that the local majority can't tolerate milk. To effect successful change, you must do at least a pilot nutritional study before you put in different types of food.

MICHEL: The first point raised by Mr. Batisse has been bothering me throughout the session. We should at least ask the question, what do we mean by international development? I would say it is a deliberate process that is either controlled or controllable. For that reason, shouldn't we ask if a certain threshold in sophistication, in education, and in organization must not be crossed before we can meaningfully talk about international development programs? In other words, if ecologists are to bring any influence to bear on this process of international development, there must be some political or administrative body that is susceptible to reason or influence.

FRASER DARLING: Wait a minute. In international development, there is AID in this country and the Ministry of Overseas Development in Britain; there is a department in France—which is helping as far as possible with Southeast Asia and French Africa.

MICHEL: I mean on the recipient end, the people we are working with. Can you reasonably speak of international development directed to the Bedouin now? Can you speak of international development directed to the Bushman in Australia? To the indigenous population in New Guinea?

FRASER DARLING: I can, insofar as they receive international aid because so-called experts are going out all the time to oversee these jobs. We are not very much pleased with some of the jobs they are doing. This is really what the whole of this conference is about.

TRAIN: I had a comment a while ago. (Laughter.)

CROWCROFT: It is out of date now. (Laughter.)

TRAIN: I have two comments. First, Dr. Borgstrom mentioned the possibility of a U.N. resolution declaring the seas to be common property of the world, and he said the U.S.S.R. might support it. I would just comment that it seems equally possible that the U.S. might oppose it.

Second, I will just mention the feed lot problem. I suggest it is not only an ecological problem. The rapid growth of feed lots in the Midwest is due in part to U.S. federal tax policy. It is a very useful tax shelter whereby if you have high income this year you can shift it to next year by buying your cattle this year in December, prepaying your interest and feed costs, selling your cattle six months later at ordinary rates, not capital gains, thereby shifting your income from one year to the other. This is a major reason for the growth, and it indicates the complexities of the environmental problem.

BORGSTROM: I had the privilege of attending the American Assembly meeting a couple of weeks ago that was attended by the Administration and their leaders in various areas. It was unanimously agreed among these American experts that this line of approach of internationalizing the seas was one that should be taken and was equally important to the U.S. The U.S. has not really pioneered the development of the oceans in the postwar period, which makes it more essential that we join in all such international efforts. They all agreed on that.

MCNEIL: I would like to come back for a moment to the problem of nomadism and the settlement of these people. Apparently most remarks here seem to imply the nomads themselves had nothing to do with this process and I think we should clarify this. In the Sudan right now, there is a question of appropriation of tremendous sums of money for the creation of water holes throughout the savannah belt. These would be deep boreholes requiring very high capital investment.

The pressure for this activity comes from the nomad councils themselves, who hope to increase their capability to produce cattle. The same people accept no controls on arranging management, so that the water holes they have are virtually useless. Indeed, they may spur serious overgrazing. I predict that, even if we spend all this money on the development of the new water holes, in a very short period of time we will be back where we started.

TALBOT: I think that the sermon by Reverend Boulding indicated—[laughter] —that some of us have not gotten our point across. It isn't a question of the ecologists being antidevelopment in these case histories we have been talking about. It is more a question of the fact that we, as ecologists, provided the methodology for this range-land development over fifty years ago. The methodology has been well known. It just wasn't accepted. Dr. Russell's point is very well taken also, that the most intensive development clearly should have been on the better lands, but the greater part of the range lands are not these better lands. We have also the choice of trying to manage ranges artificially and expensively or looking for some cheaper, better, and more natural way to get productivity. Here again, the ecologists have shown that one way to do it is through wildlife management and cropping. One problem, though, was evidenced in discussions earlier, that wildlife brings up curious emotions. It is a subject which puts funny-colored dark glasses on many people.

In 1963, when I was part of a U.N. mission looking into the development of wildlife in Eastern and Central Africa, we went to Rhodesia. We were told by some people that the game ranches had been a total failure, and others said they had been a great success. It wasn't until we got to the game ranches that we found they were indeed a success. We saw about nine at that point, four years after they had been started. This last summer I heard there were about forty such ranches. The domestic livestock industry had government veterinary facilities, cold storage facilities, and a number of other things, whereas a large number of obstacles were put in the way of game ranching. The fact that game ranches could succeed with people who were merely interested in the money indicates that there was a pretty solid ecological and economic base. This, of course, is subject to mismanagement as is any other form of land use.

MARSHALL: I would like to go back to Dr. Borgstrom's point that with half the world going hungry there is indeed something wrong, and I would like to support his contention. But I would like also to recognize what Dr. Boulding said concerning the relationship between demand and need. If you twist it around the other way, you would talk about the demand of the groups of people who would have to be the suppliers of the food and on whom most of the burden would fall. I don't feel there is any evidence whatsoever that these people have any willingness to undertake

this activity. I think this is what perhaps happens in the absence, as Dr. Boulding said, of world government.

If we consider only this country, for example, I don't think there is any real evidence that the bulk of the American people are really concerned about the problems of poor Americans, regardless of race. I don't think that there is any evidence that the British, for example, having done quite well in Africa and India for one hundred years, are very able to tolerate 1 or 2 per cent of their home island's population being poor or black right now. I think the situation in Rhodesia and South Africa and Mozambique and Angola more or less speaks for itself. I think this is sort of a massive exercise in delusion.

FRASER DARLING: I think you are making the ecologist's mistake of overgeneralization. For example, you said the British people are objecting now to 1 or 2 per cent. It is a very, very small percentage of the British people who are objecting. But when they object they object very, very vociferously.

MARSHALL: I don't think it is a poor example, Dr. Fraser Darling. I don't think it matters that a majority of the people don't agree with the minority. It is what they do about it. If they are indifferent, that is, if they do nothing, it is as if this small minority that you speak of in fact speaks for the majority of people who are silent. Indifference is just as bad as a completely negative attitude.

FRASER DARLING: I will drop this one—

COMMONER: I just want to enter an optimistic note and it is simply this: People do have a conscience. After all, the Bible was based on it. But the trouble is that the raw material, the factual substance out of which the modern conscience has to be constructed, is hidden from people. How many Americans know the terrible story that Dr. Borgstrom tells? How many of them know that when they go to the supermarket and enjoy the low price of a cage-bred broiler chicken they are literally encouraging the starvation of already starving people? We have in our country campaigns to aid the Biafrans. There *is* such a thing as conscience. It seems to me that we don't know whether Reverend Boulding is right or wrong or whether Marshall's pessimism is right or wrong, because we have not given the modern human conscience the opportunity to exercise itself. We won't know whether our people are going to come out on one side or the other until we give them the facts.

My own belief is that when we who know the facts get them before the public, a new bible—so to speak—will be written, and it will come out on the side of human welfare.

MILTON: This discussion points up the great difficulty in obtaining effective national concern and action for global or distant environmental problems. Most of the biospheric resources we are concerned with here are free, non-priced resources which traditionally have been on a first-come, first-served basis. Because they have not been priced, few people have been concerned about these "free" resources until quite recently, when the problems have become overwhelmingly obvious. However, when you try to develop local concern for distant, long-range, complex environmental resource problems, it becomes particularly hard to stir the ecological conscience. Not only are these resources considered part of the "common" environment, but the threats to them seem particularly remote and impersonal. Additionally, we should also remember that environmental reform is not yet a strong popular movement outside the minority group of rich, mass media-saturated, "over-developed" nations.

GILLHAM: Dr. West spoke about development in Rhodesia having led to a reduction in wildlife, particularly in the tribal areas. Now here we have about 400,000 families who traditionally have depended on the women producing the grain and the men producing the protein in the form of hunting. The lack of protein in this situation, and I think in many comparable situations, has arisen through the disappearance of the wildlife. This protein must be replaced at the present time, somehow, and the most obvious way appears to be some high-protein, cheap form of food.

FRASER DARLING: Many people are in for the traumatic experience of realizing that some countries can't carry the populations which they have, and nobody will really get down to this. If there is a place with only one person to the square mile like the Kasempa District in Central Africa, they say what we must do is get some people there and get something moving. Yet, there isn't the potential environmental wherewithal in that particular area to have a larger population. It would be better if there were no people at all there and it were left alone for a century or more. But we don't ever face this question of carrying capacity.

It is very cruel to think in these terms at all. But the longer we delay facing reality, the more we will have to face the question of this small planet's regional and overall carrying capacity in the future.

MYRDAL: I would like to raise my voice in support of Reverend Boulding. On the optimistic side I would first like to remind you that before the Second World War only one person in the world I know of—and it was my wife—talked much about giving aid to underdeveloped countries. Today most of the industrialized world is involved in the aid process.

I do believe we need more multilateral settlements. I think it is very wrong if you in the U.S. all the time talk about your huge expenditures on aid, particularly when you, on a per capita basis, provide so little aid. If you are honest, about one-third or one-half of this $1.8 billion from the U.S. goes to South Vietnam, which nobody in the world recognizes as an underdeveloped country, as a consequence of your involvement in that war. You now are listed as seventh in relation to your GNP, but you are giving very much less than that, in fact, to really constructive, nonmilitary aid.

Your Marshall Plan aid was once presented as being in the best interests of the U.S. I know America well enough to know that at the time the Marshall aid was given very much on humanitarian grounds; I call this a perverse puritanism, a suspicion against your own good intentions. Then of course you shifted emphasis, and now aid is indeed from the military and strategic interest.

My feeling is—and here I think I am on the same line as my friend Commoner—that ordinary Americans are not very impressed by the political and strategic interests of the U.S., and particularly not when you have such a failure of this philosophy as in the Vietnam war. I feel also that if we want to raise aid substantially and be able to run it, we have to have multilateral organizations in order to get away from highly political bilateral organizations. I feel that we will have to motivate aid-giving on moral grounds, and I say this not as a moralist but as a social scientist.

In my country, in Sweden, where we are very much the same sort of people as you, the pressure for aid is from the people on the establishment. They have compelled the politicians, when there was an election, to promise increased assistance abroad and this led to the decision that they will increase aid. I say that if we are going to raise our contribution to be able to take care of, for instance, a project like Borgstrom's, we have to argue it in terms of compassionate solidarity with poor people. And we must make people aware of the real situation in the poor countries.

DASMANN: Dr. Fraser Darling has asked me to stress some of the points in common among a group of diverse papers in this session and a discussion that has ranged even more widely. I will omit Dr. Borgstrom's paper from this consideration since it stands apart, although it has implications for the entire conference of which we must remain aware. I will discuss only the arid and semiarid range lands of the world and the attempts that have been made to develop them. These lands have a carrying capacity for domestic or wild animals that is based on the productivity of the vegetation, availability of water, and other factors. This carrying capacity sets limits on the numbers of animals that can be supported, and these limits cannot be ignored without destructive consequences. Whether nomads or sedentary people, whether domestic livestock or wild animals use these lands, the limits set by carrying capacity must be respected. If they are not, the productivity will decline, the carrying capacity will be lowered, and eventually the land can support little or nothing. This is an ecological principle that must govern development practice.

Admittedly, on some lands, we can raise carrying capacity by providing water, changing the character of the vegetation, providing some needed element in the soil, or in other ways. This permits an increase in the numbers of livestock or wild animals, and this in turn could provide a better standard of living for the existing human population, or help provide a livelihood for a growing number of people. However, the new limits of carrying capacity must then be respected, or once again productivity will be destroyed, and the lands degraded.

Many development projects, whether in Australia, Masailand, Saudi Arabia, or Rhodesia, fail because they do not take this question of carrying capacity into consideration. Water is provided, perhaps, and the land is thus enabled to support more animals and people. But seldom is provision made to hold populations at the new levels that land can support. In consequence, the land deteriorates, deserts spread or become more barren, and a greater number of people end up worse off than they were before development of the area took place.

Admittedly, political and social pressures within the developing countries can force governments to proceed with projects that are doomed in the long run to fail. One can question, however, whether responsible international development agencies should continue to play this losing game. Rather, should they not insist that carrying capacity will be respected and that the numbers of animals in these developed areas will be kept within these bounds?

Few people question the long-run desirability of controlling an insect pest such as the tsetse fly, and a disease such as foot-and-mouth, which are at present inhibiting the use of broad areas of the developing world, or greatly restricting the production of domestic animals. Yet many of us had hoped that the tsetse fly might hold out until the people of Africa acquired some good sense about land management. Now it appears that the fly may go before good sense arrives.

If the disappearance of the tsetse fly leads once more only to uncontrolled livestock grazing of the liberated areas, the future of these lands will be bleak indeed. If instead, studies were conducted to determine the most productive land uses—by wildlife, livestock, or both—and if the use of these lands were to be governed with proper respect for their long-term productive capacity, with adequate arrangement for control of the numbers of animals and men, then the development of the former tsetse lands could be a source of encouragement for the world. But one needs constantly to question whether a development project substitutes a lower value for a higher. Economists alone cannot answer that question. Social and ecological judgments are also involved.

Our technological civilization is busy blotting out indigenous cultures and separate ways of life over the earth. We say it is an inevitable price of progress, meaning that we do not want to worry about it, or to question our own concept of progress. We decide here, and in our development agencies, that nomads cannot survive as such, and so we proceed to see to it that they do not. Yet, each separate way of life, each different cultural pattern, may hold some key to human survival for the future; keys, the existence of which our narrow technological minds may have long ago forgotten. One need ask whether the welfare of today's people can be enhanced without sacrifice of these older human values.

I was impressed by Dr. Russell's statement that one must put development money into areas where it is most certain to pay off—and this could spare the marginal grazing lands where nomads and wildlife might well be left alone. More food can be produced more quickly from the better soils in the moderate rainfall belts. The experiences in the developed countries have borne this out, and in the United States we are still retiring great areas of land from agricultural use because we can get greater gains for less cost from our best lands. Yet in the developing nations we are still creating enormous problems for the future by destroying natural vegetation and wildlife in agriculturally marginal lands where neither numbers of people nor of livestock are being controlled.

The earth as a whole has a carrying capacity for people. In terms of providing for each man an adequate environment in which he can develop his full potential as a human being, we may well have already exceeded the carrying capacity for this planet. If by our development efforts we only continue to make such a situation worse, to guarantee only a less meaningful life for greater numbers of people, then we should stop and consider our aims and objectives.

V SPECIAL PROBLEMS OF ENVIRONMENTAL DEGRADATION

Gilbert F. White, Chairman

42. Ecological Hazards fom Nuclear Power Plants   *Dean E. Abrahamson*   795

43. Atomic Waste Disposal in the Sea: An Ecological Dilemma? *Joel W. Hedgpeth*   812

44. Environmental Quality and the Thermal Pollution Problem   *John Cairns, Jr.*   829

      DISCUSSION   854

45. An Ecological Overview of Caribbean Development Programs   *Carl A. Carlozzi*   858

46. Man's Effects on Island Ecosystems   *F. R. Fosberg*   869

47. Some Ecological Factors in Development Projects in the Dominican Republic
                                                        Wolfram U. Drewes   881

      DISCUSSION   892

48. Experiments with the Use of Case Histories in an Ecology Seminar
                                                        Thane Riney   903

49. Organizing Scientific Investigations to Deal with Environmental Impacts
                                                        Gilbert F. White   914

50. An Ecological Approach to International Development: Problems of Policy and
Administration   *Lynton K. Caldwell*   927

      DISCUSSION   948

A BALLAD OF ECOLOGICAL AWARENESS (continued)

A cost of exercising power is much unwanted heat,
So victory is found to be a species of defeat,
And no amount of slick brochures can cultivate a taste
For dead and tepid rivers and for radioactive waste.

The growth of population has a great deal of momentum,
Neither spirals, interruptus, or safer still, absentum
Can do much about the kids who are already on the scene,
Who will still be in the labor force in twenty-seventeen.
So there isn't very much that the developed world can do
To help that poor old woman in the very crowded shoe.

—KENNETH E. BOULDING

42. ECOLOGICAL HAZARDS FROM NUCLEAR POWER PLANTS

Dean E. Abrahamson

Environmental risks associated with the nuclear power industry are discussed in this paper. Not only is the nuclear industry expanding rapidly in the United States, but there is a major effort under way to sell the concept of large nuclear complexes in both developed and the developing countries.

Over two-thirds of the total heat generated by a nuclear power station is discharged as waste into the local environment. Should this heat be introduced into lakes, rivers, or estuaries, serious and widespread changes can be expected.

Vast quantities of radioactive wastes are formed in nuclear reactors and a portion of these wastes are presently being discharged into the local environment of the reactor. Should this practice continue as the nuclear industry expands, it will create a serious health and environmental hazard. The sources, quantities, and possible effects of the wastes, both thermal and radioactive, are outlined.

Radioactive wastes are formed in highly concentrated form. Because they are so concentrated, they could be contained and, unlike fossil fuel wastes, need not be released into the environment. As with other wastes, it costs more to contain them than to dump them into the nearest waters or into the atmosphere.

The growth of the nuclear industry in the United States has been the natural consequence of an increasing need for electrical power coupled with governmental programs dedicated to success in peaceful exploitation of nuclear energy. More than one hundred nuclear-fueled electric power plants are already planned (U.S. AEC, Nov. 14, 1968). In addition to the growing nuclear power industry in the United States, the United States Atomic Energy Commission is pressing plans for major nuclear plants in other countries. These plans are summarized in a recent AEC news release (U.S. AEC, Aug. 20, 1968):

. . . A typical industrial complex such as those studied could include interrelated industrial processes for the production of fertilizers, aluminum, phosphorus, caustic-chlorine and ammonia. The agro-industrial complex would be located on the sea coast and include large scale desalting of sea water for highly intensified irrigated agriculture. Nuclear reactors producing low cost power would serve as the energy source for the electrical and other energy requirements of the complexes.

The study indicated that the energy center concept might have application in Australia, India, Mexico, the Middle East, Peru, and the United States. Included are a number of locations where agro-industrial complexes could be attractive and provide needed food supplies to the regions. It is expected that the energy center concept may be attractive for other areas not specifically identified in the report. . . .

Detailed discussion of these plans has already been held with the governments of India, Mexico, and other nations of less industrial development. In another recent AEC news release these agro-industrial complexes are discussed with particular reference to the Middle East (U.S. AEC, June 11, 1968).

. . . The study group, including experts from Government, industry, foundations and universities, will estimate the power and water requirements of the Middle East; survey the sources and availability of raw materials for industrial products; survey the domestic and export markets including price and demand relationships for the products from such a complex; identify specific locations where the soil, climate and other conditions are suitable for agricultural development using desalted water for irrigation; design and estimate costs for agro-industrial complexes at specific locations; and define the need for experimental or pilot projects to assure the success of larger projects. . . .

In view of the tremendous potential for ecological and social change which would result from these complexes, it might be expected that the advice of ecologists, biologists, and social scientists would be sought in the planning of the programs. Little mention of these considerations is found, however, in the releases of the Atomic Energy Commission or its associated industries and agencies. The summary report (U.S. AEC, July, 1968) describing the industrial and agro-industrial complexes makes no mention of the social or environmental effects of these projects.

One does find remarks such as were made by AEC Commissioner James T. Ramey at a recent meeting (Sept. 5, 1968):

. . . Today the engineers have command (of the fast reactor development) and are busily seeing to it that a solid technical base is laid for the construction of demonstration plants. The day is near at hand when the executives, the financiers, and the lawyers will begin to play a key role in providing the management initiative, the indispensable dollars, and the sound arrangements for building these demonstration plants.

And later in the same address:

The potential of nuclear desalting is international—covering the whole rim of the Mediterranean including Spain, Italy, Greece, Israel, and the Arab countries, together with India and Pakistan, as well as our own Southwest and Latin America—and I am sure we will ultimately see this potential realized. However, the problems of management may be further complicated by the addition of foreign countries, international organization, and all of the other complexities associated with international relations.

Although these remarks were made at a meeting of the Federal Bar Association, and perhaps the emphasis on management and financing was appropriate, it does seem that mention might have been made of the biosystem which might be affected by these giant industrial complexes.

The environmental implications of the nuclear industry are not being entirely ignored. The transcript of a series of hearings before the United States Joint Committee on Atomic Energy contains a section headed

"Ecological Considerations." The entire section reads (see Hearings, April 30, May 1–3, 1968):

REPRESENTATIVE HOLIFIELD. But it [the reactor] would require more extensive cooling towers, and therefore, it would be more expensive?

MR. RAMEY. To that extent, yes, sir.

REPRESENTATIVE HOSMER. These are fads. Coming into the climate of economics of these plants are some sociological considerations, I gather. Thermal effects must be technologically zero, plants must be pretty and out of sight, and heaven knows what else, as we develop all of these things.

Regulation must be contended with in ever-increasing degrees. Doesn't that throw some variable in your economics of plants that you have to consider?

MR. RAMEY. I think these would have some effects, yes.

REPRESENTATIVE HOSMER. Let us try to get into this thing. I would like to get a feeling for this ecological basis.

When Senator Aiken's ancestors came up to Vermont they took all of the pretty stones and took them out of the fields, and piled them up to make fences out of them. And they cut down and burned up the trees, and they dragged their wagon wheels all over the country side and chased the Indians away and made other changes and they have been doing it ever since.

MR. RAMEY. There are some who love it, though.

SENATOR AIKEN. They weren't ecological at that time. Ecology is a recent part of a lot of people's vocabulary.

REPRESENTATIVE HOSMER. It is a fad.

SENATOR AIKEN. I think so.

REPRESENTATIVE HOSMER. We have gone through these dialogs and these other semantics around here but I guess it is important. Some people think it is.

How much of this nature is going to have to be left unchanged in relation to a constantly increasing population and industrialization, and all of the other things?

We can talk about ecology all we want but who is going to make the rules as to what changes are within the ballgame and what are not?

NUCLEAR REACTORS

A nuclear generating plant, (Fig. 42-1) is similar to a conventional steam plant except that the heat source, the reactor core, depends on the fission reaction in uranium, instead of burning coal, oil, or gas.

Heat is generated in the reactor core and is transferred to the primary coolant water

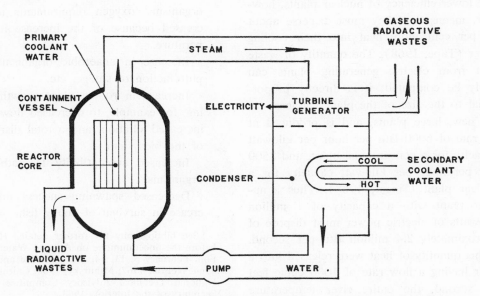

Figure 42–1 Schematic drawing of a boiling-water nuclear power reactor

surrounding the core. This water is heated, converted to steam and passed through a pipe into the turbine-generator where electricity is generated. After passing through the turbine, the water is recondensed in the condenser and is pumped back into the primary reactor vessel to complete the primary coolant loop. The single-cycle system described here is characteristic of a boiling-water reactor.

The primary coolant water, which is in direct contact with the reactor core, becomes highly radioactive. This water is contained in a closed system. However, this water is removed and replaced about once a month. It is not exchanged all at once, but in a gradual process of leaks and purposeful removal.

Cool water, the secondary coolant, passes into the condenser and removes the waste heat. For every three units of heat generated, one unit is converted into electricity and two units are waste.

QUANTITY OF THERMAL WASTE

Thermal waste is the pollutant common both to conventional and nuclear plants. The lower efficiency of nuclear plants, however, means that they must disperse about 50 per cent more heat into their cooling water (Tape, 1968). The quantity of waste heat from electric generating plants can easily be computed; it is directly proportional to the size of the plant (at least for the new, large plants, and is produced at the rate of 6000 Btu per hour per kilowatt capacity for a conventional plant, and 8500 Btu per hour per kilowatt capacity for a nuclear plant (Singer, 1968). Thus a nuclear plant with a capacity of 1 million kilowatts of electric power must dispose of approximately 2.4 million Btu per second. If this quantity of heat were released into a river having a flow rate of 1000 cubic feet per second, the entire river temperature would rise by 33 degrees Fahrenheit. This is also sufficient heat to furnish the entire heating needs of approximately 36,000 two-story houses in a subarctic climate such as found in Minnesota.

EFFECTS OF THERMAL POLLUTION

The biological and other effects associated with thermal pollution have been discussed at length in several recent publications.[1] Some of the frequently mentioned effects include:

Thermal death—the sudden death of aquatic life due directly to increased temperature.

An increased predation rate, due, for example, to changes in avoidance reactions induced by temperature changes, decrease in swimming speed and stamina, etc.

Increased susceptibility of aquatic organisms to chemical or physical toxins.

Disruption of normal biological rhythms.

Disruption of migration patterns.

Decreased oxygen concentrations in heated waters at the same time as the organisms' oxygen requirements are increased because of the increase in temperature.

Increase in anaerobic organisms with putrefaction of sludge, etc.

Increase in rooted plant growth leading, for example, to decreased flow rates, increased siltation, and a total disruption of the biosystem.

Increased susceptibility to pathogenic organisms.

Decreased spawning success and decrease in survival of young fish.

[1] See bibliography for further details. Hearings before the Subcommittee on Air and Water Pollution, February 6, 13, 14, 1968; McKee and Wolf, 1964; Nelson, 1967; Mihursky, 1968; Cairns, 1968; National Technical Advisory Committee to the Secretary of the Interior, 1968.

Death from thermal shock caused by rapid changes in water temperature.

Increased growth of taste-producing and odor-producing organisms such as blue-green algae.

Changes in efficiency of water purification and treatment methods.

Effects on various industrial processes which are temperature-dependent.

Replacement of cold-water species by other species. Effects on swimming and other recreational uses; increased decomposition of sludge, increase in sludge gas, increase in saprophytic bacteria and fungi, increase in algae formation.

Increase in incorporation of radioactive wastes into organic material and hence into the food chains when radioactive wastes are discharged along with thermal wastes (for example in association with a nuclear power plant).

It is possible that the vast quantities of heat from power plants can be used in a constructive manner. Several such possibilities have been suggested (Tape, 1968; see Hearings, Feb. 1968). Once again, however, it has been an economic question; is there more immediate economic gain from uti-

lizing the waste heat in a constructive manner or from releasing it into the river, lake, or estuary? It is only relatively recently that the true costs associated with thermal pollution have been considered.

If other nations follow the pattern set by the United States—the construction of even larger central power stations—they may benefit by counting such costs in their planning.

RADIOACTIVE WASTE PRODUCTION

To understand the processes by which the radioactive wastes can escape into the local environment, it is necessary to consider briefly the construction of a reactor. The reactor fuel, usually uranium dioxide, is formed into small pellets (Fig. 42–2). These pellets are stacked into a long, thin-walled tube, the cladding, to make up the fuel rods. Each fuel rod is approximately one-half inch in diameter and twelve feet long. The fuel rods are assembled into fuel elements which in turn are stacked into a larger mechanical structure to form the reactor core (Fig. 42–3). The core of a

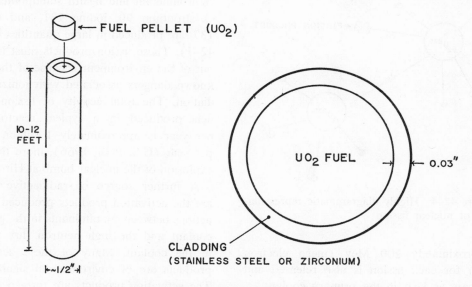

Figure 42–2 Uranium dioxide fuel pellets and fuel rods

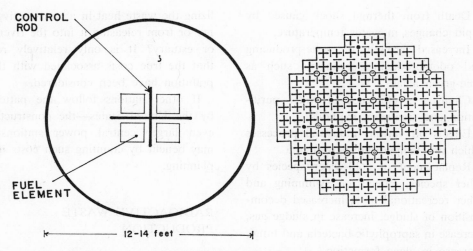

Figure 42–3   Arrangement of fuel elements and control rods in the reactor core

typical 500,000 kilowatt nuclear plant contains approximately 23,000 fuel rods. The primary coolant circulates through the spaces between the individual fuel rods.

The reaction itself is fission of uranium 235. A neutron is absorbed by the uranium nucleus resulting in an extremely unstable product which splits, producing on the average 2.5 neutrons and two new nuclei, the fission or daughter products (Fig. 42–4).

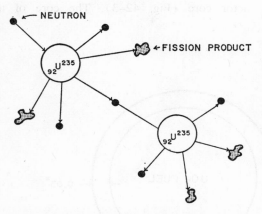

Figure 42–4   Highly diagrammatic representation of nuclear fission

Approximately 200 Mev (mega electron volt) for each fission is also released and appears as heat in the primary coolant.

The fission products cause difficulties both regarding the operation of the reactor and the contamination of the environment. Many of the fission products have a high affinity for neutrons and can ultimately poison the reactor by absorbing sufficient neutrons so that the chain fission reaction can no longer take place. The fission products are also highly radioactive.

The fission product abundance spectrum peaks in the vicinity of nuclear mass 95 and again near 140. Radioactive isotopes which are particularly significant from the environmental and health standpoints, such as strontium 90, iodine 131, and cesium 137, are produced in large quantities (Table 42–1). These fission products must be kept out of the environment because of the well-known dangers associated with ionizing radiation. The total activity of fission products produced in a typical reactor core per year is approximately 1 billion curies per year (U.S. PHS, 1966), more than the explosion of the nuclear bomb at Hiroshima.

A further source of radioactive wastes are the activation products produced by reactions between contaminants in the primary coolant and the high neutron flux present in the coolant. Many of these activation products are of environmental significance. The activation products are formed directly in the primary coolant and are released

Table 42-1

SOME FISSION PRODUCTS WHICH ARE
IMPORTANT TO PUBLIC HEALTH AND
ENVIRONMENTAL CONTAMINATION
(USPHS, 1966)

MASS	NUCLIDE AND HALF-LIFE		CRITICAL ORGAN	QUANTITY PRODUCED*
85	Krypton	10.6 years	Lung, skin	0.3
89	Strontium	51 days	Bone	58.5
90	Strontium	28 years	Bone	1.5
131	Iodine	8.1 days	Thyroid	36.0
133	Iodine	21 hours	Thyroid	36.0
137	Cesium	30 years	Total body	0.5
141	Cesium	33 days	Total body	76.5

*Millions of curies (excluding daughter products) of fission product produced in a 500 Mw(e) reactor during one year of operation followed by one day of decay.

into the environment, except as they are removed by the waste treatment system. Nuclear power stations now being planned include some treatment facilities for the effluent streams; however, it is not neces-sary to discharge any radioactive wastes from these plants. These discharges are made only because it is less expensive to re-lease the wastes than to separate them from the waste streams and retain them.

Radioactive hydrogen, tritium, is not in-cluded in Table 42–1 although it is a fission product. More tritium is formed via other reactions than via fission. The quantity of tritium produced and released is considered later as an example of a radioisotope not removed by the waste treatment systems.

RELEASE OF RADIOACTIVE WASTES INTO THE ENVIRONMENT

Some of the fission products escape into the primary coolant and are available for release into the local environment. In ad-dition, the bulk of the activation products are formed, or can diffuse into, the primary coolant. It should be emphasized that not all of the fission products which are pro-duced are available for local release. Also,

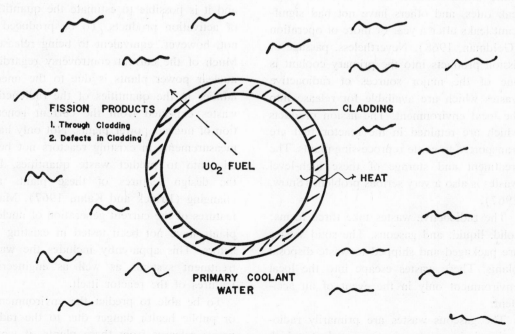

FISSION PRODUCTS
1. Through Cladding
2. Defects in Cladding

CLADDING

UO₂ FUEL

HEAT

PRIMARY COOLANT WATER

Figure 42–5 Sources of fission products which escape into the primary coolant

those radioactive wastes which are released are done so deliberately. They are released because release is cheaper than retention; the only gain is a slightly (and to date unspecified) reduced power cost to the consumer.

The fission products are produced in the uranium oxide fuel pellets. The cladding surrounding the fuel is 0.02 to 0.04 inch thick and is surrounded by the primary coolant water (Fig. 42–5). Fission products can pass through intact cladding by diffusion and other processes, or they can pass through defects in the cladding. There may be 500,000 linear feet of cladding in a reactor core. It is difficult to fabricate this amount of thin-walled tubing without leaks either initially or after prolonged exposure to high temperatures and high neutron flux.

The waste disposal systems of current power reactors are being designed with a maximum of 1 per cent of the fuel rods having cladding defects. This does not imply that 1 per cent of each of the fission products necessarily escapes, or that there will be a 2 per cent defect in each reactor core. Some initial reactor cores have had high leak rates, and others have not had significant leaks after a year or more of operation (Goldman, 1968). Nevertheless, passage of fission products into the primary coolant is one of the major sources of radioactive wastes which are available for release into the local environment. The fission products which are retained in the reactor fuel are transported to waste reprocessing plants. The treatment and storage of these high-level wastes is also a very serious problem (Snow, 1967).

The radioactive wastes take three forms: solid, liquid, and gaseous. The solid wastes are packaged and shipped to waste disposal plants. These wastes escape into the local environment only in the event of an accident.

The gaseous wastes are primarily radioactive fission and activation products which are carried over into the turbine with the steam but do not recondense as does the water. These gases are discharged into the local environment, frequently using an approximately three-hundred-foot stack to aid in their dilution.

Leaks in the primary containment structures, drains from the laboratories, and purposeful removal of the primary coolant give rise to the liquid radioactive wastes. It is usually proposed to treat this water and then to add it to the condenser cooling water (the secondary coolant) prior to discharge. The secondary coolant does not contain significant quantities of radioactive wastes; however, prior to its return to the river, these wastes are added to it.

THE QUANTITY OF RADIOACTIVE WASTE

The quantities of radioactive wastes which are discharged into the local environment are not as well known as are the quantities of thermal waste. The quantities of fission products produced in the reactor are known, and it is possible to estimate the quantities of activation products. To be produced is not, however, equivalent to being released. Much of the current controversy regarding nuclear power plants is due to the uncertainties in the quantities of the radioactive wastes expected from the current generation of nuclear power plants. Not only have measurements in existing reactors not been adequate to predict waste quantities, but the design features of these plants are changing (Brinck and Kahn, 1967). Many features of the current generation of nuclear plants have not been tested in existing reactors. This apparently includes the waste treatment systems as well as engineering features of the reactor itself.

To be able to predict the environmental or public health danger due to the radioactive releases from these plants, it would be necessary to know the quantities of each nuclide in the waste and also the chemical form of the nuclide. These data are not available (Brinck and Kahn, 1967). The release of a given quantity of strontium 90 or iodine 131 cannot be equated with the same quantity of, for example, one of the radioactive noble gases.

The manufacturer does estimate the quantities of wastes from nuclear power reactors.[2] These estimates should probably be interpreted as lower limits. Although these estimates are made for nuclear electrical generating reactors, they would probably also apply for a large reactor used, for example, for desalinization. A large boiling-water reactor (1 million kilowatts electric capacity) would discharge a minimum of 12,000 curies of gaseous waste per year. In the case of 1 per cent fuel leaks, the gaseous waste would be made up primarily of fission products and would be discharged at a rate approaching 20 million curies per year (Abrahamson and Pogue, 1968). In making these estimates it is assumed that the bulk of the gaseous discharge would be noble gases. A review of the research and development efforts of the Atomic Energy Commission shows that several are associated with the removal of iodines from reactor effluents.[3] That such research is necessary, and that all of the gaseous wastes released are not noble gases is suggested in the conclusion stated in the report of a study done at the University of Nevada (Blincoe, 1962, 1963):

This constant level [of iodine 131 in the thyroid glands of cattle] in the absence of [nuclear weapons] testing indicates that all the I-131 in the biosphere is not from nuclear explosions. Some other processes must be

[2] See, for example, the Facility Description and Safety Analysis Report for any of the reactors now operating or under construction. Available at U.S. AEC public document room, Washington, D.C.

[3] See, for example, the current events section of *Nuclear Safety*, published regularly by the Division of Technical Information, U. S. Atomic Energy Commission.

producing I-131 at a reasonably constant rate and in copious quantities. The principal known source of I-131 that could contribute to this level is exhaust gases from nuclear reactors and associated fuel reprocessing plants.

Radioactive iodine is one of the most noxious of the wastes being produced by nuclear reactors. The various radioactive isotopes of iodine are also among the most abundant of the reactor wastes. Approximately 72 million curies of I-131 are produced per year in a 1 million kilowatt (electrical) nuclear reactor (U.S. PHS, 1966). Radioiodine will not be removed from the gaseous effluent under normal operating conditions by the waste treatment system planned for power reactors now under construction in the United States.

The radioactive wastes in the liquid effluent from a plant of this size can also be estimated, but the quantity of these wastes depends critically on several factors including the extent of the waste treatment employed. The only component of the liquid waste which can be estimated with reasonable accuracy is tritium, radioactive hydrogen. No waste treatment yet proposed will remove tritium from the liquid or gaseous effluents from nuclear reactors (Smith, 1967). The total quantity of tritium which is produced by a 1 million kilowatt (electrical) nuclear plant has been estimated at 130,000 curies during its first year of operation and somewhat less in subsequent years (Abrahamson and Pogue, 1968). With present practice, all of this tritium is released either at the reactor site or at the site of the fuel reprocessing plant. The United States Public Health Service (1967) has estimated that about half of the tritium is released at the reactor site.

The phenomena associated with radioactive materials and the units used to measure quantities of radioactivity are outside of our usual experience and it is difficult to convey a feeling for these quantities. Although it is not directly applicable in terms of biological effect, it is useful to compare the quantities of radioisotopes from weapons testing or nuclear reactors with the quantity of radium which would contain the same amount of activity. A curie is equivalent to the activity in one gram of radium. We can all recall the excitement and intensive searches instituted when a capsule containing a few milligrams of radium had been lost or misplaced. Yet the quantity of radioactivity proposed for release from a single nuclear power plant each year, even under the most optimistic assumptions as to its operation, is several times the activity in the entire world supply of radium. We are being asked to dismiss lightly this discharge of radioactivity.

Tritium discharge can also be used to illustrate another point which has confused discussions of radioactive wastes and the quantities of radioisotopes already present in the environment. It has been suggested that the added tritium would not be greater than the quantity of tritium already present, in, for example, the Mississippi River. However, this tritium is itself due to pollution via the fallout from weapons testing and existing reactors, and *does not* form a part of the so-called "natural background of radiation present in the environment." Prior to the advent of weapons testing and nuclear reactors the surface waters of North America had an average tritium concentration of less than 10 picocuries per liter (Fowler, 1965). The present tritium concentration in the Upper Mississippi River is in the neighborhood of 2000 picocuries per liter.[4] It matters little to the environment or to the individuals exposed to this radiation whether it arose from weapons testing or from waste from nuclear power stations. The fact that weapons testing has increased our exposure to radiation seems a poor argument indeed for the creation of an even

greater risk by discharging radioactive wastes from nuclear power stations.

In present practice, tritium is not the only radioactive isotope which is released to the environment without any significant control. The noble gases are also released, either at the reactor site or at the fuel reprocessing plant. It has been estimated that the exposure due to only one of these isotopes, krypton 85, will approximately equal the exposure from natural sources of ionizing radiation by the year 2000 if the releases of krypton 85 continue from new reactors as they have from existing reactors (Peterson, 1967; Coleman and Liberace, 1965).

RELEASE OF RADIOACTIVE WASTES—MAJOR ACCIDENTS

It is considered normal in the operation of a nuclear reactor to discharge thousands or millions of curies per year into the local environment (Brinck and Kahn, 1967). At present, radioactive products such as the noble gases and tritium are always discharged either at the reactor site or at the fuel reprocessing plant. An attempt thus far successful, is made to retain the bulk of the other radioactive wastes, particularly those of long half-life or of particular biological significance.

The risk associated with a major reactor accident is that these radioactive fission and activation products will be suddenly released into the environment. It is essentially impossible that a reactor of the type in general use today could undergo an accident which would resemble the tremendous explosion which is associated with a fission bomb—an atomic bomb such as was used in the latter days of World War II. The accidents which can take place in water-moderated, non-breeder reactors are not these large explosions, but rather are incidents which lead to local release of the

---

[4] United States Geological Survey, unpublished results of tritium monitoring in the Mississippi River, Anoka, Minnesota.

fission products from the reactor core (U.S. AEC Report, 1957).

It was stated earlier that more than a billion curies of radioactive materials are accumulated during a year of operation in a major reactor. As has been pointed out, a fraction of these wastes are released during "normal operation" of the reactor. Another fraction of these wastes will decay. The bulk of them are, however, retained in the reactor fuel.

A major reactor accident would be possible were a reactor to lose its primary cooling water. Whether the initial event were an earthquake, sabotage, rupture of a steam line, or one of a myraid other possibilities, there would be relatively small danger of widespread dispersal of large quantities of radionuclides unless the cooling water were lost. Were cooling lost the reactor fuel would begin to melt within seconds, various chemical reactions would begin, and a fuel meltdown could continue to completion. These events would probably be accompanied by a steam explosion and chemical reactions between the remaining water, the fuel, and the structural metals of the reactor.

Were this to occur, vast quantities of volatile radioactive waste would be released from the fuel. Reactors are constructed with a heavy structural barrier called the containment, surrounding the reactor vessel. The containment would probably prevent releases of radioactivity from accidents less serious than a meltdown and from the complete meltdown of a small reactor. It is generally agreed, however, that the integrity of the containment is not assured were meltdown to occur in a large reactor.

The net result of this chain of events would be the sudden release of millions of curies of radioisotopes. The dispersion of these materials would depend on the local circumstances, meteorological conditions at the time, and other such factors.

The possibility of this accident has not been overlooked by the reactor industry and elaborate engineered safeguards have been devised to prevent a meltdown. Whether or not loss of coolant would result in a meltdown of the reactor core even if all of the engineered safeguards were to function is a matter for speculation.

Several types of major accidents are sometimes postulated; they are assumed to result in the melting or the physical disruption of the reactor core. This event would probably be accompanied by a steam explosion or a chemical reaction between the coolant, the fuel, and the structural metals of the reactor. The net result would be the sudden release of up to several million curies of radioactive wastes. The dispersion of these materials would depend on the local circumstances, local meteorology, etc.

Several years ago, the Atomic Energy Commission published a report which considered these major reactor accidents (U.S. AEC Report, 1957). It must be clearly stated that the type of accident considered in this report, and considered during the safety analysis of each reactor, is highly unlikely. The Atomic Energy Commission and its advisors devote a great deal of effort toward review of nuclear reactors to assure that they are designed so that a major accident will not occur. Various engineered safeguards are incorporated into each plant—safeguards which are said to assure that the probability of a major accident is very small. However, the probability is not negligibly small[5]; it is high enough so that insurance companies will not assume the risk. It has been questioned as to whether the public is being adequately pro-

[5] For a reasonably complete discussion of this point, the reader is referred to the various documents which relate to the Atomic Energy Commission Indemnity Legislation:

Hearings on government indemnity and reactor safety, Joint Committee on Atomic Energy, 85th Congress of the United States, First Session, 1957.

Hearings on proposed extension of AEC indemnity legislation, Subcommittee on Legislation, Joint Committee on Atomic Energy, 89th Congress of the United States, First Session, 1965 (includes discussion of major accidents, pp. 347–48).

tected by present regulations (Green, 1968; Pogue and Abrahamson, 1968).[6]

For a description of the major accidents and their result, it might be best to quote a fairly large section of the AEC report (U.S. AEC, 1957) mentioned above. After a detailed consideration of the various factors which might be involved in a major accident in a then-typical reactor near a large city, the report concludes:

OBSERVATIONS AND REMARKS

The numbers shown in the previous summary are calculated on the basis of what we believe to be the best available assumptions, data and mathematical methods. As has been stressed elsewhere, there is considerable uncertainty about many of the factors, techniques and data, so that these numbers are only rough approximations. Where information is sufficiently complete we have chosen values to represent the most probable situation but where high degrees of uncertainty exist we have chosen values believed to be on the pessimistic (high hazard) side. The results shown would be quite sensitive to variations in some of the factors which were used.

The lethal exposure (following an accident) could range from none to a calculated maximum of 3,400 [deaths]. This maximum could only occur under the adverse combination of several conditions which would exist for not more than 10 per cent of the time and probably much less.

Under the assumed accident conditions, the number of persons that could be injured could range from none to a maximum of 43,000. This high number of injuries could only occur under an adverse combination of conditions which would exist for not more than 10 per cent of the time and probably much less.

Depending upon the weather conditions and temperature of the released fission products for the assumed accident, the property damage could be as low as about one-half million dollars and as high as about $7 billion. For the assumed conditions under which there might be some moderate restrictions on the use of land or crops (Range IV), the areas affected

[6] Some of the reactor accidents which have occurred to date are described in *The Careless Atom* (Novick, 1969), which discusses radioactive pollution from reactors in some detail.

could range from about 18 square miles to about 150,000 square miles.

Perhaps considerations such as these have influenced the commercial insurance companies when they consider the question of insuring large nuclear plants. Yet this report described possible accidents in reactors which are small by today's standards. It has been reported that the report has been updated; however, the revision (if in fact it has been made) has not been released by the Atomic Energy Commission (Novick, 1969).

In addition to major accidents at the reactor site, the possibility exists for accidents during the transportation of fuel from the site. The new fuel being transported to the site is relatively free from radioactive contaminants. The spent fuel, however, contains the vast quantities of fission products described, and an accident involving it might be depressingly spectacular. A detailed evaluation of this problem would require knowledge of the quantity of spent fuel included in a single shipment, the mode of transport, and the details of the country through which shipment was being made. It is a problem which bears consideration in evaluating the risks associated with a reactor program.

BIOLOGICAL EFFECTS OF RADIATION

Since the advent of the atomic age the evidence regarding the effect of ionizing radiation has been increasing. Chadwick and Abrahams (1964) begin a paper about these effects with a general review of the situation.

Knowledge that ionizing radiation is capable of causing deleterious effects in exposed individuals followed closely the discovery of x-rays by Roentgen in 1895. The history of the various unfortunate experiences with x-rays and radioactive materials is a familiar one: repeated severe skin burns suffered by the early physicists and physicians using x-rays, skin cancers occurring in some of these same individuals at the sites of the repeated burns, bone sarcomas occurring among those who used radium-containing luminescent paints on watch and clock dials, and more recently, various neoplasms occurring in some patients receiving x-ray exposures in clinical procedures. Thus it became quickly known that large doses of radiation can cause severe acute symptoms ranging from localized skin burns to generalized severe damage to vital tissues, such as bone marrow, and at high enough doses, death. Soon it began to be noted that some of those who recovered from the acute symptoms of over-exposure went on later to develop serious sequelae such as various kinds of neoplasms including, particularly, leukemia. And finally, perhaps most significant of all, it was noted that various groups who received more than the usual exposure to radiation showed many years later a higher than normal incidence of neoplasms—analogous to the situation of those recovering from acute effects of overexposure to radiation; but this time the long-term effects occurred in individuals who had not experienced any acute manifestations of overexposure.

It can be seen that evaluation of the effects of radiation on man presents some difficulties. Of course the acute effects—the acute radiation syndrome—occurring after whole body doses of hundred of roentgens are relatively well understood. However, much more needs to be known about the long-term effects. These effects are not different from usual disease conditions: genetic defects, various kinds of neoplasms, including leukemia. They are manifest as an increased incidence of these diseases occurring usually many years after exposure. Therefore understanding the long-term effects of radiation involves follow-up of often large numbers of exposed persons and comparing their disease experience with suitable controls.

On the other hand there is a tendency to overemphasize the limitations in our knowledge of the effects of radiation on man. Unquestionably there are gaps in our knowledge. We need to know much more about the relationships between low-level radiation exposure and disease incidence, about the mechanisms of radiation damage, about subtle biochemical and physiological changes induced by radiation, and the possible relationships between these and later significant pathology. On the other hand, the very recognition of these important gaps stems from the considerable body of data currently available.

Basic to the consideration of health hazards from any toxic material is the question of the dose-response relationship and the possible threshold level of exposure—the dose below which effects are not detectable. This question is essential to the establishment of any standards for allowable exposure to ionizing radiation.

Some substances, generally considered to be quite toxic, can be taken in small quantities either acutely or chronically with no detectable effects. As the quantity is increased, a level is reached for which the most susceptible individuals begin to show the effect—this is the threshold dose for that substance. As dose is further increased a level is reached for which all subjects show the effect. Substances of this nature have a response curve as shown in curve B of Fig. 42–6.

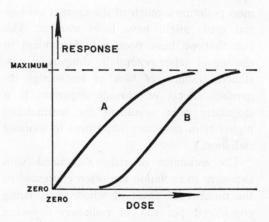

Figure 42–6 Dose-response curves: for a substance for which no threshold exists—Curve A; and for a substance which has a threshold dose—Curve B

There are other substances which may be taken into the body in small quantities without any detectable effect only so long as there is no chronic exposure. An acute exposure to such substances leads to the response indicated in curve B. If, however, these substances are taken into the body on a chronic basis, the threshold, if it exists at all, is much closer to zero. These substances are not rapidly removed by the body, but are stored such that the exposure on one day adds to that of the next day and so on. An example of such substances is lead, for which there is a fairly high threshold for an acute dose, but a very low threshold for a chronic dose, especially in children.

In the case of ionizing radiation, it is generally accepted that there is no threshold exposure below which no effects will appear. Although all of the evidence is not yet available, the Federal Radiation Council (1960) has adopted the prudent assumption that a threshold radiation does not exist, and that ". . . every use of radiation involves the possibility of some biological risk either to the individual or his descendants." (Had a correspondingly conservative approach been taken with other more common pollutants, much of the current ecological crisis might have been avoided. The fact that we have been very imprudent in the use of other potentially dangerous substances because of lack of knowledge regarding effects of chronic exposure is a singularly poor argument for maintaining higher than necessary exposures to ionizing radiation.)

The estimates of risks associated with exposure to radiation are often expressed in the number of cases of whatever is being considered per rad of radiation exposure per million people exposed. A rad is one of the units used to measure the quantity of radiation exposure. It has been shown, for example, that the average exposure to humans from naturally occurring sources of ionizing radiation is near 0.1 rad, or 100 millirads, per year (U.N. General Assembly Official Records, 1966). This natural exposure comes from cosmic rays, radioactive isotopes in the ground and building materials, and radioactive materials in our food and water. The 0.1 rad per year exposure is that which existed prior to the advent of

weapons testing with its resultant fallout and does not include medical use of ionizing radiation.

Many neoplasms have been associated with radiation exposure, and anything approaching a complete review of the current literature is beyond the scope of this paper. The International Commission on Radiological Protection (1966) has summarized much of the available data, and has computed the risk of several cancers including leukemia and thyroid carcinoma. The values given for these cancers are:

Leukemia: twenty fatalities per million persons exposed to 1 rad. Between forty and two hundred fatalities per million fetuses exposed to 1 rad.

Thyroid carcinoma: between ten and twenty cases per million children exposed to 1 rad.

Fatal cancers other than the leukemias: twenty fatalities per million persons exposed to 1 rad.

There remains, however, considerable uncertainty as to the validity of these numbers.

Difficult as it is to assess the risks of the various cancers, it is even more difficult to make a quantitative evaluation of genetic risks associated with ionizing radiation. The interested reader is referred to the International Commission for Radiological Protection Publication No. 8 (1966) and to the 1966 United Nations report. The genetic risks associated with environmental and other ionizing radiation exposure are probably of greater importance than are the somatic effects.

A reduction of life-span is also associated with exposure to radiation (Blumenthal, 1967). If recent studies (Rosenblatt and Anderson, 1967) on beagle dogs can be applied to man, they suggest that for each exposure of one rad there would be an approximately two weeks' shortening in life. The irradiated dogs tended to die of the same diseases as did nonirradiated dogs, but there was earlier onset of the diseases. To extend these results to man, however, assumes that the experiments are statistically valid, that they are directly applicable to man, that the per cent change in life shortening observed in dogs is the same as it would be for man, and that there is no threshold dose below which the effect would not be noted.

The present Federal Radiation Council recommendation is that the general public should not be exposed to greater than 0.17 rad per year in excess of natural background—without carefully considering the reasons for doing so.[7] The U. S. Atomic Energy Commission regulations nevertheless would permit the general public to be exposed to 0.5 rad per year.[8]

It is obvious that although the risk to any one individual from these exposures is relatively small, the risk to the population is large. These risks are currently being reexamined in connection with the concerns of a rapidly expanding nuclear industry.[9] Risks from exposure to ionizing radiation, as well as other environmental effects of various methods of power generation have recently been the subject of a long series of hearings before the Joint Committee on Atomic Energy, U. S. Congress. The reports of these hearings contain extensive discussions of these risks.[10]

CONCLUSION

It is apparent that the nuclear industry is creating a major challenge to the environment in the United States. Thermal wastes

from the current generation of large, nuclear power generating stations are immense in quantity and can cause drastic changes in the bodies of water involved. There is little hope for a spectacular breakthrough which would significantly improve the thermal efficiency of light-water nuclear reactors. Even if fast-breeder reactors prove safe enough for general use, the thermal efficiency would be only slightly improved over the present reactors (Tape, 1968).

If the past performance of the nuclear industry is taken as representative of what to expect, there will be vast quantities of radioactive wastes discharged both at nuclear power plant (reactor) sites and at fuel-fabricating and fuel-reprocessing plants. Even without the catastrophic releases of radioactive wastes which would result from a major accident, the introduction of these radioactive wastes in normal operation poses a major threat not only to the current generation but also to the future of the human race. Perhaps the genetic effects which would result from the wastes of the nuclear industry can be tolerated—and perhaps they cannot. It is a dangerous game to play, trading potential death and mutation for minor immediate economic gain. *There is no reason why the radioactive wastes cannot be contained, but as usual it costs more to contain wastes than to dump them into the nearest waters or into the atmosphere.*

A quantitative statement of the risks from the radioactive wastes from nuclear reactors is not possible at this time. Not only is there insufficient information to accurately predict the somatic and genetic effect of a given dose of ionizing radiation, but the quantities of radioactive wastes being released even from existing reactors are not adequately known. Although there have been several reactor-years of experience with nuclear power reactors in the United States, the measurements of the wastes from these reactors have not been adequate to permit accurate prediction of the wastes to be ex-

[7] *Background Material for the Development of Radiation Protection Standards,* Reports of the Federal Radiation Council.

[8] Code of Federal Regulations, Title 10, Part 20.

[9] "Protection or Disaster," by John W. Gofman and Arthur R. Tamplin, *Environment,* 12:3, April 1970.

[10] "Environmental Effects of Producing Electric Power," Hearing before the JCAE, U. S. Congress, Hearing reports from phases I, II, and III, available from U. S. Gov't Pr.O. etc.

pected from the current generation of large reactors (Brinck and Kahn, 1967).

There is no question, however, that substantial quantities of radioactive isotopes are being released into the environment from nuclear reactors. There is also no question that these wastes pose a major threat to health.

The nuclear reactor industry is engaged in a major effort to sell the concepts of industrial and agro-industrial complexes which would be centered around large nuclear reactors. These complexes would be situated on the seacoast and would combine electricity production with desalinization. In addition to the risks of thermal and radioactive pollution, there are the additional factors associated with the social and economic assumptions about the introduction of such engineering works in relatively undeveloped countries. The summary reports of these agro-industrial complexes contain no mention of these possible difficulties.

A realistic attempt should be made to evaluate the hidden as well as the direct costs of "going nuclear" before decisions are made in any country that might lead to irreversible changes both in the physical environment and to the life presently existing on this planet.

Perhaps the adverse as well as favorable experience with nuclear technology in the U.S. will be of use abroad. This is certainly a field in which biologists have an obligation to offset the enthusiasm of nuclear developers.

REFERENCES

Abrahamson, D. E., and Pogue, R. E. "Discharge of Radioactive and Thermal Wastes." *J. Minnesota Acad. Sci.*, 35 (1) (1968) 20–24.

Blincoe, C. AEC Contract No. AT(04-3) 34, Report TID-17229, 1963 and Report Conf-244-1. 1962.

Blumenthal, Herman T. "Radiation and Aging." *Scientist and Citizen*, 9 (2) (1967) 21–25.

Brinck, William L., and Kahn, Bernd. "Radionuclide Releases at Nuclear Power Stations." Unpublished report, Nuclear Engineering Laboratory, Environmental Surveillance and Control Program, National Center for Radiological Health, Public Health Service, U. S. Dept. of Health, Education, and Welfare, Dec. 29, 1967.

Cairns, J., Jr. "We're in Hot Water." *Scientist and Citizen*, 10 (8) (1968) 187–98.

Chadwick, D. R., and Abrahams, S. P. "Biological Effects of Radiation." *Arch. Environ. Health*, 9 (1964) 643–48.

Coleman, L. R., and Liberace, R. "Nuclear Power Production and Estimated Krypton-85 Levels." *Radiological Health Data and Reports*, 7 (11) (1965) 615–21.

Federal Radiation Council. *Background Material for the Development of Radiation Protection Standards.* Report No. 1, 1960.

Fowler, E., ed. *Radioactive Fallout, Soils, Plants, Food, Man.* New York: Elsevier Press, 1965.

Gofman, John W., and Tamplin, Arthur R. "Protection or Disaster." *Environment* 12:3. April 1970.

Goldman, M. I. "United States Experience in Management of Gaseous Wastes from Nuclear Power Stations." Paper presented to International Atomic Energy Agency Symposium on Airborne Radioactive Wastes, United Nations, New York, August 26–30, 1968.

Green, Harold P. "Reasonable Assurance of No Undue Risk: A Lawyer Dissects Reactor Licensing Procedures." *Scientist and Citizen*, 10 (5) (1968) 128–41.

Hearing before the JCAE, U. S. Congress. "Environmental Effects of Producing Electric Power." Hearing reports from phases I, II, and III. Available from U. S. Government Printing Office.

Hearings before the Joint Committee on Atomic Energy. "Participation by Small Electrical Utilities in Nuclear Power." Congress of the United States, April 30, May 1, 2, and 3, 1968. Part 1, p. 37.

Hearings before the Subcommittee on Air and Water Pollution of the Committee on Public Works, United States Senate. Thermal Pollution—1968, February 6, 13, and 14, 1968. Available from the U. S. Government Printing Office or the Subcommittee (includes an extensive bibliography).

International Commission on Radiological Protection. *The Evaluation of Risks from Radiation.* Publication No. 8. Elmsford, N.Y.: Pergamon Press, 1966.

McKee, J. E., and Wolf, H. O., eds. *Water Quality Criteria.* Publication No. 3-A of the Resources Agency of California, State Water Quality Control Board, Sacramento, California. 1964. Pp. 283 ff. deal with thermal pollution.

Mihursky, J. A. "Thermal Loading: New Threat to Aquatic Life." *Conservation Catalyst,* 2 (3) (1968) 6–9.

National Technical Advisory Committee to the Secretary of the Interior. *Report of the committee on water quality criteria.* Washington, D.C.: U. S. Government Printing Office, April 1, 1968.

Nelson, Bryce. "Thermal Pollution: Senator Muskie Tells AEC to Cool It." *Science,* 158 (1967) 755–56.

Novick, Sheldon. *The Careless Atom.* New York: Houghton Mifflin Co., 1969.

Peterson, Malcolm. "Krypton-85, Nuclear Air Pollutant." *Scientist and Citizen,* 9 (3) (1967) 54–55.

Pogue, R. E., and Abrahamson, D. E. "The Multi-Phase Problems of Pollution: I. Benefits, Risks and Regulations." *J. Minnesota Acad. Sci.,* 35 (1) (1968) 18–20.

Ramey, James T. "The Next Five Years in Nuclear Development and Regulation." U.S. AEC News Release S-33-68, Sept. 5, 1968.

Rosenblatt, L. S., and Anderson, A. C. "Survival of Control and X-Irradiated Female Beagles." 1966 Annual Report, University of California at Davis, UCD 472-113. 1967. Pp. 10–16.

Singer, S. F. "Waste Heat Management." *Science,* 159 (1968) 1184.

Smith, J. M., Jr., "The Significance of Tritium in Water Reactors." General Electric Atomic Power Equipment Dept., San Jose, California. Internal Memo dated Sept. 19, 1967.

Snow, Joel A. "Radioactive Waste from Reactors: The Problem That Won't Go Away." *Scientist and Citizen,* 9 (5) (1967) 1–8.

Tape, Gerald F. "Environmental Aspects of Central Power Plants." Commissioner U.S. AEC, AEC News Release S-54-68, Dec. 20, 1968.

United Nations General Assembly Official Records. *Report of the United Nations Scientific Committee on the Effects of Atomic Radiation,* Twenty-First Session, Supplement No. 14 (A/6314), 1966.

U. S. Atomic Energy Commission. *Theoretical Possibilities and Consequences of Major Accidents in Large Nuclear Power Plants.* Report Wash-740. 1957.

———. "AEC Studying Potential of Nuclear Energy Centers in the Middle East." News Release L-124, June 11, 1968.

———. *Nuclear Energy Centers: Industrial and Agro-Industrial Complexes.* Summary Report, ORNL-4291. July, 1968.

———. "Report on Nuclear Energy Centers for Industrial and Agro-Industrial Complexes Issued." News Release L-197, Aug. 20, 1968.

———. *The Nuclear Industry—1968.* November 14, 1968.

U. S. Public Health Service. *Routine Surveillance of Radioactivity around Nuclear Facilities.* Publication No. 999-RH-23. Washington, D.C.: U. S. Government Printing Office, 1966.

———. *Public Health Evaluation: Monticello Nuclear Generating Plant.* Environmental Facilities Section Document NF 67-12. Rockville, Md., 1967.

43. ATOMIC WASTE DISPOSAL IN THE SEA:
An Ecological Dilemma?

Joel W. Hedgpeth

A by-product of the atomic age is the addition of artificial radionuclides to the environment. Some of these occur naturally; others were previously unknown. While potentially dangerous, high-activity radionuclides must be buried or encapsuled, the greater bulk of this material is so-called low-level waste, and much of this is discharged into the sea. Research into the effect of these low-level wastes on marine life has hardly begun, but opposing points of view have already developed about these effects in the Soviet Union and the rest of the world. The Soviet researchers take the conservative view that any addition to the sea is harmful, while the "Western" researchers defend the position that the levels of artificial radioactivity from present "controlled releases" are too low to have significant effect on marine life and are less than the activity induced by bomb tests. No information is available on what might be considered permissible levels for creatures other than man, but there may be a difference in philosophy that accepts losses of a certain percentage to a fish population that would be ethically unacceptable for mankind.

The atomic age has now been with us for more than a quarter of a century, but the ecological problems associated with this development are still incompletely realized. Certainly no physicist at Los Alamos in 1945 had a clear idea of the potential effects of adding artificial radionuclides to the environment, although radiation has long been known to be dangerous to life and tissue. Now everyone is sensitive to the potential dangers of radioactive contamination to man, and we are being assured that our standards for the disposal of radioactive wastes, especially in the sea, limit quantities released to concentrations far below any conceivable danger to man. To some, it seems that the reassurances that nuclear reactors are safer than television sets and that our children may safely play upon the lawn by the front entrance to an atomic power plant are just a bit too hearty. While one need not feel concerned about the difficult task of well-paid public relations men, it is possible that with respect to our standards of waste disposal for radioactive materials and the potential contamination from power reactors, at least in the U.S.A., we are demonstrating adequate concern.[1] At least our attitude toward pollution by radioactive waste shows concern for a potential danger at the outset, a new departure in our attitude toward our environment. At this time, however, our approach is strictly anthropocentric, and, as far as the marine environment is concerned, we cannot say whether our standards for disposal of atomic wastes are reasonable or not; the "maximum permissible concentrations" are those we think permissible for ourselves, not the rest of the biosphere (Table 43–1).

Nevertheless, at the same time as we attempt to apply severe standards to peaceful uses of atomic energy, we have approached or exceeded our self-imposed limits in the sea by adding radionuclides to fallout, especially over the Northern Hemisphere, by testing bombs. The philosophical implication of this inconsistency is that man still considers it more desirable to survive as a tribe than as a species, but that is a subject for another symposium.

The earth is a ball containing radioactive materials in orbit around a comparatively small thermonuclear reactor, and its inhabitants are constantly subject to bombardment by radioactive materials from the environment, from substances within themselves, and from outer space (Fig. 43–1). Indeed, the bombardment of earth by cosmic rays may have been an important factor in stimulating the beginning of life. Uranium and thorium are among the most common radioactive materials making up the surface of the earth, and the average amount of radium in the human body is said to be 1.59×10^{-10} grams (Bugher, 1956). There is so much radioactive potassium (^{40}K) in the soil that there are almost a million disintegrations per minute in every square foot of soil, and each of us may have 27 milligrams of radioactive potassium in his system (Bugher, 1956). Data of this sort are often used to reassure us that there is nothing to be afraid of, that the atomic age is not going to turn us all into monsters or induce wholesale cancers. Perhaps the following statement was also meant to be reassuring, but it does not reassure an ecologist: "The significant alterations which man has introduced into the world are a very great acceleration in time in the processes of radioactive decay and in the changing of the proportions of the resulting radioactive elemental products, with, in some instances, the introduction of forms unrecognizable in nature" (Bugher, 1956, p. 832).

In any event it is realized that we have the problem of disposal of the products of these accelerated processes on our hands. Some of the products are dangerous radionuclides with long half-lives that must be put quietly away somewhere. They must either be buried in lead tanks in some remote and presumably unusable part of the world or sealed up in vessels impervious to pressure or the action of the sea water for a considerable period of time and dropped into some deep part of the sea. Others are "low-level" wastes either induced by the processing of radioactive materials by military or civilian installations or from reprocessing material from power reactors, or the residue of radioactive materials used in hospitals, laboratories, and industrial plants. Much of this material is now being released directly into the sea, hopefully to be diluted and dispersed in the "perpetual sink."

[1] Perhaps this is due in part to those gruesome pieces, so convincingly illustrated by Nell Brinkley, about the factory girls decaying from painting luminous watch dials, that adorned the old Hearst Sunday supplements in more innocent days.

Table 43-1

MAXIMUM PERMISSIBLE CONCENTRATIONS (MPC) FOR MAN OF RADIONUCLIDES IN WATER AND IN MARINE ORGANISMS

(From Polikarpov, 1967)

NUCLIDE	DRINKING WATER (cur/l) SOVIET STANDARD*	DRINKING WATER (cur/l) U.S. STANDARD†	SEA WATER Tentative US(a) LOCAL	SEA WATER Tentative US(a) GENERAL	SEA WATER ADOPTED IN U.S.(b)	SEA WATER TENTATIVE STD. IN U.S.(a)	SEA WATER (c)	SEA WATER (d)	SEA WATER IN INDIA (e)	CONC. FACTOR (b)	CONC. FACTOR (a)	EDIBLE Tentative US(a) LOCAL	EDIBLE Tentative US(a) GENERAL	EDIBLE ADOPTED FOR IRISH SEA (f)	EDIBLE (d)	EDIBLE IN INDIA (e)
^{3}H	3×10^{-7}	3×10^{-6}	—	—	—	—	—	—	—	—	—	—	—	—	2×10^{-3}	1×10^{-5}
^{14}C	2×10^{-7}	8×10^{-7}	—	—	—	—	—	—	—	—	—	—	—	—	3×10^{-5}	—
^{24}Na	8×10^{-8}	3×10^{-8}	—	—	—	—	—	1.6×10^{-4}	2×10^{-9}	2×10^{5}	—	—	—	—	8×10^{-5}	3×10^{-7}
^{32}P	5×10^{-9}	2×10^{-8}	—	—	9.6×10^{-11}	4.5×10^{-12}	5×10^{-12}	5×10^{-11}	2×10^{-12}	—	—	—	—	—	2×10^{-6}	5×10^{-7}
^{35}S	7×10^{-9}	6×10^{-8}	—	—	—	1.1×10^{-8}	1.2×10^{-7}	1×10^{-5}	9×10^{-8}	5	—	—	—	—	5×10^{-5}	—
^{42}K	6×10^{-9}	1×10^{-7}	—	—	—	—	—	—	—	20	—	—	—	—	1×10^{-4}	—
^{45}Ca	3×10^{-9}	9×10^{-9}	—	—	—	—	—	5×10^{-7}	4×10^{-8}	—	—	—	—	—	5×10^{-6}	1×10^{-7}
^{51}Cr	5×10^{-7}	2×10^{-6}	2×10^{-8}	7×10^{-10}	2×10^{-7}	1.2×10^{-7}	9×10^{-9}	—	4×10^{-8}	10^{3}	3×10^{2}	—	—	—	5×10^{-4}	3×10^{-5}
^{55}Fe	3×10^{-8}	8×10^{-7}	1×10^{-7}	1×10^{-11}	5.4×10^{-8}	2×10^{-8}	2×10^{-8}	—	4×10^{-8}	10^{3}	3×10^{3}	—	—	—	—	1×10^{-6}
^{59}Fe	1×10^{-8}	6×10^{-8}	7×10^{-11}	2×10^{-12}	6×10^{-11}	1.4×10^{-10}	8×10^{-10}	8×10^{-11}	7×10^{-10}	10^{4}	3×10^{3}	—	—	—	4×10^{-5}	1×10^{-6}
^{60}Co	1×10^{-8}	5×10^{-8}	3×10^{-11}	1×10^{-12}	8×10^{-10}	6×10^{-12}	6×10^{-10}	4×10^{-9}	5×10^{-11}	10^{4}	3×10^{3}	—	—	—	2×10^{-4}	8×10^{-7}
^{64}Cu	6×10^{-8}	2×10^{-6}	3×10^{-10}	3×10^{-12}	—	5×10^{-11}	5×10^{-11}	2×10^{-8}	2×10^{-9}	10^{4}	3×10^{3}	—	—	—	8×10^{-5}	—
^{65}Zn	1×10^{-8}	1×10^{-7}	3×10^{-10}	1×10^{-12}	4×10^{-10}	1.6×10^{-7}	2×10^{-10}	1.6×10^{-7}	—	5×10^{3}	3×10^{3}	—	—	—	6×10^{-4}	8×10^{-7}
^{90}Sr	3×10^{-11}	1×10^{-7}	1×10^{-10}	1×10^{-12}	2.5×10^{-8}	7×10^{-12}	5×10^{-11}	1.2×10^{-7}	2×10^{-10}	20	13	—	—	$(1\text{-}5)\times10^{-8}$	8×10^{-9}	2×10^{-7}
^{95}Zr	2×10^{-8}	6×10^{-7}	2×10^{-11}	1×10^{-10}	—	3.3×10^{-9}	—	8×10^{-10}	3×10^{-10}	—	5×10^{2}	—	—	—	—	1×10^{-6}
^{95}Nb	3×10^{-8}	1×10^{-7}	4×10^{-10}	1×10^{-10}	3×10^{-8}	—	1×10^{-9}	—	1×10^{-8}	2×10^{3}	1.2×10^{2}	—	—	—	—	2×10^{-6}
^{106}Ru	3×10^{-8}	1×10^{-7}	1×10^{-10}	3×10^{-12}	1.6×10^{-10}	—	1×10^{-10}	3×10^{-10}	2×10^{-10}	10^{3}	28	—	—	—	—	2×10^{-7}
^{131}I	6×10^{-10}	6×10^{-9}	3×10^{-10}	1×10^{-11}	1×10^{-7}	1.6×10^{-9}	2×10^{-10}	3×10^{-7}	4×10^{-9}	10^{2}	18	—	—	$(1\text{-}3)\times10^{-6}$	3×10^{-7}	2×10^{-7}
^{137}Cs	1×10^{-8}	2×10^{-8}	4×10^{-9}	3×10^{-10}	1.6×10^{-7}	1.3×10^{-11}	4×10^{-9}	3×10^{-7}	6×10^{-9}	50	—	—	—	—	—	2×10^{-7}
^{144}Ce	3×10^{-9}	1×10^{-8}	1×10^{-10}	2×10^{-8}	1.5×10^{-11}	1×10^{-11}	1×10^{-11}	—	1×10^{-8}	8×10^{3}	—	—	—	—	1.5×10^{-5}	5×10^{-8}
^{182}Ta	1×10^{-8}	4×10^{-8}	—	—	—	—	—	—	—	3×10^{2}	—	1×10^{-7}	4×10^{-9}	—	—	2×10^{-7}
^{192}Ir	1×10^{-8}	4×10^{-8}	3×10^{-10}	1×10^{-11}	—	—	—	—	—	—	—	—	—	—	—	—
Mixture of beta and gamma-emitters	5×10^{-11}	10^{-11}	—	—	—	—	—	—	—	—	—	—	—	5×10^{-6}–5×10^{-8}	—	—
Mixture of alpha-emitters	5×10^{-11}	10^{-11}	—	—	—	—	—	—	—	—	—	—	—	3×10^{-7}–1×10^{-8}	—	—

*Health regulations for "Work with radioactive substances and sources of ionizing radiations" (Russian list: Anonymous [1960]).
†0.1 of the MPC for nuclear energy workers (National Committee on Radiation Protection, [1959]).
(a) Anonymous [1960a].
(b) Anonymous [1960b].
(c) Committee on the Effects of Atomic Radiation on Oceanography and Fisheries [1959].
(d) Committee on Oceanography [1959b].
(e) Pillai and Ganguly [1961].
(f) Templeton [1962].

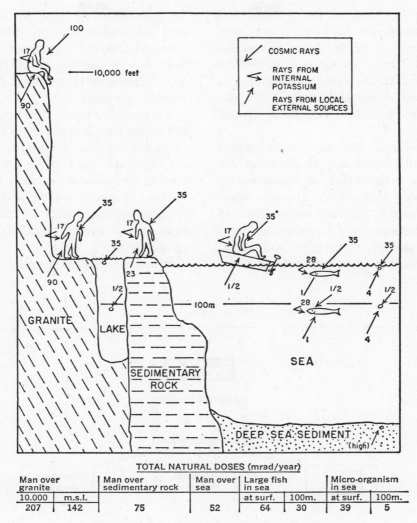

TOTAL NATURAL DOSES (mrad/year)							
Man over granite		Man over sedimentary rock	Man over sea	Large fish in sea		Micro-organism in sea	
10.000	m.s.l.			at surf.	100m.	at surf.	100m.
207	142	75	52	64	30	39	5

Figure 43–1 Comparative natural radiation
doses (From Folsom and Harley, 1957)

The two best-known sites for this release of radioactive material are the Windscale Works on the Cumberland coast and the Columbia River. The actual site of release on the Columbia is at Hanford, 250 miles upstream. While much of the radioactivity (*ca.* 3,000 curies per day) decays or is removed on sediments by the time the sea is reached, it appears that approximately 1,000 curies per day reaches the sea at the mouth of the Columbia. At the Windscale Works, about 90,000 curies a year are released through a pipeline into the Irish Sea. It is pointed out by many if not most authors discussing these situations that the total releases of artificial radionuclides from Windscale and Hanford to the oceans are less than the contribution of ^{90}Sr to the oceans by fallout from atomic weapons tests (e.g. Parker, 1967). However, if we finally abandon weapons tests, this easy excuse will no longer be available. In any event, we can expect that in the future the peaceful uses of atomic energy will provide much more potential radioactive contamination than present military uses.

It is possible that our need for energy of all sorts will stimulate us to find useful ap-

plications for some of this material and
thereby ameliorate to some extent what
now appears to be an almost insuperable
problem before we render some parts of the
earth unlivable. However, such use or conversion would probably apply to higher-
level wastes than those now being released
into the sea.

Radionuclides, like any other material
added to the ocean, may be diluted or dispersed, or concentrated or transported in
various ways (Fig. 43–2). The only essential difference is that their activity dies off
at an exponential rate; for some this decay
is such a slow process (e.g. ^{14}C with a half-
life of more than 5,000 years) that the mix-

ing processes of the ocean are more significant. Distribution of many radionuclides is
affected by biological processes, by the concentration of particles to which they may
have adhered, or by selection of substances
required for metabolism.

An important aspect of the accumulation
of radionuclides in organisms is the so-called
biological half-life, or retention time within
the organisms. An important trace element
such as zinc may be retained a few days in
oysters, to several months in fish, but we
have no precise figures for the residence
time in any marine organisms (Chipman
et al., 1958).

It seems logical to assume that there is

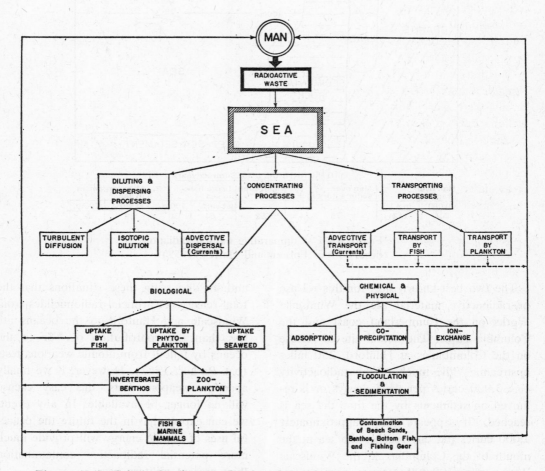

Figure 43–2 Schematic diagram showing the various marine processes acting on a
radioactive waste and the possible routes of its return to man (Waldichuk, 1961)

no preferential selection by organisms of the radionuclides over the stable element, and that the proportion accumulated by organisms will be the same as the proportion occurring in the medium, at least when the physicochemical forms are the same. It is on this assumption that Isaacs and colleagues (1962) developed the "specific activity" approach to waste disposal. In the case of such naturally abundant elements as iodine, calcium, and strontium, the radioisotopes are in comparatively low concentration in the sea and hence the possibility of accumulation of dangerous amounts by man is unlikely. According to this approach it would be impossible for an individual to exceed his allowable radiation by consuming sea food as long as the specific activity of radioisotopes is kept below the allowable limit in the regions where the potential food grows and resides.

This may not always be the case. For one thing, it remains to be demonstrated whether or not there may be preferential uptake of radionuclides as opposed to stable nuclides of some elements. Such a preferential uptake could only be related to the chemical or physical state in which the radionuclide is available to the organism, compared to the state of the stable form. The availability of a trace element in itself might stimulate biological activity, growth, or reproduction and thus prolong the residence time of the radionuclide in the region concerned. However, we have no reliable information on the effect upon organisms of adding low-level wastes to our environment, and even less on the significance of adding artificially-produced radionuclides not naturally present in the environment. The onset of the atomic age has posed significant questions in ecology and physiology that cannot be answered without critical and intensive investigation, and for many of these aspects research has already been too long delayed. If there is any saving grace to the problem of radioactive pollution it is that the radio-

nuclides released may be precisely measured and that the information from these measurements has already provided us with useful insights into ecological processes.

How little we actually know of the processes of transfer and accumulation of substances by organisms in the sea is dramatically emphasized by the appearance of perceptible amounts of DDT in penguins and seals in antarctic waters (Sladen *et al.,* 1966; George and Frear, 1966; Tatton and Ruzicka, 1967). While the concentrations are comparatively minute, in the order of 15 to 150 parts per billion, they are present, and the manner of their appearance in penguins at both Ross Island near the present intensive human activity in the Antarctic, and the remote, comparatively isolated Signy Island of the South Shetlands group suggests energy pathways in the natural system not completely understood. It seems unlikely, as Mellanby (1967) points out, that DDT is equally distributed over the entire globe, since this would require more of the material than man has manufactured so far. It is irrelevant to say that these concentrations fall "within permissible levels." The warning is clear enough. At our exponential rate of increasing pollution, how soon will it be before "unpermissible concentrations" occur? We may be in for some unpleasant surprises from our persistent and steady addition of artificial radionuclides in the sea.

What, for example, is the significance of the fact that most of the fallout from the stratosphere occurs over the Northern Hemisphere during the spring? Is this a coincidence, or is there a true relation between this seeding from the stratosphere and the spring phytoplankton blooms of the oceans?[2] Have we been tampering dangerously with a system on which our hopes for greater yields from the sea ultimately depend?

[2] I am indebted to Evan Evans for raising this question.

THE WINDSCALE WORKS

The Windscale Works are located on the Cumberland coast of the Irish Sea at Sellafield (Figure 43–3). Nuclear reactors for

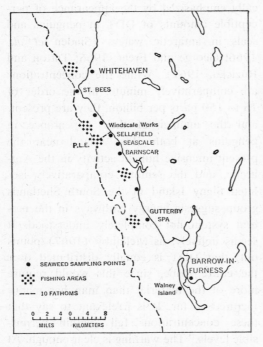

Figure 43–3 Marine Sampling Stations, Windscale Works. The Irish Sea lies to the left. (From Howells, 1966)

plutonium production for Britain's arms program are located there; at nearby Calder Hall are Britain's earliest nuclear power plants. A chemical plant at Windscale was built for the purpose of processing irradiated reactor fuel from the plutonium plants and nuclear power generating stations, and at the outset it was decided that it would be necessary to dispose of large quantities of low-level wastes by releasing them directly into the sea. For this purpose, two lines of 10-inch pipe were laid on the bottom of the sea. The discharge point is some 2,800 yards or approximately 2.5 kilometers from the shore, and at a depth of about

10 fathoms or 20 meters. The waste-containing water is fresh, and rises to the surface above the discharge point. Preliminary studies were made of the marine ecology of the shore and near-shore hydrography, and experimental releases of radioactive material were first made in 1952. After a two-year experimental period, the permissible releases were established and all discharges have been carefully monitored. The average budget of releases into the Irish Sea for the last several years is available (Table 43–2); the sharp increase in zirconium-95 and niobium-95 is due to the addition of a unit for processing uranium fuel in 1964.

In 1957, Windscale achieved notoriety from the "incident" of October 10–11, when potentially dangerous amounts of radioactive iodine and other radionuclides were released from the stack of military plutonium plant, Pile no. 1, and it was necessary to condemn quantities of milk from areas downwind (Chamberlain and Dunster, 1958). Since this incident involved dispersal by air rather than by sea, it is not directly relevant here. It is not possible to estimate the possibility of similar accidental releases to the sea, although these may never be completely ruled out. The implication of these added contaminants is not considered; probably they were not part of the original survey, and their fate in the biosphere remains to be studied.

The most abundant radionuclide released in the sea at Windscale is ruthenium-106. This isotope has a half-life of 1 year and is accumulated by marine algae at a factor of 10^3, i.e. about 1,000–2,000 times. The principal alga involved near Windscale is the intertidal *Porphyra umbilicalis,* an edible seaweed. Some 20–30 tons of *Porphyra* are gathered along the Cumberland coast and shipped to Wales annually, to be made into laver bread. Because of this, the Welsh appetite for laver bread determines the amount of radioactive wastes to be released at Windscale. The quantities to be released

Table 43-2

THE WINDSCALE WORKS
MEAN ACTIVITY DISCHARGE RATES TO SEA
(From Howells, 1966)

RADIONUCLIDE	DISCHARGE RATE—CURIES PER MONTH								
	1957	1958	1959	1960	1961	1962	1963	1964	1965
Ruthenium-106	2,218	3,522	2,956	3,302	2,095	1,916	2,781	1,924	1,752
Ruthenium-103	300	492	746	964	265	153	800	100	150
Strontium-90	137	210	129	43	41	85	46	81	97
Strontium-89	248	72	170	82	114	42	14	16	14
Cerium-144	215	497	583	74	180	200	116	267	288
Yttrium-91 and Rare Earths	300	567	506	83	201	125	90	90	73
Caesium-137	310	516	165	76	91	92	31	111	97
Zirconium-95	59	210	415	196	140	78	47	1,797	1,479
Niobium-95	535	510	845	523	658	356	272	1,735	2,803
Total Beta	5,366	6,846	7,659	6,461	3,981	3,742	4,020	5,055	4,560
Total Alpha	4.8	5.2	5.6	6.8	11.1	15.5	19.0	23.5	33.8

are based on the maximum possible amount of radioactivity the heaviest individual consumer of laver bread might possibly eat. The eating habits of laver bread consumers were studied, and it was found that while most of the nearly 600 people interviewed ate less than 25 grams per day, 11 ate 65 grams per day. Therefore the maximum rate of consumption was taken to be 75 grams per day, and the releases at Windscale must be adjusted so that 11 Welshmen in Swansea, eating all the laver bread they could possibly desire, would not be irradiated by their favorite food. The process by which the actual quantities are derived is complex and those interested in following the numbers should consult Howells (1966) for the best explanation.

In order to be certain that the releases fall within the prescribed limits, continuous monitoring is necessary. A regular sampling and analytical program is conducted. Samples of seaweed along the shore are taken twice a month; each sample is about 5 lb and is regularly analyzed for ruthenium-106 and gross alpha and beta activity, and monthly bulk analyses are made. In all, about half a ton of seaweed is gathered

and analyzed every year; this amount is about 2% of the commercial crop. In addition, sand samples are analyzed, and regular sea sampling of fish and bottom mud is carried out. All of this adds up to a sustained and expensive monitoring program which might well be emulated in some other parts of the world. It is reported on in some detail by Longley and Templeton (1965).

So far, there appears to have been no accumulation of radioactivity in the waters of the Irish Sea associated with the Windscale releases (Mauchline and Templeton, 1964). Dilution has been so effective that by the time the effluent reaches the Mull of Galloway and Anglesey it is difficult to distinguish the levels of effluent radionuclides from fallout radionuclides, but at times there is indication of a pulse of relatively unmixed water moving from Windscale toward the Mull of Galloway. According to Mauchline and Templeton, if the present rate of input of radioactivity to the Irish Sea remains constant, it will be equal to the rate of removal by currents plus the rate of radioactive decay, and the budget is roughly in balance. There are, however, detectable levels of radioactivity in bottom invertebrates in the Irish Sea associated with the Windscale releases (Fig. 43–4).

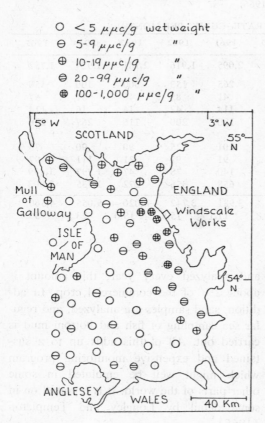

Figure 43–4 The levels of β-activity, originating from the radioactive effluent discharged from Windscale Works, present in bottom invertebrates in the Irish Sea. Corrections have been made for β-activity originating from natural and fallout sources (After Mauchline, 1963)

THE COLUMBIA RIVER PLUME

Unfortunately, there is no single comprehensive account of the disposal of radioactive wastes in the Columbia River and of their fate at sea. The radionuclides reaching the sea are mostly ^{51}Cr and ^{65}Zn (Figs. 43–5, 43–6). Since the half-life of ^{51}Cr is only 28 days, it is not a very satisfactory marker for detecting the fate of wastes very

far from the mouth of the Columbia. Detectable amounts of ^{65}Zn (which has a half-life of 245 days) have been found in pelagic and in benthic animals off the Oregon coast to depths of 2,800 meters. The amounts are stated to be "very much below hazard levels" (Carey *et al.*, 1966). During the summer months, when the plume of the Columbia River drifts to the south, ^{65}Zn is found in mussels (*Mytilus californianus*) along the coast for perhaps 200 or 300 miles, but at localities where upwelling moves the plume water away from the shore, the ^{65}Zn concentration drops quickly after earlier accumulation (Osterberg, 1965). This suggests that the biological half-life of ^{65}Zn is short in mussels. It appears to be much longer in Euphausiids, since the level of activity of ^{65}Zn in *Euphausia pacifica* does not fall to background in winter when the Columbia plume moves to the north (Osterberg, Pattullo, and Pearcy, 1964). Except in the immediate vicinity of the mouth of the Columbia, concentrations of ^{65}Zn are too low to be easily measured in the sea, and accordingly the explanation for the detectable zinc concentrations is to be sought in the biological system itself. As the authors point out:

The great affinity of marine organisms for zinc and the sensitivity of modern gamma-ray spectrographic techniques make ^{65}Zn in euphausiids easy to measure. Unfortunately, however, use of organisms as monitors introduces many uncertainties. The most important is that we do not know how accurately the radioactivity of the euphausiid reflects the radioactivity of the immediate environment. This difficulty is compounded if variations in stable zinc occur; local variations seem likely because of the affinity of marine organisms for zinc. However, no comparable data exist for stable zinc. (Osterberg, Pattullo, and Pearcy, p. 256).

The possibility suggested here, that there may be situations in which the radionuclide may be more abundant than the stable isotope, raises the question whether the "specific activity" approach recommended by

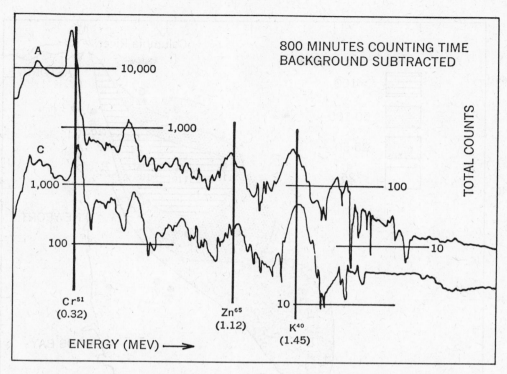

Figure 43–5 Spectra of coprecipitates from sea water from the station with most Cr[51] activity (A), and from the station at greatest distance from the mouth of the Columbia River (C). Collection sites of the two surface-water samples are points A and C respectively, on the map in Figure 43–6

Isaacs and his colleagues can be applied without some further modification. If we have a situation where the radionuclide added to the environment represents an element essential to the food chain, as zinc appears to be, and the quantities to be added exceed the quantities of the stable isotope in the environment, we cannot accept the world ocean average concentration of zinc as a standard for the computation of the specific activity. It would not be practical in such a situation to add suitably large amounts (which would be in the order of tons) of a salt containing stable zinc to ensure a low specific activity. Such addition, if feasible, might have unanticipated side effects.

Zinc occurs in virtually all marine animals sampled, and perceptible levels of ^{65}Zn have also been found in salmon from Bristol Bay, Alaska, to Eureka, California. This suggests that zinc may be a useful indicator for studying migration patterns of this fish, since it appears that the salmon from both extremes of this geographical range have at some time in their lives been within the influence of the effluent of the Columbia River (Osterberg, 1965). Zinc is evidently accumulated rapidly by fish; albacore (*Thunnus alalunga*) off the Oregon coast show an eightfold increase of ^{65}Zn in the liver between July and September (Pearcy and Osterberg, 1968).

So far, the bulk of the work with radionuclides associated with the plume of the Columbia River has been concerned with detecting radioactivity as an indicator of water movement, and to some extent with the fate of the material in the food chains. "We do not know the particular form in

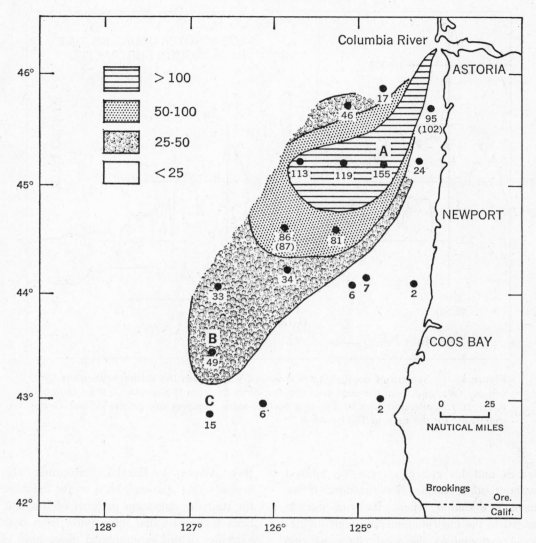

Figure 43–6   Chromium-51 (counts per minute per 100 liters of surface sea water) corrected to date of collection. June 26 to July 1, 1965 (Parentheses indicate duplicate samples. The number of counts per minute per 100 liters can be converted to picocuries per liter by multiplying by 0.861. The greatest velocity of water movement was between points A and B)

which the nuclides occurred in the sea. Their exact state and the paths by which they move through the system are unknown" (Barnes and Gross, 1966, p. 302). The whole experience with the Hanford effluent has been more in the nature of a vast unplanned marking experiment, in strong contrast. to the careful advance studies and continuing monitoring program at Wind-

scale. Indeed this unpremeditated marking experiment "homed" at Hanford itself in 1959 when an unexpectedly high ^{65}Zn level was detected in a person who had eaten oysters from Willapa Bay (just north of the Columbia) that had accumulated ^{65}Zn from the river effluent; in this case the concentration factor was 200,000 times that of the sea water (Perkins et al., 1960).

ECOLOGICAL QUESTIONS

Most of our information about the possible effects of radiation on organisms in nature is derived from experiments involving quantities or intensities that do not occur in nature upon organisms that do well under experimental conditions. It is difficult to interpret information based on experiments with such nearly indestructible organisms as the brine shrimp and fish that may survive in nature in situations not too different from hot urine (e.g., *Fundulus*). At the present time there are two schools of thought on the question of the effect of low levels of artificial radioactivity on marine organisms. Soviet workers have found, for example, that eggs of the anchovy in the Black Sea (the eggs are pelagic, i.e. in the surface layers of the sea) may be damaged by concentrations of ^{90}Sr as low as 10^{-10} curie per liter, and on this basis suggest that the maximum permissible concentration for the surface layers of the sea should be of the same order (10^{-12}) as for man, and that "further radioactive contamination of the seas and oceans is inadmissible" (Polikarpov, 1966, p. 260). The research by Soviet workers in this field is summarized by Polikarpov in his book, and this work is in fact the only attempt so far at a general summary of the problem.

The results of Soviet investigators have not been supported by research in Britain and America. Templeton (1966) studied the resistance of brown trout and plaice (*Pleuronectes platessa*) eggs to acute and chronic irradiation and found no demonstrable effect at the low levels claimed by Soviet workers. The plaice was the same species studied by Soviet investigators (their material was from the Barents Sea; Templeton used eggs from hatchery ponds at Por Erin on the Irish Sea), but the results vary so much without demonstrable effect at ^{90}Sr

concentrations of 10^{-4} curies per liter that Templeton does not consider the addition of antibiotics and controlled temperature conditions (evidently conditions not involved in the Soviet procedures) to significantly influence the results. The differences "may have afforded some degree of protection and have affected the sorptive properties of the eggs. The acute and chronic external irradiation studies suggest that the eggs of *P. platessa* are as radioresistant as other species. Nevertheless, the present data only consider that period up to hatching, and long term studies . . . will be necessary to investigate the problem more fully" (Templeton, 1966, p. 858). Commenting on the earlier contradictory results which prompted this work of Templeton's, Polikarpov (1966, p. 227) remarks: "The striking and exceptional nature of these results call for further, and if possible joint, investigation." So far there appears to have been no serious effort to undertake joint studies by Soviet and other researchers.

This subject was reviewed by Parker (1967) in a somewhat incomplete manner, since he does not clearly state that at least one species in common was investigated by Soviet and British workers (he neglects to cite Templeton's 1966 paper), but chooses rather to emphasize work done in the United States on the eggs and alevins of salmonid fishes, especially by Bonham and Donaldson (1966). Hence Parker's statement that "different species" might be in part responsible for the difference between Soviet and other results is misleading. Aside from the differences in methodology and statistical interpretation of the results, there are, of course, difficulties in comparing the reactions of such demersal fresh-water eggs as those of salmonids to those of marine pelagic or near-surface eggs of plaice and clupeid fishes. The dose response curve represented in Fig. 31 of Polikarpov's book (p. 225) indicates a little more than threefold increase of abnormal fish larvae over an increase of

^{90}Sr activity by six orders of magnitude (from 10^{-12} to 10^{-6}). In Templeton's opinion (personal communication) this is not a very sensitive system and it remains to be proven that these effects at such low levels are indeed induced by radiation.

In his review of these matters, Parker concludes with apparent equanimity: "However, whether or not harmful effects to the environment have occurred has not been determined due to diametrically opposed results of the investigations carried out to date on genetic damage to biota from the wastes released" (Parker, 1967, p. 380). This seems to say that when there is diametric disagreement between results obtained from incomparable situations, both are wrong. This attitude is disturbing in view of the incomplete and inaccurate analysis presented. It is obvious that there are too many variables involved in this "confrontation" between Soviet and other workers in this field, and the only logical approach is a program of research on identical and related species of similar life history and ecology in several parts of the world. Until critical work on comparable species proves otherwise, the results of Soviet workers must be accepted as a warning that we could be approaching a condition of saturation of the marine environment with potentially dangerous radioactive materials.

The Russian tendency to view with alarm may be based in part on the realization that comparatively small changes of natural conditions may exert a disproportionate stress upon a population that is being heavily levied by an active fishery, as most of the clupeid fishes are. Thus, while the system may not appear too sensitive under laboratory conditions, these comparatively small numbers of induced abnormalities may turn out to be much greater in proportion to the breeding stock of a heavily fished population, especially if they should coincide with other unfavorable environmental conditions such as small changes in the temperature

regime or the failure of the phytoplankton crop to coincide in phase with the larval stages of the fish. While they may sometimes be suggestive, laboratory results do not always provide us with data for predicting what may happen in the real world of the sea.

It should also be remembered that we set our standards for permissible doses for ourselves much more rigorously than we do for "less evolved" organisms. In part this may be based on the idea that "less evolved" organisms are more radioresistant, and in part it may be implicitly based on the notion that an increase in the abnormality or death rate of fishes (for example) is less serious than it would be for humans. We may not necessarily be the most important creatures on the earth, even in terms of our own survival, and it may be a dangerous error to regard other aspects of the natural system upon which we depend and of which we are a part as "less sensitive" or more tolerant to abuse.

In the real world one cannot consider the effects of radionuclides without reference to other aspects of pollution or natural factors. In the Irish Sea, ruthenium 106 is adsorbed on suspended silt which in turn is adsorbed on the *Porphyra*. What would be the effect of such an installation as Windscale combined with a massive sewer outfall, or with an industrial plant discharging large quantities of particulate matter into the sea? (Massive disposal of a fine particulate material near the mouth of the Columbia was considered by one industry.) Such "synergistic" combinations of pollutants could alter the pathways of radionuclides in food chains and produce different patterns of circulation and dilution or concentration in the sea.

Windscale and Hanford are two examples of the shape of things to come. There are several smaller-scale liquid waste disposal programs in various countries, and others are being planned. So far, all of these controlled releases are being made in regions where there is a certain amount of oceanographic sophistication and the necessary technology for continuous monitoring is available, viz., Britain, Norway, Sweden, France, Italy, and Japan. Research and surveillance are not good assurance against pollution, however. It seems obvious, for example, that even in the Pacific Ocean near the mouth of the Columbia, the residence time of such a radionuclide as ^{65}Zn in resident organisms may offset the potential for physical dispersion. What then can be expected from waste disposal in semienclosed seas and gulfs? If, for example, a large industrial-agricultural unit powered by nuclear reactors were to be placed on the shore of the Red Sea or the Persian Gulf, what might happen? If such a development would also assume increased harvest of products of the sea, has consideration of the possible effect of radioactive waste disposal in such a closed basin as the Persian Gulf been made? Or is it being assumed that there are no laver bread consumers (or their like) and that this aspect of the potential economy need not be considered?

Desalination, a logical part of such prepackaged development schemes, would add a still further complication. Desalination produces either piles of salt in quantities too vast for economic use by anyone, or more practically, concentrated brines that would be returned to the sea. John Isaacs (1964) has suggested that location of large desalination plants on steep coasts would provide another means of disposal of low-level wastes since the wastes could be mixed with the brine which is much denser than sea water and the mixture would flow along the bottom down submarine canyons to the abyssal depths of the sea. This could not happen in the Red Sea (which already has its own hot brine pool in the bottom) or the Persian Gulf or any other place that is separated from the world ocean by a comparatively shallow sill. Addition of brines to these semienclosed bodies of water is prob-

ably even more inadvisable than release of radionuclides. This aspect of nuclear-powered development schemes requires more serious consideration than it appears to have received. Some idea of the levels of oceanographic sophistication required to analyze these problems beforehand may be gained from the paper by Whipple (1964) and the appended detailed discussions to his paper.

There are many other aspects to the problem of large-scale nuclear desalination projects that have not been given adequate attention by those who have suggested them (including the United States Senate). These are discussed in some detail by Clawson, Landsberg and Alexander in an article in *Science,* June 6, 1969. Many of the difficulties appear to be related to the proposed scale of operations (it appears that we should not attempt anything of this sort except in the largest possible way), but almost no consideration is given, as these authors point out, to the matter of maintaining intakes (and they did not specifically consider problems of marine growth that impede flow, which would be most pronounced in warm-water regions), and to the problems of water storage to provide water to the fields (which would have to be on a different time schedule than production by a comparatively steady source of power). A most significant point, from the viewpoint of the country to be benefited, is that these plants would be isolated from "the mainstream of the country's culture." What is to be done, for example, with electrical energy in a region where there are not even light bulbs to turn on?

The conclusion is inescapable: the full and true costs of the proposed desalting projects, now and for the next 20 years, are at least one whole order of magnitude greater than the value of the water to agriculture.

The authors emphasize, of course, that this does not mean that we should not go on studying the matter. However, the problem of disposal of the fuel elements and other radioactive wastes from such complexes was not considered in this study of costs of producing desalinated water. These could be considerable, especially in an "undeveloped" country without industrial capacity to treat the materials. Should the most dangerous ones be buried in the land to be improved by agriculture, or will the country involved be permanently dependent on some other country for treatment of high-level wastes?

It would obviously be unwise to permit, on a world-wide basis, a development that might produce a steady discharge of radioactive materials into regions where it might build up and in turn serve as a source of pollution to larger bodies of the sea.

Reassurance that the isotope sewers of Windscale and Hanford are contributing less radioactivity to the environment than nuclear weapons tests is beside the point. As Korringa says, it is "not the accidental calamities but the general trends, the stealthy deterioration of environmental conditions in sections of the sea of vital importance to its living resources, which count most" (Korringa, 1968). Even a few more isotope sewers may be "insignificant," but the next order of magnitude may not be far off, and the research and surveillance necessary to keep such waste disposal within limits will be diluted more rapidly than the wastes may be dispersed. Can we talk of world-wide increase of the fisheries resources of the sea, at the same time as we endanger those resources with radioactive pollution that may not only alter their productivity but render them dangerous for human consumption?

The answer is, of course, that we cannot. The sea is not the inexhaustible supply of fishes that it was once thought to be, or the perpetual sink that sanitary engineers fondly hope it should be (see, e.g., Rawn, 1966). While we may be able to increase our present world fishery by perhaps four or five times, such expansion will be near

the limit of sustainable yield for many more stocks than it is now.[3] While the possible effects of adding radionuclides to the marine environment may appear to be small in terms of total populations, it must not be forgotten that when a population is heavily exploited by a fishery the reproductive stock is greatly reduced and the population becomes more susceptible to small environmental disturbances. A reduction of the genetic pool coincident with increased radioactivity might add another selective factor of unpredictable influence. The spectacular decline of the California sardine fishery may have been in part due to relatively small environmental changes acting upon an overexploited population; one of the explanations for this decline may be that small changes in

[3] Estimates of the potential yield of the sea are still more speculative than realistic. In addition to the biological problems associated with heavy fishery, the irregular, patchy occurrence of desirable species, and our hunting skills, there are the socioeconomic problems of distribution, marketing, and consumption. Taken abstractly, it is highly possible that the oceans of the world could produce more than enough protein for an exploding population; but this information is about as useful as the coal prospects of the antarctic continent. Such an exercise as that of Walter R. Schmitt (1965) makes the fundamentally dubious assertion that a complex ecological problem can be approached in the spirit of a certified public accountant (nothing is said in planning for agricultural expansion about the probability that in actual practice we would be making the world safe for schistosomiasis), although he does accept the usual informed estimate of twofold to fivefold increase in oceanic fisheries for the foreseeable future.

While the problems of total yield of fisheries and prospects of culture of marine organisms (aquiculture) are somewhat outside the scope of this paper, it should be emphasized that so far much of aquiculture has been restricted to nearshore environments, usually bays or estuaries, where the danger of recirculation of radionuclides would be greatest. Hence any increase of aquiculture would require even more rigorous control of pollutants to avoid the dangers of concentration by filter feeding organisms which might be cultured, such as mussels and oysters. Another aspect of the aquiculture problem is that of producing the fodder on which to raise the desirable species for human consumption in a closed or semienclosed system. One of the best discussions of this topic is that by John D. Isaacs (1967), who clearly states why it is impractical to consider farming the open sea.

temperature of the spawning regions reduced reproductive success of the stock at a time when it was vulnerable to other ecological influences. The story is far from simple, however, (see Murphy, 1966), and serves

to emphasize that at the present state of the art of ecology we cannot agree with the sanguine attitude that the sea is safe for any "reasonable" (or unreasonable) increase of its natural radiation background.

ACKNOWLEDGMENTS

I am pleased to acknowledge the assistance of Evan C. Evans III and W. L. Templeton in supplying information, literature, and criticism for this paper. My own opinions and interpretations are not, of course, their responsibility.

REFERENCES

Barnes, C. A., and Gross, M. G. "Distribution at Sea of Columbia River Water and Its Load of Radionuclides." In *Disposal of Radioactive Wastes into Seas, Oceans, and Surface Waters.* Symposium Proceedings, Vienna, May 16–20, 1966. International Atomic Energy Agency, STI/PUB/126. 1966. Pp. 291–302. (Cited from Parker, 1967.)

Bonham, K., and Donaldson, L. R. "Low Level of Chronic Irradiation of Salmon Eggs and Alevins." In *Disposal of Radioactive Wastes into Seas, Oceans, and Surface Waters.* Symposium Proceedings, Vienna, May 16–20, 1966. IAEA, 1966. P. 882.

Bugher, John C. "Effects of Fission Material on Air, Soil, and Living Species." In *Man's Role in Changing the Face of The Earth,* William L. Thomas, Jr., ed. Chicago: University of Chicago Press, 1956. Pp. 831–48 (Figs. 157–61).

Carey, A. G.; Pearcy, W. G.; and Osterberg, C. L. "Artificial Radionuclides in Marine Organisms in the Northeast Pacific Ocean off Oregon." In *Disposal of Radioactive Wastes into Seas, Oceans, and Surface Waters.* Symposium Proceedings, Vienna, May 16–20, 1966. IAEA. 1966. Pp. 303–19.

Chamberlain, A. C., and Dunster, H. J. "Deposition of Radioactivity in Northwest England from the Accident at Windscale." *Nature,* 182 (4636) (1958), 629–30.

Chipman, W. A.; Rice, T. R.; and Price, T. J. "Uptake and Accumulation of Radioactive Zinc by Marine Plankton, Fish, and Shellfish." *U.S. Fish and Wildlife Fishery Bulletin,* 58 (135) (1958), 279–92.

Clawson, Marion; Landsberg, Hans H.; and Alexander, Lyle T. "Desalted Seawater for Agriculture: Is It Economic?" *Science,* 164 (1969), 1141–48.

George, J. L., and Frear, D. E. H. "Pesticides in the Antarctic." *J. Applied Ecol.,* 3 (Suppl.) (1966), 155–67.

Howells, H. "Discharges of Low-Activity, Radioactive Effluent from the Windscale Works into the Irish Sea." In *Disposal of Radioactive Wastes into Seas, Oceans, and Surface Waters.* Symposium Proceedings, Vienna, May 16–20, 1966. IAEA. 1966. Pp. 769–85 (1 fig.).

Isaacs, John D. Discussion. In *Advances in Pollution Research,* E. A. Pearson, ed. Vol. 3. New York: Macmillan, 1964. Pp. 26–33.

———. "Food from the Sea." *Int. Sci. and Tech.,* April 1967, 61–68.

Isaacs, John D., ed. "Disposal of Low-Level

Radioactive Waste into Pacific Coastal Waters." National Academy of Sciences–National Research Council, Washington, D.C. *Publ.* 985, 1962. 87 pp.

Korringa, Pieter. "Biological Consequences of Marine Pollution with Special Reference to the North Sea Fisheries." *Helgolander wiss. Meeresunters,* 17 (1968), 126–40 (2 figs.).

Longley, H., and Templeton, W. L. "Marine Environmental Monitoring in the Vicinity of Windscale." In *Radiological Monitoring in the Environment.* Elmsford, N.Y.: Pergamon Press, 1965, pp. 219–47 (7 figs.).

Mauchline, J., and Templeton, W. L. "Artificial and Natural Radioisotopes in the Marine Environment." *Oceanogr. Mar.* 20, 1966. IAEA. 1966. Pp. 321–91 (6 figs.).

Mellanby, Kenneth. *Pesticides and Pollution.* The New Naturalist Series. London: Collins, 1967. 221 pp., illus.

Murphy, Garth I. "Population Biology of the Pacific Sardine (*Sardinops caerulea*)." *Proc. Calif. Acad. Sci.,* Fourth ser., 34 (1) (1966), 1–84 (17 figs.).

Osterberg, Charles. "Radioactivity from the Columbia River." *Ocean Sci. and Engr.,* 2 (1965), 968–79 (8 figs.).

Osterberg, Charles; Cutshall, N.; and Cronin, J. "Chromium-51 as a Radioactive Tracer of Columbia River Water at Sea." *Science,* 150 (3703) (1965), 1585–87 (2 figs.).

Osterberg, Charles; Cutshall, N.; Johnson, V.; Cronin, J.; Jennings, D.; and Frederick, L. In *Disposal of Radioactive Wastes into the Seas, Oceans, and Surface Waters.* Symposium Proceedings, Vienna, May 16–20, 1965. IAEA. 1966. Pp. 321–91 (6 figs.).

Osterberg, Charles; Pattullo, J. G.; and Pearcy, W. G. "Zinc-65 in Euphausiids as Related to Columbia River Water off the Oregon Coast." *Limnol. and Oceanogr.,* 9 (2) (1964), 249–57 (6 figs.).

Osterberg, Charles; Pearcy, W. G.; and Curl, H. C., Jr. "Radioactivity and Its Relationship to Oceanic Food Chains. *J. Mar. Res.,* 22 (1) (1964), 2–14 (4 figs.).

Parker, F. L. "Disposal of Low-Level Radio-active Wastes into the Oceans." *Nuclear Safety,* 8 (4) (1967), 376–82.

Pearcy, W. G., and Osterberg, C. L. "Zinc-65 and Manganese-54 in Albacore *Thunnus alalunga* from the West Coast of North America." *Limnol. Oceanogr.,* 13 (3) (1968), 490–98 (5 figs.).

Perkins, R. W.; Nielsen, J. M.; Roesch, W. C.; and McCall, R. C. "Zinc-65 and Chromium-51 in Foods and People." *Science,* 132 (3443) (1960), 1895–97.

Polikarpov, G. G. *Radioecology of Aquatic Organisms.* Trans. from the Russian by Scripta Technica Ltd., English transl. edited by Vincent Schultz and Alfred W. Klement, Jr. New York: Reinhold Book Division, 1966. xxviii, 314 pp. (36 figs.).

Rawn, A. M. "Fixed and Changing Values in Ocean Disposal of Sewage and Wastes." In *First International Conference on Waste Disposal in the Sea,* E. A. Pearson, ed. Elmsford, N.Y.: Pergamon Press, 1966. Pp. 6–11.

Schmitt, Walter R. "The Planetary Food Potential." *Ann. N.Y. Acad. Sci.,* 118 (17) (1965), 645–718.

Sladen, William J. L.; Menzie, C. M.; and Reichel, W. L. "DDT Residues in Adelie Penguins and a Crabeater Seal from Antarctica." *Nature,* 210 (5037) (1966), 670–73.

Tatton, J. O'G., and Ruzicka, J. H. A. "Organochlorine Pesticides in Antarctica." Nature, 215 (5099) (1967), 346–48.

Templeton, W. L. "Ecological Aspects of the Disposal of Radioactive Wastes to the Sea." *Ecology and the Industrial Society.* Fifth Symposium, British Ecological Society. 1965. Pp. 65–97.

———. "Resistance of Fish Eggs to Acute and Chronic Irradiation." In *Disposal of Radioactive Wastes into Seas, Oceans, and Surface Waters.* Symposium Proceedings, Vienna, May 16–20, 1966. IAEA. 1966. Pp. 847–60, 3 figs.

Whipple, R. T. P. "Considerations on the Siting of Outfalls for the Sea Disposal of Radioactive Effluent in Tidal Waters." *Advances in Water Pollution Research.* New York: Macmillan, 1964. Pp. 1–18; discussion, 19–35.

44. ENVIRONMENTAL QUALITY AND THE THERMAL POLLUTION PROBLEM

John Cairns, Jr.

The many simplified ecosystems resulting from man's various activities in the world are inherently much more unstable than the natural ecosystems they replace. This means that wise management of the environment is an increasing imperative if catastrophe is to be avoided. Management must begin with a conception of the environment as an interrelated whole. To come up with a workable method for a single environmental problem without considering the others will, at best, only delay disaster.

The rapidly increasing warming of surface waters by industrial uses of water is an example of the urgent need for basic social and policy changes so that proper management of the environment may occur. (Detailed discussions are given of present problems and techniques of observing and analyzing changes in ecological patterns in heated waters.) Electric power companies and all others using the environment for waste disposal have two alternatives: either to continue to increase stress on the environment and regard the resulting damage as a necessary product of civilization, or manage the environment so it serves the greatest number of beneficial uses. If we don't choose the second of these, we may soon have no choices at all. If we agree to manage the environment, we must set up institutions to coordinate and implement the complex decisions on environmental uses and safeguards which must be made.

If such institutions developed, there would be two not necessarily mutually exclusive alternatives of management: to adjust our society to fit the environment as it now exists so no further deterioration ensues or to deliberately modify the environment to function well under a set of conditions that we create. (A discussion of the pros and cons of both these alternatives is given, with a qualified rejection of the idea of man-created ecosystems as the sole solution to pollution problems.)

Any attempt to adjust harmoniously with the environment must deal not only with aspects of organization, attitudes, politics, and values, but with the constant changes of the environment itself. Many of the changes are man-caused, and as they continue to emerge, the ease of past assaults on the various ecosystems gives way to immense difficulties and costs. We need much quicker and more comprehensive techniques to gather and assimilate data on the many related changes before we can work out ways to best integrate our needs and those of the environment.

We have the ability to develop such techniques and others; we are also able to organize properly to employ them. But will our present attitudes continue to keep us from doing what must be done until it is too late?

The warming of our surface waters is not restricted to the present. As Wurtz (1969) points out, the early settlers destroyed the vegetational canopy which probably resulted in warmer runoff waters. Very likely, these environmental alterations affected the biota inhabiting the surface waters. One can only estimate the extent of these changes because the extensive data required to establish gradual changes in an ecosystem do not exist for most of our surface waters today—years ago such data were even rarer.

Though many industries use water to carry off heat generated by various processes and agricultural and domestic uses also warm our water, the greatest source of thermal loading is the steam-electric industry. Both fossil-fueled and nuclear-fueled plants use water as a coolant because of its high specific heat; air will not function nearly as well. Recent trends indicate that demand for electric power will double every six to ten years. Thermoelectric (as opposed to hydroelectric) power production in the United States is expected to amount to 2,000 billion kilowatt-hours by 1980 (Stroud and Douglas, 1968). Using present production methods, this will require approximately 200 billion gallons of water per day out of an estimated total supply of 1,200 billion gallons per day for the entire continental United States. Singer (1968) estimates that one-quarter of all surface waters in the United States will be used for cooling in 1985. Single existing power plants may now require up to one-half million gallons of water each minute for cooling purposes, and economic considerations apparently favor the construction of even larger plants.

Unfortunately, the distribution of water is geographically uneven and usually seasonally variable. In certain watersheds the entire volume may be required by the local power plant during low flow conditions unless cooling towers are used to permit recycling of water. An additional drawback is that this period of maximum use may coincide with the warmest period of the year when surface waters are already at or near maximum annual temperatures and the organisms inhabiting them closest to their upper temperature tolerance limit.

The literature is replete with data on the effects of temperature changes in the aquatic environment.[1] Heated waste waters may affect aquatic organisms by (1) killing them (a) directly (b) indirectly (reduced oxygen, food, decreased resistance); (2) causing internal functional aberrations (changes in respiration, growth, life history, etc.); (3)

[1] Documenting all the effects of increased temperatures in the aquatic environment would require several volumes. As I was reading a final proof of this paper, Raney and Menzel (1969) published a 469-page literature summary on this general topic. The following source references will also be useful: Kennedy and Mihursky (1967), Raney and Menzel (1967), Prosser (1967), and Holdaway et al. (1967).

competitive exclusion by more tolerant species; or (4) interference with spawning or other critical activities.

As any tropical fish fancier knows, each fish has environmental requirements that differ from those of other species. Though ranges may overlap for many species, there is something unique about the requirements of each one. The same generalization applies to aquatic species other than fish. Thus each ecosystem and drainage basin is inhabited by the mixture of species particularly suited to that environment. The ecosystem may share characteristics in common with other ecosystems but each is also significantly different from the others. All this would seem obvious to the point of triviality if laws designed to protect ecosystems were not general laws based on "average conditions"; these laws rarely consider specific regional systems as functional units with interdependent, interacting parts. However, the techniques for regional management are available (Watt, 1966, 1968) —it is our behavioral patterns and attitudes that need to be changed.

I will begin the case history portion of this paper with a pair of carefully selected, well-documented case histories of river surveys carried out by the Limnology Department of the Academy of Natural Sciences of Philadelphia. The problem simply stated was: "Could heated waste water be discharged into a stream without causing a major disruption in the aquatic community?" Or: "To what extent may industry utilize the coolant capacity of a river without damaging its other present and potential beneficial uses?" Each case history shows how ecological considerations were successfully built into the developmental and operational process of an industrial plant. After considering these studies, I wish to develop the broader consideration of environmental stress, to explore alternative means of coping with this general problem, and finally to consider how the approach

used in each of the case histories might be expanded to include entire ecosystems.

The ecological assessment consisted of a biological, chemical, and physical survey of the river above and below the discharge point, before plant operations began, followed by similar surveys after the plant had been operating. Each major increase in thermal loading was accompanied by "before and after" studies of the same type. Since the surveys were intermittent, a continually operating biological monitoring system, using Catherwood diatometers,[2] was installed as well. Both of these assessment methods were "after the fact"—that is, they were designed to detect damage after it had occurred. Since biological degradation is typically a gradual process, this system provides more protection than laymen might expect. Had any biological degradation been noted, discharge would have been reduced to levels previously tolerated by the aquatic community. The criterion for biological degradation was *reduction in the number of species present.*[3]

The first program was designed to determine whether the heated waste water from the Savannah River Plant of the Atomic Energy Commission operated by E. I. du Pont de Nemours and Company had any effect upon the aquatic organisms living in the Savannah River in the vicinity of the plant. Limnological studies began at four sites on the river a year before plant construction was complete. The first survey was

[2] A device for suspending glass slides in water as a substrate for diatoms. Slides are removed every two weeks, and the number of species as well as the number of individuals per species are counted.

[3] Although this concept (known as species diversity) is very useful as a theoretical device for coping with the analytical problems posed by environmental pollution, there are some serious valid criticisms of it. In my opinion, the primary weakness is that it gives only indirect evidence on the way the system is functioning. It also requires a number of highly trained taxonomists to identify the species that are collected. And taxonomists are in short supply and not always willing to become involved in applied research.

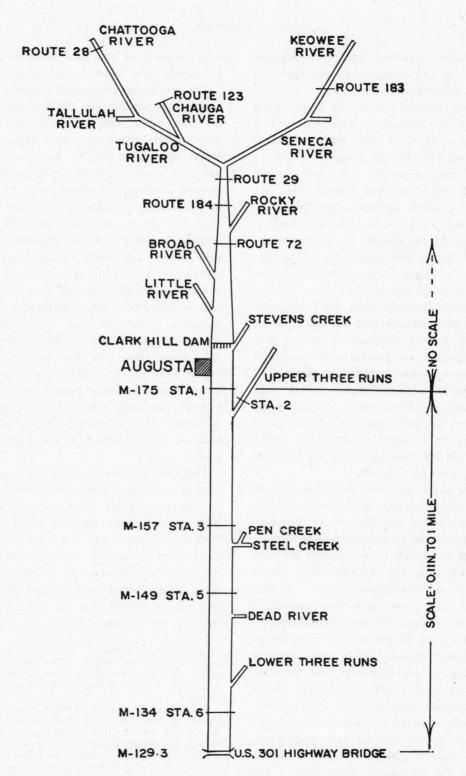

Figure 44–1 Diagrammatic map of Savannah River Basin (After Patrick, Cairns and Roback, 1967). (Station 2 was not included in the 1967 paper or in this discussion because it was only a tributary of the Savannah and ecologically distinct from the other survey stations)

carried out in the summer of 1951, and periodic surveys continue to the present. Because a control station located well above any possible effects of plant operation and three stations below the waste water discharge were selected (Fig. 44–1), any adverse effects due to plant operation could be detected.

Details of this study have been published by Patrick, Cairns and Roback (1967) and will be only briefly summarized here. It is important that stations chosen for comparative studies have comparable habitats. Because these studies were designed to detect gross reduction in species diversity (i.e., number of species), which is a usual consequence of environmental stress (Patrick, 1949; Cairns, 1966a), the quality of the environment or the types of habitat present are more important than the dimensions of the area. These surveys were carried out by field teams of specialists including an algologist, a protozoologist, a lower-invertebrate zoologist, an entomologist, an ichthyologist, a chemist-bacteriologist, and several field assistants. Usually, this team spent several weeks in the field on each survey. Upon returning to Academy laboratories, we spent several weeks to several months identifying specimens, and additional specialists were usually consulted during this period. We constantly endeavored to keep our efforts comparable both between stations and between surveys. Specimens of all species collected, except the fragile protozoans, were placed in the Academy collections.

In addition to the major surveys just described, cursory surveys were carried out periodically by two limnologists. Continuous biological monitoring was accomplished by placing Catherwood diatometers (Patrick *et al.,* 1954) at each station. These devices, which suspended microscope slides in the photosynthetic zone, provided data on the structure of the diatom community at regular intervals (Figs. 44–2, 44–3). Histograms

showing the biological changes which would be seen in case of pollution are given in Fig. 44–7 in the Appendix. Although the species composing the diatom "community" change frequently, the number of species (Table 44–1) and the structure of the curve remain very similar* as long as unusual stress (or pollution) does not develop. The curves in Figs. 44–2 and 44–3 are produced by identifying and counting several thousand diatoms on each slide removed from the diatometer. Species with one to two individuals per species are placed in the first interval, those with two to four in the second interval, etc. Enough specimens are counted to place the mode between the

Table 44–1

COMPARISON OF READINGS FROM TWO DIATOMETERS LOCATED IN THE SAME AREA OF THE SAVANNAH RIVER.[1]

DIATOMETER	DATE	SPECIES IN MODE	OBSERVED SPECIES
No. 2	Jan. 1954	19	151
No. 2	Apr. 1954	24	169
No. 2	Oct. 1954	21	142
No. 2	Jan. 1955	19	132
No. 1	Apr. 1955	25	165
No. 2	July 1955	20	132
No. 2	Oct. 1955	27	171
No. 2	Jan. 1956	30	185
No. 2	Apr. 1956	35	215
No. 2	July 1956	24	147
No. 2	Oct. 1956	23	149
No. 2	Jan. 1957	29	177
No. 2	Apr. 1957	21	132
No. 2	July 1957	29	181
No. 1	Oct. 1957	25	157
No. 2	Jan. 1958	27	152
		24	159

(January 1954–1957 averages)

* Relative to the kinds of variation which theoretically could occur with many thousands of potential colonizing species.

[1] Note the remarkable consistency of results in different seasons and different years (from Patrick, 1967).

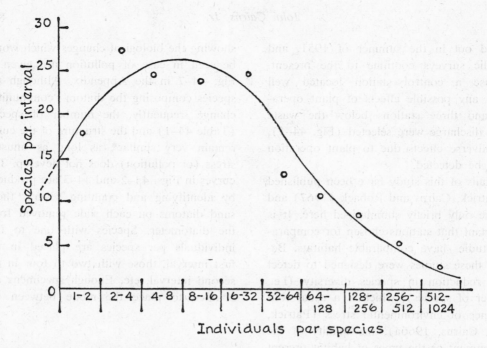

Figure 44–2 Graph of the diatom population from a stream not adversely affected by pollution (From Patrick *et al.*, 1954)

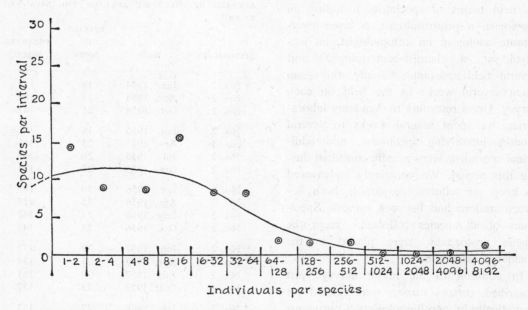

Figure 44–3 Graph of the diatom population from a "polluted" stream (From Patrick *et al.*, 1954)

third and fourth intervals. Note that the population from a "healthy" stream (Fig. 44–2) has a large number of species with comparatively few individuals per species. This distribution is characteristic of diatoms in unpolluted temperate zone streams regardless of the season or of the particular species in the community. The simplified community in Fig. 44–3 has a few species with very high numbers of individuals; it also has fewer species with lower numbers of individuals per species than does the community in Fig. 44–2. This is a characteristic response to a wide variety of environmental stresses ranging from excess heat to toxic concentrations of chemicals. Good correlations have been found between changes in the structure of the diatom community and the entire community of aquatic organisms. Literature searches and some laboratory bioassays on the effects of heated water discharge were also included in the program.

A summary of the biological results for the major surveys is given in Table 44–2, and of the chemical analyses and temperature data in Table 44–3. No gross differences were noted between the control station and the other stations, and all stations remained in the "healthy" range from 1951 to 1960 according to the system proposed by Patrick (1949). Some operational details are classified, and therefore thermal loading rates cannot be given. However, the temperature ranges in Table 44–3 indicate that the effect of plant operation on the thermal regime of the river was not great. Two points are important: (1) frequent biological assessments were made before and after plant operation began in order to determine effects upon the aquatic environment, and (2) a biologically acceptable thermal loading level was estimated from laboratory bioassays and a search of the literature, and the receiving stream was frequently checked to verify that no degradation was occurring. This procedure shows that the plant can use the river without interfering with other beneficial uses.

Although the information feedback system will be discussed in more detail in the following Potomac Electric Power Company (PEPCO) example (because it involves a series of increases in plant operating capacity), a brief outline of the planning and use of survey information should be helpful at this point. The study originated with a request from the Savannah River Plant for a preliminary study of the river above and below the proposed discharge areas. During the preliminary study, results of engineering studies of waste discharge with estimated loading rates, mixing, and other characteristics were provided in order that sampling areas or stations could be properly located. Appropriate background data on river flow, industrial and municipal waste discharge, and aquatic organisms inhabiting the river were obtained from Georgia and South Carolina state regulatory agencies and departments of fish and game as well as from federal agencies such as the U. S. Army Corps of Engineers and the U. S. Geological Survey and regional agencies such as chambers of commerce. It is important that state and regional agencies be apprised of the tentative survey plans at this stage not only because they have a role in granting permits but more importantly so that they can participate in the planning process.

The most critical sampling area or station is the one just below the discharge point, for two reasons: (1) the location of this station is primarily determined by the discharge location and the mixing characteristics of the waste rather than by ecological considerations and (2) this is likely to be the area most affected by waste discharge. This area is generally examined first, its exact location being strongly influenced by data provided by engineers. The control station location is determined primarily by ecological considerations since it can be almost anywhere above the waste discharge but must match the habitat quality of the station just below the discharge point quite closely. One or more delimiting stations are usually placed some distance downstream from the outfall so that the area damaged may be delimited in the event of serious effects immediately below the discharge point.

Once there is general agreement on the design, surveys are carried out before and

Table 44-2

	MODERATELY HIGH FLOW SUMMER, 1951				LOW FLOW FALL, 1951				WINTER, 1952				HIGH FLOW SPRING, 1952			
	1	3	5	6	1	3	5	6	1	3	5	6	1	3	5	6
ALGAE																
Division																
Cyanophyta	6	11	7	8	2	3	6	2	2	2	2	2	2	2	4	1
Chlorophyta	6	14	22	20	5	9	9	12	6	13	9	5	11	8	11	12
Rhodophyta	1	1	1	1	1	1	1	1	–	–	1	1	–	1	–	–
Bacillariophyta	93	88	60	117	89	87	103	74	77	44	58	75	50	55	39	48
Chrysophyta	1	–	–	–	–	–	–	–	1	1	1	1	1	1	–	1
TOTALS	107	114	90	146	97	100	119	89	86	60	71	84	64	67	54	62
PROTOZOA																
Class																
Mastigophora	12	9	8	14	10	11	18	20	7	4	11	19	9	13	11	18
Sarcodina	2	–	–	3	4	6	5	10	2	1	4	5	1	5	5	6
Ciliata	5	9	8	5	8	13	10	9	17	13	13	31	13	11	8	19
Suctoria	–	–	–	–	–	1	1	1	–	–	–	–	–	–	–	–
TOTALS	19	18	16	22	22	31	34	40	26	18	28	55	23	29	24	43
INVERTEBRATES																
Phylum																
Porifera	–	1	–	–	1	1	–	–	1	1	1	1	–	1	1	–
Platyhelminthes	–	1	1	–	1	1	–	–	–	1	1	–	–	1	1	–
Nemertea	–	–	–	–	–	–	–	–	–	–	1	–	–	–	–	1
Nematoda	–	–	–	–	–	–	–	–	–	–	–	–	–	–	–	–
Tardigrada	–	–	–	–	–	–	–	–	–	–	–	–	–	–	–	–
Polyzoa	–	–	–	–	–	–	–	–	–	–	–	–	–	–	–	–
Aschelminthes	7	9	4	5	5	6	7	5	11	7	17	6	5	6	3	4
Bryozoa	–	1	–	–	1	–	1	–	1	1	–	–	1	1	–	1
Annelida	2	5	2	3	5	3	3	1*	4	4	6	1	2	4	6	5
Mollusca	2	10	5	7	7	11	5	5	4	2	1	4	4	4	7	6
Arthropoda	–	1	–	–	–	2	1	2	–	3	3	1	1	4	3	3
TOTALS	11	28	12	15	20	24	17	13	21	19	30	13	13	21	21	20
INSECTS																
Order																
Odonata	6	6	3	6	2	6	5	4	2	6	11	4	6	5	5	4
Ephemeroptera	6	5	4	5	5	12	10	6	7	5	8	7	15	8	7	15
Plecoptera	1	1	3	4	2	3	4	5	5	12	9	9	3	4	4	4
Hemiptera	4	4	5	7	6	1	6	4	–	–	–	–	3	5	3	2
Megaloptera	–	1	1	2	1	1	1	2	–	1	1	–	1	–	1	–
Coleoptera	7	11	10	14	10	11	11	13	8	10	11	10	14	16	20	15
Trichoptera	6	8	1	7	1	3	2	1	3	2	11	6	6	2	4	3
Diptera	6	1	2	4	1	4	6	4	7	8	4	10	16	9	25	12
TOTALS	36	37	29	49	28	41	45	39	32	44	55	46	64	49	69	55
FISH																
Order																
Amiiformes	–	–	–	–	–	–	–	1	1	–	1	1	–	–	–	1
Lepisosteiformes	–	–	–	–	1	–	–	1	1	–	–	–	1	–	2	2
Clupeiformes	1	1	1	–	1	1	–	–	1	1	–	–	1	2	2	3
Cypriniformes	3	6	5	4	2	4	5	3	9	10	10	10	10	11	8	15
Anguilliformes	–	–	–	–	–	1	–	–	–	–	–	–	1	1	–	1
Cyprinodontiformes	–	–	1	–	–	1	–	–	1	1	–	–	1	1	1	1
Percopsiformes	–	–	–	–	–	–	–	–	1	–	–	–	1	1	1	1
Mugiliformes	–	–	–	–	1	–	–	–	1	1	–	1	1	1	–	1
Perciformes	5	8	4	7	6	4	5	5	5	6	5	7	9	6	6	7
Pleuronectiformes	–	1	1	1	–	1	1	–	1	–	1	–	–	–	1	1
Beloneiformes	–	–	–	–	–	–	–	–	–	–	–	–	–	–	–	–
TOTALS	9	16	11	13	11	12	11	10	21	19	17	19	25	23	21	33

Table 44-2 (continued)

	LOW FLOW SUMMER, 1954		LOW FLOW EARLY FALL, 1955				HIGH FLOW SPRING, 1956				HIGH FLOW SPRING, 1960				LOW FLOW EARLY FALL, 1960			
	1	6	1	3	5	6	1	3	5	6	1	3	5	6	1	3	5	6
ALGAE																		
Division																		
Cyanophyta	8	11	5	7	7	6	3	5	3	3	5	3	9	5	5	5	7	5
Chlorophyta	12	12	5	4	11	6	3	3	5	4	6	1	5	3	2	6	7	4
Rhodophyta	3	2	2	1	2	2	2	1	1	2	–	–	–	–	1	1	3	2
Bacillariophyta	79	68	85	76	82	105	89	88	87	74	84	73	76	64	66	77	85	87
Chrysophyta	1	1	1	1	1	1	1	–	1	1	1	–	–	–	1	1	1	1
TOTALS	103	94	98	89	103	120	98	97	97	84	96	77	90	72	75	90	103	99
PROTOZOA																		
Class																		
Mastigophora	25	22	25	26	25	27	20	18	19	23	24	24	33	22	23	26	25	25
Sarcodina	15	7	4	8	4	8	7	5	5	7	9	7	9	11	12	11	9	14
Ciliata	21	28	13	18	19	20	14	15	13	21	20	22	25	24	20	22	27	28
Suctoria	–	–	–	–	–	–	–	–	–	–	–	1	–	1	–	1	1	–
TOTALS	61	57	42	52	48	55	41	38	37	51	53	54	67	58	55	60	62	67
INVERTEBRATES																		
Phylum																		
Porifera	1	–	1	1	1	–	2	1	1	1	1	–	–	–	1	2	2	–
Platyhelminthes	1	1	–	–	1	–	1	1	1	–	1	–	1	1	–	1	–	1
Nemertea	–	–	–	–	–	–	–	–	–	–	1	–	–	1	–	–	–	–
Nematoda	–	–	–	–	–	–	1	–	–	–	–	–	–	–	–	–	1	–
Tardigrada	–	–	–	–	–	–	–	–	–	–	–	–	–	–	–	–	1	–
Polyzoa	–	–	–	–	–	–	–	–	–	–	1	–	1	1	1	1	2	1
Aschelminthes	2	–	2	3	2	2	1	–	–	–	–	–	–	–	–	–	–	–
Bryozoa	–	–	2	1	2	–	–	–	–	–	–	–	–	–	–	–	–	–
Annelida	2	2	2	3	4	7	2	3	2	2	3	4	4	–	3	3	4	1
Mollusca	6	3	7	5	7	7	6	4	4	5	9	11	11	10	8	11	9	11
Arthropoda	1	2	–	2	4	4	4	–	1	2	2	2	5	1	–	1	3	–
TOTALS	13	8	14	15	21	20	17	9	9	10	18	17	22	14	13	19	22	14
INSECTS																		
Order																		
Odonata	8	9	3	5	9	6	6	7	4	4	3	6	7	1	3	4	6	3
Ephemeroptera	9	7	9	7	10	9	8	7	10	9	2	2	4	8	5	4	2	4
Plecoptera	2	3	1	1	2	3	2	2	2	2	–	–	–	–	–	–	–	–
Hemiptera	2	1	2	2	1	4	4	5	4	4	5	1	2	–	1	2	2	–
Megaloptera	1	2	1	1	1	1	1	1	1	2	–	1	–	–	–	–	1	1
Coleoptera	11	20	7	8	8	11	7	7	13	11	9	13	7	5	7	8	5	6
Trichoptera	7	5	7	7	7	6	7	8	6	6	3	4	4	4	5	6	8	5
Diptera	17	19	14	10	16	18	11	10	14	8	11	8	13	7	5	10	11	9
TOTALS	57	66	44	41	54	58	46	47	54	46	33	35	37	26	26	34	35	28
FISH																		
Order																		
Amiiformes	1	–	–	–	1	–	–	1	1	1	–	–	1	1	1	1	–	1
Lepisosteiformes	–	1	1	–	–	–	1	1	1	1	2	1	2	2	2	1	2	2
Clupeiformes	3	3	6	2	3	4	3	2	2	3	3	3	4	4	4	3	5	5
Cypriniformes	3	16	10	7	9	9	7	10	11	9	8	8	10	9	13	10	12	14
Anguilliformes	–	1	1	–	1	1	1	1	1	1	1	1	1	1	1	1	1	1
Cyprinodontiformes	1	1	1	1	1	1	1	1	1	2	2	2	2	1	2	2	1	2
Percopsiformes	–	1	1	1	1	1	1	1	1	1	1	1	1	1	1	1	1	1
Mugiliformes	–	1	1	1	1	–	1	–	1	1	1	1	1	1	1	1	1	1
Perciformes	8	11	13	11	12	8	8	12	11	10	13	12	13	11	14	12	13	12
Pleuronectiformes	1	1	1	1	1	1	1	1	1	–	1	1	1	1	1	1	1	1
Beloneiformes	–	–	–	–	–	–	–	–	–	–	–	–	–	1	–	–	–	–
TOTALS	17	36	35	23	30	25	24	30	31	29	32	30	36	33	40	33	37	40

NUMBER OF SPECIES FOUND AT THE SAVANNAH RIVER SURVEY STATIONS FROM 1951 to 1960 (from Patrick, Cairns and Roback, 1967).

Table 44-3*
VARIATION ON A SURVEY

CHEMICALS	JUNE, 1951	OCTOBER, 1951	JANUARY, 1952	MAY, 1952
Alkalinity (m.o.)	21.00 - 33.60	19.10 - 21.80	18.00 - 20.00	20.00 - 21.60
Chloride	0.60 - 2.40	1.00 - 2.30	2.00 - 3.20	1.80 - 2.40
Carbon Dioxide	4.3 - 6.8	3.9 - 6.8	4.9 - 7.2	5.2 - 6.6
Dissolved Oxygen	6.74 - 6.90	7.87 - 8.17	9.48 - 10.74	7.30 - 8.50
Iron^{+++}	0.046- 0.239	0.010- 0.056	0.110- 0.160	0.050- 0.110
Hardness	8.0 - 10.4	12.50 - 15.55	9.40 - 12.20	13.30 - 15.00
Calcium	2.40 - 2.80	3.00 - 4.10	2.00 - 3.04	2.96 - 3.52
Magnesium	0.34 - 0.83	1.22 - 1.37	1.07 - 1.26	1.35 - 1.60
Ammonia Nitrogen	0.053- 0.079	0.016- 0.169	0.017- 0.046	0.017- 0.052
Nitrate Nitrogen	0.002- 0.0066	0.002- 0.004	0.001- 0.005	0.004
Nitrite Nitrogen	0.114- 0.337	0.069- 0.162	0.065- 0.098	0.077- 0.12
Phosphate	0.012- 0.103	0.069- 0.088	not done	0.031
Sulfate	not done	2.28 - 2.81	2.21 - 2.50	2.50 - 3.05
pH	7.0	6.8 - 7.0	6.7 - 6.9	6.8 - 6.9
Silicon Dioxide	8.68 - 9.54	8.34 - 9.71	8.59 - 10.13	8.39 - 8.77
Temperature (°C)	28.0 - 29.5	21.0 - 23.0	11.0 - 14.5	19.0 - 20.5
B.O.D.	0.79 - 2.01	0.48 - 1.37	0.76 - 1.07	0.55 - 0.75
Turbidity	204.0 -548.0	50.0 -120.0	110.0 -140.0	34.3 - 52.0

VARIATION ON A SURVEY

CHEMICALS	AUG.-SEPT. 1955	MAY, 1956	MAY, 1960	SEPTEMBER, 1960
Alkalinity (m.o.)	20.4 - 26.8	15.8 - 18.6	14.7 - 17.9	16.2 - 17.4
Chloride	2.8 - 3.6	3.2 - 4.2	6.1 - 7.0	5.3 - 5.9
Carbon Dioxide	6.8 - 8.0	3.6 - 5.8	4.8 - 10.6	4.7 - 6.2
Dissolved Oxygen	8.62 - 9.42	7.74 - 8.96	7.19 - 8.11	6.34 - 6.90
Iron^{+++}	0.006- 0.024	0.010- 0.037	0.447- 0.720	0.144- 0.238
Hardness	14.6 - 16.6	13.0 - 15.1	18.1 - 21.9	16.4 - 18.0
Calcium	3.60 - 5.84	2.72 - 3.36	3.28 - 3.84	3.70 - 4.36
Magnesium	1.31 - 1.65	1.31 - 1.81	2.06 - 3.33	1.31 - 1.80
Ammonia Nitrogen	0.008- 0.010	0.004	0.001	0.026- 0.047
Nitrate Nitrogen	0.001	0.001- 0.002	0.002- 0.003	0.004- 0.005
Nitrite Nitrogen	0.150- 0.203	0.144- 0.232	0.207- 0.385	0.094- 0.115
Phosphate	0.028- 0.044	0.047- 0.059	0.088- 0.469	0.022- 0.075
Sulfate	2.62 - 2.96	2.53 - 4.42	5.67 - 8.26	10.80 - 11.02
pH	6.7 - 6.8	6.8 - 6.9	6.5 - 6.8	6.8 - 6.9
Silicon Dioxide	7.85 - 8.18	7.388- 7.510	14.40 - 14.64	7.16 - 7.42
Temperature (°C)	24.3 - 26.6	19.0 - 22.9	20.8 - 24.2	24.8 - 27.5
B.O.D.	0.26 - 1.16	0.46 - 1.06	1.07 - 1.40	0.75 - 0.94
Turbidity	23.4 - 33.9	118.0 -171.0	44.85 - 53.13	26.10 -165.30

*All results are given in ppm—except pH and temperature.

THE RANGES FOR ALL STATIONS RECORDED FOR VARIOUS ENVIRONMENTAL PARAMETERS ON EACH OF THE SAVANNAH RIVER SURVEYS FROM 1951 to 1960 (from Patrick, Cairns and Roback 1967).†

† Note the rather compact temperature ranges for each survey, indicating that the operation of the Savannah River Plant had comparatively minor effects upon the temperature regime of the river. Note that the 1951 ranges, before plant operation began, are quite close to the ranges for other years.

after plant operations begin. Four seasonal (summer, fall, winter, spring) preoperational surveys were carried out on the Savannah River. In such rivers, with dramatic environmental changes during the year (i.e., high and low flow, etc.), two or more surveys should be carried out. It is also advisable to install diatometers at all stations during the first survey and to make arrangements for periodic assessment of the structure of the diatom community. Reports of survey and diatometer results are sent to the plant as soon as data have been analyzed. Changes in operations which, if continued, might have an adverse effect upon the entire aquatic community usually cause changes in the structure of the diatom community. These structural changes are detected almost at once since frequent checks are customary. The operational conditions causing biological changes can be quickly identified with continual biological monitoring systems such as the diatometer since the feedback lag time is rather short. At the moment, biological information systems do not begin to approach the speed of chemical-physical information systems, but some promising possibilities are being explored (Shirer *et al.*, 1968; Sparks *et al.*, 1969; Cairns *et al.*, in press).

During the period covered by the Patrick *et al.* (1967) paper, the upstream city of Augusta, Georgia, increased markedly in population, and its associated industrial complex also expanded and diversified as well. Control station 1 is closest to this urban-industrial complex and would be expected to be affected most. It is interesting to note that although station 1 remains in the healthy category, its species diversity relative to the other staions has declined occasionally due either to random variation or to the aggregate effects of the pollution load added to the river. If pollution load is the causative factor, presumably the stream is able to "rejuvenate" or cleanse itself, because we find that the downstream

stations have a higher number of species at these times than does station 1.

The second example of use without abuse of an aquatic environment is that of the Dickerson Plant of the Potomac Electric Power Company on the Potomac River. The approach and methodology for this study were essentially similar to those used on the Savannah River. The limnological studies on the Potomac River were carried out in the area from Point of Rocks to Whites Ferry in the vicinity of Frederick, Maryland (Fig. 44–4). Since the volume

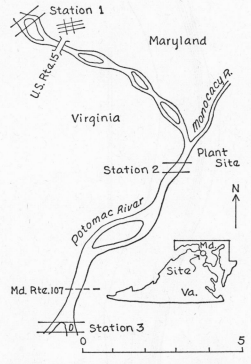

Figure 44–4 Diagrammatic map of the Potomac River Study Area (for detailed description see Cairns, 1966b) showing power plant site and three stations

of water in the river varies seasonally and the distribution of heated water depends on flow (Figs. 44–5A and 44–5B), surveys were made during both high and low flow conditions. Figures 44–5A and 5B also show

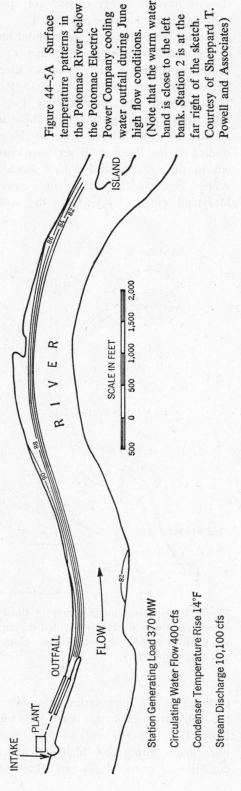

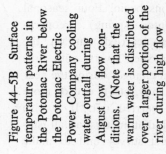

Figure 44–5A Surface temperature patterns in the Potomac River below the Potomac Electric Power Company cooling water outfall during June high flow conditions. (Note that the warm water band is close to the left bank. Station 2 is at the far right of the sketch. Courtesy of Sheppard T. Powell and Associates)

Station Generating Load 370 MW

Circulating Water Flow 400 cfs

Condenser Temperature Rise 14°F

Stream Discharge 10,100 cfs

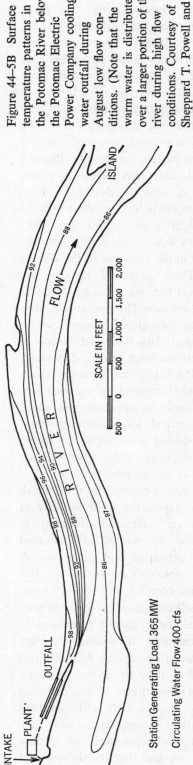

Figure 44–5B Surface temperature patterns in the Potomac River below the Potomac Electric Power Company cooling water outfall during August low flow conditions. (Note that the warm water is distributed over a larger portion of the river during high flow conditions. Courtesy of Sheppard T. Powell and Associates)

Station Generating Load 365MW

Circulating Water Flow 400 cfs

Condenser Temperature Rise 14°F

Stream Discharge 1,850 cfs

the thermal loading in the Potomac River between the discharge point and station 2. The first pair of surveys (i.e., high and low water) was carried out before plant operations began. The first power unit of the PEPCO plant at Dickerson went into operation in the spring of 1959 and the second unit in the spring of 1960. A second pair of surveys was carried out in 1960 and a third pair in 1961 to evaluate the effects of these two units. A third power unit was in operation in 1962 and a fourth pair of surveys was carried out that year to evaluate the effects of this unit. In both 1963 and 1965, a single survey was made during the period of low flow and warm water conditions to further evaluate the effects of this additional unit. Catherwood diatometers were also installed at each station to provide continual biological monitoring of river conditions between surveys. The Potomac River stations remained in the "healthy" category according to the diversity assessment methods of Patrick (1949) and Patrick *et al.* (1954). A summary of the biological data is given in Table 44–4 and chemical-physical data in Tables 44–5a and 44–5b.

Table 44-4

Algae

STATION	HIGH FLOW				LOW FLOW					
	1956	1960	1961	1962	1957	1960	1961	1962	1963	1965
1	105	93	87	86	103	85	101	60	87	84
2L*	88	82	80	81	95	84	87	76	87	78
2R	78	93	74	93	87	84	98	83	89	77
3	104	97	77	62	93	83	78	73	81	73

Protozoa

1	85	53	42	58	68	79	42	51	51	69
2L	39	59	65	51	33	52	27	59	46	58
2R	45	33	39	33	20	45	47	46	50	67
3	83	68	56	56	58	87	53	49	52	64

Invertebrates

1	24	15	22	23	29	21	31	24	22	26
2L	14	13	14	17	28	15	18	19	13	17
2R	17	12	20	14	21	15	17	19	16	16
3	15	21	24	19	26	19	30	22	27	21

Insects

1	91	71	81	74	104	81	81	74	69	65
2L	70	53	64	60	77	65	62	57	56	37
2R	41	58	59	53	52	56	51	48	53	42
3	85	76	60	63	93	90	72	66	59	57

Fish

1	18	30	29	23	28	33	29	29	23	29
2†	24	27	22	27	34	30	29	33	26	20
3	18	24	21	24	30	29	24	29	24	23

*Left bank facing downstream (i.e. below PEPCO outfall).

†Since fish move about more freely than the other organisms, no attempt was made to divide collections from Station 2 into right and left banks.

NUMBER OF SPECIES FOUND AT THE POTOMAC RIVER SURVEY STATIONS FROM 1956 to 1965.

Table 44-5a*

STATION 1

WATER CHARACTERISTIC	SERIES 1†	SERIES 2	SERIES 3	SERIES 4
Alkalinity, P	7.6	6.0	8.0	5.0
Alkalinity, m.o.	112.4	109.0	102	94
Cl	31.6	29	29	27
Hardness, total (as $CaCO_3$)	162.4	172	162	157
Hardness, calcium (as $CaCO_3$)	106	114	112	107
Hardness, magnesium (as $CaCO_3$)	56.4	58	50	50
Ca	42.4	45.6	44.8	42.8
Mg	13.7	14.1	12.15	12.15
pH	8.3	8.5	8.5	8.5
Fe (total dissolved)	0.01	0.02	0.01	0.04
NH_3–nitrogen	0.0074	<0.001	<0.001	<0.001
NO_2–nitrogen	0.0065	0.0015	0.0015	0.0027
PO_4	0.064	0.006	0.05	0.1
SO_4	101	110	101	101
SiO_2	2.0	1.6	1.5	1.66
Turbidity	22	28	77	42
Total solids	338	394	378	342
Volatile matter	90	96	106	112
Fixed residue	248	298	272	230
Specific conductivity (in mhos)	4.64×10^{-4}	4.95×10^{-4}	4.80×10^{-4}	4.57×10^{-4}
Transparency	Bottom	Bottom	Bottom	Bottom
Temperature (in °C)	24.9	24.8	26	25.5
NO_3–nitrogen	0.150	0.052	0.088	0.059

*All results are given in ppm—except pH and temperature.

†Series 1 samples were collected at all stations on the same day. Other series were collected on subsequent days.

STATION 2

WATER CHARACTERISTIC	SERIES 1	SERIES 2	SERIES 3	SERIES 4
Alkalinity, P	10.4	6.0	5.0	3.0
Alkalinity, m.o.	90.6	98.0	103.0	78.0
Cl	32.0	27.0	26.0	20.0
Hardness, total (as $CaCO_3$)	129.4	152.0	155.0	117.0
Hardness, calcium (as $CaCO_3$)	99.2	102.0	104.0	82.0
Hardness, magnesium (as $CaCO_3$)	30.2	50.0	51.0	35.0
Ca	39.7	40.8	41.6	32.8
Mg	7.3	12.5	12.4	8.5
pH	8.7	8.3	8.45	8.1
Fe (total dissolved)	0.016	0.044	0.01	0.04
NH_3–nitrogen	0.0074	<0.001	<0.001	<0.001
NO_2–nitrogen	0.0015	0.0024	0.0052	0.0123
PO_4	0.05	0.018	0.07	0.1
SO_4	90	90	90	68
SiO_2	0.84	1.68	2.1	2.94
Turbidity	46	53	41	404
Total solids	336	330	334	406
Volatile matter	116	100	106	110
Fixed residue	220	230	228	296
Specific conductivity (in mhos)	4.40×10^{-4}	4.44×10^{-4}	4.42×10^{-4}	3.38×10^{-4}
Transparency	2'1"	1'6"	1'11"	6"
Temperature (in °C)	LB RB	LB RB	LB RB	LB RB
	31.5 30.7	28 26.5	32.8 28.2	31.5 27.40
NO_3–nitrogen	0.062	0.05	0.172	0.046

Table 44-5a (continued)

STATION 3

WATER CHARACTERISTIC	SERIES 1	SERIES 2	SERIES 3	SERIES 4
Alkalinity, P	9.8	7.0	8.0	3.0
Alkalinity, m.o.	87.0	91.0	88.0	80.0
Cl	26.0	27.0	26.0	22.0
Hardness, total (as $CaCO_3$)	140.0	144.0	147.0	124.0
Hardness, calcium (as $CaCO_3$)	86.0	99.0	98.0	85.0
Hardness, magnesium (as $CaCO_3$)	54.0	45.0	49.0	39.0
Ca	34.4	39.6	39.2	34.0
Mg	13.1	10.9	11.9	9.5
pH	8.7	8.5	8.45	7.8
Fe (total dissolved)	0.016	0.01	0.01	0.03
NH_3—nitrogen	0.021	0.033	<0.001	0.026
NO_2—nitrogen	0.0013	0.0013	0.0013	0.0148
PO_4	0.04	0.022	0.056	0.154
SO_4	92	80	91.5	66
SiO_2	1.0	1.36	2.4	0.16
Turbidity	48	52	92	380
Total solids	320	294	348	390
Volatile matter	108	96	110	102
Fixed residue	212	198	238	288
Specific conductivity (in mhos)	4.30×10^{-4}	4.0×10^{-4}	4.80×10^{-4}	3.71×10^{-4}
Transparency	1'6"	1'9"	1'0"	3"
Temperature (in °C)	28.8	25.5	27.2	26.2
NO_3—nitrogen	0.039	0.062	0.104	0.319

RESULTS, IN ppm EXCEPT WHERE INDICATED, OF CHEMICAL ANALYSES FROM THE AUGUST 1965 POTOMAC SURVEY.

The interaction of limnologists, engineers, state regulatory and fish and game agencies, and power plant representatives was certainly a significant factor in the success of this project as an endeavor to study the consequences of environmental alterations. It may be of interest to the reader, then, if I discuss these interactions in more detail than is customary in an ecological paper. The Potomac Electric Power Company employed Sheppard T. Powell and Associates, consulting engineers, Baltimore, Maryland, to determine the physical, chemical, and biological consequences of the proposed discharge of heated waste waters into the Potomac River. These consulting engineers carried out the necessary chemical-physical studies (such as flow patterns, temperature gradients, dissolved oxygen concentrations, etc.), and PEPCO arranged to have the Academy of Natural Sciences of Philadelphia carry out river surveys to establish the biological condition of the river before plant operations began. The process and personnel were quite similar to those already described for the Savannah River and included the installation of diatometers. The Maryland Game and Inland Fish Commission and the Maryland Department of Water Resources were kept informed and were a part of the planning process. Whenever the Academy field team was studying the river the other organizations were invited to send representatives and almost always did so. Although Academy reports went only to PEPCO, copies were sent at once by PEPCO to the consulting engineers and state agencies. In addition, PEPCO encouraged free exchange of information so that there was a substantial informal exchange preceding the preparation of a formal report. Although this is a purely subjective opinion, I feel the critical difference between these case histories and most others

Table 44-5b

TEMPERATURES RECORDED IN AUGUST 1965
POTOMAC SURVEY—in °C.

STATION 1

	TRANSECT LEFT BANK TO RIGHT BANK					
	1	2	3	4	5	6
6:00 A.M.	25.5	25.5	25.5	25.5	25.5	25.5
Noon	26.5	26.5	26.5	26.5	27.0	27.0
3:00 P.M.	27.0	27.0	27.2	27.2	28.0	28.2
6:00 P.M.	25.5	25.2	25.2	25.5	25.0	25.0

STATION 2

	TRANSECT LEFT BANK TO RIGHT BANK					
	1	2	3	4	5	6
6:00 A.M.	30.0	30.0	29.5	28.2	28.2	27.5
Noon	31.6	32.6	30.0	31.6	31.0	29.5
3:00 P.M.	34.5	33.9	31.0	33.2	32.1	31.5
6:00 P.M.	31.6	32.2	30.0	28.9	28.2	27.6

STATION 3

	TRANSECT LEFT BANK TO RIGHT BANK					
	1	2	3	4	5	6
6:00 A.M.	28.2	28.9	28.9	28.2	28.9	27.5
Noon	28.9	28.9	28.4	27.5	28.4	27.5
3:00 P.M.	30.0	30.0	30.0	29.5	28.9	28.9
6:00 P.M.	28.2	28.2	27.5	28.2	28.2	28.9

is the contribution of an impartial fact-finding organization (the Academy of Natural Sciences).

A cluster analysis of these Potomac River survey stations based on protozoan presence-absence data has recently been prepared by Cairns and Kaesler (1969), using various combinations of Jaccard coefficients relating forty-six communities containing a total of 647 species. Essentially, cluster analysis employs the techniques used by numerical taxonomists for comparing species to compare aquatic communities. The significance is that similarities and differences between communities can be ex-

pressed numerically and similar communities will "cluster." If the control station clusters with the stations receiving heated waste water, this indicates that no significant biological changes were caused by the waste heat. These results can be expressed graphically in two dimensions as dendrograms. An example of a dendrogram prepared from this data is given in Fig. 44–6. Similarities of communities within a survey were nearly always greater than similarities among communities from different surveys, indicating linear or along-stream environmental influence. Within-survey similarities for the early and late surveys were usually higher than similarities within middle-year surveys, possibly an indication of environmental change at all stations, including the control station, and of subsequent biotic adjustment. This clustering analysis revealed no major changes in the aquatic biota that could be attributed to thermal pollution as a direct result of the operation of the electric power generating station.

The same results have been obtained with insects (Roback et al., 1969), algae (Cairns et al., in press), fish (Cairns and Kaesler, in prep.), and invertebrates other than protozoa and insects (Kaesler et al., in prep.).

In summary, the information feedback worked as follows: background data were collected before and after initial operations began as well as before and after the addition of new power-generating units. Over a period of ten years there has been a gradually increased discharge of waste heat into the Potomac River. During this time regular ecological (i.e., biological and chemical-physical) data have been gathered, and despite a definite increase of several degrees centigrade in the ambient temperature of the Potomac River below the discharge outfall, no major reduction in the number of species have occurred which could be attributed to the effects of the heated water.

Compared with the assessment of "instream" ecological effects caused by waste

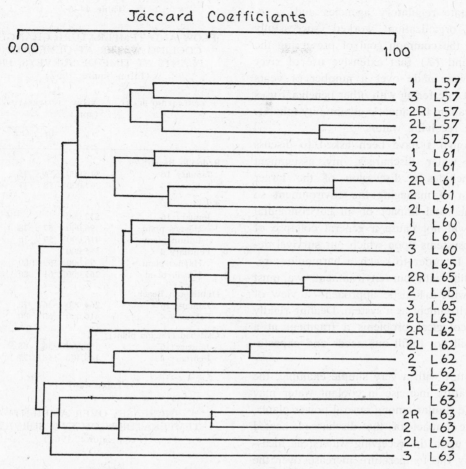

Jaccard Coefficients

0.00   1.00

1   L57
3   L57
2R L57
2L L57
2   L57
1   L61
3   L61
2R L61
2   L61
2L L61
1   L60
2   L60
3   L60
1   L65
2R L65
2   L65
3   L65
2L L65
2R L62
2L L62
2   L62
3   L62
1   L62
1   L63
2R L63
2   L63
2L L63
3   L63

Figure 44–6 Dendrogram prepared by the unweighted pair-group method showing similarities among all low-water aggregations (From Cairns and Kaesler, in press)

discharge of the average industry (particularly in 1956 when this program started), the PEPCO program was enlightened and extensive. However, the survey did not establish that the aquatic community was functioning in a normal fashion, nor do any other ecological stream surveys at the present time. With increasing use of rivers this is increasingly important. Although the presence of a normal aquatic community may imply normal function, the matter is too important to be determined indirectly. A more serious objection mentioned previously is that changes are detected only after they have occurred; a reliable predictive capability for changes in ecosystem structure and function would enable industry to make fuller use of streams without degrading them.

These situations are not dramatic—no rivers were grossly damaged with accompanying fish kills; there were no spectacular confrontations between the various groups involved; and although the communities of aquatic organisms changed, the successional pattern appeared to be similar for the areas studied in each of the rivers (of course, there were considerable differences between these two rivers). The two factors that are of interest are (1) that a truly multi-disciplinary group of administrators, plant waste disposal engineers, and ecologists from state regulatory agencies and a research organization worked successfully toward the common goal of preserving the river, and (2) that extensive use of river water was made over a number of years without interfering with other beneficial uses or degrading the aquatic community inhabiting the receiving waters.

Although I have been asked to discuss heated water discharges, my assignment also includes a discussion of the larger problem of managing the environment so that the total impact of all environmental stress will not cause a general collapse of the ecosystems upon which our survival depends. In order to reach a harmonious relationship with our environment, we must begin with a holistic approach—a view of the environment as a system. Dealing rigidly with ecological problems a fragment at a time will not fulfill our needs and expectations.

To start with a very simple example, the temperature increase in coolant water may be quite similar among several power plants, but the impact of the discharged heated waters upon the receiving waters, as measured by the temperature increase over the ambient temperature, may be quite different. An example of this distinction has been provided by Squire (1967). His data (Table 44–6) indicate that a cooling-water temperature increase of about 20° F is typical for plants in his study area. However, the temperature increase above ambient (Table 44–7) in the vicinity of outfall ranges from 4° F to 20° F. From the evidence in his paper, one would assume that the operational prerequisites of these power plants were determined more by "in-plant" effects than environmental effects. Presumably if the latter had been considered in the planning and location of the power plants in Squire's study, the temperature increase of the outfall area above ambient would only have been about 4° F instead of ranging from 4° to 20° F. In fact, if

Table 44–6

FLOW AND TEMPERATURE CHANGE OF COOLING WATER AT GENERATING PLANTS AT TIME OF SURVEYS, 1963
(From Squire, 1967)

GENERATING PLANT	FLOW (gpm)	TEMPERATURE (° F)		
		In	Out	Rise
Redondo Beach:				
January 16	310,000	56	75	+19
February 4	267,000	58	77	+19
Alamitos:				
January 16	512,000			
Haynes plant	96,000	57	78	+21
Edison plant	416,000	57	78	+21
February 4	355,000			
Haynes plant	90,000	59	80	+21
Edison plant	265,000	61	80	+19
Huntington Beach:				
January 16	264,000	56	78	+22
February 4	416,000	60	80	+20
Carlsbad (Encina plant):				
January 16	150,000	56	68.5	+12.5
February 4	149,400	58	77	+19

Table 44–7

INCREASES OVER AMBIENT TEMPERATURES ON TWO SURVEYS
(From Squire, 1967)

OUTFALL AREA	INCREASE TEMPERATURE ABOVE AMBIENT (° F) SURVEY 1	SURVEY 2	DIFFERENCE (° F), SURVEY 1 TO SURVEY 2
Redondo Beach	4.2	4.0	−0.2
Alamitos	17.0	20.0	+3.0
Huntington Beach	7.2	6.5	−0.7
Carlsbad-Encina	8.0	4.0	−4.0

the plant with the lowest increase above ambient merely reflects a lucky choice of location and the one with the highest an unfortunate choice, it is possible that sites exist where the temperature increase would be negligible. Unfortunately ecological considerations usually receive little attention when industrial sites are selected.

Another example of the danger in using

a fragmented approach to ecological problems is the summation of several environmental stresses. The stream flowing through a recently sprayed forest and receiving quantities of insecticides will have a biota less resistant to other forms of stress than an entirely uncontaminated stream. Therefore our standards and laws must in some way evaluate the total effect of all the stresses under the control of man. We must have environmental quality-control techniques functionally similar to those used in industry for producing a product. Although the assessment of environmental quality is considerably more complex than the assessment of the various components of an industrial process, the same principles apply. There must be adequate assessment, feedback of information, and a quick response procedure. The rationale and framework for this approach has already been given (Cairns, 1967, 1968a).

The related and complementary problems of increased energy production and population growth are forcing us to make a choice between a complex "quality" environment and a simplified "quantity" environment. A good example of a quality environment is a complex forest consisting of a great variety of plants and animals which will persist year in and year out with no interference from man. This ecosystem is a complex mixture of biological, chemical, and physical interactions, many of which cancel each other out. For example, if several predators are regulating the population of rodents and one disappears, the effect is often reduced by a population expansion of other predators also feeding upon the rodents. Therefore, the system is one of dynamic equilibrium, with the system itself stable but with many of its components undergoing change. A simple system such as a cornfield produces a quantity of material immediately useful to man but is notoriously unstable. Without constant care and attention it would cease to be useful and would disappear.

This history of civilization has been one of widespread simplification of the environment with consequent increased management requirements.

When man simplifies an ecosystem, he creates numerous ecological problems. When a complex natural area is cleared and planted with corn, it requires protection against insect pests. To reduce the number of these pests, insecticides are applied and the diversity of life in the soil and in the field is further reduced. Because certain of the pests may become resistant to the insecticides after repeated applications, the pesticide concentration is escalated, further simplifying the ecosystem. At the same time, other organisms including man are beginning to incorporate substantial amounts of these insecticides into their own tissues. For example, concentrations of DDT in the fat deposits of human tissues in the United States average 11 parts per million, and Israelis have been found to have as much as 19.2 parts per million (Ehrlich, 1968). So the overall question is whether we will be able to control not only thermal pollution but all the other problems producing the environmental crisis. To come up with a workable method for a single form of stress without considering the others will only cause a slight delay in the inevitable catastrophe. Only with comprehensive environmental planning, including population control, will we be able to have a meaningful ecological management program to insure a harmonious relationship with the environment.

Electric power companies and all others using the environment (including each individual since we all add to the total load) for waste disposal have two alternatives: (1) continue to increase stress on the environment and regard the resulting damage as a necessary price for our standard of living, or (2) manage the environment so that it serves the greatest number of beneficial uses. The dangers of choosing the first alternative should be abundantly clear! If they are not, there will soon be more "environmental backlashes" to provide the necessary evidence. If we agree to manage the environment to provide beneficial uses, we must first define the desired uses and then establish goals. This would require a number of regional organizations coordinated and supervised by a national organization.

Assuming that an organizational framework for environmental management has been developed, there would be two not necessarily mutually exclusive alternatives: (1) adjust our society to fit the environment as it now exists so that no further deterioration ensues, or (2) deliberately modify the environment to function well under a set of conditions that we create. Adjusting the society requires biological, chemical, and physical quality-control standards for each ecosystem. Once these social decisions have been made, an ecological surveillance system established at critical points in each ecosystem would provide continual feedback of ecological information which would be the basis for immediate action should environmental quality fall below established standards in any part of the ecosystem. Monitoring techniques have been available for years (Cairns, 1965, 1967), although the time required for biological information is many orders of magnitude greater than for chemical and physical data. New techniques are needed to reduce this lag.

Our civilization has been founded on the concept of shaping the environment to fit our needs, so the second alternative should have much appeal. "Unused" land or water seems to inspire all sorts of people and organizations to make it "useful." Against these powerful, well-financed forces, are a small but vocal group of conservationists who want primeval wilderness; this group usually loses. Most of us would probably like some of each; that is, some areas deliberately modified to suit certain of our needs and others essentially undisturbed to satisfy our other needs. I propose that when we feel it necessary to destroy an existing ecosystem that it be replaced, not by chance, but by an ecosystem containing new organisms suited to the altered environment. In the case of thermal loadings, Naylor (1965) reports on warm-water immigrants (some from fairly distant areas) which have become established in British and other European waters receiving heated effluents; he urges that if substitution is desirable, heat-tolerant species should be deliberately introduced since natural distribution methods are too dependent on chance. A deliberate attempt to establish certain plants in a heated water discharge area in California has been reported by North (1969). It is too early to determine the outcome of this particular experiment but there should be a real possibility of success. Why not stock warm-water fish and invertebrates below heated discharges into cold-water streams to enable the power plant to make fuller use of the stream and provide fishing as well? For streams which already have warm waters, one might breed selected strains of heat-tolerant aquatic organisms.

The feasibility of such management is questionable on several grounds (Cairns, 1969). First, establishing a functioning balanced aquatic community with many complex interactions requires more than throwing a few appropriate species together. Usually there is a lag period which may last five years or more before a state of dynamic equilibrium is reached. Failures are also quite likely. In areas of rapid industrial growth, new unexpected demands for environmental modification might prevent the system from ever stabilizing. An unstable system is not likely to fill as many needs as a stable one, nor is its functioning likely to be as predictable. The second disadvantage is that once the new aquatic community has become established, it will be dependent upon existing conditions—in this example, higher than normal temperatures. Should the power plant shut down in midwinter due to a strike or to replace broken or worn-out equipment, it is quite likely that some or all of the heat-tolerant and heat-dependent species will die. If aquatic environments are deliberately altered by wastes and species cultured to fit the new conditions, then our antipollution laws must be extended to include the failure to maintain the new conditions. For power plants this would mean continual discharge of heated water, which has obvious disadvantages—particularly when the plant becomes obsolete. The payment for transforming the aquatic environment would also have to be settled. There is much to be said for reaching a harmonious relationship with the present environment.

However, how does one reach a harmonious relationship with an environment that is constantly changing? Habitats and their inhabitants changed irreversibly long before the advent of man. Of course, man has modified the environment rapidly and strikingly in many areas; in most areas of the world he is a determinant, and in many areas the major determinant, of the nature and extent of these changes. Of course, man cannot exist apart from the environment and must use parts of it. Thus he contributes to the changes that occur. Unfortunately only the most selfish and superficial consideration of the consequences of these changes has characterized most uses made of the environment. For example, strip-mining is a "cheap" source of fuel if one considers only the cost of removing coal from the ground. Disruption of both terrestrial and aquatic ecological systems is enormous and no one can assess the total cost, but such assessment would prove strip-mining very expensive indeed.

We have the capacity to analyze ecological systems, to determine cause-and-effect relationships, to measure the roles of the various major components, and to estimate the consequences of various courses of action. With stress upon the environment increasing and evidence of environmental degradation all around us, we can no longer afford to tackle the problem a fragment at a time!

ACKNOWLEDGMENTS

Both the Savannah and the Potomac programs were designed by Dr. Ruth Patrick. Although I participated in them as field director and protozoologist, principal credit for their successful operation belongs to the designer. I am grateful to Mr. L. W. Cadwallader, vice-president of the Potomac Electric Power Company, for permission to publish these results and to the staff of the Potomac Electric Power Company and Sheppard T. Powell and Associates for their help and many courtesies during the course of the Potomac surveys. I am also indebted to the Atomic Energy Commission and the E. I. du Pont de Nemours and Company for permission to publish the data in Patrick *et al.* (1967), portions of which appear in this paper. Miss Jeanne Ruthven, Mr. William T. Waller and Mr. Kenneth Dickson helped prepare the rough draft of this manuscript.

APPENDIX

Constuction of Histograms

In order to make a graphic representation of conditions in each station, histograms (Fig. 44–7) were constructed according to a system devised in the Conestoga Basin studies (Patrick, 1949), with the various organisms grouped as follows:

COLUMN I[4] Column I contains species of diatoms, blue-green algae, and green algae which, according to Liebmann,[5] Kolkwitz,[6] Fjerdingstad,[7] and our own findings, are known to be tolerant of pollution.

COLUMN II Oligochaetes, leeches, and pulmonate snails.

COLUMN III Protozoa.

[4] In this report Column I has been revised because it was found that not all species of blue-green algae encountered were characteristic of pollution. This is also true of the genus *Spirogyra*. At present, the problem of classifying algae as to their tolerance to a wide range of environmental conditions is under study.

[5] Liebmann, Hans. *Handbuch der Frischwasser und Abwasserbiologie,* Vol. I. Munich: R. Oldenbourg, 1951. 539 pp.

[6] Kolkwitz, R. "Oekologie der Saprobien; . . . Verein für Wasser-, Boden-, und Lufthygiene." *Schriftenreihe,* No. 4. 1950. 64 pp.

[7] Fjerdingstad, E. "Forurening af vandlob biologisk bedomt." *Nordisk Hyg. Tskr.,* 41 (1960), 149–96.

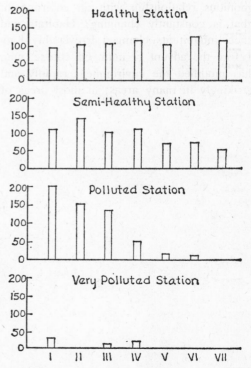

Figure 44–7 "Idealized" histograms showing changes in the structure of the aquatic "communities" following various degrees of pollution (following the system of Patrick, 1949)

COLUMN IV Diatoms, red algae, green algae other than those included in Column I.

COLUMN V Prosobranch snails, triclad worms, and a few smaller groups.

COLUMN VI Crustaceans and insects.

COLUMN VII Fish.

The number of species represented in each column determines the height of the column. So that the heights of the columns in a histogram might be comparable, they are expressed on a percentage basis. The bases used for comparison in this survey are the numbers of species for each of these columns averaged from findings in a number of similar regions of Middle Atlantic Coastal Plain rivers which are known to be free of pollution. The following numbers of species are taken to represent 100 percent:

COLUMN I	4
COLUMN II	6
COLUMN III	41
COLUMN IV	81
COLUMN V	11
COLUMN VI	47
COLUMN VII	15

DETERMINATION OF RIVER "HEALTH"

A "healthy" river is one which has a balance of organisms, i.e., one in which the biodynamic cycle is such that conditions are maintained which are capable of supporting a great variety of life forms. The algae are mostly diatoms and green algae, and the invertebrates and fish are represented by a great variety of species.

Columns I and II have been found to vary widely, depending on the ecological conditions and degree of enrichment of a station. A "healthy" station has been found to be one in which at least three of Columns IV, V, VI, and VII are 50 percent or over.

"Semi-healthy" is the condition in which the balance of life as described for a "healthy" station has been somewhat disrupted, but not destroyed. Often a given species will be represented by a large number of individuals. This condition is noted in the histograms by a double-width column and indicates that something has happened that has destroyed the

check on this species. Under other circumstances, conditions have altered so that a certain group will have a great many more species present than usually occur, while other groups will be greatly depressed. Thus the pattern is an irregular one. It may be defined as follows:

1. One or more columns double-width; two of Columns IV, V, VI, and VII under 50 percent, or
2. At least one of Columns I and II over 100 percent or less than 25 percent; at least two of Columns IV, V, VI, and VII under 50 percent or
3. At least two of Columns I, II, and III double-width or over 100 percent. Three of Columns IV, V, VI, and VII less than 75 percent, and at least one less than 50 percent.

"Polluted" is the condition in which the balance of life found in "healthy" stations is severely upset. However, conditions are favorable for some groups of organisms. Such a condition may be defined as follows:

1. Columns IV, V, VI, and VII under 50 percent; either or both Columns I and II over 100 percent or less than 25 percent, or
2. Columns IV, V, VI, and VII under 50 percent, Columns I or II double-width, or
3. Three of Columns IV, V, VI, and VII under 50 percent; Column I or II double-width and over 100 percent.

"Very polluted" is a condition which is definitely toxic to plant and animal life. Often many groups are absent. It may be defined as follows:

1. At least two of Columns V, VI, and VII absent; Column IV below 50 percent, or
2. Columns IV, V, VI, and VII present, but below 25 percent; Column I or II below 50 percent.

The histograms are used to represent graphically some of the evidence obtained during the course of the survey. It is important to note that the conclusions are not based on the histograms alone but rather on the overall biological, chemical, physical, and bacteriological results.

REFERENCES

Cairns, J., Jr. "Pollution's Eternal Triangle." *Assoc. South. Biol. Bull.*, 12 (2) (1965), 35–37.

———. "Biological Concepts and Industrial Waste Disposal Problems." *Proc. 20th Indus. Waste Conf., Ext. Series No. 118*, Purdue University. 1966a. Pp. 49–59.

———. "The Protozoa of the Potomac River from Point of Rocks to Whites Ferry." *Not. Nat. Acad. Nat. Sci. Phila.*, No. 387, pp. 1–11 plus 43 pp. supporting data deposited as document No. 8902 with the AID Aux. Pub. Proj., Photodupl. Serv., Library of Congress. 1966b. Microfilm copies $2.50.

———. "The Use of Quality Control Techniques in the Management of Aquatic Ecosystems." *Water Resources Bull.*, 3 (4) (1967), 47–53.

———. "The Need for Regional Water Resource Management." *Trans. Kans. Acad. Sci.*, 71 (4) (1968a), 480–90.

———. "We're in Hot Water!" *Scientist and Citizen* (now *Environment*), 10 (8) (1968b), 187–98.

———. Formal discussion of "The Effects of Heated Discharges on Fresh Water Benthos" by Charles B. Wurtz. *Biological Aspects of Thermal Pollution.* Edited by Peter A. Krenkel and Frank L. Parker, Vanderbilt University Press. 1969a. Pp. 214–20, informal remarks, pp. 154, 225–27.

Cairns, J., Jr., and Kaesler, Roger L. "Cluster Analysis of Potomac River Survey Stations Based on Protozoan Presence-Absence Data." *Hydrobiologia*, 34 (3–4) (1969b), 414–32.

———. "Cluster Analysis of Fish in a Portion of the Upper Potomac River." With editor.

Cairns, J., Jr.; Dickson, K. L.; Sparks, R. E.; and Waller, W. T. "Rapid Biological Information Systems for Water Pollution Control." *Jour. Water Pollution Control Federation.* In press.

Cairns, J., Jr.; Patrick, R.; and Kaesler, R. L. "Cluster Analysis of the Distribution of Diatoms and Other Algae in the Upper Potomac River." *Proc. Acad. Nat. Sciences.* In press.

Ehrlich, Paul R. *The Population Bomb.* New York: Ballantine Books, 1968. 223 pp.

Holdaway, J. L.; Resi, L. A.; Thomas, N. A.; Parrish, L. P.; Stewart, R. K.; and Mackenthun, K. M. *Temperature and Aquatic Life.* Tech. Adv. and Investigations Branch, Technical Services Program, FWPCA, U. S. Dept. of the Interior, Lab. Investigations Series, No. 6. 1967. 151 pp.

Kaesler, Roger L., and Cairns, John, Jr. "Cluster Analysis of Non-Insect Macro-Invertebrates of the Upper Potomac River." In preparation.

Kennedy, V. S., and Mihursky, J. A. "Bibliography on the Effects of Temperature in the Aquatic Environment." *Contribution* No. 326, Natural Resources Institute, University of Maryland. 1967. 89 pp. Mimeo.

Knabe, Wilhelm. "Observations on World-Wide Efforts to Reclaim Industrial Waste Land." In *Ecology and the Industrial Society*, G. T. Goodman, R. W. Edwards, and J. M. Lambert, eds. Oxford: Blackwell Scientific Publications, 1964. 395 pp. Pp. 263–96.

Naylor, E. "Effects of Heated Effluents upon Marine and Estuarine Organisms." *Adv. Mar. Biol.*, 3 (1965), 63–103.

North, Wheeler. Discussion. "Aspects of the Potential Effect of Thermal Alteration on Marine and Estuarine Benthos" by Joel W. Hedgpeth and Jefferson J. Gonor. *Biological Aspects of Thermal Pollution*, Peter A. Krenkel and Frank L. Parker, eds. Vanderbilt University Press. 1969. Pp. 119–22.

Patrick, Ruth. "A Proposed Biological Measure of Stream Conditions Based on a Survey of the Conestoga Basin, Lancaster County, Pennsylvania." *Proc. Acad. Nat. Sci. Phila.*, 101 (1949), 277–341.

———. "Natural and Abnormal Communities of Aquatic Life in Rivers." *Bull. South. Carolina Acad. Sci.*, 29 (1967), 19–28.

Patrick, Ruth; Cairns, J., Jr.; and Roback, S. S. "An Ecosystematic Study of the Fauna and Flora of the Savannah River." *Proc. Acad. Nat. Sci. Phila.,* 118 (5) (1967), 109–407.

Patrick, Ruth; Hohn, Matthew H.; and Wallace, John H. "A New Method for Measuring the Pattern of the Diatom Flora." *Notulae Naturae Acad. Nat. Sci. Phila.,* No. 259. 1954. 12 pp.

Prosser, C. Ladd. *Molecular Mechanisms of Temperature Adaptation.* Amer. Ass. Adv. Sci., Pubn. No. 84. 1967. 390 pp.

Raney, E. C., and Menzel, B. W. "A Bibliography: Heated Effluents and Effects on Aquatic Life with Emphasis on Fishes." Ithaca, N.Y.: Fernow Hall, Cornell University, 1967. 34 pp. Mimeo.

————. *Heated Effluents and Effects on Aquatic Life with Emphasis on Fishes.* Ithaca, N.Y.: Ichthyological Associates. *Bull.* No. 2, April 1969. 470 pp.

Roback, Selwyn S.; Cairns, John, Jr.; and Kaesler, Roger L. "Cluster Analysis of Potomac River Survey Stations Based on Insect Presence-Absence Data." *Hydrobiologia,* 34 (3–4) (1969), 484–502.

Shirer, Hampton W.; Cairns, J., Jr.; and Waller, W. T. "A Simple Apparatus for Measuring Activity Patterns of Fishes." *Water Resources Bull.,* 4 (3) (1968), 27–43.

Singer, S. Fred. "Waste Heat Management." *Science,* 159 (3820) (1968), 1184.

Sparks, Richard E.; Heath, Alan G.; and Cairns, John, Jr. "Changes in Bluegill EKG and Respiratory Movement Caused by Exposure to Sublethal Concentrations of Zinc." *Assn. Southeastern Biol. Bull.,* 16 (2) (1969), 69.

Squire, James L., Jr. "Surface Temperature Gradients Observed in Marine Areas Receiving Warm Water Discharges." *Tech. Paper Bureau, Sport Fisheries and Wildlife,* No. 11. 1967. 11 pp.

Stroud, R. H., and Douglas, P. A. "Thermal Pollution of Water." *Sport Fishing Institute Bulletin* No. 191. 1968. 8 pp.

Tinbergen, N. "On War and Peace in Animals and Man." *Science,* 3835 (1968), 1411–18.

Watt, Kenneth E. F. *Systems Analysis in Ecology.* New York: Academic Press, 1966. 276 pp.

————. *Ecology and Resource Management.* New York: McGraw-Hill, 1968. 450 pp.

Wurtz, Charles B. "The Effects of Heated Discharges on Fresh-Water Benthos." *Biological Aspects of Thermal Pollution,* Peter A. Krenkel and Frank L. Parker, eds. Vanderbilt University Press. 1969. Pp. 199–213.

DISCUSSION

MARSHALL: We have heard that under present circumstances much radioactive waste is washed out to sea. Dr. Abrahamson talked about much greater needs as far as waste disposal goes. What are the plans for disposing of this at the present time? What sort of method would be used?

ABRAHAMSON: A lot of waste is now being discharged. Future plans are to discharge much larger quantities of so-called low-level radioactive wastes; thermal wastes, however, are always discharged on the site. You can dump thermal wastes into the water or dissipate them into the air. Or you could use this heat energy in some useful way, but that is not economic at the moment.

Limits for radioactive waste discharge are set, at least in this country, in terms of concentrations of radioisotopes in the various effluents, not the total quantity that can be discharged. Do you have to release more? Just pump it through more water. So low concentrations, not low quantities, often are released locally. Some "low-level" waste is released locally at the site of fuel-reprocessing plants, but a lot of so-called "high-level" wastes are being stored.

These later wastes are extremely radioactive. They are very hot, both thermally and radioactively. They must be stored on the order of several hundred years because of the length of the half-life. This assumes considerable political and environmental stability in the world and also assumes that storage tanks won't leak. At the moment very hot waste is being stored in tanks, at least in this country; I understand the use of the oceans for disposal of high-level wastes is now decreasing.

The ultimate plan is to put this waste in things like salt mines, to encapsulate it in impervious ceramic materials and deposit it in salt mines. The reason for a salt mine is that its presence is evidence that it's dry there. Nevertheless, the difficulties of long-term storage are an immense problem.

CAIRNS: I would like to comment on that point. I don't think we can look for places to throw things away any longer because we are running out of "away." I think we are facing a recycling problem. Aquatic organisms are very efficient units for capturing, concentrating and recycling radioactive elements. I think we should be finding ways in which to increase the efficiency of the industrial process in treatment systems and be finding ways to use these wastes. Eventually, our goal should be to recycle and reuse all radioactive wastes within man's industrial system.

COMMONER: There is no way to get rid of radioactivity once it is cycling through ecosystems; the biological fact is that in every instance such radiation does damage. This is what makes radioactive pollution the most awesomely dangerous pollution problem.

GEORGE: Why don't we use this waste thermal heat to heat homes?

ABRAHAMSON: In the case of nuclear

plants, the reason is that nuclear power plants producing this heat are dangerous. These plants tend to be unstable and as a consequence should be located far from urban population centers.

The people who build these reactors want to put them downtown. The people who are concerned about man's health and welfare want to put them in completely unpopulated areas. So, at the moment, the problem with using waste reactor heat for heating houses is that ideally you don't want any houses around the reactors.

The possibilities of using such heat in other ways such as for heating fishponds or large areas for agriculture are still only in the discussion stage.

MILTON: Could one of the panelists sketch the overall scale of nuclear power development that is going on now worldwide and then discuss what the various existing means and potential capabilities for no-risk, non-polluting disposal are on a worldwide scale? Who has international responsibility for setting global limits to radioactive pollution? Is *anyone* worrying about this who also has the power to act?

HEDGPETH: I don't know what the British do with their very high level radioactive material. I think they bury part of it right at the Windscale Works or sink it in concrete there, but I have no clear idea what the rest of the world is going to do.

The French have decided they would put their high-level wastes at the bottom of the Mediterranean. Cousteau has opposed this. The French already release their low-level wastes from one atomic power plant directly into the Rhône. They are working on the theory that waste decay has a half-life of a year or so and that this won't do much harm. At least, that is the hope.

I don't know what the projected scale of international development of atomic power is, but there is one thing that bothers me about this, especially after reading Abrahamson's paper. I was unaware of the scale on which they planned this to be combined with desalination plants. There is a very complicated problem of dealing with high-salinity water. If you are going to desalinate on a large scale you will wind up with enormous piles of salt; it is estimated that if you process two million acre-feet a year, you come out with enough salt to ruin the world's salt, magnesium, and several other markets. If you adopt a halfway process and increase the salinity by returning brines to the sea, this changes the exchange pattern completely. This could happen in the Persian Gulf, Red Sea or other semiarid regions where there is not much exchange.

ABRAHAMSON: How much atomic development is actually being committed on an international scale, I don't know, but I do know what is being proposed is truly immense. For example, a short while ago the AEC issued an Oak Ridge Report on agro-industrial complexes. They are proposing literally to solve all our major agricultural problems with atomic technology. They listed the Southwest part of the U.S., Central America, the entire Middle East, India, Pakistan and Australia.

Another atomic development that is being pushed heavily involves immense engineering works; creating harbors; and the use of explosives for excavations underground. You name something that people extract from the earth and the promoters of atomic energy have a scheme to extract it with atomic explosives.

CALDWELL: A week from today there will be a meeting at Oak Ridge of the Senior Advisory Committee on the Agro-Industrial Complex to review the report of a team just coming back from the Middle East. The so-called Baker Resolution proposes that the political and social problems of the Middle East can be solved by the creation of large agro-industrial complexes based upon desalination and related chemical industries which will utilize some of the mineral by-products of the water.

This project was conceived largely by physicists and engineers, and politicians have been persuaded, without consulting either ecologists or social scientists, that this might be a feasible proposition. They feel the agro-industrial complex might indeed be a force for regional stability and peace.

The Oak Ridge National Labs, however, has now brought in a group of social scientists to have a look at this. I might say that I am taking to Oak Ridge with me a set of papers from this meeting. I feel much of the information from here must be brought to the attention of some of the administrative and engineering people connected with this project. They should at least hear some of the warnings from biologists with respect to the project's ecological implications.

I cite the Baker Resolution as an instance of the way in which a major technological development with important ecological implications gets into the machinery of not only domestic politics but also international politics. I would suggest the Atomic Energy Commission and the National labs are both looking for new things to do. There is an institutional momentum here that has been built up, and in the anxiety and concern of developing countries to get more power, to develop more arid land, a proposition like this can be very attractive. The dangers are not readily perceived.

WHITE: The agro-industrial complex is another illustration of the alacrity and enthusiasm with which our culture embraces a quick technological fix which is advanced as an easy and sure solution to some critical societal problem.

FOSBERG: Related to the matter of thermal pollution, in a slightly different context, there was a suggestion made two or three years ago that if the current accelerating rate of population increase continued, it would be about 720 years before the heat generated metabolically by people would make the earth uninhabitable.

I don't know whether that was a sound projection but I wonder what will be the environmental effects of pouring all the heat that we have just been hearing about into the world ecosystem. Perhaps we will be out of business long before 720 years is up.

ABRAHAMSON: When you question the proponents of nuclear power as to why this is being pushed at the moment, one argument is that the world resources of fossil fuels will be exhausted in 300 or 500 or 1,200 years, depending on who you talk to.

Now, we are talking about the thermal effects which are cumulative on a truly global scale over a period of 700 years. If these other things you people have been speaking about these last two days have any reality at all—the food and unemployment problem which will become acute in ten or twenty years—if these things are true, then it is really ridiculous to be worrying about running out of coal in 400 years or having the entire earth temperature being raised in 700 years, or so forth.

COMMONER: Far be it from me to suppress a horror story but in this case I have to; after all, the truth is even more important than horror. I don't think that the thermal problem will have any important influence on the heat balance of the earth. The energy input from the sun vastly outweighs biological and human activities and this balance is being changed drastically now in two opposite ways: one, by the accumulation of carbon dioxide from the burning of fossil fuels; secondly, in a reverse direction apparently, by the accumulation of pollution aerosols in the stratosphere. These factors are already more important than any conceivable changes in heat production on the earth.

WHITE: This still leaves us with the local problem of the disposal of waste heat. It is an immense amount to have liberated at one site.

CARLOZZI: I would like to put in one other word about a secondary effect of nuclear power. In New England, we are blessed with very active electrical companies and every day I see on TV how over the next twenty years I am about to get the benefit from eleven nuclear power plants in my area.

The production of electricity by nuclear power plants is interesting because in order for them to operate economically they can't shut down the nuclear source so they just go full tilt twenty-four hours a day. This means that you have outputs of electricity during times of the day when nobody really wants it. So for every new nuclear power plant in New England we may see a merger between a pumped storage project. In pumped storage they take the cheap electricity, pump water up to the top of some hill during the night, then during the day run it back down through tubes, using the pumps as a generator, and get their electricity back.

It is clever and simple. However, on the Connecticut River, during the summer with low flow, these proposed plants will use about 85 per cent of the total flow. What will happen to the Connecticut when there is practically no water in it for four or five hours during the day and then its flow is doubled in four hours? Is there an organism that inhabits the Connecticut that has any adaptive ability to deal with this kind of hydrology? We will have some very curious stream flow regimes to deal with in the future.

MILTON: One thing which very much disturbs me about our discussion of atomic power is that no national or international governmental body has set a clear energy use goal that takes into account *all* the important existing alternatives. At present mankind is locked into a cycle of using either hydropower, fossil fuels, or atomic energy to fuel growth. Each of these alterna-

tives has serious negative environmental impacts: hydropower floods rich alluvial soils, reduces natural fertilization by deposition of sediments during floods, destroys marine and riverine fisheries, fosters water-borne disease, increases water loss to the atmosphere, and causes massive population displacements; fossil fuels (coal, oil, natural gas) cause most of our urban air pollution problems, spill from marine tankers to pollute the oceans, and contribute to CO_2 build-up in the biosphere to initiate possible long-term changes in world climate; atomic energy's waste products of radioactive solids, gases and liquids are extremely dangerous and could seriously pollute the biosphere irreversibly. Thermal pollution is also a problem. Until we develop more efficient and clean forms of energy utilization (including better reuse and recycling of energy production wastes), we will continue to find ourselves in the dilemma of having to shift from one environmentally degrading energy source to another.

Existing powerful industrial interest groups with huge vested economic commitments to coal, oil, natural gas, atomic plants and large dams will fight any serious departure from this pattern. Nevertheless, shouldn't we be urging the powerful industrial nations of the earth to join together to initiate a crash program for developing and applying new non-polluting, efficient, economically feasible energy source alternatives? Hydrogen fusion, the fuel cell, geothermol, tidal and solar power are only a few of such potential sources that badly need to be studied. I feel such a program is critical and of the highest priority now. Without a new set of energy alternatives we will be in far more trouble a decade from now than we are today.

45. AN ECOLOGICAL OVERVIEW OF CARIBBEAN DEVELOPMENT PROGRAMS

Carl A. Carlozzi

The problems of resource development in the Caribbean region can be understood only if we investigate the relationships and dynamics of Caribbean life systems as a whole. Several basic ecological problems then emerge. The first is a situation wherein the resources of the islands are used in such a way that their productive capacities remain viable and represent an acceptable balance of cultural, economic and natural needs. These resources concern us only when possible change in the intensity of use may realistically be anticipated. For example, if the flourishing tourist industry in Barbados began to dwindle, the island might be forced to mechanize its presently labor-intensive agriculture in order to compete with other agricultural producers and thereby survive economically. Another example involves extensive virgin timber on Dominica that may soon be heavily cut and will help solve that country's economic problems for a time; yet at present, there is no sign that long-term forest, and therefore economic, survival is being planned for.

The second problem concerns the introduction of an entirely new kind of land and resource utilization when ecological knowledge is absent and there is little or no control over the quality or intensity of the new resource use. Tourism is an innovation in many of the islands and is generally the most dynamic economic force at the present time. Yet the changes of resource use and the new pollution problems wrought on the islands by this expanding and essentially grafted-on type of human activity are not being studied or considered as tourism continually expands. Alternative plans for resource use are not being developed to ward off the dramatic economic problems that future lack of tourists would cause.

A third problem is the steady attrition of unique biotic resources through extinction, extirpation, or both. It is shocking to contemplate that almost 40 per cent of all the world's vertebrate extinctions occurred in the tiny Caribbean, which has been noted for its many populations of endemic plant and animal species. Many of the existing species are now threatened as their unique environments are altered by a development process that at present does not consider their value.

The underlying question is deeply troubling: even if we can discover the ecological guidelines for a capital-intensive agriculture, a tourist industry, or the preservation of unique natural environments, will the condition of men on the islands and men elsewhere allow the guidelines to be followed? Does the marketplace or ecological criteria guide resource development? The condition at present in the Caribbean and other underdeveloped countries is one of economic dependence upon faraway industrial countries and the vagaries of their distant markets. Our wishful expectations that other men, especially those whose nations' economies are dependent on those of developed countries, will be able to display wisdom and control in applying the lessons of ecology in their own countries are to be realized only if we of the developed metropolitan nations can allow them at least as much national integrity as we have. Otherwise, their mistakes and submission to the marketplace will also be our own.

In his book, *Man, Mind and Land,* Walter Firey (1960) presents a thesis which says in short that to change any resource process the system of change must be culturally adoptable, economically gainful and ecologically possible. In the traditional sense, ecologists, I suppose, would be most interested in the third part of Firey's triad. I believe, however, that an interpretation of ecology as a holistic investigation of the relationships and dynamics of life systems would certainly fit the totality of Firey's thesis.

Within this framework I wish to discuss three ecological problems in the Caribbean. First, because of an improper balance of cultural, economic and natural factors the resources of the islands do not remain viable. These resources only concern us with respect to possible changes in the intensity of their use. The second problem is the introduction of an entirely new kind of land and resource utilization for which there is little or no documented experience to guide the necessary accommodations to an island landscape. The third problem, which has

deep historical roots, is the steady attrition of unique biotic resources through extinction or extirpation, or both.

The root of the three ecological problems is a consistent political-economic one. The eastern Caribbean region is a supplier of materials and services to the developed continental nations. Through all its recorded history it has filled this role, and it continues to fill it today. The well-being of the land and people of the islands varies in accordance with how well they supply materials and services and how strongly the market they serve makes demands upon them. This kind of existence is made doubly difficult because the capital and entrepreneurial means by which the islands may carry on their supply role are most often obtained from the market areas they serve.

The group of islands that I will discuss are all in the eastern Caribbean group known as the Lesser Antilles (Fig. 45-1). They are typically volcanic in origin, and most are oceanic. They are neotropical in the bioclimatic zonation scheme and their

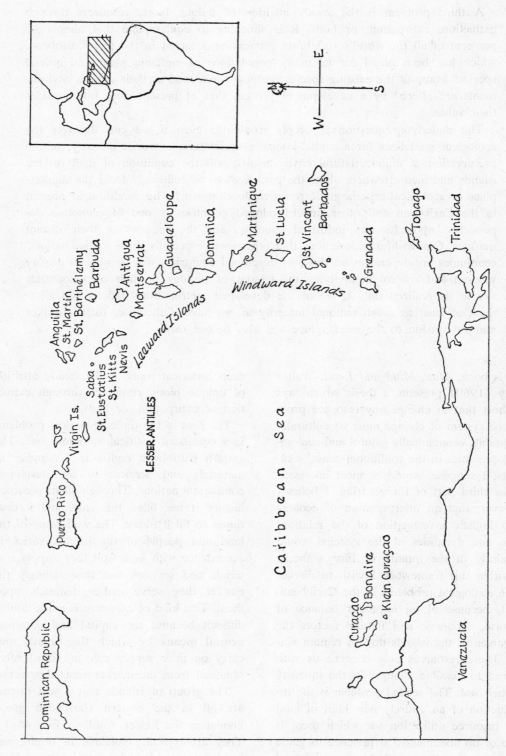

Figure 45-1 THE LESSER ANTILLES IN THE EASTERN CARIBBEAN.

natural primary productivity is expressed in an optimal climax of rain forest. Because of variations in size, topography, elevation and geomorphologic formation, some of these islands have never achieved the optimal vegetative community. J. S. Beard (1949) identifies four bioclimatic ecotypes: the optimal rain forest formation, the montane formations, the seasonal formations, and the dry evergreen formations. The gradient of island physiographic types has produced a gradient of distribution with respect to Beard's plant communities simply because the physiography of the islands introduces a variable in rainfall, one aspect of a climate that is otherwise regionally uniform and equitable. Average annual rainfall among the islands varies from approximately 500 millimeters (20 inches) on the island of Aruba to 7,500 millimeters (300 inches) on the island of Dominica.

Maximum elevation varies from approximately 75 meters (250 feet) on the island of Barbuda to 1,500 meters (5,000 feet) on the island of Dominica. A classification of physiographic types produces three kinds of islands: precipitous mountain islands with high points over 830 meters (2,750 feet), islands with somewhat steeply rolling hills with a series of high points between 230 meters and 460 meters (750 feet and 1,500 feet), and islands that are relatively flat with high points not exceeding 150 meters (500 feet). Rainfall patterns are explained by the influence of elevation on the consistent easterly trade winds.

There are some exceptions to the volcanic origins of the islands lying just off the coast of South America: Aruba, Curaçao, Bonaire, Trinidad and Tobago. All of these islands were part of the South American mainland and are separated today because of a subsidence of the coast line during the Oligocene period. Likewise, there are some exceptions to the oceanic character of the other Lesser Antilles, for the islands of the middle group were joined together by land bridges for at least some time during the Miocene and Pliocene. In terms of emergence above the sea, the volcanic islands are relatively young, the probable age of Dominica being the early Miocene and the probable age of St. Vincent as recent as the late Pliocene (Schuchert, 1945; Liddle, 1946). Volcanism is an active force today and all of the mountainous islands contain evidence of volcanic activity in the form of geysers, sulphur springs and fumeroles.

Columbus discovered these small islands of the Lesser Antilles on his second voyage in 1493. Because of greater interest in the larger islands to the north and west, the Lesser Antilles were not colonized until the first quarter of the seventeenth century. Until the 1960's, the islands were continuously controlled by people of European origin.

In the early period of occupation by the British, Dutch and French, the principal value of the islands was strategic—first as bases of operation against the Spanish, and later as jumping-off points for the exploration and settlement of the continents. By the late eighteenth century, when political contentions over continental settlement were largely resolved and sugar-cane culture was imported from South America, the islands became valued for their agricultural productivity. The lands receiving rainfall sufficient to support agriculture were cleared of their forest cover and subjected to cultivation.

Strong colonial interests were retained by Britain, France and the Netherlands until the late 1800's. Economic competition from the continents in the production of traditional crops such as sugar, cotton and tobacco and the abolition of slavery reduced potential economic returns which metropolitan mother countries could expect from the eastern Caribbean. Interest was not revived until the Second World War, when the strategic value of these islands was again obvious and some inputs toward public services and social advancement were made by improving roads, airports, docks and general communications.

Following World War II, when the world entered its current period of anticolonialism and rising nationalism, the metropolitan nations of Europe began to disengage from their interests in the eastern Caribbean. All of the islands have, since World War II, altered the political relationship with their former colonial countries, though all continue to be tied to them in varying degree by economic dependence (Carlozzi and Carlozzi, 1968).

There can be no relief felt in the present adjustments in political status, for the patterns of the islands' societies, whether independent nations or colonies, have been firmly set through prior years of experience with colonial social-economic institutions. There has been little or no alteration of agricultural activity and patterns of land use since the mid-1800's. With the exception of Dominica, all of the mountainous volcanic or steep hilly islands have been ecologically altered through extensive agricultural use that lasted for approximately 150 years. Since cultivation included even the most steeply graded forested mountain slopes, very little of virgin rain forest and montane formations remain on any of the islands. Agricultural activity, however, did not persist in the highlands of the islands because of erosion and the consequent disruption of surface soil-moisture relationships. Thus one can interpret a pattern of advancement up the mountain slopes and a gradual retreat back down to the presently cultivated lands which constitute about 50 per cent of the total surface area of the mountainous and steep hilly islands.

The effect of the established patterns of political and economic life has been to turn the attention of each island toward its metropolitan nation rather than toward its neighbors in the Caribbean. This has produced a competitiveness between the islands in their search for markets and sources of investment capital and aid. The continued dependence on cash crops for export impedes serious consideration of developing agricultural products for indigenous use and maintains a fundamental reliance upon sources of food from overseas nations (Report of the Tripartite Economic Survey, 1966). The problems of agriculture and related land use are some of the most perplexing in the region. The recently formed Caribbean Free Trade Association has not answered these fundamental problems in any important way. It has devoted most of its efforts toward intraregional trade in manufactured products.

About $250 million (U.S.) worth of staple foodstuffs are imported to the islands and Guyana per year. This constitutes approximately 20 per cent of total imports to the region. The figures here are especially significant when it is considered that this import is using the islands' small hard currency credit in foreign exchange.[1]

Since we are concerned with the utilization of resources within these island environments, it may be said that the kinds of use and the rates of use are responsive less to the concepts of sustained yield and more to the uncertain demands of traditional continental marketplaces. That this kind of influence on resource use has not produced disastrous ecological damage in modern times can be attributed to the fact that cash-crop agriculture is still an effective and needed absorber of manpower on most of the islands, and thus the political-social questions of employment sustain a labor-intensive system in spite of the push for capital-intensive agriculture.

The precarious nature of the economy throughout the region gives some measure

[1] This summarizes material from several unpublished papers. See A. McIntyre, "Aspects of Trade and Development in the Commonwealth Caribbean" (1965); and E. Armstrong, "Import Substitution in Trinidad & Tobago," the Institute of Social and Economic Research, Mona, Jamaica (1967).

of concern as to how long political exigencies may outweigh the economic requirement that agriculture compete in the world on an equal technological basis. Until now the arable land of the islands has not been subjected to very much modern equipment, and most of the agronomic research on crop productivity and soil maintenance has presupposed a continuance of labor-intensive agriculture. A diminution of income or support from outside the region would likely trigger a shift toward greater use of technology in order to increase productivity and profit.

For example, Barbados, cultivating approximately 70 per cent of its land to sugar cane, derives almost 40 per cent of its gross domestic product from sugar. Its population density is nearly 586 people per square kilometer. Its terrain is more gently rolling than in most of the other islands and thus would be amenable to agricultural machinery. The recent "Report of the Tripartite Economic Survey of the Eastern Caribbean" (1966) points out that the only feasible method of raising economic returns in sugarcane production in Barbados is by increasing mechanization, a situation which has been avoided to date by reliance on tourism, which generates almost as much economic activity as agriculture.

But tourism, like cash crops, relies on overseas markets. As a source of imported capital, tourism is equally sensitive to changes in economic conditions in uncontrollable and distant marketplaces. Today, in a period of high market demand for travel to the Caribbean, Barbados is rapidly expanding its tourism industry to encourage the flow of overseas money. A decline of the North American or western European economy would severely affect Barbados. Tourism would suffer, and much more would be required from agriculture. This would produce a shift in the mode of agricultural activity and the rate at which the soil and water resources of this island would

be used. Such a shift would be requisite for economic survival.

On the other end of the development scale, the island of Dominica is another contemporary example of resource utilization that is influenced by an external market demand. Dominica is an island of forests, much of which have never been cleared. Its population density of barely over 78 people per square kilometer is the lowest in the eastern Caribbean. Its topography is steep and rugged and precludes effective land utilization for most agricultural activities.

For many years it has been recognized that the timber resources of this island are of high economic potential. In 1962, Canadian Overseas Aid investigations placed the volume of standing timber of merchantable quality at 1,110,000 cubic meters (470 million board feet) (Report of the Tripartite Economic Survey, 1966). In 1968, the Dominica government entered into contractual agreements with a lumbering firm for the harvest and primary processing of the standing timber crop of the island, most of which was contained in Crown Land Forest Reserve. The economic potential of the forest resources of this small island country is undeniable. That utilization of the forest should be seen as a partial solution to the country's economic problems is not surprising. A market is available and outside investors are willing to develop a scale of enterprise which could profitably respond to market demand. What is significant is that rather than investigate the long-run production potential of the island forests the concerned parties have merely measured the standing timber crop available for immediate commercial harvest. Numerous inquiries during this past year by representatives from the Conservation Foundation, the American Geographical Society, the International Union for the Conservation of Nature and Natural Resources, and the Caribbean Conservation Association confirm that forest resources on Dominica will undergo a minimum rate of use that will reach 28,000 cubic meters (12 million board feet) per year, in three years. This minimum rate is stated in the contract to guarantee a minimum royalty income to the Dominica government. There is no reason to think that the minimum will be the standard for timber removal. The contract has no restriction on allowable maximum cut. The language of the contract includes such statements as "the Company shall . . . (b) conduct its timber, logging and lumber operations in accordance with the best Canadian practices. . . ." The contract further states:

The Syndicate undertakes that the Company will assist the Forestry Department of Government in undertaking studies to the determination of the rate of growth of the forests and silvicultural practices which are necessary to determine the steps to be taken to perpetuate the growth of timber in those areas of Crown Forests in which the Government desires to practice sustained yield forestry. (Agreement signed April 17, 1967, between Robert Malpas, Edward E. Osborne and John Wilson of the first part and the Honourable N. A. N. Drucreay, Minister for Trade and Industry, Government of Dominica, Xerox copy)

Considering that there are no upper limits for timber removal, the promise of research to determine forest growth rates after cutting has begun offers little hope that a serious overharvest may not ensue. The application of the best Canadian timbering practices also raises doubts, given the great differences between the Canadian forest types and the rain forest.

What needs to be examined is the automatic rate of use that may be imposed by the establishment of a forest industrial plant that is responsive to the economy of a foreign company and the demands of a distant market place rather than the ecologically determined rate of productivity of the Dominica forest.

Agriculture and, in some cases, the forest industries are the only principal users of land resources for primary production in the eastern Caribbean. The degree to which these users may cause negative ecological impacts depends on the tacit conditions of possible change in the technology of use. There is very little documented knowledge about the ecology of the islands in general and even less about the ability of the arable land to sustain mechanization. And even if we can discover the ecological guidelines for a capital-intensive agriculture or sustained-yield forestry, will the condition of men on the islands and elsewhere allow the guidelines to be followed?

The people of the eastern Caribbean seem content to avoid that question now. I think they assume that a reasonable adjustment to the land exists that partly accommodates their very real employment problem.

There is a second ecological threat facing the islands—how to adjust the impact of a newly introduced form of resource use when there is little or no ecological knowledge or control over the quality or intensity of use.

Tourism is the most dynamic economic force in the life of the islands today. Every island government wants tourists and each has been successful to some degree in getting them. A kind of tourism mystique exists among government planners. Formulae are produced to show, for example, the relationship between hotel rooms and jobs, tourist man-days and average annual per capita incomes, and jet aircraft traffic and gross domestic product. The weight of real evidence shows that economic improvement is possible by expanding tourism. The Tripartite Survey rests most of its economic development proposals on a growing tourism. The survey team also accepts the present plateau of the agricultural sector, only randomly pointing out the possibilities for improvement or growth (Agreement signed April 17, 1967, see above).

The quality of the Caribbean environment for attracting tourists needs no explanation. But the quality of the islands' environment is undergoing the same pressures that we are experiencing in the United States. The islands are becoming polluted. The tourist is usually an urban person with urban tastes, and tourism in its general effect is rather like the process of urbanization. It concentrates people and their waste products. The demands for services and comforts place strains on water supplies and sewage systems that were built with only the culture of island people in mind. Insect pests are increasingly controlled by spraying DDT to guarantee comfortable use of the beach and shoreline in all seasons. Automobile imports have risen with the need for taxis, rental cars and excursion transportation. Subdivisions fringe the towns and cities, creating seasonal home suburbias. Although agriculture has not taken on the accouterments of technology, the tourism industry has at least imposed the physical structure required by the twentieth-century American and European urban life style.

Because tourist activities and facilities tend to occupy sea-front property, most of the environmental damage is concentrated at the point where land and water meet. As might be expected, waterfront pollution is the most obvious form of environmental change. Most pollutants from land-based tourism have been organic in composition to date. The effects of this pollution on the littoral zones is virtually unstudied. Perhaps only on the island of Trinidad, where domestic and rum plant sewage discharge into a canal that feeds Caroni Wildlife Sanctuary Swamp south of Port of Spain, has there been a clearly observable effect. There the mollusk and crustacean population upon which the ibis and herons of the swamp feed have been reduced. This reduction is actually as yet unmeasured, though it was reported to me by the acting Conservator of Forests in charge of the swamp, who has

had a lifelong interest in the natural history of the area.[2]

Yachting and power boating have introduced high concentrations of domestic and petroleum pollution into harbors. No studies have been carried out on any of the islands about the ecological impact of these forms of pollution. With the increased efforts by island governments and investors to accelerate the tourism industry, it is evident that today's pollution is only a sample of what may come, given the absence of knowledge and legal controls.

In the effort to enlarge their incomes from tourism, the islands are now planning forms of waterfront and offshore use. The enlargement of yacht facilities, harbor construction, piers and wharfs and underwater tourism habitation pose possible problems for which there is no prior experience.[3]

The possibility of ecological damage is likely to be a lesser factor in island decision-making than the promise of economic reward. I have raised the problem of ecological consequences with government representatives throughout the eastern Caribbean. In every instance the answer was the same: "Ecology is a fine thing but this hotel or that yacht basin will be an important source of income and jobs." From the island governments' point of view, it is clear that ecological questions are more conveniently avoided than answered because the answer seems to promise constraint upon all hoped-for economic improvements.

St. Lucia, a mountainous island country of 610 square kilometers and ninety thousand people, is about to experience an explosive expansion of its tourist industry. Anticipating the opening of a jetport capable of handling "jumbo jets," a hotel syndicate is building a one-thousand-bed hotel.

[2] Interview with Michael Bayne, Acting Conservator of Forests, Trinidad and Tobago Forest Department, November 9, 1963.

[3] Interview with Dr. John Watts, President, Caribbean Tourist Association, July 21, 1966.

In less than two years, that one hotel will increase the island's tourist accommodations by over 300 per cent. It will concentrate a thousand visitors and one thousand tourist industry wage earners and families near the harbor at Castries, the capital. The impact of this action on the ecology of the harbor and adjacent offshore water is unknown. But would the knowledge that the hotel might generate ecological damage alter the decision about the hotel's location or construction? What I am suggesting again is that the determinants for such a decision in fact reside in the continental tourist market, not on the island. And, the market will assure its own immediate supply response simply because it contains the capital to create the supply facilities.

Of all the special characteristics of the Caribbean islands, their biotic uniqueness stands out in my own appraisals. The oceanic conditions have produced a very high degree of regional and insular endemism among the islands' flora and fauna. Richard Howard (1952), of the Arnold Arboretum, has stated that regional and insular endemic flora are the two most prevailing floral groups within the islands. J. S. Beard (1949) estimated that approximately half of the highland flora of Dominica, Martinique and Guadeloupe is endemic. Neither Howard nor Beard had any way of determining the degree of endemism in lowland areas because their investigations, along with the earliest floristic study by Grisebach (Beard, 1949), all occurred after the major period of land clearing for agriculture. Even the assessment of endemism in the highland flora is only approximate, for there has been no recent, complete floristic evaluation on any of the eastern Caribbean islands. The studies by A. L. Stoffers (1956) on *The Vegetation of the Netherlands Antilles* represent the most complete attempt to list the total vegetation of any of the islands.

Because there has been an absence of widespread human activity in the highlands of the islands for the past century, the richness of genetic material has received sanctuary. Because the vegetation has been unmolested, the highland forests have survived as an important refuge for the remaining populations of endemic animal life. The record of animal extinction is more precise than that of plants. J. H. Westermann (1953), in his monograph *Nature Preservation in the Caribbean,* presented documentation on the extinction of vertebrate fauna. His lists include eighty-seven species and subspecies of vertebrates that have become extinct throughout the Caribbean. These include forty-one mammals, twenty-one birds and twenty-five reptiles or amphibians. Most were insular endemics. It is shocking to contemplate that almost 40 per cent of all the world's vertebrate extinctions occurred in this very small region of the globe. Today there are thirty-six threatened species or subspecies of vertebrates that exist mostly in the seldom visited highland forests of the islands (Westermann, 1953).

I doubt that one can find an authoritative full-life history on any of those threatened animals. I assume that all are probably extremely vulnerable, merely because their habitats are so small and easily altered or destroyed. Two of the most spectacular of these species, the imperial parrot *Amazona imperialis* and the red-necked parrot *A. arausiaca,* inhabit the forests of Dominica. The precarious condition of these two birds in the face of imminent extensive habitat alteration illustrates how easily a threatened species may be subjected to quick extinction. It is equally apparent that alteration of these isolated environments may come, not in so dramatic a form as the timbering operation of Dominica, but rather through the introduction of foreign and toxic substances to the soil, water and air of the islands. It is sad to think that we have almost no effective understanding of how increasing pesticide application, burning of hydrocarbon fuels or pollution of the water may affect the last remaining vestiges of one of the world's most unique aggregations of living organisms.

I want to raise again the only point I intended to make. Is the rate of resource use in underdeveloped lands dependent on the economy of modern industries and the forced responsiveness to the market or is it determined by criteria derived from ecological knowledge? All my experience in the Caribbean tells me that economic scale and market demand win over ecology in almost every case. If the answer to that question is the same in other parts of the world, then surely we are all in deep trouble no matter how much we learn about ecology.

Most of the underdeveloped nations seem to lack four things: (1) money, (2) technology, (3) truly meaningful sovereignty, and (4) adequate understanding of the basis of productivity and resistance to degradation of their ecosystems.

The anxiety to acquire twentieth-century-level technology and wealth offers every opportunity to investors from wealthier nations. Having only weak international political or economic power, resources must be offered as an inducement to capital sources without any effective bargaining position for exercising control even if the potential long-run destruction of resources is understood. The controlling factors for determining resource-use rates become the "economy of scale" for the industrial plant and the ability of the market to absorb the primary resource or its elaborated product. They are, in short, susceptible to the same forces which beset the islands of Barbados, St. Lucia and Dominica.

Unless we see the full human problem implicit in each ecological problem, we are unlikely to witness very much change in the use of the world's resources. The developed countries arrange the means by which investments are made in other lands and exact the price against the sovereignty of other nations in those arrangements.

It would be comforting to retreat at this juncture to the assumed neutrality of science and scholarship and rest our case on our ability to expand the world's ecological knowledge. But we must base our assumptions on international political, economic and social realities. Our wishful expectations that other men will be able to display wisdom and control in applying the lessons of ecology may come closer to being realized only if we can allow them at least as much national integrity as we have.

REFERENCES

Beard, J. S. *The Natural Vegetation of the Windward and Leeward Islands*. Oxford Forestry Memoirs No. 21. London: Oxford University Press, 1949.

Carlozzi, Carl A., and Carlozzi, Alice A. *Conservation and Caribbean Regional Progress*. Yellow Springs, Ohio: Antioch Press, 1968.

Firey, Walter. *Man, Mind and Land*. Glencoe, Ill.: Free Press, 1960.

Howard, Richard A. "Suggestions for the Preservation of Botanical Species Endemic to the Islands of the Antilles." Paper presented to the Third General Assembly, International Union for the Protection of Nature, Caracas, Venezuela. 1952.

Liddle, Ralph. *The Geology of Venezuela and Trinidad*. Ithaca, N.Y.: Paleontological Research Institute, 1946.

Report of the Tripartite Economic Survey of

the Eastern Caribbean (to the Governments of the United Kingdom of Great Britain and Ireland, of Canada and of the United States of America). 1966.

Schuchert, Charles. *Historical Geology of the Antillean Caribbean Region.* New York: John Wiley and Sons, 1945.

Stoffers, A. L. *The Vegetation of the Netherlands Antilles,* Vol. 1. The Hague: Martinus Nijhoff, 1956.

Westermann, J. H. *Nature Preservation in the Caribbean.* Publications of the Foundation for Scientific Research in Surinam and the Netherlands Antilles, No. 9. Utrecht: Foundation for Scientific Research in Surinam and the Netherlands Antilles, 1953.

46. MAN'S EFFECTS ON ISLAND ECOSYSTEMS

F. R. Fosberg

Islands have proven to be very vulnerable to disturbance resulting from human activities. They are unique and unusually interesting scientifically. Island biotas and soils are particularly susceptible to the ravages of introduced animals. This results in the destruction of vegetation cover and the extinction of endemic plants and animals. Exotic plants tend to replace native species on islands, especially after disturbances by man or introduced animals. Fire, used in hunting and in slash-and-burn agriculture, has a profoundly degrading effect on vegetation and ultimately leads to disastrous accelerated erosion and loss of soil. Overhunting quickly eliminates useful animals. Accelerated erosion, from whatever cause, brings about degradation of the entire ecosystem. Plantation agriculture, though efficient, tends both to be vulnerable to pests and diseases and to deterioration of the quality of life for the population. Military activities, both preparatory and belligerent, are among the most destructive of all influences on islands, and the effects are long-persistent. They set the dynamic status of the system back toward the pioneer condition, and they may leave dangerous residues in the form of unexploded ammunition. Mining for phosphate and other products, if extensive, usually leaves an island in totally unusable condition for the native people. Such activity sacrifices long-term habitability to short-term gain. Medical and public health activities, while undoubtedly beneficial to the people, if un-accompanied by any instruction in methods of population regulation result in the rapid increase of human populations which soon tend to exceed the carrying capacities of small island ecosystems. Imposition of alien cultural systems, evolved in continental ecosystems, tend to bring about serious maladjustment and social problems in small islands, as well as material demands that their limited resources cannot satisfy. There seems little reason for optimism about the future of island ecosystems, so long as population growth and pressure for modernization continue.

Islands present a unique ecological situation because of their nature and the treatment they have received. Few parts of the world are as vulnerable to mismanagement, and few have suffered as grievously at the hand of man. I am going to depart from the topic of the effects of technology on islands to the extent of substituting "human activity" for "technology." Then I will be able to discuss more fully what man has done to these remarkable microcosms scattered over the seas of the world. To keep the subject manageable I will largely confine my remarks to small, mostly oceanic islands, but this does not mean that there is nothing to say about the large islands. Madagascar, by itself, would be a good case study in destruction if I were familiar enough with the details of what has happened to tell it correctly.

When I say that islands are unique, I mean more than the truism that any spot on the face of the earth is unique. Although many islands resemble each other rather closely in physical geography, islands, with the exception of coral atolls, tend to be biologically more distinct from each other and to have more unique qualities than do comparable continental areas. Almost all oceanic islands higher than sea-level atolls have some, often many, endemic plant and animal species, and relatively small biota, mostly brought together by accidents or dispersal, followed by more or less evolution. Thus, no two have the same complement of species, nor can they have identical combinations of species even locally, such as occur over and over in continental situations and form the basis of the plant association concept in phytosociology.

This uniqueness means that when an island is degraded and its biota largely destroyed, the world has lost something irreplaceable. There is no question of locating another example, as can usually be done for a continental ecosystem. It is, for example, still possible to find remnant examples of the various sorts of mid-U.S. prairie, in spite of the completeness of cultivation of the prairie regions. Not so with an island: when an insular biota is destroyed, the destruction is final. One can find another somewhat similar island, perhaps, but it will be different. A species that is lost can never be relocated. We know it existed only because of a dried fragment in an herbarium or a pickled corpse in a museum jar.

In discussing the results of man's exploitation of islands, I will depart from the currently popular idea of economic values. I cannot prove that the extinct dodo, *Clermontia halakalensis,* or Wake Island flightless rail ever had any economic value. Probably they did not, though we will never know. I am going to assume that because they existed they had value. They were a part of the fascinating diversity that makes life such an interesting and rewarding experience, and provides the basis for the remarkable stability, or homeostasis, of ecosystems that has so far protected man from completely destroying his habitat. I am going to accept as basic that the destruction of an island ecosystem causes "life to lose some of its savor" (L. H. Bailey, oral communication). The examples of destruction that I shall describe are matters that should be of serious concern to a generation that finds the world in its present condition to have little enough savor, indeed, and to promise even less in the near future.

My concept of the development of an ecosystem, island or otherwise, is that of a process of building energy into the system, reducing its randomness or entropy, and increasing order, complexity, and integration. Man's usual role has been to reverse this process and to increase very rapidly the entropy in the system. I accept as axiomatic that this role is bad, though to some extent necessary, in order that man may produce food for his outrageous numbers to eat. Even this need, however, is no excuse for his going about it in a completely thoughtless and irresponsible manner, the results of which are only now beginning to become apparent, and to worry us to the extent that we have such symposia as this.

I do not want to convey the idea, however, that the consequences of the activities I will discuss have no practical importance. If the soil of an island is washed out to sea, it cannot be cultivated. If the water storage capacity of an island is impaired, the people may suffer water shortages. If a wild species of banana becomes extinct, its disease resistance or other breeding qualities cannot be utilized. But I simply do not intend to detail all the practical consequences, many of which we do not yet know. It is sufficient to say that some of the islands that have been most mistreated are now uninhabited and, unless much energy and ingenuity are directed toward their rehabilitation, they will remain uninhabitable.

EFFECTS OF ANIMAL INTRODUCTION

The sorts of human activity that have had destructive effects on the island ecosystem are many—it is practical to discuss only a few of the more obvious. One of the worst practices has been the introduction of four-footed animals, both herbivorous and carnivorous, for various reasons—as food supplies, as agricultural and pastoral animals, as pets, and even, as in the case of rats, for no purpose at all. The resultant animal populations have been extraordinarily destructive because the vegetation of oceanic islands, and most of the species that make it up, evolved in the complete absence of such animals. These species developed no protective mechanisms at all against the browsing, bark gnawing, rooting, and even the trampling, that are the normal behavior of herbivores. The native animals—birds, reptiles, and invertebrates—on the islands, not previously subjected to predation by

cats and dogs, had no fear of them. Many had even lost the ability to fly or to run. The dodo, for example, had no chance at all against dogs.

Introduced animals found no effective enemies or diseases on the islands, so they increased exponentially until, as in the case of the rabbits on Laysan Island, they were controlled by starvation. When nothing remains for a rabbit or a goat to eat, the vegetation of an island is in bad shape indeed. And not only the vegetation. When the vegetation is gone, water is not readily absorbed; it runs off, taking the soil with it.

The sufferings of shipwrecked sailors were so real that it became standard practice to introduce goats onto any island discovered. This was done so early, and the goats were so effective, that we will never know what the vegetation of many islands was like. In the late eighteenth century, the governor of St. Helena wrote to the British Admirality that the goats were destroying the forests and asked permission to remove them. The reply was that the goats were of more value than the forests and that nothing should be done. Today we would like to know what those forests were really like.

Of course, not all introductions were so successful. Guanaco were said to have been introduced onto Tinian in the Marianas by the Spanish in the seventeenth century. They disappeared without leaving a trace, except perhaps to help various other animals destroy the forests of Tinian.

Sheep and cattle were brought into many islands for ranching. Whether they were kept under control, herded and harvested or became feral, the result was more or less the same. The native forests were destroyed and, at best, the land was converted to palatable grassland—in worse cases to weedy shrubland, and at worst to bare eroding subsoil and rocks. Richard Warner (1960) has vividly described this process in "A Forest Dies on Mauna Kea" (Hawaii). Kahoolawe

Island, in the Hawaiian group, is an example of this and other destructive processes. It is now barren and uninhabited. Easter Island, after the introduction of sheep, does not have a single living tree, at least of native species, and has few native plants of any kind. It is now nothing but a bare, wind-swept sheep ranch. Once it supported a thriving population, capable of the megalithic stone art for which the island is famous. The population is now small and the culture destroyed (Skottsberg, 1953).

EFFECTS OF PLANT INTRODUCTION

Exotic plants in many, if not most, islands have almost completely replaced the native flora, except in high mountains or cliffs. In the Hawaiian Islands, for example, a visitor unescorted by botanists, might spend three months without ever seeing a native Hawaiian plant. In the lowland populated areas, he would see gorgeous flame trees from Madagascar, frangipani trees from tropical America, shower trees from the Caribbean and the southeast Asian region, mangoes from Borneo, banyans from India and southeast Asia, samans from the Caribbean, hybrid hibiscus developed locally from largely imported parents, allamanda from Brazil, and many other memorable ornamental and food plants. In the country, he would see forests of algarroba from Peru, guava from Mexico, koa haole from Mexico, and christmas berry from South America, as well as great plantations of sugar cane and pineapples, probably from New Guinea and Paraguay respectively. Papayas from tropical America and bananas from Indonesia furnish fruit for every table. The native forests of strange island trees, without English names, that originally covered these lowlands and slopes are gone except in remote or protected pockets. The visitor does not even learn that the coconut, pineapple and lantana are not native.

The Hawaiians brought with them a considerable number of plants, only one or two of which ever occupied much more land than was specially prepared for them. But when Europeans arrived with a continuing flow of useful plants, ornamentals, and weeds, these plants took over with surprising vigor and replaced much of the native vegetation. They are now the dominant species in most habitats. This success is seldom due to any innate superiority over native species, but rather because introduced animals opened up the vegetation and allowed the newcomers to establish themselves, which they were seldom able to do alone against a closed native vegetation. Once the closed cover was broken up by browsing and trampling, the newcomers found niches that they were able to occupy more effectively, in many cases, than their rather few native competitors.

Only time will show what plants will ultimately prevail, but this must be time without continued disturbance, which in most islands now seems unlikely. Certain observations indicate that the native vegetation may, given a chance, eventually regain some ground from the exotic assemblages now prevalent. For example, in the first two decades of this century, Joseph Rock, C. N. Forbes, and others (oral communication) reported that the native wet forests of the Hawaiian island of Lanai were reduced to a few acres on top of the highest mountain. When I was on this island in 1935, George C. Munro, for years manager of the island, had long been carrying on a relentless campaign to eliminate goats, sheep, and deer and had brought the wild cattle into the domestic herds and kept them under control. There were then very few large feral herbivores on the island. The wet mountain forest had extended itself to cover hundreds of acres of the higher parts of the island (Fosberg, 1936). After the upper parts of the Waianae Range of Oahu were fenced as a water reserve in the 1920's, a few native plants began to make headway against the lantana that had dominated these mountains after it was introduced as an ornamental and spread by introduced mynah birds and perhaps doves into forest openings made by introduced cattle and goats. Its fleshy fruits are eaten by these birds and the hard seed deposited in their droppings. It forms dense thickets of a chaparral-like scrub that resists invasion by most other plants and is not eaten by herbivorous quadrupeds.

In certain cases, exotic animals and plants effect a kind of cooperation in crowding the native plants, as when livestock so effectively scattered the seeds of the introduced kiawe or mesquite tree (*Prosopis pallida*) in their droppings that this tree now dominates the lowlands in the Hawaiian Islands. Here also the introduced mynah scatters the seeds of the introduced guavas (*Psidium guajava* and *Psidium cattleianum*), the introduced lantana (*Lantana camara*) and the introduced blackberry (*Rubus penetrans*), so that these plants dominate large areas at the expense of the native plants.

The questions may be asked: Who introduced these plants and animals, when, and why? For most islands most introductions are undocumented. The Polynesians brought the pig, dog, and chicken, as well as the rat to Hawaii. Captain Vancouver introduced cattle, goats, and sheep to Hawaii in 1790. An early Spanish settler, Don Marin, brought many exotic plants, some of which are now so familiar as to be frequently thought of as Hawaiian. A priest brought the kiawe in about 1830. A Scot, homesick for Scotland, was said to have introduced gorse on Maui. The Territorial Board of Commissioners of Agriculture and Forestry introduced innumerable plants, many of which now occupy large areas (Bryan, 1947). Dr. William Hillebrand, German physician, botanist, and advisor to the Hawaiian kings in the nineteenth century, brought the mynah bird, as well as the banyan tree and many other desirable and undesirable plants. Dr. Willis Pope of the Hawaii Agricultural Experiment Station brought the blackberry. Numerous private citizens, mostly unrecorded, have made their contributions to the exotic fauna and flora, and the process still goes on throughout the island world.

EFFECTS OF FIRE AND HUNTING

Fire, set by lightning or volcanic activity, was doubtless a natural phenomenon in islands, as it was elsewhere. However, its incidence was vastly stepped up when man arrived on the scene. After game was introduced and established, fire was used in hunting. Where upland agriculture was practiced, it was usually of a slash-and-burn type, with fires spreading into vegetation not intended for destruction. Such carelessness accounts for disastrous fires on islands, as elsewhere: and deliberately set fires are common, as on Raïatéa and Guam, for example. Islands like Mangareva and large areas in Guam and Palau that were doubtless once forested, are now reduced to coarse grassland, conducive to continued burning. Not only are the forest and other vegetation destroyed, but the soil is exposed to erosion. Arid southeast Oahu is now a grassy and scrubby expanse of exposed lava ridges; once it had a fairly deep soil, traces of which were located by Dr. Frank Egler during his investigations in 1937. It will certainly take many thousands of years to reform soil on this sort of substratum, even if it is revegetated and protected from further burning. At present the area is too bare to burn very much.

Shifting agriculture or other slash-and-burn agricultural practices have a disastrous effect on islands. This sort of agriculture is defended by some ethnologists and agricultural economists as the only way to exploit soil on steep tropical slopes. Clearly it is the way that many primitive agriculturists do exploit these slopes. The practice might have been defensible so long as the population was small, only favorable spots were cultivated, and the period of rotation was long enough for vegetation and soil to recover somewhat. But populations do not remain small, especially when encouraged by modern medicine and hygiene and the elimination of tribal warfare (Taeuber, 1963). The cycles of cultivation and fallow become shorter and shorter, and clearing occurs on poorer and more marginal land. Erosion becomes catastrophic, and the island is destroyed as a favorable place to live.

Where edible or otherwise valuable animals occur—for example, birds, turtles, tortoises, or seals—they are usually overharvested. Green turtles have been almost eliminated from the Hawaiian and Bonin islands and many others where they were formerly plentiful. The Caribbean monk seal is gone. The Galapagos tortoises were hunted to dangerously low numbers and some island populations eliminated altogether. Giant tortoises were exterminated on all the western Indian Ocean islands except Aldabra.

EROSION

In most continental regions accelerated erosion is a gradual enough process that it may not be recognized until the results are catastrophic—dust bowls, dendritic mazes of gullies, and finally badlands. On many islands, the terrain is steep and the soil thin and very erodible if not held by vegetation. Destruction can become irreversible in a few years. One only has to fly over islands like Lanai and Kahoolawe in the Hawaiian group after a rainy spell to see where the

soil from the extensive bare red areas goes. There are vivid red plumes in the bright blue sea down-current from every stream mouth. Domestic and feral animals, as recounted above, have, in the last 150 years, reduced these islands to deserts, and even the subsoil is rapidly being removed by water and wind. Fortunately for the present owners of Lanai, the pineapple plant needs only enough soil to anchor itself. This soil can be very sterile, since the plants are funnel-shaped to collect rain water and may be fed by a small squirt of nutrient solution from time to time. Most other plants are not so accommodating. A large area of Lanai is a solid pineapple plantation. The rest is sad-looking. The history of Lanai would have been most instructive to a student of land utilization if it had been written down while George C. Munro, former manager of the island, still lived, as he was fond of relating it from personal remembrance.

The problem of loss of soil from mountainous areas, on continents as well as islands, is an old one. Agricultural techniques have evolved to derive some advantage from silt carried away by streams. Marsh cultures of taro and rice were developed to a high degree of productivity in valley bottoms where the silt tended to be deposited. It is no accident that wet-land taro was the staff of life on islands such as Rapa and the Hawaiian group. This is an example of a people who have evolved a technique to live with a bad situation that they may have created or at least aggravated. Rapa is a perfect example of an island "skeletonized" by erosion. This situation on Réunion has been studied and ably summarized by Gourou (1963).

MONOCULTURE

The most favorable sites on most islands have been pre-empted by plantation agriculture, producing coconuts, sugar cane, pineapples, and a few other crops. This practice has the advantage of efficiency; but its efficiency largely depends on the monoculture technique, which is extremely vulnerable to insect pests and plant diseases and puts the people completely at the mercy of market fluctuations. The diet of the people changes when they shift from a subsistence to a cash economy. Witness the trend to canned meat and fish, wheat bread, and rice in French Polynesia, and the subsequent deterioration of the natives' teeth. The change usually seems to be for the worse, though this perhaps is not wholly the fault of the system. Most people will choose a bad diet if it tastes better, or if it is merely fashionable, even though they could afford a good one. In addition to these obvious disadvantages, the plantation system also reduces the landscape to a deadly monotony, as on the island of Barbados, completely covered by sugar cane; few plants and animals are tolerated if they are even imagined to be detrimental to the crop. Those that are not detrimental are usually eliminated with those that are, as the pesticides used are seldom specific to one or a few kinds of organism. A plantation, though it may be very productive, tends to be made a "biological desert." And on islands, as noted above, this is more serious than on continents, because unique plants and animals that previously occupied these favorable habitats may not have existed elsewhere and may now be irretrievably lost.

MILITARY ACTIVITIES

Especially in relatively recent years military activities have been among the most destructive of all human interferences on many islands. Fortifications and other construction, even in periods of non-belligerency, consume and drastically alter huge areas (Hall, 1944). Most of Guam, for example, has been subject to military construction, as were certain of the Bonins, Iwo Jima, Dublon in the Truk Islands, Kwajalein, Eniwetok, and many others. During actual hostilities enormous quantities of high-explosive shells and bombs were dropped on most of these same islands. The terms "Mitcher haircut" and "Spruance haircut" vividly describe the results of these treatments (Heinland Crown, 1954, and other Marine Corps Monographs; Richard, 1957). One of the most fought-over islands during World War II was Saipan in the Marianas. Before the war, the arable land on the island was in sugar plantations. Various types of forest, some native, others planted, occupied most of the rougher areas, with some sterile soils occupied by savanna. At the onset of war, the Japanese built extensive fortifications, including caves and underground installations. The attack by the American forces was preceded by a naval and aerial bombardment of incredible intensity, and after an assault landing the island was fought over for a month. Much of the vegetation was burned or cleared and replaced by Quonset huts and other military construction. These soon disintegrated when they were abandoned after military use lessened. In 1948, an ammunition storage area exploded, throwing shells all over the northern third of the island. The unexploded shells make that part of the island dangerous even today. The sugar cane has seeded, giving rise to brakes of wild cane filling old plantations and other clearings. The forests are now mostly rather degraded second-growth of introduced species choked with weedy vines. The native upland forest, with its several endemic species, is mostly gone, though some of the species persist as occasional individuals. Native vegetation largely persists only on cliffs and in strand situations, where it readily recovered from destructive treatment. In general, the dynamic status of the vegetation has been set back toward a pioneer status and native plants have given way to exotics. Most native animals have become scarce with the reductions in their habitats.

Even areas where there was little war activity have not escaped. Some islands, such as Kahoolawe in the Hawaiian group, have been used for bombing or shelling practice and are littered with dud ammunition.

Several islands, such as Bikini, Eniwetok, Christmas Island, Mururoa, Fangatau, and Montebello have been used as test areas for atomic explosives. The results were all that might have been expected. Interestingly enough, since the vegetation of atolls, especially the drier ones, is already of a pioneer type, that is, capable of growing on new or disturbed habitats, it seems to have recovered rather promptly after the earlier of these tests, and there are now active preparations afoot for sending the Bikini people back to their atoll. Fortunately there are few, if any, local endemic species on atolls, so not too much will have been lost as a result of the tests.

MINING

One of the widespread forms of technological destruction on islands is phosphate mining, and in some cases, bauxite mining. As the result of ages of guano deposits by fish-eating birds and subsequent geochemical processes, most of the elevated atolls had large phosphate deposits, and even many low atolls had enough to repay exploitation. Especially on the raised limestone islands the mining removes all loose and semi-consolidated materials, leaving a desolate "badlands" type of pinnacled surface, utterly useless, not even supporting much vegetation, particularly where the

rainfall is low or undependable. Banaba (Ocean Island) in the central Pacific was recently abandoned by its inhabitants after it had been worked over for phosphate. Most of the soil had been removed, so that agriculture became difficult without elaborate procedures to convert coral rock to soil. Their water situation, always a marginal one, deteriorated. Water that would have been held by vegetation tended to run off. Evaporation increased from the bare surfaces. The native vegetation, on which they had depended for many essentials, was mostly eliminated. Life became so difficult that, in spite of the traditional islander's love for his home island, it became the easiest course for them to use their saved-up share of the phosphate profits to buy an island elsewhere and move to it.

The people of nearby Nauru, a similar large, but almost worked-out, elevated atoll are looking into the possibility of rehabilitating their home. Fortunately they have large funds held in trust for them—their share of the phosphate profits. It seems likely that a substantial part of these savings, perhaps all, would be used if the island were to be properly restored to a productive condition (United Nations, 1966; Anonymous, 1966, n.d.)

The phosphate islands of the western Indian Ocean are now scarcely capable of supporting anyone, except by their marine resources. A number of local species seem to have disappeared on some of them. On Christmas Island, in the eastern Indian Ocean, the last remaining colony of *Sula abbottii* (Abbott's booby) is now threatened by a stepped-up program of phosphate mining. Fortunately smaller phosphate deposits are no longer profitable because of the opening up of large continental phosphorite mines. The larger ones, however, still seem able to compete. Recently the unwelcome news was published that commercially valuable phosphate occurs on Bellona Island near the Solomons, scarcely explored botanically and the site of a most interesting primitive Polynesian or proto-Polynesian culture. Although there is every reason for leaving Bellona and nearby Rennell untouched, as has previously been the policy of the British Solomon Islands Administration, it seems a safe prediction that this discovery will provide an excuse for abandoning this intelligent policy. Thus another interesting Stone Age culture will be destroyed, and an island biota, indeed, a functioning and unique ecosystem, will be degraded.

One might ask, how is this ecosystem unique and why is it important? In addition to the consideration previously mentioned, Bellona and Rennell islands represent a special class of islands—the elevated atoll type. Elevated atolls are scattered in some numbers through tropical seas; Banaba and Nauru, mentioned above, are examples, as is Makatéa, another phosphate island in French Polynesia. However, because of the prevalence of phosphate in commercial quantities on these islands, only a very few of them remain in anything like an undisturbed condition. Henderson and Aldabra are two which are not inhabited and have not been exploited because insufficient phosphate has been found. In comparison with these uninhabited ones, Rennell and Bellona remain with intact, functioning aboriginal populations still in balance with their habitats. Understanding of these, by comparison with their uninhabited counterparts, might well be one of the most important aims of modern ecological science, since such situations could be considered as microcosms to illustrate some of the principles on which larger balanced ecosystems function. But if they are destroyed for a few million dollars' worth of phosphate, this opportunity will be lost. Some of the most beautiful scenery in Palau, both above and under water, and the hope of a tourist industry for Micronesia are now threatened by phosphate prospecting.

MEDICINE

A more insidious chain of events, but one leading to certain and serious deterioration of most islands, is set in motion by the introduction of modern hygiene and medical practice. Although few would deplore the provisions of health benefits to the charming and attractive island peoples, those responsible may certainly be severely criticized for not, at the same time, introducing effective birth control measures and educating the people as to their use. This idea is not foreign to some of these cultures, but during the recent acculturation following contact with European civilization and the accompanying reduction of population from foreign disease most such lore was either forgotten or abandoned. With effective public health measures populations are now rising at an alarming rate on many islands. Although officials point to this with pride in many cases, they have yet to come up with an effective plan to increase the resources of the islands correspondingly. And on an island the carrying capacity may be very soon exceeded by the numbers of people. Already, on a people-per-square-mile basis some of the smaller islands have an alarming population. Utilization of the resources of the productive reefs of atolls, however, greatly increases their carrying capacity and makes possible the support of present large populations. However, rapid degradation of the resource base, including the reefs, will inevitably follow any significant increase beyond the carrying capacity of any island. The case of Réunion Island studied and described by Pierre Gourou (1963) is an excellent example. The carrying capacity seems to be rapidly becoming less as the population grows. And these people have no place to go (Taeuber, 1963).

IMPOSITION OF ALIEN VALUES

Finally, we may mention something that is belatedly becoming understood about the impact of foreign cultural systems, especially the Western technological culture, on the cultures of small islands. It would seem almost a truism that any culture that has evolved on a small island or that has existed on an island long enough to reach any sort of balance, has evolved to fit the size of the environment that it occupies, as well as the other environmental characteristics. This may be readily seen in the few small island cultures that still remain relatively uninfluenced by outside cultures, for example, Satawal, Ifalik, and Woleai. The pace of life and the daily round of activities are adjusted to the dimensions of the world in which they are carried on. The system of values of such peoples is suited to the resources available and the scope for activity. They do not hurry unnecessarily and they do not accumulate wealth. Capital is not a preoccupation for most islanders.

When Western culture is thrust upon such a system, the result is in almost all cases a crumbling of the social structure and a sense of deep confusion and maladjustment. The values and demands that characterize the impinging culture cannot be satisfied by the limited environment that is available. In other words, a culture evolved in a continental situation is simply unsuited for a small island. The troubles experienced by the U.S. administration of the Trust Territory of the Pacific Islands are a good example. With the best motives in the world, with fantastic financial resources, a $50,-000,000 U.S. budget in 1970, and with a relatively immense staff, the results can only be described as a failure. The people of these far-flung islands are not happy. Many of them look back on the stern Japanese administration as "the good old days." They are being taught the virtues of a free enterprise democratic system, and their own social systems, evolved to meet the conditions prevailing in their island environments, are crumbling before the impact of a dominant system that is being forced on them by education and political pressure. An alarming proportion of the people, especially of the class that should be leaders, are rapidly becoming alcoholics. It makes one sad and depressed to see these peoples today and compare them with what they were even twenty years ago. They have acquired desires and needs with little or no chance of satisfying them, at least on any sort of long-term basis, as the resource base of their islands simply will not sustain the new levels of exploitation.

In short, almost every human activity, from those of the first arrivals to the islands, to those of contemporary Western culture, has altered or is altering the island ecosystem, and in almost all cases, altering it for the worse in the long run. And the world is becoming more impoverished thereby.

Can we arrest this process? Probably not. But if we can learn to use some self-restraint in our headlong race to seize every opportunity for resource exploitation and development, if we can preserve at least representative samples of what we are destroying, our descendents may still retain the option to restore, in some measure, these fascinating and beautiful environments, after their intangible human values are better understood and appreciated.

CONCLUSION

That there is little foundation for any optimistic predictions is indicated by my final example. Axis deer were introduced on the island of Molokai in the Hawaiian Islands at least sixty years ago. It is not easy to sort out the effects of deer from those of cattle and sheep. However, the result of the grazing, browsing, and trampling of all three herbivores has resulted in a steady deterioration of the native forests on this island. The dry lowland forest was almost gone in 1932, and by 1942 there was one tree left in the patch that had been still wooded in 1932. *Prosopis* had occupied most of the lowlands except on the plateau and windward side of west Molokai, where wind erosion was, and is, having serious consequences.

On this island, the upland wet forests were protected against cattle and sheep grazing for their watershed value. In most areas, however, the forest has been opened up by deer, allowing the entry of serious weeds—*pamakani* (*Eupatorium adenophorum*) and *Lantana camara*. Little of the rich montane rain forest and cloud forest is left intact, and the deer were, at last report, continuing their inroads (Lamoureux, personal communication, 1967). Ecologically, the island is a shambles.

This would be just another of many similar accounts, except that for the last few years there has been steady pressure by hunters to introduce these same axis deer to the island of Hawaii, where they have not previously been and where there are still a few substantial areas of native, relatively undisturbed vegetation. This pressure has been fought by all who have any interest in conservation, scientists and ranchers alike—although, with the example of Molokai, one would think that it would not even be necessary to fight. However, the facts have been misrepresented by the very officials who should know them best. It has been claimed that the deer will not enter wet forests or rough lava. The agitation has been continuous, aided and abetted by fish and game officials who feel they are in the employ of those who buy hunting licenses. Finally, there has been a decision to bring a herd of deer to be kept in a three-hundred-acre sheep pen, to observe how they reacted to this new environment. Anyone who has seen axis deer jump fences on Molokai must realize that this is merely a means of quieting the opposition until they can be presented with a *fait accompli*. If we cannot even profit by an obvious example to avoid such an unnecessary mistake, what hope is there to hand any viable island ecosystems on to our descendants? Or any other ecosystems, for that matter?

REFERENCES

Anonymous. "Background to Nauru." Prepared for the Legislative Council of Nauru (Australia). 1966. 16 pp.

————. Report to the General Assembly of the United Nations. Administration of the Territory of Nauru, 1st July 1964 to 30th June, 1965. Commonwealth of Australia. N.d.

Bryan, L. W. "Twenty-five Years of Forestry Work on the Island of Hawaii." *Hawaiian Planters Rec.*, 51 (1947), 1–80.

Carlquist, Sherwin. *Island Life: A Natural History of the Islands of the World*. New York: Natural History Press, 1965. 451 pp.

Egler, F. E. "Arid Southeast Oahu vegetation, Hawaii." *Ecol. Monogr.*, 17 (1947), 383–435.

————. "Unrecognized Arid Hawaiian Soil Erosion." *Science*, 94 (1941), 513–14.

Fosberg, F. R., ed. *Man's Place in the Island Ecosystem*. Honolulu: Bishop Museum, 1963. 264 pp.

Fosberg, F. R. "Plant Collecting on Lanai, 1935." *Mid-Pacific Mag.*, April–June 1936, pp. 119–23.

Gourou, Pierre. "Pressure on Island Environ-
ment." In *Man's Place in the Island
Ecosystem*, F. R. Fosberg, ed. Honolulu:
Bishop Museum, 1963. Pp. 207–25.

Hall, J. N. *Lost Island*. Boston: Little, Brown,
1944. 212 pp.

Heinl, R. D., and Crown, J. A. *The Marshalls:
Increasing the Tempo*. Washington, D.C.:
Government Printing Office, U. S. Marine
Corps (Marine Corps Monographs Series).
1954. 188 pp.

Richard, Dorothy E. *U. S. Naval Adminis-
tration of the Trust Territory of the
Pacific Islands*. 3 vols. Washington, D.C.:
Government Printing Office, Office of
Chief of Naval Operations, 1957.

Rock, J. *Indigenous Trees of the Hawaiian
Islands*. Honolulu: published by Rock
under patronage, 1913. 518 pp.

Skottsberg, C. *Natural History of Juan Fer-
nandez and Easter Island*. Stockholm,
1953.

Stoddart, D. R. "Ecology of Aldabra Atoll,
Indian Ocean." *Atoll Res. Bull.*, 118
(1967), 1–141.

———. "Catastrophic Human Interference
with Coral Atoll Ecosystems." *Geography*,
53 (1968), 25–40.

Taeuber, Irene B. "Demographic Instabilities
in Island Ecosystems." In *Man's Place in
the Island Ecosystem*, F. R. Fosberg, ed.
Honolulu: Bishop Museum, 1963. Pp. 226–
52.

United Nations. United Nations Trusteeship
Council Document No. T/PV. 1285, 33rd
Session. New York, July 11, 1966. Mimeo.

Warner, R. E. "A Forest Dies on Mauna
Kea." *Pacific Discovery*, 13 (2) (1960),
6–14.

47. SOME ECOLOGICAL FACTORS IN DEVELOPMENT PROJECTS IN THE DOMINICAN REPUBLIC

Wolfram U. Drewes

Many agencies have been engaged in the Alliance for Progress program since its inception. Many new roads, dams and irrigation works have been built in Latin America in the last half-dozen years, but in comparison, all too little work has taken place in the field of ecology, conservation of natural resources and the establishment or preservation of national parks or areas of interest to tourists and scientists.

An attempt was made in 1966 to incorporate ecological surveys and conservation programs into the development projects scheduled for the Dominican Republic. Although efforts to carry out specific projects in these fields were not all activated by the Dominican government, considerable headway was made in educating engineers, technicians and politicians in the values that may be derived from the use of ecological factors in evaluating the natural resource base, how they may affect project identification and execution, and of the close relationship that exists between ecology and the long-term stable operations of infrastructure installation as well as development in other sectors of the local or regional economies.

A program including general surveys and investigations of specific projects was developed to orient the Dominican government agencies and institutions dealing with resource fields. Although many problems related to resource conservation had been recognized, little had been done in the past to rectify the situation, and funds to carry out such projects were almost nonexistent. By tying conservation programs to irrigation or other infrastructure projects, a number of programs could be financed and implemented. In a similar fashion, by relating national park programs and preservation of sites of scientific or touristic value directly to the development of the tourism industry and other infrastructure projects, financial sponsorship from lending agencies could more likely be realized.

In summary, although the results of efforts by the Organization of American States (OAS) have not always reached the optimum goal, steps are being taken by the national agencies, better understanding of the close relationship between the ecology and development projects has been made possible, and the national and international financing agencies are giving serious consideration to such projects as part of the development process being carried out under the Alliance for Progress program.

International development, a two-word phrase which we have come to accept in our everyday vocabulary, was really born in the post–World War II period. Today, international organizations such as the United Nations Development Program (UNDP) and the OAS Special Fund for the Alliance for Progress are actively engaged in development projects throughout Latin America. In addition to the U.S., with its relatively large foreign aid program, a number of other countries, particularly some of the European nations, have shown increased interest in establishing bilateral programs of technical assistance with some of the less-developed countries.

Those projects which are directly related to physical development have received the highest priority. These usually include the building of roads, dams, irrigation works, potable water supplies, and others closely related to infrastructure development. Obviously, a lending agency would have much greater difficulty in determining cost-benefit ratios of a social development program than of one which clearly illustrates economic feasibility. How does one determine the impact of making institutional changes? What quantitative figures can one put on a soil erosion study or a reforestation project? What is the value of preserving scenic beauty? Can one predict the income of tourist dollars centered on national parks? What investment in ecological surveys is warranted, and which agencies might be approached to assist in financing such projects?

AN EVALUATION OF THE NATURAL RESOURCES OF THE DOMINICAN REPUBLIC

In May 1963, prior to the period of political instability, the Dominican government requested technical assistance in the natural resources sector from the OAS. A specific request was made for a soils technician and a photo interpreter. Review of the scene (OAS, 1964) indicated that very little resource mapping had been done in the past. Only small-scale geologic maps covered the country, and more meaningful larger-scale maps were available for only the western portion of the country. Twelve large-scale soil maps centering on various government-owned sugar plantations and one privately owned banana company, covering no more than approximately 6 percent of the country, were all that was available. In vegetation and land use mapping, only five mapping projects had been undertaken in the past, three at very small scale and two at larger scale, of several river valleys. To analyze the resources potential of the country without a more complete data base was impossible. Consequently, it was decided that a more thorough approach to resource investigations was warranted.

In accord with past policies, it was decided that an integrated resource investigation be undertaken, since such studies proved to be much more effective for project justification. Furthermore, whenever possible, conservation programs, ecological surveys, preservation of scenic sites and other facets of resource investigations which normally receive little direct support would be included or attached to any infrastructure development project. This orientation was purposely kept retarded to avoid distraction from those projects which might be of more specific interest to financing agencies. Sections of the report, written in Spanish (OAS, 1967), resulting from the composite effort of the integrated team[1] are presented in the following pages, translated and abbreviated.

The Dominican Republic is the first Latin American country in which a nationwide integrated survey of natural resources has been undertaken to collect, analyze and evaluate information at the reconnaissance level. Its relatively small area of 48,442 square kilometers was an important consideration in the practicality of a national survey. The serious lack of information and maps on natural resources mentioned above constituted a grave problem to long-range and short-range economic planning and was a major reason for undertaking the national study.

The small amount of information and maps that existed for the soils, forest, minerals and water resources was found to be too general for planning or project formulation. The few detailed soils surveys which existed were too limited in areal extent to be useful for regional or national planning or for the establishing of development priorities. The largest and most important agricultural region in the country, the Cibao

[1] Authors included the Field Director, P. Freeman; the resource technicians, R. Blesch, J. Montanari, O. Pretell, G. Soto, H. Tasaico; and were carried out under the direction of the Natural Resources Unit Chief, K. Rodgers, and W. U. Drewes, Assistant Director, Department of Economic Affairs.

Valley, lacked any information or maps whatsoever on its soils and present land use. The relatively large areas of forests, which had been intensively logged since Trujillo's death in 1960, had not been surveyed or inventoried and information was needed for the formulation of sound management and exploitation policy.

Limited possibilities for expanding agriculture to new lands made it imperative to relate the distribution of the rural population to the present use and to the capabilities of the natural resources base. Solid criteria for achieving better resource use and conservation practices were required. A reconnaissance survey of national scope would provide this information.

In early 1964, a mission from the World Bank was promoting the study of two large river basins, the Yaque del Norte and the Yaque del Sur, for the development of irrigation and multipurpose hydroelectric facilities. These were prefeasibility surveys of the watersheds which were to be followed by feasibility studies, but they covered only the valleys. It was understood that the Dominican government would take measures needed to provide for upper watershed management. The extensive upper watershed areas of these two rivers are located primarily in the high mountains of the Cordillera Central, and in these zones, information was needed on present land use, vegetation, and climatic conditions in order to establish a policy and program of watershed management.

Furthermore, following the overthrow of Trujillo's dictatorship, all lands belonging to Trujillo and his associates were confiscated by the government. Some of these lands were in the process of being colonized, but large tracts awaited development or settlement, and for these purposes, an evaluation of their potentials was required. A nationwide survey of these state-owned lands, scattered throughout the country, would provide the needed reconnaissance information, and other data which would determine project orientation and development.

The need to carry out a national study was obvious. The collection and integrated evaluation of data on climate, ecology, geology and land forms, soils, hydrology, present land use and forests, and population distribution would provide a basis for long-range economic planning as well as for attacking immediate problems such as development or settlement of state-owned lands and watershed management, and problems related to deforestation and shifting agriculture, especially in the upper Yaque del Norte and Yaque del Sur river basins. In order to avoid excessive time lapse between the completion of the reconnaissance survey and the initiation of more detailed development investigations, it was agreed that large-scale 1:20,000 aerial photography should be taken of the entire country as soon as it could be financed. This has now been completed.

In November 1964, the approved program was presented to the Dominican government. Arrangements for counterpart support and the provision of the existing 1:60,000 aerial photography were made, and a review of literature in the fields of botany, ecology and geology was begun. Final arrangements for a one-year survey program were completed in December 1964, and in January 1965, an OAS Natural Resources Mission was sent to Santo Domingo. Due to delays caused by the April 1965 political uprising, the survey program was subsequently extended for an additional year.

To illustrate the breadth and comprehensiveness of the Dominican study it might be noted that detailed surveys were carried of the following resource topics.

A Geomorphologic Survey was carried out to provide data and maps on land forms and their genesis, soil parent ma-

terials, and to the degree possible, subsurface lithology and structure.

An Economic Geology Survey was carried out to determine if a minerals survey program was justified, and if so, to formulate a program for financing.

A Reconnaissance Soils Survey was executed to study and map the soils associations of the country, as classified principally by parent materials, relief, land form and drainage and to make a land capability map.

A Hydrologic Survey was included to determine the movement and availability of surface and subsurface water in major watersheds and to evaluate and map climatic characteristics of the country.

An Ecologic Survey was carried out to map natural life zones of the country, to inventory the pine forests and to evaluate the forest potentials and conservation problems of the country.

A Present Land Use and Vegetation Types Survey was done to determine land use and to describe land use practices and intensity. To assist in drawing pertinent relationships a population distribution map of rural and urban population was made.

Most of the mapping was done on the 1:60,000 scale aerial photo base which covered almost all of the country. This scale of work maps was eventually reduced to 1:250,000 for final publication.

The last map, one of development projects, is based on the analysis of data presented on the respective resource maps. Recommended projects were divided into three broad groups: agriculture, forestry, and conservation programs. The agricultural projects are divided into those areas where it is felt that yields could be increased by changing land use practices and those areas where production could be increased by increasing ground or surface water supplies for irrigation. The forestry project includes a pilot reforestation program in the headwaters area of a large river (the Yaque del Norte), the basin of which is scheduled to be developed. The conservation projects include a small pilot river basin conservation project, areas that warrant being established as national parks, and scenic beach areas which should undergo controlled development for tourism and recreation purposes.

In the Dominican Republic, most of the best agricultural soils are under some form of use, and large areas with relatively low agricultural potential are being cultivated. The cartographic depiction of these agricultural lands was essential in order to assess the extent to which present land uses were in accord with productive capabilities. In spite of the relatively easy accessibility of most areas of the country, there existed only general and, in some cases, conflicting knowledge of the real extent of agricultural lands, forests and grasslands. Land use mapping was thus undertaken not only for the purpose of relating existing uses to use capability, but also to provide a tool for better orienting such programs as agricultural extension and road building, which should be related to present land use in different regions. A related objective was the determination of land use intensity and the types of agricultural systems employed in order to gain an idea of how land resources are being exploited as well as how present management systems relate to production and soils and water conservation.

The basic aims of the hydrologic investigations were a reconnaissance inventory of the water supply, water requirements, as well as flood and sediment problems. This information was then analyzed in conjunction with the other data collected by the mission for the formulation of balanced plans for the orderly development of the water resources that would help meet the energy, water needs and its control for specific areas or regions of the country.

The kind of information collected and analyzed consisted of climatic data, stream flow, flood flow, sedimentation, water quality, ground water, consumptive use–irrigation water requirements, presently irrigated land and existing irrigation systems, and a summary of past and present hydrologic investigations. As a result of these investigations, a number of areas were selected for development that previously were unused. Ecological and soil conditions of a number of extensive northern coastal tracts could be turned into productive farmland at minimum expense. On the other hand, an extensive lowland area in the Yuna valley which was scheduled for colonization and settlement was found to be a floating peat bog. Soil augers, on penetrating the surface vegetation cover, entered a layer of water many feet in depth. Had it not been for the careful soil survey and the ecological analysis made of the vegetation, it is certain that large sums of money would have been wasted on colonization of an area of limited development potential.

EVALUATION OF SURVEY DATA

Integration of different types of natural resource data was undertaken as a matter of course in most of the component parts of the national survey. The soils mapping entailed interpretation of climatic, geologic, and geomorphologic data, and, to a lesser degree, land use and vegetation data. The ecologic survey, by its very nature, required integration and use of climatic data, and observations of vegetation characteristics and agricultural conditions.

The survey of present land use and vegetation types took into consideration ecologic and climatic conditions, as well as general soils capabilities. The hydrologic survey component employed materials and data from almost all the other components for interpretation of surface and subsurface water potentials and water needs for agriculture.

In utilizing the data collected and mapped, the overall objectives of the survey were kept in mind, such as the need to intensify resource use, provide for resource conservation, formulate watershed management programs, and evaluate problems related to shifting agriculture and land settlement in general.

In order to arrive at conclusions regarding the problems and development potentials on which the programs were based, the following mapped information was compared: ecologic, population distribution, land capability, present land use, geologic, surface hydrology, and climate. For instance, zones whose ecologic conditions and rainfall values precluded any but irrigated agriculture were isolated, and areas within these with irrigable soils not in use were delimited. Reference to surface water supplies was then made, and zones with inadequate streamflow but with potentials for subsurface water were delimited and recommended for ground water exploration. In order to delimit zones needing reforestation, ecologic and land capability data were compared cartographically with present land use and forested areas. At the peripheries of the forested areas, zones were found whose ecologic and soils conditions were not suited to agriculture, but which were under scattered subsistence farming and grass cover. A check of population in these areas indicated very sparse settlement. It was thus concluded that reforestation was desirable for these zones and they were demarcated accordingly. The use of parts of these zones for grazing and agriculture (on alluvial strips) was anticipated, and further investigation of large-scale aerial photographs was recommended in order to more precisely define reforestation through protection of the natural regeneration of the pines.

A second, more detailed level of data integration was required for determining the nature of development obstacles in other areas of the country and identifying the measures which were needed to overcome these. Such was the case for most of the areas of the country under some form of agricultural use, either limited or intensive. Areas under limited agricultural use (grazing, periodic cropping with grass or brush fallow) and with marginal resource potentials (capability classes IV, V and VI, marginal rainfall or slightly excessive rainfall) required rather careful analysis to establish their potentials and identify development impediments. In the analysis of these areas, which were recognized mainly by comparing the present land use and land capability maps, reference was made to rural population averages, a 1960 farm size census, and irrigation needs, where occasional water shortage seemed to be a limiting factor. Also, limitations to agricultural production imposed by general atmospheric humidity and rainfall were identified by use of the ecologic map. A case in point was the identification of ecologic conditions excessively humid for sugar-cane cultivation in a zone of moderately good soils capabilities occupied by extensive sugar-cane plantations run by the state. This apparent incompatibility was then confirmed by production statistics, which showed extremely low yields for this area. Efforts are now being extended to convert the area to the production of crops that are ecologically compatible with the region.

With regard to overall comparisons of land capabilities and present land use, the reconnaissance data collected did not include expected or present yields, and analysis was limited to determining the compatibility of land use type or cropping systems to soils capabilities, particularly as regards conservation and other soils management measures recommended for each capability class. A summary comparison of these two factors showed that all of the soils with some degree of agricultural capability were under use, and considerable agriculture was being carried on in marginally productive or nonagricultural lands.

In summary, three factors were initially analyzed in composite in order to establish overall agricultural development potentials or problems: land capability, present land use and population distribution. Specific problems such as areas subject to accelerated erosion, frequent flooding or overpopulation were then compared to more detailed soils descriptions, ecologic conditions, hydrologic data and irrigation needs, and in some cases, agricultural census results.

Forest management and conservation problems, many of them related to the excessive deforestation of the last decade, as well as watershed management considerations were analyzed in terms of ecologic life zones, rainfall, surface configuration and location of catchment basins and present forest cover or land use. By compositing these data, conclusions were made regarding critical catchment areas, reforestation needs, and soils conservation needs in particular areas.

Use of the survey results by agricultural economists and transportation specialists was anticipated, and the final reports and maps were to be a point of departure for undertaking the agroeconomic and other interpretations which could be derived from the data. Both OAS mission specialists and national technicians utilized the survey results for formulating development plans, projects and programs. The population distribution map was especially important for these economic interpretations as it provided detailed delineation of political divisions, which in turn was related to census data, existing land use development projects and the programs for the conservation of forest, soil and water resources.

PROGRAM OF CONSERVATION OF FOREST, SOIL AND WATER RESOURCES

The Dominican government has recognized the need to protect the country's existing forest resources and to make the public aware of the vital relationship that exists between forest conservation and the control of erosion and runoff in the catchment basins for the protection of water resources. Control and management of these resources is vital to the long-term development of multipurpose hydroelectric projects and to expansion of the areas under cultivation through irrigation projects.

In spite of the concern that has been expressed with regard to these conservation problems, very little has been done up to now in the way of formulation of specific work programs to provide the necessary conservation measures. Some work has been done in the Haina-Duey catchment basin, and the organization of forest fire protection is being improved. But nothing at all has been done in the field of water and soil conservation, nor have any specific programs been established for the carrying out of the necessary measures. The nation is barely in the process of settling down from the recent political unrest, and highest priority has been given to re-establishing or improving required public facilities.

Land tenure problems. Background guidance for the organization of the conservation work is available in the form of the experiences of other countries. However, investigation of certain factors peculiar to the Dominican situation is an essential prerequisite of the formulation and execution of viable work programs.

An aspect of fundamental importance is the fact that the conservation problems affect private as well as state-owned lands. Under present law, the government can exercise control over felling trees and cultivation on both private and public domain lands. Of special significance in this connection is Law No. 5856 (*Ley de Conservación y de Arboles Frutales*), which prohibits the unauthorized felling of fruit and commercial timber trees (Article 87) and the clearing for cultivation of lands with gradients of over 25 percent (Article 36).[2] The root of the problem lies in the lack of technical personnel to enforce the law and of a clearly defined program of action supported by the necessary administrative structure.

Although it would appear that governmental intervention in conservation problems would be relatively easy in the case of state-owned lands, this does in fact present problems because of the confused situation that exists with respect to ownership of lands earmarked as forest reserves, which are under state control. Farming and stock raising is being carried out on these lands by persons who claim rights of ownership. Moreover, no complete maps exist of the Armando Bermúdez and Carmen Ramírez National Parks or of the Valle Nuevo Forest Reserve; all that is available is information concerning certain boundaries in the texts of the provisions by which they were established. It will be necessary to determine the exact locations of the public domain forest lands and to solve the tenure problems of the residents of those areas to permit the execution of the needed conservation measures. This applies both to the conservation of the forest resources and to the management of the catchment basins located in those areas.

Where conservation measures are needed, it is of fundamental importance to take into account the attitude of those who work the land. If the farmer is not the owner he will probably have no interest in the application of conservation measures

unless he is convinced that they will yield him direct benefits. Important in this connection is the definitive establishment of ownership rights, which depend largely on the cartographic demarcation of the properties. This information is needed both by the governmental representative responsible for conducting the conservation program and by the owner, who bears responsibility for the use of his land, since the program of forest, soil and water conservation projects embraces the maintenance and appropriate use of these resources on both state and privately owned lands.

Present conditions in the catchment basins. Study of the present status of the principal catchment basins in the Cordillera Central shows that not all are in good condition due to the influx of squatters and associated deforestation activities. Moreover, some are not located within national parks or forests and therefore are not under the direct administration of the Dirección Forestal or other governmental agencies.

The excessive erosion of the soil, caused mainly by the rains and in part by the clean cultivation of steeply sloping areas of the catchment basins, has resulted in obstruction of the country's major irrigation canals, which have cost a considerable amount of money to clear. Clean cultivation of steep slopes during the rainy season and the resulting excessively rapid runoff have led to severe fluctuations in the discharge rates of the rivers, with the undesirable consequence that river flow falls too low during the driest months, just when the water is most needed for irrigation of the valleys. It is not considered necessary to maintain forest cover throughout the catchment basin areas, since the land may in places be potentially suited for pasture or for certain crops. However, it is necessary that these non-forestry uses be conducted in harmony with the need to conserve the necessary conditions in the catch-

[2] Although the law specifies a limit of 25 percent, this limit is considered to be very low for many Dominican soils.

ment area to ensure controlled runoff and reduction of soil erosion. About half the land under cultivation in the Dominican Republic is very steep, of low productive capacity and is highly susceptible to erosion. To permit the government to orient and control agricultural and stock-raising activities on privately owned lands, it is necessary to determine the most suitable uses for those lands. To this end, it will be necessary to carry out soil studies and land productive capacity surveys. On lands of very broken relief, due account will have to be taken of the slope gradients.

Reforestation needs. In areas where land of low agricultural potential has been stripped of its natural vegetation for farming or has lost its vegetation cover through burning, land resources are being utilized very ineffectually. The loss of the plant cover results in erosion of the soils and a consequent reduction in the productive capability of the land, causing great irregularity in the discharge rates of the rivers, with adverse effects on water supply, particularly in the more arid areas that depend on water for irrigation. In addition, there is a serious decrease in the commercial value of the forests, since it takes a long time to replace the commercial wood trees, the average cutting age exceeding thirty years. Many of these areas can, however, be reforested, due to the existence of ecological conditions well suited to the growth of forest species and to the availability of trees that can provide seed for the natural regeneration of the forests. On the basis of these considerations, the principal areas have been indicated in which reforestation is necessary, either to provide a permanent source of marketable wood or as a means of protection of the catchment basins.

The forest, soil and water resources conservation program is closely linked to the reforestation work. The projects for the conservation of catchment basins are based chiefly on the need for plant cover, which in turn reduces soil erosion and controls runoff. It is therefore of the utmost importance that the government promote and encourage reforestation of both state and privately owned lands.

A pilot project of soil and water conservation and protection of hydrographic basins in the San José de Ocoa area has been proposed. The findings of the natural resources evaluation have highlighted the seriousness of the soil erosion problem in the Dominican Republic, particularly where cultivation is practiced on steeply sloping lands in the upper parts of the watersheds of the principal rivers. Today, the hillsides suffer seriously from accelerated soil erosion and related surface water runoff which has reduced subsurface infiltration and consequently has lowered water tables. Furthermore, the danger of flooding of the valleys has increased, which directly affects agricultural production. The progressive deterioration of agricultural conditions in the upper portions of the river basins is aggravating the general regional, and ultimately the national economic, situation.

These conditions are common to many of the higher elevations of the catchment basins of the Dominican Republic, and at the same time affect, directly and indirectly, the lower parts of the basins. It is obviously impossible to resettle all the farmers affected, because of the scarcity of good farming land. It will therefore be necessary to seek means of improving the productivity of these farming operations while at the same time conserving the soil and water resources.

The purpose of the pilot project recommended is to ascertain and put into practice the most suitable measures for the conservation of the soils and water and for the protection of a hydrographic basin, so that it may serve as an example for the formulation and execution of similar projects in other parts of the country.

The area of the pilot project selected is

located in the southeastern part of the Cordillera Central and covers about 400 square kilometers surrounding the city of San José de Ocoa.

The objectives of the project are to raise agricultural production in the area, to provide additional employment to the most needy farmers and to train Dominican personnel to form a technical nucleus for the future expansion of these activities.

In summary, the result of this project, located in an area of diverse ecological zones that produce a wide variety of agricultural products, is a recommendation that a series of practical studies and specific conservation-engineering works be carried out. Because the overall conservation practices will have to be fully accepted by the local farmers, the individual problems of each landowner are considered.

With the completion of the topographic and soils studies in the catchment basins, the necessary detailed information will be available, firstly for definitive establishment of the boundaries of the catchment basin conservation districts, and secondly for the initiation of land use control programs at the local level. During the period of validity of the temporary legislation, the government will be empowered to control land use in the most critical cases.

A total of nineteen conservation districts, corresponding to the upper basins of the major rivers, have been delineated on the basis of the present or potential utilization of their water and of the need for flood control. Almost all of the basins have an annual rainfall in excess of 1500 millimeters, include very steep slope-lands and require strict erosion and runoff control measures in connection with their utilization, in accordance with their productive potential, whether for forestry, pasture or other purposes. The basins in the area may also offer other possibilities for agriculture that could not be identified during the present reconnaissance-level study. Al-though the ecological conditions indicate that the majority of these lands are unsuitable for cleared cultivation or for perennial crops, strips of alluvial land in the valleys and isolated parcels of good land will undoubtedly exist that will have to be identified by means of more detailed studies so that a reasonable policy may be formulated with respect to their use.

Concluding comments: With the passage of one year, insufficient time has elapsed to evaluate the outcome of a project of resource evaluation such as the Dominican Republic study. A decade is usually required of such interdisciplinary studies before concrete results may be identified. However, it is always interesting to look at a program in retrospect, even if it is only a year since the completion of the reconnaissance investigation of natural resources. In this case, the problems were as numerous as they were varied. The charcoal venders and operators of portable sawmills were denuding the hills; much of the hill land was suffering from accelerated erosion, and hydroelectric plants, in operation for only a few years, had reservoirs which were being drastically reduced in size. A new plant near Constanza already could operate at only 30 percent capacity. In the valleys, the rivers, laden with silt, carried problems along with the potable waters to the towns. Also, the irrigation systems, the basis for much of the rural economy, were rapidly silting up. In the lower courses, rivers such as the Yaque del Norte, the largest in the country, which formerly were navigable, could now be waded across in the dry season and were unmanageable flooding torrents in the wet season. Former ports, such as Sánchez on Samaná Bay, now lay practically abandoned due to the recent deposition of materials carried by the Río Yuna. Most of the solutions to the problems are costly and difficult. The establishment of a polder system to save the sediments from the sea was even contemplated by a group of Dutch technicians in the country. But building dikes on nonconsolidated materials can be an expensive and never-ending process.

What has the government recently done to counter these problems? First, a decree was passed which permitted the cutting of only damaged or sick trees in the forests. Thereafter, the rash of forest-fire outbreaks was so great that the law probably did more harm than good. Consequently, a law was passed prohibiting the export of timber. Again the rush to the hills was accelerated. The timber cutters were anxious to cut and stockpile as much lumber as possible before other laws were passed which would more radically affect their livelihood.

Today laws prohibit all cutting of timber! Ironically, when hurricane Inéz cut a swatch across the Barahona peninsula in December 1966, it knocked down a large timber stand which included many almácigo (*Bursera simaruba*) trees. This particular wood is flavorless and is in high demand in the U.S. for the packing of cheese and other food products. Furthermore, the trees already knocked down by the storm were accessible and could be cut by the farmer colonist of the area affected by the storm. Through the aid of a relief program, several hundred crosscut saws were rushed to the area. But, unfortunately, by law, these damaged and drying trees could not be utilized due to the prohibition on the export of timber! By the time the laws were modified making the hurricane-affected area an exception, insects had infested the woods.

The ecological processes are indeed complex. Natural calamities and the changes in ecosystems that accompany development projects are frequently slow, but the bureaucratic processes established by man can also be slow. This, too, makes the implementation of conservation programs difficult. Furthermore, when the erosional process is already in an accelerated state as is the case in the Dominican Republic, it is difficult to control and costly to change. Consequently, the changes made in the headwater areas today, will undoubtedly not bear fruit in the valleys for many years to come. However, it is felt that by closely associating resource conservation and ecological projects to development projects scheduled to receive attention and support from national and international financing agencies, a solid step forward has been made in this collaborative effort of the Organization of American States and the Dominican government in the execution of an Alliance for Progress program.

REFERENCES

Organization of American States. *Annotated Index of Aerial Photography Coverage and Mapping of Topography and Natural Resources.* Washington, D.C., 1964.

————. *Reconocimiento y Evaluación de los Recursos Naturales de la República Dominicana.* Washington, D.C., 1967.

DISCUSSION

M. T. FARVAR: I have a question regarding Dr. Drewes's "integrated" surveys. Sometime ago I visited the Natural Resources Unit of the Pan American Union and I heard about these projects, which sound very interesting; but when I asked, "Do you have any aftereffect studies?" the answer was: "No." They indicated their job was to do preinvestment surveys and feasibility studies and things of that nature. What then is the mechanism for carrying out any aftereffect surveys and evaluations?

Many of the Unit's preinvestment surveys seem to have some of the apparent "ecological" qualifications that we have been developing in the last few days. In other words, they are integrated. They presumably use ecology. But where do you go from there? It would perhaps be reasonable to say that after the "integrated" survey, they go right ahead with development plans and never stop to evaluate and learn from mistakes. Shouldn't they have some kind of mechanism within the Organization of American States that would allow for self-correction? Don't they require the means to evaluate and see what has happened after the projects have started?

DREWES: Project aftereffects, whether good or bad, normally don't appear for five or ten years; possibly longer than that. In the case of the Peruvian projects, in which I participated, only recently were we able to see or evaluate the aftereffects quantitatively as well as subjectively.

M. T. FARVAR: Are you only "seeing" or studying the consequences too? This approach is now being undertaken by the Inter-American Development Bank, but it does take time.

RODGERS: There is no built-in mechanism for international organizations whereby the case study approach is institutionalized such that there is an automatic post-audit of applied development technologies. It is definitely needed. What we try to do in the natural resources program in the OAS, on our own initiative, is to produce case histories of our own investigations. The Dominican Republic happens to be one. Shortly after the termination of the preinvestment survey, we try to simply describe the methodologies and the results in terms of the recommendations for development programs. We then try to distribute this information to the scientific community to get comment and criticism on our methodology, try to open ourselves up to comment, to allow modification of our approach based on the reaction of people quite knowledgeable in this area. However, there is no way to actually check the results of preinvestment survey recommendations until you see what happens as a result of development.

HASKELL: There are some methods in UNDP projects for post-audit evaluation but the difficulty with these efforts is that no agency is willing to admit their mistakes.

I have often seen entomological project

evaluations that are virtually a whitewashing of numerous ecological errors made because they can't afford to say "We made an error." They fear if they admit they've done something wrong, the whole future program will be prejudiced. If we want fair post-audits, we will need an independent body to look into this, an institution not tied to anyone, who can really investigate and show the errors that have been made.

I don't think you can criticize your own wash. If you do, you wash it whiter than white.

CROWCROFT: I think the reasons for not looking into these aftereffects are purely a matter of priority. It is a matter of limited resources. You have only a few people doing work of this kind. Administrators are unwilling to allot a higher priority to going back and finding out why something went wrong, when you have a whole host of studies and projects waiting to be done with the same limited human and budgetary resources. It is a matter of administrative decisions about priorities.

TRAIN: I would like to follow up the point made by Dr. Haskell on the need for independent audits; I think this is a very obvious need. Nobody can take a look at their own affairs and come up with an objective answer. I know I can't. I am wondering whether this conference might not focus on how we could help suggest an answer for this independent environmental audit need.

What might be the most useful mechanisms for independent audits of these programs, either on a regional basis or on a selected problem basis?

WORTHINGTON: This is an important point, for we need a system capable of utilizing the huge amount of development experience now available. This information needs to be properly analyzed, not only that of the recent UNDP projects, but also that of past projects of the former Colonial era.

The five-year and ten-year development plans of countries have never been assessed in an objective and comparative way, yet these plans have been going on since the war. We tend to dash forward into new projects without learning from the experience taken from old ones.

MICHEL: Perhaps we need some new international agency, a sort of developmental ombudsman operation, to handle this problem.

FRASER DARLING: I would think that, rather than an *ad hoc* post-audit organization, what is really needed is a kind of continuous monitoring college. It should be an organization capable of constant survey, and in a position to check on what is happening all the time. This would be better than doing a project and then having a post-audit survey.

BOULDING: Development, after all, is a total process. I think we have to be careful not to overestimate the impact of governments in all this. There are only eleven countries larger than General Motors. Even Poland is only about the size of General Electric. The international corporations are really exercising a much larger impact than almost any government in the world.

You aren't only concerned with governments and international corporations. What about the individual action of individual people? This is what development involves. All governments have delusions of grandeur. They operate on the edges of an enormous human process and this total human process is what we have to understand.

MILTON: One of the most important types of international development institutions this group really has *not* focused on is the private corporation. In many ways these corporate investments are under far less adequate control (existing or potential) of their environmental impacts than bilateral and multilateral agencies. This fact is particularly important when you realize the vast sums being invested abroad by private concerns. Their ecological impacts lead all other forms of international development.

Another aspect of this dominance of private over public (particularly with Japan, the United States, Germany, Great Britain and France) economic involvement internationally is their political feedback in influencing public investments abroad, particularly bilateral ones. Because some of the strongest political supporters of U.S. foreign aid are pesticide, fertilizer, construction machinery, engineering contractor, dam-building, oil, agricultural commodity and other powerful special interest industrial groups—governmental involvements have continuous pressure on them to come up with development assistance programs closely tied to the purchase of these corporate items and services. Often, this makes it difficult, if not impossible, to get small, community-oriented, and non-profit sorts of assistance efforts started internationally. Pork barrel is one of our most important U.S. export products.

A good recent example of this problem is the tendency to increase export of pesticides in order to keep up sales as domestic demand declines and legislative prohibition spreads. Apparently, what's not good for us is good for the rest of the world. On the other hand, if these corporations can begin to produce a more ecological technology emphasizing such things as recycling of wastes, pollution control, better birth control devices, and clean, safe energy sources —the system might work to the world's advantage. But we're a long way from this now.

RUSSELL: In so far as development is financed by private corporations, they employ independent consultants afterward to see how things go. That is where the advantage of private corporations comes in.

ABRAHAMSON: But what a corporation might consider a success may not be what the people involved might consider as success.

SCUDDER: I would like to follow up on Dr. Darling's comments.

Granted the complexity of environmental changes, monitoring is absolutely essential. I notice that in the few projects that I am familiar with, if your post-audit were postponed as long as five or ten years, you would not really be able to understand why a large number of the changes which have occurred did occur; so continuous monitoring is very necessary.

On the other hand, monitoring requires more funds, more personnel, and more effort; so we have to bring in selective mechanisms to figure out what kind of projects will be monitored.

COOLIDGE: I want to shift back to something Dr. Fosberg brought up.

It seems to me that this problem of phosphate mining in Palau, which would destroy the whole possibility of having the use of that area for tourism and other purposes, means that we have to have an ecological input into planning the development of that area. We have talked about monitoring what is going on during development and about later post-audits, but this is a sort of pre-planning. The kind of critical situation in the Palaus is something we have to treat right away. We must make sure that ecological factors are included at the earliest possible time to help prevent social and environmental destruction.

RICE*: It seems to me our experience with planning is instructive in the case of evaluation. Most of planning experience now suggests that planning must be tied into the operational efforts of development. When a planning bureau is set up in the government and the work is carried out by other departments, the result is a series of paper plans which are filed and largely ignored.

* Andrew E. Rice is the Executive Secretary of the Society for International Development, Washington, D.C.

It seems to me we should learn from this in discussing evaluation. Unless evaluation and post-audit are built into the administrative system you are going to have a bunch of experts sitting around and saying you should have done better; but nobody who does the actual development job will listen attentively because it isn't part of the regular way of doing things.

DREWES: I would like to substantiate Mr. Rice's comment. There is a very close relationship between planning, project execution and monitoring, and post-audit reviews. Consequently, I feel post-audit functions should be built into or incorporated in the functions of the development agency. Staff to carry out the post-audit surveys may be assigned those functions on a rotating basis. However, if a completely independent agency is assigned to carry out the audit only great controversy will ensue. By doing their own post-audits and coming up with both the good and bad, agencies can almost automatically provide a basis for changing priorities projects and budgets. Agencies do not whitewash all their projects! Those projects which have been post-audited, and have been rated highly, will then stand to gain in future operations.

TALBOT: Throughout this conference, one of the major problems we have been facing is the need for taking ecological considerations into account before development is carried out, rather than afterward. Most of what we are reporting on here are post-audits, but hopefully what we are aiming for in the future are pre-audits.

In many cases, the pre-audit must involve a number of disciplines and a fair amount of money. Several quite massive development programs have been mentioned, among them the plans for the development of the Amazon Basin, the Mekong, and the Atlantic and Pacific sea-level canals. These present us with a unique opportunity, or perhaps a series of unique opportunities, for the ecological pre-audit—if we can take advantage of the situation, if we can train and involve enough ecologists of the right disciplines to apply themselves to these problems, and if we can work out effective institutional structures.

DREWES: I think so little has been done in the Amazon Basin that we as ecologists could well take the time now to focus on the Amazon with a little more patience. Only several years ago a leading Washington newspaper printed a series of articles advocating the development of the Amazon Basin. This became known as the "heartland theory" for the development of South America where the world's largest river system would serve as the transport link between the east and west coast of South America in a similar fashion to the way the U.S. railroad aided in the settlement of the U.S. heartland a few decades ago. Yet very few projects carried out in the Amazon Basin have taken ecological factors into consideration. Although the Johnson administration originally emphatically supported this proposal they did so with virutally no knowledge of the area. Fortunately this support was refocused on a number of better-known and more manageable river systems and no major development project involving the Amazon was initiated as yet.

Several years ago, Fernando Belaunde, the former President of Peru, proposed the construction of a north-south road along the western edge of the Amazon Basin: the Marginal Highway. Completion of such a road would undoubtedly have tremendous effects on the ecology, due to the fact that colonists will settle along the roads and clear the land in much of the area. But should this region, highly susceptible to erosion, be colonized at this time or would it be advisable to sponsor more irrigation on the coast where water and erosion can more readily be controlled? Sponsoring agriculture in tropical areas where soils are leached and acid, where heavy rains lead to accelerated erosion and where little is known about plant diseases is highly questionable at times.

Mr. Jorgenson's comments on colonization may be typical of only five nations now but undoubtedly it will affect many other nations and their inhabitants in the future. In Brazil alone, there are a number of major colonization and settlement projects involving many people.

With the present interest in the Amazon Basin being as high as it is, perhaps this may be the time to initiate studies there on a large scale. It would indeed be a splendid opportunity for ecologists to undertake the study of a large area, an integral river basin, as yet largely uninfluenced by man *before* it is modified by him. With the recent publicity on pollution, ecology and conservation, the funds for well-oriented studies of this type may now be available in the international lending agencies. It would be very desirable to study this large river basin but can we find enough ecologists and get them there before the settlers arrive in large numbers? And can one establish sound and enforceable regulations before our old mistakes in tropical resource development return to haunt us?

TIMOTHY: I would like to address myself to what Dr. Scudder has said before. On a lot of these development programs, I think one has to remember why the decisions were made to develop them, whether it was to alleviate social suffering or whether it was to bring about a means of economic gain within an area of a country for foreign exchange, etc.

I agree 100 per cent that we need ecological prefeasibility studies. The unfortunate thing is that in some cases once these studies have been carried out and the project initiated according to sound guidelines, the entire project is often managed by a complete nincompoop.

CROWCROFT: I want to speak to Dr. Timothy's remarks. He mentioned the dreadful predicament in project administration. I should have thought the answer was perfectly obvious. It is time for ecologists to stop pretending that administration is dirty work and go into administration. There is an additional incentive in my saying this. I speak from personal experience as an ecologist who indeed has become a full-time administrator. Apart from the satisfaction of bringing common sense and ecological knowledge to bear on decisions, you also have the satisfaction of being better paid. (Laughter.)

RODGERS: I would like to comment further on both John Milton's earlier remarks on the need for both ecological pre-investment and post-audit survey and on Timothy's statement about the frequent management of colonization projects by nincompoops. We have very few post-audits of colonization projects at our disposal, indicating the need is quite real. The problem is that some rather carefully thought out colonization schemes, which we have studied in their economic and physical aspects, look splendid in terms of an economic cost-benefit analysis but turn out to be perfect disasters because the criteria for selection of the project and the built-in management of the project were not as carefully thought out. The engineers have done their job, but the social scientists have not done theirs. Lending institutions do have a good deal of leverage to employ if the criteria for approving a project insist upon the proper kinds of institutional mechanisms to manage it. A good post-audit system, particularly of all projects financed by the agencies, is one way we can develop the information we need to modify our new project criteria.

MILTON: I think Kirk Rodger's commentary is very relevant to the central problem this conference is focused on. Our difficulties, I feel, are due less to a lack of ecological fact relevant to applied problems than to a fundamental lack of interest in using ecological information to improve environmental management. The bilateral and multilateral development agencies have to become much more sensitive to utilizing existing ecological information at key points in their development projects. Most past international development has given emphasis only to the narrowest sorts of economic criteria, leading to a bias toward produced, market-place goods. The majority of man's free and commonly-held resources, however, such as clean air and water, beautiful surroundings, an uncrowded habitat of maximum human and natural diversity, quiet spaces, natural production from forests and waters, and even good health—all traditionally are not included in judgments on development. Indeed, development seems to have been biased against considering these free environmental resources. We must shift our bias toward creating a better harmony with the biosphere.

I think Kirk showed that we could be far more influential if we insist development agencies must build environmental and cultural information, such as has been presented in these case histories, into the pre-investment survey process. If we can help change the way in which the World Bank and the U. N. Development Program actually make their initial project decisions, this will help redirect capital into much sounder investments. By affecting the pre-investment and criteria for selection levels, we more effectively use our energies to promote constructive alteration of the whole development process.

I think all the cases enumerated have shown that it is very difficult for governments and development institutions to extract themselves from a massive investment in a development program once it has begun. Not until much later does information come in on the bad, unanticipated side effects of various ecologically hasty programs. And, I fear, the majority of the time no ecological

or sociological post-evaluation information comes in at all, because no one is looking or responsible for such analysis. We rarely hear about our mistakes, learn from our mistakes, or even undertake any serious effort to uncover our mistakes.

For the moment, it is very important for the ecologist to become much more politically active and to urge every one of the development agencies to utilize the available ecological information in these very critical points at the pre-investment survey level. At the same time, however, we should also be urging much more intensive support for research centers for the study of tropical and arid ecosystems and the impact of human technologies on these environments. Such centers could also train more ecologists familiar with these unique ecosystems.

CALDWELL: I would like to say something about the ecologist as an administrator. I would suggest that administration is at its best a very difficult and sophisticated art that is not acquired just by going into it. The education of both scientists and engineers singularly unfits them for administration. I refer particularly to the reductionist approach that Dr. Commoner has mentioned here. To a very considerable extent administrations are a synthesis.

It seems to me there is great need for the knowledge and ability to analyze situations that ecologists could bring to the job. There is no reason why a person who is a good ecologist, environmental biologist or engineer could not be a good administrator, but the job requires something in addition to a scientific education.

One of the things we noticed in the whole business of international development, particularly in the underdeveloped countries, is that much of our frustration and disappointment and failure is due to the inability of the governments of these countries to carry on effective administrative programs. Just a few intelligent people, even a few good administrators, are not adequate to do the development job.

Administration is a process of human interaction, a systems kind of interaction. When the ecologist becomes an administrator he takes on quite a different kind of task. This task involves the intermeshing of what he has to do with many, many different kinds of people, most of whom will have no background in science whatsoever. I would suggest that if we need to have more ecologists as administrators, we are also going to have to find ways to better fit them for the job. It might be conceivable to do the other thing too, and that is to instill an ecological awareness, a greater understanding of natural systems processes into administrators who, by background, come out of fiscal management, out of business administration, out of bureaucratic environments in which they have no previous scientific backgrounds.

CROWCROFT: Can I reply to Caldwell's remark about administration? I think this view is due to a basic misconception of what ecologists are and what administrators are, as if they were different breeds. In point of fact, there are good administrators and bad administrators, and good ecologists and bad ecologists, and there is little basic difference between them.

The real question is: Do both live in the real world or in a world of fantasy? I would like to give you an example that I came across in Uganda in connection with tsetse control. I can remember being in the office of the administrator who was conducting their game elimination campaign. On his map of Uganda, in the area in which the elimination program was being carried out, he had a line of drawing pins, each representing an African hunter. He explained to me how this wall of hunters was moving forward, driving before it the game and eliminating it as they went, and further he described this operation in quasi-militaristic terms. Now, out there in the

bush each of these drawing pins, which on this map composed a "wall" was an African three miles from his nearest fellow —and he didn't hunt at night. (Laughter.) When he took a kill back, there were six miles between hunters. When another hunter went visiting his number three wife, whom he could now afford because he had this job, there were more miles between them. (Laughter.) This whole thing at the administrative level was what I referred to as administration fantasy or Ad-fan.

In actual fact, a good administrator, whether an entomologist or a man in classics or an economist or anything else, would have investigated the real situation. He would have been dealing with administrative reality, which I like to refer to as Ad-real. The real problem we are up against in our international conference is eliminating the Ad-fan. There I think is the crux of the matter. Let's not say men are trained for this or that. You can pick a good administrator in the kindergarten by how he manipulates his fellow children in the class.

RIPLEY: I would like to mention that we at Smithsonian have continually pressed for a continuing national commission on ecological monitoring. Theoretically, you could visualize such a commission eventually becoming as powerful, let us say, as the Supreme Court, with an ability to adjudicate between alternative plans to help cut a variety of Gordian knots. It seems to me the thrust of this meeting points toward the need for creating such a continuing commission which might have to be almost as powerful as a Supreme Court.

A clue to one activity of such a commission might be something we started in the last couple of years at the Smithsonian, which has attracted great interest among ecologists: the Center for Short-Lived Phenomena. It is interested in any sort of outbreak either geomorphological or biological in nature.

WHITE: Does that include conferences? (Laughter.)

RIPLEY: We haven't started collecting data on such ephemera. (Laughter.)

But in the case of short-lived phenomena, we are prepared to fly teams of ecologists, biologists, volcanologists, and so on, to where changes are occurring. Now, if such a commission could have as one of its activities monitoring function which might range broadly across the spectrum of natural events and include a center of this sort, it might indeed help fill vital needs very effectively. I hope that some thought will be given in this conference toward urging creation of a powerful continuing monitoring commission of this sort.

BUCHINGER*: Among the responsibilities of highly developed nations should be the dissemination of research results on harmful products and practices. It is immoral to maintain double standards by marketing products or promoting practices abroad where the buyers or receivers often do not have the background knowledge to justly evaluate the danger to which they are exposed. If a product is harmful in one country, it does not lose its effect by crossing borders. Nevertheless—to mention just two obvious examples—U.S. cigarette packages which are exported do not have the warnings which are printed on packages for U.S. consumers. DDT and other pesticides and insecticides which are not, or only cautiously, used in the U.S.A., are freely distributed and highly recommended by U.S. agricultural extension services in foreign countries.

MILTON: Dr. Buchinger is quite right in pointing up this double standard in technolgical applications. The philosophy behind the development of this conference was based on the observation that, in fact, no good ecological post-auditing of what happens when alien technologies are im-

* Dr. Maria Buchinger is Director, Latin American Natural Area Programs of Foresta Institute, Washington, D.C.

ported to the tropics or arid lands had been done. That is the reason for this conference and that is why these case histories have been developed.

The fact that two *private* organizations had to get together and prepare this selection of technological post-audits points up the rather great *institutional* vacuum that we are faced with in obtaining continuously responsible post-auditing in the future. The case histories we have been discussing here represent only a tiny fraction of the development process as a whole. All of it deserves the sort of re-evaluation we have been urging here. I think we must come to grips with this problem in a very serious fashion this afternoon. This is one of the major questions we are faced with.

I would like to toss out a question which is related to this whole concept of getting proper information, post-audit information, into the mainstream of development thinking. I ask not only how we can obtain better environmental information and monitoring of specific development programs but also how we can establish, on a regional basis, a continuing searching out and analysis of environmental information which may not be dramatic at the time but which will eventually provide us with absolutely basic information on the functioning of regional ecosystems. If we had such information, the ecological evaluation of various development programs within the developing countries would be much sounder. Perhaps this will require a series of environmental centers. But again, how should we establish this series of permanent regional centers of background data on the functioning of ecosystems abroad? Some such effort will be absolutely essential if we are going to have post-audit surveys that effectively anticipate environmental change. Our surveys, post-audit or preinvestment, are only as good as the ecological information we have on a regional basis; it is not good enough to send a few ecologists into a developing country on a two- or three-month basis and expect them to develop new data; they will have to evaluate projects on the basis of existing environmental information, which is often deficient.

TALBOT: I think the potential phosphate mining example in Palau that Ray Fosberg mentioned strongly supports Dr. Boulding's point on the importance of industrial pressures, and perhaps in some cases the relative importance of governments. In Palau, we found a number of the local people, including good local biologists, who recognized the importance to the future of the area of these natural tourist resources.

They and the local chief were extremely unhappy about the potential destruction of much of their area. The chief pointed out that any development like this is supposed to be approved by them and by the Congress of Micronesia through the Trust Territory and through the Department of Interior. However, checking back, it turns out that the phosphate exploration permit had been decided upon in Washington. It was then presented to the Trust Territory as a *fait accompli* and then the Congress of Micronesia found out about it sometime later.

No amount of good planning in Micronesia would have done any good. This illustrates pretty well another one of the dimensions we must consider if we are talking about ecological consequences in free planning.

WORTHINGTON: I want to emphasize a general point about islands which Ray Fosberg made. He said that an island is somehow quite different in its ecosystems, economy and sociology from a corresponding area on a continent. Islands are more brittle when it comes to development; hence, one has to be much more careful. One can, for example, afford to have a large mining development on a continent while on a island it would smash everything else to blazes.

What are the implications of this? Does it mean, for instance, that we should have more conservation areas on islands than on continents?

FOSBERG: We habitually try to impose on an island ecosystem a cultural complex developed in continents where we can more afford to make mistakes. The entire history of development of islands has been that of trying to impose such degrading activity on them. Many of these actions are not satisfactory on continents, but at least we have been able, more or less, to get away with it there. In ten years on an island you get the same results that appear after five hundred years of misuse in a continental system. I think rather than confining our concern for better island development to having more conservation areas, we had better assess the whole development idea and decide that there are some types of activity which may be appropriate on continents or very large islands that simply shouldn't be applied on small islands at all. Already, without any further experiments, we can see what many of these inappropriate processes are.

If we know that the result will be bad, let's not do it. That is the only possible solution I can see for some island problems. If we want to destroy everything and then say: "Too bad, we made a mistake," then we should continue ahead the way we are going.

BATISSE: If we are going to have any success, then we have to be realists. I hate to say this, because it sounds like a compromise, but it seems to me on the question of mining we have to recognize that mining is going to go on, whether we in this room like it or not.

I recently spent a few days in New Caledonia, where I saw the mining of nickel. This is an absolutely appalling story because nickel has to be stripped from the tops of mountains, not from the bottom. Of course, everything washes downhill. All the rivers are polluted and only recently has it become a local political problem.

Now, these problems are not going to stop the production of nickel; what we have to do there is to talk to the mining people and try to get reorganization of the operation so that minimum damage is done to the environment. This is where the ecological approach can do something really constructive in trying to modify development projects for environmental reasons but without hindering them. In many areas, there is no other alternative in fostering local governmental change in environmental policies.

FOSBERG: I think of New Caledonia as almost on a continental scale. It is a big island and you can perhaps destroy the nickel areas without destroying the rest of the island. However, my paper was considering mainly small islands; I would say that mining must be stopped due to the tremendously damaging pressures it exerts on small islands.

On Angaur, in the southeastern Palau, there was heavy phosphate mining during the Japanese period; a good portion of the island was totally destroyed. After the war, the Military Government in Japan applied tremendous pressure to continue mining phosphate to supply the phosphate deficiency in Japan.

The people left on Angaur, who had seen a large part of their available agricultural resources destroyed, protested. There were very expensive geological and a few ecological surveys that concluded it would be very expensive to rehabilitate these areas. Finally, the local people's point of view prevailed and the mining was stopped.

The people of Angaur don't want to lose the rest of their long-term means of subsistence. I think it is possible to stop mining on these small islands if the local people

think in terms of the consequences to their children and grandchildren rather than of their own immediate economic gain.

BORGSTROM: I want to speak about the Caribbean. I have been looking at these islands for five years. They now have about 21 million people. This will be doubled within approximately twenty-four or twenty-five years, and the population airlift to the U.S. is already started.

Out of these 21 million, only 7 million people are actually fed from the islands. For fish they go as far as Norway to get protein; they are dependent upon very large outside areas to produce most of their food. Furthermore, their nutrition is not improving but going downhill; if you look at Haiti today I think it is true to say that 70 per cent of the children are badly malnourished and a large portion of these show severe deficiencies.

If you look at Caribbean soil resources, it is a well-known fact that the sugar plantations have actually taken away subsistence possibilities. The forests have been destroyed and the soils eroded, but we have not been interested in stopping this. Now most of these countries are in the red. Have we ever seriously looked at the ecological balance of any of these islands?

CARLOZZI: In the Caribbean that I've studied, I see twenty-two very small islands, probably averaging between 250 and 300 square miles, and containing about 4 million people. These 4 million people have to live somehow. They aren't living very well right now. There isn't one of these islands that can exist today without government grants-in-aid. There isn't one that even comes close to maintaining its own self-sufficient indigenous source of food.

The very fact that 40 per cent of the world's vertebrate extinctions came from this tiny little part of the globe illustrates how fragile must be the habitats of those species which arose as endemics. It didn't really take very much time for man to disturb and eliminate them.

Anything that is threatened now is on some tiny little natural area tucked away high in the hills, difficult areas to reach but in a manner of weeks you could probably destroy many of these. Preservation of this natural diversity is a very delicate balance between the human needs of these islands and the question of natural areas' values to science, to the people there, and to the world. Yet we continuously maintain the open quality of their basic social-economic system by always encouraging export.

If you ask me how to change this system, I don't know, because I can't think of anything except in the classic terms of Barbara Ward's "beer, boots, and bricks." That is about the only thing they now could make for an indigenous market. As to political leadership I will quote Thoreau, who is always best quoted out of context anyway. (Laughter.)

Political leaders all "lead lives of quiet desperation." This is reflected in every decision they make and everything that they are susceptible to by the inducement and enchantment of what we from developed metropolitan nations offer them.

BOULDING: The great enemy is the concept of nature. If we want to preserve anything we have to face that it has to be in the global museum. The only answer to this problem is to turn these islands into museums. Yet you won't face this. You have this extraordinary illusion that there is something in the absence of man called "nature" and you can leave it alone. There is no such thing. If you are going to preserve anything it must be quite deliberately done through political systems and through what I call the "grant economy."

You just have to face this. There is no use bellyaching about it. If you want to preserve an island, get the people off it. Like national parks. I scandalized people by saying the object of national parks in this country is to keep poor people out of the mountains. (Laughter.)

If you want to preserve anything in the world, if you want to do anything about the Caribbean, you have to turn these natural areas into a world park. That is the only way to do it.

48. EXPERIMENTS WITH THE USE OF CASE HISTORIES IN AN ECOLOGY SEMINAR

Thane Riney

Well-intended programs of resource development which have ignored the underlying ecological basis of the area to be developed have often either created no benefits or produced disasters and reduced available resources. In 1964, an ecology seminar was begun, sponsored by the United Nations Food and Agriculture Organization (FAO) so that technical specialists might informally explore ways to improve their perspective and basic approaches to decision-making in development projects. Ecological and sociological aspects of development were emphasized to better balance the more usual and traditional importance given to economic and political considerations.

For the first year all specialists discussed the relation of their fields to ecological, sociological and economic factors of development. This resulted in a more integrated and interdisciplinary method of thinking about problems of development planning. The next phase of the seminar tried to work out practical ways in which early planning could use interdisciplinary knowledge and perspective. Check lists and other mechanisms were used to assure input from varied sources. True synthesis of disciplines was found difficult at this stage since the participants were mostly single-discipline specialists. The next phase of the seminar used case histories. It was much easier to elucidate pertinent and integrated thinking on the specific development problems presented in actual (but anonymous) cases.

The seminar also considered tactics for injecting an ecological approach into the actual field programs of development. They noted that the virtuous activity of giving outside advice often triggers very profound effects on the environment that extend far outside the scope of the single discipline responsible for the original advice. The decisions in fact quite often guarantee failure rather than success. Another principle emphasized was that in solving development problems, in planning and in execution, there is no such thing as *the* one solution. Instead there are many acceptable solutions at a given stage in history and within the limits and potential of the people, economics and environment being considered. There are also many unacceptable solutions, and the responsibility of planners is to increase the percentage of acceptable solutions.

The common-sense processes of cross-checking, learning from case histories and using interdisciplinary tools in the actual process of development will improve the effectiveness of international aid, much more so than streamlining the administrative aspects of an aid program. Our own experience has led us to feel that development within one's own organization of some mechanism for profiting from past experience is a simple enough concept which may be one of the best guarantees for continuing to improve the effectiveness of international aid.

The problems of integrated planning for development and interdisciplinary coordination of activities are major ones, and their early solution could significantly contribute to an improved methodology for aid-granting organizations at their present stage of competency in mounting successful development projects.

The problem of developing an integrated interdisciplinary methodology for dealing with the development process is essentially not an academic one but an inevitable practical consequence implicit in the basic nature of development. The theory of development is comparatively simple; the dynamics of development cause the problems.

Emphasis in the present paper is deliberately ecological and the problem considered is how we can improve our ecological competence in successfully concluding specific projects in developing countries and, at the same time, how we can develop an improved methodology for dealing with the kaleidoscopic aspects of development by integrating the ecological factors with the social and economic ones.

A case study of attempts to stimulate ecological thinking through the formation of informal seminars within the Food and Agriculture Organization of the United Nations is presented and some of the effects of the seminar and its conclusions are reviewed and discussed. To help give perspective to the circumstances under which the seminar came into being, several sources of motivation within the organization must be mentioned.

A large organization such as FAO contains a very broad range of human resources from all regions and from all disciplines related to the use of renewable natural resources for the benefit of mankind. Taking advantage of this resource within our organization, an informal group calling itself the Ecology Seminar has met over the past five years to explore ways and means of improving interdisciplinary understanding and strengthening interdisciplinary contacts within the organization and to explore together the possibilities of improving our approach toward the identification, formulation, development, execution and follow-through of successful development projects.

In terms of specific projects, possible handicaps or bottlenecks to development are innumerable because at a given point in time any one of a host of factors may arrest or prevent a desirable development trend. One of the most important tasks of advisors helping developing countries is to identify such bottlenecks and to suggest appropriate next steps to take within the context of the existing human, economic, and natural resources.

Too frequently errors are of considerable magnitude. They are in fact great enough to make one wonder sometimes how any developing country can seriously consider requesting large-scale assistance programs. At worst such programs have accelerated the spread of deserts, put formerly stable mountain or desert areas permanently out of production, lowered the basic productivity they tried to raise and thus created poorer living and feeding conditions than existed before the aid began. Other aid projects have accomplished nothing positive; money was simply wasted but at least no basic natural resource was destroyed. Fortunately many projects have been successful in that they accomplished their objectives of contributing to the development of the country, within the limitations of the available natural resources and to the social and economic benefit of the people.

A small series of case histories drawn from the semiarid regions of Africa revealed that several aid-granting organizations were involved in destroying some renewable natural resource on which specific land use depended. Interestingly enough, the kinds of aid involved were those most favored by a number of aid-granting organizations: drilling boreholes or constructing dams in regions where water is critical, elimination of tsetse fly, reducing disease and improving the breeds of cattle, and the development of large-scale irrigation projects. None of these projects are inherently bad. However, they may have disastrous results when they are developed and planned for certain economic and social reasons but ignore the ecological base on which the continuance of the program or project depends. The non-integrated approach, developing one phase of the problem and creating an imbalance in the total aspect, should be seriously questioned.

Organizations such as FAO are acutely aware of such problems in development. Any such organization assisting developing countries is involved in a series of complexly related activities, many of which are pioneering and therefore demand continuous adjustments in approach. Developing a methodology to minimize these mistakes and to improve the long-term effectiveness of international assistance is a worthy type of activity to stimulate within any such organization. Thus, involvement in the operation of large complex projects provides continuing motivation for improvement.

The question of an organization profiting from its own or similar organizations' experience has been selected for special emphasis in the present paper because it seems to fit easily within the interests of this meeting. Each organization would profit greatly by developing means of feeding back experience as an integral conscious part of its efforts to improve the effectiveness of its development programs. More specifically, effort within a single organization may usefully be put into the development of feedbacks from the country to field officers, to headquarters; from the accumulating technical experience to the administration and from one discipline to another.

Case histories provide such a feedback of experience into the organization (see Appendix). The problem is one of re-education to get those officers especially concerned with project identification, formulation and management to think beyond their specialization in order to see the broader context.

THE ECOLOGY SEMINAR

In 1964, a small nucleus group was convened consisting of men from various disciplines who were interested in exploring ways and means of improving their basic approach to the technical decisions they were constantly being called upon to make. It was their feeling that if an improvement in their own approaches could be achieved, it could be passed on, particularly to project managers who were to deal with large projects requiring a high degree of integration and coordination between various disciplines.

Our problems and aims were clear. We were interested in improving our methods for identifying appropriate forms of land use and mounting successful projects within the existing economic, social and ecological limitations of the country concerned. We were also interested in improving our capacity for problem analysis and problem solving as such difficulties arose in a project.

The group recognized the need to include sociological and ecological considerations as well as economic factors in all phases of a project. It was also recognized that the language of planning is usually the language of economists, for they are the planners traditionally consulted by governments of developing countries. Furthermore, economists, who were of course included in our nucleus group, felt they were already including sociological and ecological parameters in the planning and in the decision-making processes. However, numerous examples of failure with which we were familiar led us to the conclusion that economists could not adequately deal with sociological and ecological parameters just as sociologists and ecologists cannot satisfactorily deal with economic considerations.

For this reason, while recognizing the importance of economics in the development process, we also emphasized sociological and ecological considerations in an effort to achieve a more balanced perspective.

For the first year we dealt with descriptions of various approaches to ecology, sociology and economics. A soil scientist, for example, gave his view of the ecological approach in his discipline and how it related to the normal jobs and special problems of FAO. This was also done for range management, agricultural research, soil survey, wildlife, national parks, agroclimatol-

ogy, forestry, animal husbandry, animal health, rural sociology, economics and public relations, and extension and education. The meetings were interesting and useful in that an increased mutual understanding and collaboration were developing even at this stage.

The next phase of the seminar's development was the preoccupation with the importance of interdisciplinary consultation on technical matters. Over a period of several meetings, a usable outline was produced by those project managers in a position to recommend the desirability of starting a particular form of natural resource use in a certain area or region of a developing country. Projects rarely have an adequate interdisciplinary team in their early stages of formulation. The group, therefore, prepared three generalized check lists (social, economic and ecological) which included questions prepared by two or more representatives of each discipline. These check lists were distributed to relevant project officers.

In this phase the nucleus group, which met occasionally to discuss the progress of the seminar, observed that many of the principles discussed and accepted by the seminar members were increasingly heard in other meetings not connected with the seminar.

During this stage visiting project managers and experts from the field were occasionally available and initiated discussions on their special problems. Although all these meetings were valuable, it was difficult to progress very far with interdisciplinary thinking because the seminar was composed of largely single-discipline specialists. Frequently, as one reached a point in the discussion where the next logical step was to achieve an interdisciplinary synthesis, the discussion would revert to a member relating his discipline to ecology, as in the initial phase of the seminar.

More skillful chairmen, of course, reduced these irrelevancies somewhat, but the problem largely remained and was only solved when we moved into the next and present phase of using a case history as a basis for interdisciplinary discussion, group thinking and decision-making.

THE USE OF CASE HISTORIES

Cases were prepared in a rather special way for the particular requirements of this seminar. They were selected to illustrate a particular bottleneck retarding the success of a project. All cases used were real, although they did not necessarily involve our own organization. The normal cases were as follows: under certain terms of reference, an expert visited a country; he gave advice which was taken; and trouble resulted from following his recommendations. The new problems were normally on a much greater scale than the original difficulty the expert was to deal with (a sample case is given in the Appendix).

Cases were anonymous.[1] Participants had much experience in various regions, and it was important to put each participant on an approximately equal footing for making comments, recommendations and decisions, based only on the data presented in the case.

Cases were either presented orally or

written with numbered paragraphs to facilitate and speed discussion, criticism and decision-making. The cases were then analyzed, and the problems requiring decision were defined at the conclusion of the case presentation. The group then attempted to arrive at solutions.

Two advantages of using a short case history as a basis for discussion were apparent. We recognized that, quite normally, a visiting expert has too little time, historical knowledge and background technical evidence for making decisions which nevertheless must be made, even if they are interim working decisions. The cases duplicated this situation and had the effect of greatly facilitating relevant contributions from participating officers. In the short period of sixty to ninety minutes irrelevancies were noticeably reduced.

The second advantage was that an experienced chairman was less of a prerequisite than in the former discussions because the group had specific questions to think about, to evaluate and to decide upon.

IMPACT OF THE MEETINGS WITHIN THE ORGANIZATION

Although it is premature to make a detailed assessment of impact, the obvious inevitable by-product benefits within FAO were closer working relations between participating officers. This has been reflected in broadening the perspective of technical planning on several large projects even within the first year of the seminar meetings.

Some junior officers attended the seminars as observers to accelerate their in-service training. Several officers attending the seminar held responsible-enough positions in the organization to be required to present papers from time to time involving one aspect or another of FAO policy, and these officers consulted other members of the group in preparing the papers.

[1] The only exception to the anonymity rule was a case selected to illustrate the problem of a government being plagued by conflicting advice from outside organizations. It was difficult to present this particular case without being very specific. Through no fault of seminar members, this case, which was written, found its way into the hands of the president of the country involved, who insisted on a short mission by a seminar member to work out some system of cross-checking against conflicting external advice. While it was encouraging to recognize that our approach had a certain appeal to at least one member government, the extra seminar time spent on this case was so great that it eventually became clear that we could go into more and more depth which would convert the group into a seminar group dealing with one country. While this was recognized as a valuable experience, it was necessary, for the purposes of our seminar studies, to return to anonymous cases.

There is a feeling that genuine interdisciplinary thinking takes place at these meetings; individuals get something of value that can be translated into their own working program and there is a strong desire by participants for the meetings to continue.

A REVIEW OF SOME OF THE MAIN TECHNICAL IDEAS DISCUSSED BY THE SEMINAR AND SOME CONCLUSIONS

Since it is impossible within the scope of this paper to give an account of all the technical ideas discussed, I have selected for review two approaches to illustrate the injection of an ecological approach into field programs: the development of conservation criteria and an "alternative systems approach"—a collective term used to describe various concepts and principles which have seemed important to the group after discussing a number of specific case histories.

If we question to what extent forms of land use may be considered as appropriate for introduction or expansion, it is useful to learn to what extent present uses are meeting the social, economic and ecological requirements in a small part of the region involved or in nearby similar areas.

Conservation criteria follow logically from the assumption that while contributing to the economy and social life of a country, a successful project must not destroy the resource which it is developing.

The criterion consists simply of determining to what extent present forms of land use are meeting the minimum requirements for conservation. For example, in pastoral terms, if the habitat elements on which the domestic or wild species depend are downgrading, the animals are too numerous for the productivity of the pasture; the area is overstocked; and the present pattern of land use is thus unsatisfactory.

Much of the assistance given to developing countries has used criteria found within the teacup perimeter of various single disciplines. Within this limited horizon, decisions have often been well meaning and seemingly logical, but catastrophic in their ultimate affect on the environment. The danger comes from not realizing that the virtuous activity of giving outside advice often triggers very profound effects on the environment that extend far outside the scope of the single discipline responsible for the original advice. The decisions, in fact, quite often guarantee failure rather than success.

Equally great dangers may arise within countries through the use of seemingly sound social or political criteria. For example, consider the case of a Southern Hemisphere country, where formulation of the social and political creed "Each man must have his own land" resulted in formerly roving bands of cattle being kept inside fences. Each man would have his own cattle run which would be fenced. He would care for it, once it was his own; or so the theory went. The suggestion appeared reasonable to politicians and soon land began to be fenced. However, within four years, bush encroachment had noticeably increased along with decreasing perennial grasses. This evidence relating to conservation demonstrated that what was in fact a good political idea was rebounding because the land was rapidly downgrading.

In the same country, several years earlier, a philosophy called "Grab all you can while it lasts" produced excellent returns from livestock for a few years until the vegetation dwindled, the streams dried up and the cattle died of "drought."

To apply the conservation criterion, appropriate estimates of the present state of the vegetation are needed (including litter, bare ground, grass, shrub and tree cover). Also needed are estimates of its present trend and its potential productivity. When such results are related to past and present forms or intensities of land use, we are obtaining objective evidence facilitating the recommendation of patterns of land use that is at least ecologically sound. If the same land use pattern is acceptable on purely economic, social or political criteria, then applying conservation criteria provides a simple and easily applied cross-check.

Normally conservation criteria function as rapidly applied cross-checks on recommendations arrived at through the use of other criteria. They are rarely used alone to determine the suitability of a form of land use, although there are doubtless instances where they could be so used.

A good example of the potential usefulness of the conservation criteria is in Botswana, where the productivity of a large proportion of the country has been lowered through overgrazing by cattle. One hundred years ago, there was a good perennial grass cover. As recently as forty or fifty years ago, several important streams flowed even at the end of dry seasons, and there were reported resident populations of crocodiles and hippopotamus. Following the introduction of cattle and then boreholes, the perennial grasses were destroyed; less water was stored in the soil; runoff increased during the short heavy rains, and the proportion of shrubs and trees increased. Since outside advisors over the last fifty years have encouraged the increase of cattle numbers, the use of conservation criteria at any time in this early period could have produced evidence which hopefully would have speeded the government toward its present plan of easing away from its destructive cattle monoculture and seeking alternative ecologically acceptable forms of land use.

ALTERNATIVE SYSTEMS APPROACH

The alternative systems approach to land use planning is not a cut-and-dried approach and is not favored by those who like simple, clear-cut answers. However, development based on the renewable natural resources is seldom a simple affair. It is normally rather complicated and messy, and when dealing with a mess, we simply cannot make hard and fast rules. We can, however, be guided by certain generalizations and assumptions which conform with our past experience. Here are a few preliminary examples of practical methods and principles that have risen from a discussion of case histories within FAO.

In surveys for determining acceptable forms of land use or in missions designed to solve a major management problem, it is often useful to consider the mission in stages, the first of which is to achieve a general synthesizing definition of the problem socially, economically and ecologically. Practically, this means assessing the specific job in terms of reference, relating it to the tripartite approach here proposed.

This leads logically to increasing emphasis on rapid survey methods. It also leads to emphasis on various simplified techniques for showing local officers how they can test the validity of the outside advice.

Since we have recognized development as a many-faceted continuing process, we must also understand that in this continuum, at any given point in time, any one social, economic or ecological factor may arrest development or indeed reverse the process. Our solutions may therefore most appropriately now emphasize one aspect, three years later another and five years later still another aspect of development.

In developing countries, the present form of land use is not necessarily the future form of land use, and as a country develops socially and economically, patterns of land use are likely to be more varied and intricate.

Similarly, in solving problems there is no such thing as the one solution. Instead, at a given stage in history, there are a host of acceptable solutions. One must consider the people one works with and the limitations posed by economics and by the environment. There are also a host of unacceptable possibilities. Our responsibility is to increase the percentage of acceptable solutions.

Most of the areas that concern us can support alternative patterns of land use. Thus, good agricultural land can usually either grow a good crop of trees or can sometimes provide a site for a heavily industrialized urban area. The poorer the physical base, the fewer the land use alternatives. This is important, as it applies to many of the marginal lands.

Socially and ecologically, rapid large-scale changes are best avoided and gradual development is much to be preferred. Gradual development brings into play various inter-compensatory mechanisms or homeostatic mechanisms which, in turn, produce useful evidence for evaluating trends. Thus, if domestic or wild animals are overstocked, the imbalance between plants and animals may be detected in various ways. Observations on vegetation may be precise by recording changes in species composition, or in grosser terms, by noting the changes in the proportion of perennials, annuals, shrubs and trees. Consequent animal responses involve, for example, loss of physical condition and increased mortality of young. While changes are slow, these kinds of evidence can simply and quickly be recorded in time to recognize and arrange for a reversal of an unfavorable land use trend.

Rapid development can be ecologically dangerous. If high numbers of animals suddenly occupy land of low carrying capacity, changes can be so rapid that by the time evidence of the trend is clearly appreciated by land managers, consequences may be catastrophic and irreversible. For example, in the Ferlo region of Senegal, following rapid widespread planned distribution of boreholes in previously ungrazed savannah and without grazing control, the land was destroyed by overgrazing in two to three years. This was accomplished simply by a sudden excessive influx of pastoralists with camels, cattle, sheep, goats, fire and axes. In this case, nonintegrated, one-phase development produced not only ecological consequences but social and economic difficulties, for the families settling the area were forced by the environmental change to move elsewhere.

Governments are increasingly aware of the importance of building in cross-checks against the validity of development decisions. The ecology seminar considered that these cross-checks should be built in as an integral part of every large-scale development project.

For every serious land use plan proposed by one part of a government, there will be another part of the same government that objects. This phenomenon can be useful because governments serious about their long-term development can use these natural conflicts of interest to encourage cross-checks.

At the present state of our ability to mount successful projects, cross-checks are of obvious value because of the possibility of a mistake. They are of even greater value when designed on the assumption that one or more mistakes will be made. One objective of the follow-through operations is to identify the mistakes at as early a stage as possible and to take appropriate remedial action.

The adequacy and appropriateness of criteria for making decisions regarding land usage is an important technical aspect of large aid-granting organizations' activities. Regardless of improved efficiency in the rapid flow of paper work or other streamlined by-products of modern computerized administrative and managerial practices, without such criteria no amount of innovation in administrative procedure of reorganization will profit the lands and the people we seek to help.

Appropriate methods must be developed for feeding back to the aid-granting organizations the understanding gained from both successful and unsuccessful development projects and from problem-solving operations. Call it research, or profiting from past experience, or experiments toward an improved methodology for development, or simply efforts associated with improving the effectiveness of international aid—these efforts must be an integral part of the aid process. As efforts become less associated with the actual process of development, they become less appropriate and progressively more academic.

Those organizations actively involved in the practical operation of assistance programs are accumulating invaluable case material appropriate for review and analysis. Our own experience has led us to feel that the development within one's own organization of some mechanism for profiting from past experience is a simple common-sense concept which may be the best guarantee for continuing to improve the effectiveness of international aid.

ACKNOWLEDGMENTS

I gratefully acknowledge that many of the ideas presented in this paper are a synthesis and a summary of ideas discussed in the Ecology Seminar. I am especially grateful to R. F. E. Devred, R. G. Fontaine, J. Bleidenstein and R. A. Peterson for critical reading of the manuscript. However, I must assume responsibility for the emphasis and interpretation presented in the present paper and emphasize that the views here expressed are not necessarily the views of the FAO.

APPENDIX:
CASE HISTORY NO. 1
USED IN THE FAO ECOLOGY
SEMINAR

Introduction. When this case is considered by a research worker interested in the ecological implications of tsetse operations, it is complex and interesting insofar as it opens up many pathways for further exploration. In spite of this complexity, an advanced student should be able to devise ecologically acceptable proposals.

Approached by a specialist in land use development, the case consists largely of irrelevant information; especially for this reason it has been included in the present series.

Background. In the early 1930's, the Ministry of Agriculture of the Government of (S——) decided that in the interests of developing new lands for settlement, the tsetse fly (*Glossina morsitans*) should be removed to increase grazable lands and accelerate the growth of a small but expanding and lucrative cattle industry. The area was largely *Brachystegia* and *Combretum* woodland in hilly terrain with grassy flats bordering some watercourses and many patches of mopane (*Colophospermum mopane*) low-lying on bottom soils. The technique used for eliminating the tsetse fly was to shoot the large wild mammals of the area on which the tsetse fly was known to feed.

Thirty years later the main species of large

mammal being shot were obviously as numerous as before the shooting commenced and some species were clearly even more numerous. In the meantime, the tsetse fly had extended its range and was making increasing inroads into the health of the cattle populations living on the periphery of tsetse-infested areas. Sleeping sickness was occasionally diagnosed in the human population living in the region.

In 1959, an investigator from outside the country became interested in defining more precisely what effect the tsetse operations were having on the large mammal populations. His investigations were directed at three major aspects of the tsetse activities: (1) the changes in the populations of animals for the entire country as evidenced by the numbers of animals shot per month per hunter for tsetse operations; (2) changes over the same period for the single area recognized by the tsetse department as having the best records; and finally (3) an intensive study of the operation that the responsible government department considered their best present effort.

These investigations covered a period of two years and can be summarized as follows:

The countrywide investigation showed that the nine major mammal species involved in the spread of tsetse had either maintained the same numbers or had increased their numbers in the presence of "tsetse" shooting over a period of thirty years. Several species of mammal not involved in the spread of tsetse were quickly and completely eliminated from these areas.

The restricted area considered to be the best example of tsetse operations closely paralleled the findings of the nationwide survey. Graphs of fifty different species of animals were interchangeable for most of the species concerned, and for the major species involved in the spread of tsetse, the two sets of graphs were almost identical.

The best-organized current work of the government department was in an area 100 miles long by 17 miles wide, fenced on two sides and open at both ends. The area was divided into four sections and the central two were chosen by the investigator as a desirable area for intensive investigations. Hunters were organized and skulls of all animals shot over a sixteen-month period were collected and processed and finally placed in the local museum for study. Hunters were interviewed at their camps and accompanied on hunts to learn the quality of hunting. Checks were made of the status of the main elements of habitat on which the animals depended. The following summarizes the main results of these investigations.

For the previous twelve years, fires were started by the hunters early and as often as feasible in order to increase visibility and thus facilitate hunting. Perennial grasses had been greatly reduced and shrubby growth had markedly increased. There had been no previous human use of the area for any purpose other than sporadic hunting. The meadows and moist springs were becoming drier; streams that had been permanent at the end of the dry season became intermittent, and in some of the lowland areas large-scale erosion was taking place, the gullies being twice the height of a Land Rover or Jeep and cutting back at their heads at a rate between 50 and 75 meters per year. It was concluded that burning was the major factor responsible for decreasing perennial grasses and increased bush encroachment.

The age structure of the population, based on the aging of the three thousand skulls taken from the tsetse operations, showed an unusually large percentage of individuals under two years old. This situation was interpreted as characteristic of an expanding population. There was no indication that numbers were in the least being reduced although the value of the meat alone (excluding skins and other products) was calculated as being worth over £96,000 (sterling) for the year of the study.

Investigations of the distribution of hunters' camps and hunting tactics easily explained the reason for the ineffectiveness of the operations, for the camps were situated about ten miles apart, while each hunter rarely moved over three or four miles away from his camp in a given day. Quite unwittingly, the campaign to eliminate animals had by chance developed a system whereby the shooting operations were conducted so that they produced the maximum yield of animals on a sustained annual basis. The animals increasing in number in the intensive study area, the selected campaign area and the national campaign area were, without exception, those animals associated with shrubs, closed-canopy woodland and thicket area, and the investigator concluded that the combination of an increasingly favorable habitat (due to burning) plus a system of hunting especially suited to maintaining an annual harvest of high numbers were, in combination, responsible for the increases in animals over the previous thirty years.

The spread of the bush and thickets was also, in fact, a spread of tsetse habitat and it was only natural that, under these circumstances, the tsetse was also increasing.

The present attitude of the government is that much more research work needs to be done to determine the most appropriate method of clearing the land of tsetse. If the land were free of tsetse, it would become possible for several thousand persons to move into the area with their cattle and traditional forms of agriculture and thus provide some measure of relief for other overpopulated areas. There is, however, strong opposition to mounting a long-term expensive research program.

The political pressures are strong for making the land available for settlement. With unlimited funds there would be no hesitation in clear-felling and treating the entire area with insecticides. But the comparatively inexpensive methods of clearing are the only ones they can afford on an annual basis.

The view of a spokesman for the Department of Native Affairs was that it was hardly fair to turn the land over to his department when it was already in an advanced stage of depletion.

The Veterinary Department insisted that the control measures be increased to arrest the spread of tsetse into productive cattle areas bordering the tsetse zone. They have noticed an increase of nagana (cattle trypanosomiasis) in recent years and have been forced to increase their costly control campaigns in the bordering zones.

QUESTIONS FOLLOWING CASE EXAMPLE

The following questions were used as a basis for discussion following the presentation of the case (Appendix I) and although perhaps desirable to re-word or condense, it seems important to include these to give an idea of what the case history presentations, as used in the seminar, were all about.

The questions were as follows:

1. From the point of view of land development and using the information presented above, describe the major ecological problem that must somehow be resolved before the tsetse-infested land can be seriously considered as suitable for development.

2. Outline the major points of a new program designed to solve the problem you describe.

3. Considering only the first paragraph of the Background Information, suggest one or more programs of action that would have at least shortened the time taken for government recognition of the major ecological problem mentioned above.

NOTE: In proposing solutions, it is important to avoid grandiose and, if possible, long-term research schemes; because of political difficulties, this particular country finds it difficult to obtain large grants for development and research and the government is presently operating on an extremely slim budget.

49. ORGANIZING SCIENTIFIC INVESTIGATIONS TO DEAL WITH ENVIRONMENTAL IMPACTS

Gilbert F. White

Development projects are spreading faster than efforts to anticipate their environmental consequences. Why has more sensitive attention not been given to the ecological impacts of reservoir development in the tropics?

There are many interrelated impacts upon the environment which occur when a reservoir is built, and several ways to classify these impacts. An ideal study agenda for a proposed reservoir would include the impact on national economic efficiency, income redistribution, preservation and aesthetics, political equity, and environmental control. Planners would investigate each possible effect at least to the point where they could judge its rough range of importance to other systems; those effects which could not readily be gauged would require a judgment as to their ecological significance. The ideal agenda would also include a theoretical investigation of alternative means of reaching the same goals.

Why is it that comprehensive studies of alternatives and the possible significance and character of impacts from each alternative have never been carried out? A multiplicity of very human elements accounts for much of this lack of planning. The persons who make the decision sometimes are actually unaware of the consequences, and only study them after it is too late. This lack of foresight is due only partly to stupidity or ignorance; part of it is caused by lack of orientation and training concerning such problems, or a lack of scientific knowledge about certain ecological relationships. Sometimes there is awareness of the problems, and even preliminary planning to investigate them, but the very complexity and uncertainty of the problems create perceptual distortion, and the hazards are minimized. Often, however, it is the technicians below the official decision-makers who informally treat an ecological problem as unimportant; this is often in line with their professional traditions, the limitations of their expertise, and the failure to learn about or utilize past experience on other projects. Many economic considerations enter in; governments do not like to "waste time" in preplanning once a project is under way; the rewards of the primary planned-for impacts seem to outweigh the costs of secondary-impact damages or problems, so these are not seriously evaluated at the time; and budgets and construction costs create crises during actual implementation of a project which cause the so-called peripheral programs to be curtailed or cut out (with much higher costs often descending on the country after the damage has been done). Administrative problems, agency rivalries, the difficulties of interagency and interdisciplinary cooperation also constitute barriers to effective planning. (Examples of some of these various problems as they occurred on reservoir projects are given.)

Perhaps the most crucial aspect of resource intervention is the degree to which resource management decisions are shaped so as to take account of the theoretical range of choice open to each society in achieving its overall aims. The scene will be set to probe and weigh their consequences for all aspects of the environment only to the extent that alternative means are appraised in investigating new projects.

Some remedies for the serious and general pattern of planning omissions would include a kind of early-warning system managed by the United Nations Development Programme; investigation of what has happened in previous development projects after they were finished; serious appraisals of noneconomic consequences to the affected areas and peoples; and development of many now nonexistent or inadequate techniques for ecological investigations, as well as encouragement and extension of the existing positive steps that have been taken. If these and other steps are taken quickly and comprehensively enough, international development may yet submit to the basic question: will a project degrade or enhance the intricate environmental bases of human existence?

A puzzling aspect of many natural resource development projects is that they are not accompanied by more searching scientific investigation of their ecological consequences. To what conditions can we trace the lack of attention given to possible impacts on local fisheries in designing a hydroelectric reservoir project? The same question can be directed to schistosomiasis and soil deterioration in irrigation projects; the effects of pesticides on crops, animals, and man; the consequences of grazing and fire control; and a host of other relationships of the type canvassed in the case studies of this conference.

Failure to provide for scientific inquiry into impacts shows itself in the design of development studies, in the mode of carrying out the studies, and in the use made of the results. At each stage there is opportunity either to examine or to pass over an array of possible effects upon man and the environment which he has shaped. The papers of this conference suggest that rarely, if ever, is the full array of consequences appraised. Nor do the papers offer a satisfactory explanation of why this is common practice.

The answer which is often offered, now indignantly, now peevishly, now sadly, is simple in form. The trouble, we say, is ignorance, or stupidity, or greed, or the lack of an agency to put things right. And the correctives also put simply, range from more research or more education to running the rogues out of office and to setting up new offices for angelic practitioners of science.

Whatever the corrective measures, we are not doing conspicuously well with them. There is good reason to think that development projects are spreading faster than efforts to anticipate their environmental consequences. Perhaps we can gain a better understanding of this trend by taking an unconventional look at experience with one type of development project, the large tropical reservoir. The perspective is that of a geographer concerned with ways in which man perceives his interventions in natural systems and with his modes of adapting to them.

International development is a special and contemporary case of the broader problem of resource deterioration by man. What are the circumstances by which the human family persistently destroys its source of livelihood or fouls its nest? And what leads it to change its ways? Assessment of case histories of ecological impacts presumes that throwing light on what is happening will change the course of future events. However, more information will not in itself alter the trend.

Let us narrow the question by inquiring why more explicit and sensitive attention has not been given to the ecological impacts of reservoir development in the tropics. Analysis begins with a brief review of the theoretical relationships involved in reservoir development. It moves on to ask what might be a proper study agenda for the planning of any tropical reservoir. This theoretical ideal is compared with actual studies at three large reservoirs. Then we come to the issue of whether or not there is any myopia on the part of the engineering, scientific, and administrative fraternities in dealing practically with those relationships. Some of the current explanations for past distortions or delinquency are examined and their implications for public action are suggested.

Recognizing man to be often ignorant and sometimes stupid, we may nevertheless assume that when he avoids facing up to many consequences, as he has in the case of certain African reservoir projects, there may be reasons which seem persuasive to substantial sectors of society. In trying to understand these reasons the ground may be prepared for dealing with them in the future.

THEORETICAL RELATIONSHIPS

We begin with a large reservoir as one element in a water management system in a river basin, one of the few convenient and readily isolated units in water management. There has been more study of reservoir problems than of other units of management, such as channel regulation and irrigation distribution systems. The reservoir is a human creation, consisting of a dam or barrier intended to affect the place of water in time, space, and elevation. By its weight it creates new geophysical stresses. By its extent and fluctuation it alters the biological, physical, and human conditions in adjoining areas. Impoundment always modifies the regimen of a stream in some respect. As a minimum, it changes the elevation of available water in a channel. At maximum, a dam completely alters the distribution of water over a large area while radically changing the downstream regimen. In all but rare cases, there is daily, seasonal, and annual fluctuation in reservoir levels and in the exposed margins.

Confining attention to the reservoir itself and excluding effects of alterations downstream, the possible range of impacts of creating a reservoir may be outlined as shown in Fig. 49–1. Obviously, these are sketchy, and they will be described in more detail in another publication. Other impacts of less general significance are omitted. It is sufficient here to note their complexity and

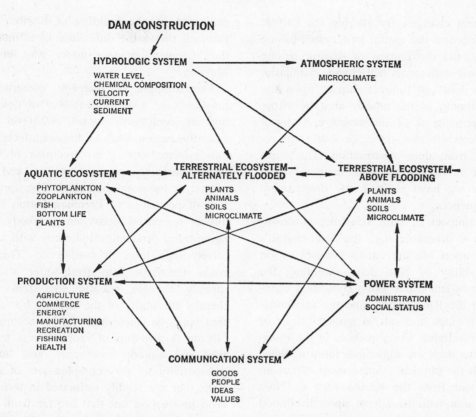

Figure 49–1 Schematic diagram of the major possible effects of a reservoir impoundment

to call attention to a few features of the relationship.

The eight systems defined consist of two physical systems of air, water and sediment movement, three distinct biological ecosystems, and three aspects of human activity. It is impossible to erect a large dam without causing some impact upon each of them.

With few exceptions the relationships are reciprocal. For example, the amount of water used for electric power production changes stream regimen and controls water levels on the margins. This, in turn, affects the growth of aquatic plants. Sediment deposition in the basin area is induced and reduces power-generating capacity.

One useful way of classifying impacts is by the systems affected. Indeed, the common idiom for reservoir projects is in terms of the primary human activity to be changed: "a storage dam for hydroelectric energy production," "a regulating reservoir for water transport," "a detention reservoir for flood control." In describing and building projects in this simple fashion, other secondary and tertiary relationships may be ignored or obscured. Thus, a power dam is seen as creating a reservoir in order to assure a certain generation of electricity and other effects of the reservoir are incidental.

A second useful classification is by the directness with which reservoir construction is related to the system's impact. The level of water in a reservoir may have a direct impact on the availability of fishing grounds to fishermen; its impact will be indirect on fish production as the aquatic ecosystem changes. By altering the habitat for snails and the spatial patterns of fishing activity, the distribution of disease among bordering settlements will change. Similarly, it may have an indirect impact upon the microclimate of the nearby area by virtue of movements of air and moisture. Many of the effects are two, three, or four steps removed from dam construction. The number of interconnections is immense even though we have omitted the downstream consequences.

The impact of dam construction downstream is dramatic: e.g., the Sadd-el-Aali's effects upon Mediterranean fisheries or on the stability of Nile delta shoreline; the growth of salt cedar along controlled channels of the Rio Grande, and the accumulation of water and salt in irrigated soils of the lower Indus. Consequences in the reservoir area itself are sometimes more obvious, as with the physical displacement of human settlement from the Kariba area or Nam Pong area with its effects upon livelihood and power structure; sometimes they are rather subtle, as with the possible results of Mekong reservoirs on fish distribution and numbers.

A third basis for classifying impact is predictability. It is possible to estimate the effect of a storage impoundment on potential electric power production with considerable accuracy. The margin of error is small. On the other hand, the effects of reservoir fluctuation on the soils and plant population of marginal lands are much less predictable. The effect of storage on the snail vector of schistosomiasis or on exotic aquatic plants finding new environmental niches is even less predictable. Certain of the climatic and hydrogeological effects are largely speculative. Some of these have been described in the Institute of Biology symposium (Lowe-McConnell, 1966) and others in the Accra symposium (Ghana Academy of Science, 1968). In this volume, Scudder examines the complex perturbations

generated by the building of Kariba, and Bardach shows the difficulties of estimating the biological changes under way in the Mekong.

The example of reservoir construction may indicate a convenient way of describing an ecological impact, whatever the causative action. Such an impact affects certain systems, varies in directness of connection with the primary project, and has greater or lesser predictability. The application of pesticides to Peruvian cotton fields affects terrestrial ecosystems directly and agricultural production indirectly with a relatively high level of confidence. Thermal waste discharge into fresh-water streams directly changes aquatic ecosystems and thereby the utility of the streams by means that can be measured fairly accurately. Nitrate fertilization of crops affects terrestrial and aquatic ecosystems and human productivity by very complex sets of reactions that are readily estimated in terms of crop production but that are far from predictable in terms of consequences for stream environment and human health.

We must add that to suggest a relationship from either theory or observation is not to specify our knowledge of it, and much of of what is outlined in the diagram is so tenuous or speculative that we cannot assert the relationship with a high degree of confidence.

DESIRABLE STUDY AGENDA

When consideration is given to building a dam at least one impact is sought explicitly. It may be power production, agricultural production, goods movement, or domestic water supply. Increasingly, dams are planned with a combination of primary purposes, and in the framework of basin or regional programs. Human manipulation presumes human ends to be served. These ends commonly are ambiguous and confused but the major ones according to the method used in the recent analysis of Colorado Basin development (National Academy of Sciences, 1968) are:

> national economic efficiency
> income redistribution
> preservation and aesthetics
> political equity
> environmental control

Only the last two of these require explanation. Political equity is the satisfaction of social commitments without primary regard for income flows or environmental quality. Environmental control is that special, oftentimes inarticulate and widespread urge to harness a stream or some other natural process because man knows how to do it.

It is usual to give national economic efficiency as the primary aim for national investment. Yet, the record is loaded with projects in which regional claims for income redistribution or political equity or the aspiration to create a monument to man's mastery of nature have figured in the final choice. In the Colorado Basin, for example, some proponents of new projects have emphasized national economic growth, others have stressed the support of central Arizona's economy, some have spoken for the preservation of the Grand Canyon, and others have called for adherence to political agreements allocating water among the basin states.

To decide what should be studied in a proposed dam construction requires, then, a conscious or tacit definition of aims. For our analysis we shall assume that these are a combination of national economic efficiency and environmental preservation, aims that may be in conflict but are susceptible to reconciliation. The preservation of environments having special aesthetic or scientific value sometimes can be achieved without loss of conventional economic efficiency; it can always be achieved at a cost

of production for other purposes. Desirable plans of study would explore each possible relationship to see how it would be affected by the construction and how this in turn would advance or retard reaching the stated aims. Water planners now are moving toward methods of taking explicit account of aesthetic values and at the same time of achieving a social aim such as food production. This involves estimating the social effects of different types and sizes of engineering works.

At once, a value judgment is required. How significant must the effect promise to be before it is investigated? One way of meeting this requirement is to specify that all possible effects shall be studied, estimating their orders of magnitude insofar as the planners are capable of identifying them. Under such a rule, the possible effect of a new water body on regional climate would be investigated far enough to reasonably judge its rough range of importance to other systems. Obviously, there are relationships so ill defined that nothing short of a long, complex, and costly investigation would suffice to determine whether or not the design of the project should take them into account. The decision to continue or not to continue with the inquiry inevitably requires a judgment as to likely payoff.

On theoretical grounds, the agenda also would include an investigation of alternative means of reaching the same goals. This would canvass, in addition to the variety of possible water management measures, the possible nonstructural measures promising similar results. Hydroelectric power would be compared with thermal sources; irrigation would be compared with fertilizer and seed programs (National Academy of Sciences, 1966).

ACTUAL STUDY PROGRAMS

A study program which examined all promising alternatives and gauged the

Table 49–1

CHARACTERISTICS OF THREE AFRICAN RESERVOIR PROJECTS

NAME	AREA OF RESERVOIR IN SQUARE MILES	ESTIMATED GENERATING CAPACITY IN Kw	ESTIMATED COST IN DOLLARS	CONSTRUCTION PERIOD
Kainji	480	320,000–880,000	140,000,000	1964–1968
Volta	3,275	512,000–882,000	156,000,000	1962–1965
Sadd-el-Aali	1,900	2,100,000	> 320,000,000	1960–

weight of possible impacts from each alternative might satisfy the ideal agenda. We must admit at once that no such study has ever been made. Experience with the planning of three reservoirs helps us see some of the reasons.

The three projects are the Kainji dam on the Niger, the Volta River dam, and the Sadd-el-Aali (High Aswan) on the Nile. Their physical and fiscal size is indicated in Table 49–1. Each is a national project supported by international financing. Each has power production as a primary purpose for advancing national economic efficiency, although Sadd-el-Aali also includes irrigation water storage as a primary purpose.

Perhaps the closest that any study of an African reservoir project has come to recognizing the theoretical relationships outlined above is in the Volta River Commission investigations (Volta River Preparatory Commission, 1956). Over a period of five years they sought to clarify problems involving physical, biological, and social processes which might be disturbed by constructing a dam at Akosambo. Table 49–2 outlines aspects of the Volta project embodied either in the investigations or in the final report of the preparatory commission. No other reservoir study approaches the Volta investigation in concept or in detail. Yet, it later required as much salvage activity as did the other two projects.

Without attempting to review the history of project planning in each case, it is possible to enumerate some of the principal

Table 49–2

OUTLINE OF MAIN TOPICS FOR INVESTIGATION BY THE VOLTA RIVER PREPARATORY COMMISSION

Technical aspects
  Dam and power installation
  Power markets, including bauxite and alumina treatment
  Landscaping
  Transport network
  Effect of reservoir on communications
  Sources of materials

Human factors
  Manpower requirements and supplies
  Productivity, health, training of labor force
  Living conditions in new communities
  Impacts on urban communities

Effects of the dam and reservoir
  Ecology, demography, and livelihood in reservoir area
  Compensation
  Resettlement and its administration
  Effects on downstream communities (agriculture, fishing, health, water, communications)
  Health and sanitation
  Agriculture, forests and fisheries

Financial and economic aspects

Other factors which could influence the projects (financial resources, overseas investment, Togoland administration, headwaters control, future of aluminum, nuclear power)

Administrative and legal framework

points at which the studies fell short of the desirable study agenda. A rigorous way to determine the deficiencies would be to compare the actual studies with the ideal agenda. Comparison is hindered by the lack of any complete history of the planning studies. We know from the available reports what findings were brought to the public or responsible officials; we cannot reconstruct the lines of investigation that were considered and then abandoned. For example, the record does not show where an engineer or administrator may have looked into a problem briefly, concluded that it did not merit further study, and moved on to another problem.

It is easier to list those relationships which were selected for further study after construction was well under way. Kainji and Volta Lakes and Lake Nasser, the portion of the Sadd-el-Aali reservoir in the United Arab Republic, are the subjects of detailed studies by teams of international experts financed jointly in each case by the respective countries and the United Nations Development Programme. The actual study plans for each project reveal the issues that seemed more significant after construction was initiated.

At Lake Nasser the investigations costing $2,600,000 over five years, include fishery biology, limnology, fishing gear technology, fish processing technology, fisheries economies; vectors of malaria, schistosomiasis, and other human diseases; vectors of animal diseases; soil, agronomic, horticultural, and economic aspects of lake shore agriculture; afforestation and wildlife conservation; geohydrology; and social and economic analysis of adjustments in community life. At Kainji, a total expenditure of $2,000,000 over six years will be divided among investigations of limnology and fish species; socioeconomic studies related to the continuation of resettlement; vectors of malaria, schistosomiasis, and onchocerciasis; and conditions for establishing a wildlife conservation zone. At Volta, a three-year investigation costing $2,700,000 is concentrating on fisheries and hydrobiology, resettlement, and public health.

For our purposes it is not necessary to discuss the intricate problems attacked by the different lines of investigation. Fisheries biology alone would call for an extensive description. What is important here is that each topic was considered sufficiently important by representatives of national and international agencies to warrant expenditure of scarce funds allocated for preinvestment surveys. The resulting program of investigations on man-made lakes defines what were regarded as significant aspects that were omitted from the construction investment.

WHY THE OMISSIONS?

Two broad sets of explanations may be advanced for the omission of more detailed studies of these problems from the original project operations. One is that those people responsible for deciding to go ahead with the construction projects were unaware of the consequences to which later studies were addressed. The other is that they were aware of possible consequences but thought it unwise to study them at that time. Lack of awareness there surely was in some quarters, either because the basic reports failed to identify possible impacts or because the readers were insufficiently prepared by training or outlook to ask about them. In some instances the scientific basis for an intelligent question was lacking, as in the case of microclimatic impacts.

To an unknown degree, there must be perceptual distortion on the part of officials dealing with these impact problems. We know that in thinking about the occurrence of floods or the hazard of drought or the recreational use of a domestic water supply, reservoir resource managers are shaped by their prior views of what it is practicable to do (Kates, 1962; Saarinen, 1966; Baumann, 1969). People who feel themselves unable to cope with a situation see it as less severe than others. A sense of efficacy in handling complexity may be a powerful aid to awareness. In the absence of knowledge of how to improve fishery or disease conditions, a responsible administrator might see them differently than he would if ready solutions were in prospect.

Probably more of the responsibility rests on conscious judgment by those planning the project. If certain officials were unaware of the complications of building the dams it was because engineers and other technicians who recognized a problem chose to treat it as insignificant. In good faith and feeling themselves loyal to their professional training and traditions, they decided that questions about fisheries or disease or resettlement need not be raised in overt fashion in their reports and advice to those higher up. As with so much natural resource management, many of the basic policy decisions are made tacitly or unconsciously by the investigator who decides which problems he will study, which options he will probe. By the time a recommended project reaches the top officials or the public arena these assumptions are plowed so deeply into the soil of the program that they are barely discernible in the construction design.

The preponderant number of decisions to exclude consideration of the full set of theoretical relationships in large tropical reservoirs may be attributed to conscious judgment that the social cost of neglecting the relationships would be smaller than the cost of attacking them frontally. Two economic considerations may be relevant.

With respect to most of the relationships, there is a high degree of scientific uncertainty as to the probable effects of investment in studies or in subsequent management. Take the case of fresh-water fisheries on new reservoirs. Although a considerable body of evidence has accumulated on the change in thermoclime once a reservoir impoundment begins, scientific information on its effects upon the biological population of the reservoir is so meager that manage-ment measures needed to increase fishery productivity can rarely be predicted. The new ecosystem is not sufficiently predictable to warrant a decision to introduce new species of fish or other life into the reservoir. Without more refined knowledge of fishery biology or suitable study methods, it is necessary to wait to see what happens.

Certain fishery experts argue that the wise and economical course of action is to observe reservoir conditions while the reservoir fills, holding off any preliminary activities until the first biological bloom has passed and the aquatic system has approached a new equilibrium. At that stage, the scene is set for more intelligent management measures involving stocking, fishing control, and measures to promote marketing and processing of the most promising variety of fish. To follow such a course might mean that the government would take negative steps to prevent undue fishing on the part of the local fishermen: it would discourage mechanical development; it would not introduce new gear, and it would try to hold the fishing industry to the existing number of fishermen and fishing boats. In these circumstances, it is asserted, the most efficient strategy for the government to follow is to do nothing during the preliminary study period with respect to fishing, to follow a modest program of observation and regulation while the reservoir is filling, and then to make a heavy input of professional study and advice after the reservoir is full. To those who insist upon base-line studies, they would reply that such studies would be useful to such a limited degree that they would not justify the expense. It would be interesting to accumulate more data, they say, but it would not result in different management practices.

The second economic consideration relates to the high risk and low probable costs attaching to secondary impacts. When a water planning agency is dealing with probable returns from sale of hydroelectric power which promises yields of at least 5 or 6 per cent per annum (with what at the moment of study approaches certainty), the probable savings of negative costs or positive benefits from secondary effects may seem relatively insignificant in monetary terms. When there is pressure to cut down total construction expenses, attention concentrates on activities promising higher returns with less chance of failure. Given the high risk involved in forecasting secondary reservoir impacts, it seems wiser to some managers to forego their consideration and take the consequences rather than to invest money and personnel in basic investigation.

There are administrative obstacles. Typically, the national agency responsible for planning a new dam does not have competence in either biological matters or those related to social organization and process. In these circumstances, it is often easier to try to solicit new personnel from a foreign environment or enlist the cooperation of other agencies in the government to share their funds. The simple bureaucratic complications of shifting funds or of supervising unfamiliar personnel may lead to a conscious decision to exclude detailed appraisal of secondary effects. It seems simpler to let others do it, and if they lack the energy or the funds, then to let the matter rest until there is public demand to revive it.

The same kind of difficulty arises with international administration of integrated resource studies. It is extremely cumbersome for two or more specialized agencies in the international family to collaborate in carrying out studies. They are highly competitive in generating new investigation and in sharing the overhead income. The Food and Agriculture Organization, which has been primarily responsible as the executing agency for the African reservoir studies, has worked out agreements for collaboration with the World Health Organization in the health field for all three reservoirs. It also seeks to work cooperatively with UNESCO, which

asserts a basic responsibility for scientific research, education, and training. Negotiating such collaboration is always more troublesome than going it alone. The same is true at the national level. A ministry of agriculture hesitates to enter into an investigation which will also involve a ministry of public works, and vice versa. Each of the ministries characteristically has its counterpart in the international specialized agency. Agriculture and fishery ministries prefer working with FAO. A ministry of public works prefers to work with the World Bank. The ministry of scientific research has ties with UNESCO. As a result, each agency is tempted to propose a project or an investigation scheme narrow enough to avoid overlapping at either the national or international level.

In a sense, obstacles to such cooperation reflect differences in approach among scientific disciplines, their educational methods, and their accompanying professional cadres. On a reservoir project, the coordination of limnologists, wildlife ecologists, sociologists, and economists may be as sticky in terms of cooperative approaches to common problems as the coordination of administrative agencies. The finger of responsiblilty should be pointed toward professional groups and to teaching and administrative agencies reflecting their orientations. When an engineer fails to examine fishery impacts it may be due to his conscious judgment that they are unimportant, but it also may reflect a deficiency in his training for work with a team that would include biological scientists.

In the case of the Volta project the negotiations for foreign financing dragged on a long time, and once they were concluded the government felt impelled to get construction under way without delay. It found itself short of funds in the bargain. Then began a process, found in numerous projects, where costs are underestimated and timing is late. Consciously and with questionable wisdom it pushed resettlement, cut out expenditures for reservoir clearing and public health investigations. As budgets were slashed, many of the activities foreseen by the Preparatory Commission were quietly dropped. Studies of basic biological changes and of potential use of the reservoir margins awaited financing through the University of Ghana with foreign assistance. Moreover, concentration on building the dam and selling electricity led the Volta River Authority to shed its responsibility for such auxiliary activity as agricultural development. When it returned to that unified role in 1967, it resumed interest in supporting the basic research on biological and social problems.

We may draw on the Volta experience as a prototype. In a number of ways the Volta River Authority failed to use the findings from its preliminary study in the final operation and construction of the reservoir. The resettlement program was initiated before the resettlement study was completed. Plans to clear the reservoir for fishing were eliminated, except for a small demonstration area about two miles long immediately adjacent to the dam. Public health measures in the reservoir area were not initiated. No detailed investigations or pilot operations were begun in the foreshore with its seasonal inundation of potentially useful agricultural land. Inadequate measures were taken to study impacts upon transportation or to experiment with simple means of maintaining passenger or freight transport from routes severed by the new lake.

In large measure, the complexity of the great reservoir's impacts had been foreseen. At various stages of the preconstruction investigations they were examined, and judgments were drawn as to their likely magnitude and ways of dealing with them. Under the pressure of getting on with the job with less funds, much of the recommended auxiliary activity was dropped, and administrative attention focused on electric power

production. When study of the secondary impacts was renewed, valuable time had been lost. In the case of resettlement, heavy expenditures were made to correct the results of hasty action. There can be little doubt that the resettlement costs to the nation were unduly heavy. It is still too early to say what the net effect was of deferring attention to the other aspects: a fair evaluation would have to compare the benefits of earlier power production with the social costs of neglecting fisheries, marginal agriculture, transport, and health during that period.

RESOURCES, ECONOMY, AND POPULATION

A similar related problem is the coordination of natural resource development with national economic policy. There is little point in preparing comprehensive river basin plans unless they are harmonized with broader national efforts to reach national goals. Just as an ideal study agenda would call for investigation of ecological impacts, it would also provide for examination of the major consequences of the proposed investment for national development.

Even more sensitive is the coordination of resource development with population policy. It is evident that much resource manipulation is intended to meet demands of growing numbers of people to be fed, clothed and housed. Thus, an irrigation component in reservoir storage is intended to provide water to support a future population. A sober canvass of alternatives would note the opportunities and limitations in influencing the options open to individuals in family planning as well as in farming.

This brings us to what may well be the crucial aspect of resource intervention in the developing world today. It may be put as the degree to which resource management decisions are shaped to take account of the theoretical range of choice open to each society in achieving its aims. To the extent that alternative means are appraised in investigating new projects the scene will be set to probe and weigh their consequences for all aspects of the environment.

SOME REMEDIES

Against this pattern of omitting and then attacking secondary impacts of reservoir development, a few remedies seem promising. If something approaching a desirable plan of study is to be achieved in the near future for major projects, a kind of early warning service must operate. The United Nations Development Programme is the appropriate agency to do this in developing countries, for it either funds or is aware of larger preinvestment studies. By identifying the emerging problems before construction planning is complete it should be able to prevent later salvage operations. Its field offices are now alert to the need for doing this with major reservoir projects.

The UNDP and FAO also have initiated in the African reservoir studies a systematic attempt to assess the social gains and losses due to studying or ignoring the secondary impacts. Methods are as yet imprecise but rough estimates are being made, and from such appraisals may come a clearer view of what payoff in understanding of environmental change may be expected from different scales and types of investigation.

We must remind ourselves that relatively little is known of the success of reservoir projects in achieving their stated primary aims. The practice is to spend huge sums on normative studies of proposed construction schemes, and little or nothing on appraisal of what happened after the bulldozers withdrew. There are only a handful of searching evaluations, and these deal primarily with the economic and fiscal aspects of the projects (King, 1967; de Wilde

et al., 1967). The appraisal of noneconomic consequences is even less advanced, and the methods of making such appraisal are crude. Suitable techniques for ecological investigation are in short supply.

The FAO has just completed a rudimentary manual pointing out the chief classes of secondary impacts which have plagued reservoir development in the past (FAO, 1969). It should be clear, however, that neither manuals nor performance evaluations can in themselves shift the prevailing approach of technical agencies to project planning. In the long run, a basic change in professional orientation and training will be required. The early warning service may be expected to call the attention both of planners and political officers to that need. This warning must be supported by evidence from concrete situations and by practical suggestions as to how the complicated and often speculative investigations of such impacts can be reconciled at reasonable cost with the studies of primary impacts.

Imposition of a special review agency or of a special study group in connection with ecological impacts of massive new projects of this nature does not seem a promising line of action. Administrative and professional resistance would be severe. Yet, means must be found to take account of the full range of consequences, and it may be that the steps already taken with regard to reservoir projects are in the right direction.

By an early warning scheme, the responsible officials can be made aware of possible secondary ecological impacts of proposed new interventions in the environment. Through manuals and case studies, the supporting evidence for confidently assessing such effects can be marshaled. These techniques, together with cooperative investigations such as those on the African reservoirs, are likely to influence the outlook of development agencies and the training of new scientific personnel. The professional groups and their teachers must broaden their outlook. The assessment of social costs and benefits from current investigations will throw light on the key problem of how much expenditure at what stage is warranted for the study of secondary effects. Over the long term, these efforts will not be effective unless they are accompanied by improvement of ecological research techniques and resource planning methods which will permit organizing scientific studies as an essential part of appraisal of environmental and social consequences from the outset of development planning.

REFERENCES

Baumann, Duane D. *The Recreational Use of Domestic Water Supply Reservoirs: Perception and Choice.* Chicago: University of Chicago Department of Geography Research Papers, 1969.

de Wilde, John C., *et al. Experiences with Agricultural Development in Tropical Africa.* 2 vols. Baltimore: Johns Hopkins Press, 1967.

Food and Agriculture Organization. *Reservoir Problems.* Rome: FAO, 1969.

Ghana Academy of Science. *Symposium on Man-made Lakes.* In press.

Kates, Robert W. *Hazard and Choice Perception in Flood Plain Management.* Chicago: University of Chicago Department of Geography Research Paper No. 78. 1962.

King, John A., Jr. *Economic Development Projects and Their Appraisal: Cases and Principles from the Experience of the World Bank.* Baltimore: Johns Hopkins Press, 1967.

Lowe-McConnell, R. H., ed. *Man-Made Lakes.* New York: Academic Press, 1966.

National Academy of Sciences. Committee on Water. *Alternatives in Water Management.* Washington: NAS, 1966.

————. Committee on Water. *Water and Choice in the Colorado Basin: An Example of Alternatives in Water Management.* Washington: NAS, 1968.

Saarinen, Thomas F. *Perception of the Drought Hazard on the Great Plains.* Chicago: University of Chicago Department of Geography Research Paper No. 106. 1966.

Volta River Preparatory Commission. *The Volta River Project.* London: Her Majesty's Stationery Office, 1956. Appendices in Vol. II.

50. AN ECOLOGICAL APPROACH TO INTERNATIONAL DEVELOPMENT:
Problems of Policy and Administration

Lynton K. Caldwell

Meaningful discussion of ecology and international development is handicapped by serious semantic difficulties. The word "development" is imprecise, normative, and teleological. Its meanings range widely but, in a practical application to international affairs, the dominant concept has been the transformation of traditional agrarian societies throughout the world into industrialized economies resembling those of the United States and Western Europe. The emphasis in international development has been on economic and technical assistance from developed to underdeveloped nations, in part through the mediation of international agencies such as the United Nations, the World Bank, FAO, WHO, and UNESCO. The word that summarizes its objectives has been "modernization."

The international development process has grown in a disjunctive and uneven manner in response to perceived needs of the so-called underdeveloped nations. These needs have seldom been adequately defined in terms of ecological circumstances or values. The complexities and inadequacies of the development process itself also have been attacked for many reasons other than ecological. A more coherent and rational global development plan under United Nations sponsorship is being advocated as preferable to the labyrinth of bilateral and multilateral arrangements now in effect. Simultaneous with this movement for development reform, have been efforts to establish an international responsibility for the protection and rational use of the biosphere. The earth is beginning to be perceived as analogous in many ways to a spaceship. The pressure of people upon resources and living space is necessitating new attitudes and behavior patterns in the interest of human civilization and survival. The inculcation of these attitudes and behaviors will require new instruments of international education and new interpretations of the rights of nations. A body of doctrine is slowly emerging that could form a basis for international environmental policy and administration. The formulation of this policy and the establishment of feasible and effective institutions to administer it is one of the major tasks of national and international politics in our time.

It has been said that "whom the gods would destroy, they first make optimists," and the saying applies with special force to the effort called "international development." Neither optimism nor development is inherently good or bad. If the optimism is justified and the development wise, the results should be beneficial. But the process of development is complex; the criteria for wisdom are seldom self-evident; and a prudent optimism must take account of the many variables that influence the outcome of any major socio-ecological change.[1] Yet prudence, pushed too far, could discourage all planned development, including measures that might restore or protect the ecological basis of a society. The hazards to happy outcomes in development projects are numerous, and while the case for development is based upon good intentions, its justification depends upon results. The uncritical assumption that good intentions necessarily produce good results has too often turned a complex process of socio-

ecological engineering into a scandal—or a disaster (Austruy, 1965).[2]

The principal thesis of this essay is that an ecological viewpoint is essential to any valid concept of development, because the development process itself—whatever its scope or complexity—is inherently ecological. It is a process of purposeful change in the systematic interrelationships of living and inanimate things as they have evolved and continue to evolve in a biosphere dominated by human society. This argument is not directly pertinent to the long familiar and often inconsequential debates over incremental versus comprehensive planning, or over harmonious versus unbalanced development. The argument is not that development, being ecological, must take all relevant interrelationships equally into account. The discovery of *which* interrelationships are more critical to human and ecological well-being and which are of lesser significance, and the discovery of *why*, is a major purpose of an ecological approach to development. This purpose is most likely to be pursued, however, when it is predicated on our basic proposition: that man's deliberate manipulation of his societies in relation to their environments is most safely and most successfully undertaken when it is understood and acted upon for what it is—a process of fundamental ecological change. But if this proposition is accepted and acted upon, far-reaching modifications in the structure and process of international

[1] Noting the shortcomings of international technical assistance in economic development, John Kenneth Galbraith (1962) observes: "This action will indeed be sound if the diagnosis of the development problem is sound. If that diagnosis is unsound we will be having a good deal of waste motion in the world. It is my unhappy feeling that the diagnosis leaves a great deal to be desired" (p. 7). Elsewhere in this essay he writes: ". . . we have probably wasted a good deal of time and effort doing things which were right in themselves but which make little or no contribution to progress because they were done in an environment which was inconsistent with advance. The environment has not been examined. It has somehow been assumed to be favorable to development" (p. 6).

[2] See also the article by Goulet (1968).

development programs are implied. Before turning to these implications, however, a closer examination of the meanings of "development" is required.

THE MEANINGS OF DEVELOPMENT

There is no easy and satisfactory way to define "development" in either its domestic or international aspects. It may be described as a complex process of purposeful change in the attitudes, behaviors, and institutions of human societies. Raymond Aron (1967) identifies three interpretations of development:

The modern, or to be precise the contemporary, theory of development stems from three sources, each of which suggests a particular interpretation of the word and the phenomenon: the long-term statistical study of economic growth; the contrast between rich and poor countries (or, to use the common terms, advanced and underdeveloped countries, the latter now being said to be "in process of development"); and, thirdly, the comparison between Soviet and Western economic and social organization (p. 8–9).

The determining element in conventional definitions of development does not appear to be the process itself, but rather the goals toward which it is directed. The term is imprecise, normative, and teleological. The process, deliberate and purposeful, implies assumptions, goals, and procedures that are open to evaluation by some criteria. But the purposes of development and the scientific criteria by which it may be evaluated are culturally determined. Technical aspects of development have been analyzed from widely separate viewpoints. There is a large volume of critical comment on economic, social, and political aspects of planned change and international technical assistance. But this comment proceeds largely from a common set of assumptions regarding the relationships of man with nature— assumptions that have been dominant in

Western technological society since the Industrial Revolution.[3] Technical and economic considerations are paramount; behavioral and ecological factors are only beginning to receive attention, and in a sharply descending order of priority.[4]

Although there is considerable difference in the definitions and interpretations of development, it is possible to ascertain what the term primarily means in actual practice. From the general literature of development and from the descriptions of development projects one may deduce that "development" represents the process through which relatively simple, traditional, agrarian societies become industrialized.[5] "Development" suggests a process of growth toward some future condition. The precise nature of that future is seldom stated explicitly, but

[3] For a sharp criticism of some current assumptions regarding development see Nedelcovic (1965, pp. 10–14).

[4] Important exceptions may be found among the French development economists and sociologists whose writings in *Economie et Humanisme* and *Tiers-Mond* frequently take a broader view of the development process than is customary in Anglo-American literature. Therefore, although the general literature of development is predominantly in English, the relative weight of the literature tends to be more nearly balanced when the behavioral and ecological aspects of development are considered. No consideration of the ecological implications of development would be adequate without recourse to the writings of Raymond Aron, Jacques Austruy, Louis-Joseph Lebret, François Perroux, and many others whose approaches to development are distinctively different from most British and American writers. There is a strong ecological or environmental emphasis in the work of some Anglo-American economists, notably those concerned with natural resources, regional science, and urban and agricultural economics. But relatively few of these have contributed to the literature on international development. However, the writings of Kenneth Boulding, John Kenneth Galbraith, and Barbara Ward, among others, take a clearly ecological approach to international affairs and development policies. For more explicit analyses of the development concept see: Montgomery, 1962; Friedrich, 1962; Papanek, 1968; also Riggs, 1964. Riggs' approach to international development and its administration is ecological in the sociological sense; he does not deal directly with the biophysical aspects of development. For a survey of the literature see De Vries (1968, pp. 43–51).

[5] *Cf.* Hoselitz, 1956. See also Riggs, 1964.

by inference one may conclude that it resembles roughly the "more advanced" West European-North American standard of living and technology. The term "development" thus carries a hidden burden of unarticulated assumptions. Implicit in its common usage are beliefs about the needs and values of people and of the forces that shape history. Few, if any, of the assumptions underlying the idea of "development" (with possible exceptions relating to public health) are supported by verified scientific evidence.

The term most commonly used to summarize the goals of development is "modernity." A number of sociologists have read specific content into the concept of "modernity," but ecological awareness or the possession of criteria for wisdom in man-environment relationships do not appear to be among its distinguishing characteristics.[6] Yet, evidence of widespread environmental destruction by traditional man and his domestic animals suggests that modernity has not necessarily made man more callous toward his environment although it has made his abuse of it more efficient.[7] Modernity has added to man's knowledge of the natural world and his relationships with it without giving him an adequate philosophy to guide these relationships toward dynamic stability and ecological renewal.

The danger in modern development is not solely in its conceptual inadequacy. Modern development, when based on inadequate diagnosis, is dangerous *because* of the likelihood that it will achieve results of some kind. Although it may fail to achieve its objectives, it may produce costly and damaging consequences. Conversely it may attain its goals, but the attainment may entail ecological backwash and unforeseen harmful side effects. Ecological disasters in development may coexist with technical success. The gross national product of a developing country may increase as the actual quality of life and the possibilities of future opportunities decrease.

Beyond this commitment to modernity, the varied interpretations of "development" demonstrate the divided and specialized state of knowledge in "modern" society. The sociologist, the political scientist, the economist, and the ecologist see the development process through disciplinary lenses that are highly selective in what they reveal and what they screen out. The beneficiaries (or victims) of development may experience it quite differently from those who administer it or observe it selectively.[8]

Although the goals of development are to some extent conceptualized by sociologists and politicians, the means to development have been prescribed primarily by economists. The planners and administrators of development are frequently professional economists and almost invariably view the development task as an exercise in applied economics. The term "development" is often shorthand for "economic development." But the economics of development tend to be the partial and specialized theories of the industrial and commercial society that were transformed by Keynes and others into the macro-theories of national and international economic control. The political-economics

---

[6] See Apter, 1965; Black, 1966; Eisenstadt, 1966; Kahl, 1968; Rustow, 1967; and Weiner, 1966.

[7] The "classic" account of the destructive proclivities of traditional societies is *Man and Nature or Physical Geography as Modified by Human Action*, written by George Perkins Marsh and first published in 1864. A 1965 edition, edited by David Lowenthal, has been published by Harvard University Press. More comprehensive records of man's ecological impact are contained in Thomas, Jr., 1956; and Fraser Darling and Milton, 1966.

[8] But there are, of course, administrators and observers with a strongly "people-oriented" outlook: e.g., Lilienthal, 1964, pp. 9–14. The official viewpoint in the Roman Catholic Church on the subject of development has emphasized the welfare of people over economic considerations: e.g., Blanc, 1967, pp. 3–14. Similarly the World Council of Churches meeting in Uppsala, July 4–20, 1968, declared "the criteria of the human being" to be the central issue of development. See *Survey of International Development*, 5, August 15, 1968, p. 2; and June 15, 1968, p. 2, reporting on an ecumenical conference on world development.

of most modern states bear the imprint of thought that was formed under conditions that have been rapidly disappearing from the present-day world.[9]

The explosive growth of human populations and technologies, and the new perceptions of man and his environment derived from the behavioral and environmental sciences, have made "economic man" obsolete. It is not the science of economics that is at fault, but rather the disassociation of economic values from other aspects of life and their unequivocal elevation to a dominant and definitive role in development planning.[10]

[9] Some economic implications of the changing world are analyzed by Boulding, 1966; Galbraith, 1958; and Ward, 1966. A good general source for interpretations of development are the proceedings of the world conferences of the Society for International Development. Note especially the Sixth World Conference (1964).

[10] "Le développement, en effet, engage la totalité des sciences humaines et sociales. L'économie du développement deviendra nécessairement sous peine de sterilité ou de malfaisance, une discipline de synthèse utilisant avec l'économie, au sens étroit, la géographie, la géologie, l'éthnologie, la démographie, la sociologie, l'écologie, sans parler des diverses disciplines plus techniques comme l'agronomie, l'hydraulique, l'hygiène, l'urbanisme, l'administration, l'animation et bien d'autres.

"Si les facteurs dits extra-économiques sont désormais considérés comme aussi importants sinon plus pour le développement que les facteurs strictement économiques, c'est dire que l'integration des sciences sociales se fera moins par les collaborations au sommet entre spécialistes que dans l'opération indivisible du développement. C'est en oeuvrant ensemble, dans l'analyse multiforme et dans l'élaboration du plan de développement d'un pays ou d'un ensemble de pays, que les divers spécialistes trouveront les conditions optimales d'une coopération féconde.

"Les essais de simple juxtaposition d'économistes, de sociologues, d'agronomes, de biologistes et d'urbanistes par exemple, au sein d'une équipe dite de planification ne sauraient suffire. Il faut qu'il y ait fusion dans la discipline du développement, par le jeu des complémentarités réquises par une analyse de la structure sous tous les aspects." Commentary by Louis-Joseph Lebret in Austruy (1965, p. 321). *Cf.* Beckerman (1956, p. 108–15).

(EDITOR'S NOTE: The following is a rough English translation of the above.)

"Development, in effect, involves the totality of social and human sciences. Development economics must, therefore, necessarily become interdisciplinary, integrating economics with geography,

The successes of development owe little to the present state of development theory, at least as it is generally understood and applied. Conventional development theory is not adequate to improve the human condition in any fundamental and lasting way. When "development theory applied" relieves traditional societies from long-endured disabilities, it too often produces new social and physical ills. The so-called underdeveloped countries seem destined to repeat the mistakes of the developed nations, plus new errors of their own making. Modernity is contagious and although some traditional societies resist acculturation by the "developed" nations, the spread of science-based technological society seems inexorable. The human problems to which "development" is addressed cry for solutions. "Development" as it has evolved thus far has provided no more than partial and sometimes misguided solutions. A better concept or instrument for improving the human condition is needed.

Some of the ingredients of a more adequate concept are implicit in the discussion thus far and can now be stated explicitly. Regardless of the scope of development projects, the conceptual framework in which they are planned and implemented should

geology, ethnography, demography, sociology, ecology, not to mention various more technical disciplines such as agronomy, hydrology, public health, urban planning, public administration, motivational psychology, and many others.

"If the said extra-economic factors are henceforth considered as equally, if not more, important for development than the strictly economic factors, then the integration of the social sciences will operationally take place less by collaboration among specialists at the top than in the indivisible process of development. It is in working together, in the multi-faceted analysis and in the elaboration of a plan of development for a country or a group of countries that the various specialists will find the optimum conditions for fruitful cooperation.

"Attempts at simple juxtaposition of economists, sociologists, agronomists, biologists, and urban planners, for example, in the heart of a planning team will not be sufficient. A fusion has to take place in the discipline of development through the interplay of required complements from the analysis of the structure from all viewpoints."

be comprehensive. It is not in the actual development plans that comprehensiveness is needed, but in a preliminary surveillance of the field of possible action. What is actually attempted may be very limited and specific. Elaborate and far-reaching plans may easily exceed the capacity of an under-developed country. Comprehensiveness that exceeds administrative capabilities could result in both economic and ecological miscarriage of development efforts. Comprehensiveness is needed primarily to determine priorities and to reduce, so far as possible, the risks of inadvertent consequences (Waterston, September, 1967, and December, 1967). But the comprehensiveness should not be a theoretical "take everything into account" assessment that could indefinitely delay all action; it should be focused and refined to identify critical factors. Systematic methods for identifying these factors and estimating their importance are urgently needed, and some possibilities for obtaining them will be discussed in the concluding section of this paper. Meanwhile there is need to direct the attention of development economists to the potentialities and significance of ecological side effects.

Even when side effects have been recognized and considered, the full range of their significance has seldom been assessed. For example, W. W. Rostow (1965) omits any mention of ecological difficulties from a survey of "Unsolved Problems of International Development." He cautiously touches upon possibilities of allocating national economic resources to retard population growth, and he prescribes chemical fertilizers and insecticides to increase agricultural yields. But he does not relate these aspects of development to any coherent concept of ecological problems or side effects. Although A. O. Hirschman's retrospective review of World Bank development projects recognizes ecological hazards, such as the flowering and death of the Bamboo forests near the Karnaphuli pulp and paper mill in East Pakistan, the failure of the East African Groundnut Scheme, and the difficulties of the Uruguayan livestock and pasture improvement project (Brookings Institution, 1967), his treatment of the side effects of development is concerned primarily with social and political benefits. Nevertheless he does recognize the possibilities of negative side effects even though he does not emphasize them. "Spelling out the probabilities of such unwelcome side-effects," he observes, "could lead to a modification of the investment decision or at least to giving the project in question a lower priority rating" (Brookings Institution, 1967, pp. 145 and 174).

THE MECHANICS OF INTERNATIONAL DEVELOPMENT

The world-wide thrust of science-based information, commerce, and technology means that development everywhere, even through a would-be autarkic national enterprise, has international implications. The mechanics of international technical assistance are obviously shaped by the political context in which the process occurs. The critical point of action is the national government of a "developing" nation. In a world political structure based on the proposition that nations are sovereign, the aid-giving nation or international agency has a much more limited role in development decisions than an aid-receiving government.[11]

Development projects and programs normally evolve out of interaction between aid-givers and aid-receivers in which the givers can sometimes enlarge the scope of their initiative after negotiations are under way. The process, as Barbara Ward (1966, p. 106) describes it, is one of bargaining

[11] For a somewhat dated but, in principle, useful analysis see International Institute of Administrative Sciences, 1951.

in which the national state holds most of the strategic advantages:

Every U.N. organ—from the Security Council to each Specialized Agency—is a bargaining center and in spite of the very real and independent authority achieved by such effective agencies as the World Bank or the International Monetary Fund, they can only hope to influence their national directors. They cannot command their support. The final decisions lie with the bargain-makers at the national level. All this means that the hard, surviving centers of decision are still the nations. In spite of all their inadequacies as instruments of either security or abundance, they have not relinquished their claim. Everything above the national level, however necessary, however beneficial, can still be revoked, except of course, reality itself.

Reality can sometimes be an effective persuader. Where nations can obviously gain more from cooperation than from competition, international initiative on behalf of a development program may be feasible (see, for example, White, 1964, pp. 32–37). Regional propositions such as the Mekong River Project or the American Marshall Plan aid to Europe are examples. The "humiliation" implicit in an offer of aid appears to be obviated by the consideration: "If others are going to receive these benefits, why not we also?"

The steps in the initiation and execution of development plans or programs are often complex and have rarely, if indeed ever, been subject to detailed and comprehensive analysis.[12] Such analysis is surely necessary to discover or to document the causes of ecological miscalculations. In some cases the origin of error is obvious; but in more instances the effective causes are obscure even though the fundamental predisposing factors are not difficult to see and are even

glaringly evident in a wide range of development efforts.

There is a cybernetic character to the entire international development movement that is essential to any realistic understanding of its mechanics. Development concepts originate largely in the developed nations and are introduced through education, example, and deliberate transplantation into the underdeveloped nations. The results are then fed back to the developed states and to international agencies such as the World Bank, the United Nations Development Program, or the Food and Agriculture Organization. Thus, in large measure, the experts of the development aid agencies are called upon to review the backwash or echo of their own ideas. This feed-back process must be considered in objectively assessing the degree to which aid authorities must or should defer to the expressed wishes of aid-receiving authorities. National sovereignty, as has been noted, is a very major factor in the mechanics of international development. But the manner in which a nation's proposals often reflect ideas generated elsewhere should be kept in mind in appraising the possibilities for changing national attitudes and policies.

Competition among aid agencies (national and international) enlarges the options available to the developing nations. Aid-givers have been known to be motivated by political and bureaucratic considerations as well as by the stated purposes of their missions. Consequently, the independence of the authorities in an aid-receiving country is strengthened by the belief, for example, that the U.S.A. and the U.S.S.R. are both anxious to assist river development in their country, or that France and the FAO are both interested in sponsoring an agricultural development project. International competition thus lessens any compulsion on national officials to accept foreign advice that they would prefer to

[12] Retrospective examination of development mechanics has been undertaken by Hirschman, 1958a, 1958b. A formal and rather summary survey of development projects has been provided by King, 1967. For additional critiques see: Adler, 1966, pp. 159–64; and Waterston, 1965, 1966, pp. 85–91.

reject. Although interagency and international rivalries in aid-giving appear to have decreased, the possibility of their occurrence ought to be recognized as a potential obstacle to an ecological approach to international development (Symonds, 1968).

As the accomplishments and failures of international technical assistance are assessed, the inadequacy of its mechanics becomes increasingly apparent. In a preliminary report on a study of the capacity of the United Nations Development Program to deliver an increased volume of technical and preinvestment assistance to developing countries, Sir Robert Jackson declared that the existing system could not be allowed to continue (Campbell, 1968). The United Nations and its affiliated organizations have not been designed for the tasks that have emerged. The inchoate complexity of the structure of international development assistance, bilateral and multilateral, combines with the efforts of sovereignty and militant nationalism to frustrate and defeat rational efforts. Sir Robert observed that "if assistance was to become increasingly multilateral, it must be proved that the international system could function effectively, and the essential requirement for that was that international and national thinking should be brought into harmony . . ." (Campbell, 1968).

THE HAZARDS OF INTERNATIONAL DEVELOPMENT

The development process is hazardous, not only to ecological variety and stability in developing areas, but to the very objectives of development itself. The process of development holds certain built-in risks that must be recognized and, where possible, insured against if the prospects for favorable outcomes are to be maximized. There is good cause for attempting to maximize the possibilities for success in development, because the opportunities for failure are more abundant. Man's interposition in nature is more likely to be harmful than good because there is an infinite number of wrong answers to any given problem. Traditional societies and natural ecosystems have passed the evolutionary test of survival. It is conjectural whether man's deliberate manipulation of his culture and his environment will, in the aggregate, produce better results in human health, happiness, and survival than the results produced by trial and error extended over millennia. It is easy to be optimistic about the possibilities of development. Man *has* used knowledge of nature to improve upon nature in specific ways, but this book demonstrates that there have been notable failures as well as notable successes; and as the number and variety of interpositions increase, the probability of synergistic effects increases. Thus, demonstrable successes of development can lead societies toward an uncritical optimism unless the risks of the process are properly appraised.

If more than half of the development efforts were either ecologically neutral or beneficial they would not extenuate the harmful effects of the remaining efforts. Development efforts that are ecologically harmful in a minority of instances are nonetheless harmful. If the objective of development is lasting improvement in the human condition, then no ecologically damaging development schemes ought to be accepted.

This discussion should not suggest that slow-moving historical changes effected by man in his environment are always ecologically safe. As we have already noted, the historical record is filled with examples of environmental deterioration occurring over extended periods. Although historical man has often maintained and, for his own purposes, improved his environmental base (e.g., West Europe and Japan), a substantial number of development efforts are intended to correct inadvertent ecological abuses growing out of unwitting traditional practices. But whether to correct human errors or to remedy real or imagined deficiencies in nature, the development process has frequently shown itself able to make bad situations worse.

To criticize the inadequacy of development concepts should not suggest that adequate concepts are readily available, waiting to be adopted by conscientious planners. It is not scandalous to fall short of identifying or achieving optimality in development goals. The very concept of optimality is so difficult to deal with that some economists and planners reject it, considering it a goal as impractical as absolute zero or perpetual motion.[13] Yet optimality, as a qualitative goal, is rejected at the very high risk of substituting means for ends, of reifying abstractions such as gross national product into development objectives without adequate regard as to how the sought-for economic growth would *actually* effect the lives of people and their prospects for future happiness and survival.

We have already noted a circularity in the relationship of development concepts to development machinery. They are mutually reinforcing. Linear or simplistic perceptions of development needs lead to organizational arrangements designed to attack narrowed concepts of the problems without seriously considering the larger and more complex reality in which these problems are embedded. There is a human tendency to define problems in a way that corresponds to our ability to deal with them, rather than to define problems as they really are. To take the latter approach may delay action while the problem is being analyzed in all its significant ramifications. This delay may be ecologically sound but politically hazardous in instances where there is popular demand for "action now!" And once an organization has been structured and staffed

to meet problems in a certain way, it is very difficult for it to abandon the assumptions underlying its creation. The self-perpetuating character of development assumptions must thus be identified as a hazard of development. The creative role of development is thus subordinated to the more conventional tasks of program formulation and execution, while opportunity for a major reorientation of the approach to development is lessened by the drag of institutional inertia.

The political structure of international development and the pressure on aid-receiving national officials to produce quick and visible results combine to form a major hazard to ecologically sound development. For national leaders, occupational survival in their political milieu is a first-order priority. If they can protect themselves or advance their personal interests by advocating development projects which promise quick results and have a mass appeal, they can be expected to do so. The popularity and ostensible feasibility of the project tend to be the determining factors. The possibility of outside financial and technical assistance (from the World Bank, for example) is also a major determinant in most countries. The "practical" attitude toward ecological consequences (if they are even considered) is to meet them if and when they arise. "When they arise" usually means "when they become apparent." At this stage the ecological damage has probably already occurred. But the public official has taken what was for him the rational course. Had he opposed or delayed the new dam, the steel mill, or the land settlement project on the grounds that possible side effects might more than offset anticipated benefits, his arguments would have needed to be reinforced by convincing evidence that is seldom available because it is obviously not the kind of evidence that ambitious officials are likely to be seeking. People are easily persuaded to accept conjecture as evidence in

[13] *Cf.* Shell, 1967. See also Austruy, "Section II, Pour l'optimum," 1965, pp. 263–95.

support of the things that they want to do. They are equally ready to dismiss impatiently evidence as conjecture when it clouds the prospect of a cherished development scheme.

A major hazard of development is, therefore, the propagation of unwise plans. These plans are an aspect of political opportunism used as a response to the restless dissatisfaction of the people and the personal insecurities or ambitions of politicians. Too often the alleged public benefits of development are used to legitimize what are, in fact, projects promoted primarily for the political or economic advantage of an influential minority. In projects of this kind the ecological costs are seldom counted.

To obtain ecologically sound development planning, it is necessary to construct procedural or institutional barriers and channels to constrain the normal operations of human behavior. The public official must be protected against the stresses of his situation by methods that will force consideration of alternative solutions to the problems of development and will establish development criteria independent of his personal judgment.

A set of hard-to-untangle interrelating hazards to international development is found in efforts to apply scientific methods to the planning and execution of development tasks. If science were a high-priority value in underdeveloped countries, it is unlikely that they would in fact be underdeveloped. The development process suffers from the lack of regard for scientific method in the developing nations and from the specialized character of science itself, which, in its present state, is much better at reductionist analysis than at creative synthesis.

Scientific investigation and pre-project comprehensive review of alternatives seldom make "good politics." Preinvestment studies or careful ecological assessment of possible side effects do little to relieve the pressures on national leaders or to enhance their reputations. This relative indifference, and indeed resistance, to science as a way of thinking and working is, of course, a part of the syndrome of "underdevelopment" and a major factor in its persistence. Underdeveloped countries share the enthusiasm of more "advanced" states for techno-science spectaculars, but rarely do these political conversation pieces (reactors, high dams, national airlines) help a nation solve any of its fundamental problems—especially the ecological problems.[14]

In addition to the risks incurred by the omission of important scientific competencies are the difficulties of communication among the specialists who may be brought together. The task of synthesis among specialists is greatly complicated by the characteristically cross-cultural character of international development. Project teams in which nationalities and languages are mixed have linguistic and semantic problems of communication, in addition to professional differences of concept and terminology.

We have identified six areas of hazard to the development process. They are: (1) the greater statistical probability of error rather than success; (2) the overextension of optimism resulting from conceptual inadequacy; (3) the dysfunctional political structure of development; (4) opportunism —personal and political; (5) the disjunctive structure of scientific professionalism; and (6) barriers to communication—intercultural and subcultural. One cannot realistically assign magnitudes to the impact of these factors because they interact synergistically. But to the extent that the harmful effects of any of them can be lessened, the prospects for effectiveness in international development can be improved. The possibilities for an ecological approach to development are dependent upon the removal or amelioration of these hazards, and it is with these possibilities that the balance of this paper is concerned.

[14] See Blackett, 1963, pp. 30–31; and White, 1966, pp. 542–43.

POSSIBILITIES AND IMPLICATIONS

A premise of an ecological approach to development is that knowledge (facts) may reshape or redefine policy choices (values). It is a highly rational attitude toward human behavior and it contrasts with the here-and-now rationalism that often characterized the judgment of practical men. There is, however, a basis for conflict between a democratic ideology concerned with helping people get what they want (as interpreted by politicians) and an ecological concern with helping people get "what is good for them" (as "good" may be understood by scientists and planners).

To the extent that "development" is the application of science and technology to the physical and socioeconomic betterment of human life, a continuing reconciliation of science and politics has become essential for success. The task of applying science through the medium of politics is unavoidable because scientific knowledge is highly selective and incomplete. There are few instances in which science can be applied automatically and directly to human affairs. An intermediary stage of selective judgment is almost invariably required, in which values other than those confirmed by science will be weighed. The outcome of this judgmental procedure is an act of synthesis or, as Austruy puts it, an act of creation. An ecological policy for development becomes doubly difficult because, *first,* the task of synthesis has not been adequately understood or cultivated in the practice of contemporary science, politics, or public administration,[15] and *second,* the science of

ecology (potentially the most complex of all sciences) is itself underdeveloped.[16]

THE TWO STRATEGIES

The conclusion that follows from the difficulties of formulating science-based policies for ecologically sound development is that two strategies for change are required. A short-run, immediate, and adaptive strategy is needed to cope with conditions as they are. A long-run and reconstructive strategy is simultaneously necessary to establish the comprehensive goals of development and to discover and perfect the means necessary to their attainment. The destructive potential of development has become so great and the misapplications of science-based technology have become so common that better policies and procedures are urgently needed to reduce the extent of damage to the biosphere until a more adequate applied ecology can be provided. Very often these strategies would be negative, designed to prevent the foreclosure of future possibilities because of present, high-risk, irreversible decisions. It would be a cautionary strategy, applied where wisdom lies chiefly in knowing what ought to be avoided.

Short-run policies are intended to help to do the best that can be done, given the mixture of critical needs, perceptions, be-

---

[15] With reference to ". . . the problem of ecological balance and its disruption by human intervention . . . ," Pierre Auger (1964) writes that ". . . no clear doctrine has emerged as yet, such as a synthesis accompanied by an appropriate evaluation of the conditions in the near future" (p. 384). The task of synthesis in policy and adminis-

tration was stated with exceptional clarity in a letter to the author (May 6, 1953) by Paul H. Appleby following his return from a consultative mission to the government of India: "Specialist after specialist pursues analysis: who pursues synthesis, or even pursues analysis with any sensible orientation to the larger function of synthesis? It is the synthesis which involves all the heavy burdens of practitioners, and these burdens are heaviest when the social-action is most complex and most complexly environed. Synthesis becomes more and more important as one goes up the hierarchy, and more and more important as one moves from the relatively specialized fields of private administration to public administration."

[16] *Cf.* comments in Fraser Darling and Milton, 1966. pp. 291–98, 402–09.

havior patterns, and institutions that now prevail. This is an uphill, against-the-grain, holding-action strategy. It would not be adequate to insure man's ecological welfare or the future safeguarding of the biosphere. Simultaneously with the formulation of a short-run strategy, the foundations should be laid for a positive ecological approach to international development.

This positive approach is dependent upon perceptions and institutions that have yet to gain general acceptance. The way that people see a situation and the arrangements that they devise for dealing with it largely determine how the problems that it presents are solved. As Kenneth Boulding has remarked, people tend to see things as they do because it has paid them to see things that way. Because man's life is short and his wants are largely immediate, there is a natural tendency among individuals and governments to take a short-range and exploitive view of environmental opportunities. To obtain ecologically sound development policies it will ultimately be necessary to cause people to perceive their environments in ecologically valid terms. "In this regard," as C. A. O. Van Nieuwenhuijze (1961, p. 51) has observed, "we still have to unlearn a considerable amount of ethnocentrism and of simplistic evolutionism, but we need not fear that our lesson will not be brought home to us."

It will also be necessary to restructure the machinery of international technical assistance to maximize the probability of adequate consideration for ecological factors. The inadequacy of existing institutions to cope with a growing global crisis of the environment is now widely recognized. And yet the unlearning, and the shaping of new concepts and institutions to govern Spaceship Earth require time—more time than the accelerating deterioration of the biosphere may permit for "modern" man to survive. Thus, the crisis of the environment is simultaneously a crisis of beliefs and of

institutions. The dilemma of an ecological approach to international development cannot be resolved by a choice between making the present development system work better or constructing a better system.[17] Both approaches must be taken.

Short-Run Adaptive Strategies. Adaptive reform measures may be taken in each of three categories: (1) behavioral change, (2) determination of priorities, and (3) technical operations. Given our premise that development *is* an ecological process, it should be evident that these measures cannot be manipulated successfully independently of one another. Efforts may be concentrated on any one of them, but the others are inevitably affected.[18]

Behavioral change to improve ecological relationships implies education and training.[19] Educational efforts are needed for all age groups and all socioeconomic sectors of a population. The introduction of meaningful ecological concepts into public education in developing countries could be undertaken within existing educational structures. Emphasis in this effort would be on perception and understanding rather than on operational technique. Yet because the purpose of the education is to change (or perhaps to reinforce) behavior, the concepts taught should be clearly related to what people actually do. The training aspect of behavioral change would apply primarily to guiding the work of public officials and industrial personnel directly engaged in environment-affecting activities. But training in ecologically desirable methods and approaches presumes criteria for ecological

[17] Cf. John P. Milton's comment (1968, p. 5) on the institutional dilemma.

[18] For a more detailed treatment of the mechanisms and effects of adaptation see Shimkin, 1966. For a discussion of adaptation of biomedical knowledge and technique to developing countries and in relation to environmental conditions see the concluding pages of Dubos, 1965.

[19] Cf. Bowman, 1964, pp. 3–7. See also *Survey of International Development,* 5 (August 15, 1968), p. 1. See also articles in *Bioscience* 18 (1968) and the article by Jordan (1968), pp. 1023–29.

desirability (see Caldwell, 1966). Some concept of desirable man-environment relationships is therefore necessary as a basis for even simple routinized training efforts.

If the determination of priorities is to reflect sound and operational ecological judgment, a precondition must be the identification of the critical factors in the environmental situation. There is already enough experience over a wide range of development efforts to make feasible a gross estimate of probable dangers in most development plans. Better means of measuring and forecasting ecological changes are certainly needed, but the papers in this volume indicate that there is more sound ecological knowledge available than is being applied. As we have previously emphasized, a major value of ecological reconnaissance in development planning is to identify what should *not* be done. To avoid unnecessary foreclosure of future opportunity and to avoid unwanted irreversible effects may be more valuable accomplishments at this stage of development thinking than formulation of comprehensive ecologically oriented programs that may not be operational.

Most of the practical suggestions for more ecologically oriented development programs have to do with specific operational methods. Most frequently mentioned among these are preinvestment and feasibility studies, project selection and evaluation, guidelines, checklists, and post-audits. Among the tools of improved decision-making in development are cost-benefit analyses.[20] There are many ways of comparing costs with benefits, and the determination of what are, in fact, costs and benefits (and to whom) is one of the major problems of development planning. The difficulty of placing a quantifiable value on many aspects of ecology has been a major impediment to the ecological approach to de-

velopment. For instance, how does one evaluate the various costs of perpetual management of artificial ecosystems (for example, by irrigation) as against the opportunity costs of reliance upon the self-renewing capabilities and limitations of natural systems? Another technique intended to assist the setting of priorities is the comparison of specific aspects of social conditions and natural resources development among a number of countries at various stages of development (Frederiksen, 1967).

Long-Run Reconstructive Strategies. Even if these incremental reforms were accomplished, major institutional difficulties would stand in the way of an ecological approach to international development. There are a large number of ecological problems now emerging that cannot easily be dealt with under existing institutional arrangements. More problems will appear as populations increase, and science and technology, in effect, shrink the size of the earth and increase the interdependency of all peoples. Some of these problems concern the use of the oceans and the upper atmosphere and are beyond effective jurisdiction of national governments. Other problems arise out of conditions and events within the territorial jurisdiction of particular national states that could adversely affect the globe.

The pre-emption of the entire globe by human society has caused it to become, in practical effect—if not in theoretical fact—a closed system. The planetary ecosystem, or biosphere, does, of course, receive inputs of energy from outer space, and men can leave it for short periods by carrying a fabricated life-support system with them. But for the great majority of the practical purposes of men, the constraints of the biosphere are those of a closed system. Until the twentieth century, men and nations could act as if the system were infinite. But now that possibility is gone forever. A totally new human condition has been created, and neither the attitudes nor institutions of men are well-

[20] *Cf.* Dorfman, 1965. For a discussion of limitations of the technique as applied in the United States see Maass, 1966, pp. 208–26; and for developing countries see Hirschman, 1958a, pp. 174–80.

adapted to meet its challenges. The nation-state system of political organization has become anachronistic in the emergent era of Spaceship Earth. As Charles Yost (1967) has forcefully asserted, the obsolete institutions of the nation-state system threaten the peace of the world and the very survival of civilization and humanity.

There is widespread dissatisfaction with the present state of international development effort,[21] and there is growing concern for the state of the biosphere (UNESCO, 1969).[22] Efforts toward institutional reform are under way on behalf of both development and global ecology. But the organizing political doctrines needed to give firm shape and direction to these efforts have not yet become clear. If the analogy of the spaceship is valid, we may conclude that a universal political order is needed that does not require men either to love or to associate with one another but does restrain their overt conduct in relation to one another and to their environment. The basic rules of conduct for passengers of a ship might afford a realistic and practical model for organizing institutions for world-wide environmental control.

Fortunately, international efforts that could lead toward a global system for protection of the biosphere have already been undertaken.[23] Clearly during the past quarter century there has been an unplanned, unstructured trend toward an international decision to establish world-wide policies and operational procedures for protecting and managing the life-support system of the earth. The Biosphere Conference of 1968 stated the issue explicitly.[24] It recommended (Recommendation 14)

. . . that Member States and governing bodies of all United Nations organizations develop comprehensive and integrated policies for management of the environment, and that international efforts and problems be considered in the formulation of such policies. (UNESCO, 1969)

The resolution specified nine aspects of the application of science and technology to the

---

[21] Cf. *Survey of International Development,* October 15, 1967; and the references to the comments of Sir Robert Jackson, 1959; Jan Tinbergen, 1968; Pierre Auger, 1964; and others.

[22] See also *Resolution 2398* (XXIII) adopted "without objection" at the 1733rd Plenary Session. See also U. N. Economic and Social Council (1968) on the question of convening an international conference on the problems of human environment.

[23] Listed in chronological order they are:

1. 1945. Establishment of the United Nations Organization, UNESCO, and FAO.

2. 1946. Establishment of the World Health Organization.

3. 1948. Establishment of the International Union for the Conservation of Nature and Natural Resources following an international conference sponsored by UNESCO and the Government of France.

4. 1949. United Nations Scientific Conference on the Conservation and Utilization of Resources. Lake Success, New York, August 17 to September 6.

5. 1955. International Technical Conference on the Conservation of the Living Resources of the Sea. Rome, April 18 to May 16.

6. 1956. Establishment of the International Atomic Energy Agency.

7. 1957–1958. International Geophysical Year.

8. 1958. Adoption of the Geneva Convention (Treaty) on Fishing and Conservation of the Living Resources of the High Seas.

9. 1959. Antarctic Treaty signed December 1 establishing the South Polar region as an international scientific reserve.

10. 1963. Conference on Application of Science and Technology for the Benefit of Less Developed Areas. Geneva, February 4 to February 20.

11. 1964. Inauguration of the International Biological Program.

12. 1966. International Treaty on the Peaceful Use of Outer Space promulgated.

13. 1967. Implementation of World Weather Watch, under sponsorship of the World Meteorological Organization.

14. 1968. UNESCO Intergovernmental Conference of Experts on the Scientific Basis for Rational Use and Conservation of the Resources of the Biosphere. Paris, September 4 to September 13.

15. 1968. United Nations General Assembly Resolution 2398 (December 3) on the Problems of Human Environment.

16. 1970. Establishment of the Scientific Committee on Problems of the Environment (SCOPE) by the International Council of Scientific Unions.

[24] Coolidge (1968), pp. 65–66, 72. See also UNESCO (1968), pp. 414–18. For the ecological thinking underlying the Biosphere Conference see UNESCO and FAO (initial draft by Raymond F. Dasmann), 1968. For a discussion of the report see *Nature and Resources,* 4 (1968), pp. 2–5.

management of the environment for which policies were needed. Several of these implied new administrative structures and procedures. Number 8, among these, called for

the establishment of an appropriate structure and mechanism to assure periodic and comprehensive review of policy and with authority, responsibility and resources to readjust guidelines and goals and to make deletions, revisions, and realignments in action programmes, based upon empirical experience, scientific and technological advance, and changes in national or world conditions. (UNESCO, 1969)

The Biosphere Conference also suggested (Recommendation 17) that the United Nations General Assembly might consider the advisability of a Universal Declaration on the Protection and Betterment of the Human Environment.

The United Nations General Assembly Resolution on the Problems of the Human Environment (December 3, 1968) marks a new stage in the growth of international policy for the biosphere. Believing it desirable to provide a framework for comprehensive consideration within the United Nations of the problems of human environment in order to focus the attention of governments and public opinion on the importance and urgency of the issue and to identify those aspects of it that can only, or best, be solved through international cooperation or agreement, the Assembly proposed to convene in 1972 a United Nations Conference on Human Environment.

Although the outcome of the Conference cannot be foreseen, some of the problems and issues with which it will almost certainly be concerned are evident. Among them are the status and protection of the oceans, the atmosphere, and the polar regions; the protection of endangered species of plants and animals; and the threats to the viability of the biosphere posed by the indiscriminate or unwise use of technology. It is highly probable that the Conference

will lead to the formulation of new provisions or principles of international law and to the establishment of new international administrative responsibilities. But the machinery of international negotiation moves slowly, and measures now in gestation may not be born in time to prevent ecological crises in one or more areas of the earth. International conferences and agencies must respect the conventional assumptions of the sovereignty of nations, and accordingly there are propositions, which, because they are inconsistent with national-state ideology, cannot easily be placed on their agendas. How, for example, would the community of nations deal with a national government that either threatened the viability of the biosphere through ecologically unwise action within its own territorial jurisdiction or mismanaged its environment to a point of collapse of its social and economic institutions. In such circumstances, which become less hypothetical daily, some generally acceptable means of international intervention would be advantageous.

There is need for a legitimized and effective means through which international action may be interposed to prevent, or to take into receivership, cases of national ecological bankruptcy. At the very least, some means is needed whereby a national government, without loss of respect, could ask for and obtain international administration of its natural resource base and its resource-based economy. Total collapse of a natural resource base in relation to human need is unlikely, but less unlikely now than in the past. Yet in many countries today, the life-support system of soil, water, air, minerals, and living things is being stressed to a degree that could result in the failure of one or more critical components. The most probable failures are the familiar ones of food or water supply, but bio-chemical manipulation of the environment could result in disastrous miscalculations through which uncontrolled quantities of insects, microorganisms, or toxic substances would be propagated in the ecosystem. But the most widespread cause of "ecological bankruptcy" may be the gradual wearing-out of the environment—the stressing of natural systems beyond their capacity for regeneration. As the viability of the resource base diminishes in relation to the demands upon it, and the margin available to compensate for misfortune lessens, an unexpected failure at some critical point in the economy or ecology of a nation could conceivably trigger the collapse of the human socio-ecological system.

Advanced nations may be as vulnerable as underdeveloped ones to this type of catastrophe, but they might be better able to take unassisted remedial action. In any case, an international organization able to cope with large-scale environmental disasters is becoming an increasingly practical proposition in a closed-system, interdependent world. If the prospect of "ecological bankruptcy" is seriously considered and timely action taken, the disaster may not occur. However, the uncertainty of the nature, scope, and timing of ecological disaster makes difficult the development of an effective operational plan for coping with it. Nevertheless, the need for an international organization to mobilize and direct measures to remedy ecological disaster is sufficiently obvious to justify its establishment at an early date.

FUNDAMENTAL AND CONTINUING PROBLEMS. If a strategy for international environmental control is to achieve the clarity of objective and the breadth of acceptance necessary to make it an effective instrument of policy, it will be necessary to extend the present area of agreement concerning *need* to the larger field of appropriate *action*. Here it will become necessary to confront some fundamental behavioral and psychological problems that must be somehow overcome if international environmental control is to become a reality. These problems are primarily those of attitudes and values as implemented through politics.

The most immediately apparent of these problems is the *design and legitimization of international institutions for environmental policy*. The concept of the absolute territorial sovereignty of nations presently stands squarely athwart any prospect for international administrative action within the boundaries of national states where ecological damage occurs or originates. If national prerogatives over territory are to be modified, an acceptable plan or principle must be available to compensate, at least psychologically, for what the nation believes it has relinquished. Reorientation and enlargement of the environmental missions of existing international organizations are the most probable courses of institutional development, with the exception of jurisdiction over the high seas. Certain aspects of the global environment are already within the defined missions of international agencies (the weather for example—a concern of the World Meteorological Organization). The living resources of the sea have been a concern of the Food and Agriculture Organization and of UNESCO. Proposals have been made to establish United Nations sovereignty over the open sea and the deep seabed and to utilize the resources of the sea, or revenues derived from their exploitation, primarily for assistance to the less-developed countries.[25] Hopefully, U.N. jurisdiction would bring a greater measure of protection to marine ecology already jeopardized by excessive harvesting of fish, whales, and other forms of marine life and by pollution. But it is equally important that funds derived from wiser use of the sea be applied with no

[25] *Survey of International Development*, V (April 15, 1968), p. 2. See also *U. N. Monthly Chronicle*, VI (January, 1969), pp. 56–62, and for background, Luther J. Carter, "Deep Seabed 'Who Should Control It?' U. N. Asks," *Science*, CLIX (January 5, 1968), pp. 66–68, and Victor Basiuk, "Marine Resources Development, Foreign Policy, and the Spectrum of Choice," *Orbis*, XII (Spring, 1968), pp. 39–72.

less wisdom to development efforts on land.

The organization most specifically concerned with the state of the biosphere on a continuing basis has been the International Union for the Conservation of Nature and Natural Resources (IUCN). The International Biological Program sponsored by the International Council of Scientific Unions and the UNESCO Man and the Biosphere Program are no less concerned with the state of the biosphere, but their efforts are largely directed toward specific research objectives rather than constituting indefinitely continuing efforts, especially in relation to the promotion of ecological awareness in the less-developed countries.

The quasi-official status of the IUCN— governments, private organizations, and individuals support its work—has mixed consequences. It may act on some issues with greater freedom than might be possible if its deliberations were determined by the political authorities of sponsoring states. And yet members of the IUCN working commissions, and delegates to its triennial general assemblies, cannot be assumed to be unmindful of political attitudes and feasibilities in their home countries. Pierre Auger contends that the IUCN and similar bodies are not effectual because of their inability to follow up on their recommendations. But this is in varying degrees the weakness of international organizations generally, especially those that have no means, through finances or favors, of inducing nations to follow their advice. Moreover, the IUCN has, in fact, been successful in more than a few international negotiations. Yet as Fairfield Osborn declared at the 7th Triennial Assembly of IUCN, perhaps its most vital function ". . . is to stimulate action by the public and by governments."[26] The strategy for effectiveness in the work of the IUCN would appear to be to strengthen its official character (and concomitantly its financial base)

[26] *AIBS Bulletin,* XI (February, 1961), p. 23.

without sacrificing its "independent" status —an effort that is now being undertaken. In addition to its relationships with national governments, its status in relation to the United Nations group of organizations and to the international scientific unions needs to be clarified and further strengthened if it is to meet the need that the growing worldwide ecological crisis presents.

A second problem area extends beyond ecology into all aspects of modern society and politics. It is the problem of *obtaining a political leadership capable of inducing rational behavior in peoples and governments.* An ecological approach to developmental issues is by implication rational. But rationality has seldom been the distinguishing characteristic of political leadership anywhere, and particularly in the developing nations. Given the limitations of human intelligence and adaptability, charismatic leadership may be necessary to bring societies through periods of social and technological transition. This leadership is not inclined toward respect for facts or science if they embarrass what it believes to be politically necessary. Prestige-gathering development projects have been used to promote the careers of many political leaders in all nations. It is understandable that these leaders are not eager to hear discouraging words about the prospects of politically advantageous projects, however dubious their ultimate ecological effects may be. What is needed is some means for making ecological good sense political good sense, and for finding ways of inducing political behavior that will confirm this relationship in action.

Third and fourth problem areas are the interrelated areas of *optimal population size and distribution* and *optimal environmental conditions.* The very concept of optimality becomes controversial when applied broadly to social issues. Adherents of absolutist ideologies reject it, convinced democrats dislike it, and many scientists view it as normative, *ergo* unscientific. Nevertheless, the concept is necessary. Whatever its epistemological deficiencies, it is necessary to find verifiable meaning in the concept if some of the most urgent problems of human ecology are to be coped with and hopefully resolved. Human numbers and distributions have become the greatest single world-wide ecological problem. If a world-wide population policy emerges, as one surely must, it will make a great difference whether it is based on broad ecological values or primarily upon the availability of food supply and shelter. Proponents of an ecological approach to international development must face the issue of optimal population or be prepared to settle for a future in which the biosphere is completely dominated by human necessities and the natural environment is progressively impoverished.[27] The problem of optimality in man-environment relationships is extremely complex, and its solutions will probably comprise a range of relationships to accommodate the varied needs and values of people. But it is a problem that any serious effort toward an international policy for the biosphere cannot ignore.

CONCLUSION

A final problem area is perhaps the most important and difficult. It is certainly the most fundamental because it is no less than the outlook of man on the quality of life and his relationship to the living world. If the beliefs and attitudes of men toward the biosphere were consistent with ecological

realities, the institutional and political problems that we have described could much more easily be resolved. Without fundamental psychological and behavioral change on the part of large numbers of peoples and governments, institutional changes, even though they occurred, would be limited in effect by the unwillingness of people to accept them. But it is through institutional mechanisms for public information, education, politics, law, and administration that beliefs and behavior are changed. And so the areas of reconstructive strategy that have been described must be simultaneously considered and acted upon as interrelating aspects of man's management of his life on earth. The construction of an international order for the human environment has now become an imperative task of philosophy and politics. It was this task of which the United States Ambassador to the United Nations, Adlai Stevenson, spoke when, in his final address in 1965 at the 39th Session of the U. N. Economic and Social Council, he said:

We travel together, passengers on a little space ship, dependent on its vulnerable reserves of air and soil; all committed for our safety to its security and peace; preserved from annihilation only by the care, the work, and I will say the love we give our fragile craft. (U.N., 1965)

When one perceives the world as a heavily stressed ecological system—the Spaceship Earth concept—the need for international measures to protect its life-sustaining capability becomes obvious. The primary threat to man's survival is now the uninhibited or misdirected behavior of man himself. The behavior of individuals has to a considerable extent been guided, and misguided, by the institutions of custom, law, and government. The behavior of national governments, however, remains largely unguided by any higher authority, unguided by an ecologically valid assessment of environmental potentialities, advantages, and limitations. The attitude of the unrestricted right of na-

---

[27] Note for example the comments of Jean-Michel von Gundertael, "People and Food in the Year 2000," *World Health,* (March, 1968), pp. 25–30. But more than ecological values are threatened, the possibilities for domestic and international peace are endangered by the social and economic inequalities that appear to be beyond the capacity of the most far-reaching development efforts to overcome. Cf. J. E. Mead, "Population Explosion: The Standard of Living and Social Conflict," *The Economic Journal,* LXXVIII (June, 1967), pp. 233–55.

Lynton K. Caldwell

945

tional decision, regardless of international consequences, has been harmful to human welfare in many respects and has been a major obstacle to world peace. Not all, but many of the disasters described in the earlier chapters of this book could have been averted had it not been for the willfulness of nations and the inadequacy or the present disjunctive system of international development to assist them to make ecologi-

cally sound analyses of development plans. As Jan Tinbergen (1968, p. 20) declares: "Other disasters will follow unless we recognize the need for international order." And I would add that this recognition must occur through action. It is not a mystery that confronts the human race; it is rather a challenge to justify its own pretensions to suzerainty over the earth.

REFERENCES

Adler, John H. "What Have We Learned About Development." *Finance and Development*, 3 (September, 1966).

Apter, David. *The Politics of Modernization.* Chicago: University of Chicago Press, 1965.

Aron, Raymond. *Industrial Society: Three Essays on Ideology and Development.* New York: Praeger, 1967.

Auger, Pierre. "Plan of an Institute of Studies for the Better Utilization of the Globe." *The Population Crisis and the Use of World Resources.* Bloomington: Indiana University Press, 1964.

Austruy, Jacques. *Le Scandale du Développement.* Paris: Éditions Marcel Rivière, 1965.

Beckerman, W. "The Economist as a Modern Missionary." *Economic Journal,* 66 (March, 1956).

Bioscience, 18 (September, 1968). Whole issue.

Black, C. E. *The Dynamics of Modernization.* New York: Harper & Row, 1966.

Blackett, P. M. S. "Sensible Shopping in the Supermarket of Science." *UNESCO Courier,* 16 (July, 1963).

Blanc, Ed. "Les voies du développement des peuples." *Economie et Humanisme,* 176 (July–August, 1967).

Boulding, Kenneth. "The Economics of the Coming Spaceship Earth." In *Environmental Quality in a Growing Economy,* Henry Jarrett, ed. Baltimore: Johns Hopkins Press for Resources for the Future, 1966.

Bowman, Mary Jean. "Perspectives on Education and Development." *International Development Review,* 6 (September, 1964).

Brookings Institution. *Development Projects Observed.* Washington: Brookings Institution, 1964 and 1967.

Caldwell, Lynton K. "Problems of Applied Ecology Perceptions: Institutions; Methods and Operational Tools." *Bioscience,* 16 (August, 1966).

Campbell, Persia. "United Nations Report: The UNDP Tools up for the Second Development Decade." *International Development Review,* 10 (December, 1968).

Coolidge, Harold J. "World Biosphere Conference: A Challenge to Mankind." *IUCN Bulletin, New Series,* 2 (October–December, 1968).

De Vries, Egbert. "A Review of Literature on Development Theory 1957–1967." *International Development Review,* 10 (March, 1968).

Dorfman, Robert, ed. *Measuring Benefits of Government Investments.* Washington: Brookings Institution, 1965.

Dubos, René. *Man Adapting.* New Haven: Yale University Press, 1965.

Eisenstadt, S. N. *Modernization: Protest and Change.* Englewood Cliffs, N.J.: Prentice-Hall, 1966.

Fraser Darling, F., and Milton, John P., eds. *Future Environments of North America.* New York: Natural History Press, 1966.

Frederiksen, Harold. "Profiles of Relative Development." *International Development Review,* 9 (December, 1967).

Friedrich, C. J., ed. *Nomos V.* New York: Atherton Press, 1962.

Galbraith, John Kenneth. "How Much Should a Country Consume." In *Perspectives on Conservation,* Henry Jarrett, ed. Baltimore: Johns Hopkins Press for Resources for the Future, 1958.

————. *Economic Development in Perspective.* Cambridge: Harvard University Press, 1962.

Goulet, Denis A. "Development for What?" *Comparative Political Studies,* 1 (July, 1968).

Hirschman, A. O. *Development Projects Observed.* New Haven: Yale University Press, 1958a.

————. *The Strategy of Economic Development.* New Haven: Yale University Press, 1958b.

Hoselitz, Bert F. "Agrarian Societies in Transition." *Annals of the American Academy of Political and Social Science,* 305 (May, 1956).

International Institute of Administrative Sciences. *National Administration and International Organization: A Comparative Survey of Fourteen Countries.* Report of an Inquiry Conducted by the International Institute of Administrative Sciences and UNESCO. Brussels, 1951.

Jackson, Sir Robert G. A. *The Case for an International Development Authority.* Syracuse, N.Y.: Syracuse University Press, 1959.

Jordan, P. A. "Ecology, Conservation and Human Behavior." *Bioscience,* 18 (November, 1968).

Kahl, Joseph A. *The Measurement of Modernism. A Study of Values in Brazil and Mexico.* Austin and London: University of Texas Press, 1968.

King, John A. *Economic Development Proj-*ects and Their Appraisal: Cases and Principles from the Experience of the World Bank.* Baltimore: Johns Hopkins Press, 1967.

Lilienthal, David E. "The Road to Change." *International Development Review,* 6 (December, 1964).

Maass, Arthur. "Benefit-Cost Analyses: Its Relevance to Public Investment Decisions." *Quarterly Journal of Economics,* 80 (May, 1966).

Marsh, George Perkins. (David Lowenthal, ed.) *Man and Nature or Physical Geography as Modified by Human Action.* Cambridge: Harvard University Press, 1965.

Milton, John P. "Resources in America: The Coming Crisis." *Population Reference Bureau* Selection No. 23. Washington: Population Reference Bureau, 1968.

Montgomery, John D. (Carl Friedrich, ed.) "Public Interest in the Ideologies of National Development." *Public Interest. Nomos V.* New York: Atherton Press, 1962.

Nature and Resources. UNESCO, Vol. 4, No. 2 (June, 1968).

Nedelcovic, Bosco. "Fallacies of Conventional Approaches to Development." *International Development Review,* 7 (December, 1965).

Papanek, Gustav F., ed. *Development Policy: Theory and Practice.* Cambridge: Harvard University Press, 1968.

Riggs, Fred. W. *Administration in Developing Countries: The Theory of Prismatic Society.* Boston: Houghton Mifflin, 1964.

Rostow, W. W. "Unsolved Problem of International Development." *International Development Review,* 7 (December, 1965), 15–18.

Rustow, Dankwart A. *A World of Nations.* Washington: Brookings Institution, 1967.

Shell, Karl, ed. *Essays on the Theory of Optimal Growth.* Cambridge, Mass.: MIT Press, 1967.

Shimkin, Demitri B. "Adaptive Strategies: A Basic Problem in Human Ecology." *Three Papers on Human Ecology,* Mills College Assembly Series 1965–1966. Oakland, Calif.: Mills College, 1966.

Society for International Development. *Motivations and Methods in Development and Foreign Aid: Proceedings of the Sixth World Conference*—March 16–18, 1964. Washington, 1964.

Survey of International Development. October 15, 1967 (whole issue); June 15, 1968, August 15, 1968, September, 1968, Vol. 6 (whole issue); November, 1968, Vol. 6 (whole issue).

Symonds, Richard. "The Relationship Between Multilateral and Bilateral Programs of Technical Assistance." *International Development Review,* 10 (March, 1968).

Thomas, William L., Jr., ed. *Man's Role in Changing the Face of the Earth.* Chicago: University of Chicago Press, 1956.

Tinbergen, Jan. "The Way Out of the Labyrinth." *Ceres,* 1 (May–June, 1968).

UNESCO. "International Conference on the Biosphere." *UNESCO Chronicle,* 14 (November, 1968).

———. Final Report. Intergovernmental Conference of Experts on the Rational Use and Conservation of the Resources of the Biosphere: Unesco House, Paris, September 4–13, 1968. SC/MD/9–Paris (January 6, 1969).

UNESCO and FAO. Report Submitted to the Economic and Social Council of the United Nations: *Conservation and Rational Use of the Environment.* New York: Economic and Social Council, U.N. (E/4458, March 12, 1968).

United Nations. U. N. Economic and Social Council. Official Records 39th Session, June 30–July 31, 1965. P. 90.

———. Economic and Social Council Resolution 1346 (XLV), July 30, 1968.

Van Nieuwenhuijze, C. A. O. *Research for Development in the Mediterranean Basin:* A Proposal. The Hague: Mouton, 1961.

Ward, Barbara. *Spaceship Earth.* New York: Columbia University Press, 1966.

Waterston, Albert. *Development Planning: Lessons of Experience.* Baltimore: Johns Hopkins Press, 1965.

———. "A Hard Look at Development Planning." *Finance and Development,* 3 (June, 1966).

———. "Pinpointing the Aims of Planning Administration." *Finance and Development,* 4 (December, 1967).

———. "Public Administration for What?" *Finance and Development,* 4 (September, 1967).

Weiner, M., ed. *Modernization.* New York: Basic Books, 1966.

White, Gilbert F. "Rivers of International Concord." *UNESCO Courier,* 18 (July–August, 1964).

White, Stanley. "Status Symbol or Stimulus." *New Scientist,* 30 (May 26, 1966).

Yost, Charles. *The Insecurity of Nations: International Relations in the Twentieth Century.* New York: Praeger, 1967.

DISCUSSION

CARLOZZI: In the case of the Caribbean, so much fits the notion that these small countries, often with newly assumed autonomy, actually can't maintain themselves. They can't make many relevant internal decisions that affect their very lives. The processes by which they are degraded are processes which are forced upon them by more developed nations.

In the absence of any institutions by which we can monitor our own behavior and can continue to respect the existence and aspirations of those people, I don't think those islands can long persist without great tragedy. Dr. Borgstrom's comment about population growth is particularly significant. Barbados already has 1,500 people per square mile and a growth rate that is about 2.8. There is just no room for expansion.

For those areas which are now fragmented, separated, mutually competitive, there is nothing but trouble waiting in the future, I think.

FOSBERG: If you are going to have global ecological planning that has any effect whatever, you are going to have to face up to the obvious need for some measure of world government. Perhaps things like the Antarctic Treaty and the proposed agency to look after the ocean may be steps in that direction. Such government has to have more than just a planning function. It has to be able to act as a world policeman. Otherwise it will be just an exercise in futility.

Commenting on the proposed receivership for ecologically bankrupt nations, I would say if we are going to wait until they are completely ecologically bankrupt, that also will be an exercise in futility. Take the case of Dominica. I don't think this island is ecologically bankrupt yet, although it is in financial difficulties, but if we could have such a receivership or something to oversee what is going on now, we might conceivably avert ecological bankruptcy. But if we wait until it happens, there is not going to be much of the environment left to save.

I was able to talk to the Mekong Advisory Commission almost two years ago. They admitted, after being a little bit scared by my comments, that certainly they should investigate the ecological consequences of what they were doing. However, they quickly added that, of course, construction money couldn't be spent for this. They would be happy to help somebody find some money to do this study but construction money couldn't be used.

At a recent Mekong seminar I asked about the relative amounts of money that had been spent on engineering planning, economic planning, ecological planning and sociological planning. I recall they admitted that some $11 million had been spent on engineering feasibility and quite a bit on economic planning. Thirty-five thousand dollars had been spent on sociology. Nothing significant had been spent on ecological planning. This means that traditional engineering practices still hold sway. And traditionally, the engineers have simply not included ecology or sociology in their scheme of values.

One other very brief comment. The matter of the Corps of Engineers coming around advancing alternatives may be fine but, being fundamentally suspicious of the Corps of Engineers, I would suspect they would put their alternatives in as smoke screens or red herrings rather than sincere alternatives that could offer people any choice other than what the engineer wants to do.

HEDGPETH: Well, the Corps of Engineers, bless them! We have been here now going on the third day and education has just been mentioned. I would like to put something in the record that was expurgated in 1947 at the National Wildlife Conference in San Antonio. We had a discussion of dam problems. I stated that one of the problems is that the engineers are not getting adequate education. To put it more bluntly, biology and ecology are not being taught at West Point.

As I say, that didn't get into the record. Of course, I am not sure it would have done any good. But this does bring up a problem. I read about a recent curriculum for engineers in which they would take, by concession, a new, "high falutin'" correspondence course in biology.

Even if biology were taught, the fashion now is in genetics and molecular biology, which are not too useful for the practical understanding of the consequences of building a dam or digging a ditch. We must concede that education is a very slow process and maybe we don't have time for it. However, in listening to descriptions of these catastrophes I have the uneasy feeling that many projects are being run by biological illiterates.

As far as costs are concerned, I brought up the fact that an architect gets 10 per cent of the cost of the building in some states and countries. In other places it is around 6 per cent. If a company plans to build a $100 million power plant, we could do very well with $10 million to investigate the possible effects. In fact, we could do with considerably less, but we're not getting it. Those responsible are not spending money on these aspects. It occurred to me in reading Gilbert White's paper that there is no clear policy that ecologists will be drawn into these projects or that their advice will be taken or acted upon.

This is a key problem in many situations. They will listen to us and say: "Well, you boys don't live in the real world. We don't believe those fairy stories." So we come back again to the urgent necessity to change people's basic attitudes.

CAIRNS: There are two small things each of us might do that would have immediate benefit. First, we can cease to tolerate multidisciplinary reports that are compartmented. Most multidisciplinary studies that I have seen have had a report by a geologist, then a biologist, then a chemist, and so forth with only a superficial attempt to interrelate the reports. I don't think we should tolerate this any more. We should force these people to write a single report so that the uninformed reader isn't forced to integrate the knowledge. This would have immediate benefits.

The second is to break down departmental barriers in the universities.

WHITE: I hope you know how to do that.

CAIRNS: I don't know how to do it. (Laughter.)

But, if one controls grant funds it should be possible. I never had any money!

We should sufficiently break down the traditional discipline orientation in most universities to allow for, at least, some student training to be problem-oriented. It should be possible for a biologist to take a course in economics without going through so many prerequisite courses that he becomes an old man.

All of us can help eliminate these barriers

so that it will be possible for a student to emerge from a university having some idea of the problems and operational prerequisites of other disciplines.

ABRAHAMSON: Having been trained in engineering earlier, I can perhaps comment on it. The training has no reality whatsoever. Engineers say they are dealing with the real world. They are not. There is no systematic or unsystematic effort to educate the engineering profession in accordance with its real responsibilities. Yet, the engineers and their equivalents in the financial world are generating most development plans themselves and in doing so they are also making the real decisions. The engineering profession had not yet become socially and environmentally responsible.

I would like to mention a second point. Two conflicting things keep turning up. One is the problem of formal education, and the other is the problem of no time. What *is* the time scale involved here? Is there going to be a catastrophic crisis of some kind in eight or ten or twenty years, or not? Is there time for education or not?

It would seem the strategy that is adopted has to reflect the answer to this question. If you have one hundred years to educate, the means of going about it would be quite different than if you have only twenty years.

CALDWELL: Certainly we need various strategies in education. I think we need multiple strategies. We certainly need basic education, and yet we don't have time to delay other effective action until we have a significant number of the people in this world that are ecologically oriented.

On the other hand, unless we have sound environmental education, we will not be able to make the kinds of reforms we are talking about stick. They will not be properly implemented if there is not understanding.

As several of you have said, the fate of most ecological critiques of development plans is to be put on a shelf some place because the people that were chosen to implement them usually don't understand them; they felt they were just not useful. We therefore must recognize that action and education are not really conflicting viewpoints. They are both consistent with the rather complex timing needed to change the whole process.

DREWES: In the development operations carried out by the Organization of American States four phases of survey intensities have been recognized:

a) The reconnaissance survey, b) The preinvestment investigation, c) the feasibility study and finally d) the detailed engineering designs. In one form or another most development projects undergo this series of treatments. It would be advantageous to all concerned if ecological factors are given their due consideration in each study phase.

The Rio Plata Development Project, a river basin project which may eventually be as important to Latin America as the Mekong Project is to Asia, is now in its initial phase of studies. In carrying out natural resource reconnaissance surveys, the ecological factors will be given consideration and every attempt will be made to incorporate this trend into the more detailed feasibility and engineering design phases of the project. However, acceptance of the inclusions of ecological factors or studies will depend largely on the funds and priorities established by the lending agencies.

In regard to ecologically bankrupt nations, I would like to nominate Haiti as deserving special attention. Haiti is subject to a vicious circle in the development process. Six or seven years ago most international lending agencies apparently abandoned that country, thinking that the economic and political situation there was so difficult that nothing could be done.

Today the U.N. has only a small program there dealing with social problems. The A.I.D. mission abandoned almost all of its operations. The Inter-American Development Bank and the International Bank of Reconstruction and Development have very modest programs going on and the Organization of American States has had limited funds for actually carrying out projects in Haiti in the past few years. Only recently have the Haitians again requested assistance, this time from the Inter-American Committee for the Alliance for Progress. The international agencies insist on certain administrative and fiscal changes before they will again become involved in Haitian development projects. Some of these recommendations may not even be very costly, yet the Haitians have absolutely no funds to carry out institutional or other changes, consequently the vicious circle is complete. The international problem has led to a stalemate. What will be Haiti's future?

In the Dominican Republic, the OAS initiated a development program just prior to their recent period of political instability. They had an operational economy which functioned somewhat better than Haiti's which permitted the Organization of American States to activate a multimillion-dollar program including some twenty-odd projects in the natural resources field. But in Haiti, the local institutions and the national economy are less well developed and the development direction is not well defined.

In Haiti, a large dam was built at the cost of more than 50 million dollars. It has a life expectancy of fifty years; yet to date, ten years after it had been built with international loan funds, it still has no turbines installed and no generators are producing electricity. Even though the reservoir behind the dam continues to silt up and much of the value of the dam is unused, the loan funds for the partially effective dam are expected to be promptly repaid by the international agencies involved. Although flood control is effective and water for irrigation is available at the dam site, no irrigation distribution system is available to provide power to local industries. This unfortunately is only one case in many related to Haiti, truly an ecologically and economically bankrupt nation. Not only should such disaster areas deserve attention from the international community, but once such agencies initiate a development program, they should understand that they have an obligation to complete it properly no matter what may be the economic or ecological consequences.

GEORGE: This point of bankruptcy raises the question whether you are talking about a national, regional, or an intellectual boundary of bankruptcy. Our major cities are ecologically bankrupt right now and thus I don't feel that we are concerned only with small, less-developed nations. Big pieces of big countries will also be involved.

We have given attention to this idea of monitoring, but I am not quite sure what we mean. I would like to make sure that we really are monitoring very closely the ecological factors emanating from our various means of production. Prior to any kind of bureaucratic monitoring, we need such ecological monitoring.

I feel that implementation of a good many of the ideas that have been brought out here are very seriously thwarted today by lobbying. Lobby processes in government in many cases act as a very severe constraint on the implementation of such good concepts. Most lobbyists stand as a very serious barrier to the implementation of many ecological principles. I think in effect what we are doing here then is recognizing that to be effective, we may have to challenge one of our country's major governmental processes.

One final point: I feel we have discussed only the engineer as the environmentally responsible party. Perhaps architects, journalists, sociologists and lawyers, for example, all might take an ecology course. Similarly, some of our ecologists might take a few engineering courses, law courses and so on.

HASKELL: There is a point of fundamental importance to this conference which is implicit in Gilbert White's paper and explicit in Lynton Caldwell's; you both say that we are irretrievably committed to the development process. In fact, this whole conference is based on that understanding.

Yesterday we had a little rumbling of discontent about this but it seems to me that no one has suggested that we are entirely on a wrong track. This seems to me something we ought to decide before we go into this afternoon's session. Are we sure that development should continue? What relevance do the values of a predominantly capitalist, predominantly Christian, predominantly temperate-climate civilization have for other countries for good or evil?

If we do decide there are overwhelming political and social reasons for development abroad, we ought to have a preamble to remind us that science can't tell us anything of value about the quality of human life or happiness. However, if properly used, it could give some of the people of the world the options to make those choices.

HARDOY: The promotion of ecological studies faces many problems which are common with my own field of work, which is planning urban and regional development. We can draw an interesting parallel in the training and application of skills for both fields.

In the last twenty years there has been a lot of progress in training urban and regional planners for the Latin American market. Today there are a good number of Latin Americans who have received degrees from the best schools in the U.S. and Europe and, since the early sixties, from Latin America. But now we have a completely different problem: How do we use them?

Our problem is that most planners work in an unsystematic way because the mechanisms for implementing planning at an urban or regional level in Latin America are extremely weak or nonexistent.

This brings us immediately to a complex problem as true for ecology as for planning. Today there are about ten thousand professionals and technicians from Bolivia living outside their country. For a country like Bolivia this is a tremendous loss. I understand there are now about two or three thousand Argentine medical doctors working in the East Coast of the U.S. alone. The number of engineers working outside of Argentina is tremendous.

However, in Argentina we continue creating new law schools and new medical schools for a country which already has some thirty thousand law students and one doctor per several hundred inhabitants. Only recently a foreign foundation started a big effort to promote agrarian economics in Argentina, a country that in the middle sixties didn't have a single economist specializing in agrarian problems. This situation in a country that largely depended on cattle export and wheat-growing is absurd. The problem the foundation is now posed with is: Where are the institutions that will use this newly trained manpower?

As many of you know, the situation in Bolivia, Paraguay, and other less-developed countries is much worse. Now, against this background, how do we deal with the whole problem of technical assistance?

We know perfectly well that when there is a technical study promoted by a foreign financial institution, for example, the lobby Professor George was talking about will press in order to select one group from outside the country that receives the assistance to do the job; perhaps 5 per cent or 10 per cent of the contract will go to local "young professionals" and for completely secondary or tertiary roles in that technical survey or preinvestment study. Thus, stimulus to promote local jobs and institutions to hold these professionals is seldom provided.

MILTON: Certainly the highly-developed

nations must be willing both to foster the creation of adequate local training centers for environmental affairs and to support the local infrastructure that will then use this expertise. This is more important than any other export the developed nations can offer.

In addition to those ecological aspects of development we have emphasized here at this conference, air, water, noise and land pollution also are serious and rapidly-growing problems abroad. The highly-developed nations of the world have a moral responsibility to diminish all forms of environmental deterioration abroad wherever these problems have been unleashed through the exportation of our own Temperate Zone technology. We have learned at home, all too well, the disastrous results of neglecting and not anticipating pollution brought on by the application of new technologies. This same pollution complex is being exported world-wide. Our assistance agencies must assume responsibility for helping to prevent the creation of pollution problems wherever we are helping to introduce industrial technology. Such reform is all the more urgent when you realize that at present virtually no attention is being given to these pollution problems in the less-developed nations.

DASMANN: I want to point out some things that other individuals here probably should point out, but they are in an awkward position to do so.

We talk about new institutional arrangements for solving some of our problems, and undoubtedly these are important. But like so many things that happen, it is much easier to set up an institution or set aside an area than it is to finance an effective operation to deal with the problem.

Some of our very worthwhile institutions, which will have to be recreated if they cease to exist, are on the verge of bankruptcy. I refer, for one, to the International Union for the Conservation of Nature, which is scratching along on a bare minimum

budget. This is the only nongovernmental organization that is really looking at this broad world picture of wildlife, national parks, endangered species and the whole host of ecological relationships tied up with these things. Just 1 per cent of most development budgets would make it possible for IUCN to function. Half a million dollars a year, perhaps, or $1 million at the most. But this money is not available.

The International Biological Program is another brave new effort that was set up and launched very effectively a while ago, except that the money was not made available and apparently will not be made available to allow the program to function in the way it was intended to function. At the Biosphere Conference in Paris in September, it was agreed that the International Biological Program was very worthwhile and we must follow up on it with a program which is now being planned by UNESCO and the other United Nations agencies and IUCN, but there is no budget for IBP and a minuscule budget for IUCN.

Perhaps we should begin shoring up some of our existing organizations before we start creating new ones.

CALDWELL: This is why I asked the question, Who owns the anchovies? Dr. Borgstrom gave us a picture of 600 per cent profit made by some organization. I submit nobody owns the anchovies or else everybody owns them.

We must stop treating nature as free goods. We are just now stopping this in the developed countries. There is a charge for pure air. I think we might well find the money if there were an international organization for custody of the oceans, the atmosphere, etc.; somebody would have to pay the world community for harvesting the blue whale or the anchovies.

There are techniques for getting the money.

BATISSE: I want to make one point here about the anchovies. There is a basic difference, in international or intergovernmental action, between the sea and the land. This is the problem of sovereignty. Whereas some kind of international arrangements can be easily reached for the sea in the near future, on the land we still have national sovereign territories to contend with.

WHITE: Friends, we have reached the hour at which we should bring this session to a close. We haven't answered a number of the questions raised here, but we have touched on a variety of what seem to be fruitful issues. We early asked ourselves: "How do we contend with the attraction of the quick technological benefits in manipulating the environment?" We then asked ourselves how society arrives at a wise judgment as to whether the external waste and other costs and hazards of nuclear generation warrant or offset the internal economies which we think are derived from such operations.

Perhaps the same problem in principle is posed by the small degraded island in the Caribbean concerning which we ask: "How do we go about assessing the full social consequences of either maintaining or, as an alternative, preserving this piece

of terrain and this group of people at the level of life to which they may aspire?"

We talked with a good deal of benefit about the necessity for, the paucity of, and possible ways of achieving post-investment evaluations—recognizing the importance of making it a continuing kind of process and trying to tie it in from the very outset of the planning operations.

We will have a chance to pursue most of these questions in our final session. I find myself, as I listen to much of our discussion, reminded of a remark that we all see our own faults most plainly in other people. I wonder if perhaps this is in part the case of the predominant culture which we represent here. We are speaking about man's degradation of the earth from a fundamental posture of very real searching and uncertainty about the validity of our way of life and our form of organization. Our basic values are very much challenged. Their expression in our daily life is unsettling to us. And as we focus on some of these specific cases of degradation we should recall a deeper and more pervasive kind of question: What is man's ultimate role on the earth?

VI THE IMPLICATIONS OF THE CONFERENCE FOR INTERNATIONAL DEVELOPMENT PROGRAMS: PANEL

Barry Commoner, Chairman

PANEL MEMBERS   Michelle Batisse

Kenneth E. Boulding

Lynton K. Caldwell

Harold J. Coolidge

Jorge E. Hardoy

Gunnar Myrdal

S. Dillon Ripley

Kirk P. Rodgers

I. S. Zonneveld

A BALLAD OF ECOLOGICAL AWARENESS (conclusion)

It's nice to be the drafter of a well-constructed plan,
For spending lots of money for the betterment of Man,
But Audits are a threat, for it is neither games nor fun
To look at plans of yesteryear and ask, "What have we done?"
And learning is unpleasant when we have to do it fast,
So it's pleasanter to contemplate the future than the past.

If it's just the noise of progress that is beating in our ears
We could look beyond the turbulence and soothe our gnawing fears.
Man is drowning in his own success, and hapless is his hope
If our science and technology is but a rotten rope.

Infinity is ended, and mankind is in a box;
The era of expanding man is running out of rocks;
A self-sustaining Spaceship Earth is shortly in the offing
And man must be its crew—or else the box will be his coffin!

—KENNETH E. BOULDING

DISCUSSION

COMMONER: Our responsibility today is to proceed to the final aspects of the problems we started out to investigate: the implementation of the insights gained from this Conference.

I wish to express my own delight in the success of the Conference thus far. We at the Center for the Biology of Natural Systems have been concerned, since our beginning in 1966, with the fact that very sweeping changes in the environment have been taking place without our being aware of their causes or even of their consequences until it was too late. It was our good fortune to contact the Conservation Foundation and to discover that we had a mutual interest in finding out the degree to which these problems had spread throughout the world.

The very existence of this Conference is already a sign of success; this collection of case histories has enabled us for the first time to bring into one place a record of what has been happening to the environment as a result of technological developments in various parts of the world. If the Conference has done nothing but generate this cohesive story I think an enormous amount has been accomplished.

We have accumulated here the results of a wide range of experience. During the past five sessions the factual record that Russell Train spoke of in his introduction to the Conference has been subjected to a process—so to speak—of scientific purification. The sometimes heated dialogues showed that if a case history was faulty, its faults were likely to have been discovered in this group. If any of the case histories needed to be changed, if there were generalizations that could not be supported by contrary case histories, it seems to me this group would have been capable of discovering that.

What we have been looking for—and what I believe we have produced—is a sound record of what has happened to ecosystems which have recently experienced the impact of the introduction of new technologies. And this alone, it seems to me, is a magnificent accomplishment. If, in this session, we can also develop some ideas as to the *causes* of environmental problems which we have documented, the Conference's accomplishments will be further enhanced.

We shall first give the members of the panel a chance to express their individual reactions, and then open the Conference for general discussion.

MYRDAL: I am the most ignorant, so perhaps it is right that I be first.

When I was invited here, I explained that I was not competent in environmental science; nevertheless I am an optimist, so when I was invited once more, I thought I could learn something. I have learned a great deal from both the horror stories and some of the nonhorror stories.

Somebody said yesterday that ecology was based on a viewpoint that you should take all things into consideration.

Really we should look on a problem from *all* relevant points of view. There are no anthropological, economic, sociological, biological, geological and ecological problems. There are only problems, and all problems are complex. What we have to do is to equip ourselves to deal with the real problems, which usually don't belong to a particular discipline and which are complex. This is a very difficult thing to do, and it is becoming more and more difficult. The disciplines we specialize in hardly understand each other. I think this is true not only for economics, but also for all the others.

Nevertheless, a new approach must be worked out. All my life, I have heard about the necessity for multidisciplinary research. Yet I have seen very little of it which was really successful.

I would like to suggest a fundamental distinction between our rich developed countries and the underdeveloped countries. One difference is that in the rich developed countries, we have organized societies to carry out strong regulations. Most underdeveloped countries, however, are what I call soft states; they write down legislation under pressure from vested interests and it is full of loopholes. Furthermore, laws are not carried out and enforced. Directives from the capital are not carried out in the villages by local authorities. Corruption comes in on all levels, from the politicians and the higher civil servants down to the man who opens the door. Surely we have some of these faults in our own countries, but, nevertheless, I think there is a large difference in magnitude.

The second difference is that in our developed countries, popular opinion means something in government. I know of no representative assembly and no government in the world which is more sensitive to public opinion than the American government. Now, however, things are going to be rather horrible in our countries, because we have not taken the many-sided view of what we are doing. We have been entirely too reductionistic.

I have no doubt that within the next five or ten years we are going to have a popular movement within the rich countries which is going to press Congress and the Administration to do many things for solving environmental problems. But the same will not be true in most, if not all, underdeveloped countries.

DASMANN: The question has been asked earlier in the conference whether the agricultural revolution, so-called, is going to help solve the population problem. I believe that the only difference it will make, if it is successful, is to buy a little time, time in which, hopefully, our efforts toward population control can begin to bear some fruit. But sometimes—and I want to say some heretical things here—I wonder if it is worthwhile buying time.

Take the example from our earlier discussion on the development of the Nile Basin. There we have had about 150 years of development effort aimed at improving and intensifying productivity in the Nile. However, if you take the average lot of the average Egyptian today and compare it with the average Egyptian lot of 150 years ago, I think you might seriously question whether the effort has been worthwhile. Perhaps we might just as well have spent the money in building a big pyramid, bigger than anything built before. In so doing, we might have forced the population of the Nile Basin to come to grips earlier with the realities of its environment.

Instead of our holding up the illusory hope that the carrying capacity of the environment can be increased indefinitely to accommodate an expanding population, Egypt should face its population problem. But, it will face the problem today with the options closed down enormously from what they were 150 years ago. Ways of living that were possible then are no longer possible. This has bothered me throughout this Conference.

In our talk about intensifying production, we seem to make the assumption that the goal of development is somehow to aim toward a maximum population of human beings subsisting on a maximum productivity. This is a goal to which ecologists can really contribute nothing. A consideration of ecology might slow the process and ameliorate some of the difficulties along the way. However, we need to change our goal away from maximizing production and toward improvement of human life—improvement of the quality of living for the individual. This should be the goal of development— not maximizing production. Development must be concerned with people.

We seem to lose sight of this and to evaluate projects only by the extent to which they have increased production. We don't evaluate the extent to which they have increased human well-being and happiness.

We mow down a thousand different ways of life toward a uniformity of life which we find suitable to our economic development programs. We could just as well aim our development programs toward increasing diversity, increasing opportunities for different ways of life, toward maintaining these nomads, perhaps, so that they could roam around the hills with their flocks, and toward maintaining the people of the Kariba Basin in the strange ways of agriculture which happen to suit them. I think this question of goals of development is one to which we haven't given enough attention here. We assume that somehow or other it is our duty to increase production in order to accommodate more and more people and provide more for those that are here. But, I think we really must reevaluate our economic development programs in terms

of how they contribute to quality of living for individual human beings.

We can do this because the development agencies—UNESCO, the FAO, the U.N. agencies, the World Bank, the Inter-American Development Bank—largely control international development. They do not have to accept projects aimed only at the goal of intensifying production. They can buy ecologically balanced programs that are aimed at improving quality of living. I suggest this should be a proposal from this Conference.

ZONNEVELD: During this Conference the words "ecology" and "ecological" are used in a rather broad way. Especially the term "ecological" was often used as a synonym for "integrated" or "holistic." I would indeed like to see all specialists of the world take on such an "ecological" point of view. We need more emphasis on holism or integration without losing our specialistic knowledge. This is particularly true of our role in development. But we ecologists have to be very careful not to be too arrogant. We should be humble. Also our profession itself (the study of the relations between living organisms and their environment) is a form of specialization. More than other specialists, the ecologist is forced to think holistically. In this is one of the unique contributions of ecological sciences to development.

Generalization and specialization are often considered as opposites. At this Conference many have made a plea for generalizers. However, I do not believe that the basic education of young people should be on being generalists. We need specialists in this complicated world, but specialists with an ability to understand and cooperate with other specialists. Therefore, at our ITC/UNESCO Centre for Integrated Survey in Delft we try to teach specialists to use their specialism in integrated survey. We teach the interdependence of natural phenomena, of cultural phenomena, the interdependence of disciplines, and the interdependence of aim and means of development and conservation. Also, management is a specialization, and we try through a special course to help them. In practice, however, managers must first be specialists and then become partial generalists by experience and additional training.

RIPLEY: It seems to me quite likely that we are heading into a sort of civil war in planning. I think that we can assume that the general thrust of all education today is sufficiently reductionistic in its emphasis, that there can be no solution to our environmental crisis so long as this emphasis persists as it does.

The quiet voices of rational students of the environment will probably not suffice to create basic changes in the system. We will all be swept aside by a ground swell of opinion from those alienated by existing processes. These people range from militant students who are unhappy about today's system of education, through middle-aged, middle-class people living in quiet desperation; each group will finally reject our social and economic goals based on subjective private initiative.

We are now living on an ecological credit card. We have seen that the average life of pesticides, as Ray Smith said, is two years now in certain areas. We have seen that we have to work out some kind of debt which farmers are incurring in order to support themselves under the present tax structure, so that they simply build one drainpipe after another facing the eventual *après nous la cloaca maxima.*

As Dr. Myrdal, Dr. Borgstrom and others have said, we must re-create aid, perhaps on moral grounds. This would require a new morality. A new kind of theocratic substitute for our present nontheocratic dominating regime. However, the implementation of such a morality will be as difficult

as the proportional benefit we hope to achieve by it.

Planning now always seems to be directed toward dollar goals. You have only to read our popular magazines to be saturated with a point of view that money is everything. Money is the only thing to have. If you have money, then you have got all you desire. If you don't have money, you don't. So long as our prominent people and dominant people intend that the world should be run this way, there is very little that we quiet simple folk can do about it.

Now it is true also that besides money we have a strong Judeo-Christian ethic. Our way is the only way. We feel uncomfortable in the presence of primitive culture. Can we possibly come to grips with the proposition that there are in effect two different sorts today and that we should preserve some sorts of gene pools, including human gene pools, which still continue to exist. There are people on earth today who do not want the patterns of education which we force upon them. These people continue to exist, and in effect they are very, very keenly attuned to the environment around them, far more so than we are. What right have we to decide our way is better than theirs and then force disruption upon them?

One of the speakers spoke about the cushioning, buffering effect from the way we grow up: isolated from the remainder of the natural environment. Can we come to grips then with the proposition that lots of people should in effect live in national parks? We think of this as sort of being on the reservation and it is very distasteful to us. If we are to have a receivership society and if large parts of the world are to become ecologically bankrupt because, as Dr. White implies, out of environmental ignorance we allow the essential pleasure principle, which impels engineers to do what they want to do, I know how they feel. I used to build little dams in brooks when

I was ten years old. It is just great fun.

Shouldn't there be some attempt to preserve that which I am perfectly willing to call, because I am not a racist, subspecific diversity of man and his cultures? Can we preserve hand skills? Can we preserve non-literate skills? Can we somehow prevent people from trampling on themselves while running to be like everybody else? If we can do all this, perhaps then we can face up to the ultimate which is some sort of rationale to prevent creating more of all the environment horror stories brought out at this Conference.

BATISSE: Mr. Chairman, I am not an ecologist. I am one of those arrogant engineers and physicists. It is not only engineers that are arrogant; economists, too, are arrogant—because they think they should run the world.

Perhaps ecologists are also arrogant, because they have not been listened to enough, and now they want to change this situation drastically.

However, I think what we really are lacking is a truly scientific approach to solving problems. This scientific approach has been particularly lacking in the application of ecology but it is not always ecological knowledge that is missing; it is the scientific approach itself, including all the consequences of such a situation.

I have been trying for many years to promote integration of various disciplines and I think we have to realize that this holistic approach is not much better carried out by the ecologist than by anybody else. The ecologist himself tends to be a specialist.

We have here to conceive how we can train people to work in teams. I would like to suggest that we need team leaders—people who are able to get other people to work together on the common problem.

But who should these team leaders be? Perhaps they should be ecologists. Certainly

geographers should be well suited to the task. Perhaps a new school of geography—call it ecological geography, or geographical ecology—could be bred to lead this important interdisciplinary work.

CALDWELL: I would like to carry that thought further with some remarks about the strategy of education and how one corrects this one-sidedness in scientific education that Barry Commoner has spoken about. We know that the configuration of knowledge is continually changing. The task now is to change it in a direction that will be useful for dealing with the situation of Spaceship Earth.

I suggest that we have more than the task of reforming science in the direction of an approach that would emphasize synthesis as well as reductionism. We also need to infuse the total educational experience with a realistic view of man's condition in the biosphere. This, of course, means we need to look closely at the hidden assumptions of contemporary education, many of which are based upon concepts that have proved to be invalid in light of present knowledge and experience.

This task of educational reform needs to be undertaken throughout the entire educational structure. However, the universities play a particularly critical role because they are the points at which new knowledge is created; they are the principal repositories of traditional knowledge, and they are the institutions that train the future teachers and researchers.

Nevertheless, we in the universities find it very difficult to reform ourselves. Within this year we have seen throughout the world a whole series of student outbreaks—protest—much of which can be explained by the university's backwardness in dealing with the realities of the environmental crisis.

I think we have a responsibility for promoting needed change on the part of government, of foundations and of professional groups. There is a saying that science is too important to be left to the scientists. I think education is too important to be left to the professional educators.

By what means can the universities be persuaded to create an environment in which you can get true disciplinary synthesis, in which you arrive at effective interdisciplinary mixture? What should be the outcome of this? We are working toward not only an infusion of this ecological awareness into the educational experience, but also toward the development of a positive attitude toward man in relation to his environment that is consistent with the Spaceship Earth situation.

For the moment we still find ourselves in a period of protest against the unanticipated results of well-intentioned action. But in the long run protest alone will not be good enough. We must create a positive outlook toward our environment. Fostering this attitude ought to be implicit in the educational experience.

SCUDDER: I would like to comment on only one general point: the need to conceptualize a much wider range of alternatives within an ecological frame of reference. By development I mean the evolution toward a single world culture based on science and technology with industrialization of the countryside and the cities. I assume this is inevitable just to support the population.

Throughout much of Africa most indigenous systems of land use have exceeded their carrying capacity. They have no other option than development. Like Dr. Darling, I regret the fact that a large number of cultures, particularly nomadic cultures and hunting and gathering cultures, are becoming extinct. This is inevitable. There is no way of protecting them. On the other hand, new cultures are evolving and let us bear in mind that in the city today there is a tremendous cultural diversity. There may even be more cultural diversity in the cities than there was in the country prior to the development of the industrial world.

This conference has largely been concerned with development from above: development which has been planned, implemented and evaluated by international development agencies, by host countries, and by various planning bodies. Such development has usually affected willy-nilly a large proportion of the local population. This is hierarchical development, all pretty much a one-way street. However, there is another kind of development which has been going on very satisfactorily in many cases, which has not been well documented: development from below. As an anthropologist, I take a people's approach here.

For example, throughout most of West Africa development of the cocoa industry was initiated and carried through by small holders without assistance from government; some assistance from government might have helped it along. Again, the successful development of maize cultivation in Northern Rhodesia was the result of development from below. In fact, frequently government from above interferes with effective development from below.

So if we wish to widen our range of alternatives, it is not an either-or proposition. It is a both-and proposition. I am trying here to emphasize, however, that we have to pay much more attention to process at the peasant and village level. Even though they usually want certain aspects of development, many people often are not aware of the true implications of development. So I think we must improve communication and integration between planning from above and from below. This is especially true if we revolutionize educational systems. If we bring in more and more education, then you can be sure there will be more and more local incentive and initiative which will need to be taken into consideration.

We must learn to conceptualize international development within an ecological frame of reference and create a much wider range of alternatives than heretofore considered.

HARDOY: I have some points to make. First, the problems of development will increasingly ask those with the power of decision to use it. Whether those decisions are right or wrong largely depends on the forethought, insight, realism, and exploration of alternatives that we can give to those with power of decision. Let me give you one example. I know of an urban planning agency operating in one of the largest metropolitan areas of Latin America which virtually has made no decisions for three years. In the meantime, the population of this metropolitan area has grown by about 600,000 people. Undoubtedly the administrators of the municipalities which form that metropolitan area have continued making decisions of all kinds.

How do we deal with such very complicated problems where scientists from different disciplines have important roles to play? How do we improve methods of detection and analysis of key development issues? This requires, above all, a working interdisciplinary team. I agree with Dr. Myrdal that interdisciplinary teams have not been very successful; but I feel this is because good scientists quite frequently are reluctant to enter and participate in interdisciplinary teams. Also, the scientists who do participate are not trained in how to make the work of an integrated team really effective.

Second, in order to get substantive decision-making, it is very important to have environmental information adequately presented from the area subject to a development program. If this is not possible, information should then be obtained from another area where there is a similar situation. Frequently we cannot wait until all the necessary information is available and must make decisions without it.

My third point is that research for action is not necessarily the same as for pure research. In underdeveloped countries, particularly among social scientists, too frequently researchers emphasize very detailed research in sectors where information is least needed.

Fourth, we must establish institutions which can assume the responsibility of implementing environmental decisions. This means that we must have an entirely different attitude in the underdeveloped countries toward development goals and the integration of new information, about social aspects, and the use of power structures. This is something that we have tended to avoid during the Conference. Many of the problems we have discussed depend upon the power structure which is guiding the underdeveloped countries.

I am an urban planner. Last year I finished a rather detailed survey for the United Nations on South American land policies and urban policies. The conclusion of this survey can be summarized in three sentences. There is no solution to the urban problem of Latin America without implementing urban policies from the national level. There is no possibility of implementing urban policies at the national level given existing land policies at the local level. Yet it is absolutely impossible to change the existing local land policies unless there is a complete change in the power structure that is controlling Latin American countries.

We have talked of creating new international institutions. Well, I would first prefer to emphasize the need for improvement of the technical and financial support for already existing national institutions. I fully agree with what Batisse said. After all, they are still countries. It is very difficult to be effective where national teams are frequently replaced. This is often overlooked. Where international and national agencies work together, too frequently the national teams grow weaker and weaker after the plan of operation has ended. We know very little about why many of these national agencies and institutions have collapsed and why they have been so ineffective after the international teams have left. The formation and consolidation of national teams should be a first priority.

COOLIDGE: Many of those here have clearly emphasized the need for scientific investigation of the ecological consequences involving various projects; I feel we should also emphasize the need for sociological studies of the peoples and areas affected, as in the case of the Mekong. Very little mention has been made here, however, of the ecological studies that should precede the setting aside of natural areas for research and study, national parks, and other reserves. I think that this form of land use can play an important part, not only in the developed countries, but also in the developing countries where it should have an increasingly important role.

For all these reasons, there is a tremendous need for more people who can use the ecological approach in development. This is going to be a challenge for the organizations that will carry forward the results of this Conference. It has been a challenge for the International Union for the Conservation of Nature over the past twenty years.

BOULDING: I would like to say something about ecology and economics. Veblen once wrote an article called: "Why Is Economics not an Evolutionary Science?" Why isn't ecology an evolutionary science? Every mutation of life has been an intrusion. Ecology has failed so far to deal effectively with the evolution of man's tools. Now these tools have brought much of the world to the edge of disaster.

The poor countries that make up the majority of this planet continue to grow poorer while the rich grow richer. If you look to see where those countries are with a growing per capita income, almost all are in the temperate zone. This is even true of relatively poor countries such as Yugoslavia and Japan which are growing fast as well as rich countries growing slowly like the United States and Canada. The trend is the same for socialist and capitalist countries alike.

Then you have the group of poor countries, largely located in the tropical areas of the globe, which are not growing. The interesting thing about developing countries is they are not developing. They are just poor. What does this suggest? It suggests that there is an evolutionary pattern here and some countries are in on it and some are not. The countries that are in on it will, as they get richer, grow more slowly. Given current trends, a nation will achieve zero growth when it reaches between five and ten thousand dollars per capita, so there may be some sort of end to the current philosophy of never-ending economic expansion.

In the meantime, the poor countries are performing a Brownian movement. They are moving in a variety of directions but not getting anywhere. The implications of this for the world are very alarming. It means that the world really is separating out into a rich temperate zone and a poor tropical zone. This, I think, is the background of our whole developmental problem. Now these people want out.

Dr. Scudder is right—they all want out. At least 90 per cent of them want out. Yet, it is very hard to get them out of economic, social and ecological regression. It is extremely hard to get on to the highly developing bandwagon. As a matter of fact, Argentina fell off it years ago.

HARDOY: Uruguay did, too. It is much easier to fall off than climb on.

BOULDING: Yes, it is quite easy to fall off. And it has pretty unfortunate results. It is not very pleasant at all. We are faced today with a profound disequilibrium; we just have to face this. It is a very dangerous process. We will be deluding the world if we don't tell them they have to change. We cannot even go back to education, really. We have eaten the apple and there is no place to go but Zion.

COMMONER: Now that we have all eaten the apple, perhaps we can participate in some of the new knowledge. This discussion is now open.

RUSSELL: I would like to take another aspect. Team leaders. One of our problems is to get an organizational setup so that people can get experience in the field working with people of other disciplines.

I was recently at a conference at which we discussed some of the problems of getting change in agriculture, the point came up that we in agricultural research must get the social scientist and others to be part of any research team.

But how do we interest a continuous stream of people in getting experience working with other people in the field? We have this great shortage of team leaders, and of ecologists able to integrate the various needed disciplines to find what is feasible and what is not feasible.

I also want to stress again that in all developments there must be a large element of faith or optimism. None of us can foresee every consequence of our actions. In development we have to accept the fact that things are almost certain to be going wrong sometime, and it is part of the leaders' job to quickly spot things that go wrong and try to remedy things before something catastrophic happens.

PHILLIPS: As you probably know, this country (U.S.A.) has taken the lead in the last few years in an attempt to bring together the planner and the ecologist. Ian McHarg, with whatever weakness there still may be in his methods of approach, has been a leader in this respect. I believe his efforts, along with those of others I know which are emerging, may be able to make a contribution toward the solution of inter-national development and planning problems. On a related point, Dr. Scudder quite rightly referred to what we might call community development: that is development from below; of the people, by the people, and for the people. The world in various parts is littered with the disasters that have come because the Western mind, particularly the American, has attempted to put into community development the concepts of Western man. We have to stop that. Western man must learn to stand back in a sympathetic manner. In parts of Africa, for example, shifting agriculture and nomadism can form a viable base for the improvement of subsistence production by using traditional approaches too.

CONWAY: I am really very upset that a number of people who are not ecologists will go away from this conference believing that ecology is just another name for a multidisciplinary approach. I want to point out the operational consequences of this belief in the scenario, "Ecologist Meets Planner."

Planner says, "What are you?"

"I am an ecologist."

"What is that?"

"A person who follows a multidisciplinary approach."

"What do you mean?"

"Well, I think of everything at once."

Planner: "Well, so do I, isn't that interesting!"

End of conversation.

This, in fact, is a real scenario because it has happened to me on a number of occasions over the last two months. Ecologists try to understand ecosystems, and the laws of energy and materials, flowing and cycling through an environment. It is this specific understanding that he has to contribute.

COMMONER: It is very obvious that there is a problem here as to what ecology is and is not. It has just struck me that a little history may be helpful here. There was a time when science was dominated by Newtonian mechanics. Science was then epitomized by mechanics and by physics. Everyone felt the world was mechanical and if you were interested in the world, you had to be competent in this realm.

I think this is a natural thing. A particular science which seems to touch the nature of the universe closely epitomizes science as a whole. What may be happening is that instead of mechanics being the metaphor of science, ecology may be the new candidate —the science most relevant to the nature of the universe as we now see it.

PHILLIPS: I also believe there is confusion as to what ecology is. Whilst some appear to think it is a science in its own right, I prefer to look on ecology as an approach, a point of view: an effort to examine all the relevant aspects of a problem and to offer advice and guidance, taking into consideration all the significant data so that whilst one strand in the web may be strengthened, there will not simultaneously be a deterioration elsewhere in the mesh. We must remember all the time that we are working with the ecosystem and, accordingly, must think, study and suggest solutions to problems holistically.

KASSAS: By way of defense of the ecologist, let's define the ecologist as a wild animal: If you want to use him, you need to let him loose on the ground and then he will come back and tell you that in this bit of the land there are such and such living things, and that such and such processes are operating within the ecosystem. He will also be able to give advice on the better use of the land. This is an ecologist. But if you go to the ecologist and say, "Come along—let us look at the Kariba Dam and make a survey of it," or, "I have got a piece of land; I would like to cultivate rice in it," then he is no more an ecologist. He has become an ordinary technologist.

When you ask an ordinary technologist to come along and assess your work after it is finished, then he is bound to do what was politely described in this Conference as a "post-audit" assessment—that which I describe in my own language as a post-mortem mourning.

That is what we have been relating in this Conference, all these horror stories are actually post-mortem mournings.

MARSHALL: This is perhaps an appropriate time to express my concern that after three days here we haven't ever asked: "For whom is the development intended?" Nobody seems to be too terribly concerned about that. I have heard much both inside and outside of this room, about the various developmental schemes and approaches that were well intentioned and designed but, unfortunately, the "natives" didn't go along with the program. I am kind of going away with the feeling that ecology and conservation is almost like patriotism. It can be used to cover a multitude of sins.

One of the papers talks about destocking the cattle of the natives in Rhodesia. This may indeed be justified on ecological or conservationist grounds, but I wonder who is the ultimate benefactor. Is this another kind of "nutritional colonialism"? We should be very careful about who actually derives the benefits from these things.

It has often been said that patriotism is the last refuge of a scoundrel and I would hope that "ecology and development" doesn't wind up being the same thing.

CARLOZZI: What I want to do is go from Marshall to Boulding to Commoner. I won't let Dr. Marshall's question sit there unresponded to, because I think it is implied in a lot of what we have talked about. Who is this development for? Dr. Boulding tells us that the trouble with the developing nations is they aren't developing. Well, I don't really agree, Dr. Boulding. There is development in the developing nations, and *we* are getting the benefit from it. I think this is the point that Dr. Marshall had in mind.

Dr. Commoner commented in his summation that somehow we have approached international development with a faulty instrument. He rests his case on the faulty instrument of our science. I couldn't disagree more. If there is a faulty instrument which moves through the Caribbean, for example, I think it is me. The faulty instruments that we carry to other countries are ourselves, because we can spend millions of dollars, expound a lot of high-minded motivations, and still arrive at Dr. Boulding's growing gulf between two worlds: one rich and the other poor. We are continuing to fill our pockets from the poor.

MILTON: I agree. Not only are we continuing to fill our pockets from the poor, but also we are making massive contributions to the multiple pollution of their environment. The rich nations of the world are a minority of the planet's population, and yet we consume the vast majority of the planet's resources. How long can or should this unequal trend continue? And of course, the more we consume in goods the more we excrete in wastes and pollution.

I feel not only must man ultimately create better distribution of world resources, stabilize world population, and create a truly ecological technology, but also he must eliminate his faulty assumption of unlimited economic growth. The GNP cannot, and should not, expand indefinitely in the natural resource-consuming sectors of the economy. Perhaps what is most needed now is a means to slow down traditional economic "progress" until we learn how to support non-environmentally consumptive growth. This might require, for example, far deeper emphasis on the service aspects of economies and on the fostering of the arts and their appreciation rather than on an

extra car, a new highway, an additional refrigerator, or an SST.

WHITE: Perhaps a qualification is in order for Barry Commoner's statement that this is the first comprehensive assessment of international development effort. We should put this conference experience down beside the experience of the United Nations Conference in 1963 on Science, Technology, and Economic Development. The emphasis in that was very heavily on science and technological inputs toward economic growth, toward the effort of the developing countries to change their status, and to a consideration of what success stories they could find in making some advances.

In that U. N. Conference, the environmental impacts of technology were largely ignored. In a complementary sense, we might say that here we have not ignored but given less attention to the tremendous and deeply frustrating drive to advance the economic growth process and to confront the problems of international organization, comparative advantage and exchange which clearly stand in the way of some changes. So I would like to see us recognize that we are here adding another side to what was previously an incomplete picture. Perhaps in uniting them we can get a more adequate view.

It is reported that at the meeting of the board of directors of a certain national game park, the director was reviewing the acquisition of new animals and then noted that they were intending to bring in an ecologist from Sweden. At that point one of the members of the board said, Why not get two? Then they might breed.

I would like to modify that statement and suggest that we should bring in both an ecologist and a social scientist. They might breed.

M. T. FARVAR: First a brief comment on Dr. White's remark about the 1963 Conference. What I gather from going through the eight volumes, since I was not present there, is that the reason for being at that Conference was primarily to talk about science and technology *for* development. There have been many other conferences like that, including the Pugwash group. Every few months another reappears. The last one was the very impressive three-volume report of the President's Science Advisory Commission.

It seems to me the main accomplishment of this Conference may indeed be to discuss and find out whether the "rope" we offer the less-developed countries is rotten. What if it is? Based on my own background in a traditional society and later experience here, the rope in fact does seem to be rotten. A good deal of what was discussed in this Conference points this up.

We have neglected to take note of some ominous warnings. Dale Newsom's description of several insects demonstrates how the technological rope promoted biological decay. Take the cabbage looper and the two-spotted spider mite. Why should we care about these funny creatures, except that they are two of several of insects that, to quote him, "can no longer be controlled with any available organochlorine, organophosphate, or carbamate insecticides. Even the most recently developed experimental materials are not effective in killing these pests." What this means to me is a realization for the first time of the possibility that we may be producing, through technology, truly indestructible insects. Maybe we are.

We also neglected to take note of LaVerne Harold's description of how the application of medical technology has produced transferable drug resistance, the exact mechanisms of which are still unclear. There, too, we may have created something that may run out of hand.

If the rope is rotten, I think the greatest service you could perform would indeed be to let us know. The people in the less-developed countries should be told about the dangers inherent in modern technology. In Africa, 90 per cent of the population may want it, but *they don't know what they are getting*. In the Middle East, I am convinced, it is a much smaller proportion of the population that "wants it." For the most part, those who "want it" are the wealthy or the educated elite. Among most of the population there is much more resistance to adoption of new technologies and lifeways. Perhaps we Middle Easterners don't want it as much as the Africans do, which may be a reflection on the nature of colonialism! What I am arriving at thereby is that we have started to make some discoveries about the nature of the rope that apparently a good many people think ought to be extended to us. There is clearly an obligation to let the world know the truth about the bill of goods we have been sold in the name of progress and improved standards of living. Unfortunately, I feel we are almost in a position of creating another haven under which one can hide under the banner of ecology. Ecology is now the new catch phrase.

It almost seems like the only practical suggestion the ecologists here have so far made (other than talking about building ecology into development) has been along the lines of destocking the stock of the natives (which amounts to destocking the natives) or of throwing natives out of islands on which they live now, because, presumably, the natives have degraded the landscape (for those who would like to enjoy it as preserves for shooting wildlife or for tourism or for what have you) or of keeping the natives from getting healthier because there may, indeed, be too many of them! I would like to know if this is what we are coming to, or whether there is a serious fundamental question here we ought to stop to ask.

TALBOT: Mr. Chairman, one of your questions at the start of this discussion was about the nature of the ecologists we are talking about. I feel our ecologists ought not to be afraid of man. I am sure many of us have attended conclaves of ecologists where we heard how bad man was and where the whole emphasis was on studying ecosystems unpolluted by man.

Fortunately, at this meeting, the emphasis hasn't been this way. Nevertheless, I believe that one of the reasons for the lack of input from ecology, has been that the ecologists who were in a position to help refused to take the step beyond basic research to apply themselves to real problem situations. They did not address themselves to the whole ecosystem, including man.

I submit that the ecologist is one who is concerned with the total ecosystem, including man. He is willing to go beyond the basic research. He is willing to direct it and apply it to these larger human environmental problems.

CROWCROFT: Could I draw your attention to the fact that an enormous and very odoriferous red herring has been dragged back and forth across the path of this Conference since it began: this question of what an ecologist is. You repeatedly refer to ecology as being really a holistic approach and Mr. Phillips says it is a point of view that takes everything into consideration.

Now, if you, as an ecologist, go to your planners and your economists and your sociologists, who are precisely these kind of people, you have nothing to contribute. In point of fact, whether you like it or not, ecology is a specialized biological science and its special field is the study of the organism in relation to the environment.

When you go to these people and you want them to listen to you and they say, "What have you got to offer?" what can you say except, "I can offer training and experience in the study of organisms in relation to their environment, and I can do something you cannot. I can look at man as an animal in this environment and tell you

what are his requirements as an animal and what are his waste products as an animal."

Surely this is something we are losing sight of, that being an ecologist does mean something specific.

RICE: I would like to make three observations. First, you are faced with the world-wide application of the ecological aspects of development. The decision-making within a country, for another country, or in an international organization all should involve taking into account these factors of man's relationship to his environment. I don't think they can be separated out except for mechanical purposes of plotting implementation strategy.

Second, I have sat through conferences where the behavioral scientists and the anthropologists have been saying very much what is said here today: "Why isn't our scientific knowledge applied to the development process? Why aren't factors involving human values, motivations, culture systems, mores, and associations cranked into the whole process of development?" I think that is also a legitimate question. These points of view should be getting into the development decision-making process as well.

Third, I would like to respond to the question raised by Dr. Marshall about the purpose of development.

It seems to me the purpose of development is to open up options for the individual, to open up opportunities. Poverty, isolation, illness, ignorance: these are what prevent people from making use of their own inborn capacity in whatever way they want, consistent with socially regulated values. The purpose of aid to development from the richer countries to the poorer countries is to eliminate these obstacles, which are not the fault of the individual, but usually are created by natural factors or by social structures. This assistance should try to eliminate restrictive factors in such a way that the individual can, as much as possible, live up to his own inborn potential.

MANDELL*: I should like to add to Dr. Ripley's comments about the learning of skills. The whole body is involved. Guiding a person's arm through a tennis swing or to an object whose image is displaced because of special eyeglasses does not teach the mind-body synchronization required to execute these tasks. Hence, education programs must provide for active participation.

Secondly, I should like to comment on the way we teach environment. Basic science texts read like the Longfellow poem *Evangeline*. They consider air as if it were pure air. They seldom inform people that they breathe in asbestos, various carcinogens, and sulfur dioxide. The books show cilia sweeping foreign matter out of the respiratory passages without mentioning the fact that these cilia become paralyzed by sulfur dioxide. Thus, a student is given a totally false picture. I submit that the environment we should be teaching about is the one that exists, not the environment of Longfellow's poem.

Thirdly, in response to Dr. Scudder, I agree that anthropology demonstrates that cultures around the world are not alike. In addition, I would add that plant physiology and plant geography show that to flourish, different plants require different environments. The world is not all like Iowa and Nebraska. We must take this into account in planning; programs must be tailored to the regions in which they are applied. Given the many cultures of the world, I think that the central job for planners is to design solutions which preserve the integrity of a culture. Because of culture man is not like other animals. The way a man walks, talks, sleeps, and breathes is all related to his culture. We

* Donald Mandell was Program Coordinator of the Center for the Biology of Natural Systems and is now Professor of Biology, Sarah Lawrence College, Bronxville, New York.

should be implementers of culture rather than propagandists for our own values and our own ideas of agriculture and technology.

KAMARCK†: I want to make a couple of comments as an economist that is engaged in trying to help development in the developing countries. I was very much impressed by the statement the chairman made that the way in which we ought to finance projects in the developing countries is to have the ecologist make a study of the project's impact on environmental systems to help avoid mistakes.

In this Conference there have been a number of papers indicating the kind of horrible mistakes that occur. In the World Bank, we have made studies of the results of some of the projects we financed to see what we could learn from them. One of the lessons we have learned is that there are mistakes that occurred that we should have been able to forecast if we had applied the available existing knowledge or if we had used better techniques. This is something that obviously we should have done. We also have learned that very often some of the things that went wrong were impossible to forecast because the basic knowledge to prevent the mistake did not exist.

I haven't read all of the papers presented at this Conference, but taking a very quick glance at them, I have not seen in these papers a clear differentiation between what went wrong that could have been avoided if one had made the proper study ahead of time, as compared to what went wrong that was impossible to forecast because we didn't have the basic knowledge then, and don't have it even today.

Albert Hirschman has written a book recently in examining the experience of a number of World Bank projects. Hirschman says that in many cases it is a very good thing that you don't know some of

† Andrew M. Kamarck directs the Economics Department of the World Bank Group.

the problems that are going to come up, because if you knew them, you would never embark on the project. And very often these are good projects, but if you knew all the problems you were going to run into, you never would have started the project at all.

I don't agree completely with Hirschman. But I do say that if you could foresee all the problems and provide all the solutions to the problems in fostering development, you might eliminate from these countries what is perhaps the most important part of the development process: problem solving. Now, I am not endorsing this completely. All I am saying is that I think humility becomes economists in the development process. I have been in this for a long time. This is one of the things I learned, but I also believe humility may be becoming to some of the other social sciences, too.

COMMONER: I think I should point out that many of the papers reveal mistakes were made because we simply didn't have basic environmental information on them. And such information is still missing. The instances of schistosomiasis, I think, are good examples of that, but there is no point in repeating the Conference. Other case histories reveal mistakes made out of ignorance of what should have been known.

TRAIN: I stated in the last sentence of my opening lines that I hoped that this Conference would go beyond the simple job of taking a look at the role of ecology in the development process, and begin to question the goals of development.

Well, we have done this, and done it in good measure. We have waxed very philosophical. We have discussed redefining our development goals in terms of some new sets of human aspirations. All of this is fine and should be done, but I think we have tended to allow the role of the ecologist to assume some rather gargantuan propor-

tions, which I think was never intended in the first place.

I don't believe the ecologist wants to assume any kind of arrogant role as a god who is able to match development to broad sets of human goals. Not at all. I don't think this Conference shoud try to define the role of the ecologist in development from that standpoint.

I think we had one very good definition of the role of ecology and that is the study of the organism in relation to its environment. From the case histories it emerges that there is a need for this, and that we have not really been meeting this need adequately.

MILTON: I think we want to emphasize here that ecology does have a discrete body of unique knowledge. The functioning of human and natural ecosystems is a field treated only by ecologists, and by no other group. The ecologist is much more than a generalist. The case histories we have accumulated here document very clearly the relevance of understanding these ecosystems before manipulating them with new technologies. If we can begin to understand, through ecology, how man actually affects ecosystems, then perhaps we can learn how to work with these same systems to produce balanced, harmonious, and sustained development in the long run.

What we ecologists want to know now is how to relate to the economist, the political scientist, the educator, and the many other disciplines which we feel have had primacy in the development process up to now. We need education. We need help from you in knowing how we can best relate our own discipline to the development process. It's a simple question, and answering it is going to take a lot of work. All this can't be done here, obviously.

Nevertheless, we hope through this Conference to open up simple lines of communication and obtain some suggestions as to where we go from here. What are the best avenues open to us now to make ecology more effective in the decision-making process?

COMMONER: Thank you. I think Dr. Batisse, who was largely responsible for UNESCO's recent Biosphere Conference, might be able to comment here.

BATISSE: Of course, one basic background question to this Conference is whether there should be development. This is a very interesting question, but I don't think we should try to answer it here. Our students in Paris in May, 1968, were raising this question, and I must say that some older people like myself were even joining in a little bit on what they were arguing about, the value of development. Perhaps we should have a conference on whether development is or is not a good thing. However, I, as an international civil servant, don't have to ask myself this question. I'm paid to help countries to develop, because that is what they say they want.

Now the question for me really is: How should they develop and yet avoid some of the mistakes which have been made in many parts of the world? Last September we held in Paris a conference on the biosphere which, in many ways, relates to the problems being discussed here. Perhaps it would be useful to summarize its main conclusions.

There were sixty-five countries represented at the Biosphere Conference; but the people there were representatives of governments. Oddly enough, they came more or less to the same conclusions about what they wanted and what was not going well. This is not common in intergovernmental conferences, so this convergence is a significant point.

Secondly, the conference was organized by UNESCO but with the close cooperation of the United Nations, FAO, WHO and from the nongovernmental agencies: the International Union for the Conservation of Nature and Natural Resources (IUCN), the Conservation Foundation and the International Biological Program.

The subject of the conference was the rational use and conservation of the resources of the biosphere. In other words, development was built into the subject "rational use." Conservation was taken to be an essential element of rational use; not opposed to use, but a part of use. There were twenty resolutions from the conference, many of them relating to research: on ecosystems, on human ecology, on monitoring of pollution, etc.

Many other resolutions related to the concept of environmental training. It was suggested that this should be injected at all levels of education.

At both this Conference and the Biosphere Conference, suggestions have been made that an appeal should be made to the financing agencies: to the World Bank and to the U.N. development programs, that they should include a more ecological approach in preinvestment surveys and the development projects. This appeal from the Biosphere Conference carries the weight, of course, of an intergovernmental body.

The main result of the Biosphere Conference is to give us a new and important task. This task is to prepare this year and next year, for submission to the next general conference of UNESCO in October, 1970, a long-term program which is to be called, probably, "Man and the Biosphere." This will be a co-operative program of research and education, to build up national and international structures for observation, research and training.

This program is going to be an heir to the International Biological Program. It is meant to implement, in a practical manner, and all over the world, the results and the methodology defined by the International Biological Program, which will be winding up in 1972.

It is important to note that UNESCO and

the other U.N. agencies are not going to implement the new program; the countries are going to do it. International organizations can't do anything but promote and coordinate. They can give, of course, a little bit of help, particularly to developing countries. But they can't do anything in place of the countries' own effort.

It is hoped that the countries will all cooperate in this international effort, this international program, *which has no set limit of time*. It's not a decade or anything like that.

This means, of course, that the countries will have to build up certain basic structures to be able to participate in the program. These structures will be primarily scientific and educational. The program should help countries to define their environmental policies on the basis of sound scientific knowledge and to help the countries build up what is called in French an *aménagement du territoire*. This will form the basis of international environmental planning.

All this will have to be done fairly rapidly. I would like to say that this particular Conference came exactly at the right moment as far as we are concerned, because all the work which has been done here, the case histories and the discussions, will be extremely helpful to those of us who are going to help prepare this long-term program.

In addition to the Biosphere Conference, the General Assembly of the United Nations has just passed a resolution for a broad conference on the human environment and its problems—scientific as well as economic, administrative, legal, and political—which will take place in 1972. This subject, therefore, has become very much a concern in the U.N. family.

COMMONER: Thank you. Dr. Coolidge, would you like to comment on IUCN, which is another international institution that has been thinking about these problems?

COOLIDGE: Gladly. The IUCN is an independent international organization made up of a membership of 27 governments and 210 organizations from 53 countries. It is now in its twentieth year. It has been called the custodian of the ecological conscience of mankind: a rather large order. The Union's basic purpose is to help define the rational use of the earth's resources to achieve the highest quality of living for mankind. It operates through six commissions: Ecology, Landscape Planning, National Parks, Conservation Education, Endangered Species (called "Survival Service"), and a Legislative Commission.

Ever since it was founded the Union has been involved with furthering the ecological point of view. Its activities include very active participation in conferences held in Africa, Southeast Asia and Latin America. The IUCN also cooperated with UNESCO, FAO and WHO in the World Biosphere Conference, and works very closely with the International Biological Program. I feel that the International Union has a valuable structure, a certain amount of experience, and is tremendously willing to cooperate in every possible way in carrying forward the recommendations that come out of this Conference. I stand ready to offer this Conference the full cooperation of the IUCN in the further development of what we have been discussing here, and I think we are in a position to be able to give very considerable help. We have 410 volunteers who are associated scientists and specialists with our various committees.

MILTON: I would like to point out that for lack of time, money and space in the program the case histories and discussion in this Conference have not dealt with a number of other important ecological consequences of technology: for example, oil, gas and coal development; mining; a host of urban pollution problems; the obliteration of biologically diverse forests and the replacement of them with introduced, homogeneous stands easier to manage; the destruction of potentially important wilderness, national park and biological reserve areas; the many problems affecting biospheric change, particularly in the atmosphere and oceans; and the development of radical new transportation technologies such as the SST. All of these subjects are of great environmental significance and deserve further intensive analysis through case studies.

What cannot be adequately examined by the case technique, however, are (a) the multiple impacts of various technologies on man and the environment in a simultaneous and cumulative sense, and (b) the long-term effects of any particular technological application on the whole biosphere.

It is important to emphasize that the combined pollutions of every nation are having an almost completely unknown effect upon world atmospheric balance and upon the productivity of the earth's oceans. Beyond the serious and important specific local problems caused by misguided development technologies, there are substantial impacts on the biosphere from these same actions. The problem of pesticide use in cotton-spraying programs extends far beyond the cotton fields, for example. The same residues are carried into the oceans, into the air and into the tissues of many species distant from the initial application. Mankind must become responsive to eliminating the long-term cumulative degradation of the biosphere, as well as the single short-term pollutions.

This will not be easy. Men are usually most concerned first, with obtaining produced wealth; second, with immediate obvious threats having simple solutions; third, with maintaining "free" resources such as good air, water and attractive surroundings; and lastly, with distant, long-term threats (to themselves, their children, their nation and their habitat) requiring complex solutions. The greatest environmental problems fall in this last category.

COMMONER: Thank you. Now, we need to consider the relevance of what we have assembled here to the actual operation of international governmental agencies. Mr. Rodgers has some comments on this subject.

RODGERS: I would like to underline three of the principal lessons I have learned in this Conference. First, we have stressed the need for better and more comprehensive preinvestment surveys before development projects are identified and initiated. Second, we need to improve our criteria for selection of development projects, particularly through the process of feasibility studies; and finally, we need to perform systematic post-audits of development projects in order to learn from our mistakes.

We have constantly stressed the need for a holistic approach in our surveys and preinvestment studies in order to avoid a piecemeal consideration of complex environmental interrelationships. Two suggestions come to mind. First, it seems that we need more broad regional studies prior to development selection. In other words, we need more reconnaissance-level studies before we jump into the selection of specific development projects. If we look at a region in terms of its physical resources, its human resources, and its needs for development and if at the outset we consider carefully the implications of certain kinds of development to the equilibrium which presently exists between human and natural influences in the region, we have a better possibility of avoiding the big mistakes (or as Dr. Boulding has characterized them, the irretrievable disasters). Second, as a method of assuring a more comprehensive approach at the survey or preinvestment stage, it has been stressed throughout the latter part of this Conference that the interdisciplinary team approach to survey seems to be justified. The few "success stories" in development have contained within them elements of at least a partial team or interdisciplinary approach. The ecologist or person knowledgeable about ecological principles may be well suited to serve as a team leader of an interdisciplinary team engaged in a regional preinvestment survey. Unfortunately, as has been pointed out here, there are very few such ecologically trained persons who are in leadership positions. It seems to me that these conference case histories demonstrate the urgent need to bring the ecologists into the hard world of the international development agencies.

There is a wide gap between the theory and practice of the integrated reconnaissance survey of regions. In the international agencies with which I am familiar there is a severe problem of bureaucratic fragmentation of the different scientific disciplines which should be teamed together for a proper integrated survey. As a result, putting together a good survey team is an extremely difficult proposition, and determining who will manage it is frequently a delicate problem. Just as in the academic environment attempts to cross over departmental lines in order to provide a student with training of a multidisciplinary nature encounters obstacles, so in international agencies the attempt to maintain a truly interdisciplinary team over a long period of time is plagued with difficulties. We can put together a team for a specific survey but most people who have been involved in such efforts have come to realize that the process of developing integration within the team is an extremely slow one, and one which sometimes is never really accomplished. Frequently it is only at the conclusion of a project that the team begins to function with some form of unity or integration, and shortly thereafter the team is disbanded.

Let me proceed now to my second point regarding the financing of development projects. I will confine my remarks here only to international agencies which are involved in financing of international develop-ment, or what the developing countries refer to as "external aid." A few general figures might be in order at this point to put this matter of international financing into perspective. A survey was recently completed by the U. S. State Department regarding the total world development financial aid, including all sources for the period covering 1962 to 1967. During this period a total of $39 billion in development financing was made available—including both loan funding and grant funding. Of this total, $23.6 billion or 60 per cent of the total was in the form of loans, while $15.4 billion or 40 per cent of the total was in the form of grants. Taking a particular region with which I am personally more familiar, the relationship between loans and grants is even more impressive. For the fiscal period 1962 to 1968 for Latin America, out of a total of $3.8 billion of U.S. assistance, $3 billion or 80 per cent was in the form of loans while $776.4 million or 20 per cent was in the form of grants. My purpose in presenting these figures is simply to point out one thing: that in international development assistance a very large proportion of the important decisions are being taken by banks. Therefore, if we wish to improve the criteria for selection of development projects, the international banking community is an important focal point. Experience dictates that one of the very critical moments regarding major investments which are financed by banks is what criteria are used to determine the economic feasibility or justification of a development project. These criteria have been established over the years by the pragmatic experience of the economists and engineers who staff banking institutions. In most cases they are in the form of manuals or internal memoranda. The consulting engineering firms which are frequently contracted to carry out feasibility studies follow these banking criteria quite religiously. For the most part only the banks' criteria for feasibility studies are taken into account in the final cost-benefit analysis in project financing. If it were possible to introduce certain considerations into these feasibility study criteria which would assure a more comprehensive or ecological approach to the analysis of a development project and its future implications, we might be able to head off some of the disasters which have occurred in the past. What I am saying, very simply, is that we need to establish a very effective dialogue between the economists and engineers who staff our international lending institutions and the kind of scientists who sit around this conference room.

My third point deals with the post-audit of development projects and development decisions. I think this Conference has demonstrated extremely well the great value of the case study approach. We have here an enormously valuable and unprecedented body of knowledge of well-documented failures in international development projects. The value of these case studies to the deliberations of this Conference suggests that some means need to be found for continuing this process on a more systematic basis. What must not be overlooked, however, is that an effective post-audit costs money and takes time. Also, as Dr. Crowcroft has pointed out, the agency carrying out the investment survey or financing the particular development project is not in the best position to execute the post-audit because it is, first of all, under constant pressure to get on with the business of more surveys and more projects. Secondly, as Dr. Haskell has pointed out, the international agency in order to protect its own future would not likely want to make public a comprehensive post-audit of any of its project failures. A number of international financing agencies, however, are at this time undertaking what amounts to internal post-audits of their own projects. This is a commendable effort and one which needs to be reinforced. So long as the results of the post-audit have a feedback to the process of selection of projects for financing, one important goal would have been achieved. To be more specific, such audits should concentrate on determining what were the key factors in success or failure of a particular project; then the agency responsible should make sure that this information results in appropriate modifications of the criteria for project selection employed by the lending institution.

One of the most discouraging aspects of this Conference has been the documented repetition of failures. It seems that our real problem is not so much the lack of knowledge as the lack of good communications. I would like therefore to point out two of many possible lines of relevant action. First, there is the matter of education. There is no doubt that we need more ecologically oriented persons in many different scientific disciplines. I do not think it is a matter of only training ecologists; it is a matter of incorporating ecological training and the holistic approach into the curriculums of economists, engineers, sociologists, anthropologists, urban and regional planners as well as physical and natural scientists. We should keep in mind also what Dr. Zonneveld has pointed out: we need a special kind of training for the individuals who will participate in interdisciplinary teams involved in surveys for development. We need to train a stronger and better group of survey team leaders.

A second immediate line of action should be the establishment of an ongoing dialogue between the type of scientists here and the economists and engineers within the development agencies who are currently making most of the important decisions regarding international development. Let us make no mistake; these economists and these engineers are presently in the center of the stage in international development. I speak not only of the economists and engineers within the banking institutions but also of those within the developing countries themselves. Unless the community of scientists represented in this room establishes communication with these individuals, I feel that much of what we have said in these last three days may have been wasted. The problem is to reach this very important body of key decision makers. The book resulting from this Conference is going to be an important vehicle for communicating our ideas, but I do not believe it will be a substitute for the continuing dialogue with development agencies that is required. I would hope that the sponsors of this Conference and the other important foundations and agencies represented here may be in a position to press forward on this important challenge.

COMMONER: Thank you very much. Mr. John C. Rothberg, who is science liaison officer from The Agency for International Development (A.I.D.), has been here during the entire Conference, and would like to make some comments now.

ROTHBERG*: Thank you. I have enjoyed the Conference, and wish to offer a few observations. Let me start with the basic premise that it is the assisted country which decides (for better or for worse) on its development goals. The countries want "development" defined as *they* perceive it. The AID can't "sell" A if the country doesn't want A. Of course AID doesn't have to accept B, which the country may want, but in fact the choice to be made is seldom so stark as either A or B: A and B usually blend into C, D, E and F.

Ecologists—or anybody else—can influence AID programs the most the closer they get to the country level. The prospects for influencing AID programs are greatest when working with the assisted government, less with the AID Mission, still less with the

AID regional bureau in Washington, and least of all with the AID central staff.

Ecologists have certain advantages in their efforts to influence AID officials. (1) They pursue an interdisciplinary approach; AID follows an integrated country program approach. Both these approaches are in contrast with the emphasis on a particular professional or technical specialty. (2) Ecologists have a basic concern with the AID basic priorities of *agriculture, education* and *family planning.* Ecologists will have a greater chance for influencing AID programs if they make their case in terms of one or another of these basic priorities, and not talk about "ecology" or "science."

This Conference shows how much we have learned, particularly in the field of ecology, but also *how much* we still have to learn, about the development process—a process that is difficult, complicated and multivariate. We have been thinking about the development problem for only a short time—perhaps a dozen years? The Marshall Plan experience was misleading—we are now working with countries which lack the institutional and technological base which the Marshall Plan countries had. It's unfortunate that the impressive and rapid performance of the Marshall Plan countries led to unrealistic expectations of AID programs, operating in less-developed countries. Ecologists—and other professionals—have an obligation to help educate the American public and the Congress on the nature of the difference. The AID hasn't done this very well.

This Conference has also added to the evidence that—with far less excuse—we have not solved analogous problems in the U.S. It may be useful to bear this in mind when considering why AID has not taken greater account of ecological factors in its programs overseas.

From the impressive evidence of the case studies discussed at this Conference, it is clear that ecological factors—along with

* Mr. Rothberg has most recently been in charge of organizing the Congressional Presentation on the Alliance for Progress Programs and other special assignments for The Agency for International Development.

others!—*do* have to be taken into account by AID policy-makers. One AID director said: "We are prisoners of the experts." He knows he needs expert advice and he seeks expert advice, but usually on a particular field of expertise rather than on the total environmental impact. One can hardly be surprised that the AID director—any more than some of the policy-makers referred to in this Conference—has not made use of the interdisciplinary insights of the ecologist. However, AID is increasing its emphasis on evaluation and on improving its information system, thus allowing for the possibility of post-audit emphasis on ecology. It is true, however, that an institutional mechanism to consider the total environment is lacking, and we would welcome suggestions on how to handle this.

The key factor in contributing to a great emphasis on ecological considerations in AID development programs is *people*—in the governments of assistance countries, in AID Missions, and among university contractors and other U.S. advisors. There are not enough good people with an understanding of the total environmental impact to go around.

COMMONER: Thank you. We now have various specific suggestions made by the previous speakers indicating ways to implement the insights which this Conference has developed. I would like to mention several of them and then turn to a general discussion of these and additional propositions.

One clear recommendation was that we ought to take the initiative in establishing a dialogue with the scientists, economists, engineers, project directors, and others who are operationally concerned with development programs.

A second suggestion was that we bring our insight into the problem before the public, before Congress, and before groups in other countries, in order to provide a more effective background understanding of ecological issues in the development process.

A third specific suggestion was that we could help to develop post-audit operations and techniques. The case histories that we have developed here could provide the starting point for such an effort.

The floor is now open to discussion on specific suggestions for implementation.

TAKAHASHI*: I think one of the problems that we face in the Bank is that we have not been in the development business very long; we still have a lot to learn about development. Some of the scientists on our staff keep reminding us that we really don't know a great deal about the ecology of the developing countries.

Most agricultural research has been done under temperate conditions. Twenty years ago development economists felt that by applying some of these techniques in tropical areas, we would get rather rapid development. Over the years, we learned the hard way that this is simply not the case; substantial research still needs to be done, particularly on responses of various types of plants and animals to tropical conditions. Here the ecologists and environmental scientists can render some valuable contributions.

We in the World Bank, like most of you here, believe in the multidisciplinary approach. Our basic work unit is a "mission," usually consisting of economists, agricultural scientists, biologists, engineers, and financial analysts. The team leader may be an economist, engineer or even a biological scientist. We are trying to move away from just reducing the problem to one of specialization. We hope rather to get the specialist to understand what some of the other problems are, and thus try to build up generalists who can perform the functions that the ecologist is aiming at.

There is one other point I would like to make in relation to post-audits. We in the Bank have been gradually building up our

* Mr. Takahashi is a development economist, working in the field of agriculture with the World Bank.

agricultural lending. Last year we made about $175 million in agricultural loans. This year we expect to do about $350 million, and over the next five years perhaps double that per-year amount. In this connection we realize the importance of post-audit activities and more and more we are trying to build reporting procedures into our projects to measure what the impacts of our investments have been.

Mr. Kamarck indicated earlier that past project results have often been quite different from those anticipated. We hope to be closer to the mark on future projects as we try to take into account various environmental factors as well as economic and technical factors.

PARELL*: Mr. Chairman, I have listened to this Conference with great interest, and have also read much of the tremendous case history evidence. This whole experience is revealing, for one who, like myself, has spent years in the field involved in the business of development. I must say this information would be extremely valuable to those responsible for designing the scope and content of the proposed 1972 U. N. Conference on the Problems of the Human Environment.

Listening here, and also based on my experience in the United Nations, I am struck by the multiplicity of views being expressed and by the projection of certain values arising out of dissimilarities in cultures and developmental experiences.

In the background discussion on the U.N. 1972 Conference, the Swedish representative emphasized the tremendous amount of legislative regulation needed in this field. Then a representative of a private enterprise economy stressed the private approach to control over the human environment, mentioning the immense amount of dollars that will ultimately have to be spent by industry and by private enterprise to overcome some of these difficulties.

* Mr. Parell is with the United Nations.

A representative of a planned economy was very quick to quote the difficulties that would arise if, as Karl Marx said, a culture develops without control rather than being directed logically: Nothing but wasteland is left behind. He was also anxious to show that degradations of the environment are much more likely in a private profit-directed economy than in the others.

On the other hand, there was a representative of an "underdeveloped" country, who emphasized the dehumanization of cultural values which all too often accompanies new technologies. He felt that measures should be taken, wherever new technologies are introduced, to overcome the resultant dehumanization.

I like the suggestions made in Professor White's paper on an early warning service system, preparation of manuals for project evaluation, and studies of the full social and environmental costs and benefits of any proposed project. Those already involved in the business of development should help in conducting these surveys.

These suggestions are extremely constructive, and are capable of being implemented at various levels: international, national or regional.

Governments might initiate such studies through their national planning commissions, functional ministries, autonomous research institutes, and professional organizations. The results could be embodied in concrete terms, in certain demonstration areas.

I think the methodology for setting certain environmental standards must be developed and the national evaluation organizations be strengthened. Let's not fool ourselves—whatever we say here will ultimately have to percolate into the national and the field levels. Certain countries have very strong policy-making organizations which should be the target for strengthening environmental quality concerns.

COMMONER: I add to my list of suggested

implementations the transmission of the information gathered here, and our methodology as it is developed, to the 1972 United Nations Conference.

Also, we should make an effort to engage in a dialogue with representatives of various nations who have different value judgments on these issues; there is also the entire assemblage of issues that Dr. White suggested.

HASKELL: Over the next few years, we have a chance to collect further information to feed into the 1972 U.N. meeting, and to take some further action. Perhaps we should consider using this group as an *ad hoc* working group for doing more of these post-audit surveys of development, and disseminating the information. Perhaps the Conservation Foundation or the Center for the Biology of Natural Systems might be ready to assume responsibility for a secretariat to organize such an effort.

You may be able to start directing attention to new development projects which are now going on or will soon begin. These projects could be evaluated, and this evaluation would form the basis for further conferences, such as the 1972 U. N. Conference.

COMMONER: What is being proposed is that some kind of secretariat be organized out of this Conference and that that group undertake to implement the various suggestions that have already been put forward here.

BORGSTROM: We are talking about the human environment and talking in terms of countries. When we are moving into a global catastrophe which already involves two and a half billion people, and where we are adding another one billion in the next ten years, we don't have any time to wait for new research. It's a question of what we can implement over the next ten years.

It is really a question of organizing a war of human survival, as I see it. We have, for example, at least 50 million people in Latin America right now which I would call ecologically displaced persons. How are they going to be moved to viable environments that can sustain survival? They are deteriorating where they are now. Talk about early warning systems. We have one country after another faced with tremendous malnutrition. We know, through nutritional research, that this is affecting their reactions, their whole pattern and approach to life. Their lethargy is a consequence of protein deficiency in the first stages of their lives.

And yet we have endless meetings where we don't formulate action programs. They often are full of good information, but I submit that most of our mistake is simply that we haven't used the information available.

Let us not forget the urgency of immediate action. We are moving toward a least common denominator where we won't have any margin left.

COMMONER: I take it you placed emphasis on the word "working" in the proposal for a *working* group.

At this point I would like to ask Russell Train whether, in view of the suggestion that has been made, and the many exhortations on the urgency of what needs to be done, how he reacts to the proposal to establish an *ad hoc* working group?

TRAIN: I react very positively to this proposal, and I would take it as a suggestion that a working *ad hoc* group should be organized from among this total group that can work cooperatively with appropriate government and other organizations.

CALDWELL: I would like to suggest that among the activities of this continuing group, which we have discussed, there be also a continuing dialogue with the representatives of the international development agencies, many of whom are based either here in Washington or in New York.

COMMONER: Thank you. I have heard a series of proposals, all directed toward a particular pattern of implementation. I have heard no negative comments on that, and

I would view the discussion here as a mandate to the organizers of this meeting to carry out the intent of these proposals. I will now recognize Dr. Phillips for a final remark.

PHILLIPS: Ladies and gentlemen, you have heard me say too much. I'm going to be very brief. I'm going to say something on your behalf. Gunnar Myrdal and I, as the two old boys, the ancients here, put our heads together and we felt that it was our responsibility to thank our hosts for the wonderful opportunity that they have given all of us to sit here to listen, to discuss, to meet one another, to experience clash of mind upon mind.

Our hosts, Russell Train, Barry Commoner, Ray Dasmann, John Milton, Taghi Farvar, and the ladies, younger and older, who looked after us have been truly ecologically minded. (Laughter.)

They have been good ecologists. Why? Because they have not only studied us as organisms, in relation to the environment (Laughter), but they have also attempted to stimulate us to look at things ecologically, synoptically, holistically.

So you see, they have been the perfect ecologists, and I ask you, therefore, to give them a hearty round of thanks for helping to make this Conference so resounding a success and so thoroughly enjoyable. (Applause.)

COMMONER: The agenda calls for closing remarks by the Chairman here. I have taken the prerogative of turning my right to comment over to our poet laureate, Kenneth Boulding.

BOULDING: A brief benediction:

Infinity is ended, and mankind is in a box;
The era of expanding man is running out of rocks;
A self-sustaining Spaceship Earth is shortly in the offing
And man must be its crew—or else the box will be his coffin!

GENERAL INDEX

A

Abbott's booby (*Sula abbottii*), 876–78

Aboriginal cultures on Bellona and Rennell Islands, 877

Abrahamson, Dean E., 1022
article by, 795–810
discussion participant, 854–57, 892–902, 948–54

Academy of Natural Sciences of Philadelphia, studies on thermal pollution, 831–46

Accidents releasing radioactive wastes, 804–7
at the Windscale Works (Eng.), 818

Accumulation and transfer of substances by organisms, 817

Achi, Kamel, 978
article by, 276–86

Adelaide University Botany Department (Australia), studies of an overstocked range, 748–50

Administrators, ecologists as, 896, 897–99
fantasy and reality and, 898

Advertising, effects of campaigns by American insecticide producers, 463, 465–66
in Cañete Valley, Peru, 462–63
creation of human need-human demand, 782–83

Aerial control of red locust, 511–12

Afghanistan. *See* Helmand Basin

Africa. *See also* specific countries
agricultural development in, 570–73
biogeographical regions of, 191–92
aquatic, 191–93
cotton production in Central Africa, 407–20, 463–64
archeological record of, 464
FAO fertilizer program in, 552–53
fish acreage in, 756
groundnut scheme in, 571
increasing animal productivity in, 783–84
lactose intolerance in, 63–64
nutrition in, 7
plant nutrient usage in, 551–52
red locust control program in, 505–15
reservoir projects in, hazards of, 920. *See also* specific reservoirs
rural malnutrition in, 84–86
semi-arid regions in, destruction of natural resources by development projects, 905

soils of, impact of development on, 568–75, 658–59
technological development and increase of disease in, 69–96
malaria, 81–84
schistosomiasis, 77–81
trypanosomiasis, 71–76
tsetse fly, its influence on, 726–41

African army worm (*Spodoptera exempta*), 520–21

Agency for International Development (AID), ways to influence, 979–80

Agricultural development, effect on pest incidence, 521–22
in East Africa, 570–73

Agricultural research, 632. *See also* Plant germ plasm

Agricultural revolution. *See also* Plant germ plasm
beginnings of, 633–34
buying time with, 960

Agriculture. *See also* specific crops and specific areas
industrialized as main polluter of environment, 657–58
heterogeneity and small holdings, 663–66
slash-and-burn, effects on island ecosystems, 873–74

Agro-ecosystem, definition of, 374, 463
of cotton, 398–401

Agro-industrial complexes, nuclear, 855–56. *See also* Radiation; Radioactive hazards of, 795–810

Aid to underdeveloped countries, competition among agencies, 933–34

from U.S., 787–88

need for multilateral organizations for, 787–88

need to recreate on moral grounds, 962

Aiken, George, 796–97

Akiba, T., 36

Albolineum (white oil), 470–71, 475–76

Aldrin, 430, 443, 450, 451, 451–52

Alfalfa, and rodent damage in Israel, 532

Alfalfa seed chalid (*Bruchophagus gibbus Boh.*), 361

Alfalfa weevil (*Hapera variabilis*), 354

Algae, tolerance for insecticides, 461

Algeria, overhead irrigation in, 365–66

Al Kholy, Abdul Rahman, 164

Allen, Robert N., 1022

article by, 318–42

discussion participant, 343–48

Alliance for Progress, 882

Almond borers (*Capnodis* spp.), 359–60

Alternative systems approach to development projects, 909–11, 964–65

Amazon Basin, proposed development of, 256, 895–96

American agriculture. *See also* specific states or areas

exploitation of Peruvian fish meal, 780–82

American Institute of Nutrition, 59

Ammonium nitrate, 553–54, 554, 555

Ammonium sulfate, 553–54ff., 570f.

Amoebiasis, in Colombia, 58–59, 141

Ampicillin, 38, 39

Anchicaya Hydroelectric Project (Colombia), 318–42

Anchicaya Dam, 322–24

Anchicaya dredge, 336–38

defects in planning, 319–21

Digua debris dams, 334–36

diversion tunnel and bottom outlet, 324

history of, 321–23

maps of, 320, 321

normal situation in Digua River before construction of dams, 332–33

outlet tower, 324–25

sedimentation of the reservoir, 325–29, 338–39

methods of preventing, 330–35

plans for future control of, 340–42

Upper Anchicaya Project, 339–40

Anchicaya River, ability to transport sediment, 333–34

Anchoveta (*Engraulis ringens* L.), biology of, 960–61

catch of, in Peru and Chile, 758

in Peru, 757–58

decline in Peruvian catch, 763–65

economics of/exploitation of Peruvian boom by wealthy nations, 781

Andean Maize Germ Plasm Bank, 649–50

Angaur (Palau), phosphate mining on, 901

Anhydrous ammonia, 554

Animals. *See also* specific animals

extinction of, in Caribbean Islands, 823

introduction of, into island ecosystems, 871–72

Anopheline mosquitoes, 20, 81ff., 465, 482–83

Antibiotics, indiscriminate use of, in agriculture, 36, 141

transferable resistance of, 35–46

Anti-locust Research Centre, 513–15

Apex bollworm (*Popocera atramen talis,* Led.), 430

Aphids (*Aphis gossypii,* Glov.), 388–89, 394–95, 411, 427, 431, 443–44ff.

resistance to insecticides, 392–93, 30–31, 443

(*Aphis pomi, A. punicae,* and *A. fabae*), 352, 360–61, 470

Appleby, Paul B., 937

Aquatic ecosystems, African, evolution of, 191–92

effect of molluscicides on microflora and microfauna of, 109–15

effect of, on epidemiology of schistosomes in Rhodesia, 102–7

effect on, of dams and barrages in the Nile catchment, 197

Aquatic species, biological changes in, due to pollution, 833–35

effect of thermal pollution on, 830–31

environmental requirements of, 830–31

Introducing suitable species into altered environments, 848–49

Arboricides, 222–23

Argentina, lack of professional institutions and manpower in, 952–53

Arid lands, 788–89

overgrazing of, in Australia, 742–52

respect for carrying capacity of, 788–89

salinity of water in, 345–46

unfavorable ecological conditions for irrigation of, 285–86

Aron, Raymond, 929

Arsenic, 427

Aruan (*Ophiocephalus striatus* Bloch,), 490, 490–91, 492

Ashanti Tribal Region (Ghana), trypanosomiasis epidemic in, 71–72

Asia, plant nutrients, usage of, 551–52

Assumptions, regarding development, 929–30

regarding relationship between man and nature, 929

Aswan Dam, 196–97

Aswan High Dam, 130–32, 196–97, 920. *See also* Lake Nasser

decrease in agricultural acreage in Egypt due to, 245–46, 252–53

destruction of fisheries of southwestern Mediterranean by, 160–76, 203–4

displacement of Egyptian Nubian population by, 374

effect on soils in Nile Valley, 245–46, 249–51

evaporation from, 245–46

planning studies for, 919–21

Atlanta, Georgia (U.S.), dysentery outbreak in, 41

Atomic Energy Commission. *See* U. S. Atomic Energy Commission

Atomic testing, effect on island ecosystems, 876

Atomic wastes. *See* Radioactive wastes

Auger, Pierre, 937

Australia, arid lands in, utilization of, 742–52

cotton production in, 398–99

drought years, 1895–1903, 745–47

future of sheep industry in, 750–52

introduction of sheep into, 744

leasehold system of land tenure in, 750–51

overgrazing of arid lands in, 744–48

rainfall in South Australia, 743–44

Royal Commission of 1898 for investigation of pastoral industry, 745–47

Royal Commission of 1927, 747–48

Automobiles, relation to incidence of urinary stones, 49–50

Axis deer, introduction of, on Molokai, 878–79

proposed introduction of, on Hawaii, 879

Azande tribe, 596–97

Azinphosmethyl, 449, 451

Azodrin, 388–89, 393

B

Bag worms (*Psychidae clania* and *P. mahasena*), 472–73, 474, 478–79

(*Cremastopsyche pendula*), 478–79

(*Metisa plana*), 478–79

Bailey, L. H., 870–71

Baker Resolution, 855–56

Ballad of Ecological Awareness, 3, 157, 371, 669, 793, 983

Banaba (Ocean Island), destruction of, by mining, 876–77

Banded-winged whitefly (*Trileurodes abutilonea*), 380–81, 444–45

Banks, as major decision mak-

ers in development, 977–78

Caja de Credito Agraria, 613–15, 618–20

Inter-American Development Bank, 610, 628

Barbados. *See also* Lesser Antilles

economic situation in, 862–63

growth rate in, 948

Bardach, John E., 1022

article by, 236–44

Barley, yield from heterogeneous populations, 652–53

Barlow, C. H., 130–31

Barn owl, influence of, on rodent population, 529–30

reproduction rate of, affected by mice population, 532–33

(Ba) Tawana Tribe, 733, 733–34

Bates, Marston, 22

Batisse, Michel, 1022

discussion participant, 245–56, 343–48, 545–48, 775–89, 892–902, 948–54, 955–83

Baylucid, 110ff.

Bedouin nomads, 673–75. *See also* Nomadism

consequences of settlement of, in Saudi Arabia, 683–92

Bee bug (*Platyngomiriodes apiformis*), 475

Beets, nitrate accumulation in, 581–82

Beet weevil (*Lixus junci*), 354

Behavioral change in man, need for, 938–39

Belaunde, Fernando, 895–96

Belgium, fish acreage of, 756

fish use in, 755f.

Bellona Island, threat of phosphate mining on, 876–77

Bengal, toxicity to fish of insecticides, 492–93

Beta-naphthylamine, as cause of bladder tumors, 47
BHC, 429, 469, 470–71, 471–72, 491
insect resistance to, 392–93, 430–31
toxicity to freshwater fish, 493–97
BHC-DDT, 444–45
BHC-DDT-Sulfur, 442–43
Big-eyed bugs, 445
Bilharziasis. *See* Schistosomiasis
Bindi (*Bassia*), 748–49
Biological control of pests, 545
of desert locusts, 516–17. *See also* Integrated control of insect pests
Biological effects of radiation, 806–9
Biology, lack of, in training of engineers, 949
Biosphere, global system for protection of, 940
Biosphere Conference (1968), 974–75
recommendations of, 940–41
Biotic uniqueness, of Caribbean Islands, 820–22
of island ecosystems, 870
Bird, A. V., 107
Birds. *See also* specific birds
diurnal birds of prey, effect of rodent control on, 528–41
thallium poisoning in, 533–34, 534–38
grain-eating birds, thallium poisoning in, 539–41
sensitivity to toxaphene, dieldrin, aldrin, 450–51
Black, C. E., 6
Black beetle (*Calosoma abreviatum* Chaud.), 431
Black Kite (*Milvus M. migrans*), effect of rodent control on, in Israel, 530–31, 531, 535 (Ta-

ble), 538–39
Bladder carcinoma, 47, 48–49
Blister beetle (*Epicauta vittata*), 376–77
Blood fluke. *See* Schistosomes
Bluebush (*Kochia*), overgrazing of, in Australia, 748–50
Blue Nile, 199–200
Boa Vista Development Project (Brazil), laterization in, 603–4
Bobwhite quail, 452–53
Bockh, Alberto, 1022
article by, 301–16
Bodenheimer, F. S., 528–29ff., 532–33
Bolin, T. D., 1022–23
article by, 61–67
Bolivia, Caranavi settlement in, 620–28
land settlement in, 609–30
determined by new roads, 660–61
map of, 621
protein deficiency in, 660–61
Bollworm (*Heliothis* spp.), 377–78ff., 392–93, 394–95, 396, 398f., 411–12ff., 427–28, 431ff., 443–44f., 476
development of control program in Central Africa, 415–18
influence of cotton production on, 411–16
resistance to insecticides, 392–93, 430, 443
Bonelli's eagle (*Hieraetus fasciatus*), effect of rodent control on, in Israel, 535 (Table), 539–40
Borgstrom, George, 1023
article by, 753–72
discussion participant, 245–56, 657–66, 775–89, 892–902, 955–83
Borkou nomads, standard of living of, 677

Borlaug, Norman E., 640–42, 643–44
Borneo States, malaria control in, 482–84
Boron, 554
Boston, Massachusetts (U.S.), *Salmonella* infection at Childrens Hospital Medical Center, 41–42
Botswana. *See* Republic of Botswana
Bottle feeding of infants in African towns, 90–91
Boulding, Kenneth, 1023
Ballad of Ecological Awareness, 3, 157, 371, 669, 793, 983
discussion participant, 137–53, 460–66, 775–89, 892–902, 955–83
Boza Barducci, Teodoro, 1023
article by, 423–38
discussion participant, 460–66
Braconid wasp (*Apanteles iphiaulux*), 473
Bragantina colonies (Brazil), lateritic soils in, 604–5
Branch borers (*Zeuzera* spp.), 470, 470–71, 472, 473
Brazil, Boa Vista Development Project, 603–4
Bragantina colonies, 604–5
lateritic soils in, 591–607
Nutrition Survey of Northeast, 56–57
President Dutra (Iata) Colony, 605–6
Tome Acu, 605–6
Brestan, 7–8, 492–93
Brody, Jane E., 91–92
Bronx, New York (U.S.) shigellosis outbreak at Albert Einstein College of Medicine, 41–42
Bruce-Chwatt, L. W., 82–83
Brucellacease, 37–38
Buchinger, Maria, 899
discussion participant, 892–902

Bud weevil or picudo (*Anthonomus vestitus*, Bohm.), 382, 392–93, 427

Bulbul (*Pycnonotus capensis*), effect of pesticides on, in Israel, 540–41

Bunce, George E., 1023
article by, 53–59
discussion participant, 137–53

Burgher John C., 813–15

Burma, Nutrition Survey of (1963), 50–51

Buzzards (*Buteo b. buteo* and *v. vulpinus*), effect of rodent control on, in Israel, 531, 535 (Table)

C

Caballo Dam (U.S.), 291–92

Cabbage, nitrate accumulation in, 581–82

Cabbage looper (*Trichoplusia ni*), 394–95, 417–18
resistance to insecticides, 430–31

Cairns, John, Jr., 1023
article by, 829–51
discussion participant, 460–66, 657–66, 775–89, 854–57, 948–54

Caja de Credito Agraria (Agricultural Credit Bank), 613–15, 618–20

Calcium arsenate, 427–28, 442–43, 443–44

Caldwell, Lynton K., 1023
article by, 927–45
discussion participant, 137–53, 343–48, 854–57, 892–902, 948–54, 955–83

California, Imperial Valley, cotton production in, 396–98
San Joaquin Valley, cotton production in, 398
sardine industry in, collapse of, 780–81

Cambodia, development plans for Mekong River, 236–44

Camels, as nomadic livestock, 675–76

Canal clearance, control method for snails, 130–31

Cancers resulting from radiation, 808–9

Cañete Valley (Peru), 426–27
advertising campaign in, and exploitation by American insecticide producers, 462–63
effect of pesticides on cotton production in, 424–38, 461–62, 462–63
programs to control cotton pests in, 428–29, 430–32

Caqueta Settlement (Colombia), 613–20
climate of, 616–17
farm incomes in, 618
land use in, 617–18
terrain and soil of, 616

Caranavi Settlement (Bolivia), 620–28
climate of, 622–23
cooperativism in, 624–25
employment opportunities in, 627–28
geographic setting of, 622–23
government programs in, 628
land use in, 625–28
settlers in, 625, 627–28
soils in, 623–24

Carbamate insecticides, insect resistance to, 396

Carbaryl, 450–51, 451–52

Caribbean Islands, animal extinction in, 823, 901–2
biotic uniqueness of, 820–22
destruction of soil and forest resources of, 901–2
development programs for, ecological view of, 858–67
Faulty economic-social system of, 902
imminence of ecological disaster in, 948
malnutrition and overpopulation in, 901

Caribbean monk seal, 874

Carlozzi, Carl A., 1023–24
article by, 858–67
discussion participant, 137–53, 245–56, 545–48, 775–89, 854–57, 892–902, 948–54, 955–83

Caroni Wildlife Sanctuary Swamp (Lesser Antilles), pollution of, 865

Carrots, as Vitamin A source, 142
nitrate accumulation in, 581–82

Case histories, experiments with, in an ecology seminar, 907–8, 911–13

Cash-cropping. *See also* Monoculture
effect of, on insects, 387
effect of, on nutrition in Africa, 84–85

Cash economy, effect on health, 874–75

Catchment basin of Cordillera Central Mountains (Dominican Republic), 888–89

Catena, definition of, 593

Cat fish (*Clarias batrachus* Linnaeus), effect of insecticides on, in rice paddies, 490, 490–91

Catla (*Catla catla*), effect of insecticides on, in rice paddies, 490

Cats, effect of mosquito spraying on, 483–84

Cattle, as nomadic livestock, 675–76
effect of proposed Jonglei Canal on, 600–1

in wildlife and tsetse areas of Rhodesia, 712–24

nagana among, in Africa, 75–76

In Kariba Lake Basin, 212–23

numbers of, in Rhodesia, 716–17

Cattle, beef, as a cause of pollution, in U. S. Midwest, 779–80

tax policies responsible for, 785

in East Africa, 574

possibility of intensive management of, 640–41

Cattle, dairy, in Kenya, 571, 572–73

Cattle egrets (*Bubulcus ibis*), effect of rodent control on, in Israel, 534, 540

Cauliflower, nitrate accumulation in, 581–82

Cedars of Lebanon, decline of, 777

Celphaloridine, 38

Center for Short-lived Phenomena, 898–99

Central Africa, archeological record of cotton production in, 463–64

cotton production and insect pests, 407–20, 463–64

insect control program, 415–18

list of major pests, 412

Central America, cotton industry in, 394–96

Cereals, effect of erratic rainfall on, 568

Ceylon, fish acreage of, 756

Chadwick, D. R., 806–8

Chalcid parasites (*Antrocephalus* spp.), 483

Chaves, Nelson, 57

Chemical dyes and bladder tumors, 48–49

Chemicals. *See also* Fertilizers, Insecticides, Mollus-cicides, Pesticides, *and* specific chemicals

effect of those used to control rodents and jackals in Israel, 527–43

interfering with reproductive physiology of locusts, 513

Chile, anchoveta catch in, 758

fish acreage in, 756

fish meal exports by, 758, 768–69

China, fish acreage in, 756

total aquatic catch by, 759

Chlordane, 447–49

Chlorinated compounds, 445, 451–52, 492–93. *See also* specific compounds

insect resistance to, 392–93, 396, 430–31, 443

corn pest resistance, 456

solubility of and storage in animal fats, 446–47

table of residues in soil and soybeans in Louisiana, 455

tolerance of algae for, 461

Chobe River area (Republic of Botswana), tsetse fly in, 733, 737ff.

Choramphenicol, 38, 39, 39–40

Christmas Island, phosphate mining on, 876–77

Chukar partridges (*Alectoris graeca*), effect of rodent control on, in Israel, 539

Cigarette packages, exported from U.S. without warning statement, 899

Cilicia, disappearance of flax germ plasm from, 635–36

Cinereous vulture (*Aegypius monachus*), effect of rodent control on, in Israel, 536 (Table), 534

Citrus trees, olive black scale, 361

Climate, influence on man, 29–30. *See also* Temperature; Rainfall

Cluster analysis of aquatic biota, 844

Coca (*Erythroxylon coca*), 660–61

Cockchafers (*Melolonthidae; lachnosterna bidentata; Psilopholis vestita*), 478, 480–83, 483–84

Cocoa, effect of fertilizer on, 554

Cocoa pests in Sabah (Malaysia), 469–78

Cocoa production, effects of, on nutrition in West Africa, 84–85

in Sabah (Malaysia), 469–70

Codfish as protein source, 754–55

Coefficient of water utilization, 284

Coffee, 568

effect of fertilizer on, 554

in Kenya, 571, 571–72

Collared dove (*Streptopelia decaocto*), effect of rodent control on, in Israel, 539

Collis, W. R. F., 84–85

Colombia, Anchicaya Hydroelectric Project, 318–42

Caqueta Settlement, 613–20

Colombian corn improvement program in, 651–52

cotton production in, 396

disappearance of corn germ plasm from, 635–36

land settlement in, 609–30

map of, 612

Neiva cotton district, 386–87

parasitological survey in, 58–59

rice varieties in, 639–45

Colonization projects. *See also* Land settlement

post-audit evaluation of, need for, 896–97

Colorado Basin (U.S.), new projects for, motives behind, 919

Columbia River (U.S.), disposal of radioactive wastes in, 813–16

Common carp (*Cyprinus carpia* Linnaeus), 490ff., 492f.

effects of γ-BHC and diazinon on, 493–97

Commoner, Barry, 1024

discussion participant, 137–53, 245–56, 343–48, 460–66, 545–48, 657–66, 775–89, 854–57, 955–83

implications of the Conference, 959–60

summary of the Conference, xxi–xxix

Communicable diseases. *See also* specific diseases

influence of "modernization" on, in Ryukyu Islands, 5–18

mass campaigns against, limitations of, 12–16

Computers and study of ecosystems, 485–86

Conjugation of bacteria cells, 36

Connecticut River (U.S.), use of, by proposed nuclear power plants, 856–57

Conservation criteria in development projects, 908–9

reconciliation with economic efficiency, 919

Conservation programs in Dominican Republic, 887–91

land turnure obstacles to, 887–89

Pilot project, 889–91

Conway, Gordon R., 1024

article by, 467–86

discussion participant, 137–

53, 245–56, 657–66, 955–83

Coolidge, Harold J., 1024

discussion participant, 137–53, 892–902, 955–83

Cooperation on development projects, difficulty of, 922–24

Cooperativism in Caranavi Settlement in Bolivia, 624–25

Copper oxychloride, 492–93

Copper sulfate, 492–93

as molluscicide, 109ff., 118–19, 126–29

cost of, 129–30

effects on fish of Nile Delta Lakes, 280–81

Corbett, G. H., 468–69

Cordillera Central Mountains (Dominican Republic), catchment basins, present condition of, 888–89

Corn, Andean Maize Germ Plasm Bank, 649–50

appearance of, 650–51

breeding of, 645–46

Colombian corn improvement program, 651–52

Cuba Yellow Flint, 647–48

disease and insect reaction to, 650–51

effect of fertilizer on, 552–53

Grain yield of varieties and crosses, 637

International Maize and Wheat Improvement Center, 640–41

maize germ plasm banks, 636–37, 647–48

total digestible nutrients (TDN) of, 639–40

Corn pests, 456

European corn borer, 415

oriental corn borer, 354–55

seed corn maggot, 358

Corps of Engineers, 949

Costa Rica, land settlement in, 611–13, 629–30

Costs of development projects, 949

Cotton. *See also* Cotton production

Acala cotton, 647

breeding for resistance to pests, 376, 416–18

economics of crop protection, 389–91

effect of heterogeneity of crops, 387–89

effect of sequence of crops, 388–89

effect of size of plantings, 389–90

effect of weeds and other plants, 382–87

fruiting characteristics of, 376–78, 410

major producing countries, 375

role of insecticides, 390–92

species and varieties of, 375–76, 411

temperature and sunlight requirements of, 381–82

tetraploid cotton, TH-149, 647

water requirements, 379–81

Cotton boll weevil (*Anthonomus grandis*), 375–76, 377–78, 378–79, 381–82, 384–85, 394–95, 414–15, 441–42, 443–45

resistance to insecticides, 392–93, 430–31, 443

Cotton fleahopper (*Psallus seriatus*), 382, 417–18, 443–44

Cotton leaf perforator (*Bucculatrix thurberiella*, Busck.), 380–81, 384–85, 397–98, 430

resistance to insecticides, 430–31

Cotton leafworm (*Alabama argillacea*), 417–18, 443–44ff.

resistance to insecticides, 392–93, 394–95, 443

Cotton pests. *See also* specific pests

and manipulation of the cotton agro-ecosystem, 373–401

effect of agronomic practices on, 385–87

effect of heterogenous crops on, 387

effect of weather and climate on, 381–82

evolutionary changes in, 378–79

in Australia, 398–99

in California, 396–98

in Central Africa, 407–20

in Central America, 394–96

in Colombia, 396

in Louisiana, 441–49

in South Texas, 396–97

integrated control, 374–75

in Turkey, 395–96

in United States, 444 (Table), 443–44

natural mortality of, 379–80

new pest in Botswana, 366

parasites, predators and pathogens of, 384–86

resistance to insecticides, 392–99

resurgence of treated pests, 445–46

Cotton production. *See also* Cotton; Cotton pests

agro-ecosystem of, 375, 398–401

effect of agro-economic practices on, 385–86

in Australia, 398–99

in California (U.S.), 396–98

in Cañete Valley (Peru), 424–26, 429, 776–83

in Central Africa, 407–20

in Central America, 394–96

in Colombia, 396

in Ecuador, 380–81, 464

in Kenya, 571

in Louisiana, 441–49

in South Texas (U.S.), 396–97

in Turkey, 395–96

on small holdings in Zambezi Valley, 664

Zande scheme for (southern Sudan), 596–98

Cotton strainer (*Dysdercus peruvianus,* Guen.), 391, 411, 427

(*Dysdercus* spp.), 411–13

Cotton whitefly (*Bemisia tabaci*), 395

Cravioto, J., 92

Crested cuckoo (*Clamator glandarius*), effect of jackal control on, in Israel, 541

Crickets, 475

Crocodiles, relation to Nile fisheries, 193–94

Cross-checks on development projects. *See* Post-audits; Pre-audits

Crowcroft, W. Peter, 1024

article by, 742–52

discussion participant, 775–89, 892–902, 955–83

Cryolite, 427–28, 447–49

Cucurbit fruit, cucurbit snout beetle, 355–56

red pumpkin beetle, 359–60

Cultural adaptation in Bolivian settlements, 660–61

Cultural diversity, 964

Cultural integrity, need to preserve, 972

Cultural systems, alien, impact on island ecosystems, 877–79

of small islands, 877–79

Culture, and relation to disease, 32–33

definition of, 32

indigenous, versus "progress," 789

Cutworm (*Agrotis ypsilon*), 352–53

Cyolane, 393

D

Dairy cattle, in Kenya, 571, 572–73

Dairy industry, European, dependence on oilseed from Africa, 780–81

Dalapon (2, 2-dichloropropionic acid), 493

Dam building. *See* Reservoir development; specific dams

Dammerman, K. W., 468–69

Dasmann, Raymond F., 1024

discussion participant, 245–56, 775–89, 948–54, 955–83

Date palm pests, 546

Date palms, effect of irrigation on, in Oued R'Hir Valley (Sahara Desert), 282–85

Davis, Alan E., 1024

article by, 61–67

discussion participant, 137–53, 775–89

DCPA, 493

DDT. *See also* BHC-DDT; BHC-DDT-Sulfur. 82–83, 219, 222, 396–97, 399, 429, 449–50, 451, 469, 470f., 471–72f., 478, 482–83f., 492, 722

in penguins and seals in Antarctic waters, 817

insect resistance to, 393, 430f.

De Bach's insecticidal check technique, 478–79

Decision-making in development, by banks, 977–78

by nations, disadvantages of, 932–33, 944–45

problems of power and information in, 964–66

Defects in development projects. Anchicaya Hydroelectric Project, 320–21

Deforestation, and lateritic soils, 591–607
by herbivores, 871–72
by slash and burn agriculture, 873–74
history of, in Rhodesia, 713–15
in Africa, 550–51
in Caribbean Islands, 901–2

De Haas, J. H., 55

Dendrograms, use of, in thermal pollution studies, 844

Denmark, fish acreage of, 756

Desalination projects, nuclear, inadvisability of, 825, 825–26, 855

Desert locust (*Schistocerca gregaraia* Forskal), 505. *See also* Locust
control program, 513–20
ecological and adaptability of, 515
invasion and recession areas, maps of, 514

Desiccation of Lake Valencia (Venezuela), 304–7, 311–12
recommendations for controlling, 315–16

Developed countries, agriculture in, dependence on imported protein from underdeveloped countries, 767–72, 780–82
fundamental differences from underdeveloped countries, 959–60, 966
main consumers of planet's resources, 969
"nutritional colonialism" of, 781, 968
popular movement in, for solving environmental problems, 960

Developers, possibility of legal action against, 274
resistance of, to drainage as part of irrigation projects, 272–73
responsibility of, 256, 465–66

Development, alternative systems approach to, 909–11
by small, independent groups, 964, 967
competition among aid agencies, 933–34
conservation criteria for, 908–9
cross-checks, importance of, 910–11
cybernetic character of, 933–34
direction of, 882
dominance of economic values in, 930–31
ecological consequences of, 914–26
lack of money and time to deal with, 922–23
lack of scientific fact concerning, 921–22
omission of, in project studies, 921–25
ways of classifying, 916–18
ecological factors in, 896–97
integration of, with social and economic factors, 904–13, 924–25
lack of interest in, in Dominican Republic, 881–91
ecological pre-audit of, importance of, 895–900
effect on pest incidence, 521–22
errors involved in, 319–21, 904–5, 972–73
financing of, 977–78
goals of, 918–19, 929–30, 971–72

diversification of ways of life, 961
gradual versus rapid development, 910
hazards and hidden costs of, 71, 347–48, 934–36
impact of private corporations on, 893–94
importance of synthesis to, 937
inherent ecological nature of, 928–29
is it desirable or not, 782–83, 952, 969–70
meanings of, 928–29ff.
nations as final decision makers in, 932–33
need for comprehensiveness in planning, 932
need to integrate all sciences in, 931
pre- and post-audit evaluation of, lack of, 892–900, 925–26
problems of policy and administration in, 927–45
reconciliation of science and politics in, 937–38
relation of, to quality of living for the individual, 960–61
strategies for sound ecological policies in, 937–39
who, in underdeveloped countries, wants it? 970
who is it for? 968–69

Development agencies. *See also* specific agencies
responsibility for proper direction of development, 961

Development theories, inadequacy of, 931, 935

Diarrhea, and lactose intolerance, 65–67

Diatoms, biological changes in, due to pollution, 833–35
tolerance for insecticides, 461

Diazinon, 471–72, 491, 497
toxicity to fresh water fish, 494–96
Dickerson Plant of the Potomac Electric Power Company, studies of thermal pollution by, 839–46
Dieldrax, 219
Dieldrin, 82–83, 219, 429–30, 442–43, 449–50ff., 452–53, 461, 469, 470–71, 471–72ff., 478, 482–83, 491ff., 510–11, 540, 722, 739
Digua River (Colombia), debris dams on, 334–36
normal situation in, before construction of dams, 332–33
Dimethoate, 471–72
Di-nitro-ortho-cresol, 509–10, 510–11
Dinka tribe (southern Sudan), and the Aweil Rice Project, 599
Dipterex, 491f.
Diquat, 493
Discussions, ecological consequences of intensification of plant productivity, 460–66 (insects), 545–48 (pests), 657–66 (fertilizers and soils)
health and nutritional consequences of selected development programs, 137–53
implications of the conference for international development programs, 959–83
intensification of animal productivity, 775–89
irrigation and water development, 245–56 (dams), 343–48 (soils), 365–67 (insects)
special problems of environmental degradation, 854–57 (atomic wastes), 892–902 (island ecosystems), 948–54 (problems of organization, policy, administration and investigation)
Disease. *See also* Communicable diseases *and* specific diseases
definition of, 28–29, 30–31
development plans for Mekong River, and, 242–43
ecology of, 19–33
effect of modernization on, in Ryukyu Islands, 6
technological development in Africa, and, 69–96
Diseases, plant, 641–44
Diversity of life patterns, proper goal of development, 961, 962–63
"Dominance," definition of, 20
Dominica. *See also* Lesser Antilles
imminence of ecological disaster in, 948
timber resources, proposed use of, 863–64
Dominican Republic, catchment basins, present conditions of, 888–89
conservation of forest, soil and water resources, program of, 887–91
land tenure disputes as obstacle to, 887–89
development projects in, 884–85, 951
natural resources survey of, 882–87
evaluation of the survey data, 885–87
hydrologic investigations, 885
land use mapping, 884–85
reforestation needs, 889–91
soil erosion in, 888–91
Drewes, Wolfram U., 1024
article by, 881–91
discussion participant, 892–902, 948–54
Drug resistance, of malaria parasites, 26–28, 82–83
transferable and the ecological effects of antibiotics, 35–46
Dubos, René, 70–71
Ducks, sensitivity to aldrin, 451–52, 452–53
Dusky stainer (*Oxycarenus* spp.), 411
Dysentery, drug-resistant organisms causing, 41–42
in Kin Son (Ryukyu Isls.), 11–13
in Sherwood Hospital (Eng.), 41–42

E

Eagles (*Aquila* spp.), effect of rodent control on, in Israel, 530–31, 536 (Table), 538–39
Earth, carrying capacity of, 787, 789
as a closed system, 939–40
East Africa, groundnut scheme in, 571
increasing animal productivity in, 783–84
Lake Edward and Lake George, trypanosomiasis epidemic near, 74–75
schistosomiasis in, 138
soils of, impact of technological development on, 568–75, 658–59
Easter Island, 871–72
Eastern Europe, fish use in, 755
Ecological approach to development. Difficulty of evaluating costs and benefits of, 939
premise of, 936–37
studies needed for successful irrigation systems, 285–86

Ecological Awareness, Ballad of, 3, 157, 371, 669, 793, 983

Ecological bankruptcy, in the Caribbean, 948
in Dominica, 948
in Haiti, 950–51
proposed receivership for, 948

Ecological consequences of development projects, investigation into, 914–26
reasons for omitting in project operations, 921–25
lack of money and time to deal with, 922–23
lack of scientific fact concerning, 921–22

Ecological control of pests
of desert locust, 516–17
of red locust, 510–11, 512–13

Ecological disasters, need for international organization to cope with, 941–42

Ecological evaluation of development projects, 273–74, 367, 606–7
See also Pre-audits; Post-audits

Ecological factors in development projects, in Dominican Republic, 881–91
in Palau (Micronesia), 894–95
lack of interest in, 896–97

Ecological hazards from nuclear power plants, 795–810

Ecological methods of farming, resistance to, 234

Ecological plunder, 781–82

Ecological problems, control over use of resources in underdeveloped countries, 866–67
dangers of fragmented approach to, 846–47

others not dealt with in this conference, 975–76

Ecologist(s), as administrators, 896, 897–99
attitude of, toward man, 970–71
definition of, 971
predictions by, 251–52, 253–56, 522
responsibility of, for preserving and understanding ecosystems, 464–66, 666

Ecology. *See also* Social ecology
as a multidisciplinary approach, 967
as an evolutionary science, 965–66
definitions of, 968, 973–74
importance of aboriginal cultures to, 877
its economic relevance in technological planning, 253–56
point of view of, 465–66
responsibility of, for decisions affecting ecosystems, 464–66, 666

Ecology Seminar of the FAO, experiments with case histories in, 903–13

Economics, of crop protection, 389–91
of fertilizers, in Nile Valley, 249–51
of large dam construction, 254–55

Economists' view of development process, 929

Ecosystems, forests versus grassland, 663–64
laws designed to protect, 830–31
relation between natural and artificial, 484–86
results of man's simplification of, 847–48

Ecosystems, island, biological uniqueness of, 870

development of, 870–71
man's effects on, 869–79

Ecuador, effect of 1967–68 drought on cotton in, 380–81
land settlement in, 611–13, 629–30
two systems of cotton culture in, 464

Education, incorporation of ecology into other curriculums, 978–79
need for generalization with specialization in, 961–62
of engineers, 949, 950
on *real* environment, 972
time required for, 950

Educational reform to foster positive attitude toward environment, 963–64

Egypt. *See also* Aswan High Dam; Nile catchment; Nile Delta; Nile River
consequences of sedentarization in, 680
fisheries in, 163
insecticide resistance in cotton pests in, 393
population of, 194–96
schistosomiasis rate in, 77
control project in, 116–35

Egyptian cotton leafworm (*Spodoptera littoralis*), 354–55, 357–58, 378, 379, 382, 393, 395–96, 460–61

Egyptian vulture (*Neophron percnopterus*), effect of rodent control on in Israel, 530–31, 536 (Table), 538–39

E. I. du Pont de Nemours and Co., Savannah River Plant of AEC, studies of thermal pollution by, 831–41

Electricity. *See also* specific dams
pumped storage of, 856–57

steam-electric industry and thermal pollution, 830

Elegant grasshopper (*Zonocerus elegans* Thub.), 411–12

Elephant Butte Dam and Reservoir, 290–92

Elephant grass (*Pennisetum purpureum*), 639–40

El Niño, 758–61

Endrin, 393–94, 396, 397, 399, 429–30, 442–43, 446–47ff., 451f., 454–55, 460, 470f., 478, 491ff.

Energy, alternative sources of, 857

pollutive sources of, 857

Engineers, education of, 949–50

impelled by pleasure principle, 962–63

Engler, Frank, 873–74

Enteric Reference Laboratory (Eng.), studies of drug resistant bacteria at, 43

Enteritis, infantile, outbreak of, in Middlesbrough, England, 42

Enterobacteria, gram-negative and transferable drug resistance, 35, 37–38

Entomophagous fungus, 473

Environment, man's relationship with, 846–49, 963–64

Environmental control, explanation of, 918–19

Environmental impacts of development projects, 914–26

Environmental risks from nuclear power plants, 795–810

Epidemiology. *See* specific diseases

EPN, 491f.

Equilibrium-disequilibrium, effect of irrigation on, 344–45, 346

Erosion, agricultural tech-

niques for use of displaced silt, 874–75

effect of, on island ecosystems, 874–75

Ethyl parathion, 395, 451

Eumolpid beetle (*Rhyparida iridipennis*), 475

Euphrates River (Syria), prospective siltation in, 346

European agriculture, dependence on Peruvian fish meal, 767–72

dependence on African oilseed, 780–81

European corn borer (*Pyrsusto nubilalis*), 415

European crane (*Megalornis grus*), effect of rodent control on, in Israel, 539–40

Evolutionary changes in cotton pests, 378–79

Extinction of Caribbean animals, 823, 901–2

F

Falconiformes, effect of rodent control on, in Israel, 535 (Table), 538–39

Fallout, possible relation to spring blossoming of phytoplankton, 817

Fallout controversy, 547–48

False (Colombian) pink bollworm (*Sacadodes pyralis*), 395

Far East, usage of plant nutrients in, 551–52

Farmers' resistance to sound ecological methods, 234

Farvar, Boyouk, 1024–25
article by, 47–51

Farvar, Mary A., 1025
article by, 671–81
discussion participant, 137–53, 245–56

Farvar, M. Taghi, 1025
discussion participant, 343–

48, 365–67, 460–66, 775–89, 892–902, 955–83

Fascioliasis, 132–34

Feed (animal), fish protein as, 754–55

Fern, aquatic (*Salvinia auriculata*), 367
in Kariba Lake, 211–12, 249

Fertilizers, chemical, cause of water pollution in Illinois, (U.S.), 657–58

ecological questions concerning, 557–58

economics of, in Nile Valley, 249–51

effect of, on corn, 552–53

effect of, on growth of plant, 554

effect of, on nutrient balance, 554–56

effect of, on nutritional value of plant, 660–62

effect of, on seed germination, 553–54

effect of, on soil acidity, 554–55

effect of, on spinach, 580, 582

effect of, on vegetation in the Highveld of the Transvaal (South Africa), 556–57

in relation to the soils of Trans-Saharan Africa, 558–65

problems in use of, 549–65

program of FAO fertilizer trials, 557–58

results of FAO Fertilizer Programme in West Africa, 552–53, 570–71

relation to nitrate-nitrite hazards, 577–89

Figueira, Fernando, 57

Filariasis, eradication of, in Miyaka Gunto (Ryukyu Islands), 8–10

Financing. *See also* Aid to underdeveloped countries
   of development projects, 977–78
   of effective organizations, 952–53
   of international locust control, 499, 519–20
   of "international pest" control, 522–23
Fire, effect on island ecosystems, 873–74
Firey, Walter, 859
Fish. *See also* Fisheries; Fish meal; specific fish
   comparison of catches in hungry world and satisfied world, 772
   effect of insecticides on, 445–47, 447–49, 461, 489–97
      in Louisiana, 454–55
      in the Nile Delta lakes, 168
      in tropical waters, 489–97
   effect of proposed Joglei Canal on, 600
   in rice paddies of Asia, 490–97
   resistance of, to cotton pest insecticides, 447–49
   sensitivity of, to azinphosmethyl, 449
   sensitivity of, to cotton pest insecticides, 445–47
   sensitivity of, to endrin, 447–49
   survey of pesticide residues in freshwater fish in Louisiana, 454–55
   use of, in Japan, United States, and Europe, 755–56
   world catch in years, 1938–66, 759
Fish acreage, 756, 757
   definition of, 756
   of selected countries, 756
Fisheries, effect of proposed

Jonglei Canal (southern Sudan) on, 600
effect of, on spread of nagana, 217
in Africa, decline of, 764
in Peru, 757–65, 765–66
   decline of, 763–65
insecticide contamination of, in Louisiana, 446–47
international agreement for control of, need for, 783–84, 785
of Aswan High Dam, 197–98
of Kariba Lake (Zambezi River), 209–12, 248–49
of Mekong catchment, 238
   effect of projected dams on, 238–41
of Nam Pong Dam Reservoir, 239–40
of Nile catchment, 200–3
of proposed Pa Mong Dam Reservoir, 240
of southeastern Mediterranean, destruction of, by Aswan High Dam, 160–76, 203–4
   introduction of Indo-Pacific species into, 169
   new developments in, 174–75
on new reservoirs, difficulties in planning for, 921–22
radioactive contamination of, 825–27
total aquatic catch of selected countries, 759
world catch, 758
Fish meal. Peruvian production and export of, 758, 762–63, 765–66
   dependence of American agriculture on, 780–82
   dependence of European and Japanese agriculture on, 767–72
   world export of, 762
Fish oil, export of, 762
"Fixation" in soils, 554–55

Flatid (*Colobesthes falcata*), 472f., 473, 475–76
Flower bugs, 445
Fluoracetamide, 528, 541, 542–43
Folidol, 430
Follow-through. *See* Post-audits
Food. *See also* Food plants; Milk; Protein; and specific animals and plants
   marine species used as, 781–82
   plants used as, 634
   resources, history of, 754–56
Food and Agriculture Organization (FAO) of the UN, Ecology seminar of, 903–13
   FAO/WHO Joint Committee on Nutrition, 57
   program of fertilizer trials, 557–58
   results of Fertilizer Programme in West Africa, 552–53, 570–71
Food plants, adaptability to environment, 641–43
   appearance, uniformity and diversity, 650–53
   diseases and pests with new varieties, 641–44
   history of, 632–34
   improvement of, 635–37
      regional approach to, 644–47, 653
   inability to escape from cultivation, 638–39
   introduction of, into new areas, 634
   major crop plants, 634
   nutrition and increased yields, 660–62
   plant germ plasm, resources and utilization, 631–56
   protein content of hybrids, 85–86
   uncultivated wild relatives of, 646–48

Food shortage, world, 632–33, 646–47
Forage grasses. *See* Grasslands; Grasses
Forbes, C. N., 872–73
Forests. *See also* Deforestation
  effect of erratic rainfall on, 568
  secondary, host to insect pests, 475–78
  versus grassland, 663–64
Forests, island, destruction of, by herbivores, 871–72
Fosberg, F. R., 1025
  article by, 869–79
  discussion participant, 854–57, 892–902, 948–54
Fouadin, 121–23
Foxes, effect on, of chemical campaign against jackals in Israel, 541
France, disposal of radioactive wastes in, 855
  fish use in, 754
Fraser Darling, Frank, 1025
  article by, 671–81
  discussion participant, 137–53, 365–67, 775–89, 892–902
Frescon, 113
Fruit trees, control of aphids on, 352, 360–61
Furazolidone, 38

G

Galapagos tortoises, 874
Galbraith, John Kenneth, 928
Gallinules, common and purple, sensitivity of, to aldrin, 451–52ff.
Gambia, schistosomiasis rate in, 77
Game animals. *See* Wildlife
Game culling, 775–76
Game farming. *See also* Wildlife, Management and cropping of
  definition of, 775–76

Game ranching. *See also* Wildlife, Management and cropping of
  definition of, 775–76
Gelgand, M., 106–7f.
Generalization in conjunction with specialization in science, 961–62
Genetic constitution and relation to environment, 31–32
Genetic studies in plant breeding, 631–54
Genghis Khan, 676
Genito-urinary disorders. Bladder carcinoma, 47ff.
  relation to new technologies and lifeways, 47–51
  stone formations, 47–48, 49–50
  vesical (urinary) schistosomiasis, 47, 49
Gentamicin, 38
George, Carl J., 1025
  article by, 160–76
  discussion participant, 137–53, 245–56, 460–66, 545–48, 775–89, 854–57, 948–54
Gerbils (*Meriones* spp. and *Gerbillus* spp.), mass outbreak of, in Israel, 538–39. *See also* Tristram's jird
Germ plasm. *See* Plant germ plasm
Ghana, results of FAO fertilizer program in, 552–53
  trypanosomiasis epidemic in Ashanti tribal region, 71–72
Ghost acreage, definition of, 756–57
  of selected countries, 757
Giant tortoises, 874
Gillham, Frederick E. M., 1025
  article by, 407–20
  discussion participant, 137–53, 460–66, 775–89

Global museums, as way to preserve islands, 902
Global system for protection of the biosphere, 90
Globe, as a closed system, 939–40
  carrying capacity of, 787, 789
Goats, as nomadic livestock, 675
  destruction of forests by, on St. Helena, 871–72
Gourou, Pierre, 877–78
Grain legumes, effect of erratic rainfall on, 568
Gram-negative enterobacteria and transferable drug resistance, 35, 37–38
Grand Banks of Newfoundland, exploitation of, 754–55
Grass. *See also* Grasslands (*Cynodon dactylos* and *Eragrotis* spp.), 556–57 (*Pennisetum flaccidum*), 637–38
Grasshopper (*Paulinia*), 367
Grasslands, 568. *See also* Nomadism
  bush encroachment on, in Rhodesia, 716–19
  cultivated grasses, 639–41
  denudation of, in Rhodesia, 719–20
  difficulty of introducing into new areas, 637–38
  ease of escape from cultivation, 638–39
  effect of Masai on, 701–3
  history of, in Rhodesia, 713–15
  increased yields through intensive management of, 639–41
  in East Africa, 574–75
  influence of fertilizers on, 556–57, 637–41
  in Masailand, 697–98
  principles for successful use of, 708–9

relation to tsetse fly, 728–29

restoration of, in Rhodesia, 720–21

toichlands of southern Sudan, 598–600

Grazing lands. *See* Grasslands

Greany, W. H., 118–19

Great Britain, dependence of agriculture on imported fish meal, 767–72

disposal of radioactive wastes in, 813–16, 818–21

dysentery outbreak in Sherwood Hospital, 41–42

fish acreage of, 756

fish use in, 755f.

ghost acreage of, 757

infantile enteritis in Middlesbrough, 42

total aquatic catch of, 759

transferable drug resistance studies in, 39–40, 43

Great Lake of Cambodia, proposed dam and reservoir on, 239–40

"Green muscardine" fungus (*Metarrhizium anisopliae*), 482–83

Green revolution, problems of. *See* Fertilizers; Insecticides; Irrigation; Pesticides; Plant germ plasm

Green turtles, 874

Griffon vultures (*Gyps fulvus*), effect of rodent control on, in Israel, 536 (Table), 541

Groundnuts (*Archis hypogaea*), 568

effect of fertilizer on, 552–53, 554

groundnut scheme in East Africa, 571

"Groundwater table," definition of, 259

Guano birds, dependence on anchoveta, 761

in competition with man for fish, 762–66

Guano industry versus fish meal industry in Peru, 762–66

Gunn, D. L., 516

Guppies, effect of dieldrin on, 461

Gusathion, 460

H

Haiti, ecological and economic bankruptcy of, 950–51

Handbook of Applied Hydraulics, 331–32

Hardoy, J., 1025–26

discussion participant, 137–53, 948–54, 955–83

Hares (*Lepus europaeus*), chemical control of, in Israel, 528, 541–42

Harlan, Jack R., 635–36

Harold, LaVerne C., 1026

article by, 35–46

discussion participant, 137–53

Harrier (*Circus macrourus*), effect of rodent control on, in Israel, 531, 536 (Table)

Harrison, A. D., 113–14

Hartley, W., 637–38

Haskell, Peter T., 1026

article by, 499–524

discussion participant, 245–56, 365–67, 545–48, 892–902, 948–54, 955–83

Hawaiian Islands. Effects of erosion on, 874–75

introduction of exotic plants into, 872–74

Hay, John, 1026

article by, 288–300

discussion participant, 343–48

Hazards, of fertilizers in relation to nitrate-nitrites in foods, 577–89

of international development, 934–37

of nuclear power plants, 795–810

Heady, Harold F., 1026

article by, 683–92

discussion participant, 775–89

health, definition of, 30–31

Heart disease among Somali nomads, 679–80

"Heartland theory for the development of South America," 895–96

Hedgpeth, Joel W., 1026

article by, 812–27

discussion participant, 460–66, 854–57, 948–54

Helmand Basin (Afghanistan), history of irrigation project in, 263–64

map of, 261

waterlogging and salinization in, 264–66

Hendricke, R. G., 92

Heptachlor, 451, 481–82

Herbicides, in control of phreatophytes, 293–94

Herero tribe (Republic of Botswana), 733–35

Hillebrand, William, 873

Hippopotamus, relation to Nile fisheries, 193–94

Hirschman, Albert, 932, 972–73

Histograms, construction of, for thermal pollution studies, 850–51

Holland, dependence of, on Peruvian fish meal, 767–72

dependence on African oilseed, 780–81

fish acreage of, 756

fish use in, 755f.

ghost acreage of, 757

Homeostasis in plants, definition of, 641–43

"Home-place" tradition, 677–78

Hooded crow (*Corvus corone*), effect of jackal control on, in Israel, 541

Hoopoe (*Upupa epops*), effect of rodent control on, in Israel, 540

Horses, as nomadic livestock, 676

House lizards (geckos or "chichaks"), in relation to malaria control and the cat population, 483–84

House mouse (*Mus musculus praetextus* Brants), cycles of mass reproduction of, 528–29

Hughes, Charles C., 1026
article by, 69–96

Human conscience, 786–87

Human need-human demand, 782, 786
role of advertising in, 782–84

Humboldt Current. *See* Peruvian Current

Hungary, transferable drug resistance studies in, 558

Hunter, John M., 1026
article by, 69–96

Hunting, effects of, on island ecosystems, 874
of large mammals in tsetse fly control, 911–13

Huxley, J., 723

Hybrid plants, 645–46. *See also* Plant germ plasm protein content in, 86

Hydrological balance, 304

Hydrologic investigation, value of, in Dominican Republic, 885

Hydromodule, definition of, 283

I

Ichneumon wasps, 478

Illinois (U.S.), water pollution in, 657–58

Immortality, as a disaster, 147–48

Imperial parrot (*Amazona imperialis*), 866–67

Inca Empire, distribution of fish protein by, 783
use of anchoveta in, 771

Indo-China, fish yield in rice paddies, 490–91

Indonesia, fish yield in rice paddies, 490–91

Indus Basin (West Pakistan) Irrigation System, history of, and future plans, 345
map of, 260
waterlogging and salinization, 262–71, 343–44

Insecticide producers (U.S.), advertising campaigns by, 463, 465–66
in Cañete Valley, Peru, 462–63
increased exports by, 463, 899
responsibility of, 486

Insecticides, contact acting, 477–80, 482–84, 485–86
economics of crop protection with, 389–91
effect on fish of Nile Delta lakes, 168
effect on tropical fish, 489–97
environmental pollution by, in Louisiana, 443, 453–55
experiences with, in Cañete Valley, Peru, 423–38
in Israel, 358, 538, 540
in Louisiana (U.S.), 439–57
in Malaysia, 470–86
in Mekong River Development, 243
for rice borer control, 491
method of application, 491–92
for tsetse fly control, 730, 739–40
effect on wildlife, 730
insect resistance to, 392–99, 430–31, 443–44, 455–

56, 520–21
proper use of, 419–20, 457, 463–64
residues of, in freshwater fish in Louisiana, 453–55
resistance of locusts to, 520–21
role of, in cotton growing, 384–85, 390–92
selectivity of, 391
sensitivity of fish to, 445–47, 447–49
sensitivity of birds to, 450
storage of, in animal fat, 446–49
synthetic organic, use of, in Louisiana, 439–57
table of relative toxicities to some wildlife and zooplankton, 451

Insect pests, 409–10. *See also* specific pests; specific crops
and the manipulation of the cotton agro-ecosystem, 373–401
biological control of, 516–17, 545
ecological control of, 510–11, 516–17
effect of irrigation on, 349–63
evolutionary changes in, 378–79
indestructible, possibility of, 970
in Malaysia, 467–86
integrated control of, 374–75, 390–92, 397, 400–1, 415–16, 418–20, 427–29, 430–32, 457, 545ff.
"international pests," 500, 505–13, 520–24, 546–47
migration of, 352–53
natural regulations of, 464–65, 468–69, 473, 479–80, 485–86

parasites, predators and pathogens of, 384–86

relationships with host plants, 366, 379, 408–9, 415

resistance of, to insecticides, 392–99, 430–31, 443–44, 455–56, 520–21

resurgence of, 445–46

secondary forests and, 475–78

selective control of, 486

Insects, useful, 383–85, 424–26, 464–65. *See also* Natural insect regulation; and specific insects

cotton fields of Cañete Valley, Peru, 431, 434–38

in Malaysia, 468–69, 473, 479–80

resurgence of treated insects, 445–46

Instituto Colombiano de Reforma Agraria (Incora), 614–20

Integrated control of insect pests, 374–75, 400–1, 545, 546

definition of, 415–16

in cotton fields, 427–28

program for, 428–29, 430–32

in Imperial Valley, California, 397

principles for, 419–20, 457

problems in developing, 418–20

relation to insecticides, 390–92

Intelligence, effect of malnutrition on, 90–92

Inter-American Development Bank, 610, 628

Interdisciplinary teams, difficulties of, 977

International Biological Program, 953

International Commission on

Radiological Protection, 808

International Maize and Wheat Improvement Center, 640–41

"International pests," control of, 520–24

difficulties in establishing, 546–47

definition of, 500

red locust control, 505–13

International Red Locust Control Service, 505–13

International Union for the Conservation of Nature, 953, 975–76

Interpenetration of crops, 464–65, 485–86

Iran, consequences of sedentarization in, 678–79

incidence of urinary tract stones, in, 49–50

Iraq, insecticide resistance in cotton pests in, 393–94

Ireland, potato famine in, 634

Ironstone Plateau. *See* Jur River District

Irrigation, 258–59. *See also* Reservoir development

and desiccation of Valencia Lake, 310–11

and salinity of water, in Tunisia, 343

and salinization, in the Upper Rio Grande, 288–98

in Juarez Valley, 298–300

as "political football," 272–73

ecological effects of, 259–62, 344–45, 346

increase in insects, 352–61

waterlogging and salinization of soil, 259

from artesian wells in Northwest Sahara Desert, 276–86

impact of, on Indus and

Helmand basins, 257–74

in combination with drainage system, 270–71

in Israel, history of, 350–52

of arid lands, 285–86

overhead sprinkling, in Israel, 361–62

in Algeria, 365–66

"pulsed," in Nile Delta lakes, 168–69

relation to spread of malaria, 81–82

relation to spread of schistosomiasis, 76–81

in Rhodesia, 102–7, 116–35

studies needed for success of, 285–86

surface-water systems, 258–59, 271

Isaacs, John D., 816–17, 820–21, 825

Island ecosystems, biological uniqueness of, 870

effect of alien values on, 877–79

effect of animal introduction into, 871–72

effect of erosion on, 874–75

effect of fire and hunting on, 873–75

effect of medicine on, 877–78

effect of military activities on, 875–76

effect of mining on, 876–77

effect of monoculture on, 874–75

man's effect on, 869–79, 900

plant introduction into, 872–74

value of, to man, 870–71

Israel, control of Parlatoria on date palms, 546–47

ecological effects of chemical control of rodents and jackals in, 527–43

effects of irrigation on insects in, 352–63

fish acreage of, 756

fisheries of, 163

fish use in, 754–55

ghost acreage of, 757

history of irrigation in, 350–52

introduction of cotton and cotton pests into, 460–61

nomadic population in, 673–75

transferable drug resistance studies in, 40

Italy, fish use in, 754

ghost acreage of, 757

ITC/UNESCO Centre for Integrated Survey in Delft, 961–62

J

Jackals (*Canis aureus*), chemical control of, in Israel, 528, 540–41

Jackdaws (*Corvus monedula*), effect of rodent control on, in Israel, 539–40

Jackson, Sir Robert, 933–34

Japan, dependence of agriculture on fish meal, 770–71

fish acreage of, 756

fish toxicity to insecticides, 492

fish use in, 754–55

fish yield in rice paddies, 490–91

floating fish meal factories, 770–71

ghost acreage of, 757

manufacture of minced fish meat, 770–71

source of protein in, 770

total aquatic catch of, 759

transferable drug resistance studies in, 39–40

Jassids (Leafhoppers) (*Em-*

poasca spp.), 411

(*Empoaesca solana*), 376, 378–79, 411–12, 416–17

resistance to insecticides, 430–31

Java, vitamin A deficiency in, 55

Jebel Aulia Dam (White Nile), 198–99

Johnson Administration (U.S.) support of "heartland theory" for development of South America, 895–96

Jonglei Canal Project (Southern Sudan), 599–603

effect of fisheries, 600

effect on Nilotic tribes and cattle raising, 600–1

effect on soils, 601–3

Jonglei Investigation Team, 600–1, 606–7

Jorgenson, Harold T., 1026

article by, 609–30

Juarez Valley (Mexico), problems of salinization in, 298–300

Judeo-Christian ethic, distrust of primitive cultures by, 962–63

Jur River District (Southern Sudan), lateritic soils in, 595–96

Jur tribe, 595–96

Juvenile hormone analogs, 391

K

Kahoolawe Island (Hawaii), 871–72

Kaiji Dam (Africa), 920

planning studies for, 919–21

Kale, nitrate accumulation in, 581–82

Kalshoven, L. G. E., 468–69

Kamarck, Andrew M., 972

discussion participant, 955–83

Kanamycin, 38

Kariba Dam (Zambezi River), 207–8

and schistosomiasis, 143

effect on agriculture in Kariba Lake Basin, 223–30

relation to trypanosomiasis among Tonga tribe, 75

Kariba Lake, 207–8

bush clearing in, 210–12

fisheries on, 209–12

fish populations, 210

reasons for decreased fish yields, 248–49

invasion of aquatic plants in, 211–12

map of, 211

Salvinia auriculata in, 211–12, 249

shore margin of, 223–28

water level graph for, 225

Kariba Lake Basin, agriculture in, 223–30

animal trypanosomiasis in, 212–23

development of, 206–34

fisheries of, 209–12

Gwenbe District, cattle population in, 216

land in relation to human population, 231

land degradation in, 230–34

Karoi Dam, use of molluscicides in, 110–13

Kartung (Gambia), schistosomiasis rate in, 77

Kassas, M., 1027

article by, 180–87

discussion participant, 137–53, 245–56, 365–67, 657–66

Kenya, agricultural development in, 571ff.

schistosomiasis rate in, 77

technological development tance of, 778–80

in, 568–69

tourism in, economic impor-

tsetse fly in Alego District
    of, 729
Kestrel (*Falco tinnunculus*),
    effect of rodent control
    on, in Israel, 531, 537
    (Table)
Kin Son (Ryukyu Isls.), dys-
    entery in, 11–13
Kok, L. T., 1027
    article by, 489–97
Kotschy, Theodore, 595
"Kotsela" (drowsiness), 734–
    35
Krader, L., 676
Krypton 85, 804–5
Kwashiorkor (protein deficien-
    cy), 54–55
    in Bolivia, 660–61

                    L

Labor migration, in Zambezi
    Valley, 664
Lactase, 61–62, 65–67
Lactose. *See* Milk
Lady beetles (*Coccinelid Hip-
    podamia   convergens*,
    Guer.), 431, 445
Lake Bardawil (Nile Delta),
    153
Lake Burullus (Nile Delta),
    166–68
  fishing techniques on, 169–
    72
Lake George, research project
    on biological productiv-
    ity, 202
Lake Idku (Nile Delta), 167
Lake Kioga, introduction of
    Nile perch into, 202–3
Lake Manzala (Nile Delta),
    168, 184–85
Lake Maryut (Nile Delta),
    167–68
Lake Nasser, 172–73. *See also*
    Aswan High Dam
  fisheries on, 160, 172–75,
    197–98, 248–49
Lake Victoria,   introduction

of Nile perch into,
    202–3
Lambrecht, Frank L., 1027
    article by, 726–41
Lanai (Hawaii), erosion on,
    874
  wet forests on, 872–73
Land. *See also* Arid lands;
    Soils
  carrying capacity of, 787
Land degradation in Kariba
    Lake Basin, 230–34
Land settlement, fully directed,
    610–11
  of frontier areas in Latin
    America, 609–30
  relation to new roads, 661
  semi-directed, 610–11
  spontaneous, 611, 615, 618–
    20, 621–22
Land Tenure Center, Univer-
    sity of Wisconsin (U.S.)
  study of Caqueta area set-
    tlements, 614–16
Land tenure disputes, obstacle
    to   conservation   pro-
    grams   in   Dominican
    Republic, 887–89
Land use, alternative systems
    approach to, 909–11
  conservation criteria in, 908–
    9
  determination of, through
    natural resources sur-
    vey in Dominican Re-
    public, 885–87
Laos, development plans for
    Mekong River, 236–44
Lappet-faced vulture (*Torgos
    tracheliotus*), effect of
    rodent control on, in
    Israel, 534 (Table), 536
Lateef, M. A., 259
Laterization of soil, 568–69,
    659
  definition of, 592–93
  in   Southern   Sudan   and
    Brazil, 591–607
  relation of climate to, 594
  relation of biota to, 594

Latin America, land settle-
    ment in, 609–30
  plant nutrients, in usage of,
    551–52
  urbanization in, 151–52
Latrines, bore-hole, as part of
    schistosomiasis   control
    in Egypt, 120–21
Laver bread, and radioactive
    contamination of *Por-
    phyra* algae, 818–19
Laysan Island, destruction on,
    by rabbits, 871
Leaching of soils, 555–56
Lead arsenate, 427–28, 470,
    475, 479
Leaf eaters (*Xanthodes grael-
    sii*), 411
Leaf   eaters   (*Cosmophila*
    spp.), 411, 411–12
Leaf-eating caterpillars, 470,
    475
Leafhopper. *See* Jassids
Leaf-roller caterpillar (*Erio-
    nota thrax*), 479–80
Leaf   rollers   (*Argyrothaenia
    sphaleropa,   Maeyrick,
    and   Platynota*),   430,
    431
Leaf worm (*Anomis texana;*
    Riley), 427, 431
  resistance   to   insecticide,
    392–93, 430
Lebanon, fisheries of, 163
  harm done by nomadism in
    forested upland, 777
Lebret, Louis Joseph, 931
Lecuna, Perez, 313–15
Lesser Antilles, agriculture on,
    862–63
  economy of, 859–64
  geography of, 859–61
  history of, 861–62
  map of, 860
  tourism on, effect of, 864–65
Lesser Kestrel (*Falco nauman-
    ni*), effect of rodent con-
    trol on, in Israel, 537
    (Table), 538
Leukemia, 808

Levant Basin, fisheries of, 162–66

Levant vole (*Microtus guentheri guentheri* Dunford and Alston), chemical control of, in Israel, 528–33, 538

Liberia, trypanosomiasis epidemic in Kissi tribal region, 71–72

Light-traps, 481–82

Limacodid (*Setora nitens*), 472ff., 477ff.

Lima Province (Peru), map of, 426

Limnology, Department of the Academy of Natural Sciences of Philadelphia, studies on thermal pollution by, 831–46

Lindane, 451, 471–72, 474–75

Lobbying as a barrier to ecological principles, 951–52

Locusts, 366–67
  biology of, 500–5
  in Malaysia, 469
  international control of, 499–524
    difficulties in establishing, 546–47
  life cycle of, 501–3
  mobility of, 502–5
  phase polymorphism in, 500–2
  resistance to insecticides, 520–21

Lofoten Banks off Norway, exploitation of, 754–55

Loftin, 376

London purple, as insecticide, 427–28

Long-eared owls (*Asio otus*), effect of mice outbreak on reproductive rate of, 532–33

Long-legged buzzard (*Buteo rufinus*), effect of rodent control on, in Israel, 535 (Table), 534–38, 538–39

Looper or geometrid (*Hyposidra talaca*), 472ff., 477

Louisiana, agricultural ecosystem of cotton in, 441–43
  cotton pest control in, 441–49
  environmental pollution from pesticides in, 453–55
  major crops in and yields, 1939–68, 441 (Tables)
  map of, 442
  rice pest control in, 449–53
  similarities to developing nations, 440–42
  sugar cane pest control in, 447–49
  use of synthetic organic insecticides in, 439–57

Lygus bugs (*Lygus lineolaris*), 378, 381–82, 384–85, 388, 411–12, 443–44

Lymnaeid snails, 132

M

McCall, A. G., 565–66

McHarg, Ian, 967

Mackenzie River (Canada), proposed development of, 255–56

McNeil, Mary, 1027
  article by, 591–607
  discussion participant, 657–66, 775–89

Magnesium deficiency, 58

Maize. *See* Corn

Major leaf worm (*Pseudoplusia rogationis*, Guen.), 430, 431

Malaria, 20, control of, in Africa, 81–84
  control of, in Borneo states, 482–84
  control of, in Malaysia, 469
  control of, in Ryukyu Islands, 137–38
  economic effect of, 83
  problems arising from an effective campaign against, 83–84

Malathion, 450–51

Malaya, oil palm pests in, 477–80
  rubber pests in, 480–83

Malaysia, effects of insecticides on fish in, 492–93
  fish yield in rice paddies of, 490–91
  map of, 468
  pest control in, 467–86

Mallards, effect of rodent control on, in Israel, 539

Mallee (*Eucalyptus* spp.), in Australia, 748–49

Malnutrition, 53–54. *See also* Kwashiorkor
  effect on intelligence and brain size, 90–92
  in Caribbean Islands, 901
  rural, in Africa, 84–86
  urban, in Africa, 89–93

Man, behavioral change needed for improving ecological relationships, 938–39
  false priorities of, 976
  human conscience, 786–87
  human need-human demand, 782, 786
  role of advertising in, 782–84
  nature of, 970–71
  relationship with nature, assumptions regarding, 929
  threatened by misguided behavior, 944–45

Man, Mind and *Land*, 859

Man Adapting, 70–71

"Man and the Biosphere" program, 974–75

Mandell, Donald, 972
  discussion participant, 955–83

Mangelsdorf, P. C., 633–34

Manila hemp (abaca) pests, 479–80

Marginal Highway proposal for Amazon Basin, 892

Marin, Don, 873

Marshall, C. L., 1027
  article by, 5–18

discussion participant, 137–53, 245–56, 460–66, 775–89, 854–57

Marshall Plan, 979

Masailand (East Africa), climate of, 697–99

ecological consequences of rangeland development in, 694–709

history of, 700–2

Ilkisongo grazing scheme in, 705–6

Konzo demonstration ranch, 704–5

livestock protection and rangeland development, 703–8

maps of, 696–97

principles for development of, 708–9

topography of, 695–97

tourism in, 707, 778–80

vegetation of, 697–98

way of life and effect on ecosystem, 701–3

wildlife of, 698–700, 709

Masai tribe, changes in way of life of, 707–8

economic importance of tourism for, 778–80

effect on ecosystem, 701–3

effect of rangeland development on, 706–7

history of, 700–2

Mason, M. H., 114

Mass-reproduction cycles, in rodents, 528–29

May, Jacques M., 1027

article by, 19–33

MCPA, 492–93

Mealy bug (*Pseudococcus citri*, Risso) 430, 470, 475

Medicine, effects of, on island ecosystems, 877–78

Mediterranean, hydrography and hydrology of, 160–62

southeastern, fisheries of, 160–76, 203–4

introduction of Indo-Pacific species into, 169

Mekong Advisory Commission, dominance of engineering in planning by, 948–49

Mekong River, effect of Nam Pong Dam on fisheries of and agriculture along, 253

planned development of, 236–44, 251

effect on agriculture, 241

effect on fisheries, 238–41

effect on spread of disease, 242–43

effect on wildlife, 243

social problems in transition to irrigation agriculture, 241–42

use of insecticides in, 243

Melon beetle, 355–56

Melons, breeding for mildew resistance, 635–36

cucurbit snout beetle, 355–56

Mendelssohn, H., 1027

article by, 527–43

discussion participant, 137–53, 245–56

Merino sheep. *See* Sheep

Merv, L., 676

Meteorology, relation of, to desert locust control, 517–19

Methemoglobinemia, 579, 658

Methyl parathion, 395ff., 442–43, 443–44, 451ff., 491ff.

Mexico, fish use in, 754–55

salinization problems in Juarez Valley, 298–300

wheat program in, 640–42

Michel, Aloys A., 1027–28

article by, 257–74

discussion participant, 343–48, 775–89, 892–902

Michigan (U.S.), "swimmer's itch" in, 139

Microclimates, changes in,

caused by irrigation, 358–61

Microwasp (*Trichogramma minutum* Riley), 431

Middlesbrough (Eng.), infantile enteritis outbreak in, 42

Migrant labor, and transmission of malaria, 81–82

and transmission of trypanosomiasis, 72

and transmission of tuberculosis, 89

Military activities, effects of, on island ecosystems, 875–76

Milk, intolerance to, in Southeast Asia, 61–67, 784

non-fortified skim and vitamin A deficiency, 53–59

powdered and infant malnutrition, in African towns, 90–91

Miller, N. C. E., 468–69

Millet, effect of fertilizer on, 552–53

Milton, John P., 1028

discussion participant, 137–53, 245–56, 460–66, 657–66, 775–89, 854–57, 892–902, 948–54, 955–83

Mineral rock phosphate, 555–56

Mining, effects of, on island ecosystems, 876–77

Minor bollworm (*Mescine peruella* Schaus.), 382, 427

Miyako Gunto (Ryukyu Isls.), eradication of filariasis in, 8–9

"Modernity," as goal of development, 929–31

modernization, effect on health and disease in Ryukyu Islands, 6. *See also* Urbanization

Mole crickets (*Gryllotalpa*), 540

Mole rat (*Spalax ehrenbergi Nehring*), as food for diurnal birds of prey, 530–31

Molluscicides, 144–45
effect on the microflora and microfauna of aquatic systems, 109–15
use of, in Egypt and Sudan, 126–29
use of, in Rhodesia, 107–15

Molokai (Hawaii), introduction of axis deer on, 878–79

Mongol Empire, 676–77

Mongooses (*Herpestes i. ichneumon*, Linnaeus), effect on, of chemical campaign against jackals in Israel, 528, 541–42
reproduction rate of, influenced by mice and vole outbreaks, 532–33

Monitoring, continuous, of development projects, 893, 894, 898–99
See also Pre-audit *and* Post-audits

Monoculture, 545–46
effect of, on insects, 387
effect of, on island ecosystems, 874–75

Monorun, 492–93

Mosquito bug (*Helopeltis clavifer*), 474–75

Mosquitoes. *See* Anopheline mosquitoes

Mosquito fish (*Gambusia affinis*), 447–49, 461

Motives behind development projects, 918–19

Mourning dove, 452–53

Multidisciplinary reports, compartmentation of, 949–50

Multiple drug resistance. *See* Drug resistance, transferable

Munro, George C., 872–74

Murchison Falls (Blue Nile), 199–200

Myrdal, Gunnar, 16, 1027
discussion participant, 137–53, 245–56, 775–89, 955–83

N

Nagana, in Africa, 75–76
in Kariba Lake Basin, 212–23

Nalidixic acid, 42–43

Nam Pong Dam reservoir, effect of, on agriculture, 253
fishery on, 239–40

Napier grass. *See* Elephant grass

Natal, schistosomiasis in, 137–38
water pollution in, 657

National institutions, need to strengthen technically and financially, 965–66

National land, in Masailand, 700
in Rhodesia, 723
in United States, 779

Nations, as anachronistic institutions in a closed global system, 939–40
as final decision-makers in development, 932–33
harm done by, 942–45

Natural insect regulation, 464–65, 485–86
in Malaysia, 468–69, 473, 479–80

Natural Resources Survey of the Dominican Republic, 882–87

Nature, as "free goods," 953
and relation to scientific systems, 462

Nature of man, 970–71

Nauru, destruction of, by mining, 876–77

Neomycin, 38

Netherlands. *See* Holland

Nettle caterpillar or limacodid (*Setora nitens*), 472ff., 477ff.

New Caledonia, nickel mining on, 900–1

Newfoundland, Grand Banks of, exploitation of, 754–55

New Guinea, plague caterpillar in, 476

New Mexico. *See* Upper Rio Grande

Newsom, L. D., 1028
article by, 439–57

N'gamiland, *kotsela* in, 734–35
population of, 733–34
tsetse fly in, 734–37
control attempts, 736–40

Nickel mining, need for an ecological operation of, 900–1
on New Caledonia, 900–1

Nicotine sulphate, as insecticide, 427

Nigeria, results of FAO fertilizer program in, 552
schistosomiasis rate in Bacita, 78
schistosomiasis rate in Yo, 78–79
trypanosomiasis in, 72–73
among Rukuba tribe of the Bauchi Plateau, 73–74

Nile Basin, harm done by development of, 960–61

Nile catchment, barrages along, 194–96
dams along, 196–200
fisheries of, 200–3
flora and fauna of, 192–94
hydrology of, 194–96
maps of, 191, 195
technological changes and aquatic biology of, 189–204

Nile Delta, geomorphology of shore, 180–82

history of, 185–86
impact of river control schemes on shoreline, 180–87, 245–46
impact of river control schemes on soils, 245–47
lakes of, 165–68, 184–85
maps of, 180, 181, 182–83, 185
Nile oyster (*Etheria eliplica*), 200
Nile perch, 202–3
Nile River, and Jonglei Canal project, 600
and the hydrography and hydrology of the Mediterranean, 160–62
barrages along, 194–96
effect of Aswan High Dam on water flow, 246–47
relation to schistosomiasis, 118
Nile Valley, effect of Aswan High Dam on level of, 246–47
effect of Aswan High Dam on soils of, 245–46, 249–51
Nilotic tribes, effect of Jonglei Canal on, 600–1
Nitrate-nitrite hazards in food, 577–79, 579–82, 657–58
Nitrogen, excess supply, effect on plants, 577–79
effect on spinach, 580
imbalance of nitrogen cycle in United States, 658
relation of climate and soil to, 579–81
relation of cultural methods to, 579–81
Nomadism, 672–81. *See also* Nomads
animals suited to, 675–76
extent of, 673–75
governmental pressures on, 677–78

harm done to Lebanese upland by, 777
harmful consequences of sedentarization, 671–81
in Egypt, 680
in Iran, 678–79
in The Sahel, 679–80
in the Soviet Union, 678–79
of Bedouins in Saudi-Arabia, 683–92
modernization of, 691–92
principles for success of, 708–9
proper land for, 777
relation to oases and sedentary populations, 676–77
role in own settlement, 785–86
standard of living, 676–77
Nomads. *See also* Nomadism
Bedouin, 673–75, 680–92
Black Arab tribes, 680–81
Borkou, 677
harmful consequences of sedentarization of, 671–81
in Lebanese upland, 777
Kazakh, 678–79
Masai, 680, 700–3
Mongols, 676–77
Somali, 679–80
Turcoman, 676
North American Water and Power Alliance, 708–9
Northern Rhodesia, development of Kariba Lake Basin, 206–34
North Vietnam, effect of housing arangements on mosquito vectors, 25
Norway, fish acreage of, 756
total aquatic catch in, 759
Notemigonus crysoleucas, 447
Nottingham (Eng.), dysentery outbreak in Sherwood Hospital, 41–42
Nuclear desalination projects, inadvisability of, 825–26

Nuclear fission, 800–1. *See also* Nuclear reactors
diagram of, 800
products of, 800–1
Nuclear power plants, and pumped storage projects, 856–57
ecological hazards from, 795–810
in New England, 856–57
wastes discharged in the sea, 812–27
Nuclear reactors, 797–98. *See also* Radioactive wastes
fuel for, 799–800
schematic drawing of, 797
thermal waste from, 797–98
Nutrient and environment interdependencies, 53–59
Nutrient cycle, 551
Nutrition. *See also* Malnutrition; Vitamin deficiency
among the Hadza and Lugbara in Tanzania, 85
among the Mabaans in Sudan, 84
effect of cash-cropping on, in West Africa, 84–85
effect of fertilizers on, 660–62
effect of urbanization on, in South African reserves, 85–86
"Nutritional colonialism," 781, 968
Nutrition Survey of Burma (1963), 50–51
Nutrition Survey of Northeast Brazil, 56–57

O

Oahu (Hawaii), effects of fire on, 873–74
lantana on, 872–73
Oats, development of crown rust resistance in, 647
Oil palm, effect of fertilizer on, 554
in Malaya, 477–78

Oil palm pests, in Malaya, 477–80

Okinawa. *See* Ryukyu Islands

Okovango Delta (Republic of Botswana), tsetse fly in, 733ff.

Okovango swamps, harmful consequences of proposed development of, 739–40

Olive black scale (*Saissetia oleae* Bern.), 361

Onion fly (*Hylemia antiqua* Meigen), 357

Orange River catchment, disequilibrium in, caused by man, 346

Orchard grass (*Dactylis*), 638

Organization of American States, 882
 Natural Resources Survey of Dominican Republic, 882–87

Organochlorine insecticides, 538–40, 540. *See also* specific compounds

Organo-phosphorus insecticides, 492–93. *See also* specific compounds
 insect resistance to, 392–93, 397–98

Oriental corn borer (*Chilo agamemnon* Bleszynski), 354–55

Osterberg, C., 820–21

Oued R'Hir Valley (Sahara Desert), agriculture and water supply in, 282–85

Overgrazing. *See also* Nomadism
 in Ferlo region of Senegal, 910
 in Republic of Botswana, 909
 on arid lands of Australia, 744–48

Overpopulation, in Caribbean Islands, 901
 in irrigated areas, 259–62
 on Reunion Island, 877–78

Owen Falls Dam (Lake Victoria), 199

P

Pacific Islands Trust Territory, impact of U.S. culture on, 878–79

Pagden, H. T., 468–69

Pakistan. *See also* Indus Basin
 wheat program in, 640–42

Palau (Micronesia), ecologic planning for, 894–95
 threat of phosphate mining on, 877
 financial and political background of, 899–900

Palestine vipers (*Vipera xanthina palaestinae*), effect of, of chemical campaign against jackals in Israel, 528, 541–42

Palm dove (*Streptopelia senegalensis*), effect of rodent control on, in Israel, 539

Pa Mong Dam, 240, 251

Paradichlorbenzene crystals, 470

Paraquat, 493

Parasites. *See also* specific names
 of insect pests, 384–86
 requiring an aquatic environment, 94–96
 survey of, in Colombia, 58–59

Parasitic wasp (*Trichogramma* sp.), 384, 479–80
 life history of, 383

Parasitological Survey in Colombia, 58–59

Parathion, 388–89, 399, 430, 461, 491, 492

Parell, 981–82
 discussion participant, 955–83

Paris green, as insecticide, 427–28

Parker, F. L., 823–24

Parlatoria, 546

Paromomycin, 38

Pastoralism, sedentary, effect on land, 677–78
 standard of living of, 677–78

Pathogens of insect pests, 379–86

Pattulo, J. G., 820–21

Peanuts. *See* Groundnuts

Pearcy, W. G., 820–21

Pellagra, 57–58

Penicillin, 38, 39–40

PCP 8 (pentachlorophenol), 493

Perthane, 398

Peru, agro-ecosystems of coastal valleys of, 380
 anchoveta catch in, 758
 Cañete Valley, cotton pest control in, 393–94
 consequence of use of pesticides in, 423–38
 economics of anchoveta boom, 781
 fishery in, 757–65
 bypassing home market, 765–70
 fish meal export and production by, 758, 762–63, 765–70
 and animal protein intake, 766–67
 fish oil exports, 762–63
 fish use in, 754–55
 insecticide resistance in cotton pests in, 392–93
 land settlement in, 611–13, 629–30
 map of, 425
 map of Lima Province, 426
 total aquatic catch in, 759

Peruvian Current, 757–61
 cross section of, 760
 exploitation of, by "well-fed" nations, 753–72

Pesticide producers (U.S.), increased exports by, 894, 899

Pesticides. *See also* Insecti-

cides; Molluscicides; and specific compounds
in Cañete Valley, Peru, 423–38
in Israel, 527–44
in Malaysia, 424–45
recommended by U.S. agricultural extension services in foreign countries, 899
Phage type, 39
Phase polymorphism, in locusts, 500–2
Philippines, fish acreage of, 756
Phillips, John V., 1028
article by, 549–65
discussion participant, 137–53, 343–48, 657–66, 955–83
Phosphamidon, 450–51
Phosphate mining, effect on island ecosystems, 876–77
on Angaur (Southeastern Palau), 901
Phreatophytes, definition of, 293
See also Salt cedars
Pineapple, 874
Pink bollworm (*Platyedra gossypiella* Sand), 361, 378f., 381–82f., 384–85, 386f., 397f., 411, 414–15f., 417–18
Pioneer type vegetation, definition of, 876
Plague caterpillar (*Tiracola plagiata*), 476
Planning, dollar as goal of, 962–63
Plant germ plasm, Andean Maise Germ Plasm Bank, 649–50
appearance, 650–51
conservation and maintenance of, 648–50, 653–54, 661–63
regional approach to, 644–47, 653

disappearance of, 635–36
evolutionary histories of outstanding germ plasm, 650–51
features needed for successful use of, 646
International Maize and Wheat Improvement Center, 640–41
International Rice Research Institute, 644
Maize Germ Plasm Banks, 636–37, 647–48
of uncultivated wild plants, 646–48
resources and utilization of, 631–54
uniformity and diversity, 651–53
Plant hopper or flatid (*Colobesthes falcata*), 472f., 473, 475–76
Plant resistance to insect pests, 416–17
Plants. *See* Food plants *and* specific plants
Poisons, dose-response relationship, 807–8
See also Radiation, biological effects of; Insecticides; Pesticides; Molluscicides
Polikarpov, G. G., 823–24
Political equity, explanation of, 918–19
Politics, and international locust control, 499
and "international pest" control, 522–23
and irrigation projects, 272–73
reconciliation of, with science in development, 937
Pollution, by beef cattle in U. S. Midwest, 779–80
tax policies responsible for, 785
caused by tourism in Lesser Antilles, 864–65
determination of, in regard to rivers, 850–51

exportation of, by highly developed nations, 952–53
in conjunction with radioactive contamination, 824–25
in Illinois, 657–58
in Ryukyu Islands, 16–18
of Lake Valencia, 307–8, 312–16
recommendations for controlling, 315–16
of Sangamon River, by nitrates, 658
of water and soil, by insecticides in Louisiana, 453–55
of waters, thermal, 829–51
Polymixin, 42–43
Polyneuropathy, 89
Pope, Willis, 873
Population, control of, importance of, to island ecosystems, 877–78
growth of, in Barbados, 948
in Caribbean Islands, 901
in Nile Basin, 960–61
in Rhodesia, 715–16
on Reunion Island, 877–78
movement of, and relation to trypanosomiasis, 71–75
and relation to malaria, 81–82
and relation to schistosomiasis, 138
relocation of, 142–43
in Jur River District, 596
in Kariba Lake Basin, 230–34
in Nile Basin, 347
in North Vietnam, 25–26
in Zandeland, 596–97
Population dynamics, of locusts, 509–10
Post-adits of development projects, 910–11, 925–26, 978
by World Bank, 980–81

See also Monitoring, continuous

Potash, 555

Potassium chloride, 553–54

Potassium sulphate, 553–54

Potomac River, diagrammatic map of, 839

studies of thermal pollution of, 839–46

Poultry production, dependence on Peruvian fish meal, 780–82

Power plants. *See also* Dams

nuclear, ecological hazards from, 795–810

in New England, 856–57

Pre-audit of development projects, 925–26

Predators of insect pests, 384–86

Predictions, ecologists and, 252, 253–56

Pre-investment studies and surveys, 975–76

Preservation of environments, reconciliation with economic efficiency, 919

President Dutra (Iata) Colony (Brazil), 605–6

lateritic soils in, 605–6

President's Science Advisory Committee, 54

"The World Food Problem" (1967), 632–33

Priorities, determination of, in development, 938–39

Private corporations, as strongest supporters of U.S. foreign aid, 894

export of harmful products to foreign countries, 899

impact of, on development projects, 893–94

Process of transfer and accumulation of substance by organisms, man's ignorance of, 817

Production, intensification of, mistaken goal of development, 960–61, 969

Professional talent, tendency to leave mother country, 952

Project Egypt 10: Schistosomiasis Control, 116–35

Propanil, 493

Protection of the biosphere, Biosphere Conference (1968), 940–41

global system for, 940

Protein, content in hybrids, 85–86

deficiency, 54–55

definition of, 54

minimum world needs of, 783–84

potential yield from the sea, 826

relation to vitamin A deficiency, 53–59

scarcity, in Rhodesia, 787

Protein supplementation programs and relation to urinary stone formation, 47–48, 49–51

Public, awareness of alternatives, 251–52

Pumped storage of electricity, 856–57

Purple herons (*Ardea purpurea*), effect of rodent control on, in Israel, 534–38

Purple veld, influence of fertilizers on, 556–57

Pyralid moth (*Herculia nigrivitta*), 483–84

R

Rabbits. *See also* Hares

destruction by, on Laysan Island, 871

effect on vegetation of arid lands in Australia, 749

Radiation, biological effects of, 806–9, 823–25

natural sources and doses of, 815

Radioactive contamination. *See also* Radioactive wastes

inconsistent American attitude toward, 812–13, 823

of fisheries, 825–27

in conjunction with other pollution sources, 824–25

Soviet researchers' view of, 812, 823–24

Radioactive hydrogen, 803–4

Radioactive iodine, 802–3

Radioactive materials. *See also* Radioactive wastes; specific elements

man's alteration of proportions of, 813–15

occurring naturally, 813–15

Radioactive wastes, 800–2

disposal in the sea, 812–27

"specific activity" approach to, 816–17, 820–21

disposal of, in England, 813–16, 818–21

in France, 855

in United States, 813–16, 820–22

distribution of, in the sea, 815–17

effect of, on fisheries, 825–27

in conjunction with other pollution sources, 824–25

marine processes acting on, 816

opposing American and Soviet views on, 812–13, 823–24

recycling of, 854–55

release of, into environment, 801–2, 854

accidents involving, 804–7

quantity of, 802–5

storage of, 854

Radionuclides. *See also* Radioactive materials

distribution of, in the sea, 815–17

maximum permissible con-

centrations of, for man, 814
relation to quantities of stable isotope in the sea, 820–22
"specific activity" approach to disposal of, 816–17, 820–21
Radishes, nitrate accumulation in, 581–82
Rainey, R. C., 503–4
Rainfall, erratic, effect of, on plants, 568
minimum needed to increase animal productivity, 783–84
Rain forests, 592, 594. *See also* Wet forest
Ramey, James T., 796–97
Rao, B. S., 480–83
Rats (*Rattus* spp.), 451, 483–84, 490
Recife (Brazil), vitamin A deficiency in, 56–58
Reconciliation of science and politics in development, 937
Red bollworm (*Diparopsis castanea* Hmps.), 411, 411–18
Red crawfish (*Procambarus clarkii*), 449–50ff.
Red locust (*Nomodacris septemfasciata* Serville), 505, 506
control program for, in Africa, 505–15
Red-necked parrot (*Amazona arausiaca*), 866–67
Red pumpkin beetle (*Rhaphidopalpa foveicollis* Lucchese), 359
Reductionist bias in science, 140–41, 547–48
Reining, C. C., 596–97
Relationship between man and nature, assumptions regarding, 929
Rennell Island, threat of phosphate mining on, 876–77

Republic of Botswana, climate of, 732–33
cotton crop in, and insect pests, 366
map of, 731
overgrazing in, 909
topography of, 731–33
tsetse fly in, 732–40
Republic of South Africa, schistosomiasis rate in Transvaal, 79–80
Republic of Sudan, cotton crop in, 380
diet of the Mabaans, 84
effect of Senna Dam on schistosomiasis rate in, 77–78, 118–19ff.
experiment in mechanized agriculture, 365–66
government attitude toward nomads in, 680
insecticide resistance in cotton pests in, 393–94
lateritic soils in, 591–607
schistosomiasis control in, 116–35
Southern Sudan, Aweil rice project, 598–600
inhabitants of, 595
Jonglei Canal Project, 599–603
Jur River District, 595–96
map of, 593
Zande scheme (cotton), 596–98
Republic of Zambia, development of Kariba Lake Basin, 206–34
Reservoir development. *See also* specific dams
ecological impacts of, 916–23
ways of classifying, 916–18
ecologists' role in, 251–52, 253–56
economics of large dams, 254–56
human ends to be served by, 918–19

in Africa, characteristics of, 920
relation to increase in vesical schistosomiasis, 47
Resistance. *See* Drug resistance; Plant resistance to insect pests; Insect pests, resistance of, to pesticides
Resistance determinant (R-d) in bacteria cells, 36ff.
Resistance Transfer Factory (RTF) in bacteria cells, 36ff.
Resources, control over use of, in underdeveloped countries, 866–67
Reunion Island, population crisis on, 877
Reynolds, Harold T., 1028
article by, 373–401
R-factor in bacteria cells, 36ff.
Rhinoceros beetle (*Oryctes rhinoceros*), 477–78
Rhodesia, bush encroachment on grasslands in, 716–19
cattle population in, 716–17
cotton production and insecticides in, 463–64
denudation of grasslands in, 719–20
fish use in, 754–55
history of domesticated cattle and grassland in, 713–16
introduction of cattle into wildlife and tsetse areas, 712–24
irrigation as cause of increase in schistosomes, 102–7
livestock population, 719–20
map of, 718
natural land in, 723
parasitic infection in, 79–80

population growth in, 715–16

protein scarcity in, 787

restoration of degraded grassland, 720–21

trypanosomiasis epidemic in Bumi River area, 75

tsetse fly in, 721–22

maps of, 717

use of molluscicides in, 107–15

wildlife in, 722–23

Rice, and fish culture in Southeast Asia, 49–91

Aweil rice project (Southern Sudan), 598–600

effect of fertilizer on, 552–53

improved variety, 145–46

nutritional quality of, 137

rat infestation of, 148–49

International Rice Research Institute, 644

production of, in Asia, 496–97

varieties of, in Colombia, 644–45

Variety IR-8, 644

Rice, Andrew E., 894

discussion participant, 892–902, 955–83

Rice borer, insecticides used against, 491

methods of application, 491–92

Rice pests. *See also* specific pests

in Louisiana, 449–53

in malaysia, 469

Rice stinkbug (*Oebalus pugnax*), 449–50, 450–51

Rice water weevil (*Lissorhoptrus cryzophilus*), 449–50, 451–52

resistance to aldrin and dieldrin, 453

Rich nations. *See* Developed countries

Rinderpest epizootic, 701, 715, 721

Riney, Thane, 1028–29

article by, 903–13

Ring bark borer (*Endoclita hosei*), 470, 472, 473–74, 475–76

Rio Plata Development Project, 950–51

Ripley, Sidney Dillon, 1029

discussion participant, 892–902, 955–83

Risks, biological, from exposure to radiation, 808–9

environmental, from nuclear power plants, 795–810

from nitrate-nitrite in foods, 577–78, 579–82, 657–58

genetic, from exposure to radiation, 808–9

River "health," determination of, 851

Riverside Handbook, 343

Rivnay, E., 1029

article by, 349–63

discussion participant, 365–67, 460–66, 545–48

Roads, and transmission of trypanosomiasis, 71–74

Relation to colonization of new areas, 661

Rock, Joseph, 872–73

Rockefeller Foundation, agricultural programs, 663

Rodents, chemical control of, in Israel, 527–43

Rodgers, Kirk P., 1029

discussion participant, 819–902, 955–83

Rooks (*Corvus frugilegus*), effect of rodent control on, in Israel, 539–40

Roseires Dam (Blue Nile), 200

Rostow, W. W., 932

Rothberg, John C., discussion participant, 955–83

Rubber pests in Malaya, 480–83

Rubber plant, effect of fertilizer on, 554

Russell, E. W., 1029

article by, 568–75

discussion participant, 251–56, 657–66, 775–89, 892–902, 955–83

Ruthenium, 26, 818–19

Rwanda, tsetse fly in Bugesera region of, 728–29

Ryania, 447–49

Ryukyu Islands, modernization in, and its effects on health and disease, 6–18

pollution in, 150–51

S

Sabah (Malaysia), cocoa pests in, 469–78

Sadd-el-Aaali. *See* Aswan High Dam

Sahara Desert, agriculture in, and water problems, 282–85

social aspects of, 284–85, 346–47

causes of waterlogging in, 281–83

exploitation of watertables in, 280–81

geology and hydrogeology of, 277–80, 279

hydroclimatology of, 277–80

map of, 278

northeastern, salinization of soils in, 276–86

quality of subterranean water in, 280–81

sedentarization in, 679–80

soils of, 558–65

standard of living in, 677

total and nomadic population in, 673–75

Saigon, slum clearance project in, 149

3

St. Helena, destruction of forests on, by goats, 871–72

St. Lucia, expanding tourist industry in, 865–66

Saipan (Marianas), effect of military activities on ecosystem of, 875–76

Salinization of soil and water, 259
  factors contributing to, 281
  in Algerian Northeast Sahara, 276–86
  social consequences of, 346–47
  in arid lands, 345–46
  in Helmand Basin, 264–66
  in Indus Basin, 262–63, 266
  in Juraez Valley, 298–300
  in Tunisia, 343
  in Upper Rio Grande Valley, 296–98
  in Valencia Lake, 311–12, 315–16

Salmonellosis infection, outbreak in Medical Center, Boston, 41–42

Saltbush (Atriplex), overgrazing of, in Australia, 748–50

Salt cedars (tamarisk), 291–94
  on Pecos River, 293
  on Upper Rio Grande, 288–300

Salton Sea (Calif.), 346

Salt-tolerant crops, breeding of, 344–45

Sand rat (*Psammomy's obesus*), extermination of, by jackals, 540–41

Sangamon River (U.S.), pollution of, by nitrates, 658

Sardines, fishery in California, collapse of, 780–81,
  fishery in Egypt, 163–64
  fishery in Levant Basin, 164–66

Saudi Arabia, climate of, 685–87
  economy of, 683–84
  history of grazing in, 687–89
  hydrology of, 689–91
  livestock numbers in, 687–89
  map of, 684
  nomadic population in, 673–75
  Bedouin settlement, consequences of, 683–92
  soils of, 685–86
  topography of, 684–86
  vegetation of, 686–87
  wildlife of, 691–92

Savannah River Basin (U.S.), diagrammatic map of, 832
  thermal pollution studies of, 831–41

Savannah River Plant (AEC) studies of thermal pollution by, 831–41

Scandinavia, fish use in, 754–55. *See also* specific countries

Schistosomes, life cycle of, 117
  (*Schistosoma haematobium*), 49, 76ff., 121–23
  (*Schistosoma mansoni*), 76ff.
  spread by irrigation systems, 102–7

Schistosomiasis, 76–81
  control methods, 120–35
  control project for, in Egypt, 116–35
  economic effect of, 80–81
  effect of, on nutrition, 80
  epidemiology of, 102–7
  in East Africa, 138
  in Natal and Zululand, 137–38
  new drug for control of, 144–45
  relation of, to aquatic systems in Rhodesia, 102–7

symptoms of, 117–18
  urinary, relation to bladder carcinoma, 49

Schmitt, W. R., 826

Schuphan, W., 1029
  article by, 577–89
  discussion participant, 137–53

Science, and importance of what is not understood, 665–66
  and international locust control, 499, 546–47
  and "international pest" control, 520–21
  importance of controversy in, 548
  reconciliation of, with politics in development, 937
  reductionist bias in, 140–41, 547–48
  transporting of, 645

Scientific approach, lack of, in solving problems, 963

Scientific system, corruption of, 465–66
  relation to nature, 462

Scoliid wasps, 482

Scudder, Thayer, 1029
  article by, 206–34
  discussion participant, 137–53, 245–56, 343–48, 365–67, 460–66, 664–66, 892–902, 955–83

Seas, atomic waste disposal in, 812–27
  internationalizing of, 783–84, 785
  potential protein yield from, 826. *See also* Fisheries

Seaweed (*Porphyra umbilicalis*), 818–19

Secondary forests, as host to insect pests, 475–78

Sedentarization of nomads, ecological consequences of, 671–81, 683–92

Sedimentation, of Anchicaya

Reservoir, 325–27, 338–39

methods of preventing, 330–35

plans for future control of, 340–42

records of, 327–30

types of, 766

Seed corn maggot (*Hylemyia cilicrura Rondani*), 358

Selective control of insects, 486

Semi-arid regions, destruction of natural resources of, by development projects, 905

Semliki Valley (Belgian Congo), trypanosomiasis epidemic in, 728–29

Senegal, malaria rate in Thiès, 82–83

overgrazing in Ferlo region, 910

results of FAO fertilizer program in, 552

Sennar Dam (Blue Nile), 199–200

and schistosomiasis increase, 77–78, 118–19

Sepat siam (*Trichogaster pectoralis* Regan), 490ff.

Serotype, 39f.

Settlement relocation. *See* Population, movement of; Population, relocation of

Sevin, 451

Shamsi, R. A., 259

Sheep, as nomadic livestock, 675

on arid lands of Australia, 744–48

Shiff, Clive Julian, 1029

article by, 102–15

Shifting cultivation, in Africa, 572–73

Shigellosis, outbreak of, at Albert Einstein Medical College in Bronx, N.Y., 41–42

Short-eared owls (*Asio flammens*), effect of mice outbreak on reproductive rate of, 532–33

Short-toed eagle (*Circaetus gallicus*), effect of rodent control on, in Israel, 528, 537, 538

Shukri, N. M., 180–81

Simazine, 492–93

Singapore, lactose intolerance in, 64–65

Sitatunga (*Tragelaphus spekei*), 740

Slash and burn agriculture, effects of on island ecosystems, 873–74

Sleeping sickness. *See* Trypanosomiasis

Smith, Ray F., 480–81, 1029

article by, 373–401

discussion participant, 137–53, 365–67, 460–66, 545–48, 657–66

Smithsonian Institution, 898–99

Smythe, P. M., 90–91

Snail survey method, 129

Snakes, effect of thallium on, 534–38

Social ecology, and the transition to irrigation agriculture, in Mekong catchment, 241–42

and Zande cash-cropping scheme, 596–97

"big money" interests and dam building, 254–55

health, disease and modernization in the Ryukyu Islands, 5–18

of African small farmer, 573, 574

of agricultural problems in Northwest Sahara Desert, 284–85, 346–47

of Aweil Rice Project, 599

of cotton production, 398–401

of development planning, 367

of farmers in Kariba Lake Basin, 234

of fishermen in Nile Delta, 165–86

of Jongeil Canal Project, 600–1

of small agricultural holdings, 664, 665

relocation of populations, 142–43

in Jur River District, 596

in Kariba Lake Basin, 230–34

in North Vietnam, 25–26

Society, definition of, 30

Sodium chlorate, 557

Sodium nitrate, 553–54, 556

Sodium pentachlorophenate, 109–10

Sodium sulphate, 556

Soils, acidity of, effect of fertilizers on, 554–55, 570

and deforestation, 550–51

condition of, necessary for high yields, 569–71

destruction of, in Caribbean Islands, 901–2

effect of rain on surface of, 569–70

erosion of, in Dominican Republic, 888–91

control efforts, 891

in East Africa, 658–59

humus content of, in Africa, 573–74

lateritic, 568–69, 659–60

in Southern Sudan and Brazil, 591–607

leaching of, 555–56

nutrient imbalance in, 554–56

of Caqueta Settlement, 616

of Caranavi Settlement, 620–28

of East Africa, impact of technological developments on 568–75, 658–59

of Nile Valley, effect of Aswan High Dam on, 245–46, 249–51

of Southern Kariba Lake Basin, 230–32

of Trans-Saharan Africa, 558–65

forest, 562–65

wooded savannah, 562–65

pollution of, by insecticides, in Louisiana, 454–55

salinization and waterlogging of, 259

in Algerian Northeast Sahara, 276–86

in Helmand Basin, 264–66

in Indus Basin, 262–63

in Juarez Valley, 298–300

in Upper Rio Grande Valley, 296–98

Somalia, nomadic population in, 673–75

government policy toward, 680

Sorghum shoot maggot (*Atherigona varia soccata*), 355

South Africa. *See also* specific countries or areas

effect of urbanization on nutrition in, 85–86

fish acreage of, 756

South America, acceptability of fish and fish products in, 771

export of fish meal related to total animal production, 766

land and urban policies in, 965

Southeast Asia, fish culture in, 490

lactose intolerance in, 61–67

Southwest Asia, impact of irrigation in, 257–74

nomadic populations in, 673–75

Sovereignty, anachronism of, in closed global system, 939–40

in decisions regarding development, 932–33, 942–45

problems of, in control of land and sea resources, 866–67, 953–54

Soviet Union, attitude of, toward radioactive contamination, 812, 823–24

consequences of sedentarization in, 678–79

fish use in, 754

total aquatic catch in, 759

Soybeans, residues of insecticides in, 455

Spain, fish acreage of, 756

fish use in, 754

total aquatic catch in, 759

Spear grass (*Stipa nitida*), 750

"Specific activity" approach to radioactive waste disposal, 816–17, 820–21

Spider mites (*Tetranychus* spp.), 381, 398–99ff., 409, 411–12, 443–44

resistance to insecticides, 392–93, 393–94, 443, 463–64

Spiders, 445

Spinach, cause of methemoglobinemia in infants, 579

effect of fertilizers on, 580

formation of nitrite in, 578, 581–82

formation of protein, amino acids, nitrate, and nitrite in, 581–89

Spiny bollworm (*Earias huegeli*), 399, 411–13, 413–14

(*Earias insulana* Boisduval), 352, 357–58, 393–94, 395–96, 411, 460–61

Stakeman, E. C., 643–44

Starlings, effect of rodent control on, in Israel, 539

Steam-electric industry as chief source of thermal pollution, 830

"Sterile-male technique" of pest control, 392

Stevenson, Adlai, 944

Stoch, M. B., 90–91

Straub, Lorenz G., 332–35, 336–37

Streptomycin, 38, 39f.

Strychnine, 540–41

Sud Swamp (Southern Sudan), 599–600

Sugar cane borer (*Diatraea saccharalis*), 448–49

resistance to insecticides, 449

Sugar cane pests in Louisiana, 447–49

Sulfate of ammonia, 658–59

Sulfathiazole, 39–40

Sulfonamides, 38, 39

Sumithion, 492

Sunfish, 461

Superphosphate, 553–54, 555–56

Surveys, Natural Resources Survey of the Dominican Republic, 882–87

Nutrition Survey of Burma (1963), 50–51

Nutrition Survey of Northeast Brazil, 56–57

types used in development projects, 950

Sweden, fish acreage of, 756

"Swimmer's itch," 139

Switzerland, fish acreage of, 756

fish use in, 754–55

Symmons, P. M., 509–10

Synthesis, importance of, in development, 937

Syria. *See also* Euphrates River

insecticide resistance in, 393–94

T

Tachinid flies, 474, 482
Taiwan, fish acreage of, 756
Takahashi, discussion participant, 955–83
Talbot, Lee M., 1029–30
  article by, 694–709
  discussion participant, 245–56, 775–89, 892–902, 955–83
Tanzania, dietary changes among the Hadza, 85
  dietary changes among the Lugbara, 85–86
  economic effect of chronic schistosomiasis in Arusha Chini, 80–81
  malaria rate in Para area, 82–83
  nutritional effects of cash-cropping in Kilimanjaro area, 84–85
  schistosomiasis, rate in, 77, 78–79
    in Rufiji Basin, 78–79
  trypanosomiasis epidemic in Kasulu District, 74
  tsetse fly in Karagwe region, 728–29
Tawes (*Puntius javanicus* Bleeker), 490, 492–93
  effect of γ-BHC and diazinon on, 493–97
TDE, 451
Tea, effect of fertilizer on, 554
  in East Africa, 571–72
  in Kenya, 571
Team leaders in development projects, shortage of, 967
Technological assistance. *See also* Aid to underdeveloped countries
  failures in, 632
  transporting of, 645

Technological development. *See also* Development
  hidden costs of, 71, 347–48
  impact of, on soils of East Africa, 568–75
  in Africa, and disease, 69–96
Temperature, effect of, on cotton and its pests, 381–82
  effect of, on locust flights, 502–3
  effect of, on man, 29–30
  effect of, on mosquito infectiousness, 22
Templeton, W. L., 823–24
Territorial Board of Commissioners of Agriculture and Forestry (Hawaii), 873
Tetracyclines, 38, 39f.
Texas. *See also* Upper Rio Grande
  cotton crop in, 380–81
    in southern Texas, 396–97
Thailand, development plans for Mekong River, 236–44
  fish acreage of, 756
  locust outbreak in, 521–22
Thallium poisoning, in birds of prey, 528, 533–34, 534–38
  in grain-eating birds, 539–41
Thallium sulfate-coated wheat, 527–28, 532–33, 534–39
Thatch-eating larvae of pyralid moth (*Herculia nigrivitta*), 483–84
Thermal pollution, 829–51, 856–57
  effects of, 798–800, 831–32
  in Savannah River Basin, 831–41
  of Potamac River, 839–46
  possibility of using waste heat, 854–55

3–5–40 insecticide formula, 429
Thyroid carcinome, 808
Tilapia (Tilapia macrochir), 210
  effects of γ-BHC and diazinon, 493–97
Timothy, David H., 1030
  article by, 631–54
  discussion participant, 137–53, 343–48, 657–66, 892–902
Tinbergen, Jan, 944–45
Tobacco, development of disease resistance in, 647
Toichlands of Southern Sudan, 598–99
  Aweil Rice Project, 599–600
Tomé Açu (Brazil), conservation of lateritic soils in, 605–6
Tonga tribe. *See* Kariba Lake Basin
Tordon, 718–19
Tothill, J. D., 597
Tourism, cause of pollution in Lesser Antilles, 864–66
  harm done by, to ecosystems and cultures, 779–80
  harm done by, to national parks in U.S., 779
  harm done by, to native populations, 777–78
  in Masailand, economic importance of, 778–80
Toxaphene, 396–97, 429, 442–43, 444–45, 449–50ff.
  insect resistance to, 392–93f., 430
Toxic materials, dose-response relationship, 807–8
Trachoma among school children in Ryukyu Islands, 10–11
Tractors, use of, in East Africa, 574

Trade acreage, 756–57
  definition of, 756
Train, Russell E., 1030
  discussion participant, 775–
      89, 892–902, 955–83
  introduction to the Confer-
      ence, xvii–xix
Transferable drug resistance.
      See Drug resistance,
      transferable
Transfer and accumulation of
      substances by organ-
      isms, 817
Transportation, effect of, on
      food resources, 755–56
Trans-Saharan Africa. Bio-
      climatic regions of,
      558–65
  soils of, 558–65
Transvaal (South Africa), in-
      fluence of fertilizers in
      Highveld, 556–57
Trichlorphon (Dipterex), 471–
      72, 473–74, 475, 479
Trifluralin, 451
  triple superphosphate, 553–
      54
Tristram's jird (*Meriones tris-
      trami* Thomas), chemi-
      cal control of, 542–43
  cycles of mass reproduc-
      tion of, 528–29, 529,
      538–39
Tritium. *See* Radioactive hy-
      drogen
Trypanosomiasis (sleeping sick-
      ness), in Africa, 71–
      76, 739–40
  animal. *See* Nagana
Tryptophan, relation to nia-
      cin, 57–58
Tsetse flies (*Glossina* spp.),
      71–72, 726–41
  as guardian of natural en-
      vironment, 740–41
  case history of attempt to
      eliminate, 911–13
  control methods for, 729–
      31
  in Kariba Lake Basin, 212–
      23

  in Okovango Delta, 733ff.
  in Republic of Botswana,
      732–40
  in Rhodesia, 717
    control attempts, 721–22
    effect on domestic cattle,
      712–24
  in Southern Africa, history
      of, 735–37
  man-made habitats for,
      728–29
Tuberculosis, failure of mass
      campaign approach, in
      Ryukyu Islands, 12–16
  in African towns, 88–89
Tunisia, irrigation and salinity
      of water in, 343
Turkey, cotton production in,
      395–96
  disappearance of flax germ
      plasm from, 635–36
  nomadic population in,
      673–75
2, 4-D, 168, 492–93, 581
2, 4, 5-T, 718–19

                  U

Uganda, administration of
      game elimination cam-
      paign, 898
  diet in the Buganda region,
      85–86
  diet of the Karamojong, 84
  diet in the northern region,
      85–86
  food taboos in Ankole area,
      84
  proposed Murchison Falls
      Dam, 199–200
  schistosomiasis rate in, 76
  trypanosomiasis epidemic
      in Dodos tribal area,
      74–78
  tsetse fly in, 728
Underdeveloped countries, con-
      trol over use of resources
      in, 866–67
  fundamental differences from
      developed countries,
      959–60, 966

  similarities between Louisi-
      ana and, 440–42
  source of protein for inten-
      sive agriculture in de-
      veloped countries, 767–
      72, 780–82
  who, in these countries,
      want development, 970
Unemployment, 347
United Arab Republic. *See*
      Egypt
United Kingdom. *See* Great
      Britain
United Nations Conference
      on Science, Technology
      and Economic Devel-
      opment (1963), 968–69
United Nations Development
      Program, 882, 933–34
United Nations General As-
      sembly, Resolution of
      the Problems of the
      Human Environment
      (Dec. 3, 1968), 941
United States, aid to underde-
      veloped countries, 787–
      88
  dependence of, on im-
      ported fish meal, 771,
      780–82
  export of cigarettes by, 899
  export of pesticides by,
      462–63, 463, 465–66,
      894, 899
  fish oil export by, 762
  fish use in, 754–55
  insecticide resistance in cot-
      ton belt, 392–93
  national parks in, harm
      done to by tourism,
      779
  pollution by beef cattle in
      Midwest, 779–80
  tax policies responsible
      for, 785
  total aquatic catch of, 759
  transferable drug resistance
      studies in, 40–41
United States Atomic Energy
      Commission, Savannah
      River Plant, studies on

thermal pollution by, 831–41

statement on accidents involving release of radioactive wastes, 806–7

statements on nuclear industrial complexes, 795–96

United States Joint Committee on Atomic Energy, "Remarks" on the ecology of nuclear power plants, 796–97

U.S.S.R. *See* Soviet Union

Universities, departmental barriers in, 949–50

need for reform in, 963–64

Upper Rio Grande, 289–90

agricultural and social history of, 290–92

map of, 289

salt cedars and salinization in, 291–94, 296–300

Upper Rio Grande Valley. Agriculture in, effect of salinization of water on, 295–98

history of, 295

Upper Volta Republic, schistosomiasis rate in, 77

trypanosomiasis among Moshie Tribe, 72–73

Uranium-dioxide fuel pellets and fuel rods, diagram, 799–800

Urbanization, effect of, on nutrition in South African reserves, 85–86

effect of, on health and disease in Ryukyu Islands, 6

in Africa, 347

in Brazil, 604

in Latin America, 151

of Egyptian Nubian population, 347

pathological effects of, in Africa, 87–93

Urea, 553–54

Urinary tract stone formations, 47–48, 49–51

Utah, "home-place" tradition and effect on the land, 677–78

Uvarov, B. P., 500, 502, 521

V

Valencia Lake and Basin (Venezuela),

decline in Lake level, 310–11

decreasing dimensions of lake, 312–13

effect of irrigation on, 310–11

El Paito Lagoon, pollution of, 307–8

geological history of, 304

hydrological balance and desiccation of, 304–7, 311–12

map of, 302–3

pollution of lake and tributaries, 312–16

recommendations for controlling problems, 315–16

salinity of, 311–12

temperature of the lake water, 308–9

Vancouver, Captain, 873

Van der Schalie, Henry, 1030

article by, 116–35

discussion participant, 137–53, 245–56

Van Nieuwenhuijze, C. A. O., 938

Variability, and improvement of food plants, 635–37, 638

Vector, characteristics of effective, 24–25

Venezuela. *See* Valencia Lake and Basin

Verticillium wilt, 395–96

Vesical (urinary) schistosomiasis, 47

Vietnam. *See also* North Vietnam

development plans for Mekong River, 236–44

Vitamin A, deficiency of, in relation to protein, 53–59

Vitamin B₆ (pyridoxine), relation to urinary tract stone formation, 47–48, 49–51

Vitamin deficiency. *See* specific vitamins

Vitamin niacin, 57–58

Volta Dam (Africa), 920

planning commission investigations, 919–21

failure to use, 924–25

W

Wales, radioactive contamination of alga used in Laver bread in, 818–19

Ward, Barbara, 933

Waste of organic fertilizer, 780

Water, and cotton productivity, 379–81

availability of, and disease transmission, 10–12

pollution of, by insecticides, in Louisiana, 453–55

thermal pollution of, 829–51

utilization, coefficient of, 284

Water hyacinth, 202–3

Waterlogging of soil, 259

in Algerian Northeast Sahara, 276–86

in Helmand Basin, 264–66

in Indus Basin, 262–63, 266

in Juarez Valley, 298–300

in Upper Rio Grande Valley, 296–98

Weeds, and coffee and tea production, 571–72

and cotton production, 382

encouraged by irrigation, 259–62

Weir, John, 117

West, Oliver, 1030

article by, 712–24

discussion participant, 775–89

West Africa, effect of cocoa production on nutrition in, 84–85

FAO fertilizer program in, 552–53

fish acreage of, 756

soils of, 568–69

West Germany, fish acreage of, 756

fish use in, 754–55

ghost acreage of, 757

transferable drug resistance studies in, 39–40

West Indies, ghost acreage of, 757

West Point, weaknesses of education at, 949

Wet forest on Lanai (Hawaii), 872–73

Wheat. Dwarf varieties used in Pakistan, 640–42

International Maize and Wheat Improvement Center, 640–61

Mexican wheat program, 640–42

wheat rust epidemics and breeding of rust resistant varieties, 643–44

Wheat rust, 643–44

West, Oliver, 1029

article by, 914–26

discussion participant, 251–56, 854–57, 892–902, 948–54, 955–83

White-breasted kingfisher (*Halcyon smyrnensis*) effect of rodent control on, in Israel, 540

White Nile, 198–99

White scale (*Hemichionaspis minor*, Mark.), 427

Wild cat (*Felis lybica tristrami* Pocock). Effect on, of chemical campaign against jackals in Israel, 541

reproduction rate influenced by mice and vole outbreaks, 532–33

Wild life, and the tsetse fly, 721–22

effect of insecticides on, 456–57, 730

effect on, of river development in Mekong catchment, 242–43

in cotton fields, 385–86

management and cropping of, 700, 730–32, 786

problems of, 775–77

of Masailand, 698–700, 709

of Rhodesia, 722–23

of Saudi Arabia, 691–92

Wind, relation to locust flights, 503–4

Windscale Works (Cumberland Coast, Eng.)

disposal of radioactive wastes at, 813–16, 818–21

marine sampling stations at, 818

monitoring program at, 819–20

Wood, B. J., 477–80

World Bank, 980

post-audit of projects by, 980–81

World Food Problem, report of PSAC, 53–54

World government, need for, in food distribution, 782

need for, in global ecological planning, 948

World Health Organization, and tsetse fly threat in Republic of Botswana, 737–38

FAO/WHO Joint Committee on Nutrition, 57

Project Egypt 10: Schistosomiasis Control, 116–35

statement on antibiotics, 43

statement on schistosomiasis, 76–77

statement on urbanization of Africa, 87–88

World parks as means of preserving "wildness," 902

Worthington, E. B., 1030

article by, 189–204

discussion participant, 137–53, 245–56, 657–66, 892–902

X

Xenylamine, as cause of bladder tumors, 48–49

Xerophthalmia, 54, 55, 56–57

Y

Yams, effect of fertilizer on, 552–53

Yei tribe (Republic of Botswana), 733, 833–34, 835

Yuna Valley (Dominican Republic), 885

Z

Zambezi River, annual flow charts, 223, 228–29

Zambezi Valley, archeological record of cotton production in, 463–64

cotton production on small holdings in, 664

Zandeland (Southern Sudan), 596–98

Zande scheme for cotton, 596–98

effect of, on soil and climate, 598

Zinc(^{65}Zn), in marine species, 820–22

Zinc, quantity of, relative to zinc isotope, 820–22

Zonneveld, I. S., 1030

discussion participant, 657–66, 955–83

Zululand, schistosomiasis in, 137–38

water pollution in, 657

INDEX OF SCIENTIFIC NAMES

A

Acacia giraffae, 738–39

Acanthocephala, 475–76

Accipiter spp., secondary poisoning of by Israel, 535 (Table)

Aegyptus monachus, 534, 536

Agrotis ypsilon, 352–53

Alabama argillacea, 417–18, 443–44

Alectoris graeca, 539

Amazona imperialis, 478–79

A. arausiaca, 866–67

Ambrosia artemisioides, 382

Anomis texana Riley, 427, 431

Anthocoridae bugs, 431

Anthonomus grandis, 375–76, 377–78, 378–79, 381–82, 384–85, 394–95, 414–15, 441–42, 443–45

Anthonomus vestitus Bohm, 382, 392–93, 427

Anthrocephalus spp., 483

Apanteles iphiaulux, 473

Aphis gossypii, Glov., 388–89, 392–93, 394–95, 411, 427, 430–31, 431, 443, 443–44

Aphis pomi, A. punicae, and A. fabae, 352, 360–61, 470

Aquila spp., 530–31, 536, 538–39

Arachis hypogaea, 568

Ardea purpurea, 534–38

Asio flemmens, 532–33

A. otus, 532–33

Atherigona varia Soccata, 355

Atriplex, 748–50

B

Bacillus thuringiensis, 385, 473–74

Bassia, 748–49

Bemisia tabaci, 395

Biomphalaria pfeifferi, 103–6, 117, 121–23ff.

Bos sauveli (Kouprey), 243

Brachiophagus gibbus Boh., 361

Bubulcus ibis, 534, 540

Bucculatrix thurberiella Busck, 380–81, 382, 396, 431–32

Bulinus (Physopsis) globosus, 103–6, 117, 121–23ff.

Buteo b. buteo; Buteo v. vulpinus, 531, 535

Bvteo rufinus, 535, 538, 538–39

C

Calosoma abreviatum Chaud., 431

Canus Aureus, 528, 540–42

Capnodis spp., 359–60

Catla catla, 490

Cervus frugilegus, 539–40

Chilo Agamemnon Besaynski, 354–55

Chrysomelids (Maecolaspis flavida, and Gastrophysa cyanea), 376–77

Chrysopa spp., 384–85, 445–46

Circaetus gallicus, 528, 537, 538

Circus aeruginosus, C. cyaneus, and C. pygargus, 536, 537

C. masrourus, 531, 536

Clamator glandarius, 541

Clarias batrachus Linnaeus, 490, 490–91

Coleomegilla maculata, 445–46

Colobesthes falcata, 472f., 473, 475–76

Corvus corone, 541

C. monedula, 539–40

Cosmophilia spp., 411, 411–12

Cremastopsyche pendula, 478–79

Cynodon dactylon (grass), 556–57

D

Dactylis, 638

Daphnia pulex, 451

Diatreae saccharalis, 447–49

Diparopsis castanea Hmps., 411, 411–12, 418

Dystercus spp., 411–13

D. peruvianus, 391, 411, 427

E

Earias huegli, 399, 411–13, 413–14

E. insulana Boisduual, 352, 357–58, 393–94, 395–96, 411, 460–61

Empoasca spp., 411

E. solana, 376, 378–79, 411–12, 416–17

Engravulis ringens L., 758, 757–58, 760–61, 763–65, 781

Enloclita hosei, 470, 472, 473–74, 475–76

Entamoeba histolytica, 58–59, 141

Epicauta vittata, 376–77

Eragrotis spp., 556–57

Erionota thrax, 479–80

Erythroxylon coca, 660–61

Escherichia coli., 35, 37–38, 39, 40–41, 41–42

Escherichia freundii, 39

Eucalyptus spp., 748–49

Euphorbia tirucalli, 729

F

Falco naumanni, 537, 538

F. tinnunculus, 531, 537

Fels lybica tristrami Pocock, 541

G

Gambusia affinis, 447–49, 461

Gastrophysa oyanea, 376–77

Geocoris punctipes, 445–46

Gerbillus spp., 538–39

Glossina spp., 71–72, 73–74, 74–75, 726–41

Grylletalpa, 540

Gypaetus barbatus, effect of rodent control on, in Israel, 536 (Table)

Gyps fulvis, 541

H

Halcyon smyrnensis, 540

Haliaetus albicilla, effect of rodent control on, in Israel, 536 (Table)

Hapera variabilis, 354

Helibthis spp., 377–78ff., 392–93, 394–95, 396, 398f., 411–12ff., 427–28, 431ff., 443–44f., 475–76

Helopeltis clavifer, 72, 474–75

Hemichienzspis minor Mark, 427

Herculia nigrtuitta, 483–84

Herpestes i. icheumon Linnaeur, 528, 541–42

Heterophyes, transmission of, 247

Hieraetus pennatus, H. fasciatus, 535 (Table), 539–40

Hippodamia convergens Guer., 445–521

Hylemiz antiqua Meigen, 357

H. cilicrura Rondani, 358

Hyposidra talaca, 472ff., 477

I

Ictalurus spp., 447

K

Klebsiella, 40–41

Kochia, 748–50

L

Lantana camara, 729

Lepomis spp., 447

  (*Lepomis machrochirus*), 451

Lepus europaeus, 528, 541–42

Lissorhoptrus cryzophilus, 449–50, 451–52

Lixus junci, 352

Lygus lineolaris, 378, 381–82, 384–85, 388

M

Macaranga, 475–76

Maecolaspis flavida, 376–77

Megaloruis gros, 539–40

Melonthidae: Lachnosterna bidentata, Psilopholis vestita, 478, 480–83, 483–84

Meriones spp., 538–39

Mescinea peruella Schauss, 382, 427

Metarrhizium anisopliae, 482–83

Metisa plana, 478–79

Microtis guentheri guentheri Dunford and Alston, 528–33, 538

Milvus m. migrans, 530–31, 531, 535, 538–39

Mugilidae, 247

Mus musculus psaetextus Brants, 528–29

N

Neophron percnopterus, 530–31, 536, 538–39

Nomodacris septemfasciata Serville, 505, 506

Notemigonus crysoleucas, 447

O

Oebalus pugnax, 449–50, 450–51

Ophiocephalus striatus Bloch., 490, 490–91, 492

Orius insidiosus, 445–46

Oryctes rhinoceros, 477–78

Oxycarenus spp., 411

P

Pandion haliaetus, effect of rodent control on, in Israel, 537 (Table)

Pangasianodon gigas, 238–39

Pasteurella, 37–38

Paulinia, 366

Pennisetum purpureum, 639–40

P. flaccidum, 637–38

Pernis apivorus, effect of rodent control on, in Israel, 535 (Table)

Pirenelle, 247–48

Plasmodium, 20, 22, 81

Platyhedra gossypiella Sand., 361, 378f., 381–82f., 384–85, 386f., 397, 411, 414–15, 417–18

Platyngomiriodes apiformis, 472, 474–75

Pleuronectes platessa, effect of irradition on, 823

Plusia argentifera, 399

Popocera atramen talis led., 430

Porphyra umbilicalis, 818–19

Procambarcus clarkii, 449–50ff.

Psallus seriatus, 382, 417–18, 443–44

Psammomy's obesus, 540–41

Pseudococcus citri Risso, 430, 470, 475

Pseudomonas, 37–38, 40–41

Pseudoplusia rogationis Guen., 430, 431

Psychidae clania; P. mahznena, 471–73, 473–74, 478–79

Purtius javanicus Bleeker, 489–90, 492–93

Pycnonotis capensis, 543

Pyrsusto nubilalis, 415

R

Rhaphidopalpa foreicollis Lucchese, 359

Rhinacloa, 382

Rhyparida iridipennis, 472, 475

Rumex crispus, 382

S

Sacadodes pyralis, 394–95

Saissetia oleae Bern., 361

Salmonella, 35, 37–38

Salvinia auriculata (aquatic fern), 367

Schistocera gregaria Forskall, 509

Schistosoma haematobium, 49, 76ff., 121–23

Schistosoma mansoni, 76ff.

Scymnus spp., 445–46

Setora nitens, 472ff., 477

Shigella, 35, 37–38, 39

Simocephalus serrulatus, 451

Spalax ehrenbergi Nebrig, 530–31

Spirillaceae, 37–38

Spodoptera exempta, 520–21

S. Littoralis, 354–55, 357–58, 378, 379, 382, 393, 395–96, 460–61

Spodoptera litura, 475–76

Stipa nitita, 750

Streptopelia decaocto, 539

Sula abbottii, 876

T

Tetranychus spp., 381, 399ff., 409, 411–12

Thrips spp., resistance to insecticides, 430–31

Tilapia mocrochir, 210, 490f., 492

Tilapia mortimeri, 210

Tilapia mossambica Peters, 490f., 492

Tiracola plagiata, 476

Torgos Tracheliotus, 534, 536

Tragelaphus specki, 738

Trichogramma minutum Riley, 431

Trichogaster pectoralis Regan, 490

Trichoplusia ni, 394–95, 417–18

Trileurodes abutilonea, 380–81, 444–45

Trypanosoma, 71–72, 727

U

Upupa epops, 540

V

Vibrio, 37–38

Vipera xanthina palaestinae, 528, 541–42

X

Xanthodes graelsii, 411

Z

Zeuzera spp., 470, 470–71, 472, 473

Zonocerus elegans Thub., 411–12

BIOGRAPHICAL INFORMATION

Abrahamson, Dean E. Dr. Abrahamson is an Associate Professor at the University of Minnesota where he was awarded an M.D. and a Ph.D. with a major in anatomy and a minor in physics. His interests embrace the technical problems of radioactive and thermal wastes and the broader aspects of the interactions of science, engineering, and society with particular attention to environmental quality.

Achi, Kamel. Mr. Achi is a lecturer in earth sciences at the University of Algiers and a geologist who has worked extensively as an FAO expert in Algeria and Tunisia. He is especially interested in arid-zone hydrology and is the author of an FAO report on the applications of hydrogeology in water resources development.

Allen, Robert N. A retired civil engineer, Mr. Allen is now engaged in private consulting. He has worked extensively in southern California and in Latin America. As an engineer with the Metropolitan Water District of Southern California, Mr. Allen worked on the design, location, construction and maintenance of the Colorado River Aqueduct. Mr. Allen then served as technical advisor and construction engineer for the Anchicaya Hydroelectric Project (until 1967) in Colombia, and has published articles relating to his work on these projects.

Bardach, John E. Dr. Bardach is Professor of Zoology and of Natural Resources at the University of Michigan. He has done extensive field work in Europe, Southeast Asia, and the Caribbean. Collaboration with other scientists has resulted in several major publications and he is the author of *Downstream* (1964) and *Harvest of the Sea* (1968). His main research interest lies in physiological ecology and its practical applications. Dr. Bardach has been honored

as a Fellow of The Academy of Zoology and of the American Association for the Advancement of Science.

Batisse, Michel. Dr. Batisse directs the Natural Resources Research Division of UNESCO in Paris. He has served previously as Scientific Officer in the Middle East Science Office and as coordinator of the Arid Zone Program. Dr. Batisse was responsible for organizing the International Hydrological Decade and the 1968 UNESCO Conference on the Rational Use and Conservation of the Resources of the Biosphere. He is presently engaged in the preparation of the intergovernmental and interdisciplinary program on "Man of the Biosphere."

Böckh, Alberto. Until his untimely death in 1969, Mr. Böckh was dedicated to the study and salvation of Lake Valencia from 1948 when he left his native Hungary to join the Office of Geological Research in Venezuela. He began work as a civil engineer in the state of Carabobo, and directed the Institute for the Conservation of Lake Valencia from its founding in 1964. He edited and published the magazine *El Lago*, which dealt with lake conservation. His book, *The Desiccation of Lake Valencia* (1956), was recently updated along with a bibliography of the Lake. He also was Vice President of the Caribbean Conservation Association.

Bolin, T. D. Dr. Bolin is Research Fellow in the School of Medicine, University of New South Wales, and a member of The Medical Staff of the Prince Henry Hospital, Little Bay, Sydney. His particular specialty is gastroenterology and he has coauthored several papers with Dr. A. E. Davis on lactose intolerance, one of which was presented at the Conference on the Ecological Aspects of International Development. He has done extensive field work throughout

Southeast Asia while compiling his scientific data.

Borgstrom, Georg. Dr. Borgstrom is a Professor of Food Science and Geography at Michigan State University and served for eight years as head of the Swedish Institute of Food Preservation Research (1948–1956). Prior to that time, he was head of the Institute for Plant Research and Food Storage. His major publications on world food issues include: *Principles of Food Science* (two volumes, 1968), *The Hungry Planet* (1965–1967), *Too Many* (1969), and *The Soviet Fishing Revolution* (in press). Dr. Borgstrom received the Socrates Prize from the Swedish Education Association in 1958 which is "awarded to anyone irrespective of race, creed, nationality who has made an outstanding contribution to adult education of lasting value." He is a fellow of some twenty-five scientific and engineering academies, among them the 300-member World Academy of Arts and Sciences.

Boulding, Kenneth E. Dr. Boulding is presently Professor of Economics at the University of Colorado (formerly Professor of Economics at the University of Michigan), a program director of the Institute of Behavioral Sciences, and past President of the American Economic Association. His scholarly interests are broad, covering general systems theory, peace research, theory of the grants economy, and general social dynamics. He was the informal Poet Laureate of the Conference, during which he composed "A Ballad of Ecological Awareness." He is also the author of many distinguished articles (over two hundred) and books (sixteen). His books include *Economic Analysis, The Meaning of the 20th Century, The Impact of the Social Sciences, Economics as a Science,* and *A Primer of Social Dynamics.*

Boza Barducci, Teodoro. Prof. Boza Barducci, Agronomist, Tropical Crops, graduated at the Institut Agronomique de Gembloux—Belgium (1930), Peruvian, is a technical advisor to the Sociedad Nacional Agraria (Lima) and Professor of Plant Breeding at the Universidad Nacional Agraria (La Molina) and the Universidad Católica in Lima, Peru. For seventeen years he directed the Agricultural Experiment Station of the Cañete Valley (sponsored by the Farmers Association), whose story he tells here. He also headed the Department of Genetics of the Agriculture Experiment Station of La Molina (Lima) for fifteen years and directed the Agriculture Experimental Station Work in Peru for the Ministry of Agriculture for three years.

Bunce, George E. Presently Assistant Professor of Biochemistry and Nutrition at Virginia Polytechnic Institute, Dr. Bunce is the co-author of *Reports on the Interdepartmental Committee on Nutrition,* for the National Nutrition Surveys of Burma and Northeast Brazil. He has published numerous articles on metabolism and trace minerals.

Cairns, John, Jr. Dr. Cairns is Research Professor of Zoology at the Virginia Polytechnic Institute and State University, Vice President of the American Microscopical Society and a Trustee of the Rocky Mountain Biological Laboratory. He has served as a research consultant to numerous state and city agencies, private organizations and congressional committees. His writings on the effects of water pollution on biological communities and the ecological consequences of large power complexes number over 130 and have appeared widely in scientific journals and periodicals.

Caldwell, Lynton Keith. Dr. Caldwell is a Professor of Political Science and Director of the Program in Science, Technology and Public Policy at Indiana University and a Fellow of the American Association for the Advancement of Science. His contributions in this field include a chapter in the *Future Environments of North America* on the administrative possibilities for environmental control (1966), a Special Report on *A National Policy for the Environment* for the Senate Committee on Interior and Insular Affairs (1968), a book, *Environment: A Challenge for Modern Society* (1970), and more than eighty scientific and scholarly papers including contributions to the *Brookhaven Biology Symposia,* the *Alaska Science Conference,* and the *Bulletin of the International Union for the Conservation of Nature and Natural Resources.*

Carlozzi, Carl A. Dr. Carlozzi is Associate Professor of Resource Planning at the University of Massachusetts and senior research associate of the Caribbean Research Institute. His current research activities concern resource and economic development in the Caribbean Islands, small water resource use and the ecologic and aesthetic values of wetlands. The most recent of his publications is the book *Conservation and Caribbean Regional Progress* (1968), written with Alice A. Carlozzi, and "An Approach to Regional Planning in Relation to Urban Areas," *Proceedings of the Latin American Conference on the Conservation of Renewable Resources* (1968).

Commoner, Barry. Dr. Commoner is Chairman of the Department of Botany and Director of the Center for the Biology of Natural Systems, Washington University, St. Louis, Missouri. Dr. Commoner has been an investigator of fundamental problems on the physiochemical basis of biological processes. His laboratory has conducted studies on free radicals in biological systems and on the mechanisms by which viruses are duplicated in the cell. He has also proposed a radical new view of the chemical base of inheritance. His keen interest in the interaction between science and social problems is noted in his recent book *Science and Survival* which deals with the serious threats to human survival that result from modern technical changes, and the responsibility of scientists and citizens in the ecological crisis.

Conway, Gordon R. Dr. Conway is presently setting up an Environmental Resource Management Research Unit at the Imperial College of Science and Technology in London, was formerly a statistician with the Institute of Ecology at the University of California at Davis. From 1961 to 1966 he was the entomologist at the Agricultural Research Centre, Tuaran, State of Sabah, Malaysia. He is working on the use of systems analysis for ecological problems which relates to his early work in the theory and practice of natural resources management, particularly pest control.

Coolidge, Harold J. Dr. Coolidge, a zoologist, is President of the International Union for the Conservation of Nature and Natural Resources, recently retired after twenty-three years as Executive Director of the Pacific Science Board, National Academy of Sciences, and is Honorary Chairman of the American Committee for International Wildlife Protection, which has been active under his guidance for forty years. His main interests are international conserva-

tion and primate mammalogy. He has authored a book and many reports and received decorations from five governments for his work, as well as many other awards.

Crowcroft, W. Peter. Dr. Crowcroft is Director of the Chicago Zoological Park in Brookfield, Illinois, and a professional lecturer in anatomy at the University of Chicago. He previously directed the South Australian Museum and worked as curator of mammals in the British Museum (Natural History). His particular interests include population dynamics of mammals and the administration of scientific institutions.

Dasmann, Raymond F. Dr. Dasmann is Senior Ecologist for The International Union for the Conservation of Nature and President of The Wildlife Society. Prior to joining the IUCN, he was Chairman of the Division of Natural Resources at Humboldt State College, Arcata, California, followed by five years at the Conservation Foundation. He also has served as a consultant to both the United Nations and UNESCO. He is the author of many books and articles; the most recent are *The Destruction of California* (1965) and *A Different Kind of Country* (1968).

Davis, Alan E. Dr. Davis is an Associate Professor at the School of Medicine, University of New South Wales. His particular specialties are gastroenterology and the absorption of nutrients, in which he has authored numerous publications.

Drewes, Wolfram U. Dr. Drewes is Assistant Director of the Department of Economic Affairs of the Organization of American States. His studies in the Latin American area have focused on the development of research methods required for evaluating resource potentials and justifying resource development by the national and international lending agencies. He is the author or contributor to several dozen professional publications on economic development, planning and exploration in the Latin American area.

Farvar, Boyouk. Dr. Farvar is Head of the Female and Pediatric Urology Division at Pahlevi Hospital No. 501, Tehran, Iran, and Consultant in Urological Surgery at Firoozgar Medical Centre, also in Tehran. He was formerly Research Associate in Urology working on "metabolic aspects of calcium oxalate stone formation" and "genito-urniary tuberculosis" at the Columbia University College of Physicians and Surgeons in New York. His areas of interest include the metabolic and nutritional causes of stones in the urinary tract. Dr. Farvar is the coauthor of the three-volume *Textbooks in General Surgery,* widely used in Iranian medical schools. He has published several original articles on urolithiasis in Iranian and foreign medical journals.

Farvar, Mary A. Mrs. Farvar is an anthropologist at Washington University, St. Louis, Missouri. She is interested in the ecological aspects of sedentarization of nomads and in nutrition and disease ecology among Middle Eastern peasant and nomadic populations. She has done field work on adaptations of urban white families to poverty in St. Louis, and nutrition and childbearing patterns in an Iranian village. She is expecting to receive her Ph.D degree from Washington University.

Farvar, M. Taghi. Dr. Farvar is Research Associate and Coordinator of Program on Ecology and International Development at the Center for the Biology of Natural Systems, Washington University, St. Louis, Missouri. He obtained his Ph.D. in 1970 in Biology and Technological Development from Washington University. Since 1969 he has also served as World Health Organization Scientist in Central America, investigating the ecological impact of insect control on agriculture, disease and development. In addition to this book, he is the author and editor of several technical and popular publications on ecology and international development, including a forthcoming book called *What Price Development?* He was born and raised in Persia, of which he is a citizen.

Fraser Darling, Frank. Dr. F. Fraser Darling is Vice President of The Conservation Foundation and of the International Union for Conservation of Nature, Fellow of the Royal Society of Edinburgh and of the Institute of Biology. He has also been appointed to serve on the Royal Commission on Environmental Pollution. He has written numerous books and papers on wildlife, agriculture and ecology. He more recently co-authored *Man and Nature in the National Parks: Reflections on Policy* (1967) for The Conservation Foundation, and was the Reith Lecturer in 1969 for the British Broadcasting Corporation.

Fosberg, F. Raymond. Dr. Fosberg is a tropical botanist and ecologist at the Museum of Natural History, Smithsonian Institution, President of the International Society for Tropical Ecology, and former Vice President of the Nature Conservancy. He was, for a number of years, a botanist for the U. S. Geological Survey during which time he did extensive research on the plant life of the Pacific islands. Dr. Fosberg has been the recipient of many scientific honors and awards. He was a Guggenheim Fellow in 1947, and has served on the Advisory Committee of the UNESCO Humid Tropics Research Programme and the Natural Research Council, National Academy of Sciences. His years of investigation into the taxonomy and distribution of higher plants have resulted in numerous scientific monographs, papers and reports, many of which have appeared in both national and international publications.

George, Carl J. Dr. George is Associate Professor of Biology at Union College, Schenectady, New York. Notable recent work is a 1967 "base line" study of the fish of the Seine Fishery of St. George Bay, Republic of Lebanon. Rockefeller and Smithsonian Fellowships have supported his studies of the delta lakes of the Nile and East Mediterranean fisheries.

Gillham, Frederick E. M. Dr. Gillham is Senior Technical Consultant to the J. L. Clark Cotton Co. (Pty.) Ltd., Johannesburg, Republic of South Africa; he works with cotton plant breeding to focus on host-plant resistance. Dr. Gillham was formerly Senior Plant Breeder (Cotton), Department of Research and Specialist Services of the Ministry of Agriculture of Rhodesia. He was Vice Chairman of the Family Planning Association of Rhodesia and has written two recent papers, "Population: the Greatest Challenge of the 20th Century" (in press, *South African Journal of Science*) and "Cotton in a Hungry World" (*South African Journal of Science*, 65, 1969, 173–79), as well as many other publications.

Hardoy, Jorge E. Dr. Hardoy directs the Centro de Estudios Urbanos Regionales, Instituto Di Tella, Buenos Aires, and is President of the Inter-American Planning Society (SIAP). An urban planner graduated at the University of Buenos Aires and Harvard, Dr. Hardoy has pursued his interest in urban history and urban regional planning as a Fellow of the Guggenheim Foundation and has published a number of books and papers on Latin American urbanization and planning.

Harold, LaVerne C. Dr. Harold is Special Assistant to the Director, Bureau of Veterinary Medicine, Food and Drug Administration, and is a student of antibiotics and food additives. His publications include two co-authorships and contributions to periodicals and professional papers concerning the medical and legal aspects of food additives.

Haskell, Peter T. Dr. Haskell is Director of the Anti-Locust Research Centre, Ministry of Overseas Development, U.K., and technical consultant to the Food and Agriculture Organization of the United Nations. He is primarily concerned with studying the behavioral physiology of insects relative to insect control. He is the recipient of the Huxley Gold Medal for biology and is the author of several books and more than fifty scientific papers.

Hay, John. Mr. Hay is a retired water engineer who worked on the Rio Grande project. His special interests encompass the problems inherent in river basin management and he is the author of "Upper Rio Grande: Embattled River," a case history published in the text *Aridity and Man* (1963).

Heady, Harold F. A specialist in range management and grasslands ecology, Dr. Heady is Professor of Forestry (Ecology) at the School of Forestry and Conservation, the University of California, Berkeley. He has worked in East Africa, Saudi Arabia, Australia, New Zealand and Brazil. He has published many papers (approximately eighty) on plant ecology, particularly on the Mediterranean annual-type grasslands in California.

Hedgpeth, Joel W. Dr. Hedgpeth is Professor of Oceanography at Oregon State University and Resident Director of the Marine Science Laboratory at Newport, Oregon. Formerly he served as Assistant Marine Biologist at Scripps Institution of Oceanography and as Director of the Pacific Marine Sta-

tion, University of the Pacific. He has acted as a consultant to the National Science Foundation and Office of Naval Research. He has been concerned about technological changes in the environment since he saw the devastating flooding of Hetch Hetchy Valley in 1919, and founded the Society for the Prevention of Progress in 1944. As a result of his involvement in the Bodega Head controversy he became interested in problems of pollution of the oceans by atomic wastes.

Hughes, Charles Campbell. Dr. Hughes is Professor of Anthropology and Psychiatry, and until recently Director of the African Studies Center at Michigan State University. Past President of the Society for Applied Anthropology, he has done extensive field work in the Arctic, Africa, and eastern Canada. He is the author of several books and numerous articles on the Eskimos, the Yoruba of Nigeria, and on topics related to culture and health.

Hunter, John Melton. Dr. Hunter, Professor of Geography at Michigan State University, is the author of numerous research studies in African geography; he formerly taught at the University of Durham, England, and at the University of Ghana, where he also served as Geographical Advisor to the Population Census Office.

Jorgenson, Harold T. Mr. Jorgenson is a land economist with the Bureau of Land Management, U. S. Department of the Interior, Washington, D.C. His career in management of land resources began with the Minnesota State Planning Board in 1938. Postwar he headed regional land planning in Alaska for many years for BLM. From time to time he has served international development agencies as an advisor on land settlement and agrarian reform. He spent two years in Egypt working in this field and on the initial feasibility investigations for the Aswan High Dam. Since 1961, he has worked on agrarian reform in Colombia, Ecuador, and Northeast Brazil for the Alliance For Progress. Most recently he has been a consultant to the Inter American Development Bank in evaluation of land settlement projects in Latin America. Listed among Mr. Jorgenson's writing credits is *The Land Resources of Alaska* (with Hugh Johnson, 1963).

Kassas, Mohammad Abdul Fattah. Dr. Kassas is Professor of Applied Botany at the University of Cairo and specializes in the ecology of arid lands. He was the recipient of the U.A.R. State prize for research in biological science in 1968, and was elected member of The Egyptian Academy of Science in 1970. He is the author of numerous papers on the ecology of the Egyptian and Sudanese deserts and Red Sea coastal land. He is co-author of the bioclimatic and vegetation maps of the Mediterranean basin published by UNESCO-FAO.

Kok, L. T. Mr. Kok is lecturer in Agricultural Entomology at the University of Malaya, Kuala Lumpur. He has written about rice pests, fish culture in rice fields, toxicity of insecticides to fish in rice paddies and symbiosis of ambrosia beetles with mutualistic fungi. In 1964 he received a research scholarship from the International Rice Research Institute. In 1968 he received a research assistantship from the Department of Entomology, University of Wisconsin. He was on the special advisory committee for the 1969 pesticide series in *Environment*— "DDT on Balance." He has several new publications, which include: "Sterol Metabolism as Basis for Mutualistic Symbiosis" (1970) and "Pupation Requirement of *Xyleborus ferrugineus*—Sterol Other than Cholesterol."

Lambrecht, Frank L. Mr. Lambrecht is a scientist for the World Health Organization. His background is in research chemistry and he is principally involved in the study of human and animal blood parasites and their vectors. He has published a number of books and is the author of some fifty papers on the epidemiology of communicable diseases, medical anthropology and the prehistory of parasitic diseases.

Marshall, Carter Lee, Jr. Dr. Marshall is Associate Professor of Community Medicine at the Mount Sinai School of Medicine in New York City, where he is the coordinator of community programs. He was trained in medicine and public health at Yale and has dealt extensively with health problems in developing countries and among the urban poor of the United States. His overseas experience includes two years in Okinawa as Chief, Medical Affairs Division, United States Civil Administration of the Ryukyu

Islands and three months at the University of Antioquia in Medellín, Colombia, where he studied the effects of urbanization on population growth. He has also traveled widely in Asia and Latin America. Dr. Marshall's domestic experience includes a year in the federal poverty program and four years in academic medicine with a focus on delivery of health services to low-income populations. Dr. Marshall is the author of a number of publications in the field of Community Medicine.

May, Jacques. Dr. May was Chief of the International Unit of the Nutrition Program of the Public Health Service until October 1969, after which date he retired. He has written nine volumes on the ecology of malnutrition, covering East Central Europe, Middle Africa, Central and Southeast Europe, Northern Africa, East and West Africa, the Far and Near East, as well as two volumes on the ecology of transmissible human disease. He is presently working on two more volumes on the ecology of malnutrition in South and Portuguese Africa and in Central America and Mexico.

McNeil, Mary. Miss McNeil is a development geologist for Lockheed Aircraft International Inc. in Los Angeles. She has served as a consultant to the National Economic Council of Brazil and has written several articles on lateritic soils for scientific journals and periodicals. She has done extensive geographical and geological research in Latin America and Africa. Much of her field results are reported in her paper for this book.

Mendelssohn, Heinrich. Dr. Mendelssohn is a member of the Department of Zoology at Tel-Aviv University where he has also served as Dean of the Faculty of Science. His special interests are ethology and physioecology of desert animals. He is Chairman of the Fauna Palaestinae Committee of the Israel Academy of Sciences.

Michel, Aloys A. Dr. Michel, Professor of Geography at the University of Rhode Island, has studied irrigation systems as infrastructural influences, analyzing changes in the organization of the regional economy due to the introduction, remodeling or expansion of modern irrigation networks. He has published *The Kabul, Kunduz, and Helmand Valleys and the National Economy of*

Afghanistan (1959) and *The Indus Rivers: A Study of the Effects of Partition* (1967).

Milton, John P. Mr. Milton is Acting Director of International Programs for The Conservation Foundation. He has served widely as a consultant in ecology, natural resource conservation and national park planning in Latin America, Africa and Asia, and as a technical specialist for the Smithsonian Institution and the Organization of American States. He has been a member of the Conservation Subcommittee for the U. S. International Biological Program at the National Academy of Sciences for the past four years. In addition, he is currently serving on the National Academy's Committee on International Environmental Protection. He is also a director of Friends of the Earth, an international membership organization concerned with environmental conservation. His articles have appeared in numerous professional journals, periodicals and books; he co-edited *Future Environments of North America* in 1966. In 1968 he was an author of the two-volume work *Galapagos: The Flow of Wildness,* and in 1970 he published a journal on the Alaskan Brooks Range, *Nameless Valleys, Shining Mountains.* Mr. Milton has a special interest in the ecology of less-developed and developing countries and in the appropriate, ecologically-sound application of local and introduced technologies. He was instrumental in the conception, organization and planning of the conference on the "Ecological Aspects of International Development" and served as conference co-secretary.

Myrdal, Gunnar Karl. Dr. Myrdal is a Professor of International Economics at the University of Stockholm and a well-known author and social scientist. He was active in public affairs in Sweden and has served as advisor to the government on economics, social and fiscal policy. He is the author of numerous books, among them *An American Dilemma: The Negro Problem and Modern Democracy* (1944), *Beyond the Welfare State* (1960), *Challenge to Affluence* (1963), the masterful *Asian Drama* (1968) and *The Challenge of World Poverty* (1970).

Newsom, L. Dale. Dr. Newsom is Head of the Department of Entomology at Louisiana State University and has served as a member of the President's Science Advisory Committee (1964), the Panel for Restoring the Quality of Our Environment and the National Academy of Sciences National Research Council. His interest in the biology and ecology of insects and the ecological consequences of pesticide use have prompted him to write extensively on the subject.

Phillips, John F. V. Professor Phillips is Senior Research Fellow in Agro-Economic Co-ordination and Applied Ecology at the University of Natal, South Africa. He has studied planning, regional development, ecosystems, the bioclimatic classifications of regions, and is concerned with ecological approaches to development. His books include *Agriculture and Ecology in Africa* (1959), *Kwame Nkrumah and the Future of Africa* (1960), *Development of Agriculture and Forestry in the Tropics* (1961, 1966), and *The Agricultural and Related Development of the Tugela Basin and Its Influent Surrounds: A Study in Subtropical Africa* (In press).

Reynolds, Harold T. Dr. Reynolds is Professor and Chairman of the Department of Entomology at the University of California, Riverside, where he has done research since 1948. He is a member of several professional societies, including the AAAS and the Entomological Society of America, and is active in international entomology. Dr. Reynolds has written nearly a hundred papers on the insects and mites which affect vegetable and field crops, including cotton, with particular reference to integrated control principles in recent years.

Riney, Thane. Mr. Riney is Chief of the Forest Conservation and Wildlife Branch in the Forest Resources Division of the Food and Agriculture Organization of the United Nations. After receiving an M.A. degree in Zoology at the University of California, Berkeley, he spent twenty years in ecological field work in the western United States, New Zealand and in over thirty African countries. In this time he has authored about a hundred scientific papers in the fields of animal behavior, ungulate ecology, animal problems and range management, given courses in various universities, held a Senior Fulbright Research Scholarship in Africa and participated in a joint FAO/IUCN project in Africa with headquarters in Switzerland. Since joining FAO he has been responsible for developing within the Organization a service for developing countries in the fields of wildlife and national park assistance, and has been active in pressing for an improved methodology for international development programs.

Ripley, Sidney Dillon. Dr. Ripley has been Secretary of the Smithsonian Institution since 1964. Currently at work (with Salim Ali) on a handbook of Indian birds, he has also written *Search for the Spiny Babbler* (1952), *A Synopsis of the Birds of India and Pakistan* (1961) and *The Land and Wildlife of Tropical Asia* (1964; with the editors of *Life* magazine). His main area of interest has been ornithology.

Rivnay, Ezekiel. Prior to his retirement Professor E. Rivnay was Head of the Plant Protection Department, the Volcani Institute of Agricultural Research, Rehovot, Israel. He has continued to be engaged in the study of the ecology of insects in arid zones and the biological control of insects and has published extensively on the results of his studies. He is now chairman of the Entomological Society of Israel.

Rodgers, Kirk P. Mr. Rodgers, as Director of the Office of Regional Development of the Organization of American States, Washington, provides technical assistance and training to Latin American countries for natural resources evaluation leading to identification of projects of economic development. Multipurpose river basin development, colonization, forestry development and training in resource management are his main areas of concentration. He has worked and traveled extensively in all countries of Latin America, and published many reports on his work.

Russell, E. Walter. Dr. Russell is Professor of Soil Science at the University of Reading, England, and former Director of the East Africa Agriculture and Forestry Resource Organization. He has concentrated on the improvement of agricultural methods in tropical countries and the management of semiarid range land. He is the author of numerous papers and books on these topics.

Schuphan, Werner. Dr. Schuphan is Professor of Applied Botany at the University of Mainz, West Germany. He also is Director of the Federal Research Institute of Plant Quality and has studied biochemical and meteorological aspects of food plants as they depend on genetics and ecology. He is particularly interested in the nutrient imbalances that can be caused by chemical fertilizers and treatments with pesticides.

Scudder, Thayer. Dr. Scudder is Professor of Anthropology in the Division of Humanities and Social Science at the California Institute of Technology and has served as consultant to FAO, the International Bank for Reconstruction and Development, the Ford Foundation and the National Academy of Sciences. He is conducting detailed long-term studies of change and continuity in the Middle Zambezi and is also concerned with cultural ecology and the sociology of tropical agriculture. He is also interested in the study of the relationship between induced social change and stress in development. He wrote *The Ecology of the Gwembe Tonga* (1962) and contributed to *Experiences with Agricultural Development in Tropical Africa* (1967), *The Next 90 Years* (1967), and *Man-made Lakes* (1966).

Shiff, Clive Julian. As Deputy Director of Blair Research Laboratories, Dr. Shiff has worked as a medical entomologist in Northern Rhodesia (now Zambia), and with tsetse fly control in (Southern) Rhodesia. He has specialized in the population dynamics of aquatic snails, the effects of molluscicides on fresh-water systems, and host attraction in schistosome miracidia. His numerous publications on these subjects have appeared in the *Bulletin* of the World Health Organization and other journals.

Smith, Ray F. Dr. Smith is Professor and Chairman of the Department of Entomology and Parasitology at the University of California in Berkeley. He has written over 170 publications since 1941 on ecology, biogeographic systematics and economic entomology, and is considered a foremost leader in integrated pest control. In his capacity as FAO consultant in Central America, he has tried to find alternatives to the indiscriminate use of chemical insecticides which is threatening the collapse of cotton-growing in that region.

Talbot, Lee M. Dr. Talbot is Field Representative for International Affairs in Ecology and Conservation for the Smithsonian Institution, and Resident Ecologist in the Smithsonian Office of Environmental Sciences. He has extensive experience in ecological research, survey, and evaluation in over seventy countries and has worked with the International Union for the Conservation of Nature, the U. N. Special Fund, and the International Biological Programme. He has been a consultant in land-use ecology, wildlife and conservation to the National Academy of Sciences–National Research Council, UNESCO, and various African and Asian governments. He has published over one hundred titles in ecology, wildlife management, and international conservation. His most recent book is *Conservation in Tropical Southeast Asia* (edited with Martha Talbot, 1968).

Timothy, David H. Dr. Timothy, Professor of Crop Science at North Carolina State University, specializes in evolution and adaptive radiation of cultivated grasses and their relatives, and the use of exotic germ plasm. Formerly as director of the Rockefeller Foundation—Colombian Corn Program, he worked on corn improvement and the preservation and classification of indigenous strains of maize. He has consulted for various institutions and governments, and contributed to professional journals and symposia in his fields of interest, and to the National Academy of Sciences—National Research Council monograph series on races of maize in Latin America.

Train, Russell E. Mr. Train, former President of The Conservation Foundation, and former Under Secretary of the U. S. Department of the Interior, is now Chairman of the new Presidential Council on Environmental Quality. He has served as an advisor to the tax committees of Congress, as Assistant to the Secretary of the Treasury and was appointed to the Tax Court by President Eisenhower in 1957. Active in conservation activities here and abroad, he has been instrumental in pioneering conservation education programs in Africa and guiding the growth of domestic and international programs of The Conservation Foundation.

van der Schalie, Henry. Dr. van der Schalie is Professor of Zoology and Curator of Mollusks in the Museum of Zoology at the University of Michigan. He has conducted bilharzia control projects for the World Health Organization, on which his paper in this book is based. His laboratories are one of the major world centers for studying the role of mollusks in transmitting helminths (pathogenic worms) to man. His most recent publication is "Man Meddles with Nature—Hawaiian Style" (1969) (*The Biologist*, 51 (4):136–46, Nov. 1969).

West, Oliver. Dr. West is Chief of the Branch of Botany and Ecology of the Ministry of Agriculture in Salisbury, Rhodesia. He has a special interest in range management and ecology and is the author of some books and numerous scientific papers.

White, Gilbert F. Dr. White is Professor of Geography and Director of the Institute of Behavioral Science at the University of Colorado and formerly at the University of Chicago. He has written extensively in the field of natural resources including such works as: *Science and the Future of Arid Lands* (1956) and *Strategies of American Water Management* (1969). He has chaired the Committee on Water of the National Research Council since 1964.

Worthington, Edgar Barton. Dr. Worthington is Scientific Director of the International Biological Programme. His primary interests are limnology, fisheries, and the relationship of science and development. He is the author of numerous research papers on hydrobiology and fisheries, particularly of Europe and Africa, and of books on inland waters and on the relationship between research and economic development. His most recent book, *Science and the Development of Africa*, was published in 1957.

Zonneveld, I. S. Dr. Zonneveld is Assistant Professor of Vegetation Survey at the International Institute for Aerial Survey and Earth Science in Delft, Netherlands and a member of the educational board of the ITC/UNESCO Center for Integrated Survey for Resources Development. He is particularly interested in the educational aspects of integrated survey for development planning.